Trainee Guide

Electrical

Level 3

National Center for Construction Education and Research

Wheels of Learning
Standardized Craft Training

Prentice Hall
Upper Saddle River, New Jersey   Columbus, Ohio

This volume is one of many in the *Wheels of Learning* craft training program. This program, covering more than 20 standardized craft areas, including all major construction skills, was developed over a period of years by industry and education specialists. Sixteen of the largest construction and maintenance firms in the U.S. committed financial and human resources to the teams that wrote the curricula and planned the national accredited training process. These materials are industry-proven and consist of competency-based textbooks and instructor guides.

The *Wheels of Learning* was developed by the National Center for Construction Education and Research in response to the training needs of the construction and maintenance industries. The NCCER is a nonprofit educational entity affiliated with the University of Florida and supported by the following industry and craft associations:

Partnering Associations
- ABC Texas Gulf Coast Chapter
- American Fire Sprinkler Association
- American Society for Training and Development
- American Welding Society
- Associated Builders and Contractors, Inc.
- Associated General Contractors of America
- Association for Career and Technical Education
- The Business Roundtable
- Carolinas AGC, Inc.
- Carolinas Electrical Contractors Association
- Construction Industry Institute
- Design Build Institute of America
- Merit Contractors Association of Canada
- Metal Building Manufacturers Association
- National Association of Minority Contractors
- National Association of Women in Construction
- National Insulation Association
- National Ready Mixed Concrete Association
- National Utility Contractors Association
- National Vocational Technical Honor Society
- North American Crane Bureau
- Painting and Decorating Contractors of America
- Portland Cement Association
- Steel Erectors Association of America
- U.S. Army Corps of Engineers
- University of Florida
- Vocational Industrial Clubs of America
- Women Construction Owners and Executives, USA

Some of the features of the *Wheels of Learning* program include:
- A proven record of success over many years of use by industry companies.
- National standardization providing "portability" of learned job skills and educational credits that will be of tremendous value to trainees.
- Recognition: upon successful completion of training with an accredited sponsor, trainees receive an industry-recognized certificate and transcript from the NCCER.
- Each level meets or exceeds Bureau of Apprenticeship and Training (BAT) requirements for related classroom training (CFR 29:29).
- Well illustrated, up-to-date, and practical information. All standardized manuals are reviewed annually in a continuous improvement process.

Acknowledgments

This manual would not exist were it not for the dedication and unselfish energy of those volunteers who served on the Technical Review Committees. A sincere thanks is extended to the:

1996 – 1999 Technical Review Committee

- Bane Allman
- Mike Basham
- Jerry Bass
- Michael E. Dahl
- Gary I. Edgington
- Timothy A. Ely
- Al Hamilton
- Don Hostetler
- E. L. Jarrell
- L.J. LeBlanc
- Jim Mitchem
- Robert Mueller
- Christine Porter
- Mike Powers
- Rob Soileau
- Joe Sullivan
- Sherry Yarbrough

1992 – 1996 Technical Review Committee

- Bane Allman
- S.A. ("Barney") Barnette
- John Brayshaw
- Gary I. Edgington
- Timothy A. Ely
- Al Hamilton
- Allen A. Hill
- Don Hostetler
- L.J. LeBlanc
- Daniel C. Miller
- Jim Mitchem
- Bob Mueller
- Burton Smith

Contents

Load Calculations – Branch Circuits

Module 26301

NATIONAL
CENTER FOR
CONSTRUCTION
EDUCATION AND
RESEARCH

LOAD CALCULATIONS—BRANCH CIRCUITS

OBJECTIVES

Upon completion of this module, the trainee will be able to:

1. Calculate loads for single-phase and three-phase branch circuits.
2. Size branch circuit overcurrent protection devices (circuit breakers and fuses) for noncontinuous duty and continuous duty circuits.
3. Understand and apply derating factors to size branch circuits.
4. Calculate ampacity for single-phase and three-phase loads.
5. Use load calculations to determine branch circuit conductor sizes.
6. Use *NEC Table 220-19* to calculate residential cooking equipment loads.
7. Select branch circuit conductors and overcurrent protection devices for electric heat, air conditioning equipment, motors, and welders.

Prerequisites

Successful completion of the following Task Modules is recommended before beginning study of this Task Module: Core Curricula; Electrical Level 1; and Electrical Level 2.

Required Trainee Materials

1. Trainee Task Module
2. Appropriate Personal Protective Equipment
3. Copy of the latest edition of the *National Electrical Code*

Note: The designations "National Electrical Code," "NE Code," and "NEC," where used in this document, refer to the *National Electrical Code®*, which is a registered trademark of the National Fire Protection Association, Quincy, MA. *All National Electrical Code (NEC) references in this module refer to the 1999 edition of the NEC.*

This course map shows all of the modules in the third level of the Electrical curricula. The suggested training order begins at the bottom and proceeds up. Skill levels increase as a trainee advances on the course map. The training order may be adjusted by the local Training Program Sponsor.

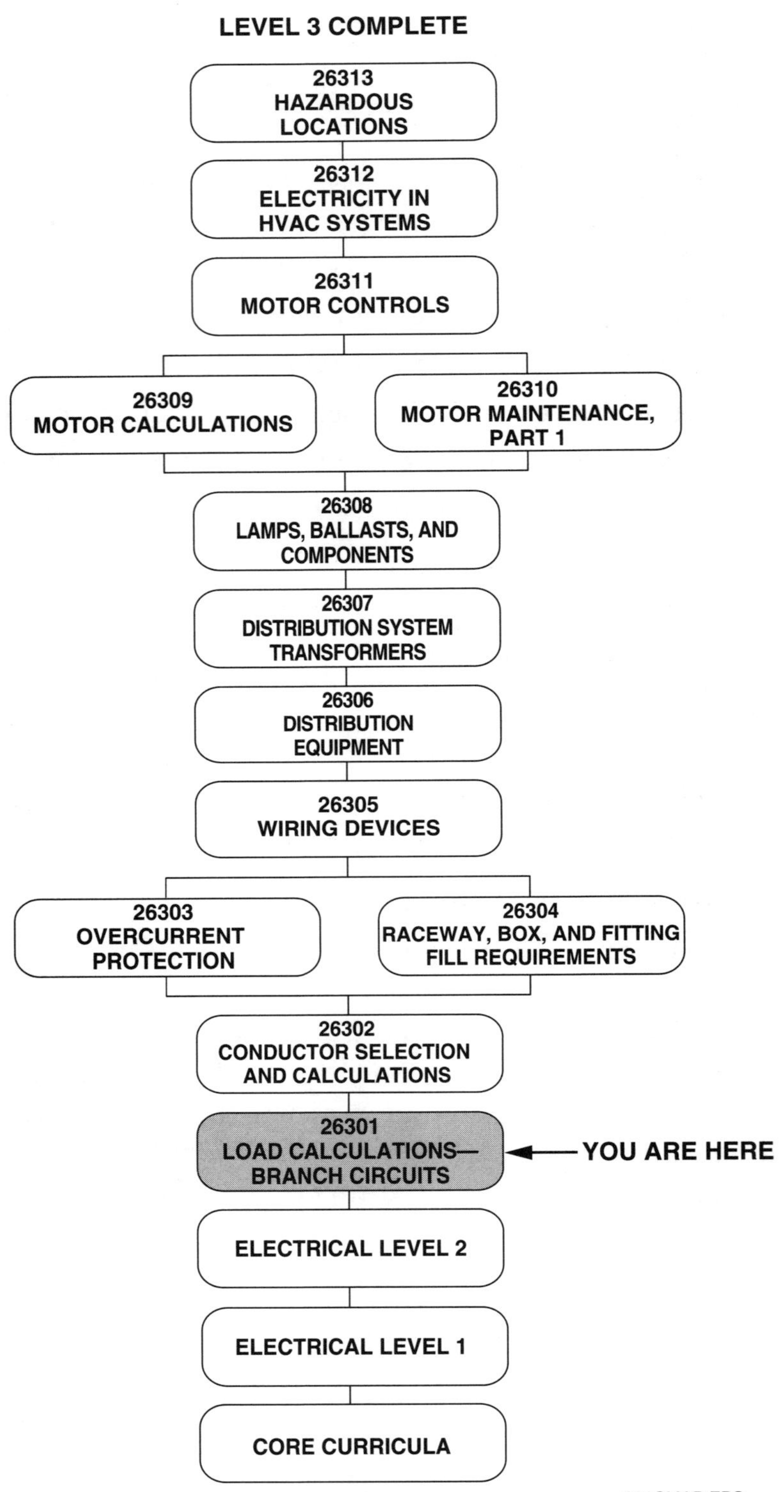

TABLE OF CONTENTS

Trade Terms Introduced In This Module

Ampacity: The current in amperes that a conductor can carry continuously under the conditions of use without exceeding its temperature rating.

Appliance: Utilization equipment, generally other than industrial, normally built-in standardized sizes or types, that is installed or connected as a unit to perform one or more functions such as clothes washing, air conditioning, food mixing, deep frying, etc.

Appliance branch circuit: A branch circuit supplying energy to one or more outlets to which appliances are to be connected. Such circuits are to have no permanently connected lighting fixtures that are not part of an appliance.

Branch circuit: The circuit conductors between the final overcurrent device protecting the circuit and the outlet(s).

Continuous load: A load in which the maximum current is expected to continue for three hours or more.

Demand factors: The ratio of the maximum demands of a system, or part of a system, to the total connected load of a system or the part of the system under consideration.

Device: A unit of an electrical system that is intended to carry but not utilize electric energy.

General-purpose branch circuit: A branch circuit that supplies a number of outlets for lighting and appliances.

Individual branch circuit: A branch circuit that supplies only one piece of utilization equipment.

Multi-outlet assembly: A type of surface or flush raceway designed to hold conductors and receptacles, assembled in the field or at the factory.

Outlet: A point on the wiring system at which current is taken to supply utilization equipment.

Overcurrent: Any current in excess of the rated current of equipment or the ampacity of a conductor. It may result from overload, short circuit, or ground fault.

Receptacle: A contact device installed at an outlet for connection as a single contact device. A single receptacle is a single contact device with no other contact device on the same yoke. A multiple receptacle is a single device containing two (duplex) or more receptacles.

Receptacle outlet: An outlet where one or more receptacles are installed.

Utilization equipment: Equipment that utilizes electric energy for electronic, chemical, heating, lighting, electromechanical, or similar purposes.

The purpose of **branch circuit** load calculations is to determine the size of branch circuit **overcurrent** protection **devices** and branch circuit conductors using *National Electrical Code* requirements. Once the branch circuit load is accurately calculated, branch circuit components may be sized to serve the load safely. Branch circuits supply **utilization equipment**. Utilization equipment is defined by the NEC as equipment that utilizes electric energy.

NEC Article 210 covers branch circuits (except for branch circuits that supply only motor loads). *NEC Section 210-2* provides a listing of other code articles for specific-purpose branch circuits. Per *NEC Section 210-3*, branch circuits are rated by the maximum rating or setting of the overcurrent device. Except for circuits serving individual utilization equipment (dedicated circuits), branch circuits shall be rated 15A, 20A, 30A, 40A, and 50A. Branch circuits designed to serve individual loads can supply any size load with no restrictions to the ampere rating of the circuit.

Per *NEC Section 210-19*, branch circuit conductors are required to be sized with an **ampacity** rating that is no less than the maximum load to be served. Branch circuit overcurrent protection is required to have a rating or setting not exceeding the rating specified in *NEC Section 240-3* for conductors, *NEC Section 240-2* for equipment, and *NEC Section 210-21* for **outlet** devices including lampholders and **receptacles**. *NEC Article 430* applies to branch circuits supplying only motor loads and *NEC Article 440* applies to branch circuits supplying only air conditioning equipment, refrigerating equipment, or both.

Branch circuit conductors must have an ampacity rating equal to, or greater than, the noncontinuous load plus 125% of the **continuous load** without the application of any adjustment or correction factors per *NEC Section 210-20(a)*.

NEC Sections 210-23(a) through (d) define permissible loads for branch circuits. This is important information because it lists the types of loads which may be served according to the size of the branch circuit. *NEC Section 210-24* and *NEC Table 210-24* summarize the branch circuit requirements.

NEC Article 220 includes the requirements used to determine the number of branch circuits required and the requirements used to compute branch circuit, feeder, and service loads. *NEC Section 210-19(a)* states that the rating of a branch circuit shall not be less than the noncontinuous load plus 125% of the continuous load. *NEC Table 220-3(a)* gives general lighting loads listed by types of occupancies. These general lighting loads are expressed as a unit load per square foot in volt-amperes (VA).

For example, the unit lighting load for a barber shop is 3VA/sq. ft.; a store is also 3VA/sq. ft.; and a storage warehouse is ¼VA/sq. ft. *NEC Sections 220-3(b)(1) through (11)* list minimum loads for **outlets** used in all occupancies—these outlets include general use receptacles and outlets not used for general illumination.

Note: Local codes may require different values than the minimum NEC values. For instance, local codes may limit the number of outlets on a branch circuit to less than the calculated value, or they may require dedicated circuits other than those that are listed in the NEC. Always check local codes before beginning any installation.

1.1.0 BRANCH CIRCUIT RATINGS

The maximum load that a branch circuit may serve is determined by multiplying the rating or setting of the overcurrent protection device (circuit breaker or fuse) by the circuit voltage. For example, the maximum load that may be supplied by a 20A, two-wire, 120V circuit is calculated by multiplying 20A by 120V.

$$20A \times 120V = 2,400VA$$

The maximum load supplied by a 20A, three-wire, 120/240V circuit is:

$$20A \times 240V = 4,800VA$$

The maximum load supplied by a 20A, 208V, three-phase circuit is determined by multiplying 20A by 208V by $\sqrt{3}$.

Note: The square root of three ($\sqrt{3}$) is approximately 1.732. You may wish to make a note of this for use in future calculations.

$$20A \times 208V \times 1.732 = 7,205.12VA$$

Branch circuits may supply noncontinuous loads, continuous loads, or a combination of noncontinuous and continuous loads. Per *NEC Section 210-19(a)*, the branch circuit rating shall not be less than the noncontinuous load plus 125% of the continuous load. A continuous load is defined by *NEC Article 100* as a load where the maximum current is expected to continue for three hours or more. Continuous loads are calculated at 125% of the maximum current rating of the load. *NEC Section 384-16(d)* states that, except where the assembly is listed for operation at 100% of its rating (exception), overcurrent devices located in panelboards shall not exceed 80% of their rating where the overcurrent device supplies a continuous duty load.

For 15A and 20A branch circuits, **NEC Section 210-23(a)** allows fastened-in-place utilization equipment to be connected in the same circuit with lighting units, cord- and plug-connected utilization equipment not fastened in place, or both. Under this condition, the fastened-in-place utilization equipment shall not exceed 50% of the branch circuit ampere rating.

Example 1:

A store has fluorescent lighting fixtures consisting of nine fluorescent ballasts rated at 1.5A at 120V. The fixtures will operate continuously during normal business hours from 9:00 A.M. until 9:00 P.M. daily.

What is the minimum size circuit breaker required for a branch circuit to serve this load?

Determine the branch circuit load:

$$9 \times 1.5A = 13.5A$$

Determine the continuous duty load (this is a continuous duty load because the lighting fixtures will stay on for more than three hours):

$$13.5A \times 125\% = 16.88A$$

The minimum size circuit breaker required is 20A.

Example 2:

What is the maximum continuous load that may be connected to a 30A, 120V fuse?

Per **NEC Section 384-16(d)**:

$$30A \times 80\% = 24A$$

The maximum continuous load cannot exceed 24A.

Example 3:

How many **receptacle outlets** can be connected to a 20A, two-wire, 120V circuit? (The receptacle outlets serve noncontinuous duty loads.)

Determine branch circuit capacity:

$$20A \times 120V = 2,400VA$$

Per **NEC Section 220-3(b)(9)**, each outlet is assigned a load of 180VA.

$$2,400VA \div 180VA = 13.33$$

Thirteen receptacle outlets can be connected to this circuit.

Example 4:

An office manager has purchased a new state-of-the-art copy machine. The nameplate rating on the copy machine is 17A, 120V.

What is the minimum size branch circuit required to serve this equipment?

This is not a continuous load, however, per **NEC Sections 210-23(a) and (b)**, the rating of any cord-connected utilization equipment shall not exceed 80% of the branch circuit ampere rating for 15A, 20A, and 30A circuits. Since the load is greater than 15A, determine the current-carrying capacity of a 20A (the smallest logical size) circuit to serve this equipment:

$$20A \times 80\% = 16A$$

A 20A circuit is not sufficient; determine the current-carrying capacity of a 30A circuit:

$$30A \times 80\% = 24A$$

The minimum size branch circuit required is 30A.

Note that the solution above assumes that only multi-receptacle 20A and 30A branch circuits exist in the office. An alternate solution would be to install a 20A **individual branch circuit** exclusively for the copy machine.

Example 5:

What is the maximum lighting load that may be connected to a 20A branch circuit supplying a piece of fixed equipment that has a rating of 8.5A, 120V?

The equipment rating is smaller than 50% of the rating of the 20A branch circuit. Therefore, 11.5A of noncontinuous lighting may be added.

$$20A - 8.5A = 11.5A$$

Example 6:

A restaurant dishwasher has a nameplate rating of 14.7A, 208V, 3Ø. During busy times in the restaurant, it is anticipated that the dishwasher will be turned on and operated for more than three hours at a time. What is the minimum size branch circuit required to supply this equipment?

This equipment is considered a continuous load (operated for more than three hours). Therefore, the load is to be multiplied by 125% to determine the branch circuit size.

$$14.7A \times 125\% = 18.38A$$

The minimum size branch circuit required is 20A.

1.2.0   DERATING

The current-carrying capacity (ampacity) of conductors may be derated (reduced) due to several conditions that may apply to branch circuits. Branch circuit conductors are derated when:

- The load to be supplied is a continuous duty load per ***NEC Sections 220-19(a) and 210-23***.

- There are more than three current-carrying conductors in a raceway per ***NEC Section 310-15(b)(2)(a)***.

- The ambient temperature that the conductors will pass through exceeds the temperature ratings for conductors listed in ***NEC Table 310-16***.

- A voltage drop exists that exceeds 3% for branch circuits or 5% for the combination of the feeder and branch circuits that is caused when the distance of branch circuit conductors becomes excessive.

- You bundle any cable assemblies more than 24" in length per ***NEC Section 310-15(b)(2)(a)***.

NEC Table 310-16 lists allowable ampacities for insulated conductors rated 0 to 2,000V. The ampacities listed apply when no more than three current-carrying conductors are installed in a raceway, are part of a cable assembly, or are for direct-buried conductors. The ampacities are based upon an ambient temperature of 30°C (86°F). If the number of current-carrying conductors in the conduit or cable exceeds three, the ampacity of the conductors must be derated using ***NEC Section 310-15(b)(2)(a)***. If the ambient temperature exceeds 30°C (86°F), the ampacity of the conductors must be derated using the temperature correction factors listed at the bottom of ***NEC Table 310-16***. Note that the multipliers listed at the bottom of ***NEC Table 310-16*** are called *correction factors*. NEC references to adjustment and correction factors mean ambient temperatures other than 30°C and more than three current-carrying conductors in a raceway or cable.

1.2.1   Temperature Derating

NEC Section 110-14(c) states that the lowest temperature rating of any component in a branch circuit (circuit breaker, fuse, receptacle, conductors, etc.) must be used to determine the ampacity rating of the branch circuit conductors. Conductors that have a higher temperature rating per ***NEC Table 310-16*** can be used for ampacity adjustment, correction, or both. For example, if the termination rating of a circuit breaker is 60°C, the ampacity rating of the branch circuit conductor rating cannot exceed the value given in the 60°C column of ***NEC Table 310-16*** for overcurrent protection. However, if the branch circuit conductor has a higher temperature rating (i.e., 90°C THHN) the higher ampacity rating can be used for ampacity adjustment, correction, or both.

Example 1:

It is determined that by combining branch circuits we can eliminate two runs of conduit. The branch circuits are to be pulled in a single conduit. All of the conductors in the conduit will be current-carrying conductors.

What is the ampacity for each of eight No. 12 THHN copper conductors in a single conduit?

Per **NEC Table 310-16**, the ampacity of No. 12 THHN is 30A. Per **NEC Table 310-15(b)(2)(a)**, the ampacity must be adjusted by 70% (seven to nine current-carrying conductors).

$$30A \times 70\% = 21A$$

Example 2:

What is the maximum load that may be connected on each of six No. 2 current-carrying THWN copper conductors in a single conduit?

Per **NEC Table 310-16**, the ampacity of No. 2 THWN is 115A. Per **NEC Table 310-15(b)(2)(a)**, the ampacity must be adjusted by 80% (four to six current-carrying conductors).

$$115A \times 80\% = 92A$$

The maximum load cannot exceed 92A.

Example 3:

A branch circuit is required to supply a noncontinuous equipment load with a nameplate rating of 55A. The equipment is located in a room with plastic extrusion equipment. The ambient temperature in the room is 92°F.

What is the minimum size THHN copper conductors required to supply the equipment?

Per **NEC Table 310-16**, No. 8 THHN copper conductors have an ampacity rating of 55A. Per correction factors to **NEC Table 310-16**, the ampacity of the conductors must be multiplied by a factor of .96.

$$55A \times .96 = 52.8A$$

The No. 8 THHN copper conductors will not meet NEC requirements. A No. 6 THHN copper conductor has a rating of 75A.

$$75A \times .96 = 72A$$

No. 6 THHN copper conductors will be required.

Example 4:

A branch circuit is needed to supply a continuous load of 19.5A. The branch circuit conductors will pass through an area that has an ambient temperature of 117°F. The project specification requires XHHW copper conductors for branch circuits.

What is the minimum size XHHW copper conductor required to supply this load and what is the minimum size fuse required as overcurrent protection?

Because this is a continuous load, the load is to be multiplied by 125%:

$$19.5A \times 125\% = 24.38A$$

The minimum size standard fuse per **NEC Section 240-6** is 25A. Per **NEC Table 310-16**, the ampacity of No. 12 XHHW copper conductors is listed as 25A. The temperature correction factor listed for 117°F is .82.

$$25A \times .82 = 20.5A$$

No. 12 XHHW will not meet NEC requirements. No. 10 XHHW copper is rated for 35A.

$$35A \times .82 = 28.7A$$

This equipment branch circuit will require No. 10 XHHW copper conductors and a 25A fuse.

1.2.2 Voltage Drop Derating For Single-Phase Circuits

NEC Section 210-19(a), FPN No. 4 states that the voltage drop for branch circuit conductors shall not exceed 3% to the farthest outlet and 5% for the combination of feeder and branch circuit distance to the farthest outlet. There are two formulas used to calculate voltage drop for single-phase circuits.

Formula 1:

$$VD = \frac{2 \times L \times R \times I}{1,000}$$

Where:

L = load center or total length in feet
R = conductor resistance per **NEC Chapter 9, Table 8**
I = current

The number 1,000 represents 1,000' or less of conductor.

Formula 2:

$$VD = \frac{2 \times L \times K \times I}{CM}$$

Where:

L = load center or total length in feet
K = constant (12.9 for copper conductors; 21.2 for aluminum conductors)
I = current
CM = area of the conductor in circular mils (from **NEC Chapter 9, Table 8**)

The result of these formulas is in volts. The result is divided by circuit voltage and the second result is multiplied by 100 to determine the % voltage drop. If the branch circuit voltage drop exceeds 3%, the conductor size is increased to compensate. For a 120V circuit, the maximum voltage drop (in volts) is 120V × 3% = 3.6V. For a 240V single-phase circuit, the maximum voltage drop (in volts) is 240V × 3% = 7.2V.

If in commercial fixed load applications, the branch circuit load is not concentrated at the end of the branch circuit but is spread out along the circuit due to multiple outlets, the load center length of the circuit should be calculated and used in the above formulas. This is because the total current does not flow the complete length of the circuit. If the full length is used in computing the voltage drop, the drop determined would be greater than what would actually occur. The load center length of a circuit is that point in the circuit where, if the load were concentrated at that point, the voltage drop would be the same as the voltage drop to the farthest load in the actual circuit. To determine the load center length of a branch circuit with multiple outlets, as shown in *Figure 1*, multiply each outlet load by its actual physical routing distance from the supply end of the circuit. Add these products for all loads fed from the circuit and divide this sum by the sum of the individual loads. The resulting distance is the load center length (L) for the total load (I) of the branch circuit.

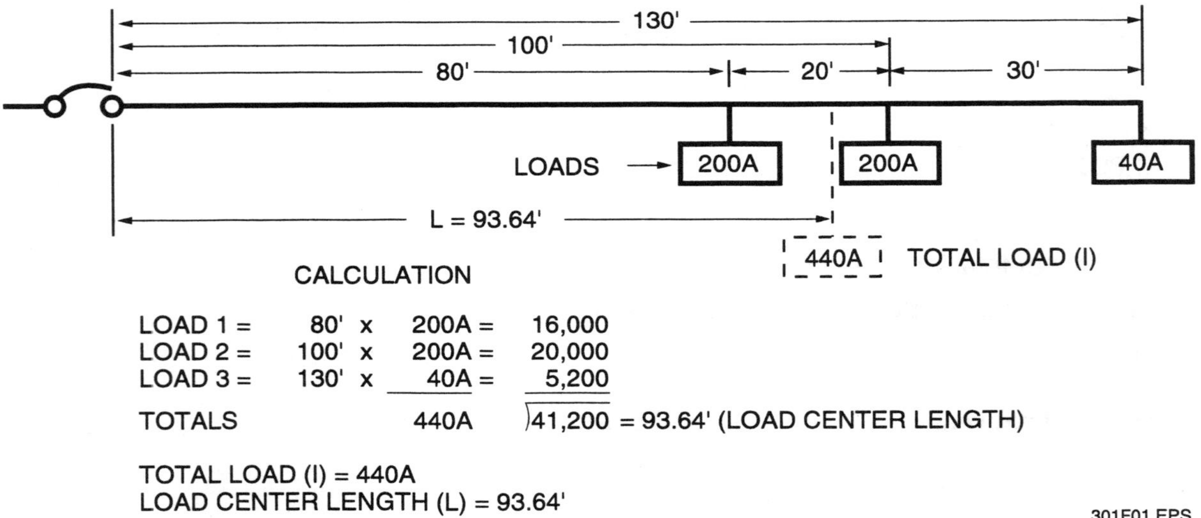

Figure 1. Calculating A Load Center Length And Total Load For Multiple Fixed Loads On A Circuit

Example 1:

The length of a 120V, two-wire branch circuit is 95'. The noncontinuous load is 14.5A.

If No. 12 THHN solid copper conductors are used, will the voltage drop for this branch circuit exceed 3%?

Use the first voltage drop formula to determine voltage drop for this branch circuit. Look up the resistance for No. 12 solid copper in *NEC Chapter 9, Table 8*. It is 1.93Ω.

$$VD = \frac{2 \times L \times R \times I}{1,000}$$

$$VD = \frac{2 \times 95' \times 1.93\Omega \times 14.5A}{1,000}$$

$$VD = 5.32$$

$$5.32V \div 120V = .0443 \times 100 = 4.43\%$$

Since this percentage exceeds the 3% allowable voltage drop, the answer to the question is yes and larger conductors would be required for this circuit. Note that this solution uses the first formula for single-phase (1Ø) voltage drop.

Example 2:

What size THHN solid copper branch circuit conductors would be required for a noncontinuous branch circuit load of 23A, 240V, 1Ø? The length of the circuit is 130'.

Use the second voltage drop formula to determine the voltage drop for this branch circuit. Since No. 10 THHN copper would be the smallest size permitted, this size will be evaluated first. Look up the area in CM for No. 10 solid conductor in *NEC Chapter 9, Table 8*.

$$VD = \frac{2 \times L \times K \times I}{CM}$$

$$VD = \frac{2 \times 130' \times 12.9 \times 23A}{10,380}$$

$$VD = 7.43$$

$$7.43V \div 240V = .031 \times 100 = 3.10\%$$

This percentage exceeds 3%; therefore, No. 10 THHN copper conductors would not meet NEC requirements, and again, larger conductors would be required.

Example 3:

What size THHN copper conductors would be required for a 240V, single-phase, three-wire branch circuit with multiple outlets consisting of three fixed 240V loads of 30A at 60', 30A at 80', and 20A at 100'?

Determine the load center length of the circuit by multiplying the outlet loads by their distance from the circuit source and then by dividing the sum of the three products by the sum of the three loads as follows:

Outlet 1 = 60' × 30A = 1,800

Outlet 2 = 80' × 30A = 2,400

Outlet 3 = 100' × 20A = 2,000

Sum the products:

1,800 + 2,400 + 2,000 = 6,200

Divide by the sum of the loads:

30A + 30A + 20A = 80A

6,200 ÷ 80A = 77.5' for the load center

For a load of 80A (per **NEC Table 310-16**), No. 4 copper THWN conductors at 75°C will be selected. Use the second formula and substitute values to check voltage drop.

$$VD = \frac{2 \times L \times K \times I}{CM}$$

$$VD = \frac{2 \times 77.5' \times 12.9 \times 80A}{41,740}$$

$$VD = 3.8V$$

Since the permissible voltage drop is 240V × 3% or 7.2V, the No. 4 THHN conductors are satisfactory for this application.

1.2.3 Voltage Drop Derating For Three-Phase Circuits

The voltage drop for balanced three-phase circuits (with negligible reactance and a power factor of 1) can be calculated using the two formulas above by substituting $\sqrt{3}$ (1.732) for the value of 2 in the formulas:

Formula 1:

$$VD = \frac{\sqrt{3} \times L \times R \times I}{1,000}$$

Formula 2:

$$VD = \frac{\sqrt{3} \times L \times K \times I}{CM}$$

Example 1:

What is the voltage drop of a 208V, 3Ø branch circuit with a load of 32A, a distance from the circuit breaker to the load of 115', and using No. 8 stranded copper conductors?

Use the first three-phase voltage drop formula to determine voltage drop for this 3Ø circuit. Look up the resistance for No. 8 stranded copper conductor in ***NEC Chapter 9, Table 8***. It is .778Ω.

$$VD = \frac{\sqrt{3} \times L \times R \times I}{1,000}$$

$$VD = \frac{1.732 \times 115' \times .778\Omega \times 32A}{1,000}$$

$$VD = 4.96V$$

The maximum voltage drop permitted for a 208V circuit is:

$$208V \times 3\% = 6.24V$$

Since, in this problem, 4.96V is less than the maximum allowable voltage drop, this circuit will not have a voltage drop problem.

Example 2:

What size THHN copper conductors would be required for a 208V, 3Ø, four-wire branch circuit with a length of 150' from the source to a fixed continuous load of 100A?

Determine load by multiplying 100A × 125% to obtain 125A. Using **NEC Table 310-16**, determine that No. 2 THHN conductors at 90°C are satisfactory for a load of 125A. Use the second three-phase voltage drop formula and substitute values.

$$VD = \frac{\sqrt{3} \times L \times K \times I}{CM}$$

$$VD = \frac{1.732 \times 150' \times 12.9 \times 125A}{66,360}$$

$$VD = 6.31V$$

Since the permissible voltage drop is 208 × 3% or 6.24V, the next larger conductor will have to be selected. AWG No. 1 THHN copper conductors will be satisfactory for this application.

1.3.0 CALCULATING BRANCH CIRCUIT AMPACITY

The branch circuit ampacity for single-phase circuits is calculated by dividing VA by the circuit voltage. For example, the ampacity of a 120V, 1Ø load rated at 1,600VA is determined by dividing 1,600VA by 120V.

$$1,600VA \div 120V = 13.33A$$

The ampacity of a 3,450VA load at 277V, 1Ø is 12.45A.

$$3,450VA \div 277V = 12.45A$$

The branch circuit ampacity for three-phase circuits is calculated by dividing VA by the circuit voltage times $\sqrt{3}$ (1.732). For example, the ampacity (I) of a 208V, three-phase load rated at 5,200VA is determined as follows:

$$I = \frac{VA}{V \times \sqrt{3}}$$

$$I = \frac{5,200VA}{208V \times 1.732}$$

$$I = 14.43A$$

Using the same equation, the ampacity of a 14,000VA three-phase load at 480V is:

$$\frac{14{,}000\text{VA}}{480\text{V} \times 1.732} = 16.84\text{A}$$

Example 1:

What is the ampacity of a single-phase load with a nameplate rating of 5.5kW, 240V?

Multiply 5.5kW by 1,000 to determine VA (watts = volt-amperes) and then divide the result by 240V.

$$5.5\text{kW} \times 1{,}000 = 5{,}500\text{VA} \div 240\text{V} = 22.92\text{A}$$

The ampacity of this load is 22.92A.

Example 2:

What is the ampacity of a three-phase electric water heater with a nameplate rating of 20kW, 208V?

Multiply 20kW by 1,000 and divide the result by (208V × 1.732).

$$20\text{kW} \times 1{,}000 = 20{,}000\text{kW} \div (208\text{V} \times 1.732) = 55.52\text{A}$$

The ampacity of this load is 55.52A.

2.0.0 LIGHTING LOADS

Lighting load branch circuit calculations are based upon the type of lighting (incandescent or electric discharge), the branch circuit voltage, and whether or not the lighting is to be used for more than three hours without an off period (continuous duty).

Branch circuit loads for incandescent lighting are determined by adding the total incandescent load (watts = VA) and dividing the total by the circuit voltage. For example, three 500W quartz lamps connected on a 120V circuit would equal 12.5A, as shown below.

$$3 \times 500\text{VA} = 1{,}500\text{VA} \div 120\text{V} = 12.5\text{A}$$

Branch circuit loads for electric discharge lighting (lighting units having ballasts, transformers, or autotransformers) are determined by multiplying the number of fixtures times the ampacity rating of the ballast. Per **NEC Section 220-4(b)**, the calculated load shall be based upon the total ampere rating of the fixture (ballast or ballasts) and not the total watts of the lamps. For example, 15 150W, high-pressure sodium fixtures connected on a 277V circuit each have a ballast of .79A. The total load is 11.85A, as shown below.

$$15 \times .79\text{A} = 11.85\text{A}$$

Example 1:

Incandescent lighting utilizing 150W medium base lamps is required for temporary lighting on a construction site. This lighting will remain on all day and all night.

How many 150W lamps can be connected on a 20A, 120V circuit?

Since the lighting will remain on for longer than three hours, this is a continuous load. For continuous duty, multiply 150VA (watts) × 125% = 187.5VA. Determine the total capacity (in VA) for the 20A circuit:

    20A × 120V = 2,400VA

Divide the circuit ampacity by the lamp demand load:

    2,400VA ÷ 187.5VA = 12.8 lamps

Twelve 150W lamps may be safely connected to a 20A, 120V circuit.

Example 2:

Two 400W metal halide high bay fixtures are required to provide additional lighting for a production machine. There is an existing, 20A, 277V lighting circuit available near the equipment and, after investigation, it is determined that the circuit has six of the same type of fixtures connected. The nameplate ampere rating for these fixtures is 2.0A at 277V. During normal operation, the fixtures are turned on for 12 hours every day.

Can two 400W fixtures be safely added to the existing circuit?

This is a continuous lighting load. The maximum continuous load that may be connected to the 20A circuit is 16A.

    20A × 80% = 16A

The load for eight fixtures (six existing and two new fixtures) is 16A.

    8 fixtures × 2.0A = 16A

Per NEC requirements, two new fixtures may safely be added to this circuit.

2.1.0   RECESSED LIGHTING

The load for recessed lighting fixtures (excluding the residential general lighting load that is calculated at 3VA per square foot) is calculated per ***NEC Section 220-3(b)(4)*** by using the maximum VA rating of the equipment (fixture) and lamps. For example, a load of 250VA would be used to calculate the load for a recessed incandescent fixture rated at 250W.

To calculate the load for a recessed fixture that uses compact fluorescent lamps, we would need to know the voltage and ampacity rating of the fluorescent ballast. To calculate the load for a recessed H.I.D. fixture (high-pressure sodium, metal halide, etc.), we would again need to know the voltage and ampacity rating of the ballast.

Example 1:

What is the load in amps for seven incandescent recessed cans that have a nameplate indicating a maximum lamp size of 150W and the fixtures are to be connected to a 120V circuit?

The number of fixtures is multiplied by the VA rating of each fixture to obtain the total VA load.

$$7 \times 150VA \text{ (watts)} = 1,050VA$$

To determine ampacity, the total VA rating is divided by the circuit voltage.

$$1,050VA \div 120V = 8.75A$$

Example 2:

What is the total load in amps for seven fluorescent recessed fixtures? Each fixture has a ballast ampacity of .20A at 277V and each fixture takes two compact fluorescent lamps rated at 26 watts each.

Because these fixtures are of the electric discharge type, we need to know the ampacity of the fixture and the number of fixtures in order to calculate the total ampacity.

$$7 \times .20A = 1.4A$$

2.2.0   HEAVY-DUTY LAMPHOLDER OUTLETS

Per ***NEC Section 220-3(b)(5)***, outlets for heavy-duty lampholders are calculated at 600VA. For example, a noncontinuous load consisting of four 120V outlets for heavy-duty lampholders could be connected to a 20A branch circuit:

$$2,400VA \div 600VA = 4 \text{ outlets}$$

3.0.0   RECEPTACLE LOADS

When the exact VA rating of a load that is to be cord- and plug-connected to a receptacle outlet is not known, a VA rating of 180VA per outlet is used per ***NEC Section 220-3(b)(9)***. For noncontinuous receptacle loads, the total noncontinuous load is calculated at 100%. For continuous loads, the total continuous load is calculated at 125%. This NEC reference does not apply to residential receptacles. Residential receptacles are included in the general illumination load (**general-purpose branch circuits**) or in specific residential loads such as receptacles required for small **appliance** and laundry loads.

For example, a 15A, 120V circuit is to be added to supply general-purpose receptacles. The receptacles are to be located above workbenches that are to be positioned against a wall. The owner states that the workers using the benches will plug small tools into the outlets, but the tools will only be occasionally used for short periods of time.

How many general-purpose duplex receptacles can be connected to a 15A, 120V circuit when the outlets are to be rated for noncontinuous duty?

Per **_NEC Section 220-3(b)(9)_**, each receptacle is assigned a value of 180VA. The capacity of a 15A, 120V circuit is 1,800VA.

$$15A \times 120V = 1{,}800VA$$

The total circuit capacity is then divided by the rating per receptacle to determine the total number that may be connected.

$$1{,}800VA \div 180VA = 10 \text{ receptacles}$$

4.0.0 MULTI-OUTLET ASSEMBLIES

A **multi-outlet assembly** is defined by **_NEC Article 100_** as a type of surface or flush raceway designed to hold conductors and receptacles, assembled in the field or at the factory. Multi-outlet assemblies may consist of single outlets wired to one or more circuits and typically spaced equally apart at distances of 6", 12", 18", etc. The NEC rules for calculating loads for multi-outlet assemblies do not apply to dwelling units.

Per **_NEC Section 220-3(b)(8)_**, each 5' of multi-outlet assembly is considered as one outlet of at least 180VA capacity. In locations where many appliances are likely to be used at one time, each 1' of multi-outlet assembly is considered as one outlet of at least 180VA capacity.

Example 1:

A total of 40' of Plugmold includes one single receptacle per foot of the assembly. The multi-outlet assembly is to be connected to a single 120V circuit.

What is the minimum size 120V circuit that would safely supply this light-duty multi-outlet assembly?

Since this is a light-duty application, the load is to be calculated at 180VA per 5' of multi-outlet assembly. Divide 40' of multi-outlet assembly by 5' and multiply the result by 180VA to obtain the total VA load. Divide the total VA load by 120V to determine the circuit ampacity and minimum circuit size.

$$40' \div 5' = 8 \times 180VA = 1,440VA$$

$$1,440VA \div 120V = 12A$$

The minimum 120V circuit size would be a 15A circuit.

Example 2:

The conditions listed for the example above have changed and it will now be necessary to feed this Plugmold with three circuits. The reason for the change is that there will now be more workers using equipment plugged into the assembly. This change means that the assembly will now be rated to supply several loads simultaneously.

How many 20A, 120V circuits would be required to safely supply this heavy-duty multi-outlet assembly?

Since this is a heavy-duty application, the load is to be calculated at 180VA per foot of multi-outlet assembly. First, determine the VA capacity for a 20A, 120V circuit.

$$20A \times 120V = 2,400VA$$

Multiply 40' of multi-outlet assembly by 180VA to obtain the total VA load.

$$40' \times 180VA = 7,200VA \text{ (total VA)}$$

Divide the total VA by 2,400VA (20A circuit capacity) to determine the number of circuits required.

$$7,200VA \div 2,400VA = 3$$

Three 20A, 120V circuits would be required to supply this assembly.

5.0.0   SHOW WINDOW LOADS

The NEC provides two options for calculating the load for show window lighting. **NEC Sections 220-3(b)(7)(b) and 220-12(a)** require a load of not less than 200VA per linear foot of show window. **NEC Section 210-62** requires one receptacle at 180VA for each 12 linear feet of show window. Since show window lighting would likely be used for more than three hours, it is considered a continuous load when using the receptacle method. The 200VA per linear foot method is not required to be increased by 125%.

Example 1:

How many receptacles would be required for a show window area that measures 67' in length?

Divide the length of show window by 12 to determine the number of receptacles required.

$67 \div 12 = 5.58$

Since **NEC Section 210-62** requires one receptacle for each 12 linear feet or major fraction thereof, six receptacles would be required.

Example 2:

What is the total load for the receptacles required in the previous example?

Multiply the number of receptacles by 180VA per receptacle and multiply the result by 125% to determine the load.

$6 \times 180VA = 1,080VA$

$1,080 \times 125\% = 1,350VA$

The load for these show window receptacles is 1,350VA.

Example 3:

What is the load for a 30' long show window?

Multiply the total length of show window area by 200VA to determine the load.

$30' \times 200VA = 6,000VA$

6.0.0   SIGN LOAD

NEC Article 600 covers requirements for signs and outline lighting. **NEC Sections 600-5(b) (1) and (2)** specify that sign circuits that supply incandescent and fluorescent lighting shall not exceed 20A, and sign circuits that supply neon tubing shall not exceed 30A. **NEC Section 600-5(a)** requires at least one 20A sign circuit that supplies no other load. This sign circuit must be provided for each commercial building and each commercial occupancy accessible to pedestrians. **NEC Section 600-5(b)(3)** requires the load for the sign circuit to be computed at a minimum of 1,200VA. Since signs for commercial occupancies are expected to operate for more than three hours at a time, the sign circuit is typically considered as a continuous load. Under this condition, the branch circuit calculation of 1,200VA is increased by 25%. The actual sign load cannot exceed 80% of the branch circuit rating.

For example, what is the maximum continuous load, in VA, which may be connected to a 20A, 120V sign circuit?

Multiply 20A by 120V to determine the total VA load for a 20A circuit.

$20A \times 120V = 2,400VA$

Multiply the result by 80% to determine the maximum continuous VA load.

$2,400VA \times 80\% = 1,920VA$

7.0.0   RESIDENTIAL BRANCH CIRCUITS

There are a number of branch circuits that are required for dwelling units. The NEC lists the requirements for these circuits including the requirements for calculating branch circuit loads for specific dwelling unit (residential) loads. These loads, which are unique to dwelling units, will be covered here.

7.1.0   SMALL APPLIANCE LOAD

NEC Sections 210-11(c) and 210-52(b) require at least two 20A small **appliance branch circuits** to be installed to supply receptacles installed in the kitchen, pantry, breakfast room, and dining room. ***NEC Section 220-16(a)*** requires that the feeder load be computed at 1,500VA for each small appliance branch circuit.

For example, what is the total feeder load for three small appliance branch circuits rated at 20A, 120V?

Multiply the number of small appliance branch circuits by 1,500VA to determine the total load.

$3 \text{ circuits} \times 1,500VA = 4,500VA$

7.2.0   LAUNDRY CIRCUIT

NEC Section 210-52(f) requires the installation of at least one receptacle to supply laundry equipment. ***NEC Section 220-16(b)*** requires that the feeder load be computed at 1,500VA for each laundry circuit.

7.3.0   DRYERS

As specified in ***NEC Section 220-18***, the load for household electric dryers is calculated at 5,000VA or the nameplate rating of the dryer, whichever is larger. ***NEC Table 220-18*** lists **demand factors** for dryers. Note that this table applies to residential dryers used in single-family dwelling units or in multi-family dwelling units. The demand factors listed do not apply to commercial dryers used in commercial facilities.

Example 1:

What is the demand load for one household electric dryer with a nameplate rating of 5,500 watts?

Per **NEC Table 220-18**, the demand factor for one dryer is 100%. Therefore, the load would be calculated as 5,500VA.

Example 2:

A new apartment building is planned. It consists of 10 dwelling units. Each unit has an electric dryer with a nameplate rating of 5,500 watts. There will be one utility transformer and one service entrance serving the building.

What is the demand load, in VA, for the 10 dryers listed above?

Per **NEC Table 220-18**, the demand factor for 10 dryers is 50%. Add the total VA for the 10 dryers and multiply the result by 50%.

10 dryers × 5,500W = 55,000VA

55,000VA × 50% = 27,500VA

7.4.0   COOKING APPLIANCES

Loads for ranges, wall-mounted ovens, counter-mounted cooking units, and other household cooking appliances are calculated using the demand factors listed in **NEC Table 220-19** and the notes to **NEC Table 220-19**. The most important single piece of information required to size the circuit for residential cooking equipment is the nameplate rating of the equipment. Although **NEC Table 220-19** lists loads in kW, **NEC Section 220-19** states that kVA shall be considered equivalent to kW for loads calculated using **NEC Table 220-19**.

Demand factors are calculated using **NEC Table 220-19** based upon the number of appliances, the maximum demand listed in Column A, and a demand factor percentage that is found using Columns B and C. Column A is used when the nameplate rating is over 8¾kW but less than 12kW. Column A is also used to calculate larger range loads per Notes 1 and 2. Column B is used when the nameplate rating is less than 3½kW. Column C is used when the nameplate rating is from 3½kW to 8¾kW. Note 3 provides a method to calculate the demand for multiple ranges, each of which has a nameplate rating of more than 1¾kW but less than 8¾kW. Note 4 provides a method to determine the size for a single branch circuit supplying one counter-mounted unit and no more than two wall-mounted ovens, provided the equipment is located in the same room.

Example 1:

What is the demand load for one range with a nameplate rating of 11.3kW?

Since the nameplate rating is greater than 8¾kW and less than 12kW, Column A is used. The demand rating for one range, not over 12kW, is listed as 8kW.

Example 2:

What is the demand load, in amps, for one range with a nameplate rating of 15.7kW, 1Ø, 240V?

Since the nameplate rating exceeds 12kW, **NEC Table 220-19, Note 1** is used. Subtract 12kW from the nameplate rating of the range to determine the number of kW exceeding 12.

$$15.7kW - 12kW = 3.7kW$$

Since .7 is a major fraction ($\geq$.5), the result is rounded off to 4kW. Multiply 5% by 4 to obtain the demand increase percentage.

$$4kW \times 5\% = 20\%$$

The maximum demand listed in Column A for one range (8kW) is then multiplied by 120% to determine the demand load for this range.

$$8kW \times 120\% = 9.6kW$$

To determine the ampacity of this load, first convert to VA (kW × 1,000), then divide VA by the circuit voltage:

$$9.6kW \times 1,000 = 9,600VA$$

$$9,600VA \div 240V = 40A$$

Example 3:

One wall-mounted oven and one counter-mounted cooking unit are to be installed in the kitchen. To reduce the cost of the electrical installation, both pieces of cooking equipment are to be connected to the same 240V, 1Ø circuit. The oven has a nameplate rating of 12.5kW and the counter-mounted unit has a nameplate rating of 8.0kW.

What is the demand load, in amps, for a single circuit to supply this cooking equipment?

NEC Table 220-19, Note 4 may be used for this calculation. First, obtain the total load by adding the nameplate ratings of the individual pieces of cooking equipment.

$$12.5kW + 8.0kW = 20.5kW$$

The equivalent of one range is 20.5kW. Using **NEC Table 220-19, Note 1**, subtract 12kW from 20.5kW to determine the number of kW exceeding 12.

$$20.5kW - 12kW = 8.5kW$$

Since .5 is a major fraction, the result is rounded off to 9kW. Multiply 5% by 9:

$$9 \times 5\% = 45\%$$

The maximum demand in Column A for one range (8kW) is then multiplied by 145% to determine the demand load.

$$8kW \times 145\% = 11.6kW$$

Divide total VA by circuit voltage to determine branch circuit ampacity.

$$11,600VA \div 240V = 48.33A$$

Example 4:

Using the resulting ampacity for the branch circuit in the previous example, what is the minimum size Type NM cable that may be used for this branch circuit and what size circuit breaker is required?

Because branch circuits of 100A or less must be terminated using the 60°C column of **NEC Table 310-16**, we will select a No. 6 copper conductor rated at 55A. A 50A circuit breaker would protect this circuit.

8.0.0   COMMERCIAL KITCHEN EQUIPMENT

Loads for commercial kitchen equipment are calculated based upon the nameplate rating of the equipment. The load is noncontinuous (100%) if operated for less than three hours at a time and continuous (125%) if operated for three hours or longer at a time. **NEC Table 220-20** lists demand factors for commercial kitchen equipment. **NEC Section 220-20** applies to commercial kitchen equipment, including cooking equipment, dishwasher booster heaters, water heaters, and other kitchen equipment.

Example 1:

What is the load, in amps, for one dishwasher booster heater? The booster heater has a nameplate rating of 15kW, 208V, 3Ø.

Under this condition, kW = kVA. Divide total kVA by voltage $\times\sqrt{3}$ (1.732).

$$15\text{kVA} \times 1{,}000 = 15{,}000\text{VA}$$

$$\frac{15{,}000\text{VA}}{208\text{V} \times 1.732} = 41.64\text{A}$$

Example 2:

What is the demand load for six pieces of commercial kitchen equipment with a total VA rating of 47,000VA?

Per *NEC Table 220-20*, the demand factor for six units is 65%. Multiply the total VA rating by 65%.

$$47{,}000\text{VA} \times 65\% = 30{,}550\text{VA}$$

The demand load is 30,550VA.

9.0.0 WATER HEATERS

As specified in *NEC Section 422-13*, fixed storage water heaters having a storage capacity of 120 gallons or less shall have the branch circuit rated at no less than 125% of the nameplate rating of the water heater.

For example, what is the minimum size circuit breaker and branch circuit conductors using Type NM cable for a water heater with a nameplate rating of 9,000VA at 240V?

Divide total VA by voltage to determine ampacity; then multiply the result by 125%.

$$9{,}000\text{VA} \div 240\text{V} = 37.5\text{A}$$

$$37.5\text{A} \times 125\% = 46.88\text{A}$$

Per *NEC Table 310-16*, 60°C column, No. 6 copper conductor is rated (for NM cable) at 55A. The circuit breaker size would be 50A.

10.0.0 ELECTRIC HEATING LOADS

NEC Article 424 covers fixed electric space heating equipment, including heating cable, unit heaters, boilers, central systems, or other approved heating equipment. This article does not apply to process heating or room air conditioning. Per *NEC Section 424-3*, branch circuits are permitted to supply any size heating equipment. If two or more outlets for heating equipment are supplied, the branch circuit size is limited to 15A, 20A, or 30A. When space heating equipment utilizes electric resistance heating elements, protection for the resistance elements shall not exceed 60A [**NEC Section 424-22(b)**]. If the equipment is rated at more than 48A, the heating elements must be subdivided and each subdivided load must not exceed 48A.

For space heating equipment consisting of resistance heating elements with or without a blower motor, the ampacity of the branch circuit shall not be less than 125% of the total load. The NEC does not require an additional increase in circuit size or conductor size for continuous load.

Example 1:

What is the minimum conductor ampacity for the following baseboard electric heaters rated 240V, 1Ø: one 1,500W unit, one 1,000W unit, and two 500W units?

First, determine the connected load by adding the load of each baseboard unit and then divide the total load in VA by the circuit voltage.

> 1,500W + 1,000W + 500W + 500W = 3,500W (VA)

> 3,500VA ÷ 240V = 14.58A

Next, multiply the load by 125% to determine the minimum conductor ampacity.

> 14.58A × 125% = 18.23A

Example 2:

What size NM conductors and circuit breaker would be required to supply the load for the previous question?

Per **NEC Table 310-16**, 60°C column, No. 12 copper conductor (for Type NM) is rated at 25A and may be connected to a 20A circuit breaker. The load, 18.23A, would require a 20A circuit breaker.

Example 3:

What is the minimum conductor ampacity for an electric forced air furnace with heating elements totaling 25kW and a blower motor with a nameplate full-load current of 4.9A? The resistance heat and the motor are rated at 240V, 1Ø.

Divide the total of the resistance heat, in VA, by the circuit voltage to determine the ampacity for the resistance heat. Add the motor ampacity to the result and multiply the total by 125% to determine total circuit ampacity.

> 25,000VA ÷ 240V = 104.17A

> 104.17A + 4.9A = 109.07A

The total circuit ampacity is 109.07A.

$$109.07A \times 125\% = 136.34A$$

Note that since this equipment is rated at more than 48A, the heating elements must be subdivided and each subdivided load cannot exceed 48A.

11.0.0 AIR CONDITIONING LOADS

Branch circuit conductors are rated at least 125% of the air conditioning compressor full-load current or the branch circuit selection current, whichever is greater, per **NEC Section 440-32**. Branch circuit selection current is determined by the equipment manufacturer and this current is required to be greater than or equal to the compressor full-load current. If the branch circuit selection current is higher, its rating shall be used instead of the compressor full-load current. Per **NEC Section 440-22(a)**, overcurrent protection devices shall not exceed 175% of the compressor full-load current or the branch circuit selection current. If this breaker is not sufficient to hold the starting current of the motor, the rating is permitted to be increased but cannot exceed 225% of the motor-rated load current or the branch circuit selection current, whichever is greater.

Example 1:

What size THHN copper conductors are required for a branch circuit supplying an air conditioner with a nameplate rating of 45A, 480V, 3Ø?

Multiply the nameplate ampacity by 125% and, using the result, select the proper THHN conductor size from **NEC Table 310-16**.

$$45A \times 125\% = 56.25A$$

NEC Table 310-16 gives an ampacity of 75A for No. 6 THHN copper. Therefore, the conductor size would be No. 6 THHN copper.

Example 2:

What size Type NM cable and circuit breaker would be required to supply an air conditioner with a nameplate rating of 16.5A, 240V, 1Ø?

Multiply the nameplate ampacity by 125% and, using the result, select the proper NM conductor size from the 60°C column of **NEC Table 310-16**.

$$16.5A \times 125\% = 20.63A$$

The 60°C column gives a rating of 25A for No. 12 copper conductors (for Type NM). Multiply the nameplate ampacity by 175% to determine the circuit breaker size.

16.5A × 175% = 28.88A

Since **NEC Section 440-22(a)** states that the rating of the overcurrent device cannot exceed 175%, a 25A circuit breaker would be required.

12.0.0   MOTOR LOADS

Branch circuit conductors and overcurrent protection devices for motors are determined by using **NEC Table 430-148** for single-phase motors and **NEC Table 430-150** for three-phase motors. To use the NEC motor tables, it is necessary to know the motor horsepower, voltage, phase, and design letter. Motor information is obtained from the motor nameplate. **NEC Section 430-6(a)(1)** requires that the values given in **NEC Tables 430-147 through 430-150** be used to determine the ampacity of branch circuit conductors and the ampere rating of switches, branch circuit short circuit and ground fault protection, etc. The motor nameplate current data is not permitted to be used in sizing these components unless otherwise specified.

To determine the branch circuit conductor size for motor circuits, the motor full-load current taken from the appropriate table is multiplied by 125% and the resulting ampacity is used to select branch circuit conductors. To determine motor full-load current using the tables, it is necessary to know the motor size in horsepower, motor voltage, and motor phase. If the motor nameplate includes a value for amps but not horsepower, **NEC Section 430-6(a)** states that the horsepower rating shall be assumed to be the value given in the tables. To assume a horsepower value, the horsepower value that most closely corresponds to the ampere value in the table is selected, using interpolation if necessary.

Example 1:

What is the motor full-load current for a 2hp, 230V, 1Ø motor?

NEC Table 430-148 is used to determine full-load current for single-phase AC motors. The left column in the table is used to find the correct motor hp and the ampacity is then determined based upon the motor voltage. A 2hp, 230V motor has a full-load current of 12A.

Example 2:

What is the motor full-load current for a 10hp, 460V, 3Ø motor?

NEC Table 430-150 is used to determine full-load current for three-phase AC motors. The left column is used to locate the motor hp and the ampacity is then obtained under the voltage column. A 10hp, 460V, 3Ø motor has a full-load current of 14A.

Example 3:

What size copper THWN branch circuit conductors would be required to supply a 25hp, 3Ø, 460V motor?

Using **NEC Table 430-150**, the full-load current for this motor is 34A. Multiply the motor full-load current by 125% to determine the minimum ampacity for branch circuit conductors.

$$34A \times 125\% = 42.5A$$

Branch circuit conductor size is then determined using **NEC Table 310-16**. No. 8 THWN copper is rated at 55A. The branch circuit conductors required to supply this 25hp motor would be No. 8 THWN copper.

Motor short circuit and ground fault protection is sized using **NEC Table 430-152**. To use this table, it is helpful to know the type of motor, horsepower, phase, motor ampacity (full-load current), and the design letter, if any.

Example 4:

What size dual-element time-delay fuse would be required for a motor with the following rating: 50hp, 3Ø, 460V, Design Letter D?

The motor full-load current is first determined using **NEC Table 430-150**. Then, using **NEC Table 430-152**, the full-load current is multiplied by the proper percentage listed for the characteristics of the motor. From **NEC Table 430-150**, the full-load current for a 50hp, 3Ø, 460V motor is 65A. From **NEC Table 430-152**, the full-load current is multiplied by 175% to select a time-delay fuse for a polyphase motor (3Ø) with a design letter other than E.

$$65A \times 175\% = 113.75A$$

Per **NEC Section 430-52(c)(1)**, the next lower standard fuse size is 110A. A fuse with a 110A rating would be used. If the 110A fuse proves to be inadequate to carry the load, **NEC Section 430-52(c)(1), Exception 1** allows the next higher size fuse to be used. In this case, the next higher size would be a 125A fuse size.

Example 5:

What size inverse-time circuit breaker would be required for a motor with the following rating: 10hp, 3Ø, 208V, Design Letter E?

The motor full-load current is 30.8A per **NEC Table 430-150**. The full-load current is multiplied by 250% per **NEC Table 430-152** to size an inverse-time circuit breaker for a 3Ø motor with Design Letter E.

$$30.8A \times 250\% = 77A$$

The next lower size circuit breaker is 70A and **_NEC Section 430-52(c)(1), Exception 1_** would permit an 80A circuit breaker if the 70A breaker is inadequate for the load.

13.0.0 WELDERS

Branch circuit conductors and overcurrent protection devices for welders are sized using the primary current and duty cycle for the welder. This information is obtained from the nameplate on the welder. Using the relevant NEC section, the multiplier (demand factor) is determined by using the nameplate duty cycle of the welder. The primary current is multiplied by the NEC multiplier to determine the ampacity that is then used to size branch circuit conductors and overcurrent protection. Typical welders include transformer arc welders, motor-generator welders, and resistance welders.

NEC Article 630 covers electric welders. Part B covers arc welders and motor-generator welders, while Part C covers resistance welders. Each NEC section lists duty cycle multipliers for individual welders based upon the type of welder. **_NEC Section 630-11(a)_** provides multipliers for arc welders and **_NEC Section 630-31(a)(2)_** provides multipliers for resistance welders.

Per **_NEC Section 630-12(a)_**, the overcurrent protection device for an individual welder branch circuit shall have a rating or setting not exceeding 200% of the primary current rating of the welder. This NEC section applies to arc welders and motor-generator welders. For resistance welders, **_NEC Section 630-32(a)_** provides that the rating or setting for the overcurrent protection device shall not exceed 300% of the primary current rating of the welder.

Note: It is advisable to check with the local inspection authority or project specifications regarding the setting or rating for welder branch circuit overcurrent protection devices. Many authorities will not permit the overcurrent device rating to exceed the rating of the branch circuit conductors.

Example 1:

What size THWN copper branch circuit conductors would be required to supply an individual arc welder with a nameplate primary current of 70A and a duty cycle of 80%?

The nameplate primary current is multiplied by .89. This multiplier is obtained from **_NEC Section 630-11(a)_** for an arc welder with a duty cycle of 80%.

70A × .89 = 62.3A

The copper THWN conductor size is selected per **_NEC Table 310-16_**. No. 6 THWN copper conductors, with a rating of 65A, would be required.

Example 2:

What size THWN copper branch circuit conductors and what size circuit breaker would be required to supply a resistance welder with a nameplate primary current of 125A and a duty cycle of 40%?

The nameplate primary current is multiplied by .63. This multiplier is obtained from **_NEC Section 630-31(a)(2)_** for an arc welder with a duty cycle of 40%.

$$125A \times .63 = 78.75A$$

Per **_NEC Table 310-16_**, No. 4 THWN conductors (85 amps) would be used. Per **_NEC Section 630-32(a)_**, the primary current is multiplied by 300% to size the overcurrent protection device. The nameplate rating for this resistance welder is 125A.

$$125A \times 300\% = 375A$$

Since this value exceeds the rating of a standard 300A overcurrent protection device, **_NEC Section 630-32_** permits the next higher standard size (400A) to be used.

SUMMARY

In order to determine the size of branch circuit overcurrent protection devices and branch circuit conductors, it is important to accurately calculate branch circuit loads using NEC requirements. When the branch circuit load is calculated, branch circuit components can be sized to safely serve the load.

NEC articles cover branch circuits ranging from lighting loads to welders. As a trainee in the electrical field, it is necessary to understand branch circuit requirements.

References

For advanced study of topics covered in this Task Module, the following books are suggested:

National Electrical Code Handbook, Latest Edition, National Fire Protection Association, Quincy, MA.

1. The general lighting load for a store is _____ VA/sq. ft.
   a. 180
   b. 4½
   c. 3½
   d. 3

2. The general lighting load (expressed as a unit load per square foot) for a warehouse is _____ VA/sq. ft.
   a. ½
   b. ¼
   c. 1
   d. 1½

3. A continuous load is defined by the NEC as a load where the maximum current is expected to continue for at least _____.
   a. 30 minutes
   b. 1 hour
   c. 8 hours
   d. 3 hours

4. What is the capacity, in amperes, for a 20A circuit breaker supplying a continuous load?
   a. 20
   b. 12
   c. 16
   d. 18

5. Branch circuit conductors supplying continuous duty loads are calculated at _____% of the rated load.
   a. 100
   b. 125
   c. 80
   d. 115

6. What is the current-carrying ampacity for each of 10 No. 10 THHN copper conductors installed in a single conduit?
   a. 20A
   b. 28A
   c. 32A
   d. 40A

7. Voltage drop shall not exceed _____% to the farthest outlet in a branch circuit.

    a. 2
    b. 3
    c. 5
    d. 10

8. The voltage drop for a 208V, 1Ø circuit with a load of 26.5A, using No. 8 stranded copper conductors at a circuit length of 145' is _____.

    a. 5.87V
    b. 5.98V
    c. 5.08V
    d. 5.18V

9. The voltage drop for a 480V, 3Ø circuit with a load of 26.5A, using No. 8 stranded copper conductors at a circuit length of 145' is _____.

    a. 5.87V
    b. 5.98V
    c. 5.08V
    d. 5.18V

10. The voltage drop for an 18A, 208V, 3Ø load with a total circuit length of 105' using No. 10 solid copper conductors is _____.

    a. 3.96V
    b. 4.57V
    c. 4.06V
    d. 4.69V

11. Load calculations for circuits supplying lighting units with ballasts are based upon _____.

    a. the total wattage of all lamps in the fixtures
    b. the circuit voltage times lamp wattage
    c. the ampere ratings of the ballasts
    d. 180VA per ballast

12. What is the total load, in amps, for a 120V circuit supplying four 150W recessed incandescent fixtures and six recessed fluorescent fixtures? (Each fluorescent ballast is rated at .65A.)

    a. 3.9A
    b. 6.07A
    c. 12.5A
    d. 8.9A

13. What is the maximum number of general-purpose noncontinuous duty duplex receptacles that can be connected to a 20A, 120V circuit in a commercial building, and what is the NEC required load rating for each receptacle?

    a.   10 receptacles; 1.5A
    b.   10 receptacles; 1.875A
    c.   16 receptacles; 150VA
    d.   13 receptacles; 180VA

14. The load for 6' of multi-outlet assembly used simultaneously is _____.

    a.   180VA per outlet
    b.   180VA per outlet times 125%
    c.   1,080VA
    d.   216VA

15. How many receptacles are required for 90 linear feet of show window area?

    a.   4
    b.   7
    c.   9
    d.   8

16. What is the total load for 55 linear feet of show window?

    a.   9,900VA
    b.   11,000VA
    c.   10,000VA
    d.   6,600VA

17. What is the total load, in VA, for two small appliance branch circuits in a single-family dwelling?

    a.   2,400VA
    b.   1,800VA
    c.   3,000VA
    d.   1,500VA

18. What is the demand load, in amps, for one household electric range with a nameplate rating of 16.75kW, 1Ø, 240V?

    a.   69.79A
    b.   41.67A
    c.   50A
    d.   33.33A

19. What is the demand load, in amps, for a single circuit supplying one wall-mounted oven rated 11.75kW, 1Ø, 240V, and a countertop cooking unit rated 9.6kW, 1Ø, 240V?

    a. 66.67A
    b. 48.33A
    c. 50A
    d. 88.96A

20. What is the demand load, in amps, for seven pieces of commercial cooking equipment with a total nameplate rating of 44.5kVA with thermostatic control operating at continuous duty? Each piece of equipment has a nameplate rating of 208V, 3Ø.

    a. 80.29A
    b. 108.08A
    c. 100.36A
    d. 123.52A

21. What is the minimum conductor ampacity for four 1,000W, 208V, 1Ø electric baseboard heaters?

    a. 24.04A
    b. 33.33A
    c. 20.83A
    d. 19.23A

22. What size THWN copper branch circuit conductors are required to supply an air conditioning unit with a nameplate rating of 33.5A, 208V, 3Ø?

    a. 10
    b. 8
    c. 6
    d. 4

23. What size time-delay fuse is required for a motor rated at 15hp, 208V, 3Ø, with a Design Letter E?

    a. 60A
    b. 80A
    c. 90A
    d. 110A

24. What is the motor full-load current for a motor rated at 5hp, 230V, and what is the minimum ampacity for branch circuit conductors?

a. 28A; 35A
b. 15.2A; 28A
c. 16.7A; 16.7A
d. 30.8A ; 28A

25. An AC nonmotor-generator arc welder on an individual circuit has a nameplate primary current of 100A and a duty cycle of 70%. The branch circuit conductors must be a minimum size _____ THHN copper.

a. No. 3
b. No. 6
c. No. 2
d. No. 4

ANSWERS TO REVIEW/PRACTICE QUESTIONS

<u>Answer</u>	<u>Section Reference</u>
1. d	1.0.0
2. b	1.0.0
3. d	1.1.0
4. c	1.1.0
5. b	1.1.0
6. a	1.2.0
7. b	1.2.2
8. b	1.2.2
9. d	1.2.3
10. a	1.2.3
11. c	2.0.0
12. d	2.1.0
13. d	3.0.0
14. c	4.0.0
15. d	5.0.0
16. b	5.0.0
17. c	7.1.0
18. b	7.4.0
19. b	7.4.0
20. a	8.0.0
21. a	10.0.0
22. b	11.0.0
23. b	12.0.0
24. a	12.0.0
25. d	13.0.0

The NCCER makes every effort to keep these manuals up-to-date and free of technical errors. We appreciate your help in this process. If you have an idea for improving this manual, or if you find an error, a typographical mistake, or an inaccuracy in the NCCER's Craft Training Manuals, please write us, using this form or a photocopy. Be sure to include the exact module number, page number, a description of the problem, and the correction, if possible. Your input will be brought to the attention of the Technical Review Committee. Thank you for your assistance.

Instructors – If you found that additional materials were necessary in order to teach this module effectively, please let us know so that we may include them in the Equipment/Materials list in the Instructor's Guide.

Write: Curriculum Development and Revision Department
National Center for Construction Education and Research
P.O. Box 141104
Gainesville, FL 32614-1104

Fax: 352-334-0932

Craft

Module Name

____

Copyright Date   Module Number   Page Number(s)

____

Description of Problem

____

____

____

____

(Optional) Correction of Problem

____

____

____

(Optional) Your Name and Address

____

____

____

Conductor Selection and Calculations

Module 26302

Electrical Trainee Task Module 26302

CONDUCTOR SELECTION AND CALCULATIONS

OBJECTIVES

Upon completion of this module, the trainee will be able to:

1. Select electrical conductors for specific applications.
2. Calculate voltage drop in both single-phase and three-phase applications.
3. Interpret and apply NEC regulations governing conductors.
4. Understand and apply NEC parallel rules.
5. Understand and apply NEC tap rules.
6. Size conductors for the load.
7. Understand and apply *NEC Tables 310-16 through 310-19*.
8. Derate conductors for fill, temperature, and voltage drop.
9. Select conductors for various temperature ranges and atmospheres.

Prerequisites

Successful completion of the following Task Modules is recommended before beginning study of this Task Module: Core Curricula; Electrical Level 1; Electrical Level 2; and Electrical Level 3, Module 26301.

Required Trainee Materials

1. Trainee Task Module
2. Appropriate Personal Protective Equipment
3. Copy of the latest edition of the *National Electrical Code*

Note: The designations "National Electrical Code," "NE Code," and "NEC," where used in this document, refer to the National Electrical Code®, which is a registered trademark of the National Fire Protection Association, Quincy, MA. *All National Electrical Code (NEC) references in this module refer to the 1999 edition of the NEC.*

COURSE MAP

This course map shows all of the modules in the third level of the Electrical curricula. The suggested training order begins at the bottom and proceeds up. Skill levels increase as a trainee advances on the course map. The training order may be adjusted by the local Training Program Sponsor.

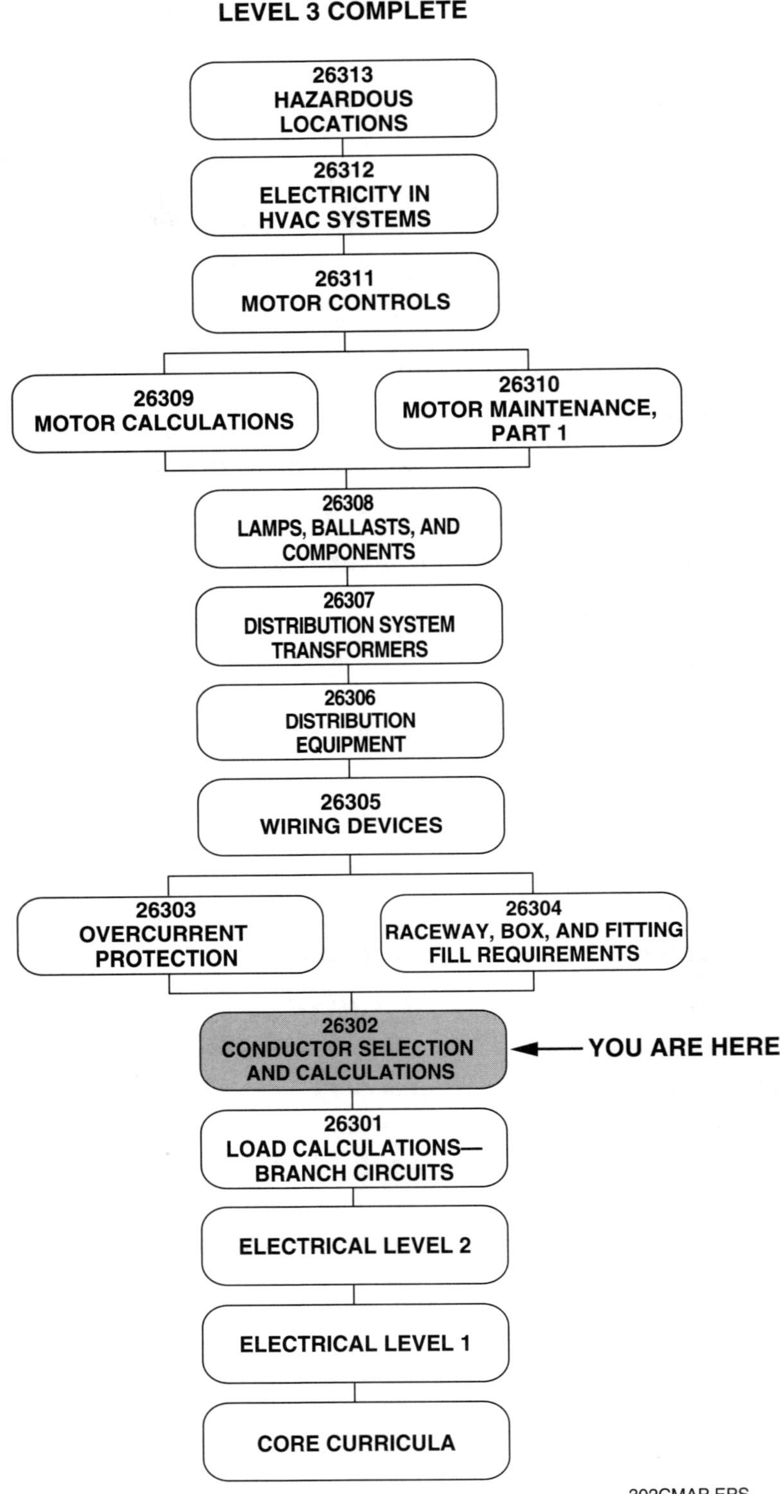

TABLE OF CONTENTS

Trade Terms Introduced In This Module

American Wire Gauge (AWG): The U.S. standard for measuring wires.

Ampacity: The current-carrying capacity of conductors or equipment, without exceeding its temperature rating, expressed in amperes.

Cable: An assembly of two or more insulated or bare wires.

1.0.0 INTRODUCTION

A variety of materials may be used to transmit electrical energy, but copper, due to its excellent cost-to-conductivity ratio, still remains the most ideal conductor. Electrolytic copper, the type used in most electrical conductors, has the following general characteristics:

- *Method of stranding* – Stranding refers to the relative flexibility of the conductor and may consist of only one strand or many strands, depending on the rigidity or flexibility required for a specific need. For example, a small-gauge wire that is to be used in a fixed installation is normally solid (one strand), whereas a wire that will be constantly flexed requires a high degree of flexibility and would contain many strands.
  - Solid wire is the least flexible form of a conductor and is merely one strand of copper.
  - Stranded refers to more than one strand in a given conductor and may vary widely, depending on size. See *Figure 1* and **NEC Chapter 9, Table 8**.
  - Flexible simply indicates that there are a greater number of strands than are found in normal stranded construction.

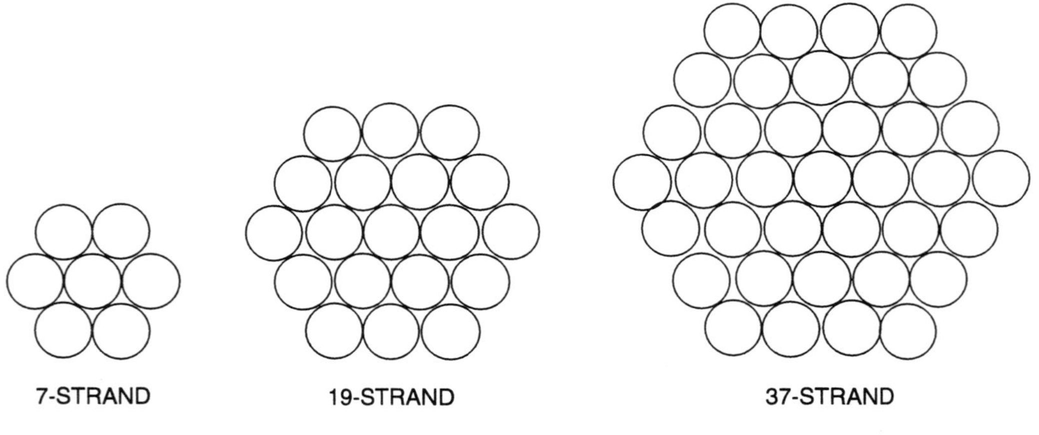

Figure 1. Common Strand Configurations

- *Degree of hardness (temper)* – Temper refers to the relative hardness of the conductor and is noted as soft drawn (SD), medium hard drawn (MHD), and hard drawn (HD). Again, the specific need of an installation will determine the required temper. Where greater tensile strength is indicated, MHD would be used over SD, and so on.

- *Bare, tinned, or coated* – Untinned copper is plain bare copper that is available in either solid or stranded types and in the various tempers just described. In this form, it is often referred to as *red copper*. Bare copper is also available with a coating of tin, silver, or nickel to facilitate soldering, impede corrosion, and prevent adhesion of the copper conductor to rubber or other types of conductor insulation. The various coatings will also affect the electrical characteristics of copper.

The **American Wire Gauge (AWG)** is used in the United States to identify the sizes of wire and **cable** up to and including No. 4/0 (0000), which is commonly pronounced in the electrical trade as *four-aught* or *four-naught*. These numbers run in reverse order as to size; that is, No. 14 AWG is smaller than No. 12 AWG and so on up to size No. 1 AWG. Up to this size (No. 1 AWG), the larger the gauge number, the smaller the size of the conductor. However, the next larger size after No. 1 AWG is No. 1/0 AWG, then 2/0 AWG, 3/0 AWG, and 4/0 AWG. At this point, the AWG designations end and the larger sizes of conductors are identified by circular mils (CM or cmil). From this point, the larger the size of wire, the larger the number of circular mils. For example, 300,000 cmil is larger than 250,000 cmil. In writing these sizes in circular mils, the *thousand* decimal is replaced by the letter *k*, and instead of writing, say, 500,000 cmil, it is usually written 500 kcmil—pronounced *five-hundred kay-cee-mil*. See *Figure 2* for a comparison of the different wire sizes.

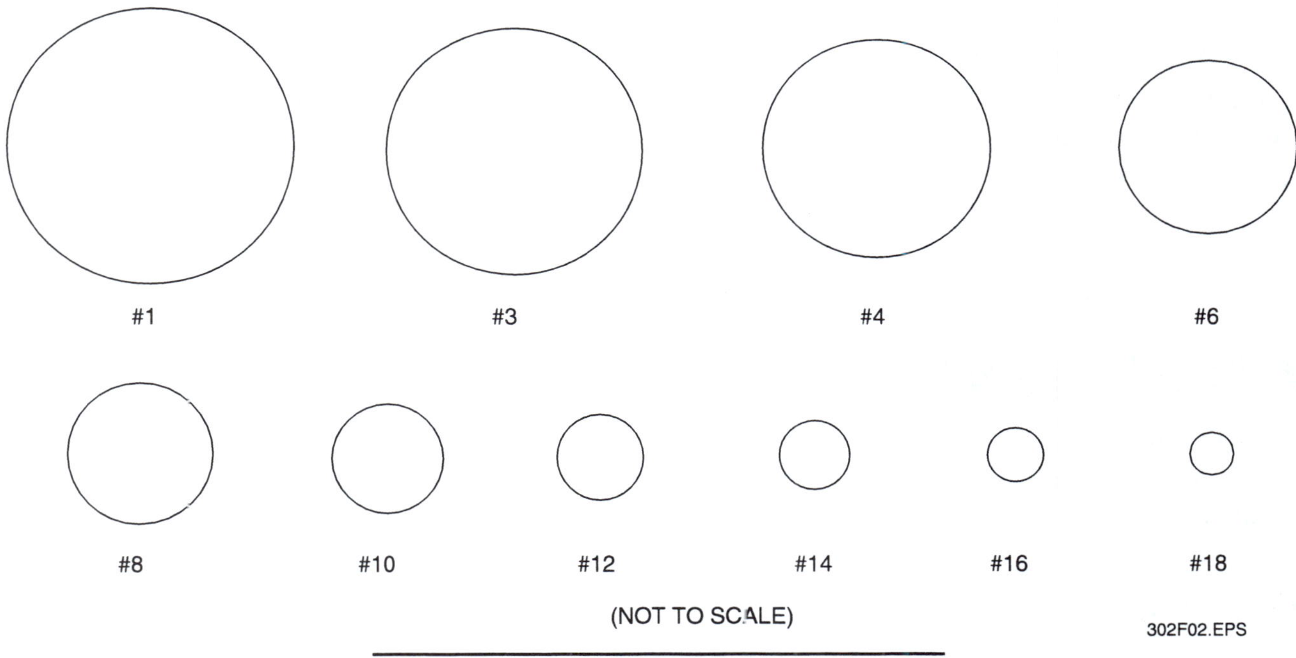

Figure 2. Comparison Of Various Wire Sizes

1.1.0   COMPRESSED CONDUCTORS

Compressed aluminum conductors are those which have been compressed so as to reduce the air space between the strands. *Figure 3* shows a cross section of a 37-strand compressed conductor.

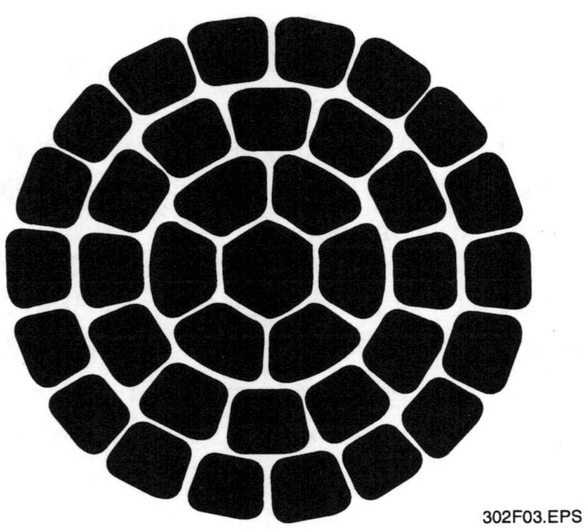

Figure 3. Cross Section Of A 37-Strand Compressed Conductor

The purpose of compressed conductors is to reduce the overall diameter of the cable so that it may be installed in a conduit that is smaller than that required for standard conductors of the same wire size. Compressed conductors are especially useful when increasing the **ampacity** of an existing service or feeder circuits.

For example, an existing service is rated at 250A and is fed with four 350 kcmil THW conductors in 3" conduit. Should it become necessary to increase the ampacity of the service to 300A, 500 kcmil THW compressed conductors may replace the 350 kcmil conductors without increasing the size of the conduit.

Both standard and compressed conductors will be covered in this module, including various types of conductor insulation and the practical applications of each type.

2.0.0   CONDUCTOR APPLICATIONS

The NEC defines a feeder as the circuit conductors between the service equipment (or other power supply source) and the final branch circuit overcurrent device. A branch circuit is defined as the circuit conductors between the final overcurrent device protecting the circuit and the outlet(s). The power riser diagram in *Figure 4* shows examples of both feeders and branch circuits.

When current-carrying conductors are used in an electrical system, the NEC requires that each ungrounded conductor be protected from damage by an overcurrent protective device such as a fuse or circuit breaker. The conductors must also be identified so that the ungrounded conductors may be distinguished from the grounded and grounding conductors. Minimum sizes or required ampacity for any of these conductors used in a circuit are selected based on NEC rules and tables. The NEC also provides tables that list the physical and electrical properties of conductors to allow the selection of the proper conductor for any application.

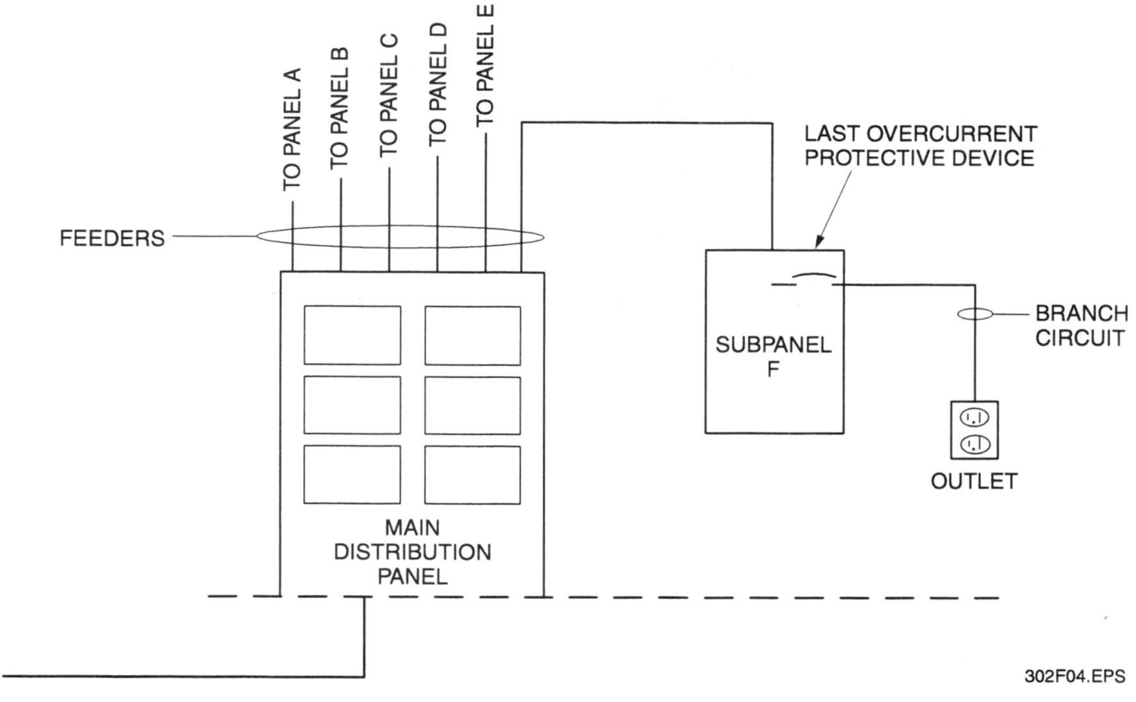

Figure 4. Power Riser Diagram Showing Feeders And Branch Circuits

NEC Section 240-3 covers the requirements for protecting conductors from excess current caused by overloads, short circuits, or ground faults. The setting or sizes of the protective device are based on the ampacity of the conductors as listed in ***NEC Tables 310-16 through 310-19***. Under certain conditions, the overcurrent device setting may be larger than the ampacity rating of the conductors as listed in the exceptions to the basic rules. For convenience, a standard rating of a fuse or circuit breaker may be used even if this rating exceeds the ampacity of the conductor as long as the rating does not exceed 800A. For example, a branch circuit with a load of 56A may be protected with a 60A overcurrent device, because 56A is not a standard overcurrent device size.

In most cases, an overcurrent device must be connected at the point where the conductor to be protected receives its supply (***NEC Section 240-21***). The most common situations are shown in *Figure 5*, which illustrates the basic rule and several exceptions, including the 10' tap rule. *Figure 6* illustrates the 25' tap rule.

Wiring systems require a grounded conductor in most installations. A grounded conductor, such as a neutral, or a grounding conductor must be identified either by the color of its insulation, by markings at the terminals, or by other suitable means (***NEC Section 200-6***). In general, a grounded conductor must have a white or natural gray finish. When this is not practical for conductors larger than No. 6 AWG, marking the terminations white is an acceptable method of identifying the conductor. Tagging is also acceptable.

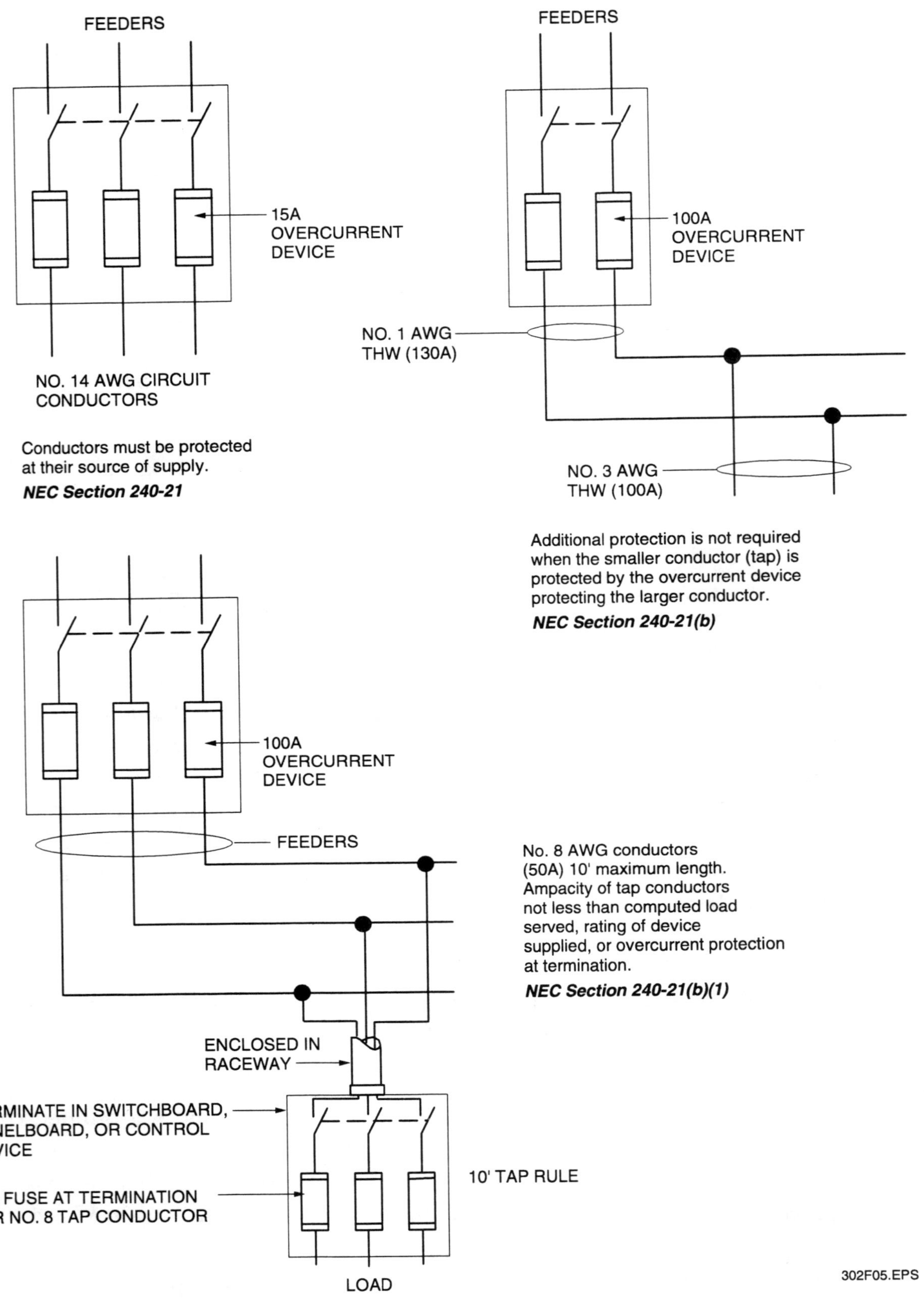

Figure 5. Location Of Overcurrent Protection In Circuits

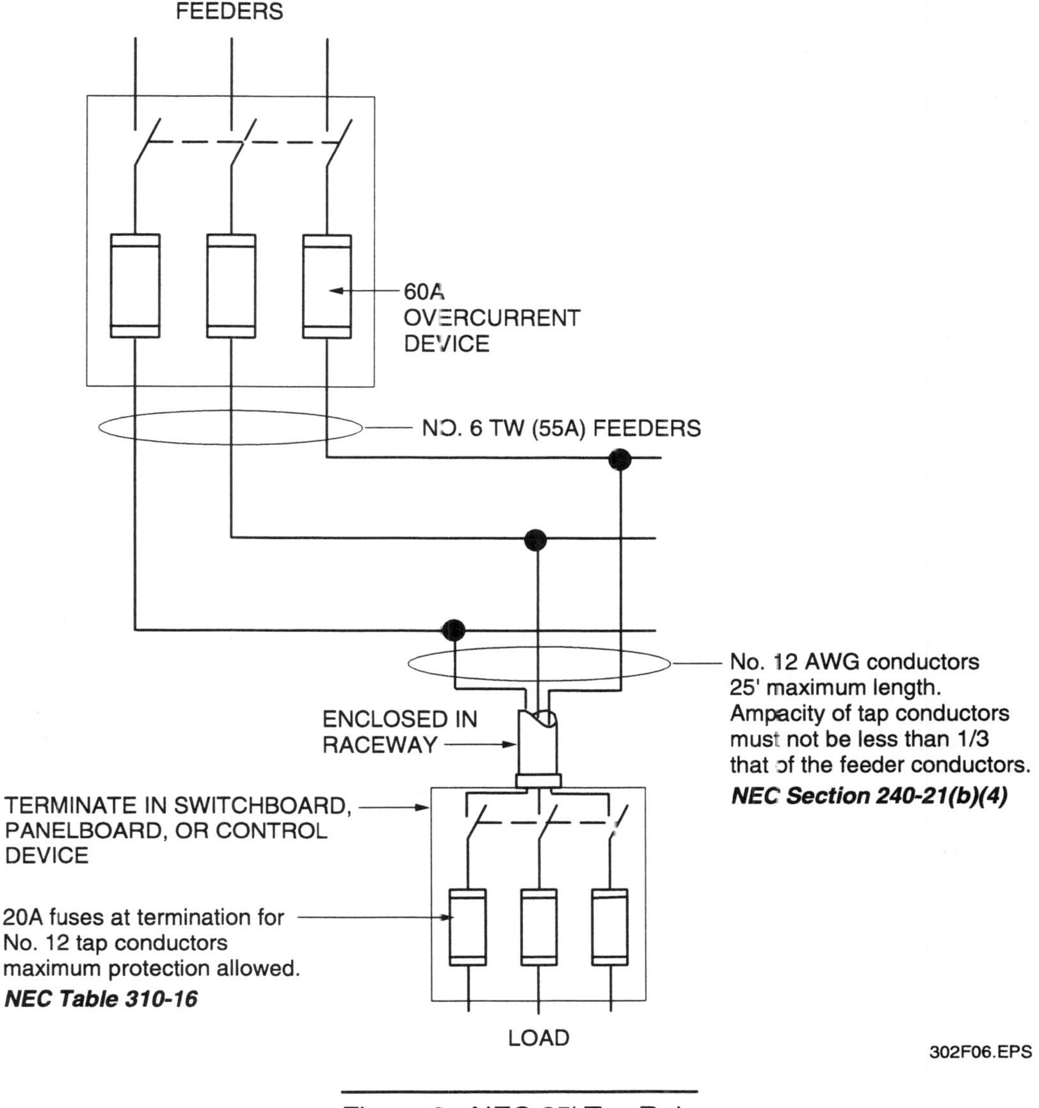

Figure 6. NEC 25' Tap Rule

2.1.0 BRANCH CIRCUITS

Now that an overview of NEC overcurrent protection has been presented, we will examine the NEC installation requirements for conductors.

In general, the ampacity (current-carrying capacity) of a conductor must not be less than the maximum load served. However, there are exceptions to this rule, namely, a branch circuit supplying a motor. Motors and motor circuits are covered in *NEC Article 430*.

The rating of the branch circuit overcurrent device determines the rating of the branch circuit (*NEC Section 210-19*). For example, if a No. 10 AWG, 30A conductor is protected by a 20A circuit breaker, then the circuit is considered a 20A branch circuit.

Furthermore, the current-carrying capacity of branch circuit conductors must not be less than the maximum load to be served. Where the branch circuit supplies receptacle outlets for use with cord- and plug-connected appliances and other utilization equipment, the conductor's ampacity must not be less than the rating of the branch circuit overcurrent device.

As mentioned previously, when the ampacity of the conductor does not match up with a standard rating of fuses or circuit breakers, the next higher standard size overcurrent device may be used, provided that the overcurrent device does not exceed 800A [***NEC Section 240-3(b)***]. This exception is not permitted, however, when the branch circuit supplies receptacles where cord- and plug-connected appliances and similar electrical equipment could be used, because too many loads plugged into the circuit could result in an overload condition. The next standard size fuse or circuit breaker may be used only when the circuit supplies a fixed load.

The allowable ampacity of conductors used on most electrical systems is found in ***NEC Tables 310-16 through 310-19***. However, the ampacities are subject to correction factors that must be applied where high ambient temperatures are encountered, that is, when the ambient temperature for the conductor location exceeds 30°C (86°F). This reduction is required even if the reduction for more than three conductors in a raceway task is also applied. For example, if six No. 10 AWG, TW current-carrying conductors are installed in a single raceway where the ambient temperature is 40°C, the ampacity of 30A must be derated or reduced to 80% because of conduit fill [***NEC Table 310-15(b)(2)(a)***] and then reduced again by a correction factor of .82 (***NEC Table 310-16***) because of the ambient temperature. Therefore, when more than three current-carrying conductors are installed in a single raceway or cable, the allowable ampacity for this condition is calculated as follows:

$$30A \times .80 \times .82 = 19.68A$$

In this situation, the listed ampacities must be reduced because of the heating effect of many current-carrying conductors in proximity. Grounding conductors are not counted as current-carrying conductors.

The rating of the branch circuit overcurrent device serving continuous loads must be not less than the noncontinuous load plus 125% of the continuous load [***NEC Section 210-20(a)***].

Note: ***NEC Article 100*** defines a continuous load as a load where the maximum current is expected to continue for three hours or more.

2.2.0 CONDUCTOR PROTECTION

According to the NEC, conductors must be installed and protected from damage (both physically and electrically). Additional requirements specify the use of boxes or fittings for certain connections, specify how connections are made to terminals, and restrict the use of parallel conductors. When conductors are installed in enclosures or raceways, additional rules apply. Finally, if conductors are installed underground, the burial depth and other installation requirements are specified by the NEC. All conductors must be protected against overcurrent in accordance with their ampacities as set forth in the NEC. They must also be protected against short circuit current damage.

According to **NEC Section 240-6**, standard overcurrent device sizes are 15A, 20A, 25A, 30A, 35A, 40A, 45A, 50A, 60A, 70A, 80A, 90A, 100A, 110A, 125A, 150A, 175A, 200A, 225A, 250A, 300A, 350A, 400A, 450A, 500A, 600A, 700A, 800A, 1,000A, 1,200A, 1,600A, 2,000A, 2,500A, 3,000A, 4,000A, 5,000A, and 6,000A. Additional standard ratings for fuses are 1A, 3A, 6A, 10A, and 601A.

Note: The small fuse ratings of 1A, 3A, 6A, and 10A were added to the NEC to provide more effective short circuit and ground fault protection for small loads.

Protection of conductors under short circuit conditions is accomplished by obtaining the maximum short circuit current available at the supply end of the conductor, the short circuit withstand rating of the conductor, and the short circuit let-through characteristics of the overcurrent device.

When a noncurrent-limiting device is used for short circuit protection, the conductor's short circuit withstand rating must be properly selected based on the overcurrent protective device's ability to protect the circuit. See *Figure 7*.

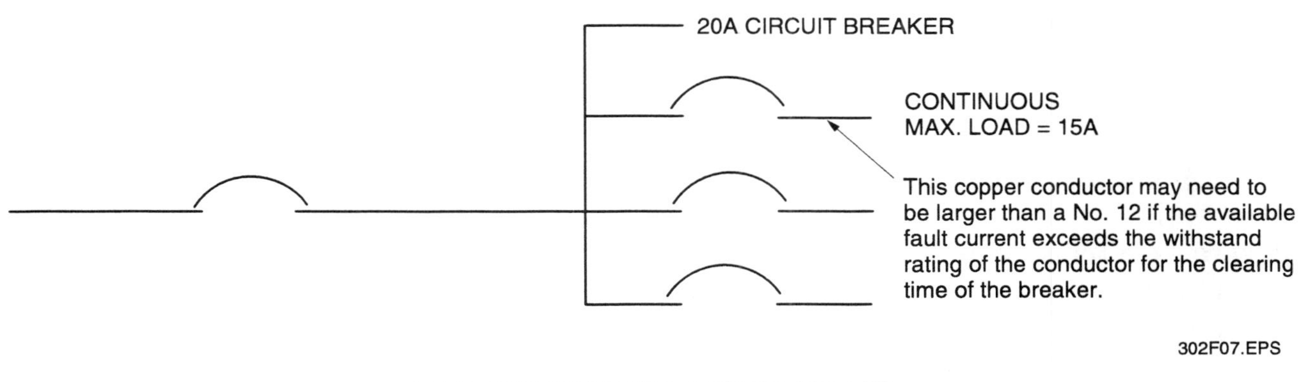

Figure 7. Noncurrent-Limiting Device

It is necessary to check the energy let-through of the overcurrent device under short circuit conditions. Select a wire size of sufficient short circuit withstand ability.

In contrast, the use of a current-limiting device permits a device to be selected which limits short circuit current to a level less than that of the conductor's short circuit withstand rating—doing away with the need for oversized ampacity conductors. See *Figure 8*.

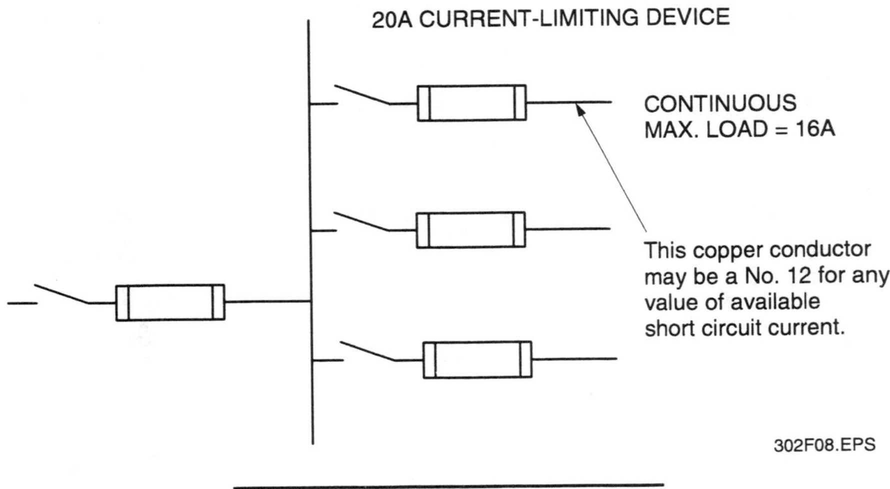

Figure 8. Current-Limiting Device

In many applications, it is desirable to use the convenience of a circuit breaker for a disconnecting means and general overcurrent protection, supplemented by current-limiting devices at strategic points in the circuits.

Flexible cords, including tinsel cords and extension cords, must be protected against overcurrent in accordance with their ampacities. Supplementary overcurrent protection is acceptable. For example, with No. 18 AWG fixture wire that is 50' in length or more, a 6A overcurrent device would provide the necessary protection. For No. 16 AWG fixture wire of 100' or more, an 8A overcurrent device would provide the necessary protection. For No. 18 AWG extension cords, a 10A overcurrent device would provide the necessary protection for a cord where only two conductors are carrying current, while a 7A overcurrent device would provide the necessary protection for a cord where three conductors are carrying current.

2.2.1 Location Of Overcurrent Protection In Circuits

In general, overcurrent protection must be installed at points where the conductors receive their supply, that is, at the beginning or line side of a branch circuit or feeder. See ***NEC Section 240-21***. Exceptions to this rule follow:

- Per ***NEC Section 240-21(b)(1)***, overcurrent protection is not required at the conductor supply if a feed tap conductor is not over 10' long; is enclosed in raceway; does not extend beyond the switchboard, panelboard, disconnecting means, or control device which it supplies; and has an ampacity not less than the combined computed loads supplied and not less than the rating of the device supplied by the tap conductors or not less than the rating of the overcurrent device at the tap conductor termination. For field-installed taps, the ampacity of the overcurrent device on the line side of the tap conductor cannot exceed 10 times the ampacity of the tap conductor.

ELECTRICAL — TRAINEE TASK MODULE 26302

- Per ***NEC Section 240-21(b)(2)***, overcurrent protection is not required at the conductor supply if a feeder tap conductor is not over 25' long; is suitably protected from physical damage; has an ampacity not less than ⅓ that of the overcurrent device protecting the feeder conductors; and terminates in a single overcurrent device.

- Per ***NEC Section 240-21(b)(3)***, overcurrent protection is not required at the conductor supply if a transformer feeder tap has primary conductors at least ⅓ ampacity and/or secondary conductors at least ⅓ ampacity when multiplied by the approximate transformer turns ratio of the overcurrent device protecting the feeder conductors; the total length of one primary plus one secondary conductor (excluding any portion of the primary conductor that is protected at its ampacity) is not over 25' in length; the secondary conductors terminate in a single overcurrent device rated at the ampacity of the tap conductors; and if the primary and secondary conductors are suitably protected from physical damage.

- Per ***NEC Section 240-21(b)(4)***, overcurrent protection is not required at the conductor supply in high bay manufacturing buildings over 35' high at walls when only qualified persons will service such a system; if the tap conductors are not over 25' long horizontally and not over 100' long total length; the ampacity of the tap conductors is not less than ⅓ of the rating of the overcurrent device protecting the feeder conductors; terminate in a single overcurrent device; are suitably protected from physical damage or are enclosed in a raceway; are at least No. 6 AWG copper or No. 4 AWG aluminum; are continuous from end-to-end and contain no splices; do not penetrate walls, floors, or ceilings; and are made no less than 30' from the floor.

WARNING!   Smaller conductors tapped to larger conductors can be a serious hazard. If not protected against short circuit conditions, these unprotected conductors can vaporize or incur severe insulation damage.

- Per ***NEC Section 240-21(c)(3)***, transformer secondary conductors of separately derived systems do not require overcurrent protection at the transformer terminals if they are installed in an industrial location; have secondary conductors that are less than 25' long; if the secondary conductor ampacity is at least equal to the secondary full-load current of the transformer and the sum of all terminating, grouped overcurrent devices; and if they are protected from physical damage.

Note: Switchboard and panelboard protection, along with transformer protection, must still be observed. See ***NEC Sections 384-16 and 450-3***.

Various NEC tables define the physical and electrical properties of conductors. Electricians use these tables to select the type of conductor and the size of conduit, or other raceway, to enclose the conductors in specific applications. NEC tables list the properties of conductors as follows:

- Name
- Operating temperature
- Application
- Insulation
- Physical properties
- Electrical resistance
- AC resistance and reactance

NEC Table 310-13 lists the name, maximum operating temperature, applications, and insulation of various types of conductors, while ***NEC Chapter 9, Table 8*** gives the physical properties and electrical resistance.

To gain an understanding of these tables and how they are used in practical applications, we will take a 4/0 THHN copper conductor and see what properties may be determined from the NEC tables.

Step 1   Turn to ***NEC Table 310-13*** and scan down the second column from the left *(Type Letter)* until THHN is found. Scan to the left in this row to see that the trade name of this conductor is heat-resistant thermoplastic.

Step 2   Scanning to the right in this row, note that the maximum operating temperature for this wire type is 90°C (194°F). Continuing to the right in this row, under the column headed *Application Provisions*, we find that this wire type is suitable for use in dry and damp locations. The next column reveals that the insulation is flame-retardant, heat-resistant thermoplastic.

Step 3   Continuing to the right in this row, the next column lists insulation thickness for various AWG or kcmil wire sizes. The insulation thicknesses for Type THHN wire, from No. 14 AWG to 1,000 kcmil, are as follows:

- 14 – 12   15 mils
- 10   20 mils
- 8 – 6   30 mils
- 4 – 2   40 mils
- 1 – 4/0   50 mils
- 250 – 500   60 mils
- 501 – 1,000   70 mils

Consequently, the insulation thickness for 4/0 THHN is 50 mils.

Step 4   Looking in the right-most column (*Outer Covering*), we see that this wire type has a nylon jacket or equivalent.

If it is desired to find the maximum current-carrying capacity of this conductor when used in a raceway, turn to *NEC Table 310-16* and proceed as follows:

Step 1   Scan down the left-hand column until the wire size is found.

Step 2   Scan to the right in this row until the 90°C column is found. This column covers the insulation types that are rated for 90°C maximum operating temperature and includes Type THHN conductor insulation.

Step 3   Note that the current-carrying rating for this size and type of conductor is 260A. This rating, however, is for not more than three conductors in a raceway. If we have more than three conductors, such as four conductors in a three-phase, four-wire feeder to a subpanel, this figure (260A) must be derated as described below.

Step 4   Refer to *NEC Section 310-15(b)(2)(a)*, which states that where the number of current-carrying conductors in a raceway or cable exceed three, the allowable ampacites shall be reduced as shown in *Table 1*.

Number of Current-Carrying Conductors	Percent of Values in Tables as Adjusted for Ambient Temperature, if Necessary
4 through 6	80
7 through 9	70
10 through 20	50
21 through 30	45
31 through 40	40
41 and above	35

Table 1. Allowable Ampacities For Current-Carrying Conductors

Since we want to know the allowable maximum current-carrying capacity of four 4/0 THHN conductors in one raceway, it is necessary to multiply the previous amperage (260A) by 80% or 0.80.

260 × .80 = 208A

These amperage tables are also based on the conductors being installed in areas where the ambient air temperature is 30°C (86°F). If the conductors are installed in areas with different ambient temperatures, a further deduction is required. For example, if this same set of four 4/0 THHN conductors were installed in an industrial area where the ambient temperature averaged 35°C, we would look in the correction factor tables at the bottom of **NEC Tables 310-16 through 310-19**. In doing so, we would find that the correction or derating factor for our situation is .96. Consequently, our present current-carrying capacity of 208A must be multiplied by 0.96 to obtain the actual current-carrying capacity of the four conductors:

$$208 \times .96 = 199.68A$$

Other sizes and types of conductors are handled in a similar manner; that is, find the appropriate table, determine the listed ampacity, and then multiply this ampacity by the appropriate factors in the correction factor tables.

It sometimes becomes necessary to know additional properties of conductors for some conductor calculations, especially for voltage drop calculations which will appear in a later section in this module. There are many useful tables in **NEC Chapter 9**. Examples of their practical use will be presented later in this module.

3.1.0   IDENTIFYING CONDUCTORS

The NEC specifies certain methods of identifying conductors used in wiring systems of all types. For example, the high leg of a 120/240V, grounded three-phase delta system must be marked with an orange color for identification; a grounded conductor must be identified either by the color of its insulation, by markings at the terminals, or by other suitable means. Unless allowed by NEC exceptions, a grounded conductor must have a white or natural gray finish. When this is not practical for conductors larger than No. 6 AWG, marking the terminals white is an acceptable method of identifying the conductors.

3.1.1   Color-Coding

Conductors contained in cables are color-coded so that identification may be easily made at each access point. *Table 2* lists the color-coding for cables up through four-wire cable. Although some control wiring and communication cables contain 60, 80, or more pairs of conductors using a combination of colors, the ones listed are the most common.

When conductors are installed in raceway systems, any color insulation is permitted for the ungrounded phase conductors except the following:

- White or gray, which is reserved for use as the grounded circuit conductor
- Green, which is reserved for use as a grounding conductor only

3.1.2   Changing Colors

Should it become necessary to change the actual color of a conductor to meet NEC requirements or to facilitate maintenance on circuits and equipment, the conductors may be reidentified with colored tape or paint.

Number of Conductors in Cable	Color of Conductors
Two-wire cable	One black (ungrounded phase conductor) One white (grounded conductor)
Two-wire cable with ground	One black (ungrounded phase conductor) One white (grounded conductor) One bare (equipment grounding conductor)
Three-wire cable	One black (ungrounded phase conductor) One white (grounded conductor) One red (ungrounded phase conductor)
Three-wire cable with ground	One black (ungrounded phase conductor) One white (grounded conductor) One red (ungrounded phase conductor) One bare (equipment grounding conductor)
Four-wire cable	One black (ungrounded phase conductor) One white (grounded conductor) One red (ungrounded phase conductor) One blue (ungrounded phase conductor)
Four-wire cable with ground	One black (ungrounded phase conductor) One white (grounded conductor) One red (ungrounded phase conductor) One blue (ungrounded phase conductor) One bare (equipment grounding conductor)

Table 2. Common Color-Coding Of Conductor Cables

For example, assume that a two-wire cable containing a black and white conductor is used to feed a 240V, two-wire, single-phase motor. Since the white-colored conductor is supposed to be reserved for the grounded conductor, and none is required in this circuit, the white conductor may be marked with a piece of black tape at each end of the circuit so that everyone will know that this wire is not a grounded conductor.

4.0.0 VOLTAGE DROP

In all electrical systems, the conductors should be sized so that the voltage drop never exceeds 3% for power, heating, and lighting loads or combinations of these. Furthermore, the maximum total voltage drop for conductors, feeders, and branch circuits combined should never exceed 5%. These percentages are recommended by the NEC but are not requirements. However, it is considered to be good practice to incorporate these percentages into every electrical installation.

In some applications, such as for circuits feeding hospital x-ray equipment, the voltage drop is even more critical—requiring a maximum of 2% voltage drop throughout. With the higher ratings on the newer types of insulation, it is extremely important to keep volt loss in mind; otherwise, some very unsatisfactory problems are likely to be encountered.

For example, the resistance and voltage drop on long conductor runs may be great enough to seriously interfere with the efficient operation of the connected equipment. Resistance elements, such as those used in incandescent lamps and electric heating units, are particularly critical in this respect; a drop of just a few volts greatly reduces their efficiency.

Electric motors are not affected by small voltage variations to the same degree as pure resistance loads, but motors will not operate at their rated horsepower if the voltage is below that at which they are rated. When loaded motors are operated at reduced voltage, the current flow actually increases, as it requires more amperes to produce a given wattage and horsepower at low voltage than at normal voltage. This current increase is also caused by the fact that the opposition of the motor windings to current flow decreases as the motor speed decreases.

From the foregoing, we can see that it is very important to have all conductors of the proper size to avoid excessive heating and voltage drop, and that, in the case of long runs, it is necessary to determine the wire size by consideration of resistance and voltage drop, rather than by the heating effect or *NEC Tables 310-16 through 310-19* alone.

To solve the ordinary problems of voltage drop requires only a knowledge of a few simple facts about the areas and resistances of conductors and the application of a few mathematical equations.

Note: The actual conductor used must also meet the other sizing requirements such as full-load current, ambient temperature, number in a raceway, etc.

4.1.0   WIRE SIZES BASED ON RESISTANCE

Earlier modules covered wire sizes and how conductors are normally specified in kcmil or AWG sizes. This numbering system was originated by the Brown & Sharpe Company and was originally called the *B & S gauge*. However, the B & S gauge quickly evolved into the American Wire Gauge (AWG) and is now standard in the United States for indicating sizes of round wires and conductors.

AWG numbers are arranged according to the resistance of the wires, with the larger numbers representing the wires of greatest resistance and smallest area. A handy rule to remember is that decreasing the gauge by three numbers gives a wire of approximately twice the area and half the resistance. Conversely, increasing the gauge by three numbers gives a wire of approximately half the area and twice the resistance.

For example, if we increase the wire gauge from No. 3 AWG, which has a resistance of 0.245 ohm per 1,000', to a No. 6 AWG, we find it has a resistance of 0.491 ohm per 1,000', which is about double. See **NEC Chapter 9, Table 8**.

Although **NEC Chapter 9, Table 8** only lists sizes down to No. 18 AWG, the American Wire Gauge numbers range from 0000 (4/0) down in size to No. 60. The 4/0 conductor is more than ½" in overall diameter and the No. 60 is as fine as a thin hair.

The most common sizes used for light and power installations range from 4/0 to No. 14 AWG. Lighting fixture wires are frequently size No. 16 or No. 18 AWG, and low-voltage control wiring sometimes drops down to size No. 22 AWG.

4.1.1 Circular Mil — Unit Of Conductor Area

In addition to AWG gauge numbers, a unit called the *mil* is also used for measuring the diameter and area of conductors. The mil is equal to $\frac{1}{1000}$ of an inch, so it is small enough to measure and express these sizes very accurately. For example, instead of saying a wire has a diameter of .055", or fifty-five thousandths of an inch, we can simply call it *55 mils*. Consequently, a wire of 250 mils in diameter is also .250", or ¼" in diameter.

Since the resistance and current-carrying capacity of conductors both depend on their cross-sectional area, a unit is necessary to express this area. Electrical conductors are commonly made in several different shapes (*Figure 9*). For square conductors, such as busbars, the square mil is used, which is a square $\frac{1}{1000}$ of an inch on each side. For round conductors, the circular mil unit is used, which is the area of a circle with a diameter of $\frac{1}{1000}$ of an inch.

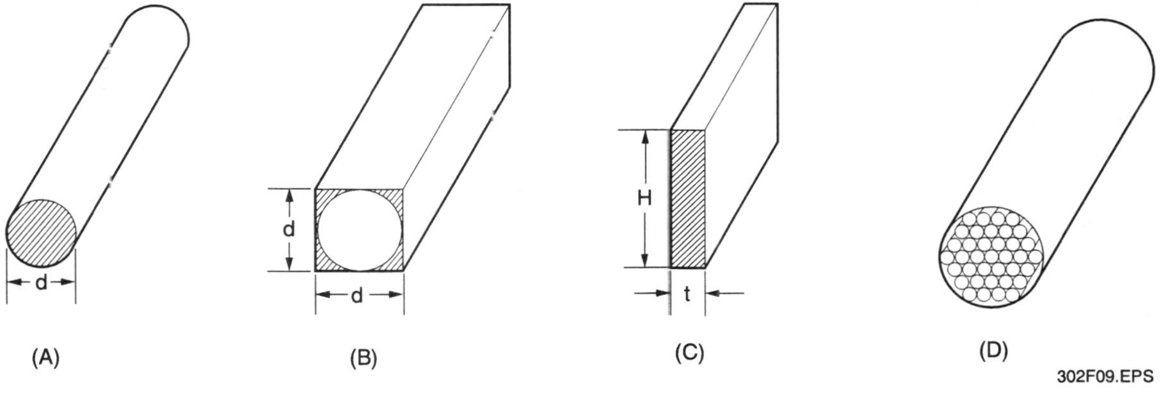

Figure 9. Electrical Conductors Are Commonly Made In Several Different Shapes

These units greatly simplify conductor calculations. For example, to determine the area of a square conductor, as shown in *Figure 9(B)*, multiply one side by the other, measuring the sides in either mils or thousandths of an inch.

To obtain the area of a round conductor in circular mils, square the diameter in mils or thousandths of an inch.

Note: To square a number, multiply the number by itself.

4.1.2 Conversion Of Square Mils To Circular Mils

When comparing round and square conductors, remember that the square mil and the circular mil are not quite the same units of area. For example, see *Figure 9(B)*, which shows a circle within a square. While the circle has the same diameter as the square, the corners of the square make it larger in area. From this, we can say that the area of one circular mil is less than that of one square mil. The actual ratio between the two is .7854, or the circle has only 78.54% of the area of a square of the same diameter. Consequently, if it is desired to find the circular mil area from the number of square mils, divide the square mils by .7854. If the reverse were true, that is, finding the square mil area from circular mils, multiply the circular mils by .7854.

For example, if the conductor in *Figure 9(A)* is a No. 4/0 conductor with a diameter of 460 mils, what is its area in both circular mils and square mils?

Circular mil area = 460 × 460 = 211,600 circular mils
Square mil area = 211,600 × .7854 = 166,190.64 square mils

If the busbar in *Figure 9(C)* is 1½" high and ¼" thick, what is its area in square mils, and what size of round conductor would be necessary to carry the same current as this busbar? First, the dimensions of a ¼" × 1½" busbar, stated in mils, are 250 mils × 1,500 mils. Therefore, the area in square mils may be determined by the following equation:

250 × 1,500 = 375,000 square mils

To find this area in circular mils, divide the square mil area (375,000) by .7854; the results are as follows:

$$\frac{375,000}{.7854} = 477,463.7 \text{ circular mils}$$

The nearest standard size to this is a round conductor 500,000 circular mils in size (500 kcmil).

Busbars of the shape shown in *Figure 9(C)* are commonly used in panelboards and switchgear. These bars normally range in thickness from .250" to .375" or more, and in heights from 1" to 12".

Stranded conductors such as the one shown in *Figure 9(D)* are used on all conductor sizes No. 6 AWG and larger. Since these conductors are not solid throughout, their area cannot be determined accurately by squaring their diameter. This diameter also varies somewhat with the twist or *lay* of the strands.

To determine the cross-sectional area of such conductors, first determine the area of each strand, either from a wire table or by calculation from its diameter, and then multiply this by the number of strands to get the total area of the cable in circular mils. ***NEC Chapter 9, Table 8*** can also be used to find the area of most conductors in circular mils. It also provides information necessary for other wiring calculations.

4.2.0   RESISTANCE OF CONDUCTORS

It is often necessary to determine the exact resistance of a conductor of a certain length in order to calculate the voltage drop under a certain current load.

The resistance per 1,000' of various conductors can be obtained from ***NEC Chapter 9, Table 8***. These conductor specifications are necessary to accurately determine the voltage drop for various sizes of conductors.

For example, to find the total resistance of a 120V, two-wire circuit consisting of two No. 10 AWG solid copper conductors, each 150' long, proceed as follows:

Step 1   The length of one conductor (150') must first be multiplied by 2 to obtain the entire length of both conductors:

$$2 \times 150' = 300'$$

Step 2   Refer to ***NEC Chapter 9, Table 8*** to find the resistance of No. 10 solid copper wire. The table gives a resistance of 1.21 ohms per 1,000' for uncoated copper wire at 75°C.

Step 3   Since our circuit is less than 1,000', we must determine the resistance of 300'. This is accomplished by dividing the actual footage (300' in this case) by 1,000'.

$$\frac{300'}{1,000'} = .30$$

Step 4   Multiply this result (.30) times the resistance of 1.21Ω:

$$.30 \times 1.21\Omega = 0.363\Omega$$

In another situation, it is desired to install an outside 120V, two-wire line between two buildings a distance of 1,650' using No. 1 AWG copper wire. What would be the total resistance of this circuit?

Step 1   Determine the total length of both conductors by multiplying the length (one way) by 2:

$$1,650' \times 2 = 3,300'$$

Step 2   Referring again to ***NEC Chapter 9, Table 8***, we see that No. 1 AWG uncoated copper wire has a resistance of 0.154 ohm per 1,000'.

Step 3 The total length of 3,300' must be divided by 1,000'.

$$\frac{3,300'}{1,000'} = 3.3$$

Step 4 Multiply this result (3.3) times the resistance found in **NEC Chapter 9, Table 8** (0.154Ω).

$$3.3 \times 0.154\Omega = .5082\Omega$$

Now we will see what happens if we apply the full current to these conductors allowed by **NEC Table 310-16**. Assuming that Type THHN conductors are used, **NEC Table 310-16** allows a maximum load on these conductors of 150A at 90°C. (Always use the 90°C column in this table when derating conductors.) If this much current flowed through this circuit for a distance of 3,300' (both ways), the voltage drop in the circuit would be:

$$\begin{aligned} \text{Voltage drop} &= I \times R \\ &= 150A \times .5082\Omega \\ &= 76.2V \end{aligned}$$

If the initial voltage is only 120V, this means that the voltage at the far end of the circuit will be only 120V − 76.2V or 43.8V and few, if any, 120V loads will operate at this low voltage. Consequently, the load will have to be reduced to make this circuit of any use.

Our goal is to keep the voltage drop within 3% of the original voltage. Therefore, since the original voltage is 120V, the allowable voltage drop may be found by using the following equation:

$$120V \times .03 = 3.6V$$

Now, what size load may be applied to this circuit to stay within this 3% range? The equation for finding the maximum current on this circuit to keep the voltage drop within 3% or 3.6V is as follows:

$$\text{Maximum current (I)} \times \text{total resistance } (\Omega) = \text{original voltage (V)} \times \text{allowable voltage drop \%}$$

Substituting our known values in this equation, we have:

$$I \times .5082\Omega = 3.6V$$

To solve for I, we divide both sides of the equation by .5082, which results in the following:

$$I = \frac{3.6V}{.5082\Omega} = 7.084A$$

Therefore, to keep the voltage drop within 3% for this length of circuit with only 120V applied, the amperage must be held to 7.084A or below.

If a larger load is connected to this circuit, and it is desired to hold the voltage drop to within 3%, then either a larger conductor will have to be used, or else the voltage will have to be increased. For example, assume that this circuit feeds a 120/240V dual-voltage pump motor. If the motor connections were rewired to accept a 240V branch circuit, then the allowable voltage drop (at 3%) would be:

$$.03 \times 240V = 7.2V$$

Continuing as before:

$$I \times \frac{7.2V}{.5082} = 14.17A$$

If 480V were applied to the circuit, the amperage would again double. These examples should show why long electric transmission lines utilize extremely high voltages—up to 250,000V or more—to keep the current, resulting voltage drop, and conductor size to the bare minimum.

4.3.0   RESISTANCE OF COPPER PER MIL FOOT

In many cases, it may be necessary to calculate the resistance of a certain length of wire or a busbar of a given size.

This can be done very easily if the unit resistance of copper is known. In doing so, a unit called the *mil foot* may be used. A mil foot represents a piece of round wire that is 1 mil in diameter and 1' in length, and is a small enough unit to be very accurate for all practical calculations. A round wire of 1 mil in diameter has an area of 1 circular mil, as the diameter multiplied by itself or *squared*, is:

$$1 \times 1 = 1 \text{ circular mil}$$

The resistance of ordinary copper is 12.9Ω per mil foot. This constant is important and should be remembered.

Suppose it is desired to determine the resistance of a piece of No. 12 copper wire that is 50' long. We know that the resistance of any conductor increases as its length increases, and decreases as its area increases. So, for a wire that is 50' long, we first multiply, and get $50' \times 12.9\Omega = 645\Omega/\text{mil ft.}^2$, which would be the resistance of a wire that is 1 circular mil in area and 50' long. Then we find in **NEC Chapter 9, Table 8** that the area of a No. 12 wire is 6,530 circular mils, which will reduce the resistance in proportion. So we now divide:

$$\frac{645}{6,530} = .0988\Omega/\text{mil ft.}^2$$

In another case, we wish to find the resistance of a coil containing 3,000' of No. 18 stranded wire. We would first multiply, and get 3,000' × 12.9Ω = 38,700Ω/mil ft.², and, as the area of No. 18 wire is 1,620 circular mils, the total resistance may be found using the following equation:

$$\frac{38,700}{1,620} = 23.89\Omega$$

Checking this with **NEC Chapter 9, Table 8**, we find a resistance of 7.95Ω per 1,000' for No. 18 stranded AWG wire. For 3,000', we use the following equation:

$$3 \times 7.95\Omega = 23.85\Omega$$

The small difference between this answer and the one obtained by the first calculation is caused by using approximate figures instead of lengthy decimal places.

The mil foot unit and its resistance of 12.9 for copper may also be used to calculate the resistance of square busbars by simply using the figure .7854 to change from square mils to circular mils.

Suppose we wish to find the resistance of a square busbar that is ¼" × 2" and 100' long. The dimensions in mils will be 250 × 2,000 = 500,000 square mils. Then, to find the circular mil area, we divide 500,000 by .7854 and get 636,618.3 circular mils. Then, we multiply, and get 100' × 12.9Ω = 1,290Ω, or the resistance of 100' of copper that is 1 mil in area. As the area of this bar is 636,618.3 circular mils, we divide:

$$\frac{1,290\Omega}{636,618.3} = .002026\Omega \text{ total resistance}$$

NEC Tables 310-16 through 310-19 list the allowable current-carrying capacities of conductors with various types of insulation. These tables, however, do not take into consideration the length of the conductors or the voltage drop. Consequently, it is often necessary to use a larger size conductor than is indicated in the tables.

4.4.0   EQUATIONS FOR VOLTAGE DROP USING CONDUCTOR AREA OR CONDUCTOR RESISTANCE

The size of the conductor required to connect an electrical load to the source of supply is determined by several factors, including:

*   Load current in amperes
*   Permissible voltage drop between source and load
*   Total length of conductor
*   Type of wire (i.e., copper, aluminum, copper-clad aluminum, etc., and its permissible load-carrying capability based on **NEC Tables 310-16 though 310-19**)

To perform voltage drop calculations, it is also necessary to recall the following:

- The resistance of a wire varies directly with its length:

  R = resistance per foot (K) × length in feet (L)

- The resistance varies inversely with its cross-sectional area:

  $$R = \frac{1}{A}$$

Combining both statements, we obtain the following equation:

$$R = \frac{L \times K}{A}$$

Where:

    A = wire size (First from **NEC Tables 310-16 through 310-19** for a given load, and then, if necessary, from **NEC Chapter 9, Table 8** for circular mils)
    L = length of wire in feet
    R = total resistance of wire
    K = resistance per mil foot

K is a constant whose value depends upon the units chosen and the type of wire (12.9 for copper and 21.2 for aluminum). Using the foot as the unit of length and the circular mil as the unit of area, the values for K represent the resistance in ohms per mil foot.

The length (L) in the above equation is the total length of a single current-carrying conductor. For a two-conductor, 120V circuit or a 240V, balanced three-wire circuit (neutral current equals zero), the length in the equation must be multiplied by 2. The equation now becomes:

$$R = \frac{2 \times L \times K}{A} \quad \text{for single-phase circuits}$$

For a three-phase, four-wire balanced circuit with a power factor near the value of 1, the equation must be multiplied by $\sqrt{3} \div 2$. (The value of $\sqrt{3}$ is approximately 1.732; you may wish to make a note of this for use in future calculations.) The equation now becomes:

$$R = \frac{\sqrt{3}}{2} \times \frac{2 \times L \times K}{A}$$

The 2's cancel each other out and the equation reduces to:

$$R = \frac{\sqrt{3} \times L \times K}{A} \quad \text{for three-phase balanced circuits}$$

Since R = E ÷ I (where E = voltage drop [VD]), substitute VD ÷ I for R in the above equations:

$$\frac{VD}{I} = \frac{2 \times L \times K}{A} \text{ for single-phase circuits}$$

and

$$\frac{VD}{I} = \frac{\sqrt{3} \times L \times K}{A} \text{ for three-phase balanced circuits}$$

Multiply each side of both equations by I:

$$VD = \frac{2 \times L \times K \times I}{A} \text{ for single-phase circuits}$$

and

$$VD = \frac{\sqrt{3} \times L \times K \times I}{A} \text{ for three-phase balanced circuits}$$

Substitute circular mils (CM) for A where CM is initially determined from the wire size ampacities listed in **NEC Tables 310-16 through 310-19** for the desired load and where **NEC Chapter 9, Table 8** is used to convert the wire size so determined to circular mils, if required. The equations become:

$$VD = \frac{2 \times L \times K \times I}{CM} \text{ for single-phase circuits}$$

and

$$VD = \frac{\sqrt{3} \times L \times K \times I}{CM} \text{ for three-phase balanced circuits}$$

You should recognize the above equations as the same ones used to calculate voltage drop for branch circuits in the previous module. Using an exercise similar to the one above, the following equations (also used in the previous module) can be derived for a given wire size resistance and load:

$$VD = \frac{2 \times L \times R \times I}{1,000} \text{ for single-phase circuits}$$

and

$$VD = \frac{\sqrt{3} \times L \times R \times I}{1,000} \text{ for three-phase balanced circuits}$$

4.5.0   USE OF VOLTAGE DROP EQUATIONS

If it is desired to determine the voltage drop on either an existing 120V, two-wire installation or a proposed project, the voltage drop of the circuit may be found by using one of the above single-phase formulas:

$$VD = \frac{2 \times L \times K \times I}{CM}$$

For example, assume we have a 120V, two-wire circuit feeding a total load of 30A and the branch circuit length is 120'.

NEC Table 310-16 allows a No. 10 AWG conductor at 60°C to carry this load. Referring to ***NEC Chapter 9, Table 8***, we find that the area (A) of a No. 10 AWG conductor is 10,380 circular mils. Then, substituting these values and a value of 12.9 (copper) for K in the equation, we have:

$$VD = \frac{2 \times 120' \times 12.9 \times 30A}{10,380}$$

$$VD = 8.95V$$

The voltage at the load is 120V − 8.95V = 111.05V, which is usually not acceptable on most installations since it exceeds the 3% recommended maximum voltage drop; that is, 3% of 120 = 3.6V. In fact, it is more than double. There are three ways to correct this situation:

- Reduce the load
- Increase the conductor size
- Increase the voltage

4.5.1   Miscellaneous Voltage Drop Equations

The final voltage drop (VD) equations discussed earlier can be solved for length (L), yielding the following equations:

$$L = \frac{VD \times CM}{2 \times K \times I} \quad \text{or} \quad L = \frac{1,000 \times VD}{2 \times R \times I} \quad \text{for single-phase circuits}$$

and

$$L = \frac{VD \times CM}{\sqrt{3} \times K \times I} \quad \text{or} \quad L = \frac{1,000 \times VD}{\sqrt{3} \times R \times I} \quad \text{for three-phase balanced circuits}$$

These equations can be used to determine the maximum circuit length for a specified voltage drop at a given load using a wire size selected from ***NEC Tables 310-16 through 310-19*** for the ampacity of the load. ***NEC Chapter 9, Table 8*** may be used to convert the selected wire size to circular mils, if required.

For example, determine the maximum circuit length for a feeder serving a 208V balanced three-phase load of 400A at a voltage drop not to exceed 3%. From **NEC Table 310-16**, determine that a 750 kcmil conductor at 60°C is rated to carry 400A. Using the three-phase length equation above containing the CM term, substitute values and calculate length:

$$L = \frac{VD \times CM}{\sqrt{3} \times K \times I}$$

$$L = \frac{208V \times 3\% \times 750,000 \; CM}{1.732 \times 12.9 \times 400A}$$

$$L = 523.6'$$

Therefore, in this example the 400A load may be positioned up to 523.6' from the source and the voltage drop will be 3% or less using 750 kcmil conductors at 60°C.

The two final voltage drop equations given earlier may also be solved for wire size in circular mils (CM) to directly determine, under certain conditions, the wire size for a given voltage drop, wire length, and load. Solving for CM yields:

$$CM = \frac{2 \times L \times K \times I}{VD} \; \text{for single-phase circuits}$$

and

$$CM = \frac{\sqrt{3} \times L \times K \times I}{VD} \; \text{for three-phase circuits}$$

The results from these two CM equations *must* be used in accordance with the following two rules:

- *Rule 1* – If the wire size calculated using the CM equation results in a wire size with less ampacity than the given load as determined from **NEC Tables 310-16 through 310-19**, discard the calculated result and use the wire size with the rated ampacity for the given load.
- *Rule 2* – If the wire size calculated using the CM equation results in a wire size equal to or greater than the wire size determined from **NEC Tables 310-16 through 310-19** for the given load, use the calculated wire size or the next larger standard wire size.

The reason for these rules is that the equation results are for non-derated bare wire. The wire sizes determined from the NEC tables are derated for the number of wires, temperature, and other factors. Calculated sizes that are smaller than those sizes rated at the desired load ampacity cannot be used. However, calculated wire sizes that are larger may be used when excessive voltage drop occurs that is a function of only the size of wire (that has already been derated) and that is caused by additional length beyond the maximum length for a specified voltage drop and load. ([L] equations above.)

To illustrate, we will solve for CM using the terms of the example given above for determining length (L) (i.e., a 400A, three-phase load at 523.6'):

$$CM = \frac{\sqrt{3} \times L \times K \times I}{VD}$$

Substituting values, we have:

$$CM = \frac{1.732 \times 523.6' \times 12.9 \times 400A}{208V \times 3\%}$$

$$CM = 749{,}916 \text{ or } 750 \text{ kcmil}$$

In this instance, of course, the length and load correlated exactly with the 3% voltage drop and a 750 kcmil conductor was obtained from the calculation. In accordance with *Rule 2*, the size obtained equaled the size of a 60°C conductor with a rated ampacity of 400A. Note that longer lengths for this same load will result in larger conductor sizes, each of which will be proven correct if cross-checked using the VD equations.

Now take the same problem but change the 523.6' to 100' and solve for CM:

$$CM = \frac{\sqrt{3} \times L \times K \times I}{VD}$$

$$CM = \frac{1.732 \times 100' \times 12.9 \times 400A}{208V \times 3\%}$$

$$CM = 143{,}223$$

From **NEC Chapter 9, Table 8**, the next largest standard conductor is 167,800 CM or a No. 3/0 AWG conductor. However, when **NEC Table 310-16** is checked, the maximum permissible ampacity of a No. 3/0 AWG conductor is found to be only 165A—far below the load of 400A.

Therefore, in accordance with *Rule 1*, the 3/0 AWG conductor solution would be discarded and 750 kcmil 60°C conductors, determined from **NEC Table 310-16** for the 400A load, would be used for the 100' run.

Even when sizing wire for low-voltage (24V) control circuits, the voltage drop should be limited to 3% because excessive voltage drop causes:

*   Failure of control coil to activate
*   Control contact chatter
*   Erratic operation of controls
*   Control coil burnout
*   Contact burnout

The voltage drop calculations described previously may also be used for low-voltage wiring, but tables are quite common and can save much calculation time.

To use *Table 3*, for example, assume a load of 35VA with a 50' run for a 24V control circuit. Referring to the table, scan the 50' column. Note that No. 18 AWG wire will carry 29VA and No. 16 wire will carry 43VA while still maintaining a maximum of 3% voltage drop. In this case, No. 16 wire would be the size to use.

AWG Wire Size	Length of Circuit (One Way in Feet)											
	25	50	75	100	125	150	175	200	225	250	275	300
20	29	14	10	7.2	5.8	4.8	4.1	3.8	3.2	2.9	2.8	2.4
18	58	29	19	14	11	9.6	8.2	7.2	6.4	5.8	5.2	4.8
16	86	43	29	22	17	14	12	11	9.6	8.7	7.8	7.2
14	133	67	44	33	27	22	19	17	15	13	12	11

Table 3. Table For Calculating Voltage Drop In Low-Voltage Wiring

The 3% voltage drop limitation is imposed to assure proper operation when the power supply is below the rated voltage. For example, if the rated 240V supply is 10% low (216V), the transformer does not produce 24V but rather 21.6V. When normal voltage drop is taken from this 21.6V, it approaches the lower operating limit of most controls. If it is assured that the primary voltage to the transformer will always be at rated value or above, the control circuit will operate satisfactorily with more than 3% voltage drop.

In most installations, several lines connect the transformer to the control circuit. One line usually carries the full load of the control circuit from the secondary side of the transformer to one control, with the return perhaps coming through several lines of the various other controls. Therefore, the line from the secondary side of the transformer is the most critical regarding voltage drop and VA capacity and must be properly sized.

When low-voltage lines are installed, it is suggested that one extra line be run for emergency purposes. This can be substituted for any one of the existing lines that may be defective. Also, it is possible to parallel this extra line with the existing line carrying the full load of the control circuit if the length of run affects control operation because of a voltage drop. In many cases, this will reduce the voltage drop and permit satisfactory operation.

SUMMARY

A great deal of valuable information about conductors, such as dimensions, resistance, and current-carrying capacity, can be obtained from convenient NEC tables; these tables should be used whenever possible as they are great time-saving devices.

There are times, however, when appropriate tables are not available, or do not give the exact information needed for a certain project or situation. This is when a knowledge of simple conductor calculations pays off.

For example, ***NEC Tables 310-16 through 310-19*** give the allowable current-carrying capacities of conductors with various types of insulation based on the heating of the conductors, but these tables do not account for voltage drop due to resistance of long circuit runs. This is very important and should always be kept in mind when planning or installing any electrical installation.

References

For advanced study of topics covered in this Task Module, the following books are suggested:

American Electricians' Handbook, Latest Edition, McGraw-Hill, New York, NY.

National Electrical Code Handbook, Latest Edition, National Fire Protection Association, Quincy, MA.

1. All things considered, the most ideal conductor is made of _____.

    a. bronze
    b. brass
    c. aluminum
    d. copper

2. Which of the following is *not* a standard configuration for stranded wire?

    a. 5-strand
    b. 7-strand
    c. 19-strand
    d. 37-strand

3. Of those listed below, the largest standard AWG wire size is _____.

    a. No. 60 AWG
    b. No. 1 AWG
    c. No. 1/0 AWG
    d. No. 4/0 AWG

4. A branch circuit is best described as _____.

    a. the circuit conductors between the service equipment and the final branch circuit overcurrent device
    b. the circuit conductors between the final overcurrent device protecting the circuit and the outlet(s)
    c. a conductor tapped onto another conductor
    d. two conductors run in parallel

5. The rating of a branch circuit is determined by the _____.

    a. type and size of the branch circuit conductors
    b. rating of the branch circuit overcurrent device
    c. total connected load
    d. characteristics of the supply circuit

6. A continuous load is best described as one in which the maximum current is expected to continue for _____ hour(s) or more.

    a. one
    b. two
    c. three
    d. four

7. Which of the following is *not* a standard rating for fuses?

    a. 600A
    b. 601A
    c. 650A
    d. 700A

8. Where in the NEC would you find information on conductor applications and descriptions of insulation types?

    a. ***NEC Table 310-15(b)(2)***
    b. ***NEC Table 310-13***
    c. ***NEC Table 310-16***
    d. ***NEC Chapter 9, Table 8***

9. Use ***NEC Table 310-16*** to find the maximum amperage for a No. 2 AWG copper wire at 90°C (assume THHN insulation).

    a. 95A
    b. 110A
    c. 130A
    d. 150A

10. What is the constant (K) for the resistance of ordinary copper?

    a. 12.9Ω
    b. 21.2Ω
    c. 1.732Ω
    d. 3.141Ω

ANSWERS TO REVIEW/PRACTICE QUESTIONS

Answer	**Section Reference**
1. d	1.0.0
2. a	1.0.0
3. d	1.0.0
4. b	2.0.0
5. b	2.1.0
6. c	2.1.0
7. c	2.2.0
8. b	3.0.0
9. c	4.2.0
10. a	4.3.0

The NCCER makes every effort to keep these manuals up-to-date and free of technical errors. We appreciate your help in this process. If you have an idea for improving this manual, or if you find an error, a typographical mistake, or an inaccuracy in the NCCER's Craft Training Manuals, please write us, using this form or a photocopy. Be sure to include the exact module number, page number, a description of the problem, and the correction, if possible. Your input will be brought to the attention of the Technical Review Committee. Thank you for your assistance.

Instructors – If you found that additional materials were necessary in order to teach this module effectively, please let us know so that we may include them in the Equipment/Materials list in the Instructor's Guide.

Write: Curriculum Development and Revision Department
National Center for Construction Education and Research
P.O. Box 141104
Gainesville, FL 32614-1104

Fax: 352-334-0932

Craft ___________________________ Module Name ___________________________

Copyright Date __________ Module Number __________ Page Number(s) __________

Description of Problem
____
____
____
____
____

(Optional) Correction of Problem
____
____
____

(Optional) Your Name and Address
____
____
____

ELECTRICAL — TRAINEE TASK MODULE 26302

Overcurrent Protection

Module 26303

OVERCURRENT PROTECTION

NATIONAL
CENTER FOR
CONSTRUCTION
EDUCATION AND
RESEARCH

OBJECTIVES

Upon completion of this module, the trainee will be able to:

1. Explain the importance of overcurrent protection.

2. Understand the key NEC requirements regarding overcurrent protection.

3. Check electrical drawings for conformance to NEC sections that cover short circuit current, fault currents, interrupting ratings, and other sections relating to overcurrent protection.

4. Determine let-through current values (peak and rms) when current-limiting overcurrent devices are used.

5. Select and size overcurrent protection for specific applications.

Prerequisites

Successful completion of the following Task Modules is recommended before beginning study of this Task Module: Core Curricula; Electrical Level 1; Electrical Level 2; and Electrical Level 3, Modules 26301 and 26302.

Required Trainee Materials

1. Trainee Task Module

2. Appropriate Personal Protective Equipment

3. Copy of the latest edition of the *National Electrical Code*

Note: The designations "National Electrical Code," "NE Code," and "NEC," where used in this document, refer to the National Electrical Code®, which is a registered trademark of the National Fire Protection Association, Quincy, MA. *All National Electrical Code (NEC) references in this module refer to the 1999 edition of the NEC.*

COURSE MAP

This course map shows all of the modules in the third level of the Electrical curricula. The suggested training order begins at the bottom and proceeds up. Skill levels increase as a trainee advances on the course map. The training order may be adjusted by the local Training Program Sponsor.

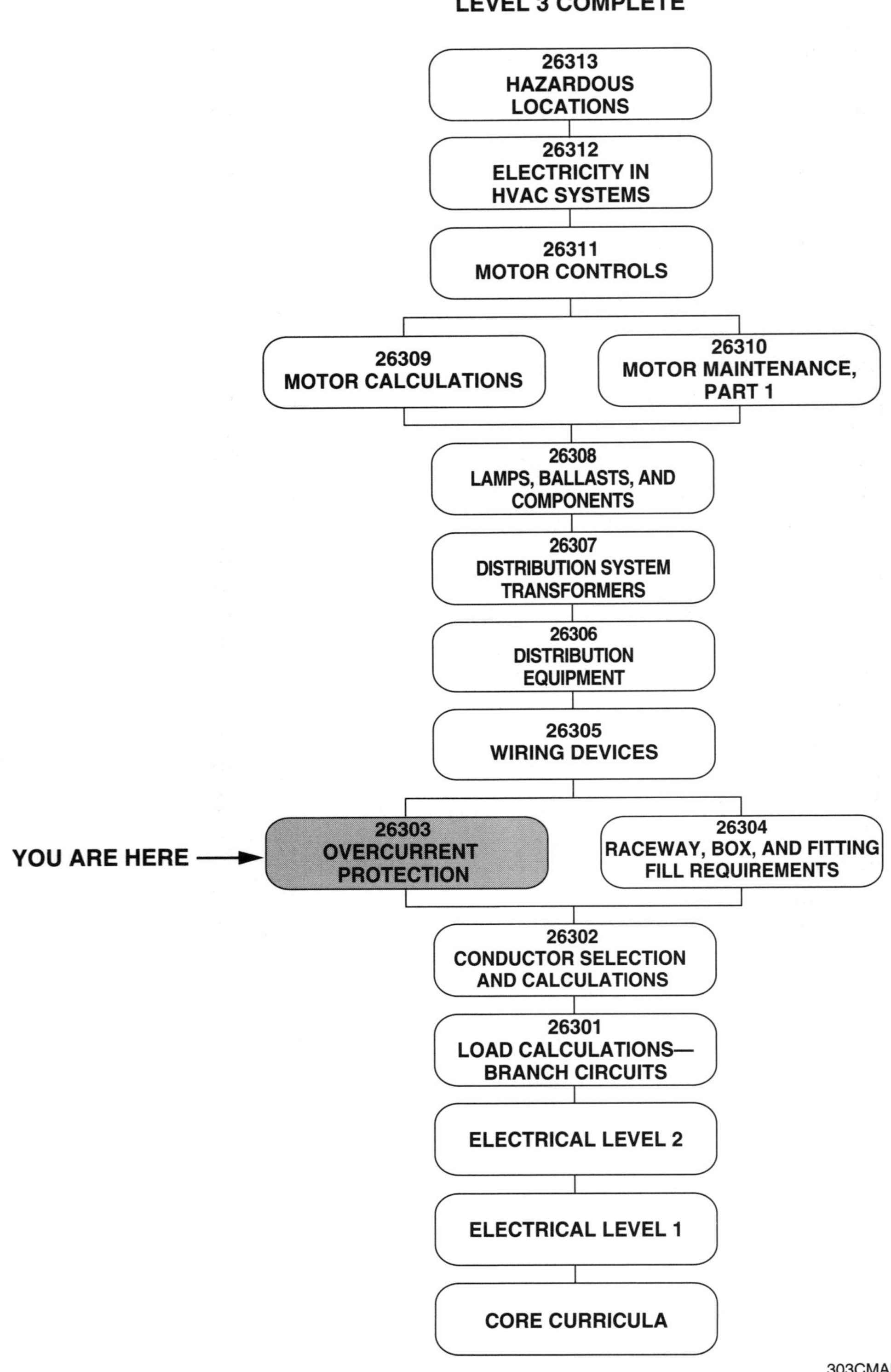

TABLE OF CONTENTS

Trade Terms Introduced In This Module

Ampere rating: The current-carrying capacity of an overcurrent protective device. The fuse or circuit breaker is subjected to a current above its ampere rating; it will open the circuit after a predetermined period of time.

Ampere squared seconds (I^2t): The measure of heat energy developed within a circuit during the fuse's clearing. It can be expressed as *melting I^2t, arcing I^2t*, or the sum of them as *clearing I^2t*. *I* stands for effective let-through current (rms), which is squared, and *t* stands for time of opening in seconds.

Arcing time: The amount of time from the instant the fuse link has melted until the overcurrent is interrupted or cleared.

Clearing time: The total time between the beginning of the overcurrent and the final opening of the circuit at rated voltage by an overcurrent protective device. Clearing time is the total of the melting time and the arcing time.

Current-limiting device: A device that will clear a short circuit in less than one half cycle. Also, it will limit the instantaneous peak let-through current to a value substantially less than that obtainable in the same circuit if that device were replaced with a solid conductor of equal impedance.

Fast-acting fuse: A fuse that opens on overloads and short circuits very quickly. This type of fuse is not designed to withstand temporary overload currents associated with some electrical loads (inductive loads).

Inductive load: An electrical load that pulls a large amount of current—an inrush current—when first energized. After a few cycles or seconds, the current declines to the load current.

Interrupting capacity: The maximum short circuit current that a circuit breaker or fuse can safely interrupt.

Melting time: The amount of time required to melt a fuse link during a specified overcurrent.

NEC dimensions: These are dimensions once referenced in the *National Electrical Code*. They are common to Class H and K fuses and provide interchangeability between manufacturers for fuses and fusible equipment of given ampere and voltage ratings.

Overload: Can be classified as an overcurrent that exceeds the normal full-load current of a circuit.

Peak let-through (Ip): The instantaneous value of peak current let-through by a current-limiting fuse when it operates in its current-limiting range.

Root-mean-square (rms): The effective value of an AC sine wave which is calculated as the square root of the average of the squares of all the instantaneous values of the current throughout one cycle. Alternating current rms is that value of an alternating current that produces the same heating effect as a given DC value.

Semiconductor fuse: Fuse used to protect solid-state devices.

Short circuit current: Can be classified as an overcurrent which exceeds the normal full-load current of a circuit by a factor many times greater than normal. Also characteristic of this type of overcurrent is that it leaves the normal current-carrying path of the circuit—it takes a shortcut around the load and back to the source.

Single phasing: That condition which occurs when one phase of a three-phase system opens, either in a low-voltage or high-voltage distribution system. Primary or secondary single phasing can be caused by any number of events. This condition results in unbalanced loads in polyphase motors and unless protective measures are taken, it will cause overheating and failure.

UL classes: Underwriters' Laboratories has developed basic physical specifications and electrical performance requirements for fuses with voltage ratings of 600V or less. These are known as *UL standards*. If a type of fuse meets with the requirements of a standard, it can fall into that UL class. Typical UL classes are R, K, G, L, H, T, CC, and J.

Voltage rating: The maximum value of system voltage in which a fuse can be used, yet safely interrupt an overcurrent. Exceeding the voltage rating of a fuse impairs its ability to safely clear an overload or short circuit.

Withstand rating: The maximum short circuit current that a component or device is capable of carrying without requiring replacement because of extensive damage.

1.0.0 INTRODUCTION

Electrical distribution systems are often quite complicated. They cannot be absolutely fail-safe. Circuits are subject to destructive overcurrents. Factors which contribute to the occurrence of such overcurrents are harsh environments, general deterioration, accidental damage or damage from natural causes, excessive expansion, or electrical distribution system overload. Reliable protective devices prevent or minimize costly damage to transformers, conductors, motors, and many other components and loads that make up the complete distribution system. Reliable circuit protection is essential to avoid the severe monetary losses which can result from power blackouts and prolonged downtime of facilities. It is the need for reliable protection, safety, and freedom from fire hazards that has made overcurrent protective devices absolutely necessary in all electrical systems, both large and small.

Overcurrent protection of electrical circuits is so important that the NEC devotes an entire article to this subject. ***NEC Article 240*** provides the general requirements for overcurrent protection and overcurrent protective devices. ***NEC Article 240, Parts A through H*** cover systems 600V (nominal) and under, while ***NEC Article 240, Part I*** covers overcurrent protection over 600V (nominal). This entire article will be covered in this module, along with practical examples.

All conductors must be protected against overcurrents in accordance with their ampacities as set forth in ***NEC Section 240-3***. They must also be protected against **short circuit current** damage as required by ***NEC Sections 110-10 and 240-1***. The two basic types of overcurrent protective devices that are in common use are fuses and circuit breakers.

1.1.0 OVERCURRENTS

An overcurrent is either an **overload** current or a short circuit current. The overload current is an excessive current relative to normal operating current but one which is confined to the normal conductive paths provided by the conductor and other components and loads of the distribution system. As the name implies, a short circuit current is one which flows outside the normal conducting paths and may be phase-to-phase or phase-to-ground.

1.2.0 OVERLOADS

Overloads are most often between one and six times the normal current level. Usually, they are caused by harmless temporary surge currents that occur when motors are started up or transformers are energized. Such overload currents or transients are normal occurrences. Since they are of brief duration, any temperature rise is trivial and has no harmful effect on the circuit components.

Continuous overloads can result from defective motors (such as worn motor bearings), overloaded equipment, or too many loads on one circuit. Such sustained overloads are destructive and must be cut off by protective devices before they damage the distribution system or system loads. However, since they are of relatively low magnitude compared to short circuit currents, removal of the overload current within a few seconds will generally prevent equipment damage. A sustained overload current results in overheating of conductors and other components and will cause deterioration of insulation which may eventually result in severe damage and short circuits if not interrupted.

1.3.0 SHORT CIRCUITS

The amperes **interrupting capacity** (AIC) rating of a circuit breaker or fuse is the maximum short circuit current which the breaker will safely interrupt. This AIC rating is at rated voltage and frequency.

Whereas overload currents occur at rather modest levels, a short circuit or fault current can be many hundreds of times larger than the normal operating current. A high level fault may be 50,000A (or larger). If not cut off within a matter of a few thousands of a second, damage and destruction can become rampant—there can be severe insulation damage, melting of conductors, vaporization of metal, ionization of gases, arcing, and fires. Simultaneously, high level short circuit currents can develop huge magnetic field stresses. The magnetic forces between busbars and other conductors can be many hundreds of pounds per lineal foot; even heavy bracing may not be adequate to keep them from being warped or distorted beyond repair.

NEC Section 110-9 clearly states that equipment intended to interrupt current at fault levels (fuses and circuit breakers) must have an interrupting rating sufficient for the nominal circuit voltage and the current that is available at the line terminals of the equipment.

Equipment intended to interrupt current at other than fault levels must have an interrupting rating at nominal circuit voltage sufficient for the current that must be interrupted.

These NEC statements mean that fuses and circuit breakers (and their related components) designed to interrupt fault or operating currents (open the circuit) must have a rating sufficient to withstand such currents. This section emphasizes the difference between clearing fault level currents and clearing operating currents. Protective devices such as fuses and circuit breakers are designed to clear fault currents and therefore must have short circuit interrupting ratings sufficient for fault levels. Equipment such as contactors and safety switches have interrupting ratings for currents at other than fault levels. Thus, the interrupting rating of electrical equipment is now divided into two parts:

- Current at fault (short circuit) levels
- Current at operating levels

Most people are familiar with the normal current-carrying **ampere rating** of fuses and circuit breakers. For example, if an overcurrent protective device is designed to open a circuit when the circuit load exceeds 20A for a given time period, as the current approaches 20A, the overcurrent protective device begins to overheat. If the current barely exceeds 20A, the circuit breaker will open normally or a fuse link will melt after a given period of time with little, if any, arcing. For example, if 40A of current were instantaneously applied to the circuit, the overcurrent protective device would open instantly, but again with very little arcing. However, if a ground fault occurs on the circuit that ran the amperage up to 5,000A, for example, an explosion effect would occur within the protective device. One simple indication of this is the blackened windows of plug fuses.

If this fault current exceeds the interrupting rating of a fuse or circuit breaker, the protective device can be damaged or destroyed; such current can also cause severe damage to equipment and injure personnel. Therefore, selecting overcurrent protective devices with the proper interrupting capacity is extremely important in all electrical systems.

For a better understanding of interrupting rating, consider the following analogy. We will use a dammed stream (*Figure 1*) as an example. Consider the reservoir capacity to be the available fault current in an electrical circuit, the flood gates (located downstream from the dam) to be the overcurrent protective device in the circuit rated at 10,000 gallons per minute (gpm) (10,000 AIC), and the stream of water coming through the discharge pipes in the dam to be the normal load current. Our drawing shows a normal flow of 100 gpm. Also note the bridge crossing the stream, downstream from the flood gates. This bridge will represent downstream circuit components or equipment connected to the circuit.

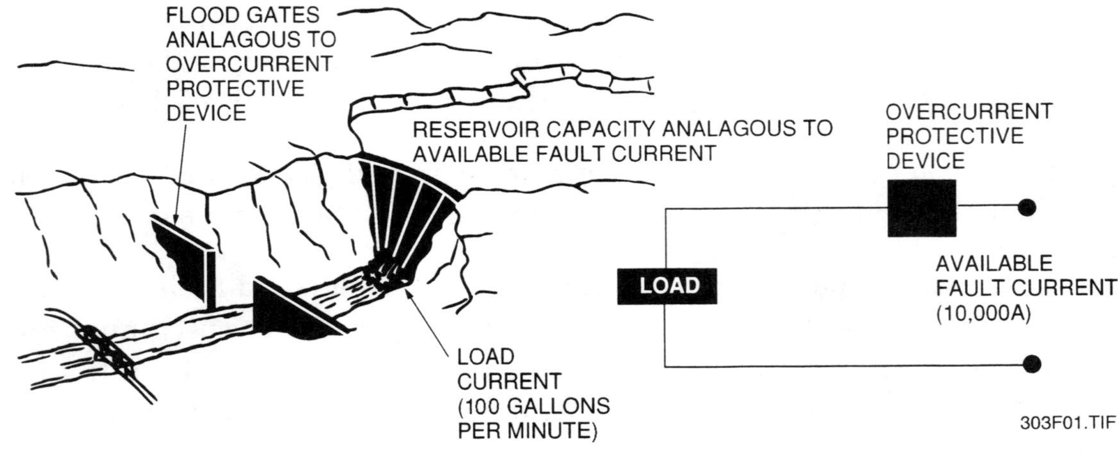

Figure 1. Normal Operating Current

Figure 2 shows this same diagram with a fault in the dam creating a water short circuit that allows 50,000 gpm to flow (50,000 fault circuit amps). Such a situation destroys the flood gates because of inadequate interrupting rating. The overcurrent protective device in the circuit will also be destroyed. With the flood gates damaged, this surge of water continues downstream, wrecking the bridge. Similarly, the downstream components may not be able to withstand the let-through current in an electrical circuit.

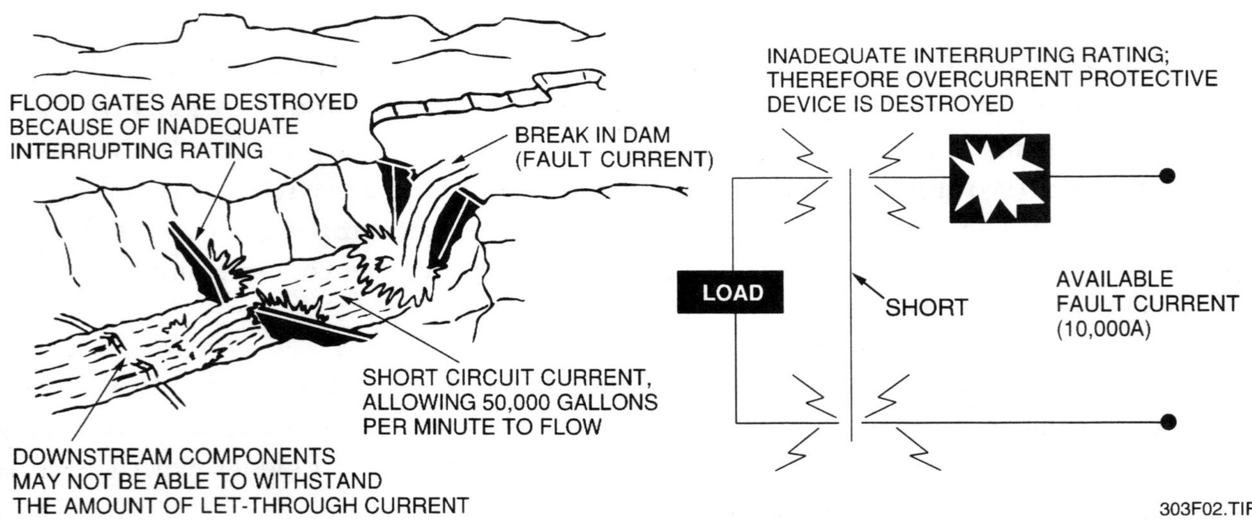

Figure 2. Inadequate Interrupting Rating

Figure 3 shows the same situation but with adequate interrupting capacity. Note that the flood gates have adequately contained the surge of water and restricted the let-through current to an amount that can be withstood by the bridge or the components downstream.

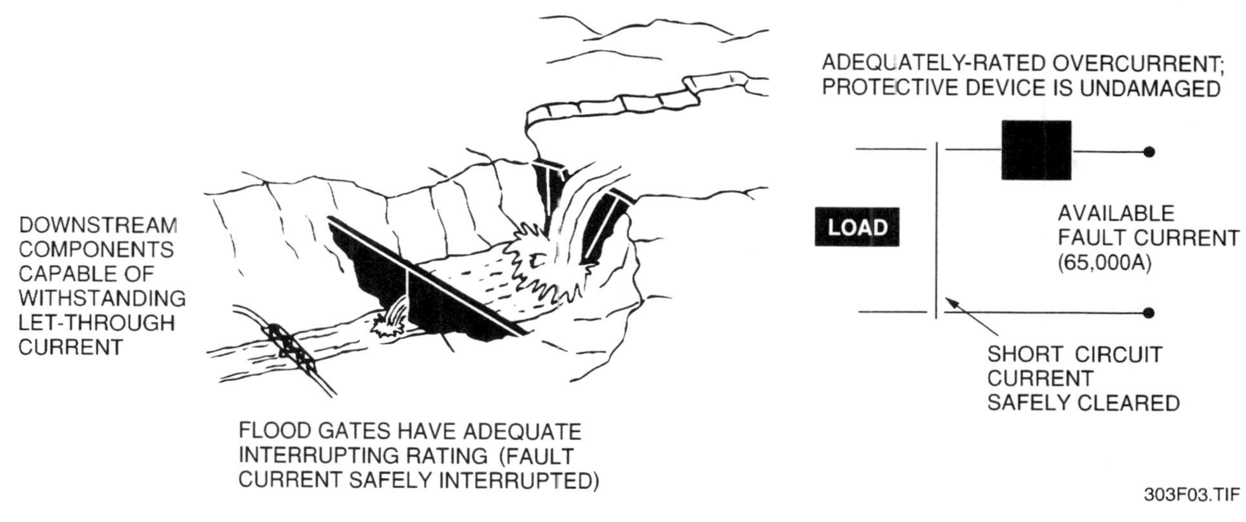

Figure 3. Adequate Interrupting Rating

There are several factors that must be considered when calculating the required interrupting capacity of an overcurrent protective device. **NEC Section 110-10** states that the overcurrent protective devices, total impedance, component short circuit current ratings, and other characteristics of the circuit to be protected shall be selected and coordinated to permit the circuit protective devices used to clear a fault to do so without extensive damage to the electrical components of the circuit. This fault shall be assumed to be either between two or more of the circuit conductors, or between any circuit conductor or the grounding conductor or enclosing metal raceway.

The component short circuit rating is a current rating given to conductors, switches, circuit breakers, and other electrical components, which, if exceeded by fault currents, will result in extensive damage to the component. The rating is expressed in terms of time intervals and/or current values. Short circuit damage can be the result of heat generated or the electro-mechanical force of a high-intensity magnetic field.

The NEC's intent is that the design of a system must be such that short circuit currents cannot exceed the **withstand ratings** of the components selected as part of the system. Given specific system components and the level of available short circuit currents that could occur, overcurrent protective devices (mainly fuses and/or circuit breakers) must be used which will limit the energy let-through of fault currents to levels within the withstand ratings of the system components.

The fuse is a reliable overcurrent protective device. It consists of a fusible link or links encapsulated in a tube and connected to contact terminals. The electrical resistance of the link is so low that it simply acts as a conductor. However, when destructive currents occur, the link quickly melts and opens the circuit to protect conductors and other circuit components and loads. Fuse characteristics are stable and do not require periodic maintenance or testing.

2.1.0   VOLTAGE RATING

Most low-voltage power distribution fuses have 250V or 600V ratings. The **voltage rating** of a fuse must be at least equal to or greater than the circuit voltage. It can be higher, but never lower. For example, a 600V fuse can be used in a 240V circuit.

The voltage rating of a fuse is a function of or depends upon its capability to open a circuit under an overcurrent condition. Specifically, the voltage rating determines the ability of the fuse to suppress the internal arcing that occurs after a fuse link melts and an arc is produced (**arcing time**). If a fuse is used with a voltage rating lower than the circuit voltage, arc suppression will be impaired and, under some fault current conditions, the fuse may not safely clear the overcurrent. Special consideration is necessary for **semiconductor fuse** applications in which a fuse of a certain voltage rating is used on a lower-voltage circuit.

2.2.0   AMPERE RATING

Every fuse has a specific ampere rating. When selecting the ampere rating, consideration must be given to the size and type of load and NEC requirements. The ampere rating of a fuse should normally not exceed the current-carrying capacity of the circuit. For instance, if a conductor is rated to carry 20A, a 20A fuse is the largest that should be used. However, there are specific circumstances in which the ampere rating is permitted to be greater than the current-carrying capacity of the circuit. A typical example is the motor circuit; dual-element fuses are generally permitted to be sized up to 175% and nontime-delay fuses up to 300% of the motor full-load amperes. Generally, the ampere rating of a fuse and switch combination should be selected at 125% of the continuous load current (this usually corresponds to the circuit capacity, which is also selected at 125% of the load current). There are exceptions, such as when the fuse-switch combination is approved for continuous operation at 100% of its rating.

2.3.0   INTERRUPTING RATING

A protective device must be able to withstand the destructive energy of short circuit currents. If a fault current exceeds a level beyond the capability of the protective device, the device may actually rupture, causing additional damage. Therefore, it is important to choose a protective device that can sustain the largest potential short circuit currents. The rating which defines the capacity of a protective device to maintain its integrity when reacting to fault currents is termed its *interrupting rating*.

NEC Section 110-9 requires equipment intended to interrupt current at fault levels to have an interrupting rating sufficient for the current that must be interrupted. Interrupting rating and interrupting capacity were covered in your Level 2 training; more advanced material is presented in this module.

2.4.0   SELECTIVE COORDINATION

The coordination of protective devices prevents system power outages or blackouts caused by overcurrent conditions. When only the protective device nearest a faulted circuit opens and larger upstream fuses remain closed, the protective devices are selectively coordinated (they discriminate). The word *selective* is used to denote total coordination (isolation of a faulted circuit by the opening of only the localized protective device).

Figure 4 shows the minimum ratios of ampere rating of low peak fuses that are required to provide selective coordination of upstream and downstream fuses.

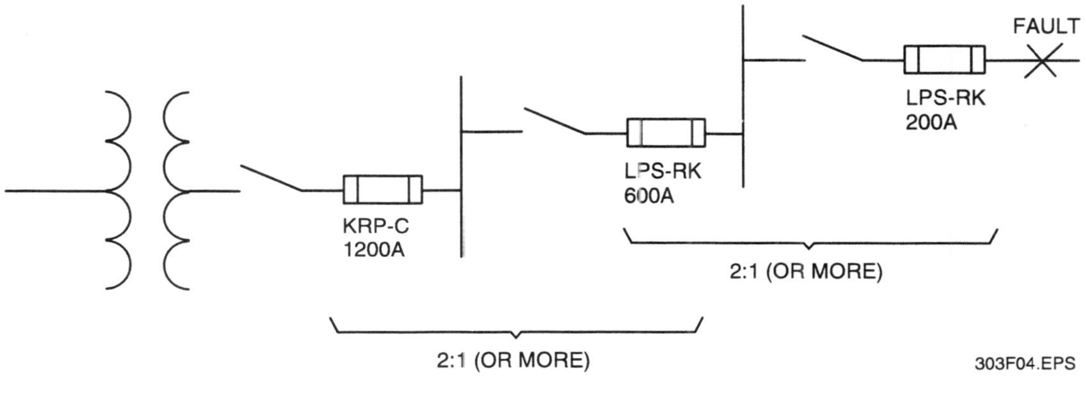

Figure 4. Selective Coordination

2.5.0   CURRENT LIMITATION

If a protective device cuts off a short circuit current in less than one half cycle, before it reaches its total available (and highly destructive) value, the device is a **current-limiting device**. Most modern fuses are current-limiting devices. They restrict fault currents to such low values that a high degree of protection is given to circuit components against even very high short circuit currents. They permit breakers with lower interrupting ratings to be used and can reduce bracing of bus structures. They also minimize the need for other components to have high short circuit current withstand ratings. If not limited, short circuit currents can reach levels of 30,000A or 40,000A or higher in the first half cycle (.008 seconds at 60Hz) after the start of a short circuit. The heat that can be produced in circuit components by the immense energy of short circuit currents can cause severe insulation damage or even an explosion. At the same time, the huge magnetic forces developed between conductors can crack insulators and distort and destroy bracing structures. Thus, it is extremely important that a protective device limit fault currents before they can reach their full potential level.

A noncurrent-limiting protective device, by permitting a short circuit current to build up to its full value, can let an immense amount of destructive short circuit heat energy through before opening the circuit, as shown in *Figure 5*. On the other hand, a current-limiting device (such as a current-limiting fuse) has such a high speed of response that it cuts off a short circuit long before it can build up to its full peak value, as shown in *Figure 6*.

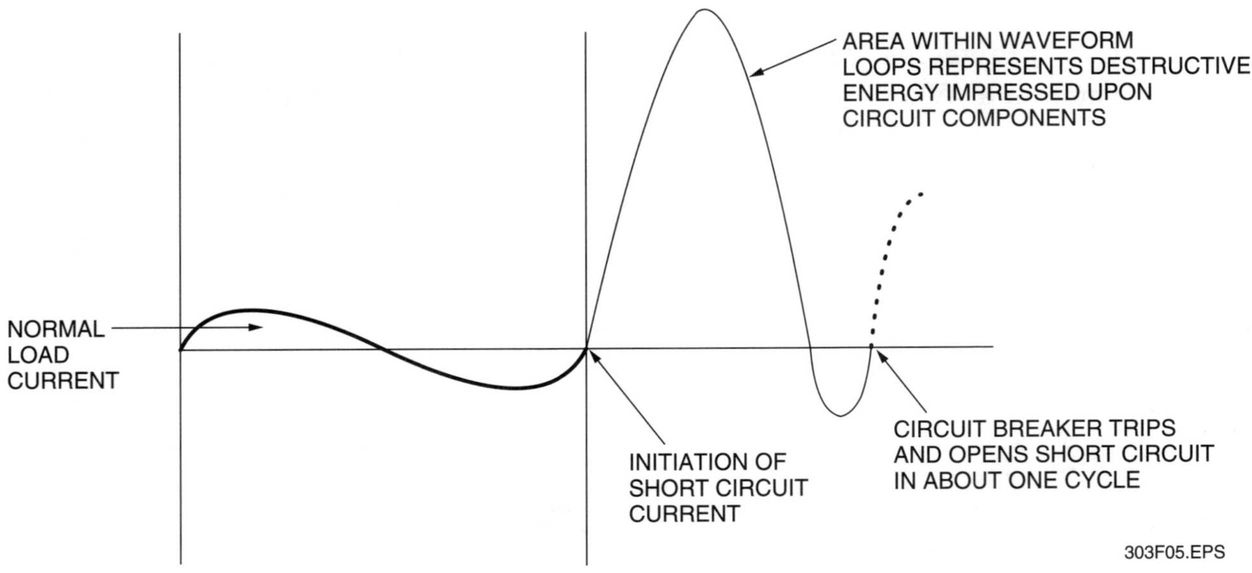

Figure 5. Characteristics Of A Noncurrent-Limiting Protective Device

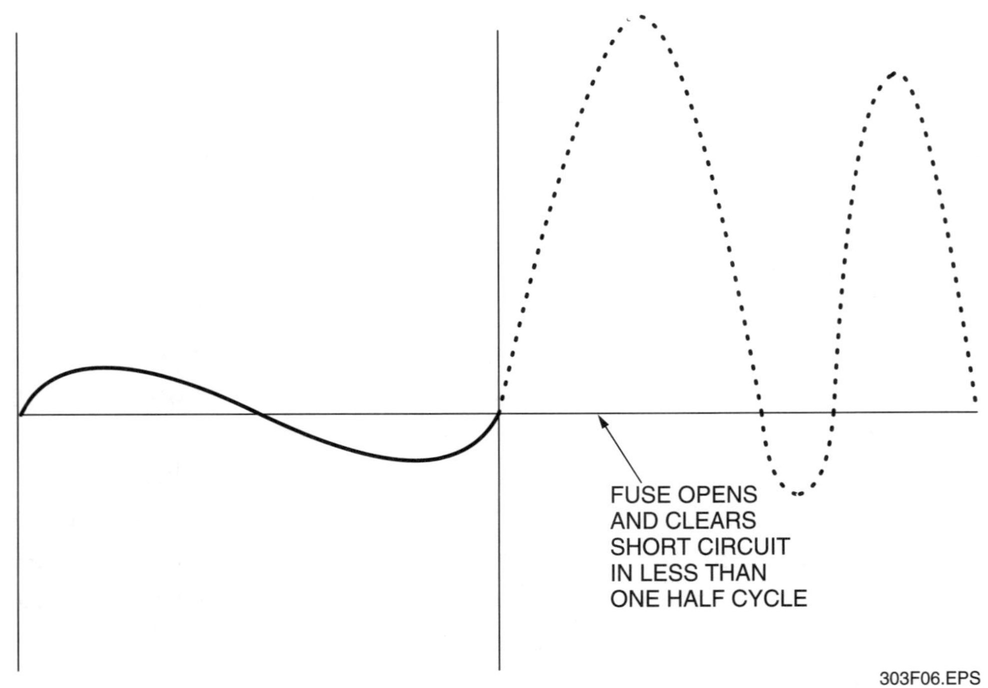

Figure 6. Characteristics Of A Current-Limiting Fuse

This section describes the operating characteristics of various types of fuses.

3.1.0   NONTIME-DELAY FUSES

The basic component of a fuse is the link. Depending upon the ampere rating of the fuse, the single-element, nontime-delay fuse may have one or more links. They are electrically connected to the end blades (or ferrules) and enclosed in a tube or cartridge surrounded by an arc-quenching filler material.

Under normal operation, when the fuse is operating at or near its ampere rating, it simply functions as a conductor. However, as illustrated in *Figure 7*, if an overload current occurs and persists for more than a short interval of time, the temperature of the link eventually reaches a level which causes a restricted segment of the link to melt; as a result, a gap is formed and an electric arc established. As the arc causes the link metal to burn back, the gap becomes progressively larger. The electrical resistance of the arc eventually reaches such a high level that the arc cannot be sustained and is extinguished; the fuse will have then completely cut off all current flow in the circuit. Suppression or quenching of the arc is accelerated by the filler material.

Overload current normally falls within the region of between one and six times normal current, resulting in currents that are quite high. Consequently, a fuse may be subjected to short circuit currents of 30,000A to 40,000A or higher. The response of current-limiting fuses to such currents is extremely fast. The restricted sections of the fuse link will simultaneously melt within a matter of two-thousandths or three-thousandths of a second in the event of a high-level fault current.

The high resistance of the multiple arcs, together with the quenching effects of the filler particles, results in rapid arc suppression and clearing of the circuit. Again, refer to *Figure 7*. The short circuit current is cut off in less than one half cycle, long before the short circuit current can reach its full value.

3.2.0   DUAL-ELEMENT, TIME-DELAY FUSES

Unlike single-element fuses, the dual-element, time-delay fuse can be applied in circuits subject to temporary motor overloads and surge currents to provide both high-performance short circuit and overload protection. Oversizing to prevent nuisance openings is not necessary with this type of fuse. The dual-element, time-delay fuse contains two distinctly separate types of elements. Electrically, the two elements are connected in series. The fuse links (similar to those used in the nontime-delay fuse) perform the short circuit protection function; the overload element provides protection against low-level overcurrents or overloads and will hold an overload which is five times greater than the ampere rating of the fuse for a minimum time of 10 seconds.

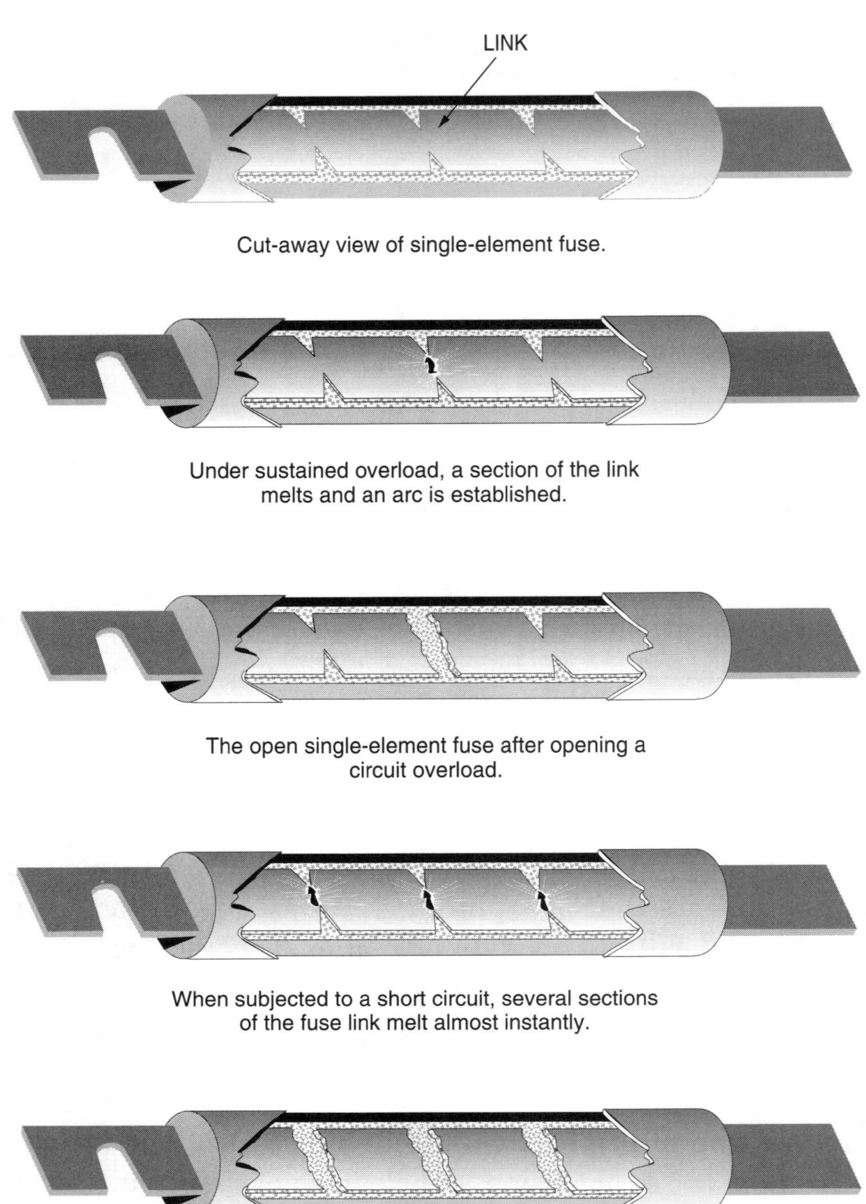

Figure 7. Characteristics Of A Single-Element Fuse

As shown in *Figure 8*, the overload section consists of a copper heat absorber and a spring-operated trigger assembly. The heat absorber bar is permanently connected to the heat absorber extension and the short circuit link on the opposite end of the fuse by the S-shaped connector of the trigger assembly. The connector electrically joins the short circuit link to the heat absorber in the overload section of the fuse. These elements are joined by a calibrated fusing alloy. An overload current causes heating of the short circuit link connected to the trigger assembly. The transfer of heat from the short circuit link to the heat absorber begins to raise the temperature of the heat absorber. If the overload is sustained, the temperature of the heat absorber eventually reaches a level which permits the trigger spring to fracture the calibrated fusing alloy and pull the connector free of the short circuit link and the heat absorber. As a result, the short circuit link is electrically disconnected from the heat absorber, the conducting path through the fuse is opened, and the overload current is interrupted. A critical aspect of the fusing alloy is that it retains its original characteristic after repeated temporary overloads without degradation.

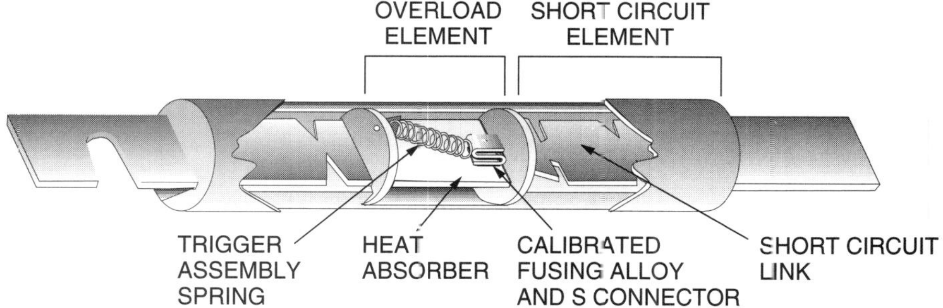

The true dual-element fuse has distinct and separate overload and short circuit elements.

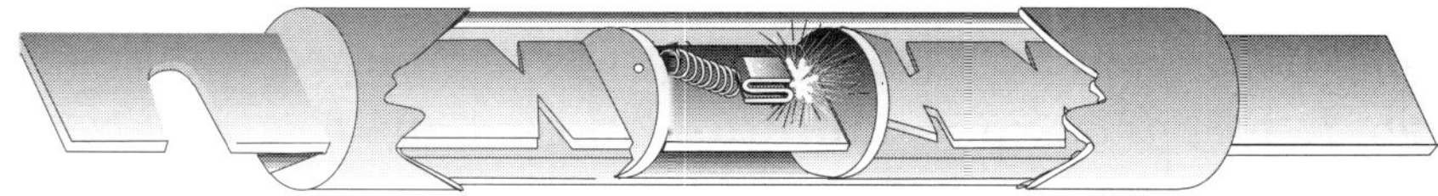

Under sustained overload conditions, the trigger spring fractures the calibrated fusing alloy and releases the connector.

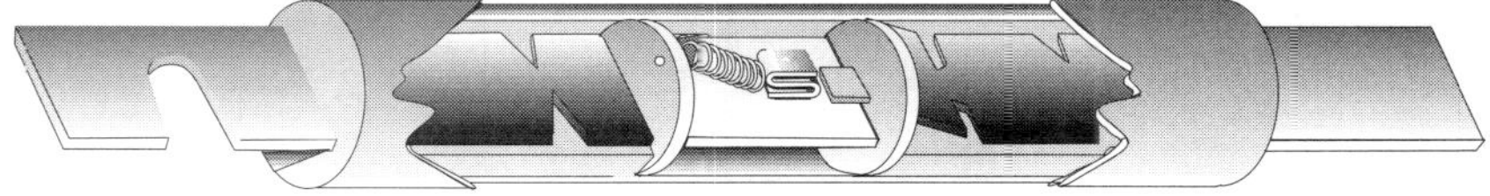

The dual-element fuse after opening under an overload.

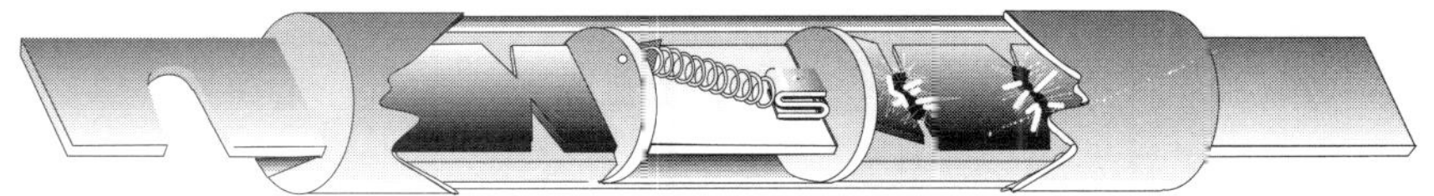

Like the single-element fuse, a short circuit current causes the restricted portions of the short circuit elements to melt and arcing to burn back the resulting gaps until the arcs are suppressed by the arc-quenching material and increased arc resistance.

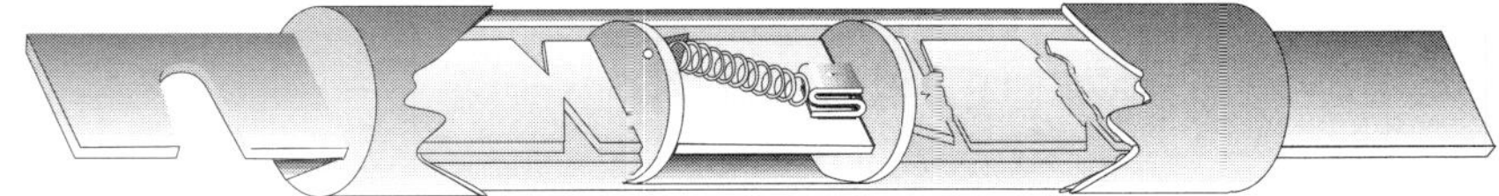

The dual-element fuse after opening under a short circuit condition.

303F08.EPS

Figure 8. Characteristics Of A Dual-Element, Time-Delay Fuse

The advantages of dual-element fuses are:

- Provide motor overload, ground fault, and short circuit protection
- Permit the use of smaller and less costly switches
- Give a higher degree of short circuit protection (greater current limitation) in circuits in which surge currents or temporary overloads occur
- Simplify and improve blackout prevention (selective coordination)

4.0.0 UL FUSE CLASSES

Safety is the primary consideration of Underwriters' Laboratories (UL). The proper selection, overall functional performance, and reliability of a product are factors that are not within the basic scope of UL activities. However, to develop its safety test procedures, UL does develop the basic performance and physical specifications of standards of a product. In the case of fuses, these standards have culminated in the establishment of distinct **UL classes** of low-voltage (600V or less) fuses. Various UL fuse classes are described below.

Class R fuses – UL Class R (rejection) fuses are high-performance ¹⁄₁₀A to 600A units, 250V and 600V, having a high degree of current limitation and a short circuit interrupting rating of up to 200,000A (**root-mean-square [rms]** symmetrical). This type of fuse is designed to be mounted in rejection-type fuse clips to prevent older Class H fuses from being installed. Since Class H fuses are not current-limiting devices and are recognized by UL as having only a 10,000A interrupting rating, serious damage could result if a Class H fuse were inserted in a system designed for Class R fuses. Consequently, ***NEC Section 240-60(b)*** requires fuseholders for current-limiting fuses to reject noncurrent-limiting fuses.

Figure 9 shows a standard Class H fuse and a Class R fuse. A grooved ring in one ferrule of the Class R fuse provides the rejection feature of the Class R fuse in contrast to the lower interrupting capacity, non-rejection type. *Figure 10* shows Class R fuse rejection clips that accept only the Class R fuses.

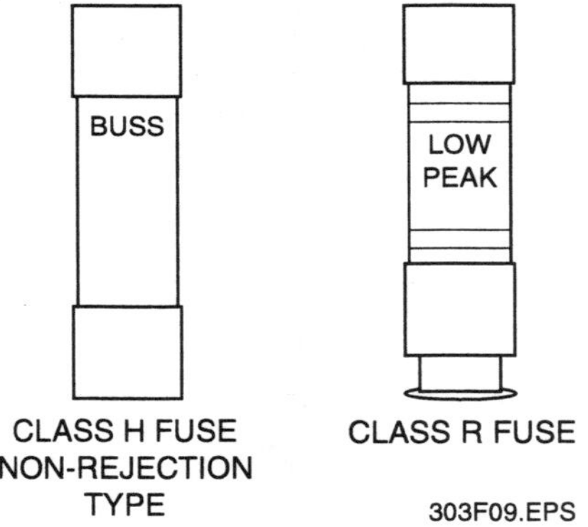

Figure 9. Comparison Of Class H And Class R Fuses

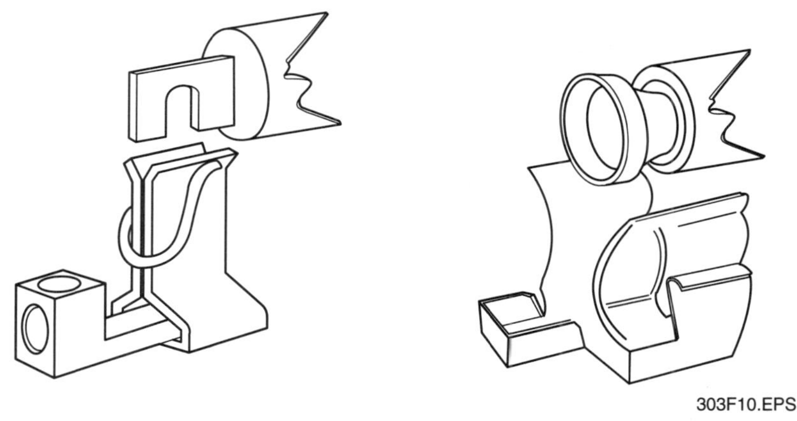

303F10.EPS

Figure 10. Class R Fuse Rejection Clips That Accept Only Class R Fuses

Class CC fuses – Class CC fuses are 600V, 200,000A interrupting rating, branch circuit fuses with overall dimensions of ¹⁵⁄₃₂" × 1½". Their design incorporates rejection features that allow them to be inserted into rejection fuseholders and fuse blocks that reject all lower voltage, lower interrupting rating ¹⁵⁄₃₂" × 1½" fuses. They are available from ¹⁄₁₀A through 30A.

Class G fuses – Class G fuses are 300V, 100,000A interrupting rating branch circuit fuses that are size rejecting to eliminate overfusing. The fuse diameter is ¹³⁄₃₂", while the length varies from 1⁵⁄₁₆" to 2¼". They are available in ratings from 1A through 60A.

Class H fuses – Class H fuses are 250V and 600V, 10,000A interrupting rating branch circuit fuses that may be renewable or nonrenewable. They are available in ampere ratings of 1A through 600A.

Class J fuses – Class J fuses are rated to interrupt 200,000A. They are UL labeled as *current limiting*, are rated for 600VAC, and are not interchangeable with other classes.

Class K fuses – Class K fuses are listed by UL as K-1, K-5, or K-9. Each subclass has designated **amperes squared seconds (I^2t)** and **peak let-through (Ip)** maximums. These are dimensionally the same as Class H fuses (**NEC dimensions**), and they can have interrupting ratings of 50,000A, 100,000A, or 200,000A. These fuses are current-limiting devices; however, they are not marked *current limiting* since they do not have a rejection feature.

Class L fuses – Class L fuses are available in ampere ratings of 601A through 6,000A, and are rated to interrupt 200,000A. They are labeled *current limiting* and are rated for 600VAC. They are intended to be bolted into their mountings and are not normally used in clips. Some Class L fuses have time-delay features for all-purpose use.

Class T fuses – Class T fuses are 300V and 600V, with ampere ratings from 1A through 1,200A. They are physically very small and can be applied where space is at a premium. They are fast-acting fuses with an interrupting rating of 200,000A.

4.1.0 BRANCH CIRCUIT LISTED FUSES

Branch circuit listed fuses are designed to prevent the installation of fuses that cannot provide a comparable level of protection to equipment. The characteristics of branch circuit fuses are as follows:

- They must have a minimum interrupting rating of 10,000A.
- They must have a minimum voltage rating of 125V.
- They must be size rejecting such that a fuse of a lower voltage rating cannot be installed in the circuit.
- They must be size rejecting such that a fuse with a current rating higher than the fuseholder rating cannot be installed in the circuit.

4.2.0 MEDIUM-VOLTAGE FUSES

As defined in ANSI/IEEE 40-1981, fuses above 600V are classified as general-purpose, current-limiting; backup current-limiting; or expulsion types.

- *General-purpose current-limiting fuses* – Fuses that are capable of interrupting all currents from the rated interrupting current down to the current that causes melting of the fusible element in one hour.
- *Backup current-limiting fuses* – Fuses that are capable of interrupting all currents from the maximum rated interrupting current down to the rated minimum interrupting current.
- *Expulsion fuses* – Vented fuses in which the expulsion effect of gases produced by the arc and lining of the fuseholder, either alone or aided by a spring, extinguishes the arc.

In the definitions just given, the fuses are defined as either expulsion or current-limiting types. A current-limiting fuse is a sealed, non-venting fuse that, when melted by a current within its interrupting rating, produces arc voltages exceeding the system voltage, which in turn forces the current to zero. The arc voltages are produced by introducing a series of high resistance arcs within the fuse. The result is a fuse that typically interrupts high fault currents within the first half cycle of the fault.

In contrast, an expulsion fuse depends on one arc to initiate the interruption process. The arc acts as a catalyst, causing the generation of de-ionizing gas from its housing. The arc is then elongated either by the force of the gases created or a spring. At some point, the arc elongates far enough to prevent a restrike after passing through a current zero. Therefore, it is not atypical for an expulsion fuse to take many cycles to clear.

4.2.1 Application Of Medium-Voltage Fuses

Many of the rules for applying expulsion fuses and current-limiting fuses are the same, but because the current-limiting fuse operates much faster on high fault currents, some additional rules must be applied.

Three basic factors must be considered when applying any fuse: voltage, continuous current-carrying capacity, and interrupting rating.

- *Voltage* – The fuse must have a voltage rating that is equal to or greater than the normal frequency recovery voltage which will be seen across the fuse under all conditions. On three-phase systems, it is a good rule of thumb that the voltage rating of the fuse be greater than or equal to the line-to-line voltage of the system.

- *Continuous current-carrying capacity* – Continuous current values that are shown on the fuse represent the level of current the fuse can carry continuously without exceeding the temperature rises as specified in ANSI C37.46. An application that exposes the fuse to a current slightly above its continuous rating but below its minimum interrupting rating may damage the fuse due to excessive heat. This is the main reason overload relays are used in series with backup current-limiting fuses for motor protection.

- *Interrupting rating* – All fuses are given a maximum interrupting rating. This rating is the maximum level of fault current that the fuse can safely interrupt. Backup current-limiting fuses are also given a minimum interrupting rating. When using backup current-limiting fuses, it is important that other protective devices are used to interrupt currents below this level.

When choosing a fuse, it is important that the fuse be properly coordinated with other protective devices located upstream and downstream. To accomplish this, one must consider the **melting time** and **clearing time** characteristics of the devices. Two curves, the minimum melting curve and the total clearing curve, provide this information. To ensure proper coordination, the following rules should be observed:

- The total clearing curve of any downstream protective device must be below a curve representing 75% of the minimum melting curve of the fuse being applied.

- The total clearing curve of the fuse being applied must lie below a curve representing 75% of the minimum melting curve for any upstream protective device.

4.3.0 CURRENT-LIMITING FUSES

To ensure proper application of a current-limiting fuse, it is important that the following additional rules be applied:

- Current-limiting fuses produce arc voltages that exceed the system voltage. Care must be taken to ensure that the peak voltages do not exceed the insulation level of the system. If the fuse voltage rating is not permitted to exceed 140% of the system voltage, there should not be a problem. This does not mean that a higher rated fuse cannot be used but points out that one must be assured that the system insulation level (BIL) will handle the peak arc voltage produced. BIL stands for *basic impulse level*, which is the reference impulse insulation strength of an electrical system.

- As with the expulsion fuse, current-limiting fuses must be properly coordinated with other protective devices on the system. For this to happen, the rules for applying an expulsion fuse must be used at all currents that cause the fuse to interrupt in 0.01 second or greater.

When other current-limiting protective devices are on the system, it becomes necessary to use I^2t values for coordination at currents causing the fuse to interrupt in less than 0.01 second. These values may be supplied as minimum and maximum values or minimum melting and total clearing I^2t curves. In either case, the following rules should be followed:

- The minimum melting I^2t of the fuse should be greater than the total clearing I^2t of the downstream current-limiting device.

- The total clearing I^2t of the fuse should be less than the minimum melting I^2t of the upstream current-limiting device.

The fuse selection chart in *Figure 11* should serve as a guide for selecting fuses on circuits of 600V or less. The dimensions of various buss fuses are shown in *Figure 12*. Both of these charts will prove invaluable on all types of projects (from residential to heavy industrial applications). Other valuable information may be found in catalogs furnished by manufacturers of overcurrent protective devices. These are usually obtainable from electrical supply houses or from manufacturers' representatives. You may also write the various manufacturers for a complete list (and price, if any) for all reference materials offered by them.

Circuit	Load	Ampere Rating	Fuse Type	Symbol	Voltage Rating (ac)	UL Class	Interrupting Rating (K)	Remarks
Main, Feeder and Branch (Conventional dimensions)	All type loads (optimum overcurrent protection)	0 to 600A	LOW PEAK® (dual-element, time-delay)	LPN-RK	250V	RK1	200	All-purpose fuses. Unequaled for combined short circuit and overload protection.
				LPS-RK	600V			
		601 to 6000A	LOW PEAK® time-delay	KRP-C	600V	L	200	
	Motors, welders, transformers, capacitor banks (circuits with heavy inrush currents)	0 to 600A	FUSETRON® (dual-element, time-delay)	FRN-R	250V	RK5	200	Moderate degree of current limitation. Time-delay passes surge currents.
				FRS-R	600V			
		601 to 4000A	LIMITRON® (time-delay)	KLU	600V	L	200	All-purpose fuse. Time-de passes surge currents.
	Non-motor loads (circuits with no heavy inrush currents)	0 to 600A	LIMITRON® (fast-acting)	KTN-R	250V	RK1	200	Same short circuit protection as LOW PEAK fuses but must be sized larger for circuits with surge currents; i.e., up to 300%.
				KTS-R	600V			
	LIMITRON fuses particularly suited for circuit breaker protection	601 to 6000A	LIMITRON® (fast-acting)	KTU	600V	L	200	A fast-acting, high-performance fuse.
	All type loads (optimum overcurrent protection)	0 to 600A	LOW-PEAK® (dual-element, time-delay)	LPJ	600V	J	200	All-purpose fuses. Unequaled for combined short circuit and overload protection.
	Non-motor loads (circuits with no heavy inrush currents)	0 to 600A	LIMITRON® (quick-acting)	JKS	600V	J	200	Very similar to KTS-R LIMITRON, but smaller.
		0 to 1200A	T-TRON™	JJN	300V	T	200	The space saver (⅓ the size of KTN-R/KTS-R).
				JJS	600V			

303F11.TIF

Figure 11. Fuse Selection Chart (600V Or Less)

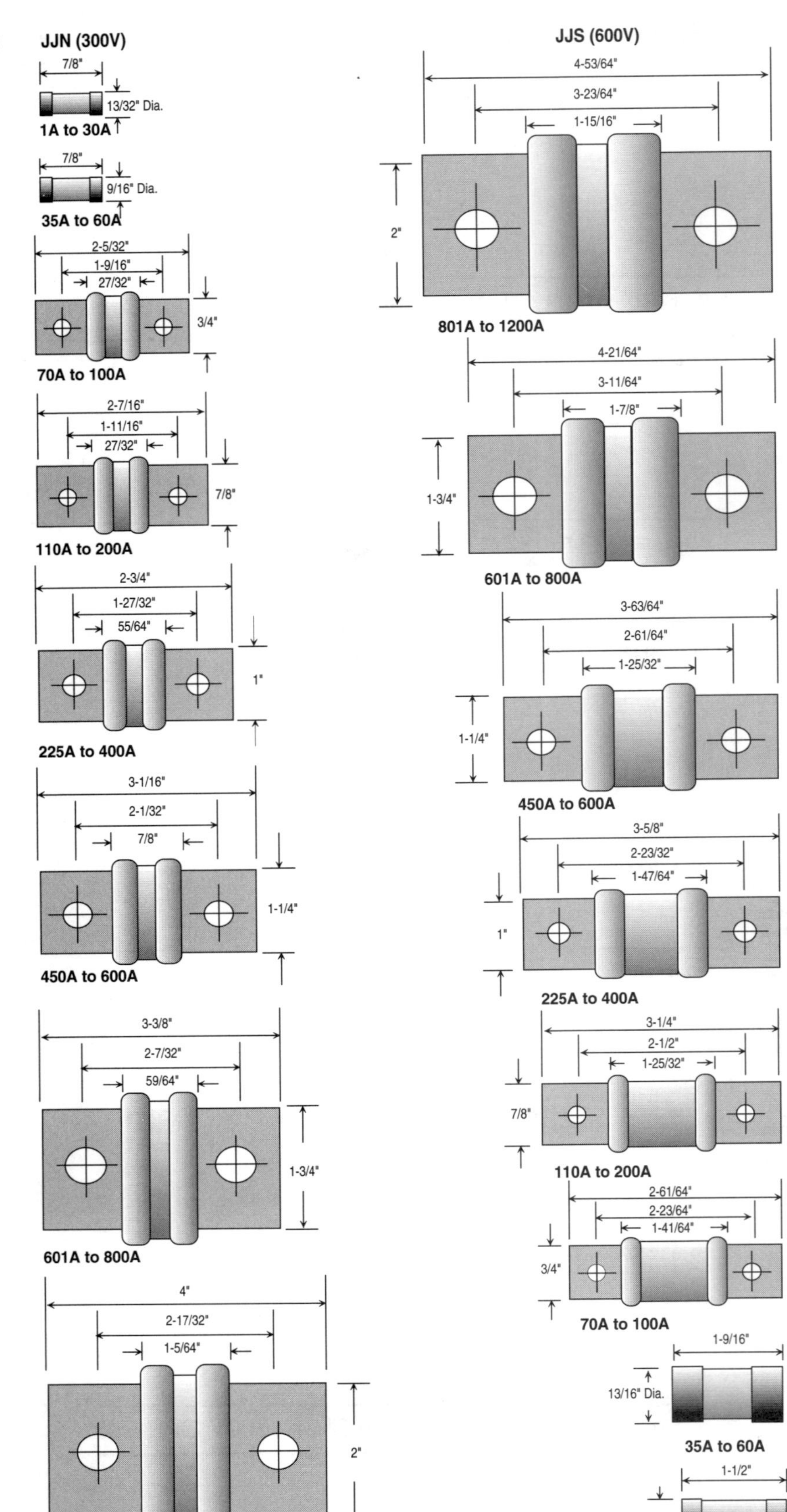

303F12A.EPS

Figure 12. Buss Fuse Dimensional Data (1 Of 3)

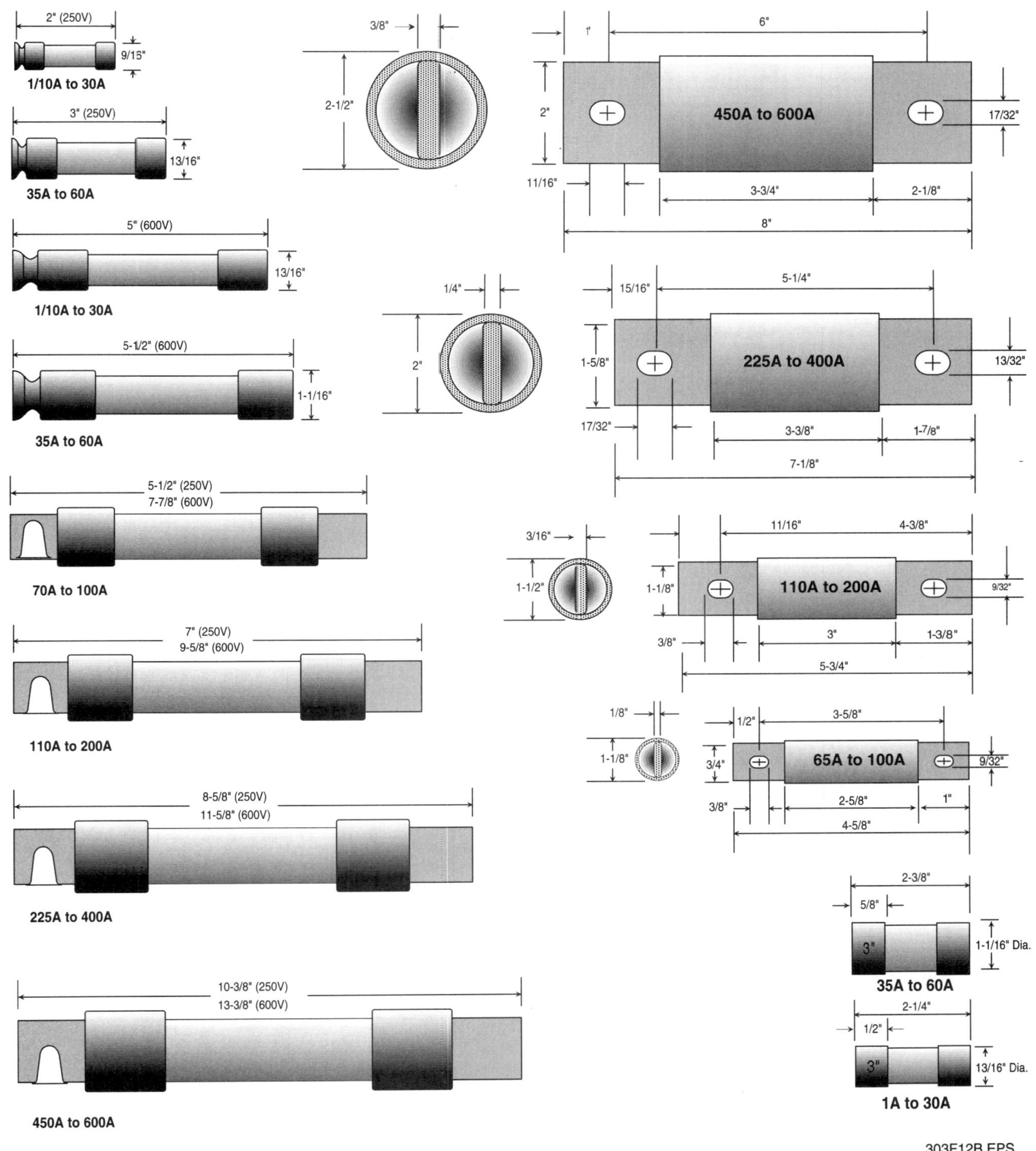

Figure 12. Buss Fuse Dimensional Data (2 Of 3)

303F12B.EPS

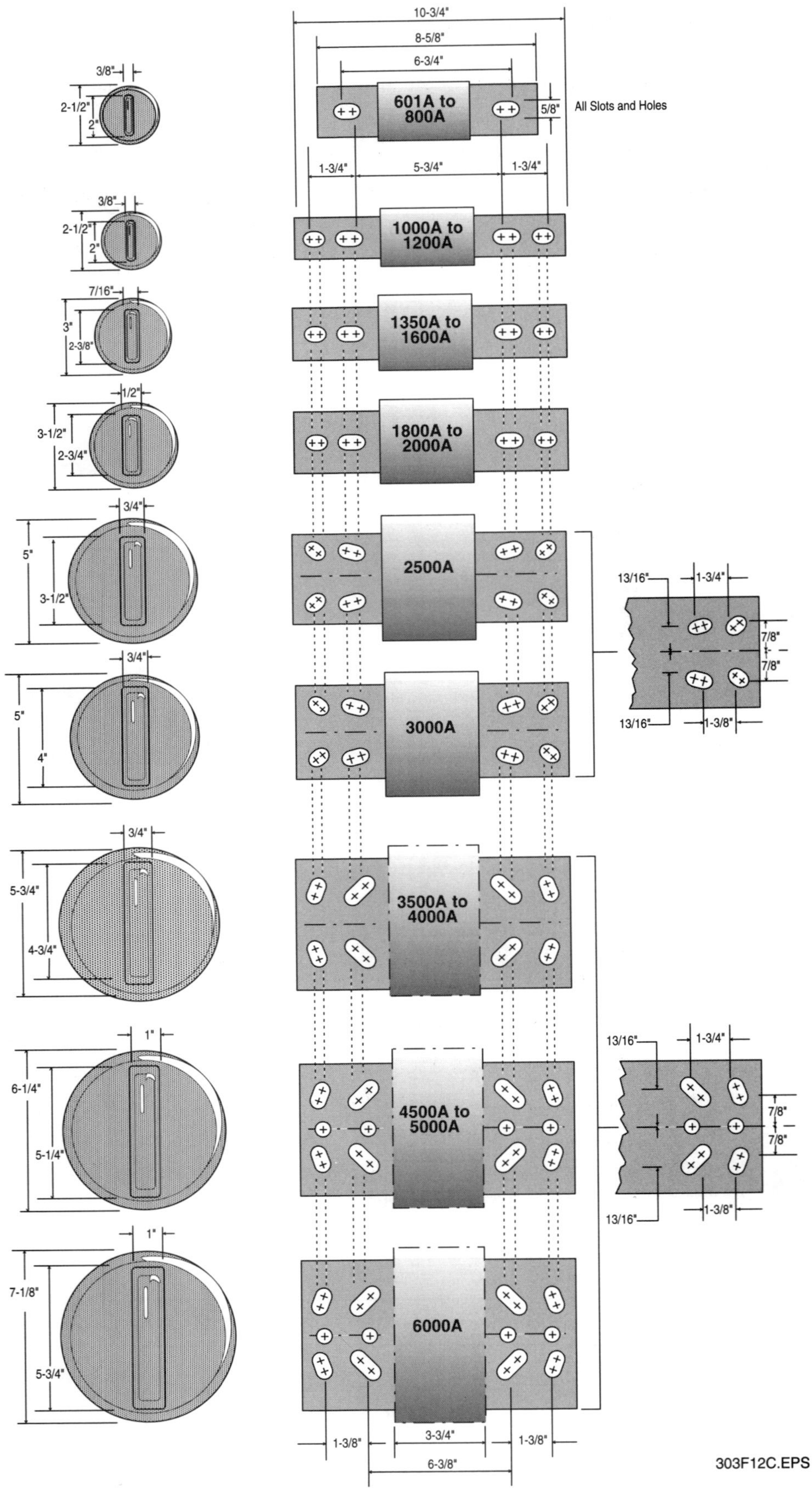

Figure 12. Buss Fuse Dimensional Data (3 Of 3)

4.4.0 FUSES FOR SELECTIVE COORDINATION

The larger the upstream fuse is relative to a downstream fuse (feeder to branch, etc.), the less possibility there is of an overcurrent in the downstream circuit causing both fuses to open. Fast action, nontime-delay fuses require at least a 3:1 ratio between the ampere rating of a large upstream, line-side, time-delay fuse to that of the downstream, load-side fuse in order to be selectively coordinated. In contrast, the minimum selective coordination ratio necessary for dual-element fuses is only 2:1 when used with low peak load-side fuses (*Figure 13*).

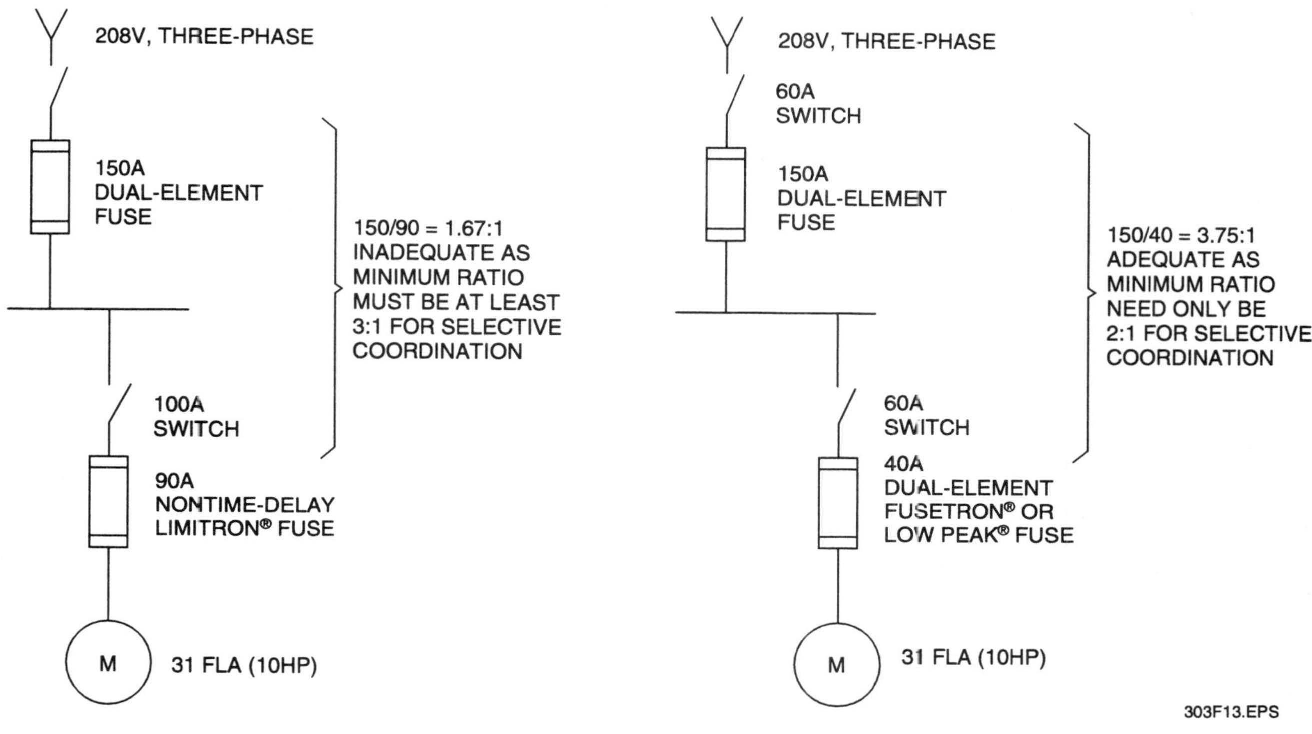

Figure 13. Fuses Used For Selective Coordination

The use of dual-element, time-delay fuses affords easy selective coordination, which hardly requires anything more than a routine check of a tabulation of required selectivity ratios. As shown in *Figure 14*, close sizing of dual-element fuses in the branch circuit for motor overload protection provides a large difference (ratio) in the ampere ratings between the feeder fuse and the branch fuse compared to the single-element, nontime-delay fuse.

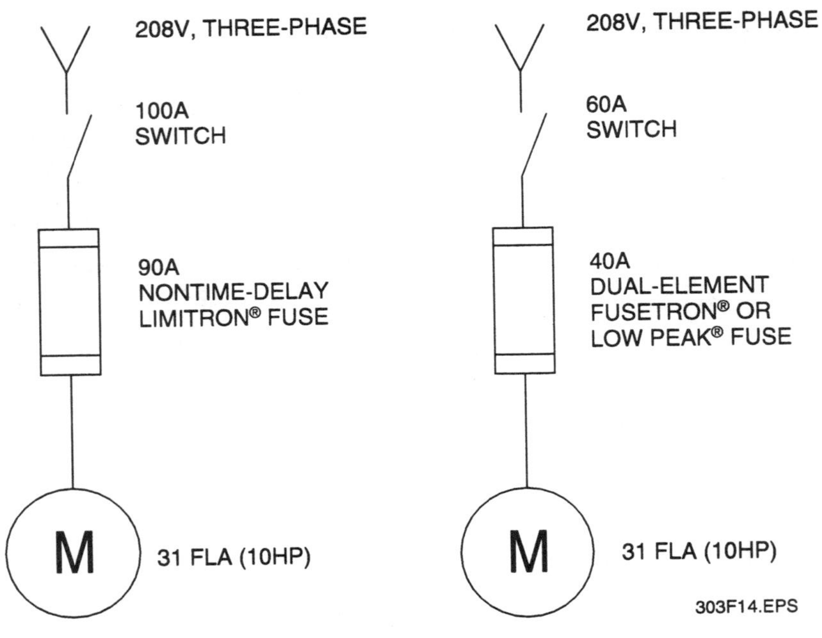

Figure 14. Comparison Of Dual-Element Fuse And Single-Element, Nontime-Delay Fuse

4.5.0   FUSE TIME-CURRENT CURVES

When a low level overcurrent occurs, a long interval of time will be required for a fuse to open (melt) and clear the fault. On the other hand, if the overcurrent is large, the fuse will open very quickly. The opening time is a function of the magnitude of the level of overcurrent. Overcurrent levels and the corresponding intervals of opening times are logarithmically plotted in graph form, as shown in *Figure 15*. Levels of overcurrent are scaled on the horizontal axis, with time intervals on the vertical axis. The curve is therefore called a *time-current* curve.

The plot in *Figure 15* reflects the characteristics of a 200A, 600V, dual-element fuse. Note that at the 1,000A overload level, the time interval which is required for the fuse to open is 10 seconds. Yet, at approximately the 2,200A overcurrent level, the opening (melt) time of the fuse is only 0.01 second. It is apparent that the time intervals become shorter and shorter as the overcurrent levels become larger. This relationship is termed an *inverse time-to-current characteristic*. Time-current curves are published or are available on most commonly-used fuses showing minimum melt, average melt, and/or total clear characteristics. Although upstream and downstream fuses are easily coordinated by adhering to simple ampere ratios, these time-current curves permit close or critical analysis of coordination.

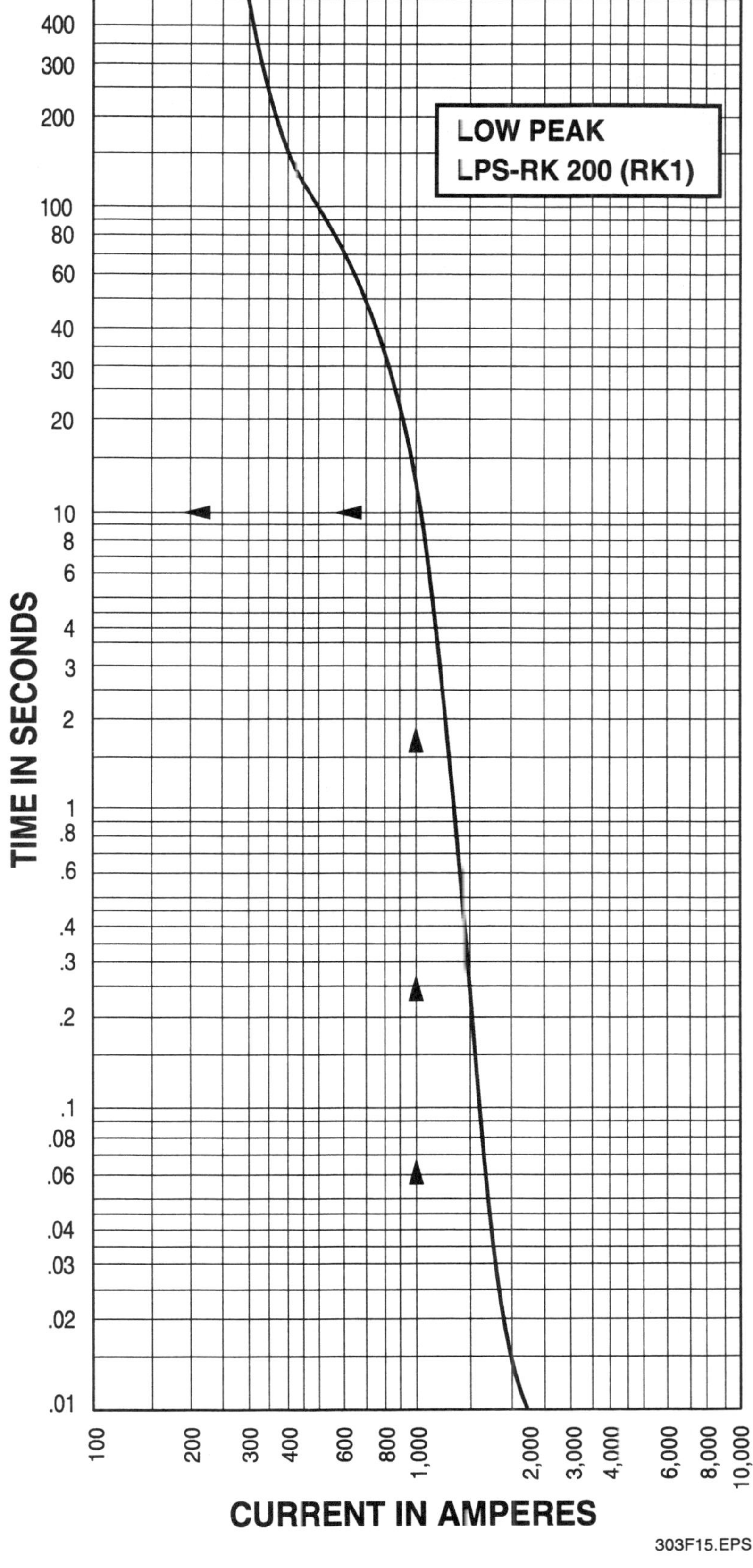

Figure 15. Typical Time-Current Curve Of A Fuse

4.5.1 Peak Let-Through Charts

Peak let-through charts enable you to determine both the peak let-through current and the apparent prospective rms symmetrical let-through current. Such charts are commonly referred to as *current limitation curves. Figure 16* shows a simplified chart with explanations of the various functions. *Figures 17 through 22* show current limitation curves for popular fuses in current use.

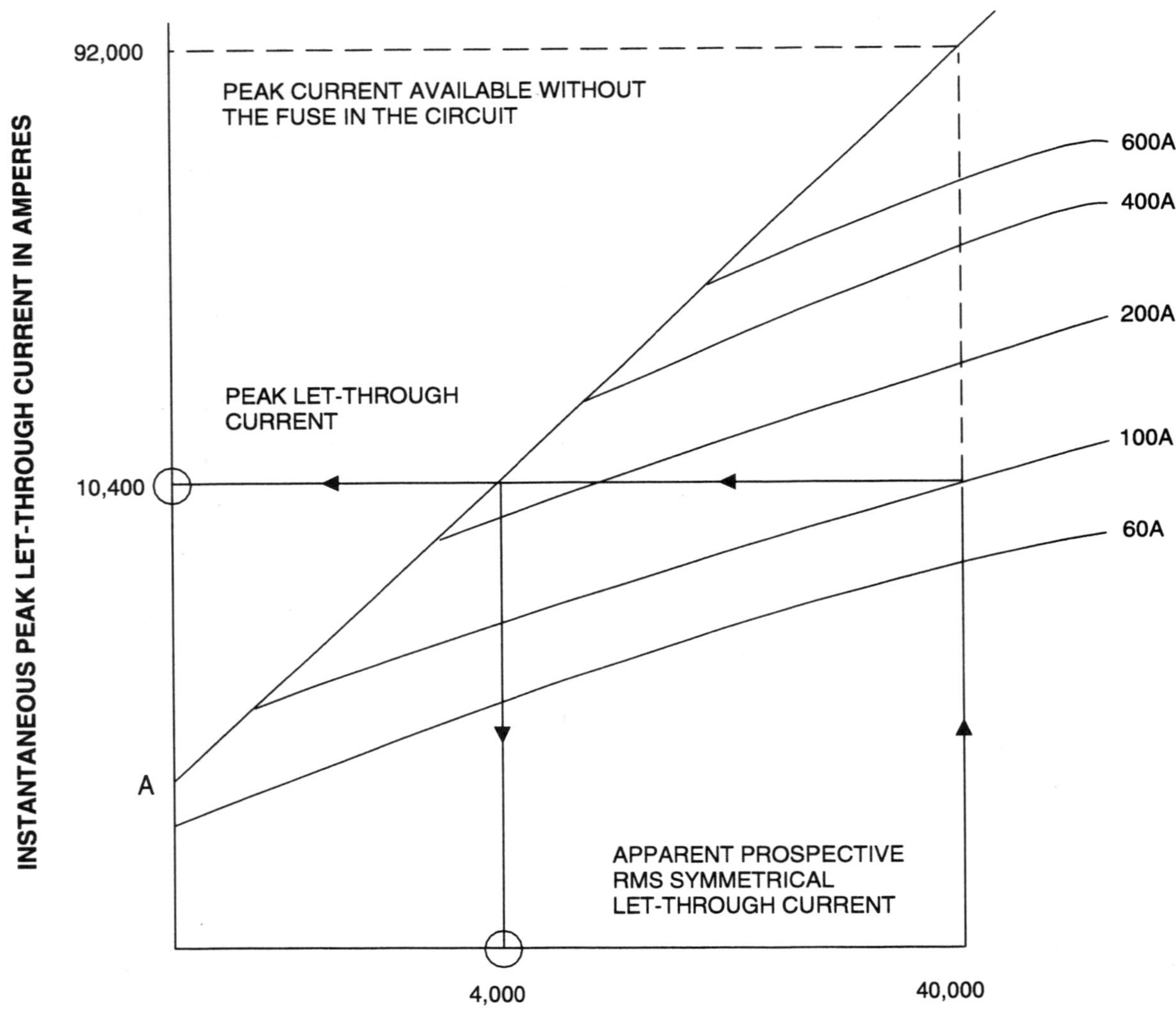

Figure 16. Principles Of Forming Current Limitation Curves

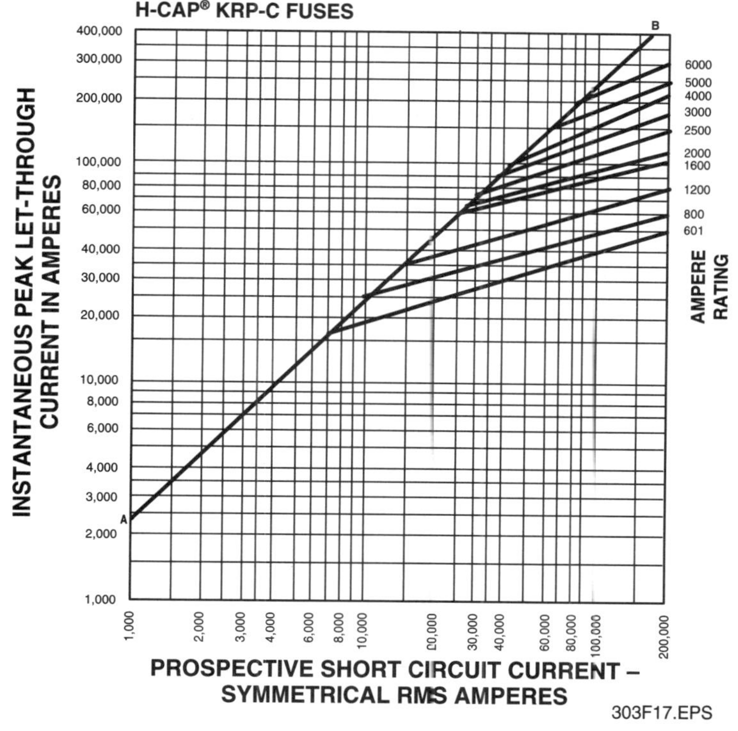

Figure 17. H-Cap® KRP-C Fuses

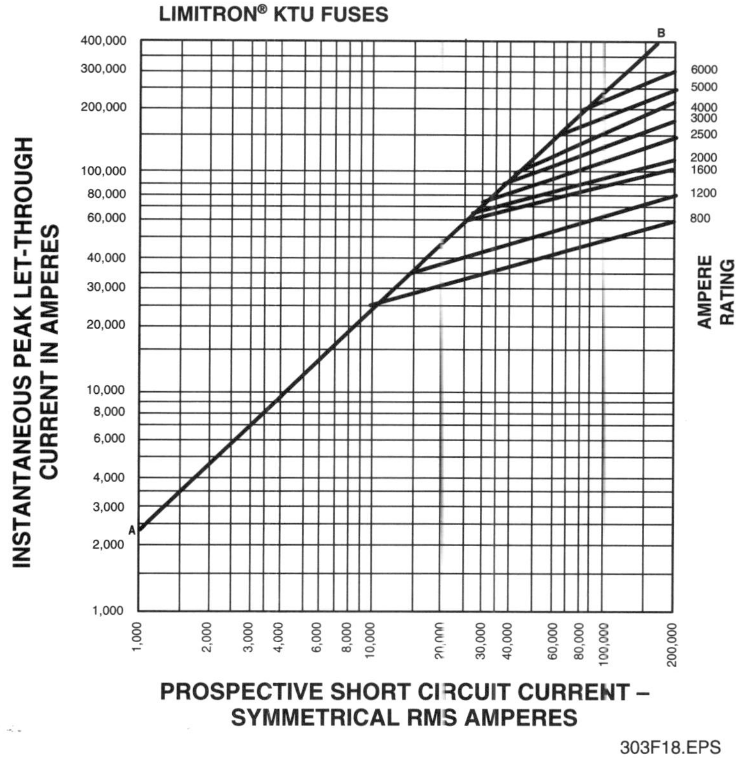

Figure 18. Limitron® KTU Fuses

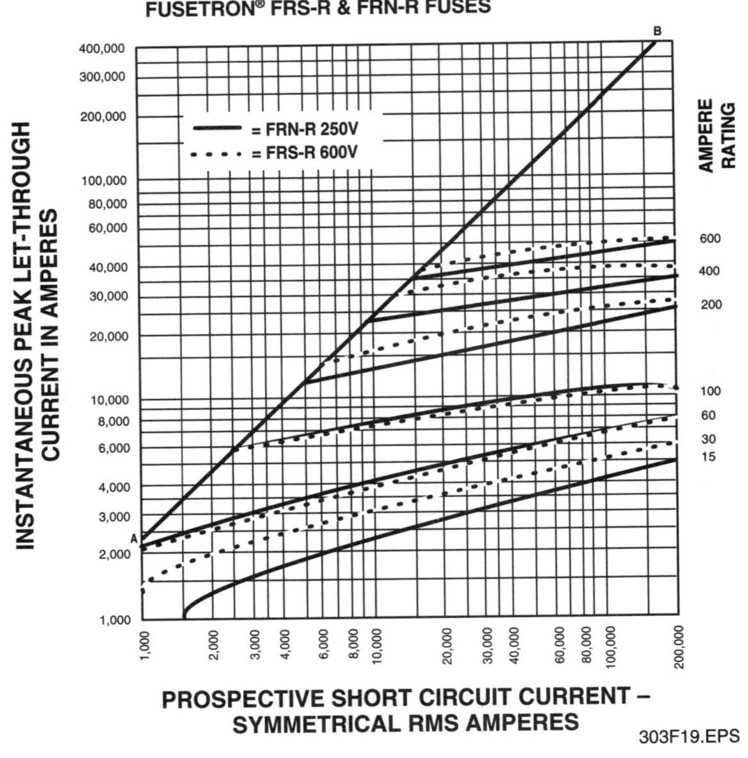

Figure 19. Fusetron® FRS-R And FRN-R Fuses

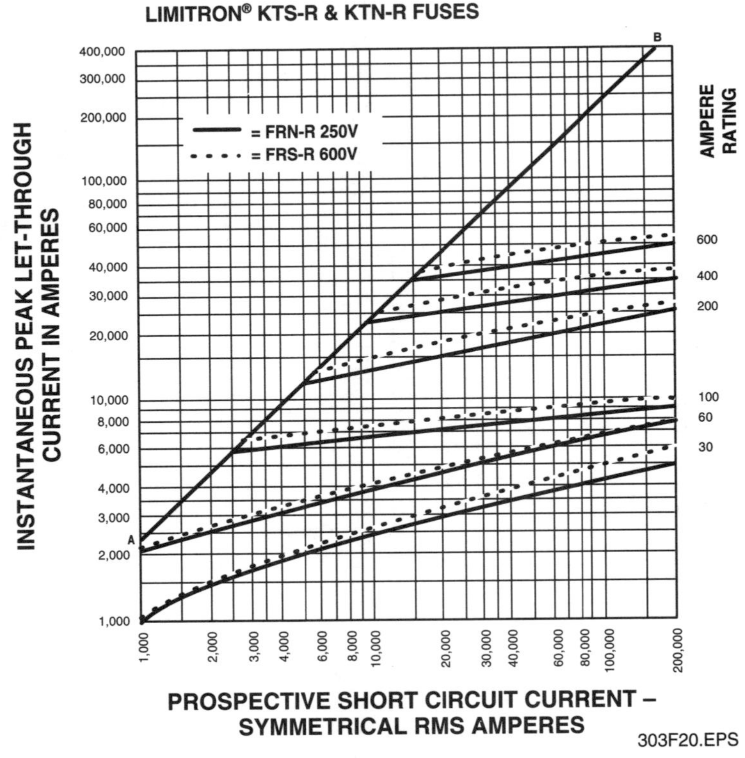

Figure 20. Limitron® KTS-R And KTN-R Fuses

ELECTRICAL — TRAINEE TASK MODULE 26303

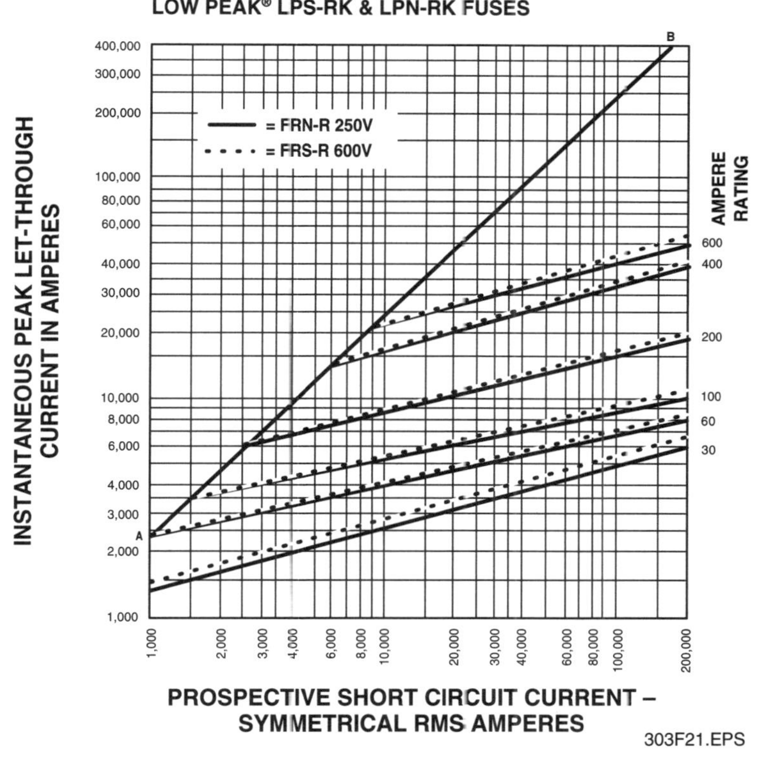

Figure 21. Low Peak® LPS-RK And LPN-RK Fuses

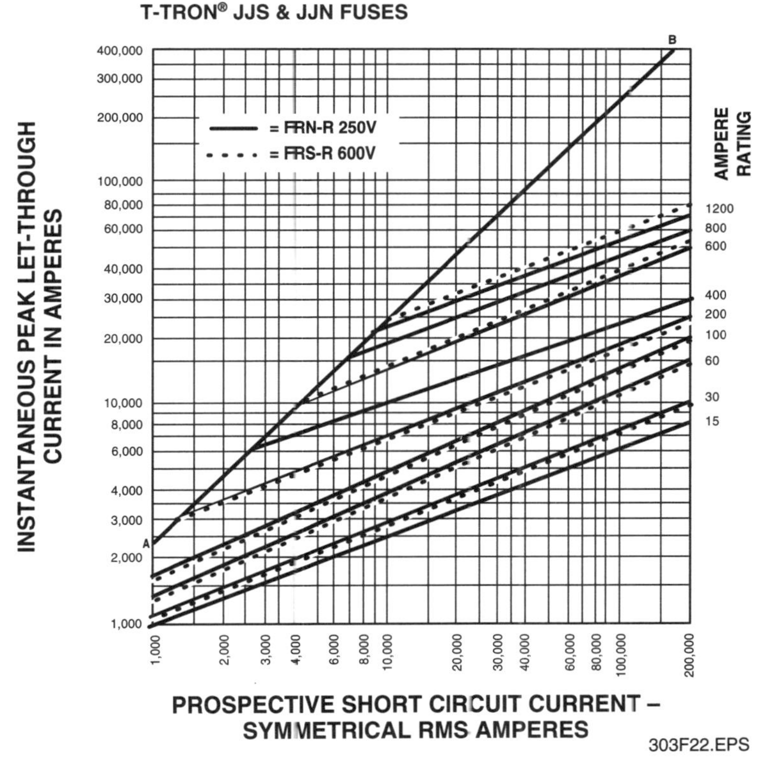

Figure 22. T-Tron® JJS And JJN Fuses

5.0.0   MOTOR OVERLOAD AND SHORT CIRCUIT PROTECTION

When used in circuits with surge currents such as those caused by motors, transformers, and other inductive components, dual-element, time-delay fuses can be sized close to full-load amperes to give maximum overcurrent protection. For example, assume that a 10hp, 208V motor has a full-load current of 31A. *Table 1* shows the fuse type, size, and switch size required by **NEC Sections 430-32 and 430-52** for a 10hp motor.

Fuse Type	Maximum Fuse Size (Amps)	Required Switch Size (Amps)
Dual-element, time-delay	45A	60A
Single-element, nontime-delay	100A	100A

Table 1. Fuse And Switch Size For A 10-Horsepower Motor (208V, 3Ø, 31 FLA)

Table 1 shows that a 45A, dual-element fuse will protect the 31A motor compared to the much larger 100A, single-element fuse necessary. It is apparent that if a sustained, harmful overload of 300% occurred in the motor circuit, the 90A, single-element fuse would never open and the motor could be damaged. The nontime-delay fuse provides only ground fault and short circuit protection—requiring separate overload protection as per the NEC.

In contrast, the 45A, dual-element fuse provides ground fault and short circuit protection plus a high degree of backup protection against motor burnout from overload or **single phasing** should other overload protective devices fail. If thermal overloads, relays, or contacts should fail to operate, the dual-element fuses will act independently to protect the motor.

Aside from providing only short circuit protection, the single-element fuse also makes it necessary to use larger size switches since a switch rating must be equal to or larger than the ampere rating of the fuse; as a result, the larger switch may cost two or three times more than would be necessary if a dual-element fuse were used (*Figure 23*).

When secondary single phasing occurs, the current in the remaining phases increases to a value of 170% to 200% of the rated full-load current. When primary single phasing occurs, unbalanced voltages that occur in the motor circuit cause excessive current. Dual-element fuses sized for motor overload protection can protect motors against the overload damage caused by single phasing.

The nontime-delay, **fast-acting fuse** must be oversized in circuits in which surge or temporary overload currents occur (**inductive load**). The response of the oversized fuse to short circuit currents is slower. Current builds up to a high level before the fuse opens, causing the current-limiting action of the oversized fuse to be less than a fuse whose ampere rating is closer to the normal full-load current of the circuit. Consequently, oversizing sacrifices some component protection and although it is permitted by the NEC, the practice is not recommended.

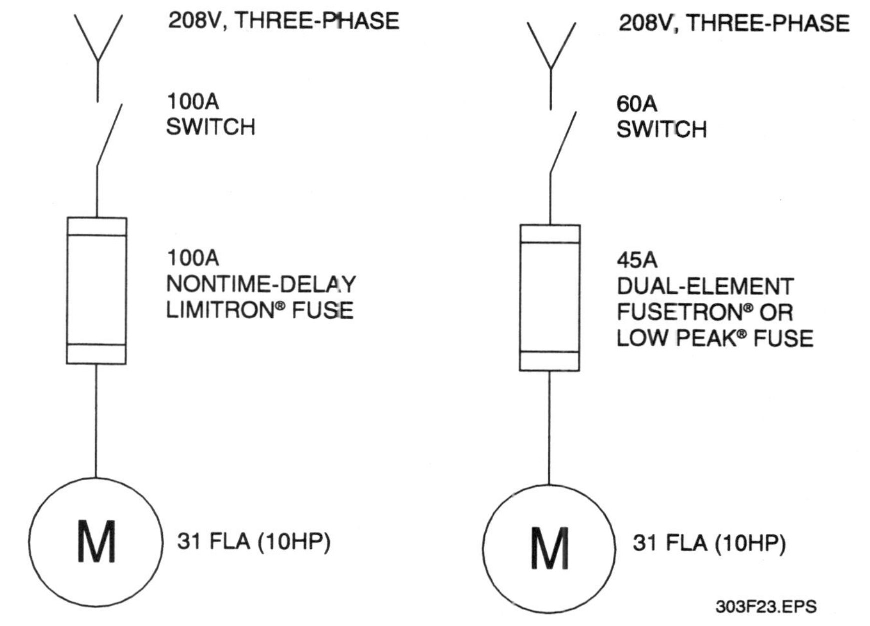

Figure 23. Dual-Element Fuses Permit The Use Of Smaller And Less Costly Switches

In actual practice, dual-element fuses used to protect motors keep short circuit currents to approximately half the value of the nontime-delay fuses, since the nontime-delay fuses must be oversized to carry the temporary starting current of motors.

6.0.0 CIRCUIT BREAKERS

Circuit breakers were covered in your Level 2 training. However, some of the more important points are worth repeating here before we cover practical applications of both fuses and circuit breakers.

Basically, a circuit breaker is a device for closing and interrupting a circuit between separable contacts under both normal and abnormal conditions. This is done manually (normal condition) by using its handle to switch it to the ON or OFF positions. However, the circuit breaker is also designed to open a circuit automatically on a predetermined overload or ground fault current without damage to itself or its associated equipment. As long as a circuit breaker is applied within its rating, it will automatically interrupt any fault and is therefore classified as an inherently safe overcurrent protective device.

The internal arrangement of a circuit breaker is shown in *Figure 24*, while its external operating characteristics are shown in *Figure 25*. Note that the handle on a circuit breaker resembles an ordinary toggle switch. On an overload, the circuit breaker opens itself or trips. In a tripped position, the handle jumps to the middle position (*Figure 25*). To reset it, turn the handle to the OFF position and then turn it as far as it will go beyond this position (RESET position); finally, turn it to the ON position.

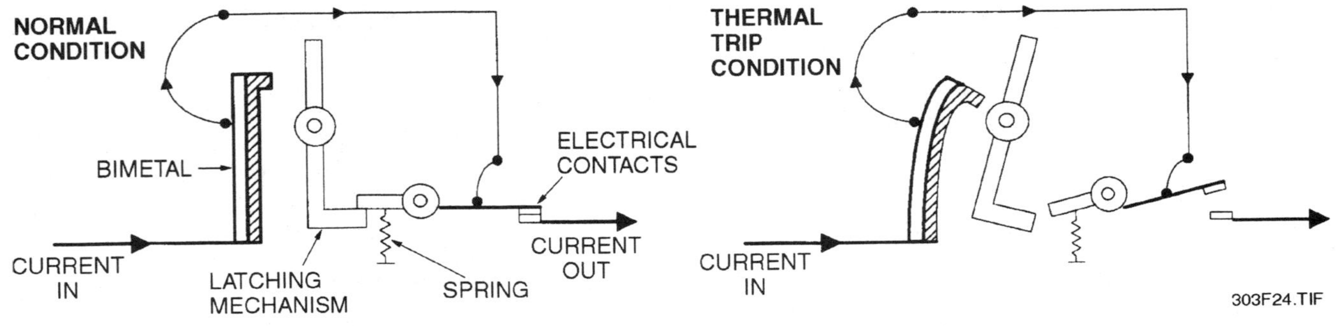

Figure 24. Internal Arrangement Of A Circuit Breaker

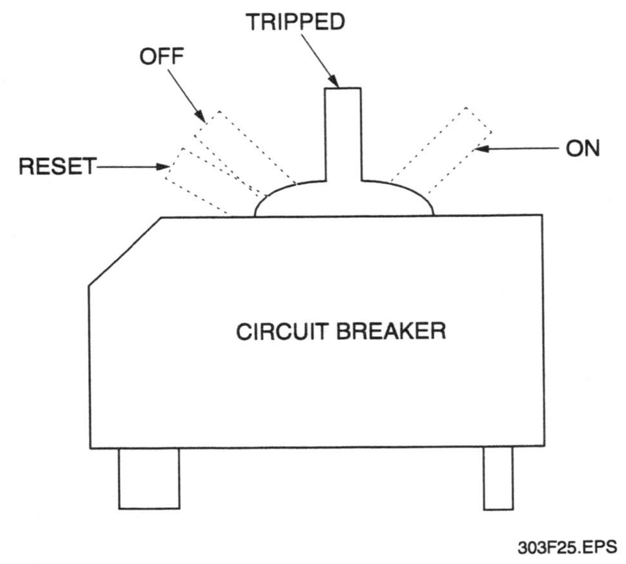

Figure 25. External Characteristics Of A Circuit Breaker

A standard molded case circuit breaker usually contains:

- A set of contacts
- A magnetic trip element
- A thermal trip element
- Line and load terminals
- Bussing used to connect these individual parts
- An enclosing housing of insulating material

The circuit breaker handle manually opens and closes the contacts and resets the automatic trip units after an interruption. Some circuit breakers also contain a manually operated push-to-trip testing mechanism.

CAUTION: When a breaker trips, always determine why it tripped before resetting it.

ELECTRICAL — TRAINEE TASK MODULE 26303

Circuit breakers are grouped for identification according to given current ranges. Each group is classified by the largest ampere rating of its range. These groups are:

* 15A – 100A
* 125A – 225A
* 250A – 400A
* 500A – 1,000A
* 1,200A – 2,000A

Therefore, they are classified as 100A, 225A, 400A, 1,000A, and 2,000A frames. These numbers are commonly referred to as *frame classifications* or *frame sizes* and are terms applied to groups of molded case circuit breakers which are physically interchangeable with each other.

6.1.0   INTERRUPTING CAPACITY RATING

In most large commercial and industrial installations, it is necessary to calculate available short circuit currents at various points in a system to determine if the equipment meets the requirements of **NEC Sections 110-9 and 110-10**. There are a number of methods used to determine the short circuit requirements in an electrical system. Some give approximate values, while others require extensive computations and are quite exacting.

The breaker interrupting capacity is based on tests to which the breaker is subjected. There are two such tests; one is set up by UL and the other by NEMA. The NEMA tests are self-certification while UL tests are certified by unbiased witnesses. UL tests have been limited to a maximum of 10,000A in the past, so the emphasis was placed on NEMA tests with higher ratings. UL tests now include the NEMA tests plus other ratings. Consequently, the emphasis is now being placed on UL tests.

The interrupting capacity of a circuit breaker is based on its rated voltage. Where the circuit breaker can be used on more than one voltage, the interrupting capacity will be shown for each voltage level. For example, the LA-type circuit breaker has 42,000A symmetrical interrupting capacity at 240V, 30,000A symmetrical at 480V, and 22,000A symmetrical at 600V.

7.0.0   CONDUCTOR PROTECTION

All conductors are to be protected against overcurrents in accordance with their ampacities as set forth in **NEC Section 240-3**. They must also be protected against short circuit current damage as required by **NEC Sections 240-1 and 110-10**.

Ampere ratings of overcurrent protective devices must not be greater than the ampacity of the conductor. There is, however, an exception. **NEC Section 240-3** states that if such conductor rating does not correspond to a standard size overcurrent protective device, the next larger size overcurrent protective device may be used, provided its rating does not exceed 800A and that the conductor is not part of a multi-outlet branch circuit supplying receptacles for cord- and plug-connected portable loads. When the ampacity of a busway or cablebus does not correspond to a standard overcurrent protective device, the next larger standard rating may be used only if the rating does not exceed 800A (***NEC Sections 364-10 and 365-5***).

Standard overcurrent device sizes stipulated in ***NEC Section 240-6*** are 15A, 20A, 25A, 30A, 35A, 40A, 45A, 50A, 60A, 70A, 80A, 90A, 100A, 110A, 125A, 150A, 175A, 200A, 225A, 250A, 300A, 350A, 400A, 450A, 500A, 600A, 700A, 800A, 1,000A, 1,200A, 1,600A, 2,000A, 2,500A, 3,000A, 4,000A, 5,000A, and 6,000A. Additional standard ratings for fuses are 1A, 3A, 6A, 10A, and 601A.

Note: The small fuse ampere ratings of 1A, 3A, 6A, and 10A were added to the NEC to provide more effective short circuit and ground fault protection for motor circuits in accordance with ***NEC Sections 430-40 and 430-52*** and UL requirements for protecting the overload relays in controllers for very small motors.

Protection of conductors under short circuit conditions is accomplished by obtaining the maximum short circuit current available at the supply end of the conductor, the short circuit withstand rating of the conductor, and the short circuit let-through characteristics of the overcurrent device.

When a noncurrent-limiting device is used for short circuit protection, the conductor's short circuit withstand rating must be properly selected based on the overcurrent protective device's ability to protect the circuit (***Figure 26***).

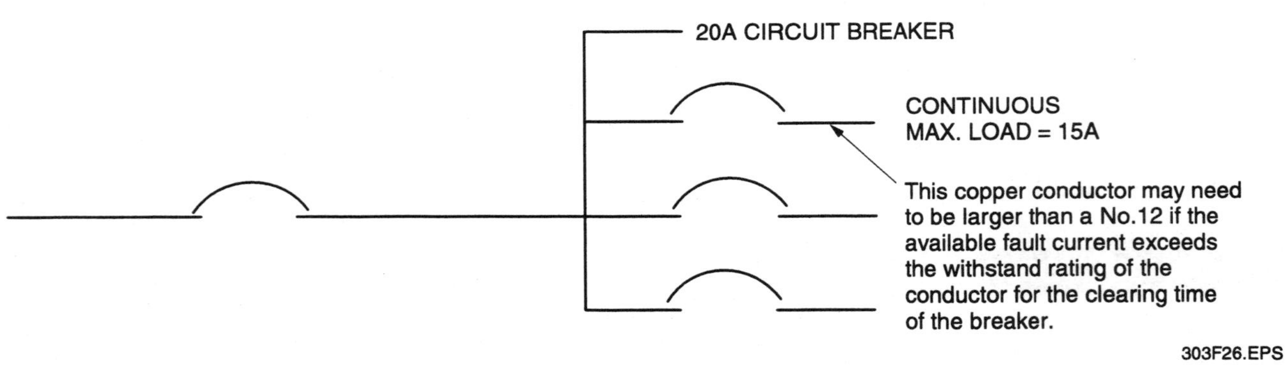

Figure 26. Conductor Protection With Noncurrent-Limiting Device

It is necessary to check the energy let-through of the overcurrent device under short circuit conditions and select a wire size of sufficient short circuit withstand ability.

In contrast, the use of a current-limiting device permits a fuse to be selected which limits short circuit current to a level less than that of the conductor's short circuit withstand rating, doing away with the need for oversized ampacity conductors (*Figure 27*).

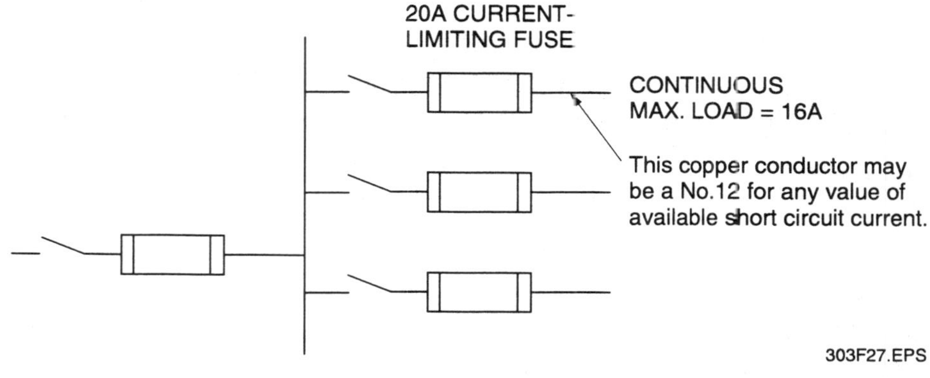

Figure 27. Circuits Protected By Current-Limiting Devices

In many applications, it is desirable to use the convenience of a circuit breaker for a disconnecting means and general overcurrent protection, supplemented by current-limiting fuses at strategic points in the circuits.

Flexible cord, including tinsel cord and extension cords, must be protected against overcurrent in accordance with their ampacities.

7.1.0 LOCATION OF OVERCURRENT DEVICES IN CIRCUITS

In general, overcurrent protection must be installed at points where the conductors receive their supply, that is, at the beginning or line side of a branch circuit or feeder. See *NEC Section 240-21*. Exceptions to this rule follow:

- Per *NEC Section 240-21(b)(1)*, overcurrent protection is not required at the conductor supply if a feed tap conductor is not over 10' long; is enclosed in raceway; does not extend beyond the switchboard, panelboard, disconnecting means, or control device which it supplies; and has an ampacity not less than the combined computed loads supplied and not less than the rating of the device supplied by the tap conductors or not less than the rating of the overcurrent device at the tap conductor termination. For field-installed taps, the ampacity of the overcurrent device on the line side of the tap conductor cannot exceed 10 times the ampacity of the tap conductor.

- Per *NEC Section 240-21(b)(2)*, overcurrent protection is not required at the conductor supply if a feeder tap conductor is not over 25' long; is suitably protected from physical damage; has an ampacity not less than ⅓ that of the overcurrent device protecting the feeder conductors; and terminates in a single overcurrent device.

- Per **NEC Section 240-21(b)(3)**, overcurrent protection is not required at the conductor supply if a transformer feeder tap has primary conductors at least ⅓ ampacity and/or secondary conductors at least ⅓ ampacity when multiplied by the approximate transformer turns ratio of the overcurrent device protecting the feeder conductors; the total length of one primary plus one secondary conductor (excluding any portion of the primary conductor that is protected at its ampacity) is not over 25' in length; the secondary conductors terminate in a single overcurrent device rated at the ampacity of the tap conductors; and if the primary and secondary conductors are suitably protected from physical damage.

- Per **NEC Section 240-21(b)(4)**, overcurrent protection is not required at the conductor supply if a feeder tap is not over 25' long horizontally and not over 100' long total length in high bay manufacturing buildings when only qualified persons will service such a system, the ampacity of the tap conductors is not less than ⅓ of the rating of the overcurrent device protecting the feeder conductors; terminate in a single overcurrent device; are suitably protected from physical damage or are enclosed in a raceway; are at least No. 6 AWG copper or No. 4 AWG aluminum; are continuous from end-to-end and contain no splices; do not penetrate walls, floors, or ceilings; and are made no less than 30' from the floor.

WARNING!	Smaller conductors tapped to larger conductors can be a serious hazard. If not protected against short circuit conditions, these unprotected conductors can vaporize or incur severe insulation damage.

- Per **NEC Section 240-21(c)(3)**, transformer secondary conductors of separately derived systems do not require overcurrent protection at the transformer terminals if they are installed in an industrial location; if they have secondary conductors that are less than 25' long; if the secondary conductor ampacity is at least equal to the secondary full-load current of the transformer and the sum of all terminating, grouped overcurrent devices; and if they are protected from physical damage.

Note:	Switchboard and panelboard protection, along with transformer protection, must still be observed. See **NEC Sections 384-16 and 450-3**.

7.1.1 Lighting/Appliance Loads

The branch circuit rating must be classified in accordance with the rating of the overcurrent protective device. Classifications for those branch circuits other than individual loads must be 15A, 20A, 30A, 40A, and 50A, as specified in **NEC Section 210-3**.

Branch circuit conductors must have an ampacity of the rating of the branch circuit and not less than the load to be served (***NEC Section 210-19***). The minimum size branch circuit conductor that can be used is No. 14 [***NEC Section 210-19(d)***]. However, there are some exceptions, as specified in ***NEC Section 210-19***.

Branch circuit conductors and equipment must be protected by an overcurrent protective device whose ampere rating conforms to ***NEC Section 210-20***. Basically, the branch circuit conductor and overcurrent protective device must be sized for the actual noncontinuous load plus 125% of the continuous load. The overcurrent protection size must not be greater than the conductor ampacity. Branch circuits rated 15A through 50A with two or more outlets (other than receptacle circuits) must be fused at their rating and the branch circuit conductor sized according to ***NEC Table 210-24***.

7.1.2   Feeder Circuits

The feeder fuse ampere rating and feeder conductor ampacity must be as follows:

- *Feeder circuit with no motor load* – The fuse size must be at least 125% of the continuous load plus 100% of the noncontinuous load. Do not size fuses larger than the ampacity of the conductor.
- *Feeder circuit with all motor loads* – Size the fuse at 125% of the full-load current of the largest motor plus the full-load current of all motors.
- *Feeder circuit with mixed loads* – Size the fuse at the sum of 125% of the full-load current of the largest motor plus 100% of the full-load current of all other motors plus 125% of the continuous, non-motor load plus 100% of the noncontinuous, non-motor load.

7.1.3   Service Equipment

Each ungrounded service entrance conductor must have an overcurrent device in series with a rating not higher than the ampacity of the conductor. The service overcurrent devices shall be part of the service disconnecting means or be located immediately adjacent to it (***NEC Section 230-91***).

Service disconnecting means can consist of one to six switches or circuit breakers for each service or for each set of service-entrance conductors permitted in ***NEC Section 230-2***. When more than one switch is used, the switches must be grouped together (***NEC Section 230-72***).

7.1.4   Transformer Secondary Conductors

Field installations indicate nearly 50% of transformers installed do not have secondary protection. The NEC *requires* overcurrent protection for lighting and appliance panelboards and *recommends* that secondary conductors be protected from damage by the proper overcurrent protective device. For example, the primary overcurrent device protecting a three-wire transformer cannot offer protection to the secondary conductors. ***NEC Section 240-3(f)*** and ***NEC Section 240-21(c)*** discuss protection of transformer secondary conductors.

7.1.5 Motor Circuit Protection

Motors and motor circuits have unique operating characteristics and circuit components. Therefore, these circuits must be dealt with differently from other types of loads. Generally, two levels of overcurrent protection are required for motor branch circuits:

- *Overload protection* – Motor running overload protection is intended to protect the system components and motor from damaging overload currents.
- *Short circuit protection (includes ground fault protection)* – Short circuit protection is intended to protect the motor circuit components such as the conductors, switches, controllers, overload relays, motor, etc., against short circuit currents or grounds. This level of protection is commonly referred to as *motor branch circuit protection.* Dual-element fuses are designed to provide this protection, as long as they are sized correctly.

There are a variety of ways to protect a motor circuit, depending upon the user's objective. The ampere rating of an overcurrent protective device selected for motor protection depends on whether the overcurrent protective device is of the dual-element, time-delay type or the nontime-delay type.

In general, nontime-delay fuses can be sized at 300% of the motor full-load current for ordinary motors so that the normal motor starting current does not affect the fuse. Dual-element, time-delay fuses are able to withstand normal motor starting current and can be sized closer to the actual motor rating than nontime-delay fuses.

A summary of NEC regulations governing overcurrent protection is covered in *Table 2,* while the table in *Figure 28* gives generalized fuse application guidelines for motor branch circuits. *Figure 29* may be used to select dual-element fuses for motor protection. *Figure 30* is a summary of overcurrent protection applications and electrical systems.

Application	Rule	NEC Reference
Scope	Overcurrent protection for conductors and equipment is provided to open the circuit if the current reaches a value that will cause an excessive or dangerous temperature in conductors or conductor insulation. See also ***NEC Sections 110-9 and 110-10*** for requirements for interrupting capacity and protection against fault currents.	***NEC Section 240-1 FPN***
Protection required	Each ungrounded service-entrance conductor must have overcurrent protection in series with each ungrounded conductor.	***NEC Section 230-90(a)***
Number of devices	Up to six circuit breakers or sets of fuses may be considered as the overcurrent device.	***NEC Section 230-90(a), Exception No. 3***
Location in building	The overcurrent device must be part of the service disconnecting means or be located immediately adjacent to it.	***NEC Section 230-91***
Accessibility	In a property comprising more than one building under single management, the ungrounded conductors supplying each building served shall be protected by overcurrent devices, which may be located in the building served or in another building on the same property, provided they are accessible to the occupants of the building served. In a multiple-occupancy building, each occupant shall have access to the overcurrent protective devices.	***NEC Sections 230-92 and 230-72(c), Exception***
Location in circuit	The overcurrent device must protect all circuits and devices, except equipment which may be connected on the supply side, including: (1) service switch; (2) special equipment, such as surge arrestors; (3) circuits for emergency supply and load management (where separately protected); (4) circuits for fire alarms or fire pump equipment (where separately protected); (5) meters with all metal housing grounded (600V or less); (6) control circuits for automatic service equipment, if suitable overcurrent protection and disconnecting means are provided.	***NEC Section 230-94 plus Exceptions***
Installation and use	Listed or labeled equipment shall be used or installed in accordance with any instructions included in the listing or labeling.	***NEC Section 110-3(b)***
Interrupting rating	Equipment intended to interrupt current at fault levels shall have an interrupting rating sufficient for the system voltage and the current which is available at the line terminals of the equipment.	***NEC Section 110-9***
Circuit impedance and other characteristics	The overcurrent protective devices, total impedance, component short circuit current ratings, and other characteristics of the circuit to be protected shall be so selected and coordinated as to permit the circuit protective devices used to clear a fault without the occurrence of extensive damage to the electrical components of the circuit.	***NEC Section 110-10***
General	Bonding shall be provided where necessary to ensure electrical continuity and the capacity to safely conduct any fault current likely to be imposed.	***NEC Section 250-2(c)***
Bonding other enclosures	Metal raceways, cable trays, cable armor, cable sheath, enclosures, frames, fittings, and other metal noncurrent-carrying parts that are to serve as grounding conductors with or without the use of supplementary equipment grounding conductors shall be effectively bonded where necessary to ensure electrical continuity and the capacity to safely conduct any fault current likely to be imposed on them. Any nonconductive paint, enamel, or similar coating shall be removed at threads, contact points, and contact surfaces or be connected by means of fittings so designed as to make such removal unnecessary.	***NEC Section 250-96(a)***

Table 2. NEC Regulations For Overcurrent Protection

Type of Motor	Dual-Element, Time-Delay Fuses			Nontime-Delay Fuses
	Desired Level of Protection			
	Motor Overload and Short Circuit	**Backup Overload and Short Circuit**	**Short Circuit Only (Based on *NEC Tables 430-147 through 430-150* current ratings)**	**Short Circuit Only (Based on *NEC Tables 430-147 through 430-150* current ratings)**
Service Factor 1.15 or Greater or 40°C Temp. Rise or Less	125% or less of motor nameplate current	125% or next standard size (not to exceed 140%)	150% to 175%	150% to 300%
Service Factor Less Than 1.15 or Greater Than 40°C Temp. Rise	115% or less of motor nameplate current	115% or next standard size (not to exceed 130%)	150% to 175%	150% to 300%

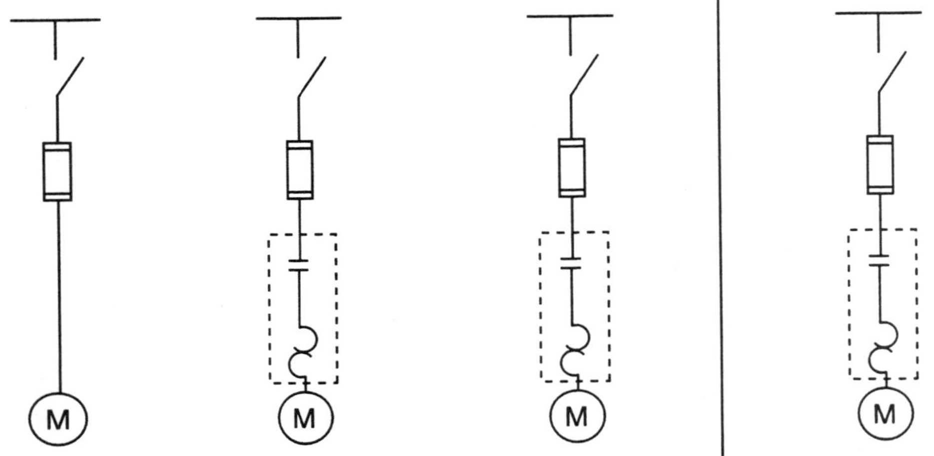

Fuses give overload and short circuit protection.

Overload relay gives overload protection and fuses provide backup overload protection.

Overload relay provides overload protection and fuses provide only short circuit protection.

Overload relay provides overload protection and fuses provide only short circuit protection.

303F28.EPS

Figure 28. Fuse Application Guidelines For Motor Branch Circuits

Dual-Element Fuse Size	Motor Protection (Used without properly sized overload relays). Motor Full-Load Amps		Backup Motor Protection (Used with properly sized overload relays). Motor Full-Load Amps	
	Motor Service Factor of 1.15 or Greater or With Temp. Rise Not Over 40° C.	Motor Service Factor Less Than 1.15 or With Temp. Rise Not Over 40° C.	Motor Service Factor of 1.15 or Greater or With Temp. Rise Not Over 40° C.	Motor Service Factor of Less Than 1.15 or With Temp. Rise Not Over 40° C.
$\frac{1}{10}$	0.08 - 0.09	0.09 - 0.10	0 - 0.08	0 - 0.09
$\frac{1}{8}$	0.10 - 0.11	0.11 - 0.125	0.09 - 0.10	0.10 -
$\frac{5}{100}$	0.12 - 0.15	0.14 - 0.15	0.11 - 0.12	0.12 - 0.13
$\frac{2}{10}$	0.16 - 0.19	0.18 - 0.20	0.13 - 0.16	0.14 - 0.17
$\frac{1}{4}$	0.20 - 0.23	0.22 - 0.25	0.17 - 0.20	0.18 - 0.22
$\frac{3}{10}$	0.24 - 0.30	0.27 - 0.30	0.21 - 0.24	0.23 - 0.26
$\frac{4}{10}$	0.32 - 0.39	0.35 - 0.40	0.25 - 0.32	0.27 - 0.35
$\frac{1}{2}$	0.40 - 0.47	0.44 - 0.50	0.33 - 0.40	0.36 - 0.43
$\frac{6}{10}$	0.48 - 0.60	0.53 - 0.60	0.41 - 0.48	0.44 - 0.52
$\frac{8}{10}$	0.64 - 0.79	0.70 - 0.80	0.49 - 0.64	0.53 - 0.70
1	0.80 - 0.89	0.87 - 0.97	0.65 - 0.80	0.71 - 0.87
$1\frac{1}{8}$	0.90 - 0.99	0.98 - 1.08	0.81 - 0.90	0.88 - 0.98
$1\frac{1}{4}$	1.00 - 1.11	1.09 - 1.21	0.91 - 1.00	0.99 - 1.09
$1\frac{4}{10}$	1.12 - 1.19	1.22 - 1.30	1.01 - 1.12	1.10 - 1.22
$1\frac{1}{2}$	1.20 - 1.27	1.31 - 1.39	1.13 - 1.20	1.23 - 1.30
$1\frac{6}{10}$	1.28 - 1.43	1.40 - 1.56	1.21 - 1.28	1.31 - 1.39
$1\frac{8}{10}$	1.44 - 1.59	1.57 - 1.73	1.29 - 1.44	1.40 - 1.57
2	1.60 - 1.79	1.74 - 1.95	1.45 - 1.60	1.58 - 1.74
$2\frac{1}{4}$	1.80 - 1.99	1.96 - 2.17	1.61 - 1.80	1.75 - 1.96
$2\frac{1}{2}$	2.00 - 2.23	2.18 - 2.43	1.81 - 2.00	1.97 - 2.17

303F29A.TIF

Figure 29. Selection Of Fuses For Motor Protection (1 Of 3)

Dual-Element Fuse Size	Motor Protection (Used without properly sized overload relays). Motor Full-Load Amps		Backup Motor Protection (Used with properly sized overload relays). Motor Full-Load Amps	
	Motor Service Factor of 1.15 or Greater or With Temp. Rise Not Over 40° C.	Motor Service Factor Less Than 1.15 or With Temp. Rise Not Over 40° C.	Motor Service Factor of 1.15 or Greater or With Temp. Rise Not Over 40° C.	Motor Service Factor of Less Than 1.15 or With Temp. Rise Not Over 40° C.
$2^6/_{10}$	2.24 - 2.39	2.44 - 2.60	2.01 - 2.24	2.18 - 2.43
3	2.40 - 2.55	2.61 - 2.78	2.25 - 2.40	2.44 - 2.60
$3^2/_{10}$	2.56 - 2.79	2.79 - 3.04	2.41 - 2.56	2.61 - 2.78
$3^1/_2$	2.80 - 3.19	3.05 3.47	2.57 - 2.80	2.79 - 3.04
4	3.20 - 3.59	3.48 - 3.91	2.81 - 3.20	3.05 - 3.48
$4^1/_2$	3.60 - 3.99	3.92 - 4.34	3.21 - 3.60	3.49 - 3.91
5	4.00 - 4.47	4.35 - 4.86	3.61 - 4.00	3.92 - 4.35
$5^6/_{10}$	4.48 - 4.79	4.87 - 5.21	4.01 - 4.48	4.36 - 4.87
6	4.80 - 4.99	5.22 - 5.43	4.49 - 4.80	4.88 - 5.22
$6^1/_4$	5.00 - 5.59	5.44 - 6.08	4.81 - 5.00	5.23 - 5.43
7	5.60 - 5.99	6.09 - 6.52	5.01 - 5.60	5.44 - 6.09
$7^1/_2$	6.00 - 6.39	6.53 - 6.95	5.61 - 6.00	6.10 - 6.52
8	6.40 - 7.19	6.96 - 7.82	6.01 - 6.40	6.53 - 6.96
9	7.20 - 7.99	7.83 - 8.69	6.41 - 7.20	6.97 - 7.83
10	8.00 - 9.59	8.70 - 10.00	7.21 - 8.00	7.84 - 8.70
12	9.60 - 11.99	10.44 - 12.00	8.01 - 9.60	8.71 - 10.43
15	12.00 - 13.99	13.05 - 15.00	9.61 - 12.00	10.44 - 13.04
$17^1/_2$	14.00 - 15.99	15.22 - 17.39	12.01 - 14.00	13.05 - 15.21
20	16.00 - 19.99	17.40 - 20.00	14.01 - 16.00	15.22 - 17.39
25	20.00 - 23.99	21.74 - 25.00	16.01 - 20.00	17.40 - 21.74
30	24.00 - 27.99	26.09 - 30.00	20.01 - 24.00	21.75 - 26.09
35	28.00 - 31.99	30.44 - 34.78	24.01 - 28.00	26.10 - 30.43

303F29B.TIF

Figure 29. Selection Of Fuses For Motor Protection (2 Of 3)

Dual-Element Fuse Size	Motor Protection (Used without properly sized overload relays). Motor Full-Load Amps		Backup Motor Protection (Used with properly sized overload relays). Motor Full-Load Amps	
	Motor Service Factor of 1.15 or Greater or With Temp. Rise Not Over 40° C.	Motor Service Factor Less Than 1.15 or With Temp. Rise Not Over 40° C.	Motor Service Factor of 1.15 or Greater or With Temp. Rise Not Over 40° C.	Motor Service Factor of Less Than 1.15 or With Temp. Rise Not Over 40° C.
40	32.00 - 35.99	34.79 - 39.12	28.01 - 32.00	30.44 - 37.78
45	36.00 - 39.99	39.13 - 43.47	32.01 - 36.00	37.79 - 39.13
50	40.00 - 47.99	43.48 - 50.00	36.01 - 40.00	39.14 - 43.48
60	48.00 - 55.99	52.17 - 60.00	40.01 - 48.00	43.49 - 52.17
70	56.00 - 59.99	60.87 - 65.21	48.01 - 56.00	52.18 - 60.87
75	60.00 - 63.99	65.22 - 69.56	56.01 - 60.00	60.88 - 65.22
80	64.00 - 71 .99	69.57 - 78.25	60.01 - 64.00	65.23 - 69.57
90	72.00 - 79.99	78.26 - 86.95	64.01 - 72.00	69.58 - 78.26
100	80.00 - 87.99	86.96 - 95.64	72.01 - 80.00	78.27 - 86.96
110	88.00 - 99.99	95.65 - 108.69	80.01 - 88.00	86.97 - 95.65
125	100.00 - 119.99	108.70 - 125.00	88.01 - 100.00	95.66 - 108.70
150	120.00 - 139.99	131.30 - 150.00	100.01 - 120.00	108.71 - 130.43
175	140.00 - 159.99	152.17 - 173.90	120.01 - 140.00	130.44 - 152.17
200	160.00 - 179.99	173.91 - 195.64	140.01 - 160.00	152.18 - 173.91
225	180.00 - 199.99	195.65 - 217.38	160.01 - 180.00	173.92 - 195.62
250	200.00 - 239.99	217.39 - 250.00	180.01 - 200.00	195.63 - 217.39
300	240.00 - 279.99	260.87 - 300.00	200.01 - 240.00	217.40 - 260.87
350	280.00 - 319.99	304.35 - 347.82	240.01 - 280.00	260.88 - 304.35
400	320.00 - 359.99	347.83 - 391.29	280.01 - 320.00	304.36 - 347.83
450	360.00 - 399.99	391.30 - 434.77	320.01 - 360.00	347.84 - 391.30
500	400.00 - 479.99	434.78 - 500.00	360.01 - 400.00	391.31 - 434.78
600	480.00 - 600.00	521.74 - 600.00	400.01 - 480.00	434.79 - 521.74

Figure 29. Selection Of Fuses For Motor Protection (3 Of 3)

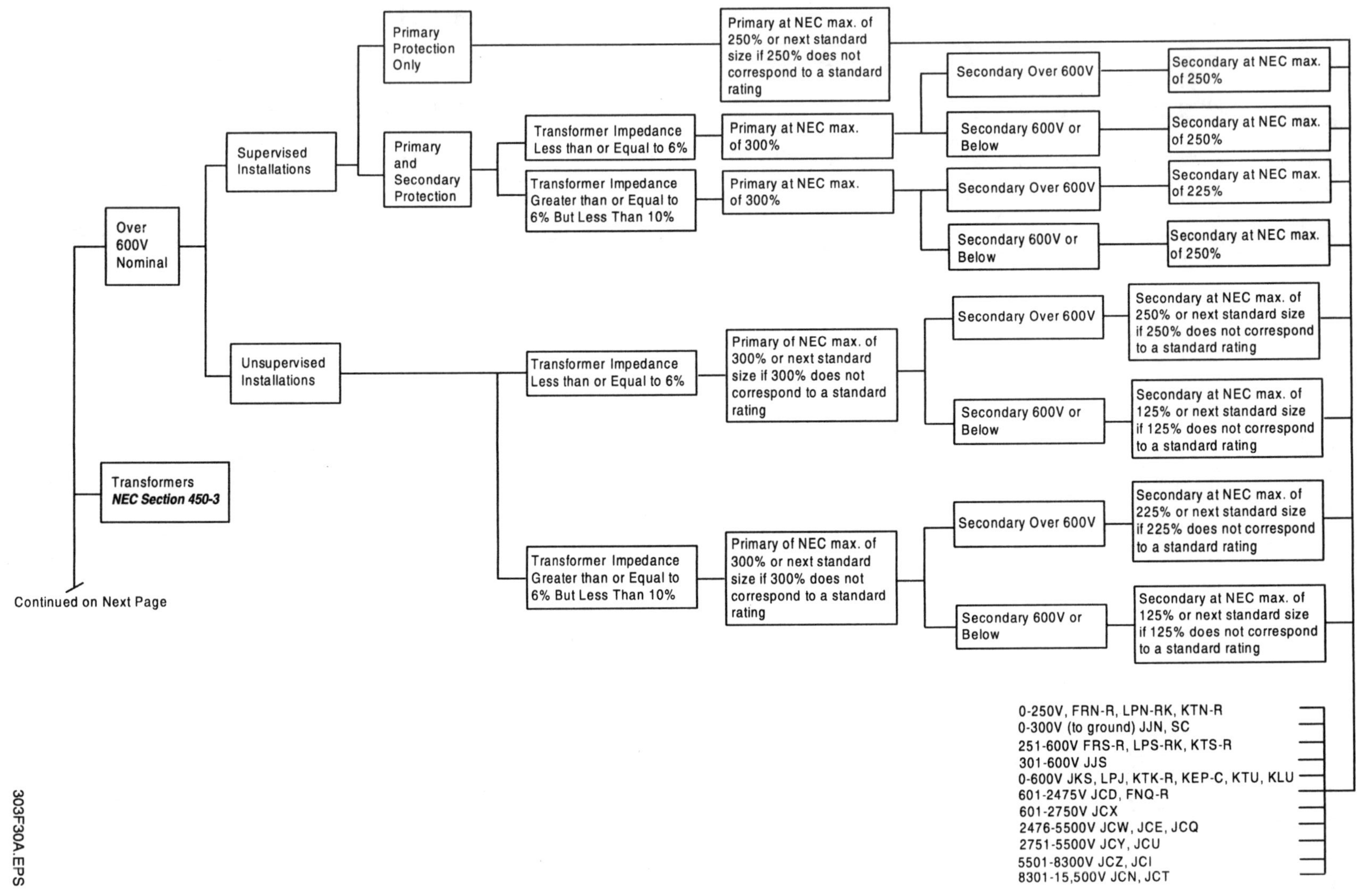

Figure 30. Summary Of Overcurrent Protection Applications (1 Of 5)

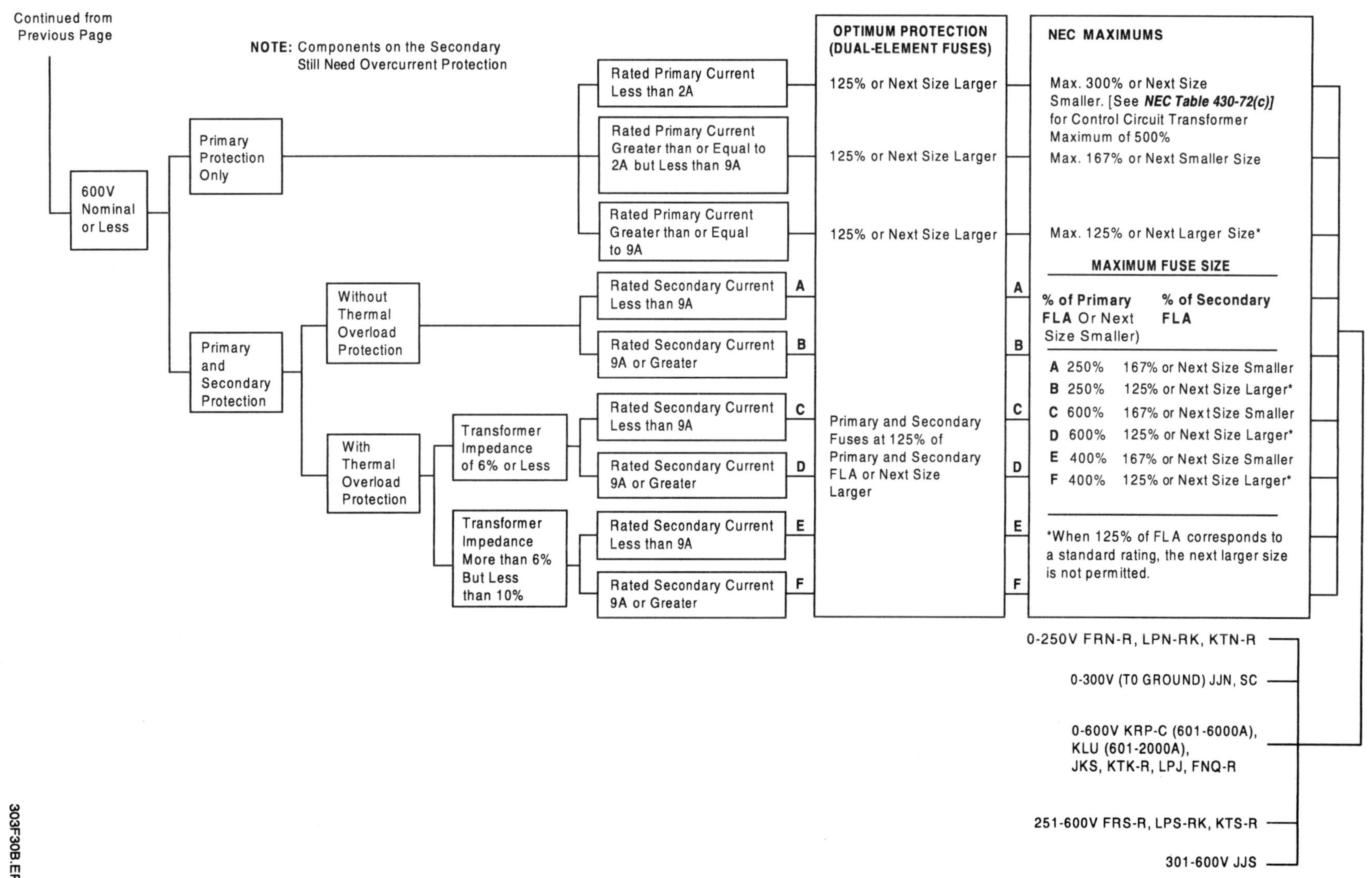

Figure 30. Summary Of Overcurrent Protection Applications (2 Of 5)

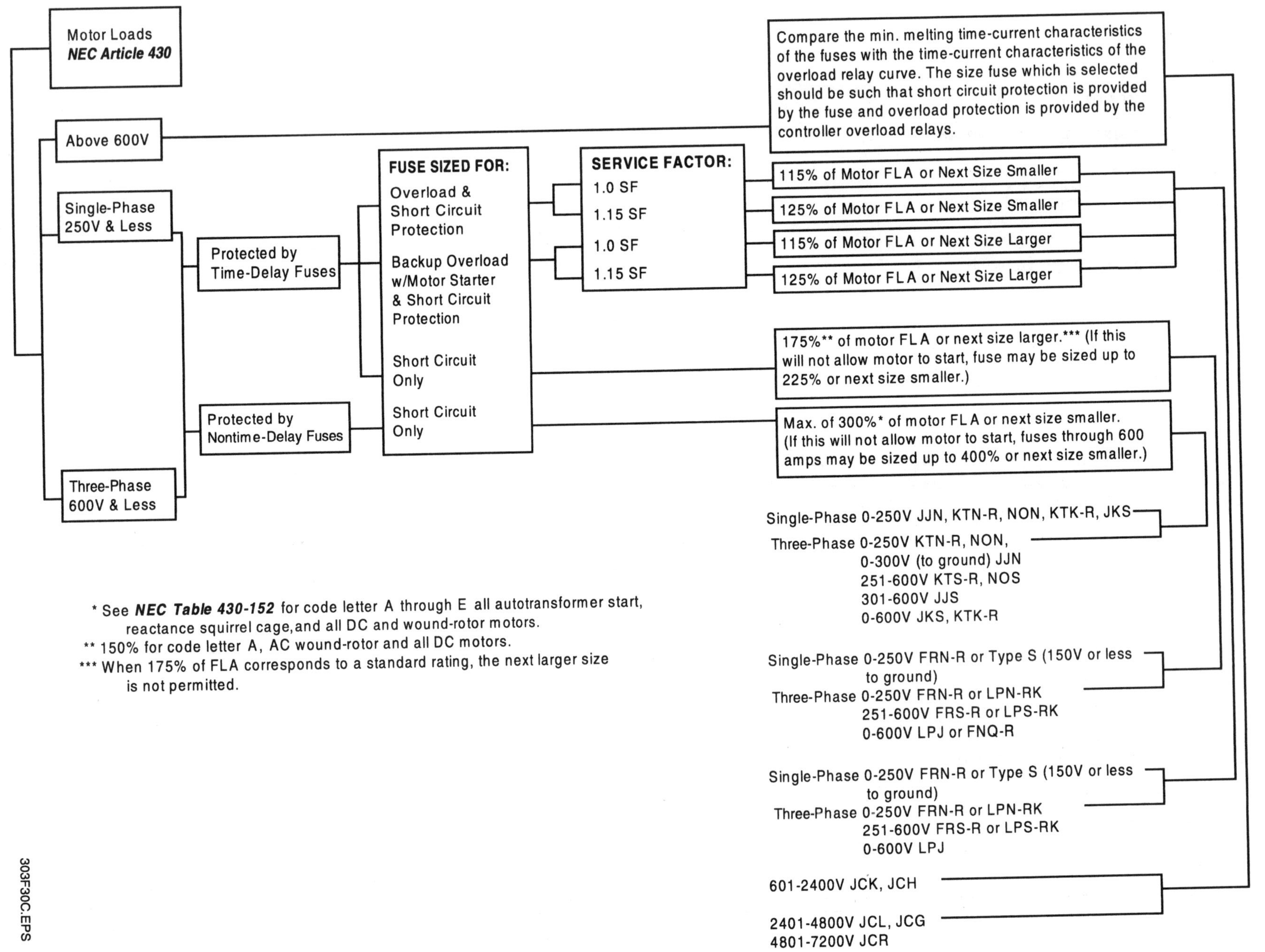

Figure 30. Summary Of Overcurrent Protection Applications (3 Of 5)

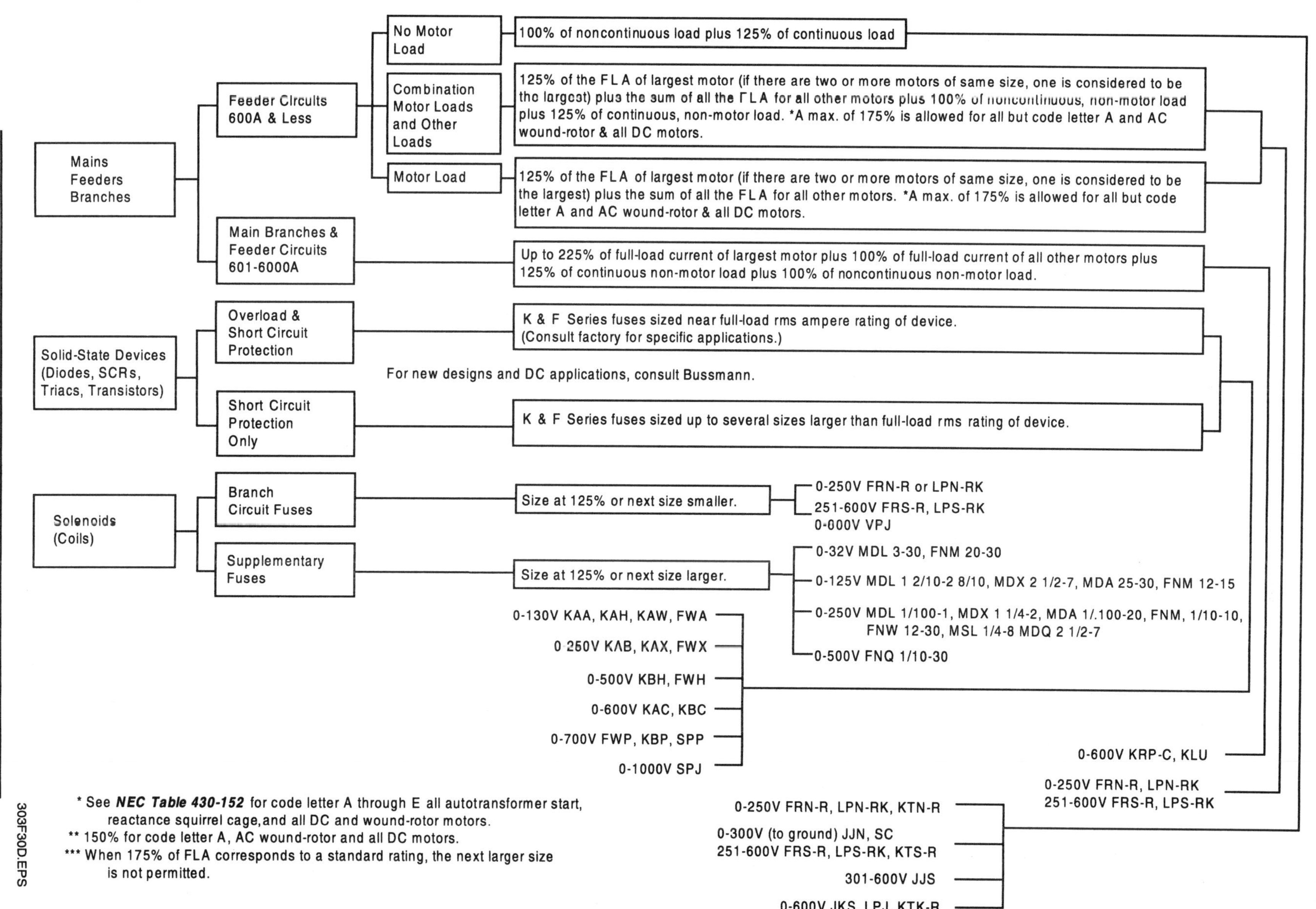

Figure 30. Summary Of Overcurrent Protection Applications (4 Of 5)

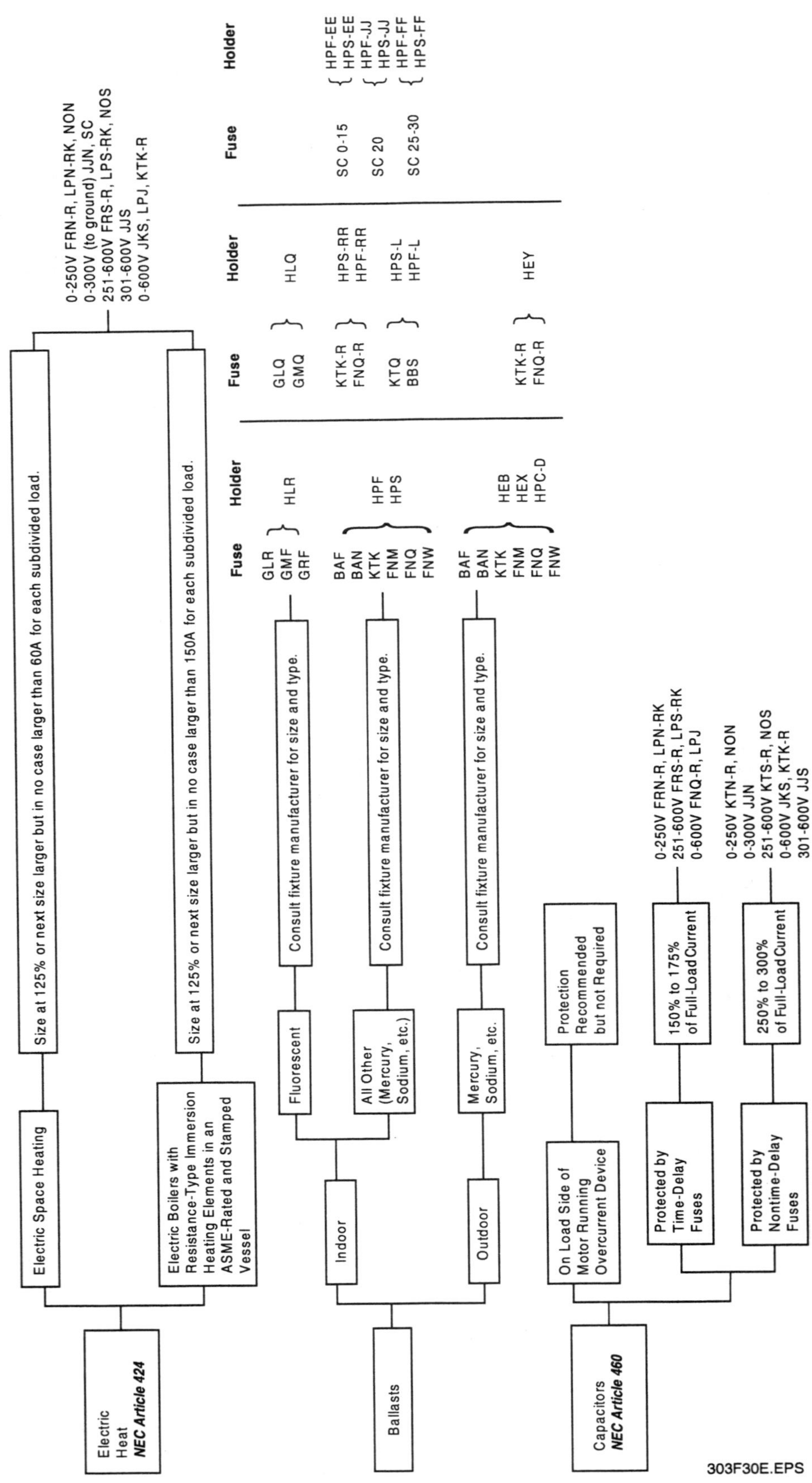

Figure 30. Summary Of Overcurrent Protection Applications (5 Of 5)

SUMMARY

Reliable overcurrent protective devices prevent or minimize costly damage to transformers, conductors, motors, and the other many components and electrical loads that make up the complete electrical distribution system. Consequently, reliable circuit protection is essential to avoid the severe monetary losses which can result from power blackouts and prolonged downtime of various types of facilities. The NEC has set forth various minimum requirements dealing with overcurrent devices and how they should be installed in various types of electrical circuits.

References

For advanced study of topics covered in this Task Module, the following books are suggested:

American Electricians' Handbook, Latest Edition, McGraw-Hill, New York, NY.

National Electrical Code Handbook, Latest Edition, National Fire Protection Association, Quincy, MA.

1. Which of the following best describes the maximum short circuit current that a fuse or circuit breaker will safely interrupt?

    a. CIA
    b. AIC
    c. SOL
    d. ICA

2. The minimum interrupting rating of branch circuit listed fuses is _____.

    a. 5,000A
    b. 10,000A
    c. 15,000A
    d. 20,000A

3. The minimum voltage rating of branch circuit fuses is _____.

    a. 24V
    b. 120V
    c. 125V
    d. 240V

4. Which of the following is *not* a classification of medium-voltage fuses?

    a. General-purpose current-limiting fuses
    b. Backup current-limiting fuses
    c. Expulsion fuses
    d. Proportion fuses

5. An expulsion fuse is best described as a _____.

    a. fuse capable of interrupting all currents from the rated interrupting current down to the current that causes melting of the fusible element in an hour
    b. fuse capable of interrupting all currents from the maximum rated interrupting current down to the rated minimum interrupting current
    c. strap-mounted device
    d. vented fuse in which the expulsion effect of gases produced by the arc and lining of the fuseholder, either alone or aided by a spring, extinguishes the arc

6. Which of the following is *not* a basic factor to consider when applying any fuse?

    a. Voltage
    b. Continuous current-carrying capacity
    c. Interrupting rating
    d. Manufacturer's brand name

7. The total clearing time of any downstream protective device must be below a curve representing _____ of the minimum melting curve of the fuse being applied.

    a. 10%
    b. 20%
    c. 50%
    d. 75%

8. When a common circuit breaker trips, the handle is in the _____ position.

    a. OFF
    b. ON
    c. middle
    d. RESET

9. Circuit breakers are grouped for identification according to given current ranges. How is each group classified?

    a. The largest ampere rating of its range
    b. The smallest ampere rating of its range
    c. The absolute lowest ampere rating of its range
    d. The overall average ampere rating of its range

10. When circuit breakers are classified as 100A through 2,000A frames, these numbers are normally referred to as the _____.

    a. frame size
    b. overload protective current
    c. maximum voltage allowed on the circuit
    d. physical size of the circuit breaker

ANSWERS TO REVIEW/PRACTICE QUESTIONS

<u>Answer</u>		<u>Section Reference</u>
1.	b	1.3.0
2.	b	4.1.0
3.	c	4.1.0
4.	d	4.2.0
5.	d	4.2.0
6.	d	4.2.1
7.	d	4.2.1
8.	c	6.0.0
9.	a	6.0.0
10.	a	6.0.0

The NCCER makes every effort to keep these manuals up-to-date and free of technical errors. We appreciate your help in this process. If you have an idea for improving this manual, or if you find an error, a typographical mistake, or an inaccuracy in the NCCER's Craft Training Manuals, please write us, using this form or a photocopy. Be sure to include the exact module number, page number, a description of the problem, and the correction, if possible. Your input will be brought to the attention of the Technical Review Committee. Thank you for your assistance.

Instructors – If you found that additional materials were necessary in order to teach this module effectively, please let us know so that we may include them in the Equipment/Materials list in the Instructor's Guide.

Write: Curriculum Development and Revision Department
National Center for Construction Education and Research
P.O. Box 141104
Gainesville, FL 32614-1104
Fax: 352-334-0932

Craft

Module Name
____

Copyright Date   Module Number   Page Number(s)
____

Description of Problem
____

____

____

____

(Optional) Correction of Problem
____

____

____

(Optional) Your Name and Address
____

____

____

Raceway, Box, and Fitting Fill Requirements

Module 26304

RACEWAY, BOX, AND FITTING FILL REQUIREMENTS

OBJECTIVES

Upon completion of this module, the trainee will be able to:

1. Size raceways according to conductor fill and NEC installation requirements.
2. Size and install outlet boxes according to NEC installation requirements.
3. Size, select, and install pull and junction boxes according to NEC installation requirements.
4. Size conduit and conduit bodies using tables in *NEC Chapter 9* and *Appendix C*.
5. Calculate conduit fill using a percentage of the trade size conduit inside diameter (ID).
6. Calculate the required bending radius in boxes and cabinets.
7. Determine when cable must be racked in pull or junction boxes.

Prerequisites

Successful completion of the following Task Modules is recommended before beginning study of this Task Module: Core Curricula; Electrical Level 1; Electrical Level 2; and Electrical Level 3, Modules 26301 through 26302.

Required Trainee Materials

1. Trainee Task Module
2. Appropriate Personal Protective Equipment
3. Copy of the latest edition of the *National Electrical Code*

Note: The designations "National Electrical Code," "NE Code," and "NEC," where used in this document, refer to the National Electrical Code®, which is a registered trademark of the National Fire Protection Association, Quincy, MA. *All National Electrical Code (NEC) references in this module refer to the 1999 edition of the NEC.*

This course map shows all of the modules in the third level of the Electrical curricula. The suggested training order begins at the bottom and proceeds up. Skill levels increase as a trainee advances on the course map. The training order may be adjusted by the local Training Program Sponsor.

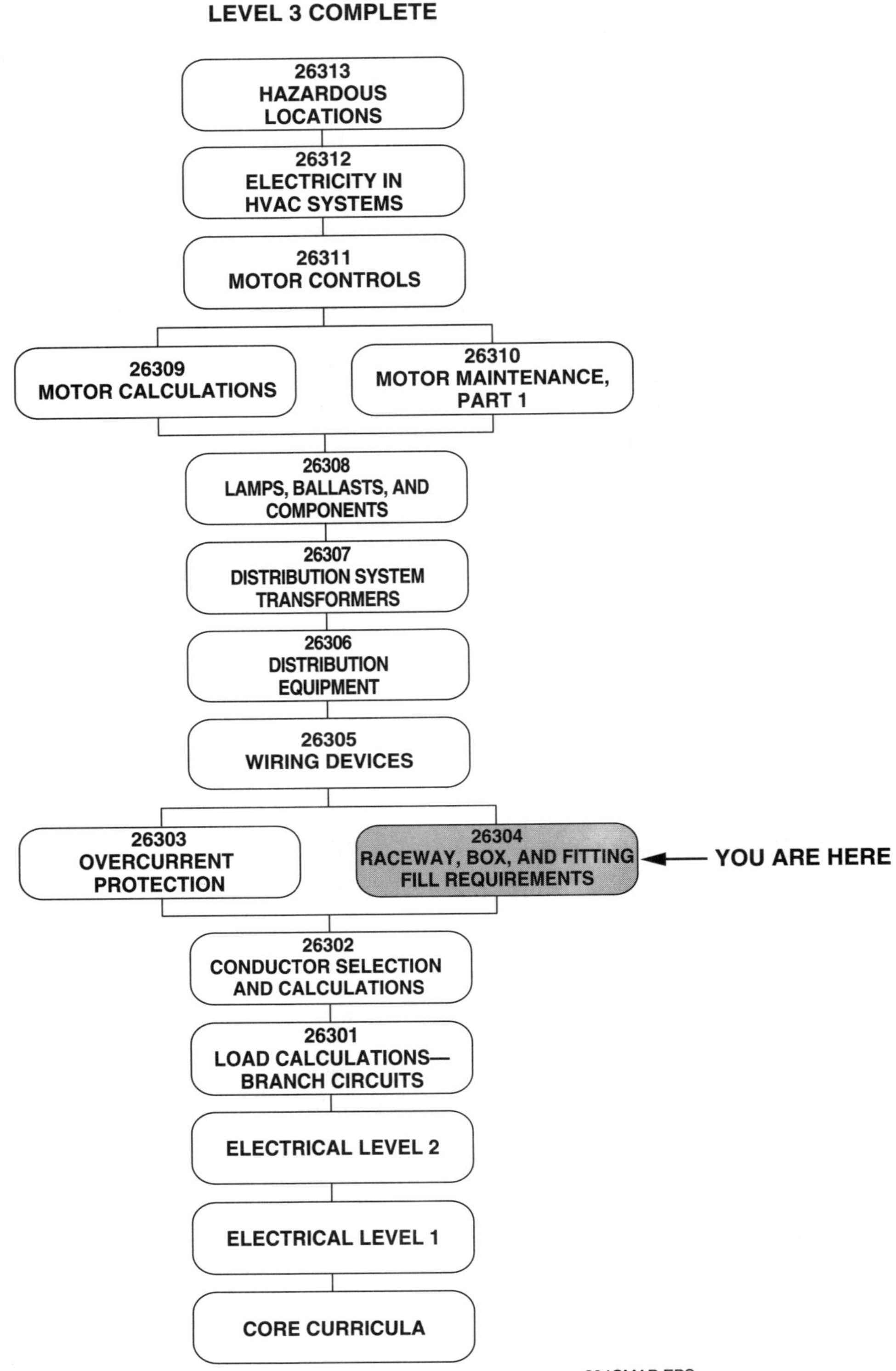

304CMAP.EPS

TABLE OF CONTENTS

Trade Terms Introduced In This Module

American wire gauge (AWG): The U.S. standard for wire measurement.

Ampacity: The current-carrying capacity of conductors or equipment, expressed in amperes.

Cable: An assembly of two or more conductors which may be insulated or bare.

Clearance: The vertical space between a cable and its conduit.

Conduit fill: Amount of cross-sectional area used in a raceway.

Jacket: A nonmetallic, polymeric, close-fitting protective covering over conductor insulation; the cable may have one or more conductors.

Junction box: A group of electrical terminals housed in a protective box or container.

Knockout: A portion of an enclosure designed to be easily removed for raceway installation.

Triangular configuration: The geometric pattern which cables will take in a conduit when the cables are triplexed or are pulled in parallel with the ratio of the conduit inside diameter (ID) to the single-conductor cable outside diameter (OD) less than 2.5.

1.0.0 INTRODUCTION

A raceway is any channel which is designed and used for the sole purpose of holding wires, **cables**, or busbars. Raceways are constructed of either metal or insulating material.

Types of raceways include:

- Rigid metal conduit
- Intermediate metal conduit (IMC)
- Rigid nonmetallic conduit
- Flexible metal conduit
- Liquid-tight flexible metal conduit
- Electrical metallic tubing (EMT)
- Underfloor raceways
- Cellular metal floor raceways
- Cellular concrete floor raceways
- Surface metal raceways, wireways, and auxiliary gutters

Raceways provide mechanical protection for the conductors that run in them and prevent accidental damage to insulation and the conducting metal. They also protect conductors from the harmful chemical attack of corrosive atmospheres and prevent fire hazards to life and property by confining arcs and flame due to faults in the wiring system.

One of the most important functions of metal raceways is to provide a path for the flow of fault current to ground, thereby preventing voltage buildup on conductor and equipment enclosures. This feature, of course, helps to minimize shock hazards to personnel and damage to electrical equipment. To maintain this feature, it is extremely important that all metal raceway systems be securely bonded together into a continuous conductive path and properly connected to a grounding electrode such as a water pipe or a ground rod.

A box or fitting must be installed at:

- Each conductor splice point
- Each outlet, switch point, or junction point
- Each pull point for the connection of conduit and other raceways

Furthermore, boxes or other fittings are required when a change is made from conduit to open wiring. Electrical workers also install pull boxes in raceway systems to facilitate the pulling of conductors.

The NEC specifies specific maximum fill requirements for raceways, outlet boxes, pull boxes, and **junction boxes**. Fill requirements specify the area of conductors in relation to the box, fitting, or raceway system. This module is designed to cover these NEC requirements and apply these rules to practical applications.

2.0.0 CONDUIT FILL REQUIREMENTS

NEC Article 370 provides rules on the maximum number of conductors permitted in raceways. In conduits, for either new work or rewiring of existing raceways, the maximum **conduit fill** must not exceed 40% of the conduit cross-sectional area. In all such cases, fill is based on using the actual cross-sectional areas of the particular types of conductors used.

Other derating rules are specified in *NEC Article 310*. For example, if more than three conductors are used in a single conduit, a reduction in **ampacity** is required. Ambient temperature is another consideration that may call for derating of wires below the values given in NEC tables.

2.1.0 FACTORS INFLUENCING FIT

Besides the NEC requirements, five factors influence a cable's mechanical fit in a raceway:

- Configuration
- Weight
- **Clearance**
- Jam ratio
- Coefficient of friction

2.1.1 Configuration

The configuration of the cable in the raceway is measured by the ratio of the inner diameter of the conduit to the overall diameter of one of the cables within the conduit:

$$\frac{D}{d}$$

Where:

D = overall diameter

d = inner diameter

A cradled configuration (*Figure 1*) occurs when cables with a ratio of 2.5 or greater are pulled in parallel from individual reels. A **triangular configuration** (*Figure 1*) occurs when cables with a ratio of less than 2.5 are pulled in parallel from individual reels or when cables are assembled.

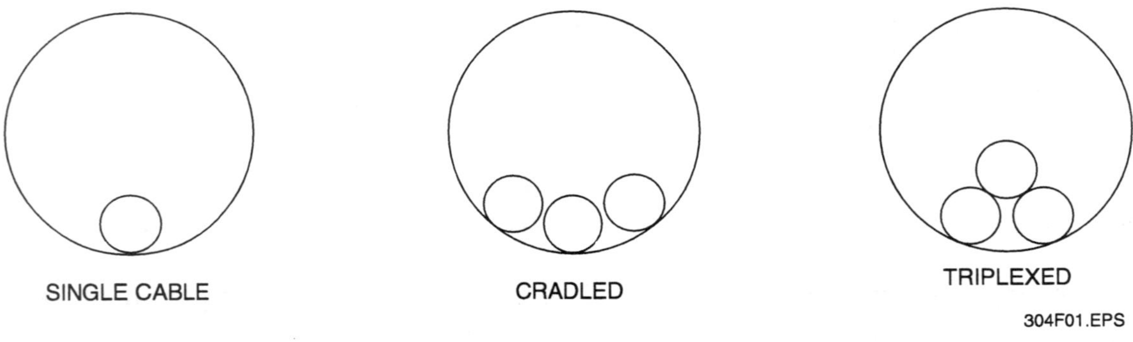

Figure 1. Cable Raceway Configurations

Configuration directly affects drag, which is computed as the weight correction factor (w).

2.1.2 Weight

When making installation calculations, use the total weight per unit length of the cables being pulled. Cabled assemblies will weigh more than paralleled cables unless the cables were specially ordered to have several paralleled cables wound on a reel.

Due to its geometric configuration, a cable is subjected to uneven force when it is pulled into a conduit. This imbalance results in additional frictional drag which must be calculated and allowed for if the installation is to be a success (see *Figure 2*).

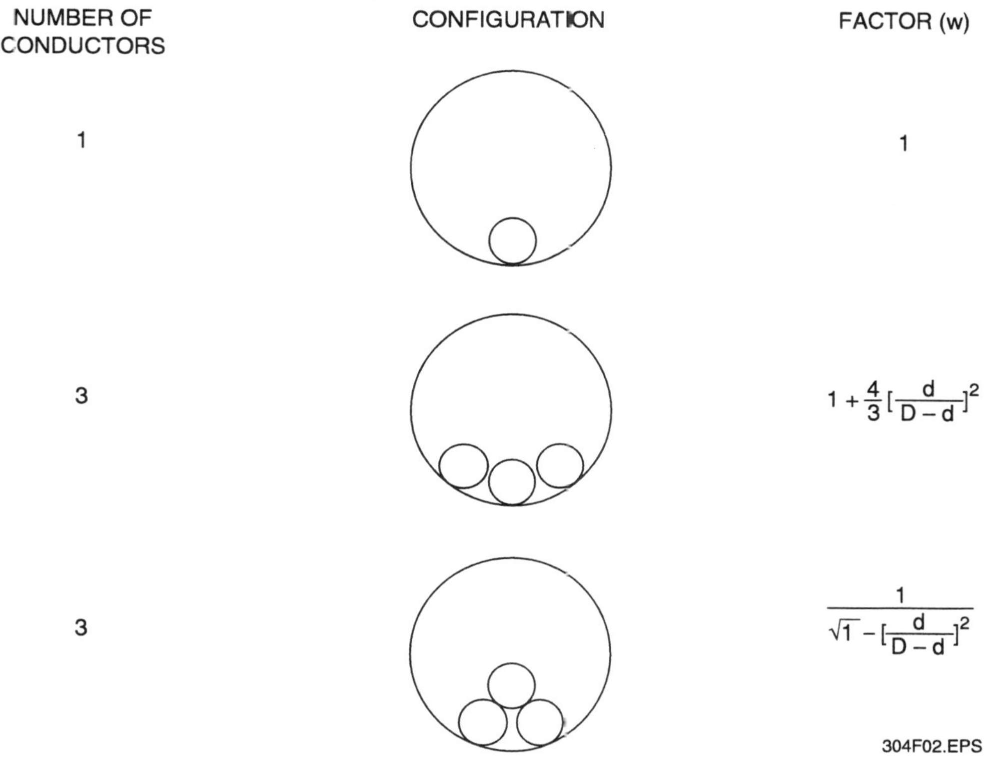

Figure 2. Weight Correction Factors For Various Cable Configurations

The graph in *Figure 3* illustrates the weight correction factor.

When computing the weight correction factor, ensure that all cable diameters are equal. When in doubt, use the cradled configuration equation.

The cables may be in either a single- or multiple-conductor construction. However, when only one cable (whether a single conductor or multiple conductors under a common **jacket**) is being pulled, no weight correction factor is needed.

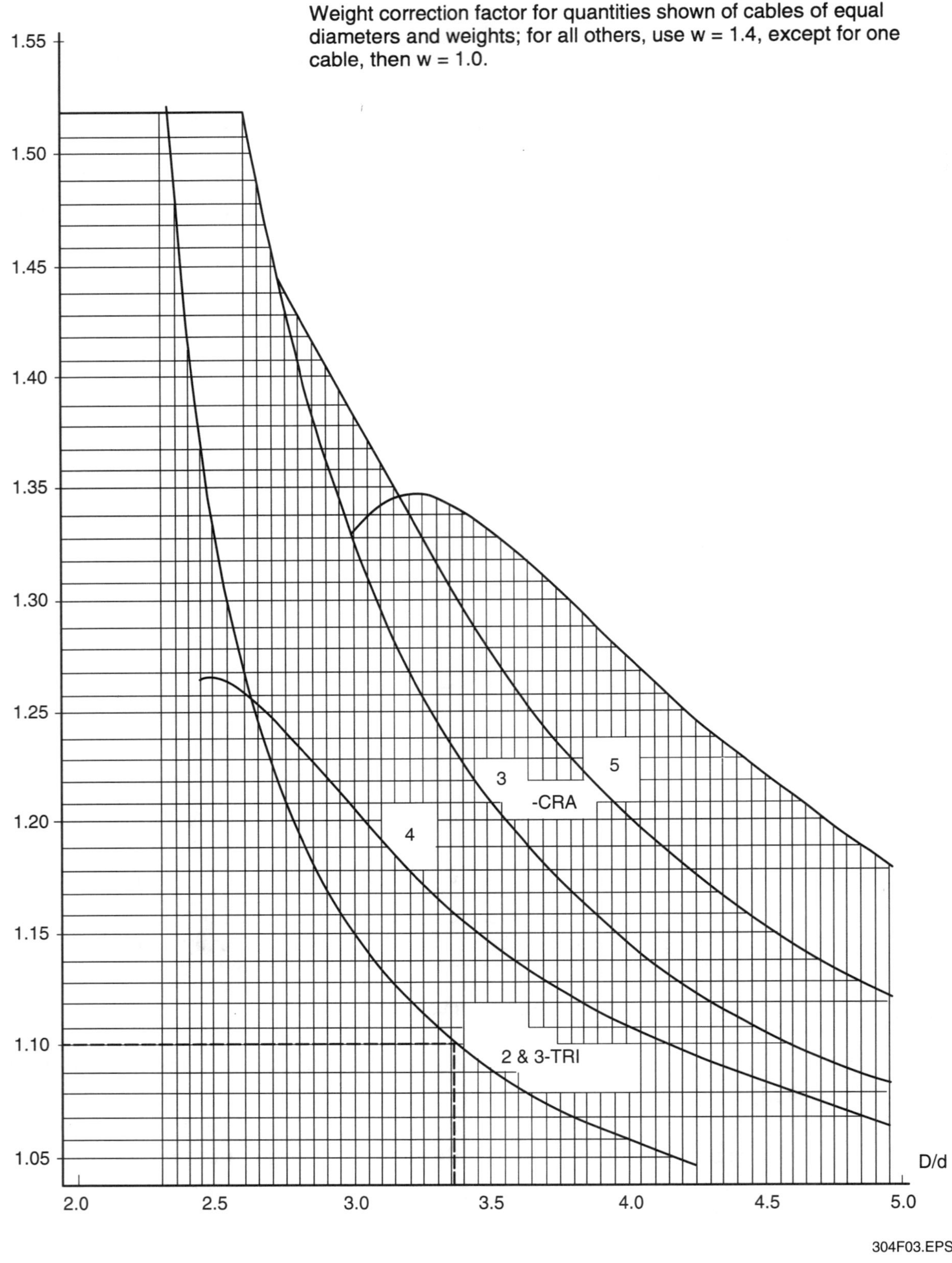

Figure 3. Weight Correction Factors

2.1.3 Clearance

Clearance refers to the distance between the uppermost cable in the conduit and the inner top of the conduit. Clearance should be ¼" at minimum and up to 1" for large cable installations or installations involving numerous bends. It is calculated as follows:

- When calculating clearance, ensure all cable diameters are equal. Use the triplexed configuration equation (*Figure 4*) if you are in doubt. Again, the cables may be of single- or multiple-conductor construction.

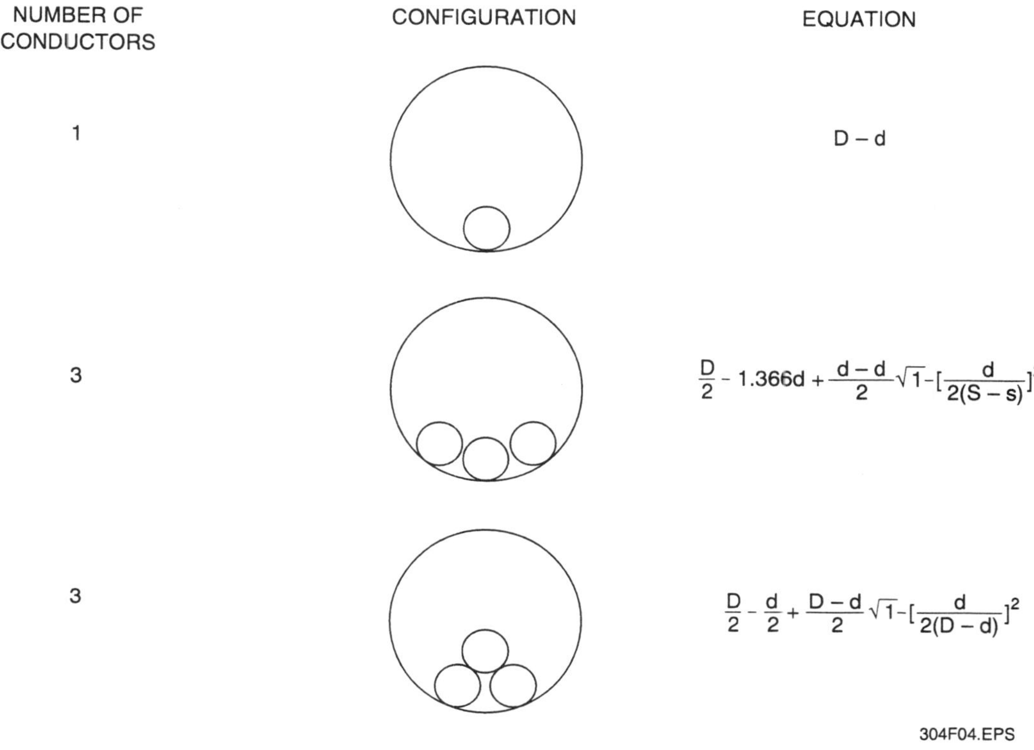

For 1 conductor:
$$D - d$$

For 3 conductors (first configuration):
$$\frac{D}{2} - 1.366d + \frac{d-d}{2}\sqrt{1-[\frac{d}{2(S-s)}]^2}$$

For 3 conductors (second configuration):
$$\frac{D}{2} - \frac{d}{2} + \frac{D-d}{2}\sqrt{1-[\frac{d}{2(D-d)}]^2}$$

Figure 4. Principles Of Calculating Cable Clearances

2.1.4 Jam Ratio

Jamming is the wedging of three cables lying side by side in a conduit. (See **NEC Chapter 9, Table 1, FPN No. 2**.) This usually occurs when cables are being pulled around bends or when cables twist. The jam ratio is calculated by slightly modifying the ratio used to measure configuration (D/d). A value of 1.05D is used for the inner diameter of the conduit because bending a cylinder creates an oval cross-section in the bend (1.05D/d). If the value of 1.05D/d is:

- Larger than 3.2, jamming is impossible
- Between 2.8 and 3.2, serious jamming is probable
- Less than 2.8, jamming is impossible but clearance should be checked

Since there are manufacturing tolerances on cable, the actual overall diameter should be measured prior to computing the jam ratio.

2.1.5 Coefficient Of Dynamic Friction

The coefficient of dynamic friction (f) is a measure of the friction between the cable and the conduit or roller, and can vary from 0.03 to 0.8, even with lubrication. Typical values are shown in *Table 1*.

Cable Exterior	Type of Conduit			
	M[1]	PVC[2]	FIB[3]	ASB[4]
Polyvinyl chloride (PVC)	0.4	0.35	0.5	0.5
Low-density HMW polyethylene (PE)	0.35	0.35	0.5	0.5
Chlorinated polyethylene (CPE)	0.35	0.35	0.5	0.5
Hypalon (chlorosulfonated PE or CSPE)	0.5	0.5	0.7	0.6
Neoprene (chloroprene or N)	0.5	0.5	0.7	0.6
Flame-retardant EP (FREP)	0.4	0.4	0.5	0.5
Cross-linked PE (XLPE)	0.35	0.35	0.5	0.5
Lead	0.5	0.5	0.5	0.5

[1] Metallic, steel, or aluminum

[2] Polyvinyl chloride, thinwall, or heavy Schedule 40

[3] Fiber conduit (Orangeburg or Nocrete)

[4] Asbestos cement (Transite or Korduct)

Table 1. Typical Coefficients Of Dynamic Friction

The coefficient of friction of a duct or conduit varies with the type of cable covering, condition of the duct or conduit internal surface, type and amount of pulling lubricant used, and ambient installation temperature.

High ambient temperatures (80°F and over) can increase the coefficient of dynamic friction for cable having a nonmetallic jacket.

Pulling lubricants must be compatible with the cable components and be applied while the cable is being pulled.

2.2.0 CONDUIT FILL

The allowable number of conductors in a raceway system is calculated as percentage of fill, as shown in *Table 2*. When using this table, remember that equipment grounding or bonding conductors, where installed, must be included when calculating conduit fill or tubing fill. The actual dimensions of the equipment grounding or bonding conductor (insulated or bare) must be used in the calculation.

Number of Conductors	1	2	Over 2
All conductor types	53%	31%	40%

Table 2. Percent Of Cross-Section Of Conduit For Conductors

Note: If all of the conductors are of the same size, refer to **NEC Appendix C, Tables C1 through C12**, being careful to identify the type of raceway and conductor being used. If you are using compact aluminum conductors, refer to **NEC Tables C1(A) through C12(A)**.

To calculate how many No. 6 THW wires you can install in a 2" EMT conduit, proceed as follows:

Step 1   Refer to **NEC Appendix C, Table C1**.

Step 2   Locate the section of the table listing THW wire.

Step 3   Move right across the table until you reach the *2" Trade Size* column.

Step 4   Move down this column until you are lined up with conductor size No. 6.

Step 5   The total quantity of No. 6 THW wire in a 2" EMT conduit is determined to be 18.

You can also use these tables if you know the size and type of wire and need to know the size of a raceway required.

To find the size of rigid metallic conduit required for four 500 kcmil THHN conductors, proceed as follows:

Step 1   Refer to **NEC Appendix C, Table C8**.

Step 2   Locate the section of the table listing THHN insulation.

Step 3   Move down the table until you reach 500 kcmil.

Step 4   Move right across the table from 500 kcmil until you reach the column with the number 4, indicating 4 conductors. Look up to the top of this column to find that you would need a trade diameter of 3". (If the quantity of conductors is not listed in the row, you must use the next higher listed quantity.)

If you have more than one size of conductor installed in the same raceway, use **NEC Chapter 9, Tables 4 and 5** to determine the proper conduit size and fill requirements. Follow the procedure shown below.

Step 1   Using **NEC Chapter 9, Table 5**, select the type and size of conductors being used.

Step 2   Move right to the *Approx. Area Sq. In.* column to find the area required for each conductor size.

Step 3   Multiply the number of each size of conductors by the quantity to determine the total sq. in. required for each conductor size. Add the total sq. in. required for each conductor size together to determine the total area required.

Step 4   Determine the type and size of raceway being used (e.g., EMT, IMC, rigid, etc.).

Step 5   Refer to **NEC Chapter 9, Table 4** to locate the type of raceway.

Step 6   Once the appropriate raceway is identified, move right across the row to the column that corresponds to the number of conductors in the raceway.

Step 7   Go down this column until you reach a value that is equal to or greater than the amount calculated in Step 3.

Step 8   Move left across the table to find the trade size of conduit required.

For example, take a situation in which a 1,000A service-entrance conductor is to be installed using three parallel conduits, each containing three 500 kcmil THHN ungrounded conductors and one 350 kcmil THHN grounded conductor (neutral), as shown in *Figure 5*. What size of rigid conduit is required?

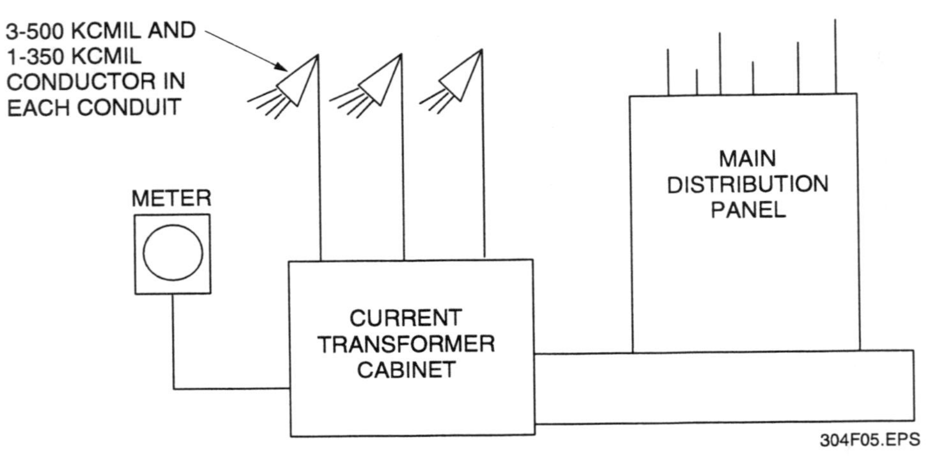

Figure 5. Power Riser Diagram Of A 1,000A Service-Entrance Conductor

Step 1   Refer to **NEC Chapter 9, Table 5** to determine the area (in sq. in.) of a 500 kcmil THHN conductor. The area is found to be .7073 sq. in.

Step 2   Repeat Step 1 to find the area for 350 kcmil THHN. The area is found to be .5242 sq. in.

Step 3   Multiply the number of conductors of each size by their corresponding areas.

.7073 × 3 = 2.1219 (total area required for 500 kcmil conductors)

.5242 × 1 = .5242 (total area required for 350 kcmil conductor)

ELECTRICAL — TRAINEE TASK MODULE 26304

Step 4   Add the totals together to obtain the total area required for all conductors.

       2.1219 + .5242 = 2.6461 sq. in.

Step 5   Refer to **_NEC Chapter 9, Table 4_** and locate _Rigid Metal Conduit_.

Step 6   Looking in the _Over 2 Wires_ column, scan down until you find a number equal to or greater than 2.6461. The value found is 3.000. Now scan back to the left to determine that the conduit size required is 3".

Therefore, each of the three conduits containing three 500 kcmil THHN conductors and one 350 kcmil THHN conductor must be at least 3" trade size to comply.

**Note:**   You may have noticed that the internal diameter of a raceway does not match the trade size in all cases, nor does it match the internal diameter of different raceways in the same trade size. The trade size is a size given to a raceway with an internal diameter close to that size. In recognizing the difference in internal diameters, the NEC has expanded **_NEC Chapter 9, Table 4_** and added the tables in **_Appendix C_**.

3.0.0   CONDUIT BODIES, PULL BOXES, AND JUNCTION BOXES

The NEC specifically states that at each splice point or pull point for the connection of conduit or other raceways, a box or fitting must be installed. The NEC specifically considers conduit bodies, pull boxes, and junction boxes, and specifies the installation rules as listed in _Table 3_.

Conduit bodies provide access to the wiring through removable covers. Typical examples are Types T, C, X, L, and LB. Conduit bodies enclosing No. 6 or smaller conductors must have an area twice that of the largest conduit to which they are attached, but the number of conductors within the body must not exceed that allowed in the conduit. If a conduit body has entry for three or more conduits such as Type T or X, splices may be made within the conduit body. Splices may not be made in conduit bodies having one or two entries unless the volume is sufficient to qualify the conduit body as a junction box or device box.

When conduit bodies or boxes are used as junction boxes or pull boxes, a minimum size box is required to allow conductors to be installed without undue bending. The calculated dimensions of the box depend on the type of conduit arrangement and the size of the conduits involved.

Application	Installation Requirements	NEC Reference
Conduit bodies	Conduit bodies enclosing No. 6 conductors or smaller must have a cross-sectional area twice that of the largest conduit or tubing to which it is attached. The maximum number of conductors allowed in the conduit body must not exceed the allowable fill for the attached conduit. Conduit bodies must not contain splices, taps, or devices unless they are durably and legibly marked by the manufacturer with their cubic inch capacity. Conduit bodies must be supported in a rigid and secure manner.	*NEC Section 370-16(c)*
Minimum sizes	Boxes and conduit bodies used as pull or junction boxes must comply with (a) through (d) below: (a) For raceways containing conductors of No. 4 or larger, the minimum dimensions of pull or junction boxes installed in a raceway or cable run must comply with the following: • In straight pulls, the length of the box must not be less than eight times the trade diameter of the largest conduit. • Where angle or U-pulls are made, the distance between each raceway entry inside the box and the opposite wall of the box must not be less than six times the trade diameter of the largest raceway in a row. This distance must be increased for additional entries by the amount of the sum of the diameters of all other raceway entries in the same row on the same wall of the box. Each row must be calculated individually, and the single row that provides the maximum distance must be used. • The distance between raceway entries enclosing the same conductor must be less than six times the trade diameter of the largest raceway. (b) If pull boxes or junction boxes have any dimension over 6', all conductors must be cabled or racked up in an approved manner. (c) All boxes and fittings must be provided with covers compatible with the box, and if metal, must comply with *NEC Section 250-110*. (d) Where permanent barriers are installed in a box, each section shall be considered a separate box.	*NEC Section 370-28*
Accessibility	Junction, pull, and outlet boxes must be accessible without removing any part of a building or digging.	*NEC Section 370-29*
Over 600V	Special requirements apply to boxes used on systems of over 600V.	*NEC Article 370, Part E*

Table 3. Installation Requirements For Conduit Bodies, Pull Boxes, And Junction Boxes

3.1.0 SIZING PULL AND JUNCTION BOXES

Figure 6 shows a junction box with several conduits entering it. Since 4" conduit is the largest size in the group, the minimum length required for the box can be determined by the following calculation:

4" (trade size of conduit) × 8 [per **NEC Section 370-28(a)(1)**] = 32" (minimum length of box)

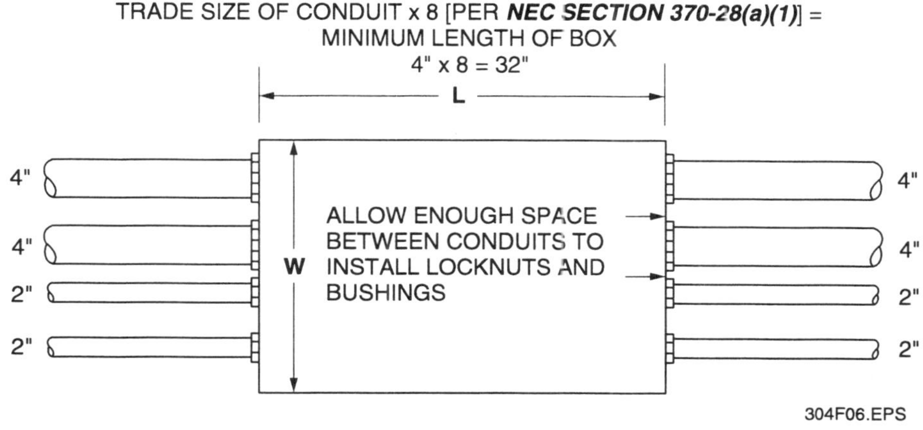

Figure 6. Pull Box Used On Straight Pulls

Therefore, this particular pull box must be at least 32" in length. The width of the box, however, need be only of sufficient size to enable locknuts and bushings to be installed on all the conduits or connectors entering the enclosure.

Junction or pull boxes in which the conductors are pulled at an angle, as shown in *Figure 7*, must have a distance of not less than six times the trade diameter of the largest conduit. The distance must be increased for additional conduit entries by the amount of the sum of the diameter of all other conduits entering the box on the same side (the wall of the box). The distance between raceway entries enclosing the same conductors must not be less than six times the trade diameter of the largest conduit.

Since the 4" conduit is the largest in this case:

$$L_1 = 6 \times 4 + (3 + 2) = 29"$$

Since the same number and sizes of conduit are located on the adjacent wall of the box, L_2 is calculated in the same way; therefore, $L_2 = 29$.

The distance (D) = 6 × 4 or 24". This is the minimum distance permitted between conduit entries enclosing the same conductor.

The depth of the box need only be of sufficient size to permit locknuts and bushings to be properly installed. In this case, a 6" deep box would suffice.

If the conductors are smaller than No. 4, the length restriction does not apply.

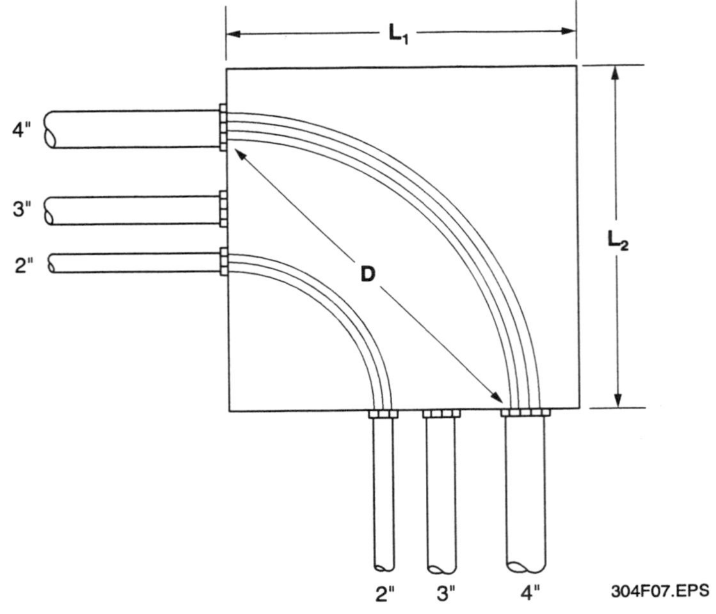

Figure 7. Junction Box With Conduit Runs Entering At Right Angles

Figure 8 shows another straight pull box. What is the minimum length if the box has one 3" conduit and two 2" conduits entering and leaving the box? Again, refer to **NEC Section 370-28(a)(1)** and find that the minimum length is eight times the largest conduit size. In this case, it is:

$8 \times 3" = 24"$

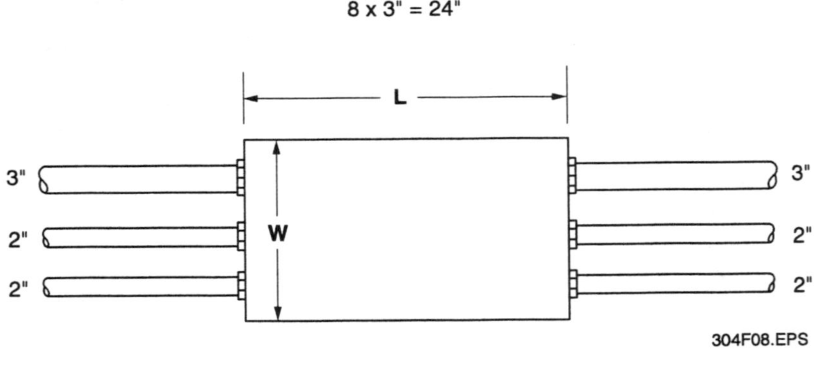

Figure 8. Typical Straight Pull Box

Let us review the installation requirements for pull or junction boxes with angular or U-pulls [**NEC Section 370-28(a)(2)**]. Two conditions must be met in order to determine the length and width of the required box:

- The minimum distance to the opposite side of the box from any conduit entry must be at least six times the trade diameter of the largest raceway.
- The sum of the diameters of the raceways on the same wall must be added to this figure.

    ELECTRICAL — TRAINEE TASK MODULE 26304

Figure 9 shows the minimum length of a box with two 3" conduits, two 2" conduits, and two 1½" conduits in a right-angle pull. The minimum length based on this configuration is:

$$6 \times 3" \quad = 18'$$
$$1 \times 3" \quad = 3'$$
$$2 \times 2" \quad = 4'$$
$$2 \times 1\tfrac{1}{2}" = \underline{3'}$$
$$\phantom{2 \times 1\tfrac{1}{2}" = } 28'$$

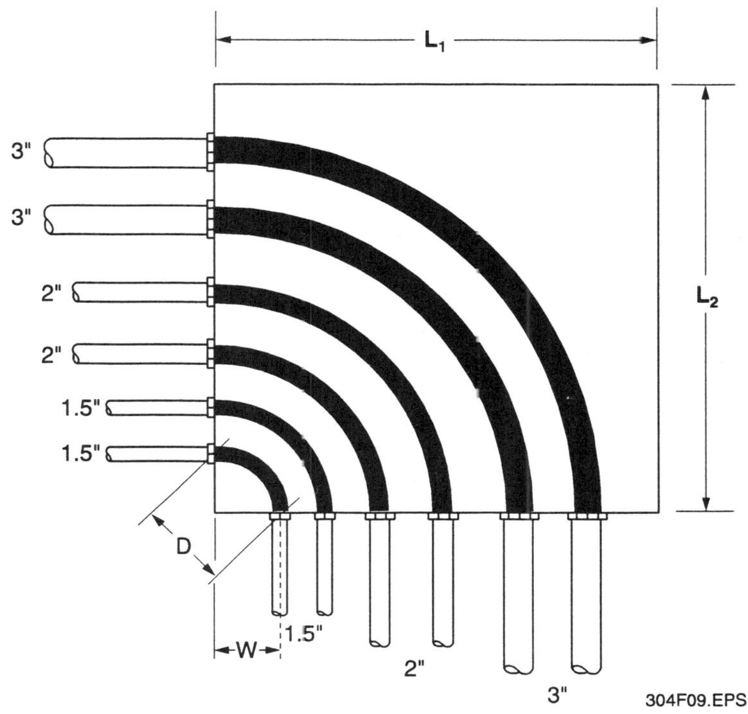

Figure 9. Minimum Size Pull Box For Angle Conduit Entries

Since the number and size of conduits on the two sides of the box are equal, the box is square and has a minimum size dimension of 28". However, the distance between conduit entries must now be checked to ensure that all NEC requirements are met; that is, the spacing (D) between conduits enclosing the same conductor must not be less than six times the conduit diameter. Again, refer to *Figure 9* and note that the 1½" conduits are the closest to the left-hand corner of the box. Therefore, the distance (D) between conduit entries must be:

$$6 \times 1\tfrac{1}{2}" = 9"$$

The next group, the two 2" conduits, is calculated in a similar fashion:

$$6 \times 2 = 12"$$

The remaining raceways in this example are the two 3" conduits and the minimum distance between the 3" conduit entries must be:

$6 \times 3 = 18"$

A summary of the conduit entry distances is shown in *Figure 10*. However, some additional math is required to obtain the spacing (w) between the conduit entries. For example, the distance from the corner of the pull box to the center of the conduits (w) may be found by the following equation:

$$\text{Spacing} = \frac{\text{diagonal distance (D)}}{\sqrt{2}}$$

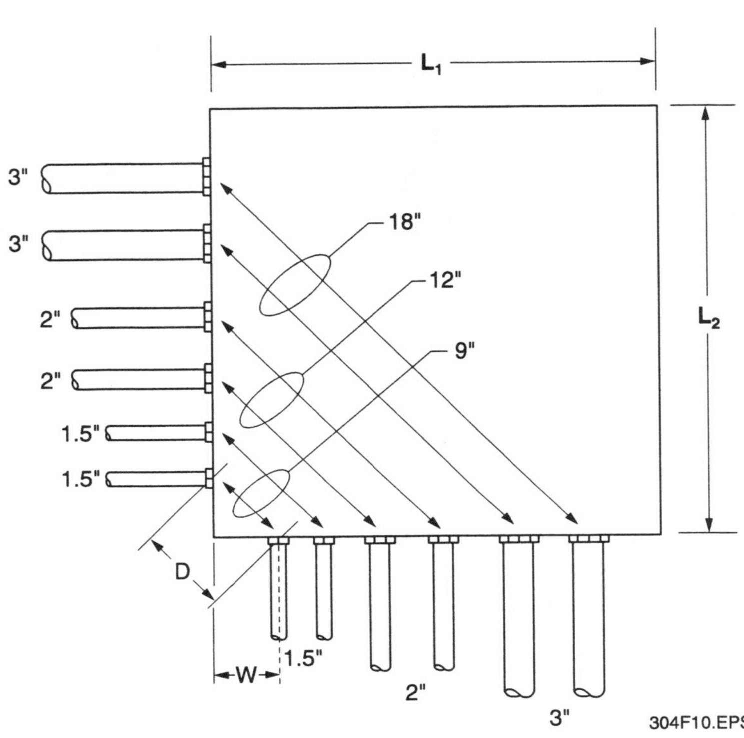

Figure 10. Required Distances Between Conduit Entries

Consequently, the spacing (w) for the 1½" conduit may be determined using the following equation:

$$\frac{9}{\sqrt{2}} = \frac{9}{1.414} = 6.4"$$

Therefore, the spacing (w) is 6.4". This distance is measured from the left lower corner of the box in each direction, both vertically and horizontally, to obtain the center of the first set of 1½" conduits. This distance must be added to the spacing of the other conduits, including locknuts or bushings.

Note: A rule of thumb is to allow ½" clearance between locknuts.

Using all information calculated thus far and using *Figure 10* as reference, the required measurements of the pull box may be further calculated as follows:

Step 1   Calculate space (w):

$$D = 6 \times 1\tfrac{1}{2}" = 9"$$

Step 2   Divide this number (9") by the square root of 2 (1.414) and make the following calculation:

$$w = \frac{9"}{1.414} = 6.4"$$

Step 3   Measure from the left, lower corner of the pull box over 6.4" to obtain the center of the **knockout** for the first 1½" conduit. Measure up (from the lower left corner) to obtain the center of the knockout for this same cable run on the left side of the pull box.

Step 4   Since there are two 3" (inside diameter) conduits, each with a measured outside diameter of approximately 4.25", the space for these two conduits can be found using the following equation:

$$2 \times 4.25" = 8.5"$$

Step 5   The space required for the two 2" (inside diameter) conduits, each with a measured outside diameter of approximately 3.25", may be determined in a similar manner:

$$2 \times 3.25" = 6.5"$$

Step 6   The space required for the two 1.5" (inside diameter) conduits, each with a measured outside diameter of approximately 2.75", may be determined using the same equation:

$$2 \times 2.75" = 5.5"$$

Step 7   To find the required space for locknuts and bushings, multiply 0.5" by the total number of conduit entries on one side of the box. Since there are a total of six conduit entries, use the following equation:

$$6 \times 0.5" = 3.0"$$

Step 8   Add all figures obtained in Steps 2 through 7 together to obtain the total required length of the pull box.

Clear space (w)	=	6.4"
1.5" conduits	=	5.5"
2" conduits	=	6.5"
3" conduits	=	8.5"
Space between locknuts	=	3.0"
Total length of box	=	29.9"

Since the same number and size of conduits enter on the bottom side of the pull box and leave, at a right angle, on the left side of the pull box, the box will be square. Although a box exactly 29.9" will suffice for this application, the next larger standard size is 30"; this should be the size pull box selected. Even if a custom pull box is made in a sheet metal shop, the workers will still probably make it an even 30" unless specifically ordered otherwise.

3.2.0   CABINETS AND CUTOUT BOXES

NEC Article 373 deals with the installation requirements for cabinets, cutout boxes, and meter sockets. In general, where cables are used, each cable must be secured to the cabinet or cutout box by an approved method. Furthermore, the cabinets or cutout boxes must have sufficient space to accommodate all conductors installed in them without crowding.

NEC Table 373-6(a) gives the minimum wire bending space at terminals, along with the width of sizing gutter in inches.

Figure 11 gives a summary of NEC requirements for the installation of cabinets and cutout boxes.

Other basic NEC requirements for cabinets and cutout boxes are as follows:

- *NEC Table 373-6(a)* applies when the conductor does not enter or leave the enclosure through the wall opposite its terminal.

- *NEC Section 373-6(b), Exception No. 1* states that a conductor must be permitted to enter or leave an enclosure through the wall opposite its terminal, provided the conductor enters or leaves the enclosure where the gutter joins an adjacent gutter that has a width that conforms to *NEC Table 373-6(b)* for that conductor.

- *NEC Section 373-6(b), Exception No. 2* states that a conductor not larger than 350 kcmil must be permitted to enter or leave an enclosure containing only a meter socket(s) through the wall opposite its terminal, provided the terminal is a lay-in type where either: (a) the terminal is directly facing the enclosure wall, and the offset is not greater than 50% of the bending space specified in *NEC Table 373-6(a)*, or (b) the terminal is directed toward the opening in the enclosure and is within a 45° angle of directly facing the enclosure wall.

- *NEC Table 373-6(b)* must apply where the conductor enters or leaves the enclosure through the wall opposite its terminal.

NEC Article 374 covers the installation requirements for auxiliary gutters, which are permitted to supplement wiring spaces at meter centers, distribution centers, and similar points of wiring systems and may enclose conductors or busbars, but must not be used to enclose switches, overcurrent devices, appliances, or other similar equipment.

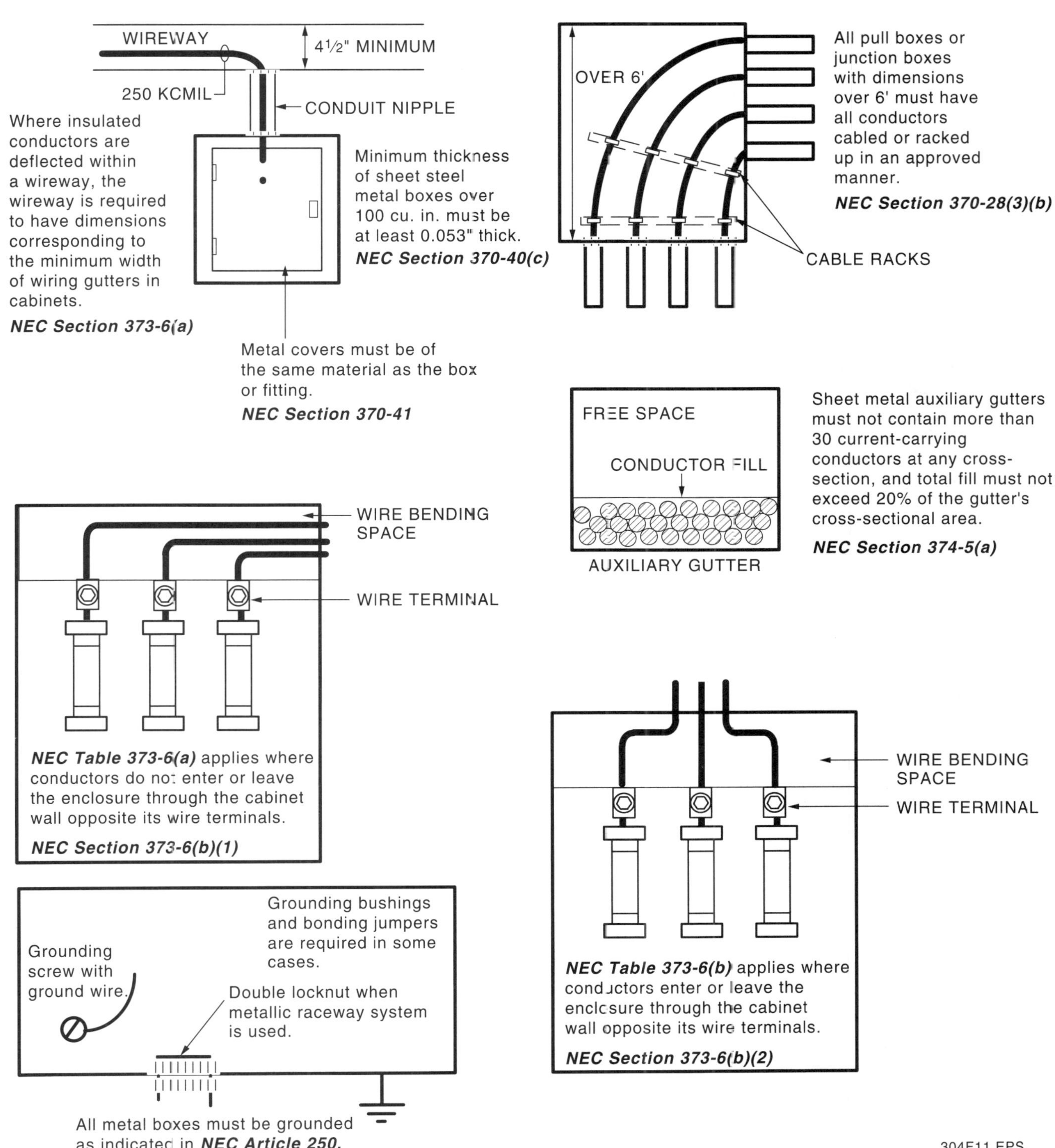

Figure 11. Installation Requirements For Cabinets And Cutout Boxes

In general, auxiliary gutters must not contain more than 30 current-carrying conductors at any cross-section. The sum of the cross-sectional areas of all contained conductors at any cross-section of an auxiliary gutter must not exceed 20% of the interior cross-sectional area of the auxiliary gutter. We discussed earlier that conductors installed in conduits and tubing must not exceed 40% fill. Auxiliary gutters are limited to only 20%.

When dealing with auxiliary gutters, always remember the number 30. This is the maximum number of conductors allowed in any auxiliary gutter regardless of the cross-sectional area. This question will be found on almost every electrician's examination in the country. Refer to *Figure 11* for a summary of NEC installation requirements for auxiliary gutters.

4.0.0 OUTLET BOXES

On every job, a lot of boxes are required for outlets, switches, pull boxes, and junction boxes. All of these must be sized, installed, and supported to meet current NEC requirements. Since the NEC limits the number of conductors allowed in each outlet or switch box according to its size, electricians must install boxes large enough to accommodate the number of conductors that must be spliced in the box or fed through. Therefore, a knowledge of the various types of boxes and the volume of each is essential.

4.1.0 SIZING OUTLET BOXES

In general, the maximum number of conductors permitted in standard outlet boxes is listed in **NEC Table 370-16(a)**. These figures apply where no fittings or devices such as fixture studs, cable clamps, switches, or receptacles are contained in the box and where no grounding conductors are part of the wiring within the box. Obviously, in all modern residential wiring systems, there will be one or more of these items contained in the outlet box. Therefore, where one or more of the above-mentioned items are present, the number of conductors is reduced by one less than that shown in the table for each type of fitting and by two for each device strap. For example, a deduction of two conductors must be made for each strap containing a device such as a switch or duplex receptacle; a further deduction of one conductor shall be made for one or more grounding conductors entering the box. For example, a 3" × 2" × 3½" box is listed in the table as containing a maximum number of eight No. 12 wires. If the box contains cable clamps and a duplex receptacle, three wires will have to be deducted from the total of eight—providing for only five No. 12 wires. If a ground wire is used, only four No. 12 wires may be used, which might be the case when a three-wire cable with ground is used to feed a three-way wall switch.

Figure 12 illustrates one possible wiring configuration for outlet boxes and the maximum number of conductors permitted in them as governed by **NEC Section 370-16**. This example shows two single-gang switch boxes joined or ganged together to hold a single-pole toggle switch and a duplex receptacle. This type of arrangement is likely to be found above kitchen countertops whereas the duplex receptacle is provided for small appliances and the single-pole switch could be used to control a garbage disposal. This arrangement is also useful above a workbench—the receptacle for small power tools and the switch to control lighting over the bench.

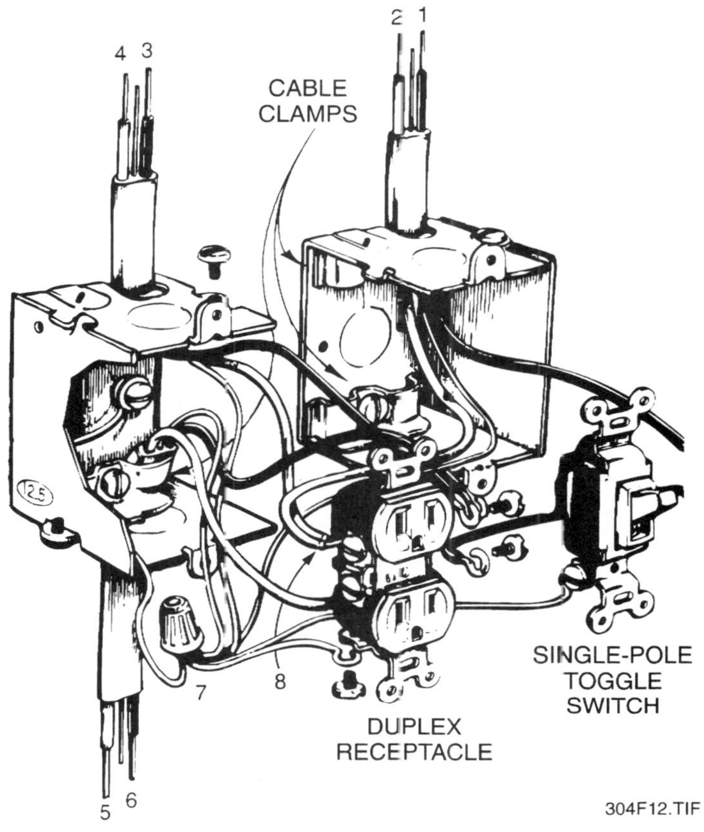

Figure 12. One Possible Box Sizing Configuration

Since **NEC Table 370-16(a)** gives the capacity of one 3" × 2" × 2½" device box as 12.5 cu. in., the total capacity of both boxes in *Figure 12* is 25 cu. in. These two boxes have a capacity to allow 10 No. 12 **American Wire Gauge (AWG)** conductors, or 12 No. 14 AWG conductors, less the deductions as listed below.

- Per **NEC Section 370-16(b)(4)**, two conductors must be deducted for each strap-mounted device based on the largest size conductor connected to the device. Since there is one duplex receptacle and one single-pole toggle switch, four conductors must be deducted from the total number stated in the above paragraph.

- Per **NEC Section 370-16(b)(2)**, the combined boxes contain one or more cable clamps, another conductor must be deducted based on the largest size conductor in the box. Note that only one deduction is made for similar clamps, regardless of the number. However, any unused clamps may be removed to facilitate the electrical worker's job (i.e., to allow for more work space).

- Per *NEC Section 370-16(b)(5)*, the equipment grounding conductors, regardless of the number, count as one conductor only. Therefore, deduct one conductor based on the largest size grounding conductor in the box.

Therefore, to comply with the NEC, and considering the combined deduction of six conductors, only four No. 12 AWG conductors (six No. 14 AWG conductors) may be installed in the outlet box configuration in *Figure 12*.

Figure 12 shows three types of nonmetallic-sheathed (NM) cables, designated 12/2 with ground, entering the ganged outlet boxes. This is a total of six current-carrying conductors and three ground wires, for a total of nine. This arrangement is in violation of the NEC because the total number of conductors exceed the NEC limits. However, if No. 14 AWG conductors were installed rather than No. 12, the configuration will comply with the NEC. Another alternative is to go to 3" × 2" × 3½" device boxes, which would then have a total of 36 cu. in. for the two boxes.

Also note the jumper wire in *Figure 12* (numbered 8 in the drawing). Conductors that both originate and end in the same outlet box are exempt from being counted against the allowable capacity of an outlet box [*NEC Section 370-16(b)(1)*]. This jumper wire (8) taps off one terminal of the duplex receptacle to furnish a hot wire to the single-pole toggle switch. Therefore, this wire originates and terminates in the same set of ganged boxes and is not counted against the total number of conductors. By the same token, the three grounding conductors extending from the wire nut to the individual grounding screws on the devices originate and terminate in the same set of boxes. These conductors are also exempt from being counted with the total. Incidentally, the wire nut has a crimp connector beneath; wire nuts alone are not allowed to connect equipment grounding conductors.

A pictorial definition of stipulated conditions as they apply to *NEC Section 370-16* is shown in the following illustrations. *Figure 13* illustrates an assortment of raised covers and outlet box extensions. These components, when combined with the appropriate outlet boxes, serve to increase the usable work space. Each type is marked with their cu. in. capacity which may be added to the figures in *NEC Table 370-16(a)* to calculate the increased number of conductors allowed.

Figure 14 shows typical wiring configurations which must be counted as conductors when calculating the total capacity of outlet boxes. A wire passing through the box without a splice or tap is counted as one conductor. Therefore, a cable containing two wires that passes in and out of an outlet box with a splice or tap is counted as two conductors. However, wires which enter a box and are either spliced or connected to a terminal, and then exit again, are counted as two conductors. In the case of two 2-wire cables, the total conductors charged will be four. Wires that enter and terminate in the same box are charged as individual conductors and in this case, the total charge would be two conductors. Remember, when one or more grounding wires enter the box and are joined, a deduction of only one conductor is required, regardless of their number.

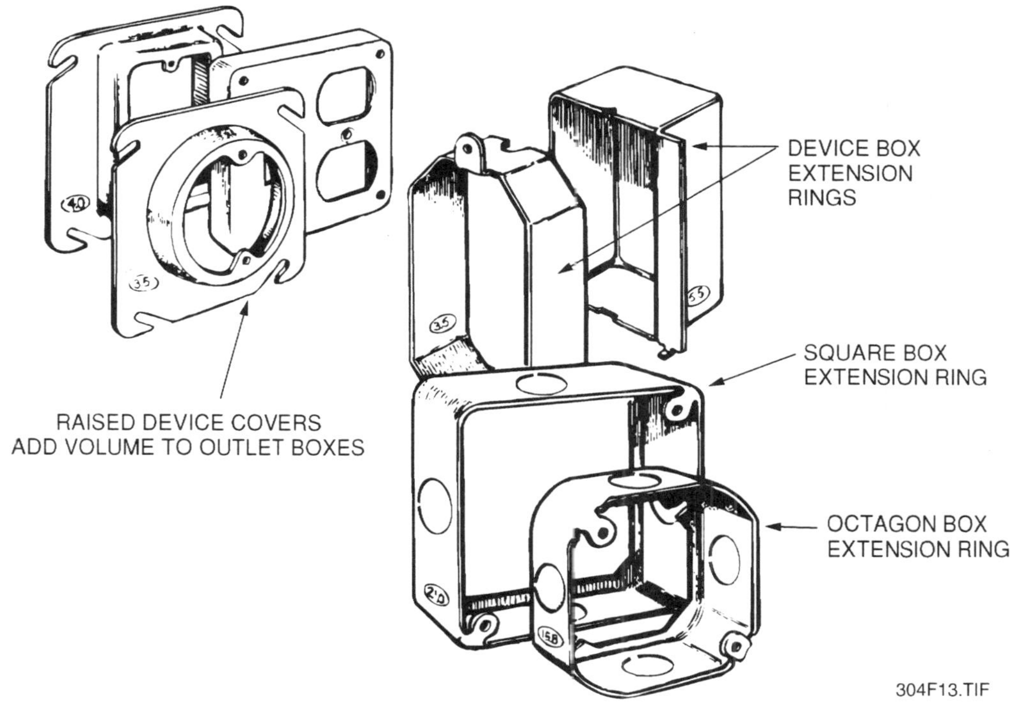

Figure 13. Raised Box Covers Add To The Box Capacity

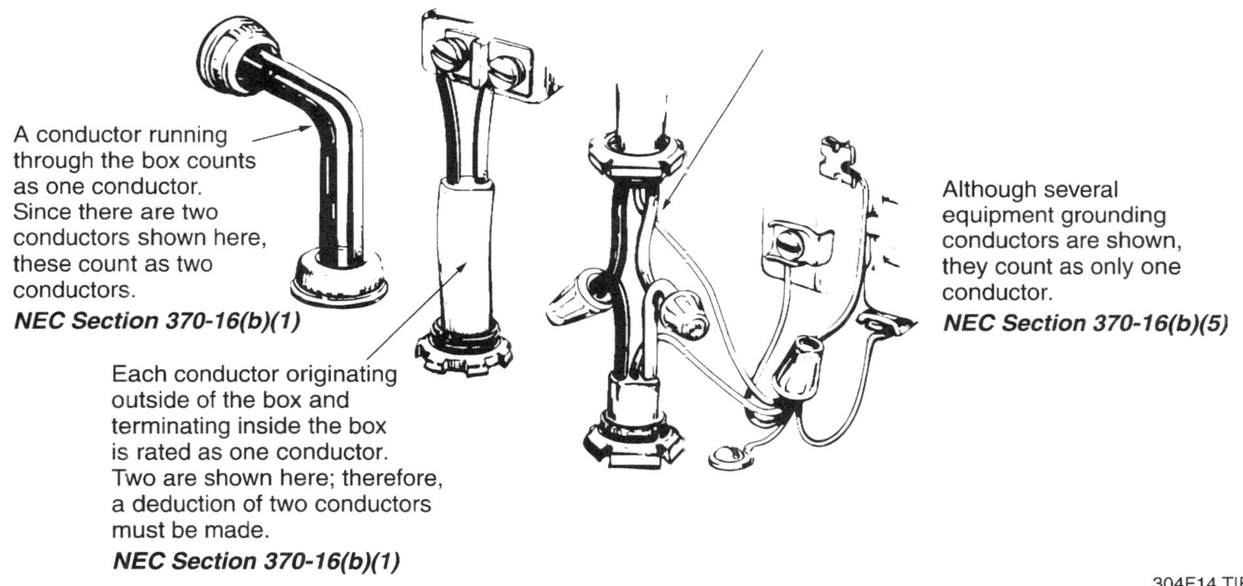

Figure 14. Wiring Configurations That Must Be Counted As Conductors When Calculating Box Capacity

Further components that require deduction adjustments from those specified in **NEC Table 370-16(a)** include fixture studs, hickeys, and fixture stud extensions [**NEC Section 370-16(b)(3)**]. One conductor must be deducted from the total for each type of fitting used. Two conductors must be deducted for each strap-mounted device, such as duplex receptacles and wall switches; a deduction of one conductor is made when one or more internally mounted cable clamps are used.

Figure 15 shows components which may be used in outlet boxes without affecting the total number of conductors. Such items include grounding clips and screws, wire nuts, and cable connectors when the latter is inserted through knockout holes in the outlet box and secured with locknuts. Pre-wired fixture wires are not counted against the total number of allowable conductors in an outlet box, nor are conductors originating and ending in the box.

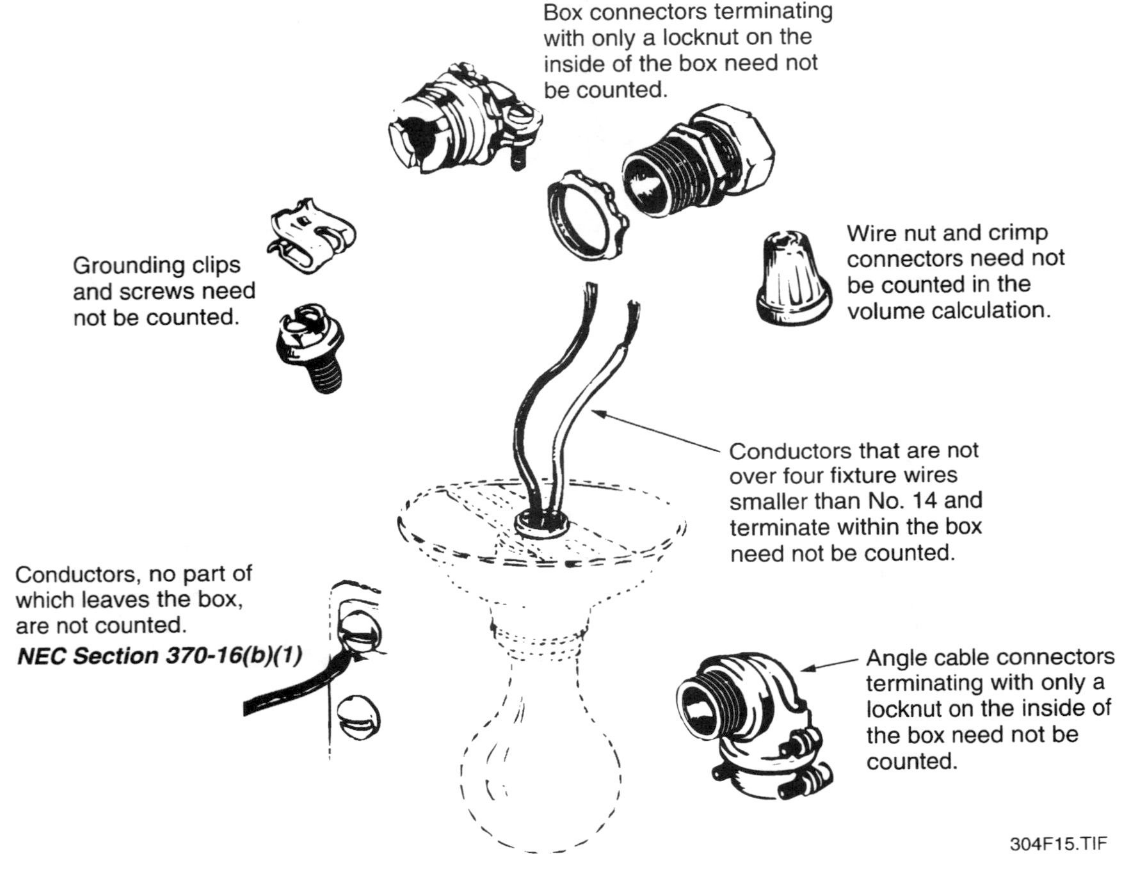

Figure 15. Components That Do Not Affect The Capacity Of An Outlet Box

To better understand how outlet boxes are sized, we will take two No. 12 AWG conductors installed in ½" EMT and terminating into a metallic outlet box containing one duplex receptacle. What size outlet box will meet NEC requirements?

ELECTRICAL — TRAINEE TASK MODULE 26304

Step 1   Use **NEC Section 370-16** to calculate the total number of conductors and equivalents.

> One receptacle = 2
>
> Two No. 12 conductors = 2
> ___________________________
>
> Total No. 12 conductors = 4

Step 2   Determine the amount of space required for each conductor.

> **NEC Table 370-16(b)** gives the box volume required for each conductor:
>
> No. 12 AWG = 2.25 cu. in.

Step 3   Calculate the outlet box space required by multiplying the number of cu. in. required for each conductor by the number of conductors found in Step 1.

> 4 x 2.25 = 9.00 cu. in.

Once you have determined the required box capacity, again refer to **NEC Table 370-16(a)** and note that a 3" × 2" × 2¼" box comes closest to our requirements. This box size is rated for 10.5 cu. in.

Where four No. 12 conductors enter the box, two additional No. 12 conductors must be added to our previous count for a total of six conductors.

> 6 × 2.25 = 13.5 cu. in.

Again, refer to **NEC Table 370-16(a)** and note that a 3" × 2" × 2¾" device box with a rated capacity of 14.0 cu. in. is the closest device box that meets NEC requirements. Of course, any box with a larger capacity is permitted.

SUMMARY

The NEC specifies certain fill requirements for raceways, outlet boxes, pull and junction boxes, cabinets, cutout boxes, auxiliary gutters, and similar conductor-containing housings. In some cases, NEC tables may be used to determine the proper size of housing; in other cases, calculations are required in conjunction with tables and manufacturers' specifications.

This module should provide a firm foundation for determining the proper size of raceway, box, or fitting for any given application. However, it is recommended that you carefully review the NEC requirements pertaining to all such fill requirements.

References

For advanced study of topics covered in this Task Module, the following books are suggested:

American Electricians' Handbook, Latest Edition, McGraw-Hill, New York, NY.

National Electrical Code Handbook, Latest Edition, National Fire Protection Association, Quincy, MA.

1. Any channel used for holding wires, cables, or busbars is called a _____.
    a. knockout
    b. raceway
    c. junction box
    d. conduit fill

2. Which of the following is *not* a factor influencing a cable's mechanical fit in a raceway?
    a. Clearance
    b. Jam ratio
    c. Age
    d. Weight

3. If you have more than one size of conductor installed in the same raceway, refer to _____ to determine the proper conduit and fill requirements.
    a. ***NEC Appendix A***
    b. ***NEC Section 380-6(d)***
    c. ***NEC Article 310***
    d. ***NEC Chapter 9, Tables 4 and 5***

4. What special procedures must be taken with cables installed in a pull box that is 6' high or over?
    a. The cables must be racked in the box in an approved manner.
    b. The cables must terminate within the box.
    c. The cables must not terminate within the box.
    d. Cable clamps of any kind are not allowed.

5. When calculating pull box size, _____ is the standard amount of clearance that should be allowed between locknuts.
    a. 1"
    b. ½"
    c. ¼"
    d. ⅛"

6. If a straight pull box contains two 4" conduits entering one end and leaving the other end, what is the minimum length of the box?
    a. 12"
    b. 24"
    c. 32"
    d. 36"

7. If a straight pull box contains one 4" conduit and one 3" conduit (both sizes entering and leaving from opposite ends), what is the minimum length of the box?

   a.   24"
   b.   32"
   c.   36"
   d.   38"

8. The maximum number of conductors allowed in any auxiliary gutter is ______.

   a.   30
   b.   20
   c.   40
   d.   25

9. What is the maximum percentage of fill allowed in an auxiliary gutter?

   a.   10%
   b.   20%
   c.   30%
   d.   40%

10. What is the minimum wire bending space that must be provided in a cabinet or cutout box in which three No. 1/0 THWN conductors terminate?

   a.   7"
   b.   12"
   c.   14"
   d.   18"

11. What effect do extension rings have on outlet box fill capacity?

   a.   The box capacity remains the same.
   b.   The box capacity decreases.
   c.   The box capacity increases.
   d.   This only applies to NM boxes, and the box capacity decreases.

12. How many conductor deductions must be allowed for three bare equipment grounding conductors in an outlet box?

   a.   1
   b.   2
   c.   3
   d.   4

13. How many conductor deductions must be allowed for a BX box connector terminating with only a locknut on the inside of the outlet box?

   a. 6
   b. 4
   c. 2
   d. 0

14. How many conductor deductions must be counted for three No. 16 AWG fixture wires that terminate within an outlet box?

   a. 1
   b. 2
   c. 0
   d. 3

15. How many conductor deductions must be counted for two wire nuts used for splicing conductors inside an outlet box?

   a. 0
   b. 1
   c. 2
   d. 3

ANSWERS TO REVIEW/PRACTICE QUESTIONS

<u>Answer</u>	<u>Section Reference</u>
1. b	1.0.0
2. c	2.1.0
3. d	2.2.0
4. a	3.0.0
5. b	3.1.0
6. c	3.1.0
7. b	3.1.0
8. a	3.2.0
9. b	3.2.0
10. a	3.2.0
11. c	4.1.0
12. a	4.1.0
13. d	4.1.0/Fig. 15
14. c	4.1.0/Fig.15
15. a	4.1.0

The NCCER makes every effort to keep these manuals up-to-date and free of technical errors. We appreciate your help in this process. If you have an idea for improving this manual, or if you find an error, a typographical mistake, or an inaccuracy in the NCCER's Craft Training Manuals, please write us, using this form or a photocopy. Be sure to include the exact module number, page number, a description of the problem, and the correction, if possible. Your input will be brought to the attention of the Technical Review Committee. Thank you for your assistance.

Instructors – If you found that additional materials were necessary in order to teach this module effectively, please let us know so that we may include them in the Equipment/Materials list in the Instructor's Guide.

Write: Curriculum Development and Revision Department
National Center for Construction Education and Research
P.O. Box 141104
Gainesville, FL 32614-1104
Fax: 352-334-0932

Craft ___________________ Module Name _______________________

Copyright Date __________ Module Number __________ Page Number(s) __________

Description of Problem
____
____
____
____

(Optional) Correction of Problem
____
____
____

(Optional) Your Name and Address
____
____
____

WIRING DEVICES

NATIONAL
CENTER FOR
CONSTRUCTION
EDUCATION AND
RESEARCH

OBJECTIVES

Upon completion of this module, the trainee will be able to:

1. Select wiring devices according to the National Electrical Manufacturers' Association (NEMA) classifications.
2. Size wiring devices according to NEC and NEMA requirements.
3. Select the proper box or enclosure for wiring devices.
4. Follow NEC regulations governing the installation of wiring devices.
5. Explain the types and purposes of grounding wiring devices.
6. Determine the maximum load allowed on specific wiring devices.

Prerequisites

Successful completion of the following Task Modules is recommended before beginning study of this Task Module: Core Curricula; Electrical Level 1; Electrical Level 2; Electrical Level 3, Modules 26301 through 26304.

Required Trainee Materials

1. Trainee Task Module
2. Appropriate Personal Protective Equipment
3. Copy of the latest edition of the *National Electrical Code*

Note: The designations "National Electrical Code," "NE Code," and "NEC," where used in this document, refer to the National Electrical Code®, which is a registered trademark of the National Fire Protection Association, Quincy, MA. *All National Electrical Code (NEC) references in this module refer to the 1999 edition of the NEC.*

This course map shows all of the modules in the third level of the Electrical curricula. The suggested training order begins at the bottom and proceeds up. Skill levels increase as a trainee advances on the course map. The training order may be adjusted by the local Training Program Sponsor.

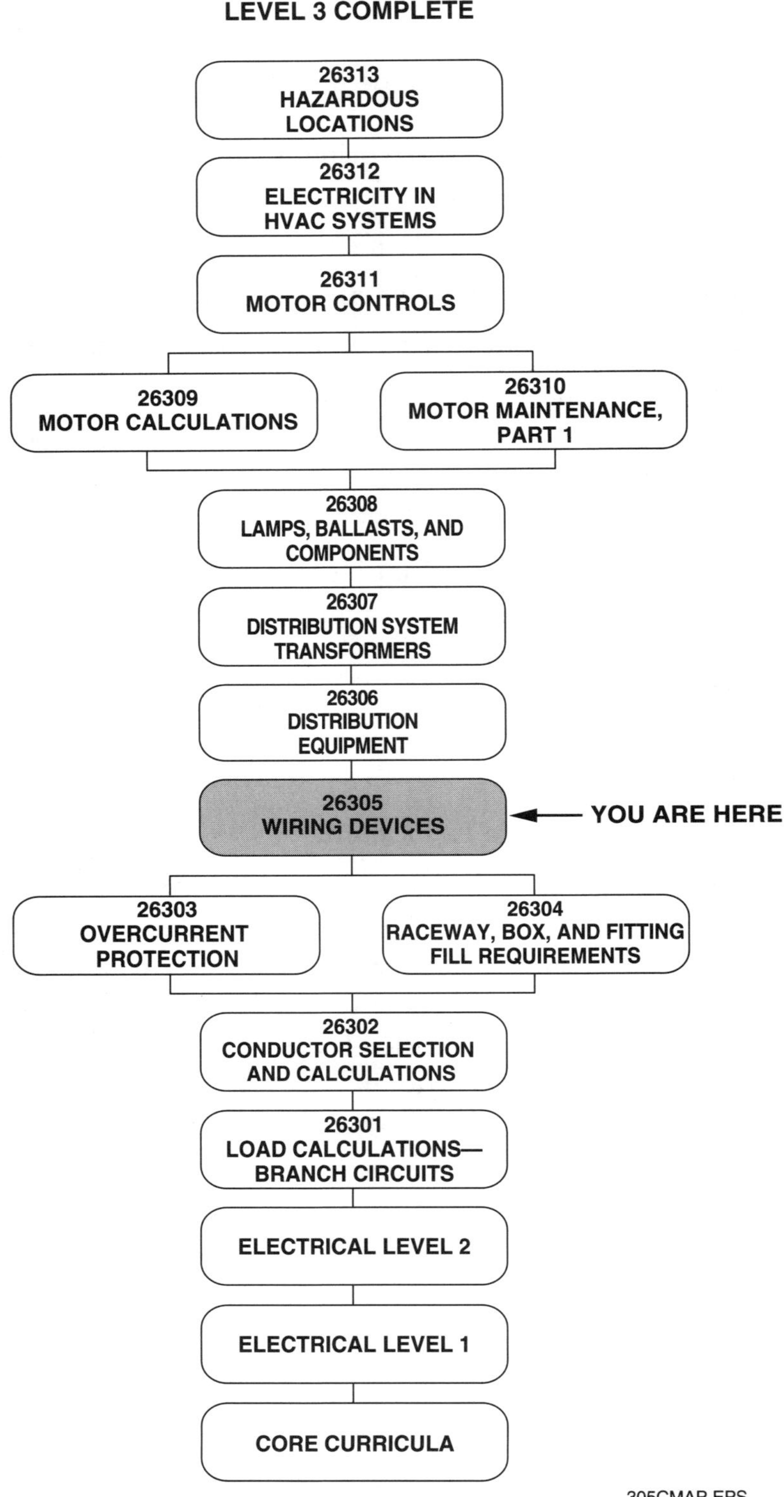

305CMAP.EPS

TABLE OF CONTENTS

Trade Terms Introduced In This Module

Attachment plug: The male connector for electrical cords.

Cord: A small, flexible conductor assembly, usually jacketed.

Device: An item intended to carry or help carry but not utilize electric energy.

Four-way switch: A device which, when used in conjunction with two three-way switches, offers control of an electrical outlet (usually lighting) at three or more locations.

Gang switch: A unit of two or more switches that allows control of two or more circuits from one location. The entire mechanism is mounted in one box under one cover.

Receptacle: A contact device installed at an outlet for the connection of an attachment plug and flexible cord to supply portable equipment.

Switch: A device used to open, close, or change the connection of a circuit.

Three-way switch: A switch used to control a light or set of lights from two different locations.

1.0.0 INTRODUCTION

The NEC defines a **device** as a unit of an electrical system that is intended to carry or help carry but not utilize electric energy. This covers a wide assortment of system components that include (but are not limited to) the following:

- **Switches**
- Relays
- Contactors
- **Receptacles**
- Conductors

This module covers switching devices and receptacles. Both are commonly known as *wiring devices*. Other devices, such as relays, contactors, etc., are covered in other modules.

2.0.0 RECEPTACLES

A receptacle is a contact device installed at an outlet for the connection of a single **attachment plug**. Several types and configurations are available for use with many different attachment plugs, each designed for a specific application (*Figure 1*). For example, receptacles are available for two-wire, 120V, 15A and 20A circuits; others are designed for use on two-wire and three-wire; 240V/20A, 30A, 40A, and 50A circuits. There are also a variety of other types, many of which are discussed in this module.

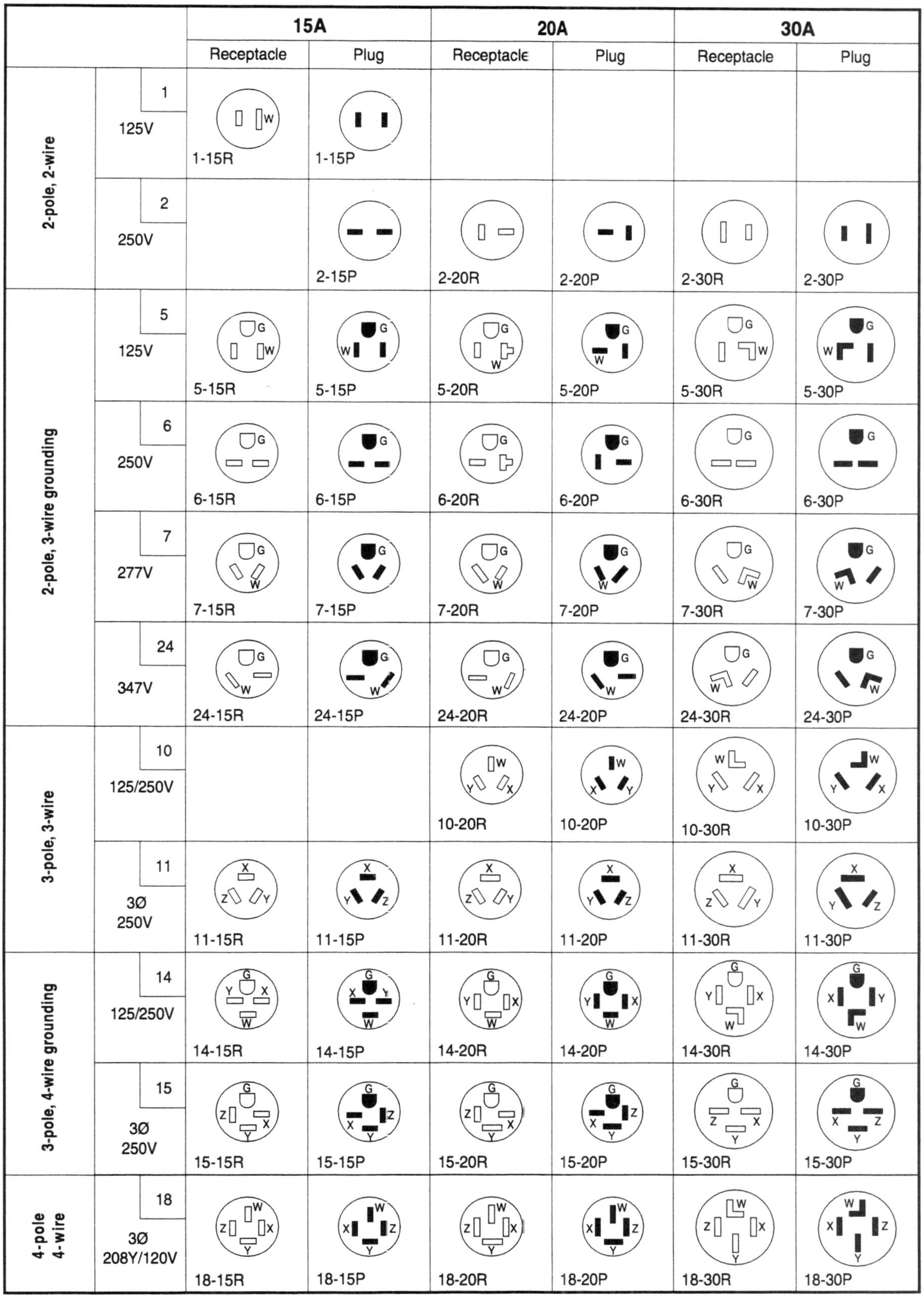

		15A		20A		30A	
		Receptacle	Plug	Receptacle	Plug	Receptacle	Plug
2-pole, 2-wire	1 125V	1-15R	1-15P				
	2 250V		2-15P	2-20R	2-20P	2-30R	2-30P
2-pole, 3-wire grounding	5 125V	5-15R	5-15P	5-20R	5-20P	5-30R	5-30P
	6 250V	6-15R	6-15P	6-20R	6-20P	6-30R	6-30P
	7 277V	7-15R	7-15P	7-20R	7-20P	7-30R	7-30P
	24 347V	24-15R	24-15P	24-20R	24-20P	24-30R	24-30P
3-pole, 3-wire	10 125/250V			10-20R	10-20P	10-30R	10-30P
	11 3Ø 250V	11-15R	11-15P	11-20R	11-20P	11-30R	11-30P
3-pole, 4-wire grounding	14 125/250V	14-15R	14-15P	14-20R	14-20P	14-30R	14-30P
	15 3Ø 250V	15-15R	15-15P	15-20R	15-20P	15-30R	15-30P
4-pole 4-wire	18 3Ø 208Y/120V	18-15R	18-15P	18-20R	18-20P	18-30R	18-30P

305F01A.EPS

Figure 1. Common Receptacles And Plugs (1 Of 2)

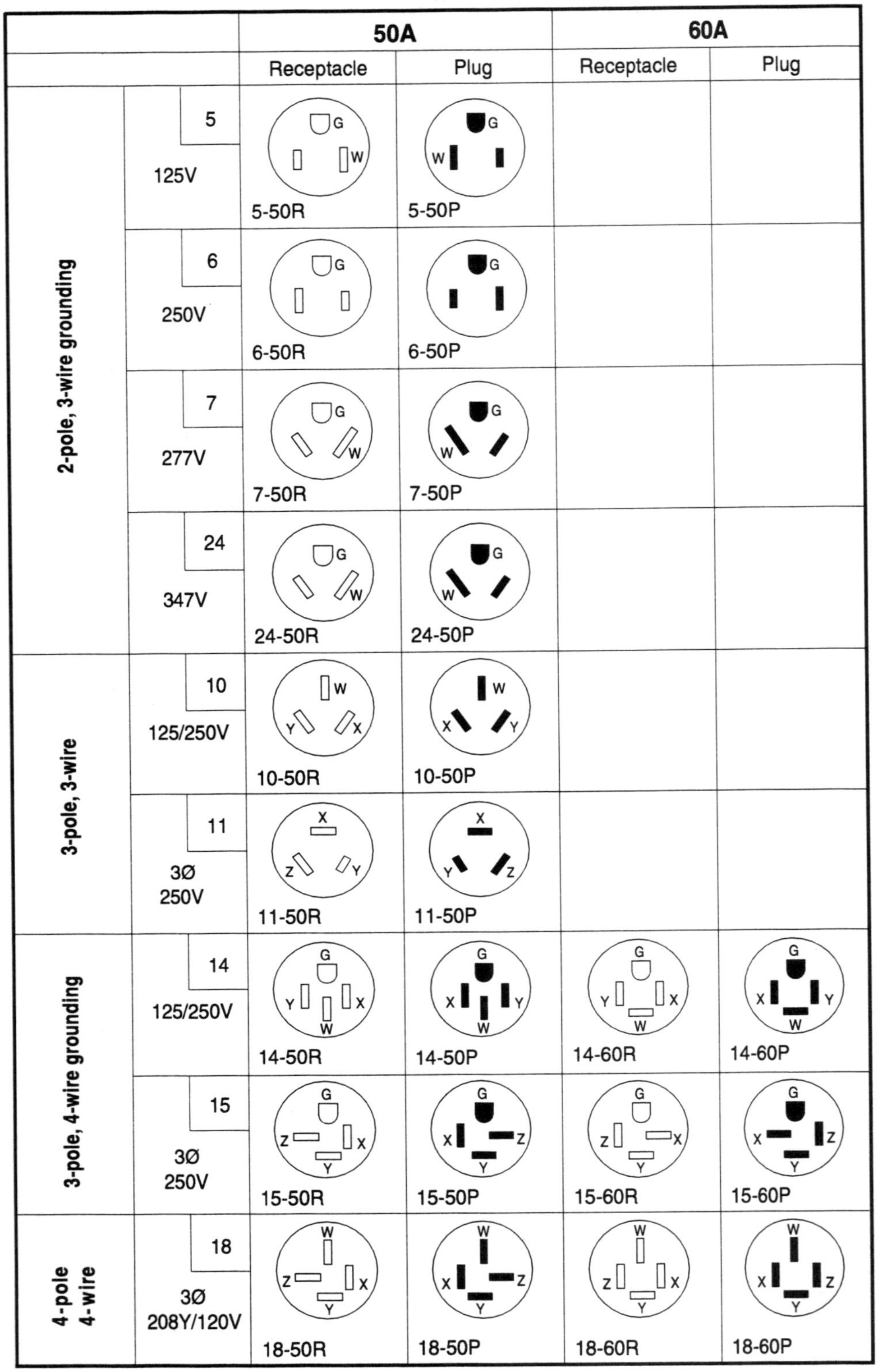

			50A		60A	
			Receptacle	Plug	Receptacle	Plug
2-pole, 3-wire grounding	5	125V	5-50R	5-50P		
	6	250V	6-50R	6-50P		
	7	277V	7-50R	7-50P		
	24	347V	24-50R	24-50P		
3-pole, 3-wire	10	125/250V	10-50R	10-50P		
	11	3Ø 250V	11-50R	11-50P		
3-pole, 4-wire grounding	14	125/250V	14-50R	14-50P	14-60R	14-60P
	15	3Ø 250V	15-50R	15-50P	15-60R	15-60P
4-pole 4-wire	18	3Ø 208Y/120V	18-50R	18-50P	18-60R	18-60P

305F01B.EPS

Figure 1. Common Receptacles And Plugs (2 Of 2)

ELECTRICAL — TRAINEE TASK MODULE 26305

Receptacles are rated according to their voltage and amperage capacity. This rating determines the number and configuration of the contacts, both on the receptacle and the receptacle mating plug. This chart was developed by the Wiring Device Section of the National Electrical Manufacturers' Association (NEMA) and illustrates various voltage and current ratings. Note that all configurations in *Figure 1* are for general-purpose, straight blade, nonlocking devices. Locking-type receptacles and plugs are covered later in this module.

Unsafe interchangeability has been eliminated by assigning a unique configuration to each voltage and current rating. All dual ratings have been eliminated, and interchangeability exists only where it does not present an unsafe condition.

Each configuration is designated by a number composed of the chart line number, the amperage, and either R for receptacle or P for plug cap. For example, a 5-15R is found on line 5 and represents a 15A receptacle.

A clear distinction is made between system grounds and equipment grounds. System grounds, referred to as *grounded conductors*, normally carry current at ground potential, and terminals for such conductors are marked *W* for white in the chart. Equipment grounds, referred to as *grounding conductors*, carry current only during ground fault conditions. The terminals for such conductors are marked *G* for grounding in the chart.

2.1.0   RECEPTACLE CHARACTERISTICS

Receptacles have various symbols and information inscribed on them that help to determine their proper use and ratings. For example, *Figure 2* shows a standard duplex receptacle and contains the following printed inscriptions:

- Testing laboratory label
- Canadian Standards Association (CSA) label
- Type of conductor for which the terminals are designed
- Current and voltage ratings listed by maximum amperage, maximum voltage, and current restrictions

The testing laboratory label is an indication that the device has undergone extensive testing by a nationally recognized testing lab and has met with certain minimum safety requirements. The label does not indicate any type of quality rating. The receptacle in *Figure 2* is marked with the UL label which indicates that the device type was tested by Underwriters' Laboratories, Inc. of Northbrook, IL. ETL Testing Laboratories, Inc. of Cortland, NY is another nationally recognized testing laboratory. These laboratories provide labeling, listing, and follow-up service for the safety testing of electrical products to nationally recognized safety standards or specifically designated requirements of jurisdictional authorities.

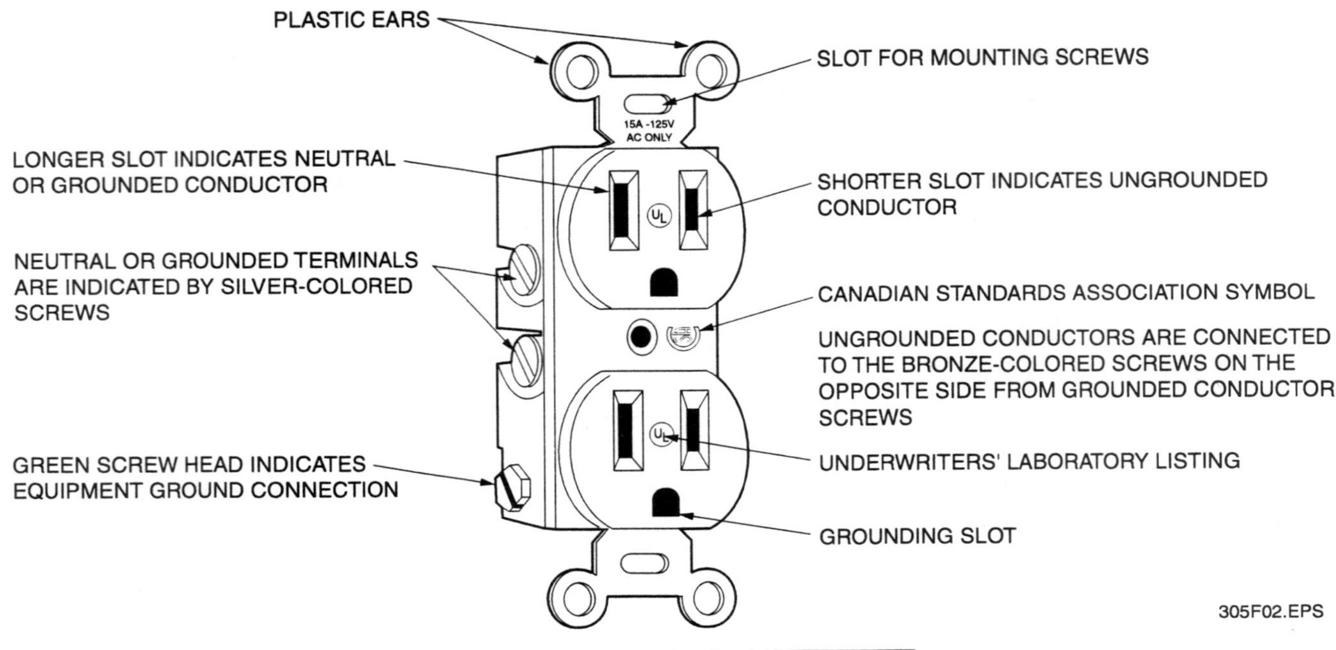

Figure 2. Typical Duplex Receptacle

The CSA label is an indication that the material or device has undergone a similar testing procedure by the Canadian Standards Association and is acceptable for use in Canada.

Current and voltage ratings are listed by maximum amperage, maximum voltage, and current restriction. On the device shown in *Figure 2*, the maximum current rating is 15A. The maximum voltage allowed on this device is 125V.

Conductor markings are also usually found on duplex receptacles. Receptacles with quick-connect wire clips will be marked *USE #12 OR #14 SOLID WIRE ONLY*. If the inscription CO/ALR is marked on the receptacle, either copper, aluminum, or copper-clad aluminum wire may be used. The letters ALR stand for aluminum revised. Receptacles marked with the inscription CU/AL should be used for copper only, although they were originally intended for use with aluminum also. However, such devices frequently failed when connected to 15A or 20A circuits. Consequently, devices marked with CU/AL are no longer acceptable for use with aluminum conductors.

The remaining markings on duplex receptacles may include the manufacturer's name or logo, the words *WIRE RELEASE* inscribed under the wire release slots, and the letters GR beneath or beside the green grounding screw.

The screw terminals on receptacles are color-coded. For example, the terminal with the green screw head is the equipment ground connection and is connected to the U-shaped slots on the receptacle. The silver-colored terminal screws are for connecting the grounded or neutral conductors and are associated with the longer of the two vertical slots on the receptacle. The brass-colored terminal screws are for connecting the ungrounded or hot conductors and are associated with the shorter vertical slots on the receptacle.

Note: The long vertical slot accepts the grounded or neutral conductor, while the shorter vertical slot accepts the ungrounded or hot conductor.

2.2.0 MOUNTING RECEPTACLES

Although no actual NEC requirements exist on mounting heights and positioning of receptacles, there are certain installation methods that have become standard in the electrical industry. *Figure 3* shows common mounting heights of duplex receptacles used on conventional residential and small commercial installations. However, these dimensions are frequently varied to suit the building structure. For example, ceramic tile might be placed above a kitchen or bathroom countertop. If the dimensions in *Figure 3* put the receptacle part of the way out of the tile (i.e., half in and half out), the mounting height should be adjusted to either place the receptacle completely in the tile or completely out of the tile, as shown in *Figure 4*.

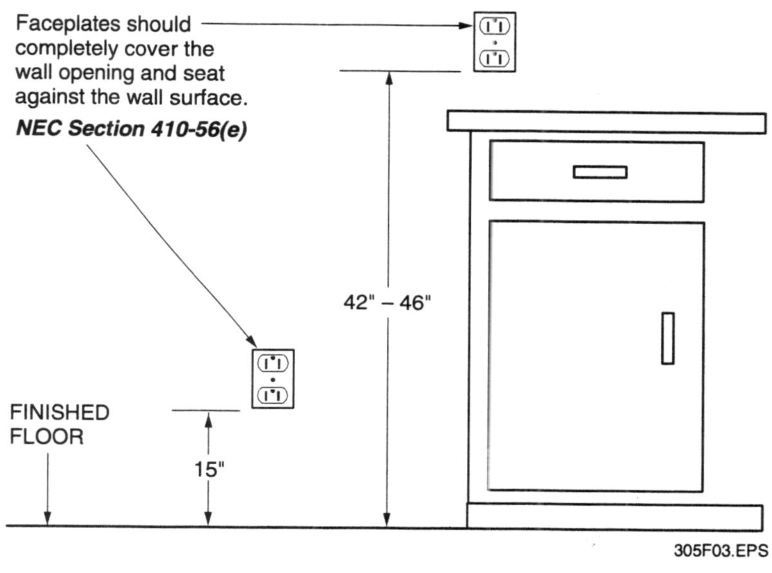

Figure 3. Mounting Heights Of Duplex Receptacles

Figure 4. Adjusting Mounting Heights

Refer again to *Figure 3* and note that the mounting heights are given to the bottom of the outlet box. Many dimensions on electrical drawings are given to the center of the outlet box or receptacle. However, during the actual installation, workers installing the outlet boxes can mount them more accurately (and in less time) by lining up the bottom of the box with a chalk mark rather than trying to eyeball this mark to the center of the box.

A decade or so ago, most electricians mounted receptacle outlets 12" from the finished floor to the center of the outlet box. However, a recent survey taken of over 500 homeowners shows that they prefer a mounting height of 15" from the finished floor to the bottom of the outlet box. It is easier to plug and unplug the **cord** assemblies at this height, especially for senior citizens and those homeowners who are confined to wheelchairs. However, always check the working drawings, written specifications, and details of construction for measurements that may affect the mounting height of a particular receptacle outlet.

Note: Be sure to check local codes as well as the job specifications for specific receptacle mounting requirements.

NEC Section 370-20 requires all outlet boxes installed in walls or ceilings of concrete, tile, or other noncombustible material such as plaster or drywall to be installed in such a manner that the front edge of the box or fitting is not set back from the finished surface by more than ¼". Where walls and ceilings are constructed of wood or other combustible materials, outlet boxes and fittings must be flush with the finished surface of the wall. See *Figure 5*.

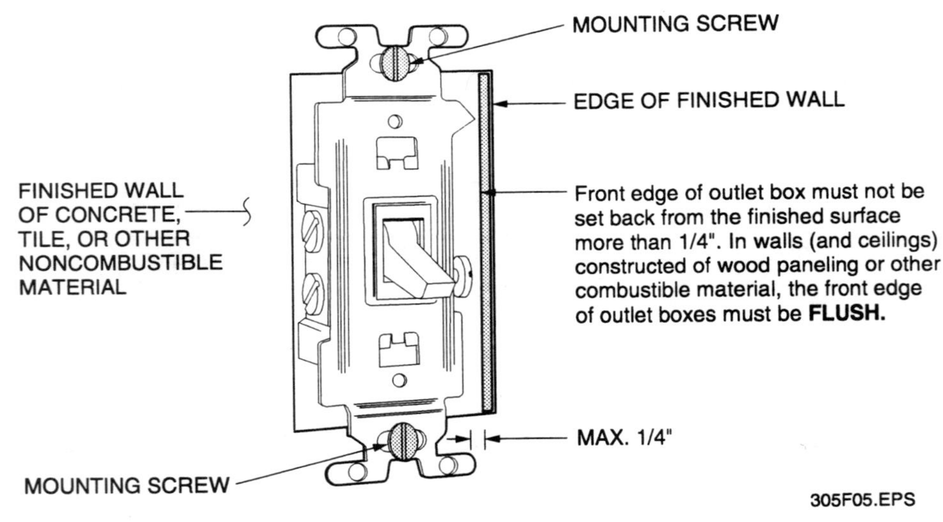

Figure 5. NEC Requirements For Mounting Outlet Boxes In Walls Or Ceilings

Wall surfaces such as drywall, plaster, etc., that contain wide gaps or are broken, jagged, or otherwise damaged must be repaired so there will be no gaps or open spaces greater than ⅛" between the outlet box and the wall material. These repairs should be made prior to installing the faceplate. Such repairs are best made using a noncombustible caulking or spackling compound. See *Figure 6*.

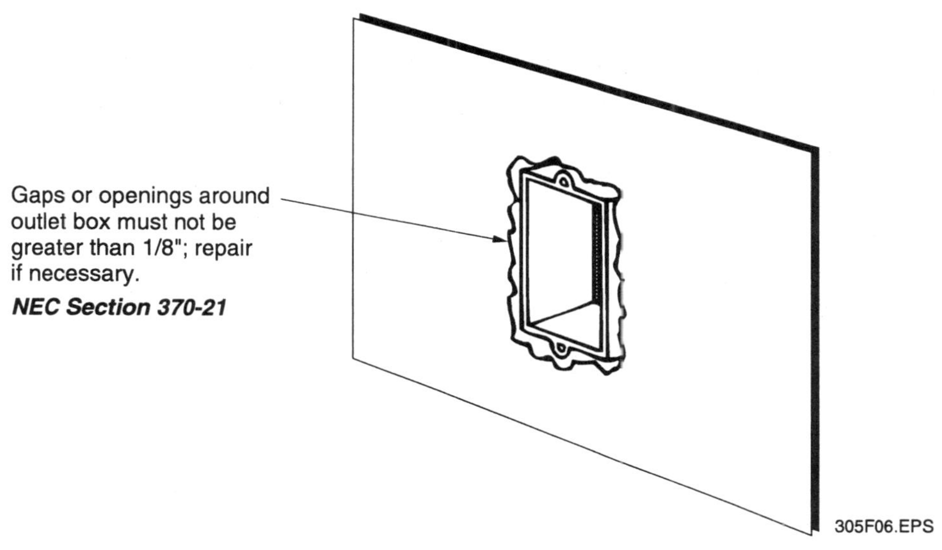

Figure 6. Gaps Or Openings Around Outlet Boxes Must Be Repaired

2.3.0   TYPES OF RECEPTACLES

There are many types of receptacles. For example, the duplex receptacles discussed previously are the straight-blade type which accepts a straight blade connector or plug. This is the most common type of receptacle in the U.S. and can be found on virtually all electrical projects from residential to large industrial installations.

- *Twist lock receptacles* – Twist lock receptacles are designed to accept a slightly curved blade connector or plug. The plug/connector and the receptacle lock together with a slight twist. This prevents accidentally unplugging the equipment.

- *Pin-and-sleeve receptacles* – Pin-and-sleeve devices have a unique locking feature. These receptacles are made with an extremely heavy-duty plastic housing. They are manufactured with long brass pins for long life and are color-coded according to voltage for easy identification.

- *Low-voltage receptacles* – These receptacles are designed for both AC and DC systems where the maximum potential is 50V. Receptacles used for low-voltage systems must have a minimum current-carrying capacity of 15A.

- *440V receptacles* – Portable electrical equipment operating at 440V to 460V is common on many industrial installations. This includes welders, battery chargers, and other types of portable equipment. Special 440V plugs and receptacles are used to connect and disconnect such equipment from a power source. 440V receptacles are available in two-wire, single-phase; three-wire, three-phase; and four-wire, three-phase. Equipment grounding is required in all cases, and provisions are provided in each receptacle for such grounding.

WARNING!	Make certain that the plug-and-cord assembly is compatible with both the equipment and receptacle before connecting to a 440V receptacle. Polarity and equipment grounding checks on the plug-and-cord assembly should be made on a monthly basis or more often if subjected to hard use.

3.0.0 LOCATING RECEPTACLES

Several NEC sections specify requirements for locating receptacles in all types of installations. This section presents a summary of these requirements.

3.1.0 RESIDENTIAL OCCUPANCIES

NEC Section 210-52 should be referred to when laying out outlets for residential and some commercial installations. This section details the general provisions along with small appliance circuit requirements, laundry requirements, unfinished basements, attached garages, and other areas of the home. *Figure 7* illustrates various NEC requirements for locating receptacles.

In general, every dwelling—regardless of its size—must have receptacles located in each habitable area so that no point along the floor line in any wall space (2' wide or wider) is more than 6' from an outlet in that space. The purpose of this requirement is to prevent the need for extension cords and to minimize the use of cords across doorways, fireplaces, and similar openings.

In addition, a minimum of two 20A small appliance branch circuits are required to serve all receptacle outlets, including refrigeration equipment, in the kitchen, pantry, breakfast room, dining room, or similar area of the dwelling unit. Such circuits, whether two or more are used, must have no other outlets connected to them.

ELECTRICAL — TRAINEE TASK MODULE 26305

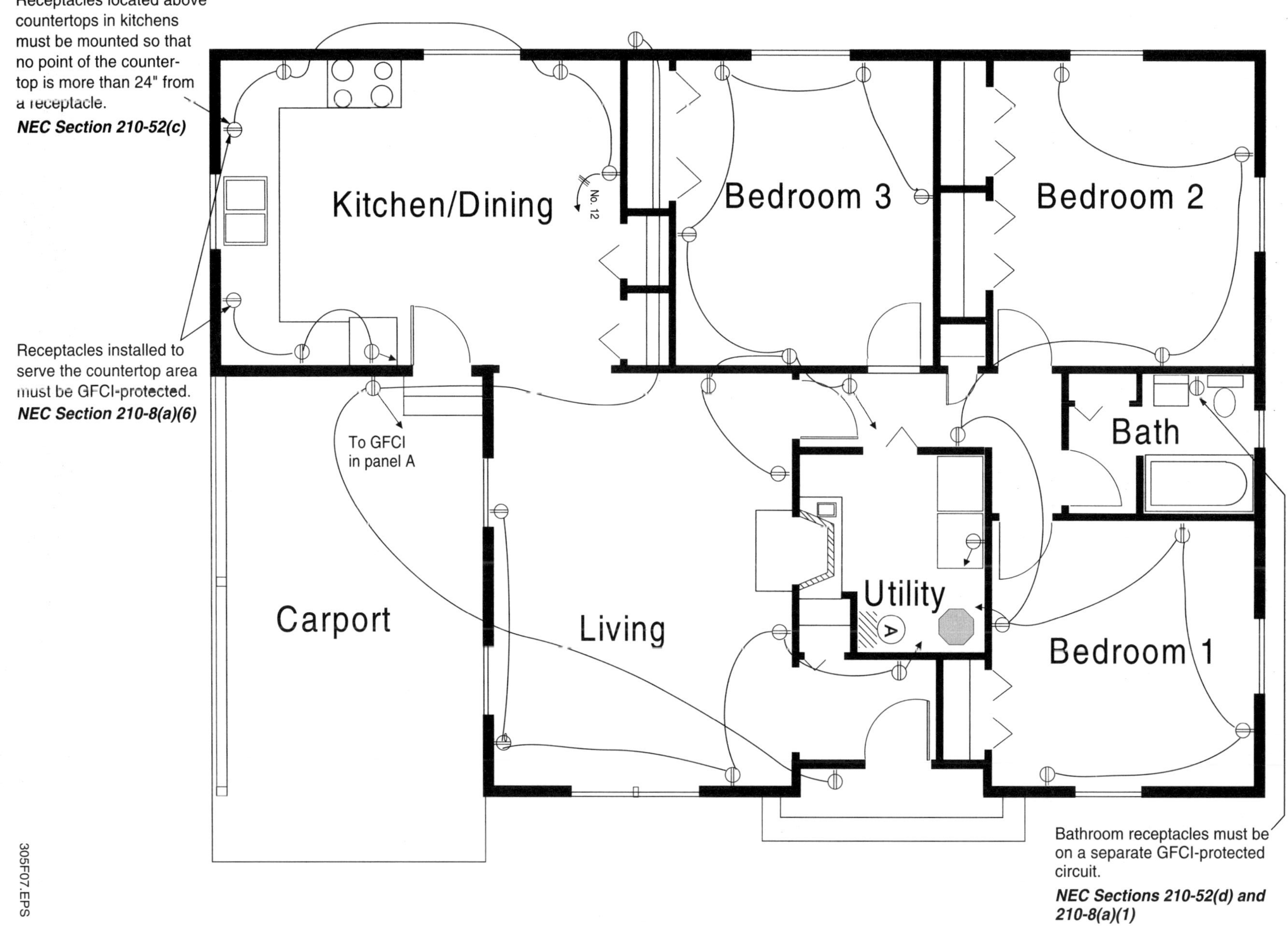

Figure 7. Summary Of NEC Requirements For Locating Receptacles

At least one receptacle is required in each laundry area, on the outside of the building at the front and back, in each basement, in each attached and detached garage, in each hallway 10' or more in length, and at an accessible location for servicing any HVAC equipment. *Figures 8 and 9* summarize these and other NEC requirements regarding the installation of receptacles in dwelling units.

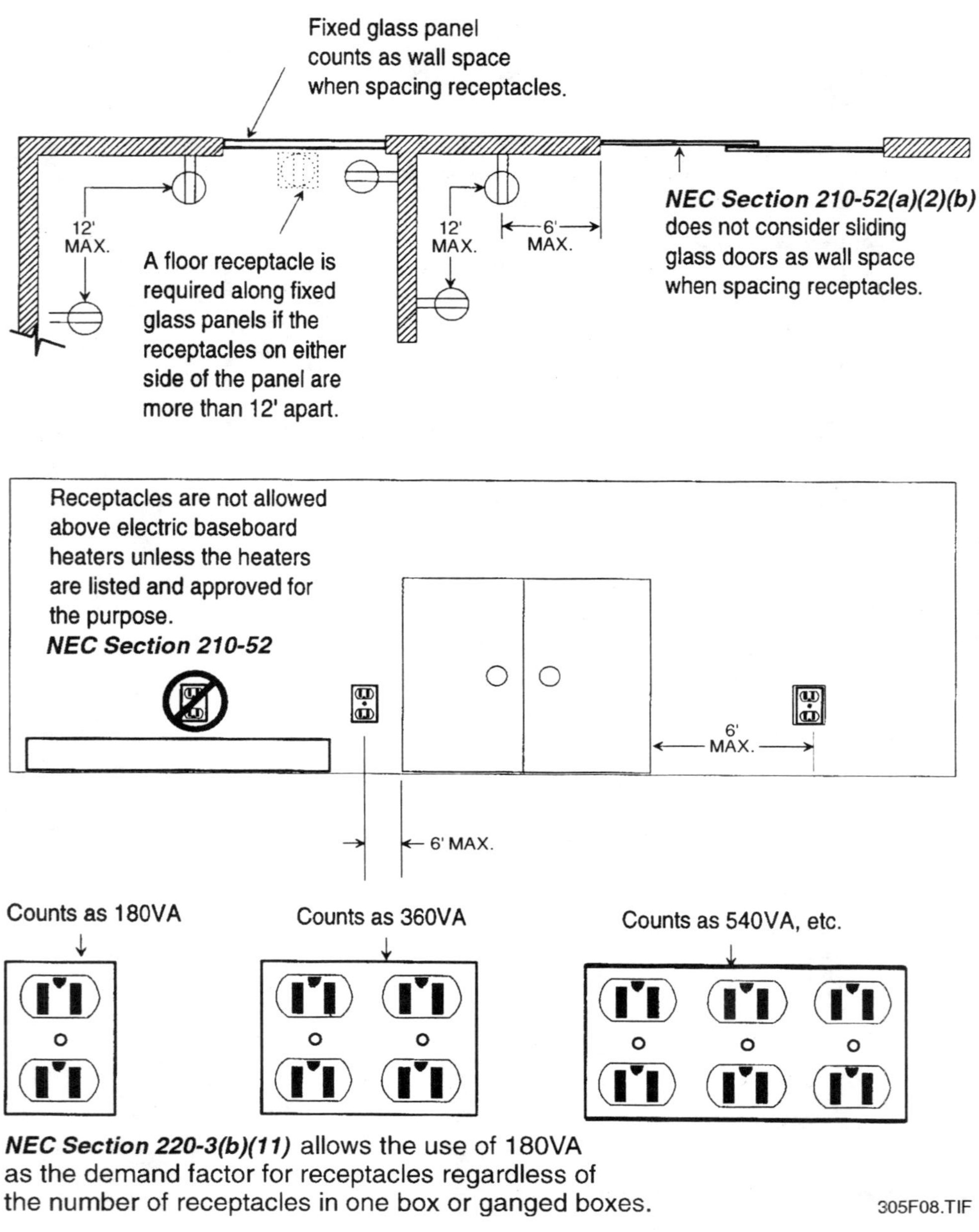

Figure 8. NEC Requirements For Receptacles

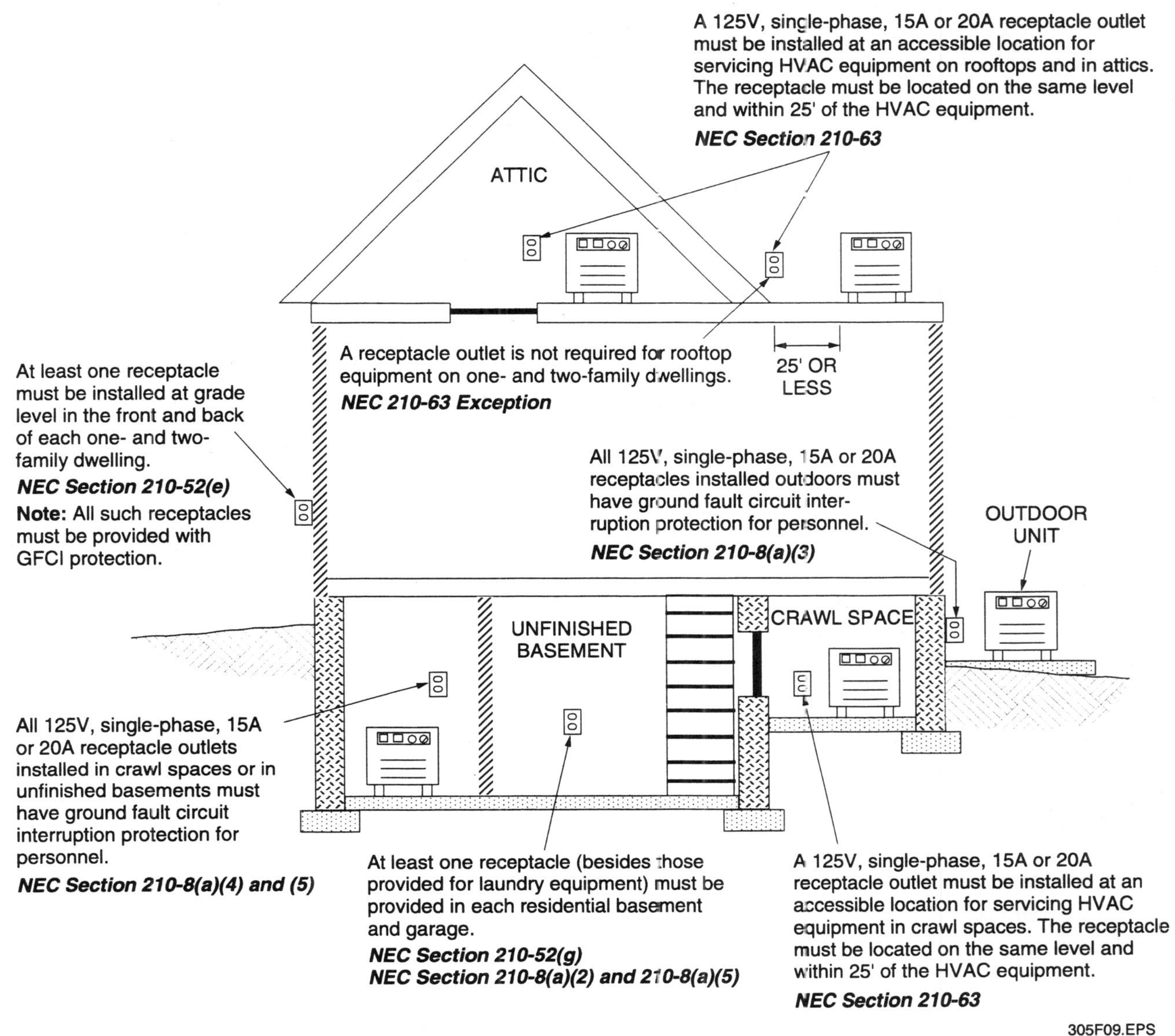

Figure 9. NEC Requirements For Placement Of Receptacles

When upgrading existing electrical systems, the NEC permits the use of a GFCI receptacle in place of a grounded receptacle. With such an arrangement, additional grounded receptacles may be connected on the downstream side of the GFCI, as shown in *Figure 10*.

Other receptacles and related circuits are provided as needed according to the load to be served. For example, receptacles are normally provided in residential occupancies for electric ranges, clothes dryers, and similar appliances. Most operate on 120/240V branch circuits using 30A to 60A receptacles.

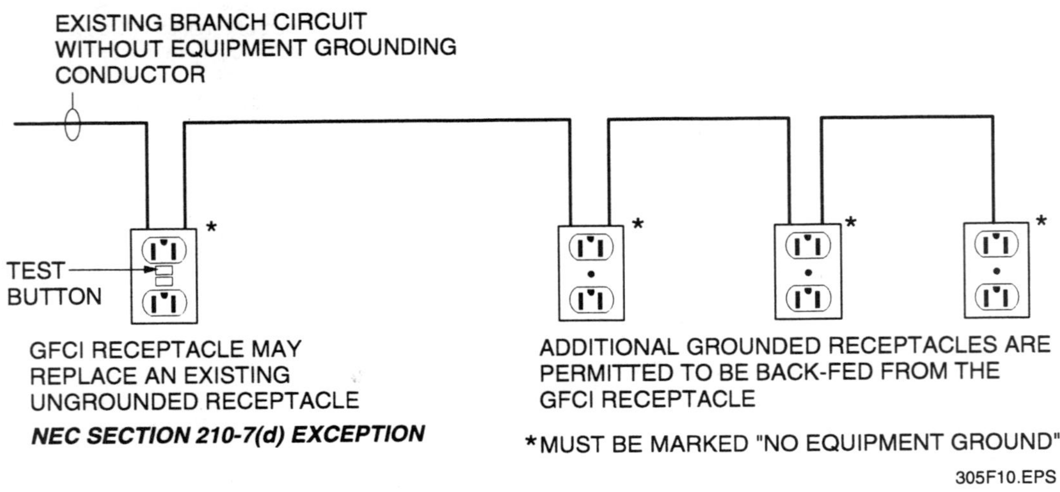

Figure 10. A GFCI May Replace An Ungrounded Receptacle

3.2.0   COMMERCIAL APPLICATIONS

Receptacle requirements for commercial installations follow the same general requirements set forth for residential occupancies, with some exceptions. For example, guest rooms in hotels, motels, and similar occupancies must have receptacle outlets installed in accordance with **NEC Section 210-52**. However, some leeway is given to commercial installations. **NEC Section 210-60(b)** permits receptacle outlets to be located conveniently for permanent furniture layout.

The only other requirement for commercial installations deals with the placement of receptacle outlets in show windows. **NEC Section 210-62** requires at least one receptacle for each 12 linear feet of show window area measured horizontally at its maximum width. See *Figure 11*. To calculate the number of receptacles required at the top of any show window, measure the total linear feet and then divide this figure by 12. Any remainder or major fraction thereof requires an additional receptacle. For example, the show window in *Figure 11* is 18' in length. Consequently, the number of receptacles required may be calculated as follows:

$$\frac{18'}{12'} = 1.5 \text{ receptacles}$$

To comply with **NEC Section 210-62**, two receptacles are required in this area. Had the calculation resulted in a figure of 1.01, the local inspection authorities would probably require only one receptacle in the show window.

Of course, GFCIs are required on all 15A and 20A receptacles installed in commercial bathrooms or toilets, in commercial garages, receptacles installed outdoors, crawl spaces, boathouses, and all receptacles installed on roofs.

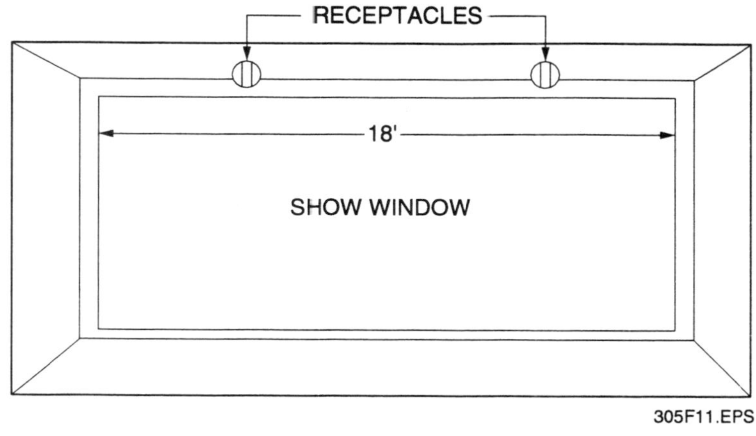

Figure 11. Commercial Show Window Receptacle Placement

Other receptacles and related circuits are provided as needed according to the load to be served.

The purpose of a switch is to make and break an electrical circuit in a safe and convenient manner. In doing so, a switch may be used to manually control lighting, motors, fans, and various other items connected to an electrical circuit. Switches may also be activated by light, heat, chemicals, motion, and electric energy for automatic operation. **NEC Article 380** covers the installation and use of switches.

The NEC switch definitions are as follows:

- *Bypass isolation switch* – This is a manually operated device used in conjunction with a transfer switch to provide a means of directly connecting load conductors to a power source and of disconnecting the transfer switch.

- *General use switch* – A switch intended for use in general distribution and branch circuits. It is rated in amperes and is capable of interrupting its rated current at its rated voltage.

- *General use snap switch* – A form of general use switch that is designed for installation in flush device boxes or on outlet box covers, or otherwise used in conjunction with wiring systems recognized by the NEC.

- *Isolation switch* – A switch intended for isolating an electric circuit from the source of power. It has no interrupting rating and is intended to be operated only after the circuit has been opened by some other means (see *Figure 12*).

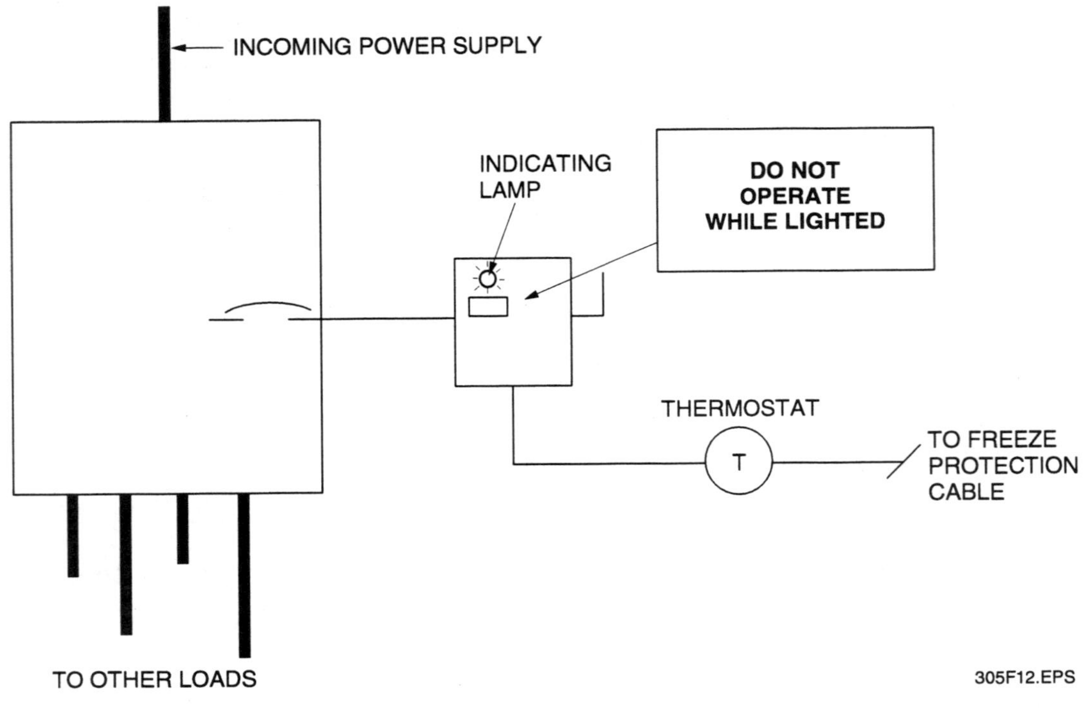

Figure 12. Isolation Switch

- *Motor circuit switch* – A switch that is rated in horsepower and is capable of interrupting the maximum operating overload current of a motor of the same horsepower rating as the switch at its rated voltage.
- *Transfer switch* – A device used to transfer one or more load conductor connections from one power source to another. This type of switch may be either automatic or nonautomatic.

4.1.0 SWITCH CONFIGURATIONS

Although basic switch terms are covered to some extent in earlier modules, a brief review is warranted here. In general, the major terms used to identify the characteristics of switches are *pole* and *throw*.

The term *pole* refers to the number of conductors that the switch will control in the circuit. For example, a single-pole switch breaks the connection to only one conductor in the circuit. A double-pole switch breaks the connection to two conductors, and so forth.

The term *throw* refers to the number of internal operations that a switch can perform. For example, a single-pole, single-throw switch will make one conductor when thrown in one direction (the ON position) and break the circuit when thrown in the opposite direction (the OFF position). The common ON/OFF toggle switch is a single-pole, single-throw (SPST) switch. The single-pole, double-throw (SPDT) switch, also known as the **three-way switch**, is used to control a single load, such as a lamp, from two locations. A double-pole, single-throw

(DPST) switch opens or closes two conductors at the same time. Both conductors are either open or closed, that is, in the ON or OFF position. A double-pole, double-throw (DPDT) switch is used to direct a two-wire circuit through one of two different paths. One application of a double-pole, double-throw switch is an electrical transfer switch in which certain circuits may be energized from either the main electric service or from an emergency standby generator. The double-pole, double-throw switch makes the circuit from one or the other and prevents the circuit from being energized from both sources at once. *Figure 13* shows common switch configurations.

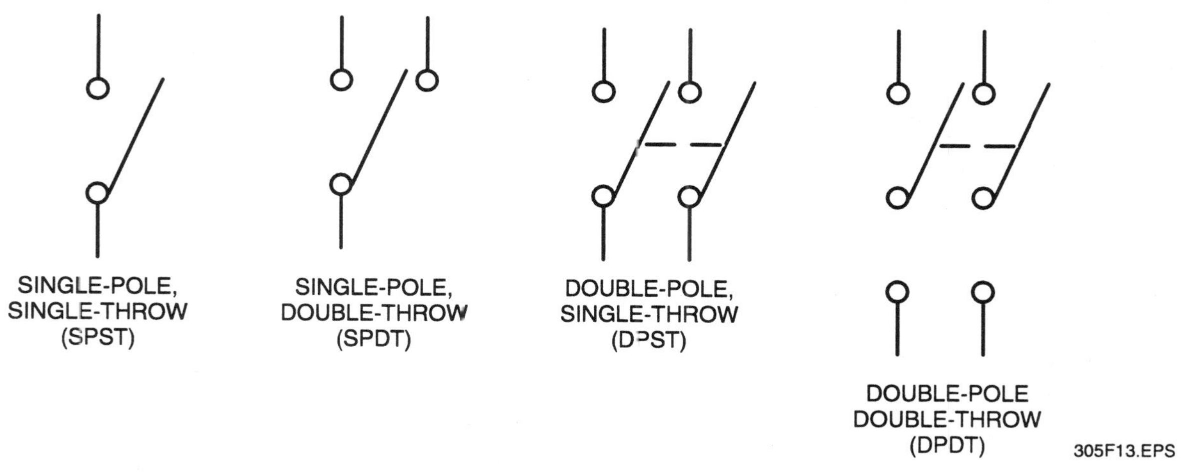

Figure 13. Common Switch Configurations

4.2.0   SWITCH IDENTIFICATION

Switches vary in grade, capacity, and purpose. It is very important that the proper type of switch is selected for the given application. For example, most single-pole toggle switches used for the control of lighting are restricted to AC use only and are not suitable for use on DC circuits, such as a 32VDC emergency lighting circuit. A switch rated for AC only will not extinguish a DC arc quickly enough. Not only is this a dangerous practice (causing arcing and heating of the device), the switch contacts would probably burn up after only a few operations of the handle, if not the first time.

Figure 14 shows a typical single-pole toggle switch—the type most often used to control AC lighting in all installations. Note the identifying marks. They are similar to those on the duplex receptacle discussed previously.

Screw terminals are also color-coded on conventional toggle switches. Switches are typically constructed with a ground screw attached to the metallic strap of the switch. The ground screw is usually a green-colored hex head screw. This screw is for connecting the equipment grounding conductor to the switch. On three-way switches, the common or pivot terminal usually has a black or bronze screw head.

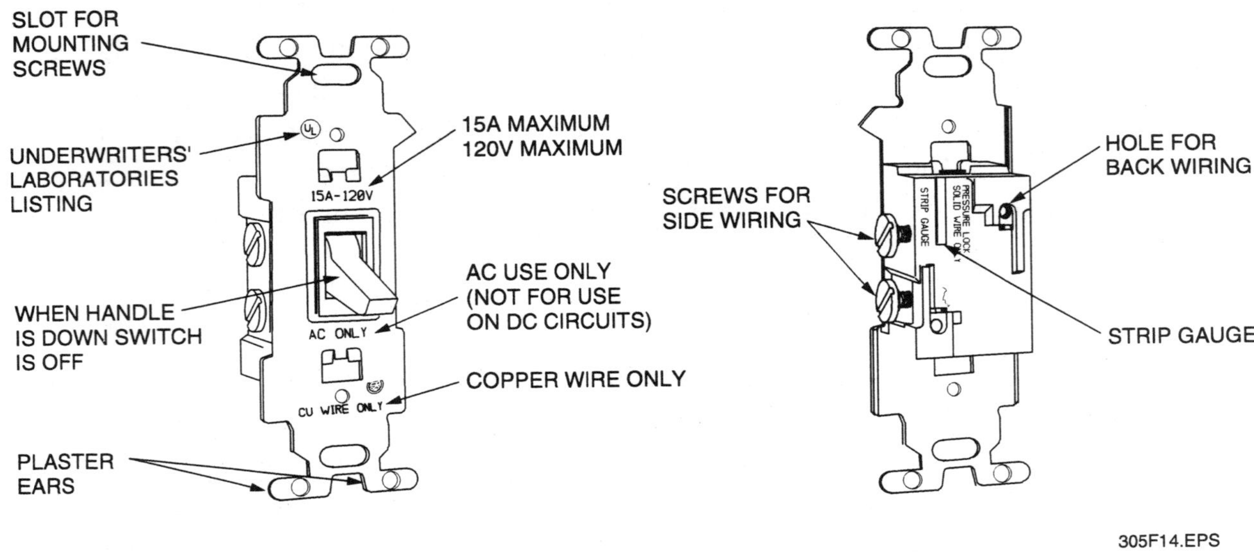

Figure 14. Identifying Marks On A Single-Pole Toggle Switch

The switch shown is the type normally used for residential construction. Heavy-duty switches are normally used on commercial wiring. Some heavy-duty switches are rated for use on 277V circuits with current-carrying ratings up to 30A. It is important to check the rating of each switch before it is installed.

The exact type and grade of switch to be used on a specific installation is often dictated by the project drawings or written specifications. Sometimes wall switches are specified by manufacturer and catalog number; other times they are specified by type, grade, voltage, current rating, etc., leaving the contractor or electrician to select the manufacturer. The naming of a certain brand of switch for a particular project does not necessarily mean that this brand must be used. A typical paragraph from an electrical specification (concerning the substitution of materials) may read as follows:

The naming of a certain make or manufacturer in the Specifications is to establish a quality standard for the article desired. The Contractor is not restricted to the use of the specific brand of the manufacturer named unless so indicated in the Specifications. However, where a substitution is requested, a substitution will be permitted only with the written approval of the Architect-Engineer. No substitute material or equipment shall be ordered, fabricated, shipped, or processed in any manner prior to the approval of the Architect-Engineer. The Contractor shall assume all responsibility for additional expenses as required in any way to meet changes from the original material or equipment specified. If notice of substitution is not furnished to the Architect-Engineer within ten days after the contract is awarded, the equipment and materials named in the Specifications are to be used.

Electrical specifications dealing with wall switches are covered in at least two sections of the specifications:

- 16100, *Basic Materials and Methods*
- 16500, *Lighting*

Brief excerpts from these two sections follow.

SECTION 16B – BASIC MATERIALS AND WORKMANSHIP

*SWITCH OUTLET BOXES: Wall switches shall be mounted approximately 54" above the finished floor (AFF) unless otherwise noted. When the switch is mounted in a masonry wall, the bottom of the outlet box shall be in line with the bottom of a masonry unit. Where more than two switches are located, the switches shall be mounted in a **gang switch** outlet box with gang cover. Dimmer switches shall be individually mounted unless otherwise noted. Switches with pilot lights, switches with overload motor protection, and other special switches that will not conveniently fit under gang wall plates may be individually mounted.*

EQUIPMENT AND INSTALLATION WORKMANSHIP

a. *All equipment and material shall be new and shall bear the manufacturer's name and trade name. The equipment and material shall be essentially the standard product of a manufacturer regularly engaged in the production of the required type of equipment and shall be the manufacturer's latest approved design.*

b. *The Electrical Contractor shall receive and properly store the equipment and material pertaining to the electrical work. The equipment shall be tightly covered and protected against dirt, water, chemical or mechanical injury, and theft. The manufacturer's directions shall be followed completely in the delivery, storage, protection, and installation of all equipment and materials.*

c. *The Electrical Contractor shall provide and install all items necessary for the complete installation of the equipment as recommended or as required by the manufacturer of the equipment or required by code without additional cost to the Owner, regardless of whether the items are shown on the plans or covered in the Specifications.*

d. *It shall be the responsibility of the Electrical Contractor to clean the electrical equipment, make necessary adjustments, and place the equipment into operation before turning the equipment over to the Owner. Any paint that was scratched during construction shall be touched up with factory color paint to the satisfaction of the Architect. Any items that were damaged during construction shall be replaced.*

WIRING DEVICES

a. *GENERAL: The wiring devices specified below with ARROW HART numbers may also be the equivalent wiring device as manufactured by BRYANT ELECTRIC, HARVEY HUBBELL, or PASS & SEYMOUR. All other items shall be as specified.*

   (1) Single Pole AH#1991

   (2) Three-Way AH#1993

   (3) Four-Way AH#1994

   (4) Switch with pilot light AH#2999-R

   (5) Motor Switch – Surface AH#6808

   (6) Motor Switch – Flush AH#6808-F

b. *WALL SWITCHES: Where more than one flush wall switch is indicated in the same location, the switches shall be mounted in gangs under a common plate.*

c. *WALL PLATE: Stainless steel wall plates with satin finish minimum .030 inches shall be provided for all outlets and switches.*

In general, the preceding electrical specifications give the grade of materials to be used on the project and the manner in which the electrical system must be installed. Most specification writers use an abbreviated language; although it is relatively difficult for beginners to understand, experience makes possible a proper interpretation with little difficulty. However, electricians involved with any project should make certain that everything is clear. If it is not, contact the architectural or engineering firm and clarify the problem prior to performing the work, not after a system has been completed.

5.0.0 NEC REQUIREMENTS FOR SWITCHES

There are many NEC requirements for installing light switches (*Figure 15*). For example, wall switch-controlled lighting outlets are required in each habitable room of all residential occupancies. Wall switch-controlled lighting is also required in each bathroom, hallways, stairways, attached garages, and at outdoor entrances. A wall switch-controlled receptacle may be used in place of the lighting outlet in habitable rooms other than the kitchen and bathrooms. Providing a wall switch for room lighting is intended to prevent an occupant's groping in the dark for table lamps or pull chains. In stairways with six or more steps, the stairway lighting must be controlled at two locations—at both the top and bottom of the stairway. This is accomplished by using two three-way switches, as discussed in previous modules.

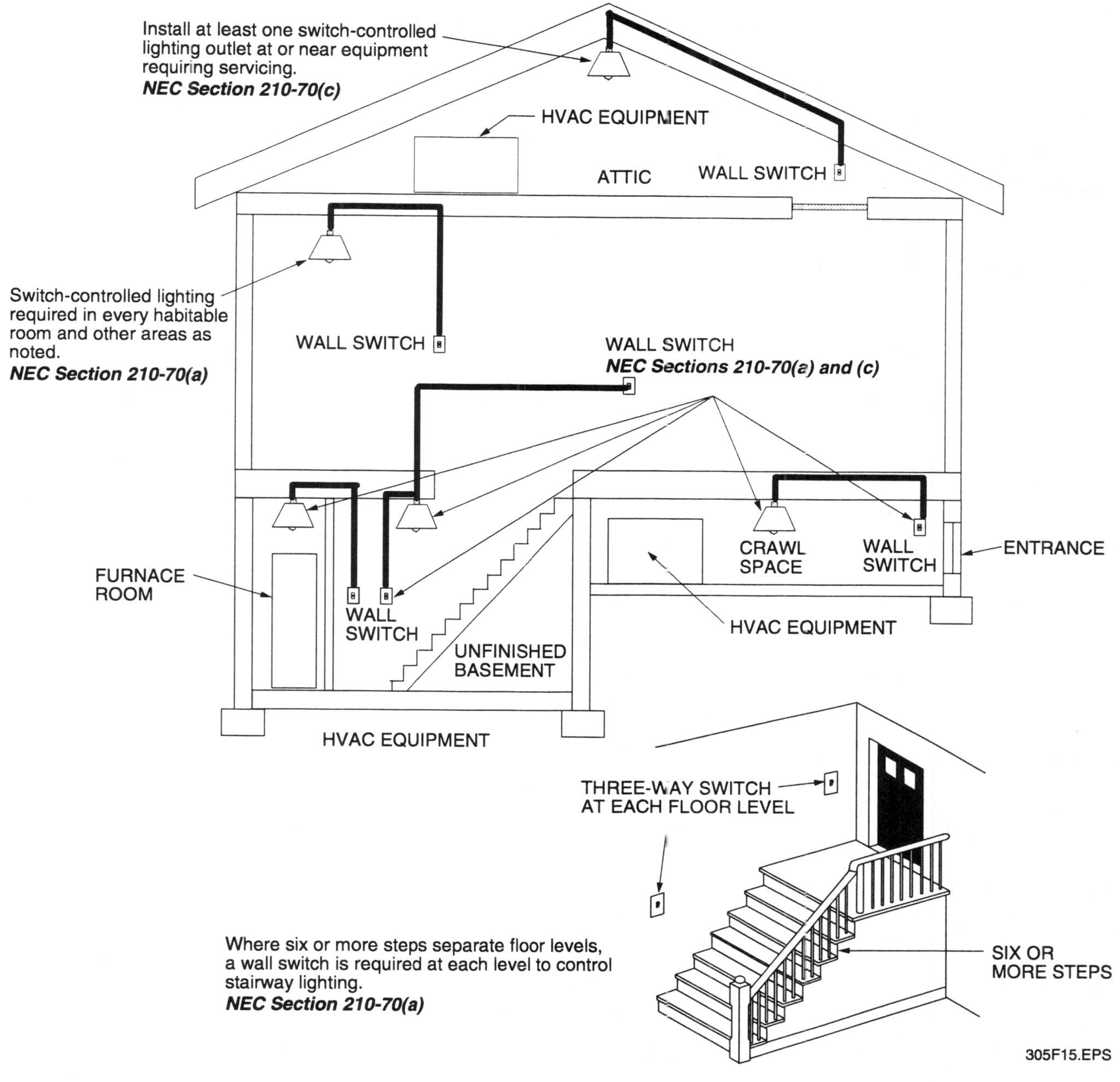

Figure 15. NEC Requirements For Residential Wall Switches

Lighting outlets are also required in attics, crawl spaces, utility rooms, and basements when these spaces are used for storage or contain equipment requiring servicing, such as HVAC equipment. Again, if the basement or attic stairs have more than six steps, a three-way switch is required at each landing.

At least one wall switch-controlled lighting outlet is required in each guest room in hotels, motels, or similar locations, as shown in *Figure 16*. Note that a wall switch-controlled receptacle is permitted in lieu of the lighting outlet.

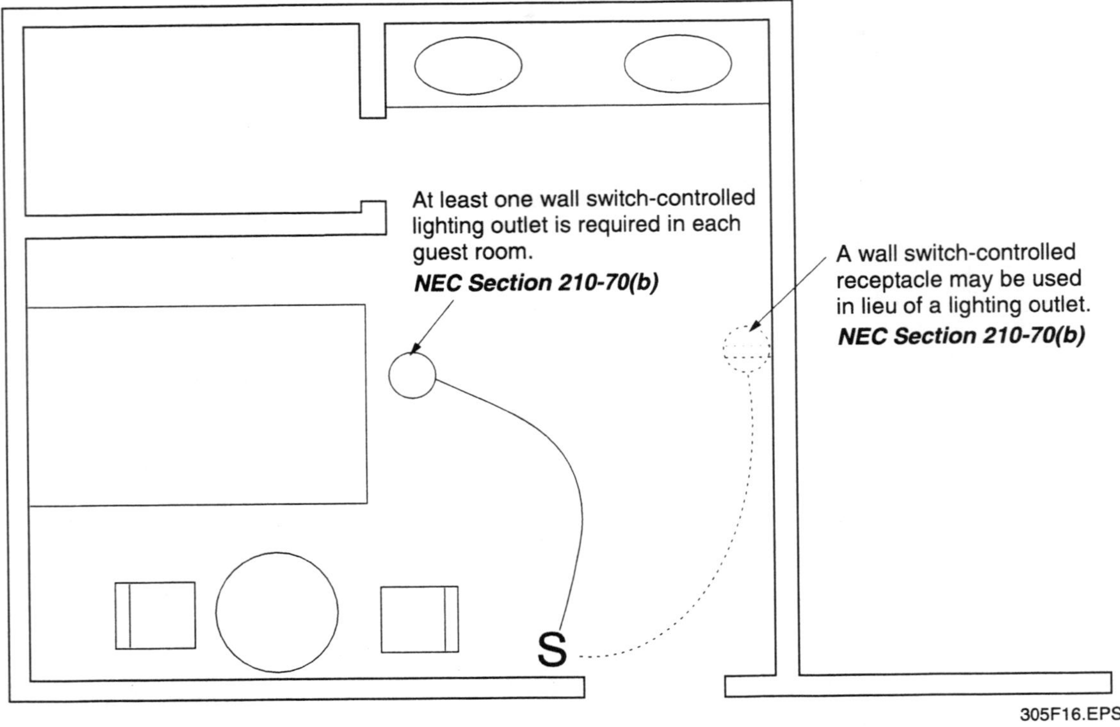

Figure 16. Wall Switch Requirements For Guest Rooms

In many commercial installations, circuit breakers in panelboards are permitted to control main area lighting where the areas are constantly illuminated during operating hours. Consequently, wall switches are not required in these areas. However, wall switches are normally installed at outdoor entrances, entrances to storerooms, small offices, toilets, and similar locations.

Wiring diagrams of switch circuits (single-pole, three-way, and **four-way switches**) were thoroughly discussed in previous modules and these diagrams will not be repeated here. However, it is recommended that the trainee review these diagrams at this time if deemed necessary.

6.0.0   SAFETY SWITCHES

Enclosed single-throw safety switches are manufactured to meet industrial, commercial, and residential requirements. See *Figure 17*. The two basic types of safety switches are:

* General-duty
* Heavy-duty

Double-throw switches are also manufactured with enclosures and features similar to the general-duty and heavy-duty single-throw designs.

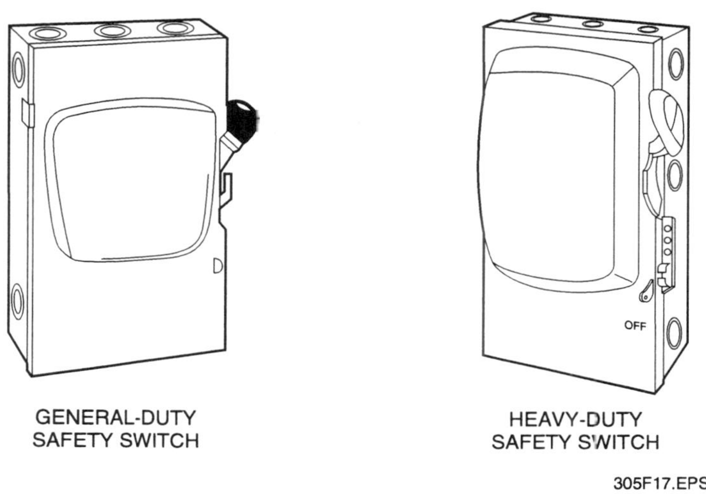

Figure 17. Typical Safety Switches

The majority of safety switches have visible blades and safety handles. The switch blades are in full view when the enclosure door is open and there is visually no doubt when the switch is off. The only exceptions are NEMA Type 7 and 9 enclosures; these do not have visible blades. The switch handles on all types of enclosures are an integral part of the box, not the cover, so that the handle is in control of the switch blades under normal conditions. ***NEC Table 430-91*** provides a complete listing of enclosure types.

6.1.0 HEAVY-DUTY SWITCHES

Heavy-duty switches are intended for applications where ease of maintenance, rugged construction, and continued performance are primary concerns. They can be used in atmospheres where general-duty switches would be unsuitable, and are therefore widely used in industrial applications. Heavy-duty switches are rated 30A through 1,200A and 240V to 600VAC or VDC. Switches with horsepower ratings are capable of opening a circuit up to six times the rated current of the switch. When equipped with Class J or Class R fuses for 30A through 600A switches, or Class L fuses in 800A and 1,200A switches, many heavy-duty safety switches are UL-listed for use on systems with up to 200,000 rms symmetrical amperes available fault current. This, however, is about the highest short circuit rating available for any heavy-duty safety switch. Applications include use where the required enclosure is NEMA Type 1, 3R, 4, 4X, 5, 7, 9, 12, or 12K.

6.1.1 Switch Blade And Jaws

Two types of switch contacts are used in today's safety switches: the butt contact and the knife blade and jaw. On switches with knife blade construction, the jaws distribute a uniform clamping pressure on both sides of the blade contact surface. In the event of a high-current fault, the electromagnetic forces which develop squeeze the jaws tightly against the blade. In the butt-type contact, only one side of the blade's contact surface is held in tension against the conducting path. Electromagnetic forces due to high current faults force the contacts apart, causing them to burn severely. Consequently, the knife blade and jaw construction is the preferred type for use on all heavy-duty switches. The action of the blades moving in and out of the jaws aids in cleaning the contact surfaces. All current-carrying parts of these switches are plated to reduce heating by keeping oxidation to a minimum. Switch blades and jaws are made of copper for high conductivity. Spring-clamped blade hinges are another feature that help ensure clean contact surfaces and cool operation. Visible blades are used to provide visual evidence that the circuit has been opened.

WARNING!   Before changing fuses or performing maintenance on any safety switch, always visibly check the switch blades and jaws to ensure that they are in the OFF position and verify with a voltage tester.

6.1.2 Fuse Clips

Fuse clips are plated to control corrosion and to keep heating to a minimum. All fuse clips on heavy-duty switches have steel reinforcing springs for increased mechanical strength and firmer contact pressure. See *Figure 18*.

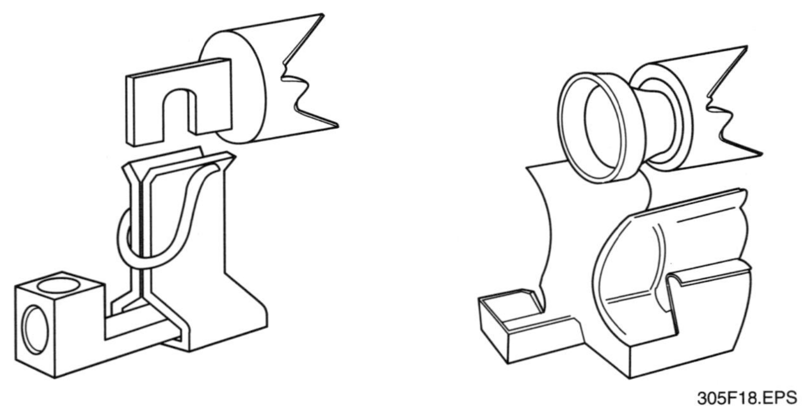

Figure 18. Detail Of Safety Switch Fuse Clips

6.1.3 Terminal Lugs

Most heavy-duty switches have front removable, screw-type terminal lugs. Most switch lugs are suitable for copper or aluminum wire except NEMA Type 4, 4X, 5 stainless, 12, and 12K switches, which have all-copper current-carrying parts and lugs designated for use with copper wire only. Heavy-duty switches are suitable for the wire sizes and number of wires per pole as listed in *NEC Tables 373-6(a) and (b)*.

6.1.4   Insulating Material

As the voltage rating of switches is increased, arc suppression becomes more difficult and the choice of insulation material becomes more critical. Arc suppressors are usually made of insulation material and magnetic suppressor plates when required. All arc suppressor materials must provide proper control and extinguishing of arcs.

6.1.5   Operating Mechanism And Cover Latching

Most heavy-duty safety switches have a spring-driven, quick-make, quick-break mechanism. A quick-break action is necessary to safely switch the mechanism OFF under a heavy load.

The spring action, in addition to making the operation quick-make, quick-break, firmly holds the switch blades in the ON or OFF position. The operating handle is an integral part of the switching mechanism and is in direct control of the switch blades under normal conditions.

The switching mechanism should include a one-piece crossbar connected to all switch blades. This adds to the overall stability and integrity of the switching assembly by promoting proper alignment and uniform switch blade operation.

Dual cover interlocks are standard on most heavy-duty switches where the NEMA enclosure permits. However, NEMA Type 7 and 9 enclosures have bolted covers and obviously cannot contain dual cover interlocks. The purpose of a dual interlock is to prevent the enclosure door from being opened when the switch handle is in the ON position and prevent the switch from being turned ON while the door is open. A means of bypassing the interlock is provided to allow an energized switch to be inspected by qualified personnel. However, this practice is extremely dangerous and should be avoided if at all possible. Heavy-duty switches can be padlocked in the OFF position with up to three padlocks.

6.1.6   Enclosures

Heavy-duty switches are available in a variety of enclosures which have been designed to conform to specific industry requirements based upon the intended use. Sheet metal enclosures (NEMA Type 1) are constructed from cold-rolled steel which is usually phosphatized and finished with an electrode-deposited enamel paint. NEMA Type 3R rainproof and Type 12 and 12K dusttight enclosures are manufactured from galvanized sheet steel and painted to provide better weather protection. NEMA Type 4, 4X, and 5 enclosures are made of corrosion-resistant Type 304 stainless steel and require no painting. NEMA Type 7 and 9 enclosures are cast from copper-free aluminum and finished with an enamel paint. NEMA Type 1 switches are general-purpose devices designed for use indoors to protect personnel from live parts and the enclosed equipment from dirt. Switches rated through 200A are provided with ample knockouts; 400A through 1,200A switches are provided without knockouts.

The following are the NEMA enclosure types that will be encountered most often. Always make certain that the proper enclosure is chosen for the application.

NEMA Type 3R switches are designated rainproof and are designed for use outdoors. See *Figure 19*. NEMA Type 3R enclosures for switches rated through 200A have provisions for interchangeable bolt-on hubs at the top endwall. NEMA Type 3R switches rated higher than 200A have blank top endwalls. Knockouts are provided (below live parts only) on enclosures for 200A and smaller Type 3R switches. Type 3R switches are available in ratings through 1,200A.

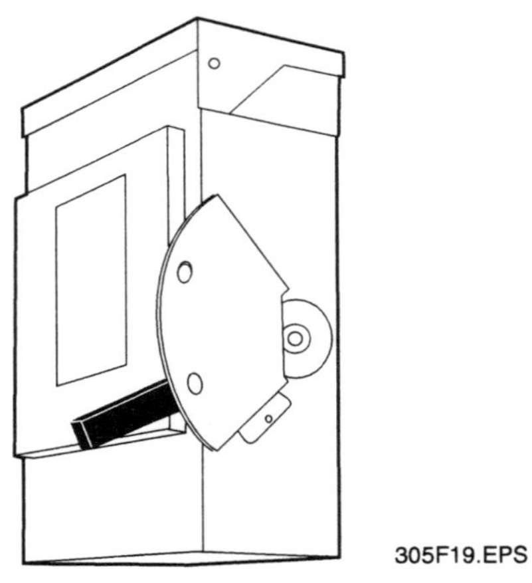

Figure 19. NEMA Type 3R Enclosure

NEMA Type 4, 4X, and 5 stainless steel switches are designated dusttight, watertight, and corrosion-resistant and designed for indoor and outdoor use. Common applications include commercial kitchens, dairies, canneries, and other types of food processing facilities, as well as areas where mildly corrosive liquids are present. All NEMA Type 4, 4X, and 5 stainless steel enclosures are provided without knockouts. Use of watertight hubs is required. Available switch ratings are 30A through 600A.

NEMA Type 12 and 12K switches are designated dusttight (except at knockout locations on Type 12K) and are designed for indoor use. In addition, NEMA Type 12 safety switches are designated as raintight for outdoor use when the supplied drain plug is removed. Common applications include heavy industrial use where the switch must be protected from dust, lint, flying material, oil seepage, etc. NEMA 12K switches have knockouts in the bottom and top endwalls only. Available switch ratings are 30A through 600A in Type 12 and 30A through 200A in Type 12K.

NEMA Type 4, 4X, 5, 12, and 12K switch enclosures have positive sealing to provide a dusttight and raintight (watertight with stainless steel) seal. Enclosure doors are supplied with oil-resistant gaskets. Switches rated 30A through 200A incorporate spring-loaded, quick-release latches. 400A and 600A switches feature single-stroke sealing by operation of a cover-mounted handle. 30A, 60A, and 100A switches in these enclosures are provided with factory-installed fuse pullers.

6.1.7 Interlocked Receptacles

Heavy-duty, 60A NEMA Type 1 and 12 switches with an interlocked receptacle are also available. This receptacle provides a means of connecting and disconnecting loads directly to the switch. A non-defeating interlock prevents the insertion or removal of the receptacle plug while the switch is in the ON position. It also prevents operation of the switch if an incorrect plug is used.

6.1.8 Accessories

Accessories for field installation include Class R fuse kits, fuse pullers, insulated neutrals with grounding provisions, equipment grounding kits, watertight hubs for use with NEMA Type 4, 4X, 5, or 12 switches, and interchangeable bolt-on hubs for Type 3R switches.

An electrical interlock consists of auxiliary contacts for use where control or monitoring circuits need to be switched in conjunction with the safety switch operation. Kits can be either factory-installed or field-installed, and they contain either one normally open and one normally closed contact or two normally open and two normally closed contacts. The electrical interlock is actuated by a pivot arm which operates directly from the switch mechanism. The electrical interlock is designed so that its contacts disengage before the blades of the safety switch open and engage after the safety switch blades close.

6.2.0 GENERAL-DUTY SWITCHES

General-duty switches for residential and light commercial applications are used where operation and handling are moderate and where the available fault current is 10,000 rms symmetrical amperes or less. Some general-duty safety switches, however, exceed this specification in that they are UL-listed for use on systems having up to 100,000 rms symmetrical amperes of available fault current when Class R fuses and Class R fuse kits are used. Class T fusible switches are also available in 400A, 600A, and 800A ratings. These switches accept 300VAC Class T fuses only. Some examples of general-duty switch applications include residential, farm, and small business service entrances and light-duty branch circuit disconnects.

General-duty switches are rated up to 600A at 240VAC in general-purpose (Type 1) and rainproof (Type 3R) enclosures. Some general-duty switches are horsepower-rated and capable of opening a circuit up to six times the rated current of the switch; others are not. Always check the switch specifications under a horsepower-rated condition before use.

6.2.1 Switch Blades And Jaws

All current-carrying parts of general-duty switches are plated to minimize oxidation and reduce heating. Switch jaws and blades are made of copper for high conductivity. Where required, a steel reinforcing spring increases the mechanical strength of the jaws and contact pressure between the blade and jaw. Good pressure contact maintains the blade-to-jaw resistance at a minimum, which in turn promotes cool operation. All general-duty switch blades feature visible blade construction. With the door open, there is visually no doubt when the switch is OFF. However, you should always verify this with a voltage tester.

6.2.2   Fuse Clips

Fuse clips are normally plated to control corrosion and keep heating to a minimum. Where required, steel reinforcing springs are provided to increase the mechanical strength of the fuse clip. The result is a firmer, cooler connection to the fuses as well as superior fuse retention.

6.2.3   Terminal Lugs

Most general-duty safety switches are furnished with mechanical set screw lugs which are suitable for aluminum or copper conductors.

6.2.4   Insulating Material

Switch and fuse bases are made of a strong, non-combustible, moisture-resistant material which provides the required phase-to-phase and phase-to-ground insulation for applications on 240VAC systems.

6.2.5   Operating Mechanism And Cover Latching

Although not required by either the UL or NEMA standards, some general-duty switches have spring-driven, quick-make, quick-break operating mechanisms. Operating handles are an integral part of the operating mechanism and are not mounted on the enclosure cover. The handle provides an indication of the status of the switch. When the handle is up, the switch is ON. When the handle is down, the switch is OFF. A padlocking bracket is provided which allows the switch handle to be locked in the OFF position. Another bracket is provided which allows the enclosure to be padlocked closed.

6.2.6   Enclosures

General-duty safety switches are available in either a NEMA Type 1 enclosure for general-purpose indoor applications or a NEMA Type 3R enclosure for rainproof outdoor applications. Enclosure types were discussed in detail earlier in this module.

6.3.0   DOUBLE-THROW SAFETY SWITCHES

Double-throw switches are used as manual transfer switches and are not intended for use as motor circuit switches; thus, horsepower ratings are generally unavailable.

Double-throw switches are available as either fused or nonfusible devices. Two general types of switch operation are available:

- Quick-make, quick-break (for use where fast action is the most desirable feature)
- Slow-make, slow-break (for use where the application might expose the switch to voltage fluctuations or current surges on startup)

Figure 20 shows a practical application of a double-throw safety switch used as a transfer switch in conjunction with a standby emergency generator system.

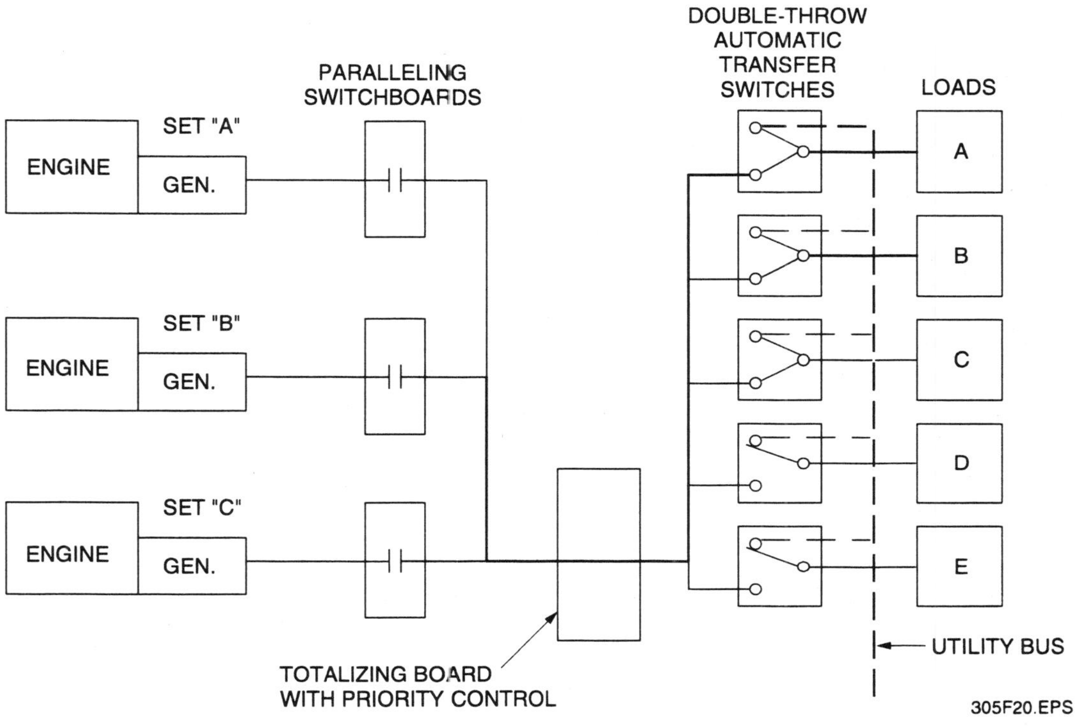

Figure 20. Practical Application Of A Double-Throw Safety Switch

6.4.0 NEC SAFETY SWITCH REQUIREMENTS

Safety switches, in both fusible and nonfusible types, are used as a disconnecting means for services, feeders, and branch circuits. Installation requirements involving safety switches are found in several places throughout the NEC, including the following:

- *NEC Article 373*
- *NEC Article 380*
- *NEC Article 430, Part H*
- *NEC Article 440, Part B*
- *NEC Section 450-8(c)*

When used as a service disconnecting means, the major installation requirements are listed in *Table 1*.

Application	Installation Requirements	NEC Reference or Comment
General	A means must be provided to disconnect all conductors serving the premises from service-entrance conductors. Each disconnecting means must be permanently identified. Disconnecting means must be installed at a readily accessible location nearest the service-entrance conductors. Service disconnecting means cannot be installed in bathrooms. Each service disconnecting means must be suitable for the prevailing conditions.	*Section 230-70*
Number of disconnects	Service disconnecting means can consist of no more than six switches for each service.	*Section 230-71*
Working space	Requirements for any electrical equipment apply; that is, the minimum head room of working spaces around service equipment must be 6.5' or more. The dimensions of working space in the direction of access to live parts operating at 600V nominal or less to ground and likely to require examination, adjustment, servicing, or maintenance while energized must not be less than indicated in *NEC Table 110-26(a)*.	*Section 110-26*
Type of disconnect	Disconnects may include either a manually operated or power-operated safety switch, provided the switch can be opened by hand in the event of a power supply failure.	*Section 230-76*
Connections to terminals	Service conductors must be connected to the disconnecting means by pressure connectors, clamps, or other approved means. Soldered connections are forbidden. A second service drop is permitted where the existing service capacity is over 2,000A at a supply voltage of 600V or less.	*Sections 230-81 and 230-2(c)*
More than one building on the same premises	In industrial establishments, the disconnecting means for several buildings may be conveniently located if NEC conditions are met.	*Section 225-32, Exception 1*

Table 1. NEC Installation Requirements Governing Switches Used For Service Disconnects

SUMMARY

The NEC defines a device as a unit of an electrical system that is intended to carry or help carry but not utilize electric energy. This covers a wide assortment of system components that include (but are not limited to) the following:

- Switches
- Relays
- Contactors
- Receptacles
- Conductors

The purpose of a switch is to make and break an electrical circuit in a safe and convenient manner. ***NEC Article 380*** covers most of the installation requirements for switches.

A receptacle is a contact device installed at the outlet for the connection of a single attachment plug. A single receptacle is a single contact device with no other contact device on the same yoke. A multiple receptacle is a single device containing two or more receptacles, with the most common being the duplex receptacle. ***NEC Sections 210-50, 210-52, 210-60, 210-62, and 220-4*** cover many of the requirements for receptacles.

References

For advanced study of topics covered in this Task Module, the following books are suggested:

American Electricians' Handbook, Latest Edition, McGraw-Hill, New York, NY.

National Electrical Code Handbook, Latest Edition, National Fire Protection Association, Quincy, MA.

REVIEW/PRACTICE QUESTIONS

1. Which of the following statements is true concerning duplex receptacles?
    a.   CU/AL markings indicate the use of both copper and aluminum wire.
    b.   CU/AL markings indicate the use of aluminum or copper-clad wire.
    c.   CO/ALR markings indicate the use of both copper and aluminum wire.
    d.   CO/ALR markings indicate the use of copper wire only.

2. The _____ in a duplex receptacle is for connection to a grounded conductor.
    a.   long slot
    b.   short slot
    c.   grounding slot
    d.   slot connected to the green screw

3. Which of the following wire sizes may usually be used in quick-connect wire clips in 15A receptacles and switches?
    a.   No. 12 AWG
    b.   No. 6 AWG
    c.   No. 4 AWG
    d.   No. 2 AWG

4. What is the maximum distance that outlet boxes may be set back from the finished surface in concrete walls?
    a. $\frac{1}{16}$"
    b. $\frac{1}{8}$"
    c. $\frac{1}{4}$"
    d. $\frac{1}{2}$"

5. What is the maximum distance that outlet boxes may be set back from the finished surface in wood-paneled walls?
    a. $\frac{1}{16}$"
    b. $\frac{1}{8}$"
    c. $\frac{1}{4}$"
    d.   0"

6. The intent of *NEC Section 210-52* is to _____.
    a.   prevent the need for extension cords
    b.   ensure ample amperage for cord-and-plug appliances
    c.   prevent the use of more appliances than the circuit can handle
    d.   enable extension cords longer than 6' to be used

7. Receptacles installed to serve _____ must be protected with a GFCI.

   a. crawl spaces above ground level
   b. bedrooms
   c. living rooms
   d. kitchen countertop areas

8. The NEC requires at least one receptacle for every _____ of show window in a store building.

   a. 3'
   b. 6'
   c. 12'
   d. 18'

9. In a set of electrical specifications, you would most likely find information concerning wall switches for lighting control in _____.

   a. Section 15408
   b. Section 16500
   c. Section 16700
   d. Section 16800

10. The _____ is the preferred contact for use in heavy-duty switches.

   a. butt-type
   b. knife blade and jaw
   c. clip-type
   d. None of the above.

ANSWERS TO REVIEW/PRACTICE QUESTIONS

Answer	Section Reference
1. c	2.1.0
2. a	2.1.0
3. a	2.1.0
4. c	2.2.0
5. d	2.2.0
6. a	3.1.0
7. d	3.1.0/Figure 7
8. c	3.2.0
9. b	4.2.0
10. b	6.1.1

ELECTRICAL — TRAINEE TASK MODULE 26305

The NCCER makes every effort to keep these manuals up-to-date and free of technical errors. We appreciate your help in this process. If you have an idea for improving this manual, or if you find an error, a typographical mistake, or an inaccuracy in the NCCER's Craft Training Manuals, please write us, using this form or a photocopy. Be sure to include the exact module number, page number, a description of the problem, and the correction, if possible. Your input will be brought to the attention of the Technical Review Committee. Thank you for your assistance.

Instructors – If you found that additional materials were necessary in order to teach this module effectively, please let us know so that we may include them in the Equipment/Materials list in the Instructor's Guide.

Write: Curriculum Development and Revision Department
National Center for Construction Education and Research
P.O. Box 141104
Gainesville, FL 32614-1104
Fax: 352-334-0932

Craft ___________________________ Module Name ___________________________

Copyright Date __________ Module Number __________ Page Number(s) __________

Description of Problem

____

____

____

____

(Optional) Correction of Problem

____

____

____

(Optional) Your Name and Address

____

____

____

Distribution Equipment

Module 26306

DISTRIBUTION EQUIPMENT

NATIONAL
CENTER FOR
CONSTRUCTION
EDUCATION AND
RESEARCH

OBJECTIVES

Upon completion of this module, the trainee will be able to:

1. List the voltage classifications used in the industry.
2. Describe the purpose of switchgear.
3. Describe the basic physical makeup of a switchboard.
4. Describe the four general classifications of circuit breakers and list the major circuit breaker ratings.
5. Describe switchgear construction, metering layouts, wiring requirements, and maintenance.
6. List NEC requirements pertaining to switchgear.
7. Describe the visual and mechanical inspections and electrical tests associated with low-voltage and medium-voltage cables, metal-enclosed busways, and metering and instrumentation.
8. Describe a ground fault relay system and explain how to test it.
9. Describe an HVL switch.
10. Describe a bolted pressure switch and list its maintenance requirements.
11. Describe a typical switchgear transformer and lists its testing and maintenance requirements.
12. List the safety precautions associated with instrument transformers and describe their maintenance requirements.

Prerequisites

Successful completion of the following Task Modules is recommended before beginning study of this Task Module: Core Curricula; Electrical Level 1; Electrical Level 2; and Electrical Level 3, Modules 26301 through 26305.

Required Trainee Material

1. Trainee Task Module
2. Appropriate Personal Protective Equipment
3. Copy of the latest edition of the *National Electrical Code*

COURSE MAP

This course map shows all of the modules in the third level of the Electrical curricula. The suggested training order begins at the bottom and proceeds up. Skill levels increase as a trainee advances on the course map. The training order may be adjusted by the local Training Program Sponsor.

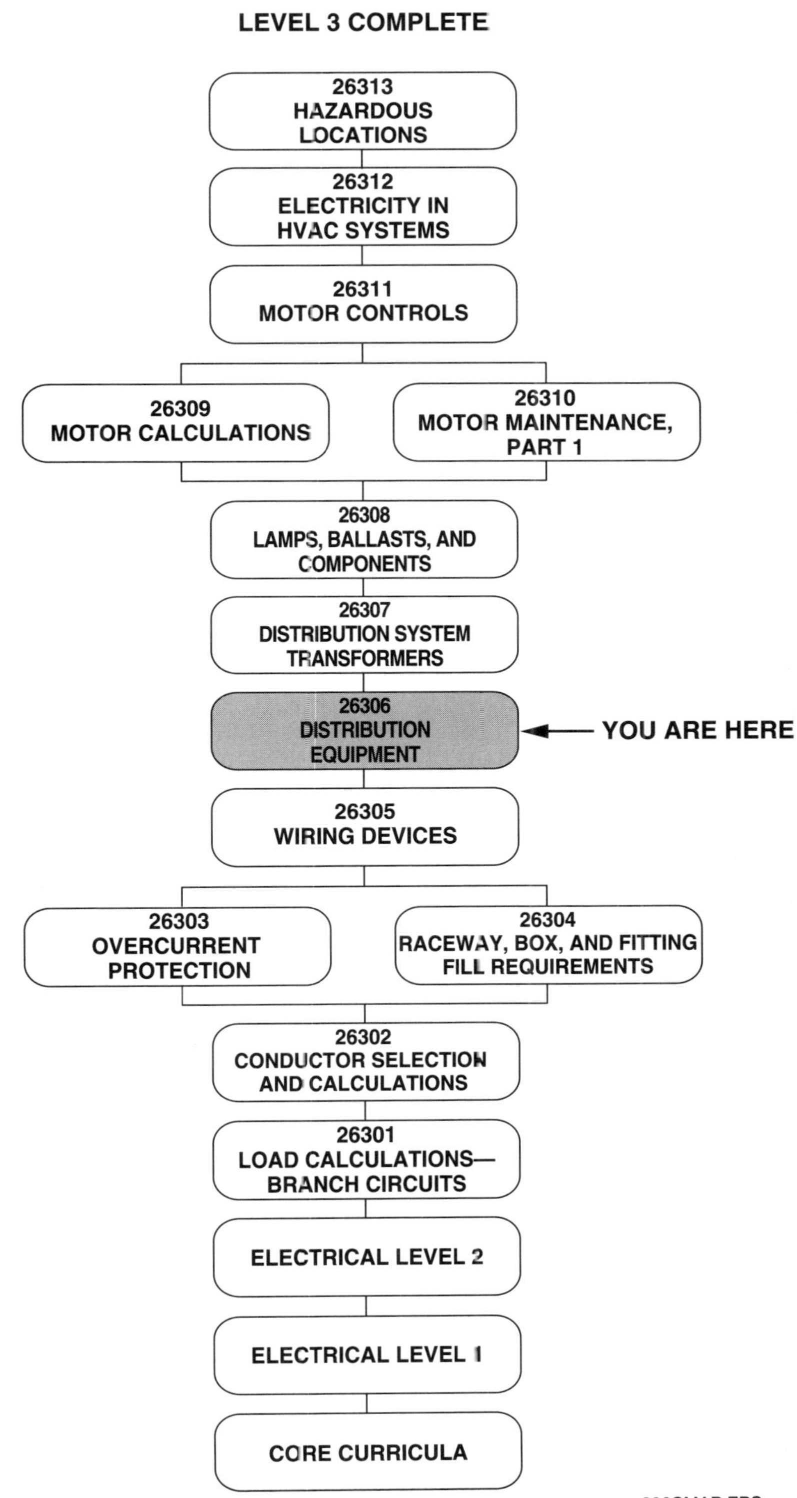

TABLE OF CONTENTS

TABLE OF CONTENTS (Continued)

Trade Terms Introduced In This Module

Air circuit breaker: A circuit breaker in which the interruption occurs in air.

Ampacity: The current rating in amperes, as of a conductor.

Basic impulse insulation level (BIL): The maximum impulse voltage the winding insulation can withstand without failure.

Branch circuit: A set of conductors that extend beyond the last overcurrent device in the low-voltage system of a given building.

Bus: A conductor or group of conductors that serves as a common connection for two or more circuits in a switchgear assembly.

Bushing: An insulating structure including a through conductor, or providing a passageway for such a conductor, for the purpose of insulating the conductor from the barrier and conducting from one side of the barrier to the other.

Capacity: The rated load-carrying ability expressed in kilovolt-amperes or kilowatts of generating equipment or other electric apparatus.

Circuit breaker: A device that interrupts a circuit without injury to itself so that it can be reset and reused over again.

Contactor: An automatic electric power switch designed for frequent operation.

Distribution system equipment: Switchboard equipment that is downstream from the service-entrance equipment.

Distribution transformer: A transformer that is used for transferring electric energy from a primary distribution circuit to a secondary distribution circuit. Distribution transformers are usually rated between 5kVA and 500kVA.

Feeder: A set of conductors originating at a main distribution center and supplying one or more secondary distribution centers, one or more branch circuit distribution centers, or any combination of these two types of load.

Fuse: An overcurrent protective device with a circuit opening fusible part that is heated and severed by the passage of overcurrent.

Metal-enclosed switchgear: Switchgear that is primarily used in indoor applications up to 600V.

Service-entrance equipment: Equipment located at the service entrance of a given building that provides overcurrent protection to the feeder and service conductors and also provides a means of disconnecting the feeders from the energized service equipment.

Switchboard: A large single panel, frame, or assembly of panels on which switches, fuses, buses, and instruments are mounted.

Switchgear: A general term covering switching or interrupting devices and any combination thereof, with associated control, instrumentation, metering, protective, and regulating devices.

1.0.0   INTRODUCTION

An electrical power system consists of several subsystems on both the utility (supply) side and the customer (user) side. Electricity generated in power plants is stepped up to transmission voltage and fed into a nationwide grid of transmission lines. This power is then bought, sold, and dispatched as needed. Local utility companies take power from the grid and reduce the voltage to levels suitable for subtransmission and distribution through various substations to the customer. This may range from the common 200A, 120/240V residential service to hundreds of thousands of amps at voltages from 480V to 69kV in an industrial facility.

From the point of service, the customer must control, distribute, and manage the power to supply their electrical needs. This module will discuss how this is done using a typical industrial facility as an example. We will discuss the various components of the distribution system and their interdependence. An understanding of single-line diagrams will allow analysis of a facility's distribution system.

Note: The voltage conventions used in this module are industry standards for distribution systems.

2.0.0   VOLTAGE CLASSIFICATIONS

Electrical equipment is usually divided by voltage. The various voltage levels are classified as low, medium, high, extra high, and ultra high, and are discussed in the following paragraphs.

- *Low voltage (LV)* – Low voltage is considered to be 600V and below. It is typically used to supply nominal voltage directly to electrical loads. Common voltages in this category are 120V, 208V, 240V, and 480V.
- *Medium voltage (MV)* – Medium voltage ranges from 601V to 15kV. It is mainly used for distribution purposes and for supplying large electrical loads.
- *High voltage (HV)* – High voltage ranges from 15kV to 230kV. It is mainly used for transmission purposes.
- *Extra high voltage (EHV) or very high voltage (VHV)* – Extra high voltage or very high voltage ranges from 230kV to 800kV. It is used only for transmission purposes.
- *Ultra high voltage (UHV)* – Ultra high voltage is any voltage greater than 800kV. Presently, the common voltages in this category range between 1,100kV and 1,500kV.

According to the National Electrical Code, the term **switchboard** may be defined as a large single panel, frame, or assembly of panels on which switches, overcurrent and other protective devices, **buses**, and instruments may be mounted, either on the face or back, or both. Switchboards are generally accessible from both the rear and from the front, and are not intended to be installed in cubicles. The design of switchboards enables convenient and safe electrical power delivery to the customer.

3.1.0 APPLICATIONS

Switchboards are used in modern distribution systems to subdivide large blocks of electrical power. One location for switchboards is typically where the main power enters the building. In this location, the switchboard would be referred to as **service-entrance equipment**. The other location common for switchboards is downstream from the service-entrance equipment. In the downstream location, the switchboard is commonly referred to as **distribution system equipment**.

3.2.0 GENERAL DESCRIPTION

A switchboard consists of a stationary structure that includes one or more freestanding units of uniform height that are mechanically and electrically joined to make a single coordinated installation. These cubicles contain circuit interrupting devices. They take up less space in a plant, have more eye appeal, and eliminate the need for a separate room to protect personnel from contact with lethal voltages.

The main portion of the switchboard is formed from heavy-gauge steel welded with members across the top and bottom to provide a rigid enclosure. Most switchboard enclosures are divided into three sections: the front section, the bus section, and the cable section. These three sections are physically separated from one another by metal partitions. This confines any damage that may occur to any one section and keeps it from affecting the other sections.

Typical switchboard components include:

- **Circuit breakers**
- **Fuses**
- Motor starters
- Ground fault systems
- Instrument transformers
- Switchboard metering
- Control power transformers

Switchboards are used in modern distribution systems to subdivide large blocks of electrical power.

Electrical ratings include three-phase, three-wire and three-phase, four-wire systems with voltage ratings up to 600V and current ratings up to 4,000A.

A switchboard enclosure is described as a *dead front panel*; however, it contains energized breakers. Busbars can be a standard size or customized. Standard sizes are made of silver-plated or tin-plated copper or tin-plated aluminum. Conventional bus sizing is .25" × 2" through .375" × 7". Bussing is also fabricated in custom sizes. Copper provides 1,000A/sq. in. of cross-sectional area. When using aluminum, the amperage value is 750A/sq. in.

When two busbars are bolted together using Grade S hardware with the proper torque, the **ampacity** of the connection is 200A/sq. in. of the lapped portion for aluminum or copper bussing. Bussing joints must be bolted together to the specified torque and include Belleville washers or Keps nuts. Aluminum busbars must be tin-plated, and copper busbars over 600A, must be plated with tin or silver.

3.3.0 SWITCHBOARD FRAME HEATING

Table 1 shows guidelines that should be observed in order to keep heat losses in the iron switchboard frame members to a safe minimum. The dimensions are recommended values and should be adhered to whenever possible. There are some standards that deviate from these values, but these have been tested and cannot be applied to custom bussing.

Amperes	Minimum Distance From Phase Bus to Closest Steel Member	Minimum Distance From Neutral Bus to Closest Steel Member
3,000	4"	2"
4,000	6"	3"
5,000 and over	12"	see below
5,000 to 6,000	An aluminum or non-magnetic material should be used in place of steel frame sections. Wherever possible, you must maintain 12" to steel members and 6" to aluminum or non-magnetic members. Neutral spacing can be 6" and 3", respectively. If the main bus is tapered, it is permissible (at 4,000A and below) to use steel frames for those sections containing the tapered bus.	
6,000 and over	You must use an aluminum or non-magnetic material for frame sections, and maintain 12" to steel members and 6" to aluminum or non-magnetic members. Neutral spacing can be 6" and 3", respectively. The use of any steel frame members is to be discouraged. If the main bus is tapered, it is permissible (at 4,000A and below) to use steel frames for those sections containing the tapered bus.	

Note: For amperages above 8,000A, the neutral spacing must be 12" wherever possible.

Table 1. Switchboard Frame Heating Guidelines

3.4.0 LOW-VOLTAGE SPACING REQUIREMENTS

To minimize tracking or arcing from energized parts to ground, switchboard construction includes spacing requirements. These spacing requirements are measured between live parts of opposite polarity and between live parts and grounded metal parts. *Figure 1* illustrates switchboard spacing requirements.

VOLTAGE INVOLVED		MINIMUM SPACING BETWEEN LIVE PARTS OF OPPOSITE POLARITY		MINIMUM SPACING THROUGH AIR AND OVER SURFACE BETWEEN LIVE PARTS AND GROUNDED METAL PARTS
GREATER THAN	MAX.	THROUGH AIR	OVER SURFACE	BOTH THROUGH AIR AND OVER SURFACE
0 -- 125		1/2"	3/4"	1/2"
125 -- 250		3/4"	1-1/4"	1/2"
250 -- 600		2"	2"	1*

* A THROUGH AIR SPACING OF NOT LESS THAN 1/2" IS ACCEPTABLE (1) AT A MOLDED-CASE CIRCUIT BREAKER OR A SWITCH, OTHER THAN A SNAP SWITCH, (2) BETWEEN UNINSULATED LIVE PARTS OF A METER MOUNTING OR GROUNDED DEAD METAL, AND (3) BETWEEN GROUNDED DEAD METAL AND THE NEUTRAL OF A 480Y/277V, THREE-PHASE, FOUR-WIRE SWITCHGEAR SECTION.

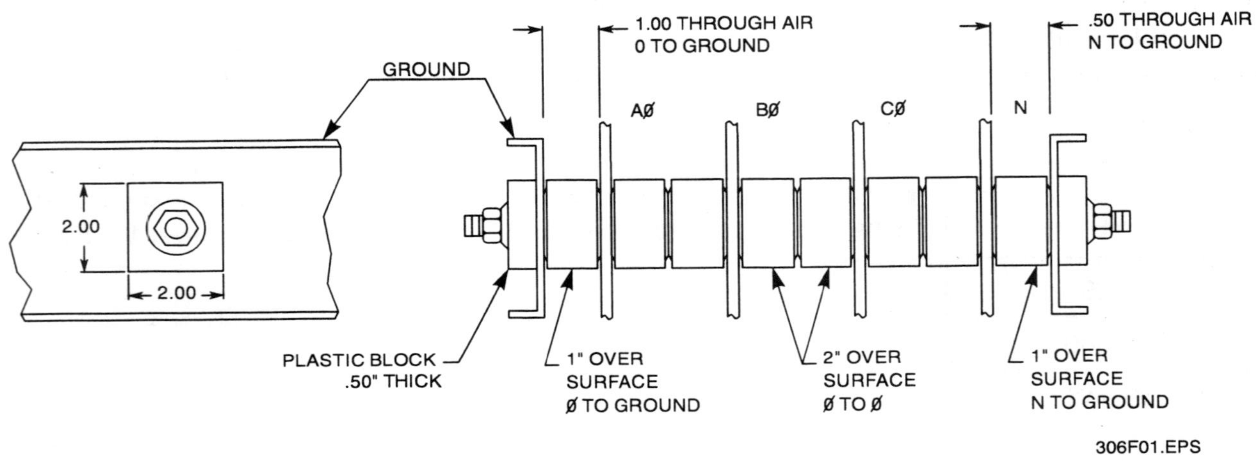

Figure 1. Switchboard Spacing Requirements

An isolated dead metal part, such as a screwhead or washer, interposed between uninsulated live parts of opposite polarity, or between an uninsulated live part and grounded dead metal, is considered to reduce the spacing by an amount equal to the dimension of the interposed part along the path of measurement.

When measuring over-surface spacing, any slot, groove, and the like that is 0.013" (0.33mm) wide or less and in the contour of the insulating material is to be disregarded.

When measuring spacing, an air space of 0.013" or less between a live part and an insulating surface is to be disregarded, and the live part is to be considered in contact with the insulating material. A pressure wire connector shall be prevented from any turning motion that would result in less than the minimum acceptable spacings. The means for turn prevention shall be reliable, such as a shoulder or boss. A lock washer alone is not acceptable.

A means of turn prevention need not be provided if spacings are not less than the following minimum accepted values:

- When the connector, and any connector of opposite polarity, have each been turned 30° toward the other
- When the connector has been turned 30° toward other live parts of opposite polarity and toward grounded dead metal parts

3.5.0   CABLE BRACING

All construction employing conductors and having a short circuit current rating greater than 50,000 rms symmetrical amperes requires a cable brace positioned as close to the supply lugs as possible. The cable brace is intended to be mounted in the same area that is allotted for wire bending. It is not necessary to provide additional mounting height to accommodate the cable brace.

The cable brace requirement does not apply to load-side cables, main breakers, or switches. It only applies when cables are connected directly to an unprotected line-side bus.

The bus restrictions for a line-side bus include:

- There can be no splice in edgewise bus mounting of 2,100A or less rated at 50,000 rms symmetrical amperes.
- There can be no splice in flatwise bus mounting of 600A or less rated over 50,000 rms symmetrical amperes.

Note: This does not apply to connections made from the through bus to a switch or circuit breaker.

The cable restrictions for a line-side bus include:

- Bussing of 600A or less that is rated over 50,000 rms symmetrical amperes cannot use cables. It must be bus connected.
- If cabling is required, 800A minimum bussing must be used.

Cable bracing requirements may be excluded if the bussing is able to fully withstand the total available short circuit current.

4.0.0　SWITCHGEAR

Switchgear is a general term used to describe switching and interrupting devices, and assemblies of those devices containing control, metering, protective, and regulatory equipment, along with the associated interconnections and supporting structures.

Switchgear performs two basic functions:

- Provides a means of switching or disconnecting power system apparatus
- Provides power system protection by automatically isolating faulty components

Switchgear can be classified as:

- **Metal-enclosed switchgear** (low voltage)
- Metal-clad switchgear (low and medium voltage)
- Metal-enclosed interrupters
- Unit substations

The low-voltage and medium-voltage switchgear assemblies are completely enclosed on all sides and topped with sheet metal, except for ventilating openings and inspection windows. They contain primary power circuit switching or interrupting devices, buses, connections, and control and auxiliary devices. *Figure 2* shows a typical low-voltage, metal-clad switchgear.

The station-type cubicle switchgear consists of indoor and outdoor types with power circuit breakers rated from 14.4kV to 34.5kV, 1,200A to 5,000A, and 1,500kVA to 2,500kVA interrupting **capacity**.

4.1.0　DESCRIPTION OF SWITCHGEAR

Switchgear consists of a stationary structure that includes one or more freestanding units of uniform height that are mechanically and electrically joined to make a single coordinated installation. These units, commonly referred to as *cubicles*, contain circuit interrupting devices such as circuit breakers. They take up less space in a plant or installation, have more eye appeal, and eliminate the need for a separate room to protect personnel from contact with lethal voltages.

The main portion of switchgear is formed from heavy-gauge sheet steel that has been welded or bolted together. Structural members across the top, sides, and bottom provide a rigid enclosure. Metal-clad switchgear enclosures are divided into three sections: the front section, the bus section, and the cable or termination section.

These three sections are physically separated from one another by metal partitions. This confines any damage that may occur to any one section and keeps it from affecting the other sections. It also separates power between the sections for ease and safety of maintenance.

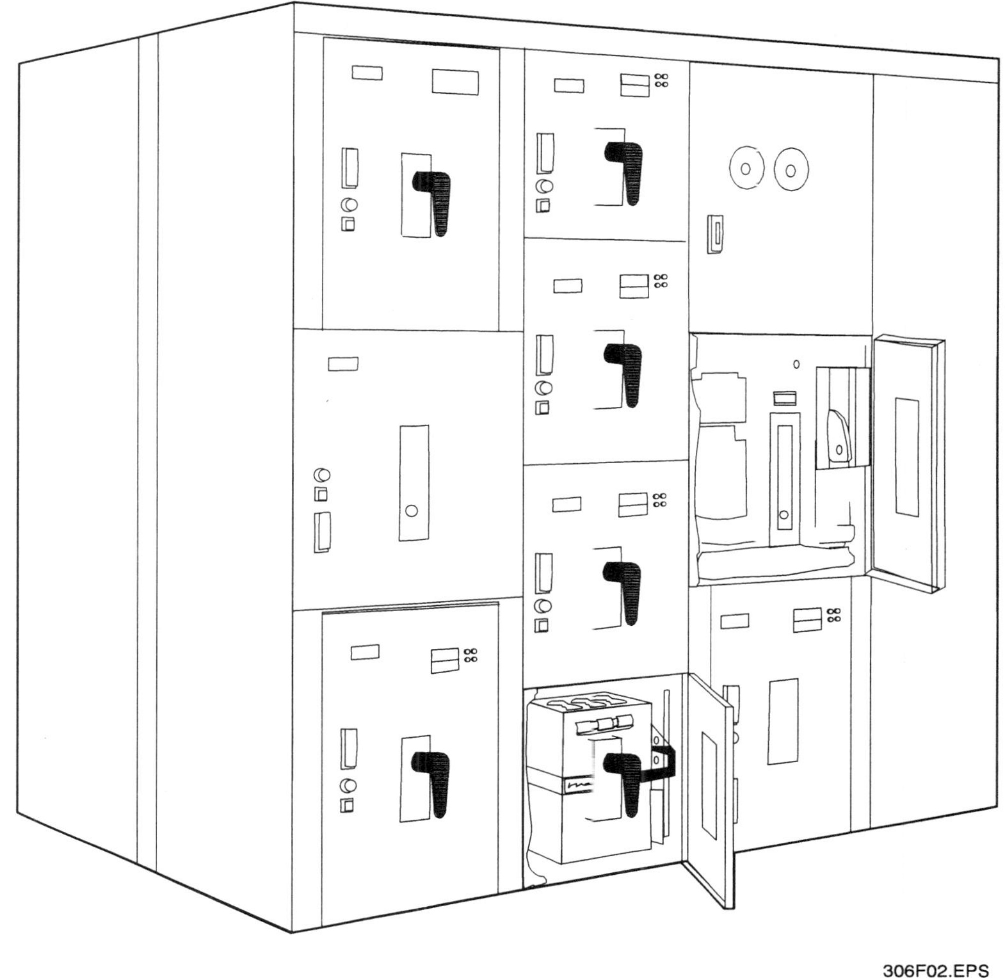

Figure 2. Typical Metal-Clad Switchgear

The rigid enclosure provides primary structural strength of the switchgear assembly and the means by which the switchgear is fastened to its foundation. The strength of the enclosure and its mounting system will vary depending on its intended use. For example, switchgear used in a nuclear application must meet certain seismic qualifications.

The enclosure also provides the required supports and mounts for items to be located in the switchgear and provides for the necessary interconnections between the switchgear and other plant systems.

The number of sections and physical makeup of switchgear varies depending on the voltage and current ratings, plant specifications, and specific manufacturer.

4.2.0 SWITCHGEAR CONSTRUCTION

Square D two-high, metal-clad switchgear is designed for use on electrical distribution systems rated from 2,400V to 13,800V nominal (see *Figures 3, 4,* and *5*).

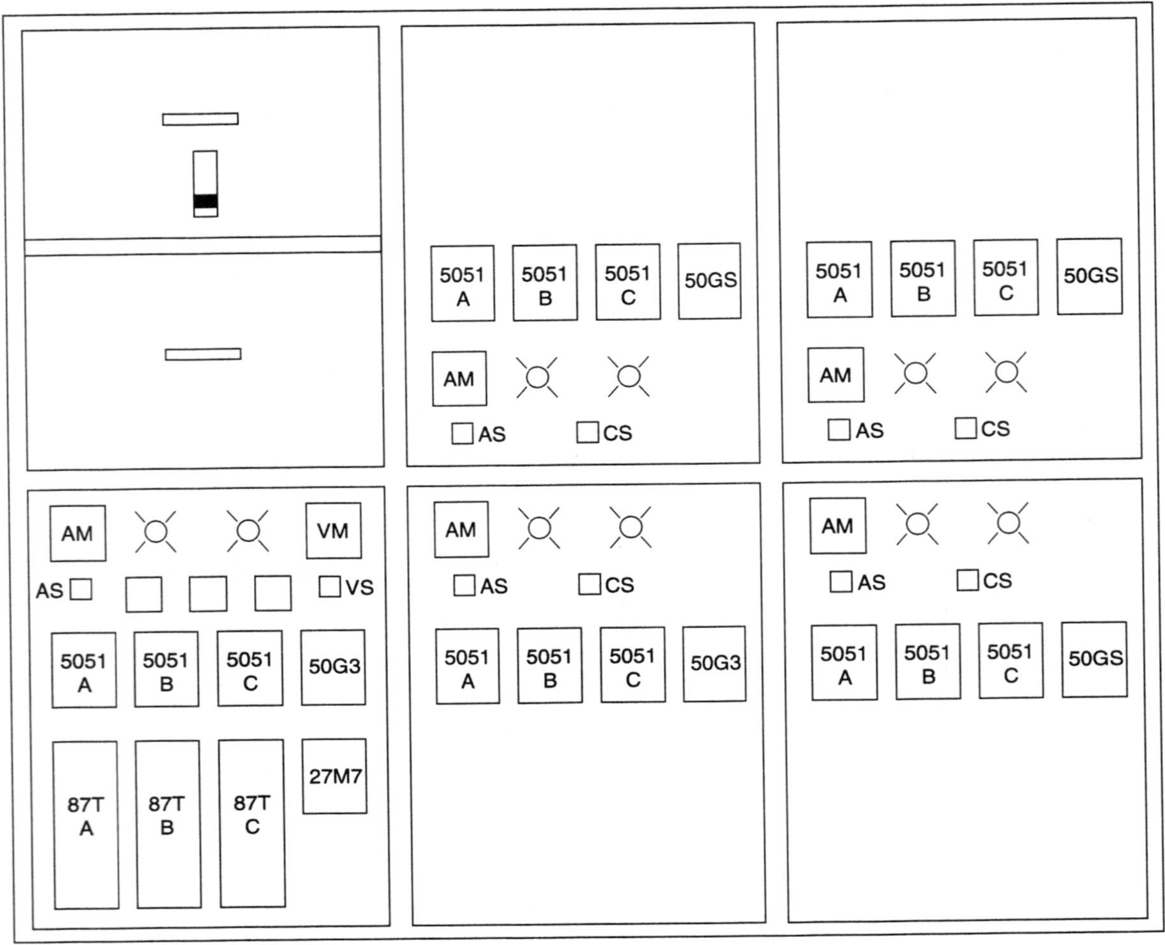

Figure 3. Square D Two-High, Metal-Clad Switchgear

The ratings for the Square D two-high, metal-clad switchgear include:

- 2.4kV to 13.8kV
- 1,200A to 3,000A (3,500A with cooling fans)
- 250kVA to 750kVA interrupting capacity
- 60kV and 95kV **basic impulse insulation level (BIL)**
- Stored energy operating mechanism
- Drawout construction
- Insulated bussing
- Indoor NEMA Size 1

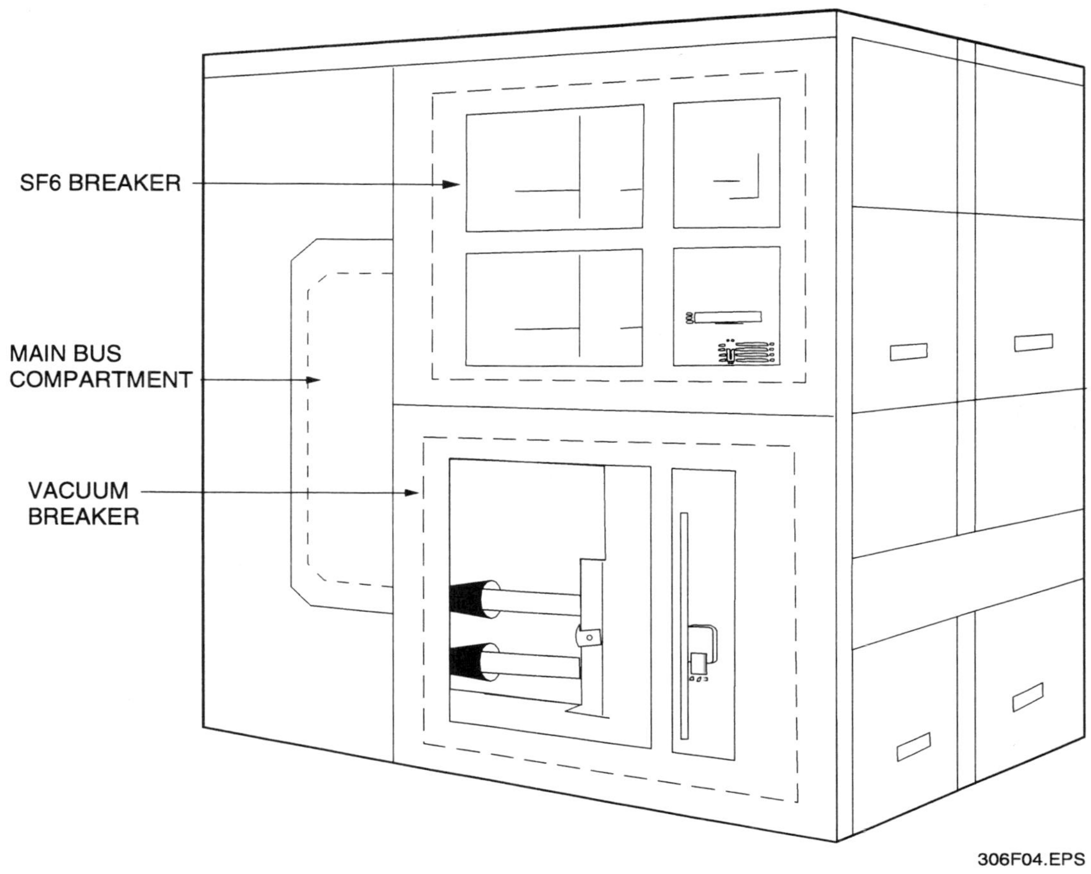

Figure 4. Square D Two-High, Metal-Clad Switchgear (Side View)

4.3.0 PRINCIPAL COMPONENTS

The principal components of the Square D two-high, metal-clad switchgear are as follows:

- *Hinged front door* – Relays, instruments, and meters are mounted on the door space in a standardized arrangement.

- *Horizontal drawout circuit breaker* – Circuit breakers have a horizontal drawout design. Disconnect, test, and connect positions are provided with the door in the closed position.

- *Main bus barriers* – Main bus barriers (not shown) between bays are track-resistant, flame-retardant, glass polyester, with porcelain inserts at 8.25kV and 15kV ratings.

- *Current transformers (CTs)* – Space is available for four front-accessible, bushing-type current transformers per phase. Two of these current transformers may be placed on the line side of the breaker and two on the load side on each phase.

- *Cable space* – The switchgear allows top or bottom cable entry with adequate space for four 750MCM cables per phase, potheads, cable supports, and surge arrestors.

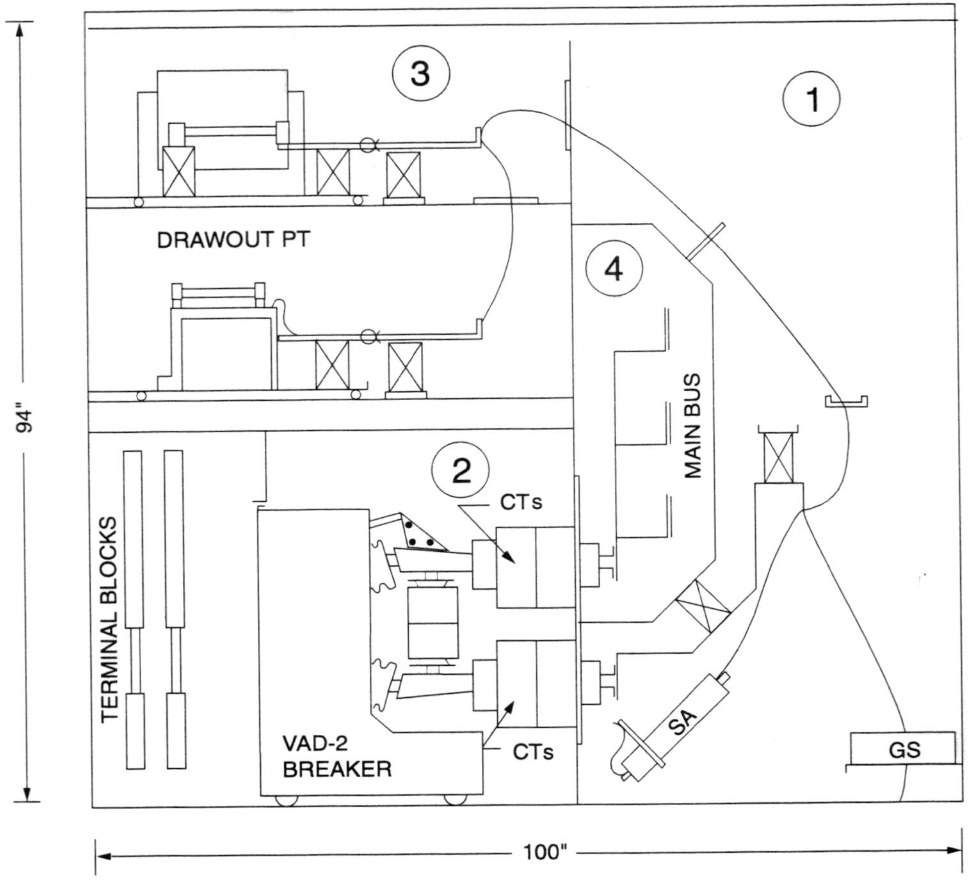

AVAILABLE OPTIONS

① **CABLE COMPARTMENT**

- Bottom or top cable entry
- Ground sensor current transformer (zero sequence)
- Space for stress cone termination
- 1/C or 3/C pothead
- Surge arrestors, if required
- Fixed-mounted control power transformer (CPT), with no cable entry at the bottom

② **BREAKER COMPARTMENT**

- 1200/2000 SF6 or vacuum circuit breaker in two-high construction
- Side space available for terminal block connections
- Maximum 4 CTs per phase (two on either side of breaker pole)

③ **AUXILIARY COMPARTMENT**

- Fused drawout PTs or single-phase CPT (15kVA maximum)
- Drawout fuses

④ **MAIN BUS COMPARTMENT**

- 1200/2000A insulated aluminum (copper optional) main bus

Figure 5. Square D Two-High, Metal-Clad Switchgear (Internal View)

- *Automatic shutters* – When the circuit breaker is withdrawn from the connected position, the breaker forces the steel shutter to rotate automatically into a position which covers the energized components.

- *Main bus and supports* – An insulated bus is provided with fluidized bed epoxy insulation, and with a special design combination of porcelain and main bus supports. Porcelain or glass polyester bus supports and insulators (as specified) are provided in the cable and auxiliary compartments.

- *Insulating tubes* – Porcelain insulating tubes are used to insulate the primary stationary contacts and breaker runbacks at both 5kV and 15kV ratings.

- *Compartment barriers* – All main compartments are separated by grounded metal barriers.

- *Racking mechanism* – The gear-driven racking system incorporates safety interlocks. The racking mechanism is an internal part of the breaker. It consists of a self-engaging, self-aligning screw device that becomes spin-free in the connected position at the end of the breaker travel. This prevents possible damage due to overtightening. Safety interlocks, as required by ANSI, are provided to prevent electrical or mechanical operation of the breaker during the racking procedure.

- *Frame and housing* – Steel frames provide a strong, rigid structure. The structure is engineered for flexibility to allow for modifications and future addition of equipment.

- *Voltage transformers* – Front-accessible, drawer-mounted voltage transformers can be completely withdrawn through the use of rollers and drawer-mounted cantilever rails. For safety, the voltage transformers are grounded when moved to the withdrawn position.

- *Control power transformers (CPTs)* – Control power transformers rated up to 15kVA are drawer-mounted and can be completely withdrawn from the front for ease of accessibility.

- *Circuit breakers* – FG-2 and VAD-2 circuit breakers using SF6 and vacuum interrupters offer application flexibility. The breakers are designed, manufactured, and tested per ANSI standards, and are of a compact size and weight.

- *Breaker lift truck* – A portable lifter device is required to install the breaker in the upper-tier breaker compartment. This device uses a height-adjustable platform and is latched to the cell for safety. All breakers located in the bottom compartments can be rolled directly on the floor and the use of a breaker lifting truck is not required.

- *Breaker compartment* – The stationary primary disconnect contacts are automatically covered by bright orange steel shutters when the breaker is withdrawn. Accidental contact with primary voltage live parts is prevented. The shutters should not be forced into the open position or removed for inspection or maintenance when the unit is energized.

- *Doors* – Relays, instruments, indicating lights, control switches, and other control devices may be mounted on the front door of the breaker and auxiliary components.

4.4.0   CONTROL AND METERING WIRE STANDARDS

Switchboard control and meter wiring standards must meet the requirements of *Machine Tool Wires and Cables Safety Standard UL 1063, Switchboard Safety Standard UL 891,* and *Service Equipment Safety Standard UL 869,* with the following highlights:

- Stranded copper conductor with thermoplastic insulation, UL and CSA approved
- Insulation thickness for No. 16 – No. 10 AWG size conductor is .030" ($\frac{1}{32}$")
- 600V, 90°C minimum rating for dry locations; 60°C minimum rating when exposed to oil and moisture
- Conductors no smaller than No. 14 AWG for control wiring

4.5.0   WIRING SYSTEM

The NEC requires wiring to be supported mechanically to keep the wiring in place. Wire harnessing is generally used within the switchboard with the following restrictions:

- Each bundle or cable of wires must be run in a vertical or horizontal direction, securing the harness by means of plastic cable ties or cable clips.
- Plastic wire cable clamps shall be placed at strategic locations along the harnessing to hold the harness firmly in place to prevent interference with the control components' required electrical, mechanical, and arcing clearances.
- Apply wire ties to the harnessed wiring every 3" to 4", with self-adhesive cable ties spaced at every 12".
- Some precautions to be observed when wiring the switchboard electrical components are as follows:
  - Keep control wires at least $\frac{1}{2}$" from moving parts.
  - Avoid running wires across sharp metal edges. To protect the wiring from mechanical damage, use approved cable protectors, such as a nylon clip cable guard, a wire guard for edge protection, or special edge protection molding.
  - Wires must not touch exposed bare electrical parts of opposite polarity.
  - Wires must not interfere with the adjustment or replacement of components.
  - Wires should be as straight and as short as possible.
  - Wires shall not be spliced.
  - To eliminate possible strain on the control wire, a certain amount of slack should be given to the individual or harnessed conductor terminated at a component connection.
  - The equipment ground busbar shall not be used as a portion of the control or metering circuits.
  - Do not use pliers for bending control wiring. Use your hands or an approved wire bending device.

4.5.1   Door-Mounted Wiring Restrictions

No incoming wiring connections may be made directly to the door-mounted devices. Wires from the door-mounted equipment to the panel terminal block should be a minimum of 19-strand wire.

Wires from the door must be neatly cabled so that the door can be opened easily without placing excessive strain on the wire terminal connections. In some cases, the cable must be separated into two bundles to accomplish this. Insulated sleeving, tubing, or vinyl tape must be used to bundle and protect the flexible wires.

4.5.2   Terminal Connections

All control or metering wiring entering or leaving the switchboard should terminate at terminal blocks, leaving one side of the terminal block free for the user's connections. No factory connections are allowed on the user's terminal connection point. For factory wiring, allow a maximum of two control wires on the same side of a terminal block. No more than three connections are allowed on terminals of control transformers, meters, meter selector switches, and metering equipment.

Since bolted pressure switches or any 100% current-rated, molded-case circuit breaker's line and load power terminals are allowed a higher maximum operating temperature than the recommended insulated conductor's operating temperature, the control wires cannot be placed directly on the 100%-rated disconnect device's line and load connections.

In all cases, control wires cannot touch any exposed part of opposite electrical polarity.

4.6.0   METERING CURRENT AND POTENTIAL TRANSFORMERS

Ground connections on a potential transformer (PT) or current transformer (CT) secondary terminal must be connected to the ground bus. CT secondary terminals must be shorted if no metering equipment is connected to the current transformer.

PTs are required to have primary and secondary fusing. If protective circuits such as ground fault or phase failure protective systems are placed in the secondary circuit of the potential transformer, no secondary fusing is required.

Metering circuit connections made directly to the incoming bus must be provided with current-limiting fuses that are equal in rating to the available interrupting capacity.

Note: CTs and PTs will be discussed later.

4.7.0 SWITCHGEAR HANDLING, STORAGE, AND INSTALLATION

The following is a basic guideline for the handling of switchgear. It is important to emphasize that these recommendations only supplement the manufacturer's instructions. Manufacturers include instruction books and drawings with their equipment. It is absolutely imperative that you read and understand these documents before handling any equipment.

- *Switchgear handling* – Immediately upon receipt of switchgear, an inspection for damage during transit should be performed. If any damage is noted, the transportation company should be notified immediately.

- *Switchgear rigging* – Instructions for switchgear should be found in the manufacturer's instruction books and drawings. Verify that the rigging is suitable for the size and weight of the equipment.

- *Switchgear storage* – Indoor switchgear that is not being installed should be stored in a clean, dry location. The equipment should be level and protected from the environment if construction is proceeding. The longer equipment is in storage, the more care is required for protection of the equipment. If a temporary cover is used to protect the equipment, this cover should not prevent air circulation. If the building is not heated or temperature controlled, heaters should be used to prevent moisture/condensation buildup. Outdoor switchgear that cannot be installed immediately must be provided with temporary power. This power will allow operation of the space heaters provided with the equipment.

- *Bus connections* – The main bus that is usually removed during shipping should be reconnected. Ensure that the contact surfaces are clean and pressure is applied in the correct manner. The conductivity of the joints is dependent on the applied pressure at the contact points. The manufacturer's torque instructions should be referenced.

- *Cable connections* – When making cable connections, verify the phasing of each cable. This procedure is done in accordance with the connection diagrams and the cable tags. When forming and mounting cables, ensure that the cables are tightened per the manufacturer's instructions.

- *Grounding* – Any sections of ground bus that were previously disconnected for shipping should be reconnected when the units are installed. All secondary wiring should be connected to the switchgear ground bus. The ground bus should be connected to the system ground with as direct a connection as possible. If it is to be run in metal conduit, adequate bonding to the circuit is required. The ground connection is necessary for all switchgear and should be of sufficient ampacity to handle any abnormal condition.

5.0.0 SWITCHBOARD MAINTENANCE

When working on switchboards or any piece of electrical equipment, you must always be aware of and follow all applicable safety procedures. If you are not sure if the procedures you are following are safe, contact your supervisor. It is better to check the procedure than to go ahead and follow unsafe work practices.

Always follow established procedures for grounding and locking out a circuit, and ensure that you have control over the switchboard voltage source(s).

5.1.0   GENERAL MAINTENANCE GUIDELINES

To perform a visual inspection:

Step 1   Check the exterior for the proper fit of doors and covers, paint, etc.

Step 2   Check the interior, particularly the current-carrying parts, including the following:

- Inspect the busbars for dirt, corrosion, or overheating.
- If necessary, perform an infrared or thermographic test. Note any discoloration which would represent a poor bus joint.
- Check the busbar supports for cracks.
- Check for correct electrical spacing.
- Check the torque of all joints.

To clean the switchboard:

Step 1   Vacuum the interior (do not use compressed air).

Step 2   Wipe down the interior using a clean, lint-free cloth. Use nonconductive, non-residue solution such as contact cleaner or denatured alcohol.

To check equipment operation:

Step 1   Manually open and close circuit breakers and switches.

Step 2   Electrically operate all components such as ground fault detectors, sure trip metering, current transformers, test blocks, ground lights, blown main fuse detectors, and phase failure detectors.

To perform a megger test:

Step 1   Isolate the bus by opening all circuit breakers and switches.

Step 2   Disconnect any devices such as relays and transformers that may be connected to the busbars.

Step 3   Make sure all personnel are clear of the switchboard.

Step 4   Use a 1,000V megger to check the phase-to-phase and phase-to-ground resistance. Megger readings should be one megohm per kV rating of the equipment with a minimum of one megohm corrected to 68°F.

Step 5   If low readings are found and moisture is thought to be a problem, apply heat to the switchboard (200W per section). Retest in eight hours. Readings should improve substantially.

5.2.0 SPECIFIC GUIDELINES

5.2.1 Thermographic Survey

A thermographic survey involves checking switches, busways, open buses, switchgear, cable and bus connections, circuit breakers, rotating equipment, and load tap changers.

Infrared surveys should be performed during periods of maximum possible loading and not at less than 40% of the rated load of the electrical equipment being inspected.

Negative test results include the following:

- Temperature gradients of 1°C to 3°C indicate a possible deficiency and require investigation.
- Temperature gradients of 4°C to 15°C indicate a deficiency. Repair as time permits.
- Temperature gradients of 16°C and above indicate a major deficiency. Secure power and repair as soon as possible.

5.2.2 Metal-Enclosed Switchgear And Switchboards

To perform a visual and mechanical inspection:

Step 1 Inspect the physical, electrical, and mechanical condition of the equipment.

Step 2 Compare the equipment nameplate information with the latest single-line diagram and report any discrepancies.

Step 3 Check for proper anchorage, required area clearances, physical damage, and proper alignment.

Step 4 Inspect all doors, panels, and sections for missing paint, dents, scratches, fit, and missing hardware.

Step 5 Inspect all bus connections for high resistance. Use a low-resistance ohmmeter or check tightness of bolted bus joints using a calibrated torque wrench.

Step 6 Test all electrical and mechanical interlock systems for proper operation and sequencing.

- A closure attempt must be made on all locked-open devices. An opening attempt must be made on all locked-closed devices.
- A key exchange must be made with all devices operated in normally off positions.

Step 7 Clean the entire switchgear using the manufacturer's approved methods and materials.

Step 8 Inspect insulators for evidence of physical damage or contaminated surfaces.

Step 9 Inspect the lubrication:

- Verify appropriate contact lubricant on moving current-carrying parts.
- Verify appropriate lubrication of moving and sliding surfaces.
- Exercise all active components.
- Inspect all indicating devices for proper operation.

To perform electrical testing:

Step 1 Perform ratio and polarity tests on all current and voltage transformers.

Step 2 Perform ground resistance tests.

Step 3 Perform insulation resistance tests on each bus section (phase-to-phase and phase-to-ground) for one minute. Refer to *Table 2*.

Minimum Voltage Rating of Equipment	Minimum Test Voltage (VDC)	Recommended Minimum Insulation Resistance (in Megohms)
2 – 250V	500	50
251 – 600V	1,000	100
601 – 5,000V	2,500	1,000
5,001 – 15,000V	2,500	5,000
15,001 – 39,000V	5,000	20,000

Table 2. Insulation Resistance Tests On Electrical Apparatus And Systems At 68°F

Step 4 Perform an overpotential test on each bus section (phase-to-ground) for five minutes. Refer to *Table 3*.

Step 5 Perform an insulation resistance test on the control wiring. (Do not perform this test on wiring connected to solid-state components.)

Step 6 Calibrate all meters at mid-scale. Calibrate watt-hour meters to one-half percent (0.5%). Verify multipliers.

Step 7 Perform a phasing check on double-ended switchgear to ensure proper bus phasing from each source.

CAUTION: You must be certified and authorized to perform these tests; care should be taken to ensure that there is no voltage present.

Nominal System (Line) Voltage*	Insulation Class	Minimum AC Factory Test	Applied AC Test	Field-Applied DC Test
1.2kV	1.2	10kV	6kV	8.5kV
2.4kV	2.5	15kV	9kV	12.7kV
4.8kV	5	19kV	11.4kV	16.1kV
8.3kV	8.7	26kV	15.6kV	22.1kV
14.4kV	15	34kV	20.4kV	28.8kV
18kV	18	40kV	24kV	33.9kV
25kV	25	50kV	30kV	42.4kV
34.5kV	35	70kV	42kV	59.4kV
46kV	46	95kV	57kV	80.6kV
69kV	69	140kV	84kV	118.8kV

*Intermediate voltage ratings are placed in the next higher insulation class.

Table 3. Overpotential Test Voltage For Electrical Apparatus Other Than Inductive Equipment

Any values of insulation resistance less than those listed in *Table 2* or in the manufacturer's literature should be investigated. Overpotential tests should not proceed until insulation resistance levels are raised above minimum values.

Overpotential test voltages must be applied in accordance with *Table 3*.

Test results are evaluated on a go/no-go basis by slowly raising the test voltage to the required value. The final test voltage is applied for five minutes for DC test potentials and one minute for AC test potentials.

5.2.3 Low-Voltage Cables (600V Maximum)

To perform a visual and mechanical inspection:

Step 1 Inspect cables for physical damage and proper connection in accordance with the single-line diagram.

Step 2 Test cable mechanical connections to the manufacturer's recommended values using a calibrated torque wrench.

Step 3 Check color-coded cable against the applicable engineer's specifications and NEC standards.

To perform electrical testing:

Step 1 Perform an insulation resistance test on each conductor with respect to ground and adjacent conductors. The applied potential should be 1,000VDC for one minute.

Step 2 Perform a continuity test to ensure proper cable connection. The minimum insulation resistance values must not be less than two megohms.

5.2.4 Medium-Voltage Cables (15kV Maximum)

To perform a visual and mechanical inspection:

Step 1 Inspect exposed sections for physical damage.

Step 2 Inspect for shield grounding, cable support, and termination.

Step 3 Inspect for proper fireproofing in common cable areas.

Step 4 If cables are terminated through window-type CTs, make an inspection to verify that neutrals and grounds are properly terminated for normal operation of the protective devices.

Step 5 Visually inspect the jacket and insulation condition.

Step 6 Inspect for proper phase identification and arrangement.

5.2.5 Metal-Enclosed Busways

To perform a visual and mechanical inspection:

Step 1 Inspect the bus for physical damage.

Step 2 Inspect for proper bracing, suspension, alignment, and enclosure.

Step 3 Check the tightness of bolted joints using a calibrated torque wrench.

Step 4 Check for proper physical orientation per the manufacturer's labels to ensure proper cooling. Perform continuity tests on each conductor to verify that proper phase relationships exist.

Step 5 Check outdoor busways for removal of weep-hole plugs, if applicable, and also for the proper installation of a joint shield.

To perform electrical testing:

Step 1 Perform an insulation resistance test. Measure the insulation resistance on each bus run (phase-to-phase and phase-to-ground) for one minute.

Step 2 Perform AC or DC overpotential tests on each bus run, both phase-to-phase and phase-to-ground.

Step 3   Perform a contact resistance test on each connection point of the uninsulated bus. On an insulated bus, measure the resistance of the bus section and compare values with adjacent phases.

Step 4   Insulation resistance test voltages and resistance values must be in accordance with the manufacturer's specifications or *Table 1*.

Step 5   Apply overpotential test voltages in accordance with *Table 2*.

5.2.6 Metering And Instrumentation

To perform a visual and mechanical inspection:

Step 1   Examine all devices for broken parts, indication of shipping damage, and wire connection tightness.

Step 2   Verify that meter connections are in accordance with appropriate diagrams.

To perform electrical testing:

Step 1   Check the calibration of meters at all cardinal points.

Step 2   Calibrate watt-hour meters to one-half of one percent (0.5%).

Step 3   Verify all instrument multipliers.

6.0.0 NEC REQUIREMENTS

This section is designed to provide a brief description of the NEC articles that are applicable to switchboard construction, installation, and accessories.

6.1.0 REQUIREMENTS FOR ELECTRICAL INSTALLATIONS

NEC requirements for electrical installations include the following:

- *Interrupting rating* – The interrupting rating is the maximum current a device is intended to interrupt under standard test conditions. ***NEC Section 110-9*** defines the equipment interrupting rating as sufficient to interrupt the current that is available at the line-side terminals of the equipment.

- *Deteriorating agents* – ***NEC Section 110-11*** provides for the protection of equipment and conductors from environments which could cause deterioration (such as gases, vapors, liquids, or moisture) unless specifically designed for such environments.

- *Mechanical execution of work* – ***NEC Section 110-12*** states that electrical equipment is to be installed in a neat and professional manner. Any openings provided by the equipment manufacturer or at the time of installation that are not being used must be sealed equivalent to the structure wall. This section also forbids the use of electrical equipment with damaged parts that may affect the safe operation or mechanical strength of the equipment.

- *Mounting and cooling* – ***NEC Section 110-13*** states that electrical equipment shall be securely fastened to its mounting surface by mechanical fasteners excluding wooden plugs driven into concrete, masonry, plaster, or similar materials. Equipment shall be located so as not to restrict air flow required for convection or forced-air cooling.

- *Electrical connections* – Due to the resistive oxidation created when dissimilar metals are connected, splicing devices and pressure connectors must be identified for the conductor material with which they are to be used (***NEC Section 110-14***). Dissimilar metal conductors may not be mixed in terminations or splices. Fluxes, solders, and antioxidation compounds must be suitable for use and must not adversely affect conductors, installation, or equipment. Terminals for use with more than one conductor or aluminum must be identified as such.

- *Markings* – The manufacturer's trademark or logo, as well as system ratings including voltage, current, wattage, etc., must be permanently attached to the equipment (***NEC Section 110-21***).

- *Disconnect identification* – Each disconnecting means (e.g., circuit breaker, fused switch, **feeder**, or unfused disconnects) must be clearly marked as to its purpose at its point of origin unless located in such a manner that its purpose is evident (***NEC Section 110-22***).

- *Working space* – Suitable access and working space shall be maintained around electrical equipment to permit safe operation and maintenance (***NEC Section 110-26***). A minimum clearance of 3' is required in front of all electrical enclosures; in all cases, space must be adequate to allow doors or hinged parts to open to a 90° angle. In special case installations, the clearances in ***NEC Table 110-26(a)*** must be adhered to. Storage of any kind is not permitted within the clearance area. At least one entrance of ample size must be provided to access the work area. In cases of services over 1,200A and over 6' wide, two entrances are required. The work space must be adequately illuminated.

6.2.0 REQUIREMENTS FOR CONDUCTORS

NEC conductor requirements include the following:

- *Neutrals* – Grounded conductors (neutrals) size No. 6 AWG and smaller are color-coded with a solid white or gray marking for the entire length of the conductor. Conductors size No. 6 and larger may be color-coded with a solid white marking tape at termination points at the time of installation. Where different electrical systems are run together, each system's grounded conductor must be distinctively identified (***NEC Section 200-6***).

- *Protection* – **Branch circuit** conductors must be protected by overcurrent devices, as specified in ***NEC Section 240-3***.

- *Loading* – ***NEC Section 210-19(a)*** states that protective device calculations for continuous duty circuits are calculated at 125% of the continuous load. This equates to an 80% loading factor on the branch circuit.

- *Tap rules* – Tap conductors are conductors which are tapped onto the line-side bus of the switchboard to feed control circuits, control power transformers, metering devices, etc. Overcurrent devices (typically fuses) are connected where the conductor to be protected receives its supply. Per ***NEC Section 240-21***, tap conductors do not require protection if the following conditions are met:

  - The length of the conductor is not over 10'.
  - The ampacity of the conductor is not less than the combined loads supplied by the conductor.
  - The conductors do not extend beyond the switchboard.
  - The conductors are enclosed in a raceway except at the point of connection to the bus.
  - For field installations where the tap conductors leave the enclosure or vault in which the tap is made, the rating of the overcurrent device on the line side of the tap conductors does not exceed 10% of the tap conductor's ampacity.

- *Markings* – All conductors and cables shall be permanently marked to indicate the manufacturer, voltage, AWG size, and insulation type (***NEC Sections 310-11, 310-12, and 384-3***).

  - Grounded conductors (neutrals) size No. 6 and smaller shall have a continuous marking of white or gray for the entire length of the conductor. Larger conductors may be marked at each termination with white marking tape.
  - Grounding conductors (ground wires) shall be permitted to be bare wire. In cases of insulated grounding conductors, the conductor will have a continuous marking of green for the entire length of the conductor. Larger conductors may be marked at each termination with marking tape.
  - Ungrounded conductors (phase wires) must be distinguishable from grounded or grounding conductors with colors other than white, gray, or green. Typical ungrounded conductor identification colors are black, red, blue, brown, orange, and yellow. Conductors size No. 6 or smaller must have a continuous marking. Larger cables may be marked at each termination.
  - In switchboards fed by a four-wire, delta system in which one phase is grounded at its midpoint, the phase having the higher voltage must be marked with an orange color.

- *Ampacities* – The ampacities of cable are determined by the cable size and insulation type (***NEC Section 310-15***).

6.3.0   GROUNDING

NEC grounding requirements include the following:

- *Grounding* – ***NEC Section 250-20*** states that AC systems between 50V and 1,000V must be grounded when any of the following conditions are met:

  - Where the system can be grounded in such a way that the maximum phase-to-ground voltage does not exceed 150V

- When the system is three-phase, four-wire, wye-connected and the neutral is used as a circuit conductor

- When the system is three-phase, four-wire, delta-connected and the midpoint of a phase is used as a conductor (developed neutral)

- *Grounding electrode conductor* – **NEC Sections 250-24, 250-28, and 250-66** state that a grounding electrode (ground rod) conductor of the proper size must be used to connect the equipment grounding conductors (ground bus) and the service equipment enclosure. For grounded systems (delta or wye), an unspliced main bonding jumper in the service equipment must be used to connect the grounding conductor to the equipment grounding conductor and enclosure.

Note: Some systems are ungrounded and will not blow fuses.

- *Made electrodes* – **NEC Sections 250-52 and 250-56** state that made electrodes (such as rod or pipe electrodes) must extend a minimum of 8' into the soil. The electrode must be no less than ¾" in diameter for pipe and ⅝" in diameter for rods. It must be galvanized metal or copper-coated to resist corrosion. Underground structures such as water piping systems may be used as the made electrode. Underground gas piping systems must not be used. Aluminum electrodes are not permitted. Made electrodes must maintain a resistance of no more than 25Ω to ground. If the resistance is above 25Ω, an additional electrode is required to maintain the minimum resistance.

- *Grounding of ground wire conduits* – **NEC Section 250-64(e)** states that a grounding conductor or its enclosure must be securely mounted to the surface which it runs along. In cases where the conductor is enclosed, the enclosure must be electrically continuous and firmly grounded.

- *Ground connection surfaces* – Nonconducting coatings such as paint, enamel, or insulating materials must be thoroughly removed at any point where a grounding connection is made (**NEC Section 250-12**).

6.4.0 SWITCHBOARDS AND PANELBOARDS

NEC requirements for switchboards and panelboards include the following:

- *Dedicated space* – **NEC Sections 110-26(f) and 384-4** state that panelboards and switchboards may only be installed in spaces specifically designed for such purposes. No other piping, ducts, or devices may be installed or pass through such areas, except equipment that is necessary to the operation of the electrical equipment.

- *Inductive heating* – **NEC Section 384-3(b)** states that busbars and conductors must be arranged so as to avoid overheating due to inductive forces.

- *Phasing* – **NEC Section 384-3(f)** states that phasing in switchboards must be arranged A, B, C from front to back, top to bottom, and left to right, respectively, when facing the front of the switchboard. In systems containing a high leg, the B phase must be the phase conductor having a higher voltage to ground.

- *Wire bending space* – **NEC Section 384-35** states that the wire bending space must be in accordance with **NEC Tables 373-6(a) and (b)**.

- *Minimum spacing* – **NEC Section 384-36** states that the spacing between bare metal parts and conductors must be as specified in **NEC Table 384-36**.

- *Conductor insulation* – Insulated conductors within switchboards must be listed as flame-retardant and rated at not less than the voltage applied to them or any adjacent conductors they may come in contact with (**NEC Section 384-9**).

7.0.0   GROUND FAULTS

Ground faults exist when an unintended current path is established between an ungrounded conductor and ground. These faults can occur due to deteriorated insulation, moisture, dirt, rodents, foreign objects such as tools, and careless installation.

Ground faults are usually high arcing and low level in nature, which conventional breakers will not detect. Ground fault protection is used to protect equipment and cables against these low-level faults.

Ground fault protection is required per the NEC on solidly-grounded wye services of more than 150V to ground but not exceeding a phase-to-phase voltage of 600V with each service disconnecting means of 1,000A or more.

7.1.0   GROUND FAULT SYSTEMS

Generic types of ground fault systems include:

- Ground strap
- Residual
- Zero sequence

The ground-powered ground fault relay is a solid-state device designed for industrial environments. Ground-powered ground fault relays are intended for use only on power systems which include a grounded conductor (neutral or ungrounded phase). The grounded conductor must be grounded at the service equipment, but the neutral may or may not be used in the feeder or branch circuits.

7.2.0   SYSTEM OPERATION

When circuit conditions are normal, the currents from all the phase and neutral (if used) conductors add up to zero, and the sensor current transformer produces no signal. When any ground fault occurs, the currents add up to equal the ground fault current, and the sensor produces a signal proportional to the ground fault. This signal provides power to the ground fault relay, which trips the circuit breaker.

A ground fault lasting for less than the time-delay period will not pick up the ground trip coil, thus eliminating nuisance tripping of self-clearing faults.

The ground fault relay is a high-reliability device due to its solid-state construction. The use of redundant, self-protecting, and high-reliability components further improves the performance.

Self-protection against failure is provided through an internal fuse which will blow and result in a tripping function if the solid-state circuitry fails during a ground fault situation.

7.3.0 SENSOR MOUNTING

The sensor current transformer (sensor) should be mounted so that all phase and neutral (if used) conductors pass through the core window once. The ground conductor (if used) must not pass through the core window. The neutral conductors must be free of all grounds after passing through the core window (see *Figure 6*).

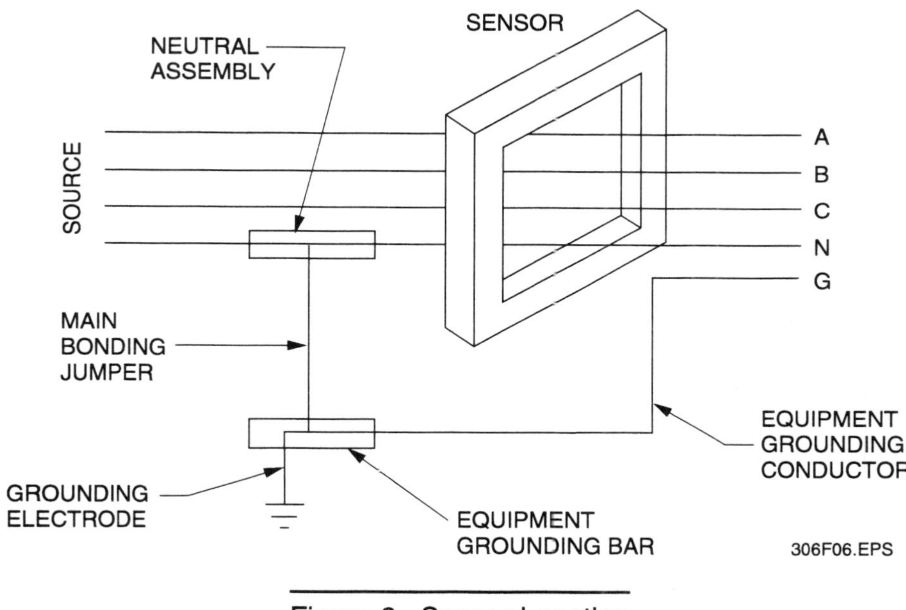

Figure 6. Sensor Location

When so specified by the system design engineer, the sensor may be mounted so that only the conductor connecting the neutral to ground at the service equipment passes through the core window. In such cases, the sensor must provide power to the particular ground fault relay which is associated with the main circuit breaker.

Maintain at least two inches of clearance from the iron core of the sensor to the nearest busbar or cable to avoid false tripping. Cable conductors should be bundled securely and braced to hold them at the center of the core window.

The sensor should be mounted within an enclosure and protected from mechanical damage.

7.4.0 RELAY MOUNTING

The ground fault relay should be mounted in a vertical position within an enclosure with the terminal block at the lower end. The location of the relay should be such that the trip setting knob is accessible without exposing the operator to contact with live parts or arcing from disconnect operation.

7.5.0 CONNECTIONS

Connections for standard application should be made according to the wiring diagram in *Figure 7*. Wires from the sensor to the ground fault relay should be no longer than 25' and no smaller than No. 14 AWG wire. Wires from the ground fault relay to the trip coil should be no longer than 50' and no smaller than No. 14 AWG wire. All wires should be protected from arcing fault and physical damage by barriers, conduit, armor, or location in an equipment enclosure. Do not disconnect or short circuit wires to the circuit breaker trip coil at any time when the power is turned on.

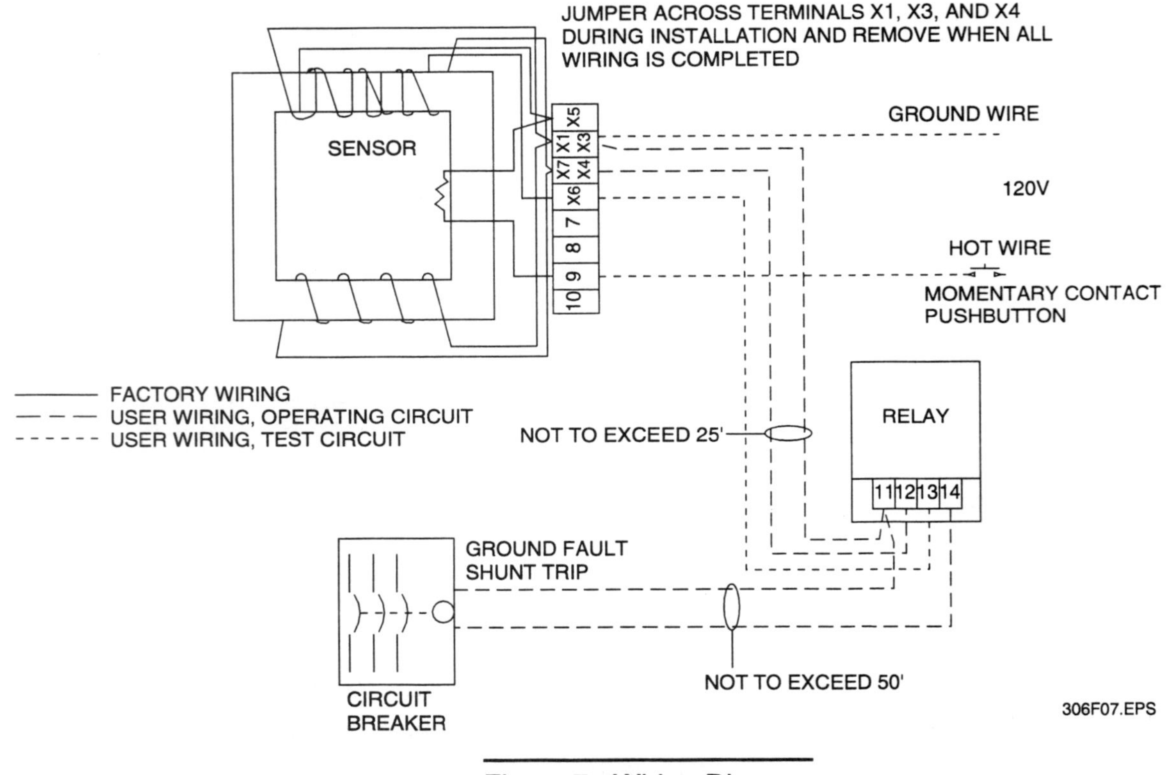

Figure 7. Wiring Diagram

7.6.0 RELAY SETTINGS

The ground fault relay has an adjustable trip setting. The amount of time delay is factory set and is available in nominal time delays of 0.1, 0.2, 0.3, and 0.5 second. When ground fault protection is used in downstream steps, the feeder should have the next lower time-delay curve than the main, the branch the next lower curve than the feeder, and so on.

High trip settings on main and feeder circuits are desirable to avoid nuisance tripping. High settings usually do not reduce the effectiveness of the protection if the ground path impedance is reasonably low. Ground faults usually quickly reach a value of 40% or more of the available short circuit current in the ground path circuit.

7.6.1 Coordination With Downstream Circuit Breakers

It is recommended that the magnetic trips of any downstream circuit breakers that are not equipped with ground fault protection be set as low as possible. Likewise, the ground fault relay trip settings for main or feeder circuits should be higher than the magnetic trip settings for unprotected downstream breakers, where possible. This will minimize nuisance tripping of the main or feeder breaker for ground faults occurring on downstream circuits.

7.6.2 Instantaneous Trip Feature

Standard ground-powered ground fault relays have a built-in instantaneous trip feature. This instantaneous trip has a fixed time delay of approximately 1½ cycles, and the fixed trip setting is higher than found on most feeder or branch breakers to avoid nuisance tripping. Its purpose is to interrupt very high-current ground faults on main disconnects as quickly as possible and to protect the ground fault relay components.

7.7.0 GENERIC NATIONAL ELECTRICAL TESTING ASSOCIATION GROUND FAULT SYSTEM TEST

7.7.1 Procedures

Perform a visual inspection:

Step 1 Inspect the components for physical damage.

Step 2 Determine if a ground sensor was located properly around the appropriate conductor(s).

- Zero sequence sensing requires all phases and the neutral to be encircled by the sensor(s).
- Ground return sensing requires the sensor to encircle the main bonding jumper.

Step 3 Inspect the main bonding jumper to ensure:

- Proper size
- Termination on the line side of the neutral disconnect link
- Termination on the line side of the sensor on zero sequence systems

Step 4 Inspect the grounding electrode conductor to ensure:

- Proper size
- Correct switchboard termination

Step 5   Inspect the ground fault control power transformer for proper installation and size. When the control transformer is supplied from the line side of the ground fault protection circuit interrupting device, overcurrent protection and a circuit disconnecting means must be provided.

Step 6   Visually inspect the switchboard neutral bus downstream of the neutral disconnect line to verify the absence of ground connections.

Perform electrical tests:

Step 1   Check for proper ground fault system performance, including correct response of the circuit interrupting device confirmed by primary/secondary ground sensor current injection.

- Measure the relay pickup current.
- Ensure that the relay time delay is measured at two values above the pickup current.

Step 2   Test system operation at 57% of the rated voltage.

Step 3   Functionally check the operation of the ground fault monitor panel for:

- Trip test
- No-trip test
- Nonautomatic reset

Step 4   Verify proper sensor polarity on the phase and neutral sensors for residual systems.

Step 5   Measure the system neutral insulation resistance downstream of the neutral disconnect link to verify the absence of grounds.

Step 6   Test systems (zone interlock/time coordinates) by simultaneous ground sensor current injection and monitor for the proper response.

Test result evaluation:

- The system neutral insulation resistance should be above 100Ω and preferably one megohm or greater.
- The maximum pickup setting of the ground fault protection must be 1,200A and the maximum time delay must be one second for ground fault currents equal to or greater than 3,000A (***NEC Article 230-95***).
- The relay pickup current should be within 10% of the manufacturer's calibration marks or fixed setting.
- The relay timing should be in accordance with the manufacturer's published time-current characteristics.

Figure 8 shows the general appearance of an HVL (high-voltage limiting) switch. The HVL switch is a switching device for primary circuits up to the full interrupting current of the switch. The switches are single-throw devices designed for use on 2.4kV to 34.5kV systems.

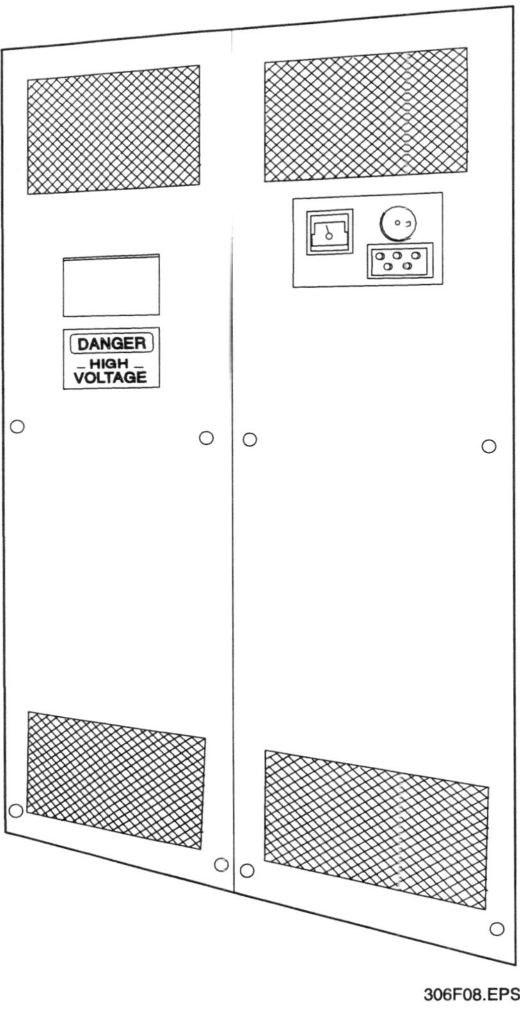

306F08.EPS

Figure 8. HVL Switch

HVL switches may provide both switching and overcurrent protection. HVL switches are commonly used as a service disconnect in unit substations and for sectionalizing medium voltage feeder systems. The HVL switch is designed to conform to ANSI standards for metal enclosed switchgear.

8.1.0   RATINGS

Switch ratings are as follows:

- *Switch kV* – The design voltage for the switch. Of course, nominal system voltage is the normal application method; thus, a 5kV switch may be used for nominal system voltages of 2.4kV or 4.16kV, etc.

- *BIL (kV)* – The maximum voltage pulse that the equipment will withstand.

- *Frequency (Hertz)* – All HVL switches may be used in either 50Hz or 60Hz power systems.

- *Withstand (kV)* – The maximum 60Hz voltage that can be applied to the switch for one minute without causing insulation failure.

- *Capacitor switching (kVAR)* – The maximum capacitance expressed in kVAR that can be switched with the HVL.

- *Fault close* – The maximum, fully offset fault current that the switch can be closed into without sustaining damage. The term *fully offset* means that the fault current will have a delaying DC component in addition to the AC component.

- *Short time current* – The amount of current that the switch will carry for 10 seconds without sustaining any damage.

- *Continuous current (amps)* – The amount of current that the switch will carry continuously.

- *Interrupting current (amps)* – The maximum amount of current that the switch will safely interrupt.

8.2.0 VARIATIONS

There are six main types of switches:

- *Upright* – The upright switch design is the most common type. The upright construction of the service entry, jaws, and arc chutes are located near the top of the cubicle. The hinge point is below the jaws and arc chutes.

- *Inverted* – The inverted switch design has the terminals, jaws, and arc chutes located near the bottom of the cubicle. The hinge point is above the jaws and arc chutes. This type of switch is used primarily as a main switch to a lineup of other switches. Its handle operation is identical to that of an upright switch: to close the switch, the handle is moved up; to open it, the handle is moved down.

- *Fused/unfused* – HVL switches are available in both fused and unfused models. If equipped with fuses, the entire HVL switch has the fault interrupting capacity of the fuse and therefore provides fault protection. Either current-limiting or boric acid fuses may be used in the HVL switch.

- *Duplex* – A duplex switch is actually two switches, each in its own bay. The bays are mechanically connected and the switches are electrically connected on the load side. This switch may be used to supply power to a single load from two different sources.

- *Selector* – A selector allows an HVL switch to have double-throw characteristics. The selector switch is a single switch with a load connected to the moving or switch mechanism. Throwing the switch to one side connects the load to one source, while throwing it the other way connects it to a second source. The selector switch will be interlocked with another switch to prevent the selector switch from interrupting current flow. The selector serves a purpose similar to the duplex switch. However, the selector switch is not an interrupter; it is a disconnect.

- *Motor-operated* – This type of switch is most commonly used as the major component in an automatic transfer scheme. It can also be used when open and close functions are to be initiated from remote locations.

8.3.0 OPENING OPERATION

In the closed position, the main switch blade is engaged on the stationary interrupting contacts. The circuit current flows through the main blades.

As the switch operating handle is moved towards the open position, the stored energy springs are charged. After the springs become fully charged, they toggle over the dead center position, discharging force to the switch operating mechanism.

The action of the switch operating mechanism forces the movable main blade off the stationary main contacts while the interrupting contacts are held closed, momentarily carrying all the current without arcing. Once the main contacts have separated well beyond the striking distance, the interrupting blade contact which was held captive has charged the interrupter blade hub spring, and the interrupter blade is suddenly forced free and flips open.

The resulting arc drawn between the stationary and movable interrupting contacts is elongated and cooled as the plastic arc chute absorbs heat and generates an arc-extinguishing gas to break up and blow out the arc. The combination of arc stretching, arc cooling, and extinguishing gas causes a quick interruption with only minor erosion of the contacts and arc chutes.

The movable main and interrupting contacts continue to the fully open position and are maintained there by spring pressure.

8.4.0 CLOSING

When the switch operating handle is moved towards the closed position, the stored energy springs are being charged and the main blades begin to move. As the main and interrupter blades approach the arc chute, the stored energy springs become fully charged and toggle over the dead center position.

When the main and movable blades approach the main stationary contacts, a high voltage arc leaps across the diminishing air gap in an attempt to complete the circuit. The arc occurs between the tip of the stationary main contacts and a remote corner of the movable main blades. This arc is short and brief since the fast-closing blades minimize the arcing time.

The spring pressure and momentum of the fast-moving main blades completely close the contacts. The force is great enough to cause the contacts to close even against repelling short circuit magnetic forces if a fault exists. At the same time, the interrupter blade tip is driven through the twin stationary interrupting contacts, definitely latching and preparing them for an interrupting operation when the switch is opened.

8.5.0   MAINTENANCE

Maintenance tasks for an HVL switch include the following:

Step 1   The HVL switch should be operated several times. Observe the mechanism and check for binding.

Step 2   Inspect the interrupting and main blades every 100 operations for excessive wear or damage. Replace as necessary. Also, inspect the arc chutes for damage.

Step 3   Clean the switch and its compartment thoroughly. Use a clean cloth and avoid solvents.

Step 4   Lubricate the switch. The pivot points on the switch should be greased. The switch contacts should also be lubricated with a light film of grease after being cleaned.

Step 5   Final maintenance checks include phase-to-ground and phase-to-phase megger testing. If the results are satisfactory, then a DC high potential test is performed.

8.6.0   SLUGGISH OPERATION

A switch that is operating sluggishly hesitates on the opening cycle. This contrasts with the normal snapping action. Observing the interrupter blade during the opening operation is the proper way to determine sluggish operation. Sluggishness must be repaired to prevent the switch from locking up completely. Perform the following procedure:

Step 1   Tease the switch closed and then open again while watching the interrupter blades closely. Sluggishness on close will be noted by the main blade's being engaged behind the contacts of the arc chute. On opening, the interrupter blades may hesitate momentarily.

Step 2   Disconnect the links from the operating shaft. Never operate the switch with the links off as this may break the handle crank casting. This is because the main spring energy is absorbed by the handle crank rather than the main blades.

Step 3   Rotate the handle approximately 45° and hold it in this position while trying to operate the switch by hand. Excessive binding will prevent rotation of the shaft.

Step 4   Check the contact adjustment at the jaw and hinge.

Step 5   Check for binding between the interrupter blade and the arc chute.

Step 6   Remove the front panel over the operating mechanism and disconnect the spring yoke from the cam. Check for binding between the spring pivot and the sides of the operator. Check the spring for breaks.

9.0.0   BOLTED PRESSURE SWITCHES

Bolted pressure switches (*Figures 9* and *10*) are used frequently on service-entrance feeders. They are often used in lieu of circuit breakers because they are inexpensive. Bolted pressure switches can be manually-operated or motor-operated types. However, unlike a circuit breaker, they can only be automatically tripped by three events: a ground fault, a phase failure, or a blown main fuse detector.

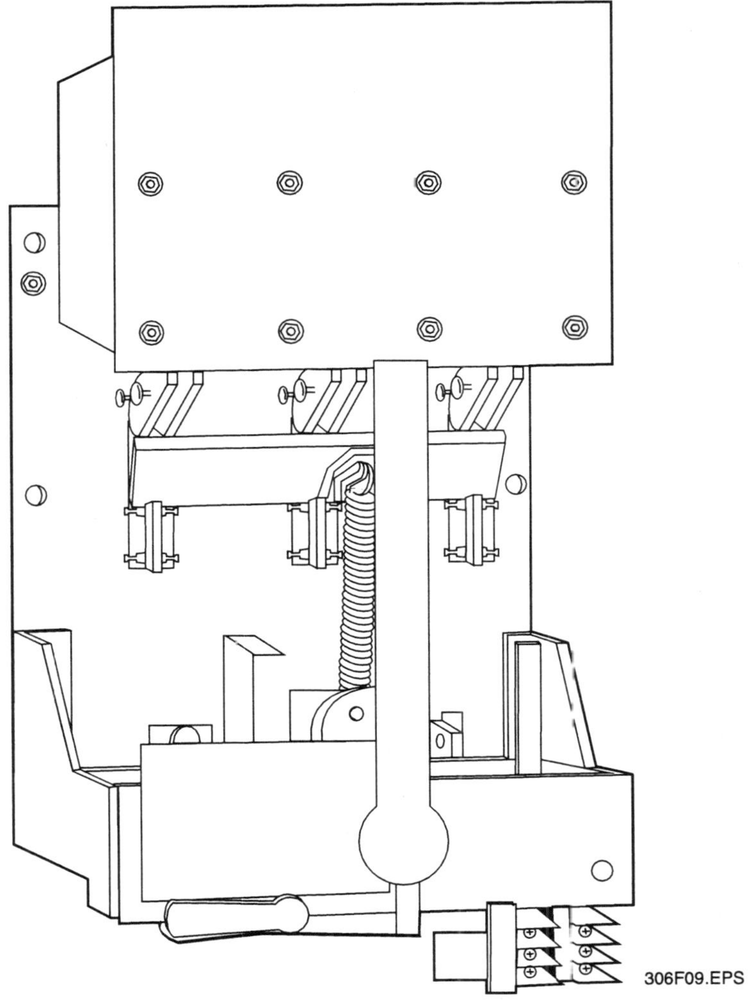

Figure 9. Bolted Pressure Switch

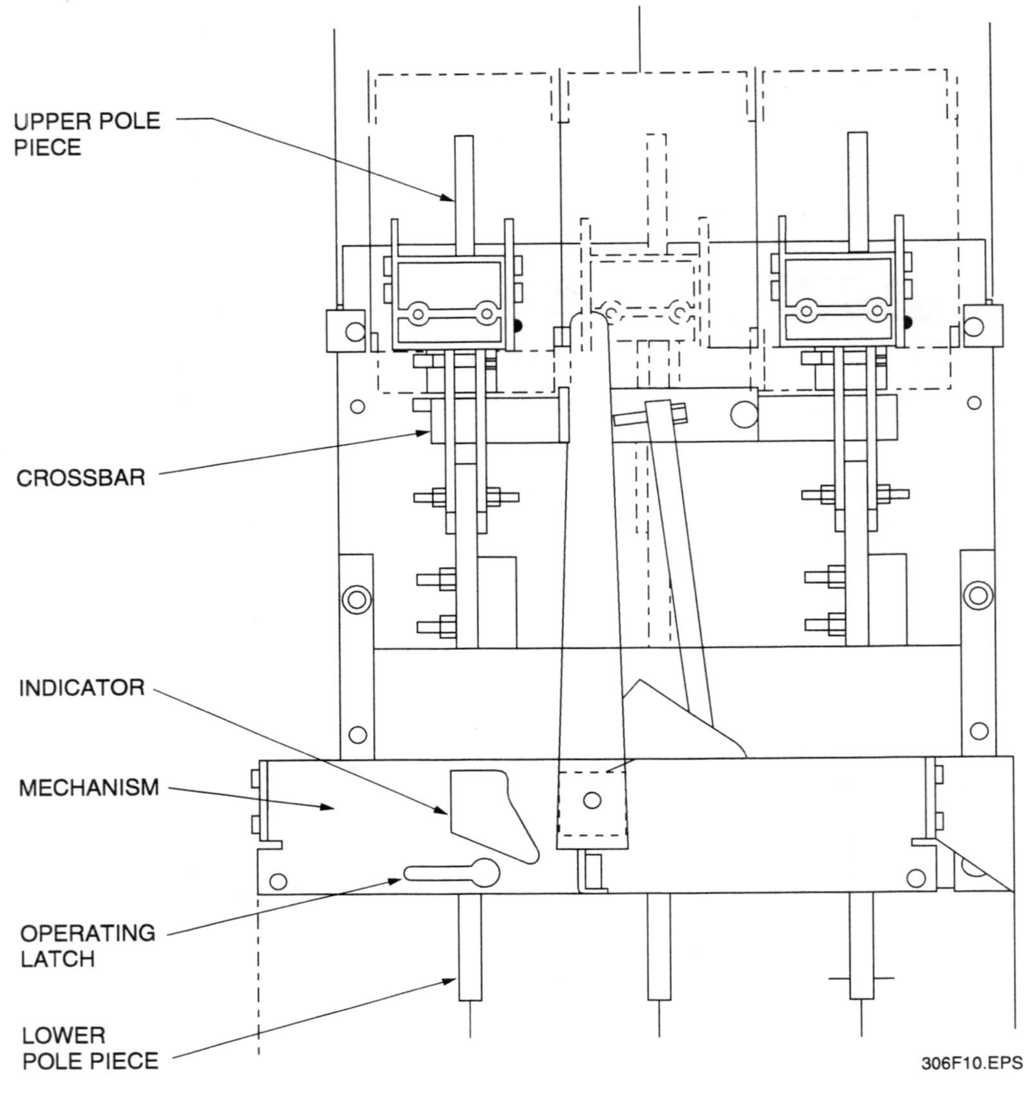

Figure 10. Bolted Pressure Switch (Front View)

9.1.0 GROUND FAULT

Under normal conditions, the currents in all conductors surrounded by the ground fault CT equal zero. When a ground fault occurs, this sensed current increases, eventually reaching the ground fault relay pickup point and causing the bolted pressure switch to trip.

The ground fault system may also be tested. By depressing the test button, a green test light will illuminate, indicating correct circuit operation. To actually test the switch, press the TEST and RESET buttons simultaneously. This sends an actual trip signal through the current sensor, thus tripping the switch. Whenever a bolted pressure switch is tripped, a red light or a red flag will trip. Additionally, the ground fault relay must be reset before the switch can be reclosed.

9.2.0 PHASE FAILURE

If a phase failure relay is installed, it will cause a trip of the bolted pressure switch if a phase is lost. This could occur when a tree limb knocks a line down.

Under this condition, the phase failure relay will sense the lost phase and trip the bolted pressure switch, thus preventing a single-phasing condition.

9.3.0 BLOWN MAIN FUSE DETECTOR

If one of the in-line main fuses were to blow, the blown main fuse detector would detect it and cause a trip of the bolted pressure switch. The trip signal generated comes from a capacitor trip unit. This ensures that power is always available to trip the switch.

9.4.0 MAINTENANCE

These switches have a high failure rate due to lack of maintenance. All manufacturers of bolted pressure switches recommend annual maintenance. Lack of annual maintenance will eventually result in a switch that is stuck shut. Since these switches are often used as service-entrance equipment, a stuck switch can pose immediate personnel safety hazards, as well as equipment failures.

CAUTION: When performing any maintenance, always follow the safety procedures of your company.

Due to the high interrupting capacity of the switch when operated under load, the grease that is used on the movable blades deteriorates over time and eventually turns into an adhesive. Even when the switch is not operated on a recurring basis, the grease still deteriorates due to the high temperatures associated with the current drawn by the phase. The deterioration of this grease has been shown to cause the switch to stick shut. The grease must be cleaned off yearly with denatured alcohol and replaced.

Note: Regular electrical grease cannot be used; use only the grease specifically recommended by the switch manufacturer.

Additionally, infrared scanning of in-service bolted pressure switches has revealed a marked heating concern in switches. A digital low resistance ohmmeter (DLRO) is used to ensure that all three phases carry similar current loads. DLRO readings should never be greater than 75 microhms and there should not be more than a 5% difference between the phases.

Typical annual maintenance includes:

Step 1 Deenergize the switch, lock and tag it, and perform a preliminary operational check.

Step 2   Record pre-maintenance DLRO readings.

Step 3   With the switch open, disassemble the crossbar to free all three phases.

Step 4   Clean off all old grease with denatured alcohol or a similar solvent.

Step 5   Inspect the arc tips and arc chutes for damage.

Step 6   Adjust all pivotal connections on each blade to within the manufacturer's recommended tolerances.

Step 7   Apply an appropriate grease to the movable blades and the area where the blades come in contact with the stationary assembly.

Step 8   Check the pullout torque on each individual blade prior to crossbar reassembly. It should be in accordance with the manufacturer's prescribed limits. Too much torque will result in a switch that will be unable to open under load.

Step 9   Record the DLRO readings.

Step 10   Reassemble the crossbar assembly.

Step 11   Close and open the switch manually several times. Ensure that no phases hang up on the arc chute assembly.

Step 12   Megger the switch.

Step 13   Energize and test all accessories (e.g., ground fault detector, phase failure detector, blown main fuse detector, etc.).

Remember, if the switch is physically stuck shut, deenergize the switch from the incoming power supply and take extra precautions when trying to unstick the switch. It is acceptable to pry the blades open with a large screwdriver, but beware of the excessive outward force that will result from a charged opening spring. To alleviate this, discharge the opening spring before commencing any work on the switch.

10.0.0   TRANSFORMERS

Transformers are used to step voltage up and down in the power transmission and distribution system.

The reason for such high transmission voltages is twofold. First, as a transformer increases transmission voltage, the required current decreases in the same proportion; therefore, larger amounts of power can be transmitted and line losses reduced. Second, to send large amounts of power over long distances at a high current and a low voltage requires a very large diameter wire. The reduction in current reduces the conductor size, which results in a cost reduction.

A transformer is an electrical device that uses the process of electromagnetic induction to change the levels of voltage and current in an AC circuit, without changing the frequency and with very little loss of power.

10.1.0   TRANSFORMER THEORY

As current flows through a conductor, a magnetic field is produced around the conductor. This magnetic field begins to form at the instant current begins to flow, and expands outward from the conductor as the current increases in magnitude.

When the current reaches its peak value, the magnetic field is also at its peak value. When the current decreases, the magnetic field also decreases.

Alternating current (AC) changes direction twice per cycle. These changes in direction or alternation create an expanding and collapsing magnetic field around the conductor.

If the conductor is wound into a coil, the magnetic field expanding from each turn of the coil cuts across other turns of the coil. When the source current starts to reverse direction, the magnetic field collapses, and again the field cuts across the other turns of the coil.

The result in both cases is the same as if a conductor is passed through a magnetic field. An electromotive force (EMF) is induced in the conductor. This EMF is called a *self-induced EMF* because it is induced in the conductor carrying the current.

The direction of this induced EMF is always opposite the direction of the EMF which caused the current to flow initially. This principle is known as Lenz's Law:

- An induced EMF always has such a direction as to oppose the action that produced it.
- For this reason, the EMF induced is also known as a *counter-electromotive force (CEMF)*.

The counter-electromotive force reaches a value nearly equal to the applied voltage; thus, the primary current is limited when the secondary is open circuited.

10.1.1   No-Load Operation

The operation of a transformer is based on the principle that electrical energy can be transferred efficiently by mutual induction from one winding to another. When the primary winding is energized from an AC source, an alternating magnetic flux is established in the transformer core. This flux links the turns of the primary with the secondary, thereby inducing a voltage in them. Since the same flux cuts both windings, the same voltage is induced in each turn of both windings. Whenever the secondary of a transformer is left disconnected (or open), there is no current drawn by the secondary winding. The primary winding draws the amount of current required to supply the magnetomotive force, which produces the transformer core flux. This current is called the *exciting* or *magnetizing current*.

The exciting current is limited by the CEMF the primary and a small amount of resistance which cannot be avoided in any current-carrying conductor.

10.1.2 Load Operation

When a load is connected to the secondary winding of a transformer, the secondary current flowing through the secondary turns produces a counter-magnetomotive force. According to Lenz's Law, this magnetomotive force is in a direction that opposes the flux which produced it. This opposition tends to reduce the transformer flux and is accompanied by a reduction in the CEMF in the primary. Since the primary current is limited by the internal impedance of the primary winding and the CEMF in the winding, whenever the CEMF is reduced, the primary current continues to increase until the original transformer flux reaches a state of equilibrium.

10.2.0 TRANSFORMER TYPES

Transformers can be divided into two main categories: power transformers and **distribution transformers**. Power transformers handle large amounts of power and are generally used at transmission level voltages. Distribution transformers are designed to handle larger currents at lower voltage levels. Distribution transformers have smaller kVA ratings and are physically much smaller than power transformers. Power transformers often have an auxiliary means of cooling, such as fans and radiators. Distribution transformers are usually self-cooled, with no fans or other cooling methods. Where distribution transformers may be pole-mounted or pad-mounted, power transformers are always pad-mounted.

Although there is some overlap between power and distribution transformers, a transformer that is rated at more than 500kVA and/or 34.5kV is generally a power transformer. A transformer rated below these values can be considered a distribution transformer. Remember, there is an overlap in kVA capacity and voltage, depending on the system and power requirements.

10.3.0 DRY TRANSFORMERS (AIR-COOLED)

Many transformers do not use an insulating liquid to immerse the core and windings. Dry or air-cooled transformers are used for many jobs where small, low-kVA transformers are required. Large distribution transformers are usually oil-filled for better cooling and insulating. However, for installations in buildings and other locations where the oil in oil-filled transformers would be a serious fire hazard, dry transformers are used. These transformers are generally of the core form. The core and coils are similar to those of other transformers. A three-phase, dry-type transformer is shown in *Figure 11*. The enclosing side plates on the high-voltage side have been removed to show the baffles which control the direction of air circulation.

The case is made of sheet metal and provided with ventilating louvers for the circulation of cooling air. To increase the output, fans can be installed to draw cooling air through the coils at a faster rate than is possible with natural circulation.

Figure 11. Dry-Type Transformer

Either Class B or Class H insulation is used for the windings. Class B insulation may be operated safely at a hot-spot temperature of 130°C. Class H insulation may be operated safely at a hot-spot temperature of 180°C. The use of these materials makes it possible to manufacture smaller transformers. Both Class B and Class H insulation consist of mica, asbestos, fiberglass, and similar inorganic material. Temperature-resistant organic varnishes are used as the binder for Class B insulation. Silicone or fluorine compounds or similar materials are used as the binder for Class H insulation. Such transformers use high-temperature insulation only in locations where the high temperature requires such insulation.

10.4.0   SEALED DRY TRANSFORMERS

Hermetically-sealed dry transformers are constructed in large sizes for voltages above 15kV. They are used for installations in buildings and other locations where oil-filled transformers would be a serious fire hazard, but may also be used for lower voltages and kVA ratings, and for water-submersible transformers in locations subject to floods.

Nitrogen is typically used for the insulation and cooling of sealed dry transformers.

10.5.0 TRANSFORMER NAMEPLATE DATA

Transformer nameplate data includes the following:

- *Electrical ratings* – The information relating to the transformer electrical parameters can be found on the nameplate.
- *Voltage ratings* – The voltage rating identifies the nominal root mean square (rms) voltage value at which the transformer is designed to operate. A transformer can operate within a ±5% range of its rated primary voltage. If the primary voltage is increased to more than +5%, the windings of the transformer can overheat. Operation of the transformer at more than –5% decreases its power output proportional to the percent voltage reduction. Transformer windings are rated as follows:
  - Phase-to-phase and phase-to-neutral for wye windings (e.g., 480Y/277VAC)
  - Phase-to-phase for delta windings (e.g., 480VAC)
  - Dual-voltage windings (e.g., 480VAC × 240VAC)

When transformers are equipped with a tap changer, the voltage ratings in the nameplate indicate the nominal voltages.

- *BIL* – This identifies the maximum impulse voltage the winding insulation can withstand without failure.
- *Phase* – The phase information indicates the number of phase windings contained in a transformer tank.
- *Frequency* – The frequency rating of a transformer is the normal operating system frequency. When a transformer is operated at a lower frequency, the reactance of the primary winding decreases. This causes a higher exciting current and an increase in flux density. In addition, there is an increase in core loss, which results in overall heating.
- *Class* – Transformers are classified by the type of cooling they employ.
- *Temperature rise* – The temperature rise rating is the maximum elevation above ambient temperature that can be tolerated without causing insulation damage.
- *Capacity* – The capacity of a transformer to transfer energy is related to its ability to dissipate the heat produced in the windings. The capacity rating is the product of the rated voltage and the current that can be carried at that voltage without exceeding the temperature rise limitation.
- *Impedance* – Impedance identifies the opposition of a transformer to the passage of short circuit current.
- *Phasor diagrams* – Phasor diagrams show phase and polarity relationships of the high and low windings. They can be used with the schematic connection diagram to provide test connection points and to provide proper external system connections.

10.6.0   TRANSFORMER CASE INSPECTIONS

When inspecting the inside of a transformer case, look for the following:

- Bent, broken, or loose parts
- Debris on the floor or in the coils
- Corrosion of any part
- Worn or frayed insulation
- Shifted core members
- Damaged tap changer mounts or mechanisms
- Misaligned core spacers and loose coil elements
- Broken or loose blocking

Upon the completion of the inspection, replace the covers and bolt securely. All information should be recorded on appropriate inspection sheets.

10.7.0   TRANSFORMER TESTS

The following list of tests are the recommended minimum tests that should be included as part of a maintenance program. These tests are conducted to determine and evaluate the present condition of the transformer. From the results of these tests, a determination is made as to whether the transformer is suitable for service.

- *Continuity and winding resistance test* – There should be a continuity check of all windings. If possible, measure the winding resistance and compare it to the factory test values. An increase of more than 10% could indicate loose internal connections.
- *Insulation resistance test* – To ensure that no grounding of the windings exist, a 1,000V insulation resistance test should be made.
- *Ratio test* – A turns ratio test should be made to ensure proper transformer ratios and that all connections were made. If equipped with a tap changer, all positions should be checked.
- *Core ground* – This test is performed in the same way as the insulation resistance test, except the measurement is made from the core to the frame and ground bus. Remove the core ground strap before the test.
- *Heat scanning* – After the transformer is energized, a heat scan test should be done to detect loose connections. This test is performed using an infrared scanning device which shows or indicates hot spots.

For all practical purposes, the voltages and currents used in the primary circuits of substations are much too large to be used to provide operating quantities to relaying or metering circuits. In order to reduce voltage and currents to usable levels, instrument transformers are employed.

Instrument transformers are used to:

- Protect personnel and equipment from the high voltages and/or currents used in electric power transmission and distribution.

- Provide reasonable use of insulation levels and current-carrying capacity in relay and metering systems and other control devices.

- Provide a means to combine voltage and/or current phasors to simplify relaying or metering.

Instrument transformers are manufactured with a multitude of different ratios to provide a standard output for the many different system primary voltage levels and load currents.

There are two major classifications of instrument transformers: potential (voltage) transformers and current transformers.

11.1.0   POTENTIAL TRANSFORMERS

A potential transformer is designed to reduce high primary system voltages down to usable levels. Potential transformers are used whenever the system primary voltage exceeds 600V, and also on many 240V and 480V systems.

The standard secondary circuit voltage level for a potential transformer circuit is 120V for circuits below 25kV and 115V for circuits above 25kV at the potential transformer's rated primary voltage. These voltages correspond to typical transformation ratios of standard transmission voltages. The current flowing in the secondary of the potential transformer circuit is very low under normal operating conditions, typically less than one ampere.

Potential transformers are constructed as lightly-loaded distribution transformers with the design emphasis on winding ratio accuracy rather than thermal ratings. Potential transformer construction can be of the air-insulated dry type, case epoxy-insulated, oil-filled, or SF6-insulated, depending upon the primary circuit voltage level.

The standard output voltage of potential transformers is either 120V or 69.3V, depending on whether its primary uses phase-to-phase or phase-to-neutral connections. Understanding the operation of a potential transformer is simplified by the inspection of its equivalent circuit.

Potential transformers must have their secondary circuits grounded for safety reasons in the event that a short circuit develops between the primary and secondary windings, and to negate the effects of parasitic capacitance between the primary and the secondary. *Figure 12* shows the connection of an ideal potential transformer circuit.

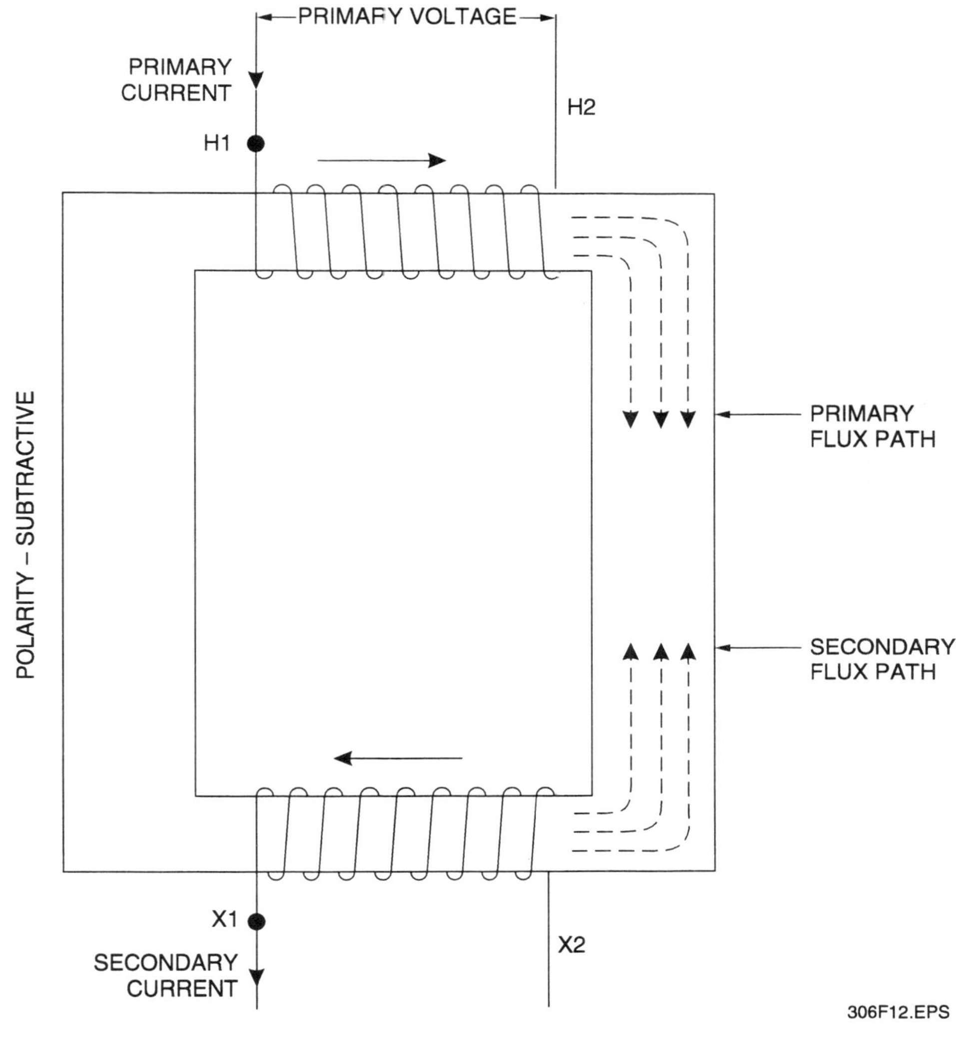

Figure 12. Potential Transformer Construction

11.2.0   CURRENT TRANSFORMERS

A current transformer is designed to reduce high primary system currents down to usable levels.

Current transformers are used whenever system primary voltage isolation is required.

The standard secondary circuit current for a current transformer circuit is 5A with full-rated current flowing in the primary circuit. The voltage level in the secondary circuit is typically very low under normal operating conditions; however, the voltage level across a current transformer's secondary terminals can rise to a very dangerous level if the secondary circuit becomes opened while the primary circuit is energized.

The primary considerations in current transformer design are the current-carrying capability and saturation characteristics. Insulation systems are of the same generic types as potential transformers; however, SF6 insulation is infrequently used in current transformer construction.

Current transformers are manufactured in four basic types: oil-filled (e.g., donut type), bar, window, and **bushing** type. The bushing-type transformer is normally applied on circuit breakers or power transformers. The other types are used for the remaining indoor and outdoor installations. *Figure 13* illustrates some common types of current transformer construction.

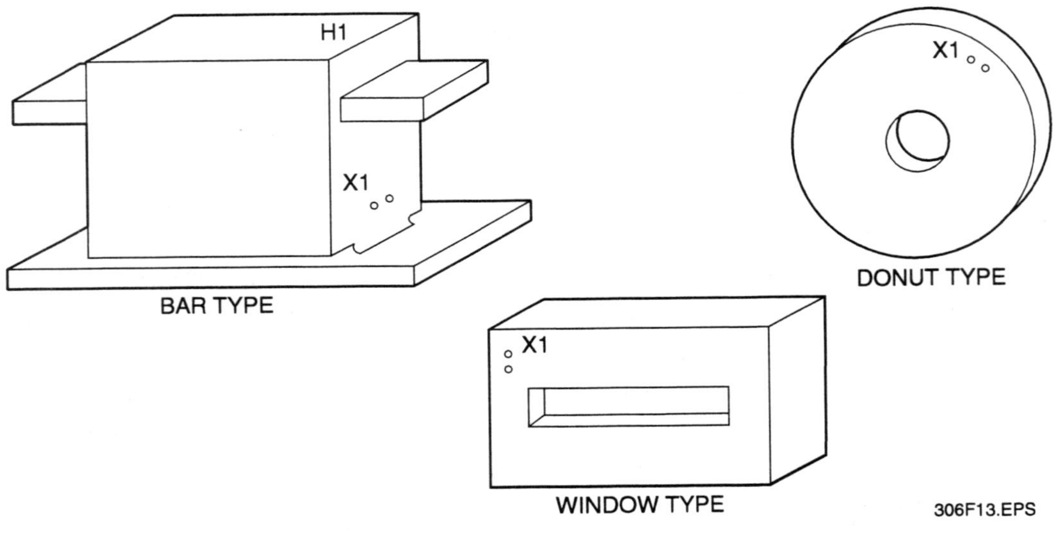

Figure 13. Types Of Current Transformer Construction

The major criterion for the selection of the current transformer for relaying is its primary current rating, maximum burden, and saturation characteristics. Saturation is particularly important in relaying due to the fact that many relays are called upon to operate only under fault conditions.

Current transformer circuits operate at a very low voltage. Connected loads (burdens) range from 0.2Ω to 2Ω. These small impedances, together with a maximum continuous current of up to 5A, keep these circuits at low potentials. The voltage can become high momentarily during faults when large secondary currents flow. This voltage is a function of the current, burden, and transformer VA capability.

As with potential transformers, current transformers must also have their secondary windings grounded in the event of an insulation breakdown between the primary and secondary, and to negate the effects of parasitic capacitance.

ELECTRICAL — TRAINEE TASK MODULE 26306

11.3.0   INSTRUMENT TRANSFORMER MAINTENANCE

Instrument transformers require regular inspection and maintenance. The inspection should cover the following points:

Step 1   Inspect for physical damage and check the nameplate information for compliance with instructions and specification requirements.

Step 2   Verify the proper connection of transformers against the system requirements.

Step 3   Verify the tightness of all bolted connections and ensure that adequate clearances exist between the primary circuits and the secondary circuit wiring.

Step 4   Verify that all required grounding and shorting connections provide good contact.

Step 5   Test for proper operation of the transformer withdrawal mechanism (trip out) and grounding operation, when applicable.

12.0.0   CIRCUIT BREAKERS

Circuit breakers are the only circuit interrupting devices which combine a full fault current interruption rating and the ability to be manually or automatically opened or closed.

A circuit breaker is defined as a mechanical switching device that is capable of making, carrying, and breaking currents under normal circuit conditions and also making, carrying (for a specified time), and breaking currents under specified abnormal circuit conditions, such as a short circuit (according to IEEE).

The four general classifications of circuit breakers are:

- **Air circuit breakers** (ACBs)
- Oil circuit breakers (OCBs)
- Vacuum circuit breakers (VCBs)
- Gas circuit breakers (GCBs)

Circuit breakers may conveniently be divided into low-voltage, medium-voltage, and high-voltage classes. Although there is considerable overlap among these classes, each one has certain characteristic features.

12.1.0   CIRCUIT BREAKER RATINGS

Circuit breaker ratings are given on the breaker nameplate. The information from the nameplate should be reviewed when considering any breaker selection problem. The same rating information should be included in any documentation for breaker applications. The rating information includes some of the following items:

- *Rated voltage* – The rated voltage is the maximum voltage for which the circuit breaker is designed.

- *Rated current* – This is the continuous current that the circuit breaker can carry without exceeding a standard temperature rise (usually 55°C).

- *Interrupting rating* – This is the maximum value of current at rated voltage that the circuit breaker is required to successfully interrupt for a limited number of operations under specified conditions. The term is usually applied to abnormal or emergency conditions.

13.0.0 ELECTRICAL DRAWING IDENTIFICATION

Before looking at actual plant diagrams, it is necessary to understand the symbology used to condense electrical drawings. The designer uses symbols and abbreviations as a type of shorthand. This section will present the standard symbols, abbreviations, and device numbers which make up the designer's shorthand.

13.1.0 ELECTRICAL DIAGRAM SYMBOLOGY

It is imperative that every line, symbol, figure, and letter is a diagram have a specific purpose and that the information be presented in its most concise form. For example, when the rating of a current transformer is given, a transformer symbol is shown, and an abbreviation such as CT is not needed; the information is implied by the symbol itself. Writing the unit of measure (amp) in this case is also unnecessary, since a current transformer is always rated in amperes. Thus, the numerical rating and the transformer symbol are sufficient. The key to reading and interpreting electrical diagrams is to understand and use the electrical legend. The legend shows the symbols used in the diagram, and also contains general notes and other important information. Most electrical legends are very similar; however, there are some variations between the legends developed by different companies. Only the legend specifically designed for a given set of drawings should be used for those drawings.

The legend prevents the necessity of memorizing all the symbols presented on a diagram and can be used as a reference for unfamiliar symbols. Typically, the legend will be found in the bottom right corner of a print or on a separate drawing. In addition to symbols, abbreviations are an important part of the designer's shorthand. For example, a circle can be used to symbolize a meter, relay, motor, or indicating light. A circle's application can generally be distinguished by its location in the circuit; however, the designer uses a set of standard abbreviations to make the distinction clear. The following abbreviations are used to represent meters:

A	Ammeter
AH	Ampere-hour meter
CRO	Oscilloscope
DM	Demand meter
F	Frequency meter

GD	Ground detector
OHM	Ohmmeter
OSC	Oscillograph
PF	Power factor meter
PH	Phase meter
SYN	Synchroscope
TD	Transducer
V	Voltmeter
VA	Volt-ammeter
VAR	VAR meter
VARH	VAR hour meter
W	Wattmeter
WH	Watt-hour meter

As mentioned earlier, indicating lamps may also be represented by a circle. The following abbreviations are used to represent indicating lamps:

A	Amber
B	Blue
C	Clear
G	Green
R	Red
W	White

Relays are another component commonly represented by a circle. The following abbreviations are used for relays:

CC	Closing coil
CR	Closing/control relay
TC	Trip coil
TR	Trip relay
TD	Time-delay relay
TDE	Time-delay energize
TDD	Time-delay deenergize
X	Auxiliary relay

Still another component that is commonly represented by a circle is the motor. Motors usually have the horsepower rating in or near the circle representing them. The abbreviation for horsepower is HP (or hp). Any other piece of equipment represented by a circle will be identified in the legend, notes, or spelled out on the diagram itself.

Contacts and switches are also identified using standard abbreviations. The following is a list of these abbreviations:

a	Breaker A contact
b	Breaker B contact
BAS	Bell alarm switch
BLPB	Backlighted pushbutton
CS	Control switch
FS	Flow switch
LS	Limit switch
PB	Pushbutton
PS	Pressure switch
PSD	Differential pressure switch
TDO	Time-delay open
TDC	Time-delay closed
TS	Temperature switch
XSH	Auxiliary switch

The following figures illustrate examples of these abbreviations and symbols.

Figure 14 shows A and B contacts in their normally deenergized state. If relay CR is deenergized, contact A is open and contact B is shut. When relay CR is energized, contact A is shut and contact B is open.

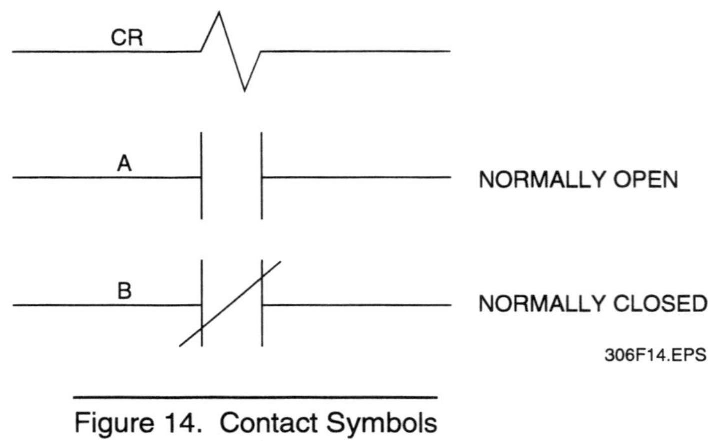

Figure 14. Contact Symbols

Figure 15 illustrates a control switch and its associated contacts. Contacts 1 through 4 open and close as a result of the operation of control switch 1 (CS1).

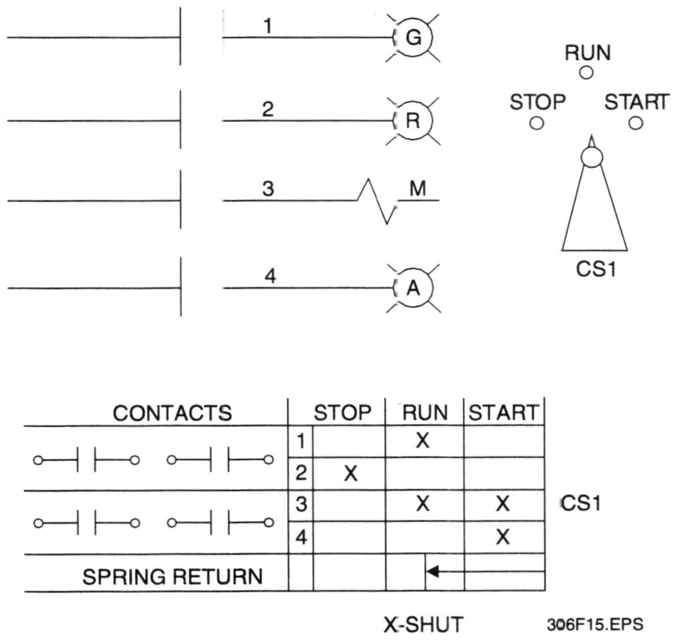

Figure 15. Switch Development

In the stop position, contact 2 is shut and the red indicating lamp is lit. In the start position, contacts 3 and 4 are shut, energizing the M coil and the amber indicating lamp, respectively. When the switch handle is released, the spring returns to the run position and contact 4 opens, deenergizing the amber lamp and closing contact 1 to energize the green lamp.

There are many abbreviations used on electrical drawings. The designer makes an effort to use standard abbreviations; however, you will encounter nonstandard abbreviations. Nonstandard abbreviations will typically be defined in the diagram notes or legend. *Figure 16* defines abbreviations commonly used in wiring prints and specifications. The symbols further illustrate descriptions of the abbreviations.

SPST N.O.		SPST N.C.		SPDT		TERMS	
SINGLE BREAK	DOUBLE BREAK	SINGLE BREAK	DOUBLE BREAK	SINGLE BREAK	DOUBLE BREAK	SPST	SINGLE-POLE SINGLE-THROW
						SPDT	SINGLE-POLE DOUBLE-THROW
DSPT 2N.O.		DSPT 2N.C.		DPDT		DPST	DOUBLE-POLE SINGLE-THROW
SINGLE BREAK	DOUBLE BREAK	SINGLE BREAK	DOUBLE BREAK	SINGLE BREAK	DOUBLE BREAK	DPDT	DOUBLE-POLE DOUBLE-THROW
						N.O.	NORMALLY OPEN
						N.C.	NORMALLY CLOSED

Figure 16. Supplementary Contact Symbols

This section will cover the specific types of electrical prints that you need to be familiar with in order to install and maintain electrical systems.

14.1.0 SINGLE-LINE DIAGRAMS

Analyzing and reading complex electrical circuits can be very difficult. Diagrams are simplified to single-line (one-line) diagrams to aid in reading the prints.

A one-line diagram is defined as a diagram that indicates by means of single lines and standard symbology the paths, interconnections, and component parts of an electric circuit or system of circuits. This type of drawing uses a single line to represent all conductors (phases) of the system. All components of power circuits are represented by symbols and notations. One-line diagrams are valuable tools for system visualization during planning, installation, operation, and maintenance, and they provide a basic understanding of how a portion of the electrical system functions in terms of the physical components of the circuit.

There are two types of single-line diagrams: the overall plant single-line diagram and the project single-line diagram. Overall plant single-line diagrams show the electrical power distribution system, in simplified form, from the utility or generated supply to the load side of the substation protection devices. The overall plant single-line diagrams do not include distribution panels, motor control centers, motors, or similar electrical equipment located on the load side of the substation. Project single-line diagrams show the electrical power distribution and utilization for a particular project or local plant area. These diagrams are the continuation of overall plant single-line diagrams and indicate the power distribution from the load side of the substation protective device to the final point of utilization on a branch circuit. This diagram will generally be of more use than the overall plant diagram. An example of a single-line diagram is shown in *Figure 17*.

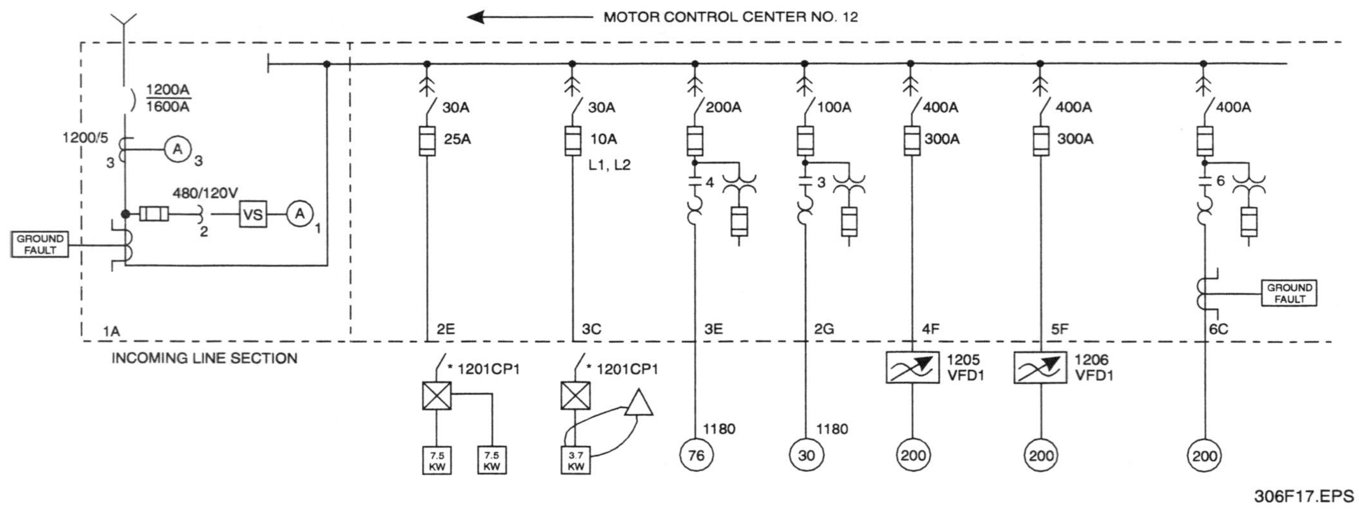

Figure 17. One-Line Diagram

14.2.0 ELEMENTARY DIAGRAMS

An elementary diagram is a drawing that falls between one-line diagrams and schematics in terms of complexity. An elementary diagram is a wiring diagram showing how each individual conductor is connected. *Figure 18* is an example of an elementary diagram.

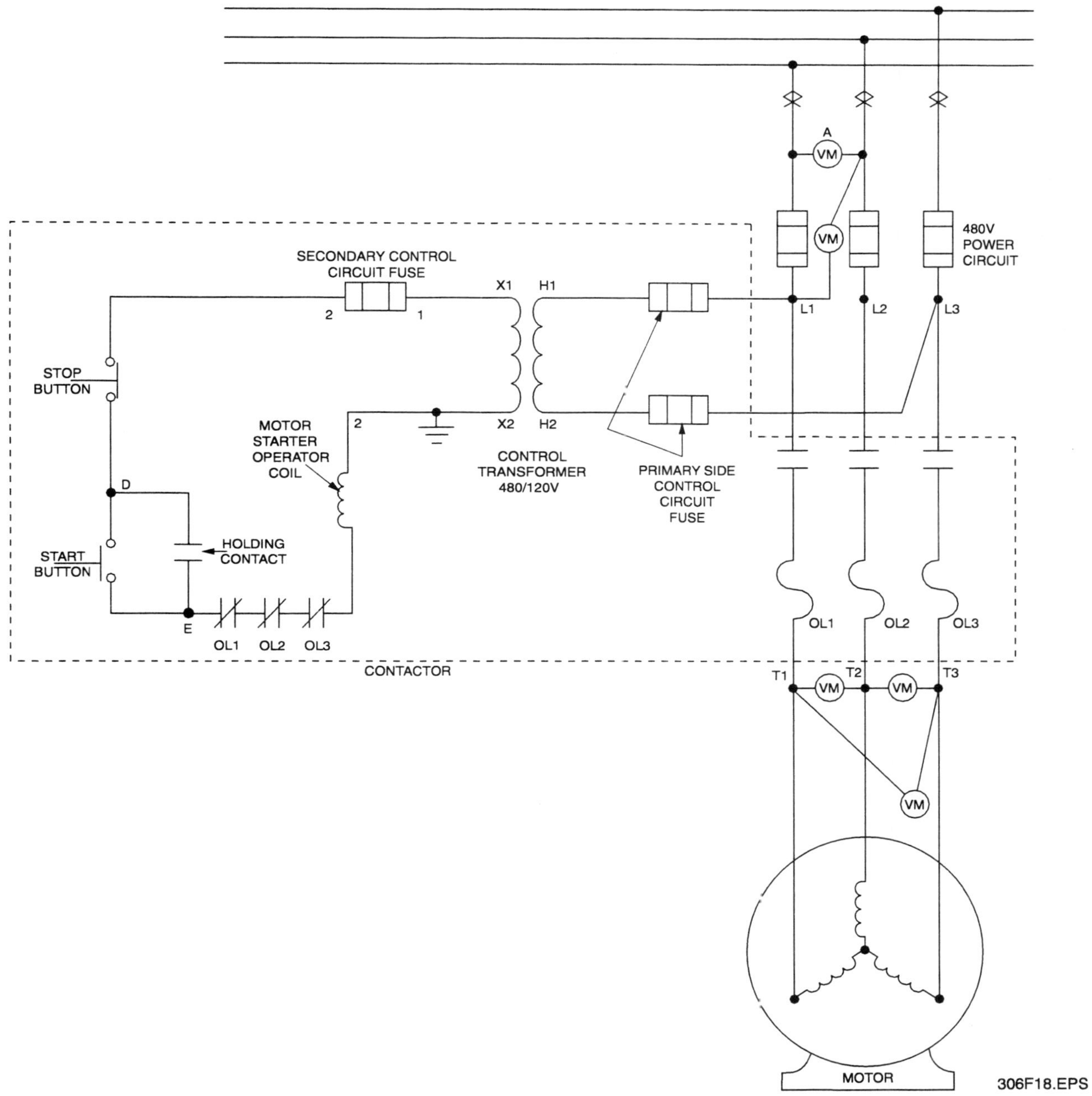

Figure 18. Elementary Diagram

Elementary diagrams, interconnection diagrams, and connection diagrams all illustrate individual conductors. Elementary diagrams are used to show the wiring of instrument and electrical control devices in an elementary ladder or schematic form. The elementary diagram reflects the control wiring required to achieve the operation and sequence of operations described in the logic diagram. When presented in ladder form, the vertical lines in each ladder diagram represent the hot and neutral wires of a 120VAC circuit. If a number of schemes are connected to the same 120VAC circuit, the vertical lines are continuous from the top to the bottom of the ladder. The hot wire is always shown on the left side of the ladder and the neutral on the right. A ground symbol is normally not shown on the neutral wire.

The hot and neutral wire numbers are shown at the top of the vertical lines on each ladder diagram. The circuit identification number and source of the 120VAC circuit are also shown at the top center of each ladder. If two or more 120VAC circuits are represented in a single ladder, the vertical lines are broken, and the wire numbers and circuit identification are entered, at the top of each ladder segment. Each horizontal line in a ladder diagram represents a circuit path. All devices shown on a single horizontal line represent a series circuit path; parallel circuit paths are shown on two or more horizontal lines.

14.3.0   INTERCONNECTION DIAGRAMS

When troubleshooting electrical circuits, you may use an elementary circuit diagram to determine the cause of a failure; however, since elementary diagrams are drawn without regard to physical locations, connection diagrams should be used to aid in locating faulty components. Interconnection and connection diagrams are structured in such a way that they present all the wires which were shown in the elementary drawing in their actual locations. These drawings show all electrical connections within an enclosure, with each wire labeled to indicate where each end of the wire is terminated.

The interconnection diagram is made to show the actual wiring connections between unit assemblies or equipment. Internal wiring connections within unit assemblies or equipment are usually omitted. The interconnection diagrams will appear adjacent to the schematic diagram or on a separate drawing, depending upon the format chosen when making the schematic diagram. The development of the interconnection diagram is integrated with that of the schematic diagram and only the equipment, terminal blocks, and wiring pertinent to the accompanying schematic diagram appear in the interconnection diagram.

A typical interconnection diagram will contain the following information:

- An outline of the equipment involved in its relative physical location
- Terminal blocks in the equipment that are concerned with the wiring illustrated on the schematic
- Wire numbers, cable sizes, cable numbers, cable routing, and cable tray identification (should not be repeated on the interconnection diagram except where necessary)

- Wiring between equipment (normally shown as individual cables, but may be combined on complex drawings)
- Equipment identification information

14.4.0 CONNECTION DIAGRAMS

The connection diagram shows the internal wiring connections between the parts that make up an apparatus. It will contain as much detail as necessary to make or trace any electrical connections involved. A connection diagram generally shows the physical arrangement of component electrical connections. It differs from the interconnection diagram by excluding external connections between two or more unit assemblies or pieces of equipment.

The schematic diagram shows the arrangement of a circuit with the components represented by conventional symbols. Its intent is to show the function of a circuit. The schematic, like the elementary drawing, is not laid out with respect to physical locations.

A wiring diagram also shows the physical locations of all electrical equipment and/or components with all interconnecting wiring. It shows the actual connection point of every wire and the color of the wires connected to each terminal of every component. It allows the electrician to easily locate terminals and wires. A wiring diagram in conjunction with a schematic greatly aids in troubleshooting a given piece of equipment. Connection diagrams can be shown in various forms.

The following sections illustrate two types of connection diagrams.

14.4.1 Point-To-Point Method

This form is used for the simpler diagrams where sufficient space is available to show each individual wire without sacrificing the clarity of the diagram. *Figure 19* is a point-to-point connection diagram.

14.4.2 Cable Method

In complex diagrams, individual wires are cabled so as to conserve drawing space. *Figure 20* is a cable method connection diagram.

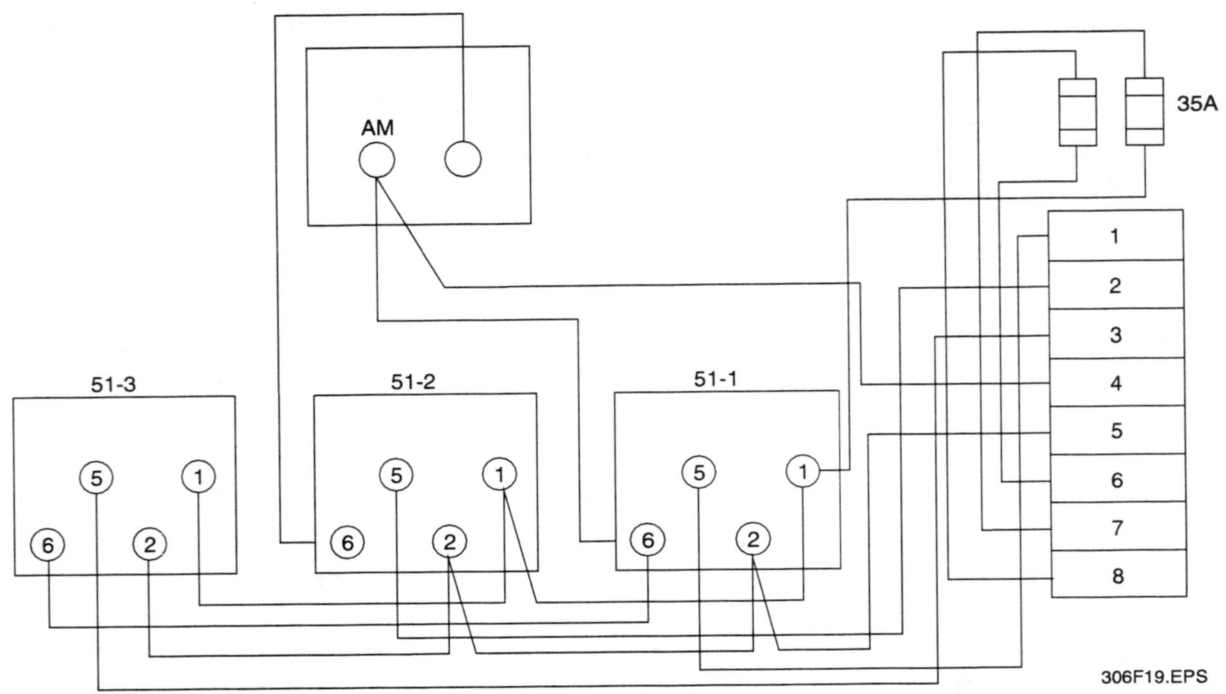

Figure 19. Point-To-Point Connection Diagram

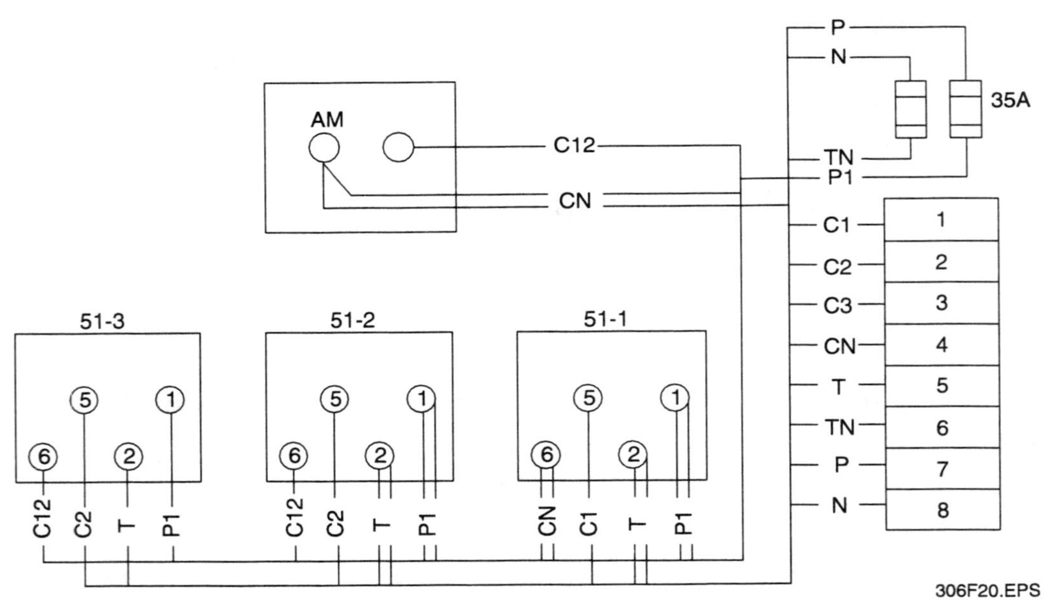

Figure 20. Cable Method Connection Diagram

ELECTRICAL — TRAINEE TASK MODULE 26306

The one-line diagram in *Figures 21* and *22* is typical of those used to show how an electrical system is to be installed. In general, a one-line diagram is never drawn to scale. Such drawings show the major components in an electrical system and then use only one drawing line to indicate the connections between these components. Even though only one line is used between components, this single line may indicate a raceway of two, three, four, or more conductors. Notes, symbols, tables, and detailed drawings are used to supplement and clarify a one-line diagram. Refer again to *Figures 21* and *22*. These drawings were prepared by an electrical manufacturing company to give workers at the job site an overview of a 2,000kVA substation utilizing a 13.8kV primary and a 4.16kV, three-phase, three-wire, 60Hz secondary. Note that this drawing sheet is divided into the following sections:

- Service order (S.O.) numbers
- Unit numbers
- One-line diagram
- Title block
- Revision notes

Service order numbers are arranged at the top of the drawing sheet in a time sequence, bar-chart type arrangement. For example, S.O. #58454 deals with the primary side of the 2,000kVa transformer, including the transformer itself. This section includes a high-voltage switchgear with an indoor/outdoor enclosure. The switchgear itself consists of two HLP-C interrupter switches, each rated at 15kV, 600A, with 150E current-limiting fuses (CLF).

Service order #58455 deals with the wiring and related components on the secondary side of the transformer and begins with a low-voltage switchgear with an indoor/outdoor enclosure.

Service order #58454 is further subdivided into three units which are indicated as such on the drawing immediately under the S.O. number. Unit #1 deals with incoming line #1; Unit #2 deals with incoming line #2; and Unit #3 covers the 2,000kVA transformer and its related connections and components.

Service order #58455 is further subdivided into two units: Unit #4 and Unit #5. Basically, Unit #4 covers grounding, the installation of current transformers, various meters, potential transformers, a 10kVA, 4,160/240V transformer, and a six-circuit panel, all derived from a 600A, 4,160V, three-wire, 60Hz main bus.

Unit #5 continues with the main bus and covers the installation and connection of a complete motor control center, along with another fully-equipped future space, less **contactors**.

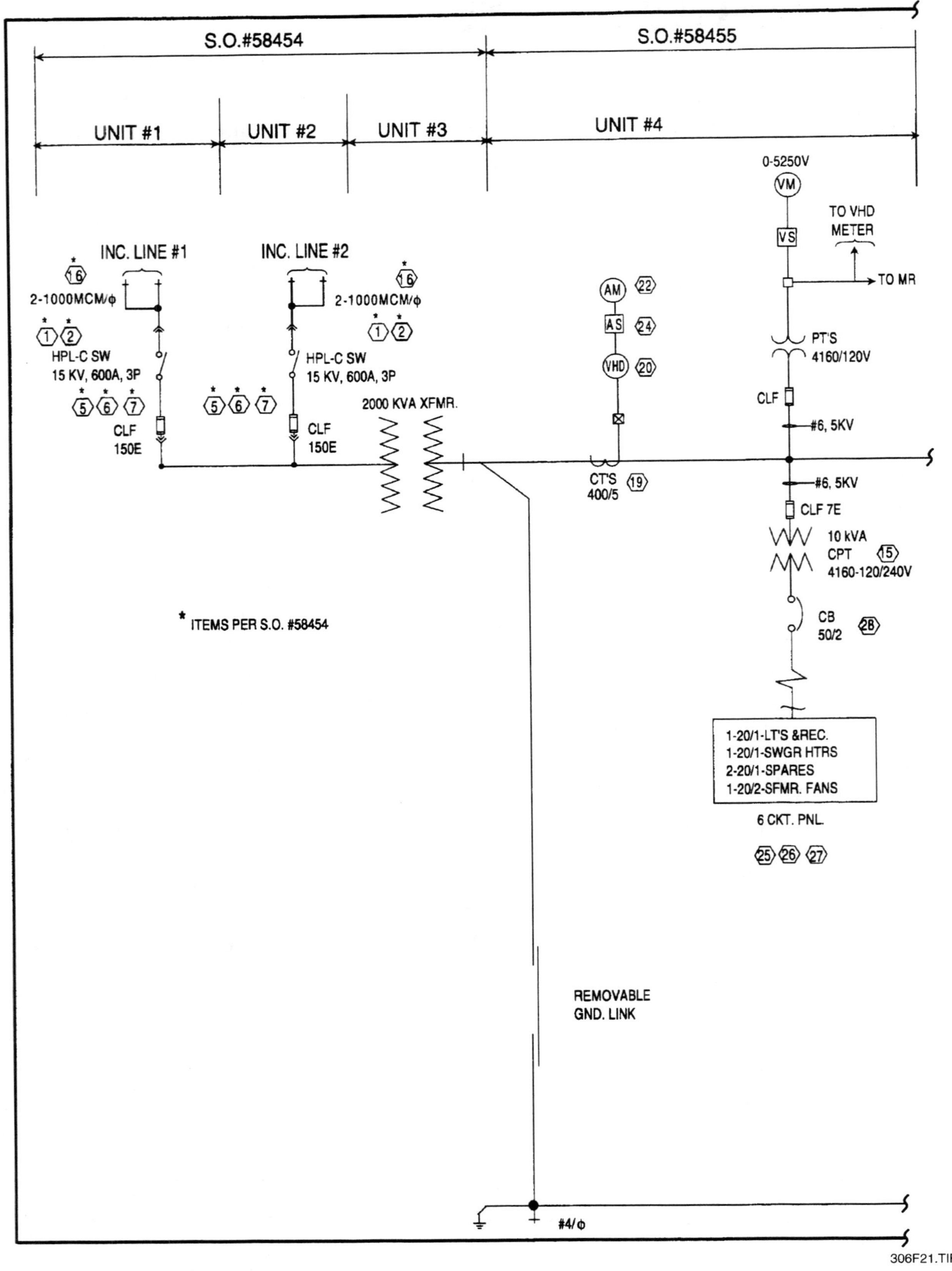

Figure 21. One-Line Diagram Of A 2,000kVA Substation (Left Side)

ELECTRICAL — TRAINEE TASK MODULE 26306

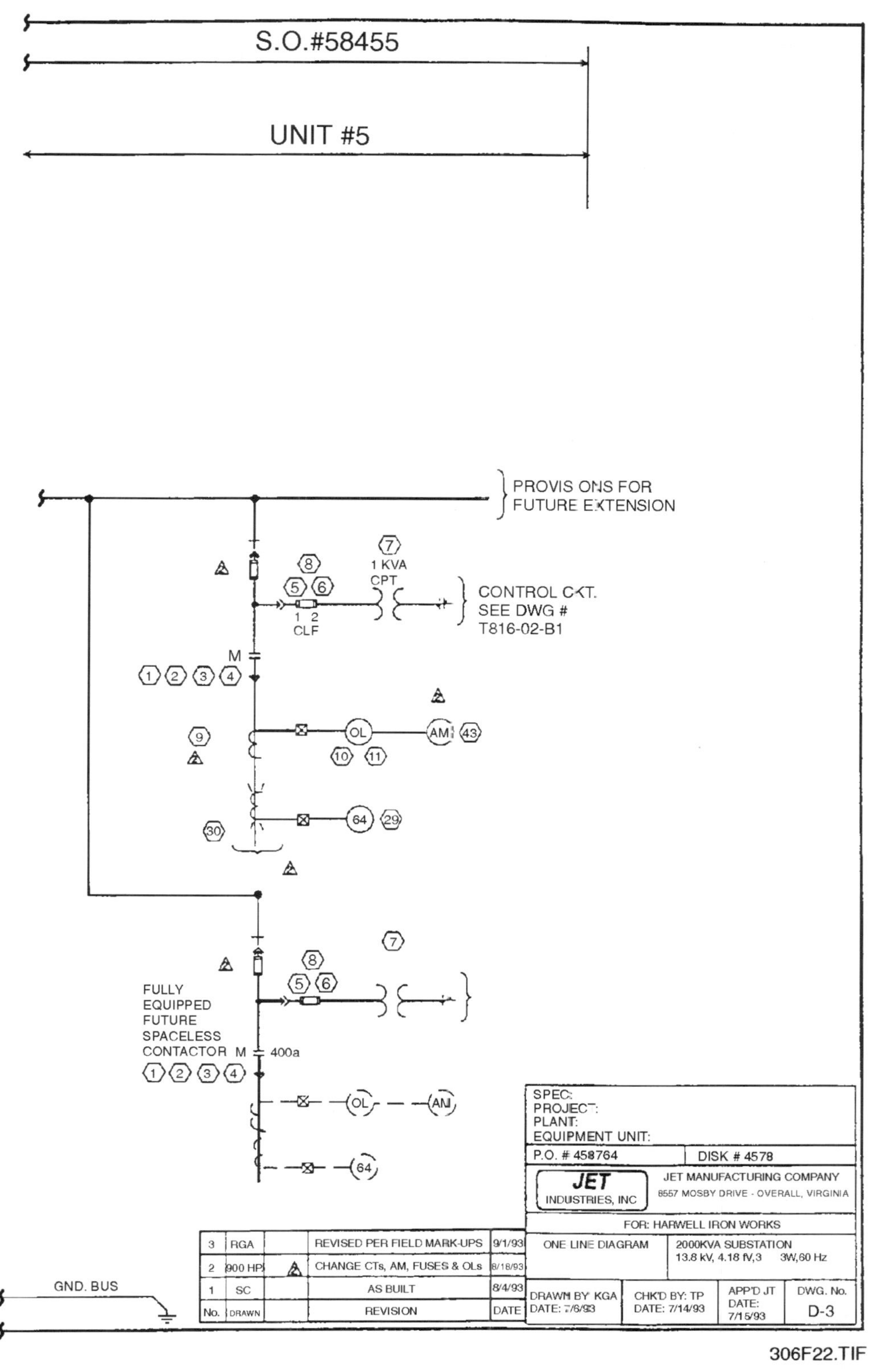

Figure 22. One-Line Diagram Of A 2,000kVA Substation (Right Side)

The one-line diagram takes up most of the drawing sheet and gives an overview of the entire installation. We will begin at the left side of the drawing where incoming line #1 is indicated. This section of the drawing is shown in *Figure 23*.

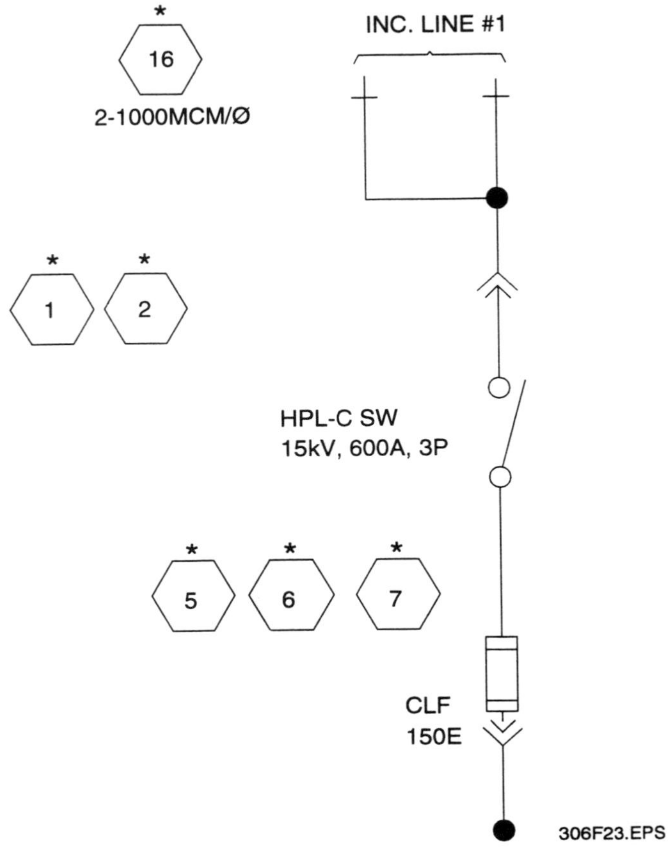

Figure 23. Incoming High-Voltage Line

Incoming line #1 (partially abbreviated on the drawings as INC. LINE #1) consists of two, 1,000MCM (kcmil) conductors per phase as indicated by note 2-1000MCM/Ø (i.e., parallel 1,000kcmil conductors). Since this is a three-phase system, a total of six 1,000kcmil conductors are used.

The single-line continues to engage separable connectors at the single-throw, 15kV, 600A, three-pole switch. Overcurrent protection is provided by current-limiting fuses as indicated by the fuse symbol combined with a note. The single-line continues to the high-voltage bus, which connects to the primary side of the 2,000kVA transformer. Incoming line #2 (partially abbreviated on the drawings as INC. LINE #2) is identical to line #1. This line also connects to the high-voltage bus, which connects to the primary side of the 2,000kVA transformer. Notice the numerals, each enclosed by a hexagon, placed near various components in these two high-voltage primaries. Note also that an asterisk is placed above each of these marks. A note on the drawing indicates the following:

*ITEMS PER S.O. #58454

These marks appear in a supplemental schedule known as the *Bill of Materials*, which describes the marked items, lists the number required, manufacturer, catalog number, and a brief description of each. Such schedules are extremely useful to estimators, job superintendents, and workers to ensure that each required item is accounted for and installed.

Every electrical drawing should have a title block, normally located in the lower right-hand corner of the drawing sheet; the size of the block varies with the size of the drawing and also with the information required.

In general, the title block for an electrical drawing should contain the following:

- Name of the project
- Address of the project
- Name of the owner or client
- Name of the person or firm who prepared the drawing
- Date the drawing was made
- Scale(s), if any
- Initials of the drafter, checker, designer, and engineer, with dates under each
- Job number
- Drawing sheet number
- General description of the drawing

The title block for the project in question is shown in *Figure 24*.

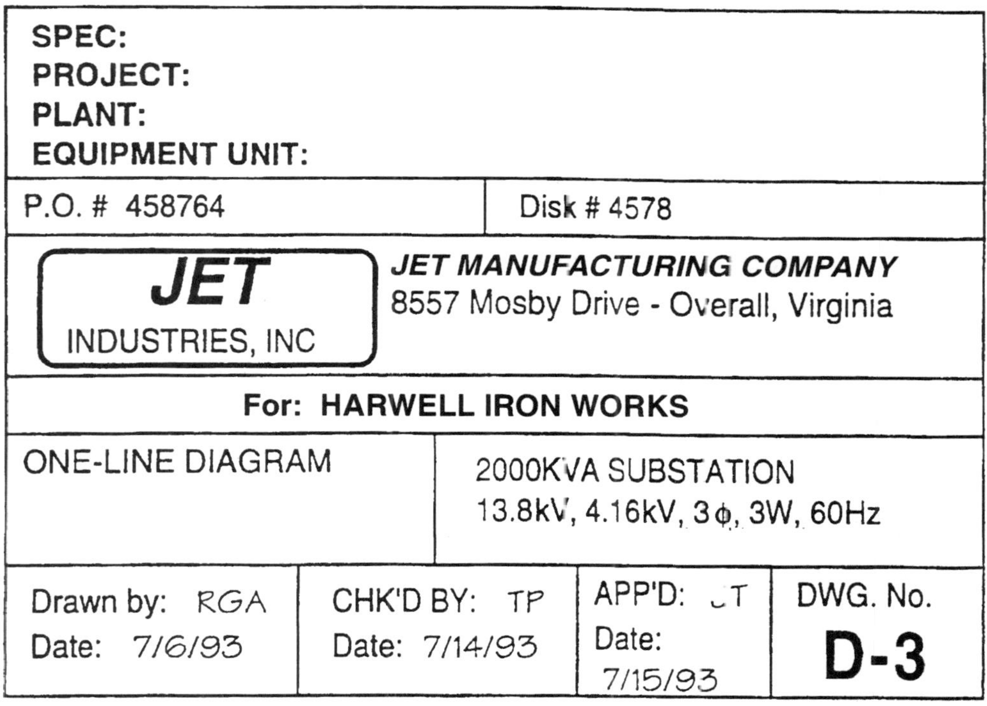

306F24.TIF

Figure 24. Typical Drawing Title Block

Sometimes, electrical drawings will have to be partially redrawn or modified during the planning or construction of a project. It is extremely important that such modifications are noted and dated on the drawings to ensure that all workers have an up-to-date set of drawings. In some situations, sufficient space is left near the title block for the dates and descriptions of revisions, as shown in *Figure 25*.

3	RGA		Revised per field mark-ups	9/1/93
2	900HP	2	Change CTs, AM, fuses & OLs	8/18/93
1	SC		As built	8/4/93
No.	**Drawn**		**Revision**	**Date**

306F25.EPS

Figure 25. Typical Drawing Revision Block

CAUTION: When a set of electrical drawings has been revised, always make certain that the most up-to-date set is used for all future layout work. Either destroy the obsolete set of drawings, or else clearly mark on the affected drawing sheets: *Obsolete Drawing – Do Not Use*. Also, when working with a set of working drawings and written specifications for the first time, thoroughly check each page to see if any revisions or modifications have been made to the originals. Doing so can save much time and expense for all concerned with the project.

15.1.0 INTERPRETING SECONDARY ONE-LINE DIAGRAMS

Referring again to *Figure 21*, note that a 600A, 4,160V, three-phase, three-wire, 60Hz aluminum main bus is used to feed the remaining secondary elements. Also note the removable ground link between the transformer and the grounding bus connection. The drawing shows this conductor as a No. 4/0 AWG. Looking back at the 2,000kVA transformer, note that the main bus continues in a horizontal line to the right of the transformer symbol. The first equipment encountered is the metering section. Note the current transformers (CTs), which are designated by both symbol and note. The 400/5 note indicates that the CTs have a ratio of 400 to 5; that is, if 400A are flowing in the main bus, only 5A will flow to the meters. Again, numerals enclosed in hexagons are placed at each component in this section. Referring to the Bill of Materials schedule in *Figure 26*, we see a description of Item (Mark) #19 as CTs 400/5 Type JAF-0. Two are required; the catalog number is 750X10G304 and the manufacturer is GE (General Electric). Continuing from the CTs down to Item #20, the schedule describes this as a three-phase, three-wire, watt-hour meter with a 15-minute demand. It is designed to register with CTs with a ratio of 400/5 and PTs with a primary/ secondary at 4,160V/240V. Locate the remaining numerals in this group and find their descriptions in the schedule in *Figure 26*.

ELECTRICAL — TRAINEE TASK MODULE 26306

	Mark	Req'd	Cat. No.	Mfg.	Description	
○	1	2	IC2957B103C	GE	Disc. Handle & Elec. Interlock ASM.	○
○					(400A) (CAT#116C9928G1)	○
○	2	2	IC2957B108E	GE	Vert. Bus (CAT#195B4010G1)(400A)	○
○					Shutter ASM. (CAT#116C9927G1) (400A)	○
○	3	2	1C2957B10BF	GE	Coil Finger ASM. (CAT#194A6949G1) (400A)	○
○					Safety Catch (CAT#194A6994G1) (400A)	○
○					Stab Fingers (CAT#232A6635G) (400A)	○
○	4	1		Toshiba	5kV, 300A, 3P, Vacuum Contactor	○
○					120VAC Rectified Control	○
○					Type CV461J-GAT2	○
○	5	4	2033A73G03	W	5kV Fuse MTG (2/CPT)	○
○	6	4	677C592G09	W	5kV, CLF, 2E Fuses Type CLE-PT	○
○	7	2	HN1K0EG15	Micron	1kVA, 4160-120 CPT	○
○	8	3	9F60LJD809	GE	CLF Size 9R (170A) Type EJ-2 (600HP)	○
○	9	3	615X3	GE	CT'S 150/5A Type JCH-0	○
○	10	1	CR224C610A	GE	200 Line Block O.L. Rly. 3 Elements	○
○					Ambient Compensated W/INC. Contact	○
○	11	0	CR123C3.56A	GE	O.L. HTR (600HP)	○
○	11A	3	CR123C3.26A	GE	O.L. HTR. (2.79A) (700HP)	○
○	12	1	7022AB	AG	Off Delay R.Y .5-5 SEC.	○
○	13	0	CR2810A14A	GE	Machine Tool RLY. 1NO&1NC 120VAC (MR)	○
○	14	1	CR294OUM301	GE	Emergency Stop PB (Push to Stop Pull to Reset) W/NP	○
○	15	1	9T28Y5611	GE	10kVA CPT. 4160-120/240V	○
○	16	2	643X92	GE	PT'S 4160/120V Type JVM-3/2FU	○
○	17	2	9F60CED007	GE	CLF 7E, 4.8kV Type EJ-1	○
○	18	2	9F61BNW451	GE	Fuse Clips Size C	○

306F26A.TIF

Figure 26. Bill Of Materials Schedule (1 Of 2)

Mark	Req'd	Cat. No.	Mfg.	Description
19	2	750X10G304	GE	CT'S 400/5 Type JAF-0
20	1	700X64G885	GE	DWH-Meter 3ϕ, 3W, 60HZ, Type DSM-63 W/15MIN. Demand Register CT'S Ratio 400/5 & PT'S 4160-120V
21	1	50-103021P	GE	VM Scale 0-5250V Type AB-40
22	1	50-103131L	GE	AM Scale 0-400A Type AB-40
23	1	10AA004	GE	VS Type SBM
24	1	10AA012	GE	AS Type SBM
25	1	TL612FL	GE	6 CKT. PNL.
26	4	TQL1120	GE	20/1 C/B Type TQL.
27	1	TQL2120	GE	20/2 C/B Type TQL.
28	1	TEB12050WL	GE	50/2 C/B Type TEB
29	1	3512C12H02	W	Type GR Groundgard RLY. Solid State
30	1	3512C13H03	W	GRD. Sensor
31	2	H	Smout Hollman	1/2 LT. REC.
32	2	7604-1	GE	LT. SW. & Receptacle
33	2	4D846G20	GE	120VAC, 250W HTR
34	1		Econo	Econo Lift for Contactor
35	11	Lot	Cook	NP/Schedule DWG. 58455-A1
36	3	Hold	T & B	Lug
37	0	50250440LSPK	GE	AM Scale 0-100A PNL. Type 2% ACC. Type 250 4-1/2 Case
38	1	NON10	Bus	10A, 250V Fuse
39	1	CP232	AH	2P, 250V Pull-Apart Fuse Block
40	1		Cook	SWGR NP S.O.#58455

306F26B.TIF

Figure 26. Bill Of Materials Schedule (2 Of 2)

The two taps from the main bus in the drawing in question are for feeding two motor control centers (MCC); one is to be put into use immediately, while the other is a fully-equipped MCC (less contactors) for future use. First, look at the complete MCC. An enlarged view of this section is shown in *Figure 27*. This feeder is provided with overcurrent protection by means of current-limiting fuses (CLF), which are fuse type EJ-2 rated at 170A (see Item #8, *Figure 26*).

Immediately beneath this device, note that a tap is taken from the main line, fused with 5kV MTG fuses (Item #5) and also 5kV, CLF, 2E fuses (Item #6) before terminating at a 1kVA, 4,160V/120V CPT transformer (Item #7). This transformer is provided to accommodate the 120V control circuit shown in *Figure 27*. Since motor controls and motor control circuits are covered later in your training, the circuit in *Figure 27* will not be explained in depth in this module. It is presented here to give you a visual knowledge of a motor control circuit, not necessarily to explain how it functions. Now backtrack to the main feeder and continue downward to a contactor before another group of current transformers are installed in the circuit. These CTs are accompanied by notes and Item #9. Referring to the schedule in *Figure 26* for a description of Item #9, we see that these three CTs have a ratio of 150/5—that is, when the circuit is drawing 150A, the metering devices will receive only 5A, but the meter itself will indicate 150A. This circuit continues to a 200-line block overload relay with three elements, and then on to an ammeter with a range of 0A to 150A.

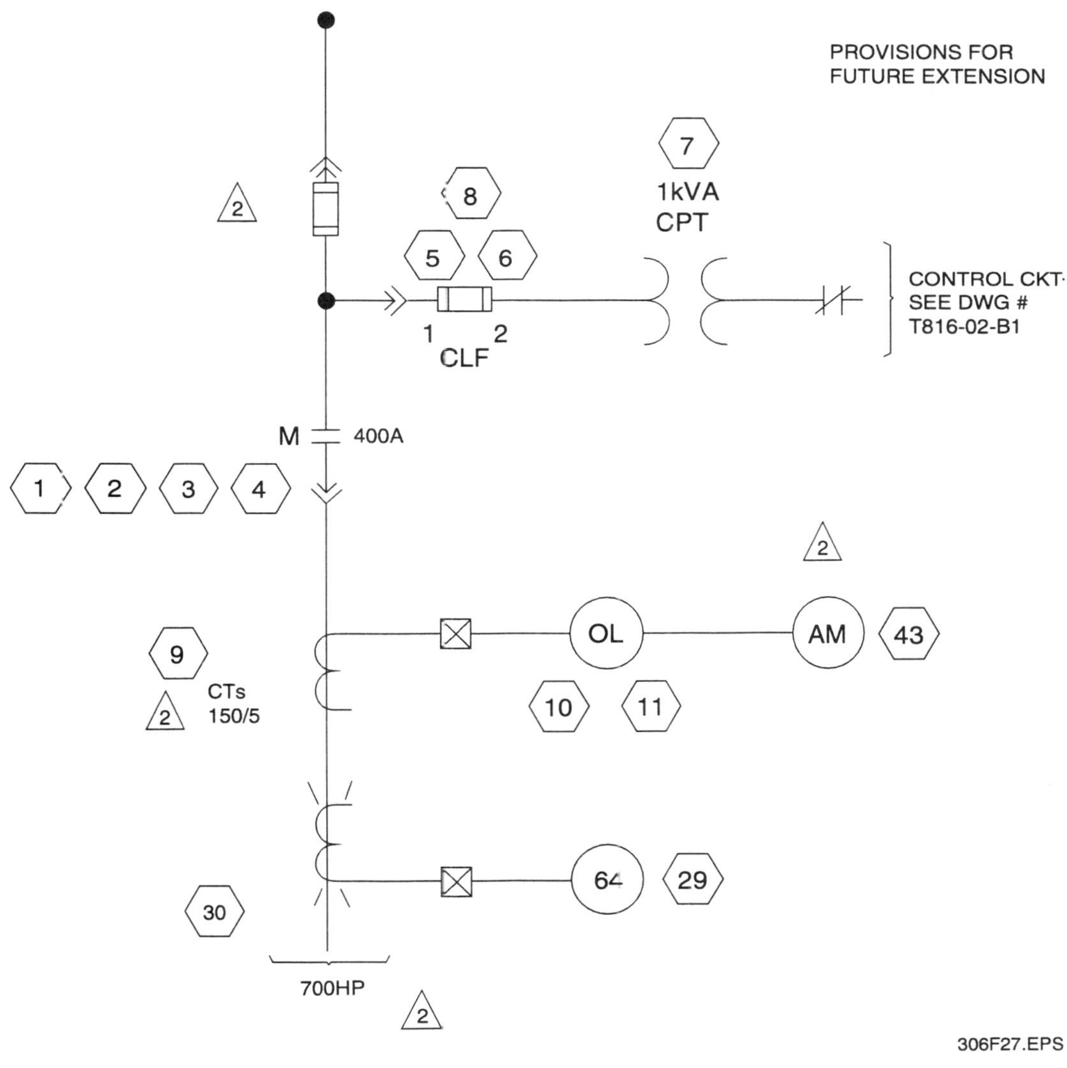

Figure 27. Enlarged View Of The MCC Feeder

The next item on this main vertical feeder is a ground sensor, which is connected to a solid-state ground guard relay. The feeder then enters and connects to the busbars in a motor control center (MCC) enclosure, as shown in *Figure 28*. The remaining feeder in this one-line wiring diagram is for future use and is similar to the circuit just described.

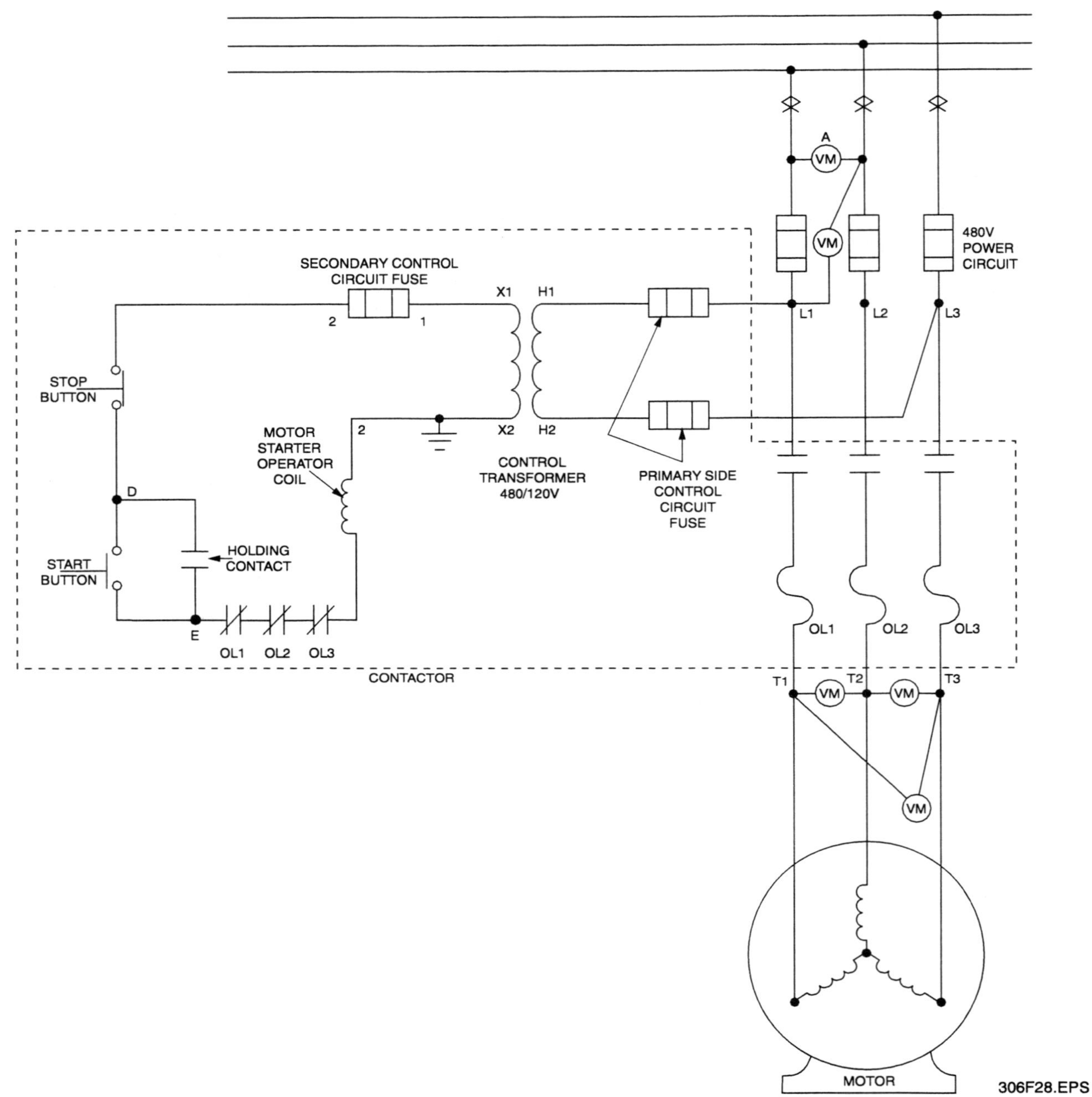

Figure 28. Motor Control Circuit Diagram

15.2.0 SHOP DRAWINGS

When large pieces of electrical equipment are needed, such as high-voltage switchgear and motor control centers, most are custom built for each individual project. In doing so, shop drawings are normally furnished by the equipment manufacturer prior to shipment to ensure that the equipment will fit the location at the shop site, and also to instruct workers on the job as to how to prepare for the equipment (e.g., rough-in conduit, cable tray, etc.).

The drawing in *Figure 29* is one page of a shop drawing showing an isometric pictorial view of the enclosure.

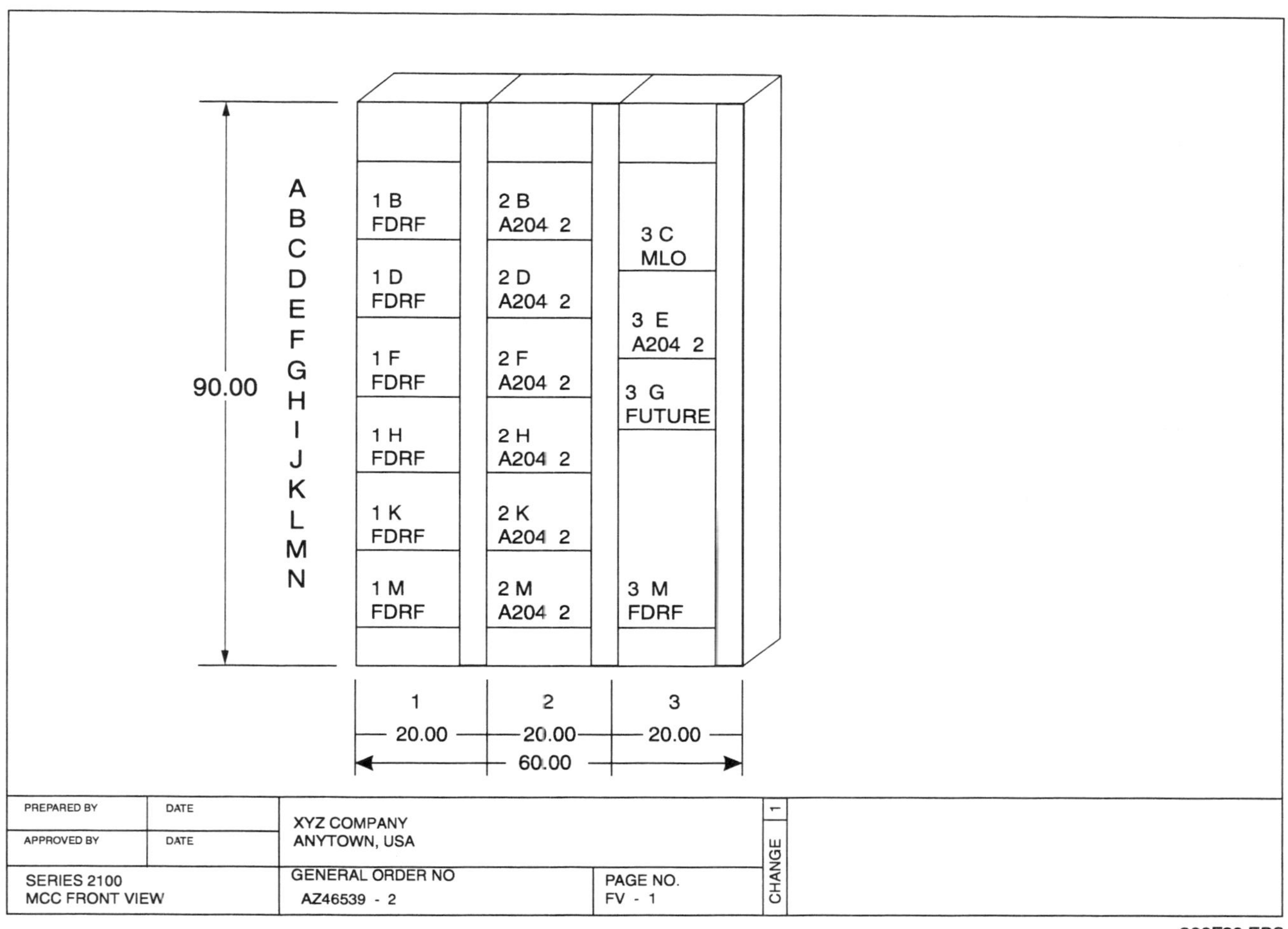

Figure 29. Isometric View Of A Motor Control Center

Shop drawings will also usually include connection diagrams for all components that must be field wired or connected.

As-built drawings, including detailed factory-wired connection diagrams are also included to assist workers and maintenance personnel in making the final connections, and then troubleshooting problems once the system is in operation.

Typical drawings are shown in *Figures 30* and *31*.

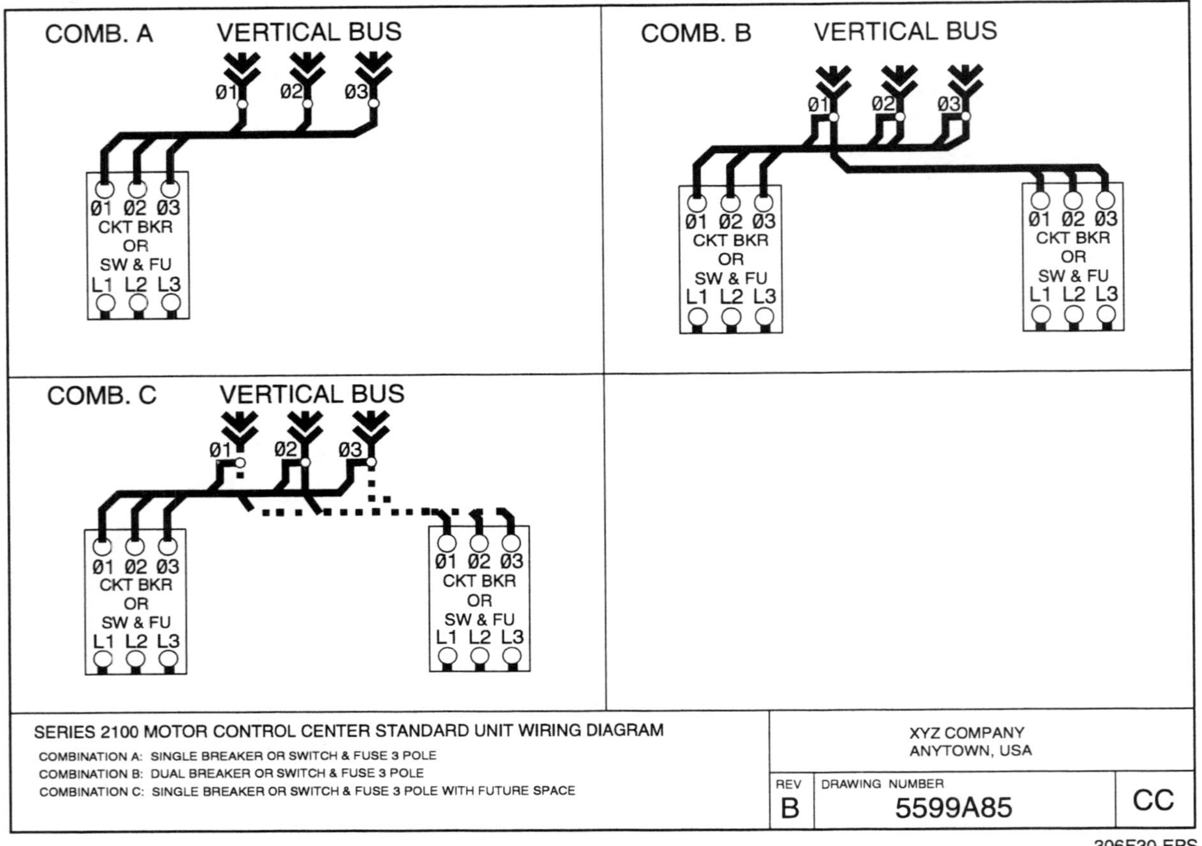

Figure 30. Motor Control Center Standard Unit Wiring Diagram

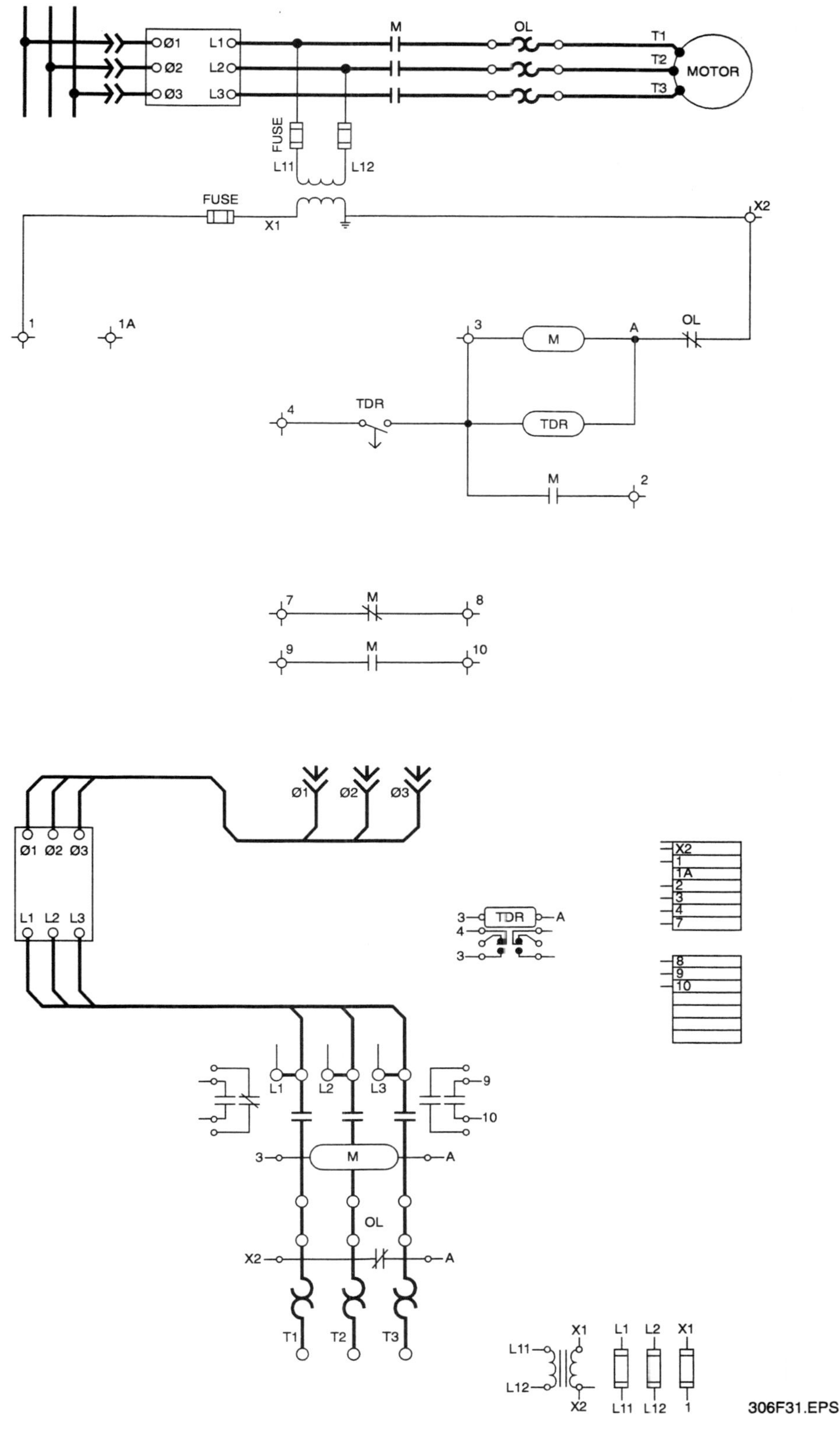

Figure 31. Unit Diagrams For Motor Control Center

16.1.0   PANELBOARD LIGHTING

Circuit control and overcurrent protection must be provided for all circuits and the power-consuming devices connected to these circuits. Lighting and power panels located throughout large buildings being supplied with electrical energy provide this control and protection. *Figure 32* shows fifteen panelboards provided in a typical industrial building to feed electrical energy to the various circuits.

PANEL NO.	LOCATION	MAINS	VOLTAGE RATING	NO. OF CIRCUITS	BREAKER RATINGS	POLES	PURPOSE
P-1	BASEMENT N. CORRIDOR	BREAKER 100A	208/120V 3Ø, 4W	19 2 5	20A 20A 20A	1 2 1	LIGHTING AND RECEPTACLES SPARES
P-2	BASEMENT N. CORRIDOR	BREAKER 100A	208/120V 3Ø, 4W	24 2 0	20A 20A	1 2	LIGHTING AND RECEPTACLES SPARES
P-3	2ND FLOOR N. CORRIDOR	BREAKER 100A	208/120V 3Ø, 4W	24 2 0	20A 20A	1 2	LIGHTING AND RECEPTACLES SPARES
P-4	BASEMENT S. CORRIDOR	BREAKER 100A	208/120V 3Ø, 4W	24 2 0	20A 20A	1 2 1	LIGHTING AND RECEPTACLES SPARES
P-5	1ST FLOOR S. CORRIDOR	BREAKER 100A	208/120V 3Ø, 4W	23 2 1	20A 20A 20A	1 2 1	LIGHTING AND RECEPTACLES SPARES
P-6	2ND FLOOR S. CORRIDOR	BREAKER 100A	208/120V 3Ø, 4W	22 2 2	20A 20A 20A	1 2 1	LIGHTING AND RECEPTACLES SPARES
P-7	MFG. AREA S. WALL E.	BREAKER 100A	208/120V 3Ø, 4W	5 7 2	20A 20A 20A	1 1 1	LIGHTING AND RECEPTACLES SPARES
P-8	MFG. AREA S. WALL W.	BREAKER 100A	208/120V 3Ø, 4W	5 7 2	20A 20A 20A	1 1 1	LIGHTING AND RECEPTACLES SPARES
P-9	MFG. AREA S. WALL E.	BREAKER 100A	208/120V 3Ø, 4W	5 7 2	50A 20A 20A	1 1 1	LIGHTING AND RECEPTACLES SPARES
P-10	MFG. AREA S. WALL W.	BREAKER 100A	208/120V 3Ø, 4W	5 7 2	50A 20A 20A	1 1 1	LIGHTING AND RECEPTACLES SPARES
P-11	MFG. AREA EAST WALL	LUGS ONLY 225A	208/120V 3Ø, 4W	6	20A	3	BLOWERS AND VENTILATORS
P-12	BOILER ROOM	BREAKER 100A	208/120V 3Ø, 4W	10 4	20A 20A	1 1	LIGHTING AND RECEPTACLES SPARES
P-13	BOILER ROOM	LUGS ONLY 225A	208/120V 3Ø, 4W	6	20A	3	OIL BURNERS AND PUMPS
P-14	MFG. AREA EAST WALL	LUGS ONLY 400A	208/120V 3Ø, 4W	3 2 1	175A 70A 40A	3 3 3	CHILLERS FAN COIL UNITS FAN COIL UNITS
P-15	MFG. AREA WEST WALL	LUGS ONLY 600A	208/120V 3Ø, 4W	5	100A	3	TROLLEY BUSWAY AND ELEVATOR

306F32.EPS

Figure 32. Schedule Of Electric Panelboards For An Industrial Building

16.2.0   PANELBOARD CONSTRUCTION

In general, panelboards are constructed so that the main feed busbars run the height of the panelboard. The buses to the branch circuit protective devices are connected to the alternate main buses. In an arrangement of this type, the connections directly across from each other are on the same phase and the adjacent connections on each side are on different phases. As a result, multiple protective devices can be installed to serve the 208V equipment. An example of a panelboard is shown in *Figure 33*.

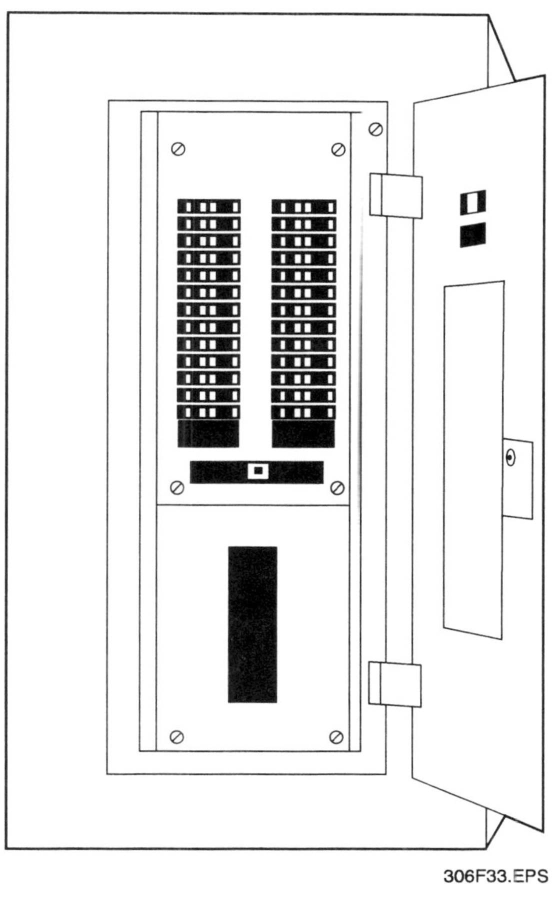

306F33.EPS

Figure 33. Lighting And Appliance Panelboard With Main Breaker

16.2.1   Identification Of Conductors

The ungrounded conductors may be any color except green (or green with a yellow stripe), which is reserved for grounding purposes only; or white or natural gray, which are reserved for the grounded circuit conductor. See ***NEC Section 200-6***.

NEC Section 210-4(d) requires that where different voltages exist in a building, the ungrounded conductors for each system must be identified at each accessible location. Identification may be by color-coding, marking, tape, tagging, or other approved means. The means of identification must be permanently posted at each branch circuit panelboard.

For example, this situation may occur when the building is served with 277/480V and step-down transformers are used to provide 120/208V for lighting and receptacle outlets. Examples of panelboard wiring connections are shown in *Figures 34, 35, 36,* and *37.*

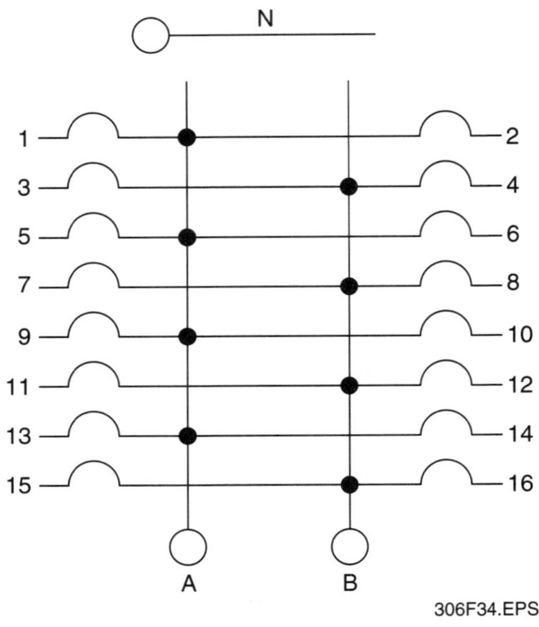

Figure 34. Lighting And Appliance Branch Circuit Panelboard – Single-Phase, Three-Wire Connections

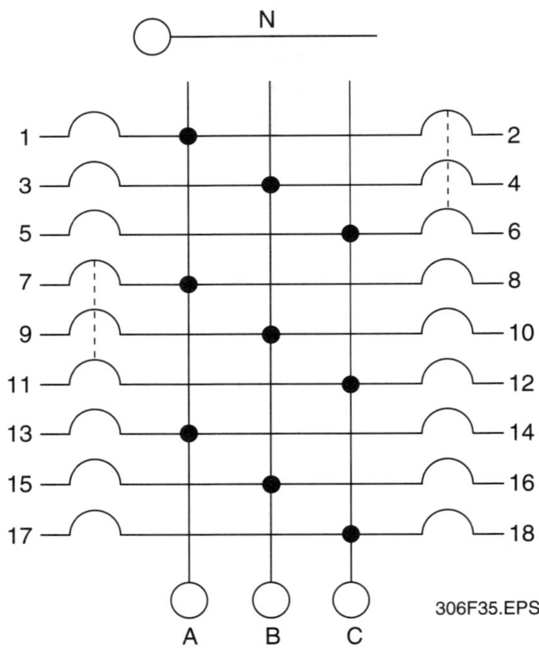

Figure 35. Lighting And Appliance Branch Circuit Panelboard – Three-Phase, Four-Wire Connections

ELECTRICAL — TRAINEE TASK MODULE 26306

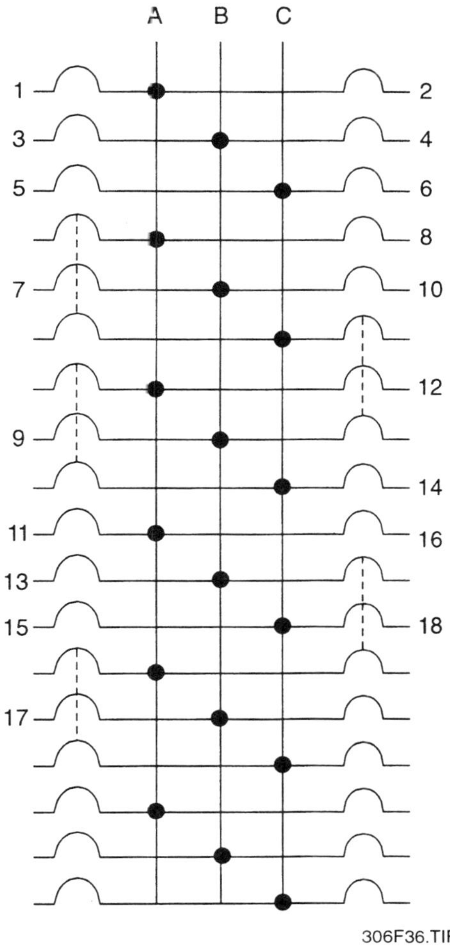

Figure 36. Bakery Panelboard Circuit Showing Alternate Numbering Scheme

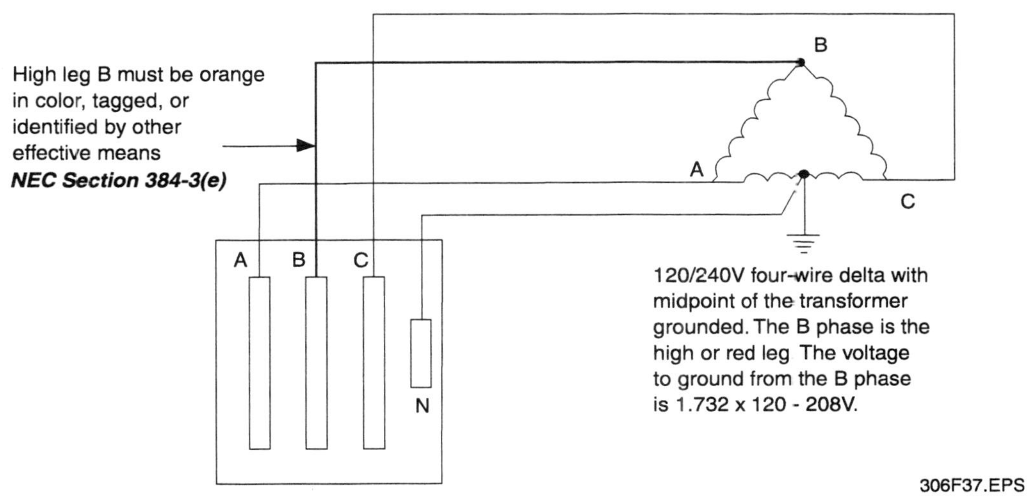

Figure 37. Panelboards And Switchboards Supplied By Four-Wire, Delta-Connected Systems Must Have The B Phase Connected To The Phase Having The Higher Voltage To Ground

16.2.2   Number Of Circuits

The number of overcurrent devices in a panelboard is determined by the needs of the area being served. Using the bakery panelboard in *Figure 36* as an example, there are 13 single-pole circuits and five three-pole circuits. This is a total of 28 poles. When using a three-phase supply, the incremental number is six (a pole for each of the three phases on both sides of the panelboard). The minimum number of poles that could be specified for the bakery is 30. This would limit the power available for growth and would not permit the addition of a three-pole lead. The reasonable choice is to go to 36 poles, which provides flexibility for growth loads.

16.3.0   PANELBOARD PROTECTIVE DEVICES

The main protective device for a panelboard may be either a fuse or a circuit breaker. This section concentrates on the use of circuit breakers. The selection of the circuit breaker should be based on the necessity to:

* Provide the proper overload protection
* Ensure a suitable voltage rating
* Provide a sufficient interrupting current rating
* Provide short circuit protection
* Coordinate the breaker(s) with other protective devices

The choice of the overload protection is based on the rating of the panelboard. The trip rating of the circuit breaker cannot exceed the amperage capacity of the busbars in the panelboard. The number of branch circuit breakers is generally not a factor in the selection of the main protective device except in a practical sense. It is a common practice to have the total amperage of the branch breakers greatly exceed the rating of the main breaker; however, it makes little sense for a single branch circuit breaker to be the same size as, or larger than, the main breaker.

The voltage rating of the breaker must be higher than that of the system. Breakers are usually rated at 250V to 600V.

The importance of the proper interrupting rating cannot be overstressed. You should recall that if there is ever any question as to the exact value of the short circuit current available at a point, the circuit breaker with the higher interrupting rating is to be installed.

Many circuit breakers used as the main protective device are provided with an adjustable magnetic trip (*Figure 38*). Adjustments of this trip determine the degree of protection provided by the circuit breaker if a short circuit occurs. The manufacturer of this device provides exact information about the adjustments to be made. In general, a low setting may be 10 or 12 times the overload trip rating.

Two rules should be followed whenever the magnetic trip is set:

- The magnetic trip must be set to the minimum practical setting.
- The setting must be lower than the value of the short circuit current available at that point.

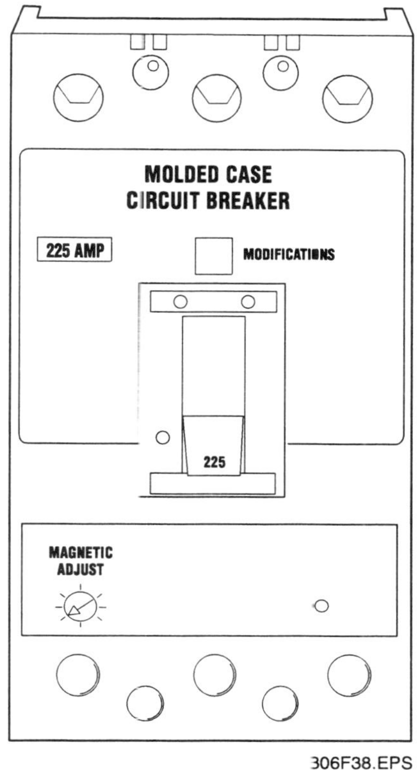

Figure 38. Circuit Breaker With Adjustable Magnetic Trip

If subfeed lugs are used, ensure that the lugs are suitable for making multiple breaker connections, as required by **NEC Section 110-14(a)**. In general, this means that a separate lug is to be provided for each conductor being connected.

If taps are made to the subfeeder, they can be reduced in size according to **NEC Section 240-21**. This specification is very useful in cases such as that of panel P-12 in *Figure 32*. For this panel, a 100A main breaker is fed by a 350MCM conductor. Within the distances given in **NEC Section 240-21**, a conductor with a 100A rating may be tapped to the subfeeder and connected to the 100A main breaker in the panel.

Per **NEC Section 110-14(c)**, the temperature rating of conductors must be selected and coordinated so as not to exceed the lowest temperature rating of any connected termination, conductor, or device.

16.4.0   BRANCH CIRCUIT PROTECTIVE DEVICES

The schedule of panelboards for the industrial building (*Figure 32*) shows that lighting panels P-1 through P-6 have 20A circuit breakers, including double-pole breakers to supply special receptacle outlets. A double-pole breaker requires the same installation space as two single-pole breakers. Breakers are shown in *Figure 39*.

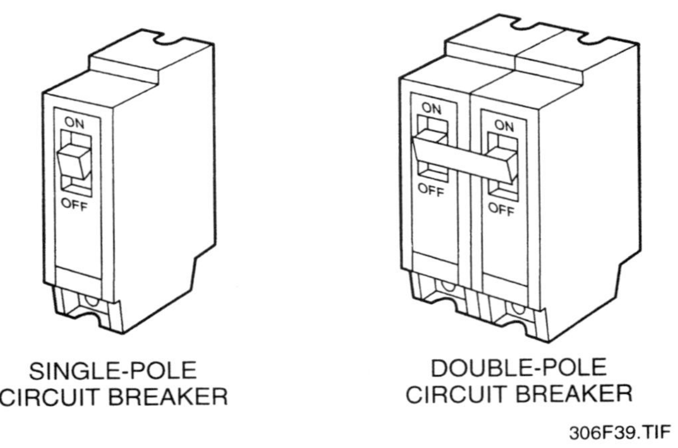

Figure 39. Branch Circuit Protective Devices

SUMMARY

This module covered the wiring requirements of distribution systems, including component selection, interdependence, and maintenance. It also explained the NEC requirements for these systems and provided a basic understanding of how to apply them. It also covered the various wiring diagrams related to distribution system transformers.

References

For advanced study of topics covered in this Task Module, the following books are suggested:

American Electricians' Handbook, Latest Edition, McGraw-Hill, New York, NY.

National Electrical Code Handbook, Latest Edition, National Fire Protection Association, Quincy, MA.

1. Voltages classified as medium voltage are in the range of _____.

   a. 120V to 240V
   b. 120V to 600V
   c. 601V to 15kV
   d. 15kV to 230kV

2. The term *interrupting rating* refers to the _____.

   a. trip setting of a circuit breaker
   b. voltage rating of a fuse
   c. highest voltage level a device can withstand
   d. maximum current a device will safely interrupt at rated voltage

3. Which of the following is a color that can be used to designate an ungrounded conductor?

   a. Green
   b. White
   c. Gray
   d. Red

4. When an unintended path is established between an ungrounded conductor and ground, it is called a _____.

   a. phase fault
   b. open circuit
   c. ground fault
   d. short circuit

5. A device that is designed to protect industrial equipment from ground faults is a _____.

   a. molded-case circuit breaker
   b. dual-element fuse
   c. ground-powered ground fault relay
   d. ground fault circuit interrupter

6. The maximum voltage which a piece of equipment can withstand is known as its _____.

   a. interrupting capacity
   b. basic impulse level (BIL)
   c. current limit
   d. frequency

7. A transformer rated at more than 500kVA is considered a(n) ______ transformer.

    a. power
    b. control
    c. distribution
    d. isolation

8. The term *capacity* on a transformer nameplate refers to ______.

    a. its voltage rating
    b. its ability to transfer energy
    c. the voltage produced by the secondary
    d. the number of secondary windings

9. The term *class* on a transformer nameplate refers to ______.

    a. its use (control, power, etc.)
    b. the type of cooling it uses
    c. whether it is step-up or step-down
    d. its range of operating frequencies

10. Of the following, which statement is *incorrect*?

    a. Instrument transformers are available in many ratios.
    b. Instrument transformers make it possible to use reasonable insulation ratings in relays.
    c. Instrument transformers protect personnel and equipment from distribution voltages.
    d. Instrument transformers are more accurate than direct monitoring of power system voltages and currents.

11. Of the following types of current transformers, which is normally used with circuit breakers or power transformers?

    a. Bar
    b. Bushing
    c. Oil-filled
    d. Window

12. Which of the following is *not* a general classification of circuit breakers?

    a. Fuse circuit breaker
    b. Air circuit breaker
    c. Oil circuit breaker
    d. Gas circuit breaker

13. What type of diagram shows the actual wiring connections between unit assemblies or equipment?

a. Schematic diagram
b. Front panel diagram
c. Interconnection diagram
d. Block diagram

14. The trip rating of a circuit breaker used as the main protective device in a panelboard cannot exceed _____.

a. the total amperage of the branch breakers
b. the amperage capacity of the busbars in the panelboard
c. the amperage of the individual branch fuses
d. 250V

15. If Device Number 51 is indicated on an electrical print, it would be a(n) _____.

a. circuit breaker
b. reverse power relay
c. field circuit breaker
d. AC time overcurrent relay

ANSWERS TO REVIEW/PRACTICE QUESTIONS

<u>Answer</u>	<u>Section Reference</u>
1. c	2.0.0
2. d	6.1.0
3. d	6.2.0
4. c	7.0.0
5. c	7.1.0
6. b	8.1.0
7. a	10.2.0
8. b	10.5.0
9. b	10.5.0
10. d	11.0.0
11. b	11.2.0
12. a	12.0.0
13. c	14.3.0
14. b	16.3.0
15. d	Appendix

The devices in switching equipment are referred to by numbers, with appropriate suffix letters when necessary, according to the functions they perform.

These numbers are based on a system adopted as standard for automatic switchgear by IEEE, and incorporated in American Standard C37.2-1970. This system is used in connection diagrams, instruction books, and specifications.

Device Number	Definition and Function
1	**Master Element** — The initiating device, such as a control switch, voltage relay, float switch, etc., which serves either directly, or through such permissive devices as protective and time-delay relays, to place equipment in or out of operation.
2	**Time-Delay Starting or Closing Relay** — A device that functions to give a desired amount of time delay before or after any point of operation in a switching sequence or protective relay system, except as specifically provided by device functions 48, 62, and 79 described later.
3	**Checking or Interlocking Relay** — A device that operates in response to the position of a number of other devices (or to a number of predetermined conditions) in equipment to allow an operating sequence to proceed, to stop, or to provide a check of the position of these devices or of these conditions for any purpose.
4	**Master Contactor** — A device, generally controlled by device No. 1 or equivalent, and the required permissive and protective devices, that serves to make and break the necessary control circuits to place equipment into operation under the desired conditions and to take it out of operation under other or abnormal conditions.
5	**Stopping Device** — A control device used primarily to shut down equipment and hold it out of operation. (This device may be manually or electrically actuated, but excludes the function of electrical lockout [see device function 86] on abnormal conditions.)
6	**Starting Circuit Breaker** — A device whose principal function is to connect a machine to its source of starting voltage.
7	**Anode Circuit Breaker** — A device used in the anode circuits of a power rectifier for the primary purpose of interrupting the rectifier circuit if an arc-back should occur.
8	**Control Power Disconnecting Device** — A disconnective device such as a knife switch, circuit breaker, or pullout fuse block that is used for the purpose of connecting and disconnecting the source of control power to and from the control bus or equipment. *Note:* Control power is considered to include auxiliary power which supplies such apparatus as small motors and heaters.
9	**Reversing Device** — A device used for the purpose of reversing a machine field or for performing any other reversing functions.
10	**Unit Sequence Switch** — A device used to change the sequence in which units may be placed in and out of service in multiple-unit equipment.
11	Reserved for future application.
12	**Over-Speed Device** — Usually a direct-connected speed switch which functions on machine over-speed.
13	**Synchronous-Speed Device** — A device such as a centrifugal-speed switch, slip-frequency relay, voltage relay, undercurrent relay, or other device that operates at approximately the synchronous speed of a machine.
14	**Under-Speed Device** — A device that functions when the speed of a machine falls below a predetermined value.
15	**Speed- or Frequency-Matching Device** — A device that functions to match and hold the speed or frequency of a machine or of a system equal to, or approximately equal to, that of another machine, source, or system.

Device Number	Definition and Function
16	Reserved for future application.
17	**Shunting or Discharge Switch** — A device that serves to open or close a shunting circuit around any piece of apparatus (except a resistor), such as machine field, machine armature, capacitor, or reactor. *Note:* This excludes devices which perform such shunting operations as may be necessary in the process of starting a machine by devices 6 or 42, or their equivalent, and also excludes the device 73 function, which serves for the switching of resistors.
18	**Accelerating or Decelerating Device** — A device used to close or to cause the closing of circuits which are used to increase or decrease the speed of a machine.
19	**Starting-to-Running Transition Contactor** — A device that operates to initiate or cause the automatic transfer of a machine from the starting to the running power connection.
20	**Electrically Operated Valve** — An electrically operated, controlled, or monitored valve in a fluid line. *Note:* The function of the valve may be indicated by the use of suffixes.
21	**Distance Relay** — A device that functions when the circuit admittance, impedance, or reactance increases or decreases beyond predetermined limits.
22	**Equalizer Circuit Breaker** — A breaker that serves to control or to make and break the equalizer or the current-balancing connections for a field, or for regulating equipment, in a multiple-unit installation.
23	**Temperature Control Device** — A device that functions to raise or lower the temperature of a machine or other apparatus, or of any medium, when its temperature falls below, or rises above, a predetermined value. *Note:* An example is a thermostat which switches on a space heater in a switchgear assembly when the temperature falls to a desired value as distinguished from a device which is used to provide automatic temperature regulation between close limits and would be designated as 90T.
24	Reserved for future application.
25	**Synchronizing or Synchronism-Check Device** — A device that operates when two AC circuits are within the desired limits of frequency, phase angle, or voltage, to permit or to cause the paralleling of these two circuits.
26	**Apparatus Thermal Device** — A device that functions when the temperature of the shunt field or the armortisseur winding of a machine, or that of a load limiting or load shifting resistor, or of a liquid or other medium, exceeds a predetermined value; or if the temperature of the protected apparatus, such as a power rectifier, or any medium decreases below a predetermined value.
27	**Undervoltage Relay** — A device that functions on a given value of undervoltage.
28	**Flame Detector** — A device that monitors the presence of the pilot or main flame in such apparatus as a gas turbine or steam boiler.
29	**Isolating Contactor** — A device used expressly for disconnecting one circuit from another for the purposes of emergency operation, maintenance, or testing.
30	**Annunciator Relay** — A nonautomatically reset device that gives a number of separate visual indications upon the functioning of protective devices, and which may also be arranged to perform a lockout function.
31	**Separate Excitation Device** — A device that connects a circuit, such as the shunt field of a synchronous converter, to a source of separate excitation during the starting sequence; or one which energizes the excitation and ignition circuits of a power rectifier.

Device Number	Definition and Function
32	**Directional Power Relay** – A device that functions on a desired value of power flow in a given direction, or upon reverse power resulting from arc-back in the anode or cathode circuits of a power rectifier.
33	**Position Switch** – A device that makes or breaks its contacts when the main device or piece of apparatus, which has no device function number, reaches a given position.
34	**Master Sequence Device** – A device such as a motor-operated multi-contact switch, or the equivalent, or a programming device such as a computer, that establishes or determines the operating sequence of the major devices in equipment during starting and stopping or during other sequential switching operations.
35	**Brush-Operating or Slip-Ring Short-Circuiting Device** – A device used for raising, lowering, or shifting the brushes of a machine, or for short-circuiting its slip rings, or for engaging or disengaging the contacts of a mechanical rectifier.
36	**Polarity or Polarizing Voltage Device** – A device that operates or permits the operation of another device on a predetermined polarity only, or verifies the presence of a polarizing voltage in equipment.
37	**Undercurrent or Underpower Relay** – A device that functions when the current or power flow decreases below a predetermined value.
38	**Bearing Protective Device** – A device that functions on excessive bearing temperature, or on other abnormal mechanical conditions such as undue wear, which may eventually result in excessive bearing temperature.
39	**Mechanical Condition Monitor** – A device that functions upon the occurrence of an abnormal mechanical condition (except that associated with bearings as covered under device function 38), such as excessive vibration, eccentricity, expansion, shock, tilting, or seal failure.
40	**Field Relay** – A device that functions on a given or abnormally low value or failure of machine field current, or on an excessive value of the reactive component of armature current in an AC machine indicating abnormally low field excitation.
41	**Field Circuit Breaker** – A device that functions to apply or remove the field excitation of a machine.
42	**Running Circuit Breaker** – A device whose principal function is to connect a machine to its source of running or operating voltage. This function may also be used for a device, such as a contactor, that is used in series with a circuit breaker or other fault protecting means, primarily for frequent opening and closing of the circuit.
43	**Manual Transfer or Selector Device** – A device that transfers the control circuits so as to modify the plan of operation of the switching equipment or of some of the devices.
44	**Unit Sequence Starting Relay** – A device that functions to start the next available unit in multiple-unit equipment on the failure or non-availability of the normally preceding unit.
45	**Atmospheric Condition Monitor** – A device that functions upon the occurrence of an abnormal atmospheric condition, such as damaging fumes, explosive mixtures, smoke, or fire.
46	**Reverse-Phase or Phase-Balance Current Relay** – A device that functions when the polyphase currents are of reverse-phase sequence, or when the polyphase currents are unbalanced or contain negative phase-sequence components above a given amount.
47	**Phase-Sequence Voltage Relay** – A relay that functions upon a predetermined value of polyphase voltage in the desired phase sequence.
48	**Incomplete Sequence Relay** – A relay that generally returns the equipment to the normal or off position and locks it out if the normal starting, operating, or stopping sequence is not properly completed within a predetermined time. If the device is used for alarm purposes only, it should preferably be designated as 48A (alarm).

Device Number	Definition and Function
49	**Machine or Transformer Thermal Relay** – A relay that functions when the temperature of a machine armature, or other load-carrying winding or element of a machine, or the temperature of a power rectifier or power transformer (including a power rectifier transformer), exceeds a predetermined value.
50	**Instantaneous Overcurrent or Rate-of-Rise Relay** – A relay that functions instantaneously on an excessive value of current, or on an excessive rate of current rise, thus indicating a fault in the apparatus or circuit being protected.
51	**AC Time Overcurrent Relay** – A relay with either a definite or inverse time characteristic that functions when the current in an AC circuit exceeds a predetermined value.
52	**AC Circuit Breaker** – A device that is used to close and interrupt an AC power circuit under normal conditions or to interrupt this circuit under fault or emergency conditions.
53	**Exciter or DC Generator Relay** – A relay that forces the DC machine field excitation to build up during starting or which functions when the machine voltage has built up to a given value.
54	Reserved for future application.
55	**Power Factor Relay** – A relay that operates when the power factor in an AC circuit rises above or below a predetermined value.
56	**Field Application Relay** – A relay that automatically controls the application of the field excitation to an AC motor at some predetermined point in the slip cycle.
57	**Short-Circuiting or Grounding Device** – A primary circuit switching device that functions to short-circuit or ground a circuit in response to automatic or manual means.
58	**Rectification Failure Relay** – A device that functions if one or more anodes of a power rectifier fail to fire, or to detect an arc-back, or on failure of a diode to conduct or block properly.
59	**Overvoltage Relay** – A relay that functions on a given value of overvoltage.
60	**Voltage or Current Balance Relay** – A relay that operates on a given difference in voltage, or current input or output of two circuits.
61	Reserved for future application.
62	**Time-Delay Stopping or Opening Relay** – A time-delay relay that serves in conjunction with the device that initiates the shutdown, stopping, or opening operation in an automatic sequence.
63	**Pressure Switch** – A switch that operates on given values or on a given rate of change of pressure.
64	**Ground Protective Relay** – A relay that functions on failure of the insulation of a machine, transformer, or other apparatus to ground, or on flashover of a DC machine to ground. ***Note:*** This function is assigned only to a relay which detects the flow of current from the frame of a machine or enclosing case or structure of a piece of apparatus to ground, or detects a ground on a normally ungrounded winding or circuit. It is not applied to a device connected in the secondary circuit or secondary neutral of a current transformer connected in the power circuit of a normally grounded system.
65	**Governor** – The assembly of fluid, electrical, or mechanical control equipment used for regulating the flow of water, steam, or other medium to the prime mover for such purposes as starting, holding speed or load, or stopping.

Device Number	Definition and Function
66	**Notching or Jogging Device** — A device that functions to allow only a specified number of operations of a given device or equipment, or a specified number of successive operations within a given time of each other. It also functions to energize a circuit periodically or for fractions of specified time intervals, or is used to permit intermittent acceleration or jogging of a machine at low speeds for mechanical positioning.
67	**AC Directional Overcurrent Relay** — A relay that functions on a desired value of AC overcurrent flowing in a predetermined direction.
68	**Blocking Relay** — A relay that initiates a pilot signal for blocking of tripping on external faults in a transmission line or in other apparatus under predetermined conditions, or cooperates with other devices to block tripping or to block reclosing on an out-of-step condition or on power swings.
69	**Permissive Control Device** — Generally a two-position, manually-operated switch that in one position permits the closing of a circuit breaker, or the placing of equipment into operation, and in the other position prevents the circuit breaker or the equipment from being operated.
70	**Rheostat** — A variable resistance device used in an electric circuit which is electrically operated or has other electrical accessories, such as auxiliary, position, or limit switches.
71	**Level Switch** — A switch that operates on given values, or on a given rate of change of level.
72	**DC Circuit Breaker** — A circuit breaker used to close and interrupt a DC power circuit under normal conditions or to interrupt this circuit under fault or emergency conditions.
73	**Load-Resistor Contactor** — A contactor used to shunt or insert a step of load limiting, shifting, or indicating resistance in a power circuit, or to switch a space heater in a circuit, or to switch a light, or regenerative load resistor of a power rectifier or other machine in and out of a circuit.
74	**Alarm Relay** — A device other than an annunciator, as covered under device No. 30, which is used to operate, or to operate in connection with, a visual or audible alarm.
75	**Position Changing Mechanism** — A mechanism that is used for moving a main device from one position to another in equipment (for example, shifting a removable circuit breaker unit to and from the connected, disconnected, and test positions).
76	**DC Overcurrent Relay** — A relay that functions when the current in a DC circuit exceeds a given value.
77	**Pulse Transmitter** — A device used to generate and transmit pulses over a telemetering or pilot-wire circuit to remove the indicating or receiving device.
78	**Phase Angle Measuring or Out-of-Step Protective Relay** — A relay that functions at a predetermined phase angle between two voltages, or between two currents, or between voltage and current.
79	**AC Reclosing Relay** — A relay that controls the automatic reclosing and locking out of an AC circuit interrupter.
80	**Flow Switch** — A switch which operates on given values, or a given rate of change of flow.
81	**Frequency Relay** — A relay that functions on a predetermined value of frequency, either under or over or on normal system frequency, or rate of change of frequency.
82	**DC Reclosing Relay** — A relay that controls the automatic closing and reclosing of a DC circuit interrupter, generally in response to load circuit conditions.
83	**Automatic Selective Control or Transfer Relay** — A relay that operates to select automatically between certain sources or conditions in equipment, or performs a transfer operation automatically.

Device Number	Definition and Function
84	**Operating Mechanism** – The complete electrical mechanism or servo-mechanism, including the operating motor, solenoids, position switches, etc., for a tap changer, induction regulator, or any similar piece of apparatus which has no device function number.
85	**Carrier or Pilot-Wire Receiver Relay** – A relay that is operated or restrained by a signal used in connection with carrier-current or DC pilot-wire fault directional relaying.
86	**Locking-Out Relay** – An electrically-operated relay that functions to shut down and hold equipment out of service on the occurrence of abnormal conditions. It may be reset either manually or electrically.
87	**Differential Protective Relay** – A protective relay that functions on a percentage of phase angle or other quantitative difference of two currents or of some other electrical quantities.
88	**Auxiliary Motor or Motor Generator** – A device used for operating auxiliary equipment such as pumps, blowers, exciters, rotating magnetic amplifiers, etc.
89	**Line Switch** – A switch used as a disconnecting load-interrupter, or isolating switch in an AC or DC power circuit, when this device is electrically operated or has electrical accessories, such as an auxiliary switch, magnetic lock, etc.
90	**Regulating Device** – A device that functions to regulate a quantity or quantities such as voltage, current, power, speed, frequency, temperature, and load, at a certain value or between certain (generally close) limits for machines, tie lines, or other apparatus.
91	**Voltage Directional Relay** – A relay that operates when the voltage across an open circuit breaker or contactor exceeds a given value in a given direction.
92	**Voltage and Power Directional Relay** – A relay that permits or causes the connection of two circuits when the voltage difference between them exceeds a given value in a predetermined direction and causes these two circuits to be disconnected from each other when the power flowing between them exceeds a given value in the opposite direction.
93	**Field Changing Contactor** – A device that functions to increase or decrease in one step the value of field excitation on a machine.
94	**Tripping or Trip-Free Relay** – A device that functions to trip a circuit breaker, contactor, or equipment, or to permit immediate tripping by other devices, or to prevent immediate reclosure of a circuit interrupter in case it should open automatically even though its closing circuit is maintained closed.
95 96 97	Used only for specific applications on individual installations where none of the assigned numbered functions from 1 to 94 is suitable.

The NCCER makes every effort to keep these manuals up-to-date and free of technical errors. We appreciate your help in this process. If you have an idea for improving this manual, or if you find an error, a typographical mistake, or an inaccuracy in the NCCER's Craft Training Manuals, please write us, using this form or a photocopy. Be sure to include the exact module number, page number, a description of the problem, and the correction, if possible. Your input will be brought to the attention of the Technical Review Committee. Thank you for your assistance.

Instructors – If you found that additional materials were necessary in order to teach this module effectively, please let us know so that we may include them in the Equipment/Materials list in the Instructor's Guide.

Write: Curriculum Development and Revision Department
National Center for Construction Education and Research
P.O. Box 141104
Gainesville, FL 32614-1104

Fax: 352-334-0932

Craft ________________________ Module Name ________________________

Copyright Date __________ Module Number __________ Page Number(s) __________

Description of Problem

____

____

____

____

(Optional) Correction of Problem

____

____

____

(Optional) Your Name and Address

____

____

____

Distribution System Transformers

Module 26307

NATIONAL
CENTER FOR
CONSTRUCTION
EDUCATION AND
RESEARCH

DISTRIBUTION SYSTEM TRANSFORMERS

OBJECTIVES

Upon completion of this module, the trainee will be able to:

1. Describe transformer operation.
2. Explain the principle of mutual induction.
3. Describe the operating characteristics of various types of transformers.
4. Connect a multi-tap transformer for the required secondary voltage.
5. Explain NEC requirements governing the installation of transformers.
6. Compute transformer sizes for various applications.
7. Explain types and purposes of grounding transformers.
8. Connect a control transformer for a given application.
9. Size the maximum load allowed on open delta systems.
10. Describe how current transformers are used in conjunction with watt-hour meters.
11. Apply capacitors and rectifiers to practical applications.
12. Calculate the power factor of any given electrical circuit.

Prerequisites

Successful completion of the following Task Module is recommended before beginning study of this Task Module: Core Curricula; Electrical Level 1; Electrical Level 2; Electrical Level 3, Modules 26301 through 26306.

Required Trainee Materials

1. Trainee Task Module
2. Appropriate Personal Protective Equipment
3. Copy of the latest edition of the *National Electrical Code*

Note: The designations "National Electrical Code," "NE Code," and "NEC," where used in this document, refer to the National Electrical Code®, which is a registered trademark of the National Fire Protection Association, Quincy, MA. *All National Electrical Code (NEC) references in this module refer to the 1999 edition of the NEC.*

COURSE MAP

This course map shows all of the modules in the third level of the Electrical curricula. The suggested training order begins at the bottom and proceeds up. Skill levels increase as a trainee advances on the course map. The training order may be adjusted by the local Training Program Sponsor.

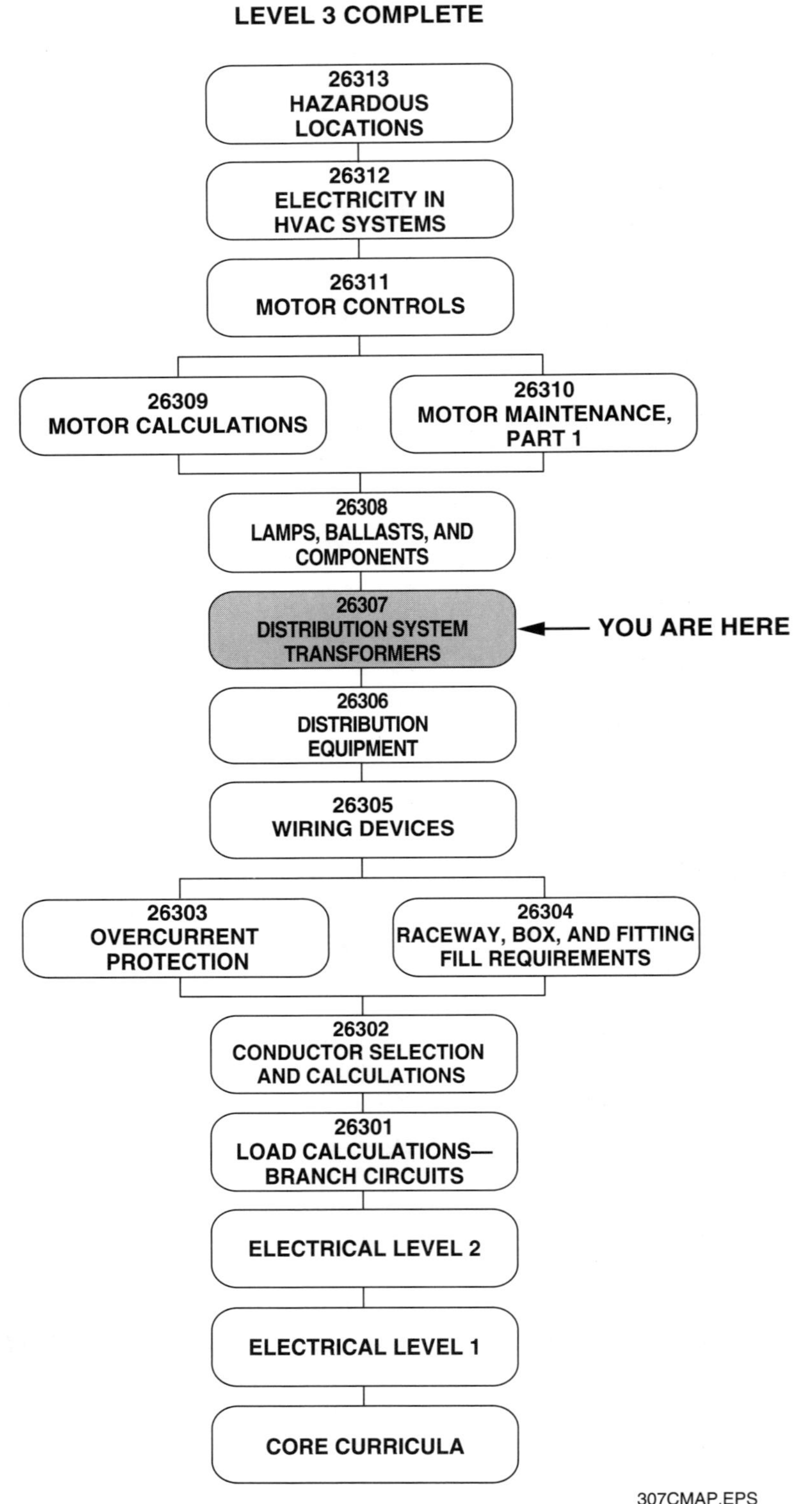

TABLE OF CONTENTS

Trade Terms Introduced In This Module

Ampere turn: The product of amperes times the number of turns in a coil.

Autotransformer: Any transformer in which primary and secondary connections are made to a single coil. The application of an autotransformer is a good choice where a 480Y/277V or 208Y/120V, three-phase, four-wire distribution system is used.

Capacitance: The storage of electricity in a capacitor or the opposition to voltage change. Capacitance is measured in farads (f) or microfarads (μf).

Current transformer: A single-phase instrument transformer connected in series in a line that carries the full-load current. The turns ratio is designed to produce a reduced current in the secondary suitable for the current coil of standard measuring instruments and in proportion to the load current.

Flux: The rate of energy flow across or through a surface. Also, a substance used to promote or facilitate soldering or welding by removing surface oxides.

Hertz (Hz): The derived SI unit for frequency. One Hertz equals one cycle per second.

Induction: The production of magnetization or electrification in a body by the mere proximity of magnetized or electrified bodies, or of an electric current in a conductor by the variation of the magnetic field in its vicinity.

Kilovolt-amperes (kVA): 1,000 volt-amperes (VA).

Loss: The power expended without doing useful work.

Magnetic field: The area around a magnet in which the effect of the magnet can be felt.

Magnetic induction: The number of magnetic lines or the magnetic flux per unit of cross-sectional area perpendicular to the direction of the flux.

Mutual induction: The condition of voltage in a second conductor because of current in another conductor.

Potential transformer: A special transformer designed for use in measuring high voltage; normally, the secondary voltage is 120V.

Power transformer: A transformer that is designed to transfer electrical power from the primary circuit to the secondary circuit(s) to step up the secondary voltage at less current or step down the secondary voltage at more current, with the voltage-current product being constant for either the primary or secondary.

Reactance: The opposition to AC due to capacitance and/or inductance.

Rectifiers: Devices used to change alternating current to direct current.

Transformer: A static device consisting of one or more windings with a magnetic core. Transformers are used for introducing mutual coupling by induction between circuits.

Turn: The basic coil element that forms a single conducting loop comprised of one insulated conductor.

Turns ratio: The ratio between the number of turns between windings in a transformer; normally the primary to the secondary, except for current transformers, in which it is the ratio of the secondary to the primary.

1.0.0   INTRODUCTION

The electric power produced by alternators in a generating station is transmitted to locations where it is utilized and distributed to users. Many different types of **transformers** play an important role in the distribution of electricity. The main purpose of a transformer is to change the output voltage. **Power transformers** are located at generating stations to step up the voltage for more economical transmission. Substations with additional power transformers and distribution equipment are installed along the transmission line. Finally, distribution transformers are used to step down the voltage to a level suitable for utilization.

Transformers are also used quite extensively in all types of control work to raise and lower AC voltage on control circuits. They are also used in 480Y/277V systems to reduce the voltage for operating 208Y/120V lighting and other electrically-operated equipment. Buck-and-boost transformers are used for maintaining appropriate voltage levels in certain electrical systems.

It is important for anyone working with electricity to become familiar with all aspects of transformer operation—how they work, how they are connected into circuits, their practical applications, and precautions to take during the installation or while working on them. This module is designed to cover these items as well as overcurrent protection and grounding. Other subjects include correcting power factor with capacitors and the application of **rectifiers**.

2.0.0   TRANSFORMER BASICS

A very basic transformer consists of two coils or windings formed on a single magnetic core, as shown in *Figure 1*. Such an arrangement will allow transforming a large alternating current at a low voltage into a small alternating current at a high voltage, or vice versa.

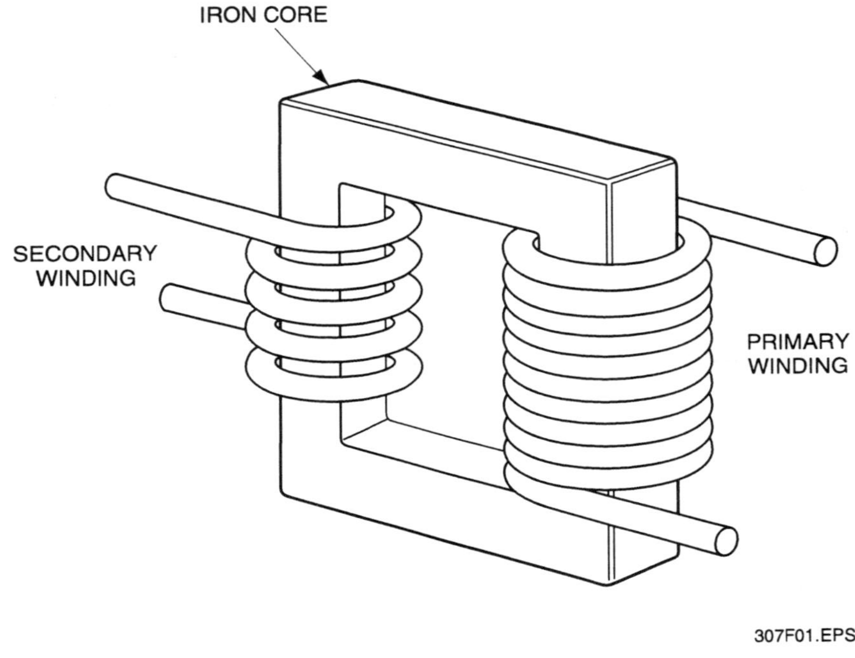

Figure 1. Basic Components Of A Transformer

2.1.0   MUTUAL INDUCTION

The term **mutual induction** refers to the condition in which two circuits are sharing the energy of one of the circuits. It means that energy is being transferred from one circuit to the other.

Consider the diagram in *Figure 2*. Coil A is the primary circuit which obtains energy from the battery. When the switch is closed, the current starts to flow and a **magnetic field** expands out of coil A. Coil A then changes the electrical energy of the battery into the magnetic energy (**induction**) of a magnetic field. When the field of coil A is expanding, it cuts across coil B, the secondary circuit, inducing a voltage in coil B. The indicator (a galvanometer) in the secondary circuit is deflected and shows that a current, developed by the induced voltage, is flowing in the circuit.

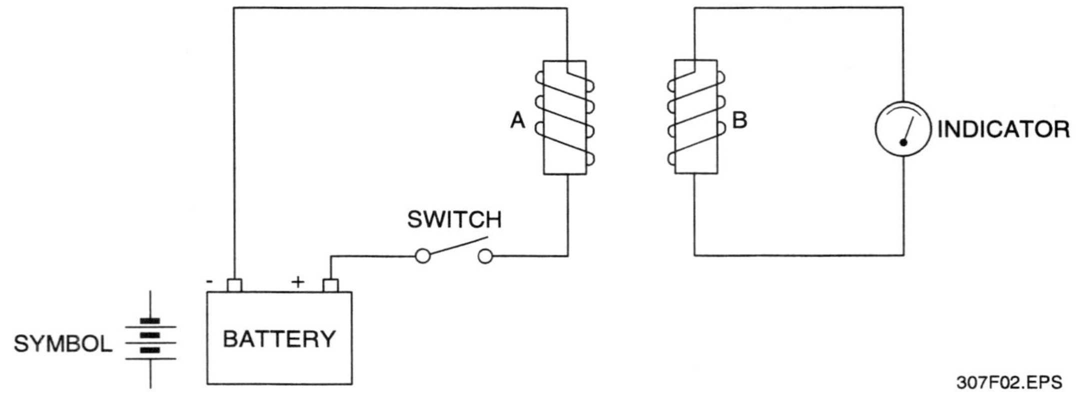

Figure 2. Mutual Induction Circuits

ELECTRICAL — TRAINEE TASK MODULE 26307

The induced voltage may be generated by moving coil B through the **flux** of coil A. However, this voltage is induced without moving coil B. When the switch in the primary circuit is open, coil A has no current and no field. As soon as the switch is closed, current passes through the coil, and the magnetic field is generated. This expanding field moves or cuts across the wires of coil B, thus inducing a voltage without the movement of coil B.

The magnetic field expands to its maximum strength and remains constant as long as full current flows. Flux lines stop their cutting action across the **turns** of coil B because the expansion of the field has ceased. At this point, the indicator needle on the meter reads zero because the induced voltage no longer exists. If the switch is opened, the field collapses back to the wires of coil A. As it does so, the changing flux cuts across the wires of coil B, but in the opposite direction. The current present in the coil causes the indicator needle to deflect, showing this new direction. Therefore, the indicator shows current flow only when the field is changing, either building up or collapsing. In effect, the changing field produces an induced voltage in the same way as a magnetic field moving across a conductor. This principle of inducing voltage by holding the coils steady and forcing the field to change is used in innumerable applications. The transformer is particularly suitable for operation by mutual induction. Transformers are the ideal components for transferring and changing AC voltages as needed.

Transformers are generally composed of two coils placed close to each other, but not connected. Refer once more to *Figure 1*. The coil that receives energy from the line voltage source is called the *primary,* and the coil that delivers energy to a load is called the *secondary*. Even though the coils are not physically connected, they manage to convert and transfer energy as required by a process known as *mutual induction.*

Transformers, therefore, enable changing or converting power from one voltage to another. For example, generators that produce moderately large alternating currents at moderately high voltages use transformers to convert the power to a very high voltage and proportionately small current in transmission lines, permitting the use of smaller cable and producing less power **loss**.

When alternating current (AC) flows through a coil, an alternating magnetic field is generated around the coil. This alternating magnetic field expands outward from the center of the coil and collapses into the coil as the AC through the coil varies from zero to a maximum and back to zero again, as discussed in an earlier module. Since the alternating magnetic field must cut through the turns of the coil, a self-inducing voltage occurs in the coil, which opposes the change in current flow.

If the alternating magnetic field generated by one coil cuts through the turns of a second coil, voltage will be generated in this second coil just as voltage is induced in a coil which is cut by its own magnetic field. The induced voltage in the second coil is called the *voltage of mutual induction* and the action of generating this voltage is called *transformer action*. In transformer action, electrical energy is transferred from one coil (the primary) to another (the secondary) by means of a varying magnetic field.

2.2.0 INDUCTION IN TRANSFORMERS

As stated previously, a simple transformer consists of two coils located very close together and electrically insulated from one another. The primary coil generates a magnetic field which cuts through the turns of the secondary coil and generates a voltage in it. The coils are magnetically coupled to each other, and consequently, a transformer transfers electrical power from one coil to another by means of an alternating magnetic field.

Assuming that all the magnetic lines of force from the primary cut through all the turns of the secondary, the voltage induced in the secondary will depend on the ratio of the number of turns in the primary to the number of turns in the secondary. For example, if there are 100 turns in the primary and only 10 turns in the secondary, the voltage in the primary will be 10 times the voltage in the secondary. Since there are more turns in the primary than there are in the secondary, the transformer is called a *step-down transformer*. Transformers are rated in **kilovolt-amperes (kVA)** because it is independent of power factor. *Figure 3* shows a diagram of a step-down transformer with a **turns ratio** of 100:10 or 10:1.

$$\frac{10 \text{ turns}}{100 \text{ turns}} = 0.10 = .10 \times 120V = 12V$$

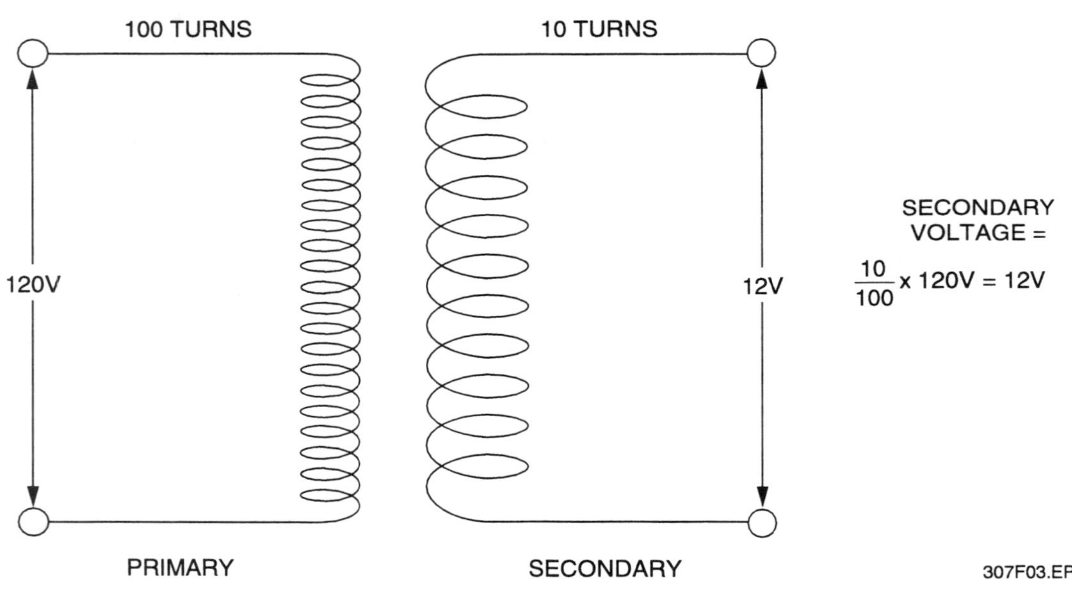

Figure 3. Step-Down Transformer With A 10:1 Turns Ratio

Assuming that all the primary magnetic lines of force cut through all the turns of the secondary, the amount of induced voltage in the secondary will vary with the ratio of the number of turns in the secondary to the number of turns in the primary.

If there are more turns in the secondary winding than in the primary winding, the secondary voltage will be higher than that in the primary and by the same proportion as the number of turns in the winding. The secondary current, in turn, will be proportionately smaller than the primary current. With fewer turns in the secondary than in the primary, the secondary voltage will be proportionately lower than that in the primary, and the secondary current will be proportionately larger. Since alternating current continually increases and decreases in value, every change in the primary winding of the transformer produces a similar change of flux in the core. Every change of flux in the core and every corresponding movement of the magnetic field around the core produce a similarly changing voltage in the secondary winding, causing an alternating current to flow in the circuit that is connected to the secondary.

For example, if there are 100 turns in the secondary and only 10 turns in the primary, the voltage induced in the secondary will be 10 times the voltage applied to the primary. See *Figure 4*. Since there are more turns in the secondary than in the primary, the transformer is called a *step-up transformer*.

$$\frac{100}{10} = 10 \times 12V = 120V$$

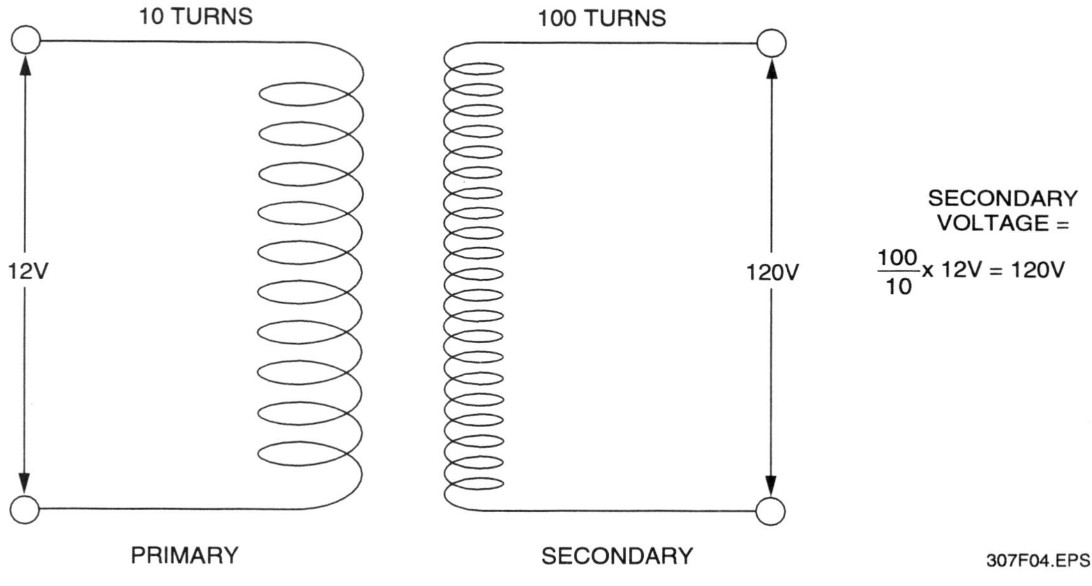

Figure 4. Step-Up Transformer With A 1:10 Turns Ratio

Note: A transformer does not generate electric power. It simply transfers electric power from one coil to another by **magnetic induction**. Transformers are rated in either volt-amperes (VA) or kilovolt-amperes (kVA).

2.3.0   MAGNETIC FLUX IN TRANSFORMERS

Figure 5 shows a cross-section of what is known as a *high-leakage flux transformer*. In these transformers, if no load were connected to the secondary or output winding, a voltmeter would indicate a specific voltage reading across the secondary terminals. If a load were applied, the voltage would drop, and if the terminals were shorted, the voltage would drop to zero. During these circuit changes, the flux in the core of the transformer would also change; it is forced out of the transformer core and is known as *leakage flux*. Leaking flux can actually be demonstrated with iron filings placed close to the transformer core. As the changes take place, the filings will shift their position, clearly showing the change in the flux pattern.

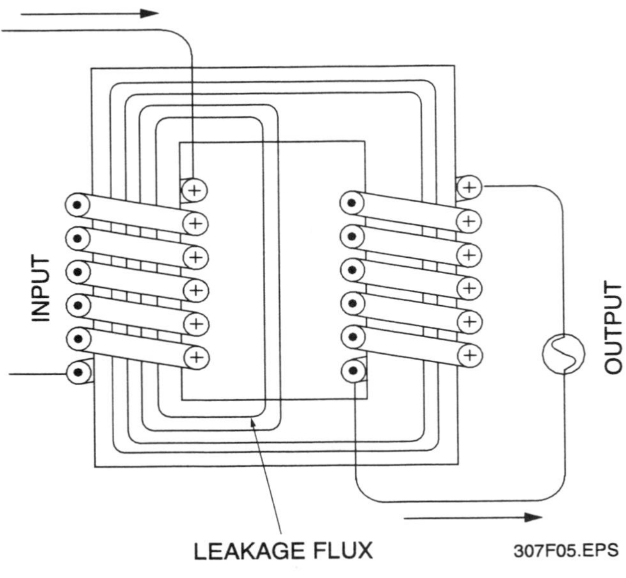

Figure 5. Transformer With High-Leakage Flux

What actually happens is that as the current flows in the secondary, it tries to create its own magnetic field which is in opposition to the original flux field. This action, like a valve in a water system, restricts the flux flow, which forces the excess flux to find another path, either through the air or in adjacent structural steel as in transformer housings or supporting clamps.

Note that the coils in *Figure 5* are wrapped on the same iron core, but are separated from each other, while the transformer in *Figure 6* has its coils wrapped around each other, which results in a low-leakage transformer design.

3.0.0 TRANSFORMER CONSTRUCTION

Transformers that are designed to operate on low frequencies have their coils, called *windings*, wound on iron cores. Since iron offers little resistance to magnetic lines, nearly all the magnetic field of the primary flows through the iron core and cuts the secondary.

Iron cores of transformers are constructed in three basic types: the open core, the closed core, and the shell type. See *Figure 7*. The open core is the least expensive to manufacture as the primary and secondary are wound on one cylindrical core. The magnetic path, as shown in *Figure 7*, is partially through the core and partially through the surrounding air. The air path opposes the magnetic field, so that the magnetic interaction or linkage is weakened. Therefore, the open core transformer is highly inefficient.

ELECTRICAL — TRAINEE TASK MODULE 26307

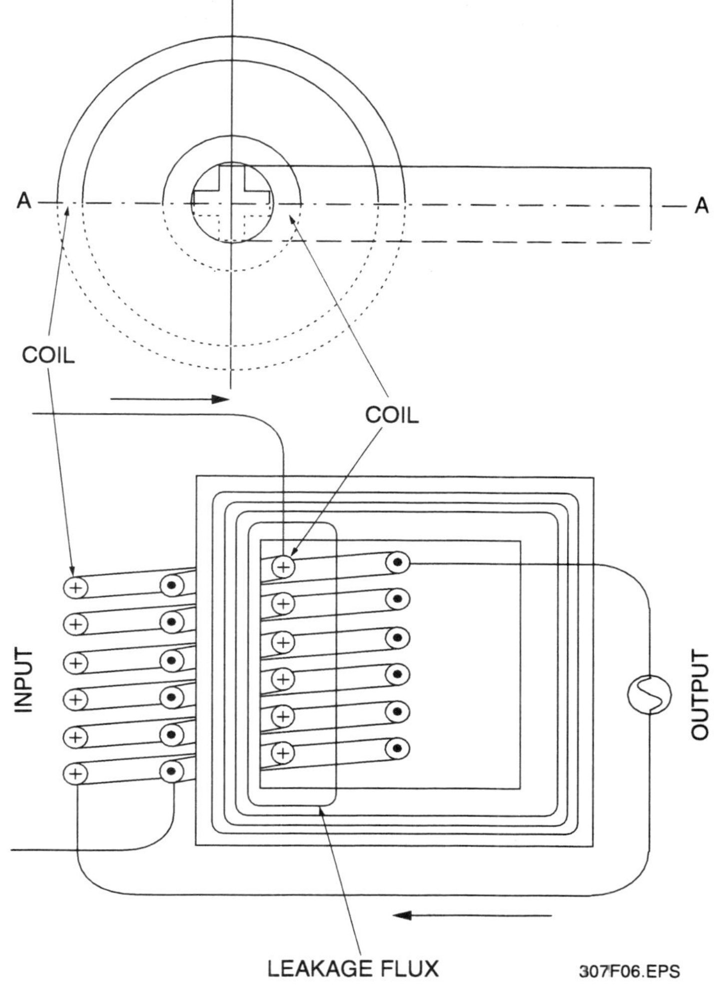

Figure 6. Low-Leakage Transformer

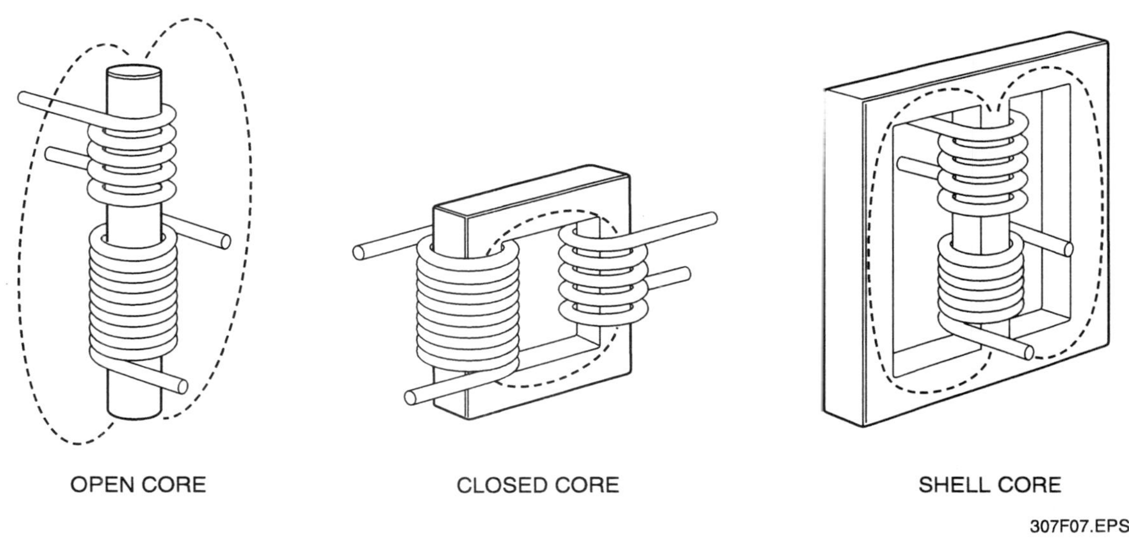

Figure 7. Three Types Of Iron Core Transformers

The closed core improves the transformer efficiency by offering more iron paths and a reduced air path for the magnetic field. The shell-type core further increases the magnetic coupling and therefore, the transformer efficiency is greater due to two parallel magnetic paths for the magnetic field, providing maximum coupling between the primary and the secondary.

3.1.0 CORES

Special core steel is used to provide a controlled path for the flow of magnetic flux generated in a transformer. In most practical applications, the transformer core is not a solid bar of steel, but is constructed of many layers of thin sheet steel called *laminations*.

While the specifications of the core steel are primarily of interest to the transformer design engineer, the electrical worker should at least have a conversational knowledge of the materials used.

The steel used for transformer core laminations will vary with the manufacturer, but a popular size is .014" thick and is called *29-gauge steel*. It is processed from silicon iron alloys containing approximately 3¼% silicon. The addition of silicon to the iron increases its ability to be magnetized and also renders it essentially non-aging.

The most important characteristic of electrical steel is core loss. It is measured in watts per pound at a specified frequency and flux density. The core loss is responsible for the heating in the transformer and also contributes to the heating of the windings. Much of the core loss is a result of eddy currents which are induced in the laminations when the core is energized. To hold this loss to a minimum, adjacent laminations are coated with an inorganic varnish.

Cores may either be of the core type, as shown in *Figure 8*, or the shell type, as shown in *Figure 9*. Of the two, the core type is favored for dry-type transformers for the following reasons:

- Only three core legs require stacking, thus reducing cost.
- Steel does not encircle the two outer coils; this provides better cooling.
- The required floor space is reduced.

3.2.0 TYPES OF CORES

Transformer cores are normally available in three types:

- Butt
- Wound
- Mitered cores

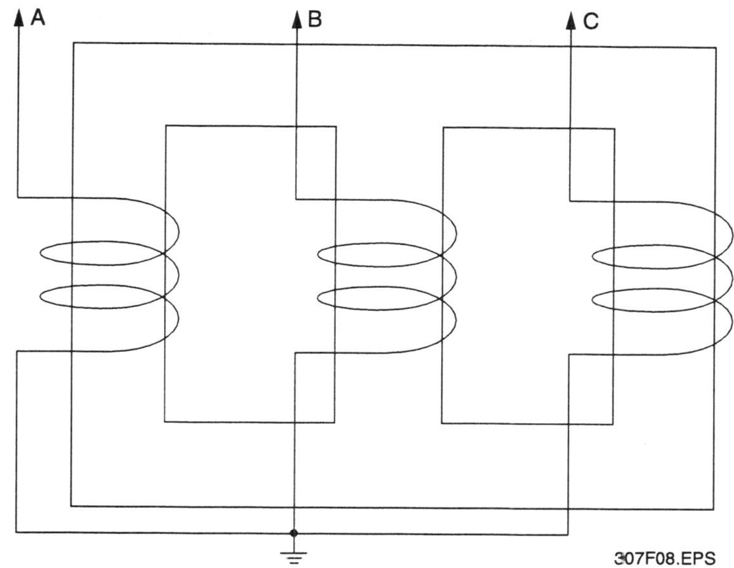

Figure 8. Core-Type Transformer Construction

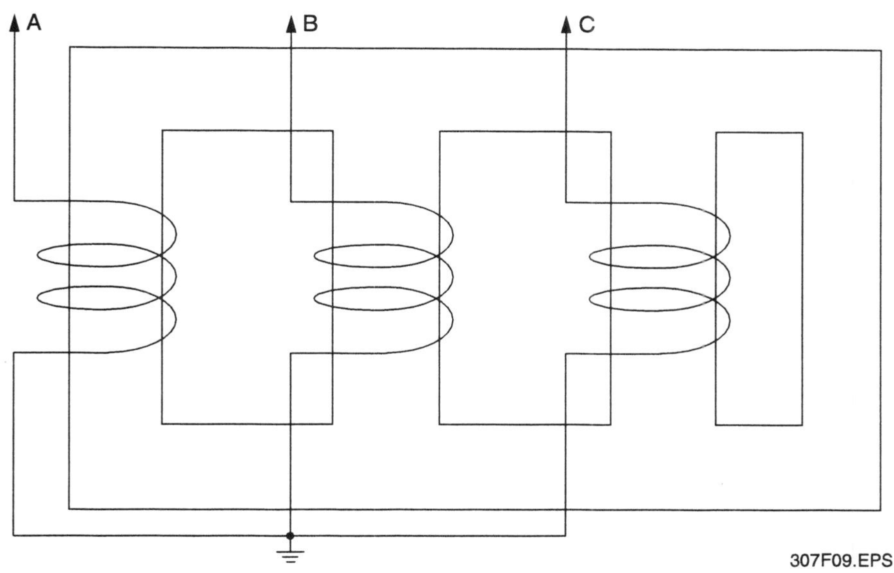

Figure 9. Shell-Type Transformer Core

The butt-and-lap core is shown in *Figure 10*. Only two sizes of core steel are needed in this type of core due to the lap construction shown at the top and right side. For ease of understanding, the core strips are shown much thicker than the .014" thickness mentioned earlier. Each strip is carefully cut so that the air gap indicated in the lower left corner is as small as possible. The permeability of steel to the passage of flux is about 10,000 times as effective as air, hence the air gap must be held to the barest minimum to reduce the **ampere turns** necessary to achieve adequate flux density. Also, the amount of sound produced by a transformer due to magneto-striction is a function of the flux density, which produces a difference between this construction and other types.

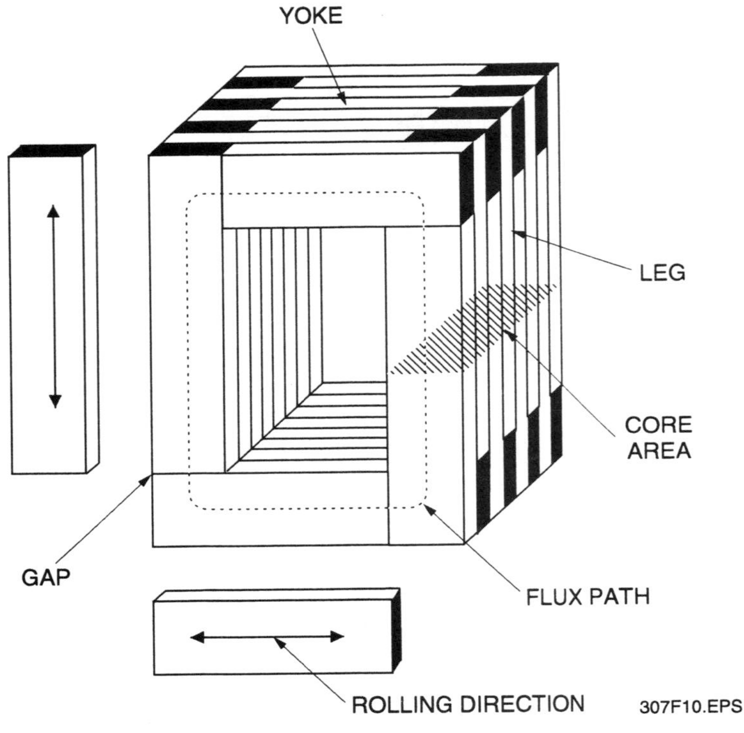

Figure 10. Butt-And-Lap Transformer Core

Another phenomenon in core steel is that the flux flows more easily in the direction in which the steel was rolled. This also varies between hot-rolled steel and cold-rolled steel. For example, the core loss due to flux passing at right angles to the rolling direction is almost 1½ times as great in hot-rolled steel and 2½ times as great in cold-rolled steel when compared with the core loss in the direction of rolling. The difference in exciting current is more dramatic, with ratios of two to one in hot-rolled steel and almost 40 to 1 in cold-rolled steel. These are primarily the designer's concern, but you should know that there is a difference.

Eddy currents are restricted from passage from one lamination to another due to the inorganic insulating coating. However, the magnetic lines of flux easily transfer at adjacent laminations in the lap area but in so doing, they are forced to cross at an angle to the preferred direction.

3.3.0 WOUND CORES

Because of the unique characteristics of core steel, some core designs are made to take advantage of these differences. One such type is shown in *Figure 11*. The core loops are cut to predetermined lengths so that the gap locations do not coincide. These cuts permit assembling the core around a prewound coil that passes through both openings. Another design, now discontinued because of unfavorable cost, used a continuous core with no cuts. Separate coils had to be wound on each of the vertical legs of the completed core. You may encounter transformers of this type in existing installations.

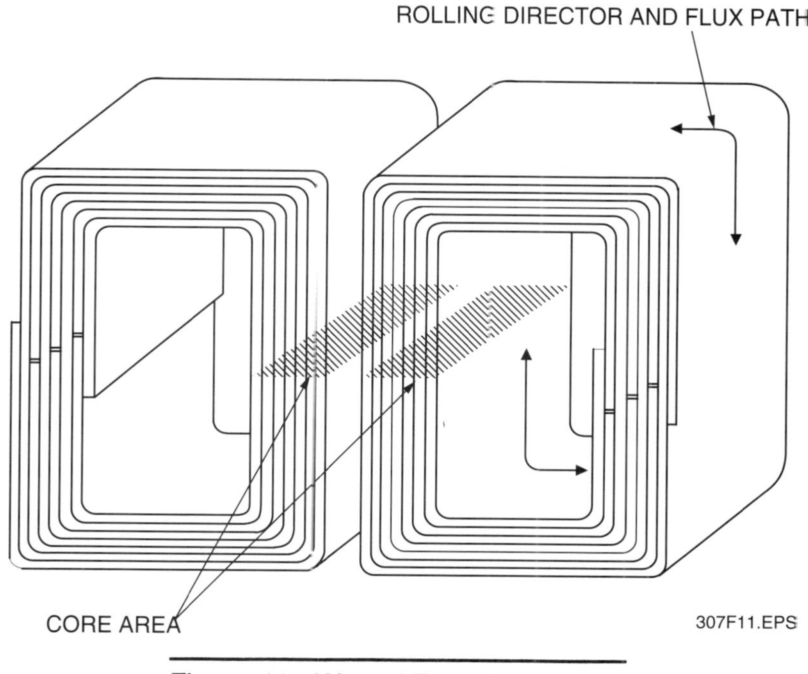

Figure 11. Wound Transformer Coil

3.4.0   MITERED CORES

Figure 12 shows a mitered core design. It is basically a butt-lap core with the joints made at 45° angles.

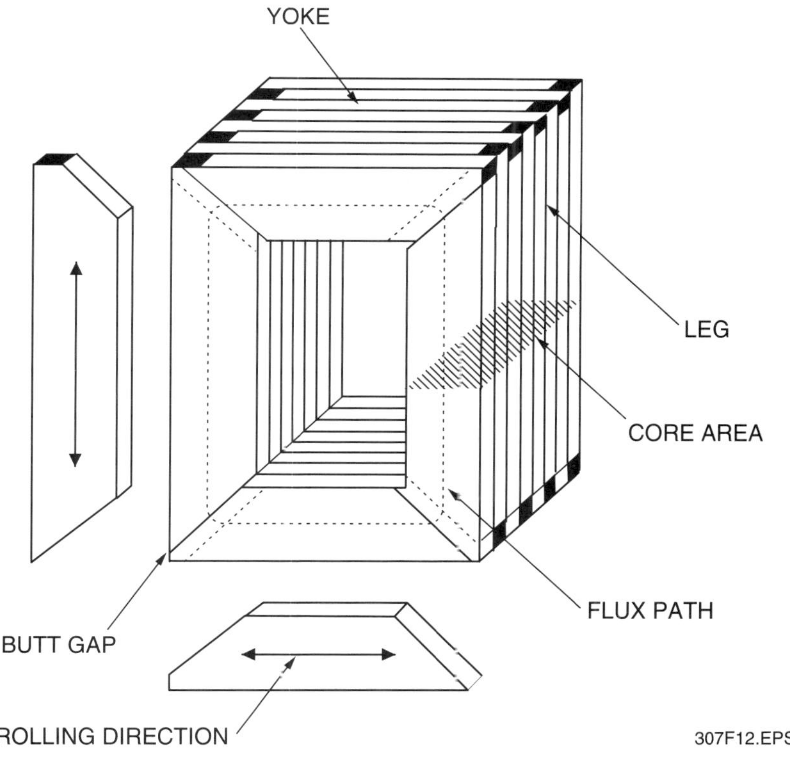

Figure 12. Mitered Transformer Core

There are two benefits derived from this type of joint:

- It eliminates all cross grain flux, and thereby improves the core loss and exciting current values.
- It reduces the flux density in the air gap, resulting in lower sound levels.

This type of core is normally used only with cold-rolled, grain-oriented steel, and permits this steel to be used to its fullest capability.

3.5.0 TRANSFORMER CHARACTERISTICS

In a well-designed transformer, there is very little magnetic leakage. The effect of the leakage is to cause a decrease of secondary voltage when the transformer is loaded. When a current flows through the secondary in phase with the secondary voltage, a corresponding current flows through the primary in addition to the magnetizing current. The magnetizing effects of the two currents are equal and opposite.

In a perfect transformer (i.e., one having no eddy current losses, no resistance in its windings, and no magnetic leakage), the magnetizing effects of the primary load current and the secondary current neutralize each other, leaving only the constant primary magnetizing current effective in setting up the constant flux. If supplied with a constant primary pressure, such a transformer would maintain constant secondary pressure at all loads. Obviously, the perfect transformer has yet to be built; the best transformers available today have a very small eddy current loss where the drop in pressure in the secondary windings is not more than 1% to 3%, depending on the size of the transformer.

4.0.0 TRANSFORMER TAPS

If the exact rated voltage could be delivered at every transformer location, transformer taps would be unnecessary. However, this is not possible, so taps are provided on the secondary windings to provide a means of either increasing or decreasing the secondary voltage.

Generally, if a load is very close to a substation or power plant, the voltage will consistently be above normal. Near the end of the line, the voltage may be below normal.

In large transformers, it would naturally be very inconvenient to move the thick, well-insulated primary leads to different tap positions when changes in source voltage levels make this necessary. Therefore, taps are used, such as those shown in the wiring diagram in *Figure 13*. In this transformer, the permanent high-voltage leads would be connected to H_1 and H_2, and the secondary leads, in their normal fashion, to X_1 and X_2, and X_3 and X_4. Note, however, the tap arrangements available at taps 2 through 7. Until a pair of these taps is interconnected with a jumper wire, the primary circuit is not completed. If this were a typical 7,200V primary, the transformer would normally have 1,620 turns. Assume 810 of these turns are between H_1 and H_6 and another 810 between H_3 and H_2. Then, if taps 6 and 3 are connected with a flexible jumper on which lugs have already been installed, the primary circuit is completed and we have a normal ratio transformer that could deliver 120/240V from the secondary.

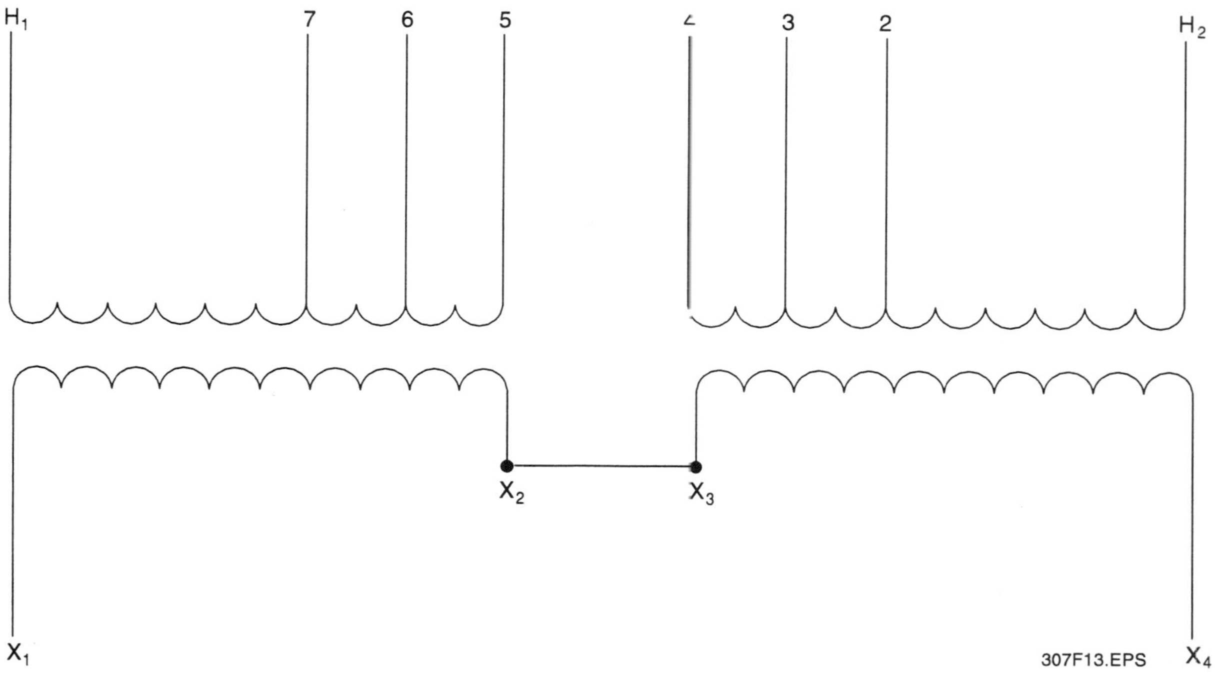

Figure 13. Transformer Taps To Adjust Secondary Voltage

Between taps 6 and either 5 or 7, 40 turns of wire exist. Similarly, between taps 3 and either 2 or 4, 40 turns are present. Changing the jumper from 3 to 6 to 3 to 7 removes 40 turns from the left half of the primary. The same condition would apply on the right half of the winding if the jumper were between taps 6 and 2. Either connection would boost secondary voltage by 2½%. Had taps 2 and 7 been connected, 80 turns would have been omitted, and a 5% boost would result. Placing the jumper between taps 6 and 4 or 3 and 5 would reduce the output voltage by 5%.

5.0.0 BASIC TRANSFORMER CONNECTIONS

Transformer connections are many, and space does not permit the description of all of them here. However, an understanding of a few connection types will give the basic requirements and make it possible to use manufacturer's data for others should the need arise.

5.1.0 SINGLE-PHASE LIGHT AND POWER

The diagram in *Figure 14* is a transformer connection used extensively in residential and small commercial applications. It is the most common single-phase distribution system in use today. It is known as the three-wire, 120/240V single-phase system and is used where 120V and 240V are used simultaneously.

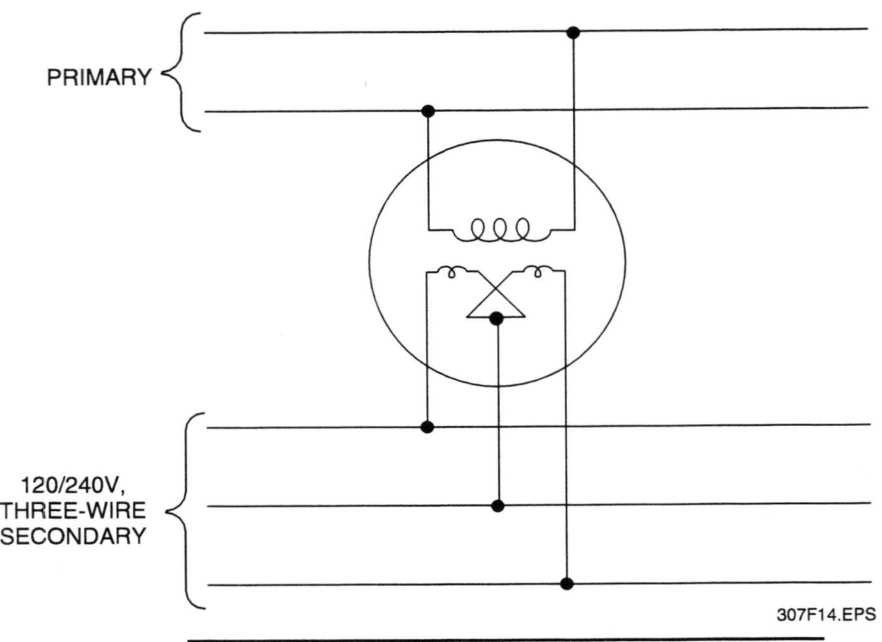

Figure 14. Single-Phase Transformer Connection

5.2.0 Y-Y SYSTEM FOR LIGHT AND POWER

The primaries of the transformer connection in *Figure 15* are connected in a wye configuration, which is sometimes called a *star connection*. When the primary system is 2,400/4,160Y volts, a 4,160V transformer is required when the system is connected in a delta Y configuration. However, with a Y-Y (wye-wye) system, a 2,400V transformer can be used, offering a savings in transformer cost.

It is necessary that a primary neutral be available when this connection is used, and the neutrals of the primary system and the transformer bank are tied together, as shown in the diagram. If the three-phase load is unbalanced, part of the load current flows in the primary neutral. For these reasons, it is essential that the neutrals be tied together as shown. If this tie were omitted, the line-to-neutral voltages on the secondary would be very unstable (i.e., if the load on one phase were heavier than on the other two, the voltage on this phase would drop excessively, and the voltage on the other two phases would rise).

Also, varying voltages would appear between the lines and the neutral, both in the transformers and in the secondary system, in addition to the 60 **hertz (Hz)** component of voltage. This means that for a given value of rms voltage, the peak voltage would be much higher than for a pure 60Hz voltage. This overstresses the insulation both in the transformers and in all apparatus connected to the secondaries.

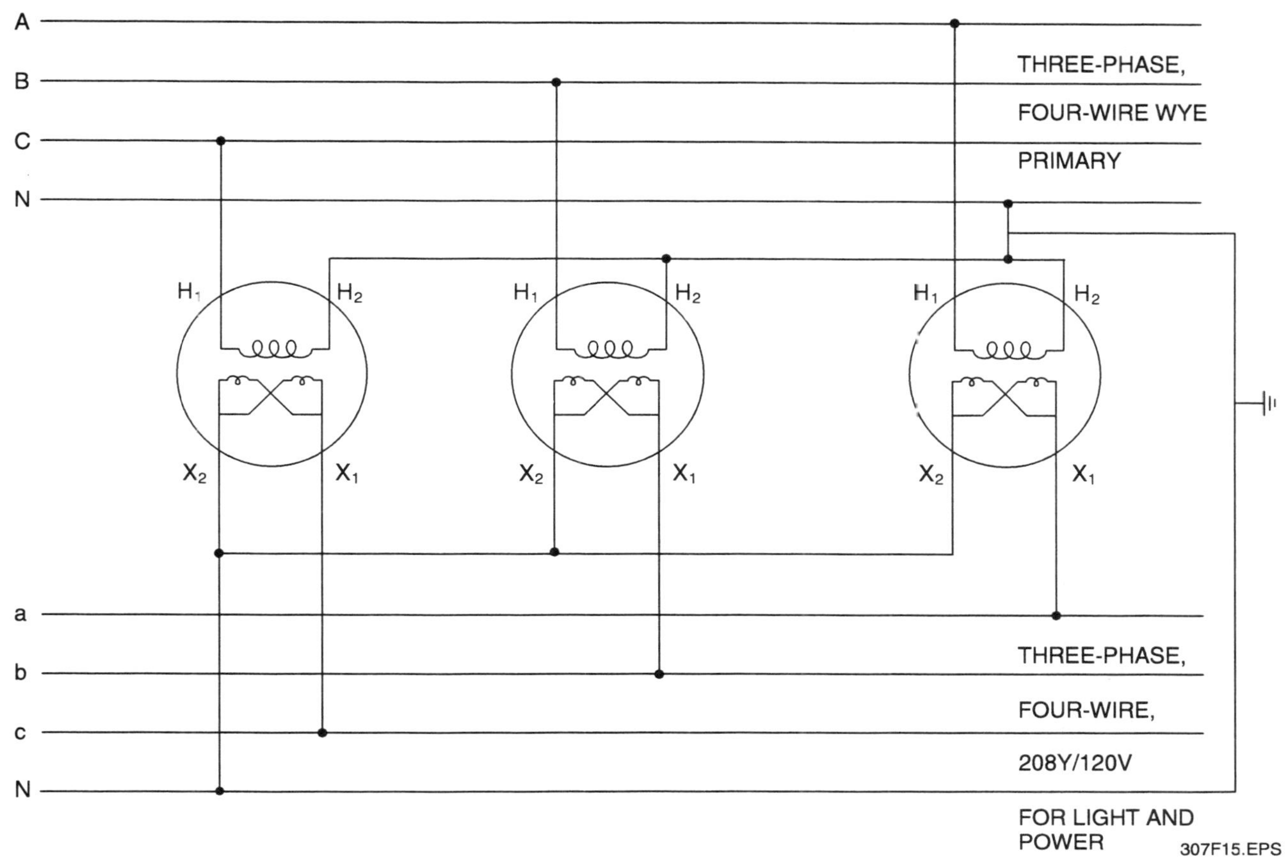

Figure 15. Y-Y Transformer System

5.3.0 DELTA-CONNECTED TRANSFORMERS

The delta-connected system in *Figure 16* operates a little differently from the previously described wye-wye system. While the wye-connected system is formed by connecting one terminal from each of three equal voltage transformer windings together to make a common terminal, the delta-connected system has its windings connected in series, forming a triangle or the Greek symbol delta (Δ). In *Figure 17*, a center-tapped terminal is used on one winding to ground the system. A 120/240V system has 120V between the center-tapped terminal and each ungrounded terminal on either side (i.e., phases A and C), and 240V across the full winding of each phase.

Refer to *Figure 17* and note that a high leg results at point *B*. This is also known as the *red leg* or *wild leg*. This high leg has a higher voltage to ground than the other two phases. The voltage of the high leg can be determined by multiplying the voltage to ground of either of the other two legs by the square root of 3, which we round to a value of 1.732. Therefore, if the voltage between phase A to ground is 120V, the voltage between phase B to ground may be determined as follows:

$$120V \times 1.732 = 207.84V = 208V$$

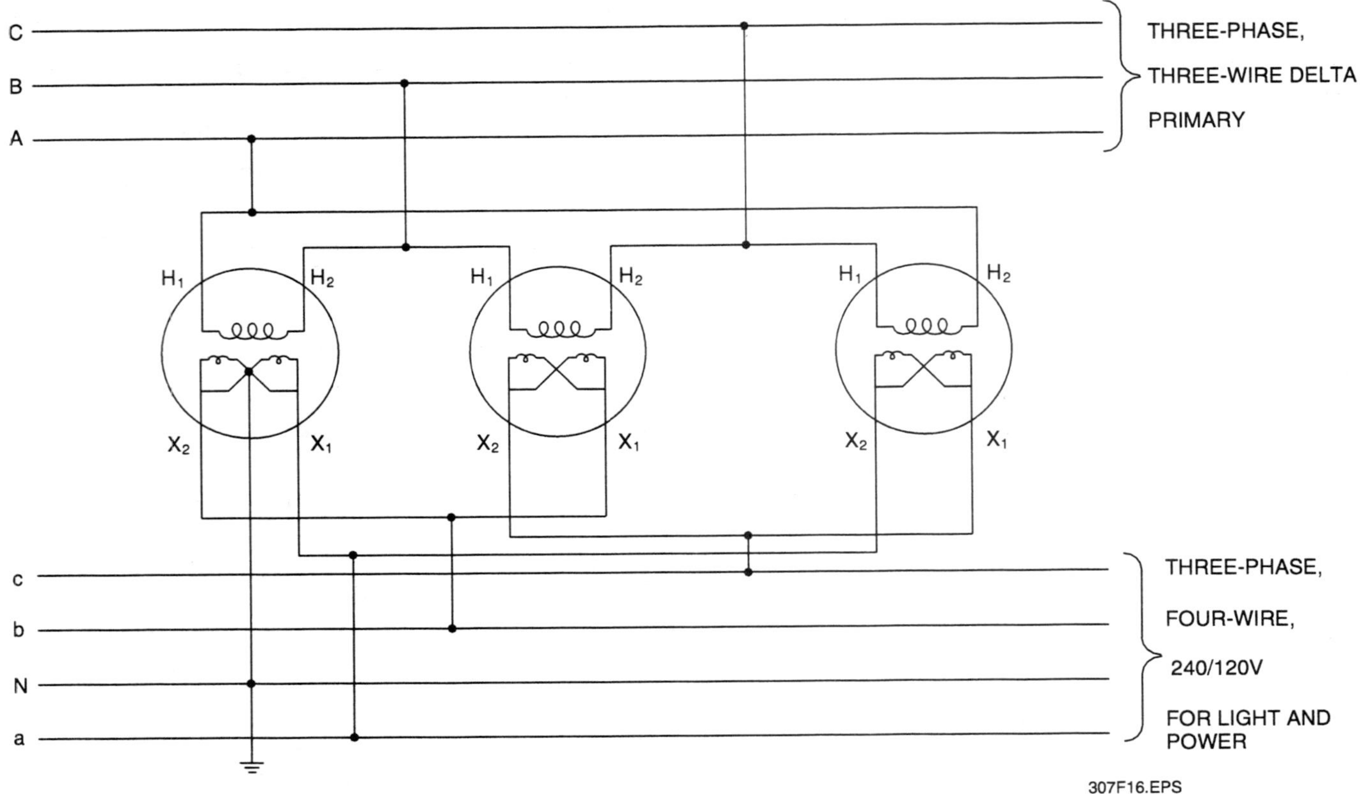

Figure 16. Delta-Connected Secondary

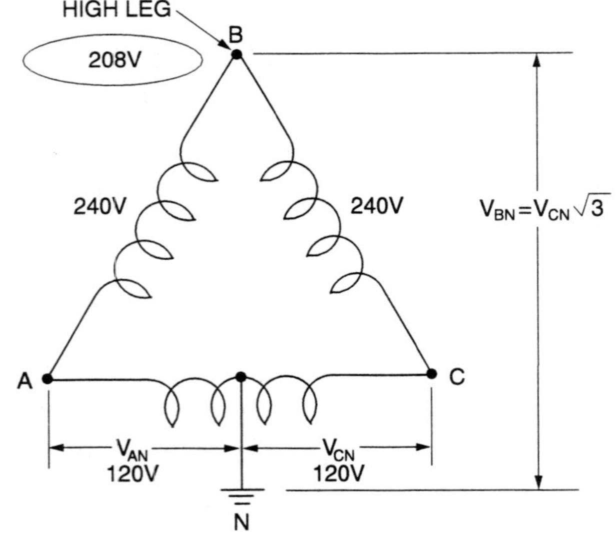

On a three-phase, four-wire, 120/240V delta-connected system, the midpoint of one phase winding is grounded to provide 120V between phase A and ground; also between phase C and ground. Between phase B and ground, however, the voltage is higher and may be calculated by multiplying the voltage between C and ground (120V) by the square root of 3 or 1.732. Consequently, the voltage between phase B and ground is approximately 208V (thus, the term *high leg*).

The NEC requires that conductors connected to the high leg of a four-wire delta system be color-coded with orange insulation or tape.

Figure 17. Characteristics Of A Center-Tapped, Delta-Connected System

ELECTRICAL — TRAINEE TASK MODULE 26307

From this, it should be obvious that no single-pole breakers should be connected to the high leg of a center-tapped, four-wire, delta-connected system. In fact, **NEC Sections 215-8 and 384-3(e)** require that the phase busbar or conductor having the higher voltage to ground be permanently marked by an outer finish that is orange in color. This prevents future workers from connecting 120V single-phase loads to this high leg, which would probably damage any equipment connected to the circuit. Remember the color orange; no 120V loads are to be connected to this phase.

WARNING!

Always use caution when working on a center-tapped, four-wire, delta-connected system. Phase B has a higher voltage to ground than phases A and C. Never connect 120V circuits to the high leg. Doing so will result in damage to the circuits and equipment.

5.3.1   Open Delta

Three-phase, delta-connected systems may be connected so that only two transformers are used; this arrangement is known as an *open delta system*, as shown in *Figure 18*. It is frequently used on a delta system when one of the three transformers becomes damaged. The damaged transformer is disconnected from the circuit, and the remaining two transformers carry the load. In doing so, the three-phase load carried by the open delta bank is only 86.6% of the combined rating of the remaining two equal sized units. It is only 57.7% of the normal full-load capability of a full bank of transformers. In an emergency, however, this capability permits single-phase and three-phase power at a location where one unit burned out and a replacement was not readily available. The total load must be curtailed to avoid another burnout.

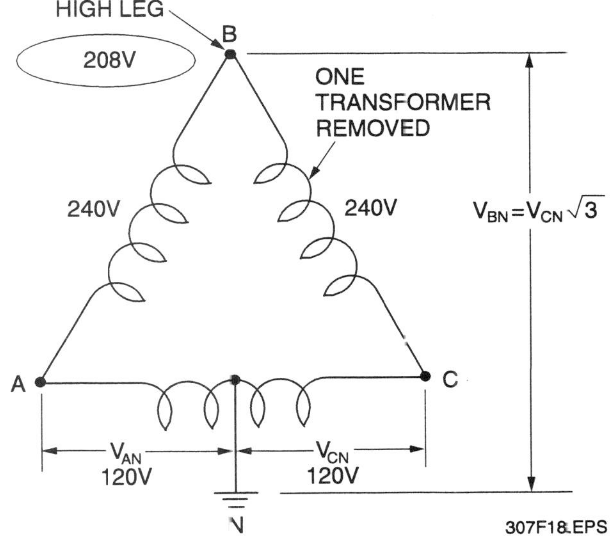

Figure 18. Open Delta System

5.4.0   TEE-CONNECTED TRANSFORMERS

When a delta-wye transformer is used, we would usually expect to find three primary and three secondary coils. However, in a tee-connected, three-phase transformer, only two primary and two secondary windings are used, as shown in *Figure 19*. If an equilateral triangle is drawn (see dotted lines in *Figure 19*) so that the distance between H_1 and H_3 is 4.8", you would find that the distance between H_2 to the midpoint of $H_1 - H_3$ measures 4.16", for a ratio of .866 (4.16" ÷ 4.8"). Therefore, if the voltage between outside phases is 480V, the voltage between H_2 to the midpoint of $H_1 - H_3$ will equal 480V × .866 = 415.68V or 416V. Also, if you were to place an imaginary dot exactly in the center of this triangle, it would lay on the horizontal winding—the one containing 416V. If you measured the distance from this dot to H_2, you would find it to be twice as long as the distance between the dot and the midpoint of H_1 to H_3. The measured distances would be 2.77" and 1.385" or the equivalent of 277V and 138½V, respectively.

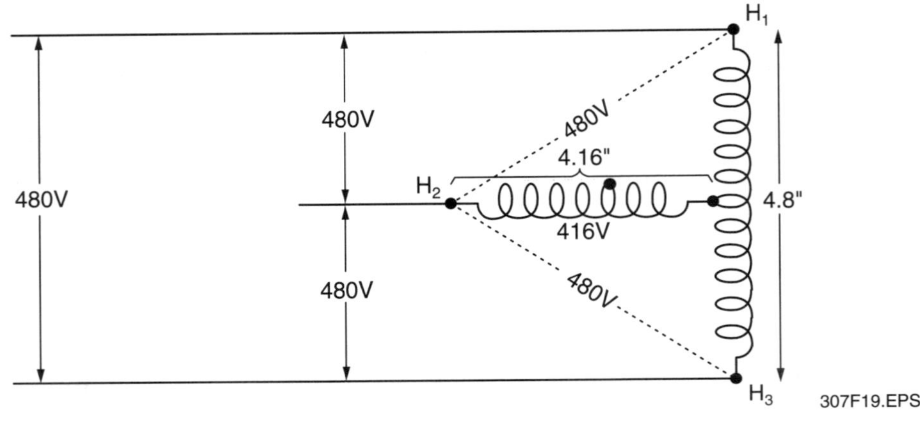

Figure 19. Typical Tee-Connected Transformer

Now, look at the secondary winding in *Figure 20*. By placing a neutral tap X_0 so that ⅓ the number of turns exist between it and the midpoint of X_1 and X_3 as exist between it and X_2, we then can establish X_0 as a neutral point that may be grounded. This provides 120V between X_0 and any of the three secondary terminals and the three-phase voltage between X_1, X_2, and X_3 will be 208V.

5.5.0   PARALLEL OPERATION OF TRANSFORMERS

Transformers will operate satisfactorily in parallel on a single-phase, three-wire system if the terminals with the same relative polarity are connected together. However, the practice is not very economical because the individual cost and losses of the smaller transformers are greater than one larger unit giving the same output. Therefore, paralleling of smaller transformers is usually done only in an emergency. In large transformers, however, it is often practical to operate units in parallel as a regular practice. See *Figure 21*.

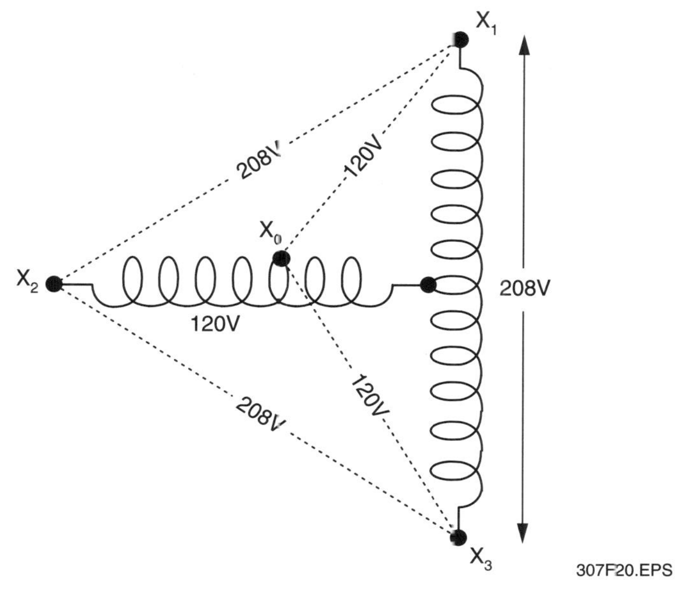

Figure 20. Secondary Voltage On A Tee-Connected System

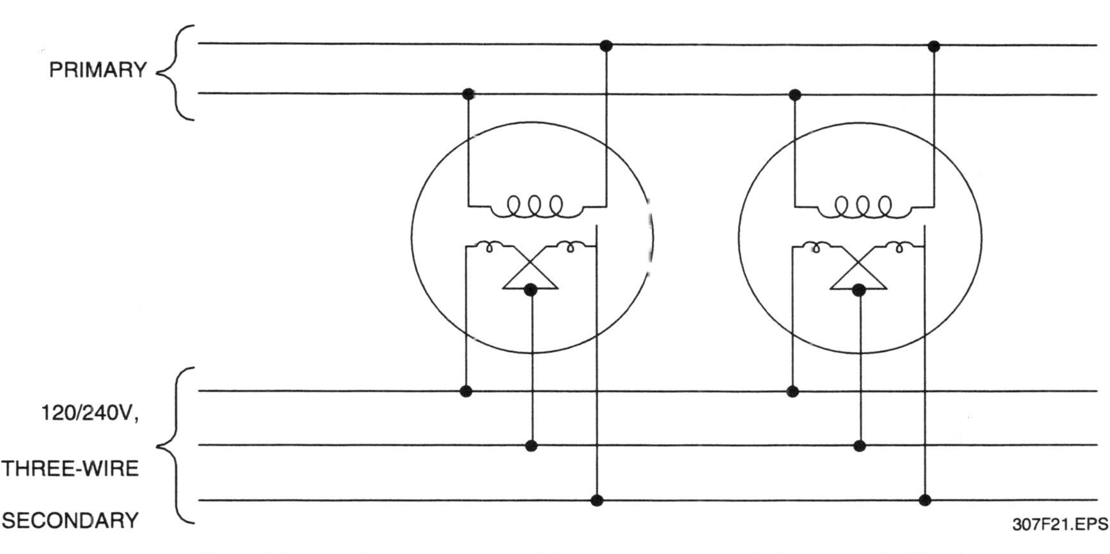

Figure 21. Parallel Operation Of Single-Phase Transformers

When connecting large transformers in parallel, especially when one of the windings is for a comparatively low voltage, the resistance of the joints and interconnecting leads must not vary significantly between the different transformers or it will cause an unequal division of load.

Two three-phase transformers may also be connected in parallel, provided they have the same winding arrangement, are connected with the same polarity, and have the same phase rotation. If two transformers—or two banks of transformers—have the same voltage ratings, the same turns ratios, the same impedances, and the same ratios of **reactance** to resistance, they will divide the load current in proportion to their kVA ratings, with no phase difference between the currents in the two transformers. However, if any of the preceding conditions are not met, then it is possible for the load current to divide between the two transformers in proportion to their kVA ratings. There may also be a phase difference between currents in the two transformers or banks of transformers.

Some three-phase transformers cannot be operated properly in parallel. For example, a transformer having both its primary and secondary windings connected in delta cannot be connected in parallel with another transformer that is connected either with a primary delta or a secondary Y. However, a transformer with a delta primary and a Y secondary can be made to parallel with transformers having their windings joined in certain ways; that is, a Y primary connection and a delta secondary connection.

To determine whether or not three-phase transformers will operate in parallel, connect them as shown in *Figure 22*, leaving two leads on one of the transformers unjoined. Test with a voltmeter across the unjoined leads. If there is no voltage between the points shown in the drawing, the polarities of the two transformers are the same, and the connections may then be made and the transformer put into service.

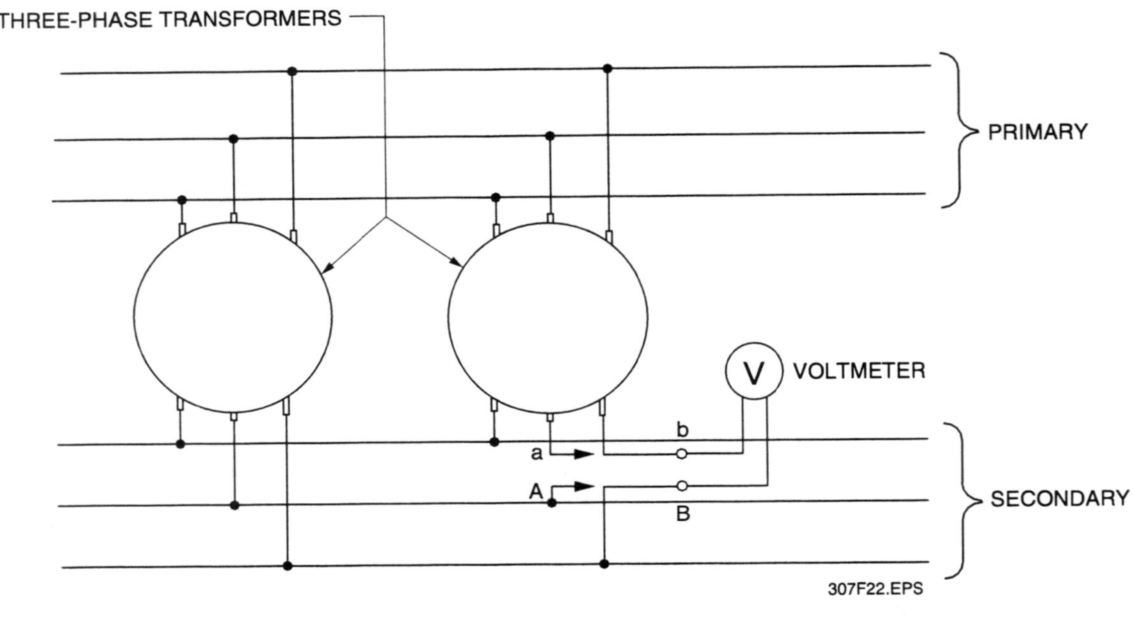

Figure 22. Testing Three-Phase Transformers For Parallel Operation

If a reading indicates a voltage between the points indicated in the drawing (either one of the two or both), the polarities of the two transformers are different. Should this occur, disconnect transformer lead A successively to mains 1, 2, and 3, as shown in *Figure 22*, and at each connection, test with a voltmeter between b and B and the legs of the main to which lead A is connected. If with any trial connection the voltmeter readings between b and B and either of the two legs is found to be zero, the transformer will operate with leads b and B connected to those two legs. If no system of connections can be discovered that will satisfy this condition, the transformer will not operate in parallel without changes to its internal connections or it may not operate in parallel at all.

In parallel operation, the primaries of the two or more transformers involved are connected together, and the secondaries are also connected together. With the primaries so connected, the voltages in both primaries and secondaries will be in certain directions. It is necessary that the secondaries be so connected that the voltage from one secondary line to the other will be in the same direction through both transformers. Proper connections to obtain this condition for single-phase transformers of various polarities are shown in *Figure 23*. In *Figure 23(A)*, both transformers A and B have additive polarity; in *Figure 23(B)*, both transformers have subtractive polarity; and in *Figure 23(C)*, transformer A has additive polarity and B has subtractive polarity.

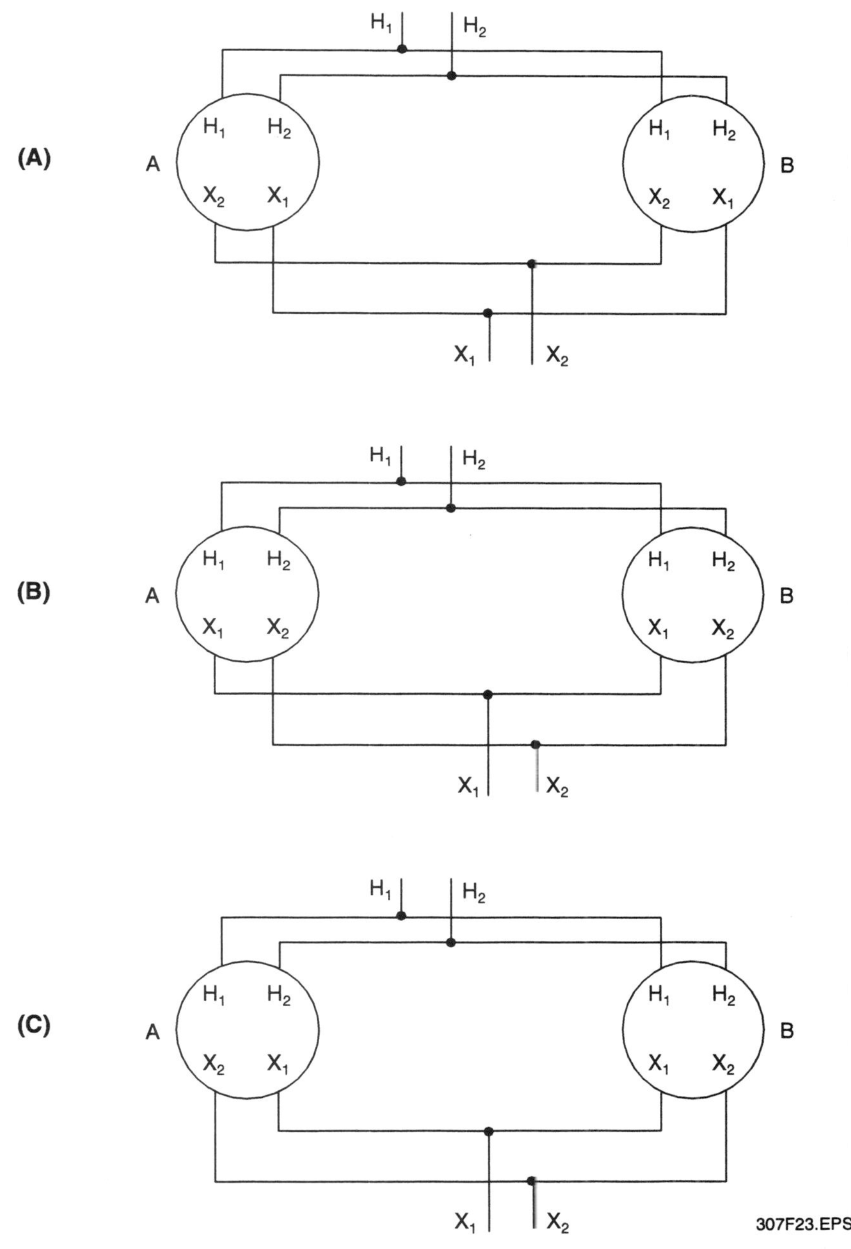

Figure 23. Transformers Connected In Parallel

Transformers, even when properly connected, will not operate satisfactorily in parallel unless their transformation ratios are very close to being equal and their impedance voltage drops are also approximately equal. A difference in transformation ratios will cause a circulating current to flow, even at no load, in each winding of both transformers. For example, in a loaded parallel bank of two transformers of equal capacities, if there is a difference in the transformation ratios, the load circuit will be superimposed on the circulating current. The result in such a case is that in one transformer, the total circulating current will be added to the load current, whereas in the other transformer, the actual current will be the difference between the load current and the circulating current. This may lead to unsatisfactory operation. Therefore, the transformation ratios of transformers for parallel operation must be definitely known.

When two transformers are connected in parallel, the circulating current caused by the difference in the ratios of the two is equal to the difference in the open circuit voltage divided by the sum of the transformer impedances, because the current is circulated through the windings of both transformers due to this voltage difference. To illustrate, let I represent the amount of circulating current—in percent of full-load current—and the equation will be:

$$I = \frac{\text{percent voltage difference} \times 100}{\text{sum of percent impedances}}$$

Assume an open circuit voltage difference of 3% between two transformers connected in parallel. If each transformer has an impedance of 5%, the circulating current (in percent of full-load current) is:

$$I = \frac{3 \times 100}{5 + 5} = 30\%$$

A current equal to 30% of the full-load current therefore circulates in both the high-voltage and low-voltage windings. This current adds to the load current in the transformer having the higher induced voltage and subtracts from the load current of the other transformer. Therefore, one transformer will be overloaded, while the other may or may not be, depending on the phase angle difference between the circulating current and the load current.

5.5.1   Impedance In Parallel-Operated Transformers

Impedance plays an important role in the successful operation of transformers connected in parallel. The impedance of the transformers must be such that the voltage drop from no load to full load is the same in all transformer units in both magnitude and phase. In most applications, you will find that the total resistance drop is relatively small when compared with the reactance drop, and the total percent impedance drop can be taken as approximately equal to the percent reactance drop. If the percent impedances of the given transformers at full load are the same, they will, of course, divide the load equally.

The following equation may be used to obtain the division of loads between two transformer banks operating in parallel on single-phase systems:

$$\text{Power} = \frac{kVA^1 \div Z^1}{(kVA^1 \div Z^1) + (kVA^2 \div Z^2)} \times \text{total kVA load}$$

Where:

kVA^1 = kVA rating of transformer 1
kVA^2 = kVA rating of transformer 2
Z^1 = percent impedance of transformer 1
Z^2 = percent impedance of transformer 2

In this equation, it can be assumed that the ratio of resistance to reactance is the same in all units since the error introduced by differences in this ratio is usually so small as to be negligible.

The preceding equation may also be applied to more than two transformers operated in parallel by adding, to the denominator of the fraction, the kVA of each additional transformer divided by its percent impedance.

5.5.2 Parallel Operation Of Three-Phase Transformers

Three-phase transformers, or banks of single-phase transformers, may be connected in parallel, provided each of the three primary leads in one three-phase transformer is connected in parallel with a corresponding primary lead of the other transformer. The secondaries are then connected in the same way. The corresponding leads are the leads which have the same potential at all times and the same polarity. Furthermore, the transformers must have the same voltage ratio and the same impedance voltage drop.

When three-phase transformer banks operate in parallel and the three units in each bank are similar, the division of the load can be determined by the same method previously described for single-phase transformers connected in parallel on a single-phase system.

In addition to the requirements of polarity, ratio, and impedance, paralleling of three-phase transformers also requires that the angular displacement between the voltages in the windings be taken into consideration when they are connected together.

Phasor diagrams of three-phase transformers that are to be paralleled greatly simplify matters. With these, all that is required is to compare the two diagrams to make sure they consist of phasors that can be made to coincide, then connect the terminals corresponding to coinciding voltage phasors. If the phasor diagrams can be made to coincide, leads that are connected together will have the same potential at all times. This is one of the fundamental requirements for paralleling. Phasor diagrams are covered in more detail later in this module.

An **autotransformer** is a transformer whose primary and secondary circuits have part of a winding in common; therefore, the two circuits are not isolated from each other. See *Figure 24*. The application of an autotransformer is a good choice where a 480Y/277V or 208Y/120V, three-phase, four-wire distribution system is used. Some of the advantages are:

- Lower purchase price

- Lower operating cost due to lower losses

- Smaller size; easier to install

- Better voltage regulation

- Lower sound levels

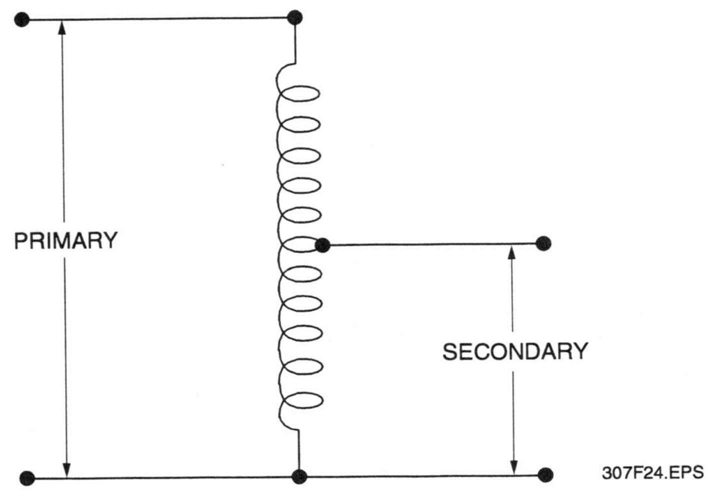

Figure 24. Step-Down Autotransformer

For example, when the ratio of transformation from the primary to the secondary voltage is small, the most economical way of stepping down the voltage is by using autotransformers, as shown in *Figure 25*. For this application, it is necessary that the neutral of the autotransformer bank be connected to the system neutral.

An autotransformer, however, cannot be used on a 480V or 240V, three-phase, three-wire delta system. A grounded neutral phase conductor must be available in accordance with ***NEC Sections 210-9 and 215-11***, which require that branch circuits and feeders derived from autotransformers be electrically connected to a grounded conductor of the system supplying the autotransformer.

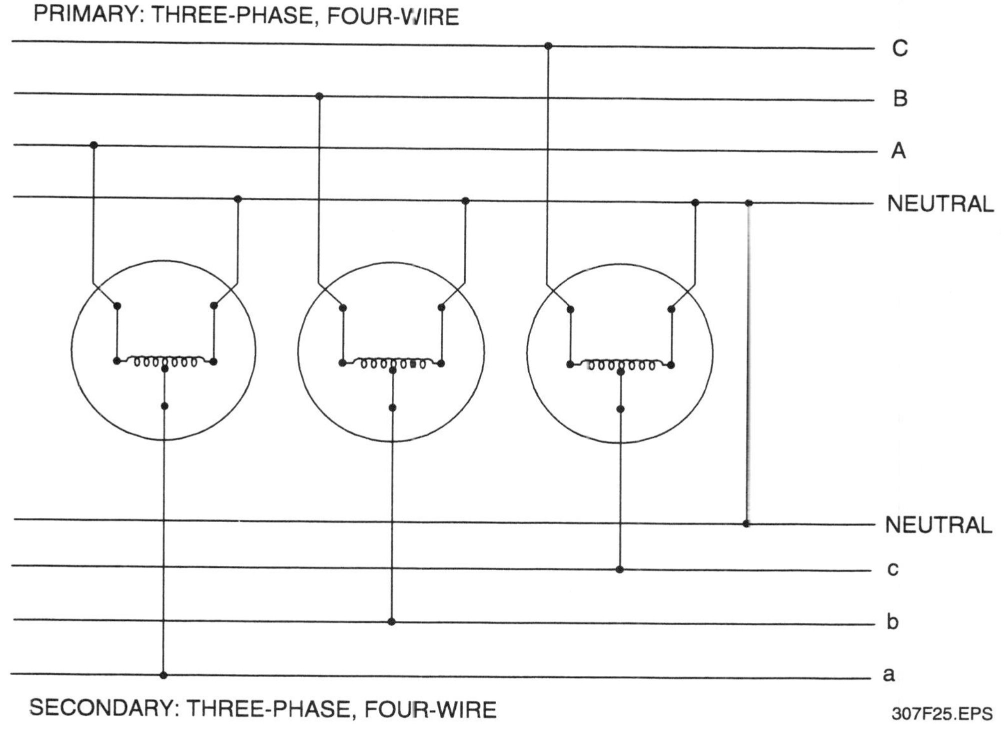

Figure 25. Autotransformers Supplying Power From A Three-Phase, Four-Wire System

7.0.0 DRY-TYPE TRANSFORMER CONNECTIONS

Electricians performing work on commercial and industrial installations will be concerned with the installation and connections of dry-type transformers. Dry-type transformers are available in both single-phase and three-phase types, with a wide range of sizes from small control transformers to those rated at 500kVA or more. Such transformers have wide application in electrical systems of all types.

NEC Section 450-11 requires that each transformer must be provided with a nameplate giving the manufacturer, rated kVA, frequency, primary and secondary voltage, impedance of transformers 25kVA and larger, required clearances for transformers with ventilating openings, and the amount and type of insulating liquid (where used). In addition, the nameplate of each dry-type transformer must include the temperature class for the insulation system. See *Figure 26*.

In addition, most manufacturers include a wiring diagram and a connection chart, as shown in *Figure 27* for a 480V delta primary to 208Y/120V secondary. It is recommended that all transformers be connected as shown on the manufacturer's nameplate.

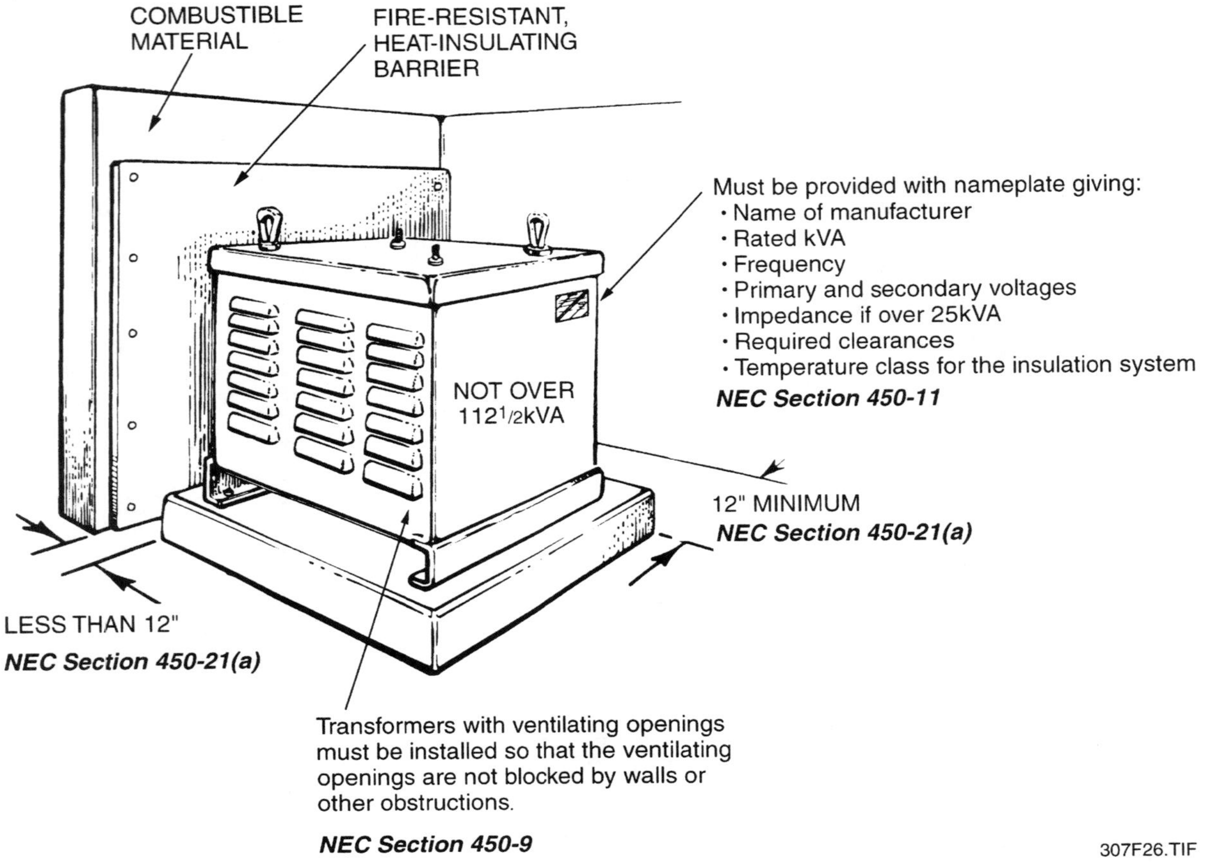

Figure 26. Dry-Type Transformer Installed Indoors

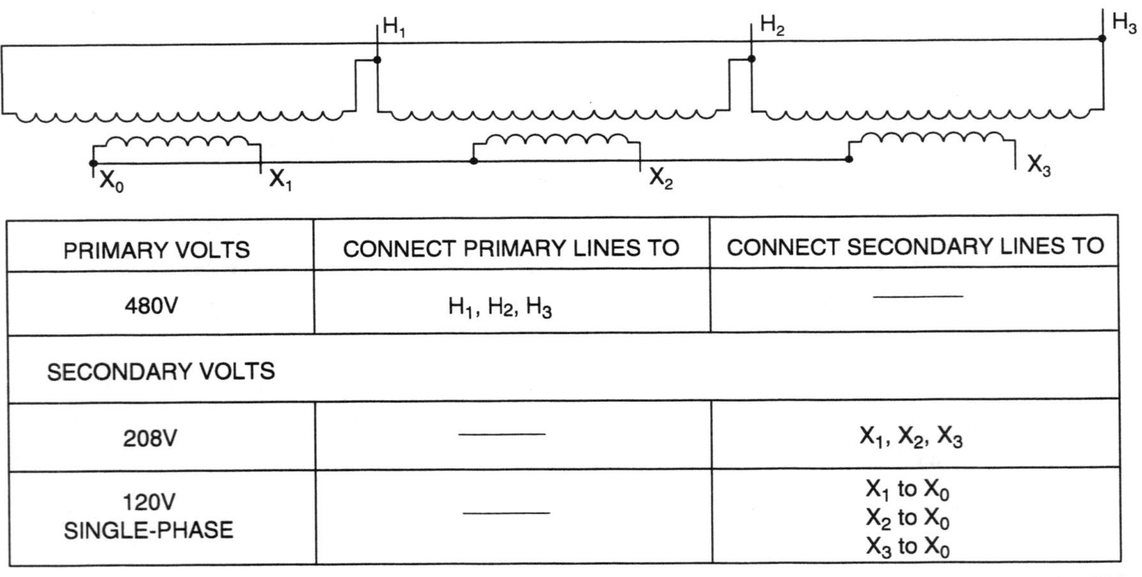

PRIMARY VOLTS	CONNECT PRIMARY LINES TO	CONNECT SECONDARY LINES TO
480V	H_1, H_2, H_3	———
SECONDARY VOLTS		
208V	———	X_1, X_2, X_3
120V SINGLE-PHASE	———	X_1 to X_0 X_2 to X_0 X_3 to X_0

Figure 27. Typical Manufacturer's Wiring Diagram For A Delta-Wye Transformer

In general, this wiring diagram and accompanying table indicate that the 480V, three-phase, three-wire primary conductors are connected to terminals H_1, H_2, and H_3, respectively—regardless of the desired voltage on the primary. A neutral conductor, if required, is carried from the primary through the transformer to the secondary. Two variations are possible on the secondary side of this transformer: 208V, three-phase, three-wire or four-wire; or 120V, single-phase, two-wire. To connect the secondary side of the transformer as a 208V, three-phase, three-wire system, the secondary conductors are connected to terminals X_1, X_2, and X_3; the neutral is carried through with conductors usually terminating at a solid neutral bus in the transformer.

Another popular dry-type transformer connection is the 480V primary to 240V delta/120V secondary. This configuration is shown in *Figure 28*. Again, the primary conductors are connected to transformer terminals H_1, H_2, and H_3. The secondary connections for the desired voltages are made as indicated in the table.

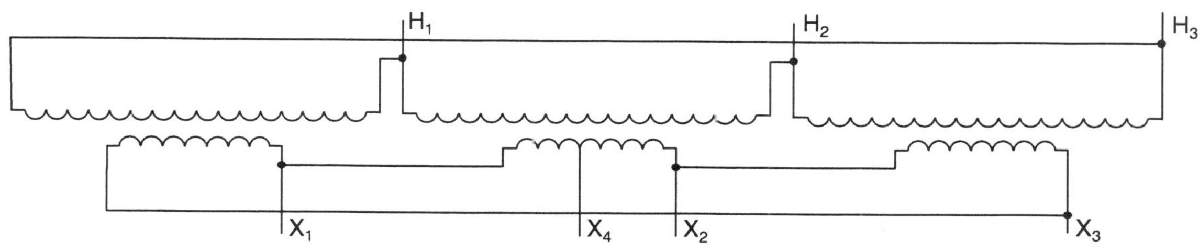

PRIMARY VOLTS	CONNECT PRIMARY LINES TO	CONNECT SECONDARY LINES TO
480V	H_1, H_2, H_3	———
SECONDARY VOLTS		
240V	———	X_1, X_2, X_3
120V	———	X_1, X_4 or X_2, X_3

307F28.EPS

Figure 28. 480V Delta To 240V Delta Transformer Connections

7.1.0   ZIG-ZAG CONNECTIONS

There are many situations in which it is desirable to upgrade a building's lighting system from 120V fixtures to 277V fluorescent fixtures. Often, these buildings have a 240/480V, three-phase, four-wire delta system. One way to obtain 277V from a 240/480V system is to connect 240/480V transformers in a zig-zag fashion, as shown in *Figure 29*. In doing so, the secondary of one phase is connected in series with the primary of another phase, thus changing the phase angle.

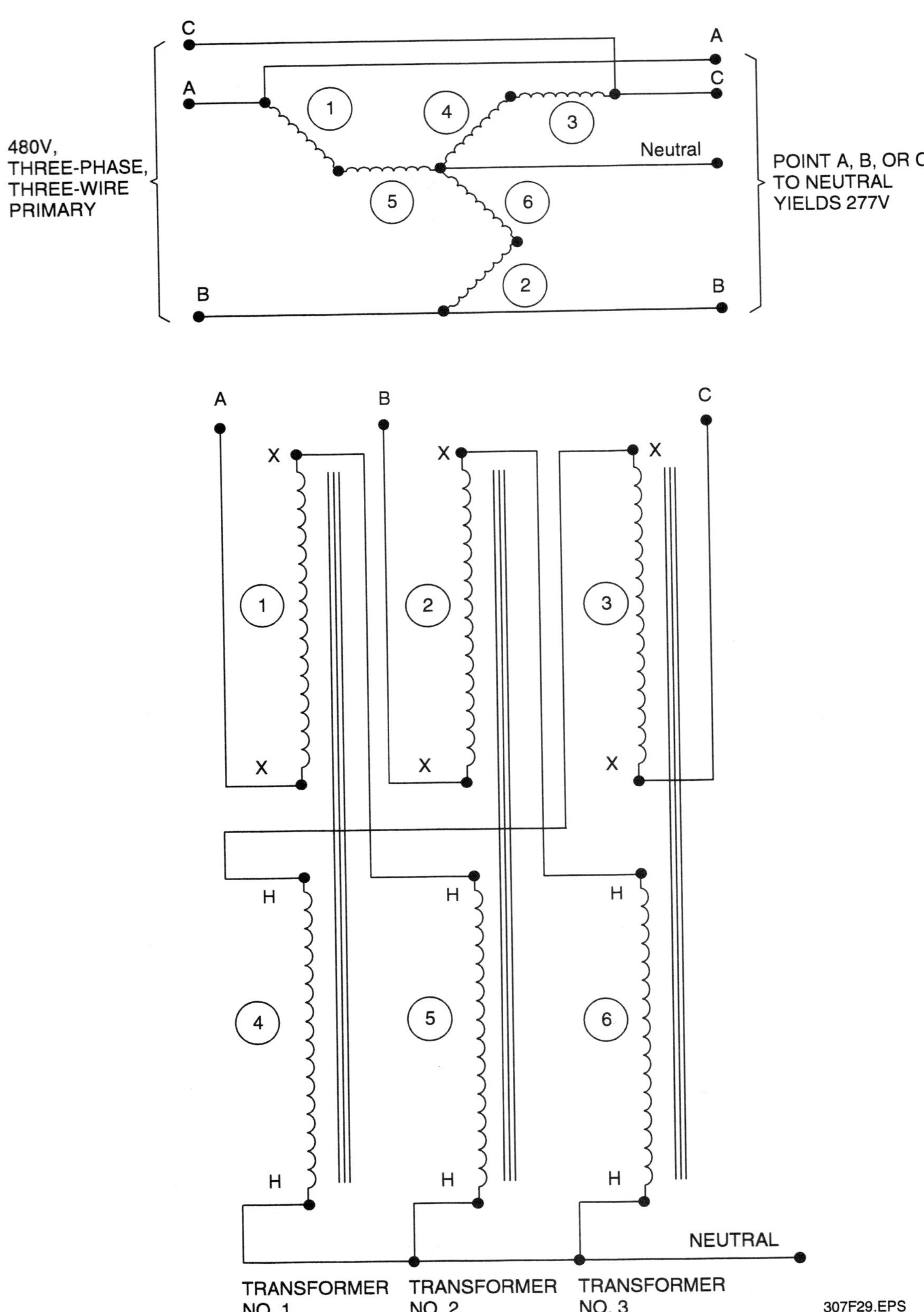

Figure 29. Zig-Zag Connection

ELECTRICAL — TRAINEE TASK MODULE 26307

The zig-zag connection may also be used as a grounding transformer where its function is to obtain a neutral point from an ungrounded system. With a neutral being available, the system may then be grounded. When the system is grounded through the zig-zag transformer, its sole function is to pass ground current. A zig-zag transformer is essentially six impedances connected in a zig-zag configuration.

The operation of a zig-zag transformer is slightly different from that of the conventional transformer. We will consider current rather than voltage. While a voltage rating is necessary for the connection to function, this is actually line voltage and is not transformed. It provides only exciting current for the core. The dynamic portion of the zig-zag grounding system is the fault current. To understand its function, the system must also be viewed backward—that is, the fault current will flow into the transformer through the neutral, as shown in *Figure 30*.

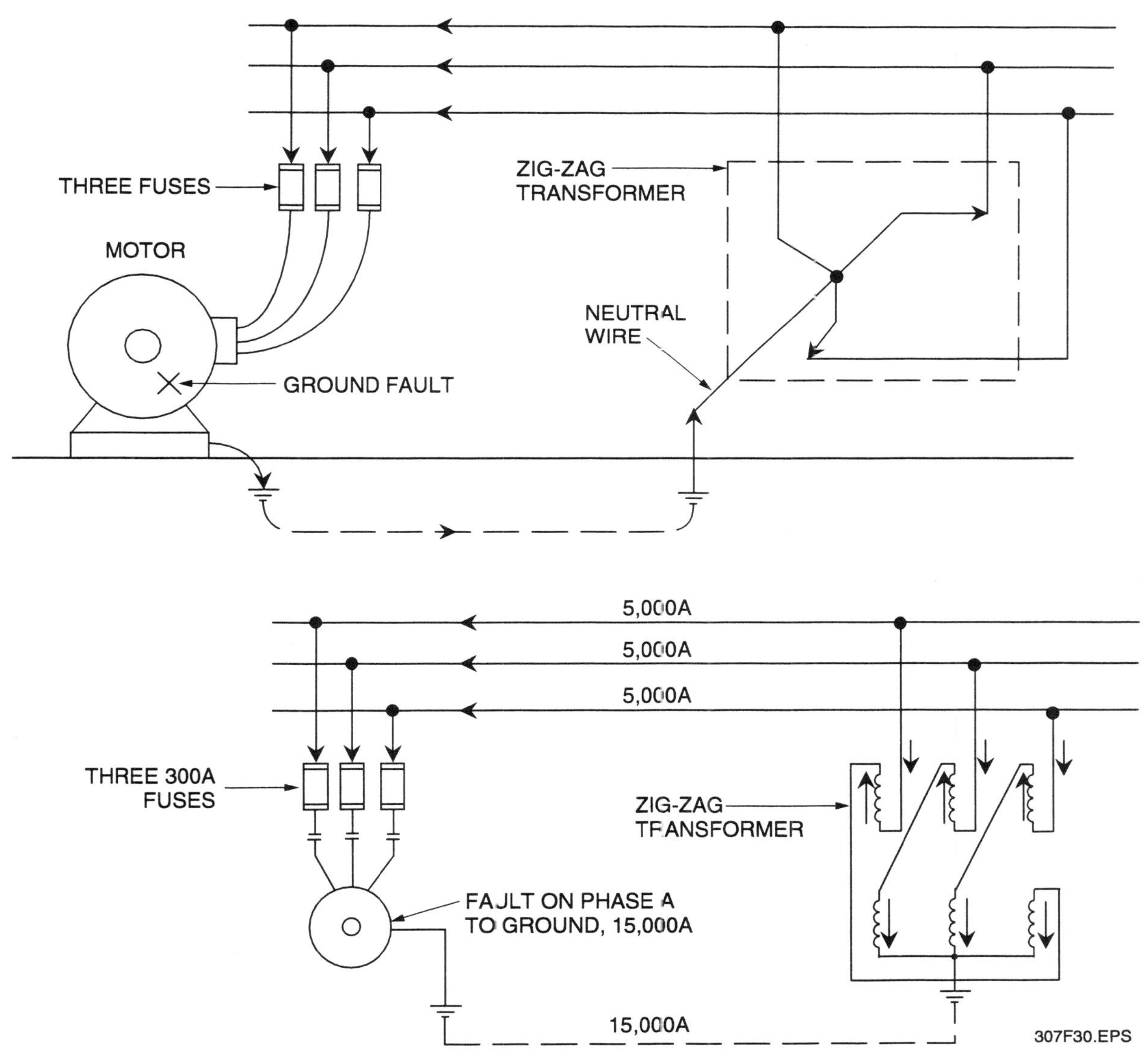

Figure 30. Fault Current Paths For A Three-Phase System

The zero sequence currents are all in phase in each line (i.e., they all hit the peak at the same time). In reviewing *Figure 30*, we see that the current leaves the motor, goes to ground, flows up the neutral, and splits three ways. It then flows back down the line to the motor through the fuses, which then open, shutting down the motor.

The neutral conductor will carry full fault current and must be sized accordingly. It is also time rated (0–60 seconds) and can therefore be reduced in size. This should be coordinated with the manufacturer's time/current curves for the fuse. See the Level 3 module entitled *Overcurrent Protection*.

To determine the size of a zig-zag grounding transformer, proceed as follows:

Step 1   Calculate the system line-to-ground asymmetrical fault current.

Step 2   If relaying is present, consider reducing the fault current by installing a resistor in the neutral. If fuses or circuit breakers are the protective device, you may need all the fault current to quickly open the overcurrent protective devices.

Step 3   Obtain the time/current curves of the relay and the fuses or circuit breakers.

Step 4   Select the zig-zag transformer for:

- Fault current (line-to-ground fault)
- Line-to-line voltage
- Duration of fault (determined from time/current curves)
- Impedance per phase at 100% (for any other, contact the manufacturer)

7.2.0 BUCK-AND-BOOST TRANSFORMERS

The buck-and-boost transformer is a very versatile unit for which a multitude of applications exist. Buck-and-boost transformers, as the name implies, are designed to raise (boost) or lower (buck) the voltage in an electrical system or circuit. In their simplest form, these insulated units will deliver 12V or 24V when the primaries are energized at 120V or 240V, respectively. However, their prime use and value lies in the fact that the primaries and secondaries can be interconnected, permitting their use as an autotransformer.

Assume that an installation is supplied with a 208Y/120V service, but one piece of equipment in the installation is rated for 230V. A buck-and-boost transformer may be used on the 230V circuit to increase the voltage from 208V to 230V (*Figure 31*). With this connection, the transformer is in the boost mode and delivers 228.8V at the load. This is close enough to 230V that the load equipment will function properly.

If the connections were reversed, this would also reverse the polarity of the secondary with the result being a voltage of 208V − 20.8V = 187.2V. The transformer is now operating in the buck mode.

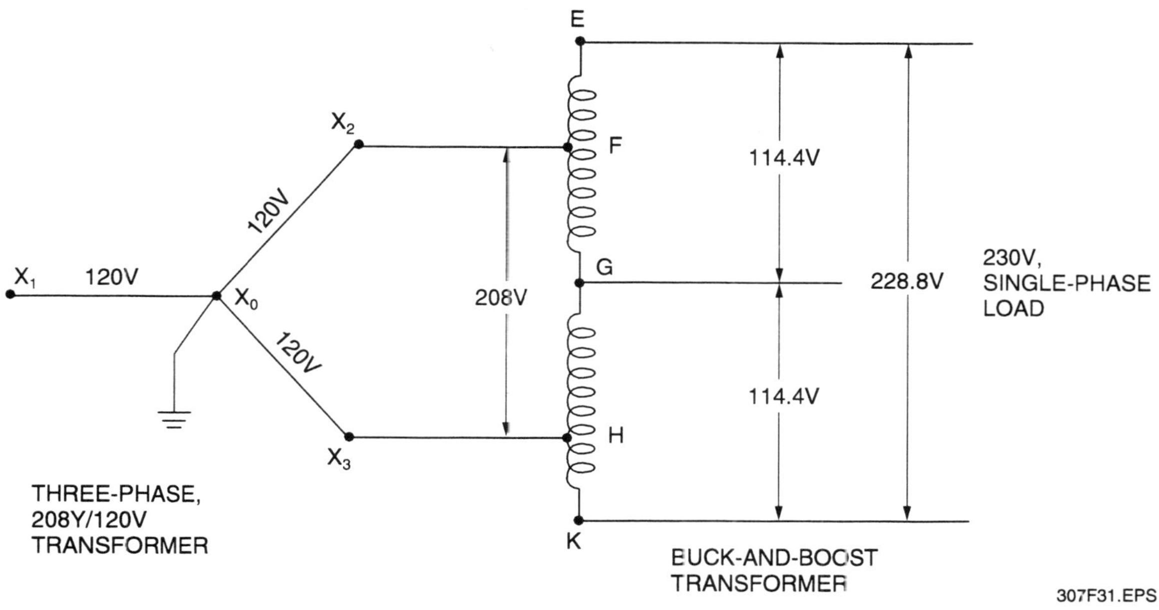

Figure 31. Buck-And-Boost Transformer Connected To A 208V System To Obtain 230V

It is important to know how to calculate sizes of buck-and-boost transformers for any given application. However, due to the amount of basic material covered in this module, advanced sizing and application techniques for buck-and-boost transformers are presented in Level 4 of your training. Still, you should be familiar with the basic buck-and-boost wiring diagrams at this time. Transformer connections for typical three-phase, buck-and-boost, open delta transformers are shown in *Figure 32*. The connections shown are in the boost mode; to convert to the buck mode, reverse the input and output connections.

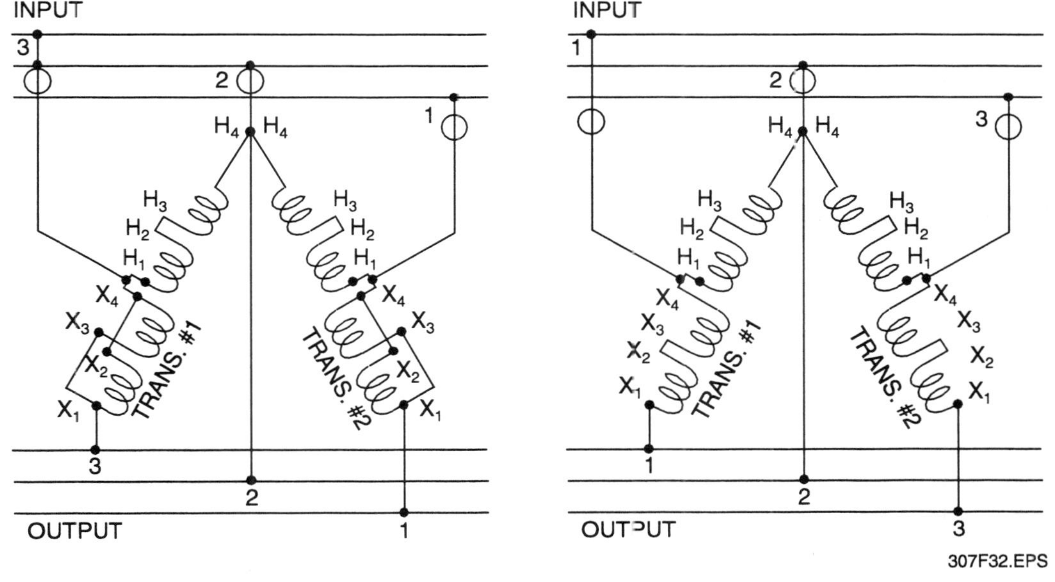

Figure 32. Open Delta, Three-Phase, Buck-And-Boost Transformer Connections

Another three-phase buck-and-boost transformer connection is shown in *Figure 33*; this time it is a wye-connected type. While the open delta transformers (*Figure 32*) can be converted from buck to boost or vice versa by reversing the input/output connections, this is not the case with the three-phase, wye-connected transformer. The connection shown in *Figure 33* is for the boost mode only.

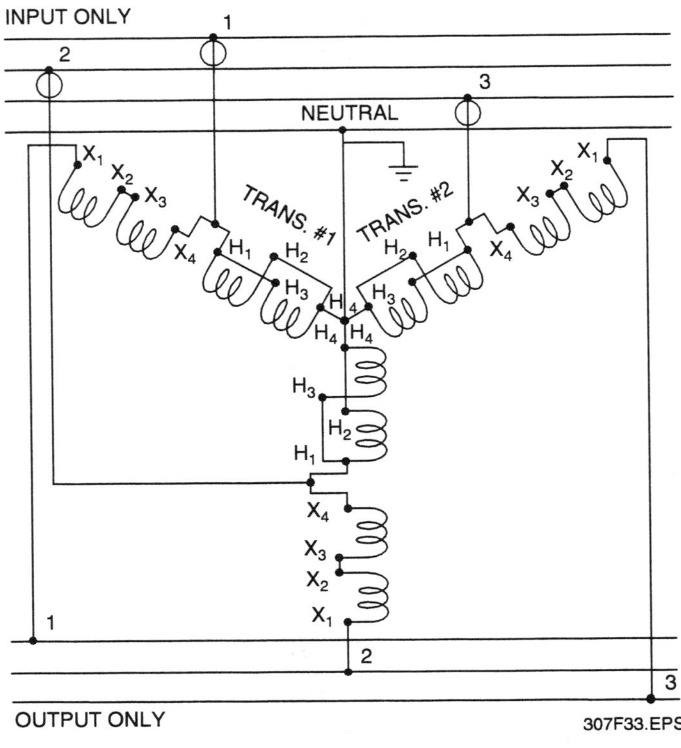

Figure 33. Three-Phase, Wye-Connected, Buck-And-Boost Transformer In The Boost Mode

Several typical single-phase, buck-and-boost transformer connections are shown in *Figure 34*. Other diagrams may be found on the transformer's nameplate or in the manufacturer's instructions supplied with each new transformer.

8.0.0 CONTROL TRANSFORMERS

Control transformers are available in numerous types, but most are dry-type, step-down units with the secondary control circuit isolated from the primary line circuit to ensure maximum safety. See *Figure 35*. These transformers and other components are usually mounted within an enclosed control box or control panel, which has a pushbutton station or stations independently grounded as recommended by the NEC. Industrial control transformers are especially designed to accommodate the momentary current inrush caused when electromagnetic components are energized, without sacrificing secondary voltage stability beyond practical limits. See ***NEC Section 430-72(c)***.

     ELECTRICAL — TRAINEE TASK MODULE 26307

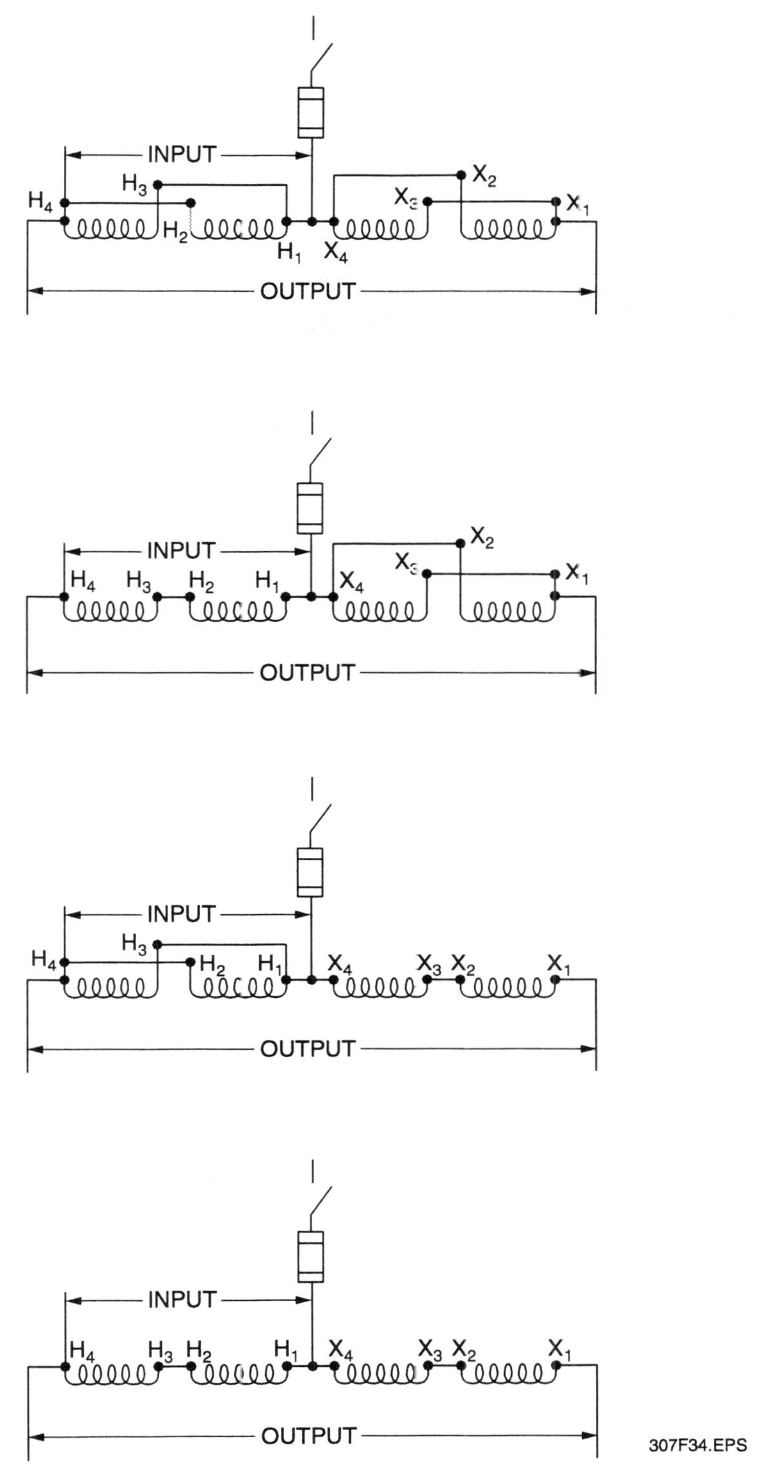

Figure 34. Typical Single-Phase, Buck-And-Boost Transformer Connections

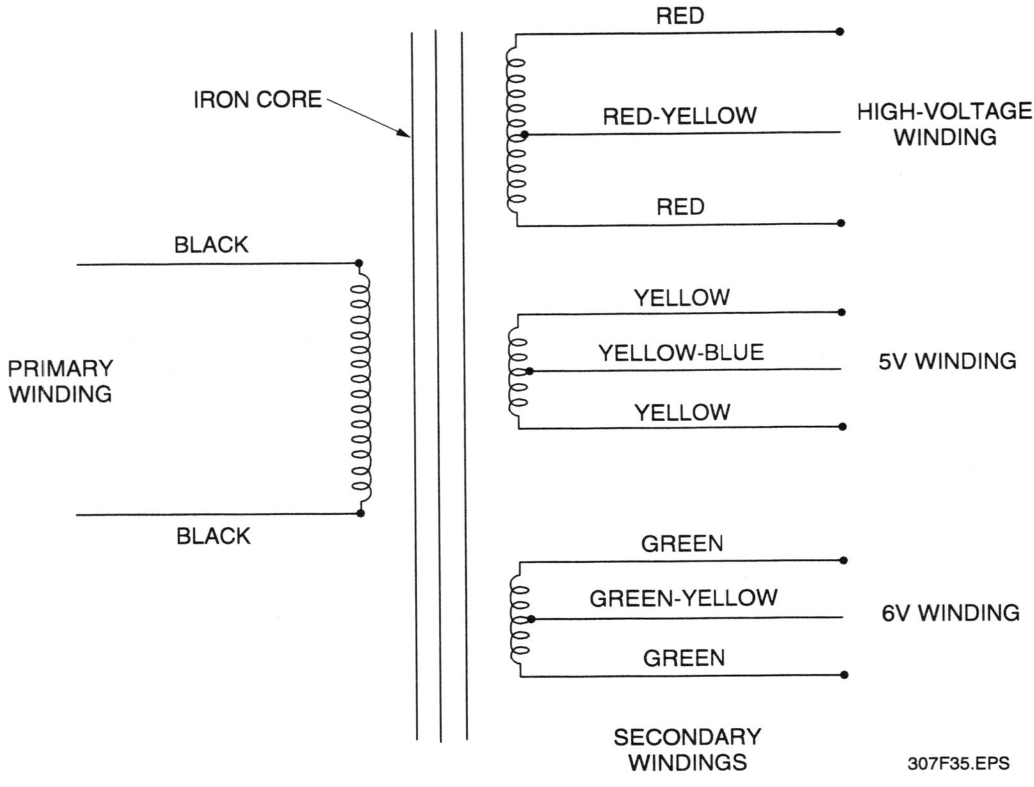

Figure 35. Typical Control Transformer Wiring Diagram

Other types of control transformers, sometimes referred to as *control and signal transformers*, normally do not have the required industrial control transformer regulation characteristics. Rather, they are constant-potential, air-cooled transformers used for the purpose of supplying the proper reduced voltage for control circuits of electrically operated switches or other equipment and, of course, for signal circuits. Some are of the open type with no protective casing over the winding, while others are enclosed with a metal casing over the winding.

When choosing control transformers for any application, the loads must be calculated and completely analyzed before the proper transformer selection can be made. This analysis involves every electrically-energized component in the control circuit. To select an appropriate control transformer, first determine the voltage and frequency of the supply circuit. Next, determine the total inrush volt-amperes (watts) of the control circuit. In doing so, do not neglect the current requirements of indicating lights and timing devices that do not have inrush volt-amperes, but are energized at the same time as the other components in the circuit. Their total volt-amperes should be added to the total inrush volt-amperes.

Again, control transformers will be covered in more detail in Level 4, as will other types of transformers. The material presented in this module is designed to introduce you to these devices; additional study of practical applications is forthcoming.

In general, a **potential transformer** (*Figure 36*) is used to supply voltage to instruments such as voltmeters, frequency meters, power factor meters, and watt-hour meters. The voltage is proportional to the primary voltage, but it is small enough to be safe for the test instrument. The secondary of a potential transformer may be designed for several different voltages, but most are designed for 120V. The potential transformer is primarily a distribution transformer especially designed for voltage regulation so that the secondary voltage (under all conditions) will be as close as possible to a specified percentage of the primary voltage.

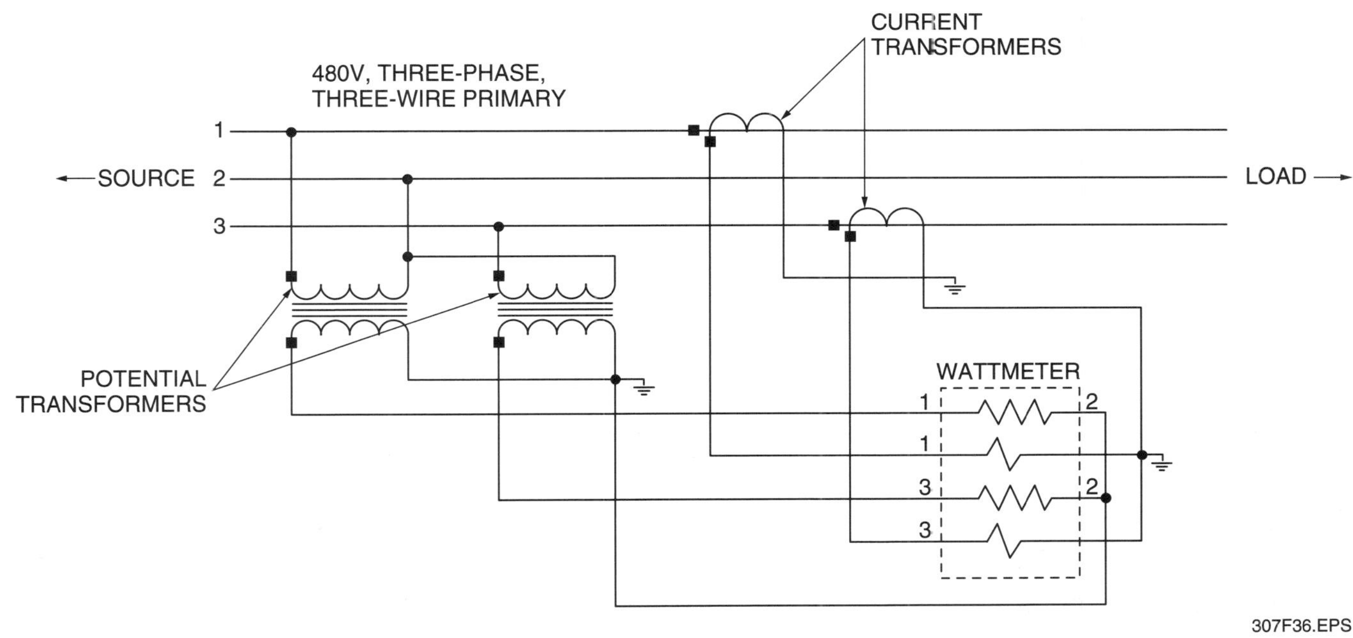

Figure 36. Current And Potential Transformers Connected For Watt-Hour Metering Of A Three-Phase Circuit

A **current transformer** is used to supply current to an instrument connected to its secondary, with the current being proportional to the primary current, but small enough to be safe for the instrument. The secondary of a current transformer is usually designed for a rated current of 5A.

A current transformer operates in the same way as any other transformer in that the same relation exists between the primary current, the secondary current, and voltage. A current transformer is connected in series with the power lines to which it is applied so that line current flows in its primary winding. The secondary of the current transformer is connected to current devices such as ammeters, wattmeters, watt-hour meters, power factor meters, some forms of relays, and the trip coils of some types of circuit breakers.

When no instruments or other devices are connected to the secondary of the current transformer, a short circuit device or shunt is placed across the secondary to prevent the secondary circuit from being opened while the primary winding is carrying current.

10.0.0   NEC REQUIREMENTS

Transformers must normally be accessible for inspection, except for dry-type transformers under certain specified conditions. Certain types of transformers with a high voltage or kVA rating are required to be enclosed in transformer rooms or vaults when installed indoors. The construction of these vaults is covered in ***NEC Sections 450-41 through 450-48*** and described in *Figure 37* and *Table 1*.

In general, the NEC specifies that the walls and roofs of vaults must be constructed of materials that have adequate structural strength for the conditions with a minimum fire resistance of three hours. However, where transformers are protected with an automatic sprinkler system, water spray, carbon dioxide, or halon, the fire resistance construction may be lowered to only one hour. The floors of vaults in contact with the earth must be of concrete and not less than 4" thick. If the vault is built with a vacant space or other floors (stories) below it, the floor must have adequate structural strength for the load imposed thereon and a minimum fire resistance of three hours. Again, if the fire extinguishing facilities are provided, as outlined above, the fire resistance construction need only be one hour. The NEC does not permit the use of studs and wallboard construction for transformer vaults.

10.1.0   OVERCURRENT PROTECTION FOR TRANSFORMERS

The overcurrent protection for transformers is based on their rated current, not on the load to be served. The primary circuit may be protected by a device rated or set at not more than 125% of the rated primary current of the transformer for transformers with a rated primary current of 9A or more.

Instead of individual protection on the primary side, the transformer may be protected only on the secondary side if all of the following conditions are met:

- The overcurrent device on the secondary side is rated or set at not more than 125% of the rated secondary current.

- The primary feeder overcurrent device is rated or set at not more than 250% of the rated primary current.

ELECTRICAL — TRAINEE TASK MODULE 26307

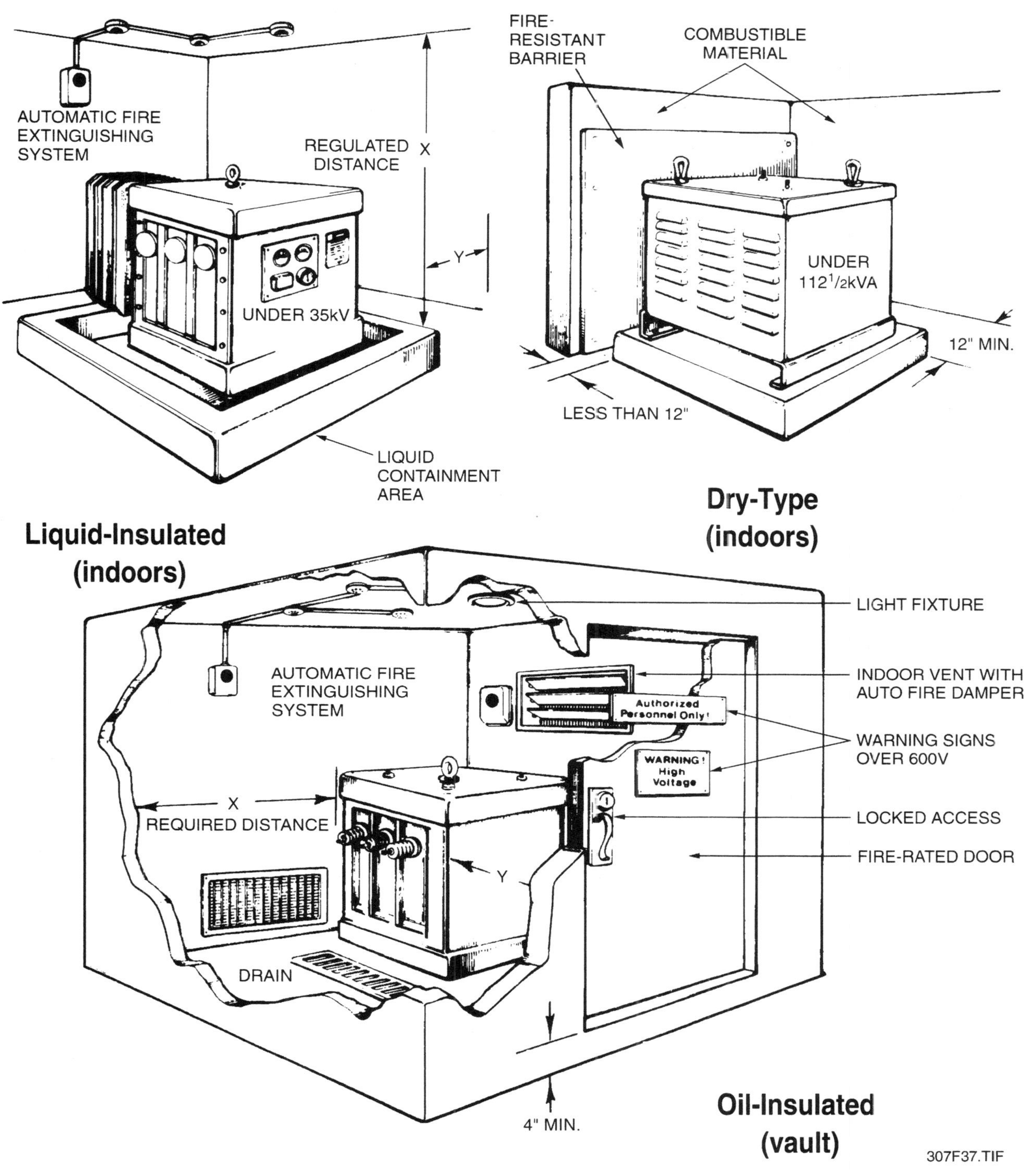

Figure 37. Transformer Installation Requirements

Application	NEC Regulation	NEC Reference
Location	Transformers must be readily accessible to qualified personnel for maintenance and inspection. Dry-type transformers may be located out in the open. Dry-type transformers not exceeding 600V and 50kVA are permitted in fire-resistant hollow spaces of a building under the conditions specified in the NEC. Liquid-filled transformers must be installed as specified in the NEC and usually in vaults when installed indoors.	*NEC Section 450-13* *NEC Article 450, Part B*
Overcurrent protection	The primary protection must be rated or set as follows: • 9A or more – 125% • Less than 9A – 167% • Less than 2A – 300% If the primary current (line side) is 9A or more, the next higher standard size overcurrent protective device greater than 125% of the primary current is used. For example, if the primary current is 15A, 125% of 15A = 18.75A. The next standard size circuit breaker is 20A. Therefore, this size (20A) may be used. Conductors on the secondary side of a single-phase transformer with a two-wire secondary may be protected by the primary overcurrent device under certain NEC conditions.	*NEC Section 450-3(b)*
Over 600V	Special NEC rules apply to transformers operating at over 600V.	*NEC Section 450-3(a)*

Table 1. Summary Of NEC Transformer Installation And Overcurrent Protection Requirements

For example, if a 12kVA transformer has a primary current rating of 480V, calculate the amperage as follows:

$$\frac{12,000W}{480V} = 25A$$

With a secondary current rated at 120V, the amperage becomes:

$$\frac{12,000W}{120V} = 100A$$

The individual primary protection must be set at:

$$1.25 \times 25A = 31.25A$$

ELECTRICAL — TRAINEE TASK MODULE 26307

In this case, a standard 30A cartridge fuse rated at 600V could be used, as could a circuit breaker approved for use on 480V. However, if certain conditions are met, individual primary protection for the transformer is not necessary if the feeder overcurrent protective device is rated at not more than:

$$2.5 \times 25A = 62.5A$$

In addition, the protection of the secondary side must be set at not more than:

$$1.25 \times 100A = 125A$$

In this case, a standard 125A circuit breaker could be used.

Note: The example cited is for the transformer only, not the secondary conductors. The secondary conductors must be provided with overcurrent protection as outlined in **NEC Section 210-20**.

The requirements of **NEC Section 450-3** cover only transformer protection; in practice, other components must be considered when applying circuit overcurrent protection. Circuits with transformers must meet the requirements for conductor protection in **NEC Articles 240 and 310**, while panelboards must meet the requirements of **NEC Article 384**.

Primary fuse protection only – If secondary fuse protection is not provided, then the primary fuses must not be sized larger than 125% of the transformer primary full-load amperes (FLA), except if the transformer primary FLA is that shown in **NEC Section 450-3(b)**. See *Figure 38*.

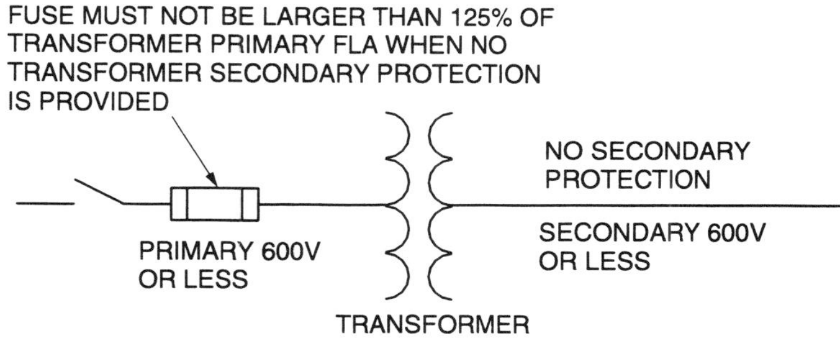

PRIMARY CURRENT	PRIMARY FUSE RATING
9A or more	125% or next higher standard rating if 125% does not correspond to a standard fuse size
2A to 9A	167% maximum
Less than 2A	300% maximum

307F38.EPS

Figure 38. Transformer Circuit With Primary Fuse Only

Individual transformer primary fuses are not necessary where the primary circuit fuse provides this protection.

Primary and secondary protection – In unsupervised locations with a primary over 600V, the primary fuse can be sized at a maximum of 300%. If the secondary is also over 600V, the secondary fuses can be sized at a maximum of 250% for transformers with impedances not greater than 6% and 225% for transformers with impedances greater than 6% and not more than 10%. If the secondary is 600V or below, the secondary fuses can be sized at a maximum of 125%. Where these settings do not correspond to a standard fuse size, the next higher standard size is permitted.

In supervised locations, the maximum settings are as shown in *Figure 39*, except for secondary voltages of 600V or below, where the secondary fuses can be sized at a maximum of 250%.

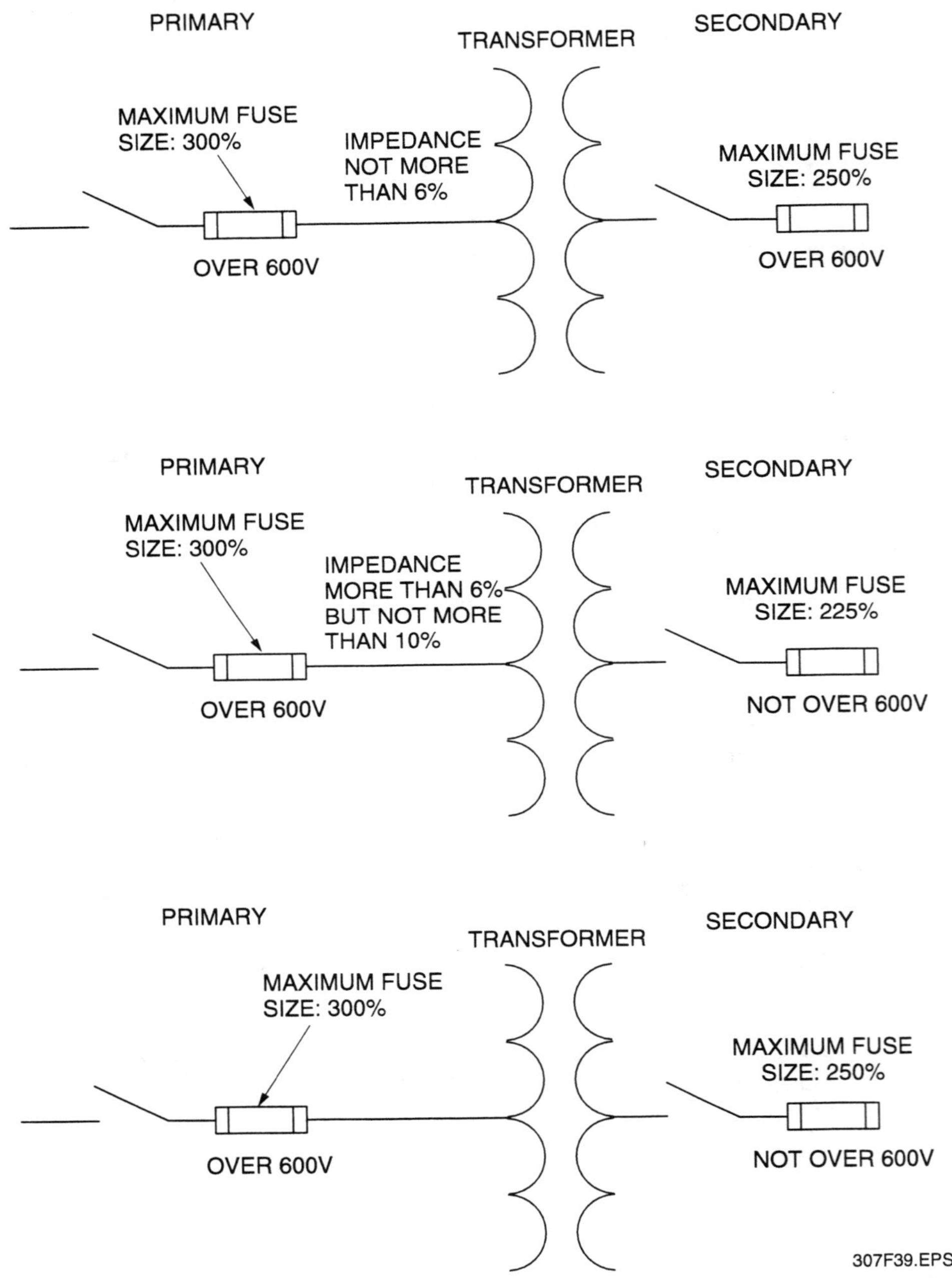

Figure 39. Minimum Overcurrent Protection For Transformers In Supervised Locations

Primary protection only – In supervised locations, the primary fuses can be sized at a maximum of 250% or the next larger standard size if 250% does not correspond to a standard fuse size.

Note: The use of primary protection only does not remove the requirements for compliance with ***NEC Articles 240 and 384***. See FPN No. 1 in ***NEC Section 450-3***, which references ***NEC Sections 240-3 and 240-100*** for proper protection of secondary conductors.

10.1.1   Overcurrent Protection For Small Power Transformers

Low-amperage, E-rated, medium-voltage fuses are general-purpose, current-limiting fuses. The E rating defines the melting time current characteristic of the fuse and permits electrical interchangeability of fuses with the same E rating. For a general-purpose fuse to have an E rating, the current responsive element shall melt in 300 seconds at an rms current within the range of 200% to 240% of the continuous current rating of the fuse, fuse refill, or link (ANSI C37.46).

Low-amperage, E-rated fuses are designed to provide primary protection for potential, small service, and control transformers. These fuses offer a high level of fault current interruption in a self-contained, non-venting package which can be mounted indoors or in an enclosure.

As for all current-limiting fuses, the basic application rules found in the NEC and the manufacturer's literature should be adhered to. In addition, potential transformer fuses must have sufficient inrush capacity to successfully pass through the magnetizing inrush current of the transformer. If the fuse is not sized properly, it will open before the load is energized. The maximum magnetizing inrush currents to the transformer at system voltage and the duration of this inrush current vary with the transformer design. Magnetizing inrush currents are usually denoted as a percentage of the transformer full-load current (i.e., 10X, 12X, 15X, etc.). The inrush current duration is usually given in seconds. Where this information is available, an easy check can be made on the appropriate minimum melting curve to verify proper fuse selection. In lieu of transformer inrush data, the rule of thumb is to select a fuse size rated at 300% of the primary full-load current or the next larger standard size.

For example, a transformer manufacturer states that an 800VA, 240V, single-phase potential transformer has a magnetizing inrush current of 12X lasting for 0.1 second. Therefore:

$$I = \frac{800VA}{2,400V} = 0.333A$$

Inrush current = 12A × 0.333A = 4A

Since the voltage is 2,400V, we can use either a JCW or a JCD fuse. Using the 300% rule of thumb:

300% of .333A = .999A

Therefore, we would choose a JCW-1E or JCD-1E fuse.

Typical potential transformer connections – Typical potential transformer connections can be grouped into two categories:

- Those connections that require the fuse to pass only the magnetizing inrush of one potential transformer. See *Figure 40*.
- Those connections that must pass the magnetizing inrush of more than one potential transformer. See *Figure 41*.

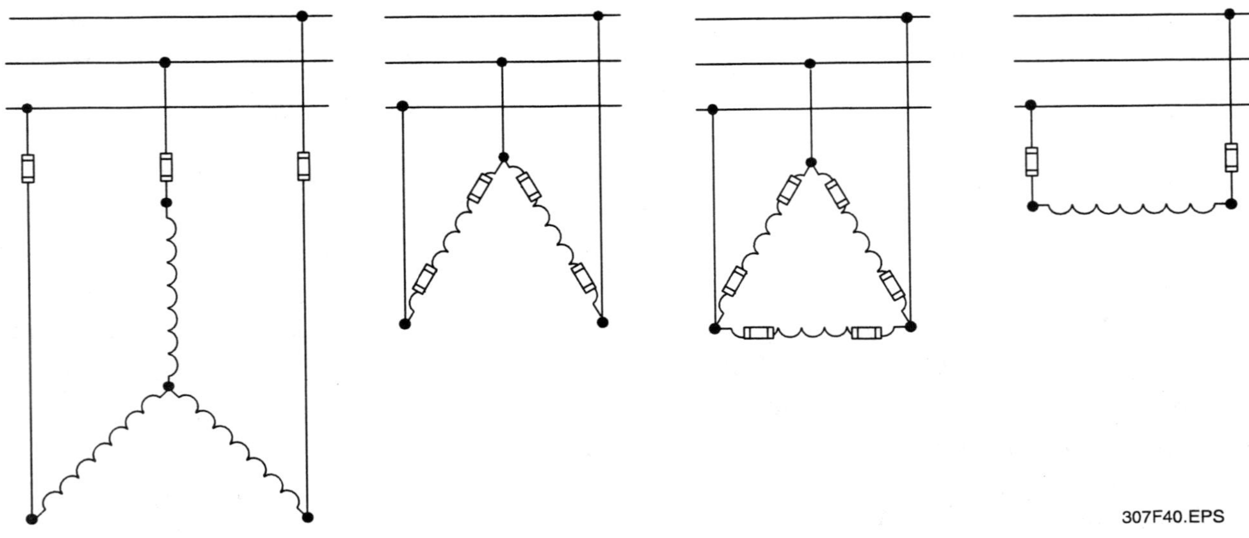

Figure 40. Connections Requiring Fuses To Pass Only The Magnetizing Inrush Of One Transformer

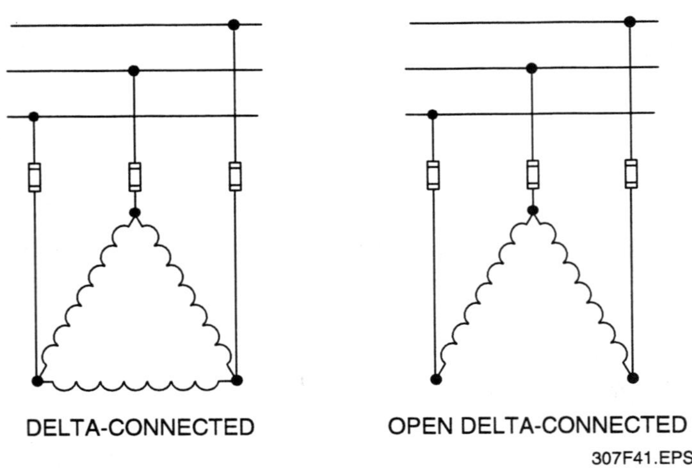

Figure 41. Connections Requiring Fuses To Pass The Magnetizing Inrush Of More Than One Transformer

ELECTRICAL — TRAINEE TASK MODULE 26307

Fuses for medium-voltage transformers and feeders – E-rated, medium-voltage fuses are general-purpose, current-limiting fuses. The fuses carry either an E or an X rating, which defines the melting time current characteristic of the fuse. The ratings are used to allow electrical interchangeability among different manufacturers' fuses.

For a general-purpose fuse to have an E rating, the following conditions must be met:

- Current responsive elements with ratings 100A or below shall melt in 300 seconds at an rms current within the range of 200% to 240% of the continuous current rating of the fuse unit (ANSI C37.46).
- Current responsive elements with ratings above 100A shall melt in 600 seconds at an rms current within the range of 220% to 264% of the continuous current rating of the fuse unit (ANSI C37.46).

A fuse with an X rating does not meet the electrical interchangeability for an E-rated fuse, but offers the user other ratings that may provide better protection for the particular application.

Transformer protection is the most popular application of E-rated fuses. The fuse is applied to the primary of the transformer and is solely used to prevent rupture of the transformer due to short circuits. It is important, therefore, to size the fuse so that it does not clear on system inrush or permissible overload currents. Magnetizing inrush must also be considered when sizing a fuse. In general, power transformers have a magnetizing inrush current of 12X, which is the full-load rating for a duration of $\frac{1}{10}$ second.

10.2.0 TRANSFORMER GROUNDING

Grounding is necessary to remove static electricity and also as a precautionary measure in case the transformer windings accidentally come in contact with the core or enclosure. All transformers should be grounded and bonded to meet NEC requirements and also local codes, where applicable.

The tank of every power transformer should be grounded to eliminate the possibility of obtaining static shocks from it or being injured by accidental grounding of the winding to the case. A grounding lug is provided on the base of most transformers for the purpose of grounding the case and fittings.

The NEC specifically states the requirements for grounding and should be followed in every respect. Furthermore, certain advisory rules recommended by manufacturers provide additional protection beyond that of the NEC. In general, the code requires that separately derived alternating current systems be grounded as stated in ***NEC Section 250-30***.

Figure 42 summarizes NEC regulations governing the grounding of transformers to provide for fault current to trip overcurrent protective devices.

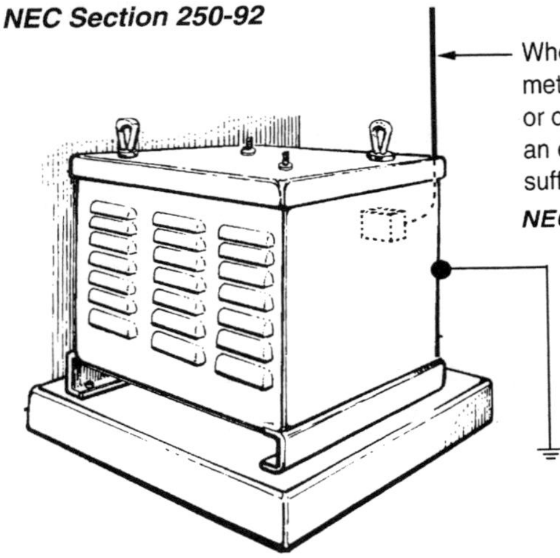

Figure 42. Summary Of NEC Requirements For Transformer Grounding

11.0.0 POWER FACTOR

Power factor was covered in the Level 2 module entitled *Alternating Current*, so a brief review of the subject should suffice here. The equation for power factor is:

$$\text{power factor (pf)} = \frac{kW}{kVA}$$

Where:

kW = kilowatts

kVA = kilovolt-amperes

Calculating the power factor of an electrical system requires that the true power, inductive reactance, and capacitive reactance of the system be determined. An analogy should enhance your understanding of these terms.

Imagine a farm wagon to which three horses are hitched, as shown in *Figure 43*. The horse in the middle (#1) is pulling straight ahead; we will call this horse *true power* because all of the effort is in the direction that the work should be done. Horse #2 wants to nibble at the grass growing along the side of the road. This horse does not contribute an ounce of pull in the desired direction, but causes a problem by pulling the wagon toward the ditch. We will call horse #2 *inductance*. The third horse has about the same strength as horse #2 and enjoys the grass on the opposite side of the road, which causes this horse to pull in the exact opposite direction of horse #2. Horse #3 also contributes nothing to the forward motion. This horse is called **capacitance**.

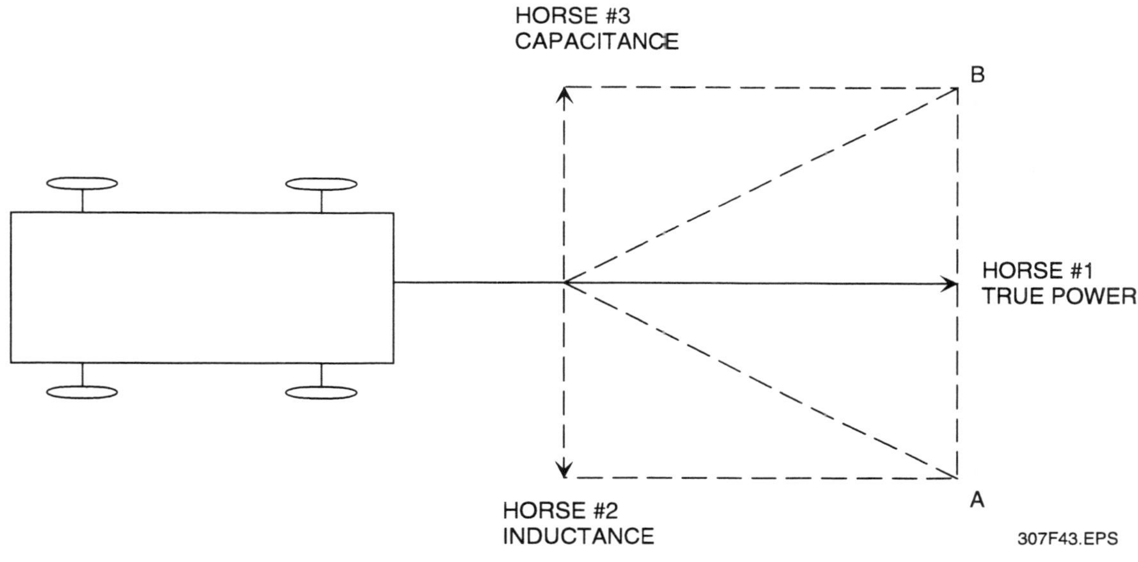

Figure 43. Depicting Power Factor

We will forget about horse #3 for the moment. If only horse #1 and horse #2 were pulling, the wagon would go in the direction of dotted line A. Notice that the length of that line is greater than the line to #1, so the horse named *inductance* has an effect on the final result. The direction and length of A might well be called *apparent power* and happens to be the hypotenuse (or diagonal) of a right angle triangle.

If the #2 horse were unhitched, then horses #1 and #3 would cause the wagon to move in the direction of B and the length of that line would also be *apparent power*. If all three horses were pulling, horses #2 and #3 would cancel one another out, and the only useful animal would be reliable horse #1—true power.

In an AC circuit, there are always three forces working in varying lengths. Inductance (horse #2) is present in every magnetic circuit and always works at a 90° angle with true power. Therefore, we have a power factor of less than 100% because the wagon does not move straight ahead, but travels towards the right due to the pull of horse #2. However, we can improve the power factor by adding horse #3, capacitance, which tends to cancel out the pull of inductance, enabling the wagon to travel straight ahead.

11.1.0   CAPACITORS

NEC Article 460 states specific rules for the installation and protection of capacitors other than surge capacitors or capacitors that are part of another apparatus. The chief use of capacitors is to improve the power factor of an electrical installation or an individual piece of electrically operated equipment. In general, this efficiency lowers the cost of power. The NEC requirements for capacitors operating under 600V are summarized in *Table 2*.

Application	NEC Regulation	NEC Reference
Enclosing and guarding	Capacitors must be enclosed, located, or guarded so that persons cannot come into accidental contact or bring conducting materials into accidental contact with exposed energized parts, terminals, or buses associated with them. However, no additional guarding is required for enclosures accessible only to authorized and qualified persons.	***NEC Section 460-2(b)***
Stored charge	Capacitors must be provided with a means of draining the stored charge. The discharge circuit must be either permanently connected to the terminals of the capacitor or capacitor bank, or provided with automatic means of connecting it to the terminals of the capacitor bank on removal of voltage from the line. Manual means of switching or connecting the discharge circuit shall not be used.	***NEC Section 460-6***
Capacitors on circuits over 600V	Special NEC regulations apply to capacitors operating at over 600V.	***NEC Articles 460, Part B and 490***
Conductor ampacity	The ampacity of capacitor circuit conductors must not be less than 135% of the rated current of the capacitor.	***NEC Section 460-8(a)***
Capacitors on motor circuits	The ampacity of conductors that connect a capacitor to the terminals of a motor or to motor circuit conductors shall not be less than one-third the ampacity of the motor circuit conductors and in no case less than 135% of the rated current of the capacitor.	***NEC Section 460-8(a)***
Overcurrent protection	Overcurrent protection is required in each ungrounded conductor unless the capacitor is connected on the load side of a motor running overcurrent device. The setting must be as low as practicable.	***NEC Section 460-8(b)***
Disconnecting means	A disconnecting means is required for a capacitor unless it is connected to the load side of a motor controller. The rating must be not less than 135% of the rated current of the capacitor.	***NEC Section 460-8(c)***
Overcurrent protection for improved pf	If the power factor is improved, the motor running overcurrent device must be selected based on the reduced current draw, not the full-load current of the motor.	***NEC Section 460-9***
Grounding	Capacitor cases must be grounded except when the system is designed to operate at other than ground potential.	***NEC Section 460-10***

Table 2. NEC Capacitor Installation Requirements

Since capacitors may store an electrical charge and hold a voltage that is present even when a capacitor is disconnected from a circuit, capacitors must be enclosed, guarded, or located so that persons cannot accidentally contact the terminals. In most installations, capacitors are installed out of reach or are placed in an enclosure accessible only to qualified persons. The stored charge of a capacitor must be drained by a discharge circuit either permanently connected to the capacitor or automatically connected when the line voltage of the capacitor circuit is removed. The windings of a motor or a circuit consisting of resistors and reactors will serve to drain the capacitor charge.

Capacitor circuit conductors must have an ampacity of not less than 135% of the rated current of the capacitor. This current is determined from the VA rating of the capacitor as for any other load. For example, a 100kVA (100,000VA) three-phase capacitor operating at 480V has a rated current of:

$$I = \frac{100,000\text{VA}}{1.732 \times 480\text{V}} = 120.3\text{A}$$

The minimum conductor ampacity is then:

$$I = 1.35 \times 120.3\text{A} = 162.4\text{A}$$

When a capacitor is switched into a circuit, a large inrush current results to charge the capacitor to the circuit voltage. Therefore, an overcurrent protective device for the capacitor must be rated or set high enough to allow the capacitor to charge. Although the exact setting is not specified in the NEC, typical settings vary between 150% and 250% of the rated capacitor current.

In addition to overcurrent protection, a capacitor must have a disconnecting means rated at not less than 135% of the rated current of the capacitor unless the capacitor is connected to the load side of the motor running overcurrent device. In this case, the motor disconnecting means would serve to disconnect the capacitor and the motor.

A capacitor connected to a motor circuit serves to increase the power factor and reduce the total kVA required by the motor capacitor circuit. As stated earlier, the power factor (pf) is defined as the true power in kilowatts divided by the total kVA or:

$$pf = \frac{\text{kW}}{\text{kVA}}$$

A power factor of less than one represents a lagging current for motors and inductive devices. The capacitor introduces a leading current that reduces the total kVA and raises the power factor to a value closer to unity (one). If the inductive load of the motor is completely balanced by the capacitor, a maximum power factor of unity results and all of the input energy serves to perform useful work.

The capacitor circuit conductors for a power factor correction capacitor must have an ampacity of not less than 135% of the rated current of the capacitor. In addition, the ampacity must not be less than one-third the ampacity of the motor circuit conductors.

The connection of a capacitor reduces the current in the feeder up to the point of connection. If the capacitor is connected on the load side of the motor running overcurrent device, the current through this device is reduced and its rating must be based on the actual current, not on the full-load current of the motor.

11.2.0   RESISTORS AND REACTORS

NEC Article 470 covers the installation of separate resistors and reactors on electric circuits. However, this article does not cover such devices that are component parts of other machines and equipment.

In general, the NEC requires resistors and reactors to be placed where they will not be exposed to physical damage. Therefore, such devices are normally installed in a protective enclosure, such as a controller housing or other type of cabinet. When these enclosures are constructed of metal, they must be grounded as specified in *NEC Article 250*. Furthermore, a thermal barrier must be provided between resistors and/or reactors and any combustible material that is less than 12" away. A space of 12" of more between the devices and combustible material is considered a sufficient distance so as not to require a thermal barrier.

Insulated conductors used for connections between resistors and motor controllers must be rated at not less than 90°C (194°F) except for motor starting service. In this case, other conductor insulation is permitted, provided other sections of the NEC are not violated.

11.3.0   DIODES AND RECTIFIERS

The diode and the rectifier are the simplest form of electronic components. The only difference between the two is their size; a component that is rated less than 1A is called a *diode*, while a similar component rated above 1A is called a *rectifier*. The main purpose of either device is to convert or rectify alternating current to direct current.

Diodes and rectifiers are composed of two material types: P and N. One has free electrons, while the other has a shortage of electrons. When the two types of material are bonded together, a solid-state component is produced that will allow electrons to flow in one direction and act as an insulator when the voltage is reversed.

Diodes and rectifiers are used extensively in control circuits. For example, *Figure 44* shows an AC voltage supplying a control transformer which must supply a DC electronic controller.

Consequently, two rectifiers are installed on the secondary side of the transformer to change AC to DC. The rectifiers allow current to flow in one direction, but will not allow the normal alternating current reversal—simulating direct current.

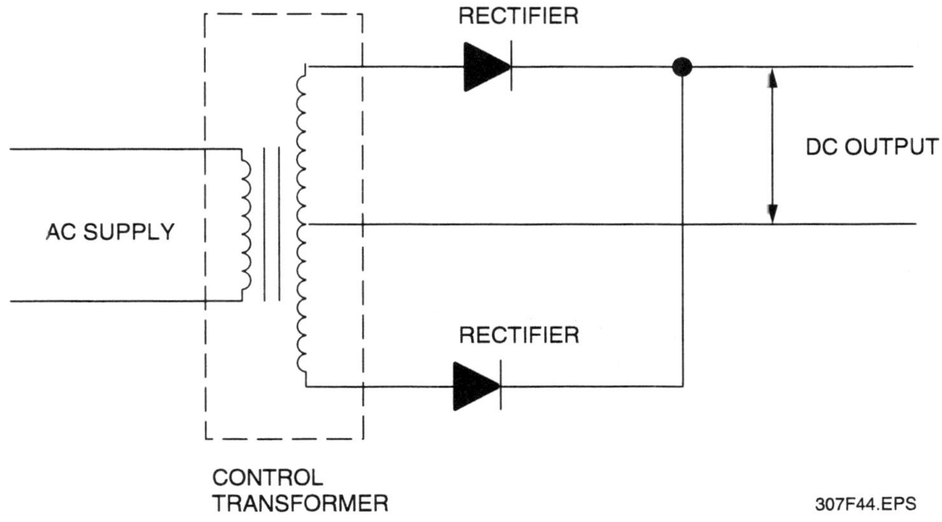

Figure 44. Rectifiers Used In A Control Circuit To Change AC To DC

12.0.0 VECTORS

The theoretical study of transformers includes the use of phasor diagrams (vectors) that graphically represent voltages and currents in transformer windings.

A vector or phasor diagram is a line with direction and length. Reading a vector diagram is like reading a road map and is not much more difficult, just a bit more refined. For example, road directions that instruct you to go east 40 miles, then south 30 miles to get to your destination are simple to understand. In other words, you had to drive 70 miles to get there. However, had you been able to drive as the crow flies, the distance would have been shorter— only 50 miles. See *Figure 45(A)*. If the miles were converted into electrical terms, this same triangle would be the classic 3/4/5 triangle or the 80% power factor relationship, as shown in *Figure 45(B)*.

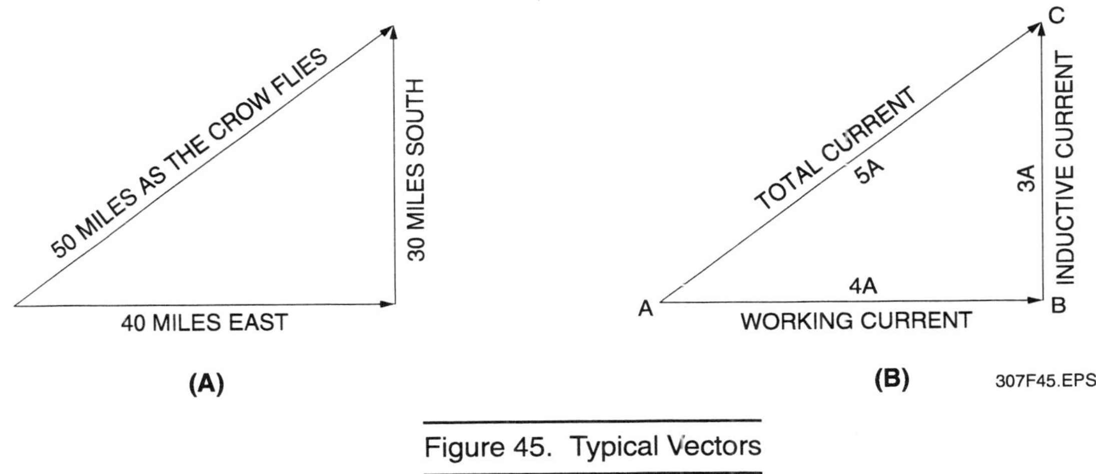

Figure 45. Typical Vectors

Referring to *Figure 45(B)*, if the working current (line A-B) is 4A and the inductive current (line B-C) is 3A, then the diagonal line A-C or hypotenuse will be 5A. This value may be proven by drawing lines A-B and B-C to scale and then connecting line A-C and measuring it. However, the same results may be obtained mathematically using the Pythagorean theorum, which states that the hypotenuse is equal to the square root of the sum of the squares of the other two sides:

$$AC = \sqrt{AB^2 + BC^2}$$
$$AC = \sqrt{4^2 + 3^2} = \sqrt{16 + 9} = \sqrt{25}$$
$$AC = 5$$

In this example, the working current is related to kilowatts (kW) and the total current is related to kVA; the ratio between the two is $4 \div 5 = 0.80$. Since the power factor equals $kW \div kVA$, the power factor of this circuit is 80%.

12.1.0   PRACTICAL APPLICATIONS OF PHASOR DIAGRAMS

When three single-phase transformers are used as a three-phase bank, the direction of the voltage in each of the six phase windings may be represented by a voltage phasor. A voltage phasor diagram of the six voltages involved provides a convenient way to study the relative direction and amounts of the primary and secondary voltages.

The same is true for one three-phase transformer, which also has six voltages to be considered, because its phase windings on the high-voltage and low-voltage sides are connected together in the same way as the phase windings of three single-phase transformers.

To show how a phasor diagram is drawn, consider the three-phase transformer shown in *Figure 46*. Here we have a Y delta-connected three-phase transformer with three legs, with each leg carrying a high-voltage and low-voltage winding. The high-voltage windings are connected in Y (with a common neutral point at N) with the leads to the high-voltage terminals designated H_1, H_2, and H_3. The three low-voltage windings are connected in delta. The junction points of the three windings serve as low-voltage terminals X_1, X_2, and X_3.

The voltages in the low-voltage windings are assumed to be equal to each other in amount, but are displaced from each other by 120°.

When drawing the phasor diagram for the low-voltage windings, phasor X_1X_2 is drawn first in any selected direction and to any convenient scale. The arrowhead indicates the instantaneous direction of the alternating voltage in winding X_1X_2 and the length of the phasor represents the amount of voltage in the winding. The broken lines that extend past the arrowheads represent reference lines for phase angles.

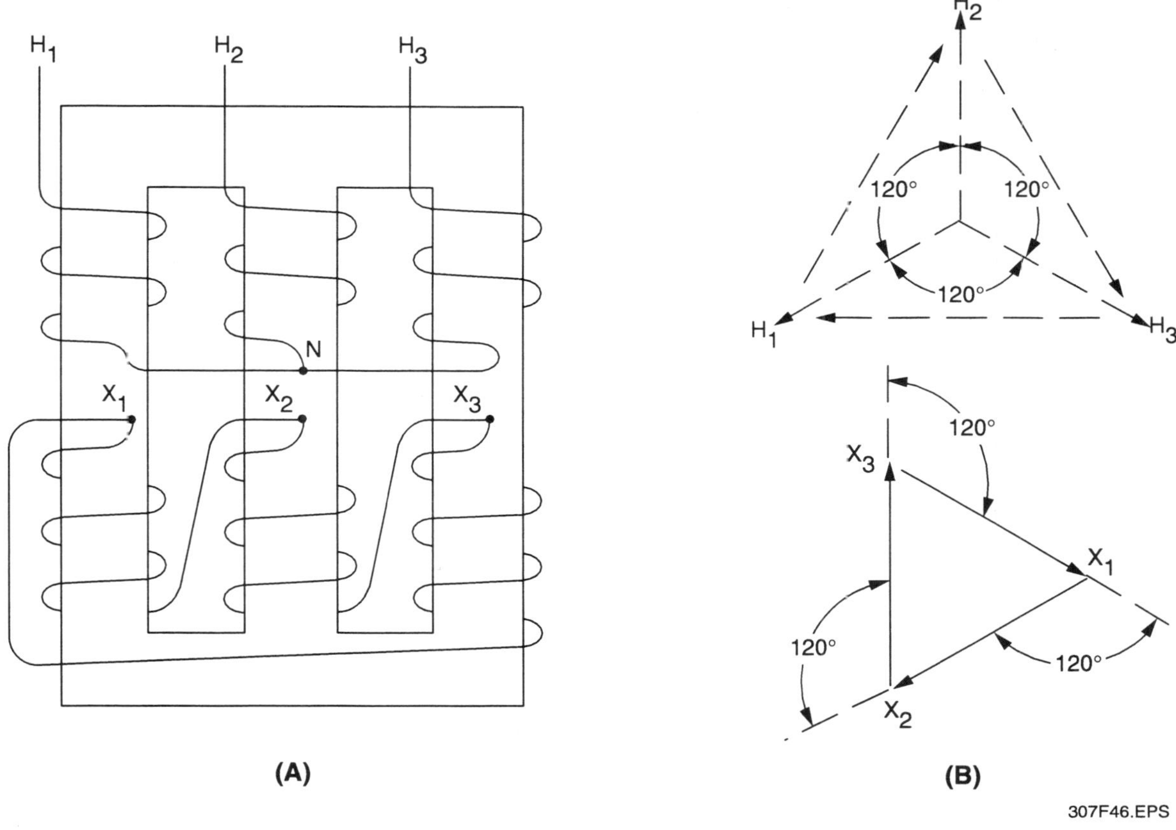

(A)   (B)

307F46.EPS

Figure 46. Windings And Phasor Diagrams Of A Three-Phase Transformer

Since winding X_2X_3 is physically connected to the end of X_2 in the X_1X_2 winding, phasor X_2X_3 will be started at point X_2, 120° out of phase with phasor X_1X_2 in the clockwise direction. The length of phasor X_2X_3 is equal to the length of phasor X_1X_2. Winding X_3X_1 is drawn in a similar manner.

The high-voltage phasor comes next. Since the low-voltage winding X_1X_2 is wound on the same leg as the high-voltage winding NH_1, the voltages in these two windings are in phase and are represented by parallel voltage phasors. Therefore, the phasor NH_1 is drawn from a selected point N parallel to X_1X_2. Note that all three high-voltage windings are physically connected to a common point N. Therefore, the phasors representing the voltages NH_1, NH_2, and NH_3 will all start at the common (point N in the phasor diagram). Again, the high-voltage phasors are all of the same length, but are displaced from each other by 120°, as shown.

The high-voltage phasors have the same length as the low-voltage phasors. Each phase of the high voltage is, however, proportional to the low voltage in the same phase according to the turns ratio, making the line voltage 1.732 times higher than the phase voltage in any one winding. It can be geometrically proven, for example, that $H_1H_2 \times NH_1 = 1.732 \times NH_2$ and so forth for each line voltage.

When comparing three-phase transformers for possible operation in parallel, draw the voltage phasor diagram for transformer bank A and mark the terminals as shown in *Figure 47(A)*. Next, draw the phasor diagram for bank B on drafting or other transparent paper; then draw a heavy reference line m-n, as shown in *Figure 47(B)*. Cut the transparent diagram into two parts, as indicated by the dashed lines in the drawing. The two parts of the reference line are now marked m and n. Place diagram m on the high-voltage diagram in *Figure 47(A)* so that the terminals which are desired to be connected together coincide. Place diagram n on the low-voltage diagram in *Figure 47(A)* so that the heavy reference line of n is parallel to the heavy reference line of m. If the terminals of n can be made to coincide with the low-voltage terminals, the terminals which coincide can be connected together for parallel operation. If the low-voltage terminals cannot be made to coincide, parallel operation is not possible with the assumed high-voltage connection.

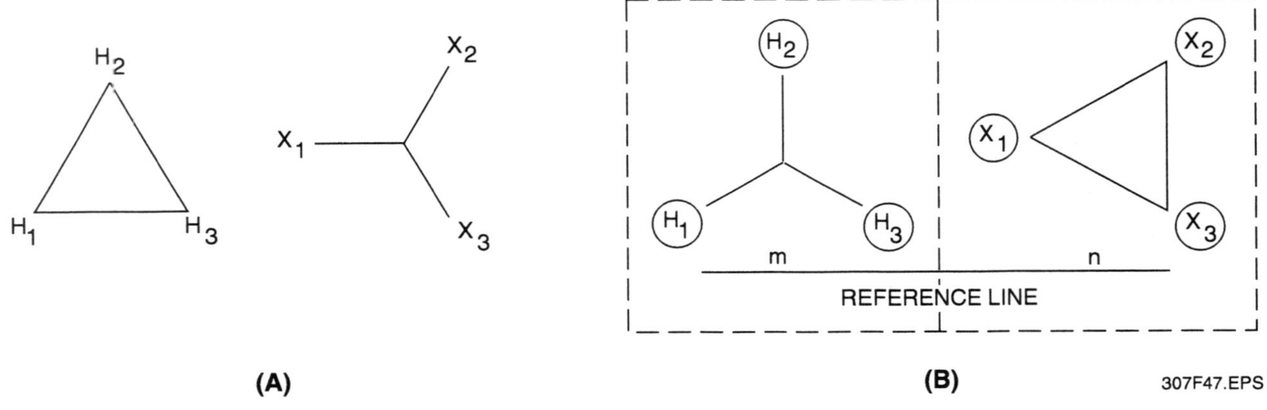

Figure 47. Phasor Diagrams For Three-Phase Transformer Banks In Parallel

12.2.0   VOLTAGE DROP

Figure 48 shows a simple 100% power factor circuit in which a 1Ω resistance appears between the source of power and the load. The current in this series circuit is 10A and the voltage at the source is 120V. Because Ohm's Law states that $E = IR$, we must have a voltage drop across the resistance equal to 10 times 1 or 10V. With the voltage and current in phase, only 110V will be available at the load because we must subtract the resistance drop from the source voltage. Voltage drop was covered more thoroughly earlier in your training.

Voltage drop, however, becomes a little more complicated when inductance is introduced into the circuit, as shown in *Figure 49*. In this case, the load voltage will be equal to the source voltage minus the voltage drops through R and X, but they cannot be added arithmetically. The vector diagram in *Figure 50* shows that the dotted line A-C is the combination of the two voltages across R and X, and represents the voltage drop in the line only.

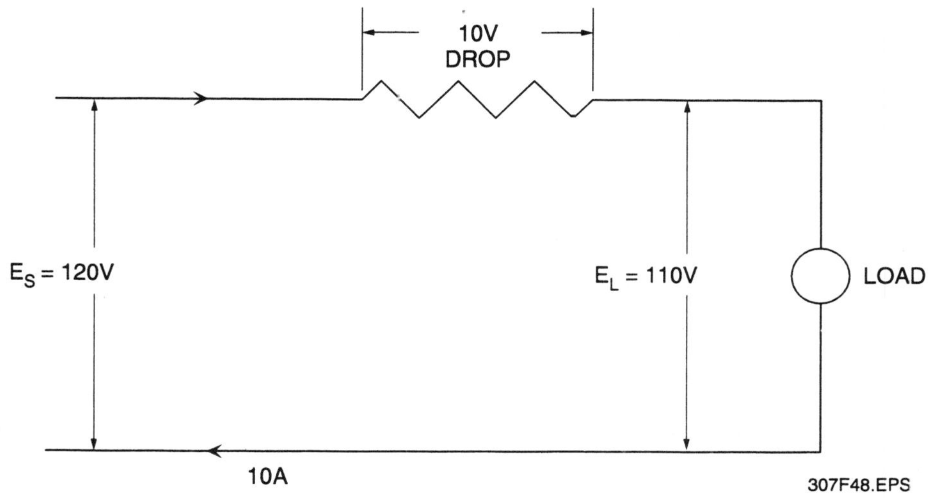

Figure 48. Circuit Containing Resistance Only

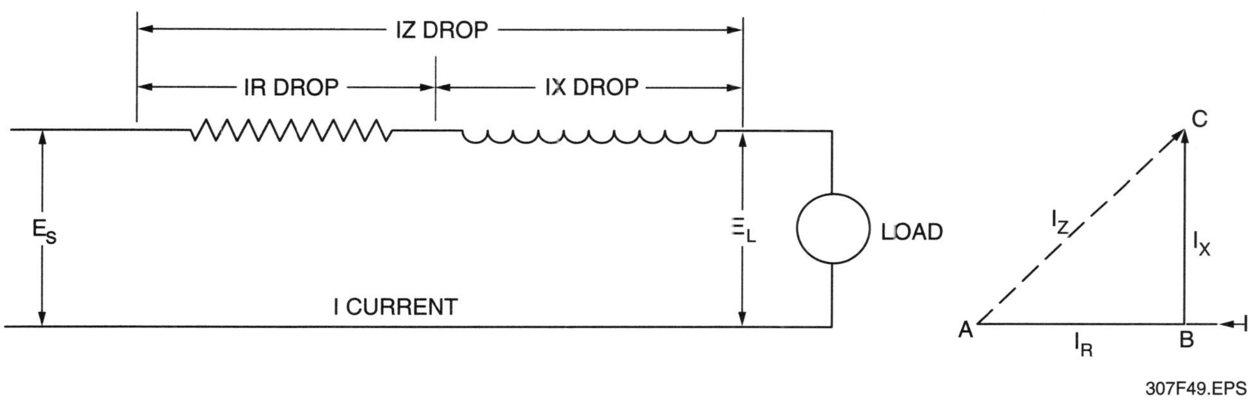

Figure 49. Electrical Circuit With Both Resistance And Inductance

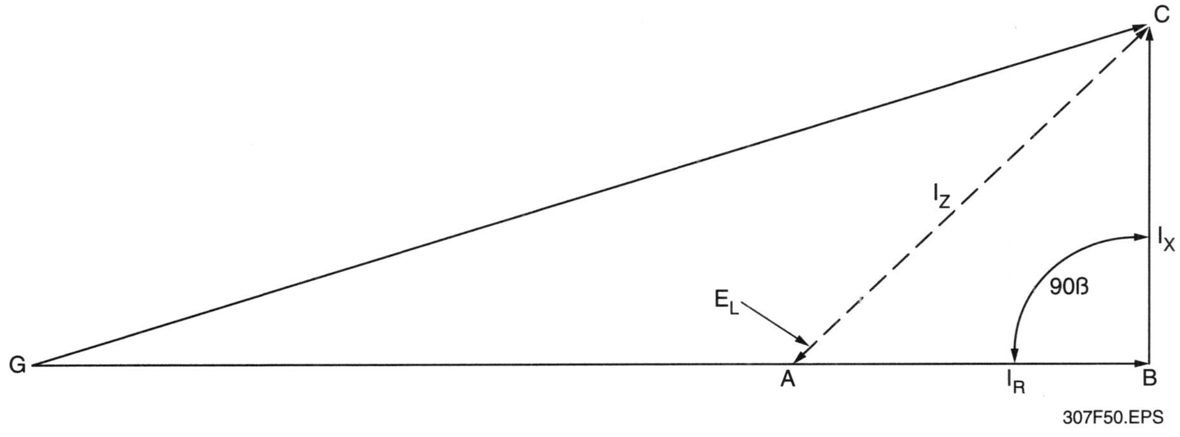

Figure 50. Effect Of Voltage Drop In An AC Circuit

Figure 50 shows that line G-A, which is the load voltage E_L, is less than the source voltage G-C due to the voltage drop in line A-C. Because of the effect of the reactance in the line, this voltage drop cannot be subtracted arithmetically from the source voltage to obtain the load voltage; vectors must be used.

Calculations of impedance can be simplified by using equivalent circuits. The reactance voltage drop is governed by the leakage flux, and the voltage regulation depends on the power factor of the load. To determine transformer efficiency at various loads, it is necessary to first calculate the core loss, hysteresis loss, eddy current loss, and load loss.

However, for all practical purposes in electrical construction applications, a transformer's efficiency may be considered to be 100%. Therefore, for our purposes, a transformer may be defined as a device that transfers power from its primary circuit to the secondary circuit without any significant loss.

Since power (W) equals voltage (E) times current (I), if $E_P I_P$ represents the primary power and $E_S I_S$ represents the secondary power, then $E_P I_P = E_S I_S$ (the subscript P = primary and the subscript S = secondary). See *Figure 51*. If the primary and secondary voltages are equal, the primary and secondary currents must also be equal. Assume that E_P is twice as large as E_S. For $E_P I_P$ to equal $E_S I_S$, I_P must be one-half of I_S. Therefore, a transformer that steps voltage down always steps current up. Conversely, a transformer that steps voltage up always steps current down. However, transformers are classified as step-up or step-down only in relation to their effect on voltage.

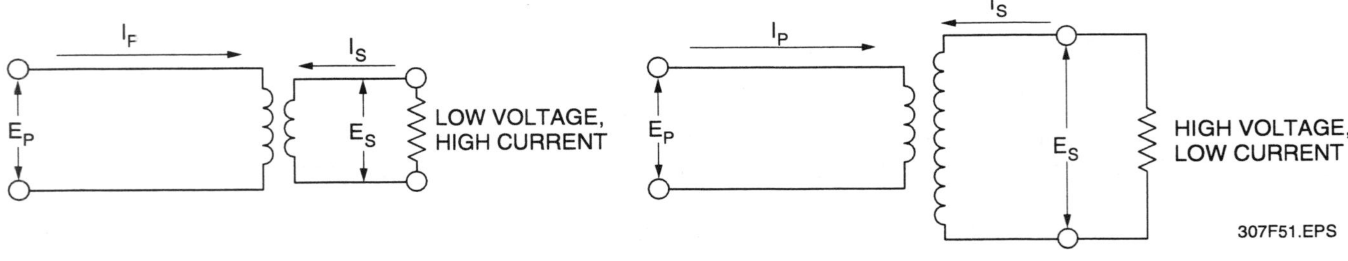

Figure 51. When Voltage Is Stepped Down, Current Is Stepped Up (And Vice Versa)

13.0.0 TROUBLESHOOTING

Since transformers are an essential part of every electrical installation, electricians must know how to test and locate problems that develop in transformers—especially in the smaller power supply or control transformers. The procedure for accomplishing this is commonly known as *troubleshooting*.

The term *troubleshooting*, as used in this module, covers the investigation, analysis, and corrective action required to eliminate faults in electrical systems, including circuits, components, and equipment. Most problems are simple and easily corrected (e.g., an open circuit, a ground fault or short circuit, or a change in resistance).

ELECTRICAL — TRAINEE TASK MODULE 26307

There are many useful troubleshooting charts available. Most charts list the complaint on the left side of the chart, then the possible cause, followed by the proper corrective action.

When troubleshooting, think before acting, study the problem thoroughly, then ask yourself these questions:

- What were the warning signs preceding the trouble?
- What previous repair and maintenance work has been done?
- Has similar trouble occurred before?
- If the circuit, component, or piece of equipment still operates, is it safe to continue operation before further testing?

The answers to these questions can usually be obtained by:

- Questioning the owner of the equipment
- Taking time to think the problem through
- Looking for additional symptoms
- Consulting troubleshooting charts
- Checking the simplest things first
- Referring to repair and maintenance records
- Checking with calibrated instruments
- Double-checking all conclusions before beginning any repair

Note: Always check the easiest and most obvious things first; following this simple rule will save time and trouble.

13.1.0   DOUBLE-CHECK BEFORE BEGINNING

The source of many problems can be traced not to one part alone but to the relationship of one part with another. For instance, a tripped circuit breaker may be reset to restart a piece of equipment, but what caused the breaker to trip in the first place? It could have been caused by a vibrating hot conductor momentarily coming into contact with a ground, a loose connection, or any number of other causes.

Too often, electrically-operated equipment is completely disassembled in search of the cause of a certain complaint and all evidence is destroyed during disassembly. Check again to be certain an easy solution to the problem has not been overlooked.

13.2.0   FIND AND CORRECT THE BASIC CAUSE OF THE TROUBLE

After an electrical failure has been corrected in any type of electrical circuit or piece of equipment, be sure to locate and correct the cause so the same failure will not be repeated. Further investigation may reveal other faulty components.

Also be aware that although troubleshooting charts and procedures greatly help in diagnosing malfunctions, they can never be complete. There are too many variations and solutions for any given problem.

To solve electrical problems consistently, you must first understand the basic parts of electrical circuits, how they function, and for what purpose. If you know that a particular part is not performing its job, then the cause of the malfunction must be within this part or series of parts.

13.3.0 TROUBLESHOOTING TRANSFORMERS

This section discusses common transformer problems.

Open circuit – Should one of the windings in a transformer develop a break or open condition, no current can flow and therefore, the transformer will not deliver any output. The main symptom of an open circuit in a transformer is that the circuits which derive power from the transformer are deenergized or dead. Use an AC voltmeter or a volt-ohm-milliammeter (VOM) to check across the transformer output terminals, as shown in *Figure 52*. A reading of zero volts indicates an open circuit.

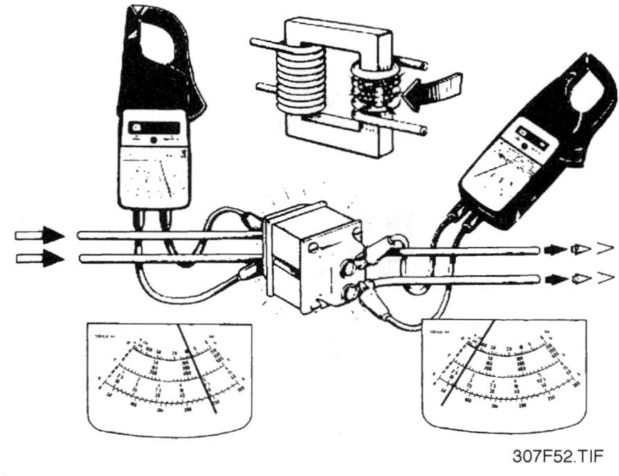

Figure 52. Checking A Transformer For An Open Winding Using A VOM

Next, take a voltage reading across the input terminals. If a voltage reading is present, then the conclusion is that one of the windings in the transformer is open. However, if no voltage reading is on the input terminals either, then the conclusion is that the open is elsewhere on the line side of the circuit; perhaps a disconnect switch is open.

WARNING!   Make absolutely certain that your testing instruments are designed for the job and are calibrated for the correct voltage. Never test the primary side of any transformer over 600V unless you are qualified, have the correct high-voltage testing instruments, and the test is made under the proper supervision.

If voltage is present on the line or primary side and is not present on the secondary or load side, open the switch to deenergize the circuit and place a warning tag (tagout and lock) on this switch so that it is not inadvertently closed again while someone is working on the circuit. Disconnect all of the transformer primary and secondary leads, then check each winding in the transformer for continuity, as indicated by a resistance reading taken with an ohmmeter (*Figure 53*).

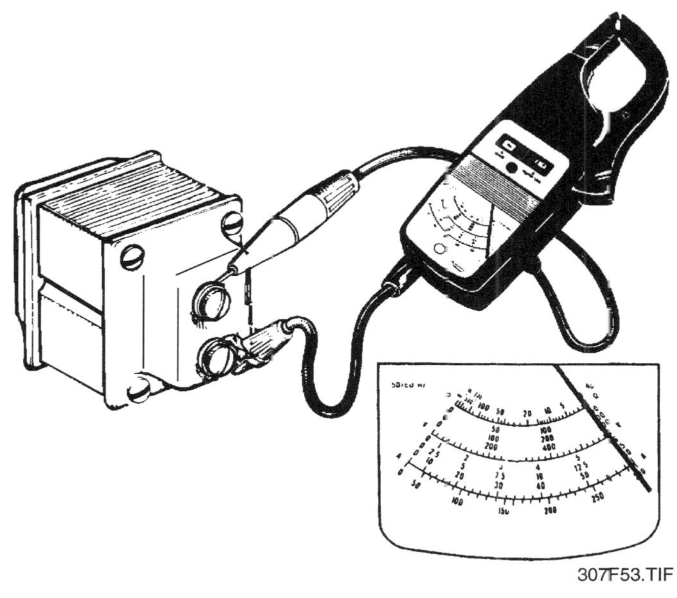

Figure 53. Checking For An Open Winding With A Continuity Test Using A VOM

Continuity is indicated by a relatively low resistance reading on control transformers, while an open winding will be indicated by an infinite resistance reading on the ohmmeter. In most cases, small transformers will have to be replaced, unless the break is accessible and can be repaired.

Shorted turns — Sometimes a few turns in the secondary winding of a transformer will acquire a partial short, which in turn will cause a voltage drop across the secondary. The symptom of this condition is usually overheating of the transformer caused by large circulating currents flowing in the shorted windings. The most accurate way to check for this condition is with a transformer turns ratio tester (TTR). However, another way to check for this condition is with a VOM set at the proper voltage scale (*Figure 54*). Take a reading on the line or primary side of the transformer first to make certain normal voltage is present, then take a reading on the secondary side. If the transformer has a partial short or ground fault, the voltage reading should be lower than normal.

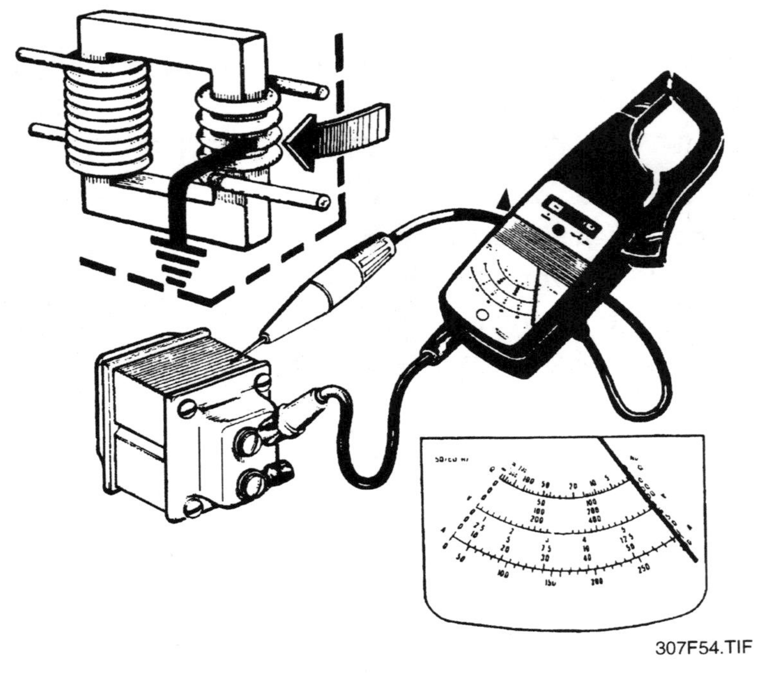

Figure 54. Testing A Transformer For A Ground Fault Using A VOM

Replace the faulty transformer with a new one and again take a reading on the secondary. If the voltage reading is now normal and the circuit operates satisfactorily, leave the replacement transformer in the circuit, and either discard or repair the original transformer.

A highly sensitive ohmmeter may also be used to test for this condition when the system is deenergized and the leads are disconnected; a lower than normal reading on the ohmmeter indicates this condition. However, the difference will usually be so slight that the average ohmmeter is not sensitive enough to detect it. Therefore, the recommended method is to use the voltmeter test.

Complete short – Occasionally, a transformer winding will become completely shorted. In most cases, this will activate the overload protective device and deenergize the circuit, but in other instances, the transformer may continue trying to operate with excessive overheating due to the very large circulating current. This heat will often melt the wax or insulation inside the transformer, which is easily detected by the odor. Also, there will be no voltage output across the shorted winding and the circuit across the winding will be dead.

The short may be in the external secondary circuit or it may be in the transformer's winding. To determine its location, disconnect the external secondary circuit from the winding and take a reading with a voltmeter. If the voltage is normal with the external circuit

ELECTRICAL — TRAINEE TASK MODULE 26307

disconnected, then the problem lies within the external circuit. However, if the voltage reading is still zero across the secondary leads, the transformer is shorted and will have to be replaced.

Grounded windings – Insulation breakdown is quite common in older transformers, especially those that have been overloaded. At some point, the insulation breaks or deteriorates, and the wire becomes exposed. The exposed wire often comes into contact with the transformer housing and grounds the winding.

If a winding develops a ground and a point in the external circuit connected to this winding is also grounded, part of the winding will be shorted out. The symptoms will be overheating (which is usually detected by heat or a burning smell) and a low-voltage reading, as indicated on a voltmeter (*Figure 55*). In most cases, transformers with this condition will have to be replaced.

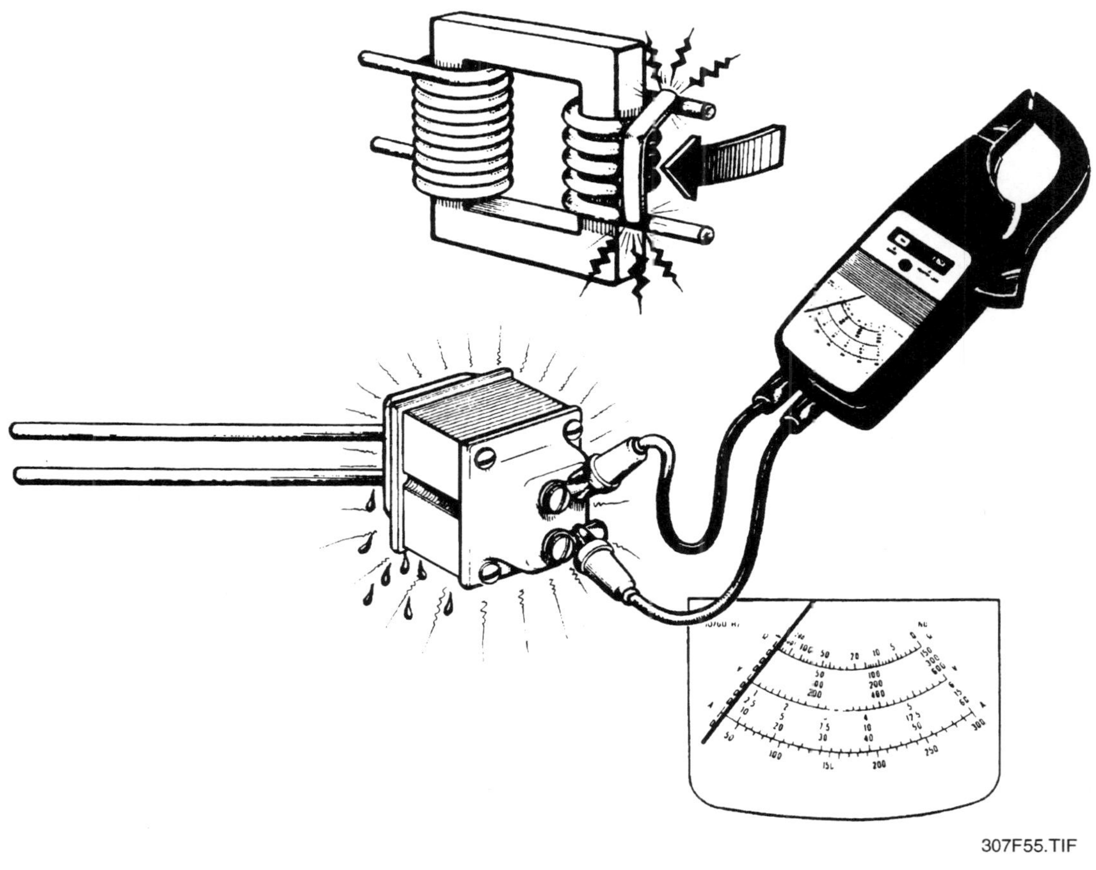

307F55.TIF

Figure 55. Transformers That Overheat Usually Have A Partial Short In The Windings

A megohmmeter (megger) is the best test instrument to check for this condition. Disconnect the leads from both the primary and secondary windings. Tests can then be performed on either winding by connecting the megger negative test lead to an associated ground and the positive test lead to the winding to be measured.

WARNING!   Do not use a megger unless you are qualified and properly supervised.

The insulation resistance should then be measured between the windings themselves. This is accomplished by connecting one test lead to the primary and the second test lead to the secondary and ground. After that, connect the first lead to the secondary and the second test lead to the primary and ground. All such tests should be noted on a record card under the proper identifying labels.

SUMMARY

This module covered the basic components and applications of distribution system transformers. When the AC voltage needed for an application is lower or higher than the voltage available from the source, a transformer is used. The essential components of a transformer are the primary winding, which is connected to the source, and the secondary winding, which is connected to the load. Both are wound on an iron core. The two windings are not physically connected. The alternating voltage in the primary winding induces an alternating voltage in the secondary winding. The ratio of the primary and secondary voltages is equal to the ratio of the number of turns in the primary and secondary windings. Transformers may step up the voltage applied to the primary winding and have a higher voltage at the secondary terminals, or they may step down the voltage applied to the primary winding and have a lower voltage available at the secondary terminals.

References

For advanced study of topics covered in this Task Module, the following books are suggested:

American Electricians' Handbook, Latest Edition, McGraw-Hill, New York, NY.

National Electrical Code Handbook, Latest Edition, National Fire Protection Association, Quincy, MA.

1. The main purpose of a transformer is to _____.
   a. change the current
   b. improve the power factor
   c. change the voltage
   d. enter impedance into the circuit

2. The three parts of a basic transformer are the _____.
   a. housing, lifting hooks, and base
   b. dry, oil-filled, and gas-filled chambers
   c. shell, open winding, and closed winding
   d. primary winding, secondary winding, and core

3. When AC flows through a transformer coil, a _____ field is generated around the coils.
   a. magnetic
   b. non-magnetic
   c. high-impedance
   d. rotating

4. When the field from one coil cuts through the turns of a second coil, what will occur in the second coil?
   a. The second coil will not be affected.
   b. The coils will rotate.
   c. Voltage will be generated.
   d. No current will flow in the circuit.

5. What causes voltage to be induced in a transformer?
   a. Transformer taps
   b. Mutual induction
   c. Reluctance
   d. Capacitance

6. In a transformer with a turns ratio of 5:1 (primary has 5 times the number of turns as the secondary), what will be the voltage on the secondary if the primary voltage is 120V?
   a. 12V
   b. 24V
   c. 48V
   d. 60V

7. The three basic types of iron core transformers are ______.
   a. dry, oil-filled, and auto
   b. closed, open, and shell
   c. control, power, and lighting
   d. metal, nonmetallic, and high-temperature

8. One effect caused by magnetic leakage in transformers is a ______.
   a. reactance voltage drop
   b. low impedance
   c. higher secondary voltage
   d. lower secondary voltage

9. A symptom of a transformer with an open circuit is ______.
   a. high voltage on the secondary
   b. excessive overheating
   c. no output on the secondary
   d. voltage drop across the secondary

10. To check for insulation resistance, a(n) ______ should be used.
    a. ammeter
    b. megger
    c. voltmeter
    d. TTR

ANSWERS TO REVIEW/PRACTICE QUESTIONS

Answer		Section Reference
1.	c	1.0.0
2.	d	2.0.0
3.	a	2.1.0
4.	c	2.1.0
5.	b	2.1.0
6.	b	2.2.0
7.	b	3.0.0
8.	d	3.5.0
9.	c	13.3.0
10.	b	13.3.0

The NCCER makes every effort to keep these manuals up-to-date and free of technical errors. We appreciate your help in this process. If you have an idea for improving this manual, or if you find an error, a typographical mistake, or an inaccuracy in the NCCER's Craft Training Manuals, please write us, using this form or a photocopy. Be sure to include the exact module number, page number, a description of the problem, and the correction, if possible. Your input will be brought to the attention of the Technical Review Committee. Thank you for your assistance.

Instructors – If you found that additional materials were necessary in order to teach this module effectively, please let us know so that we may include them in the Equipment/Materials list in the Instructor's Guide.

Write: Curriculum Development and Revision Department
National Center for Construction Education and Research
P.O. Box 141104
Gainesville, FL 32614-1104

Fax: 352-334-0932

Craft ___________________________ Module Name _____________________________

Copyright Date __________ Module Number __________ Page Number(s) __________

Description of Problem

____

____

____

____

(Optional) Correction of Problem

____

____

____

(Optional) Your Name and Address

____

____

____

notes

Lamps, Ballasts, and Components
Module 26308

LAMPS, BALLASTS, AND COMPONENTS

NATIONAL
CENTER FOR
CONSTRUCTION
EDUCATION AND
RESEARCH

OBJECTIVES

Upon completion of this module, the trainee will be able to:

1. Recognize incandescent, fluorescent, and high-intensity discharge (HID) lamps and describe how each type of lamp operates.
2. Recognize ballasts and describe their purpose for use in fluorescent and HID lighting fixtures.
3. Explain the relationship of Kelvin temperature to the color of light produced by a lamp.
4. Recognize basic occupancy sensors, photoelectric sensors, and timers used to control lighting circuits and describe how each device operates.
5. Use troubleshooting checklists to troubleshoot fluorescent and HID lamps and lighting fixtures.

Prerequisites

Successful completion of the following Task Modules is recommended before beginning study of this Task Module: Core Curricula; Electrical Level 1; Electrical Level 2; Electrical Level 3, Modules 26301 through 26307.

Required Trainee Materials

1. Trainee Task Module
2. Appropriate Personal Protective Equipment
3. Copy of the latest edition of the *National Electrical Code*

Note: The designations "National Electrical Code," "NE Code," and "NEC," where used in this document, refer to the National Electrical Code®, which is a registered trademark of the National Fire Protection Association, Quincy, MA. *All National Electrical Code (NEC) references in this module refer to the 1999 edition of the NEC.*

This course map shows all of the modules in the third level of the Electrical curricula. The suggested training order begins at the bottom and proceeds up. Skill levels increase as a trainee advances on the course map. The training order may be adjusted by the local Training Program Sponsor.

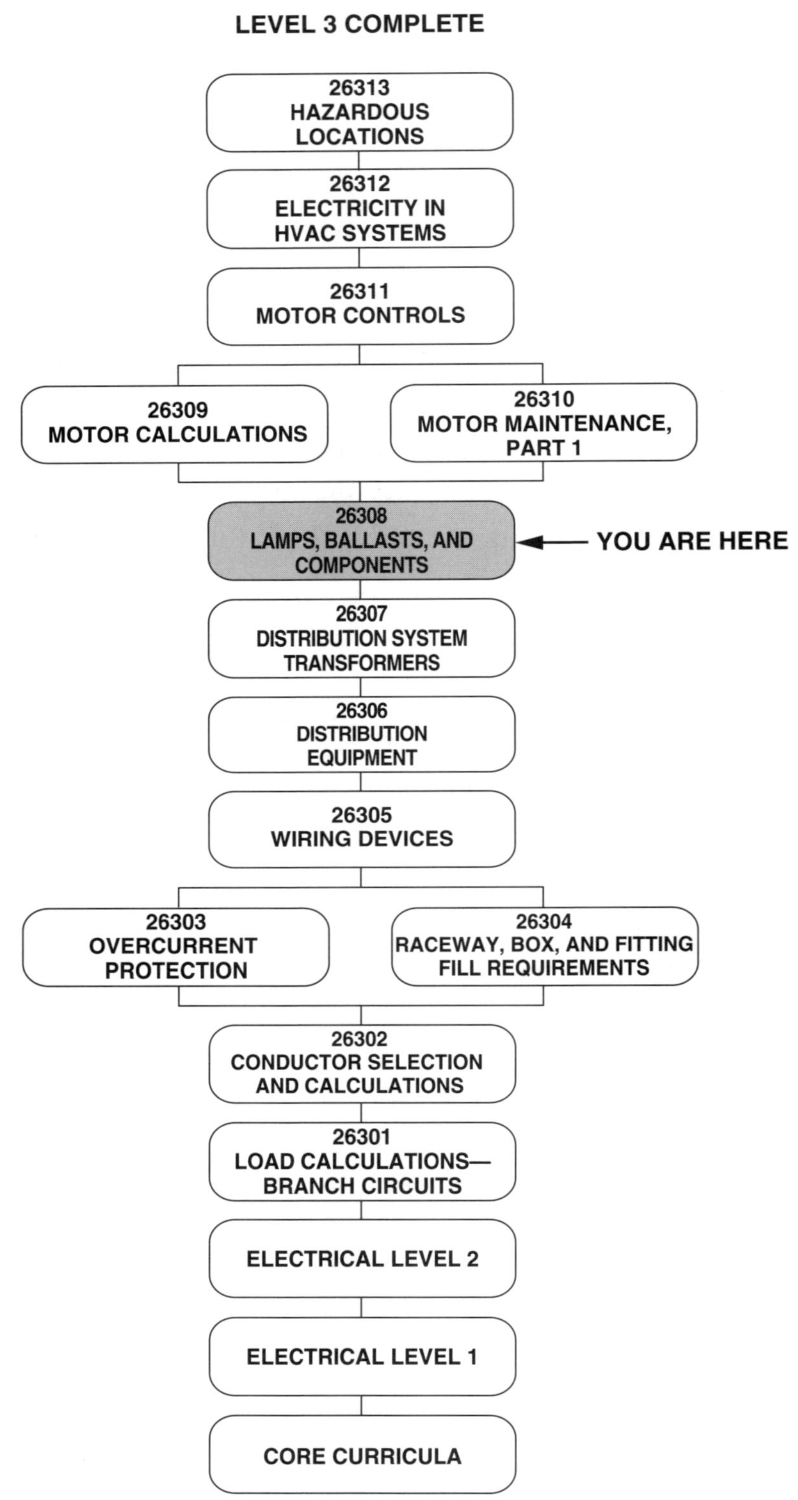

TABLE OF CONTENTS

Trade Terms Introduced In This Module

Color rendering index (CRI): A scale from 0 to 100 used by lamp manufacturers to indicate how normal and natural a light source makes objects appear in full sunlight or in incandescent light. Generally, the higher the CRI, the better it makes people and objects appear.

Dip tolerance: The ability of an HID lamp or lighting fixture circuit to ride through voltage variations without the lamp extinguishing and cooling down.

Efficacy: The light output of a light source divided by the total power input to that source. It is expressed in *lumens per watt (LPW)*.

Incandescence: The self-emission of radiant energy in the visible light spectrum resulting from thermal excitation of atoms or molecules such as occurs when an electric current is passed through the filament in an incandescent lamp.

Lumen maintenance: A measure of how a lamp maintains its light output over time. It may either be expressed as a graph of light output versus time or numerically.

Lumens per watt (LPW): A measure of the efficiency, or, more properly, the efficacy of a light source. The efficacy is calculated by taking the lumen output of a lamp and dividing by the lamp wattage. For example, a 100W lamp producing 1,750 lumens has an efficacy of 17.5 lumens per watt.

1.0.0 INTRODUCTION

This is the second of three modules that cover the subject of electric lighting. This module builds on the information and lighting principles previously covered in the first module, *Electric Lighting*. The third module, presented later in your training, will provide detailed technical information on the applications for the different types of lighting fixtures.

This module provides information on the operation of specific types of incandescent, fluorescent, and high-intensity discharge (HID) lamps and related lighting fixture components. Also introduced are some common lighting circuit control devices and energy conservation schemes used to control lighting. Guidelines for troubleshooting fluorescent and HID lighting fixtures are also covered.

2.0.0 STANDARD INCANDESCENT LAMPS

Incandescent lamps, also called *filament lamps*, are used for general lighting and typically provide a warm and natural light. Incandescent lamps were invented over a century ago. With some refinements, the basic construction of a standard incandescent lamp remains the same today. Incandescent lamps consist of a thin coiled or shaped tungsten-wire filament (*Figure 1*) supported inside an evacuated glass envelope (bulb) filled with an inert gas, typically a mix of argon and nitrogen. The inert gas helps to prevent the filament from combining with oxygen and burning out. The envelopes of most lamps are made of regular lead or soda lime (soft) glass. Envelopes of lamps that must withstand higher temperatures are typically made of borosilicate heat-resistant (hard) glass. The lamp's base supports the lamp envelope and filament and provides the electrical connection between the lamp and its power source.

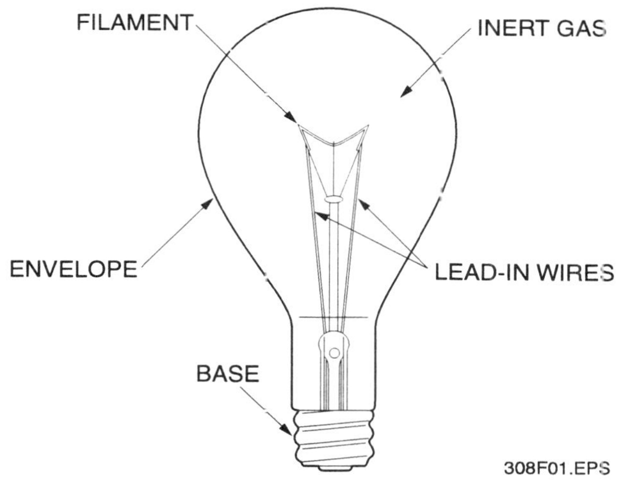

Figure 1. Components Of An Incandescent Lamp

In an incandescent lamp, light is generated by passing an electric current through the filament, and its resistance causes it to heat to **incandescence**. The hotter the filament gets, the more efficient it is in converting electricity to light output. Tungsten has a positive resistance characteristic that makes its resistance at operating temperature much greater than its cold resistance (typically 12 to 16 times greater). It should be pointed out that when a filament operates hotter, its life is shortened. This makes the design of each type of lamp a tradeoff between efficiency and lamp life. This is why lamps of equal wattage may have different lumen and life ratings.

Of all the lamp types, standard incandescent lamps are the most inefficient. Because they produce light by heating the filament until it glows, most of the energy they consume is given off as heat, resulting in a low efficiency (**efficacy**) of typically 5 to 22 **lumens per watt (LPW)**. Incandescent lamps also have the shortest life expectancy of all lamp types, typically between 750 and 2,000 average hours, depending on the type. This is because tungsten from the filament evaporates over time and is deposited on the walls of the bulb, thus reducing the light output. Also, the filament gets thinner and thinner with use and eventually breaks, causing the lamp to fail.

Incandescent lamps are made in numerous sizes and shapes, with different filament form arrangements and mounting bases. *Figure 2* shows some examples of typical lamp sizes and shapes. Lamps are identified by a letter referring to their shape and a number that indicates the maximum diameter stated in eighths of an inch. For example, A-40 identifies a lamp with an A-shape which is $^{40}/_8$ (5") in diameter. Lamps with standard, tubular, and similar envelope shapes provide lighting in all directions (omni-directional). Those with shapes designated as

R, *ER*, and *PAR* are all reflector-type lamps. They direct their light out in front by reflecting it from their cone-shaped inside walls.

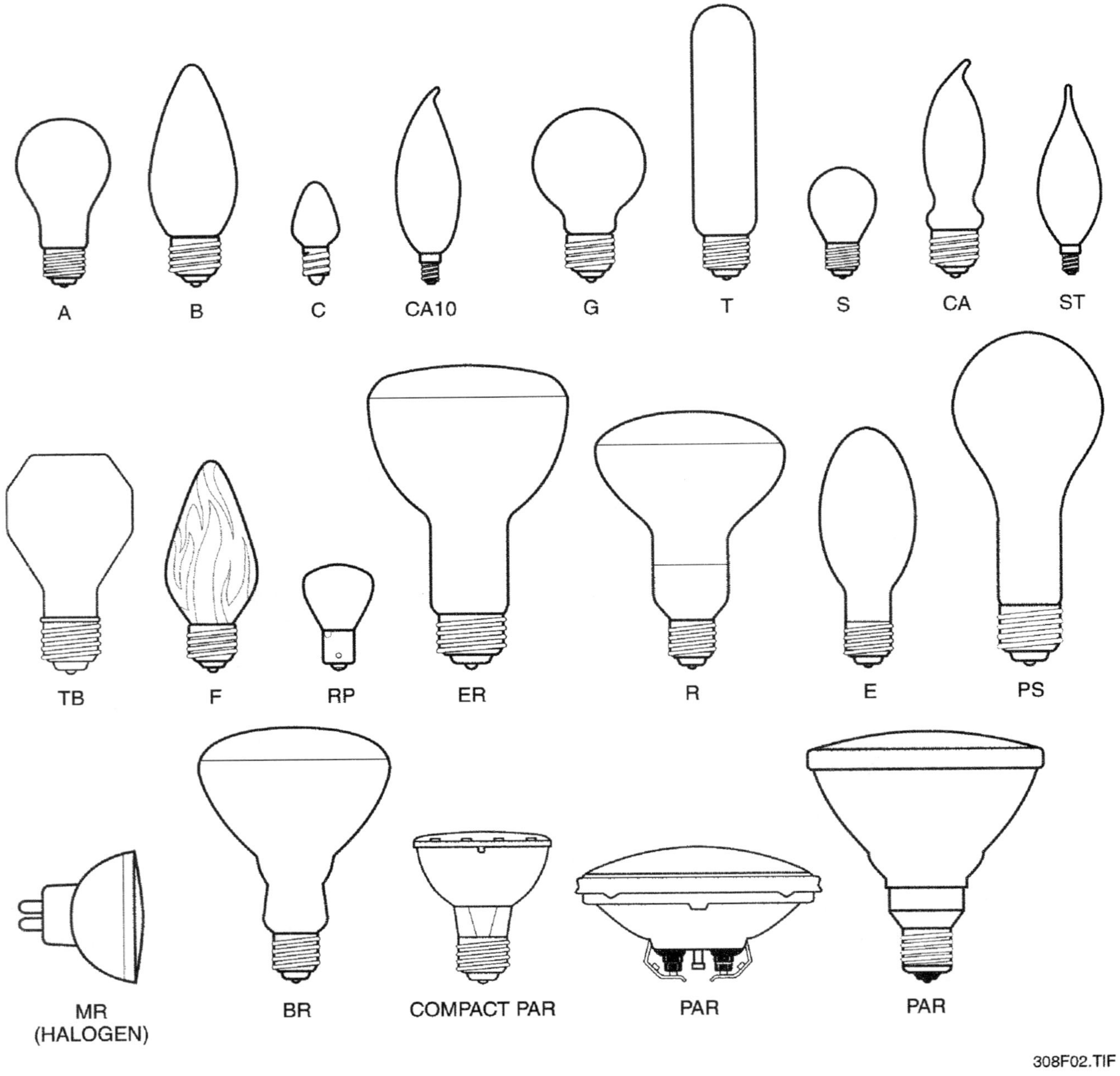

Figure 2. Incandescent Lamp Shapes

Figure 3 shows some examples of incandescent lamp filament forms used by one lamp manufacturer. The form of a filament is determined mainly by service requirements. Filament forms are identified by a letter or letters followed by an arbitrary number. Commonly used letters are: C (coiled), indicating that the filament wire is wound into a helical coil; CC (coiled coil), indicating the coil itself is wound into a helical coil; and S (straight), indicating that the filament wire is uncoiled. The numbers shown in *Figure 3* indicate the arrangement of the filament on the supports.

ELECTRICAL — TRAINEE TASK MODULE 26308

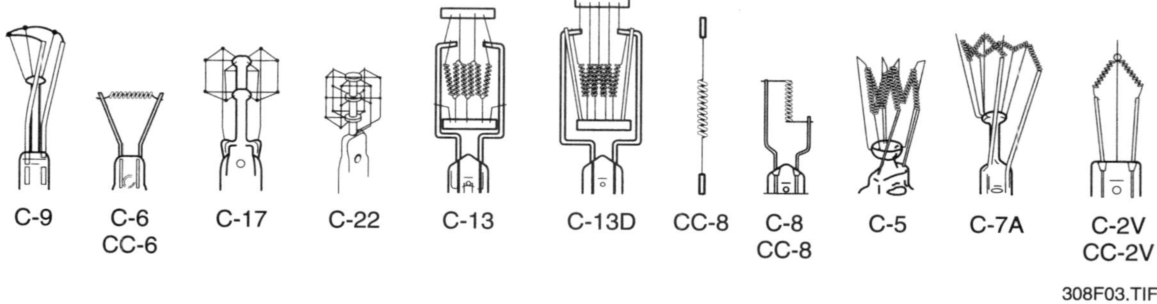

Figure 3. Examples Of Incandescent Lamp Filament Forms

The lamp base supports the lamp and provides the connection between the lamp and the power source. *Figure 4* shows some examples of common incandescent lamp bases.

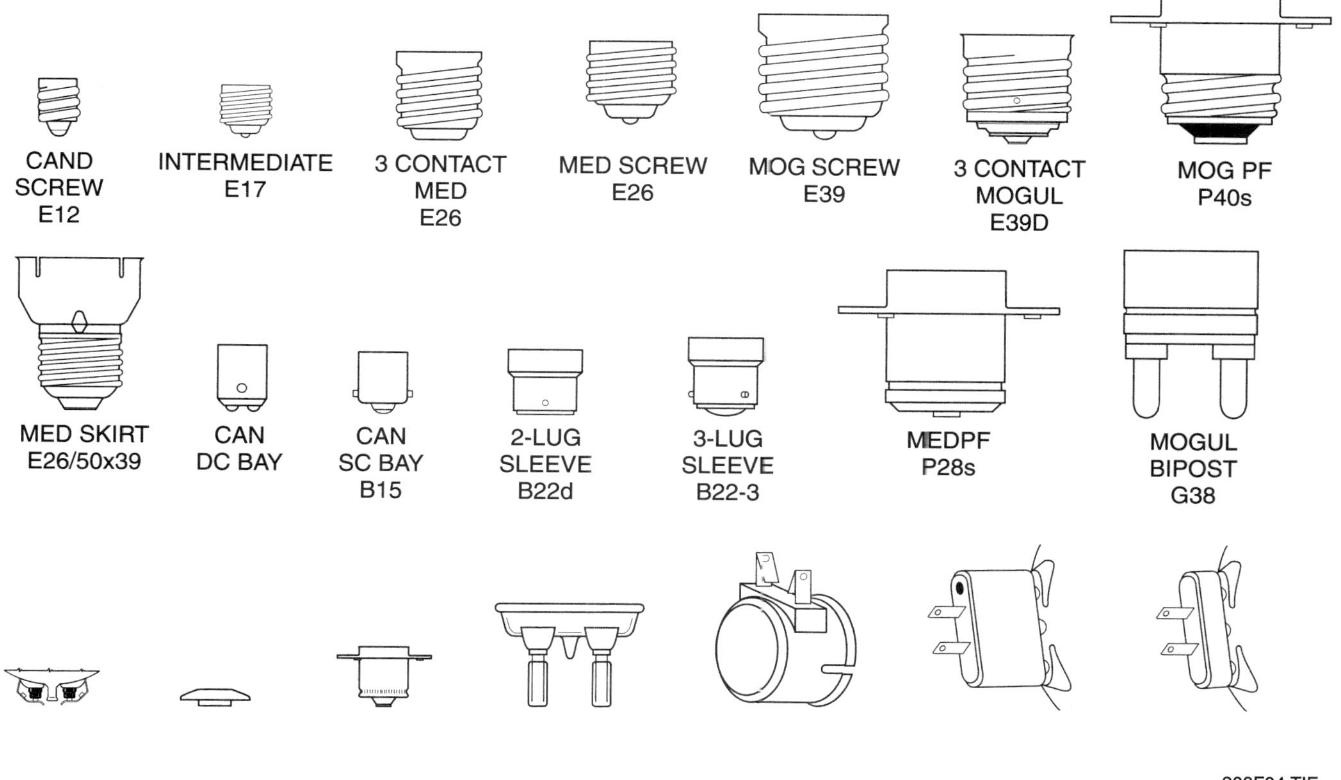

Figure 4. Examples Of Incandescent Lamp Bases

Incandescent lamps and other types of lamps are available in many different voltage and wattage ratings. When installing incandescent lamps, it is important to make sure that the correct voltage rating is selected. This is because a small difference between the rating and the actual supply voltage has a great effect on the lamp life and light output. The wattage rating is an indication of the consumption of electrical energy used by a lamp to produce its rated light output. It is not a measure of the lamp's light output. For example, a standard 100W lamp may produce 1,600 lumens, while a typical 31W fluorescent lamp may produce about 2,600 lumens. *Figure 5* shows the relationships between watts, lumens, and lamp life for a typical lamp when operated at different percentages of its rated voltage. For example, reducing the supply voltage for a 120V lamp to approximately 94% (113V) will increase its life by 220%, but reduce the light output to 80% and the wattage to about 90%.

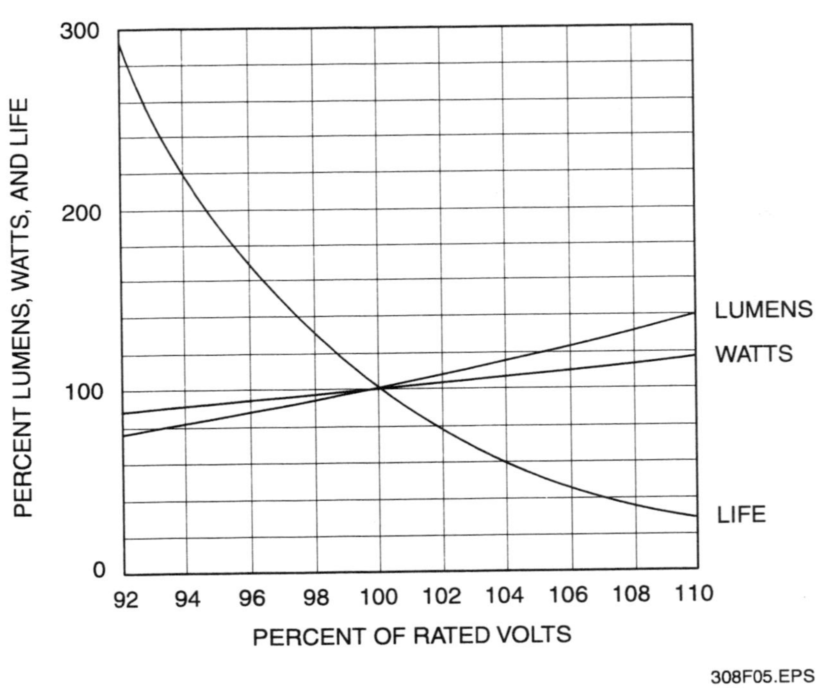

Figure 5. Relationship Of Rated Lamp Voltage To Watts, Lumens, And Lamp Life

3.0.0 TUNGSTEN HALOGEN INCANDESCENT LAMPS

Tungsten halogen incandescent lamps (halogen lamps) are a refinement over the standard incandescent lamp. Like standard incandescent lamps, halogen lamps are made in many sizes, shapes, and wattages. When compared to the standard incandescent lamp, they provide greater efficacy (12 to 36 LPW), longer service life (2,000 to 5,000 average hours), and improved light quality. Their light output contains more blue and less yellow than standard incandescent lamps, making their light appear whiter and brighter.

Halogen lamps (*Figure 6*) typically have a short, thick tungsten filament encased in a capsule filled with halogen gases, such as iodine or bromine, that allow the filaments to operate at higher temperatures than a standard incandescent lamp. This increases their efficacy (LPW) by more than 20%. The use of halogen gas in the lamp accounts for the longer life and excellent **lumen maintenance**. During operation, tungsten atoms evaporated from the filament combine with halogen atoms to form a gaseous compound that circulates inside the lamp, causing the tungsten atoms to be redeposited on the hot filament, rather than on the inside surface of the lamp envelope. The halogen atoms are then released, allowing them to combine with additional tungsten atoms, thus repeating the process. This action slows down any deterioration of the filament, thereby improving lumen maintenance and extending the lamp's life.

Halogen Lamp Technology

All halogen lamps feature a short, thick tungsten filament encased in a capsule filled with halogen gas. The regeneration cycle described below is the key to the long life and excellent lument maintenance of these lamps.

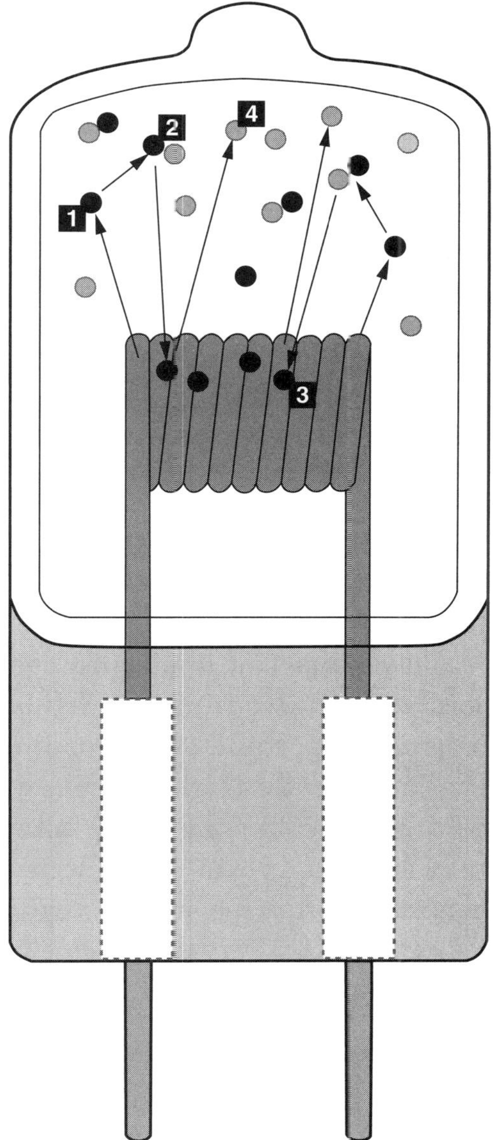

1. Tungsten atoms evaporate from filement
2. Tungsten atoms combine with halogen atoms
3. Gaseous compound returns to hot filament, redepositing tungsten atoms
4. Halogen atoms are released to combine with additional tungsten atoms.

308F06.EPS

Figure 6. Basic Tungsten Halogen Lamp

Because of the higher filament operating temperatures, there is more ultraviolet (UV) radiation generated from a halogen lamp than from standard incandescent lamps. The amount of UV radiation emitted is determined by the lamp envelope material. Fused quartz and high-silica glass transmit most of the UV radiation emitted by the filament, while special high-silica glass and aluminosilicate glasses absorb UV radiation. For general lighting applications, it is recommended that lighting fixtures for halogen lamps have a lens or cover glass which will, in addition to providing the required safety protection, filter out most of the UV radiation.

CAUTION: Operating halogen lamps at voltages above and below the manufacturer's recommendations can have adverse effects on the internal chemical process because the temperature will differ from the design value. Also, it is important to follow the manufacturer's instructions as to burning position, lamp handling, and lighting fixture temperatures.

4.0.0 FLUORESCENT LAMPS

Fluorescent lamps are low-pressure mercury discharge lamps which are very energy efficient (75 to 100 LPW) and have a long service life (12,000 to more than 24,000 average hours). Each requires a ballast to effectively start the lamp and regulate its operation. Light is produced by passing an electric arc between two tungsten cathodes at opposite ends of a glass tube filled with a low-pressure mercury vapor and other gases (*Figure 7*). The arc excites the atoms of mercury. This generates UV radiation, which causes the phosphor coating on the inside of the tube to fluoresce and produce visible light. By using different phosphor coatings, the spectral light output of a fluorescent lamp can be made to produce warm, intermediate, or cool color temperatures. The color temperatures of lamps are covered later in this module.

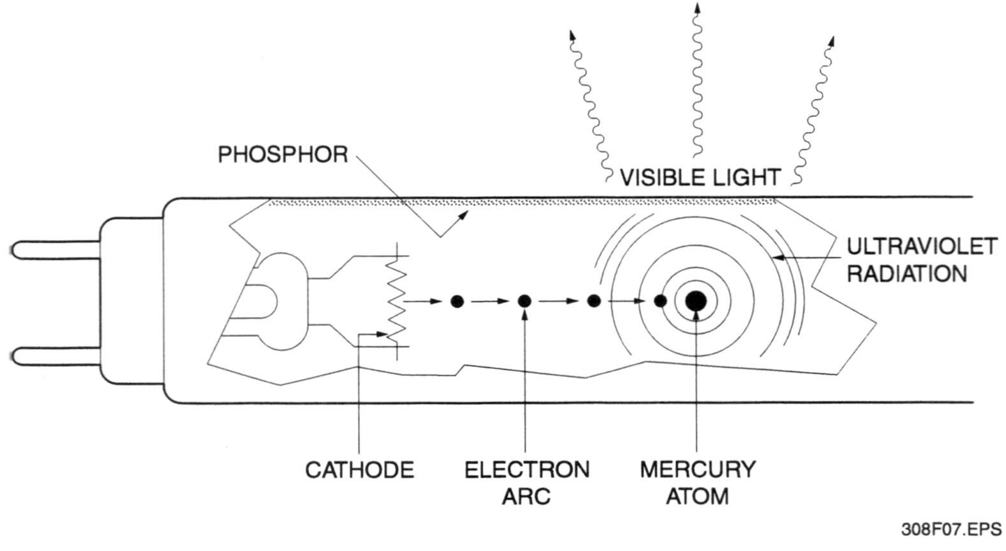

Figure 7. Basic Fluorescent Lamp

ELECTRICAL — TRAINEE TASK MODULE 26308

Fluorescent bulbs are made in straight, U-bent, circular, and compact varieties, several of which are shown in *Figure 8*. Not only do they come in a wide variety of wattages, sizes, and bases, but they are also available in several color temperatures and color rendition capabilities. Fluorescent lamps are designated by the letter T followed by the diameter of the lamp tube expressed in eighths of an inch. They vary in diameter from T-5 (⅝") to PG (power groove)-17 (2⅛"). In overall length, straight fluorescent lamps range from 6" to 96". Higher wattages go with longer tubes. For example, a 20W straight T-12 tube is shorter than a 40W T-12 tube.

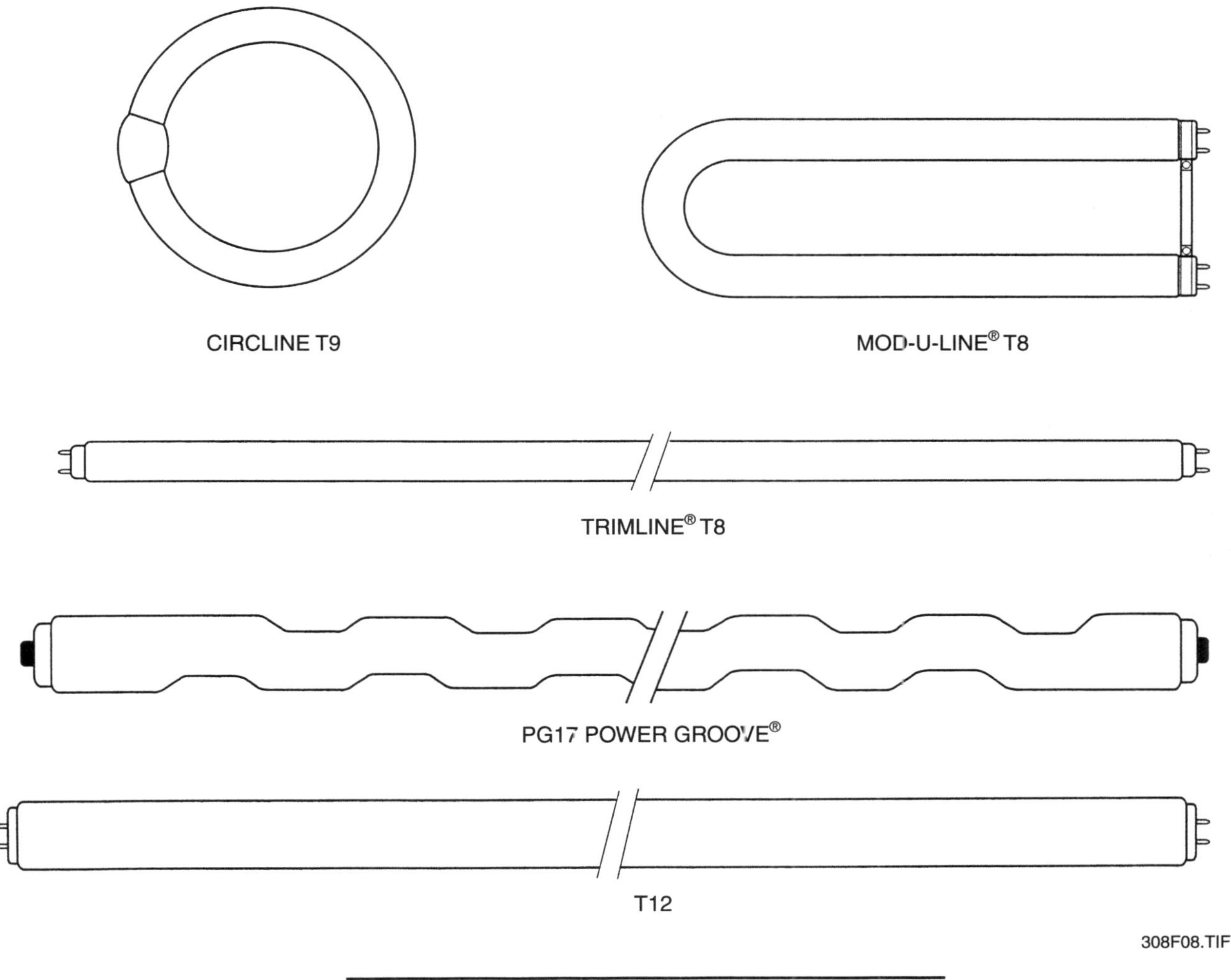

Figure 8. Fluorescent Lamp Shapes And Bases

Fluorescent lamps have two electrical requirements. To start the lamp, a high-voltage surge is needed to establish an arc in the mercury vapor. Once the lamp is started, the gas offers a decreasing amount of resistance, which means that current must be regulated to match this drop. Otherwise, the lamp would draw more and more power and rapidly burn itself out. This is why fluorescent lamps are operated in lighting fixture circuits containing a ballast that provides the required voltage surge at startup and then controls the subsequent flow of current to the lamp. Ballasts are covered in detail later in this module.

There are three electrical classes of fluorescent lamps and lighting fixtures: preheat, rapid start, and instant start. The term *preheat* refers to a lighting fixture circuit used with fluorescent lamps wherein the lamp electrodes are heated or warmed to a glow stage by a replaceable starter separate from the ballast. When power is applied to the lighting fixture, the starter functions to preheat the lamp's cathodes before the lamp is started. Note that preheat lamps and lighting fixtures are nearly obsolete and are not used in new construction. The term *rapid start* refers to a lighting fixture circuit designed to start the lamp by continuously heating or preheating the lamp electrodes. Unlike the preheat circuit, the ballast does not require a separate starter. During operation, standard rapid-start lamps draw about 430mA of current. The term *instant start* refers to a lighting fixture circuit used to start specially designed lamps without the aid of a starter. To strike the arc instantly, the circuit uses a higher open circuit voltage than is required for a preheat or rapid-start lamp of the same length. Both preheat and rapid-start lamps have a bi-pin (2-pin) base at each end. Instant-start lamps have a single pin at each end of the lamp. Normally, lamps identified as preheat, rapid-start, or instant-start types should be used only with the corresponding type of ballast. Other terms commonly used to designate types of fluorescent lamps include:

- *Slimline lamps* – A group of lamps which are instant starting, with single-pin bases.
- *High-output (HO) lamps* – A group of rapid-start lamps designed to operate at higher operating currents (800mA to 1,000mA) that produce higher levels of light output. Because of the higher operating currents involved, the lamps have a recessed double-contact base. HO lamps are typically used in industrial areas and retail stores with high ceilings.
- *Very high-output (VHO) lamps* – A group of rapid-start lamps designed to operate at high currents (1,500mA) in order to produce high light output levels. Because of the higher operating currents involved, the lamps have a recessed double-contact base. VHO lamps are typically used in factories, warehouses, gymnasiums, and open areas.

Note: While the bases on HO and VHO lamps are the same, each must be matched to the correct ballast.

- *Compact lamps* – Lamps made of ½" to ⅝" single or multiple U-shaped tubes terminated in a plastic base (*Figure 9*). The base contains the cathodes and, in some versions, a magnetic or electronic ballast. Some have replaceable tubes. A few of the newer versions are dimmable and others, using a tight-spiral tube, look much like a standard lamp in size and shape. They are used both to replace incandescent lamps and in lighting fixtures designed for their use. They can provide up to 75% energy cost savings when compared to incandescent lamps of comparable light output. They also have a lifespan of up to 13 times longer than standard incandescent lamps.
- *T-8 lamps* – Newer and more energy-efficient lamps than older T-12 lamps. For example, a 32W, T-8 lamp uses 20% less energy to provide the same light output as a 40W, T-12 lamp. T-8 lamps use special triphosphor coatings that improve control over the lamp's color properties.

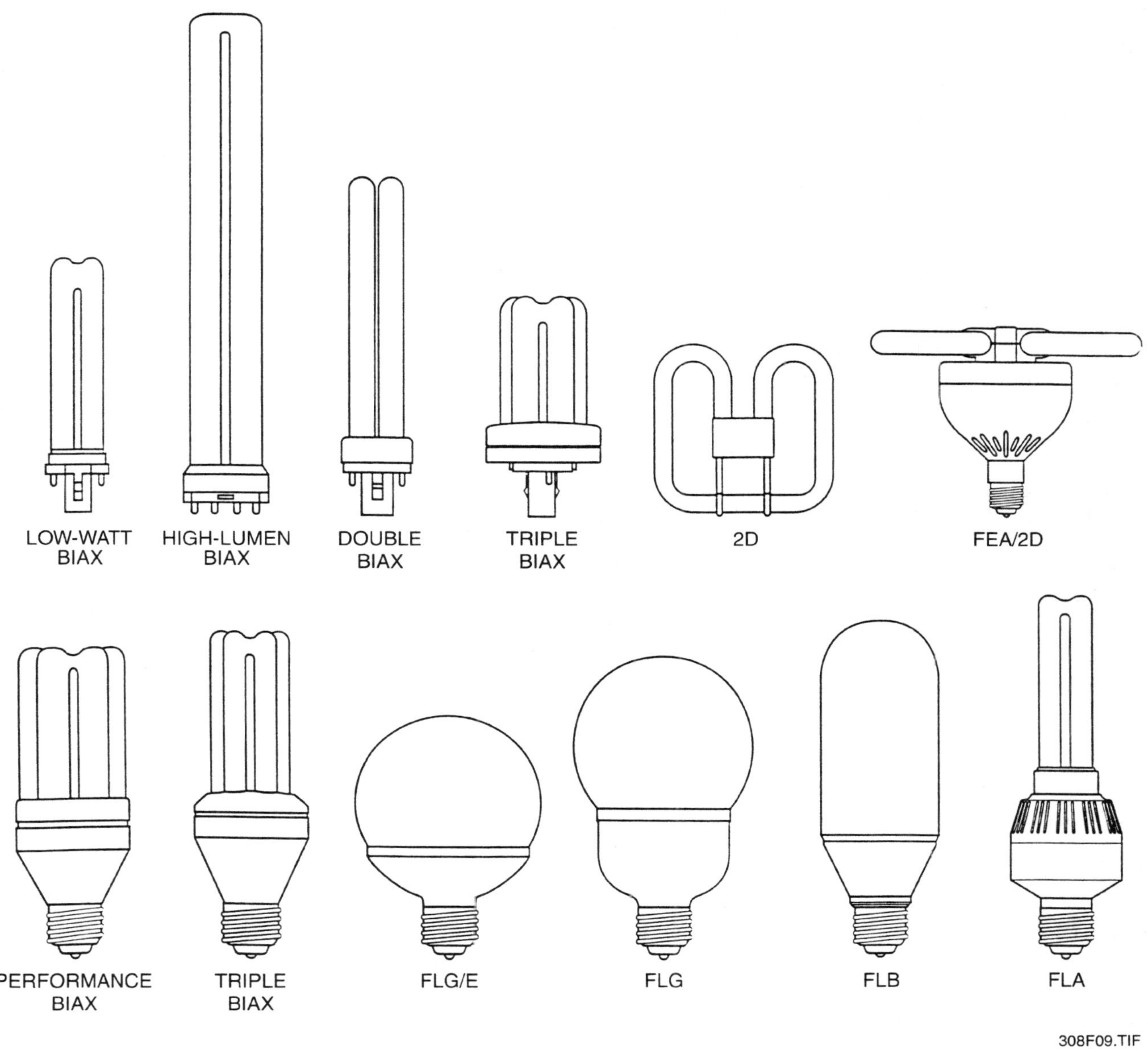

Figure 9. Compact Fluorescent Lamps

Lamp holders (*Figure 10*) are made in several variations for each lamp base style to allow for various spacings and mounting methods in luminaires. When fluorescent lamps are used in circuits providing an open circuit voltage in excess of 330V, or in circuits which may permit a lamp to ionize and conduct current with only one end inserted in the lamp holder, electrical codes require some automatic means for deenergizing the circuit when the lamp is removed. This is usually accomplished by the lamp holder so that upon removal, the ballast primary circuit is opened. Note that the use of recessed contact bases for HO and VHO lamps has eliminated the need for this disconnect feature in the lamp holders for these lamps.

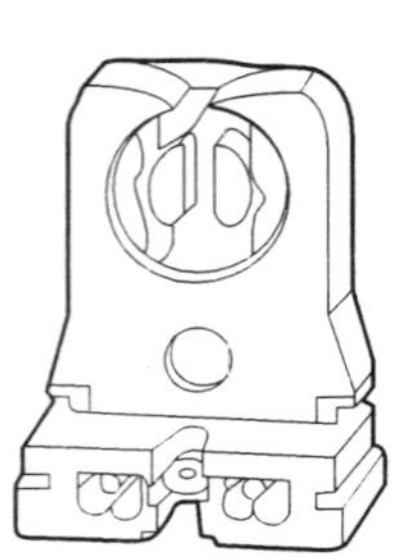
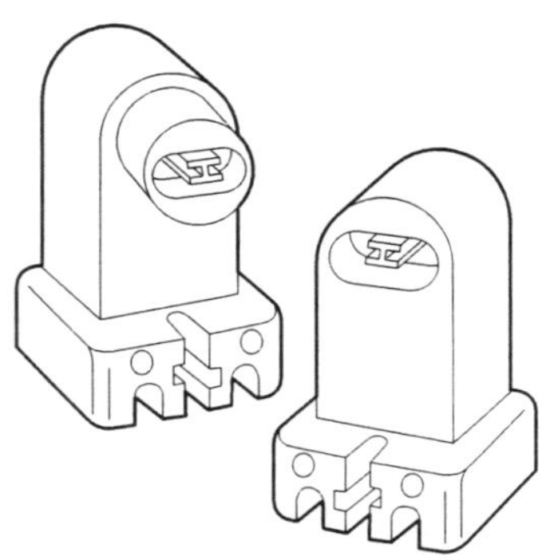
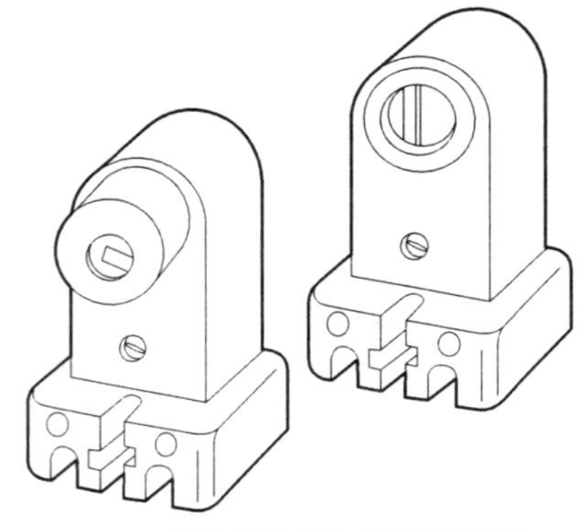

BI-PIN SLIDE-ON
AND SCREW MOUNT LAMP HOLDER

HIGH-OUTPUT (HO) LAMP HOLDER

SINGLE-PIN (SLIMLINE)
LAMP HOLDER

308F10.EPS

Figure 10. Typical Fluorescent Lamp Holders

5.0.0   HIGH-INTENSITY DISCHARGE (HID) LAMPS

High-intensity discharge (HID) lamps provide long life and high efficiency. They are somewhat similar to fluorescent lamps in that they produce light when electricity excites specific gases in pressurized bulbs. An arc is established between two electrodes in a gas-filled tube, which causes mercury vapor to produce radiant energy. Unlike a fluorescent lamp, a combination of factors shifts the wavelength of much of the energy to within the visible range, so light is produced without phosphors. First, the electrodes are only a few inches apart at opposite ends of a sealed arc tube (*Figure 11*) and the gases in the tube are highly pressurized. This allows the arc to generate extremely high temperatures, causing metallic elements within the gas atmosphere to vaporize and release large amounts of visible radiant energy. Like fluorescent lamps, HID lamps must be used in matched lighting fixtures with a ballast specifically designed for the lamp type and wattage. In addition, HID lamps require a warmup period to achieve full light output.

There are three types of HID lamps: mercury vapor, metal halide, and high-pressure sodium. The names refer to elements that are added to the gases in the lamp, which cause each type to have somewhat different color characteristics and efficiency. Mercury vapor lamps are the oldest HID technology. They are energy efficient (50 to 60 LPW) and have a long service life (12,000 to more than 24,000 average hours). These lamps produce light energy by radiation from excited mercury vapor in both the visible and ultraviolet range. They normally have specially formulated glass outer jackets to filter the UV energy. The phosphor coatings used in some mercury vapor lamp types add additional light and improve color rendering. Today, the use of mercury vapor lamps is limited mainly to the replacement of existing lamps and landscape lighting of evergreen trees. Other HID lamps that have better efficiency and color properties are being used for new construction.

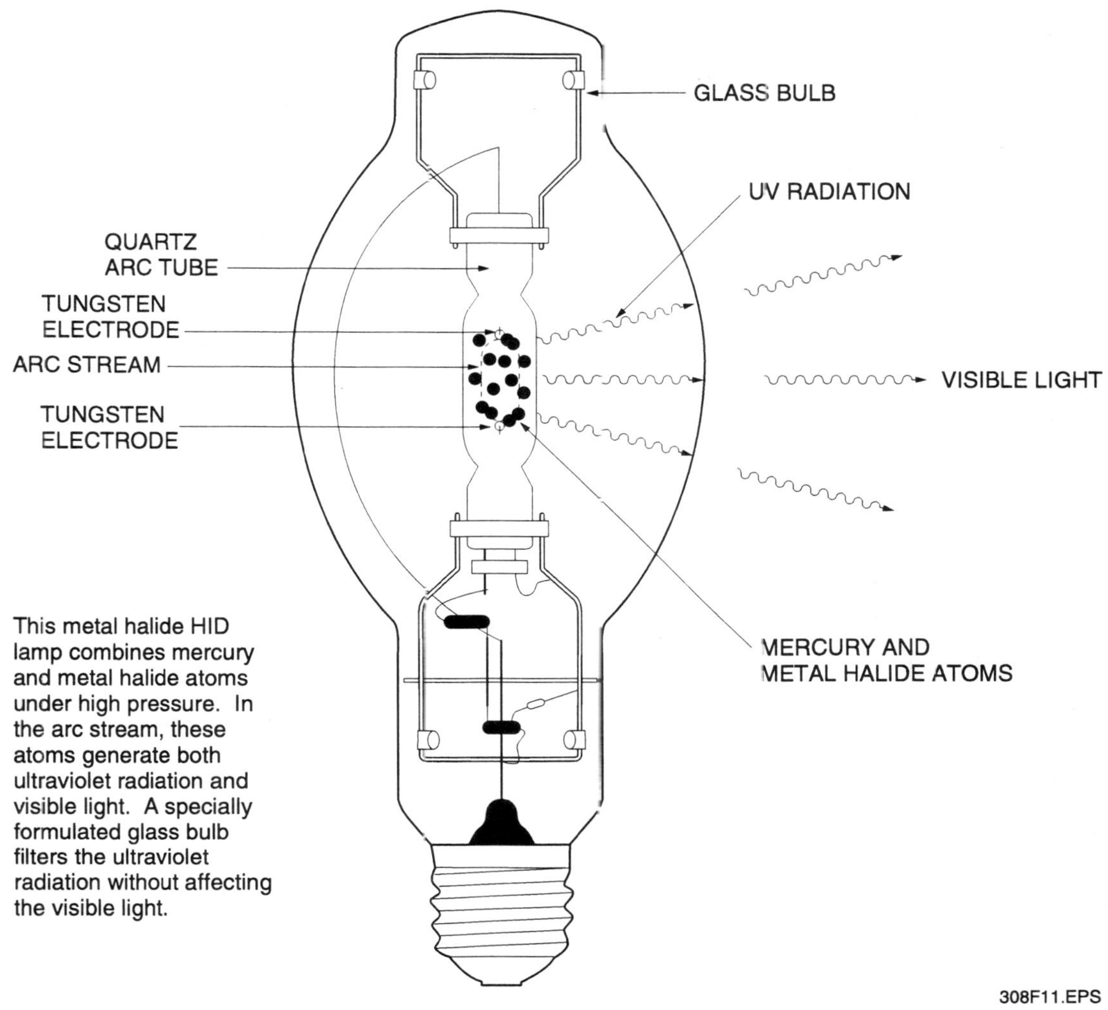

Figure 11. Basic Metal Halide Lamp

Metal halide lamps are the most energy-efficient source of white light. They have high efficacy (80 to 115 LPW), excellent color rendition, long service life (10,000 to more than 20,000 average hours), and good lumen maintenance (longevity). The metal halide HID lamp combines mercury and metal halide atoms under high pressure. In the arc stream, these atoms generate both UV radiation and visible light. A special glass bulb filters the UV radiation without affecting the visible light.

High-pressure sodium HID lamps use mercury and sodium in the arc stream contained within a tube made of a special ceramic material. They have extremely high efficacy (90 to 140 LPW) and exceptionally long service life, typically up to 24,000 hours. However, they produce light that is concentrated in the yellow/orange portion of the spectrum, which causes them to render colors poorly.

Low-pressure sodium lamps use sodium in a low-pressure arc stream and produce light that is limited to a single wavelength in the yellow portion of the spectrum. These lamps are the most efficient of any lamp type, but are used only where energy efficiency and long life are the only requirements. It should be pointed out here that technically speaking, low-pressure sodium lamps are not actually a type of HID lamp.

6.0.0 LAMP COLOR RENDERING AND COLOR TEMPERATURE CHARACTERISTICS

Colors appear differently under various light sources. The **color rendering index (CRI)**, a scale from 0 to 100, is used by lamp manufacturers to indicate how normal and natural a specific lamp makes objects appear. Generally, the higher the CRI, the better it makes people and objects appear. Note that the CRI of different lamps can be compared only if the sources have approximately the same color temperature. Also, CRI differences among lamps are not usually visible to the eye unless the difference is greater than 3 to 5 points.

Lamps can create atmospheres which are warm or cool in appearance. The color temperature, expressed in Kelvins (K), is one way lamp manufacturers describe the color tone (warmth or coolness) produced by a lamp. For example:

* Color temperatures of 3,000K and lower are described as warm in tone and slightly enhance reds and yellows.
* A color temperature of 3,500K is considered moderate in tone, producing a balance between warmth and coolness.
* Color temperatures of 4,100K and higher are considered cool in tone, slightly biased towards blues and greens.

Some typical color temperatures are: 2,200K for high-pressure sodium lamps, 2,800K for incandescent lamps, 3,000K for halogen lamps, 3,500K for metal halide lamps, 4,100K for cool white fluorescent lamps, and 5,000K for daylight simulating fluorescent lamps.

Fluorescent lamps have more options in terms of light quality than any other lamp type. This is because of the variations (formulations) available in the composition of the phosphor coating on the inside of the lamp tube. Early fluorescent lamps used a single halophosphor coating and could offer improved color quality with only a decrease in efficacy (LPW). With the newer lamps, triphosphor coatings are used that allow precise control over the generation of red, green, and blue (the primary colors of light). This enables the manufacture of high-LPW lamps in a variety of color temperatures that provide excellent color rendition.

7.0.0 FLUORESCENT AND HID LIGHTING FIXTURE BALLASTS

Ballasts are a main component of fluorescent and HID lighting fixtures. They are used to start and properly control the flow of power to the fluorescent or HID lamps.

ELECTRICAL — TRAINEE TASK MODULE 26308

7.1.0 FLUORESCENT LIGHTING FIXTURE BALLASTS

In fluorescent lighting fixtures, the ballasts perform the following functions:

- Provide the proper voltage to establish an arc between two electrodes
- Regulate the electric current flowing through the lamp to stabilize the light output
- Supply the correct voltage required for proper lamp operation and compensate for voltage variations in the electrical current
- Provide continuous voltage to maintain heat in the lamp electrodes while the lamp operates (rapid-start circuits)

Fluorescent ballasts (*Figure 12*) are made to operate in the three basic fluorescent lighting fixture operating circuits: preheat, rapid start, and instant start.

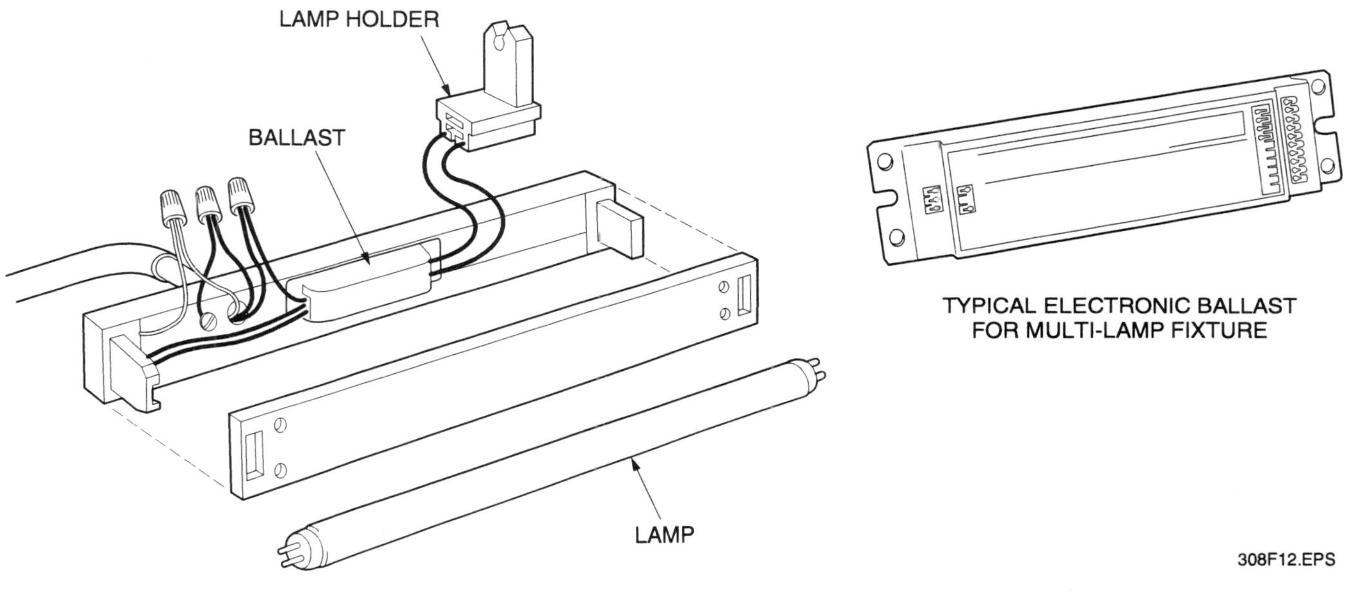

Figure 12. Components Of A Basic Fluorescent Lamp Fixture

7.1.1 Preheat Lamp And Ballast Operation

In preheat circuits, such as the one shown in *Figure 13(A)*, the lamp electrodes (cathodes) are heated before application of the high voltage across the lamp(s). The preheating requires a few seconds, and the necessary delay is provided by an automatic switch called a *starter*. When power is first applied to the lamp circuit, the starter places the lamp's electrodes in series across the ballast, causing current to flow through both electrodes, heating them. After the electrodes are sufficiently preheated, the switch opens and applies the voltage across the lamp. Because the switch opens under load, a transient voltage (inductive spike) is developed in the circuit, which aids in the ignition of the lamp. Note that the first fluorescent lamps developed were of the preheat type. This type of lamp is now obsolete and is seldom used except in smaller sizes, such as those used in desk lamps and similar fixtures.

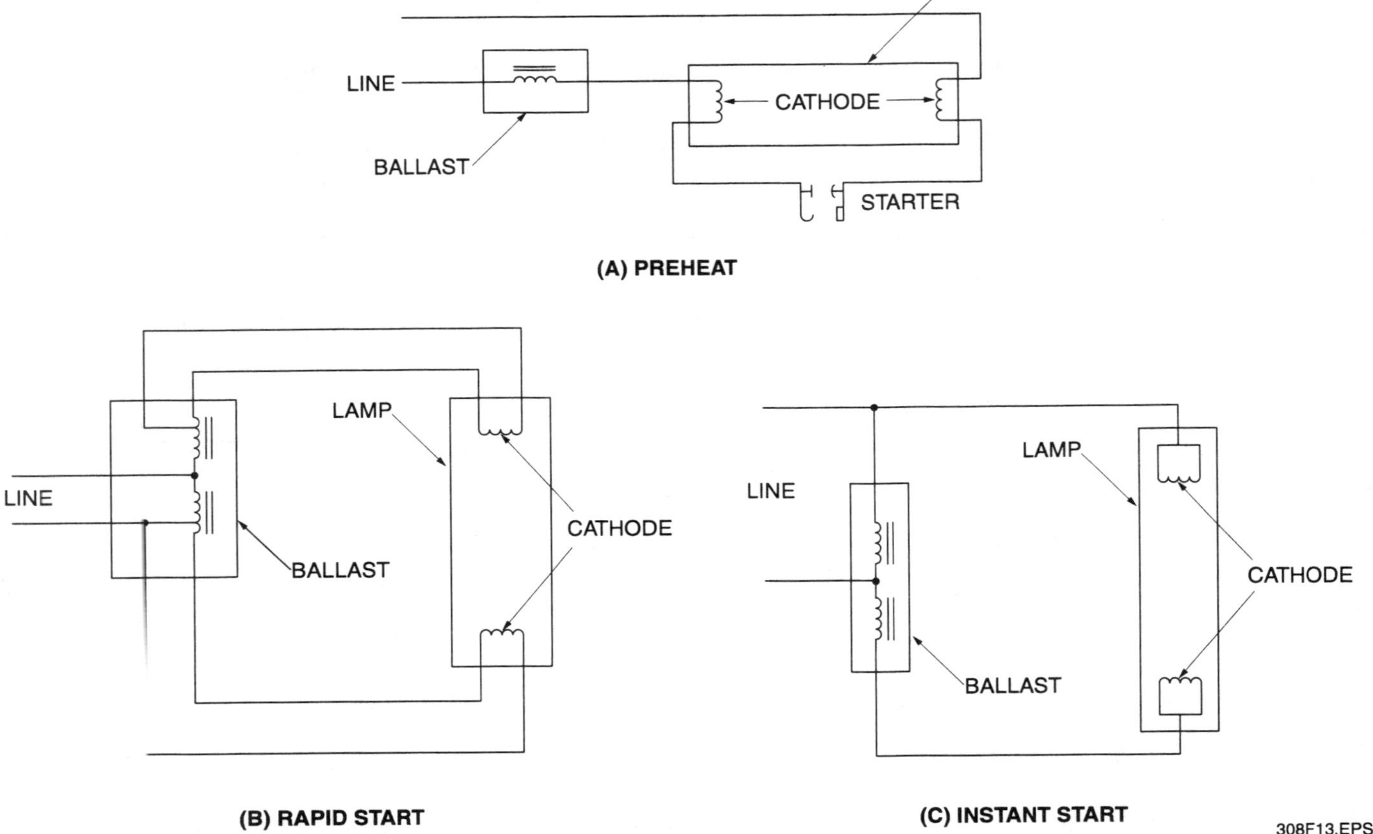

Figure 13. Basic Fluorescent Lighting Fixture Circuits

7.1.2 Rapid-Start Lamp And Ballast Operation

This is probably the most common type of lamp and fixture used today. Lamps designed for rapid-start operation, such as the one shown in *Figure 13(B)*, normally have low-resistance electrodes. These remain energized by low-voltage applied from the ballast while the lamps are in operation. They usually start in one second, the time required to bring the electrodes up to proper temperature. The standard rapid-start circuit operates with a typical lamp current of about 430mA. Rapid-start circuits used with high-output (HO) and very high-output (VHO) lamps draw currents of about 800mA and 1500mA, respectively. In some energy-saving circuits, the electrode voltage is reduced or disconnected after the starting of the lamps. Heating is accomplished through low-voltage windings built into the ballast or through separate low-voltage transformers designed for this purpose. Fluorescent lamps used with rapid-start ballasts are bi-pin lamps. Rapid-start lamps can be dimmed using special dimming ballasts. These are covered later in this module.

Another version of a rapid-start ballast is the trigger-start ballast. Trigger-start ballasts are used with preheat fluorescent lamps up to 32W without the need for a starter.

7.1.3 Instant-Start Lamp And Ballast Operation

The lamp electrodes in instant-start lamps are not preheated. The ballasts provide a high voltage (100V to 1,000V) across the electrodes that causes electrons to be emitted from the electrodes, as shown in *Figure 13(C)*. These electrons flow through the tube, ionizing the gas and initiating an arc discharge. Thereafter, the arc current provides electrode heating. Because no preheating of electrodes is required, instant-start lamps need only a single contact at each end. Thus, a single pin is used on most instant-start lamps, commonly called *slimline lamps*. However, T-8 bi-pin lamps can be operated with either rapid-start or instant-start electronic ballasts. When used with an instant-start ballast, the terminals in the lamp holders must be connected together. New fixtures come with the lamp holders wired in this way.

7.1.4 Types Of Fluorescent Ballasts

Each fluorescent lamp must be operated by a ballast that is specifically designed to provide the proper starting and operating voltage required by the particular lamp. Lamp and lighting fixture manufacturers make a wide variety of ballasts designed for use in lighting fixtures that operate in all three of the lamp starting modes described above. Ballasts are made for single-lamp, two-lamp, three-lamp, and four-lamp operation. The names used to identify the different types of ballasts can vary by manufacturer. Some common categories of ballasts are:

- *Standard ballast* – Lowest priced, least efficient, and highest wattage ballast. Their use is obsolete.
- *High-efficiency ballast* – Lower wattage, better efficiency, and longer life than a standard ballast.
- *Hybrid ballast* – Lower wattage, higher efficiency, and longer life than a standard high-efficiency ballast.
- *Electronic rapid-start ballast* – Low wattage and longest life available with various ballast factors and wattage packages for T-12 and T-8 lamps.
- *Electronic instant-start ballast* – Lowest system wattage and highest system efficiency. The lamp life is slightly shorter than with rapid-start ballasts.

High-efficiency ballasts can be of the magnetic or electronic type. The magnetic type usually contains coils, capacitors, transformers, and a thermal protector installed in a metal case. The coils and transformers are generally made with steel laminations and copper wire. Once assembled, the ballast components are encapsulated in the ballast case with a potting compound to improve the heat dissipation and reduce ballast noise.

If the ballasts are of the electronic type, they may be made with discrete electronic components and/or with integrated circuits. Some of those with integrated circuits are compatible for use with dimming systems, occupancy sensors, and daylight sensors. Electronic ballasts are quieter, more efficient, and weigh less, but are also more expensive. With electronic ballasts, the power input is 50Hz to 60Hz, but the ballast operates the lamps at 20kHz to 50kHz, with resulting improvements in ballast and lamp efficacy. The operating frequency is selected so that it is high enough to increase the lamp's efficacy and to shift the ballast noise to the inaudible range, but not so high as to cause electromagnetic interference (EMI) problems. Note that many electronic ballasts do not come equipped with wire leads. These ballasts are connected into the circuit using wire harnesses specifically designed for that purpose.

NEC Section 410-73(e) requires that all fluorescent fixture ballasts used indoors, including any replacement ballasts, have a thermal protection device integral within the ballast. All such ballasts are marked *Class P*. The exceptions to this requirement include simple reactance ballasts used with fluorescent fixtures using straight tubular lamps, ballasts used with exit fixtures and so identified, and egress lighting energized only during an emergency. Class P ballasts with thermal protection operate to open the circuit at a predetermined temperature in order to prevent abnormal heat buildup caused by a fault in one or more of the ballast components, or by some lamp holder or wiring fault.

High-efficiency, energy-saving ballasts have a high power factor rating. The power factor is the ratio of watts to volt-amperes. To be classified as a high power factor ballast, a ballast must have a power factor of at least 90%. Anything less is considered normal or low power factor. A ballast's power factor rating is marked on the ballast nameplate. Energy saving high power factor ballasts cost more than low power factor ballasts, but over time, the savings in energy consumption far exceeds the higher initial cost. In any application where there are to be a large number of ballasts, it is best to install ballasts with a high power factor. When compared to magnetic ballasts, electronic ballasts are more energy efficient.

Ballasts can emit a hum, especially the magnetic types. This is caused by magnetic vibration in the ballast core. Ballast manufacturers give their ballasts a sound rating ranging from A to F, with A being the quietest. The need for quiet ballast operation is determined mainly by the desired ambient noise level of the location where the ballast is to be installed. For example, a ballast with an A rating might be used in a doctor's office, while one with an F rating might be suitable for a factory application.

When installing a replacement ballast, make sure to dispose of the old ballast in a proper manner. Unless you see a label stamped *No PCBs* on the failed ballast you are disposing of, you must assume that it contains toxic PCBs and must be disposed of in accordance with the prevailing EPA and local requirements. Failure to do so can expose you and your employer to potential liability for cleanup in the event of PCB leakage.

7.1.5 Fluorescent Dimming Ballasts

To dim fluorescent lamps, the use of special dimming ballasts and dimmer switches is required. The dimmer control allows the dimming ballast to maintain a voltage to the lamp's electrodes that will maintain the electrodes' proper operating temperature. It also allows the dimming ballast to vary the current flowing in the arc. This in turn varies the intensity of light coming from the lamp. Dimming fluorescent lamps differs from dimming incandescent lamps in two main ways: first, fluorescent dimmers do not provide dimming to zero light as do incandescent dimmers; and second, when dimming fluorescent lamps, the color temperature does not vary much over the dimming range. This is unlike incandescent lamps, which tend to turn yellower when dimmed.

Most fluorescent dimming ballasts are of the electronic type. However, older autotransformer magnetic types are also available. Electronic dimming ballasts are normally more efficient and less bulky than magnetic ballasts. *Figure 14* shows a wiring diagram for an electronic dimmer used with a dimming ballast for rapid-start lamps. The dimmer shown is a slider type and allows a wide range (20% to 100%) of light output adjustment for the fluorescent lamp. It is important to point out that the performance of a dimming system may not be satisfactory if the lamp is not correctly matched with the dimming ballast and the controller. Also, when connecting such dimmer circuits, always check the dimmer and ballast manufacturer's wiring diagrams to determine the proper connections.

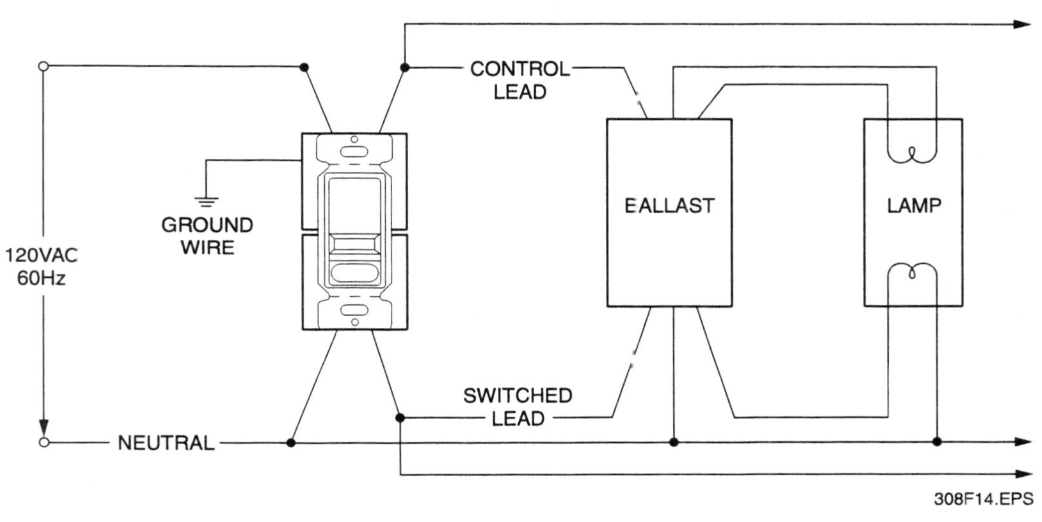

Figure 14. Dimmer Circuit Using Dimming Ballast For Rapid-Start Lamp

7.1.6 Emergency Lighting Ballasts

Special emergency ballasts with self-contained battery-operated power packs are made for use in some fluorescent lighting fixtures. Upon the loss of input power to the lighting fixture, these ballasts typically function to operate one 8' lamp at emergency lighting levels for about 90 minutes, or one 4' lamp for about 120 minutes.

7.2.0 HID LIGHTING FIXTURE BALLASTS

HID lamps require the use of a ballast to provide enough voltage to strike the arc in the lamp. This function may be accomplished by the ballast itself or in conjunction with a separate electronic ignitor circuit. An ignitor (*Figure 15*) is an electronic device used in the circuitry for high-pressure sodium and some metal halide HID lamps. It provides a pulse of at least 2,500V peak root mean square (rms) to initiate the lamp arc. When the system is energized, the ignitor provides the required pulse until the lamp is completely lit and then automatically stops pulsing.

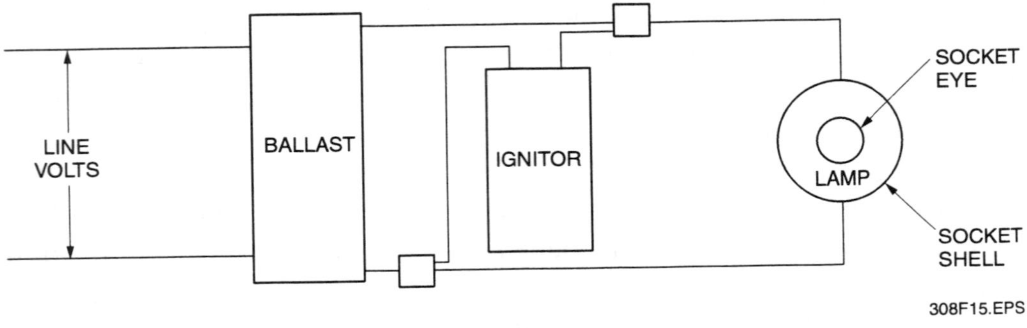

Figure 15. Simplified HID Lamp Ignitor Circuit

The HID lamp ballast also acts to control the arc wattage during warmup and normal operation. In addition, some ballasts may also provide a line voltage matching transformer function, enhance lamp wattage regulation with respect to changes in line voltage and/or lamp voltage, and dimming or other control interface functions.

Physically, there are numerous types and shapes of ballasts used with HID lamps (*Figure 16*). The same is true electrically. Some ballasts are made with primary leads that allow the ballast to be connected to different supply voltages, such as 120V, 208V, 240V, or 277V. Such ballasts are called *multi-tap ballasts*. It is extremely important that only the proper voltage lead be connected to the supply voltage. The types of ballasts used by a major HID lighting fixture manufacturer (Hubbell) are described here. The ballasts used by other manufacturers are similar. HID ballasts can be grouped into three basic categories:

- Linear, non-regulating circuit ballasts
- Constant wattage autotransformer ballasts
- Three-coil ballasts

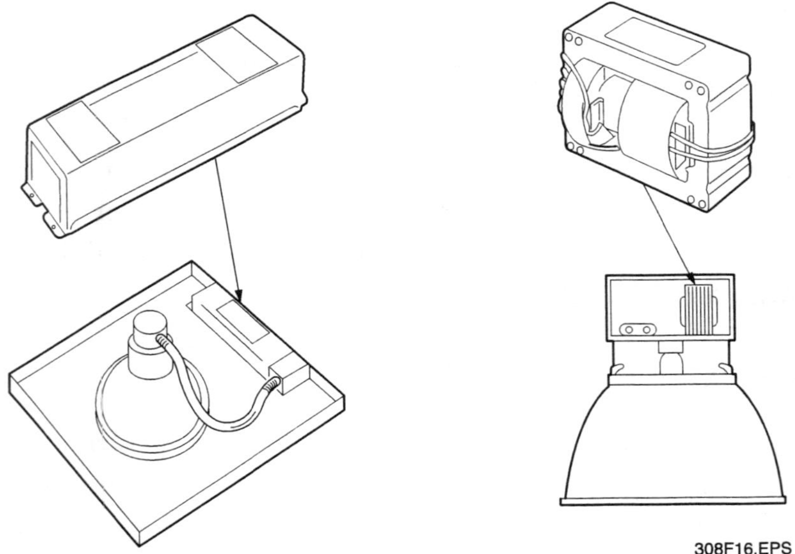

Figure 16. Examples Of HID Ballasts

ELECTRICAL — TRAINEE TASK MODULE 26308

7.2.1　Linear, Non-Regulating Circuit Ballasts

Linear, non-regulating circuits include reactor ballasts and auto-lag ballasts. These provide for the basic operation of some mercury and high-pressure sodium HID lamps. With the exception of the self-ballasted lamp, the reactor ballast is the most basic form of ballast. See *Figure 17(A)*. It consists of a single coil wound on an iron core placed in series with the lamp. The only function performed by the reactor is to limit the current delivered to the lamp. This type of ballast can only be used when the line voltage applied to the lamp is within the required starting voltage range of the lamp. The power factor for a reactor ballast is typically in the 40% to 50% range. However, a capacitor is normally added to the circuit to improve the power factor to better than 90%. Because this type of ballast provides for no line voltage regulation, outages due to line dips and brown-outs are typical. The auto-lag ballast, as shown in *Figure 17(B)*, is a reactor ballast combined with a step-up or step-down autotransformer, which provides for some input voltage regulation.

7.2.2　Constant-Wattage Autotransformer Ballasts

The constant-wattage autotransformer (CWA) ballast, shown in *Figure 17(C)*, is a ballast circuit that uses magnetic saturation to maintain better lamp wattage regulation and improved **dip tolerance**. CWA ballasts are used mainly with mercury and high-pressure sodium lamps. A variation of the CWA, called the peaked lead auto-regulator (PLA), is used with metal halide lamps. Another variation, called the constant-wattage isolated (CWI) ballast, shown in *Figure 17(D)*, is an isolated winding version of the PLA. It is typically used with mercury lamps.

The term *dip tolerance* used above relates to the dips in line voltage experienced by all power systems as loads are switched in and out, or as other transitory conditions occur. A well-regulated distribution system will seldom experience voltage dips of more than 10%, but on some circuits, dips of 20% or more may occur. If a ballast is not capable of riding through the voltage dip and sustaining the lamp, it will extinguish and have to cool down before reignition. Lamp dropout due to line voltage dips generally increases with lamp age. The use of ballasts with improved dip tolerance may delay the onset of such lamp dropout problems.

7.2.3　Three-Coil Ballasts

Three-coil ballasts are isolated winding ballasts in which the input and lamp windings are separated (isolated) by a third winding, which helps to eliminate drastic changes in the demands of the lamp on the supply system and maintains lamp stability during supply system variations. See *Figure 17(E)*. This type of circuit provides the highest degree of lamp operating stability and waveform control, with the lowest harmonics and best performance consistency through the life of the lamp. A magnetic regulator version is used with high-pressure sodium lamps and an electro-regulator version is used with metal halide lamps.

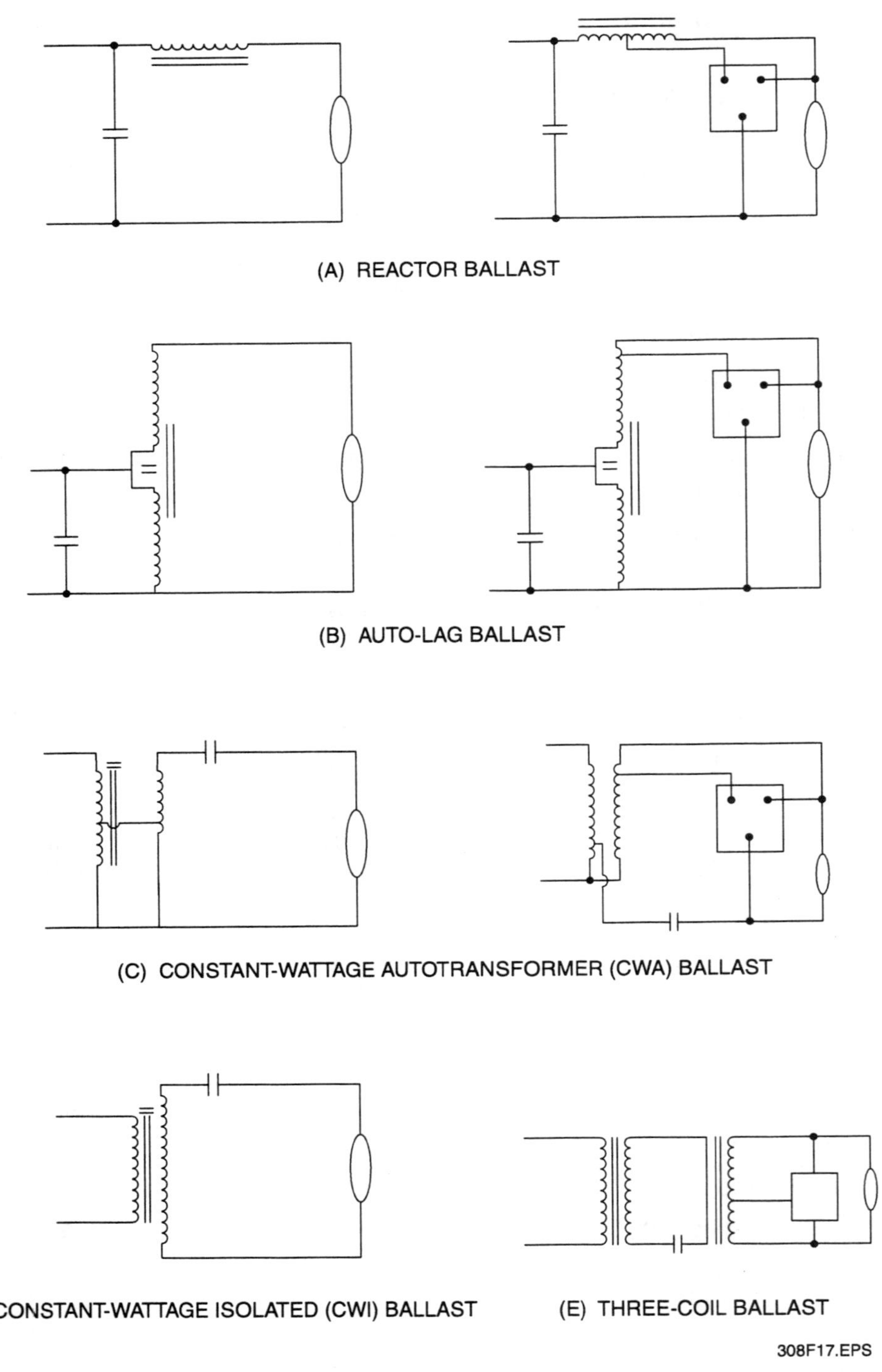

Figure 17. Simplified HID Ballast Circuits

7.2.4 Dimming HID Lamps

HID lamps can be controlled using equipment similar to that used for dimming fluorescent lamps. However, the long warmup and restrike times associated with HID lamps may limit their applications. Multi-level ballasts are made for HID lamps that allow their light to be reduced. This type of ballast is typically used in lighting fixtures for warehouses, parking garages, tunnels, and daytime lighting applications. Some equipment is made that allows HID lamps to be dimmed to less than 20% of their full light output; however, most lamp manufacturers will not guarantee full life expectancy if their lamps are operated below 50%. Also, color shifts in the light output of the lamps may limit their use in some applications.

Fluorescent and HID lamps and lighting fixtures are normally very reliable; however, problems do occur that require troubleshooting the lamps and/or lighting fixtures. *Appendix A* contains guidelines and checklists that can be used to aid you when troubleshooting problems with fluorescent and HID lighting systems.

Because of high energy costs, the use of lighting controls to manage the application of lighting is common. Several devices can be used to control lighting circuits in order to conserve energy. These include occupancy sensors, photosensors, timers, and similar devices.

9.1.0   OCCUPANCY SENSORS

Occupancy sensors (*Figure 18*) are devices that can be used to turn lights on and off automatically in an individual space such as a private office, restroom, or storage area. Occupancy sensors can be motion detecting (ultrasonic), heat sensing (infrared), or sound sensing. They can be recessed or surface-mounted on a wall or ceiling, they can replace wall switches, or they can plug into receptacles. The sensor turns the lights on when it senses someone coming into the room or area and turns the lights off some time after no longer sensing anyone present. Units come either with fixed, preset time delays and sensitivity levels, or with adjustable ones.

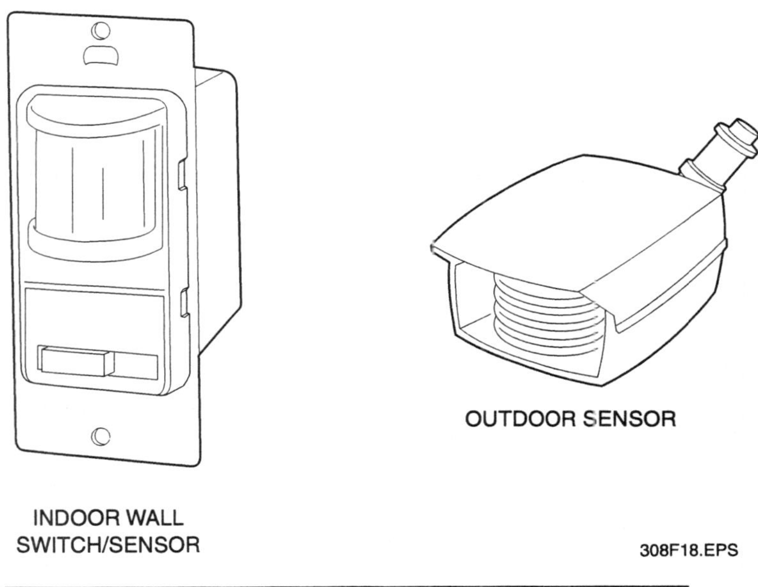

Figure 18. Examples Of Infrared Occupancy Sensors

Ultrasonic sensors transmit ultrasound and receive a reflected signal to sense the presence of occupants in a space. They typically operate at a frequency between 25kHz and 40kHz. Passive infrared sensors detect the changes in infrared patterns across their segmented detection regions. The type of sensor used must be compatible with the application. For example, a motion detector or sound detector may not be the right choice if occupants of the space sit very quietly at desks. People in such situations have been known to complain that they must deliberately move or make noise from time to time to prevent the sensor from turning off the lights. On the other hand, infrared sensors must be placed so that no obstruction blocks their sensing field.

9.2.0 PHOTOSENSORS

Electronic photosensors (*Figure 19*) sense the level of visible light in the surrounding area and convert this level into an electrical signal. This signal can be used in one of two ways, depending on the type of system. In the first type, the signal can be used to activate a simple ON/OFF switch or relay that functions to control the power to the related lighting fixtures. In the second type, a variable output signal is produced that can be sent to a controller that operates to continuously adjust the output of electric lighting in the area.

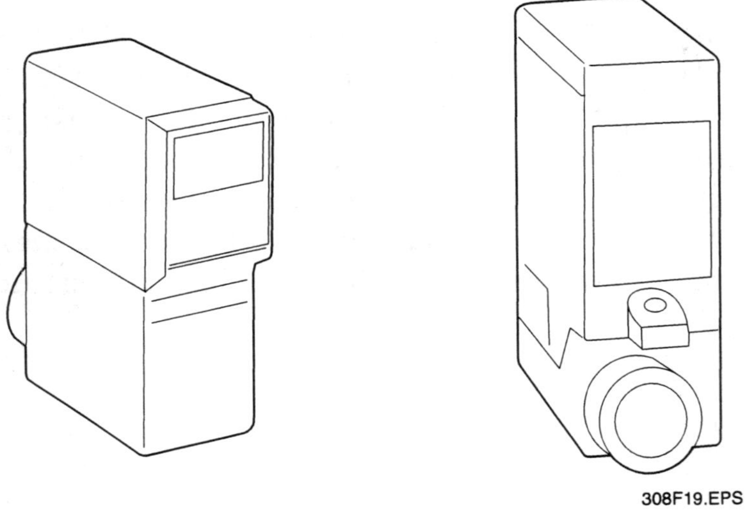

Figure 19. Examples Of Photoelectric Sensors

Photosensors can be an integral part of a lighting fixture, remote from the lighting fixture, or may control a circuit relay that operates several lighting fixtures. It is important that the area controlled by one photosensor have the same daylight illumination conditions (amount and direction) and that the area be contiguous with no high walls or partitions to divide it. When photosensors are used outdoors, the sensor should be aimed due north.

9.3.0 TIMERS

Timers are used to turn lighting on or off in response to known or scheduled sequences of events. Timers can be very simple clock-like mechanisms or they can be microprocessors that can program a sequence of events for years at a time. With a simple timer, the load is switched on and held energized for a preset period of time. Timer limits can range from a few minutes to 12 hours. Some models have a hold position for continuous service.

An electromechanical time clock/timer (*Figure 20*) is driven by an electric motor, with contactors actuated by mechanical stops or arms attached to the clock face. Time clocks have periods ranging from 24 hours to seven days. They can initiate many operations. Some can actuate a momentary contact switch to provide on and off pulses for actuating relays or contactors. Electronic time clocks/timers provide programmable selection of many switching operations and can typically be controlled to the nearest minute over a seven-day period. Most can control multiple channels and have time-of-day scheduling, holiday programming, daylight savings time adjustment, leap year correction, annual override, and battery carryover for protection against power outages.

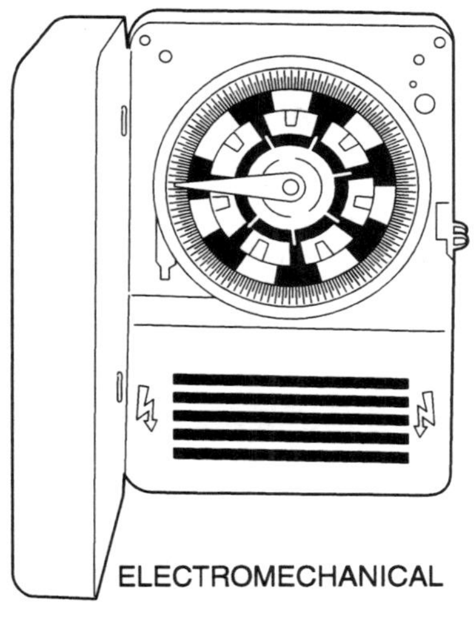

Figure 20. Typical Timer Controls

Time clocks are often used in conjunction with photosensors in order to turn off lighting when there is no longer a need for it. For example, an industrial building may use a photosensor signal to activate outdoor lighting at dusk, then a time clock is used to turn off that lighting after the last worker has left the facility. Another example is when a photosensor is used to signal when to turn the lights on, then a time clock is used to initiate dimming the lights when a high level of lighting is no longer needed.

Modern buildings normally use some form of an energy management system (EMS) to economically control the amount of energy consumed by the building's lighting circuits and HVAC equipment. An EMS can be a fairly simple stand-alone unit connected to one or more pieces of equipment (e.g., room lighting, a heat pump or rooftop HVAC unit, etc.), or it can be more extensive and control all the lights and equipment throughout an entire large facility.

Whether large or small, an EMS typically consists of a computer or control processor, energy management and scheduling software, sensors and controls located where needed, and, in large systems, a communications network. When programmed, an EMS can automatically control lighting to:

- Turn off lights in unoccupied areas
- Maintain partial lighting before and after working hours or public use hours
- Schedule lighting operation by hour of day and time of year

You will recognize the tasks performed by an EMS as being similar to those performed by the sensors and timers that were discussed earlier. The EMS simply receives signal inputs applied from these devices and processes them so as to perform tasks more reliably and precisely than can be performed by manual methods. Lighting control can be implemented in a building by a local approach, a central system, or both. The method used is determined both by the size of the controlled areas and how the control inputs are integrated into the system. A local lighting system is divided into small, independently controllable zones based on size, environment, etc., or according to functional need. The inputs from the sensors located in the zone are wired directly to a control that is also located in the zone (*Figure 21*). In central systems, the sensor inputs from the individual zone sensors are all wired to a central control.

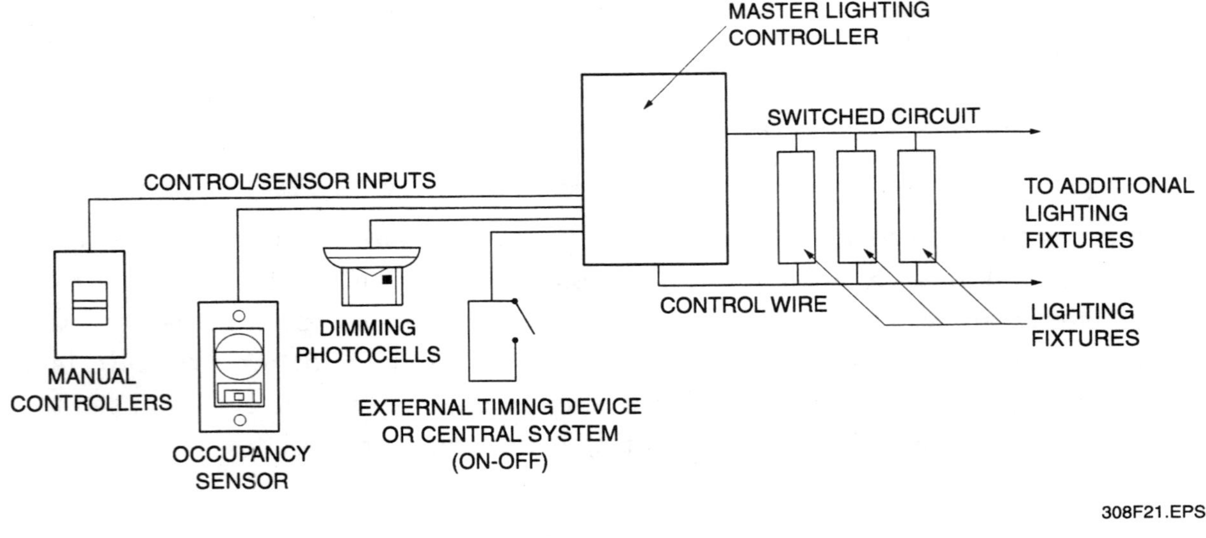

Figure 21. Simplified Zone Lighting Control Circuit

An EMS commonly turns lights on and off and/or initiates partial lighting in an area via relays that are activated or deactivated by the EMS control unit. *Figure 22* shows a typical lighting switching scheme involving the use of split-wired, multi-ballasted lighting fixtures. By split-wiring three-lamp and four-lamp lighting fixtures, multiple light intensities can be provided in a single zone. The relay-based control system provides full lighting for specific times of the day, while allowing a reduced lighting level and reduced power for those times when less lighting is needed.

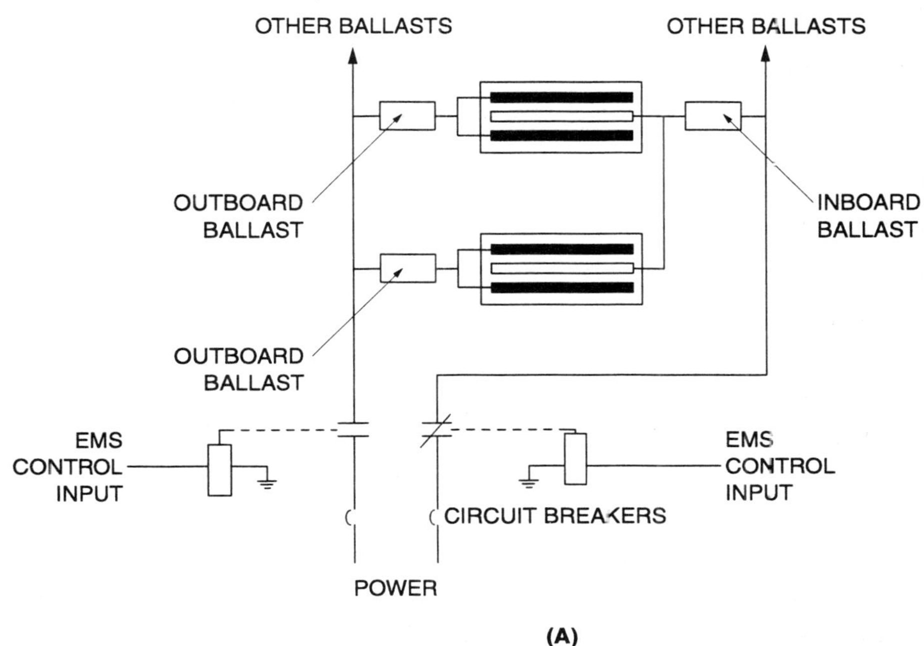

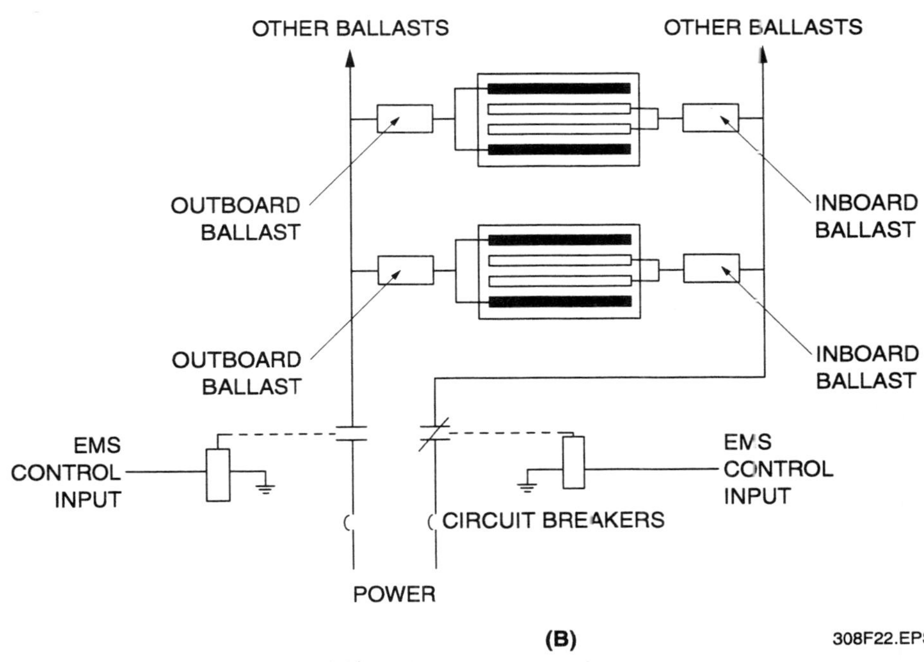

Figure 22. Simplified Wiring Diagrams Of Relay-Controlled Lighting Fixture Circuits

Figure 22(A) shows a relay-controlled split-wiring system connected to two three-lamp lighting fixtures. This arrangement allows for four levels of lighting: 0%, 33⅓%, 66⅔%, and 100%. As shown, the relay to the inboard ballasts is closed, allowing two of the six lamps to be turned on, thus providing light at the 33⅓% level.

Figure 22(B) shows a similar relay-controlled split-wiring system connected to two four-lamp lighting fixtures. This arrangement allows for three levels of lighting: 0%, 50%, and 100%. As shown, the relay to the inboard ballasts is closed, allowing four of the eight lamps to be turned on, thus providing light at the 50% level.

SUMMARY

This module covered the construction and theory of operation for incandescent, fluorescent, and high-intensity discharge (HID) lamps and lighting fixtures. It also introduced some common types of equipment and methods widely used for controlling the use of electric lighting in order to conserve energy. Understanding the construction and characteristics of the different kinds of lamps and lighting fixtures and how to control them for increased efficiency and economy will enable you to better install and/or maintain lighting systems so that they will provide a maximum of comfort and a minimum of eyestrain and fatigue.

References

For advanced study of topics covered in this Task Module, the following books are suggested:

American Electricians' Handbook, Latest Edition, McGraw-Hill, New York, NY.

Lighting Handbook, Latest Edition, Illuminating Engineering Society Of North America (IESNA), New York, NY.

National Electrical Code Handbook, Latest Edition, National Fire Protection Association, Quincy, MA.

ACKNOWLEDGMENTS

Figures 2, 3, 4, 8, and 9 courtesy of GE Lighting Systems, Inc.
Figures 6, 7, and 11 courtesy of OSRAM Sylvania, Inc.
Appendix A courtesy of Hubbell Lighting, Inc.

1. In an incandescent lamp, the filament resistance is _______.

    a. much higher when the lamp is turned on
    b. lower when the lamp is turned on
    c. somewhat higher when the lamp is turned on
    d. the same whether the lamp is turned on or off

2. The filament of a tungsten halogen lamp is encased in a capsule containing _______ gas.

    a. nitrogen
    b. argon
    c. halogen
    d. sodium

3. The diameter of a 4', T-12 fluorescent lamp is _______ .

    a. 1"
    b. $1\frac{1}{8}$"
    c. $1\frac{1}{4}$"
    d. $1\frac{1}{2}$"

4. During operation, a high-output (HO) fluorescent lamp typically has a current draw of _______.

    a. 430mA
    b. 800mA
    c. 1,100mA
    d. 1,500mA

5. The type of high-intensity discharge (HID) lamp that uses the oldest HID technology is the _______ lamp.

    a. low-pressure sodium
    b. high-pressure sodium
    c. mercury vapor
    d. metal halide

6. Lamps with color temperatures of _______ and lower are considered to produce a light that is warm in tone.

    a. 3,000K
    b. 3,500K
    c. 4,100K
    d. 5,000K

7. An electronic ballast typically operates the connected fluorescent lamps at a frequency of
    _____ to improve both ballast efficiency and lamp efficacy.

    a. 50Hz to 60Hz
    b. 10kHz to 20kHz
    c. 20kHz to 50kHz
    d. 60kHz to 100kHz

8. A fluorescent lamp is blinking off and on in very short cycles. The most probable cause is
    _____.

    a. the lamp itself
    b. incorrect supply voltage
    c. low ambient temperature
    d. a loose socket connection

9. Which sensor is *not* normally used as an occupancy sensor?

    a. Motion detector
    b. Infrared sensor
    c. Photosensor
    d. Sound sensor

10. If the contacts of both relays are closed in the circuit shown in *Figure 22(A)*, what
    percentage of lighting will be produced by the lighting fixtures?

    a. 0%
    b. 33⅓%
    c. 66⅔%
    d. 100%

ANSWERS TO REVIEW/PRACTICE QUESTIONS

<u>Answer</u>	<u>Section Reference</u>
1. a	2.0.0
2. c	3.0.0
3. d	4.0.0
4. b	4.0.0
5. c	5.0.0
6. a	6.0.0
7. c	7.1.4
8. a	8.0.0, Appendix A
9. c	9.1.0
10. d	10.0.0

TROUBLESHOOTING GUIDELINES AND CHECKLISTS

Troubleshooting Guide

HID

This guide is prepared to assist electricians with normal routine maintenance and to help them understand the operation of different lamp sources and electrical systems.

Caution: High voltages, currents, and temperatures are required to operate gas discharge lamps. Shock and burn hazards exist, and testing or evaluating fixtures or components should be done by qualified individuals only.

Light Sources:

Fluorescent

Mercury Vapor (MV)

Metal Halide (MH)

High Pressure Sodium (HPS)

Lamps

Fluorescent lamps come in many sizes, shapes and colors. This lamp source can provide numerous advantages, depending on the needs and requirements of end users. These lamps are generally used when low mounting heights and quiet operation are required. Note that many new, more efficient lamps and electronic ballasts offer the customer many energy saving opportunities.

Mercury Vapor lamps were the first to be developed in the family of high intensity discharge (HID) lamps. Their advantage is that they offer long life. Their disadvantages are poor color rendition, poor lumen maintenance, and low efficiency.

MH lamps are similar to MV lamps in design and operation. Their lumen output is double that of MV lamps of the same wattage. MH lamps are used in installations that require high efficiency, and white light. Lamp life historically has been less than MV and HPS, however new MH systems are now changing this by providing excellent life, lumen maintenance and color control.

A. HPS lamps offer long life and more lumens per watt than MV or MH sources. HPS lamps emit a pale amber color compared to other whiter light sources. Energy savings is the main HPS advantage. New high-xenon HPS lamps offer even higher LPW, longer life and improved lumen maintenance.

Ballasts

All HID light sources require some form of ballast because:

Most require a starting voltage that is higher than the line voltage.

They all have a characteristic known as negative resistance. This means that once the arc is initiated, the lamp's resistance continually decreases as current increases. For all practical purposes, the lamp becomes a short circuit. The ballast limits and controls the current wave form through the lamp

They provide voltage transformation to allow the use of many line voltages.

There are many different types of ballasts used with different lamps. Within a lamp type, ballasts vary in lamp operating wattage and regulation caused by changes in line voltage and lamp voltage. Better regulation and control normally results in higher initial cost, but may greatly improve operating characteristics and overall performance.

Capacitors

Capacitors are used for power factor correction or as current regulation devices which provide the control necessary to ensure proper lamp and ballast operation. Different wattages, voltages, and ballast types require a variety of different capacitors. The ballast ID label specifies the microfarad and voltage rating required for proper operation. If the capacitor is incorrectly wired, improper operation of the fixture as well as other component failures could result.

Ignitors/Starters

These devices are utilized to provide the proper voltage and energy to start the lamp. They are predominantly used with HPS lamps as well as some Metal Halide and Fluorescent systems.

Electrical Testing Procedures

Caution: High voltages, currents, and temperature are required to operate lamps. Therefore, shock and burn hazards exist, and testing or evaluating fixtures or components should be done only by qualified individuals.

A. Testing Lamps

The easiest method of troubleshooting a fixture is to try a **known** good lamp in the inoperative fixture. If the lamp being replaced exhibits any of the following conditions, replace with a new lamp.

1. **Sodium Leaker Lamp** - will have a brown/golden coating on the inside of the lamp envelope other than at the base of the lamp.

2. **Amalgam Leaker Lamp** - the lamp envelope will have a smoked bronze appearance on the inside of the envelope.

3. **Faulty Base to Lamp Envelope Seal** - a white powdery substance will appear at the base of the lamp where oxygen has leaked inside the lamp.

4. **End of Lamp Life** - the arc tube will be black on both ends or the entire length of the arc tube will be black.

5. **Broken Welds or Arc Tube Support Brackets** - mechanical breaks occasionally occur due to rough handling or internal thermal stresses. Broken welds in evacuated (HPS) lamps can also create a problem known as vacuum switching. Extremely high voltage surges occur in the lamp circuit if the weld opens while the lamp is operating. Secondary coil burnout, ignitor arcing and socket arcing can occur. Rewelding may occur and the lamp may **appear** to be satisfactory; however, if left in operation, failure of the ballast and/or ignitor is likely.

B. Ignitors/Starters

The starter provides the necessary voltage and energy required to initiate the arc in the lamp. The easiest way to check the ignitor on 35W to 150W HPS units is to install a 120V incandescent lamp in the fixture. If the incandescent lamp operates but a known good HPS lamp will not ignite,

308A01.TIF

Troubleshooting/Fluorescent Service Checklist

replace starter. In 200W to 1000W HPS fixtures, install a mercury lamp of similar wattage. If the mercury lamp lights and the HPS lamp will not, replace the starter.

Do not operate Incandescents or mercury lamps used to check the starter for extended periods of time (more than ½ hour).

C. Capacitors

Testing Capacitors may be accomplished by:

1. **Visual Inspection for swollen capacitors.** If the capacitor is swollen or bulged on the sides or top where the terminals are located, remove and replace with a new one.

2. **Verify the correct microfarad rating** as specified on the ballast I.D. label.

3. **Using an ohmmeter to check capacitors:**
discharge capacitor by shorting between the terminals

disconnect capacitor from circuit

remove bleed resistor

4. **Set ohmmeter to highest resistance scale** and connect leads to capacitor terminals.
   - if resistance starts low and gradually increases, the capacitor is good.
   - if resistance starts low and doesn't increase, the capacitor is shorted and should be replaced.
   - if resistance is high and remains relatively the same, the capacitor is open and should be replaced.

D. Ballast

Visual inspection of the coil for burned or charred windings is the easiest method for checking the ballast. If lamps, ignitors and capacitors test good, replace the ballast. Testing the voltage at the socket is another method of checking the ballast. However, to use this procedure you must know specific ballast/lamp voltage and amperage requirements. The starting aid (if present) should be disconnected prior to testing the voltage at the socket. Failure to remove the starting aid could damage the test equipment

Fluorescent Service Checklist

(Identify problem and test for cause in numerical sequence.)

PROBLEM	End of Lp. Life	Incorr. Lamp	Def. Blst.	Incorr. Blst.	Incorrect Supply Voltage	No Supply Voltage	Incomp. Lamp Seating	(B) Dirty Lamps	Incorr. Fixt. Wiring	Loose Socket Connect.	(C) Low Amb Temp.	High Amb. Temp.
Failure to Start (A)	1	5	4	10	6	7	8	2	9	11	3	
Slow Starting		3			4			2			1	
Blinking Off and On - Very Short Duration Cycles	1				2					4	3	
Long Duration Cycles - Several Minutes to Hours(D)		3	2		4				5			1
Short Lamp Life		2	1	3	4		5		6		7	
Lamp End Blackening - One End Only (A)			4				1		2	3		
Lamp End Blackening - Both Ends(A)	1	2	3	6	7		4		5			
Lamp Ends Only Lighted		1	2	3					4			

A. Generally indicates lamp cathode heat is missing. Problem source must be identified and corrected.

B. In humid weather or when air conditioning systems are operated only during working hours, dust on the lamps may gather condensation and prevent reliable starting. Lamps and fixtures must be cleaned and the lamp waxed with a good silicone wax.

C. Energy saving lamp, ballast combinations will not reliably start near or below 60°F; all others 50°F unless low temperature systems are used.

D. Indicates ballast thermal protector is cycling. May be the result of high ambient temperature, fixture misapplication or restricted air circulation. With recessed fixtures, check to be sure insulation has not been placed directly on the recessed fixture body. With surface mounted fixtures mounted against insulated ceiling, make sure they are rated for such applications.

All service checklists detail the more probable problem causes. It is important to keep in mind that other elements may be involved or more than one cause present. All electrical service work must begin with a careful and detailed evaluation of the problem and thorough inspection of all components, paying special attention to all wiring connections.

The ability to field test ballasts is very limited. The normal verification is to substitute a known good ballast in the problem fixture.

On rapid start systems only, cathode heater voltage may be verified by a voltage reading between **the contacts on each socket.** (A voltage of 3.5 to 5 is considered normal.)

Caution - Voltages in excess of 500V may be present between the lamp socket parts and ground.

Mercury Vapor And Metal Halide Service Checklist

Identify problem and test for cause in numerical sequence.

	A	B	C	D	E	F	G	H	I	J	K
PROBLEM	End of Lamp Life	Incorrect Lamp	Open Cap.	Def. Starter (if app.)	Incorrect Supply Voltage	Photo- Cont.	New Lamp Repl.	Line Voltage Dips	Shorted. Cap.	Burned Ballast Windings	Incorrect Ballast
FAILURE TO OPERATE	1	5	3	4	2						6
LAMP CYCLING		1			2	3					
COLOR SHIFT							1	2			
LOW LIGHT OUTPUT		2			1						
TRIPPED BREAKER OR BLOWN FUSE									1	2	3

A. End of Lamp Life

At lamp's end of life, the voltage requirements of the lamp exceeds the output ability of the ballast. The usual failure mode for mercury is low light output followed by failure to operate, and for Metal Halide low light levels, color shifts, and lamp operating instability (cycling). Replace end of life lamp as dictated by lamp testing procedure.

B. Incorrect Lamp

Lamp wattage, voltage, burning position, and type must be checked against the fixture label to be sure the proper lamp has been installed.

C. Open Capacitor

This is the usual result of electrical failure or mechanical damage. Very often the capacitor can will be bulged or distorted. Where the capacitor is used in series with the lamp, the lamp will not operate. See tests for capacitors or replace with a known good capacitor.

D. Defective Starter

The function of the starter is to provide a high voltage pulse to ignite the lamp. To test, replace with a known good lamp. (Also see Ignitor/Starter testing procedure)

E. Incorrect Supply Voltage

When investigating problems of low light output or cycling, voltage readings first must be taken at the fixture to properly identify power distribution problems. In the case of multiple supply type ballasts, verification that the supply voltage is connected to the appropriate input lead is advised.

F. Photocontrol

Problems may result from electrical failure, incorrect wiring, or from an incorrect amount of light reaching the cell. First cover the eye of the cell with electrical tape to verify fixture and cell operation. If the fixture fails to operate, the cell must be bypassed electrically to identify the problem source. Problems of incorrect amount of light usually can be resolved by repositioning the fixture or by using cell caps to regulate the light level.

G. New Lamp Replacement

New lamps, when installed, go through a period of burn-in or seasoning which may extend for a period of 100 hours or more. The usual result is noticeable color variation between lamps. While metal-halide lamps are noted for this, the system will stabilize as the burn-in period ends. It is important to understand that some variation in color may be noted between lamp manufacturers, or between old and new lamps.

H. Line Voltage Dips

When investigating voltage dips, it is important to identify distribution system loading. The usual cause is the starting of large motors or the use of electric welding equipment. Line voltage recorders will usually identify the problem. It is important to understand that mild dips will cause a color shift, while severe dips will cause the lamp to go out. Dip tolerance depends on lamp type, lamp age and ballast type.

I. Shorted Capacitor

This is the direct result of electrical failure or mechanical damage. The most common result of a shorted capacitor is ballast failure. In all cases of shorted capacitors, both capacitor and transformer should be replaced. See tests for capacitors or replace with a known good capacitor.

J. Burned Ballast Coils

1. Burned Primary Coils

This is the usual result of fixture connection to incorrect supply voltage. Repeated failure often in conjunction with capacitor failure may indicate short duration high voltage spikes on the distribution system. The use of a scope along with power company assistance is generally required to identify these spikes. Equally important as a cause of failure is a shorted capacitor (See "I" above - Shorted Capacitor). See tests for ballasts on preceding page and replace if necessary.

2. Burned Secondary Coils

This may be caused by a short circuit in the lamp circuit wiring or by mechanical failure in the lamp. Carefully inspect all lamp circuit wiring. See tests for ballasts on preceding page and replace it if necessary. **In all cases, replace the lamp.**

K. Incorrect Ballast

The requires checking only a new fixture or if a recurring problem is encountered. Carefully compare details on the transformer to the fixture label and lamp used in the circuit. Change components as required.

308A03.TIF

High-Pressure Sodium Service Checklist

Identify problem and test for cause in numerical sequence.

PROBLEM	A End of Lamp Life	B Incorrect Supp. Voltage	C Incorrect Lamp	D Shorted Capacitor	E Photo-Control	F Line Volt. Dip	G Defective Lamp	H Defective Starter	I Open Capacitor	J Burned Ballast Windings
LAMP CYCLING SINGLE FIXTURE	1	3	2		4					
LAMP CYCLING GROUP OF FIXTURES					2	1				
FAILURE TO START		2	3				4	1	5	6
LOW LIGHT OUTPUT		2	3	1			4			

A. End of Lamp Life

At a lamp's end of life, the operating voltage requirements of the lamp exceed the output ability of the ballast. This results in the lamp cycling off and on. It is important to understand that in the early stages of failure, the lamp may operate for several hours before cycling off. As the lamp nears total failure, the on time will decrease until the lamp fails to ignite at all. Cycling lamps should immediately be replaced to avoid starting aid damage. See lamp tests or replace with a known good lamp.

B. Incorrect Supply Voltage

When investigating problems of low light output, cycling, or failure to start, voltage readings must be taken *at the fixture* to properly identify distribution system problems. For multiple supply type ballasts, proper lead connection must be verified.

C. Incorrect Lamp

Lamp wattage, voltage, burning position, and type must be checked against fixture label to be sure the proper lamp has been installed in the fixture.

D. Shorted Capacitor

This is the direct result of electrical failure or mechanical damage. The most common result is low light output; cycling may also occur.

E. Photocontrol

Problems may result from electrical failure or from an incorrect amount of light reaching the cell. First cover the eye of the cell with electrical tape to verify fixture and cell operation. If the fixture fails to operate, the cell must be bypassed electrically to identify the problem source. Problems of incorrect amount of light usually can be resolved by repositioning the fixture or by using cell caps to regulate the light level. Occasionally, the cell will see light from the fixture reflected off a nearby object and turn itself off. Repositioning the cell or reflecting object may be required.

F. Line Voltage Dip

When investigation voltage dips, it is important to identify distribution system loading. The usual cause is the starting of large motors or the use of electric welding equipment. Line voltage recorders will usually identify the problem. It is important to understand that lamps nearing end of life will be more susceptible to voltage dips than new lamps, and lamp operating on reactor ballasts are more sensitive to voltage dips than those on regulating ballasts.

G. Defective Lamp

This is normally the result of some mechanical failure in the lamp. This can often be determined by brown or silver coating on the lamp outer jacket, or by deposits at the base of the lamp. See lamp testing procedures or replace with a known good lamp.

H. Defective Starter

The function of the starter is to provide a high voltage pulse to ignite the lamp. Failure to operate generally results from electrical failure in the starter. See tests for starters or replace with a known good starter.

I. Open Capacitor

This generally results from electrical failure or mechanical damage. Very often the capacitor can will be bulged or distorted. When the capacitor is used in the secondary (lamp) circuit, the fixture will not operate. See tests for capacitors or replace with a known good capacitor.

J. Burned Ballast Windings

This is often the result of fixture being connected to incorrect supply voltage. Repeated primary winding failures often in conjunction with capacitor failures may indicate short duration high voltage spikes on the distribution system. The use of a scope in conjunction with power company assistance is generally required to identify these spikes. See tests for ballasts and replace if necessary.

308A04.TIF

Light Output Service Checklist

(Investigate in numerical sequence)

A	B	C	D	E	F	G	H	I	J
Voltage	Socket Position	Lamps	Reflector	Reflectance	Obstruct.	Light Meters	Dirt	Line Current Harmonics	Spacing & Mount. Height
2	6	3	7	4	8	1	9	10	5

Voltage

Measurements must be checked a) at the fixture b) at the end of the distribution line. Confirm correct ballast voltage tap connection to supply voltage.

Socket Position

If adjustable, check fixture instructions and confirm correct position has been selected.

Lamps

Check for (a) correct wattage (b) correct burn position (c) high output vs. standard (d) color that appears to be correct (after burn in).

Reflector

Has the correct reflector been installed? If adjustable, has the proper mounting position been selected? Verify whether reflector should be open or enclosed.

Reflectance

Recheck original calculations and confirm correct reflectance was used for walls, ceiling and floor. Ratio of incident light to reflected light is a measure of reflectance.

Obstructions

Note obstructions in the air and at the floor level that would restrict normal light distribution. In the air this would include piping, heating, crane rails, steel structure, fog, or other airborne contaminants. At floor level work in progress, racks, cabinets, machinery and partitions. In addition consideration must be given to guards, visors and other fixtures.

Light Meters

Use a second meter to confirm out of spec readings. Be sure the meter is not shadowed, not receiving reflected light, and held in the correct plane, and calibrated.

Dirt

Be sure the reflector lamp and lens (if involved) are clean and free of construction dust.

Current/Wave Form

Check for hot panels, conduit and feeder wiring indicating harmonics and overloading.

Spacing & Mounting Height

Confirm the installation is per the original design for fixture spacing mounting height and aiming (if involved). Check for pole spacing, pole heights, and setbacks.

308A05.TIF

The NCCER makes every effort to keep these manuals up-to-date and free of technical errors. We appreciate your help in this process. If you have an idea for improving this manual, or if you find an error, a typographical mistake, or an inaccuracy in the NCCER's Craft Training Manuals, please write us, using this form or a photocopy. Be sure to include the exact module number, page number, a description of the problem, and the correction, if possible. Your input will be brought to the attention of the Technical Review Committee. Thank you for your assistance.

Instructors – If you found that additional materials were necessary in order to teach this module effectively, please let us know so that we may include them in the Equipment/Materials list in the Instructor's Guide.

Write: Curriculum Development and Revision Department
National Center for Construction Education and Research
P.O. Box 141104
Gainesville, FL 32614-1104

Fax: 352-334-0932

Craft ___________________________ Module Name ___________________________

Copyright Date __________ Module Number __________ Page Number(s) __________

Description of Problem

____

____

____

____

(Optional) Correction of Problem

____

____

____

(Optional) Your Name and Address

____

____

____

Motor Calculations

Module 26309

MOTOR CALCULATIONS

NATIONAL
CENTER FOR
CONSTRUCTION
EDUCATION AND
RESEARCH

OBJECTIVES

Upon completion of this module, the trainee will be able to:

1. Size branch circuits and feeders for electric motors.
2. Size, select, and install overcurrent protective devices for motors.
3. Size, select, and install overload relays for electric motors.
4. Calculate and install devices to improve the power factor at motor locations.
5. Size motor short circuit protectors.
6. Size multi-motor branch circuits.
7. Size motor disconnects.
8. Protect motor circuits with transformers.

Prerequisites

Successful completion of the following Task Modules is recommended before beginning study of this Task Module: Core Curricula, Electrical Level 1; Electrical Level 2; Electrical Level 3, Modules 26301 through 26308.

Required Trainee Materials

1. Trainee Task Module
2. Appropriate Personal Protective Equipment
3. Copy of the latest edition of the *National Electrical Code*

Note: The designations "National Electrical Code," "NE Code," and "NEC," where used in this document, refer to the National Electrical Code®, which is a registered trademark of the National Fire Protection Association, Quincy, MA. *All National Electrical Code (NEC) references in this module refer to the 1999 edition of the NEC.*

This course map shows all of the modules in the third level of the Electrical curricula. The suggested training order begins at the bottom and proceeds up. Skill levels increase as a trainee advances on the course map. The training order may be adjusted by the local Training Program Sponsor.

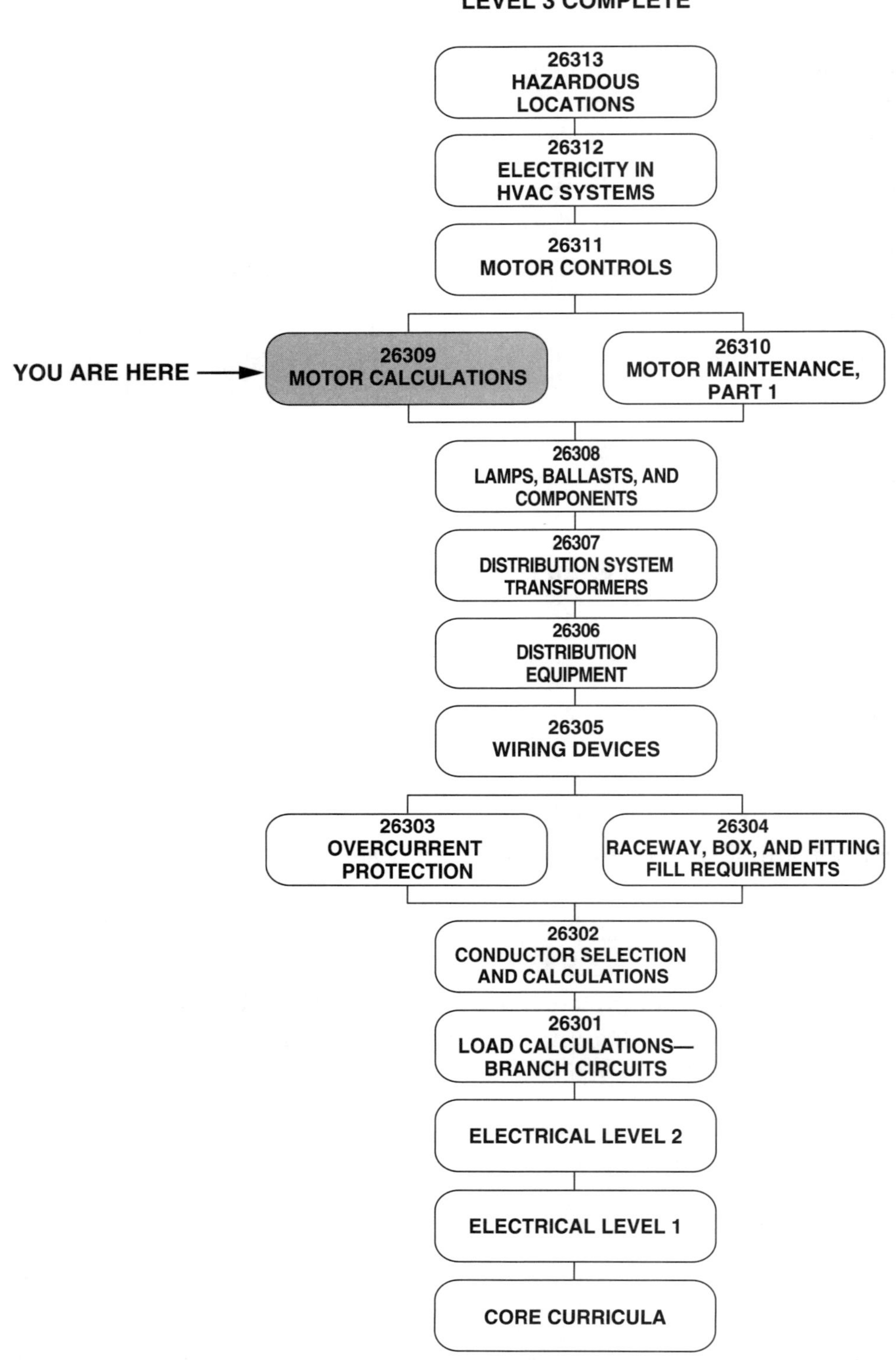

309CMAP.EPS

Trade Terms Introduced In This Module

Circuit interrupter: A non-automatic, manually operated device designed to open a current-carrying circuit without injury to itself.

Rating: A designated limit of operating characteristics based on definite conditions. Such operating characteristics as load, voltage, frequency, etc., may be given in the rating.

Service factor: The number by which the horsepower rating is multiplied to determine the maximum safe load that a motor may be expected to carry continuously at its rated voltage and frequency.

Terminal: A point at which an electrical component may be connected to another electrical component.

Torque: A force which produces or tends to produce rotation. Common units of measurement of torque are foot-pounds and inch-pounds.

1.0.0   INTRODUCTION

Electric motors are used in almost every type of installation imaginable, from residential appliances to heavy industrial machines. Many types of motors are available, from small shaded-pole motors (used mostly in household fans) to huge synchronous motors for use in large industrial installations. There are numerous types in between to fill every conceivable niche. None, however, have the wide application possibilities of the three-phase motor. This is the type of motor that electricians encounter most frequently. Therefore, the majority of the material in this module will deal with three-phase motors.

There are three basic types of three-phase motors:

- Squirrel cage induction motor
- Wound-rotor induction motor
- Synchronous motor

The type of three-phase motor is determined by the rotor or rotating member (*Figure 1*). The stator winding is basically the same for all three motor types.

The principle of operation for all three-phase motors is the rotating magnetic field. There are three factors that cause the magnetic field to rotate:

- The voltages of a three-phase electrical system are 120° out of phase with each other.
- The three voltages change polarity at regular intervals.
- The stator windings around the inside of the motor are arranged in a specific manner to induce rotation.

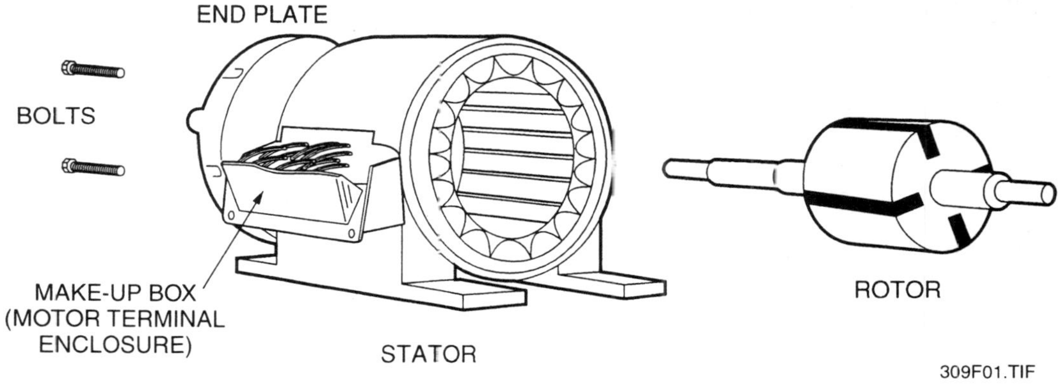

Figure 1. Basic Parts Of A Three-Phase Motor

The NEC plays an important role in the installation of electric motors. ***NEC Article 430*** covers the application and installation of motor circuits and motor control connections, including conductors, short circuit and ground fault protection, controllers, disconnects, and overload protection.

NEC Article 440 contains provisions for motor-driven air conditioning and refrigerating equipment, including the branch circuits and controllers for the equipment. It also takes into account the special considerations involved with sealed (hermetic) motor compressors, in which the motor operates under the cooling effect of the refrigeration. When referring to ***NEC Article 440***, be aware that the rules in this article are in addition to, or are amendments to, the rules given in ***NEC Article 430***. Motors are also covered to some degree in ***NEC Articles 422 and 424***.

2.0.0   MOTOR BASICS

The rotor of an AC squirrel cage induction motor (*Figure 2*) consists of a structure of steel laminations mounted on a shaft. Embedded in the rotor is the rotor winding, which is a series of copper or aluminum bars, short circuited at each end by a metallic end ring. The stator consists of steel laminations mounted in a frame. Slots in the stator hold stator windings that can be either copper or aluminum coils or bars. These are connected to form a circuit.

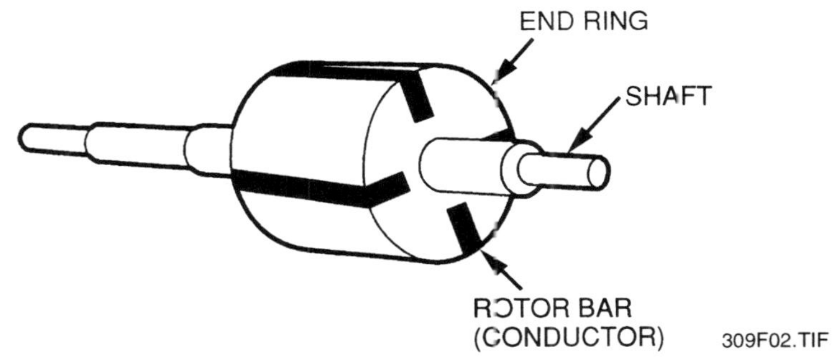

Figure 2. Squirrel Cage Rotor

Energizing the stator coils with an AC supply voltage causes current to flow in the coils. The current produces an electromagnetic field that causes magnetic poles to be created in the stator iron. The strength and polarity of these poles vary as the AC current flows in one direction, then the other. This change causes the poles around the stator to alternate between being south and north poles, thus producing a rotating magnetic field.

The rotating magnetic field cuts through the rotor, inducing a current in the rotor bars. This induced current only circulates in the rotor, which in turn causes a rotor magnetic field. As with two conventional bar magnets, the north pole of the rotor field attempts to line up with the south pole of the stator magnetic field, and the south pole attempts to line up with the north pole. However, because the stator magnetic field is rotating, the rotor chases the stator field. The rotor field never quite catches up due to the need to furnish **torque** to the mechanical load.

2.1.0   SYNCHRONOUS SPEED

The speed at which the magnetic field rotates is known as the *synchronous speed*. The synchronous speed of a three-phase motor is determined by two factors:

- Number of stator poles
- Frequency of the AC line in Hertz (Hz)

The synchronous speeds for various 60Hz motors are as follows:

- Two poles – 3,600 rpm
- Four poles – 1,800 rpm
- Six poles – 1,200 rpm
- Eight poles – 900 rpm

From the above, we can see that the rpm of a three-phase motor decreases as the number of poles increases.

2.2.0   STATOR WINDINGS

The stator windings of three-phase motors are connected in either a wye or a delta configuration (*Figure 3*). Some motor stators are designed to operate both ways; that is, they are started as a wye-connected motor to help reduce starting current and then changed to a delta configuration for running.

Many three-phase motors have dual-voltage stators. These stators are designed to be connected to either 240V or 480V. The leads of a dual-voltage stator use a standard numbering system. *Figure 4* shows a dual-voltage, wye-connected stator.

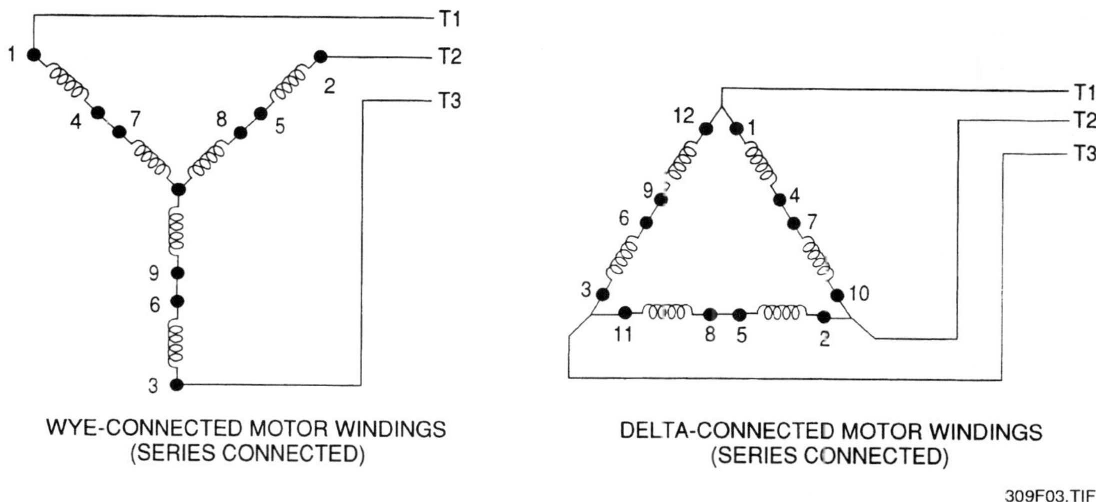

WYE-CONNECTED MOTOR WINDINGS
(SERIES CONNECTED)

DELTA-CONNECTED MOTOR WINDINGS
(SERIES CONNECTED)

309F03.TIF

Figure 3. Types Of Windings Found In Three-Phase Motors

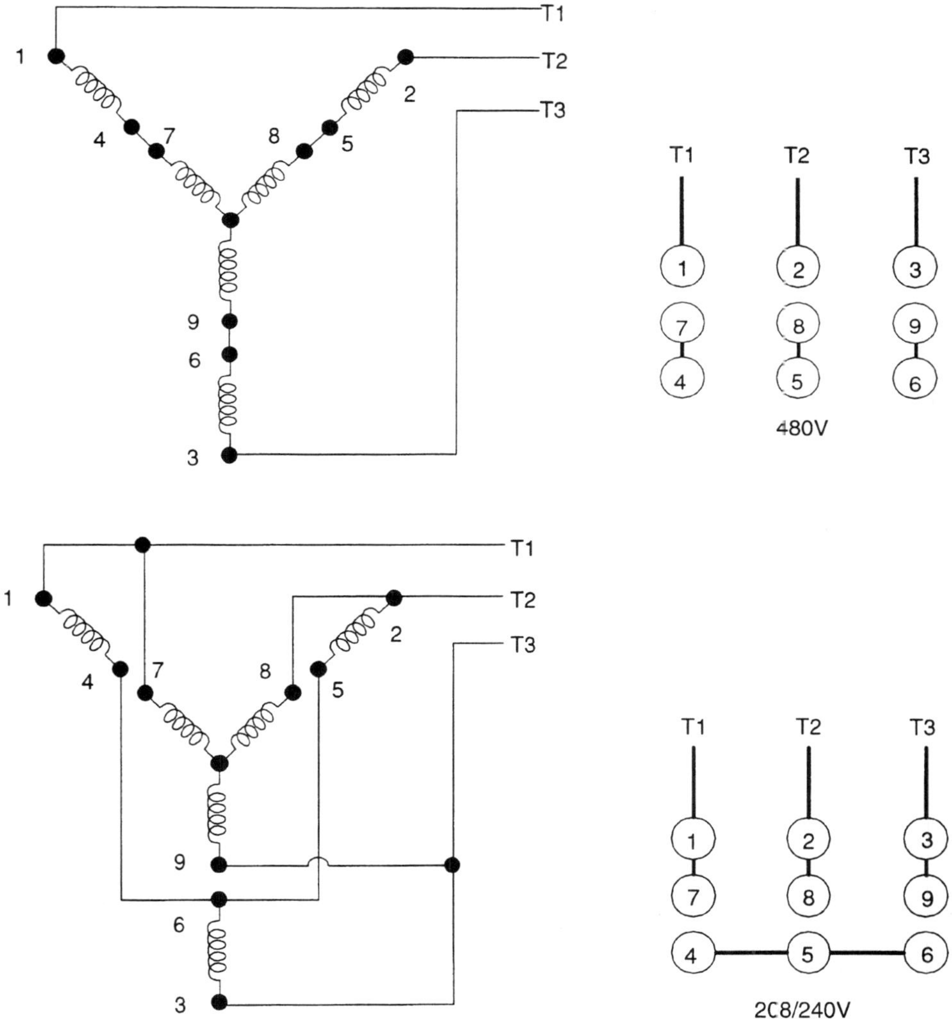

480V

208/240V

309F04.TIF

Figure 4. Dual-Voltage, Wye-Connected, Three-Phase Motors

Note that the nine motor leads are numbered in a spiral. The leads are connected in series for use on the higher voltage and in parallel for use on the lower voltage. Therefore, for the higher voltage, leads 4 and 7, 5 and 8, and 6 and 9 are connected together. For the lower voltage, leads 4, 5, and 6 are connected together; further connections are 1 and 7, 2 and 8, and 3 and 9, which are then connected to the three-phase power source. *Figure 5* shows the equivalent parallel circuit when the motor is connected for use on the lower voltage.

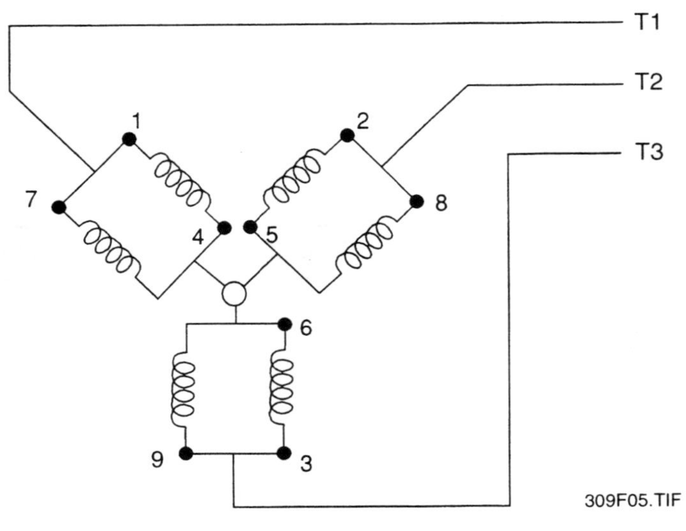

Figure 5. Equivalent Parallel Circuit

The same standard numbering system is used for delta-connected motors, and many delta-wound motors also have nine leads, as shown in *Figure 6*. However, there are only three circuits of three leads each. The high-voltage and low-voltage connections for a three-phase, delta-wound, dual-voltage motor are shown in *Figure 7*.

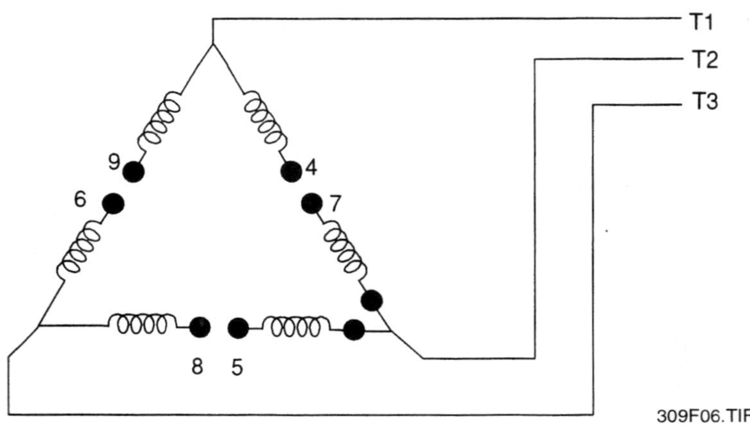

Figure 6. Arrangement Of Leads In A Nine-Lead, Delta-Wound, Dual-Voltage Motor

ELECTRICAL — TRAINEE TASK MODULE 26309

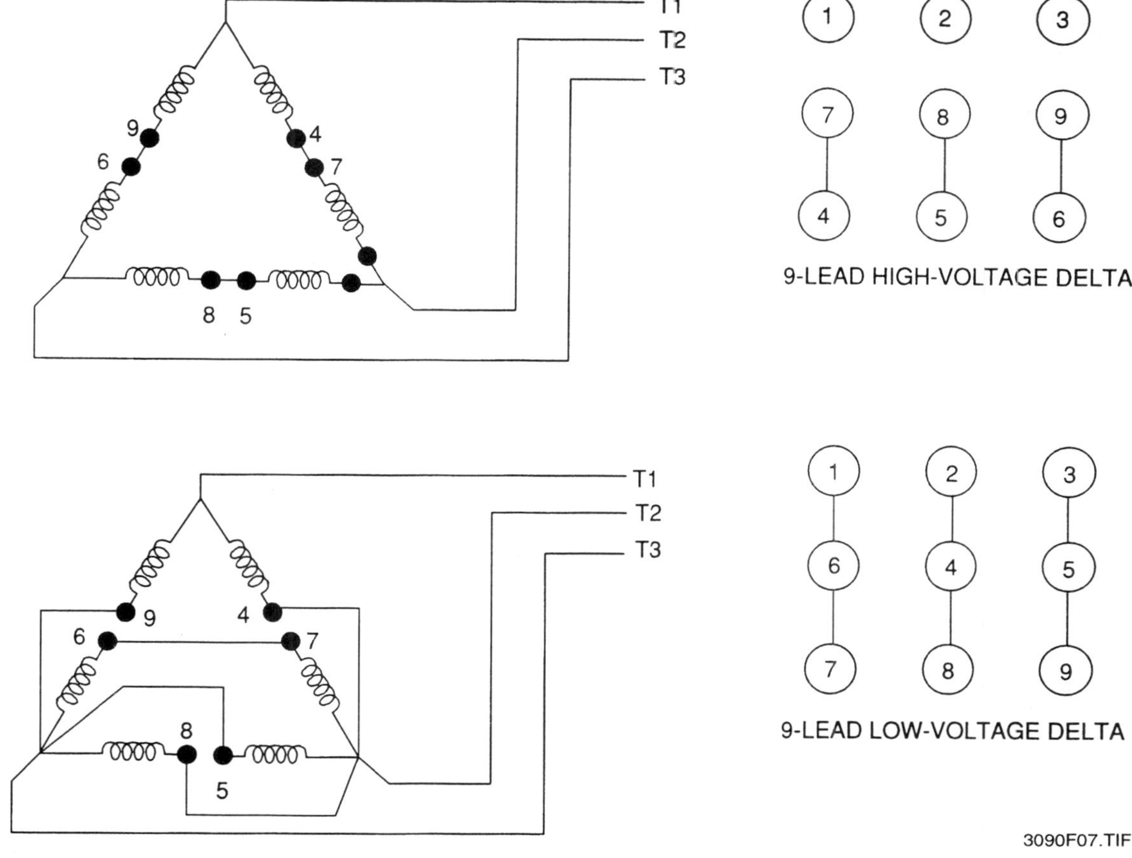

Figure 7. Lead Connections For A Three-Phase, Dual-Voltage, Delta-Wound Motor

In some instances, a dual-voltage motor connected in a delta configuration will have 12 leads instead of nine. *Figure 8* shows the high-voltage and low-voltage connections for a dual-voltage, 12-lead, delta-wound motor.

2.2.1 Principles Of Dual-Voltage Connections

When a motor is operated at 240V, the current draw of the motor is double the current draw of a 480V connection. For example, if a motor draws 10A of current when connected to 240V, it will draw only 5A when connected to 480V. The reason for this is the difference of impedance in the windings between a 240V connection and a 480V connection. Remember that the low-voltage windings are always connected in parallel, while the high-voltage windings are connected in series.

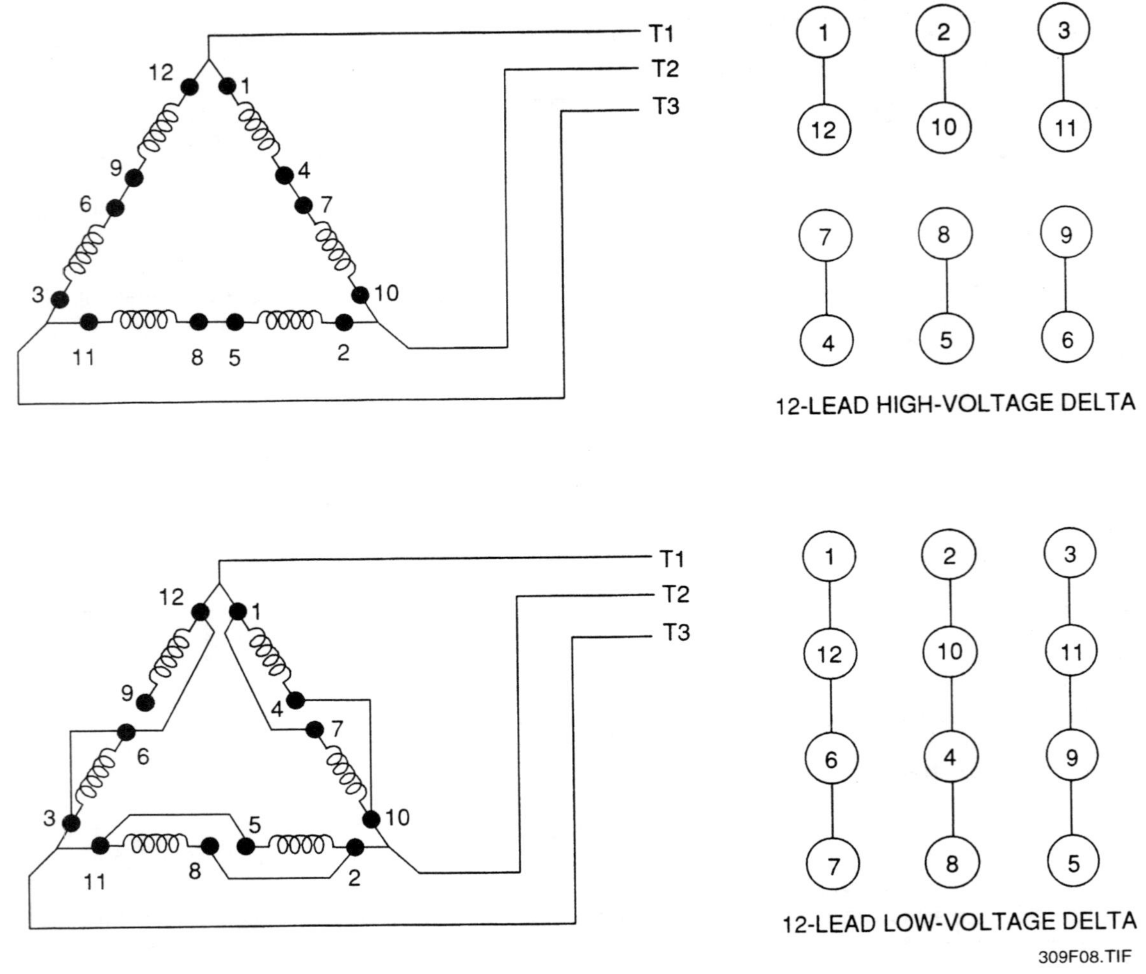

Figure 8. Lead Connections For A 12-Lead, Dual-Voltage, Delta-Wound Motor

For instance, assume that the stator windings of a motor (R1 and R2) both have an impedance of 48Ω. If the stator windings are connected in parallel, the total impedance (R_t) may be found as follows:

$$R_t = \frac{R1 \times R2}{R1 + R2}$$

$$R_t = \frac{48\Omega \times 48\Omega}{48\Omega + 48\Omega}$$

$$R_t = \frac{2,304\Omega}{96\Omega}$$

$$R_t = 24\Omega$$

Therefore, the total impedance (R) of the motor winding connected in parallel is 24Ω, and if a voltage (E) of 240V is applied to this connection, the following current (I) will flow:

$$I = \frac{E}{R}$$

$$I = \frac{240V}{24\Omega}$$

$$I = 10A$$

If the windings are connected in series for operation on 480V, the total impedance of the winding is:

$$R_t = R1 + R2$$
$$R_t = 48\Omega + 48\Omega$$
$$R_t = 96\Omega$$

Consequently, if 480V is applied to this winding, the following current will flow:

$$I = \frac{E}{R}$$

$$I = \frac{480V}{96\Omega}$$

$$I = 5A$$

It is obvious that twice the voltage means half the current flow, or vice versa.

2.3.0   SPECIAL CONNECTIONS

Some three-phase motors designed for operation on voltages higher than 600V may have more than 12 leads. Motors with 15 or 18 leads are common in high-voltage installations. A 15-lead motor has three coils per phase, as shown in *Figure 9*. Notice that the leads are numbered in the same spiral sequence as a nine-lead, wye-wound motor.

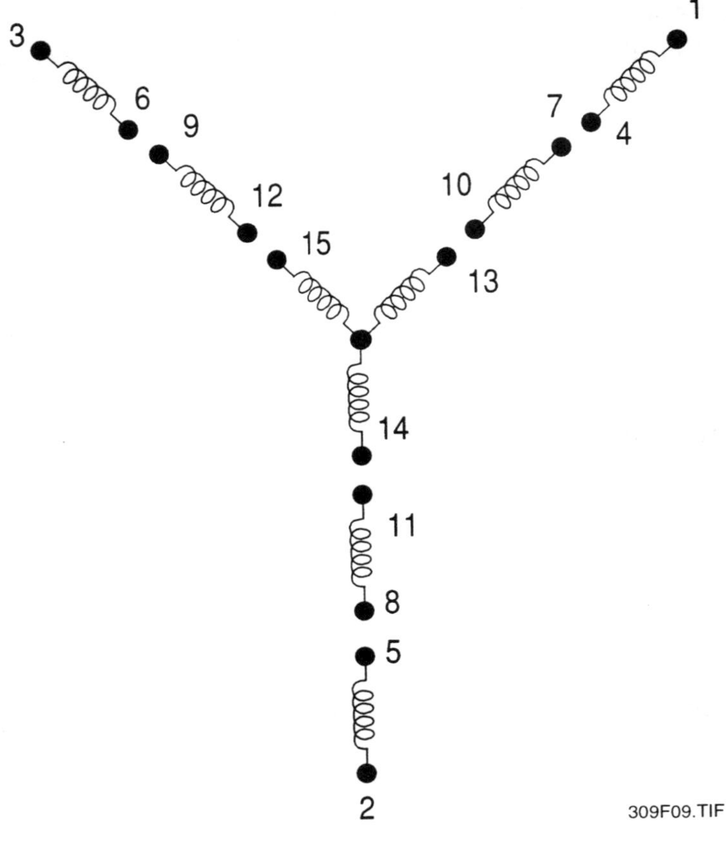

Figure 9. Fifteen-Lead Motor

3.0.0 CALCULATING MOTOR CIRCUIT CONDUCTORS

The basic elements of a motor circuit are shown in *Figure 10*. Although these elements are shown separately in this illustration, there are certain cases in which the NEC permits a single device to serve more than one function. For example, in some cases, one switch can serve as both the disconnecting means and the controller. In other cases, short circuit protection and overload protection can be combined in a single circuit breaker or set of fuses.

Note: ***NEC Section 430-22(a)*** states that when sizing conductors supplying a single motor used for continuous duty, the conductors must have a current-carrying capacity of not less than 125% of the motor full-load current **rating**. Conductors on the line side of the controller supplying multi-speed motors must be based on the highest of the full-load current ratings shown on the motor nameplate. Conductors between the controller and the motor must have a current-carrying rating based on the current rating for the speed of the motor being fed by each set of conductors.

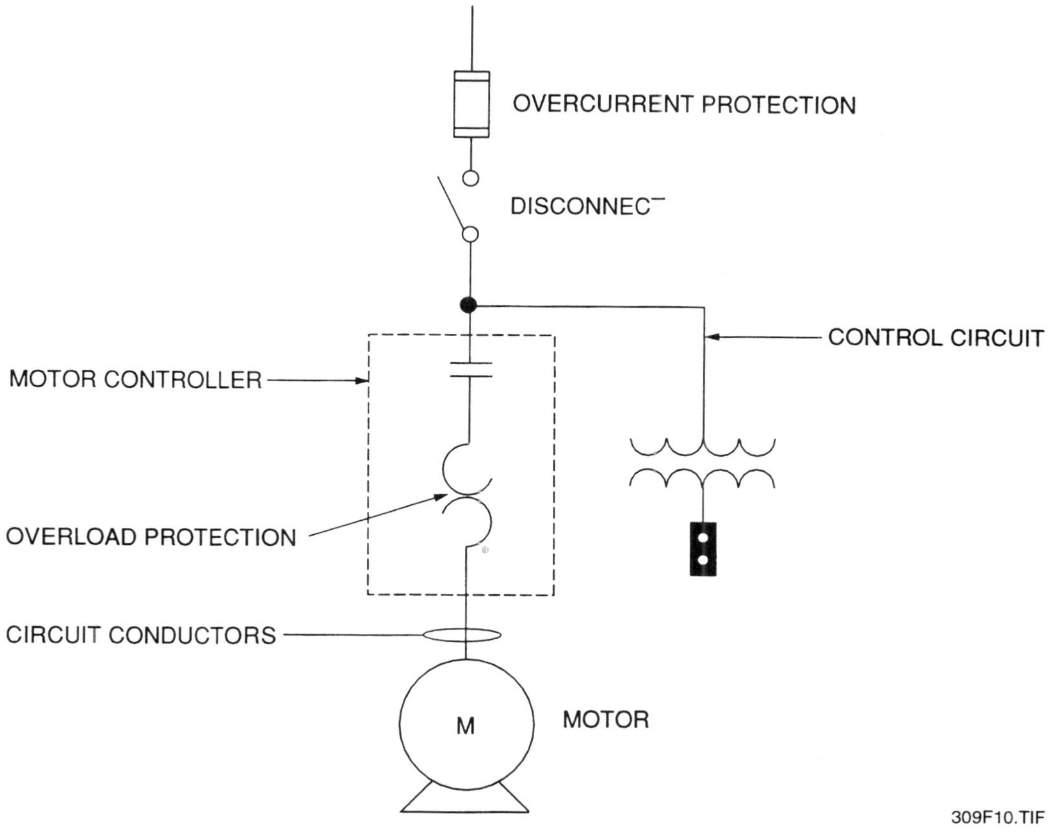

Figure 10. Basic Elements Of Any Motor Circuit

A typical motor control center and branch circuits feeding four different motors are shown in *Figure 11*. We will see how the feeder and branch circuit conductors are sized for these motors.

Step 1   Refer to **NEC Table 430-150** for the full-load current of each motor.

Step 2   Determine the full-load current of the largest motor in the group.

Step 3   Calculate the sum of the full-load current ratings for the remaining motors in the group.

Step 4   Multiply the full-load current of the largest motor by 1.25 (125%) and then add the sum of the remaining motors to the result (**NEC Section 430-24**). The combined total will give the minimum feeder size.

When sizing feeder conductors for motors, be aware that the procedure previously described will give the minimum conductor rating based on temperature rise only. Consequently, it is often necessary to increase the size of conductors to compensate for voltage drop and power loss in the circuit.

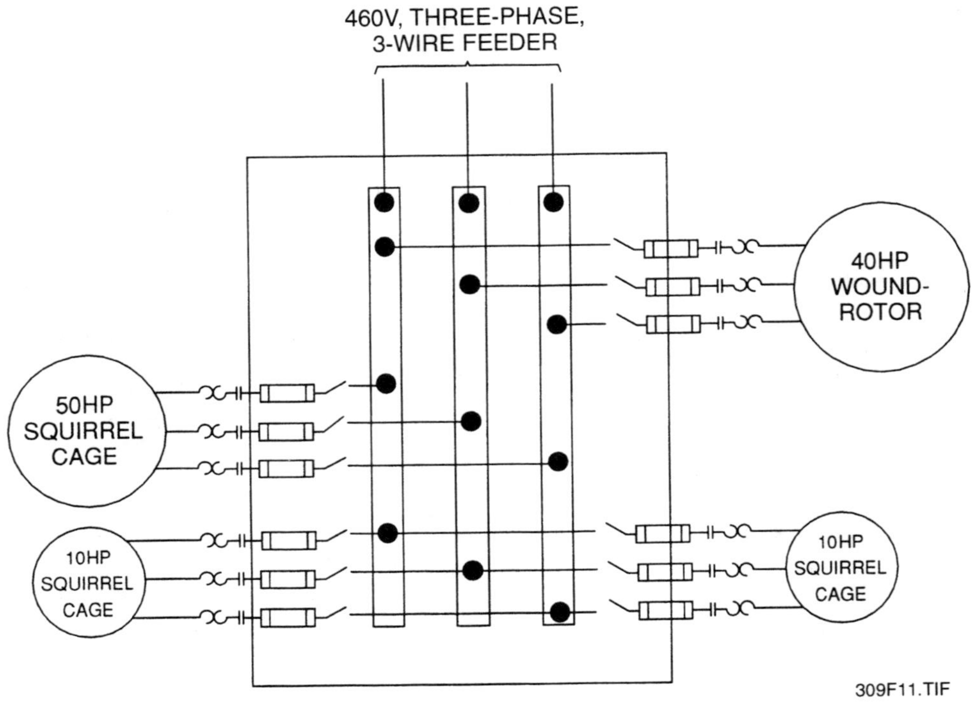

Figure 11. Typical Motor Control Center

Now we will complete the conductor calculations for the motor circuits in *Figure 11*.

Referring to **NEC Table 430-150**, the motor horsepower is shown in the far left-hand column. Follow across the appropriate row until you come to the column titled *460V*, which is the voltage of the motor circuits in *Figure 11*. We find that the ampere ratings for the motors in question are as follows:

*   50hp = 65A
*   40hp = 52A
*   10hp = 14A

The largest motor in this group is the 50hp squirrel cage motor, which has a full-load current of 65A.

The sum of the remaining motors is:

52A + 14A + 14A = 80A

Now, multiply the full-load current of the largest motor by 125% (1.25) and then add the total amperage of the remaining motors:

$(1.25 \times 65A) + 80A = 161.25A$

Therefore, the minimum feeder size for the 460V, three-phase, three-wire motor control center will be 161.25A. Referring to **NEC Table 310-16** under the column headed 75°C, the closest conductor size is 2/0 copper (rated at 175A) or 4/0 aluminum (rated at 180A).

The branch circuit conductors feeding the individual motors are calculated somewhat differently. **NEC Section 430-22(a)** requires that the ampacity of branch circuit conductors supplying a single continuous-duty motor must not be less than 125% of the motor full-load current rating. Therefore, the current-carrying capacity of the branch circuit conductors feeding the four motors in question are calculated as follows:

50hp motor = 65A × 1.25 = 81.25A
40hp motor = 52A × 1.25 = 65A
10hp motor = 14A × 1.25 = 17.5A

Referring to **NEC Table 310-16**, the closest size 75°C THWN copper conductors that will be permitted to be used on these various branch circuits are as follows:

- A 50hp motor at 81.25A requires No. 4 AWG THWN conductors.
- A 40hp motor at 65A requires No. 6 AWG THWN conductors.
- A 10hp motor at 17.5A requires No. 12 AWG THWN conductors [see **NEC Section 240-3(d)**].

Refer to *Figure 12* for a summary of the conductors used to feed our example motor control center, along with the branch circuits supplying the individual motors.

If voltage drop and/or power loss must be taken into consideration, please refer to the *Conductor Selection and Calculations* module.

For motors with other voltages (up to 2,300V) or for synchronous motors, refer to **NEC Table 430-150**.

In accordance with **NEC Section 430-22(b)**, branch circuit conductors serving motors used for short-time, intermittent, or other varying duty must have an ampacity not less than the percentage of the motor nameplate current rating shown in **NEC Table 430-22(b)**. However, to qualify as a short-time, intermittent motor, the nature of the apparatus that the motor drives must be arranged so that the motor cannot operate continuously with a load under any condition of use. Otherwise, the motor must be considered continuous duty. Consequently, the majority of motors encountered in the electrical trade must be rated for continuous duty, and the branch circuit conductors sized accordingly.

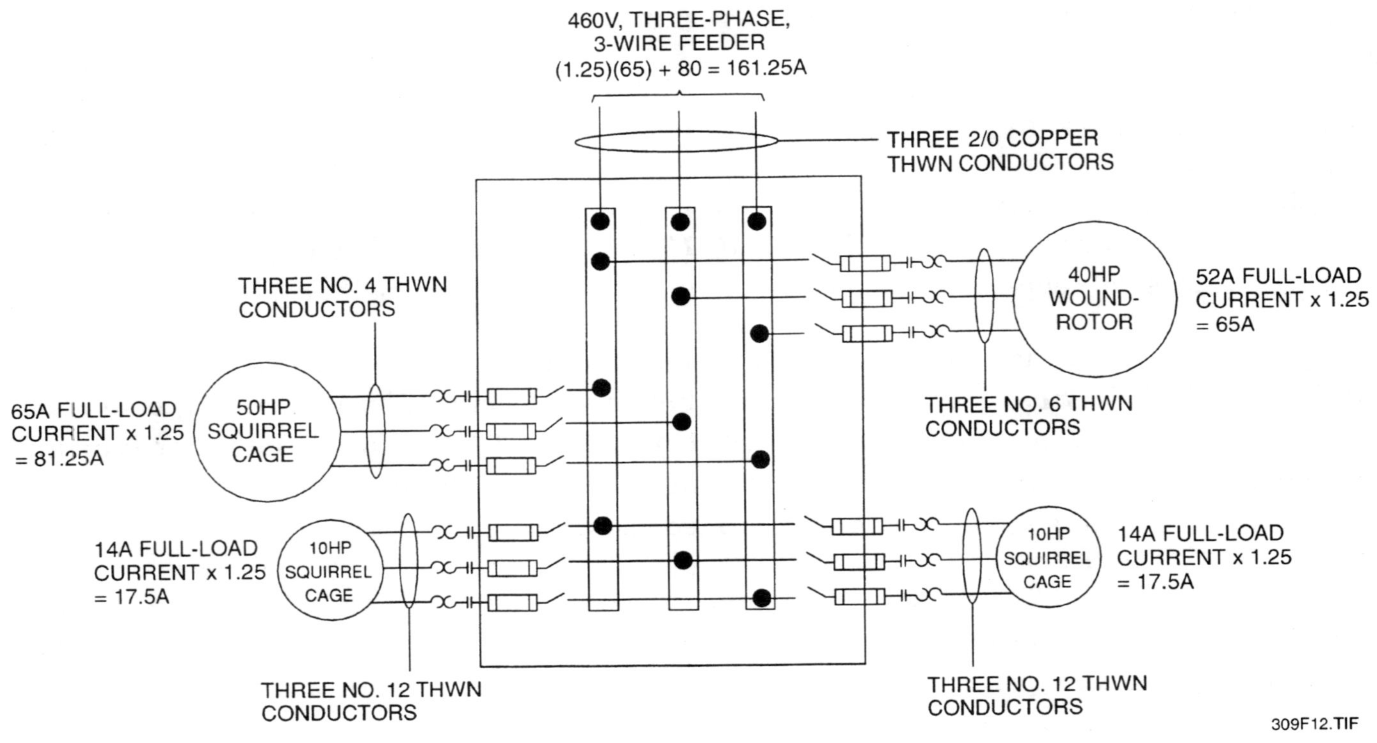

Figure 12. Sizing Motor Branch Circuits

3.1.0 WOUND-ROTOR MOTORS

The primary full-load current ratings for wound-rotor motors are listed in **NEC Table 430-150** and are the same as those for squirrel cage motors. Conductors connecting the secondary leads of wound-rotor induction motors to their controllers must have a current-carrying capacity at least equal to 125% of the motor full-load secondary current if the motor is used for continuous duty. If the motor is used for less than continuous duty, the conductors must have a current-carrying capacity of not less than the percentage of the full-load secondary nameplate current given in **NEC Table 430-22(b)**. Conductors from the controller of a wound-rotor induction motor to its starting resistors must have an ampacity in accordance with **NEC Table 430-23(c)**.

Note: *NEC Section 430-6(a)(1)* specifies that for general motor applications (excluding applications of torque motors and sealed hermetic-type refrigeration compressor motors), the values given in *NEC Tables 430-147, 430-148, 430-149, and 430-150* should be used instead of the actual current rating marked on the motor nameplate when sizing conductors, switches, and overcurrent protection. Overload protection, however, is based on the marked motor nameplate.

     ELECTRICAL — TRAINEE TASK MODULE 26309

3.2.0   CONDUCTORS FOR DC MOTORS

NEC Sections 430-22(a), Exception 1 and 430-29 cover the rules governing the sizing of conductors from a power source to a DC motor controller and from the controller to separate resistors for power accelerating and dynamic braking. ***NEC Section 430-29***, with its table of conductor ampacity percentages, assures proper application of DC constant-potential motor controls and power resistors. However, when selecting overload protection, the actual motor nameplate current rating must be used.

3.3.0   CONDUCTORS FOR MISCELLANEOUS MOTOR APPLICATIONS

NEC Section 430-6 should be referred to for torque motors, shaded-pole motors, permanent split capacitor motors, and AC adjustable-voltage motors.

NEC Section 430-6(b) specifically states that the motor's nameplate full-load current rating is used to size ground fault protection for a torque motor. However, both the branch circuit conductors and the overcurrent protection are sized by the provisions listed in ***NEC Section 430-52(b)***, and the full-load current ratings listed in ***NEC Tables 430-147 through 430-150*** are used instead of the motor's nameplate rating.

For sealed (hermetic) refrigeration compressor motors, the actual nameplate full-load running current of the motor must be used in determining the current rating of the disconnecting means, controller, branch circuit conductor, overcurrent protective devices, and motor overload protection.

4.0.0   MOTOR PROTECTIVE DEVICES

NEC Sections 430-51 through 430-58 require that the branch circuit protection for motor controls protect the circuit conductors, control apparatus, and the motor itself against overcurrent due to short circuits or ground faults.

Motors and motor circuits have unique operating characteristics and circuit components. Therefore, these circuits must be dealt with differently from other types of loads. Generally, two levels of overcurrent protection are required for motor branch circuits:

- *Overload protection* – Motor running overload protection is intended to protect the system components and motor from damaging overload currents.
- *Short circuit protection (includes ground fault protection)* – Short circuit protection is intended to protect the motor circuit components such as the conductors, switches, controllers, overload relays, motor, etc., against short circuit currents or grounds. This level of protection is commonly referred to as *motor branch circuit protection*. Dual-element fuses are designed to provide this protection, provided they are sized correctly.

There are a variety of ways to protect a motor circuit, depending upon the application. The ampere rating of a fuse selected for motor protection depends on whether the fuse is of the dual-element, time-delay type or the nontime-delay type.

In general, *NEC Table 430-152* specifies that short circuit/ground fault protection nontime-delay fuses can be sized at 300% of the motor full-load current for ordinary motors, while those for wound-rotor or direct current motors may be sized at 150% of the motor full-load current. The sizes of nontime-delay fuses for the four motors previously mentioned are listed in *Figure 13*. Because none of these sizes are standard, *NEC Section 430-52(c), Exception No. 1* permits the size of the fuses to be increased to a standard size. Also, where absolutely necessary to permit motor starting, the size of the overcurrent device may be further increased, but must never be more than 400% of the full-load current [*NEC Section 430-52(c), Exception No. 2*]. In actual practice, most electricians would use a 200A nontime-delay fuse for the 50hp motor, a 175A fuse for the 40hp motor, and 45A fuses for the 10hp motors. If any of these fuses do not allow the motor to start without blowing, the fuses for the 50hp motor may be increased to a maximum of 260A; the 40hp motor to 208A, and the 10hp motors to 56A. Standard sizes are 250A, 200A, and 50A, respectively.

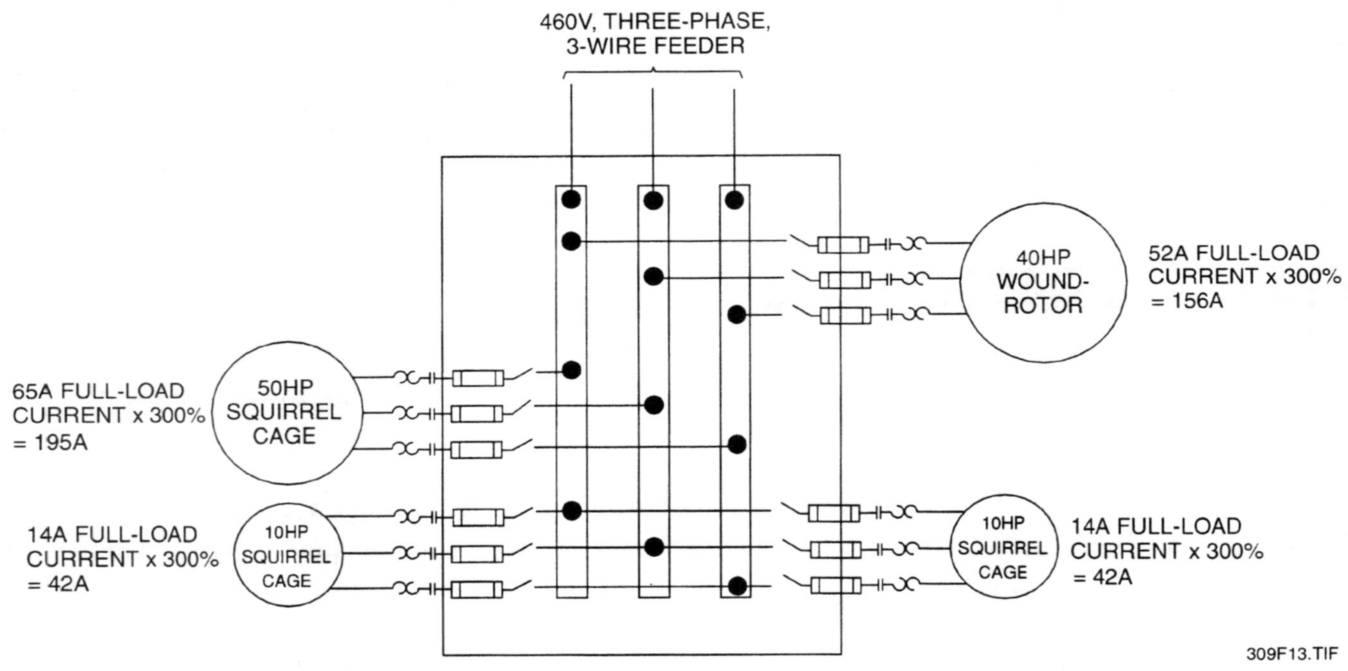

Figure 13. Ratings Of Nontime-Delay Fuses For Typical Motor Circuits

Per *NEC Table 430-152*, dual-element, time-delay fuses are able to withstand normal motor starting current and can be sized closer to the actual motor rating than nontime-delay fuses. If necessary for proper motor operation, dual-element, time-delay fuses may be sized up to 175% of the motor's full-load current for all standard motors with the exception of wound-rotor and direct current motors. These motors must not have fuses sized for more than 150% of the motor's full-load current rating. Where absolutely necessary for proper operation, the

ELECTRICAL — TRAINEE TASK MODULE 26309

rating of dual-element, time-delay fuses may be increased, but must never be more than 225% of the motor full-load current rating [**NEC Section 430-52(c), Exception No. 2**]. To size dual-element fuses at 175% for the four motors in *Figure 13*, proceed as follows:

50hp motor = 65A × 175% = 113.75A

40hp motor = 52A × 175% = 91A

10hp motors = 14A × 175% = 24.5A

Figure 14 gives general fuse application guidelines for motor branch circuits (**NEC Article 430, Part C**). Bear in mind that in many cases, the maximum fuse size depends on the motor design letter, motor type, and starting method.

Type of Motor	Dual-Element, Time-Delay Fuses			Nontime-Delay Fuses
	Desired Level of Protection			
	Motor Overload and Short Circuit	Backup Overload and Short Circuit	Short Circuit Only (Based on *NEC* Tables 430-147 through 430-150 current ratings)	Short Circuit Only (Based on *NEC* Tables 430-147 through 430-150 current ratings)
Service Factor 1.15 or Greater or 40°C Temp. Rise or Less	125% or less of motor nameplate current	125% or next standard size (not to exceed 140% of motor nameplate current)	150% to 175%	150% to 300%
Service Factor Less Than 1.15 or Greater Than 40°C Temp. Rise	115% or less of motor nameplate current	115% or next standard size (not to exceed 130% of motor nameplate current)	150% to 175%	150% to 300%

Fuses give overload and short circuit protection.

Overload relay gives overload protection and fuses provide backup overload protection.

Overload relay provides overload protection and fuses provide only short circuit protection.

Overload relay provides overload protection and fuses provide only short circuit protection.

309F14.EPS

Figure 14. Fuse Application Guidelines For Motor Branch Circuits

4.1.0 PRACTICAL APPLICATIONS

For various reasons, motors are often oversized. For instance, a 5hp motor may be installed when the load demand is only 3hp. In these cases, a much higher degree of overload protection can be obtained by sizing the overload relay elements and/or dual-element, time-delay fuses based on the actual full-load current draw. In existing installations, the procedure for providing the maximum overcurrent protection for oversized motors is as follows:

Step 1 With a clamp-on ammeter, determine the running rms current when the motor is at normal full-load, as shown in *Figure 15*. (Be sure this current does not exceed the nameplate current rating). The advantage of this method is realized when a lightly loaded motor (especially those over 50hp) experiences a single-phase condition. Even though the relays and fuses may be sized correctly based on the motor nameplate, circulating currents within the motor may cause damage. If unable to meter the motor current, take the current rating off the motor nameplate.

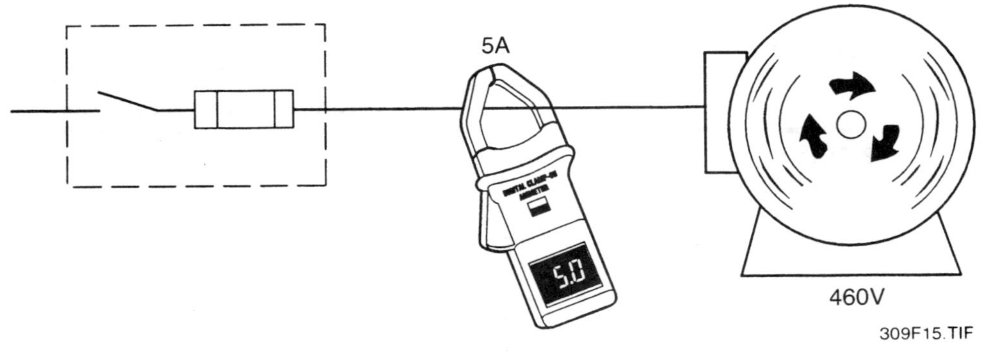

Figure 15. Determining Running Current With An Ammeter

Step 2 Size the overload relay elements and/or overcurrent protection based on this current. *Table 1* may be used to assist in sizing dual-element fuses.

Step 3 Use a labeling system to mark the type and ampere rating of the fuse that should be in the fuse clips. This simple system makes it easy to run spot checks for proper fuse replacements.

Note: When installing the proper fuses in the switch to give the desired level of protection, it is often advisable to leave spare fuses on top of the disconnect or starter enclosure, or in a cabinet adjacent to the motor control center. This way, if the fuses open, the proper fuses can be readily reinstalled.

Individual motor disconnect switches must have an ampere rating of at least 115% of the motor full-load ampere rating [**NEC Section 430-110(a)**] or as specified in **NEC Section 430-109**. The next larger size switches with fuse reducers may sometimes be required.

Dual-Element Fuse Size	Motor Protection (used without properly-sized overload relays). Motor Full-Load Amps		Backup Motor Protection (used with properly-sized overload relays). Motor Full-Load Amps	
	Motor Service Factor of 1.15 or Greater or With Temp. Rise Not Over 40° C.	Motor Service Factor Less Than 1.15 or With Temp. Rise Not Over 40° C.	Motor Service Factor of 1.15 or Greater or With Temp. Rise Not Over 40° C.	Motor Service Factor of Less Than 1.15 or With Temp. Rise Not Over 40° C.
$\frac{1}{10}$	0.08 - 0.09	0.09 - 0.10	0 - 0.08	0 - 0.09
$\frac{1}{8}$	0.10 - 0.11	0.11 - 0.125	0.09 - 0.10	0.10 - 0.11
$\frac{5}{100}$	0.12 - 0.15	0.14 - 0.15	0.11 - 0.12	0.12 - 0.13
$\frac{2}{10}$	0.16 - 0.19	0.18 - 0.20	0.13 - 0.16	0.14 - 0.17
$\frac{1}{4}$	0.20 - 0.23	0.22 - 0.25	0.17 - 0.20	0.18 - 0.22
$\frac{3}{10}$	0.24 - 0.30	0.27 - 0.30	0.21 - 0.24	0.23 - 0.26
$\frac{4}{10}$	0.32 - 0.39	0.35 - 0.40	0.25 - 0.32	0.27 - 0.35
$\frac{1}{2}$	0.40 - 0.47	0.44 - 0.50	0.33 - 0.40	0.36 - 0.43
$\frac{6}{10}$	0.48 - 0.60	0.53 - 0.60	0.41 - 0.48	0.44 - 0.52
$\frac{8}{10}$	0.64 - 0.79	0.70 - 0.80	0.49 - 0.64	0.53 - 0.70
1	0.80 - 0.89	0.87 - 0.97	0.65 - 0.80	0.71 - 0.87
$1\frac{1}{8}$	0.90 - 0.99	0.98 - 1.08	0.81 - 0.90	0.88 - 0.98
$1\frac{1}{4}$	1.00 - 1.11	1.09 - 1.21	0.91 - 1.00	0.99 - 1.09
$1\frac{4}{10}$	1.12 - 1.19	1.22 - 1.30	1.01 - 1.12	1.10 - 1.22
$1\frac{1}{2}$	1.20 - 1.27	1.31 - 1.39	1.13 - 1.20	1.23 - 1.30
$1\frac{6}{10}$	1.28 - 1.43	1.40 - 1.56	1.21 - 1.28	1.31 - 1.39
$1\frac{8}{10}$	1.44 - 1.59	1.57 - 1.73	1.29 - 1.44	1.40 - 1.57
2	1.60 - 1.79	1.74 - 1.95	1.45 - 1.60	1.58 - 1.74
$2\frac{1}{4}$	1.80 - 1.99	1.96 - 2.17	1.61 - 1.80	1.75 - 1.96
$2\frac{1}{2}$	2.00 - 2.23	2.18 - 2.43	1.81 - 2.00	1.97 - 2.17

309T01A.TIF

Table 1. Dual-Element Fuses For Motor Protection (1 Of 3)

Dual-Element Fuse Size	Motor Protection (used without properly-sized overload relays). Motor Full-Load Amps		Backup Motor Protection (used with properly-sized overload relays). Motor Full-Load Amps	
	Motor Service Factor of 1.15 or Greater or With Temp. Rise Not Over 40° C.	Motor Service Factor Less Than 1.15 or With Temp. Rise Not Over 40° C.	Motor Service Factor of 1.15 or Greater or With Temp. Rise Not Over 40° C.	Motor Service Factor of Less Than 1.15 or With Temp. Rise Not Over 40° C.
$2^{6}/_{10}$	2.24 - 2.39	2.44 - 2.60	2.01 - 2.24	2.18 - 2.43
3	2.40 - 2.55	2.61 - 2.78	2.25 - 2.40	2.44 - 2.60
$3^{2}/_{10}$	2.56 - 2.79	2.79 - 3.04	2.41 - 2.56	2.61 - 2.78
$3^{1}/_{2}$	2.80 - 3.19	3.05 - 3.47	2.57 - 2.80	2.79 - 3.04
4	3.20 - 3.59	3.48 - 3.91	2.81 - 3.20	3.05 - 3.48
$4^{1}/_{2}$	3.60 - 3.99	3.92 - 4.34	3.21 - 3.60	3.49 - 3.91
5	4.00 - 4.47	4.35 - 4.86	3.61 - 4.00	3.92 - 4.35
$5^{6}/_{10}$	4.48 - 4.79	4.87 - 5.21	4.01 - 4.48	4.36 - 4.87
6	4.80 - 4.99	5.22 - 5.43	4.49 - 4.80	4.88 - 5.22
$6^{1}/_{4}$	5.00 - 5.59	5.44 - 6.08	4.81 - 5.00	5.23 - 5.43
7	5.60 - 5.99	6.09 - 6.52	5.01 - 5.60	5.44 - 6.09
$7^{1}/_{2}$	6.00 - 6.39	6.53 - 6.95	5.61 - 6.00	6.10 - 6.52
8	6.40 - 7.19	6.96 - 7.82	6.01 - 6.40	6.53 - 6.96
9	7.20 - 7.99	7.83 - 8.69	6.41 - 7.20	6.97 - 7.83
10	8.00 - 9.59	8.70 - 10.00	7.21 - 8.00	7.84 - 8.70
12	9.60 - 11.99	10.44 - 12.00	8.01 - 9.60	8.71 - 10.43
15	12.00 - 13.99	13.05 - 15.00	9.61 - 12.00	10.44 - 13.04
$17^{1}/_{2}$	14.00 - 15.99	15.22 - 17.39	12.01 - 14.00	13.05 - 15.21
20	16.00 - 19.99	17.40 - 20.00	14.01 - 16.00	15.22 - 17.39
25	20.00 - 23.99	21.74 - 25.00	16.01 - 20.00	17.40 - 21.74
30	24.00 - 27.99	26.09 - 30.00	20.01 - 24.00	21.75 - 26.09
35	28.00 - 31.99	30.44 - 34.78	24.01 - 28.00	26.10 - 30.43

309T01B.TIF

Table 1. Dual-Element Fuses For Motor Protection (2 Of 3)

Dual-Element Fuse Size	Motor Protection (used without properly-sized overload relays). Motor Full-Load Amps		Backup Motor Protection (used with properly-sized overload relays). Motor Full-Load Amps	
	Motor Service Factor of 1.15 or Greater or With Temp. Rise Not Over 40° C.	Motor Service Factor Less Than 1.15 or With Temp. Rise Not Over 40° C.	Motor Service Factor of 1.15 or Greater or With Temp. Rise Not Over 40° C.	Motor Service Factor of Less Than 1.15 or With Temp. Rise Not Over 40° C.
40	32.00 - 35.99	34.79 - 39.12	28.01 - 32.00	30.44 - 37.78
45	36.00 - 39.99	39.13 - 43.47	32.01 - 36.00	37.79 - 39.13
50	40.00 - 47.99	43.48 - 50.00	36.01 - 40.00	39.14 - 43.48
60	48.00 - 55.99	52.17 - 60.00	40.01 - 48.00	43.49 - 52.17
70	56.00 - 59.99	60.87 - 65.21	48.01 - 56.00	52.18 - 60.87
75	60.00 - 63.99	65.22 - 69.56	56.01 - 60.00	60.88 - 65.22
80	64.00 - 71.99	69.57 - 78.25	60.01 - 64.00	65.23 - 69.57
90	72.00 - 79.99	78.26 - 86.95	64.01 - 72.00	69.58 - 78.26
100	80.00 - 87.99	86.96 - 95.64	72.01 - 80.00	78.27 - 86.96
110	88.00 - 99.99	95.65 - 108.69	80.01 - 88.00	86.97 - 95.65
125	100.00 - 119.99	108.70 - 125.00	88.01 - 100.00	95.66 - 108.70
150	120.00 - 139.99	131.30 - 150.00	100.01 - 120.00	108.71 - 130.43
175	140.00 - 159.99	152.17 - 173.90	120.01 - 140.00	130.44 - 152.17
200	160.00 - 179.99	173.91 - 195.64	140.01 - 160.00	152.18 - 173.91
225	180.00 - 199.99	195.65 - 217.38	160.01 - 180.00	173.92 - 195.62
250	200.00 - 239.99	217.39 - 250.00	180.01 - 200.00	195.63 - 217.39
300	240.00 - 279.99	260.87 - 300.00	200.01 - 240.00	217.40 - 260.87
350	280.00 - 319.99	304.35 - 347.82	240.01 - 280.00	260.88 - 304.35
400	320.00 - 359.99	347.83 - 391.29	280.01 - 320.00	304.36 - 347.83
450	360.00 - 399.99	391.30 - 434.77	320.01 - 360.00	347.84 - 391.30
500	400.00 - 479.99	434.78 - 500.00	360.01 - 400.00	391.31 - 434.78
600	480.00 - 600.00	521.74 - 600.00	400.01 - 480.00	434.79 - 521.74

309T01C.TIF

Table 1. Dual-Element Fuses For Motor Protection (3 Of 3)

Some installations may require dual-element fuses of a larger size than those shown in *Table 1*, providing only short circuit protection. This may occur when:

- The motor uses dual-element fuses in high ambient temperature environments.
- The motor is started frequently or rapidly reversed.
- The motor is directly connected to a machine that cannot be brought up to full speed quickly (e.g., centrifugal machines such as extractors and pulverizers, machines having large fly wheels such as large punch presses, etc.).
- The motor has a Design Letter E with full-voltage start.

4.2.0 MOTOR OVERLOAD PROTECTION

A high-quality electric motor that is properly cooled and protected against overloads can be expected to have a long life. The goal of proper motor protection is to prolong motor life and postpone the failure that ultimately takes place. Good electrical protection consists of providing both proper overload protection and current-limiting short circuit protection. AC motors and other types of high inrush loads require protective devices with special characteristics. Normal, full-load running currents of motors are substantially less than the currents that result when motors start or are subjected to temporary mechanical overloads. This is illustrated by the typical motor starting current curve shown in *Figure 16*.

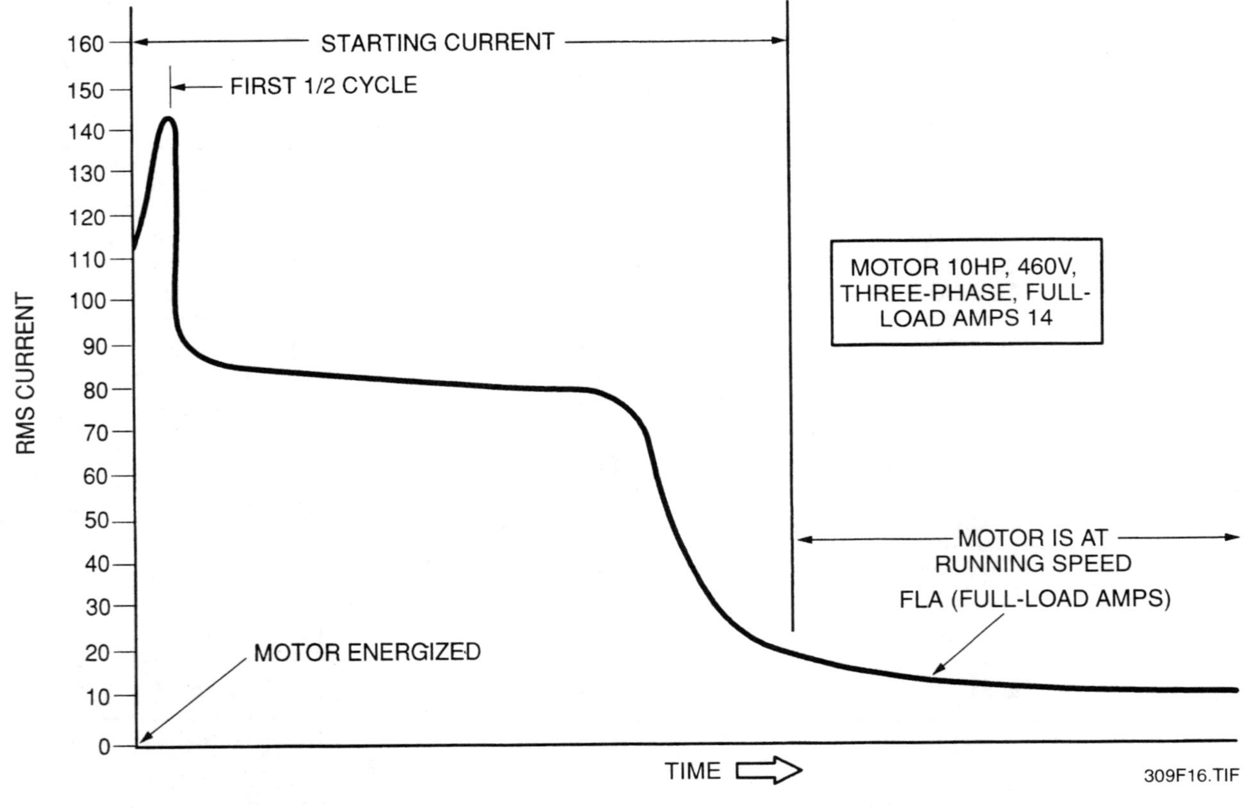

Figure 16. Motor Starting Current Characteristics

At the moment an AC motor circuit is energized, the starting current rapidly rises to many times the normal running current and the rotor begins to rotate. As the rotor accelerates and reaches running speed, the current declines to the normal running current. Thus, for a period of time, the overcurrent protective devices in the motor circuit must be able to tolerate the rather substantial temporary overload. Motor starting currents can vary substantially, depending on the motor type, load type, starting methods, and other factors. For the first half cycle, the momentary transient rms current may be 11 times the normal current, or even higher. After this first half cycle, the starting current subsides to 4 to 8 times (typically 6 times) the normal current and remains there for several seconds. This is called the *locked-rotor current*. When the motor reaches running speed, the current then subsides to its normal running level.

Motor overload protective devices must withstand the temporary overload caused by motor starting currents, and, at the same time, protect the motor from continuous or damaging overloads. The main types of devices used to provide motor overload protection include:

- Overload relays
- Fuses
- Circuit breakers

There are numerous causes of overloads, but if the overload protective devices are properly responsive, such overloads can be removed before damage occurs. To ensure this protection, the motor running protective devices should have time-current characteristics similar to motor damage curves but should be slightly faster. This is illustrated in *Figure 17*.

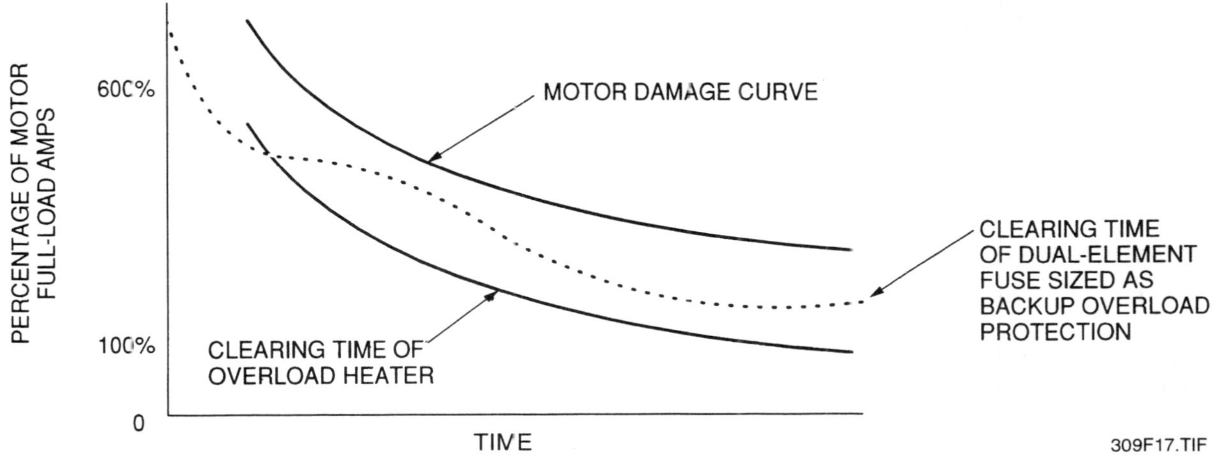

Figure 17. Time-Current Characteristics Of Dual-Element Fuses And Overload Heaters

Note: Heaters (thermal overload relays) are discussed later in this module.

For example, we will take a 10hp motor and determine the proper circuit components that should be employed (refer to *Figure 18*).

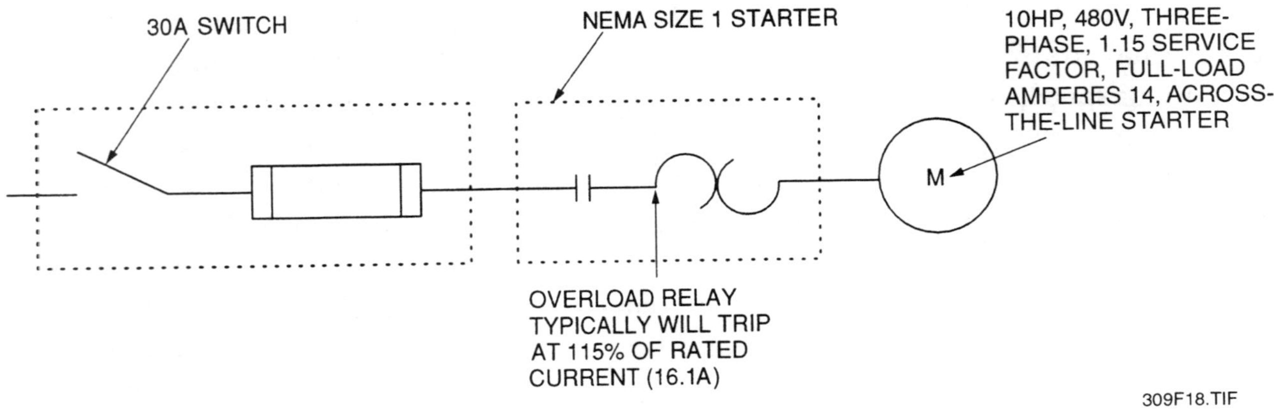

Figure 18. Circuit Components Of A Typical 10-Horsepower Motor

To begin, select the proper size overload relays. Typically, the overload relay is rated to trip at about 115% of the rated current (in this case, 1.15 × 14A = 16.1A). The correct starter size (using NEMA standards) is a NEMA Type 1. The switch size that should be used is 30A. Switch sizes are based on NEC requirements; dual-element, time-delay fuses allow the use of smaller switches.

For short circuit protection on large motors with currents in excess of 600A, low-peak time-delay fuses are recommended. Most motors of this size will have reduced voltage starters, and the inrush currents are not as rigorous. Low-peak fuses should be sized at approximately 150% to 175% of the motor full-load current.

Motor controllers with overload relays commonly used on motor circuits provide motor running overload protection. The overload relay setting or selection must comply with **NEC Section 430-32**. On overload conditions, the overload relays should operate to protect the motor. For motor backup protection, size dual-element fuses at the next ampere rating greater than the overload relay trip setting. This can typically be achieved by sizing dual-element fuses at 125% for 1.15 **service factor** motors and 115% for 1.0 service factor motors. The service factor is the number by which the horsepower rating is multiplied to determine the maximum safe load that a motor may be expected to carry continuously at its rated voltage and frequency.

5.0.0   CIRCUIT BREAKERS

The NEC recognizes the use of instantaneous trip circuit breakers (without time delay) for short circuit protection of motor branch circuits. Such breakers are acceptable only if they are adjustable and are used in combination motor starters. Such starters must have overload protection for each conductor and must be approved for the purpose. This permits the use of smaller circuit breakers than would be allowed if a standard thermal-magnetic circuit breaker was used. In this case, smaller circuit breakers offer faster operation for greater protection against grounds and short circuits. *Figure 19* shows a schematic diagram of magnetic-only circuit breakers used in a combination motor starter.

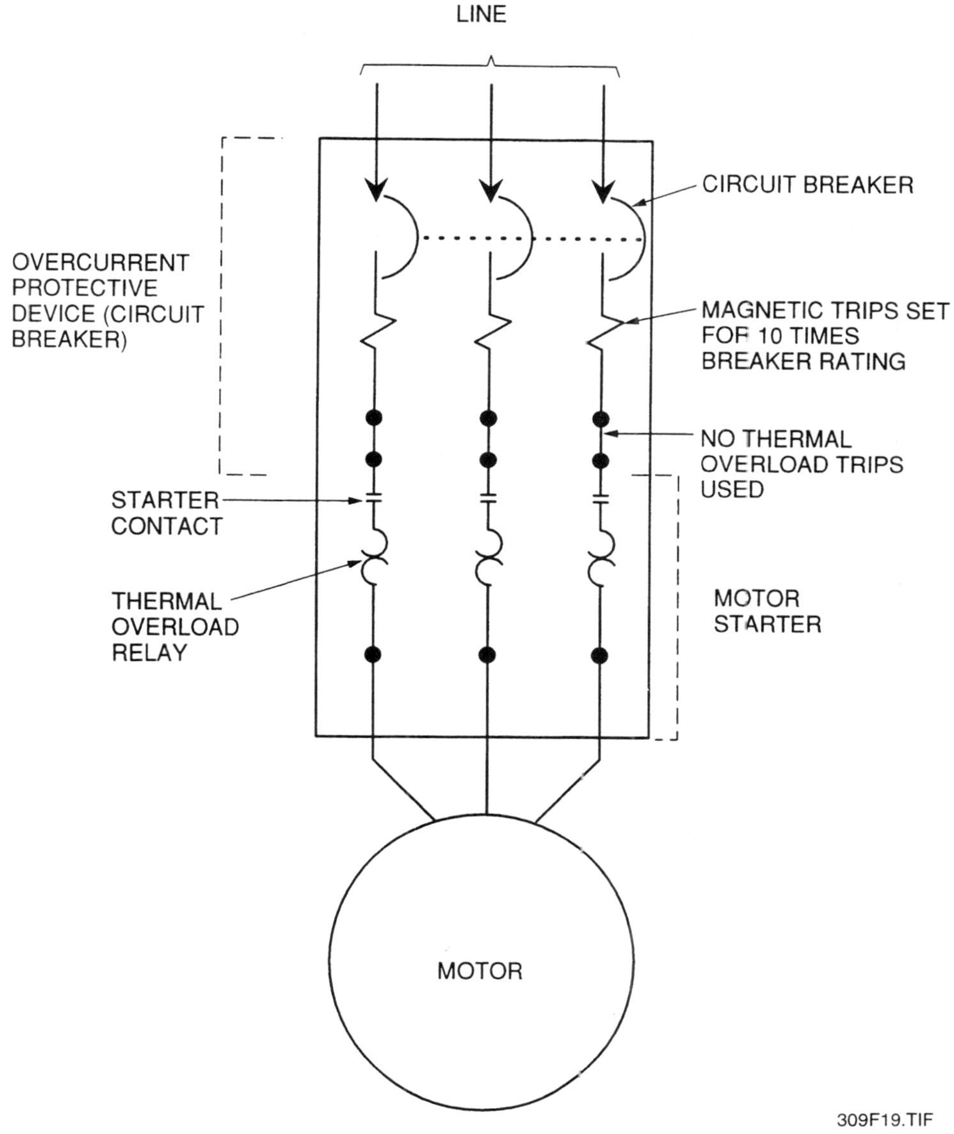

Figure 19. Combination Motor Starter With Magnetic-Only Circuit Breakers

The use of magnetic-only circuit breakers in motor branch circuits requires careful consideration due to the absence of overload protection up to the short circuit trip rating that is normally available in thermal elements in circuit breakers. However, heaters in the motor starter protect the entire circuit and all equipment against overloads up to and including locked-rotor current. Heaters (thermal overload relays) are commonly set at 115% to 125% of the motor full-load current.

In dealing with such circuits, an adjustable circuit breaker can be set to take over the interrupting task at currents above locked-rotor current and up to the short circuit duty of the supply system at the point of the installation. The magnetic trip in such breakers can typically be adjusted from 3 to 13 times the breaker current rating. For example, a 100A circuit breaker can be adjusted to trip anywhere between 300A and 1,300A. Consequently, the circuit breaker may serve as motor short circuit protection.

5.1.0 APPLICATION OF MAGNETIC-ONLY CIRCUIT BREAKERS

We will compare the use of both thermal-magnetic and magnetic-only circuit breakers in the motor circuit shown in *Figure 20*. In doing so, our job is to select a circuit breaker that will provide short circuit protection and also qualify as the motor circuit disconnecting means.

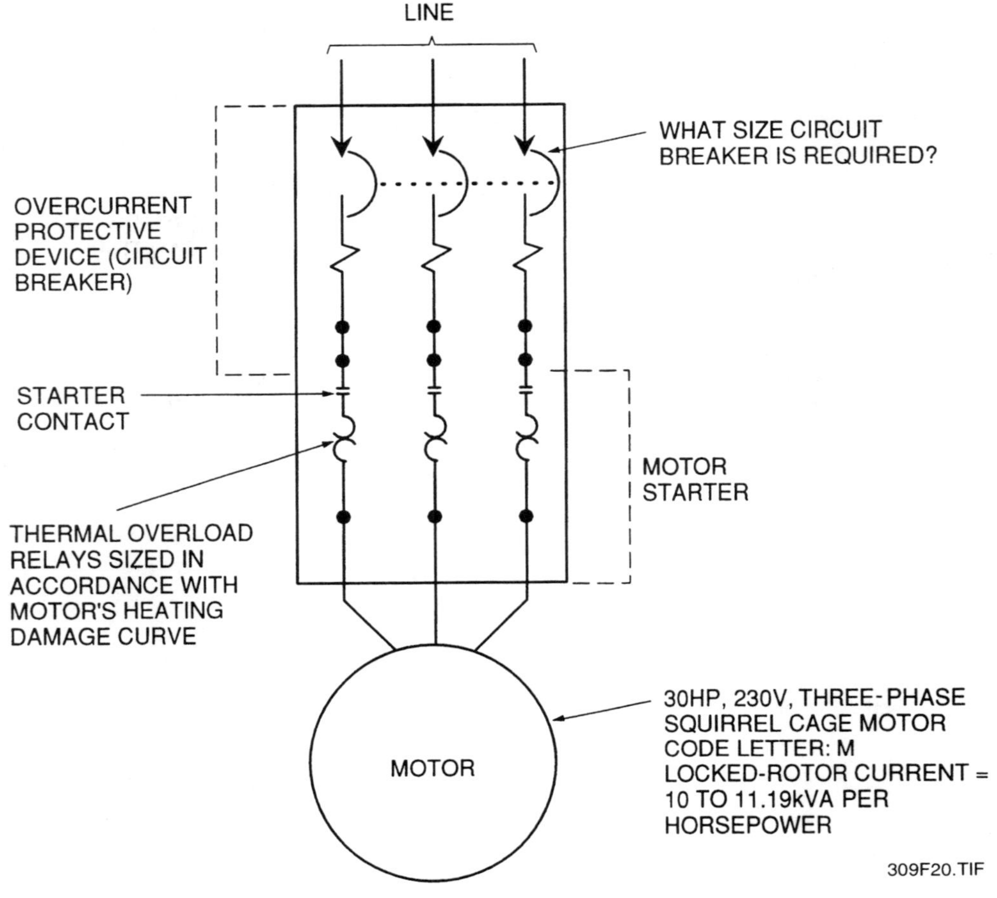

Figure 20. Typical 30-Horsepower Motor Circuit

Step 1   Determine the motor full-load current from *NEC Table 430-150*. This is found to be 80A.

Step 2   A circuit breaker suitable for use as a motor disconnecting means must have a current rating of at least 115% of the motor full-load current. Therefore:

$$1.15 \times 80A = 92A$$

Note: *NEC Table 430-152* permits the use of an inverse-time circuit breaker rated at not more than 250% of the motor full-load current. However, a circuit breaker could be rated as high as 400% of the motor full-load current if necessary to hold the motor starting current without opening.

Step 3 Assuming that a circuit breaker rated at 250% of the motor full-load current will be used, perform the following calculation:

$$2.5 \times 80A = 200A$$

Step 4 Select a regular thermal-magnetic circuit breaker with a 225A frame that is set to trip at 200A.

Step 5 Refer to *Figure 20* and note that this is a NEMA Design Letter E motor. Refer to **NEC Table 430-152** and note that an instantaneous breaker for a Design Letter E motor should be 1,100% of the motor full-load current.

Step 6 Determine the circuit breaker rating by multiplying the full-load current by 1,100%:

$$80A \times 1,100\% \ (11.00) = 880A$$

The thermal-magnetic circuit breaker selected in Step 4 will provide protection for grounds and short circuits without interfering with motor overload protection. Note, however, that the instantaneous trip setting of a 200A circuit breaker will be about 10 times the current rating, or:

$$200A \times 10 = 2,000A$$

Now consider the use of a 100A circuit breaker with thermal and adjustable magnetic trips. The instantaneous trip setting at 10 times the normal current rating would be:

$$100A \times 10 = 1,000A$$

Although this 1,000A instantaneous trip setting is above the 880A locked-rotor current of the 30hp motor in question, the starting current would probably trip the thermal element and open the circuit breaker.

This problem can be solved by removing the circuit breaker's thermal element and leaving only the magnetic element in the circuit breaker. Then the conditions of overload can be cleared by the overload devices (heaters) in the motor starter. If the setting of the instantaneous trip circuit breaker will not hold under the starting load in **NEC Section 430-52(c)(3)**, then **Exception No. 1** will, under engineering evaluation, permit increasing the trip setting up to, but not exceeding, 1,300% (1,700% for NEMA Design Letter E).

Therefore, since it has been determined that the 30hp motor in question has a full-load ampere rating of 80A, the maximum trip must not be set higher than:

$$80A \times 17 = 1,360A \text{ or about } 1,300A$$

This circuit breaker would qualify as the circuit disconnect because it has a rating higher than 115% of the motor full-load current ($80A \times 1.15 = 92A$). However, the use of a magnetic-only circuit breaker does not protect against low-level grounds and short circuits in the branch circuit conductors on the line side of the motor starter overload relays—such an application must be made only where the circuit breaker and motor starter are installed as a combination motor starter in a single enclosure.

5.2.0 MOTOR SHORT CIRCUIT PROTECTORS

Motor short circuit protectors (MSCPs) are fuse-like devices designed for use only in a special type of fusible-switch combination motor starter. The combination offers short circuit protection, overload protection, disconnecting means, and motor control, all with assured coordination between the short **circuit interrupter** and the overload devices.

The NEC recognizes MSCPs in *NEC Section 430-40 and 430-52*, provided the combination is identified for the purpose (i.e., a combination motor starter equipped with an MSCP and listed by Underwriters' Laboratories or another nationally recognized third-party testing lab as a package called an *MSCP starter*).

6.0.0 MULTI-MOTOR BRANCH CIRCUITS

NEC Sections 430-53(a) and (b) permit the use of more than one motor on a branch circuit, provided the following conditions are met:

- Two or more motors, each rated at not more than 1hp, and each drawing a full-load current not exceeding 6A, may be used on a branch circuit protected at not more than 20A at 125V or less, or 15A at 600V or less. The rating of the branch circuit protective device marked on any of the controllers must not be exceeded. Individual overload protection is necessary in such circuits unless the motor is not permanently installed, or is manually started and is within sight of the controller location, or has sufficient winding impedance to prevent overheating due to locked-rotor current, or is part of an approved assembly which does not subject the motor to overloads and which incorporates protection for the motor against locked-rotor current, or the motor cannot operate continuously under load.

- Two or more motors of any rating, each having individual overload protection, may be connected to a single branch circuit that is protected by a short circuit protective device (MSCP). The protective device must be selected in accordance with the maximum rating or setting that could protect an individual circuit to the motor of the smallest rating. This may be done only where it can be determined that the branch circuit device so selected will not open under the most severe normal conditions of service that might be encountered. This NEC section offers wide application of more than one motor on a single circuit, particularly in the use of small integral-horsepower motors installed on 208V, 240V, and 480V, three-phase industrial and commercial systems. Only such three-phase motors have full-load operating currents low enough to permit more than one motor on circuits fed from 15A protective devices.

Using these NEC rules, we will take a typical branch circuit (*Figure 21*) with more than one motor connected and see how the calculations are made.

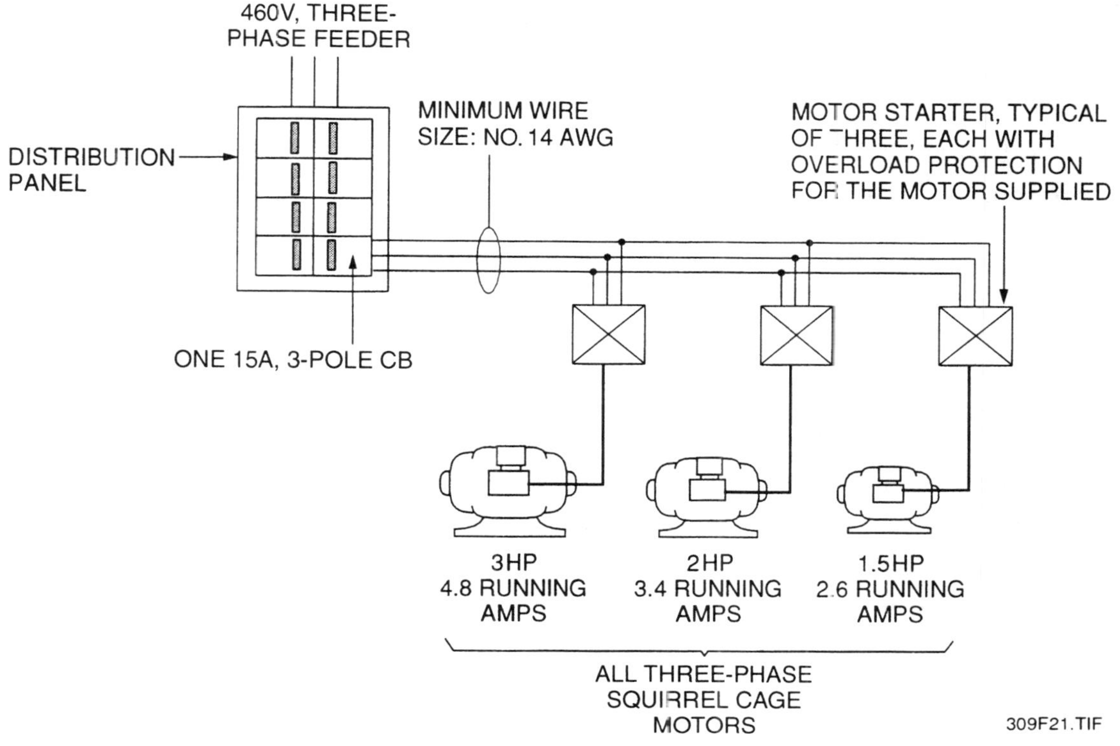

Figure 21. Several Motors On One Branch Circuit

The full-load current of each motor is taken from **NEC Table 430-150** as required by **NEC Section 430-6(a)**. A circuit breaker must be chosen that does not exceed the maximum value of short circuit protection (250%) required by **NEC Section 430-52** and **NEC Table 430-152** for the smallest motor in the group (in this case, 1.5hp). Since the listed full-load current for the smallest motor (1.5hp) is 2.6A, the calculation is made as follows:

2.6A × 2.5 (250%) = 6.5A

Note: **NEC Section 430-52, Exception No. 1** allows the next higher size rating or setting for a standard circuit breaker. Since a 15A circuit breaker is the smallest standard rating recognized by **NEC Section 240-6**, a 15A, three-pole circuit breaker may be used.

The total load of the motor currents must be calculated as follows:

4.8A + 3.4A + 2.6A = 10.8A

The total full-load current for the three motors (10.8A) is well within the 15A circuit breaker rating, which has a sufficient time delay in its operation to permit starting of any one of these motors with the other two already operating. The torque characteristics of the loads on starting are not high. Therefore, the circuit breaker will not open under the most severe normal service.

Make certain that each motor is provided with the properly rated individual overload protection in the motor starter.

Branch circuit conductors are sized in accordance with **NEC Section 430-24**. In this case:

$$4.8A + 3.4A + 2.6A + [25\% \text{ of the largest motor } (4.8A \times .25 = 1.2A)] = 12A$$

No. 14 AWG conductors rated at 75°C will fully satisfy this application.

Another multi-motor situation is shown in *Figure 22*. In this case, smaller motors are used. In general, **NEC Section 430-53(b)** requires branch circuit protection to be no greater than the maximum amperes permitted by **NEC Section 430-52** for the lowest rated motor of the group, which in this case is 1.1A for the ½hp motors. With this information in mind, we will size the circuit components for this application.

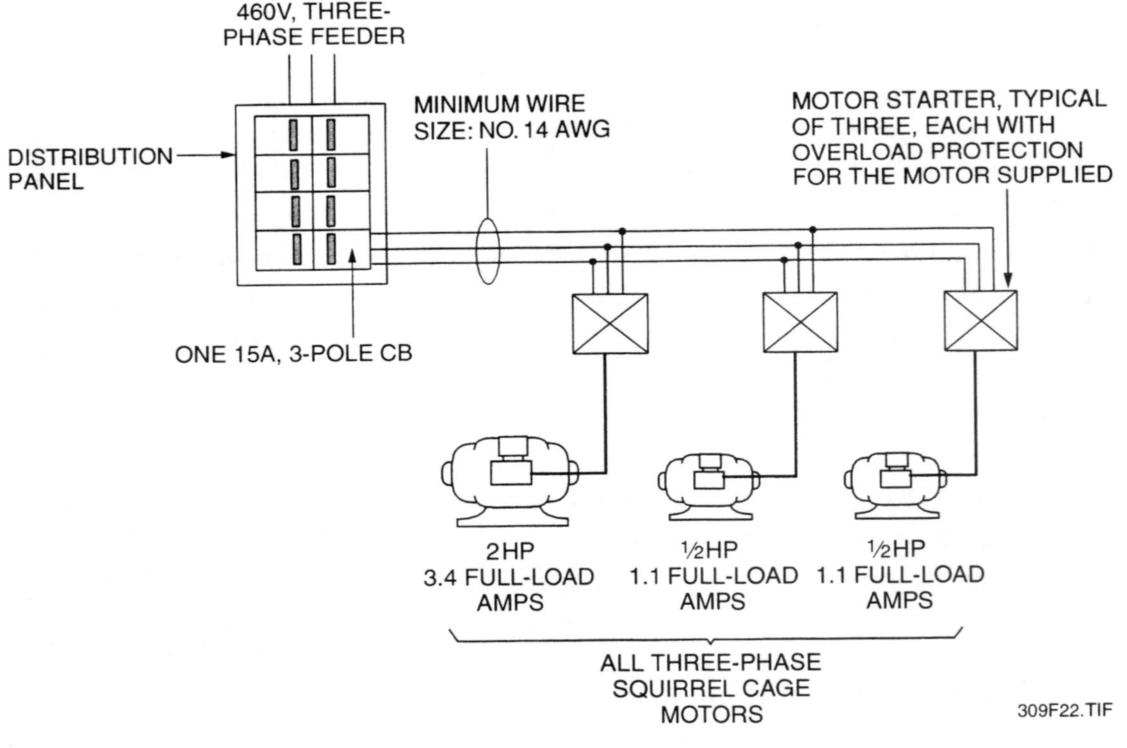

Figure 22. Several Smaller Motors Supplied By One Branch Circuit

From *NEC Section 430-52* and *NEC Table 430-152*, the maximum protection rating for a circuit breaker is 250% of the lowest rated motor. Since this rating is 1.1A, the calculation is performed as follows:

2.5 × 1.1A = 2.75A

Note: Since 2.75A is not a standard rating for a circuit breaker (*NEC Section 240-6*), *NEC Section 430-52(c)(1), Exception No. 1* permits the use of the next higher rating. Because 15A is the lowest standard rating of circuit breakers, it is the next higher device rating above 2.75A and satisfies NEC rules governing the rating of the branch circuit protection.

These two previous applications permit the use of several motors up to the circuit capacity, based on *NEC Sections 430-24 and 430-53(b)* and on starting torque characteristics, operating duty cycles of the motors and their loads, and the time delay of the circuit breaker. Such applications greatly reduce the number of circuit breakers and panels and the amount of wire used in the total system. One limitation, however, is placed on this practice in *NEC Section 430-52(c)(2)*, which specifies that where maximum branch circuit short circuit and ground fault protective device ratings are shown in the manufacturer's overload relay table for use with a motor controller or are otherwise marked on the equipment, they shall not be exceeded even if higher values are allowed, as shown in the preceding examples.

7.0.0   POWER FACTOR CORRECTION AT MOTOR TERMINALS

Generally, the most effective method of power factor correction is the installation of capacitors at the cause of the poor power factor—the induction motor. This not only increases the power factor, but also releases system capacity, improves voltage stability, and reduces power losses.

When power factor correction capacitors are used, the total corrective kVAR on the load side of the motor controller should not exceed the value required to raise the no-load power factor to unity. Corrective kVAR in excess of this value may cause over-excitation that results in high transient voltages, currents, and torques that can increase safety hazards to personnel and possibly damage the motor or driven equipment.

Do not connect power factor correction capacitors at motor **terminals** on elevator motors; multi-speed motors; plugging or jogging applications; or open transition, wye-delta, autotransformer starting, and some part-winding start motors.

If possible, capacitors should be located at position No. 2, as shown in *Figure 23*. This does not change the current flowing through the motor overload protectors.

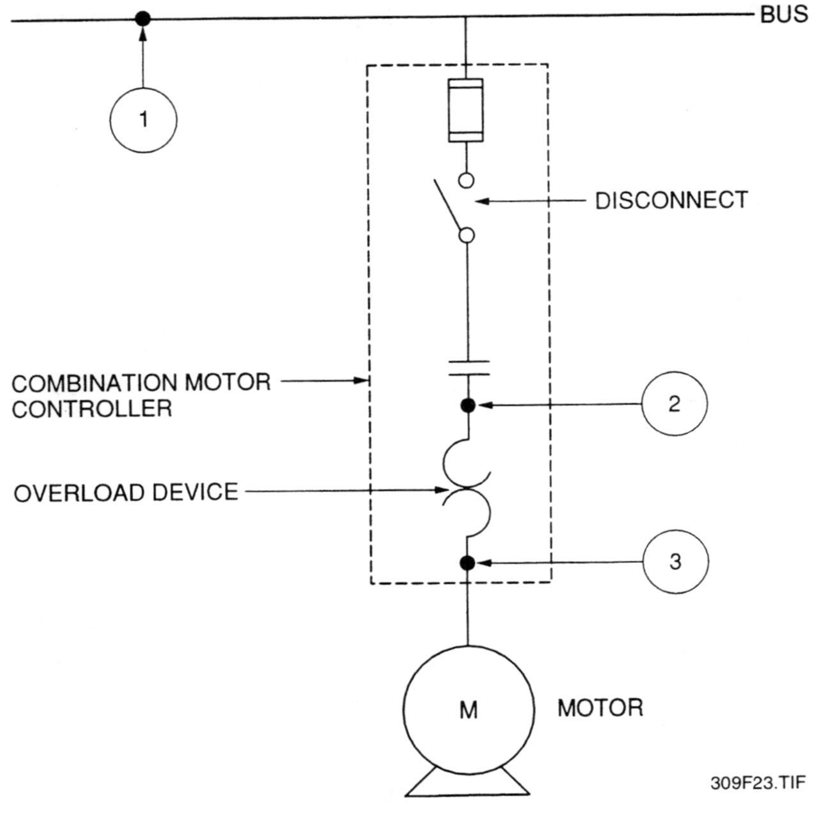

Figure 23. Placement Of Capacitors In Motor Circuits

The connection of capacitors at position No. 3 requires a change of overload protectors. Capacitors should be located at position No. 1 for any of the following applications:

- Elevator motors
- Multi-speed motors
- Plugging or jogging applications
- Open transition, wye-delta, autotransformer starting motors
- Some part-winding motors

Note: To avoid over-excitation, make sure that the bus power factor is not increased above 95% under all loading conditions.

Table 2 allows the determination of corrective kVAR required where capacitors are individually connected at motor leads. These values should be considered the maximum capacitor rating when the motor and capacitor are switched as a unit. The figures given are for three-phase, 60Hz, NEMA Class B motors to raise the full-load power factor to 95%.

Nominal Motor Speed in RPM

Induction Motor Horsepower Rating	3600		1800		1200		900		720		600	
	Capacitor Rating kVAR	Line Current Reduction %	Capacitor Rating kVAR	Line Current Reduction %	Capacitor Rating kVAR	Line Current Reduction %	Capacitor Rating kVAR	Line Current Reduction %	Capacitor Rating kVAR	Line Current Reduction %	Capacitor Rating kVAR	Line Current Reduction %
3	1.5	14	1.5	15	1.5	20	2	27	2.5	35	3.5	41
5	2	12	2	13	2	17	3	25	4	32	4.5	37
7½	2.5	11	2.5	12	3	15	4	22	5.5	30	6	34
10	3	10	3	11	3.5	14	5	21	6.5	27	7.5	31
15	4	9	4	10	5	13	6.5	18	8	23	9.5	27
20	5	9	5	10	6.5	12	7.5	16	9	21	12	25
25	6	9	6	10	7.5	11	9	15	11	20	14	23
30	7	8	7	9	9	11	10	14	12	18	16	22
40	9	8	9	9	11	10	12	13	15	16	20	20
50	12	8	11	9	13	10	15	12	19	15	24	19
60	14	8	14	8	15	10	18	11	22	15	27	19
75	17	8	16	8	18	10	21	10	26	14	32.5	18
100	22	8	21	8	25	9	27	10	32.5	13	40	17
125	27	8	26	8	30	9	32.5	10	40	13	47.5	16
150	32.5	8	30	8	35	9	37.5	10	47.5	12	52.5	15
200	40	8	37.5	8	42.5	9	47.5	10	60	12	65	14
250	50	8	45	7	52.5	8	57.5	9	70	11	77.5	13

309T02.TIF

Table 2. Motor Power Factor Correction Table

SUMMARY

The NEC plays an important role in the selection and application of motors, including branch circuit conductors, disconnects, controllers, overcurrent protection, and overload protection. For example, *NEC Article 430* covers the application and installation of motor circuits and motor control connections, including conductors, short circuit and ground fault protection, controllers, disconnects, and overload protection.

NEC Article 440 contains provisions for motor-driven air conditioning and refrigerating equipment, including the branch circuits and controllers for the equipment. It also takes into account the special considerations involved with sealed (hermetic) motor compressors, in which the motor operates under the cooling effect of the refrigeration. When referring to *NEC Article 440*, be aware that the rules in this article are in addition to, or are amendments to, the rules given in *NEC Article 430*.

References

For advanced study of topics covered in this Task Module, the following books are suggested:

American Electricians' Handbook, Latest Edition, McGraw-Hill, New York, NY.

National Electrical Code Handbook, Latest Edition, National Fire Protection Association, Quincy, MA.

REVIEW/PRACTICE QUESTIONS

1. A squirrel cage motor rotor is best described as ______.

    a. a structure of copper or aluminum wire coils
    b. insulating fibers mounted on a shaft
    c. copper bars mounted on a spindle
    d. steel laminations mounted on a shaft

2. Stator windings can best be described as ______.

    a. a structure of copper or aluminum wire coils
    b. insulating fibers mounted on a shaft
    c. copper bars mounted on a spindle
    d. steel wires mounted on a shaft

3. What is the speed of a 60Hz, three-phase induction motor with two poles?

    a. 3,600 rpm
    b. 1,800 rpm
    c. 1,200 rpm
    d. 900 rpm

4. The two most common three-phase motor configurations are ______.

    a. synchronous and rms
    b. box and star
    c. wye and delta
    d. star and wye

5. What is the most common number of motor leads found on a three-phase, wye-wound motor?

    a. 3
    b. 6
    c. 9
    d. 12

6. What is the total impedance of the stator windings in a three-phase motor if the windings are connected in parallel and the impedance of each winding is 96Ω?

    a. 48Ω
    b. 96Ω
    c. 192Ω
    d. 220Ω

7. If a squirrel cage induction motor draws 2A of current at 240V, what will the amperage be if connected for use on 120V?

    a.   1A
    b.   2A
    c.   3A
    d.   4A

8. Which of the following motors is most likely to have 15 to 18 motor leads?

    a.   Single-phase capacitor-start motor
    b.   120V shaded-pole motor
    c.   480V three-phase squirrel cage motor
    d.   2,100V three-phase motor

9. The main purpose of motor overload protection is to protect the motor ______.

    a.   against short circuits
    b.   against ground faults
    c.   from damaging overload currents
    d.   against locked-rotor current

10. A circuit breaker suitable for use as a motor disconnecting means must have a current rating of at least ______% of the motor full-load current.

    a.   250
    b.   175
    c.   300
    d.   115

ANSWERS TO REVIEW/PRACTICE QUESTIONS

<u>Answer</u>	<u>Section Reference</u>
1. d	2.0.0
2. a	2.0.0
3. a	2.1.0
4. c	2.2.0
5. c	2.2.0
6. a	2.2.1
7. d	2.2.1
8. d	2.3.0
9. c	4.0.0
10. d	5.1.0

The NCCER makes every effort to keep these manuals up-to-date and free of technical errors. We appreciate your help in this process. If you have an idea for improving this manual, or if you find an error, a typographical mistake, or an inaccuracy in the NCCER's Craft Training Manuals, please write us, using this form or a photocopy. Be sure to include the exact module number, page number, a description of the problem, and the correction, if possible. Your input will be brought to the attention of the Technical Review Committee. Thank you for your assistance.

Instructors – If you found that additional materials were necessary in order to teach this module effectively, please let us know so that we may include them in the Equipment/Materials list in the Instructor's Guide.

Write: Curriculum Development and Revision Department
National Center for Construction Education and Research
P.O. Box 141104
Gainesville, FL 32614-1104
Fax: 352-334-0932

Craft ________________________ Module Name ________________________

Copyright Date ________ Module Number ________ Page Number(s) ________

Description of Problem

____

____

____

____

(Optional) Correction of Problem

____

____

____

(Optional) Your Name and Address

____

____

____

Motor Maintenance, Part 1

Module 26310

MOTOR MAINTENANCE, PART 1

NATIONAL
CENTER FOR
CONSTRUCTION
EDUCATION AND
RESEARCH

OBJECTIVES

Upon completion of this module, the trainee will be able to:

1. Properly store motors and generators.
2. Test motors and generators.
3. Make connections for specific types of motors and generators.
4. Clean open-frame motors.
5. Lubricate motors that require this type of maintenance.
6. Collect and record motor data.
7. Select tools for motor maintenance.
8. Select instruments for motor testing.

Prerequisites

Successful completion of the following Task Modules is recommended before beginning study of this Task Module: Core Curricula; Electrical Level 1; Electrical Level 2; Electrical Level 3, Modules 26301 through 26308.

Required Trainee Materials

1. Trainee Task Module
2. Appropriate Personal Protective Equipment
3. Copy of the latest edition of the *National Electrical Code*

Note: The designations "National Electrical Code," "NE Code," and "NEC," where used in this document, refer to the National Electrical Code®, which is a registered trademark of the National Fire Protection Association, Quincy, MA. *All National Electrical Code (NEC) references in this module refer to the 1999 edition of the NEC.*

This course map shows all of the modules in the third level of the Electrical curricula. The suggested training order begins at the bottom and proceeds up. Skill levels increase as a trainee advances on the course map. The training order may be adjusted by the local Training Program Sponsor.

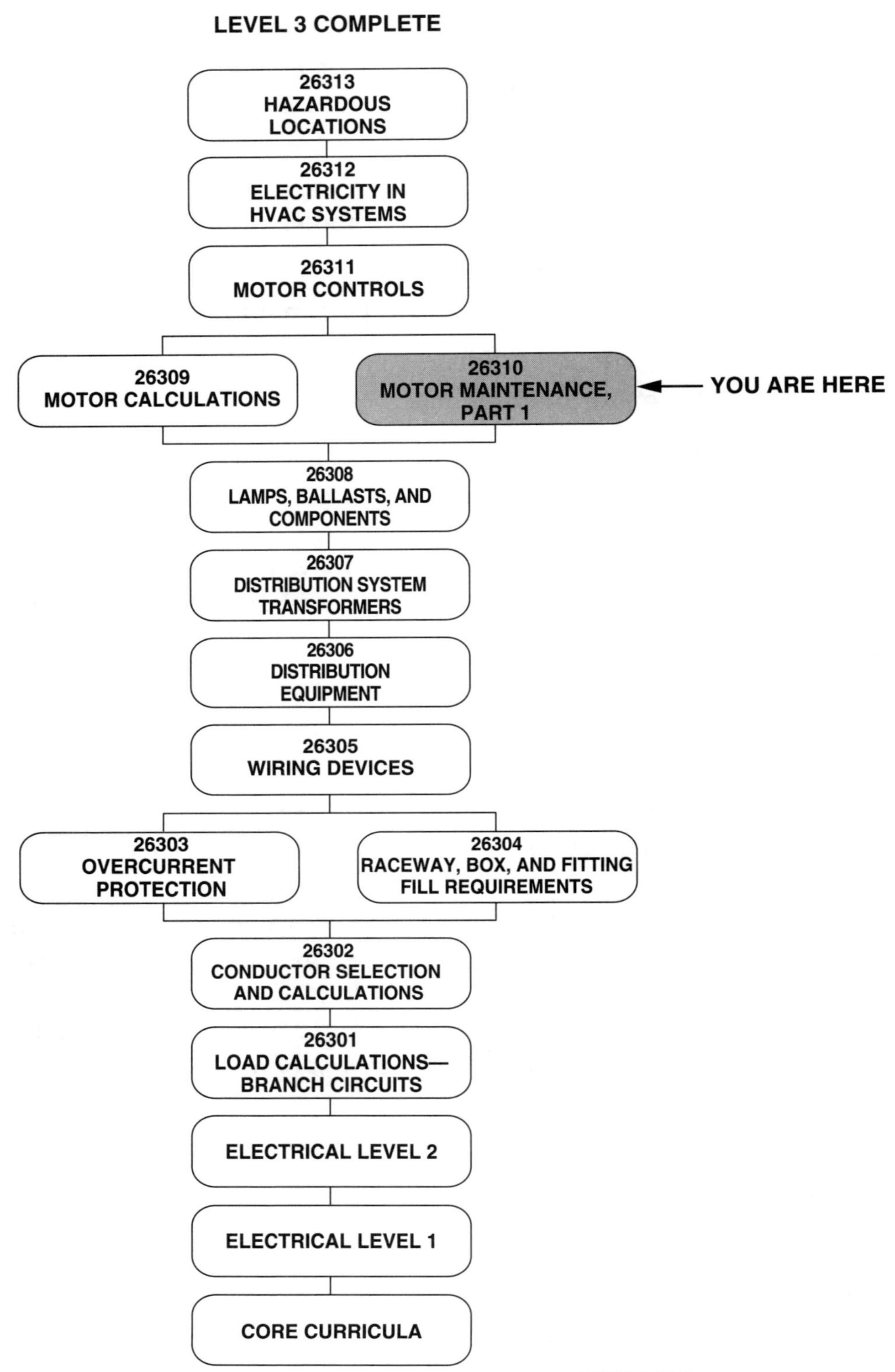

TABLE OF CONTENTS

Trade Terms Introduced In This Module

Armature: 1. Rotating machine: the member in which alternating voltage is generated. 2. Electromagnetic: the member that is moved by magnetic force.

Brush: A conductor between the stationary and rotating parts of a machine; usually made of carbon.

Brush holders: Adjustable arms for holding the commutator brushes of a generator against the commutator, feeding them forward to maintain proper contact as they wear, and permitting them to be lifted from the contact when necessary.

Commutator: A device used on electric motors or generators to maintain a unidirectional current.

Commutator pole: An electromagnetic bar inserted between the pole pieces of a generator to offset the cross-magnetization of the armature currents.

Generator: 1. A rotating machine that is used to convert mechanical energy to electrical energy. 2. General apparatus, equipment, etc., that is used to convert or change energy from one form to another.

Slip rings: The means by which the current is conducted to a revolving electrical circuit.

Starting winding: A winding in an electric motor used only during the brief period when the motor is starting.

1.0.0 INTRODUCTION

AC motor failure accounts for a high percentage of electrical repair work. The care given to an electric motor while it is being stored and operated affects the life and usefulness of the motor. A motor that receives good maintenance will outlast a poorly treated motor many times over. Actually, if a motor is initially installed correctly and has been properly selected for the job, very little maintenance is necessary—provided it does receive a little care at regular intervals. The basic care consists of:

- Cleaning
- Lubrication

Cleaning – The frequency for cleaning an AC motor depends on the type of environment in which it is used. In general, keep both the interior and exterior of the motor free from dirt, water, oil, and grease. Motors operating in dirty areas should be periodically disassembled and thoroughly cleaned.

ELECTRICAL — TRAINEE TASK MODULE 26310

If the motor is totally enclosed (fan-cooled or nonventilated), such as the one shown in *Figure 1*, and is equipped with automatic drain plugs, they should be free of oil, grease, paint, grit, and dirt so they do not clog up.

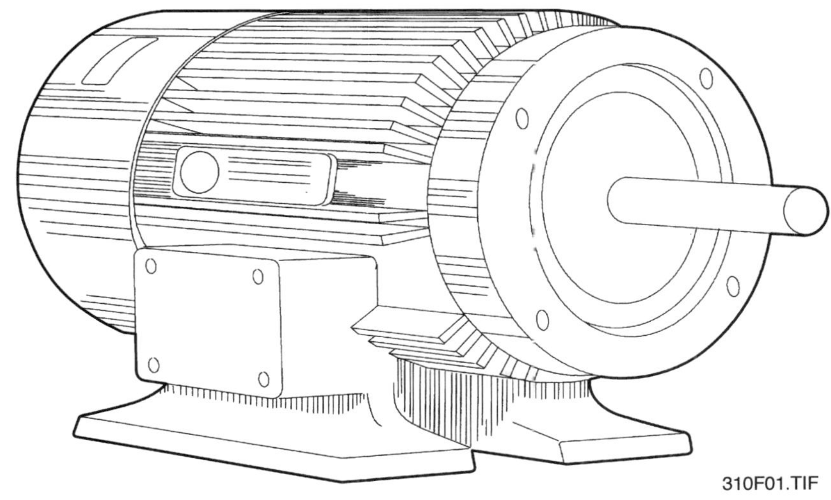

Figure 1. Totally Enclosed, Fan-Cooled Motor

Lubrication – Most motors are properly lubricated at the time of manufacture, and it is not necessary to lubricate them at the time of installation. However, if a motor has been in storage for a period of six months or longer, it should be relubricated before starting.

To lubricate conventional motors:

Step 1   Stop the motor.

Step 2   Wipe clean all grease fittings (filler and drain).

Step 3   Remove the filler and drain plugs (A and B in *Figure 2*).

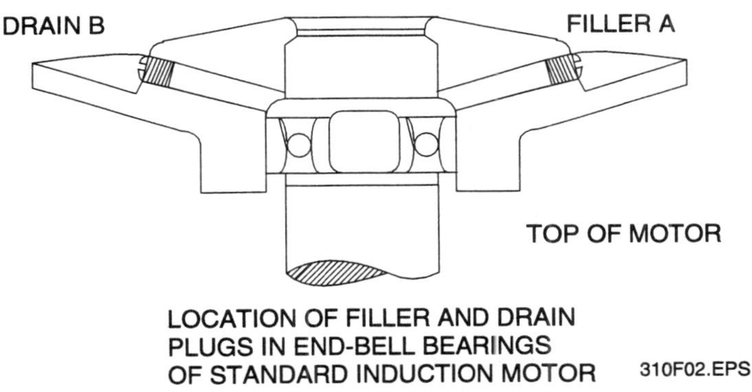

Figure 2. Location Of Motor Filler And Drain Plugs

Step 4   Free the drain hole of any hard grease (use a piece of wire if necessary).

Step 5   Add grease using a low-pressure grease gun.

Step 6   Start the motor and let it run for approximately 30 minutes.

Step 7   Stop the motor, wipe off any drained grease, and replace the filler and drain plugs.

Step 8   The motor is now ready for operation.

Every four years (every year in the case of severe duty), motors with open bearings should be thoroughly cleaned, washed, and repacked with grease. *Table 1* shows the relubrication periods for various motors. Standard conditions mean operation of 8 hrs./day, normal or light loading, and at 100°F maximum ambient. Severe conditions represent operation of 24 hrs./day, shock loadings, vibration, dirty or dusty areas, or areas at 100°F to 150°F ambient temperature. Extreme conditions are defined as heavy shock or vibration, large amounts of dirt or dust, or high ambient temperatures (above 150°F).

Frame Size	Relubrication Period		
900 rpm, 1,200 rpm, and Variable Speed	**Standard Conditions**	**Severe Conditions**	**Extreme Conditions**
140 – 180	4.5 years	18 months	9 months
210 – 280	4.0 years	16 months	8 months
320 – 400	3.5 years	14 months	7 months
440 – 508	3.0 years	12 months	6 months
510	2.5 years	11.5 months	6 months
1,800 rpm	**Standard Conditions**	**Severe Conditions**	**Extreme Conditions**
140 – 180	3.0 years	1 year	6 months
210 – 280	2.5 years	10.5 months	5.5 months
320 – 400	2.0 years	9 months	4.5 months
440 – 508	1.5 years	8 months	4 months
510	1 year	6 months	3.5 months
Over 1,800 rpm	6 months	3 months	3 months

Table 1. Relubrication Periods For Various Sizes And Types Of Motors

Bearings provide minimum resistance and align the motor rotor during operation. Therefore, the quantity of grease is important to correct bearing operation. The grease cavity should be filled one third to one half full. Always remember that too much grease is as detrimental as insufficient grease. *Table 2* shows the amount of grease required and *Table 3* give the recommended grease for a Class B or F motor. However, always check with the motor manufacturers for their recommendations and specifications for greasing motors.

Bearing Number	Amount in Cubic Inches	Approximate Equivalent Teaspoons
203	.15	.5
205	.27	.9
206	.34	1.1
207	.43	1.4
208	.52	1.7
209	.61	2.0
210	.72	2.4
212	.95	3.1
213	1.07	3.6
216	1.49	4.9
219	2.8	7.2
222	3.0	10.0
307	.53	1.8
308	.66	2.2
309	.81	2.7
310	.97	3.2
311	1.14	3.8
312	1.33	4.4
313	1.54	5.1
314	1.76	5.9
316	2.24	7.4
318	2.78	9.2

Table 2. Typical Amount Of Grease Required When Regreasing Electric Motors

Insulation Class Shown on Nameplate	Grease Designation	Grease Supplier
B or F	Chevron SRI-2	Standard Oil of California or Equivalent

Table 3. Recommended Grease For Motor Lubrication

WARNING!	The amount of grease added to motor bearings is very important. Only enough grease should be added to replace the grease used by the bearings. Too much grease can be as harmful as insufficient grease.

2.0.0 PRACTICAL MAINTENANCE TECHNIQUES

Once the motor has been sized and installed properly, the key to long, trouble-free motor life is proper maintenance. Maintaining a motor in good operating condition requires periodic inspection to determine if any faults exist, and then promptly correcting these faults. The frequency and thoroughness of these inspections depend on such factors as:

- Number of hours and days the motor operates
- Importance of the motor in the production scheme
- Nature of service
- Environmental conditions

Each week, every motor in operation should be inspected to see if the windings are exposed to any dripping water, acid, or alcohol fumes as well as excessive dust, chips, or lint on or about the motor. Make certain that objects that will cause problems with the motor's ventilation system are not placed too near the motor and do not come into direct contact with the motor's moving parts.

In sleeve-bearing motors, check the oil level frequently (at least once a week) and fill the oil cups to the specified line with the recommended lubricant. If the journal diameter is less than 2", always stop the motor before checking the oil level. For special lubricating systems such as forced, flood-and-disc, and wool-packed lubrication, follow the manufacturer's recommendations. Oil should be added to the bearing housing only when the motor is stopped, and then a check should be made to ensure that no oil creeps along the shaft toward the windings where it may harm the insulation.

Always be alert to any unusual noise which may be caused by metal-to-metal contact (bad bearings, etc.), and also learn to detect any abnormal odor which might indicate scorching insulation varnish.

Feel the bearing housing each week for evidence of excess heat and vibration. Listen for any unusual noise. A standard screwdriver with the blade on the bearing housing and the handle clasped with the hand while the ear is positioned so as to rest on the cupped hand will magnify the noise. Also inspect the bearing housing for the possibility of creeping grease on the inside of the motor which might harm the insulation.

Commutators and **brushes** should be checked for sparking and should be observed through several cycles if the motor is on cycle duty. A stable copper oxide carbon film—as distinguished from a pure copper surface—on the commutator is an essential requirement for good commutation. Such a film, however, may vary in color from copper to straw or from chocolate brown to black. The commutator should be clean and smooth and have a high polish. All brushes should be checked for wear and connections should be checked for looseness. The commutator surface may be cleaned by using a piece of dry canvas or other hard, nonlimiting material which is wound around and securely fastened to a wooden stick and held against the rotating commutator.

The air gap on sleeve-bearing motors should be checked frequently, especially if the motor has recently been rewound or otherwise repaired. After new bearings have been installed, for example, make sure that the average reading is within 10%, provided the reading should be less than .020". Check the air passages through punchings and make sure they are free of all foreign matter.

Compressed air may be used to blow motor windings clean, provided too much pressure is not used. Industrial-type vacuum cleaners have also been used with success. However, before performing either of these cleaning operations, make certain that the motor is disconnected from the line. Then the windings may be wiped off with a dry cloth. In doing so, check for moisture, and see if any water has accumulated in the bottom of the motor frame. Check also to see if any oil or grease has worked its way up to the rotor or **armature** windings. If so, clean with AWA 1,1,1 or a similar cleaning solution.

CAUTION: When using compressed air, exercise caution, wear Appropriate Personal Protective Equipment, and be sure to use a limited airflow tip or pulse nozzle. Excess pressure can cause damage to the windings.

When performing any of the preceding maintenance operations, always disconnect the power and lockout/tagout. Check other motor parts and accessories such as the belt, gears, flexible couplings, chain, and sprockets for excessive wear or improper location. Also check the starter and check that the motor comes up to proper speed each time it is started.

Once every month or so, check the shunt, series, and commutating field windings for tightness. Do this by trying to move the field spools on the poles, as drying out may have caused some play. If this condition exists, the motor should be serviced immediately. Also check the motor cable connections for looseness and tighten if necessary.

At the same time the preceding checks are made, check the brushes in their holders for fit and free play. The brush spring pressure should also be checked. Tighten the brush studs in the holders to take up slack from the drying out of washers, making sure that studs are not displaced, particularly on DC motors. All worn or damaged brushes should be replaced at this time. Look for chipped toes or heels and for heat cracks during the inspection.

Each month, examine the commutator surface for high bars and high mica or evidence of scratches or roughness. See that the risers are clean and have not been damaged in any way.

Where motors are subjected to hard use, all ball or roller bearing motors should be serviced by purging out the old grease through the drain hole and applying new grease once each month or more frequently if circumstances dictate. After each grease change, check to make sure grease or oil is not leaking out of the bearing housing. If so, correct this condition before starting the motor, or the insulation may be damaged.

Check the sleeve bearings for wear about six to eight times each year. Clean out the oil wells if there is evidence of dirt or sludge. Flush with lighter oil before refilling.

For motors with enclosed gears, open the drain plug and check the oil flow for the presence of metal scale, sand, grit, or water. If the condition of the oil is poor, drain, flush, and refill as recommended by the manufacturer of the motor. Rock the rotor to see if slack or backlash is increasing.

Loads being driven by motors have a tendency to change from time to time due to wear on the machine or the product being processed through the machine. Therefore, all loads should be checked from time to time for a changed condition, bad adjustment, and poor handling or control.

During the monthly inspection, note if belt-tightening adjustments are all used up. If they are, the belts may be shortened. Also see if the belts run steadily and close to the inside edge of the pulley. On chain-driven machines, check the chain for evidence of wear and stretch, and clean the chain thoroughly. Check the chain lubricating system and note the incline of the slanting base to make sure it does not cause oil rings to rub on the housing.

Once or twice each year, all motors in operation should be given a thorough inspection consisting of the following:

- *Windings* – Check the insulation resistance by using the instruments and techniques described later in this module. The windings should also be given a visual inspection; look for dry cracks and other evidence of a need for coating insulating material. Clean all surfaces thoroughly, especially ventilating passages. Also examine the frame to see if any mold is present or if water is standing in the bottom. Either will suggest dampness and may require that the windings be dried out, varnished, and baked.

- *Air gap and bearings* – Check the air gap to make sure that average readings are within 10% provided the readings should be less than .020". All bearings (ball, roller, and sleeve) should be thoroughly checked and defective ones replaced. Waste-packed and wick-oiled bearings should have waste or wicks renewed if they have become glazed or filled with metal, grit, or dirt, making sure that the new material bears well against the shaft.

- *Squirrel cage rotors* – Check for broken parts or loose bars as well as evidence of local heating. If the fan blades are not cast in place, check for loose blades. Also look for marks on the rotor surface which may indicate the presence of foreign matter in the air gap or a worn bearing or bearings.

- *Wound rotors* – Wound rotors should be cleaned thoroughly, especially around collector rings, washers, and connections. Tighten all connections. If rings appear to be rough, spotted, or eccentric, they should be refinished by qualified personnel. Make certain that all top sticks or wedges are tight; tighten those which are not.

- *Armatures* – Clean all armature air passages thoroughly. In doing so, look for oil or grease creeping along the shaft back to the bearing. Check the commutator surface condition, looking for high bars, high mica, or eccentricity. If necessary, turn down the commutator to secure a smooth, fresh surface. This operation is performed in a lathe of suitable size, as shown in *Figure 3*.

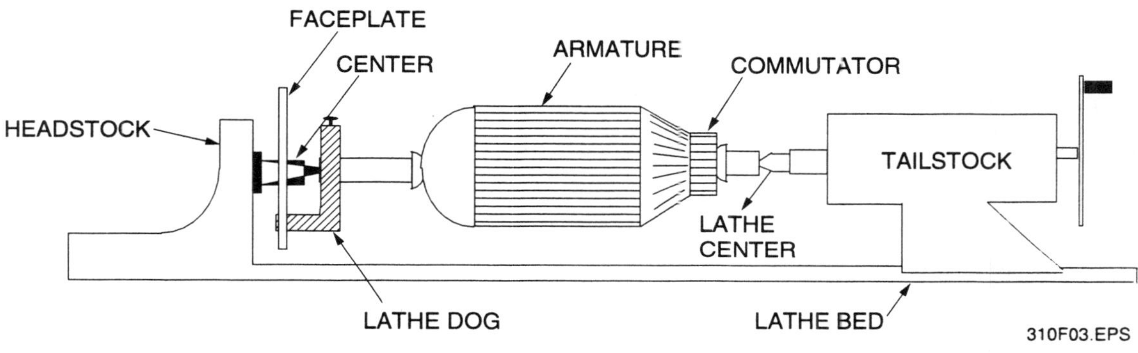

Figure 3. Motor Armature Secured In Lathe Between Centers

For armatures with drilled center holes, put a lathe dog on the shaft opposite the commutator and tighten it. If it is necessary to put the lathe dog on a bearing surface, put a piece of thin copper around the shaft to protect it. Put a faceplate on the spindle end of the lathe along with centers in both the headstock and tailstock. Apply some white lead or oil on the tailstock center and then place the commutator between centers and tighten the tailstock firmly, but not so tight as to spread the end of the shaft.

Use a sharp-pointed lathe cutting tool in the tool holder to turn the commutator down, running the lathe at medium speed (around 700 rpm). Finish the job with a fine file and abrasive paper.

Armatures without drilled center holes will necessitate the use of chucks. The armature shaft opposite the commutator should be chucked in a three-jaw universal chuck in the headstock. Chuck a bearing of proper size in a drill-type chuck and place it in the tailstock of the lathe. Oil this bearing and then place the commutator end shaft into it. See *Figure 4*. The commutator is then turned in the same manner as described previously.

 11

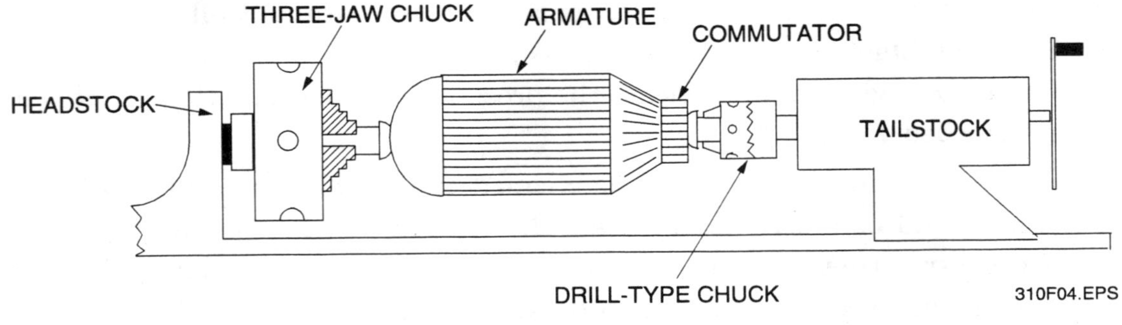

Figure 4. Motor Armature Secured In Lathe With Lathe Chucks

When turning down an armature, always use a pointed tool with a sharp and smooth edge to obtain the cleanest cut possible. Take only a fine cut each time to prevent tearing the commutator. To finish the job, smooth down the surface with a soft file while the armature is revolving in the lathe between centers. While the armature is still turning, you may polish its surface using various grits of abrasive paper.

When the armature has been turned, clean between the bars if necessary and then test with a growler or other test instrument to determine if any shorts are present. The vibration of a hacksaw blade on any coil means that the coil is shorted at the leads or commutator. Clean between the **commutator poles** and test again. As soon as the armature tests okay, it is ready to put back into service.

Motor loads should be re-evaluated from time to time, as they will vary for several reasons. Use an ammeter and take an ampere reading on the motor, first with no load and then at a full load—or through an entire cycle. This should provide a good idea as to the mechanical condition of the driven machine.

Without proper maintenance, no motor can be expected to perform well for any length of time or to remain in service as long as it should. Although motor maintenance is costly, it is far less expensive than continually replacing or overhauling motors.

3.0.0 MOTOR BEARING MAINTENANCE

AC motors account for a high percentage of electrical repair work, and most of these failures can be traced to faulty bearings. Consequently, most industrial establishments place heavy emphasis on the proper handling, repair, and maintenance of various types of sleeve and ball bearings. As a result, plants are finding that electric motors last longer and perform better when a carefully planned motor lubrication schedule is followed.

If AC motor failure occurs, the first step is to find out why the motor failed. There are various causes of motor breakdowns, such as excessive load, binding or misalignment of motor drives, wet or dirty surroundings, and bearing failure. Bearing failure can occur in newer motors with high-quality bearings as frequently as in older motors equipped with less reliable bearings. A notable exception is motors equipped with sealed bearings, which are much less prone to failure.

Considering this information, particularly the fact that sealed bearings are shielded from contamination and do not require lubrication, it stands to reason that contamination of bearings is one of the major causes of bearing failure. Consequently, most plant maintenance departments are updating the lubrication methods and bearing maintenance techniques, emphasizing cleanliness in procedures for all types of motor bearings.

3.1.0   TYPES OF BEARINGS

There are many types of bearings, but ball bearings are probably the most common. This type of bearing is found on various-size motors, and construction types may include:

- Open
- Single-shielded
- Double-shielded
- Sealed
- Double-row and other special types

Open bearings, as the name implies, are open construction and must be installed in a sealed housing. These bearings are less apt to cause churning of grease and are therefore used mostly on large motors.

The single-shield bearing has a shield on one side to keep grease from the motor windings. Double-shielded bearings have a shield on both sides of the bearing. This type of bearing is less susceptible to contamination and, because of its design, reduces the possibility of over-greasing. Sealed bearings have a double shield on each side of the bearing which forms an excellent seal. This bearing requires no maintenance, affords protection from contamination at all times, and does not require regreasing. It is normally used on small or medium motor sizes.

The largest motors are usually furnished with oil-ring sleeve bearings, while some of the smallest fractional-horsepower motors are equipped with plain sleeve bearings.

Each bearing type has characteristics which make it the best choice for a certain application. Replacement should be made with the same type of bearings. The following list provides a basic understanding of bearing applications and a guide to analysis of bearing problems due to misapplication.

Figure 5 shows several types of bearings used in electric motors.

Figure 5. Various Types Of Bearings

The following is a brief description of each bearing type:

- *Self-aligning ball bearing* – The self-aligning ball bearing, with two rows of balls rolling on the spherical surface of the outer ring, compensates for angular misalignment resulting from errors in mounting, shaft deflection, and distortion of the foundation. It is impossible for this bearing to exert any bending influence on the shaft—a most important consideration in applications requiring extreme accuracy at high speeds. Self-aligning ball bearings are used for radial loads and moderate thrust loads in either direction.

- *Single-row, deep-groove ball bearing* – The single-row, deep-groove ball bearing will sustain, in addition to radial load, a substantial thrust load in either direction, even at very high speeds. This advantage results from the intimate contact existing between the balls and the deep, continuous groove in each ring. When using this type of bearing, careful alignment between the shaft and housing is essential. This bearing is also available with seals and shields which serve to exclude dirt and retain lubricant.

- *Angular-contact ball bearings* – The angular-contact ball bearing supports a heavy thrust load in one direction, sometimes combined with a moderate radial load. A steep contact angle, assuring the highest thrust capacity and axial rigidity, is obtained by a high thrust-supporting shoulder on the inner ring and a similar high shoulder on the opposite side of the outer ring. These bearings can be mounted singly or, when the sides are flush ground, in tandem for constant thrust in one direction. They can also be mounted in pairs when the sides are flush ground; this provides for a combined load, either face-to-face or back-to-back.

- *Double-row, deep-groove ball bearing* – The double-row, deep-groove ball bearing embodies the same principle of design as the single-row bearing. However, this bearing has a lower axial displacement than occurs in the single-row design, substantial thrust capacity in either direction, and high radial capacity due to the two rows of balls.

- *Spherical-roller bearing* – The spherical-roller bearing, due to the number, size, and shape of the rollers, and the accuracy with which they are guided, has maximum capacity. Since the bearing is inherently self-aligning, angular misalignment between the shaft and housing has no detrimental effect, and the full capacity is always available for useful work. The design and proportion are such that, in addition to radial load, thrust loads may be carried in either direction.

- *Cylindrical-roller bearing* – This type of bearing has high radial capacity and provides accurate guiding of the rollers, resulting in a close approach to true rolling. Consequent low friction permits operation at high speed. Those types which have flanges on one ring only allow a limited free axial movement of the shaft in relation to the housing. They are easy to dismount even when both rings are mounted with a tight fit. The double-row type is particularly suitable for machine-tool spindles.

- *Ball-thrust bearing* – The ball-thrust bearing is designed for thrust load in one direction only. The load line through the balls in parallel to the axis of the shaft results in high thrust capacity and minimum axial deflection. Flat seats are preferred for heavy loads or for close axial positioning of the shaft.

- *Spherical-roller thrust bearing* – The spherical-roller thrust bearing is designed to carry heavy thrust loads or combined loads which are predominantly thrust. This bearing has a single row of rollers which roll on a spherical outer race with full self-alignment. The cage, centered by an inner ring sleeve, is constructed so that lubricant is pumped directly against the inner ring's unusually high guide flange. This bearing operates best with relatively heavy oil lubrication.

- *Tapered-roller bearings* – Since the axes of its rollers and raceways form an angle with the shaft axis, the tapered-roller bearing is especially suitable for carrying radial and axial loads acting simultaneously. A bearing of this type usually must be adjusted toward another bearing capable of carrying thrust loads in the opposite direction. Tapered roller bearings are separable—their cones (inner rings) with rollers and their cups (outer rings) are mounted separately.

Recommendations for ball bearing assembly, maintenance, inspection, and lubrication are shown in *Table 4*. Refer to this list often when working with electric motors.

3.2.0   FREQUENCY OF LUBRICATION

The frequency of motor lubrication depends not only on the type of bearing, but also on the motor application. Small- and medium-size motors equipped with ball bearings (except sealed bearings) are greased every three to six years if the motor duty is normal. On severe applications (high temperature, wet or dirty locations, or corrosive atmospheres), lubrication may be required more often. In severe applications, past experience and condition of the grease are the best guides as to the frequency of lubrication.

The lubrication in sleeve bearings should be changed at least once a year or more often when the motor duty is severe or the oil appears dirty.

Do	Do Not
DO work with clean tools in clean surroundings.	DO NOT work under the handicap of poor tools, a rough bench, or dirty surroundings.
DO remove all outside dirt from the housing before exposing the bearing.	DO NOT use dirty, brittle, or chipped tools.
DO treat a used bearing as carefully as a new one.	DO NOT handle bearings with dirty or moist hands.
DO use clean solvents and flushing oils.	DO NOT spin uncleaned bearings.
DO lay bearings out on clean paper or cloth.	DO NOT spin any bearings with compressed air.
DO protect disassembled bearings from dirt and moisture.	DO NOT use the same container for both cleaning and the final rinse of the bearings.
DO use clean, lint-free rags to wipe bearings.	DO NOT scratch or nick the bearing surfaces.
DO keep bearings wrapped in oil-proof paper when not in use.	DO NOT remove grease or oil from new bearings.
DO clean the outside of the housing before replacing the bearings.	DO NOT use the incorrect kind or amount of lubricant.
DO keep bearing lubricants clean when applying and cover containers when not in use.	DO NOT use a bearing as a gauge to check either the housing bore or the shaft fit.
DO be sure the shaft size is within the specified tolerances recommended for the bearing.	DO NOT install a bearing on a shaft that shows excessive wear.
DO store bearings in their original unopened cartons in a dry place.	DO NOT open the carton until the bearing is ready for installation.
DO use a clean, short-bristle brush with firmly embedded bristles to remove dirt, scale, or chips.	DO NOT judge the condition of a bearing until after it has been cleaned.
DO be certain that, when installed, the bearing is square with and held firmly against the shaft shoulder.	DO NOT pound directly on a bearing or ring when installing as this may cause damage to the shaft and bearing.
DO follow lubricating instructions supplied with the machinery. Use only grease where grease is specified; use only oil where oil is specified. Be sure to use the exact kind of lubricant called for.	DO NOT overfill when lubricating. Excess grease and oil will ooze out of the overfilled housings past seals and closures, collect dirt, and cause problems. Too much lubricant will also cause overheating, particularly where bearings operate at high speeds.
DO handle grease with clean paddles or grease guns. Store grease in clean containers. Keep grease containers covered.	DO NOT permit any machine to stand inoperative for months without turning it over periodically. This prevents moisture which may condense in a standing bearing from causing corrosion.

Table 4. Ball Bearing Assembly, Maintenance, And Lubrication Recommendations

3.2.1 Lubrication Procedure

For effective motor lubrication, cleanliness and use of the proper lubricant are of paramount importance.

When greasing a ball bearing motor, the bearing housing, grease gun, and fittings are wiped clean. Great care must be taken to keep dirt out of the bearing when greasing. Next, the relief plug is removed from the bottom of the bearing housing. This is done to prevent excessive pressure from building up inside the bearing housing during greasing. Grease is then added, with the motor running if possible, until it begins to flow from the relief hole. The motor is allowed to run for 5 to 10 minutes to expel any excess grease. The relief plug is replaced and the bearing housing is cleaned.

It is important to avoid over-greasing. When too much grease is forced into a bearing, a churning of the lubricant occurs, resulting in high temperatures and eventual bearing failure.

On motors that do not have a relief hole, grease should be applied sparingly. If possible, disassemble the motor and repack the bearing housing with the proper amount of grease. During this procedure, always maintain strict cleanliness.

The importance of adherence to these procedures cannot be overemphasized. Contamination and overgreasing of bearings can both cause bearing failure.

For sleeve bearings, use only the recommended oil for the particular service conditions. Observing careful cleanliness, old oil is removed and new oil is added until the oil level reaches the full line on the oil sight gauge. This is done only when the motor is not running.

3.3.0 TESTING BEARINGS

Two of the most effective tests are what might be called the *feel* test and the *sound* test. If performing the feel test while the motor is running and the bearing housing feels overly hot to the touch, it is probably malfunctioning.

Note: Some bearings may operate safely up to about 85°C.

During the sound test, listen for foreign noises coming from the motor. Also, one end of a steel rod (about 3' long and ½" in diameter) may be placed on the bearing housing while the other end is held against the ear. The rod acts as an amplifier, transmitting unusual sounds such as thumping or grinding, which would indicate a failing bearing. Special listening devices, such as a transistorized stethoscope, can also be used for this purpose.

It is also important to check the air gap on sleeve-bearing motors periodically. This test is performed with a feeler gauge and indicates when a bearing begins to wear. Four measurements should be taken about 90° apart around the rotor periphery. These measurements are recorded and compared with earlier readings; deviations from previous readings may indicate bearing wear.

Motors should also be checked for end play. Ball bearing motors should have about ½₂" to ½₆" end play. Sleeve-bearing motors may have up to ½" end play.

On large sleeve bearings, the oil level should be checked periodically and the oil visually inspected for contamination. If possible, the oil rings should be checked when the motor is operating.

Other inspections include checking for misaligned or bent shafts and for excessive belt pressure.

4.0.0 TROUBLESHOOTING MOTORS

To detect defects in electric motors, the windings are normally tested for ground faults, opens, shorts, and reverses. The exact method of performing these tests will depend on the type of motor being serviced.

WARNING!   Before performing troubleshooting, disconnect power, then lockout/tagout.

Before we can begin our study of troubleshooting, it is important to clarify some basic terms. These include the following:

* *Ground* – A winding becomes grounded when it makes an electrical contact with the metal frame of the motor. The usual causes of grounds include the following: bolts securing the end plates come into contact with the winding; the wires press against the laminations at the corners of the slots, which is likely to occur if the slot insulation tears or cracks during winding; and the centrifugal switch may be grounded to the end plate.
* *Open circuits* – Loose or dirty connections or a broken wire can cause an open circuit in an electric motor.
* *Shorts* – Two or more turns of the coil that contact each other electrically will cause a short circuit. This condition may develop in a new winding if the winding is tight and much pounding is necessary to place the wires in position. In other cases, excessive heat developed from overloads will degrade the insulation and cause shorts. A short circuit is usually detected by observing smoke from the windings as the motor operates or when the motor draws excessive current at no load.

4.1.0 TOOLS FOR TROUBLESHOOTING

This section describes some of the tools used for troubleshooting motors of all types.

In addition to small portable devices such as voltmeters, ammeters, brush-spring tension testers, and a transistorized stethoscope for checking motor bearings, maintenance equipment should include a 500V insulation resistance tester (megger), a spark gap oil dielectric tester, and a portable oil-filtering unit.

The use of some of these tools has been covered in previous modules, so only the ones that have not been previously covered will be discussed here.

- *Transistorized stethoscope* – This type of testing instrument is equipped with a transistor-amplifier and is used to ascertain the condition of motor bearings. A little practice in interpreting what is heard through it may be required, but, in general, it is relatively simple to use. If, when the stethoscope is applied to a motor bearing, a purring sound is heard, the bearing is usually normal. On the other hand, a thumping sound or a rough grinding sound indicates a failing bearing.

- *Insulation resistance tests* – High-voltage cables, such as those rated at 2,300V, should be tested periodically. Circuits carrying 480V should be tested annually; this includes transformers, motors, motor starters, **generators**, and switches. Also, certain high-power process equipment such as electric furnaces and die casting machines should receive insulation resistance tests annually.

When performing an insulation resistance test, first make a careful safety check and ensure that all circuits and equipment are rated at the voltage of the megger. Furthermore, all equipment scheduled for testing must be disconnected from all power sources. All safety switches should be opened and locked out to make certain that motor starters or other control equipment cannot accidentally energize the apparatus.

Before continuing, also check the megger and other testing instruments for proper operation. This is accomplished by first testing for an infinity reading by operating the megger with the test leads disconnected. A second test is made with the megger leads shorted and the megger handle turned very slowly; this time, the meter should read zero.

Following these checks, insulation resistance readings should be obtained by testing between a conductor and ground or between two conductors, or both. Insulation readings from conductor to ground are obtained by connecting the line test lead to the conductor and the earth test lead to ground. For the test between conductors, the test leads are connected to the two conductors to be tested.

After the proper connections have been made, the megger handle is turned at an even speed for about one minute. At the end of this time, the insulation resistance value is recorded.

Because temperature and humidity have profound effects on insulation resistance readings, the temperature and humidity at the apparatus should be recorded immediately after the test. In addition, pertinent considerations should be noted such as the condition of the immediate area (wet location or excessive dust) and whether the apparatus has been in operation prior to the test or at rest for a prolonged period of time.

After the readings have been recorded, they are corrected for temperature using a temperature correction chart (supplied with most meggers). As a rule of thumb, most maintenance departments feel that 600V winding insulation is acceptable if the corrected resistance value is one megohm or more. Higher resistance readings which show a continuing downward trend over a period of time indicate failing insulation.

Table 5 provides a list of practical tools and equipment for effective electrical maintenance, both for motors and other electrical apparatus.

Tools or Equipment	Application
Multimeters, voltmeters, ohmmeters, clamp-on ammeters, wattmeters, clamp-on power factor meter	Measure circuit voltage, resistance, current, and power. Useful for circuit tracing and troubleshooting.
Potential and current transformers, meter shunts	Increase range of test instruments to permit the reading of high-voltage and high-current circuits.
Tachometer	Checks rotating machinery speeds.
Recording meters	Provide a permanent record of voltage, current, power, temperature, etc., on charts for analytic study.
Insulation resistance tester, thermometer, psychrometer	Test and monitor insulation resistance; use a thermometer and psychrometer for temperature and humidity correction.
Portable oil dielectric tester, portable oil filter	Test OCB, transformer oil, or other insulating oils. Recondition used oil.
Transistorized stethoscope	Detect faulty rotating machinery bearings and leaky valves.
Air gap feeler gauges	Check motor or generator air gap between rotor and stator.
Cleaning solvent	Removes grease or dirt from motor windings or other electrical parts.
Hand stones (rough, medium, fine), grinding rig, canvas strip	Used for grinding, smoothing, and finishing commutators or slip rings.
Spring tension scale	Checks brush pressure on DC motor commutators or on AC motor skip rings; tests electrical contact pressure on relays, starters, or contacts.

Table 5. Tools For Electrical Maintenance

4.2.0 GROUNDED COILS

The usual effect of one grounded coil in a winding is the repeated blowing of a fuse or tripping of the circuit breaker when the line switch is closed, provided that the machine frame and the line are both grounded. Two or more grounds will give the same result and will also short out part of the winding in that phase in which the grounds occur. A quick and simple test to determine whether or not a ground exists in the winding can be made with a conventional continuity tester. Before testing with this instrument, first make certain that the line switch is open and locked out, causing the motor leads to be deenergized. Place one test lead on the frame of the motor and the other in turn on each of the line wires leading from the motor. If there is a grounded coil at any point in the winding, the lamp of the continuity tester will light, or in the case of a meter, the dial will swing toward infinity.

To locate the phase that is grounded, test each phase separately. In a three-phase winding, it will be necessary to disconnect the star or delta connections, if accessible. After the grounded phase is located, the pole group connections in that phase can be disconnected and each group tested separately. When the leads are placed (one on the frame and the other on the grounded coil group), the lamp will indicate the ground in this group by lighting. The stub connections between the coils and this group may then be disconnected and each coil tested separately until the exact coil that is grounded is located.

Sometimes moisture in the insulation around the coils on old and defective insulation will cause a high-resistance ground that is difficult to detect with a test lamp. A megger can be used to detect such faults, but in many cases, a megger may not be available. If not, use a test outfit consisting of a headphone set (telephone receiver) and several dry cell batteries connected in series, as shown in *Figure 6*. Such a test set will detect a ground of very high resistance by producing an audible clicking sound through the receiver, and will often be effective when the ordinary test lamp fails to locate the trouble.

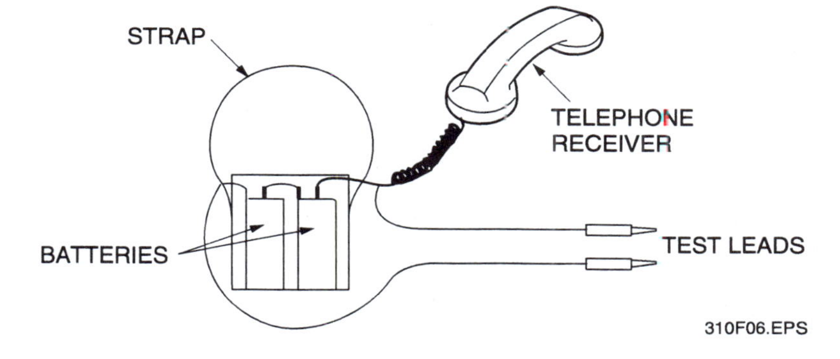

Figure 6. When Used For Testing, A Clicking Sound Indicates A Fault

Armature windings and the commutator of a motor may be tested for grounds in a similar manner. On some motors, the **brush holders** are grounded to the end plate. Consequently, before the armature is tested for grounds, the brushes must be lifted away from the commutator.

When a grounded coil is located, it should be either removed and reinsulated or cut out of the circuit. At times, however, it may be inconvenient to stop a motor long enough for a complete rewinding or permanent repairs. In such cases, when trouble develops, it is often necessary to make a temporary repair until a later time when the motor may be taken out of service.

To temporarily repair a defective coil, a jumper wire of the same size as that used in the coil is connected to the bottom lead of the coil immediately adjacent to the defective coil and run across to the top lead of the coil on the other side of the defective coil, leaving the defective coil entirely out of the circuit. The defective coil should then be cut at the back of the winding and the leads taped so that they cannot function when the motor is started again. If the defective coil is grounded, it should also be disconnected from the other coils.

4.3.0 SHORTED COILS

Shorted turns within coils are usually the result of failure of the insulation on the wires. This is frequently caused by the wires being crossed and having excessive pressure applied on the crossed conductors when the coils are being inserted in the slot. Quite often it is caused by using too much force when driving the coils down in the slots. In the case of windings that have been in service for several years, failure of the insulation may be caused by oil, moisture, etc. If a shorted coil is left in a winding, it will usually burn out in a short time, and if it is not located and repaired promptly, it will probably cause a ground and the burning out of a number of other coils.

One inexpensive way of locating a shorted coil is by the use of a growler and a thin piece of steel. *Figure 7* shows a growler in use in a stator. Note that the poles are shaped to fit the curvature of the teeth inside the stator core. The growler should be placed in the core as shown, and the thin piece of steel should be placed the distance of one coil span away from the center of the growler. Then, by moving the growler around the bore of the stator and always keeping the steel strip the same distance away from it, all of the coils can be tested.

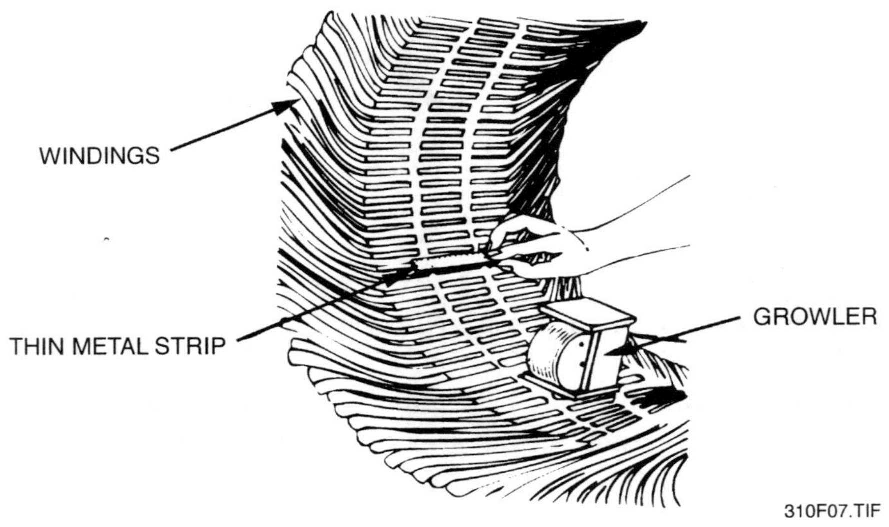

Figure 7. Growler Used To Test A Stator Of An AC Motor

If any of the coils has one or more shorted turns, the piece of steel will vibrate very rapidly and cause a loud humming noise. By locating the two slots over which the steel vibrates, both sides of the shorted coil can be found. If more than two slots cause the steel to vibrate, they should all be marked, and all shorted coils should be removed and replaced with new ones or cut out of the circuit, as previously described.

Sometimes one coil or a complete coil group becomes short circuited at the end connections. The test for this fault is the same as that for a shorted coil. If all the coils in one group are shorted, it will generally be indicated by the vibration of the steel strip over several consecutive slots, corresponding to the number of coils in the group.

The end connections should be carefully examined, and those that appear to have poor insulation should be moved during the time that the test is being made. It will often be found that when the shorted end connections are moved during the test, the vibration of the steel will stop. If these ends are reinsulated, the trouble should be eliminated.

4.4.0   OPEN COILS

When one or more coils become open due to a break in the turns or a poor connection at the end, they can be tested with a continuity tester, as previously explained. If this test is made at the ends of each winding, an open can be detected by the lamp failing to light. The insulation should be removed from the pole group connections, and each group should be tested separately.

An open circuit in the **starting winding** may be difficult to locate, since the problem may be in the centrifugal switch as well as the winding itself. (The starting winding is only in the circuit when the motor is starting.) In fact, the centrifugal switch is probably more apt to cause trouble than the winding since parts become worn, defective, and (most likely) dirty. Insufficient pressure of the rotating part of centrifugal switches against the stationary part will prevent the contacts from closing and thereby produce an open circuit.

If the trouble is a loose connection at the coil ends, it can be repaired by resoldering the splices, but if it is within the coil, the coil should either be replaced or a jumper should be connected around it until a better repair can be made.

4.5.0   REVERSED CONNECTIONS

Reversed coils cause the current to flow through them in the wrong direction. This fault usually manifests itself, as do most irregularities in winding connections, by a disturbance of the magnetic circuit which results in excessive noise and vibration. The fault can be located by the use of a magnetic compass and some source of low-voltage direct current. This voltage should be adjusted so it will send about one-fourth to one-sixth of the full-load current through the winding, and the DC leads should be placed on the start and finish of one phase. If the winding is three-phase, star-connected, this would be at the start of one phase and the star point. If the winding is delta-connected, the delta must be disconnected and each phase tested separately.

Place a compass on the inside of the stator and test each of the coil groups in that phase. If the phase is connected correctly, the needle of the compass will reverse as it is moved from one coil group to another. However, if any one of the coils is reversed, the reversed coil will build up a field in the direction opposite to the others, thus causing a neutralizing effect which will be indicated by the compass needle refusing to point definitely to that group. If there are only two coils per group, there will be no indication if one of them is reversed, as that group will be completely neutralized.

When an entire coil group is reversed, it causes the current to flow in the wrong direction in the whole group. The test for this fault is the same as that for reversed coils. The winding should be magnetized with direct current, and when the compass needle is passed around the coil groups, they should indicate alternately north/south, north/south, etc. If one of the groups is reversed, three consecutive groups will be of the same polarity. The remedy for either reversed coil groups or reversed coils is to make a visual check of the connections at that part of the winding, locate the wrong connection, and reconnect it properly.

When the wrong number of coils are connected in two or more groups, the trouble can be located by counting the number of ends on each group. If any mistakes are found, they should be remedied by reconnecting properly.

4.6.0 REVERSED PHASE

Sometimes in a three-phase winding, a complete phase is reversed by either having taken the starts from the wrong coils or by connecting one of the windings wrong in relation to the others when making the star or delta connections. If the winding is connected in a delta configuration, disconnect any one of the points where the phases are connected together and pass current through the three windings in series. Place a compass on the inside of the stator and test each coil group by slowly moving the compass one complete revolution around the stator.

The reversals of the needle in moving the compass one revolution around the stator should be three times the number of poles in the winding.

When testing a star-connected or wye-connected winding, connect the three starts together and place them on one DC lead. Then connect the other DC lead and star point, thus passing the current through all three windings in parallel. Test with a compass as explained for the delta winding. The result should then be the same, or the reversals of the needle in making one revolution around the stator should again be three times the number of poles in the winding.

These tests for reversed phases apply to full-pitch windings only. If the winding is fractional pitch, a careful visual check should be made to determine whether there is a reversed phase or mistake in connecting the star or delta connections.

Table 6 is an AC troubleshooting chart that may be used by qualified personnel who have the proper tools and equipment. These instructions do not cover all details or variations in equipment, nor do they provide for every possible condition to be met in actual practice. Always refer to the manufacturer's instructions before testing any motor.

Malfunction	Probable Cause	Corrective Action
Slow speed	Open primary circuit	Locate fault with testing device and repair
Slow to accelerate	Excess loading Poor circuit Defective squirrel-cage rotor Applied voltage too low	Reduce load Check for high resistance Replace Get power company to increase voltage tap
Wrong rotation	Wrong sequence of phases	Reverse connections at motor or at switchboard
Motor overheats	Overloaded motor Clogged blowers or air shields Motor may have one phase open Grounded coil Unbalanced terminal voltage Unbalanced terminal voltage Shorted stator coil Faulty connection High voltage Low voltage	Reduce load Clean to restore proper ventilation of motor Check to make sure that all leads are well connected Locate and repair Check to make sure that all leads are well connected Check for faulty leads Repair and then check wattmeter reading Indicated by high resistance; locate and repair Check terminals of motor with voltmeter Same as above
Motor stalls	Wrong application Overloaded motor Low motor voltage Open circuit Incorrect control resistance of wound rotor	Change type or size (consult manufacturer) Reduce load See that nameplate voltage is maintained Fuses blown Check control sequence; replace broken resistors; repair open circuits
Motor does not start	One phase open Defective rotor Poor stator coil connection	See that no phase is open; reduce load Look for broken bars or rings; repair or replace Remove end bells
Motor runs, then quits	Power failure	Check for loose connections to line, fuses, and control

Table 6. General Troubleshooting Chart For AC Motors (1 Of 2)

Malfunction	Probable Cause	Corrective Action
Slow speed	Not applied properly	Consult supplier for proper type
	Voltage too low at motor terminals because of line drop	Use higher voltage on transformer terminals or reduce load
	If wound rotor, improper control operation of secondary	Correct secondary control
	Starting load too high	Check load that the motor is supposed to carry upon starting
	Low pull-in torque of synchronous motor	Change rotor starting resistance or change rotor design
	Check that all brushes are riding on rings	Check secondary connections; leave no leads poorly connected
	Broken rotor bars	Look for cracks near the rings; a new rotor may be required
Motor vibrates	Motor misaligned	Realign
	Weak foundation	Strengthen base
	Coupling out of balance	Balance coupling
	Driven equipment unbalanced	Rebalance driven equipment
	Defective ball bearing	Replace bearing
	Bearing not in line	Line up properly
	Balancing weights shifted	Rebalance rotor
	Wound rotor coils replaced	Rebalance rotor
	Polyphase motor running single phase	Check for open circuit
	Excessive end play	Adjust bearing or add washer
Unbalanced line current	Unequal terminal volts	Check leads and connections
	Single-phase operation	Check for open circuit
	Poor rotor contacts in control wound rotor resistance	Check for control devices
	Brushes not in proper position in wound rotor	See that brushes are properly seated and shunts in good condition
	Fan rubbing air shield	Remove interference
	Fan striking insulation	Clear fan
	Loose on bedplate	Tighten holding bolts
Magnetic noise	Air gap not uniform	Check and correct bracket fits or bearing

Table 6. General Troubleshooting Chart For AC Motors (2 Of 2)

If a split-phase motor fails to start, the trouble may be due to one or more of the following faults:

- Tight or frozen bearings
- Worn bearings, allowing the rotor to drag on the stator
- Bent rotor shaft
- One or both bearings out of alignment
- Open circuit in either the starting or running windings
- Defective centrifugal switch
- Improper connections in either winding
- Grounds in either winding or both
- Shorts between the two windings

Tight or worn bearings – Tight or worn bearings may be due to the lubricating system failing, or when new bearings are installed, they may run hot if the shaft is not kept well oiled.

If the bearings are worn to such an extent that they allow the rotor to drag on the stator, this will usually prevent the rotor from starting. The inside of the stator laminations will be worn bright where they are rubbed by the rotor. When this condition exists, it can generally be easily detected by close observation of the stator field and rotor surface when the rotor is removed.

Bent shaft and bearings out of line – A bent rotor shaft will usually cause the rotor to bind in a certain position and then run freely until it returns to that position. An accurate test for a bent shaft can be made by placing the rotor between centers on a lathe and turning the rotor slowly while a tool or marker is held in the tool post close to the surface of the rotor. If the rotor wobbles, it is an indication of a bent shaft.

Bearings out of alignment are usually caused by uneven tightening of the end shield plates. When placing end shields or brackets on a motor, the bolts should be tightened alternately, first drawing up two bolts which are directly opposite one another. These two should be drawn up only a few turns and then the others tightened an equal amount all the way around. When the end shields are drawn up as far as possible with the bolts, they should be tapped tightly against the frame with a mallet and the bolts tightened again.

Open circuits and defective centrifugal switches – Open circuits in either the starting or running winding will cause the motor to fail to start. This fault can be detected by testing in series with the start and finish of each winding using a test lamp or ohmmeter.

A defective centrifugal switch will often cause considerable trouble that is difficult to locate unless one has good knowledge of the operating characteristics of these switches. If the switch fails to close when the rotor stops, the motor will not start when the line switch is closed.

Failure of the switch to close is generally caused by dirt, grit, or some other foreign matter getting into the switch. The switch should be thoroughly cleaned with a degreasing solution such as AWA 1,1,1 and then inspected for weak or broken springs.

If the winding is on the rotor, the brushes sometimes stick in the holders and fail to make good contact with the **slip rings**. This causes sparking at the brushes. There will probably also be a certain place where the rotor will not start until it is moved far enough for the brush to make contact on the ring. The brush holders should be cleaned and the brushes carefully fitted so they move more freely with a minimum of friction between the brush and the holders. If a centrifugal switch fails to open when the motor is started, the motor will probably growl and continue to run slowly, causing the starting winding to burn out if it is not promptly disconnected from the line. In most cases, however, the heaters in the motor control will take care of this before any serious damage occurs. This fault is likely to be caused by dirt or hardened grease in the switch.

Reversed connections and grounds – Reversed connections are caused by improperly connecting a coil or group of coils. The wrong connections can be found and corrected by making a careful check of the connections and reconnecting those that are found at fault. The test with a DC power source and a compass can also be used for locating reversed coils. Test the starting and running windings separately, exciting only one winding at a time with direct current. The compass should show alternate poles around the winding.

The operation of a motor that has a ground in the winding will depend on where the ground is and whether or not the frame is grounded. If the frame is grounded, then when the ground occurs in the winding, it will usually blow a fuse or trip the overcurrent device.

A test for grounds can be made using a test lamp or continuity tester. One test lead should be placed on the frame and the other on a lead to the winding. If there is no ground, the lamp will not light, nor will any deflection be present when a meter is used. If the light does light, it indicates a ground due to a defect somewhere in the insulation.

Short circuits – Short circuits between any two windings can be detected by the use of a test lamp or continuity tester. Place one of the test leads on one wire of the starting winding and the other test lead on the wire of the running winding. If these windings are properly insulated from each other, the lamp should not light. If it does, it is a certain indication that a short exists between the windings. Such a short will usually cause part of the starting winding to burn out. The starting winding is always wound on top of the running winding, so if it becomes burned out due to a defective centrifugal switch or a short circuit, the starting winding can be conveniently removed and replaced without disturbing the running winding.

6.0.0   STORING MOTORS

There are many reasons for storing motors, but the two major ones are:

- The project on which they are to be used is not complete.
- Spare motors are often kept as backups on most industrial installations.

The first consideration when storing motors for any length of time is the location. A dry location (one that does not undergo severe changes in temperature over a 24-hour period) should be selected whenever possible. When the ambient temperature changes frequently during a 24-hour period, condensation is certain to form on the motor, and moisture is one of the worst enemies of motor insulation. Therefore, guarding against moisture is one of the chief concerns when storing motors of any type.

A means for transporting the motor from the place of storage to the place where it will be used, or else shifted around in the storage area, is also of importance. Motors should not be lifted by their rotating shafts. Doing so can damage the alignment of the rotor in relationship to the stator. Even picking up the smaller fractional horsepower motors by the shaft is not recommended. Many workers have received bad cuts from the sharp keyways on motor shafts when picked up with bare hands.

CAUTION: Never lift a motor by its shaft. The sharp edges of keyways are not unlike sharp kitchen knives and can cause deep cuts if handled carelessly.

When an electric motor is received at the job site, always refer to the manufacturer's instructions and follow them to the letter. Failure to do so could result in serious injury to both the workers and the motor.

Once the motor has been uncrated, check to see if any damage has occurred during shipping and handling. Be sure that the motor shaft and armature turn freely. This is also a good time to determine if the motor has been exposed to dirt, grease, grit, or excessive moisture in either shipment or storage.

Note: Motors in storage should have their shafts turned over once each month to redistribute grease in the bearings.

Clean the motor of any dirt or grit before putting it into service.

WARNING!   Never start a motor which has been wet unless it has been thoroughly dried.

Eyebolts of lifting lugs on motors are intended only for lifting the motor and factory motor-mounted standard accessories. These lifting devices should never be used when lifting or handling the motor when the motor is attached to other equipment.

The eyebolt lifting-capacity rating is based on a lifting alignment coincident with the eyebolt center line. The eyebolt capacity reduces as deviation from this alignment increases.

The following is a list of items that must be considered when storing motors for any length of time:

- Make sure motors are kept clean.
- Make sure motors are kept dry.
- Supply supplemental heating in the storage area, if necessary.
- Motors should be stored in an orderly fashion (i.e., grouped by horsepower, etc.).
- Motor armatures should be rotated periodically.
- Lubrication should be checked periodically.
- Protect shafts and keyways during storage and also while transporting motors from one location to another.
- Test motor winding resistance upon receiving; test again after placing in storage.

7.0.0 IDENTIFYING MOTORS

Electrical workers will sometimes come across a motor with no identification (no nameplate or lead tags) which must be put back into service or else repaired. The experienced electrician should know how to positively identify the motor's characteristics, even with no written data.

The NEMA standard method of motor identification is easy to remember by drawing the coils to form a wye. Identify one outside coil end with the number 1, and then draw a decreasing spiral and number each coil end in sequence, as shown in *Figure 8*.

By using an ohmmeter or other continuity tester, the individual circuits can be located as follows:

Step 1   Connect one probe of the tester to any lead, and check for continuity to each of the other eight leads. A reading from only one other lead indicates one of the two-wire circuits. A reading to two other leads indicates the three-wire circuit that makes up the internal wye connection.

Step 2   Continue checking and isolating leads until all four circuits have been located. Tag the wires of the three lead circuits T-7, T-8, and T-9 in any order. The other leads should be temporarily marked T-1 and T-4 for the circuit, T-2 and T-5 for the second circuit, and T-3 and T-6 for the third and final circuit.

Note: The following test voltages are for the most common dual voltage range of 230/460V. For other motor ranges, the voltages listed should be changed in proportion to the motor rating.

ELECTRICAL — TRAINEE TASK MODULE 26310

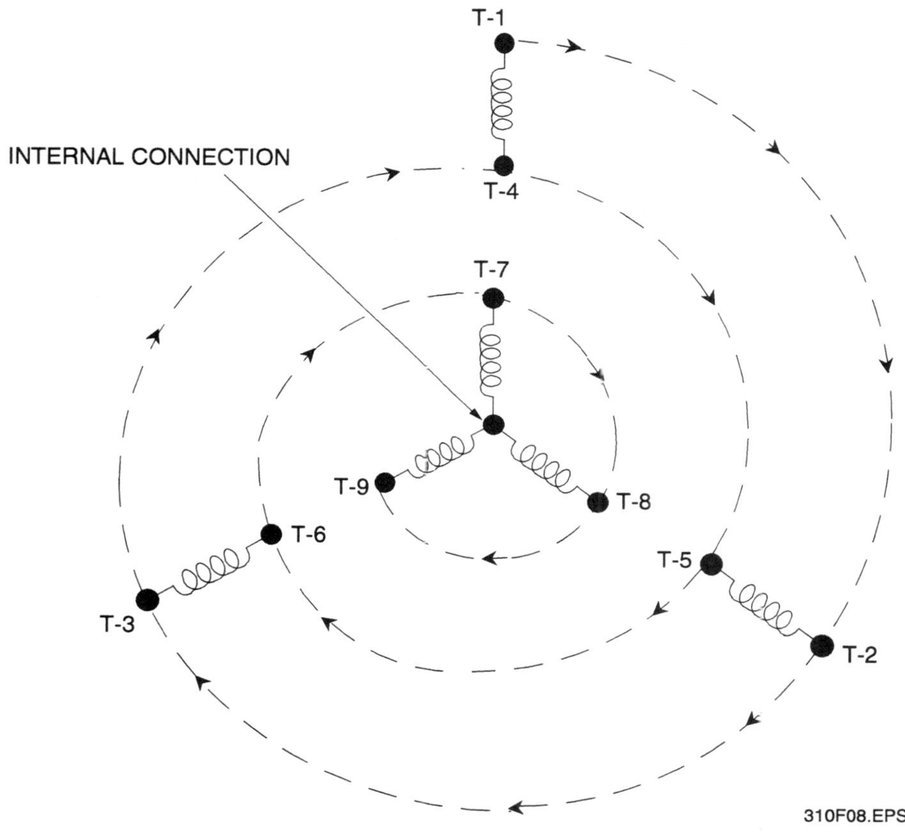

Figure 8. Identify One Outside Coil And Then Draw A Decreasing Spiral And Number Each Coil

As all the coils are physically mounted in slots on the same motor frame, the coils will act almost like the primary and secondary coils of a transformer. *Figure 9* shows a simplified electrical arrangement of the coils. Depending on which coil group power is applied to, the resulting voltage readings will be additive, subtractive, balanced, or unbalanced, depending on their physical location with regard to the coils themselves.

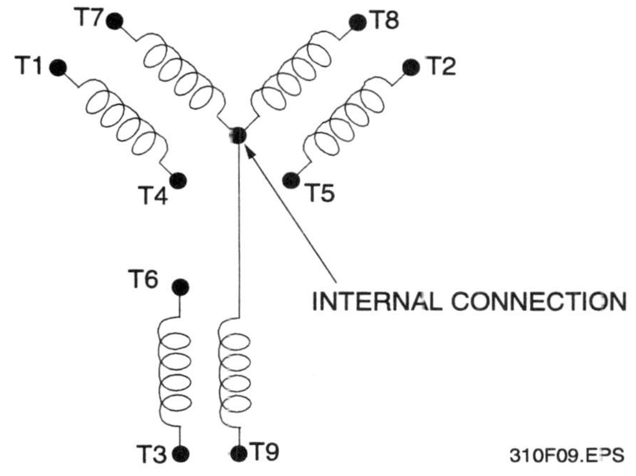

Figure 9. Simplified Electrical Arrangement Of Wye-Wound Motor Coils

Step 3 The motor may be started on 230V by connecting leads T-7, T-8, and T-9 to the three-phase source. If the motor is too large to be connected directly to the line, the voltage should be reduced by using a reduced voltage starter or other suitable means.

Step 4 Start the motor with no load connected and bring it up to normal speed.

Step 5 With the motor running, a voltage will be induced in each of the open two-wire circuits that were tagged T-1 and T-4, T-2 and T-5, and T-3 and T-6. With a voltmeter, check the voltage reading of each circuit. The voltage should be approximately 125V to 130V and should be the same on each circuit.

Note: The voltages referred to in this section are for reference only and will vary greatly from motor to motor, depending on size, design, and manufacturer. If the test calls for equal voltages of 125V to 130V and the reading is only 80V to 90V, that is acceptable as long as the voltage readings are nearly equal.

Step 6 With the motor still running, carefully connect the lead that was temporarily marked T-4 with the T-7 and line lead. Read the voltage between T-1 and T-8 and also between T-1 and T-9. If both readings are of the same value and are approximately 330V to 340V, leads T-1 and T-4 may be disconnected and permanently marked T-1 and T-4.

Step 7 If the two voltage readings are of the same value and are approximately 125V to 130V, disconnect and interchange leads T-1 and T-4 and mark them permanently (original T-1 changed to T-4 and original T-4 changed to T-1).

Step 8 If the readings between T-1 and T-8 and also between T-1 and T-9 are of unequal values, disconnect T-4 from T-7 and reconnect T-4 to the junction of T-8 and the line.

Step 9 Measure the voltage between T-1 and T-7 and also between T-1 and T-9. If the voltages are equal and approximately 330V to 340V, tag T-1 is permanently marked T-2 and T-4 is marked T-5 and disconnected. If the readings taken are equal but are approximately 125V to 130V, leads T-1 and T-4 are disconnected, interchanged, and marked T-2 and T-5 (T-1 changed to T-5, and T-4 changed to T-2). If both voltage readings are different, the T-4 lead is disconnected from T-8 and moved to T-9. Voltage readings are taken again (between T-1 and T-7, and T-1 and T-8) and the leads permanently marked T-3 and T-6 when equal readings of approximately 330V to 340V are obtained.

Step 10 The same procedure is followed for the other two circuits that were temporarily marked T-2 and T-5, and T-3 and T-6 until a position is found where both voltage readings are equal and approximately 330V to 340V and the tags change to correspond to the standard lead markings, as shown in *Figure 10*.

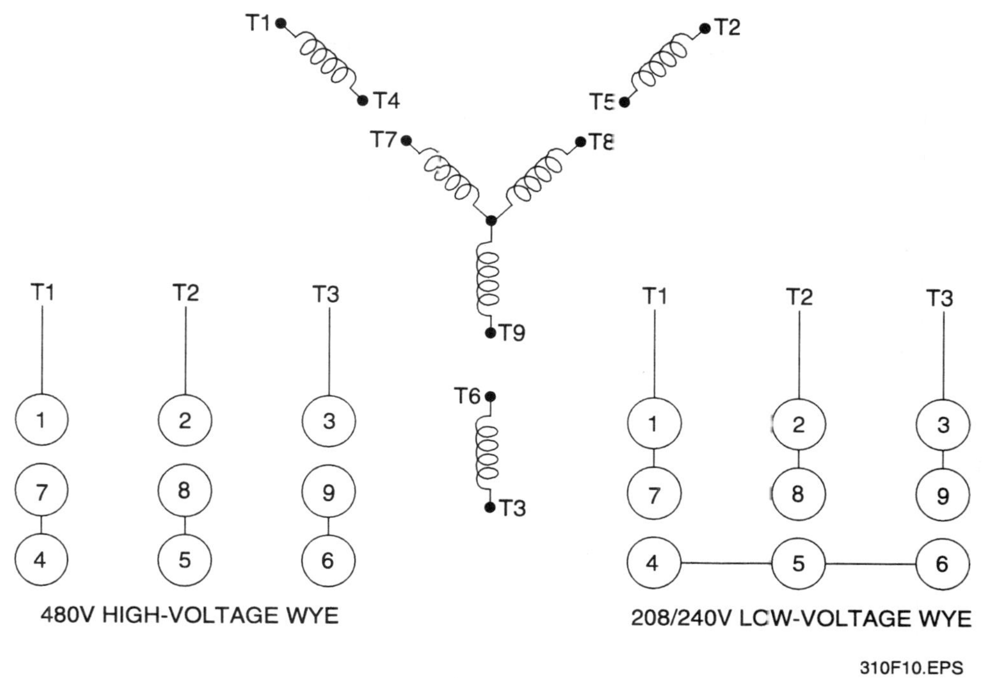

Figure 10. NEMA Standard Lead Markings For Dual-Voltage, Wye-Wound Motors

Step 11 Once all leads have been properly and permanently tagged, leads T-4, T-5, and T-6 are connected together and voltage readings are taken between T-1, T-2, and T-3. The voltages should be equal and approximately 230V.

Step 12 As an additional check, the motor is shut down and leads T-7, T-8, and T-9 are disconnected, and leads T-1, T-2, and T-3 are connected to the line. Connect T-1 to the line lead T-7 was connected to, T-2 to the same line that T-8 was connected to, and T-3 to the same lead to which T-9 was connected. With T-4, T-5, and T-6 still connected together to form a wye connection, the motor can again be started without a load. If all lead markings are correct, the motor rotation with leads T-1, T-2, and T-3 connected will be the same as when T-7, T-8, and T-9 were connected.

The motor is now ready for service and is connected in series for high voltage or parallel for low, as indicated by the NEMA connections shown in *Figure 10*.

Note: This procedure may not work on some wye-wound motors with concentric coils.

7.1.0   THREE-PHASE, DELTA-WOUND MOTORS

Most dual-voltage, delta-wound motors also have nine leads, as indicated in *Figure 11*, but there are only three circuits of three leads each.

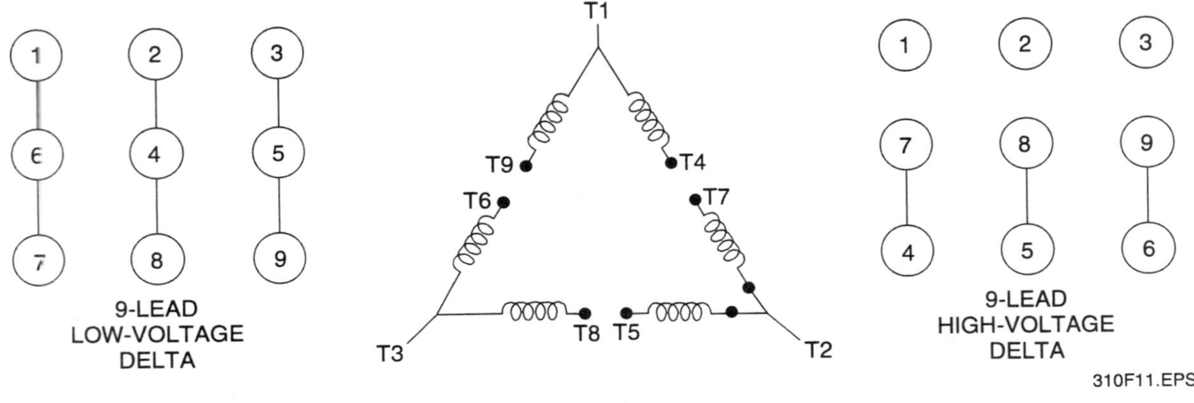

Figure 11. NEMA Standard Lead Markings For Dual-Voltage, Delta-Wound Motors

Continuity tests are used to find the three coil groups as was done for the wye-wound motor. Once the coil groups are located and isolated, further resistance checks must be made to locate the common wire in each coil group. As the resistance of some delta wound motors is very low, a digital ohmmeter, Wheatstone bridge, or other sensitive device may be needed.

Each coil group consists of two coils tied together with three leads brought out to the motor junction or terminal box. Reading the resistances carefully between each of the three leads shows that the readings from one of the leads to each of the other two leads will be the same (equal), but the resistance reading between those two leads will be double the previous readings. *Figure 12* may help to clarify this technique.

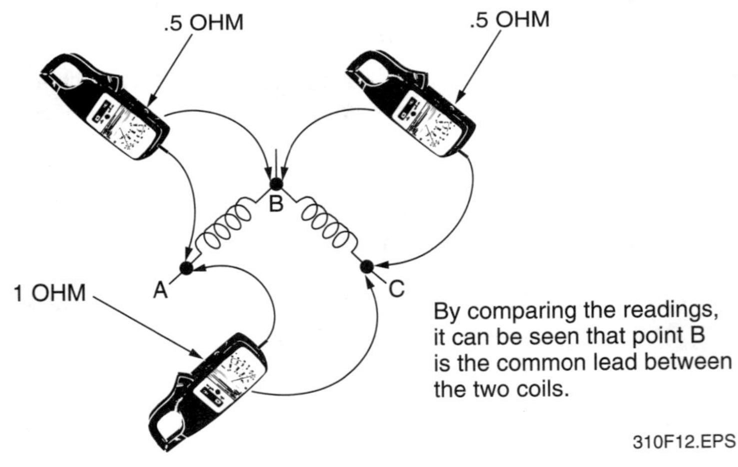

Figure 12. Using An Ohmmeter To Test Motor Leads

The common lead found in the first coil group is permanently marked T-1, and the other two leads are temporarily marked T-4 and T-9. The common lead of the next coil group is found and permanently marked T-2, and the other leads are temporarily marked T-5 and T-7. The common lead of the last coil group is located and marked T-3, with the other leads temporarily marked T-6 and T-8.

After the leads have been marked, the motor may be connected to a 230V, three-phase line using leads T-1, T-4, and T-9. Lead T-7 is connected to the line and T-4, and the motor is started with no load connected. Voltage readings are taken between T-1 and T-2. If the voltage is approximately 460V, the markings are correct and may be permanently marked.

If the voltage reading is 400V or less, interchange T-5 and T-7 or interchange T-4 and T-9 and read the voltage again. If the voltage is approximately 230V, interchange both T-5 with T-7 and T-4 with T-9. The readings should now be approximately 460V between leads T-1 and T-2. The leads connected together now are actually T-4 and T-7 and are marked permanently. The remaining lead in each group can now be marked T-9 and T-5.

Connect one of the leads of the last coil group (not T-3) to T-9. If the reading is approximately 460V between T-1 and T-3, the lead may be permanently marked T-6. If the reading is 400V or less, interchange T-6 and T-8. A reading of 460V should exist between T-1 and T-3. T-6 is changed to T-8 and marked permanently and temporary T-8 is changed to T-6.

If all leads are now correctly marked, equal readings of approximately 460V can be obtained between leads T-1, T-2, and T-3.

To double-check the markings, the motor is shut off and reconnected using T-2, T-5, and T-7. T-2 is connected to the same line lead as T-1, lead T-5 is connected where T-4 was, and T-7 is hooked where T-9 was previously connected. When started, the motor should rotate in the same direction as before.

Stop the motor and connect leads T-3, T-6, and T-8 to the line leads previously connected to T-2, T-5, and T-7, respectively, and when the motor is started, it should still rotate in the same direction.

The motor is now ready for service and is connected in series for high or parallel for low voltage, as indicated by the NEMA standard connections.

7.2.0 RECORDKEEPING

The first step towards establishing a reliable maintenance program is to prepare accurate records. As a minimum, records on each motor should include:

- A complete description, including age and nameplate data
- Location and application, keeping such notations up to date if motors are transferred to different areas or used for different purposes
- Notations of scheduled preventive maintenance and previous repair work performed
- Location of duplicate or interchangeable motors
- An estimate of the motor's importance in the production process to which it relates

SUMMARY

This module covered various motor maintenance techniques, including lubrication, storage, and elementary troubleshooting.

In determining which motors are likely to fail first, it is important to remember that motor failures are generally caused by loading, age, vibration, contamination, or commutation problems.

Advanced motor maintenance techniques will be presented in your Level 4 training.

References

For advanced study of topics covered in this Task Module, the following books are suggested:

American Electricians' Handbook, Latest Edition, McGraw-Hill, New York, NY.

National Electrical Code Handbook, Latest Edition, National Fire Protection Association, Quincy, MA.

1. Which of the following provides minimum resistance and aligns the motor rotor while turning?

    a. Compensator
    b. Brushes
    c. End bells
    d. Bearings

2. Which of the following is true concerning lubricating motor bearings?

    a. Always add a little more grease than is needed.
    b. Too much grease can be as harmful as insufficient grease.
    c. No grease is better than too much grease.
    d. Too much grease is better than insufficient grease.

3. Which of the following is *not* a concern of good motor maintenance?

    a. Number of hours and days the motor operates
    b. Manufacturer of the motor
    c. Environmental conditions
    d. Importance of the motor in the production scheme

4. Which of the following is usually an indication of a bad motor bearing?

    a. Hot bearing housing
    b. Cold bearing housing
    c. No unusual vibration
    d. No unusual noise while the motor is running

5. When using compressed air to clean motors, which of the following precautions should be taken?

    a. Make sure the air is warmer than the ambient motor temperature.
    b. Make sure not to use too much pressure.
    c. Make sure the air is colder than the ambient motor temperature.
    d. Use only a high-velocity nozzle.

6. When cleaning wound rotor motors, the _______ should receive the most attention.

    a. lifting eyebolt
    b. end bells
    c. collector rings
    d. motor terminal enclosure

7. Which of the following is the name of the motor conductor(s) that is (are) used only during the brief period when the motor is starting?

    a. Motor leads
    b. Drum armature
    c. Starting winding
    d. Shunt-field winding

8. If a split-phase motor fails to start, which of the following is *not* a likely cause?

    a. Tight or frozen bearings
    b. Bent rotor shaft
    c. Defective centrifugal switch
    d. Improper air gap

9. Which of the following statements is true concerning motors in storage?

    a. Rotors should not be moved or turned until the motor is put in use.
    b. Rotors should be turned once a month to distribute bearing grease.
    c. Rotors should be turned once a year to distribute bearing grease.
    d. Rotors should be turned once every three years to keep them from rusting.

10. The best attachment point for lifting heavy motors is (are) the ______.

    a. eyebolt
    b. shaft
    c. base
    d. end bells

notes

ANSWERS TO REVIEW/PRACTICE QUESTIONS

<u>Answer</u>		<u>Section Reference</u>
1.	d	1.0.0
2.	b	1.0.0
3.	b	2.0.0
4.	a	2.0.0
5.	b	2.0.0
6.	c	2.0.0
7.	c	4.4.0
8.	d	5.0.0
9.	b	6.0.0
10.	a	6.0.0

The NCCER makes every effort to keep these manuals up-to-date and free of technical errors. We appreciate your help in this process. If you have an idea for improving this manual, or if you find an error, a typographical mistake, or an inaccuracy in the NCCER's Craft Training Manuals, please write us, using this form or a photocopy. Be sure to include the exact module number, page number, a description of the problem, and the correction, if possible. Your input will be brought to the attention of the Technical Review Committee. Thank you for your assistance.

Instructors – If you found that additional materials were necessary in order to teach this module effectively, please let us know so that we may include them in the Equipment/Materials list in the Instructor's Guide.

Write: Curriculum Development and Revision Department
National Center for Construction Education and Research
P.O. Box 141104
Gainesville, FL 32614-1104
Fax: 352-334-0932

Craft ___________________________ Module Name ___________________________

Copyright Date __________ Module Number __________ Page Number(s) __________

Description of Problem

____

____

____

____

(Optional) Correction of Problem

____

____

____

(Optional) Your Name and Address

____

____

____

Motor Controls

Module 26311

MOTOR CONTROLS

NATIONAL
CENTER FOR
CONSTRUCTION
EDUCATION AND
RESEARCH

OBJECTIVES

Upon completion of this module, the trainee will be able to:

1. Describe the operating principles of motor controls and control circuits.
2. Select motor controls for specific applications.
3. Connect motor controllers for specific applications.
4. Explain NEC regulations governing the installation of motor controls.
5. Follow NEC requirements when installing motor control circuits.
6. Interpret motor control diagrams.
7. Size and select thermal overload relays and other protective devices for motor controls.
8. Connect control transformers in conjunction with motor control circuits.

Prerequisites

Successful completion of the following Task Modules is recommended before beginning study of this Task Module: Core Curricula; Electrical Level 1; Electrical Level 2; Electrical Level 3, Modules 26301 through 26310.

Required Trainee Materials

1. Trainee Task Module
2. Appropriate Personal Protective Equipment
3. Copy of the latest edition of the *National Electrical Code*

Note: The designations "National Electrical Code," "NE Code," and "NEC," where used in this document, refer to the National Electrical Code®, which is a registered trademark of the National Fire Protection Association, Quincy, MA. *All National Electrical Code (NEC) references in this module refer to the 1999 edition of the NEC.*

COURSE MAP

This course map shows all of the modules in the third level of the Electrical curricula. The suggested training order begins at the bottom and proceeds up. Skill levels increase as a trainee advances on the course map. The training order may be adjusted by the local Training Program Sponsor.

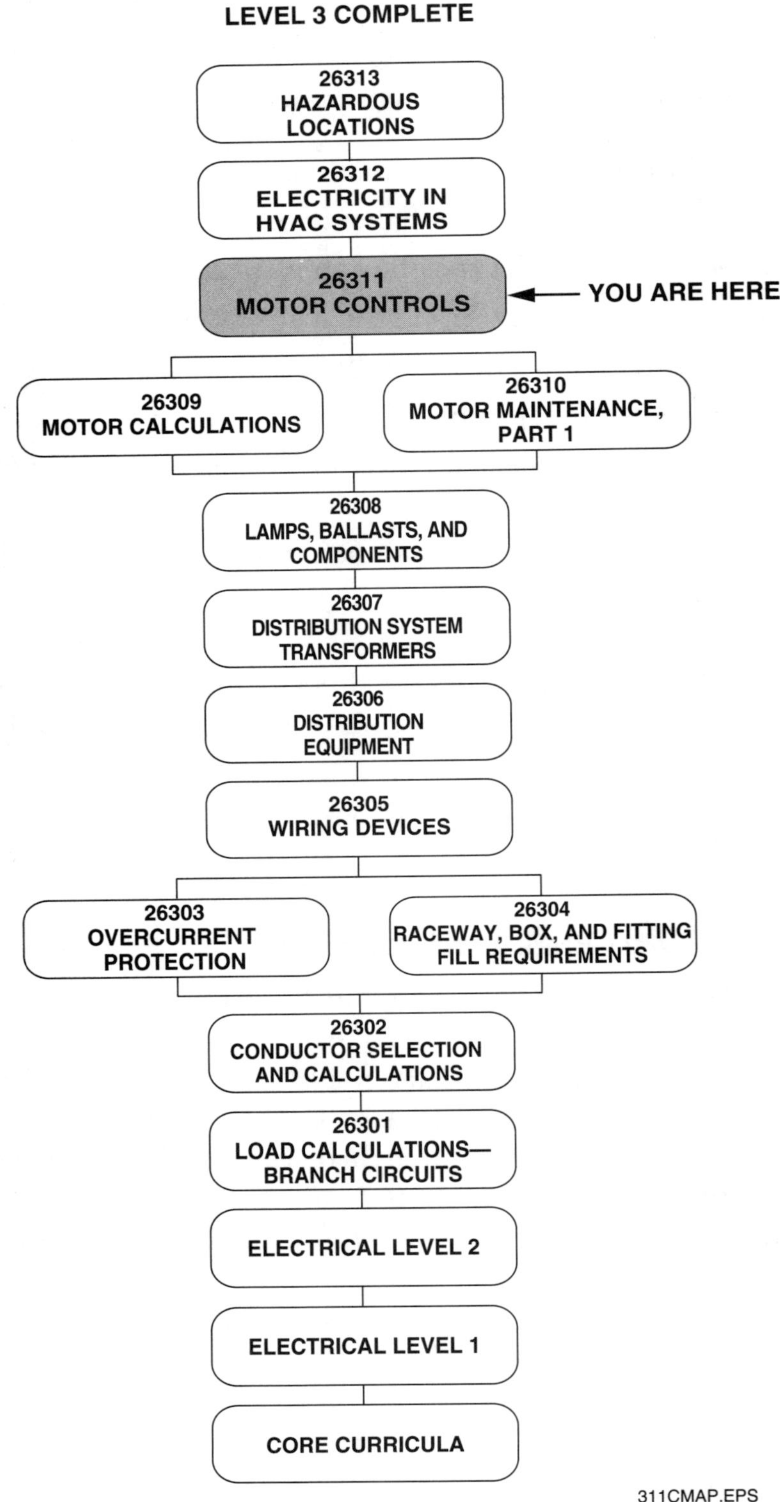

ELECTRICAL — TRAINEE TASK MODULE 26311

TABLE OF CONTENTS

Trade Terms Introduced in This Module

Ambient temperature: The temperature of the air where a piece of equipment is situated.

Bimetal strip: A temperature regulating or indicating device that works on the principle that when two dissimilar metals with unequal expansion rates are welded together, they will bend as the temperature changes.

Control: An automatic or manual device used to start, stop, and/or regulate the flow of gas, liquid, and/or electricity.

Controller: A device or group of devices that serves to govern in some predetermined manner the electric power delivered to the apparatus to which it is connected.

Float switch: A switch that is opened and closed by a float that rises and falls with the level of the liquid in a tank.

Inching: The momentary activation of machinery used for inspection or maintenance. The controls for such activation usually consist of start, stop, and inch. The device used to operate such machinery is usually a single-phase or three-phase induction motor.

Induction motor: An AC motor that does not run exactly in step with the alternations. The currents supplied are led through the stator coils only; the rotor is rotated by the currents induced by the varying field set up by the stator coils.

Interlock: A safety device used to ensure that a piece of apparatus will not operate until certain conditions have been satisfied.

Jogging: The repeated starting and stopping of a motor at frequent intervals for short periods of time. See *inching*.

Magnetic coil: The winding of an electromagnet, which consists of a coil of wire wound in one direction, producing a dense magnetic field capable of attracting iron or steel when carrying an electric current.

Motor control: A device used to start and/or stop a motor at certain temperature or pressure conditions.

Motor starter: An electric controller used to accelerate a motor from rest to normal speed and also to stop the motor.

Plugging: Braking an induction motor by reversing the phase sequence of the power to the motor. This reversal causes the motor to develop a counter torque, which results in the exertion of a retarding force. Plugging is used to secure both rapid stop and quick reversal.

Relay: A device designed to abruptly change a circuit because of a specified control input.

Temperature rise: The difference between the winding temperature of a motor when it is running and the ambient temperature.

Thermal protector: A protective device that is assembled as an integral part of a motor or motor compressor and that, when properly applied, protects the motor against dangerous overheating due to an overload or failure to start.

1.0.0   INTRODUCTION

Electric motors provide one of the principal sources for driving all types of equipment and machinery, and every motor in use must have some type of **control** mechanism, if only to start and stop it.

Motor controls cover a wide range of types and sizes, from a simple toggle switch to a complex system with such components as **relays**, timers, and switches. The common function, however, is the same in any case—that is, to control some operation of an electric motor.

A motor **controller** will include some or all of the following functions:

- Starting and stopping
- Overload protection
- Overcurrent protection
- Reversing
- Changing speed
- **Jogging**
- **Plugging**
- Sequence control
- Pilot light indication

The controller can also provide the control for auxiliary equipment such as brakes, clutches, solenoids, heaters, and signals, and may be used to control a single motor or a group of motors.

The term **motor starter** is often used and means practically the same thing as a controller. Strictly, a motor starter is the simplest form of controller and is capable of starting and stopping the motor and providing it with overload protection.

See *Figure 1* for a review of the electrical symbols used in the wiring diagrams in this module.

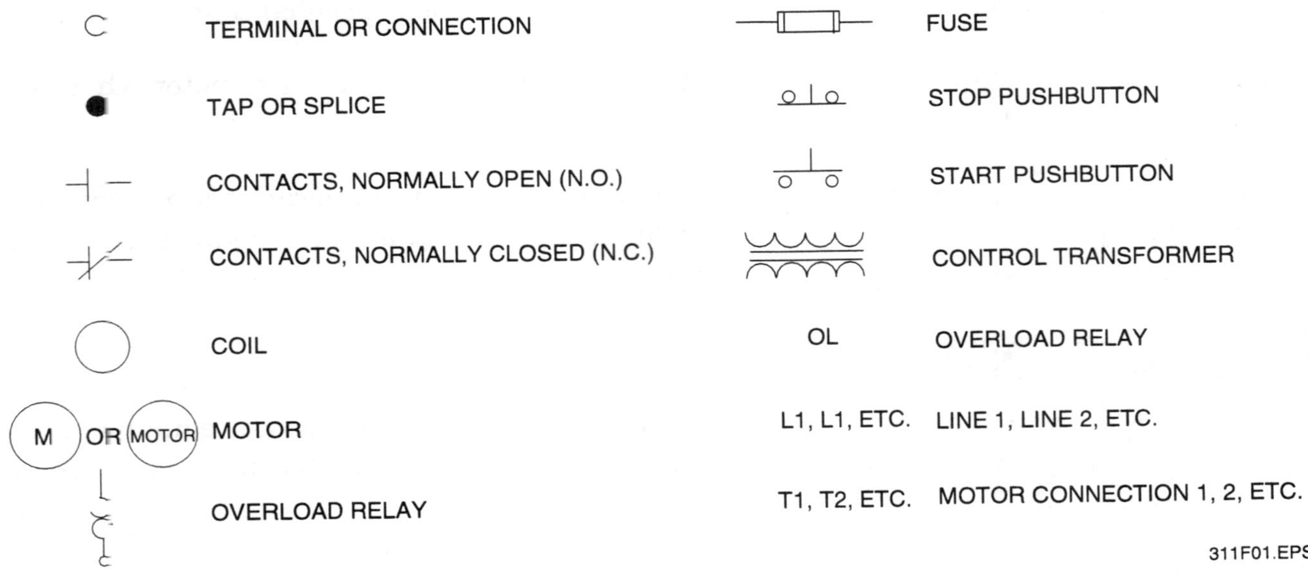

Figure 1. Symbols Used In Wiring Diagrams

2.0.0 TYPES OF MOTOR CONTROLLERS

A large variety of motor controllers are available that will handle almost every conceivable application. However, all of them can be grouped into the following categories:

- Plug and receptacle assemblies
- Manual starters
- Magnetic controllers

2.1.0 PLUG AND RECEPTACLE ASSEMBLIES

NEC Section 430-81 defines a controller as any switch or device normally used to start and stop a motor by making and breaking the motor circuit current. The simplest form of controller allowed by the NEC is an attachment plug and receptacle (*Figure 2*). However, this arrangement is limited to portable motors rated at ⅓hp or less.

Figure 2(A) is a pictorial view of a portable motor with a cord and plug assembly attached. If this motor is portable and less than ⅓hp, then the plug and receptacle may act as the motor controller, as permitted by *NEC Section 430-81(c)*.

Figure 2(B) is the same circuit depicted in the form of a wiring diagram. Note that symbols have been used to represent the various circuit items rather than actually drawing the items themselves; yet they are arranged on the basis of their physical relationship to each other. This simplifies the drawing, both from a drafter's point of view and also for those who must interpret it.

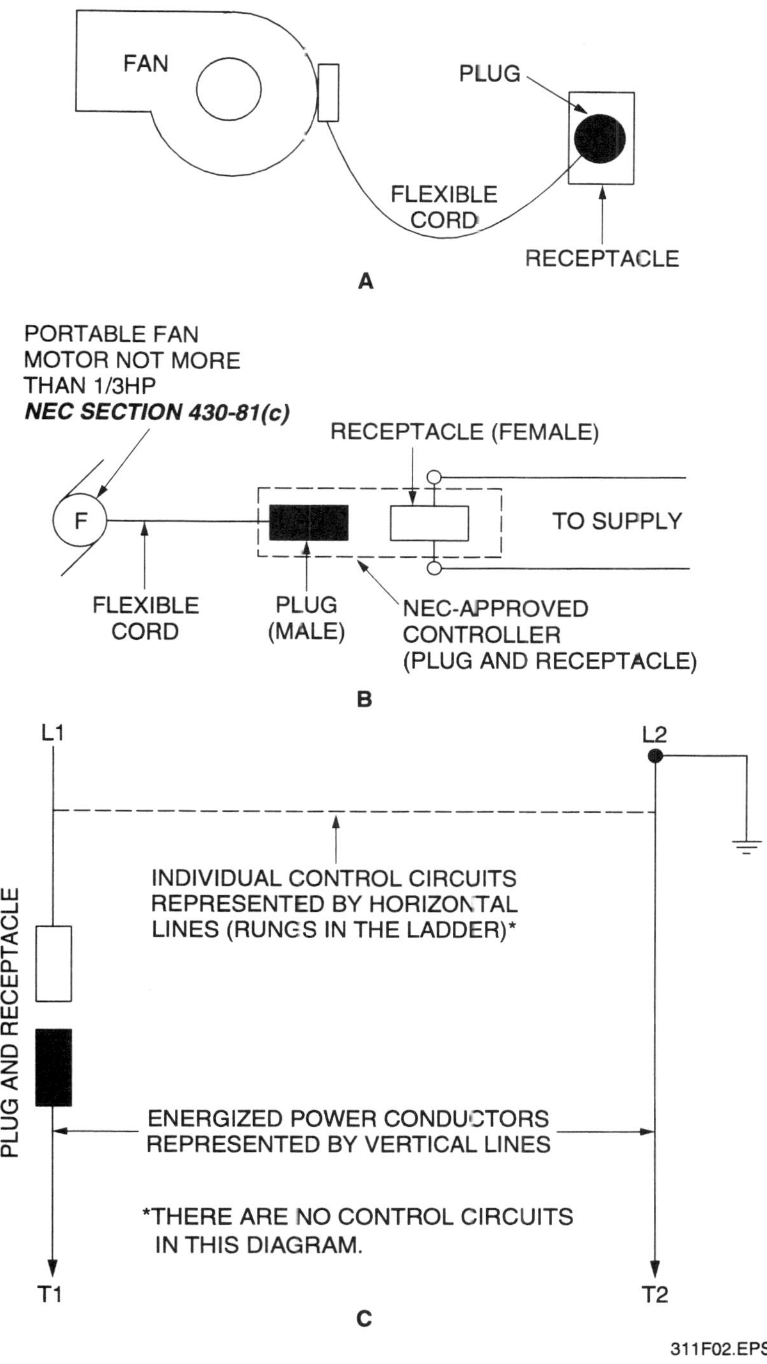

Figure 2. Plug And Receptacle Motor Controllers

Another form of drawing for this same circuit is shown in *Figure 2(C)*. This type of drawing
has become known as the *ladder diagram*; it is a schematic representation of the electrical
circuit. Ladder diagrams are drawn in an H format with the energized power conductors
represented by vertical lines and the individual circuits represented by horizontal lines.
Rather than physically representing the circuit items, as in *Figure 2(B)*, a ladder diagram
arranges the conductors and electrical components schematically according to their electrical

function in the circuit. Therefore, ladder diagrams merely represent the current paths (shown as the rungs of a ladder) to each of the controlled or energized output devices.

Where stationary motors rated at ⅛hp or less are normally left running (clock motors, fly fans, etc.), and are constructed so that they cannot be damaged by an overload or failure to start, the branch circuit protective device may serve as the controller. Consequently, the branch circuit breaker or fusible disconnect serves as both branch circuit overcurrent protection and motor controller. Such a circuit is shown in *Figure 3*.

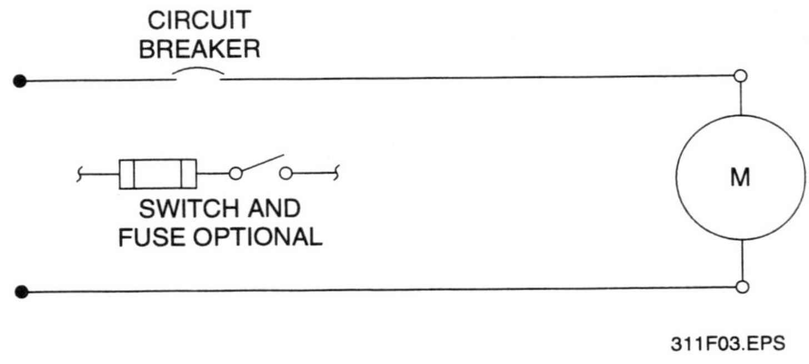

Figure 3. Branch Circuit Protective Device Serving As The Motor Controller

2.2.0 MANUAL STARTERS

A manual starter is a motor controller whose contact mechanism is operated by a mechanical linkage from a toggle handle or pushbutton, which is in turn operated by hand. A **thermal protector** unit and direct-acting overload mechanism provide motor running overload protection. Basically, a manual starter is an ON/OFF switch with overload relays.

Manual starters are used mostly on small machine tools, fans and blowers, pumps, compressors, and conveyors. They have the lowest cost of all motor starters, have a simple mechanism, and provide quiet operation with no AC magnetic hum. The contacts, however, remain closed and the lever stays in the ON position in the event of a power failure, causing the motor to automatically restart when the power returns. Therefore, low-voltage protection and low-voltage release are not possible with these manually-operated starters. However, this action is an advantage when the starter is applied to motors that run continuously.

2.2.1 Fractional-Horsepower Manual Starters

Fractional-horsepower manual starters are designed to control and provide overload protection for motors of 1hp or less on 120V or 240V single-phase circuits. They are available in single-pole and two-pole versions, and are operated by a toggle handle on the front. When a serious overload occurs, the thermal unit trips to open the starter contacts, disconnecting the motor from the line. The contacts cannot be reclosed until the overload relay has been reset by moving the handle to the full OFF position, after allowing about two minutes for the thermal unit to cool. The open-type starter will fit into a standard outlet box and can be used with a standard flush plate. The compact construction of this type of device makes it possible to mount it directly on the driven machinery and in various other places where the available space is small. *Figure 4* shows fractional-horsepower (FHP) manual motor starter wiring diagrams for both 120V and 240V single-phase motors, along with a pictorial representation.

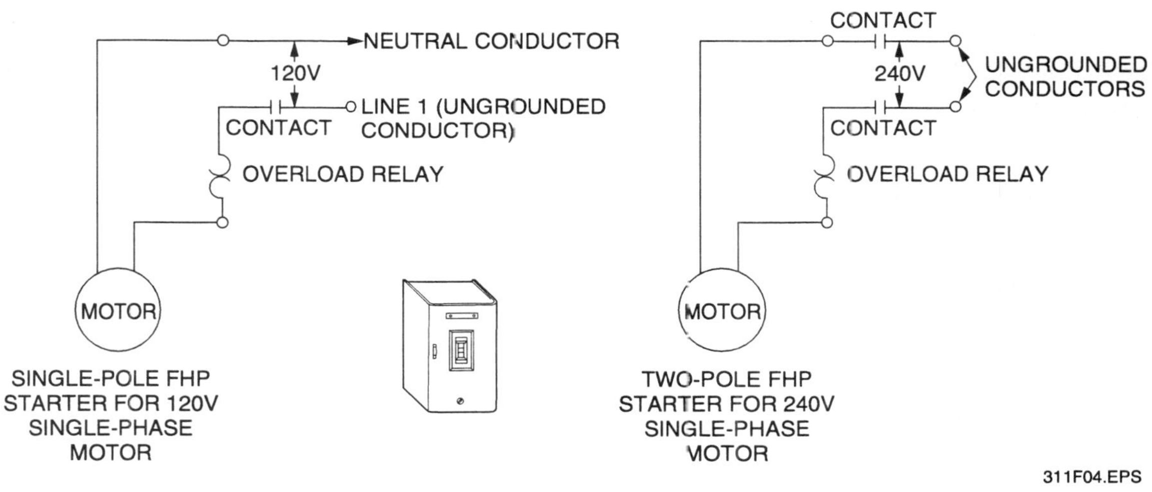

Figure 4. Wiring Diagrams Of Fractional-Horsepower Manual Starters

Note that the single-pole FHP starter has only one contact to trip and disconnect the motor from the line; the grounded or neutral conductor is not opened when the handle is in the **OFF** position. This single-pole starter also has one overload relay connected in series with the ungrounded conductor.

The two-pole FHP starter has two contacts to open both phases when connected to a 240V circuit. When the toggle handle is in the **OFF** position, no current flows to the motor. However, only one overload relay is needed, since one will shut down the motor if the relay detects an overload and opens.

2.2.2   Manual Motor Starting Switches

Manual motor starting switches provide ON/OFF control of single-phase or three-phase AC motors where overload protection is not required or is provided separately. Two-pole and three-pole switches are available, with ratings up to 10hp, 600V, three-phase power. The continuous current rating is 30A at 250V maximum and 20A at 600V maximum. The toggle operation of the manual switch is similar to the fractional-horsepower starter, and typical applications of the switch include pumps, fans, conveyors, and other electrical machinery that have separate motor protection. They are particularly suited to switch nonmotor loads, such as resistance heaters.

2.2.3   Integral-Horsepower Manual Starters

The integral-horsepower manual starter is available in two-pole and three-pole versions to control single-phase motors up to 5hp and polyphase motors up to 10hp, respectively.

Two-pole starters have one overload relay and three-pole starters usually have three overload relays. When an overload relay trips, the starter mechanism unlatches, opening the contacts to stop the motor. The contacts cannot be reclosed until the starter mechanism has been reset by pressing the STOP button or moving the handle to the RESET position, after allowing time for the thermal unit to cool.

Integral-horsepower manual starters with low-voltage protection prevent automatic startup of motors after a power loss. This is accomplished with a continuous-duty solenoid, which is energized whenever the line voltage is present. If the line voltage is lost or disconnected, the solenoid deenergizes, opening the starter contacts. The contacts will not automatically close when the voltage is restored to the line. To close the contacts, the device must be manually reset. This manual starter will not function unless the line terminals are energized. This is a safety feature that can protect personnel or equipment from damage and is used on such equipment as conveyors, grinders, metalworking machines, mixers, woodworking equipment, etc. *Figure 5* shows a wiring diagram of an integral-horsepower manual starter with low-voltage protection.

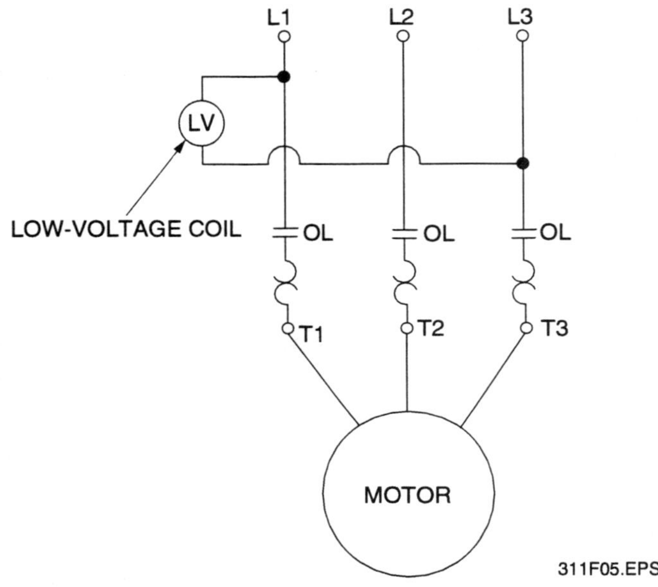

Figure 5. Integral-Horsepower Manual Starter With Low-Voltage Protection

2.3.0 MAGNETIC CONTROLLERS

Unlike manual motor controllers, magnetic motor controllers use electromagnetic energy for closing switches. The electromagnet consists of a coil of wire placed on an iron core. When current flows through the coil, the iron of the magnet becomes magnetized and attracts the iron bar, called the *armature*. An interruption of the current flow through the coil of wire causes the armature to drop out due to the presence of an air gap in the magnetic circuit.

Line voltage magnetic motor starters are electromechanical devices that provide a safe, convenient, and economic means of starting and stopping motors. The majority of motor controllers are of this type. Therefore, the operating principles and applications of magnetic motor controllers should be fully understood.

In the construction of a magnetic controller, the armature is mechanically connected to a set of contacts so that when the armature moves to its closed position, the contacts also close. When the coil has been energized and the armature has moved to the closed position, the controller is said to be *picked up* and the armature is said to be *seated* or *sealed in*. Some of the magnetic armature assemblies in current use are as follows:

- *Clapper* – In this type, the armature is hinged. As it pivots to seal in, the movable contacts close against the stationary contacts.
- *Vertical action* – The action is a straight line motion with the armature and contacts being guided so that they move in a vertical plane.
- *Horizontal action* – Both the armature and the contacts move in a straight line through a horizontal plane.
- *Bell crank* – A bell crank lever transforms the vertical action of the armature into a horizontal contact motion. The shock of armature pickup is not transmitted to the contacts, resulting in minimum contact bounce and longer contact life.

These four types of assemblies are shown in *Figure 6*.

The magnetic circuit of a controller consists of the magnet assembly, the coil, and the armature. The coil and the current flowing in it cause a magnetic flux to be set up through the iron in a similar manner to a voltage causing current to flow through a system of conductors. The changing magnetic flux produced by alternating currents results in a **temperature rise** in the magnetic circuit. The heating effect is reduced by laminating the magnet assembly and armature. By placing a coil of many turns of wire around a soft iron core, the magnetic flux set up by the energized coil tends to be concentrated; therefore, the magnetic field effect is strengthened. Since the iron core is the path of least resistance to the flow of the magnetic lines of force, magnetic attraction will concentrate according to the shape of the magnet.

The magnet assembly is the stationary part of the magnetic circuit. The coil is supported by and surrounds part of the magnet assembly in order to induce magnetic flux into the magnetic circuit.

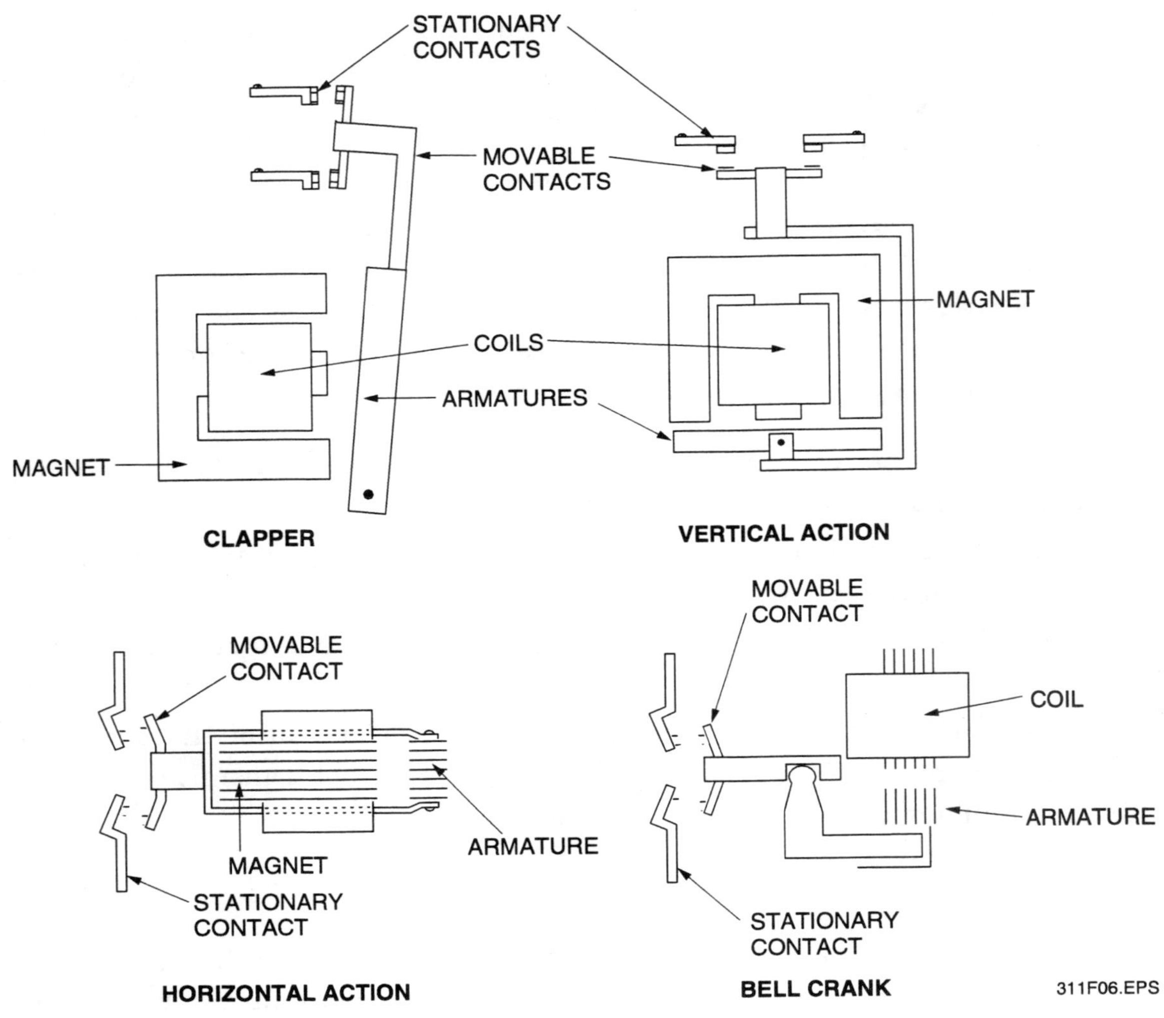

Figure 6. Several Types Of Magnetic Armature Assemblies

The armature is the moving part of the magnetic circuit. When it has been attracted into its sealed-in position, it completes the magnetic circuit. To provide maximum pull and help ensure quiet operation, the faces of the armature and the magnet assembly are ground to a very close tolerance.

When a controller's armature has sealed in, it is held closely against the magnet assembly. However, a small gap is always deliberately left in the iron core circuit. When the coil becomes deenergized, some magnetic flux (residual magnetism) always remains, and if it were not for the gap in the iron circuit, the residual magnetism might be sufficient to hold the armature in the sealed-in position. See *Figure 7*.

The shaded-pole principle is used to provide a time delay in the decay of flux in DC coils, but it is used more frequently to prevent chatter and wear in the moving parts of AC magnets.

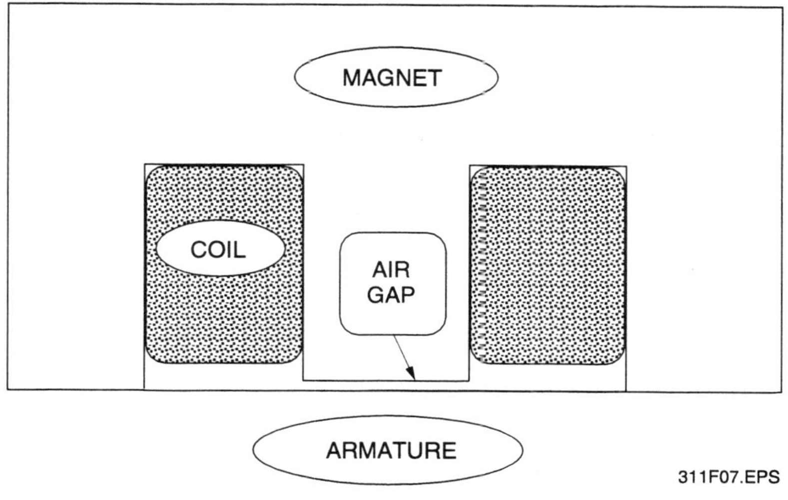

Figure 7. Armature Assembly Air Gap

A shading coil is a single turn of conductive material mounted in the face of the magnet assembly or armature. The alternating main magnetic flux induces currents in the shading coil, and these currents set up an auxiliary magnetic flux that is out of phase from the pull due to the main flux. This keeps the armature sealed in when the main flux falls to zero, which occurs 120 times per second with 60-cycle AC. Without the shading coil, the armature would tend to open each time the main flux goes through zero, resulting in excessive noise, wear on the magnet faces, and heat. See *Figure 8*. A magnet assembly and armature showing shading coils is shown in *Figure 9*.

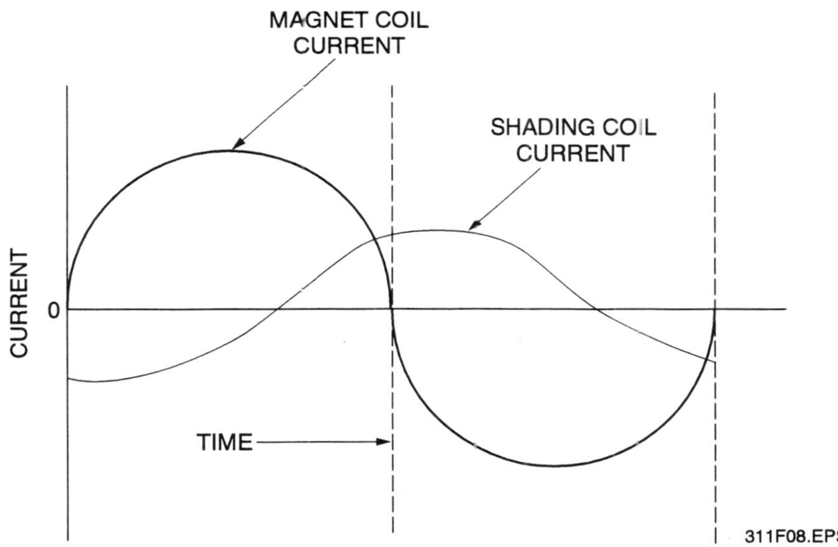

Figure 8. Auxiliary Flux Produces A Magnetic Pull Out Of Phase From The Main Flux

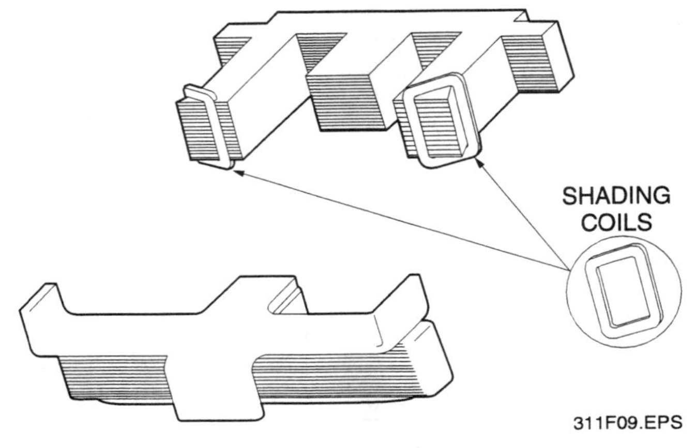

Figure 9. Magnet Assembly And Armature With Shading Coils

For a further explanation of shaded coil principles, see *Figure 10*, which illustrates an exaggerated view of a pole face with a copper band or short circuited coil of low resistance connected around a portion of the pole tip. When the flux is increasing in the pole from left to right, the induced current in the coil is in a clockwise direction.

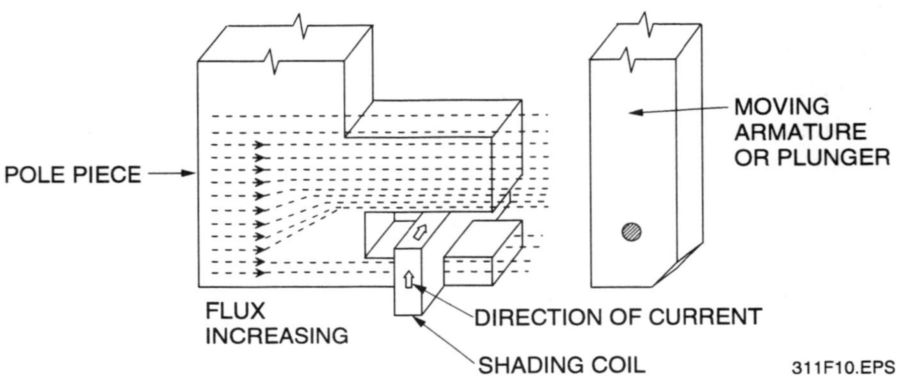

Figure 10. Section Of Pole Face With Current In Clockwise Direction

The magnetomotive force produced by the coil opposes the direction of the flux of the main field. Therefore, the flux density in the shaded portion of the iron will be considerably less, and the flux density in the unshaded portion of the iron will be more than would be the case without the shading coil.

Figure 11 shows the pole with the flux still moving from left to right, but decreasing in value. Now the current in the coil is in a counterclockwise direction. The magnetomotive force produced by the coil is in the same direction as the main unshaded portion, but less than it would be without the shading coil. Consequently, if the electric circuit of a coil is opened, the current decreases rapidly to zero, but the flux decreases much more slowly due to the action of the shading coil.

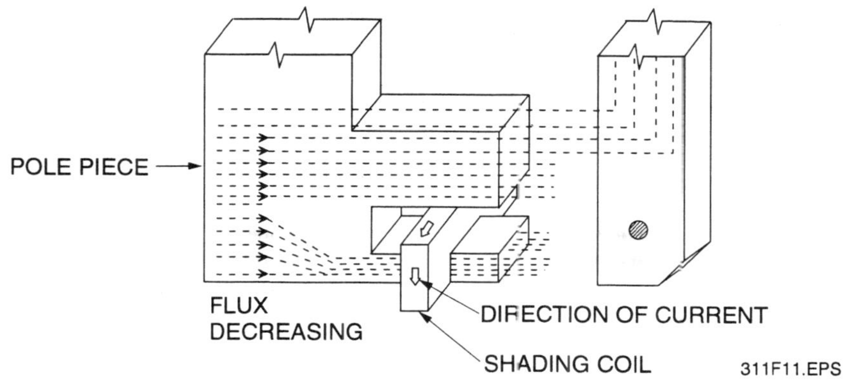

Figure 11. Section Of Pole Face With Current In Counterclockwise Direction

3.0.0 MAGNETIC COILS

The magnetic coil used in motor controllers has many turns of insulated copper wire wound on a spool. Most coils are protected by an epoxy molding, which makes them very resistant to mechanical damage.

When the controller is in the open position, there is a large air gap (not to be confused with the built-in gap discussed previously) in the magnet circuit; this is when the armature is at its furthest distance from the magnet. The impedance of the coil is relatively low due to this air gap, so that when the coil is energized, it draws a fairly high current. As the armature moves closer to the magnet assembly, the air gap is progressively reduced, and with it, the coil current, until the armature has sealed in. The final current is referred to as the *sealed current*. The inrush current is approximately 6 to 10 times the sealed current. (The ratio varies with individual designs.) After the controller has been energized for some time, the coil will become hot. This will cause the coil current to fall to approximately 80% of its cold value.

AC magnetic coils should never be connected in series. If one device were to seal in ahead of the other, the increased circuit impedance will reduce the coil current so that the slow device will not pick up; or, having picked up, will not seal. Consequently, AC coils are always connected in parallel.

Magnetic coil data is usually given in volt-amperes (VA). For example, given a magnetic starter whose coils are rated at 600VA inrush and 60VA sealed, a 120V coil draws 600VA ÷ 120A or 5A inrush and 60VA ÷ 120V or .5A sealed. The same starter with a 480V coil will only draw 600VA ÷ 480V or 1.25A inrush and 60VA ÷ 480V or .125A sealed.

The minimum voltage which will cause the armature to start to move is called the *pickup voltage*. The seal-in voltage is the minimum control voltage required to cause the armature to seat against the pole faces of the magnet. On devices using a vertical action magnet and armature, the seal-in voltage is higher than the pickup voltage to provide additional magnetic pull to ensure good contact pressure.

Control devices using the bell crank armature and magnet arrangement are unique in that they have different force characteristics. Devices using this operating principle are designed to have a lower seal-in voltage than pickup voltage. Contact life is extended, and contact damage under abnormal voltage conditions is reduced, for if the voltage is sufficient to pick up, it is also high enough to seat the armature.

If the control voltage is reduced sufficiently, the controller will open. The voltage at which this happens is called the *drop-out voltage*. It is somewhat lower than the seal-in voltage.

3.1.0   VOLTAGE VARIATION

The National Electrical Manufacturers' Association (NEMA) standards require that magnetic devices operate properly at varying control voltages from a high of 110% to a low of 85% of rated coil voltage. This range, which is established by the coil design, ensures that the coil will withstand given temperature rises at voltages up to 10% over rated voltage, and that the armature will pick up and seal in, even though the voltage may drop to 15% under the nominal rating.

3.1.1   Effects Of Voltage Variation

If the voltage applied to the coil is too high, the coil will draw more than its designed current. Excessive heat will be produced and will cause early failure of the coil insulation. The magnetic pull will be too high, which will cause the armature to slam home with excessive force. The magnet faces will wear rapidly, leading to a shortened life for the controller. In addition, contact bounce may be excessive, resulting in reduced contact life.

Low control voltage produces low coil currents and reduced magnetic pull. On devices with vertical action assemblies, if the voltage is greater than the pickup voltage but less than the seal-in voltage, the controller may pick up but it will not seal. With this condition, the coil current will not fall to the sealed value. As the coil is not designed to continuously carry a current greater than its sealed current, it will quickly get very hot and burn out. The armature will also chatter and cause excess wear on the magnet faces.

In both vertical action and bell crank construction, if the armature does not seal, the contacts will not close with adequate pressure. Excessive heat, with arcing and possible welding of the contacts, will occur as the controller attempts to carry current with insufficient contact pressure.

3.2.0   AC HUM

All AC devices which incorporate a magnetic effect produce a characteristic hum. This hum or noise is due mainly to the changing magnetic pull (as the flux changes) inducing mechanical vibrations.

Contactors, starters, and relays could become excessively noisy as a result of some of the following operating conditions:

*   Broken shading coil
*   Operating voltage too low
*   Misalignment between the armature and magnet assembly—the armature is then unable to seat properly
*   Wrong coil
*   Dirt, rust, filings, etc. on the magnet faces (the armature is unable to seal in completely)
*   Jamming or binding of moving parts so that full travel of the armature is prevented
*   Incorrect mounting of the controller (as on a thin piece of plywood fastened to a wall) may cause a sounding board effect

4.0.0   POWER CIRCUITS IN MOTOR STARTERS

The power circuit of a starter includes the stationary and movable contacts, and the thermal unit or heater portion of the overload relay assembly. The number of contacts (or poles) is determined by the electrical service. For example, in a three-phase, three-wire system, a three-pole starter is required. See *Figure 12*.

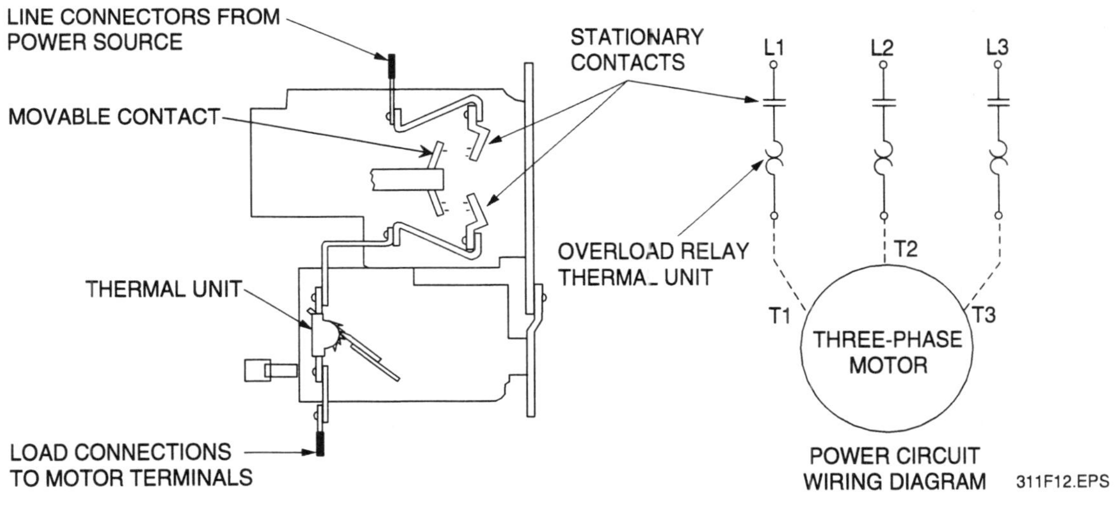

Figure 12. Power Circuit In A Typical Three-Pole Magnetic Starter

To be suitable for a given motor application, the magnetic starter selected should equal or exceed the motor horsepower and full-load current ratings. For example, assume that we want to select a motor starter for a 50hp motor to be supplied by a 240V, three-phase service, and the full-load current of the motor is 125A. Referring to *Table 1*, it can be seen that a NEMA Size 4 starter would be required for normal motor duty. If the motor is to be used for jogging or plugging duty, a NEMA Size 5 starter should be chosen.

CAUTION: For three-phase motors having a locked rotor kVA/hp in excess of that for the motor NEMA size in *Table 1*, do not apply the controller at its maximum rating without consulting the manufacturer. In most cases, the next higher horsepower-rated controller should be used. Per **NEC Section 430-83(a)(1)**, controllers for NEMA Design E motors of more than 2hp shall be marked for use with a Design E motor or shall have a horsepower rating of no less than 1.4 times the rating of a motor rated 3hp through 100hp, or no less than 1.3 times the rating of a motor over 100hp.

NEMA Size	Volts	Maximum Horsepower Rating—Non-plugging and Nonjogging Duty		Maximum Horsepower Rating—Plugging and Jogging Duty		Continuous Current Rating, amperes—600 Volt Max.	Service-Limit Current Rating, Amperes *	Tungsten and Infrared Lamp Load, Amperes—250 Volts Max. *	Resistance heating Loads, kW—other than Infrared Lamp Loads		KVA Rating for Switching Transformer Primaries at 50 or 60 Cycles		3-Phase Rating for Switching Capacitors
		Single Phase	Poly-Phase	Single Phase	Poly-Phase				Single Phase	Poly-phase	Single Phase	Poly-Phase	Kvar
00	115	⅓	...	...	...	9	11	5	...	...	...	...	...
	200	...	1½	...	...	9	11	5	...	...	...	...	...
	230	1	1½	...	...	9	11	5	...	...	...	...	...
	380	...	1½	...	...	9	11	...	...	...	...	...	...
	460	...	2	...	...	9	11	...	...	...	...	...	...
	575	...	2	...	...	9	11	...	...	...	...	...	...
0	115	1	...	½	...	18	21	10	...	...	0.9	1.2	...
	200	...	3	...	1½	18	21	10	...	...	...	1.4	...
	230	2	3	1	1½	18	21	10	...	...	1.4	1.7	...
	380	...	5	...	1½	18	21	...	...	...	...	2.0	...
	460	...	5	...	2	18	21	...	...	...	1.9	2.5	...
	575	...	5	...	2	18	21	...	...	...	1.9	2.5	...

311T01A.TIF

Table 1. Electrical Ratings For AC Magnetic Contactors And Starters (1 Of 3)

NEMA Size	Volts	Maximum Horsepower Rating—Non-plugging and Nonjogging Duty		Maximum Horsepower Rating—Plugging and Jogging Duty		Continuous Current Rating, amperes—600 Volt Max.	Service-Limit Current Rating, Amperes *	Tungsten and Infrared Lamp Load, Amperes—250 Volts Max. *	Resistance heating Loads, kW—other than Infrared Lamp Loads		KVA Rating for Switching Transformer Primaries at 50 or 60 Cycles		3-Phase Rating for Switching Capacitors
		Single Phase	Poly-Phase	Single Phase	Poly-Phase				Single Phase	Poly-phase	Single Phase	Poly-Phase	Kvar
	115	2	...	1	...	27	32	15	3	5	1.4	1.7	...
	200	...	7½	...	3	27	32	15	...	9.1	...	3.5	...
	230	3	7½	2	3	27	32	15	6	10	1.9	4.1	...
1	380	...	10	...	5	27	32	...	...	16.5	...	4.3	...
	460	...	10	...	5	27	32	...	12	20	3	5.3	...
	575	...	10	...	5	27	32	...	15	25	3	5.3	...
1P	115	3	...	1½	...	36	42	24	...	...	...	...	...
	230	5	...	3	...	36	42	24	...	...	...	...	...
	115	3	...	2	...	45	52	30	5	8.5	1.0	4.1	...
	200	...	10	...	7½	45	52	30	...	15.4	...	6.6	11.3
	230	7½	15	5	10	45	52	30	10	17	4.6	7.6	13
2	380	...	25	...	15	45	52	...	...	28	...	9.9	21
	460	...	25	...	15	45	52	...	20	34	5.7	12	26
	575	...	25	...	15	45	52	...	25	43	5.7	12	33
	115	7½	...	...	...	90	104	60	10	17	4.6	7.6	...
	200	...	25	...	15	90	104	60	...	31	...	13	23.4
	230	15	30	...	20	90	104	60	20	34	8.6	15	27
3	380	...	50	...	30	90	104	...	...	56	...	19	43.7
	460	...	50	...	30	90	104	...	40	68	14	23	53
	575	...	50	...	30	90	104	...	50	86	14	23	67

311T01B.TIF

Table 1. Electrical Ratings For AC Magnetic Contactors And Starters (2 Of 3)

NEMA Size	Volts	Maximum Horsepower Rating—Non-plugging and Nonjogging Duty		Maximum Horsepower Rating—Plugging and Jogging Duty		Continuous Current Rating, amperes—600 Volt Max.	Service-Limit Current Rating, Amperes *	Tungsten and Infrared Lamp Load, Amperes—250 Volts Max. *	Resistance heating Loads, kW—other than Infrared Lamp Loads		KVA Rating for Switching Transformer Primaries at 50 or 60 Cycles		3-Phase Rating for Switching Capacitors
		Single Phase	Poly-Phase	Single Phase	Poly-Phase				Single Phase	Poly-phase	Single Phase	Poly-Phase	Kvar
4	200	...	40	...	25	135	156	120	...	45	...	20	34
	230	...	50	...	30	135	156	120	30	52	11	23	40
	380	...	75	...	50	135	156	...	...	86.7	...	38	66
	460	...	100	...	60	135	156	...	60	105	22	46	80
	575	...	100	...	60	135	156	...	75	130	22	46	100
5	200	...	75	...	60	270	311	240	...	91	...	40	69
	230	...	100	...	75	270	311	240	60	105	28	46	80
	380	...	150	...	125	270	311	...	...	173	...	75	132
	460	...	200	...	150	270	311	...	120	210	40	91	160
	575	...	200	...	150	270	311	...	150	260	40	91	200
6	200	...	150	...	125	540	621	480	...	182	...	79	139
	230	...	200	...	150	540	621	480	120	210	57	91	160
	380	...	300	...	250	540	621	...	...	342	...	148	264
	460	...	400	...	300	540	621	...	240	415	86	180	320
	575	...	400	...	300	540	621	...	300	515	86	180	400
7	230	...	300	...	...	810	932	720	180	315	...	...	240
	460	...	600	...	...	810	932	...	360	625	...	...	480
	575	...	600	...	...	810	932	...	450	775	...	...	600
8	230	...	450	...	...	1215	1400	1080	...	...	...	...	360
	460	...	900	...	...	1215	1400	...	...	...	...	...	720
	575	...	900	...	...	1215	1400	...	...	...	...	...	900

311T01C.TIF

Table 1. Electrical Ratings For AC Magnetic Contactors And Starters (3 Of 3)

Power circuit contacts handle the motor load. The ability of the contacts to carry the full-load current without exceeding a rated temperature rise and their isolation from adjacent contacts correspond to NEMA standards established to categorize the NEMA size of the starter. The starter must also be capable of interrupting the motor circuit under locked rotor current conditions.

4.1.0   MOTOR NAMEPLATES

Much information about sizing motor starters can be found on the motor nameplate. Consequently, a review of motor nameplates is in order.

A typical motor nameplate is shown in *Figure 13*. A nameplate is one of the most important parts of a motor since it gives the motor's electrical and mechanical characteristics (e.g., the horsepower, voltage, rpm, etc.). Always refer to the motor nameplate before connecting it to an electric system or selecting the motor starter and related components. The same is true when performing preventive maintenance or troubleshooting.

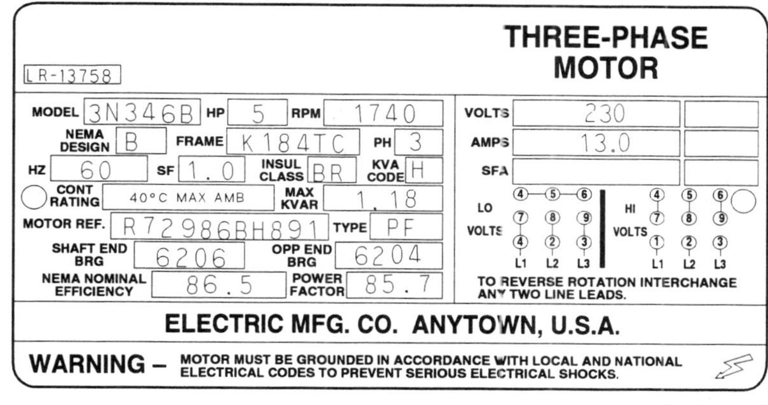

311F13.EPS

Figure 13. Typical Motor Nameplate

On the motor nameplate shown in *Figure 13*, the model number identifies the particular motor. The type or class specifies the insulation used to ensure the motor will perform at the rated horsepower and service factor load. The phase indicates whether the motor has been designed for single-phase or three-phase use.

When selecting motor starters for a given motor, the motor code letter and NEMA design letter on the nameplate both play important roles. *Table 2* may be used as a guide when selecting motor controllers. For Design Letter E motors, refer to ***NEC Section 430-83(a)(1)***.

Controller HP Rating	Maximum Allowable Motor Code Letter
1¹/₂	L
3 to 5	K
7¹/₂ and above	H

Table 2. Using Motor Code Letters To Size Motor Controllers

5.0.0 OVERLOAD PROTECTION

Overload protection for an electric motor is necessary to prevent burnout and ensure maximum operating life. If permitted, an electric motor will operate at an output of more than its rated capacity. Conditions of motor overload may be caused by an overload on driven machinery, a low line voltage, or an open line in a polyphase system that results in single-phase operation. Under any condition of overload, a motor draws excessive current that causes overheating. Since motor winding insulation deteriorates when subjected to overheating, there are established limits on motor operating temperatures. To protect a motor from overheating, overload relays are employed on motor controls to limit the amount of current drawn. This is known as *overload protection* or *running protection*.

The ideal overload protection for a motor is an element with current-sensing properties that are very similar to the heating curve of the motor (*Figure 14*), which would act to open the motor circuit when the full-load current is exceeded. The operation of the protective device should be such that the motor is allowed to carry harmless overloads, but is quickly removed from the line when an overload has persisted for too long.

Single-element, nontime-delay fuses are not designed to provide overload protection. Their basic function is to protect against short circuits (overcurrent protection). Motors draw a high inrush current when starting and conventional single-element fuses have no way of distinguishing between this temporary and harmless inrush current and a damaging overload. Such fuses, if chosen on the basis of motor full-load current, will blow every time the motor is started. On the other hand, if a fuse is chosen large enough to pass the starting or inrush current, it will not protect the motor against small, harmful overloads that might occur later.

Dual-element, time-delay fuses can provide motor overload protection, but suffer the disadvantages of being nonrenewable and must be replaced.

The overload relay is the heart of motor protection. It has inverse trip-time characteristics, permitting it to hold in during the accelerating period (when inrush current is drawn), yet providing protection on small overloads above the full-load current when the motor is running. Unlike dual-element fuses, overload relays are renewable and can withstand repeated trip and reset cycles without requiring replacement. They cannot, however, take the place of overcurrent protective equipment.

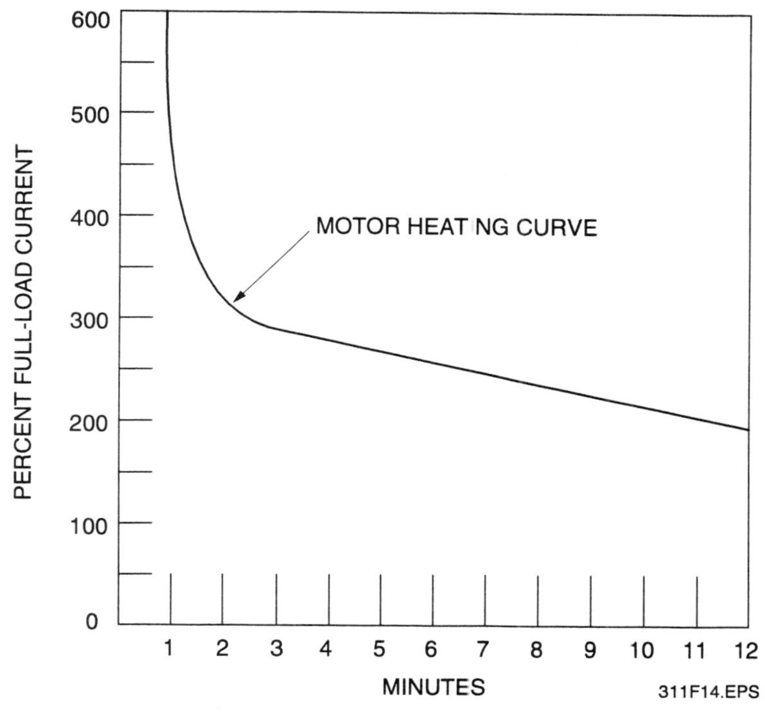

Figure 14. Ideal Overload Protection Follows The Motor's Heating Curve

The overload relay consists of a current-sensing unit connected in line with the motor, plus a mechanism that is actuated by the sensing unit and serves to directly or indirectly break the circuit. In a manual starter, an overload trips a mechanical latch and causes the starter contacts to open and disconnect the motor from the line. In magnetic starters, an overload opens a set of contacts within the overload relay itself. These contacts are wired in series with the starter coil in the control circuit of the magnetic starter. Breaking the coil circuit causes the starter contacts to open, disconnecting the motor from the line.

Overload relays can be either thermal or magnetic. Magnetic overload relays react only to current excesses and are not affected by temperature. As the name implies, thermal overload relays rely on the rising temperatures caused by the overload current to trip the overload mechanism. Thermal overload relays can be further subdivided into melting alloy and bimetallic types.

5.1.0 MELTING ALLOY THERMAL OVERLOAD RELAYS

The melting alloy assembly of the heater element overload relay and solder pot is shown in *Figure 15*. Excessive overload motor current passes through the heater element, thereby melting an eutectic alloy solder pot. The ratchet wheel will then be allowed to turn in the molten pool, and a tripping action of the starter control circuit results, stopping the motor. A cooling off period is required to allow the solder pot to harden before the overload relay assembly may be reset and motor service restored.

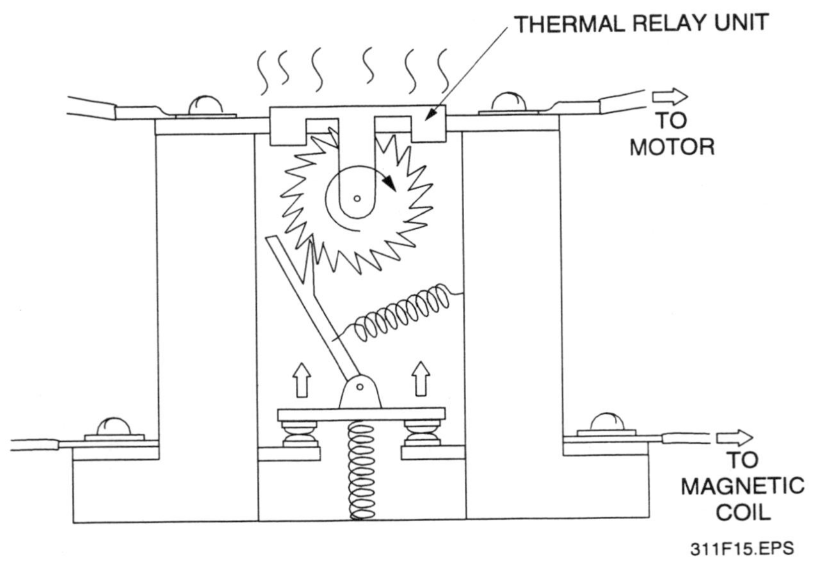

Figure 15. Operating Characteristics Of A Melting Alloy Overload Relay

Melting alloy thermal units are interchangeable and of a one-piece construction, which ensures a constant relationship between the heater element and solder pot and allows factory calibration, making them virtually tamperproof in the field. These important features are not possible with any other type of overload relay construction.

A wide selection of interchangeable thermal units is available to provide precise motor overload protection for any full-load current.

5.2.0 BIMETALLIC THERMAL OVERLOAD RELAYS

Bimetallic overload relays have two advantages:

- The automatic reset feature is an advantage when devices are mounted in locations that are not easily accessible for manual operation.
- These relays can easily be adjusted to trip within a range of 85% to 115% of the nominal trip rating of the heater unit. This feature is useful when the recommended heater size might result in unnecessary tripping, while the next larger size would not provide adequate protection.

Ambient temperatures affect overload relays operating on the principle of heat. *Figure 16* is a bimetallic overload relay with the side cover removed, showing the location of the contact, heater coil, and **bimetal strip**.

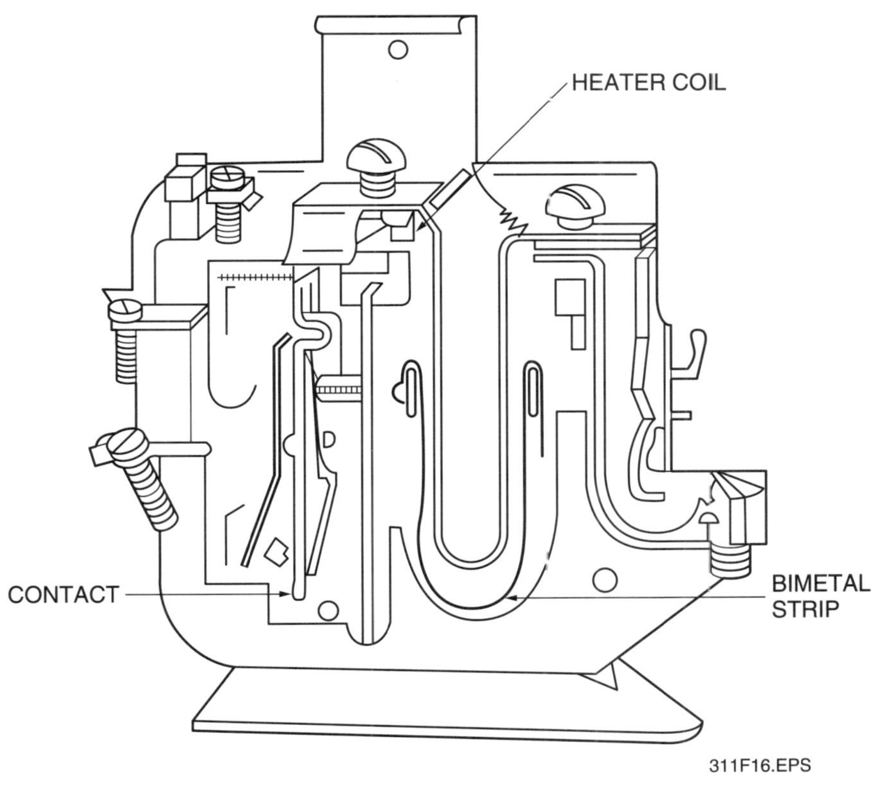

Figure 16. Bimetallic Overload Relay With Side Cover Removed

5.3.0 AMBIENT COMPENSATION

Ambient-compensated bimetallic overload relays were designed for a particular situation in which the motor is at a constant temperature and the controller is in a separate location that experiences varying temperatures. In this case, if a standard thermal overload relay were used, it would not trip consistently at the same level of motor current if the controller temperature changed. This thermal overload relay is always affected by the surrounding temperature.

To compensate for the temperature variations experienced by the controller, an ambient-compensated overload relay is applied. Its trip point is not affected by temperature and it performs consistently at the same value of current.

Melting alloy and bimetallic overload relays are designed to approximate the heat actually generated in the motor. As the motor temperature increases, so does the temperature of the thermal unit. The motor and relay heating curves in *Figure 17* show this relationship. From this graph, we can see that no matter how high the current draw, the overload relay will provide protection, yet the relay will not trip unnecessarily.

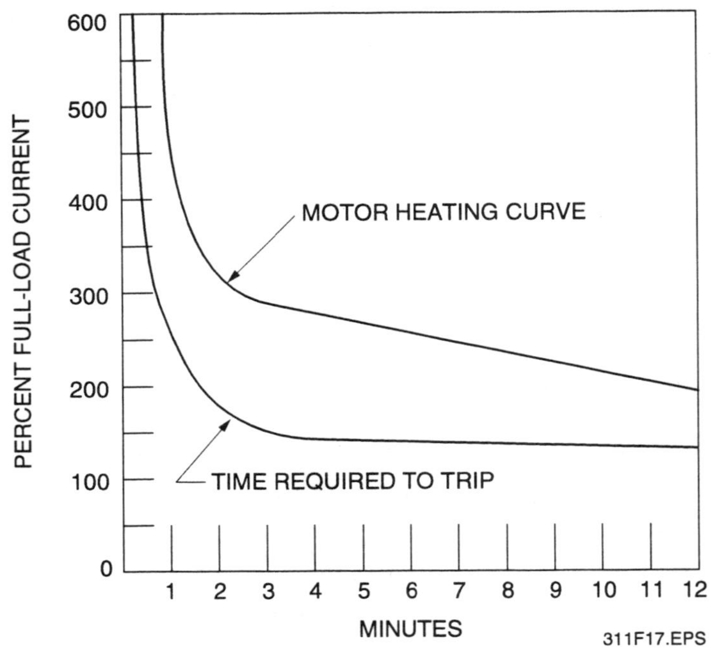

Figure 17. Comparison Of Motor Heating Curve And Overload Relay Trip Curve

5.4.0   SELECTING OVERLOAD RELAYS

When selecting thermal overload relays, the following items must be considered:

- Motor full-load current
- Type of motor
- Difference in ambient temperature between the motor and controller

Motors of the same horsepower and speed do not all have the same full-load current, and the motor nameplate must always be checked to obtain the full-load amperes for a particular motor. Do not use a published table. Thermal unit selection tables are published on the basis of continuous-duty motors with a 1.15 service factor operating under normal conditions. The tables are shown in the manufacturer's catalog and also appear on the inside of the door or cover of the motor controller. These selections will properly protect the motor and permit it to develop its full horsepower, allowing for the service factor, if the ambient temperature is the same at the motor as it is at the controller. If the temperatures are not the same, or if the motor service factor is less than 1.15, a special procedure is required to select the proper thermal unit. Standard overload relay contacts are closed under normal conditions and open when the relay trips. An alarm signal is sometimes required to indicate when a motor has stopped due to an overload trip. Also, with some machines (particularly those associated with continuous processing) it may be required to signal an overload condition rather than have the motor and process stop automatically. This is done by fitting the overload relay with a set of contacts that close when the relay trips, thus completing the alarm circuit. These contacts are appropriately called *alarm contacts*.

A magnetic overload relay has a movable magnetic core inside a coil that carries the motor current. The flux set up inside the coil pulls the core upward. When the core rises far enough, it trips a set of contacts on the top of the relay. The movement of the core is slowed by a piston working in an oil-filled dashpot mounted below the coil. This produces an inverse-time characteristic. The effective tripping current is adjusted by moving the core on a threaded rod. The tripping time is varied by uncovering oil bypass holes in the piston. Because of the time and current adjustments, the magnetic overload relay is sometimes used to protect motors having long accelerating times or unusual duty cycles.

6.0.0 PROTECTIVE ENCLOSURES

The correct selection and installation of an enclosure for a particular application can contribute considerably to the length of life and troublefree operation. To shield electrically live parts from accidental contact, some form of enclosure is always necessary. This function is usually filled by a general-purpose, sheet-steel cabinet. Frequently, however, dust, moisture, or explosive gases make it necessary to employ a special enclosure to protect the motor controller from corrosion or the surrounding equipment from explosion. When selecting and installing control apparatus, it is always necessary to carefully consider the conditions under which the apparatus must operate; there are many applications in which a general-purpose enclosure does not afford the required protection.

Underwriters' Laboratories has defined the requirements for protective enclosures according to various hazardous conditions, and NEMA has standardized enclosures from these requirements. NEMA enclosure types include the following:

- *General-purpose (NEMA Type 1)* – A general-purpose enclosure is intended primarily to prevent accidental contact with the enclosed apparatus. It is suitable for general-purpose applications indoors where it is not exposed to unusual service conditions. A NEMA Type 1 enclosure serves as protection against dust, light, and indirect splashing, but is not dust-tight.

- *Dust-tight, raintight (NEMA Type 3)* – This enclosure is intended to provide suitable protection against rain and sleet. It is suitable for application outdoors, such as for construction work.

- *Rainproof, sleet-resistant (NEMA Type 3R)* – This enclosure protects against interference in operation of the contained equipment due to rain and resists damage from exposure to sleet. It is designed with conduit hubs and external mounting, as well as drainage provisions.

- *Watertight (NEMA Type 4)* – This enclosure is designed to withstand a hose test which consists of a stream of water from a hose with a 1" nozzle delivering at least 65 gallons per minute. The water is directed on the enclosure from a distance of not less than 10' for a period of five minutes. During this period, it may be directed in one or more directions, as desired. There should be no leakage of water into the enclosure under these conditions.

- *Watertight, corrosion-resistant (NEMA Type 4X)* – These enclosures are similar to NEMA Type 4 enclosures except that they are made of a material that is highly resistant to corrosion. They are ideal in applications such as meatpacking and chemical plants, where contaminants would ordinarily destroy a steel enclosure over a period of time.

- *Hazardous locations, Class I (NEMA Type 7)* – These enclosures are designed to meet the application requirements of NEC Class I hazardous locations in which flammable gases or vapors are or may be present in the air in quantities sufficient to produce explosive or ignitable mixtures. In this type of equipment, the circuit interruption occurs in air.

- *Hazardous locations, Class II (NEMA Type 9)* – These enclosures are designed to meet the application requirements of NEC Class II locations for operation in the presence of combustible dust. The letter(s) following the type number indicate the particular group(s) of hazardous locations (as defined in the NEC) for which the enclosure is designed. The designation is incomplete without the suffix letter(s).

- *Industrial use (NEMA Type 12)* – This type of enclosure is designed to exclude dust, lint, fibers and other flying materials, and oil or coolant seepage. There are no conduit openings or knockouts in the enclosure, and mounting is by means of flanges or mounting feet.

- *Oil-tight, dust-tight (NEMA Type 13)* – These enclosures are generally made of cast iron and are used in the same areas as NEMA Type 12 enclosures. The main difference is that due to its cast housing, a conduit entry is provided as an integral part of the NEMA Type 13 enclosure, and mounting is by means of blind holes rather than mounting brackets.

7.0.0 MOTOR CONTROL CIRCUITS

A complete wiring diagram is best used when making the initial connections of a circuit or when tracing a fault in a circuit. It shows the devices in symbol form and indicates the actual connections of all wires between the devices. Ladder diagrams use the same symbols to represent the individual devices, but indicate by only one line the fact that these devices are in the same circuit. Such schematic diagrams are simple and can be quickly prepared when principles of motor control are being studied.

A motor control circuit is represented by its complete wiring diagram in *Figure 18* and by a ladder diagram in *Figure 19*. In the wiring diagram (*Figure 18*), the three supply conductors are indicated by L1, L2, and L3, and the motor terminals by T1, T2, and T3. Each line has a terminal overload protective device (OL) connected in series with the normally open line contactors (M1, M2, and M3), which are controlled by the **magnetic coil** (C). Each contactor has a pair of contacts that close or open during operation. The control station, consisting of START/STOP pushbuttons, is connected across lines L1 and L2. An auxiliary contactor (M) is connected in series with the STOP pushbutton and in parallel with the START pushbutton. The control circuit also has a normally closed overload contactor (OC) connected in series with the starter coil (C).

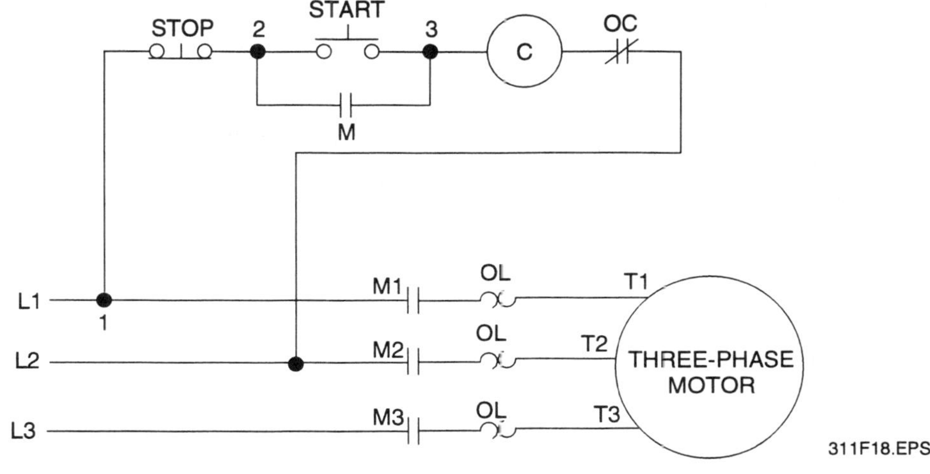

Figure 18. Wiring Diagram Of A Simple Motor Control Circuit

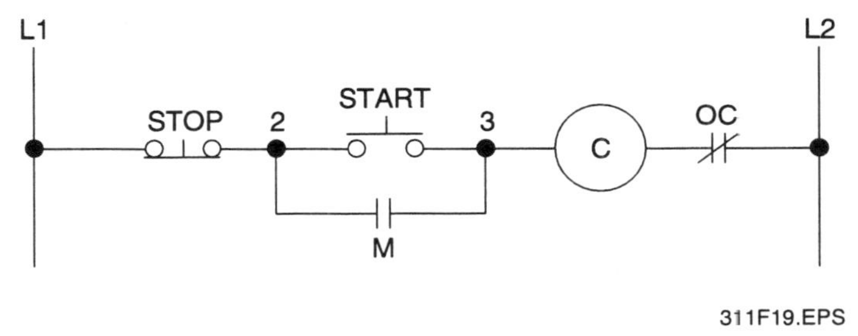

Figure 19. Ladder Diagram Of A Simple Motor Control Circuit

The same connections are represented in *Figure 19* by a ladder diagram showing the two main lines (L1 and L2) vertically, with a horizontal line representing the control circuit with a control station containing two pushbuttons, an auxiliary interlocking contactor, the starter coil (C), and the normally closed overload contactor (OC). The diagram depicts when the control circuit is not energized and the normally open contactors are open. There is no complete path for the current unless the START button is pushed.

Always read a ladder diagram from left to right (i.e., from L1 to L2). For example, when the START pushbutton is momentarily pressed, the path is complete from L1 through the closed STOP button, START button, normally closed overload contactor, and coil C to line L2. Current will flow through this circuit and energize coil C. Coil C closes the auxiliary or sealing contactor. The spring-actuated START button may be released, but the auxiliary contacts of contactor M **interlock** (or seal) the circuit and keep it closed as long as coil C is energized.

When the contacts of the control device close, they complete the coil circuit of the motor starter, causing it to pick up and connect the motor to the lines. When the control device contacts open, the starter is deenergized, stopping the motor.

The line contactors (M1, M2, and M3) in *Figure 18* close when coil C is energized, causing the circuit to the motor terminals to be completed. The wiring diagrams in *Figures 18* and *19* do not show the motor starter, speed controller, or similar control devices, only the pushbutton arrangement for starting and stopping the motor. They may be referred to as *basic motor control circuits.*

When the STOP pushbutton is pressed or the circuit is opened, coil C is deenergized, and the auxiliary and line contactors open. There is no path for the current to the motor, and the motor stops.

A similar wiring diagram is shown in *Figure 20*, this time with a slight modification to the control circuit. The only change in the control circuit is that the auxiliary contactor (M) interlocks the circuits to the motor side of the line, or to T2 instead of L2. The function of the control circuit and pushbuttons is the same as for the circuit in *Figures 18* and *19*. A ladder diagram of the control circuit in *Figure 20* is shown in *Figure 21*.

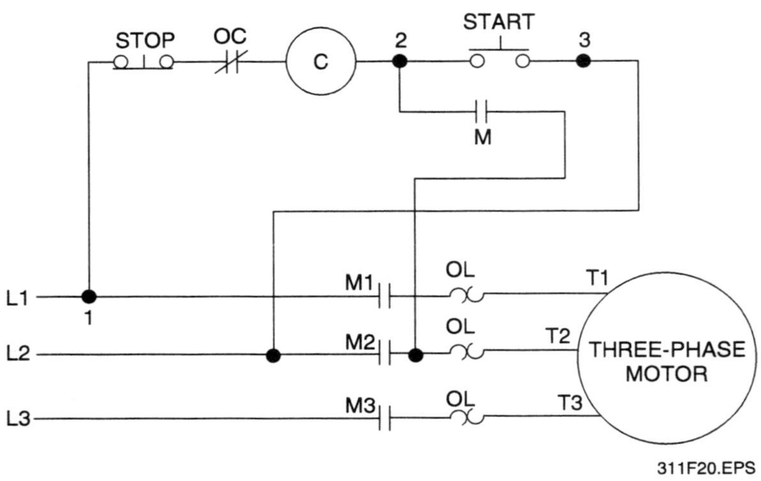

Figure 20. Interlocking Control Circuit

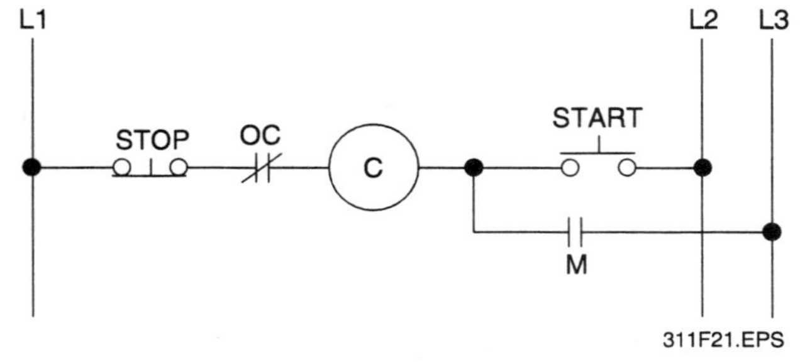

Figure 21. Ladder Diagram Of An Interlocking Control Circuit

ELECTRICAL — TRAINEE TASK MODULE 26311

Two-wire control provides low-voltage release but not low-voltage protection. When wired as illustrated, the starter will function automatically in response to the direction of the control device, without the attention of an operator. In this type of connection, a holding circuit interlock is not necessary.

A three-wire control circuit is shown in *Figure 22*. This circuit uses momentary contact START/STOP buttons and a holding circuit interlock wired in parallel with the START button to maintain the circuit.

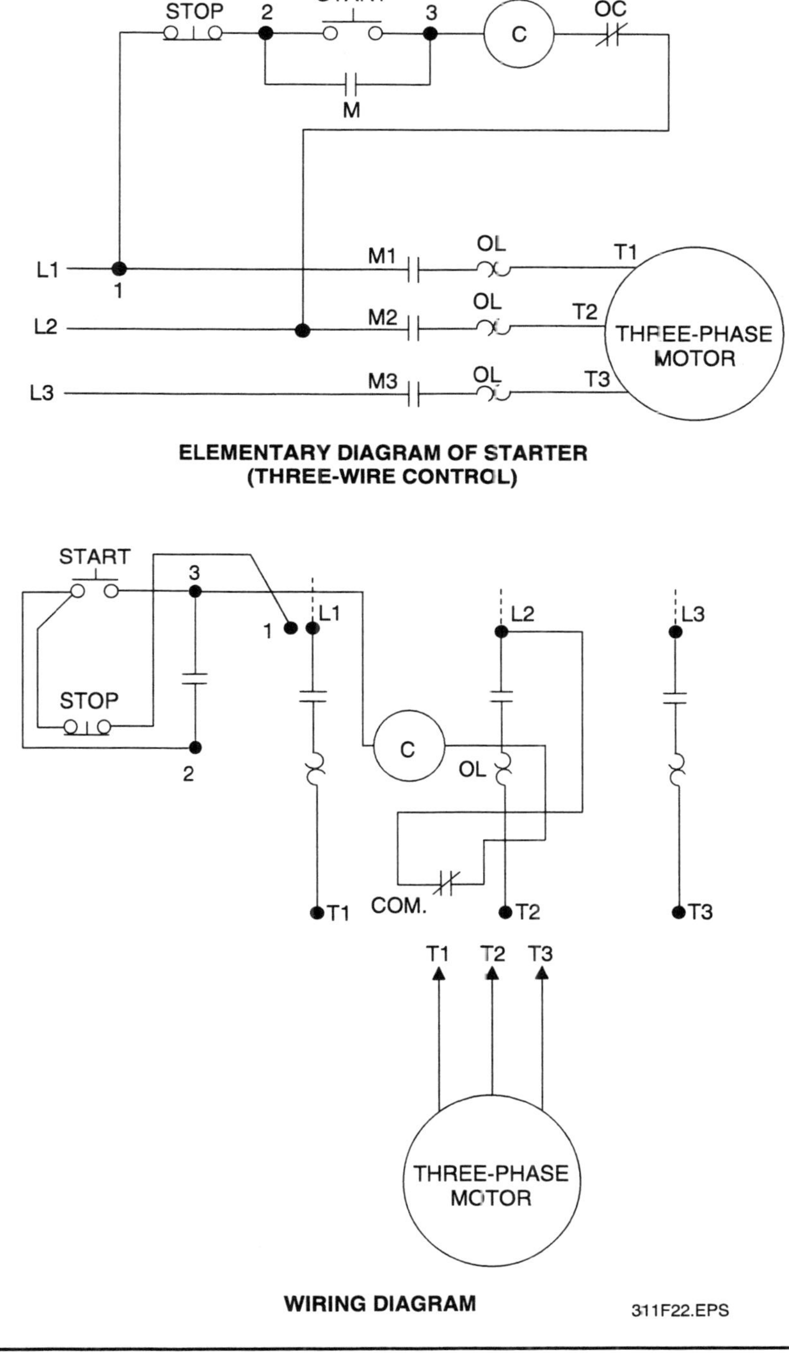

Figure 22. Wiring Diagrams Of A Three-Wire Motor Control Circuit

Pressing the normally open (N.O.) START button completes the circuit to the coil. The power circuit contacts in lines L1, L2, and L3 close, completing the circuit to the motor, and the holding circuit contact also closes. Once the starter has picked up, the START button can be released, as the now closed interlock contact provided an alternative current path around the reopened start contact.

Pressing the normally closed (N.C.) STOP button will open the circuit to the coil, causing the starter to drop out. The starter can also be deenergized by an overload condition that causes the overload contact to open, a power failure, or a drop in voltage to less than the seal-in value. When the starter drops out, the interlock contact reopens, and both current paths to the coil (through the START button and the interlock) are now open.

Since three wires from the pushbutton station are connected to the starter—at points 1, 2, and 3—this wiring scheme is commonly referred to as *three-wire control*.

The holding circuit interlock is a normally open auxiliary contact provided on standard magnetic starters and contactors. It closes when the coil is energized to form a holding circuit for the starter after the START button has been released.

In addition to the main or power contacts which carry the motor current and the holding circuit interlock, a starter can be provided with external auxiliary contacts, commonly called *electrical interlocks*. Interlocks are rated to carry only control circuit currents, not motor currents. Both N.O. and N.C. versions are available. Among a wide variety of applications, interlocks can be used to control other magnetic devices where sequential operation is desired, to electrically prevent another controller from being energized at the same time, and to make and break circuits to indicating or alarm devices such as pilot lights, bells, or other signals.

7.1.0   MULTIPLE PUSHBUTTONS

If motors are required to be started from more than one location, additional pushbutton stations may be connected to the circuit. In doing so, additional START buttons must be connected in parallel with the original START button, and the additional STOP buttons must be connected in series with the original STOP button, as shown in *Figure 23*. The auxiliary contactor must also be in parallel with the second START button if buttons should be only momentarily pressed for starting. For three control stations, there should be three START buttons in parallel with the auxiliary contactor and three STOP buttons in series.

Note: Any control device connected in the control circuit to start the motor must be connected in parallel with the START button and be of the normally open type. Every device which has the function of stopping the motor must be in series with the STOP button and be normally closed. By adding elements to the circuit in this manner, a complex control circuit may be obtained.

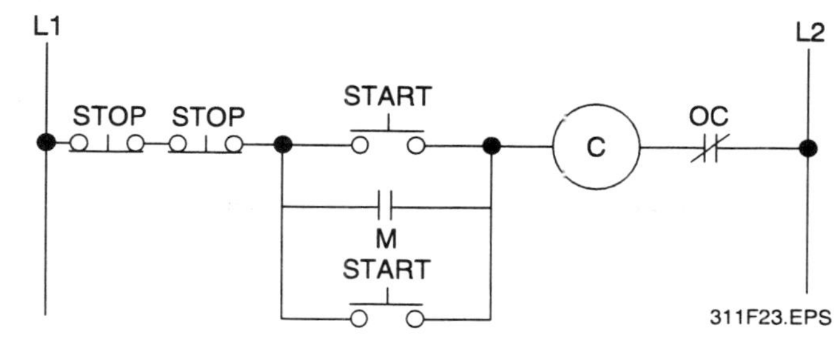

Figure 23. Control Circuit With Two Pushbutton Stations

Another modification of the control circuit is used for **inching** the motor to provide for intermittent operation through unequal short time intervals. The modified circuit is shown in *Figure 24*. The STOP button is connected across the START button, but in series with the auxiliary interlock contactor. The STOP button is latched open and keeps the circuit of the interlocking contactor open. Releasing the START button stops the motor because the STOP button keeps the interlock branch open. The motor runs only as long as the START button is held down. This type of control enables the application of short movement (inching) of the motor in order to make adjustments.

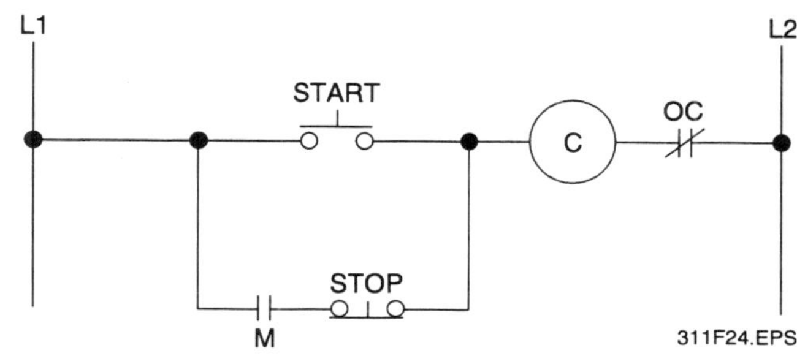

Figure 24. Control For Inching A Motor

7.2.0   REVERSING MOTOR ROTATION

When the control circuit is being designed for reversing the motor direction as well as for starting the motor, such as the one shown in *Figure 25*, a REVERSE-START button with its interlock contactor, normally closed overload contactor, and reverse contact coil must be added to the basic forward control circuit. Since the added REVERSE-START button is a starting device, it must be connected in parallel with the original FORWARD-START button. The REVERSE-START button is connected behind the STOP button so that the same STOP button can stop both the forward and reverse rotation of the motor. When the FORWARD-START button is momentarily pressed, the forward coil (FC) is energized, which closes the normally open contactor (FC1) and opens the normally closed contactor (FC2) in the reverse control circuit. The now open contactor (FC) in the reverse control circuit ensures that even if the REVERSE-START button is pressed, the reverse circuit will remain open and not active. After the motor has been stopped by the STOP button, it may be started in the reverse direction by pressing the REVERSE-START button. This action energizes the reverse coil (RC), which keeps the normally open contactor (RC1) closed and the normally closed contactor (RC2) open, so that the motor cannot be started in the forward direction.

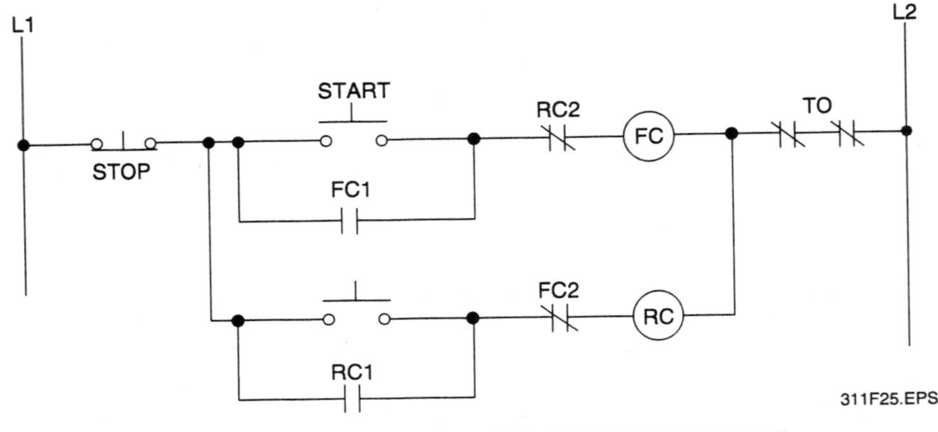

Figure 25. Control For Reversing Motor Rotation

A modified reversing motor control circuit is shown in *Figure 26* drawn as a full wiring diagram. A ladder diagram of the same circuit is shown in *Figure 27*. Instead of two starting buttons for forward and reverse rotation, one selector switch (1) is used with one START button (2) and one STOP button (3). When the selector switch is first turned to the forward (F) position and the START pushbutton is pressed, the motor runs in the forward direction. To reverse the direction of the motor, the selector switch is turned to the reverse (R) position. The STOP button stops the motor in either direction. For actual connections of wires, *Figure 26* is more useful, but for studying the principles of control, *Figure 27* will be more convenient.

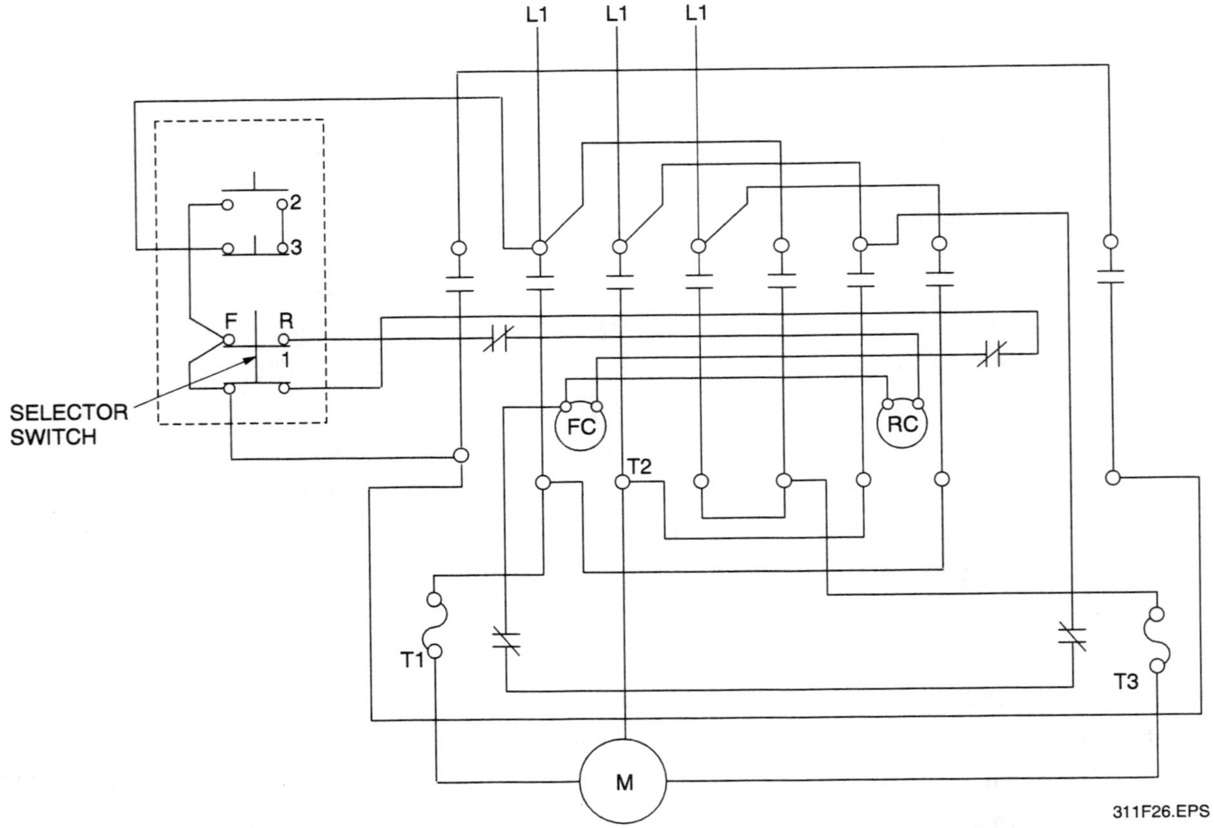

Figure 26. Wiring Diagram Of A Reversing Motor Control Circuit

ELECTRICAL — TRAINEE TASK MODULE 26311

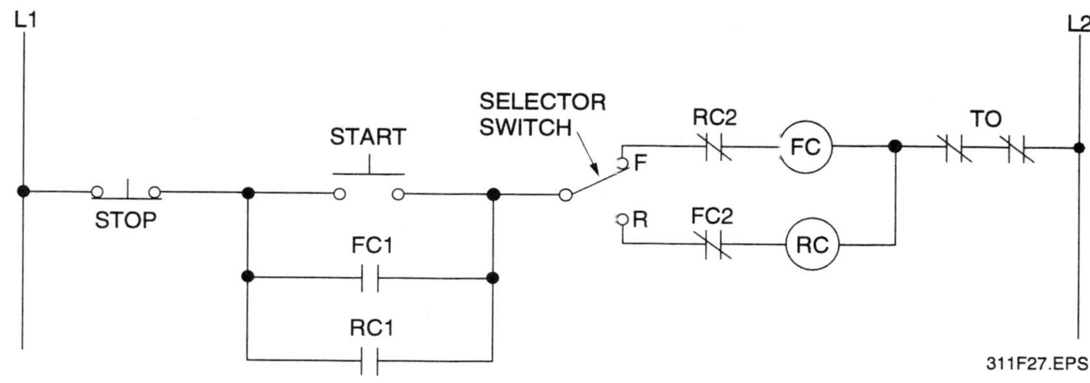

Figure 27. Ladder Diagram Of A Reversing Motor Control Circuit

The circuit in *Figure 28* shows a three-pole reversing starter used to control a three-phase motor. Three-phase squirrel-cage motors can be reversed by reconnecting any two of the three line connections to the motor. By interwiring two contactors, an electromagnetic method of making the reconnection can be obtained.

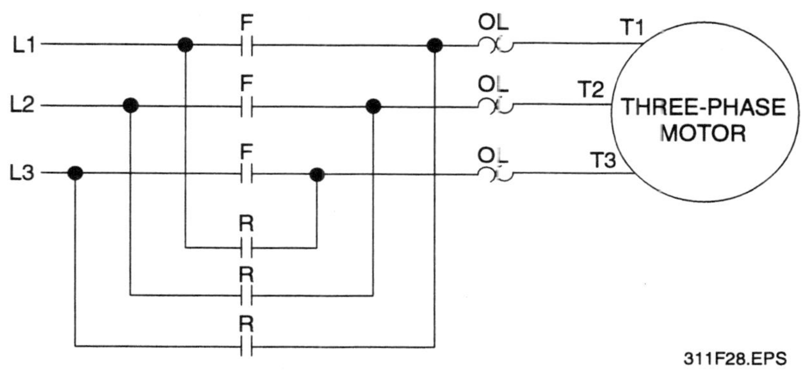

Figure 28. Three-Pole Reversing Starter Used To Control A Three-Phase Motor

As seen in the power circuit (*Figure 28*), the contacts (F) of the forward contactor (when closed) connect lines L1, L2, and L3 to the motor terminals T1, T2, and T3, respectively. As long as the forward contacts are closed, mechanical and electrical interlocks prevent the reverse contactor from being energized.

When the forward contactor is deenergized, the second contactor can be picked up, closing its contacts (R), which reconnect the lines to the motor. Note that by running through the reverse contacts, line L1 is connected to motor terminal T3, and line L3 is connected to motor terminal T1. The motor will now run in reverse.

Manual reversing starters (employing two manual starters) are also available. As in the magnetic version, the forward and reverse switching mechanisms are mechanically interlocked, but since coils are not used in the manually-operated equipment, electrical interlocks are not furnished.

The ladder diagram in *Figure 29* shows the basic components of a control circuit for two motors. One motor must already be running before the other can be started, and both should stop at the same time. Basic control circuits for both motors are connected between lines L1 and L2. When the first START button closes the control circuit of the first motor, its control coil (M1) closes not only the interlock contacts (M1) in the first control circuit, but also a normally open contactor (M) in the control circuit of the second motor. If the START button for the second motor is now pushed, it energizes coil M2, and closes the normally open contactor (M2) in the second control circuit. Now, both motors will run until the STOP button is pressed. The second motor is prevented from starting when its own START button is pressed unless the first motor is already running. Both motors can be stopped at the same time by using the STOP button.

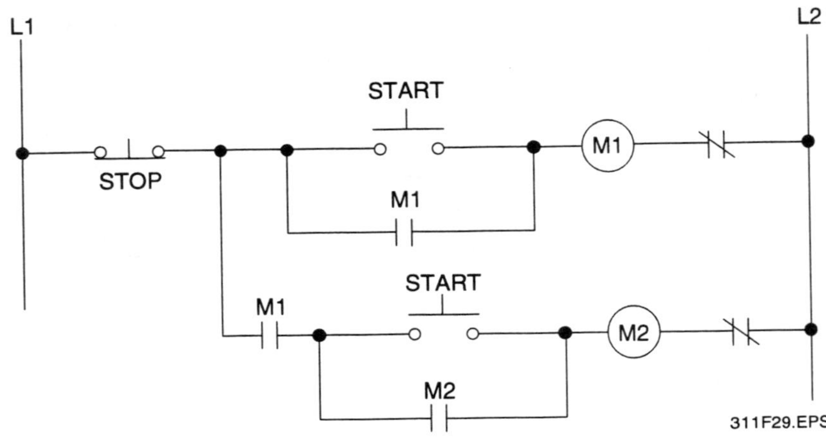

Figure 29. Control Of Two Motors Running Alternately

7.4.0 **AUTOMATIC CONTROL CIRCUIT**

When completely automatic control of a motor is required, two pilot switches (PS1 and PS2) are connected into the basic control circuit, as shown in *Figure 30*. The starting pilot switch (PS1) is connected in parallel with the START button. The pilot switch may be a floating switch, pressure switch, or time switch, and will close automatically when a preset condition occurs. For the **float switch**, a certain level of the liquid closes the switch; for the pressure switch, a gas pressure of a certain value closes the switch; and for the time switch, a timer closes the switch after a certain preset time interval.

When the automatic starting switch closes the control circuit, coil M is energized and closes the interlock contactor (M). The automatic stopping switch (PS2) is normally closed, and like the automatic starting switch, opens automatically at a preset condition and stops the control circuit.

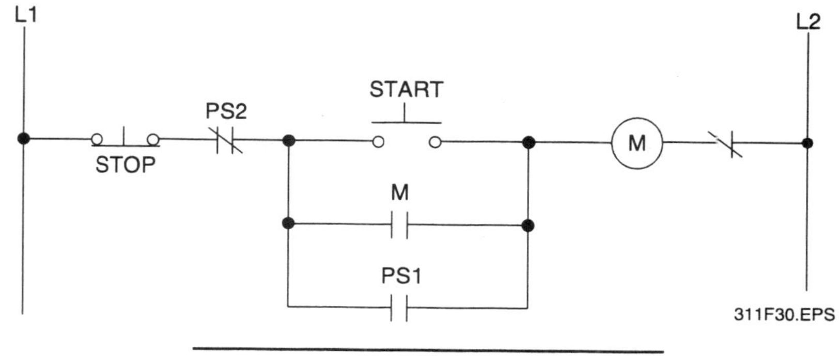

Figure 30. Automatic Motor Control

There are several variations of the motor control circuits previously described. There are also different types of motor starters. Some of these starters are becoming obsolete and are seldom used on new construction. However, electricians will often work on existing installations where some of the older motor starters are still in use, and an identifying knowledge of them is warranted.

8.1.0   ACROSS-THE-LINE MOTOR STARTERS

Induction-type and synchronous AC motors have a high starting current; therefore, they are mostly started at reduced voltage, although there are many quite large AC motors which are started across the line (i.e., by applying the full-rated voltage). A basic circuit diagram of a full-voltage starter for a three-phase **induction motor** is shown in *Figure 31*. Overload protection relays (OL) are in all three lines, and the motor is started by the basic control circuit, which uses a control station with START and STOP buttons.

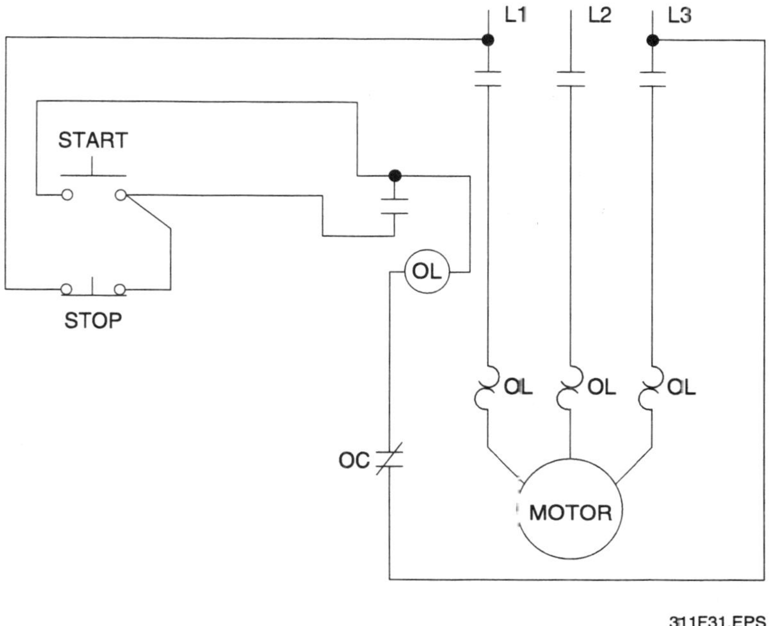

Figure 31. Full-Voltage Starter For A Three-Phase AC Motor

8.2.0 REDUCED-VOLTAGE STARTING OF AC MOTORS

The starter shown in *Figure 32* uses autotransformers to provide reduced-voltage starting of a squirrel-cage induction motor. The motor (1) is connected to the three lines (L1, L2, and L3) by means of the movable lever (2). When the lever is moved from the middle (OFF position), to the START position, the autotransformers (3) are connected in the circuit by means of the oil-immersed contacts (4). The low-voltage taps from the autotransformers are then connected to the motor and the motor starts. When the motor is up to speed, the lever is thrown from the START position to the RUN position, disconnecting the autotransformers and connecting the supply directly to the motor by the contacts (5).

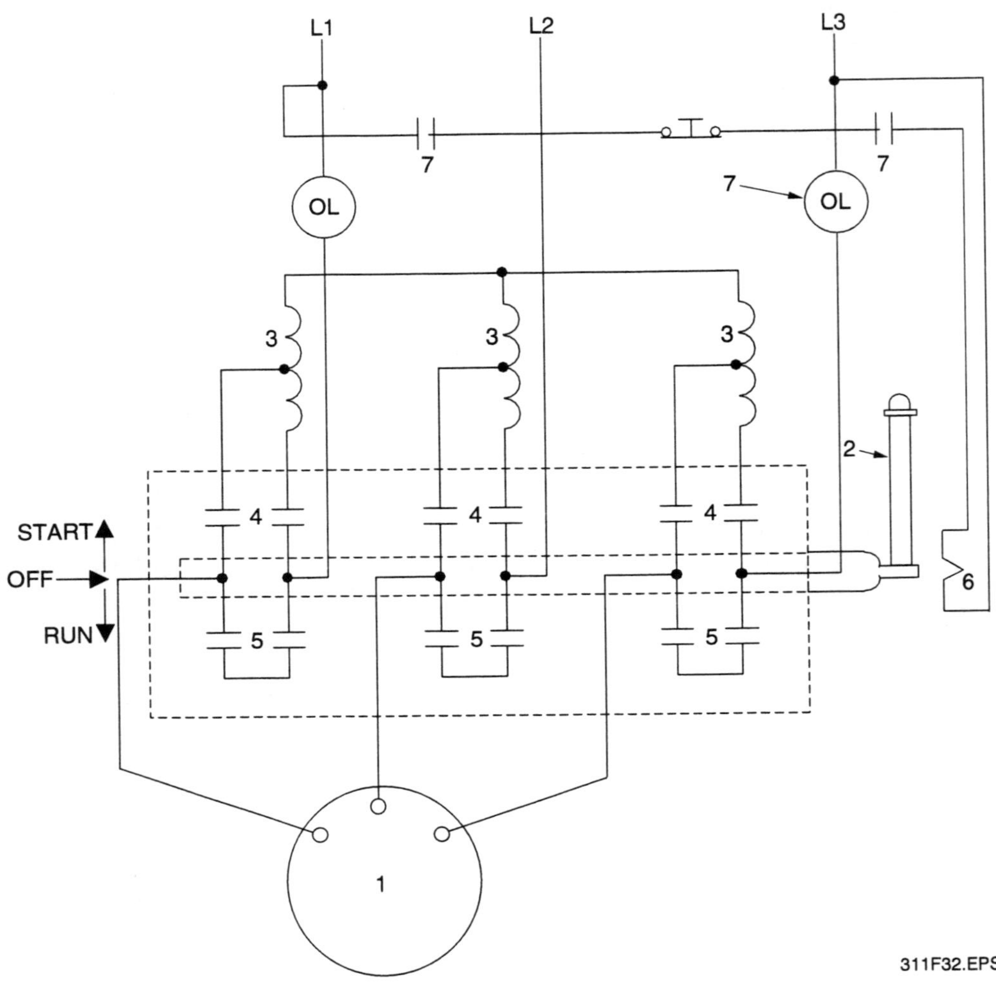

Figure 32. Autotransformers Used To Start A Three-Phase Induction Motor

The lever is held closed by the holding coil (6), which is connected across one phase of the supply through the relay contacts (7) of the overload relays and the STOP button. The relays are built with dashpots, which delay the operation of the relays during the starting period and for momentary overloads. Operation of the relays, or of the STOP pushbutton, opens the holding coil circuit and allows the lever to come to the OFF position, breaking the circuit made by the relay contacts (7).

Autotransformers with several taps may be used for multi-speed control of a squirrel-cage motor. All squirrel-cage motors use controllers in the primary or stator winding.

8.3.0 RESISTANCE MAGNETIC STARTERS

A resistance-type starter used with a three-phase squirrel-cage induction motor is shown in *Figure 33*. The motor is started by pressing the START button to energize coil M, which closes the three line contactors (M1, M2, and M3) and the interlock (M4) to maintain power to the coil after the START button is released.

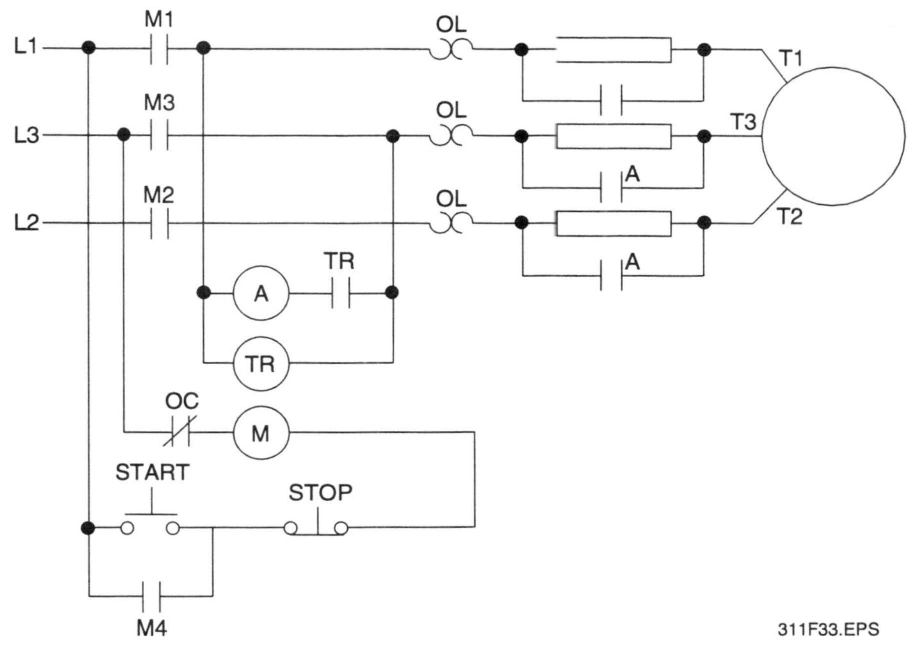

Figure 33. Resistance Starter Used For A Squirrel-Cage Induction Motor

When the contactor is closed, the timing relay (TR) becomes energized and immediately starts to measure the time for which it is adjusted. At the end of the timing period, the contacts (TR) close to energize coil A of the accelerating contactor (A). When the three-pole contactor (A) closes, the starting resistors will be short circuited and the motor will be connected directly to the AC power lines. The heater elements of either of the thermal-type overload relays open the normally closed contactor (OC) in case of overload.

8.4.0 STARTER FOR WOUND INDUCTION MOTORS

The wound three-phase induction motor differs from the squirrel-cage induction motor in that it uses wound coils in the rotor instead of bars, and three sets of brushes to collect the current from the three collector rings, which are not used in the squirrel-cage motor. To start a wound motor, it is necessary to connect the brushes to external resistors, as shown in *Figure 34*. The three-phase star-connected stator (1) is connected to a three-phase source (2), and the three-phase star-connected rotor (3), or secondary, is connected through the slip rings and brushes to the three resistors (4), which are also star-connected. They increase the resistance of the rotor, which in turn increases the torque of the rotor and decreases its speed. When the resistance is gradually cut out, the speed gradually increases and the torque decreases. With no secondary resistance, the wound motor operates at maximum speed. The starter and controller are built with combinations of basic control circuits. Manuals provided by manufacturers show control circuits for each specific type.

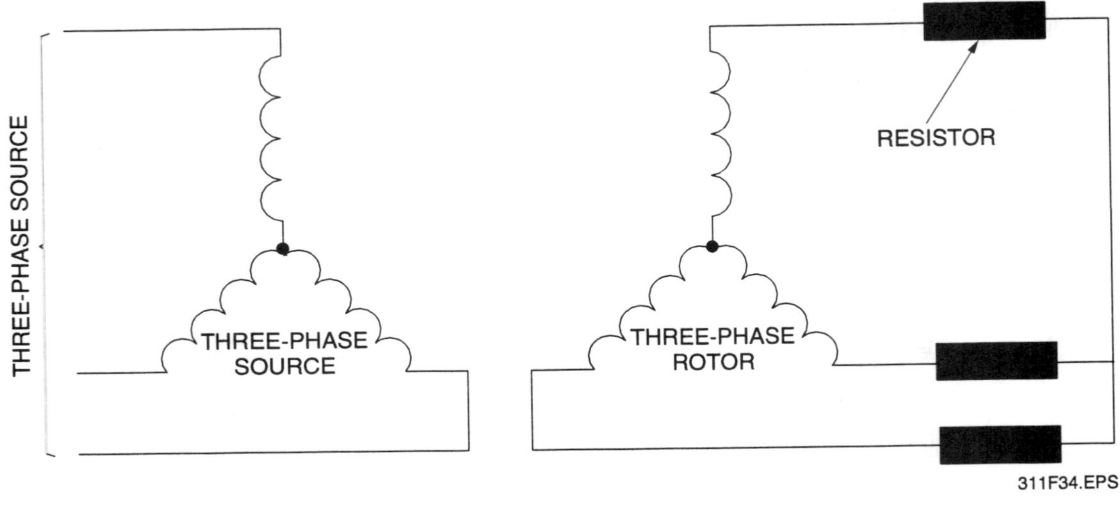

Figure 34. Wound Motor And Secondary Resistors

8.5.0   STARTING AND BRAKING SYNCHRONOUS MOTORS

The main electrical connections for a large high-voltage synchronous motor are shown in *Figure 35*. The high-voltage, three-phase lines (L1, L2, and L3) supply 13,800V to the synchronous motor (1) through a main (running) circuit breaker (2). This breaker is electrically interlocked with the starting breakers (3) and (4), and when the starting breakers are closed, the running breaker must be open. The starting breakers connect the starting autotransformer (5), which reduces the voltage to about 50% or 6,900V, and energizes the motor. When the motor comes up to speed, the starting breaker (4) is open and the running breaker connects the motor directly to the high-voltage line. The primary of a current transformer (6) is connected to one supply line and its secondary is connected to an ammeter (7) to measure the motor current at any time. The field winding (8) is energized by the exciter (9) through the field rheostat (10). The exciter may be a shunt-wound DC generator with its own field rheostat (not shown). The field discharge resistor (11) and field switch (12) serve a double purpose in that they provide a low-resistance path for the induced currents in the motor field when the motor is started and discharge the induced currents when the field breaker is opened.

Dynamic braking is obtained by braking resistors (13) through the braking contactors (14). The field is left energized and the motor is disconnected from the line and connected to the braking resistors. By using quick-acting control sequences, the motor can be stopped within approximately one second, without shock or high stresses.

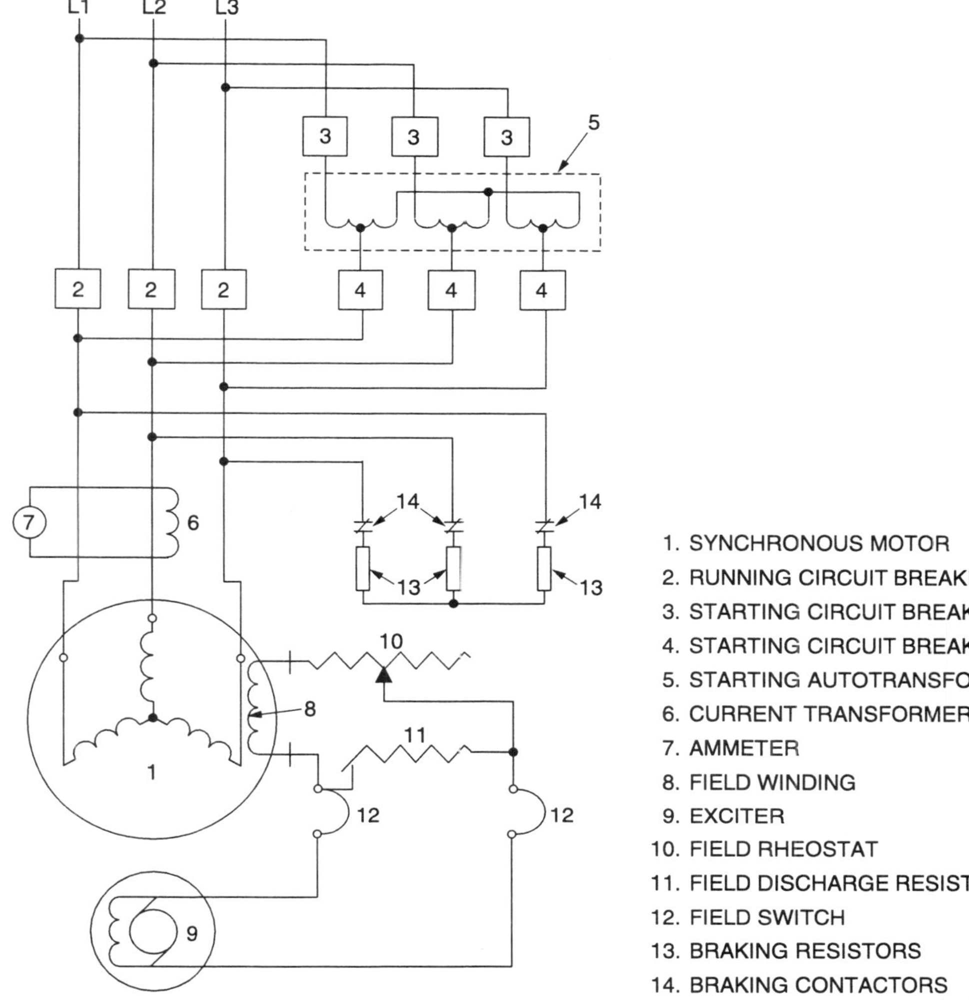

Figure 35. Connections For A Three-Phase Synchronous Motor

9.0.0 CONTROL RELAYS

A control relay is an electromagnetic device used in the control circuits of magnetic starters, contactors, solenoids, timers, and other relays. They are generally used to amplify the contact capability or to multiply the switching functions of a pilot device.

The wiring diagram in *Figure 36* demonstrates how a relay amplifies contact capacity. *Figure 37(A)* represents a current amplification. The relay and starter coil voltages are the same, but the ampere rating of the temperature switch is too low to handle the current drawn by the starter coil (M). A relay is interposed between the temperature switch and the starter coil. The current drawn by the relay coil (CR) is within the rating of the temperature switch and the relay contact (CR) has an adequate rating for the current drawn by the starter coil.

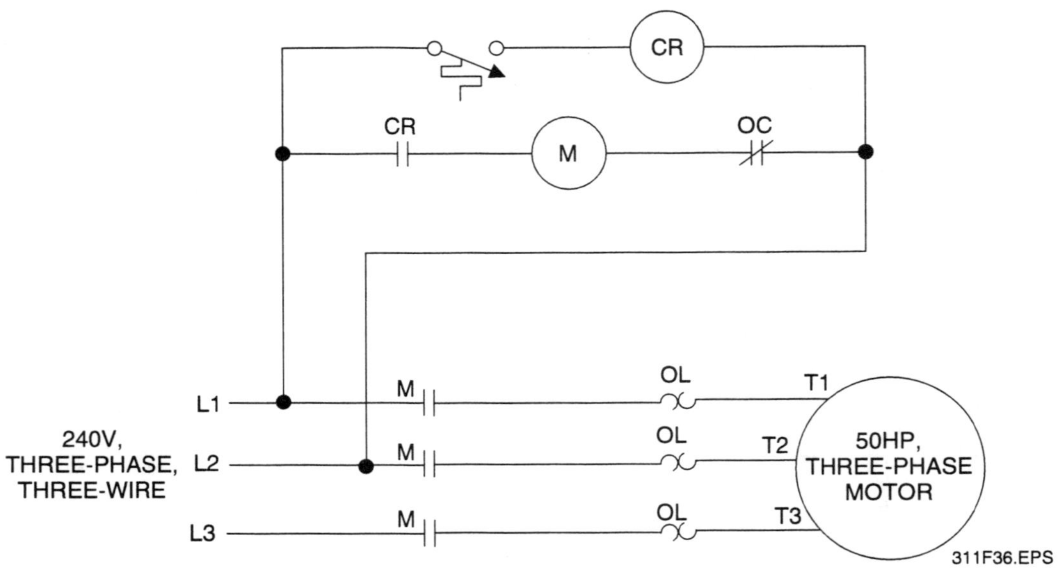

Figure 36. Relay Amplifying Contact Capacity

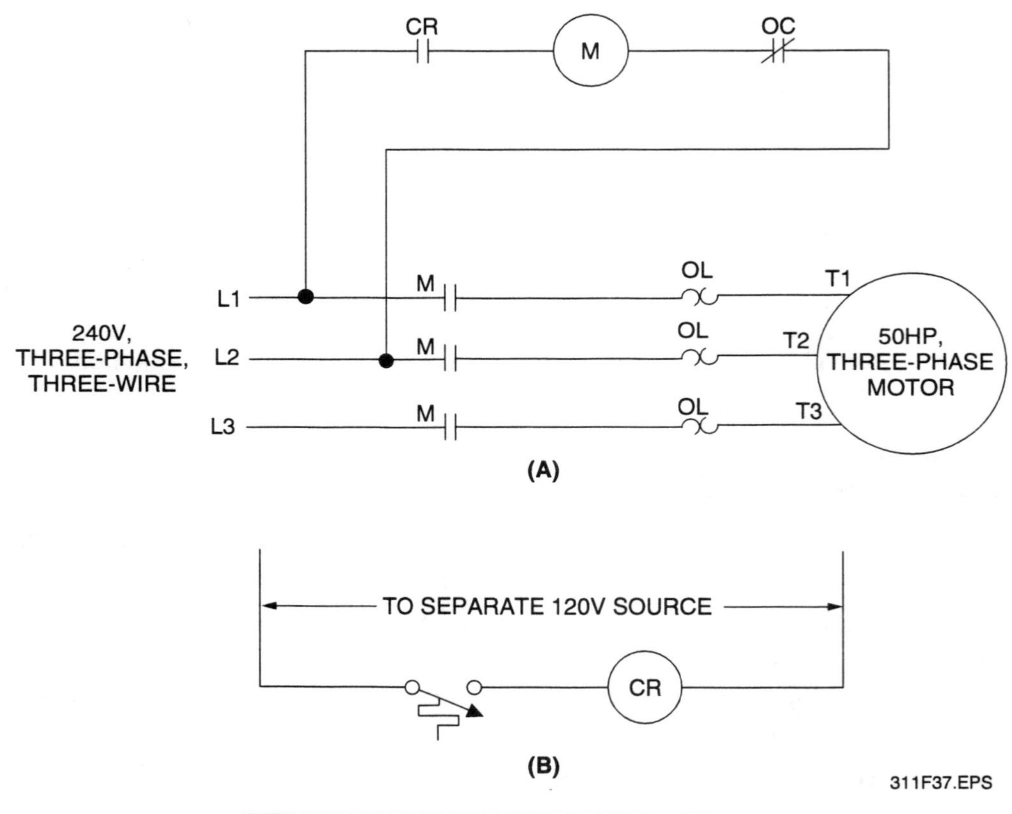

Figure 37. Circuit Amplifying Voltage

Figure 37(B) represents a voltage amplification for use when the voltage rating of the temperature switch is too low to permit its direct use in a starter control circuit operating at a higher voltage. In this application, the coil of the interposing relay and the pilot device are wired to a low-voltage power source that is compatible with the rating of the pilot device. The relay contact, with its higher voltage rating, is then used to control the operation of the starter.

Relays are commonly used in complex controllers to provide the logic necessary to set up and initiate the proper sequencing and control of a number of interrelated operations. When selecting a relay for a particular application, one of the first steps should be a determination of the control voltage at which the relay will operate. Once the voltage is known, the relays that have the necessary contact rating can be further reviewed and a selection made based on the number of contacts and other characteristics.

10.0.0   ADDITIONAL CONTROLLING EQUIPMENT

Additional equipment controls are as follows:

- *Timers and timing relays* – A pneumatic timer or timing relay is similar to a control relay, except that timer contacts are designed to operate at a preset time interval after the coil is energized or deenergized. A delay on energization is referred to as an *on delay*, while a delay on deenergization is called an *off delay*.

  A timed function is useful in such applications as the lubrication system of a large machine, in which a small oil pump must deliver lubricant to the bearings of the main motor for a set period of time before the main motor starts.

  In pneumatic timers, the timing is accomplished by the transfer of air through a restricted orifice. The amount of restriction is controlled by an adjustable needle valve, permitting changes to be made to the timing period.

- *Drum switch* – A drum switch is a manually-operated, three-position, three-pole switch which carries a horsepower rating and is used for manual reversing of single-phase or three-phase motors. Drum switches are available in several sizes and can be either spring return (momentary contact) or maintained contact. Separate overload protection using manual or magnetic starters must usually be provided, as drum switches do not include this feature.

- *Pushbutton station* – A control station may contain pushbuttons, selector switches, and pilot lights. Pushbuttons may be momentary or maintained contact. Selector switches are usually maintained contact, or can be spring return to provide momentary contact operation. Standard duty stations will handle the coil currents of contactors up to NEMA Size 4. Heavy-duty stations have higher contact ratings and provide greater flexibility through a wider variety of operators and interchangeability of units.

- *Foot switch* – A foot switch is a control device operated by a foot pedal. It is used where the process or machine requires that the operator have both hands free. Foot switches usually have momentary contacts but are available with latches which enable them to be used as maintained contact devices.

- *Limit switch* – A limit switch is a control device that converts mechanical motion into an electrical control signal. Its main function is to limit movement, usually by opening a control circuit when the limit of travel is reached. Limit switches may be momentary contact (spring return) or maintained contact types. Among other applications, limit switches can be used to start, stop, reverse, slow down, speed up, or recycle machine operation.

- *Snap switch* – Snap switches for motor control purposes are enclosed, precision switches which require low operating forces and have a high repeat accuracy. They are used as interlocks and as the switch mechanism for control devices such as precision limit switches and pressure switches. They are also available with integral operators for use as compact limit switches, door-operated interlocks, and so on. Single-pole, double-throw and double-pole, double-throw versions are available.

- *Pressure switch* – The control of pumps, air compressors, and machine tools requires control devices that respond to the pressure of a medium such as wire, air, or oil. The control device that does this is a pressure switch. It has a set of contacts which are operated by the movement of a piston, bellows, or diaphragm against a set of springs. The spring pressure determines the pressures at which the switch closes and opens its contacts.

11.0.0 TROUBLESHOOTING CONTROLLING EQUIPMENT

Table 3 lists various motor control problems, along with their causes and remedies. This table is of a general nature and covers only the main causes of trouble.

Note: Misapplication of a device is a major cause of motor control trouble and should always be checked when a device is not functioning properly.

Actual physical damage or broken parts can usually be found quickly and replaced. Damage due to water or flood conditions requires special treatment.

There are two types of contact wear: electrical and mechanical. The majority of wear to contact tips is due to electrical wear. The mechanical wear is insignificant and requires no further mention.

Arcing causes electrical wear by eroding the contacts. During arcing, a small part of each contact melts, then vaporizes and is blown away.

Malfunction	Possible Cause	Corrective Action
Constant chatter	Broken pole shader	Replace
	Poor contact in control circuit	Improve contact or use holding circuit interlock (three-wire control)
	Low voltage	Correct voltage condition; check momentary voltage dip during starting
Contactor welding or freezing	Abnormal inrush of current	Use larger contactor or check for grounds
	Rapid jogging	Install larger device rated for jogging service
	Insufficient tip pressure	Replace contact springs; check contact carrier for damage
	Low voltage preventing magnet from sealing	Correct voltage condition; check momentary voltage dip during starting
	Foreign matter preventing contacts from closing	Clean contacts with approved solvent
	Short circuit	Remove fault and check to be sure fuse or breaker size is correct
Short contact life or tip overheating	Filing or dressing	Do not file silver-faced contacts; rough spots or discoloration will not harm contacts
	Interrupting excessively high	Install larger device or check currents for grounds, shorts, or excessive motor currents; use silver-faced contacts
	Excessive jogging	Install larger device rated for jogging
	Weak contact pressure	Adjust or replace contact springs
	Dirt or foreign matter on contact surface	Clean contacts with approved solvent
	Short circuit	Remove fault and check for proper fuse or breaker size
	Loose connection	Clean and tighten
	Sustained overload	Install larger device or check for excessive load current
Coil overheated	Overvoltage or high ambient temperature	Check application and circuit
	Incorrect coil	Check rating and if incorrect, replace with proper coil
	Shorted turns caused by mechanical damage or corrosion	Replace coil
	Undervoltage, failure of magnet to seal in	Correct system voltage
	Dirt or rust on pole faces increasing air gap	Clean pole faces

Table 3. Motor Control Troubleshooting Chart (1 Of 2)

Malfunction	Possible Cause	Corrective Action
Overload relays tripping	Sustained overload	Check for grounds, shorts, or excessive currents
	Loose connection on load wires	Clean and tighten
	Incorrect heater	Relay should be replaced with correct size heater unit
Failure to trip causing motor burnout	Mechanical binding, dirt, corrosion, etc.	Clean or replace
	Wrong heater or heaters omitted and jumper wires used	Check ratings; apply proper heater
	Motor and relay in different temperatures	Adjust relay rating accordingly
	Wrong calibration or improper calibration adjustment	Consult factory
Magnetic and mechanical parts inoperative	Broken shading coil	Replace shading coil
Noisy magnet humming	Magnet faces not mating	Replace magnet assembly; realign
	Dirt or rust on magnet faces	Clean and realign
	Low voltage	Check system voltage and voltage dips during starting
Failure to pick up and seal	Low voltage	Check system voltage and voltage dips during starting
	Coil open or shorted	Replace
	Wrong coil	Check coil number
	Mechanical obstruction	With power off, check for free movement of contact and armature assembly
Failure to drop out	Gummy substance on pole faces	Clean with solvent
	Voltage not removed	Check coil circuit
	Worn or rusted parts causing binding	Replace parts
	Residual magnetism due to lack of air gap in magnet path	Replace worn magnet parts

Table 3. Motor Control Troubleshooting Chart (2 Of 2)

When a device is new, the contacts are smooth and have a uniform silver color. As the device is used, the contacts become pitted and the color may change to blue, brown, or black. These colors result from the normal formation of metal oxide on the contact surfaces and are not detrimental to contact life and performance. Therefore, contacts should not be filed to restore the original color. This practice only shortens contact life and may cause welding.

The contacts should be replaced under the following conditions:

- *Insufficient contact material* – This is when the amount of contact material remaining is inadequate. When less than $\frac{1}{64}$" remains, replace the contacts.

- *Irregular surface wear* – This type of wear is normal. However, if a corner of the contact material is worn away and a contact may mate with the opposing contact support member, the contacts should be replaced. This condition can result in contact welding.

- *Pitting* – Under normal wear, contact pitting should be uniform. This condition occurs during arcing, as described above. The contacts should be replaced if the pitting becomes excessive and little contact material remains.

- *Curling of contact surface* – This condition results from severe service that produces high contact temperatures and causes separation of the contact material from the contact support member.

The measurement procedure for checking the contact tip material requires a continuity checker and a $\frac{1}{32}$" feeler gauge. The procedure is as follows:

Step 1 Place the feeler gauge between the armature and the magnet frame, with the armature held tightly against the magnet frame.

Step 2 Check the continuity of each phase.

If there is continuity in all phases, the contacts are in good condition. If not, all contacts should be replaced. Even though the contacts have sufficient material, any of the other problems listed above would necessitate replacement of the contacts.

Note: Contacts should only be replaced when necessary; too frequent replacement is a waste of money and natural resources.

SUMMARY

This module presented the terms and concepts which are fundamental to an understanding of motor control equipment and its applications. A knowledge of the definitions, symbols, diagrams, and illustrations will give you a sound background in the language, basic principles, and applications associated with motor controls.

References

For advanced study of topics covered in this Task Module, the following books are suggested:

American Electricians' Handbook, Latest Edition, McGraw-Hill, New York, NY.

Electricians' Guide to AC Motor Controls, Latest Edition, COXCO, Spokane, WA.

National Electrical Code Handbook, Latest Edition, National Fire Protection Association, Quincy, MA.

1. Which of the following is *not* a function of a motor controller?
   a. Plugging
   b. Jogging
   c. Changing speed
   d. Gapping

2. A fractional-horsepower manual motor starter for a 240V, single-phase motor uses _____ contact(s).
   a. one
   b. two
   c. three
   d. four

3. A fractional-horsepower manual motor starter for a 240V, single-phase motor uses _____ thermal overload device(s).
   a. one
   b. two
   c. three
   d. four

4. The main purpose of an integral-horsepower manual starter with low-voltage protection is to prevent the _____.
   a. motor from stopping during a voltage dip
   b. motor from slowing down during a voltage dip
   c. motor from overheating during a voltage dip
   d. automatic startup of a motor after a power loss

5. The main feature that distinguishes a magnetic starter from a manual starter is _____.
   a. it is colored gray
   b. an electromagnet
   c. it has a threadless lug
   d. it is rated in motor horsepower

6. When a controller's armature has sealed in and fits closely against the magnet assembly, _____ is always deliberately left in the iron core circuit.
   a. excess wire
   b. a small gap
   c. some minor defect
   d. a gap of 2" or more

7. Which of the following is *not* a cause of excessive magnetic hum in a magnetic motor starter?

    a. Temperature fluctuations
    b. Incorrect mounting
    c. Misalignment between the armature and magnet assembly
    d. Dirt or rust

8. To provide overcurrent protection for motors, ______ are used.

    a. circuit breakers or fuses
    b. lightning arrestors
    c. heaters
    d. overload relays

9. To provide overload protection for motors, ______ are used.

    a. general-purpose, current-limiting fuses
    b. backup current-limiting fuses
    c. overload relays
    d. timing relays

10. What is the name given to the part of a melting alloy thermal overload relay that provides accurate response to overload current?

    a. Bimetal element
    b. Solder pot
    c. Air gap
    d. Terminals

11. The basic components of a bimetallic thermal overload relay include a ______.

    a. contact, bimetallic strip, and heater coil
    b. fuse capable of interrupting all currents from the maximum rated interrupting current down to the rated minimum interrupting current
    c. timer and contactor
    d. vented fuse with a time-delay element

12. Which of the following is *not* a consideration when selecting overload relays?

    a. Type of motor
    b. Full-load current rating of the motor
    c. Possible difference in ambient temperature between the motor and the controller
    d. Manufacturer of the motor

13. The term used to describe the repeated starting and stopping of a motor at frequent intervals for short periods of time is ______.

    a. plugging
    b. inching
    c. air gapping
    d. limiting

14. The main purpose of control relays when used in motor starters is to ______.

    a. amplify the contact capability or multiply the switching functions of a pilot device
    b. back up current-limiting fuses
    c. back up overcurrent and overload devices
    d. prevent the motor starter from functioning automatically

15. The device that converts mechanical motion into an electrical control signal is known as a ______.

    a. mechanical interlock
    b. pilot light
    c. limit switch
    d. contactor

ANSWERS TO REVIEW/PRACTICE QUESTIONS

<u>Answer</u>	<u>Section Reference</u>
1. d	1.0.0
2. b	2.2.1
3. a	2.2.1
4. d	2.2.3
5. b	2.3.0
6. b	2.3.0
7. a	3.2.0
8. a	5.0.0
9. c	5.0.0
10. b	5.1.0
11. a	5.2.0
12. d	5.4.0
13. b	7.1.0
14. a	9.0.0
15. c	10.0.0

The NCCER makes every effort to keep these manuals up-to-date and free of technical errors. We appreciate your help in this process. If you have an idea for improving this manual, or if you find an error, a typographical mistake, or an inaccuracy in the NCCER's Craft Training Manuals, please write us, using this form or a photocopy. Be sure to include the exact module number, page number, a description of the problem, and the correction, if possible. Your input will be brought to the attention of the Technical Review Committee. Thank you for your assistance.

Instructors – If you found that additional materials were necessary in order to teach this module effectively, please let us know so that we may include them in the Equipment/Materials list in the Instructor's Guide.

Write: Curriculum Development and Revision Department
National Center for Construction Education and Research
P.O. Box 141104
Gainesville, FL 32614-1104

Fax: 352-334-0932

Craft ____________________ Module Name ____________________

Copyright Date ____________ Module Number ____________ Page Number(s) ____________

Description of Problem

____

____

____

____

(Optional) Correction of Problem

____

____

____

(Optional) Your Name and Address

____

____

____

notes

Electricity In HVAC Systems
Module 26312

ELECTRICITY IN HVAC SYSTEMS

NATIONAL
CENTER FOR
CONSTRUCTION
EDUCATION AND
RESEARCH

OBJECTIVES

Upon completion of this module, the trainee will be able to:

1. Describe the basic operating principles of air conditioning systems.
2. Explain how refrigeration systems operate.
3. Interpret nameplate data on heating, ventilation, and air conditioning (HVAC) equipment.
4. Describe the various types of heating systems used in residential and commercial applications.
5. Explain the role of the NEC in HVAC power and control wiring.
6. Describe the operating principles of compressors as they relate to refrigeration.
7. Troubleshoot HVAC systems.
8. Install electrical circuits and related components to HVAC equipment in accordance with ***NEC Articles 220, 424, and 440***.

Prerequisites

Successful completion of the following Task Modules is recommended before beginning study of this Task Module: Core Curricula; Electrical Level 1; Electrical Level 2; Electrical Level 3, Modules 26301 through 26311. The trainee should also read ***NEC Articles 424 and 440***.

Required Trainee Materials

1. Trainee Task Module
2. Appropriate Personal Protective Equipment
3. Copy of the latest edition of the *National Electrical Code*

Note: The designations "National Electrical Code," "NE Code," and "NEC," where used in this document, refer to the National Electrical Code®, which is a registered trademark of the National Fire Protection Association, Quincy, MA. *All National Electrical Code (NEC) references in this module refer to the 1999 edition of the NEC.*

COURSE MAP

This course map shows all of the modules in the third level of the Electrical curricula. The suggested training order begins at the bottom and proceeds up. Skill levels increase as a trainee advances on the course map. The training order may be adjusted by the local Training Program Sponsor.

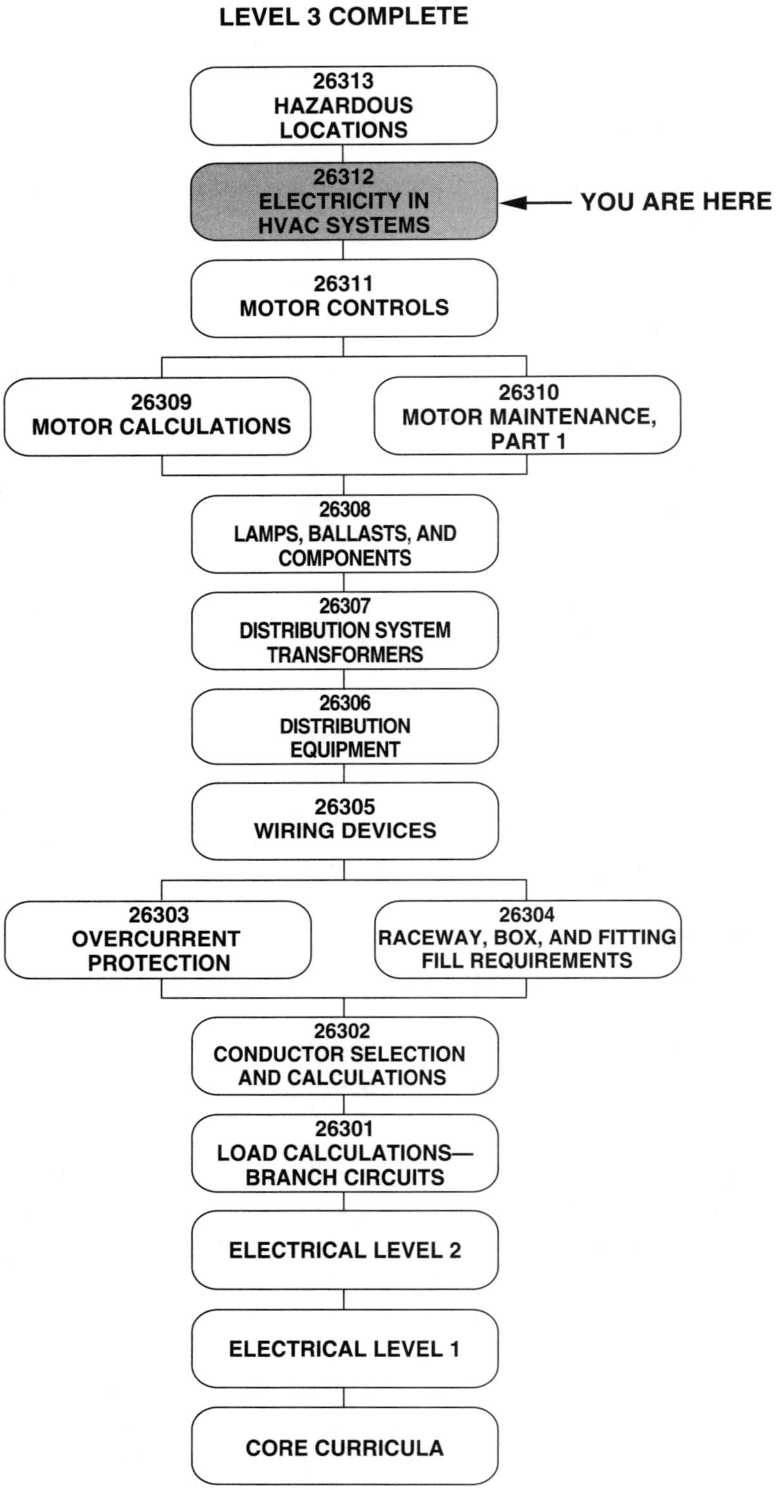

LEVEL 3 COMPLETE

- 26313 HAZARDOUS LOCATIONS
- 26312 ELECTRICITY IN HVAC SYSTEMS ← YOU ARE HERE
- 26311 MOTOR CONTROLS
- 26309 MOTOR CALCULATIONS
- 26310 MOTOR MAINTENANCE, PART 1
- 26308 LAMPS, BALLASTS, AND COMPONENTS
- 26307 DISTRIBUTION SYSTEM TRANSFORMERS
- 26306 DISTRIBUTION EQUIPMENT
- 26305 WIRING DEVICES
- 26303 OVERCURRENT PROTECTION
- 26304 RACEWAY, BOX, AND FITTING FILL REQUIREMENTS
- 26302 CONDUCTOR SELECTION AND CALCULATIONS
- 26301 LOAD CALCULATIONS— BRANCH CIRCUITS
- ELECTRICAL LEVEL 2
- ELECTRICAL LEVEL 1
- CORE CURRICULA

312CMAP.EPS

TABLE OF CONTENTS

TABLE OF CONTENTS

Trade Terms Introduced In This Module

Absolute pressure scale: Positive pressure measurements that start at zero (no pressure at all); also, the gauge pressure plus the pressure of the atmosphere (14.7 psi at sea level at 70°F).

Air cleaner: A device used for the removal of airborne impurities.

Air conditioning: A process that heats, cools, cleans, and circulates air and controls its moisture content. Ideally, it performs all of these functions simultaneously on a year-round basis.

Air diffuser: An air distribution outlet that is designed to direct air flow into desired patterns.

Area (A): The square footage of any plane surface or cross-section of a duct, the air inlet or outlet from a room, or the circular plane of rotation of a propeller.

Atmospheric pressure: The pressure exerted on all things on the Earth's surface as a result of the weight of the atmosphere. It is 14.7 psi at sea level at 70°F.

Back pressure: The pressure in the low side of a refrigerating system; also called the *suction pressure* or *low-side pressure*.

Balance point: The lowest outside temperature at which the refrigeration cycle of a heat pump will supply the heating requirements without the aid of a supplementary heat source.

Bimetal: A temperature-regulating or indicating device that works on the principle that when two dissimilar metals with unequal expansion rates are welded together, they will bend as the temperature changes.

British thermal unit (Btu): The quantity of heat required to raise the temperature of one pound of water 1° Fahrenheit (F).

Centigrade (C): The temperature scale used in the metric system. The freezing point of water is 0°C; the boiling point is 100°C.

Cold: A relative term for temperature. Cold means having less heat energy than another object against which it is being compared.

Compressor: A component of a refrigeration system that converts low-pressure, low-temperature refrigerant gas into high-temperature, high-pressure refrigerant gas.

Condenser: A heat exchanger that transfers heat from the refrigerant flowing inside it to the air or water flowing over it.

Conduction: A means of heat transfer in which heat is moved from one substance to another by means of direct contact.

Conductor: A material in which the transfer of heat by conduction occurs easily.

Convection: The transfer of heat by the flow of liquid or gas.

Damper: A valve used for controlling air flow.

Evaporator: A heat exchanger that transfers heat from the air flowing over it to the cooler refrigerant flowing through it.

Expansion device: A device that provides a pressure drop that converts the high-temperature, high-pressure liquid refrigerant from the condenser into the low-temperature, low-pressure liquid refrigerant entering the evaporator; also known as the *liquid metering device* or *metering device*.

Expansion valve: A type of refrigerant control that maintains a pressure difference between high-side and low-side pressure in a refrigerating mechanism. The valve operates by pressure in the low or suction side.

Gauge pressure: The pressure measured on a gauge, expressed as *psig* or *in. Hg. vac*; also, pressure measurements that are made in comparison to atmospheric pressure.

Heat: A form of energy. It causes molecules to be in motion and raises the temperature of a substance. Other forms of energy such as electricity, light, and magnetism deteriorate into heat.

Heat content: The amount of heat energy contained in a substance. Heat content is measured in Btu's.

Heat transfer: The transfer of heat from a warmer substance to a cooler substance.

Insulators: Materials that resist heat transfer by conduction.

Latent heat: The heat energy absorbed or rejected when a substance is changing state (solid to liquid, liquid to gas, or vice versa) and there is no change in the measured temperature.

Mechanical refrigeration: The use of machinery to provide cooling.

Noxious: Harmful to health.

Pressure: Force per unit of area.

Radiation: The movement of heat in the form of invisible rays or waves, similar to light.

Refrigerant: A fluid (liquid or gas) that picks up heat by evaporating at a low temperature and pressure and gives up heat by condensing at a higher temperature and pressure.

Refrigeration: The transfer of heat from a space or object where it is not wanted to a space or object where it is not objectionable (e.g., from indoors to outdoors).

Refrigeration cycle: The process by which a circulating refrigerant absorbs heat from one location and transfers it to another location.

Sensible heat: Heat that can be measured by a thermometer or sensed by touch. Sensible heat is the energy of molecular motion.

Space heater: A heater used in enclosed spaces.

Subcooling: The temperature of a liquid when it is cooled below its condensing temperature.

Superheat: The measurable heat added to the vapor or gas produced after a liquid has reached its boiling point and completely changed into a vapor.

Temperature: The dry-bulb temperature of either ambient or exhaust air.

Thermocouple: A device made of two different metals that generates electricity when there is a difference in temperature from one end to the other.

Thermostat: A device that is responsive to ambient temperature conditions.

Ton of refrigeration: The quantity of refrigeration that can remove heat at the rate of 12,000 Btu's per hour.

Total heat: Sensible heat plus latent heat.

Toxic: Poisonous.

1.0.0 INTRODUCTION

Since ancient times, people have sought ways to make the buildings in which they live, work, and play more comfortable. Today, heating, ventilation, and **air conditioning** (HVAC) systems provide the means to control the **temperature**, humidity, and even the cleanliness of the air in our homes, schools, offices, and factories. This module covers the basic processes of heating, ventilation, and air conditioning, including applicable NEC requirements and electrical troubleshooting.

1.2.0 HEATING

Early humans burned fuel as a source of **heat**. That has not changed; what is different between now and then is the way it is done. We no longer need to huddle around a wood fire to keep warm. Instead, a central heating source such as a furnace or boiler does the job using the **heat transfer** principle. That is, heat is created in one place and carried to another place by means of air or water.

For example, in a common household furnace, fuel oil or natural gas is burned to create heat, which warms metal plates known as *heat exchangers (Figure 1)*. Air from living spaces is circulated over the heat exchangers and returned to the living spaces as heated air. This type of system is known as a *forced-air system*.

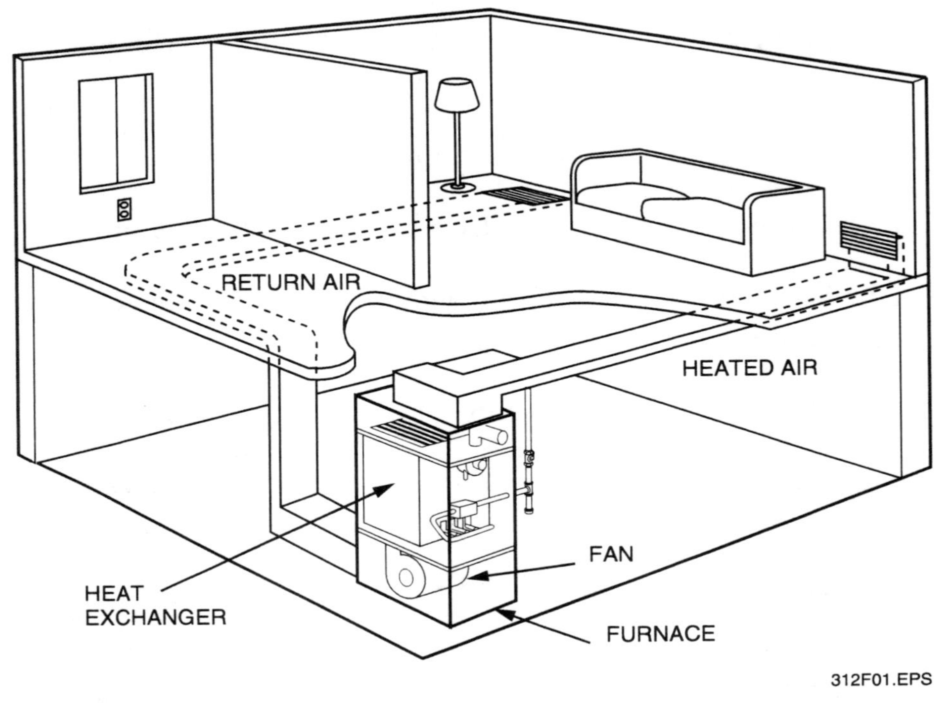

Figure 1. Forced-Air Heat

Water is also used as a heat exchange medium. The water is heated in a boiler (*Figure 2*), then pumped through pipes to heat exchangers, where the heat it contains is transferred to the surrounding air. The heat exchangers are usually baseboard heating elements located in the space to be heated.

Natural gas and fuel oil are the most widely used heating fuels. Electricity is also used as a heat source. In an electric heating system, electricity flows through coils of heavy wire, causing the coils to become hot. Air from the conditioned space is passed over the coils and the heat from the coils is transferred to the air. Because electricity is expensive to use for heating, this method is no longer common in **cold** climates. It is more likely to be used in warm climates where heat is seldom required.

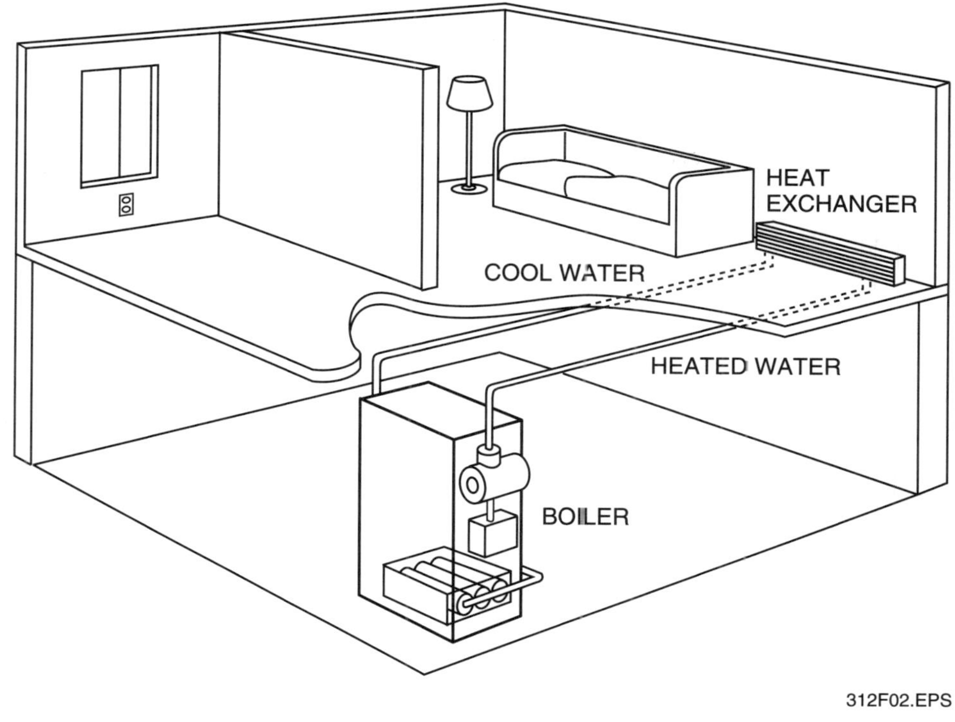

Figure 2. Hot Water Heat

1.3.0   VENTILATION

Ventilation is the introduction of fresh air into a closed space in order to control air quality (*Figure 3*). Fresh air entering a building provides the oxygen we breathe. In addition to fresh air, we want clean air. The air in our homes, schools, and offices contains dust, pollen, and molds, as well as vapors and odors from a variety of sources. Relatively simple air circulation and filtration methods, including natural ventilation, are used to help keep the air in these environments clean and fresh. Many industrial environments, on the other hand, require special ventilation and air management systems. Such systems are needed to eliminate **noxious** or **toxic** particles and fumes that may be created by the processes and materials used at the facility.

The U.S. Government has strict regulations governing indoor air quality in industrial environments and the release of toxic materials to the outside air. Where noxious or toxic fumes may be present, the indoor air must be constantly replaced with fresh air. Fans and other ventilating devices are normally used for this purpose. Special filtering devices may also be required; these not only protect the health of building occupants, but also prevent the release of toxic materials to the outside air.

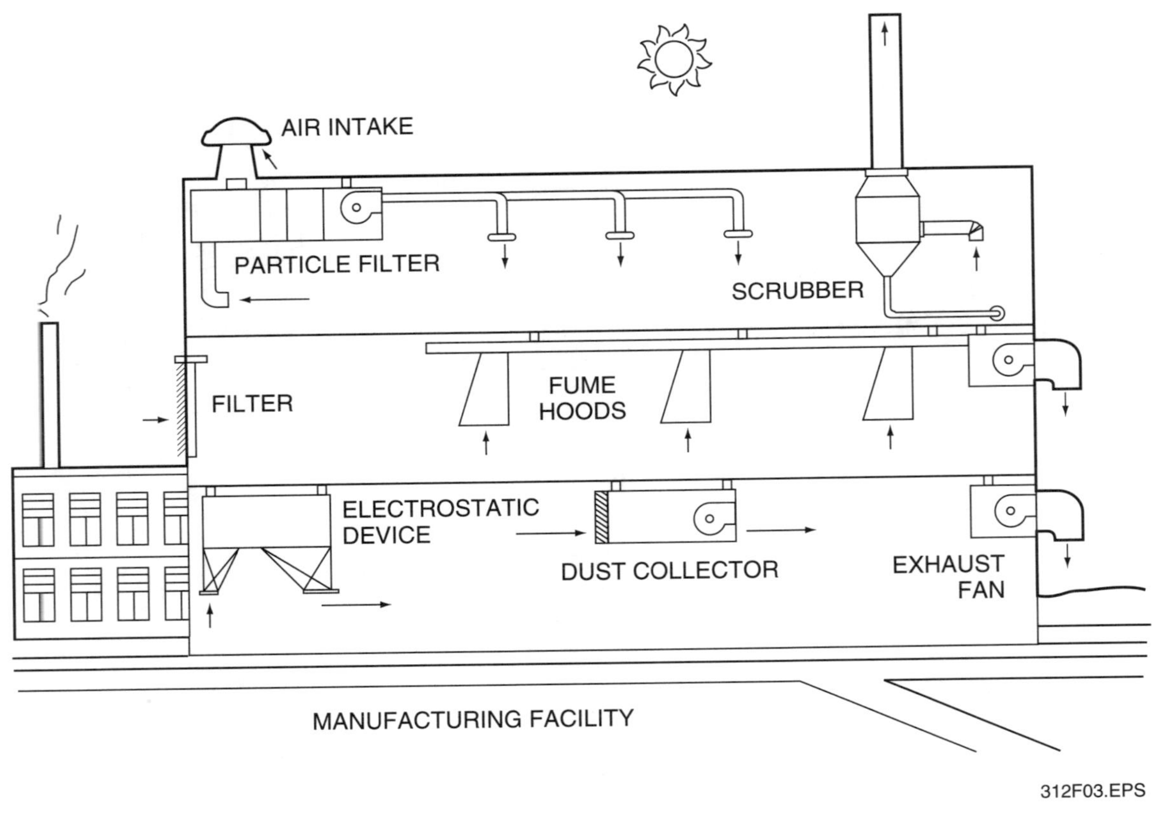

Figure 3. Ventilation System

1.4.0 AIR CONDITIONING

Mechanical refrigeration, which came into use in the twentieth century, is based on a process known as the **refrigeration cycle** (*Figure 4*).

Simply stated, the refrigeration cycle relies on the ability of chemical **refrigerants** to absorb heat. If a cold refrigerant flows through a warm space, it will absorb heat from the space. Having given up heat to the refrigerant, the space becomes cooler. The colder the refrigerant, the more heat it will absorb, and the cooler the space will become. If the super-hot refrigerant flows to a cooler location (e.g., the outdoors), the refrigerant will give up the heat it absorbed from the indoors and become cool again.

A mechanical refrigeration system is a sealed system operating under high **pressure**. The main elements of a mechanical refrigeration system include the following:

- *Compressor* – Provides the force that circulates the refrigerant and creates the high pressure necessary for the refrigeration cycle to work. A special refrigerant compressor is used.

- *Evaporator* – A heat exchanger in which the heat in the warm indoor air is transferred to the cold refrigerant.

ELECTRICAL — TRAINEE TASK MODULE 26312

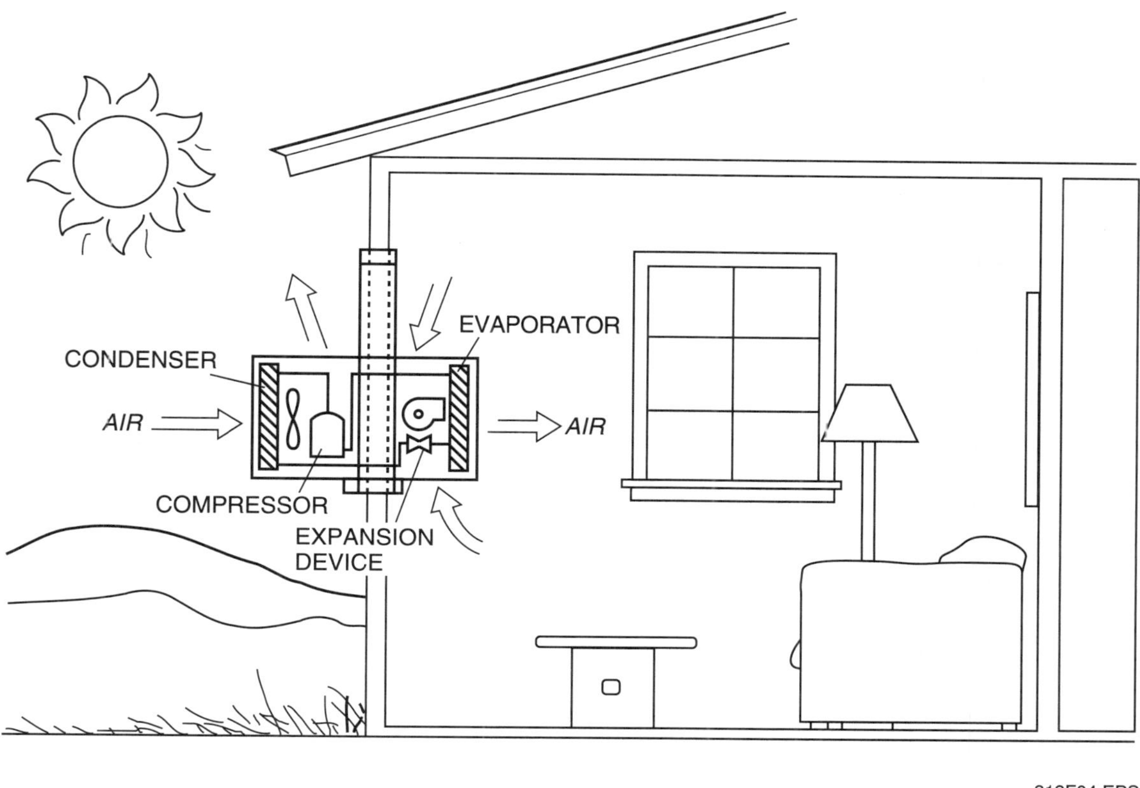

Figure 4. Basic Refrigeration Cycle

- ***Condenser*** – A heat exchanger in which the heat absorbed by the refrigerant is transferred to the cooler outdoor air or to a water supply.
- ***Expansion device*** – Provides a pressure drop that lowers the boiling point of the refrigerant as it enters the evaporator. This allows the refrigerant to absorb heat in the evaporator.

The relationship between temperature and pressure is critical to mechanical refrigeration. As you study the process, you will learn that the same refrigerant can be very cold at one point in the system (the evaporator input) and very hot at another (the condenser input). These two points are often only inches apart. This is possible because of pressure changes caused by the compressor and expansion device. In addition to the circulation of refrigerant, air must also circulate. Fans are used to move air across the condenser and evaporator.

This is a simple explanation of the refrigeration cycle. It is meant to give you a basic idea of how an air conditioner works. Later in the module, you will explore this subject in greater detail. The relationship between temperature and pressure will also be studied in more detail. It is the key to understanding and troubleshooting mechanical refrigeration systems.

The refrigeration cycle is the same in all refrigeration equipment, from the small air conditioner in your car to the huge system that cools the largest office building. The difference is in the size and construction of the components and piping and the amount and type of refrigerant.

2.0.0 AIR CONDITIONING FUNDAMENTALS

In nature, there is nothing from which heat or temperature is totally absent. Cold is a relative term for temperature. It means an object has less heat energy (making it colder) than another object to which it is being compared. For ease of understanding, it is helpful to define cold as being the absence of heat.

Refrigeration is the transfer of heat from a place or object where it is not wanted to a place or object where it is not objectionable. Simply defined, refrigeration is cooling by the removal of heat. Air conditioners do not pump cold into a space. They take heat out of the space or object to be cooled and move it outside (*Figure 5*). A chemical fluid known as *refrigerant* circulates through a refrigerator or air conditioning system. The refrigerant absorbs heat from the refrigerated space, then carries it to a location outside the space. You will learn more about refrigerant later in this module.

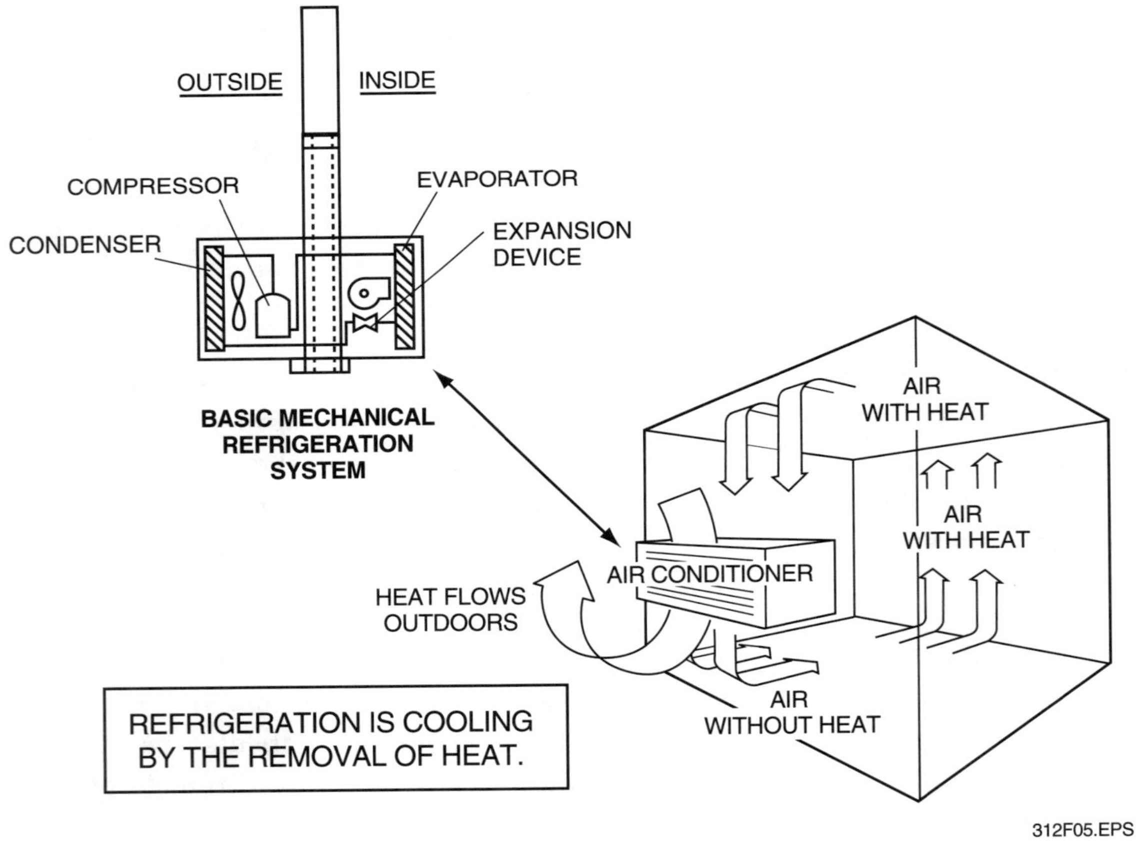

Figure 5. Refrigeration – Transfer Of Heat

ELECTRICAL — TRAINEE TASK MODULE 26312

2.1.0 HEAT

To understand refrigeration, you must understand heat. Like light, electricity, and magnetism, heat is a form of energy. Heat can be measured and controlled. Like other forms of energy, it can do work. Its ability to do work depends on two characteristics: temperature and **heat content** (quantity).

2.1.1 Temperature

Temperature compares the degree of hotness or coldness of any object or substance. The intensity of heat is measured in degrees (°) with a thermometer. Two temperature scales are normally used for measuring temperature. These include the Fahrenheit (F) scale and the Celsius or **Centigrade (C)** scale (*Figure 6*).

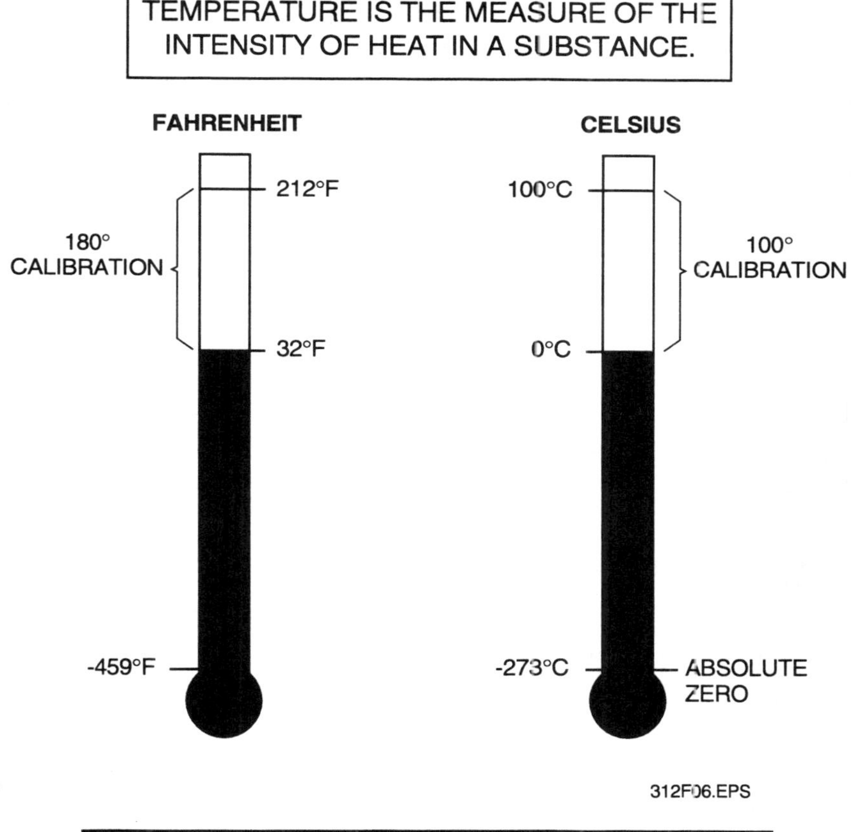

Figure 6. Fahrenheit And Celsius Temperature Scales

Under normal atmospheric pressure, water boils at 212°F and freezes at 32°F. The distance between the two points is divided into 180 equal parts. On the Celsius scale, water boils at 100°C and freezes at 0°C. The distance between the two points is divided into 100 equal parts. The absolute zero point shown on the temperature scale is the theoretical point at which all molecular motion stops, resulting in zero heat content.

2.1.2 Heat Content

Heat content or the quantity of heat is the amount of heat energy contained in a substance. Heat content is measured in **British thermal units (Btu's)**. One Btu is the amount of heat needed to raise the temperature of one pound of water 1°F. (One pound of water is equal to about a pint of water.) For example, by heating 10 pounds of water from 40°F to 50°F (a difference of 10°F), 100 Btu's of heat are added to the water. The opposite is also true. If the 10 pounds of water had been cooled 10°F, 100 Btu's would have been removed.

2.1.3 Sensible And Latent Heat

Depending on the heat content and temperature, substances can exist in three states: solid, liquid, and gas.

Using water as an example, the three states are ice (solid), water (liquid), and steam or vapor (gas). In a refrigeration system, the refrigerant exists in either a liquid or gas state, depending on its heat content. For this reason, these two states are the ones you will be most concerned with in your study of refrigeration.

When a substance such as water changes from one state to another, something peculiar happens (*Figure 7*). If heat is added to one pound of ice at 0°F, a thermometer will show a rise in temperature until the reading reaches 32°F. This is the point at which the ice starts changing into water. If heat is continually added, the thermometer reading remains fixed at 32°F instead of rising as expected. It continues to read 32°F until the entire pound of ice is melted. The increase in temperature from 0°F to 32°F as registered by the thermometer is called **sensible heat**. The heat that was added to the ice and caused its change in state from a solid to a liquid but did not register on the thermometer is called **latent heat**. To review:

- Sensible heat is heat that can be sensed by a thermometer or by touch.
- Latent heat is the heat energy absorbed or rejected when a substance is changing state (solid to liquid, liquid to gas, or vice versa) without a change in the measured temperature.
- Sensible heat plus latent heat equals **total heat**.

If we continue to add heat to the pound of water after all the ice has melted, the thermometer will once again show an increase in temperature until the temperature reaches 212°F. At this point, the water starts boiling and changes state from water into steam or water vapor. As even more heat is added, the thermometer reading remains at 212°F until all the water has turned into steam. If we continue to add heat, the thermometer will once again register sensible heat; this is called **superheat**. Superheat is the measurable heat added to the vapor or gas once a liquid has reached its boiling point and has been completely changed into a vapor.

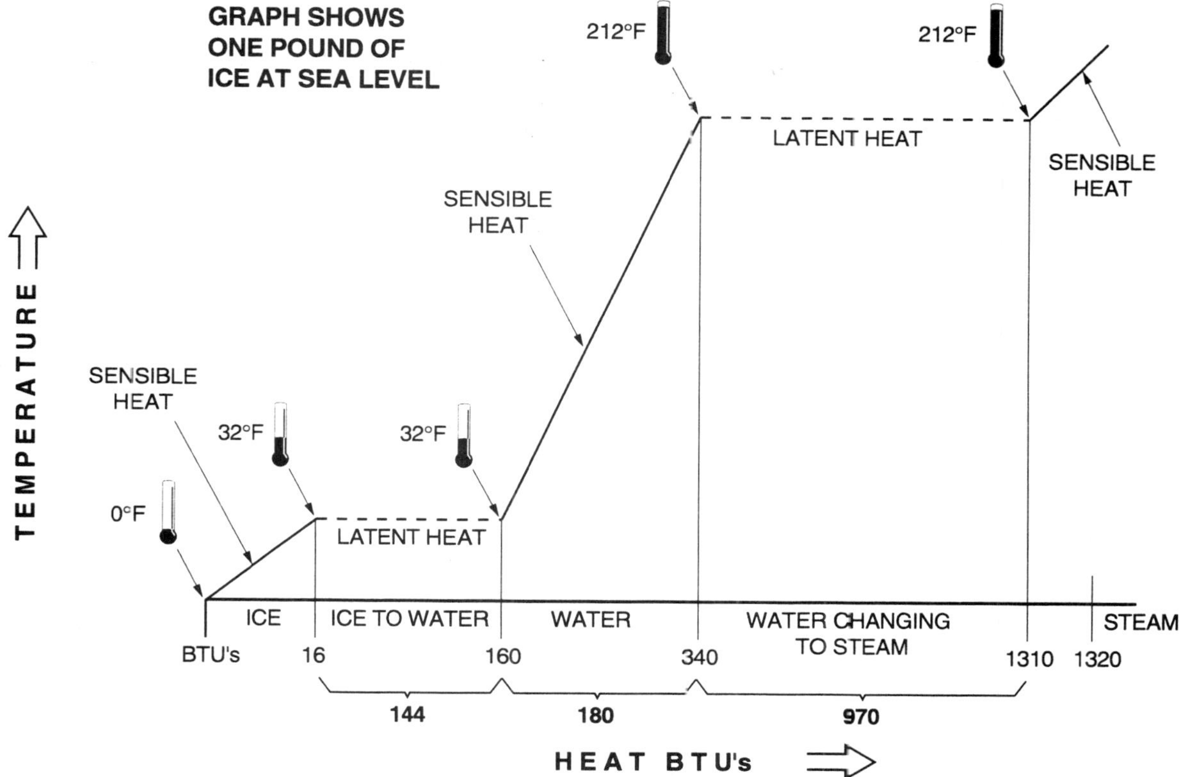

SENSIBLE HEAT:

HEAT THAT CAUSES A TEMPERATURE CHANGE AND CAN BE SENSED BY A THERMOMETER OR BY TOUCH.

LATENT HEAT:

HEAT THAT PRODUCES A CHANGE IN STATE WITHOUT A CHANGE IN TEMPERATURE.

312F07.EPS

Figure 7. Changing States Of Water

As shown in *Figure 7*, it takes a great deal more heat to cause a change in state than is needed for a degree change in temperature. It required 144 Btu's of latent heat to melt the pound of ice before the temperature began to rise. This is 144 times as much heat as is needed to raise the temperature of water one degree. The change from water to steam required an even greater amount of latent heat. It took 970 Btu's to change the water to steam. It is important to remember that none of this latent heat registered on the thermometer.

As mentioned previously, the two states you are most concerned with in learning about refrigeration are the liquid and gas states. Another term used in refrigeration work concerning changes in the state of matter is **subcooling**. Subcooling is the reverse of superheat. It is the temperature of a liquid when it is cooled below its condensing temperature. For example, the condensing temperature of water is 212°F. If the water is subcooled 10°, the temperature is cooled to 202°F.

2.2.0 HEAT TRANSFER

Heat transfer is the movement of heat from one place to another, either within a substance or between substances. Heat always flows from a warmer location to a cooler location. It is important to remember that in order to have heat flow, there must be a difference in temperature. There are three ways to move or transfer heat. These are listed below and shown in *Figure 8*:

- **Conduction**
- **Convection**
- **Radiation**

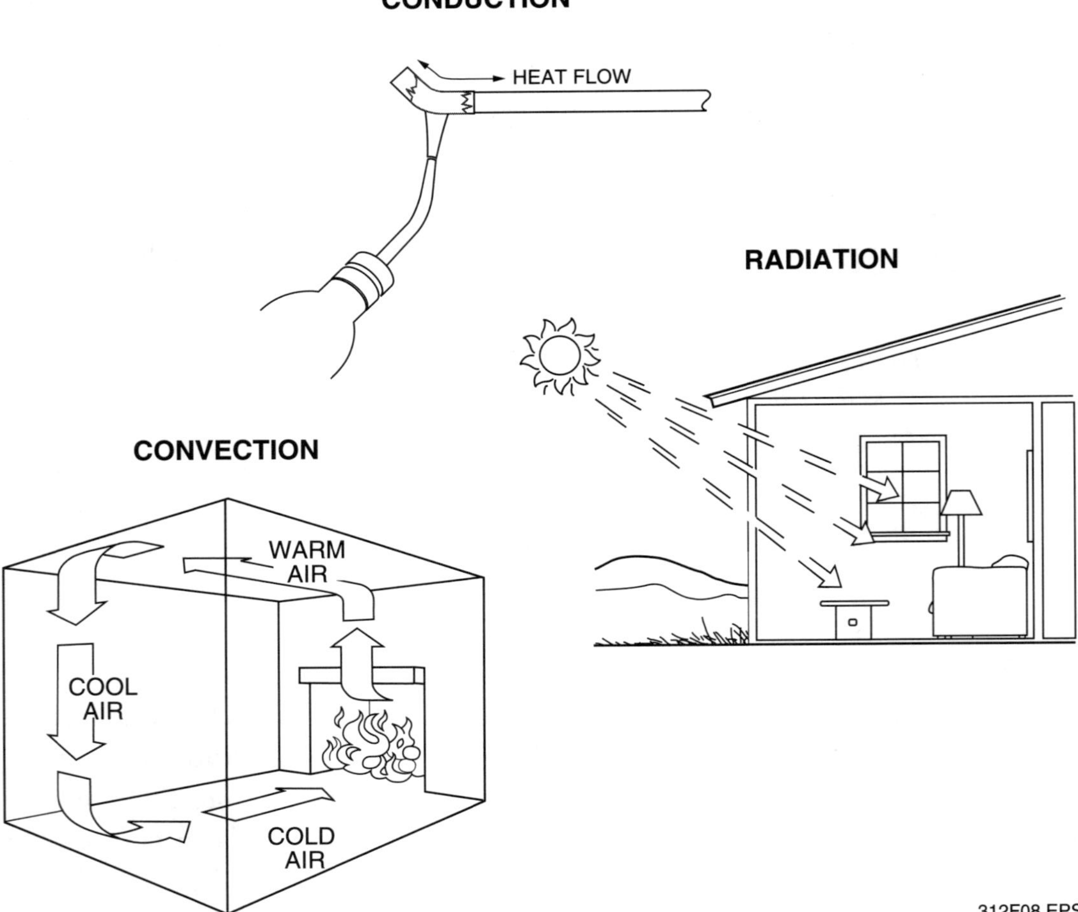

Figure 8. Heat Movement

2.2.1   Conduction

Conduction is a means of heat transfer in which heat is moved from molecule to molecule within a substance. When these molecules are heated, they move about, colliding with one another. These collisions continue in a direction towards the cooler part of the material, causing the movement of heat in the same direction. For example, when copper tubing is being heated by a torch, the molecules in the tubing nearest the torch get heated first and begin to move and collide with the nearby molecules in the tubing. These molecules then collide with other molecules, causing the tubing to become heated. The result is that the heat is carried by conduction from the end being heated by the torch toward the cold end.

2.2.2   Convection

Convection is the transfer of heat by the flow of liquid or gas. As shown in *Figure 8*, air near the fireplace is heated by conduction and becomes warmer than the air in the rest of the room. Since warm air rises, the heated air moves upward toward the ceiling. In doing so, it gives up heat as it travels and then settles back down to the floor as it cools. The cooler air at the floor level moves towards the fireplace to replace the rising warm air. It too will warm, rise, give off heat, and settle back down. This circulation of air is accomplished via convection. Convection can be either natural or forced. Natural convection is shown by the example of the fireplace. Forced convection uses fans or pumps to speed up the circulation process, such as those found in home heating and air conditioning systems.

2.2.3   Radiation

Radiation is the movement of heat in the form of invisible rays or waves, similar to light. Like light, it needs no medium on which to travel. Radiation takes place free of convection. It travels in straight lines from the heat source to the point where it is absorbed without heating the space in between. Heat from the sun travelling through space and warming our homes is a good example of heat transfer by radiation. The solar radiation comes through the windows in a building; strikes the walls, floors, furniture, and people; and is absorbed.

2.2.4   Conductors And Insulators

The rate of heat conduction varies for different substances. Some materials support the transfer of heat, while others restrict it. Materials in which the transfer of heat by conduction occurs easily are called **conductors**. **Insulators** are materials that resist heat transfer by conduction. Cork, fiberglass, and polyurethane foam are examples of insulators. Most metals are good conductors of heat. Copper and aluminum are used in both wiring and refrigeration systems because of their good heat conduction ability.

2.2.5 Rate Of Heat Transfer

The rate of heat transfer describes how fast heat can be added to or removed from an object or between objects. It is usually expressed in two ways: one way is in Btu's per hour or Btuh and another way is by the ton (a much larger unit of measure). The ton is commonly used in refrigeration work to describe the heating or cooling load for a space, or the capacity of a piece of equipment or system.

One **ton of refrigeration** is defined as 12,000 Btu's per hour or 12,000 Btuh (*Figure 9*). The ton is based on the amount of heat required to melt one ton of ice in a 24-hour period. As mentioned earlier, one pound of ice at 32°F absorbs 144 Btu's of heat while melting. Assuming that it takes one hour to melt, the rate of heat transfer is 144 Btuh. Since a ton of ice contains 2,000 pounds, a total of 288,000 Btu's per day or 12,000 Btu's per hour (288,000 ÷ 24) is the amount of heat required to melt the ice.

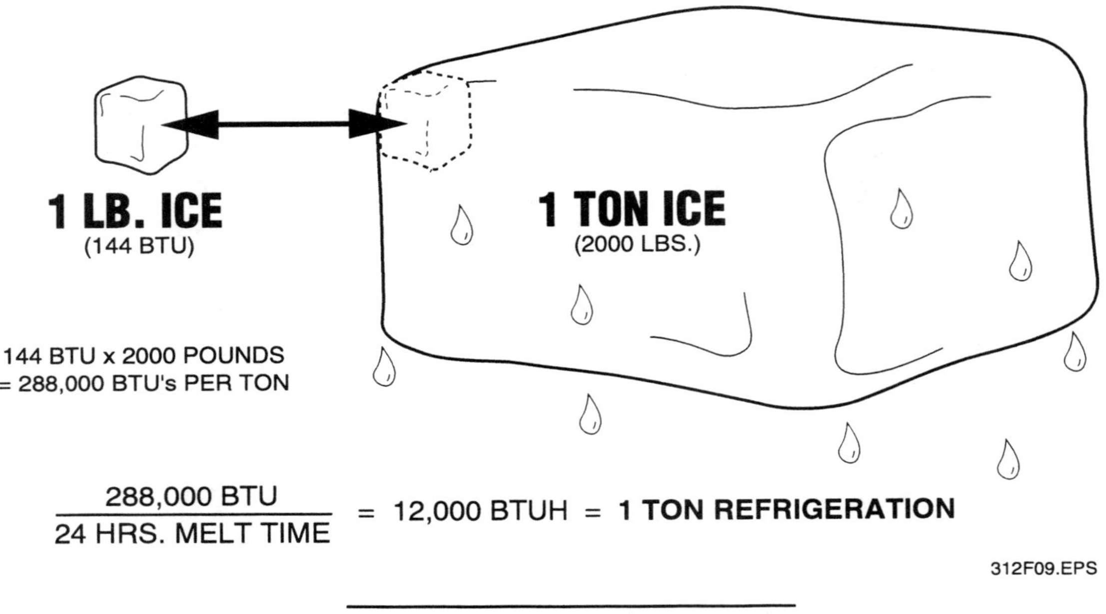

Figure 9. One Ton Of Refrigeration

2.3.0 PRESSURE

Pressure is defined as force per unit area. This is normally expressed in *pounds per square inch, inches of mercury,* or for very low pressures, *inches of water.* Depending on the state of a substance, pressure may be exerted in one direction, several directions, or all directions (*Figure 10*). Using the three states of water as an example, ice (a solid) exerts pressure only in a downward direction. The same is true for all solid materials. As a liquid, water exerts pressure against all sides of the container in contact with it. As a gas (water vapor), it exerts pressure on all the surfaces of the container because it completely fills the container. In refrigeration work, the term *fluid* is generally used when describing pressure. Fluid means the liquid or gaseous state of a material such as a refrigerant. Fluids tend to exert pressure equally in all directions like the water vapor given in the example.

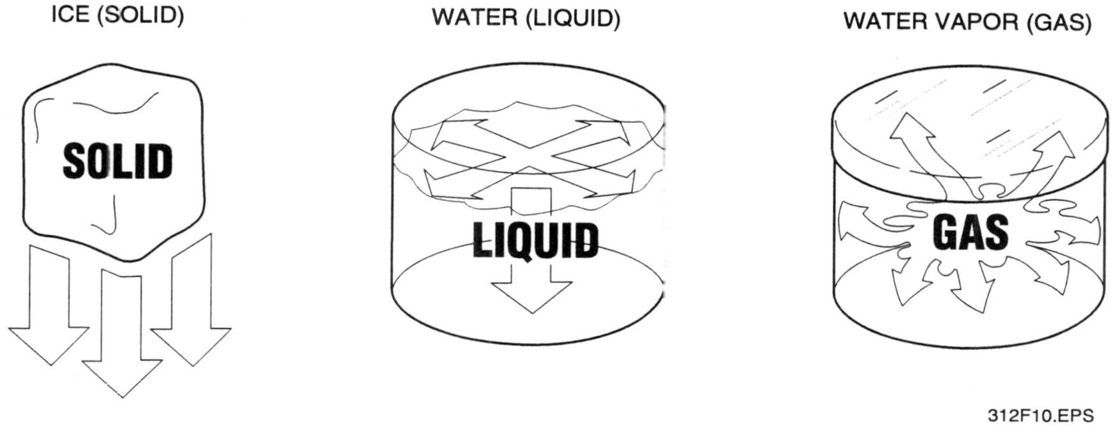

Figure 10. The Directions Of Pressure

2.3.1 Atmospheric Pressure

The earth is surrounded by a blanket of air called the *atmosphere*. Air is matter consisting of oxygen, nitrogen, and water vapor. It has weight and exerts a force called **atmospheric pressure** on all things on the Earth's surface. Atmospheric pressure can be measured with a barometer. For this reason, it is often referred to as *barometric pressure*. The barometer compares the pressure of the atmosphere to the pressure of no atmosphere.

Figure 11 shows a simple mercury tube barometer. The top of the barometer tube is sealed, while the open end at the bottom rests in a container of mercury. Air pressure pushing down on the mercury in the container causes the column of mercury in the tube to rise. The extent of the rise is determined by the amount of pressure applied to the mercury.

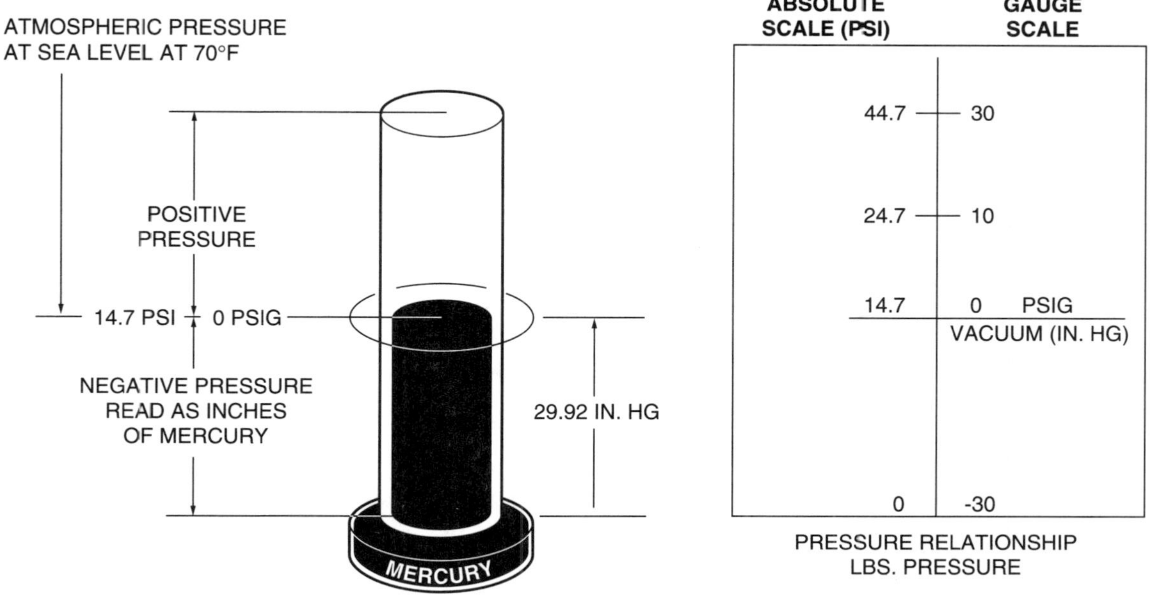

Figure 11. Absolute And Gauge Pressure Scale Comparison

Visualize a column of air with a cross-sectional area of one square inch and extending from the Earth's surface at sea level to the limits of the atmosphere. Also, assume that the temperature at sea level is 70°F. If this column of air is applied to the mercury tube barometer, the height of the mercury in the tube will be slightly less than 30" (29.92"). Its weight will be 14.7 pounds. This means that every square inch of any surface at sea level has 14.7 pounds of air pressure pushing down on it. These values of 29.92" of mercury and 14.7 pounds per square inch at sea level at 70°F are standards that are used frequently in refrigeration work. A pressure scale, called the **absolute pressure scale**, is based on the barometer measurements just described. On this scale, pressures are expressed as *pounds per square inch (psi)* or *pounds per square inch absolute (psia)*, starting from zero, which represents a complete absence of pressure.

2.3.2　Gauge Pressure

Another scale, called **gauge pressure**, is normally used for refrigeration work. Gauge pressure scales use atmospheric pressure as their zero starting point. Positive gauge pressures, which are those above zero (14.7 psi), are expressed in pounds per square inch gauge or psig. Negative pressures (those below 0 psig) are expressed in inches of mercury vacuum or in. Hg. vac. Gauge pressures can easily be converted to absolute pressures by adding 14.7 to the gauge pressure value. For example, a gauge pressure of 10 psig equals an absolute pressure of 24.7 (10 + 14.7). A comparison of the gauge and absolute pressure scales is shown in *Figure 11*.

2.3.3　Pressure/Temperature Relationships

Pressure and temperature have a special relationship. Two things are important to remember. First, the temperature at which a liquid or gas changes state is dependent on the pressure. Second, the boiling temperature of a liquid will drop as the pressure on it decreases. It will rise as the pressure increases. Using our water example, water boils at 212°F at sea level (14.7 psia). With a lower atmospheric pressure of about 11.6 psia that exists at 5,000' above sea level, the same water would boil at the lower temperature of about 203°F. At the higher pressure of about 29.7 psia (15 psig + 14.7 atmospheric pressure) such as can be reached in a pressure cooker, the water boils at the higher temperature of about 250°F. *Figure 12* shows the temperature/pressure relationship of water.

If the pressure on a liquid can be lowered enough, its boiling point need not be a high temperature. This relationship is basic to the refrigeration process. Each refrigerant used with cooling equipment has its own temperature/pressure relationship. Like water, the boiling temperature of refrigerants rises as the pressure is increased, and drops as the pressure is decreased.

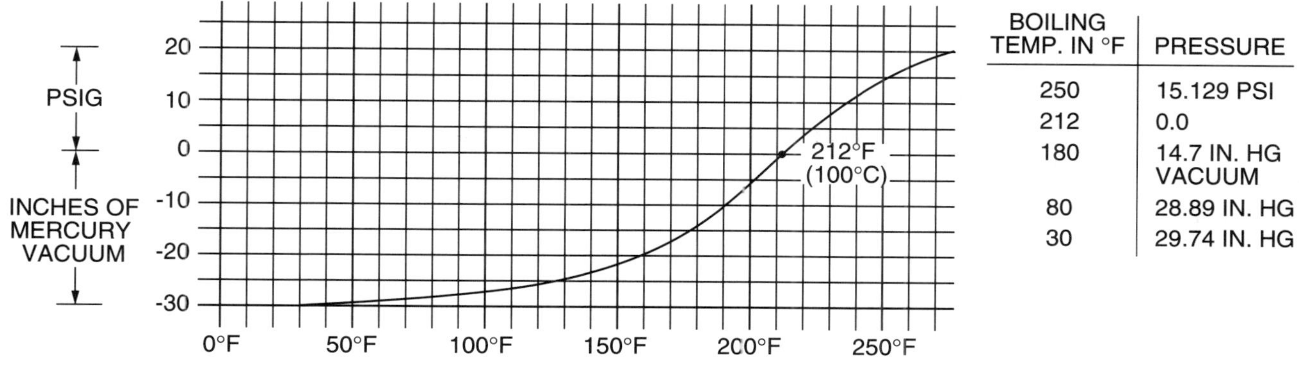

Figure 12. Temperature/Pressure Relationship Of Water

2.3.4 Movement Of Fluids

Differences in pressure cause the flow of fluids. This flow is always from a higher pressure to a lower pressure. Just as heat moves from a higher temperature to a lower temperature, so too does a liquid or gas move from a higher pressure to a lower pressure. The result is that liquids and gases can be made to move by adjusting or changing the pressure around them. In refrigeration, a compressor is used to create the pressure differential that causes refrigerant to flow in a system.

3.0.0 COOLING SYSTEMS

This section covers the basic components and processes of cooling systems. A fundamental knowledge of these items is required in order to perform effective troubleshooting.

3.1.0 MECHANICAL REFRIGERATION SYSTEM

There are many types of systems used to provide cooling for personal comfort, food preservation, and industrial processes. Each of these uses a mechanical refrigeration system. *Figure 13* shows a basic system. As discussed earlier, basic refrigeration components include the following:

- Evaporator
- Compressor
- Condenser
- Expansion device

Also shown in *Figure 13* is the piping, called *lines*, used to connect the basic components in order to provide the path for refrigerant flow. Together, the components and lines form a closed refrigeration system. The lines are:

- *Suction line* – The tubing that carries heat-laden refrigerant gas from the evaporator to the compressor.

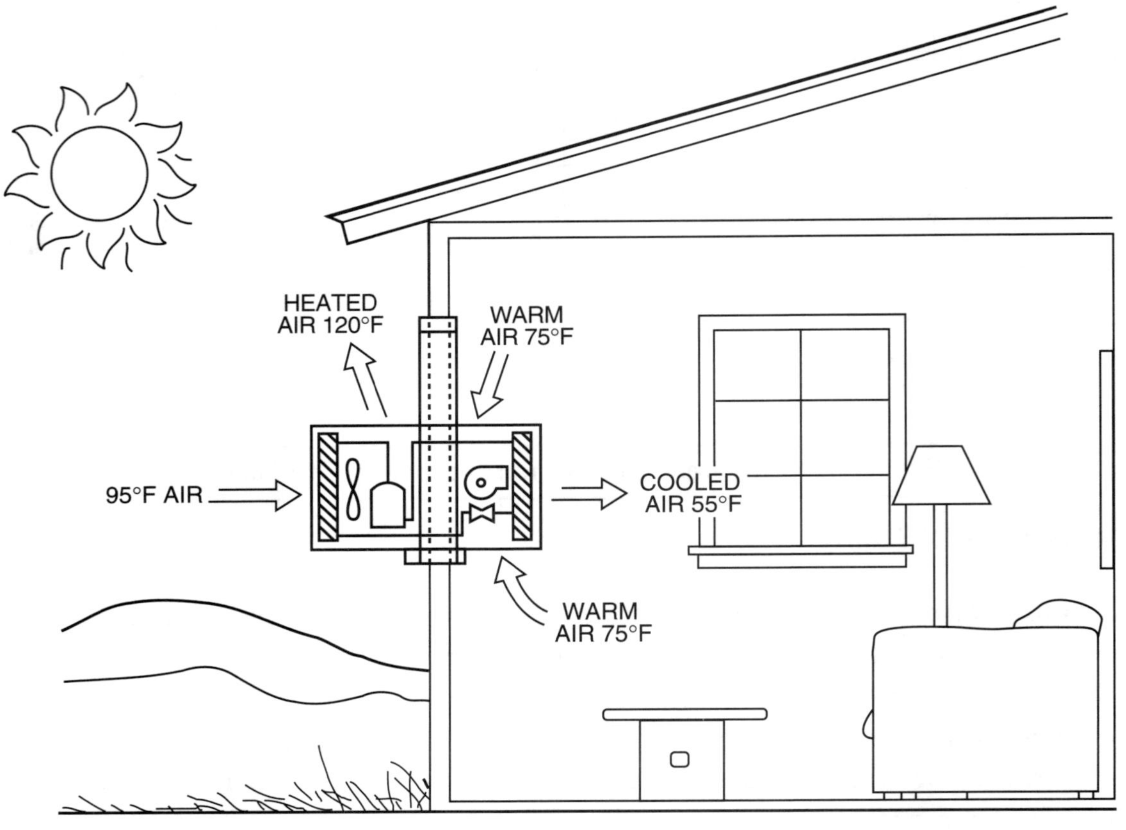

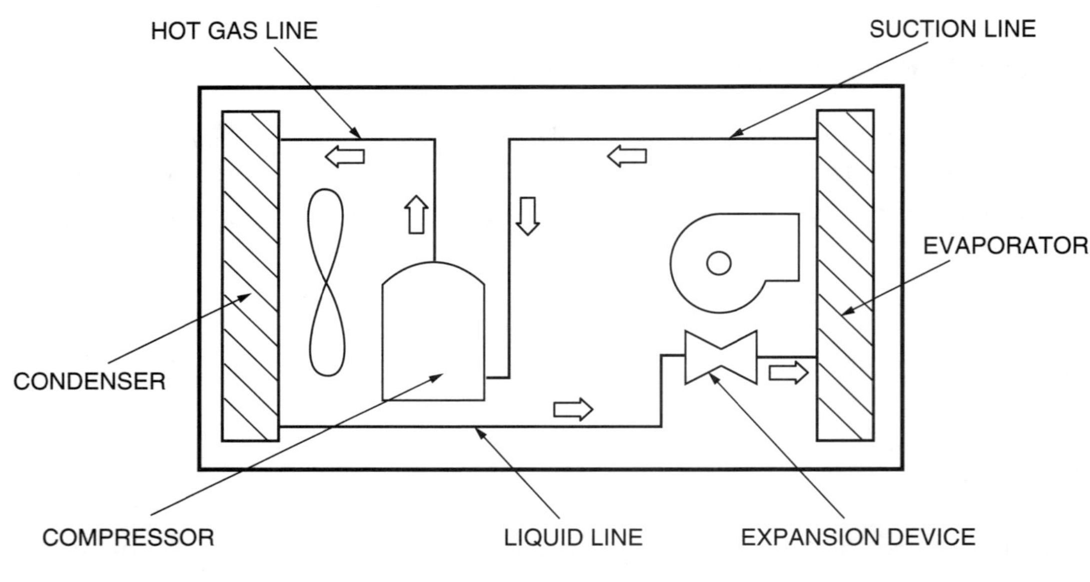

Figure 13. Air And Refrigerant Flow In A Refrigeration Cycle

- *Hot gas line (discharge line)* – The tubing that carries hot refrigerant gas from the compressor to the condenser.

- *Liquid line* – The tubing that carries the liquid refrigerant formed in the condenser to the expansion device.

The arrows on *Figure 13* show the direction of flow through the system. The purpose of the refrigerant is to move heat. It is the medium by which heat can be moved into or out of a space or substance. A refrigerant is any fluid (liquid or gas) that picks up heat by evaporating at a low temperature and pressure and gives up heat by condensing at a higher temperature and pressure. Refrigerants often boil at very low temperatures (as low as -21°F).

Remember that the operation of a mechanical refrigeration system is the same for all systems. Only the type of refrigerant used, the size and style of the components, and the installed locations of the components and the lines will change from system to system. Other devices, called *accessories*, may be used in some systems to gain the desired cooling effect. The events that take place within the system happen again and again in the same order. This repeating series of events is called the *refrigeration cycle*.

3.2.0   REFRIGERATION CYCLE

3.2.1   Basic Operation

The refrigeration cycle is based on two principles:

- As liquid changes to a gas or vapor, it is capable of absorbing large quantities of heat.

- The boiling point of a liquid can be changed by changing the pressure exerted on the liquid.

As shown in *Figure 13*, the refrigerant flows through the system in the direction indicated by the arrows. We will begin with the evaporator. It receives low-temperature, low-pressure liquid refrigerant from the expansion device. The evaporator is a series of tubing coils that expose the cooler liquid refrigerant to the warmer air passing over them. Heat from the warmer air is transferred through the tubing to the cooler refrigerant. This causes it to boil or vaporize. It is important to realize that even though it has just boiled, it is still not considered hot because refrigerants boil at such low temperatures. So, it is a low-temperature, low-pressure refrigerant vapor that travels through the suction line to the compressor.

The compressor receives the low-temperature, low-pressure vapor and compresses it. It then becomes a high-temperature, high-pressure vapor. This travels to the condenser via the hot gas line.

Like the evaporator, the condenser is a series of tubing coils through which the refrigerant flows. As cooler air moves across the tubing, the hot refrigerant vapor gives up superheat and cools. As it continues to give up heat to the outside air, it cools to the condensation point, where it begins to change from a vapor into a liquid. As more cooling takes place (subcooling), all of the refrigerant becomes a liquid. This high-temperature, high-pressure liquid travels through the liquid line to the input of the expansion device.

The expansion device regulates the flow of refrigerant to the evaporator. It also decreases its pressure and temperature. By the use of a built-in restriction, such as a small hole or orifice, it converts the high-temperature, high-pressure refrigerant from the condenser into the low-temperature, low-pressure refrigerant needed to absorb heat in the evaporator.

3.2.2 Refrigeration Cycle In A Typical Air Conditioning System

Refrigeration components are divided into two sections based on pressure. The high-pressure side includes all of the components where the pressure of the refrigerant is at or above the condensing pressure. This is often referred to as the *head pressure, discharge pressure,* or *high-side pressure.* The low-pressure side includes all of the components where the pressure of the refrigerant is at or below the evaporating pressure. This is the **back pressure**, which is also known as the *suction pressure* or *low-side pressure.* The dividing point between the sections cuts through the compressor and the expansion device.

We will now discuss the refrigeration cycle in more detail. We will describe a typical air conditioner that uses HCFC-22 (R-22) as the refrigerant. R-22 boils at 40°F when under a pressure of 69 psig. R-22 is one of the many refrigerants used in air conditioning and refrigeration. Each has its own boiling point and temperature and pressure characteristics.

This example will demonstrate the concepts and temperature/pressure relationships you have learned so far. For our example, assume an air temperature of 75°F for the room being cooled and an outdoor air temperature of 95°F. These values will vary due to equipment and load conditions. Follow along on *Figure 14* as we describe this system.

1. A mixture (75% liquid, 25% vapor) of R-22 is supplied from the expansion device to the evaporator. This mixture is at a pressure of 69 psig, which corresponds to the 40°F boiling point of R-22 refrigerant. (This information is commonly available in pressure/temperature charts from the refrigerant manufacturer.) The 40°F boiling point is used here because it is typical of the temperatures normally used for evaporators in air conditioning systems.

2. Because the refrigerant flowing through the evaporator is cooler (40°F) than the warmer inside room air (75°F), it absorbs heat, causing the liquid refrigerant to boil and turn into a vapor. After traveling about 90% of the way through the evaporator tubing, all the refrigerant has boiled into a vapor known as the *saturated vapor.*

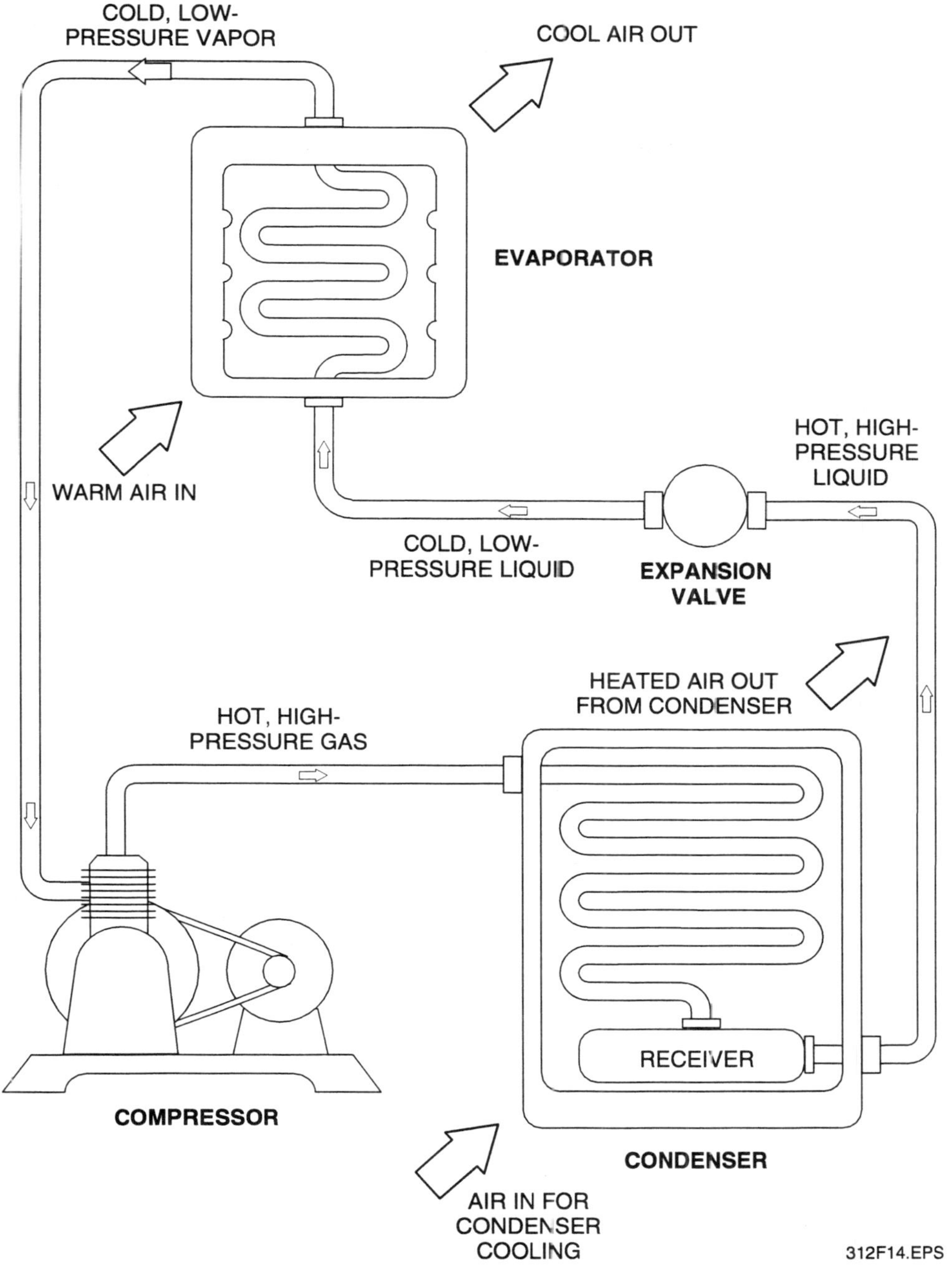

Figure 14. Typical Air Conditioning Cycle For HCFC-22 (R-22) Refrigerant

3. During the remaining 10% of travel through the evaporator, the saturated vapor continues to absorb heat from the warmer air, thus raising its temperature to 50°F. In other words, the saturated vapor is superheated 10°F (50°F – 40°F). This superheated vapor flows through the suction line and is drawn into the low-pressure side of the compressor. The cooled inside room air is recirculated by the evaporator fan back into the room at a temperature of about 55°F.

4. The superheated vapor applied at the suction input of the compressor typically picks up an additional 10°F superheat (60°F − 50°F) because the vapor in the suction line absorbs more heat from the warmer surrounding air as it travels from the evaporator to the compressor.

5. After compression, the highly superheated gas from the compressor flows through the hot gas line to the condenser. This hot gas may be close to 200°F at 300 psig. The saturated temperature corresponding to 300 psig is 130°F; therefore, the hot gas line has gained about 70°F (200°F − 130°F) superheat. This superheat must be removed before the vapor can be condensed into a liquid. The 200°F refrigerant in the hot gas line easily gives up some of its superheat to the surrounding 95°F air. The hot gas line is normally not insulated, and the tubing is a good conductor of heat.

6. Because the refrigerant in the condenser is still hotter than the warmer outside air passing over the condenser, it easily gives up the remaining superheat. This drops its temperature to 130°F. As heat continues to be transferred from the vapor to the cooler outside air, the vapor begins to subcool and condense into a liquid. After the refrigerant has travelled about three quarters of the way through the condenser, all of the refrigerant has condensed into a liquid. The 130°F condensing temperature is set by the condenser design. A standard condenser is designed to have a condensing temperature about 35°F higher than the surrounding air. In this case, 95°F outside air is used to absorb the heat, so 95°F + 35°F = 130°F condensing temperature.

7. During the remaining one quarter of travel through the condenser, the liquid refrigerant continues to drop in temperature (subcool). This lowers its temperature about 15°F to 115°F. In other words, the liquid refrigerant is subcooled 15°F (130°F − 115°F).

8. The subcooled liquid refrigerant from the condenser travels through the liquid line to the expansion device. The liquid line is usually not insulated and may be long. Thus, the 115°F liquid refrigerant is further subcooled and continues to drop in temperature as it gives up more heat to the cooler outside air. This drop could increase the subcooling by another 5°F, lowering the temperature of the liquid refrigerant to 110°F.

9. The expansion device controls the flow of liquid refrigerant to the evaporator. Subcooled liquid from the condenser enters at the high temperature of 110°F and high pressure of 300 psig. It leaves the expansion device at the low temperature of 40°F and low pressure of 69 psig, thereby lowering the boiling point of the liquid refrigerant supplied to the evaporator. In the expansion device, the subcooled liquid refrigerant at 300 psig is passed through a small opening or orifice. This changes the pressure of the liquid refrigerant from 300 psig to 69 psig, causing some of it to flash into a vapor. This flash gas cools the remaining liquid to produce a mixture of about 75% liquid and 25% vapor. The pressure of this mixture is 69 psig, which corresponds to the 40°F boiling point needed for correct evaporator operation. This low-temperature, low-pressure mixture from the expansion device then travels to the evaporator.

10. The refrigerant has now completed its cycle and is ready to start over again.

3.3.0 COMPRESSORS

The compressor is the keystone of the refrigeration system. It creates the pressure difference that causes refrigerant flow around the system. In the process, it takes refrigerant vapor at a low temperature and pressure and raises the vapor to a higher temperature and pressure.

Compressors are usually driven by an electric motor (*Figure 15*). Very large compressors can be driven by internal combustion engines or steam turbines. Compressors are divided into three groups based on the way they are joined to their motors or engines: open, hermetic, and semi-hermetic.

COMPRESSORS TAKE REFRIGERANT VAPCR AT A LOW TEMPERATURE AND PRESSURE AND RAISE IT TO A HIGHER TEMPERATURE AND PRESSURE.

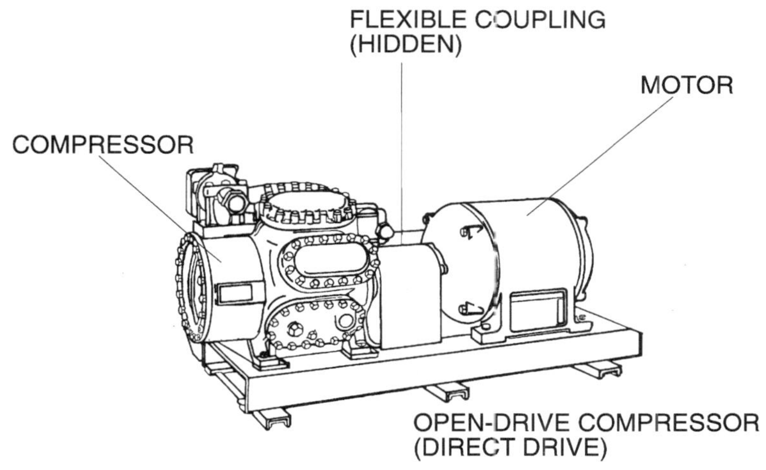

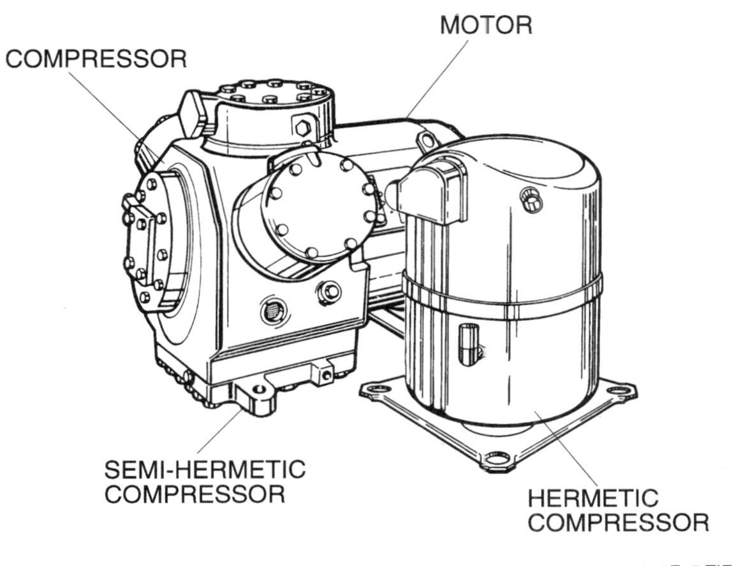

Figure 15. Compressors

- *Open compressor* – The compressor is separate from its motor. One end (the shaft) extends outside the case. A mechanical seal is used with the rotating shaft to prevent leakage of the refrigerant. The compressor motor drives the compressor using a belt (belt drive) or flexible coupling (direct drive). Belt-driven arrangements allow the motor to run at one speed, while the compressor can run at another. The proper combination of pulleys (also called drives) produces the desired speed of the compressor. Most direct-drive systems use an electric motor to drive the compressor. This means that the compressor also runs at the speed of the drive motor.

- *Hermetic (welded hermetic) compressor* – The compressor and motor have a common drive shaft. They are sealed in a welded steel enclosure or shell. Hermetic compressors are more compact, less noisy, and require less maintenance than open-type compressors because they have no belts or couplings to break or wear out. Because they are sealed, the entire unit must be replaced when they fail.

- *Semi-hermetic (serviceable hermetic) compressor* – Similar to the hermetic compressor, the compressor and motor share the same housing and a common drive shaft. When they fail, access to the compressor or motor for repair is possible by removing the heads and/or the bottom and end plates.

Five types of compressors are commonly used in mechanical refrigeration systems:

- Reciprocating
- Rotary
- Scroll
- Screw
- Centrifugal

3.3.1 Reciprocating Compressors

Reciprocating compressors are the most common type. They use one or more pistons moving back and forth within a cylinder or cylinders (*Figure 16*). Piston movement is synchronized with the opening and closing of suction and discharge valves. These valves control the intake and discharge of the refrigerant. Reciprocating compressors are typically used in refrigerators, air conditioners, and commercial processing equipment. Welded hermetic reciprocating compressors are most popular below 10 tons, but their use is increasing in the 10- to 20-ton range. Serviceable semi-hermetic compressors are used in commercial air conditioning and heat pumps above 10 tons. Open reciprocating compressors are used mostly for refrigeration work and on industrial and large commercial air conditioning and heat pumps anywhere in the 5- to 150-ton range.

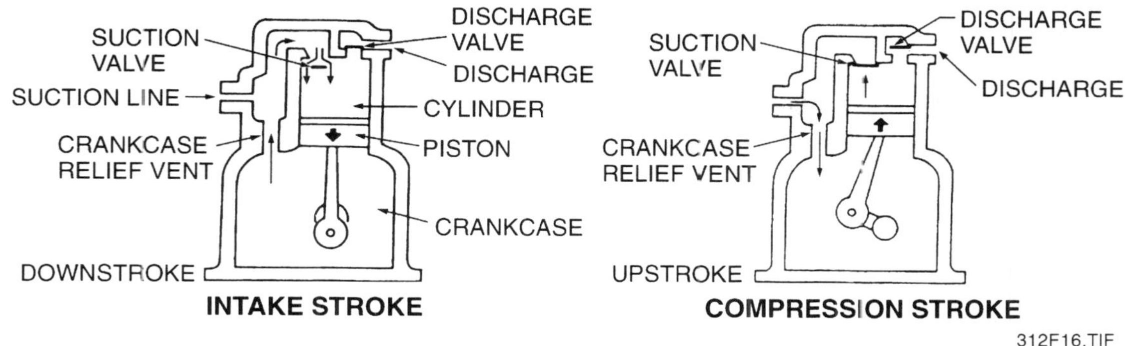

Figure 16. Reciprocating Compressor

3.3.2   Rotary Compressors

Rotary compressors are usually welded hermetic compressors. They are frequently used on appliances, room air conditioners, and central air conditioning below 5 tons. Rotary compressors are of two types: stationary vane and rotary vane.

In the stationary vane compressor (*Figure 17*), a shaft with an attached off-center (eccentric) rotor rotates or rolls around the cylinder. A stationary vane mounted in the compressor housing slides in and out, and follows the rotating motion of the rotor as it moves within the cylinder. This vane also separates the suction and discharge sides of the cylinder. As the shaft turns, the rotor rolls around the cylinder, drawing suction gas in the intake opening, while at the same time compressing the gas against the cylinder wall on the discharge or compression side. A valve at the discharge keeps the compressed gas from leaking back into the cylinder and into the suction side during the off cycle. This process continues as long as the compressor is running.

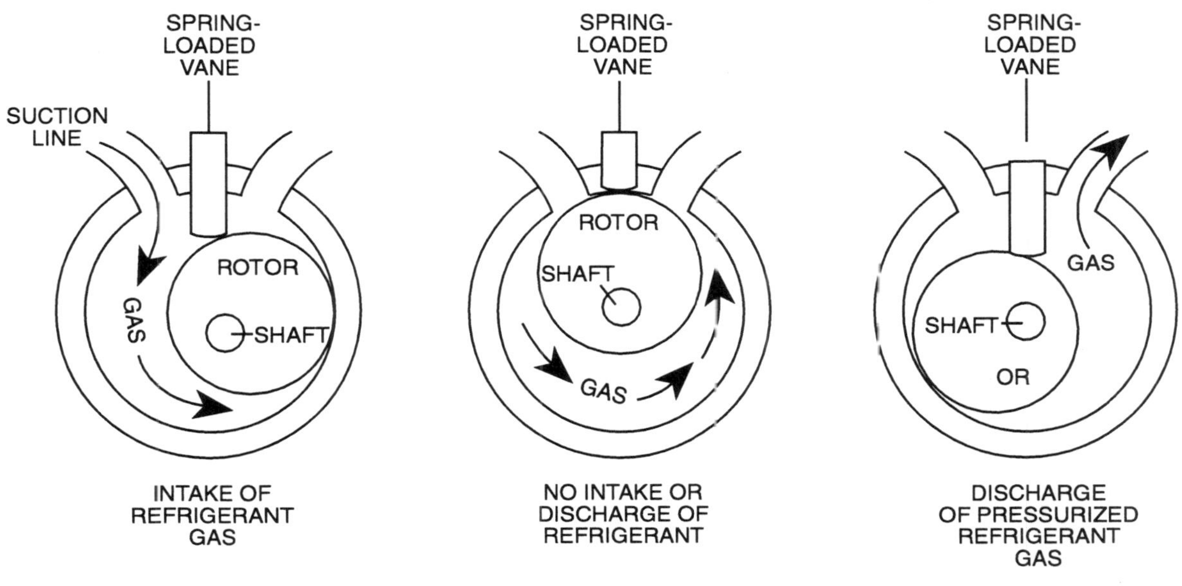

Figure 17. Stationary Vane Rotary Compressor

Rotary vane compressors have a rotor centered on the drive shaft. However, the drive shaft is positioned off-center in the cylinder. Mounted on the rotor are two or more vanes that slide in and out to follow the shape of the cylinder. As the rotor turns, these vanes trap low-pressure suction gas and compress it against the cylinder wall, then force it out the discharge opening. The vanes also keep the compressed gas from mixing with the incoming low-pressure gas.

3.3.3 Scroll Compressors

Scroll compressors are usually welded hermetic compressors. Of all the compressor types, scroll compressors have the fewest working parts. They operate efficiently even in applications that have large changes in refrigerant pressures, such as with commercial refrigeration and heat pumps.

No suction or discharge valves are used in a scroll compressor (*Figure 18*). It achieves compression by the use of two spiral-shaped parts called *scrolls*. One is fixed; the other is driven and moves in an orbiting action inside the fixed one. There is contact between the two. Refrigerant gas enters the suction port at the outer edge of the scroll and after compression, it is squeezed out a separate discharge port at the center of the stationary scroll. The orbiting action draws gas into pockets between the two spirals. As this action continues, the gas opening is sealed off and the gas is compressed and forced into smaller pockets as it progresses toward the center.

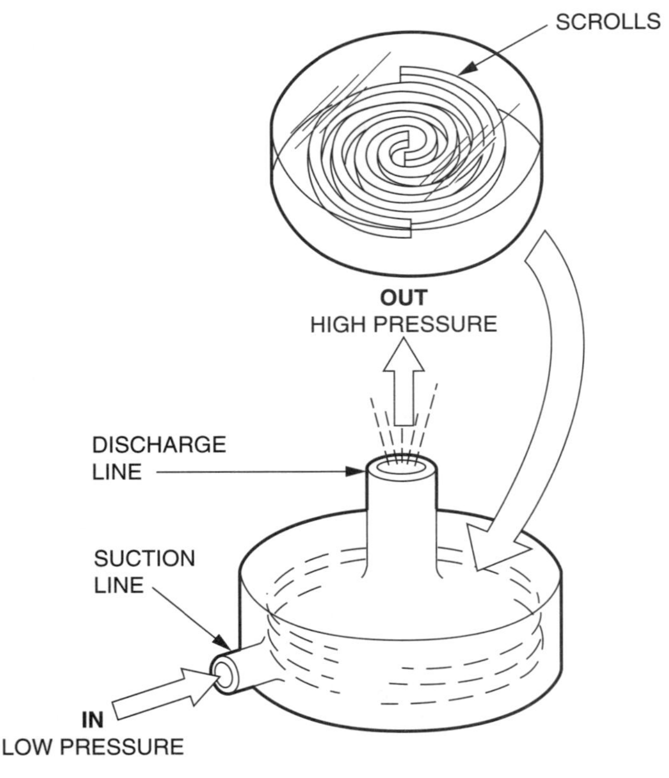

312F18.EPS

Figure 18. Scroll Compressor

3.3.4 Screw Compressors

Screw compressors are used in large commercial and industrial applications requiring capacities from 20 to 750 tons. They are made in both open and hermetic styles.

Screw compressors use a matched set of screw-shaped rotors, one male and one female, enclosed within a cylinder (*Figure 19*). The male rotor is driven by the compressor motor. In turn, it drives the female rotor. Normally the driven male rotor turns faster than the female rotor because it has fewer lobes than the female rotor. Typically, the male has four lobes and the female has six. As these rotors turn, they mesh with each other and compress the gas between them. The screw threads form the boundaries separating several compression chambers which move down the compressor at the same time. In this way, the gas entering the compressor is moved through a series of progressively smaller compression stages until the gas exits at the compressor discharge in its fully compressed state.

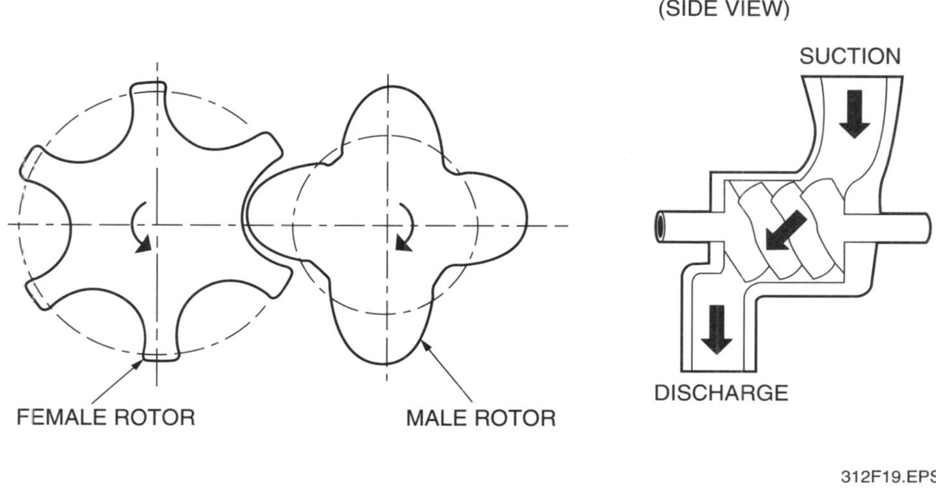

Figure 19. Screw Compressor

3.3.5 Centrifugal Compressors

Centrifugal compressors are made in open and hermetic designs. They are typically used on commercial and industrial refrigeration and air conditioning systems with capacities larger than 100 tons. Standard models range up to 10,000 tons of capacity with custom models exceeding 20,000 tons.

Centrifugal compressors use a high-speed impeller with many blades that rotate in a spiral-shaped housing (*Figure 20*). The impeller is driven at high speeds (typically 10,000 rpm) inside the compressor housing. Refrigerant vapor is fed into the housing at the center of the impeller. The impeller throws this incoming vapor in a circular path outward from between the blades and into the compressor housing. This action, called *centrifugal force*, creates pressure on the high-velocity gas and forces it out the discharge port. Often, several impellers are put in series to create a greater pressure difference and to pump a sufficient volume of vapor. A compressor that uses one impeller is called a *single-stage compressor*, one that uses two impellers is called a *double-stage* or *two-stage compressor*, and so on. When more than one stage is used, the discharge from the first stage is fed into the inlet of the next stage. The NEC requirements applicable to compressors will be discussed later in this module.

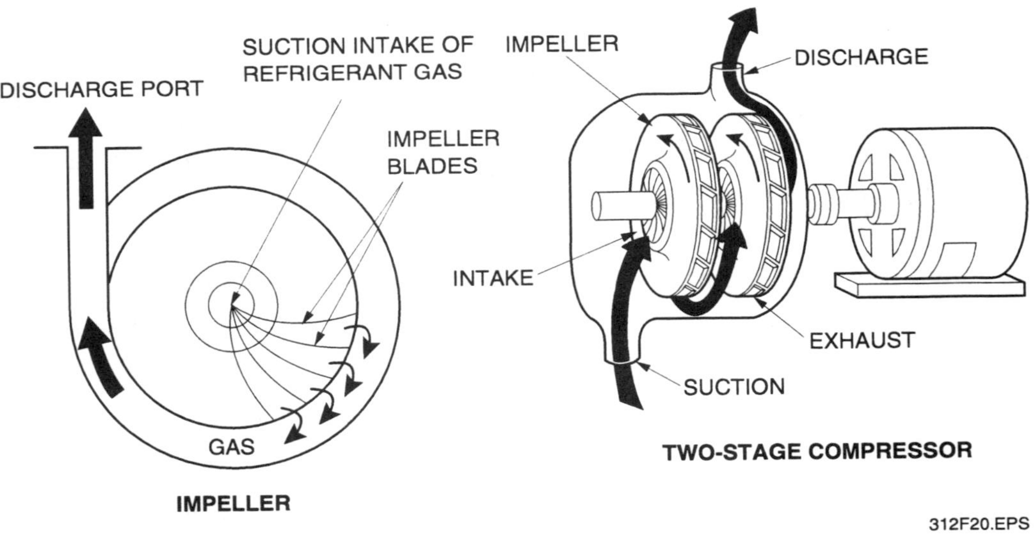

Figure 20. Centrifugal Compressor

3.4.0 CONDENSERS

Condensers (*Figure 21*) are used for removing heat from the refrigeration system. They take in high-pressure, high-temperature refrigerant gas from the compressor and change it into a high-temperature, high-pressure liquid. They do this by transferring the heat from the refrigerant to the air, to water, or both. As the refrigerant flow progresses through the condenser, it first rejects the superheat and then fully condenses into a subcooled, high-temperature, high-pressure liquid. For the condenser to operate properly, the condensing medium of air or water must always be at a lower temperature than the refrigerant it is condensing. Condensers are grouped according to the medium used to carry the heat away from the refrigerant vapor. These groups are:

* Air cooled
* Water cooled
* Evaporative (a combination of air and water cooling)

3.4.1 Air-Cooled Condensers

Air-cooled condensers reject the heat absorbed by the system directly to the outdoor air. At normal design (peak load) conditions, the refrigerant flowing through the condenser is about 25°F to 35°F warmer than the outside air to which it is rejected. This means that a saturation temperature of 120°F to 130°F is typical in the condenser when the outside air is 95°F. Because the medium is outside air, this temperature tends to be greater than is needed for condensers used in water-cooled systems.

ELECTRICAL — TRAINEE TASK MODULE 26312

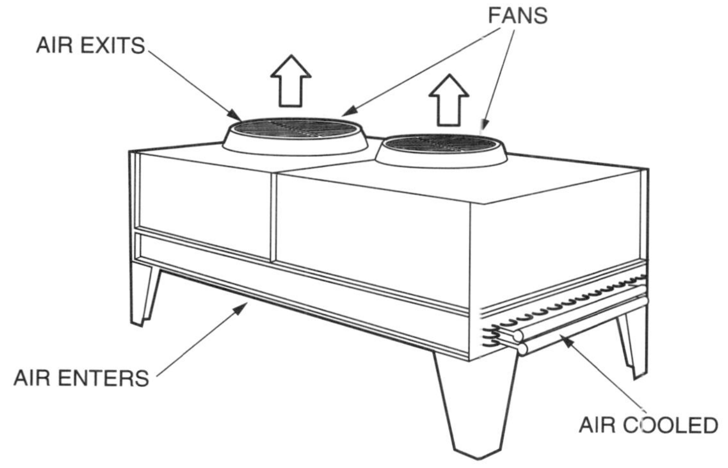

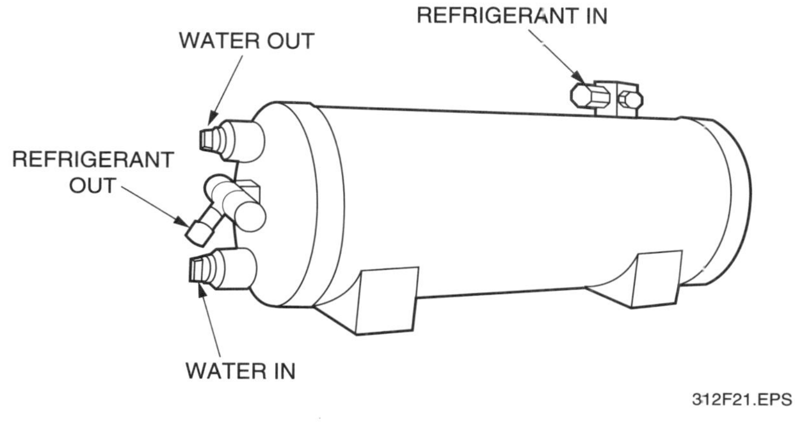

Figure 21. Condensers

Propeller (axial) fans are used with most air-cooled condenser units to increase the amount of air being circulated across the condenser. This increases its capacity to reject heat. Because air-cooled condensers require the circulation of air over their surfaces, their location and the temperature of the surrounding air are very important to proper operation. It is important to note that the higher the temperature of the condensing air, the more work the system compressor must do to provide refrigerant vapor at an even higher temperature so heat can then be transferred from the gas out of the condenser. This causes the compressor to use more power. Air-cooled condensers are typically used in residential air conditioning up to about five tons and in commercial air conditioning up to about 50 tons. Air-cooled condensers are generally of two types: tube and fin condensers and plate condensers (*Figure 22*).

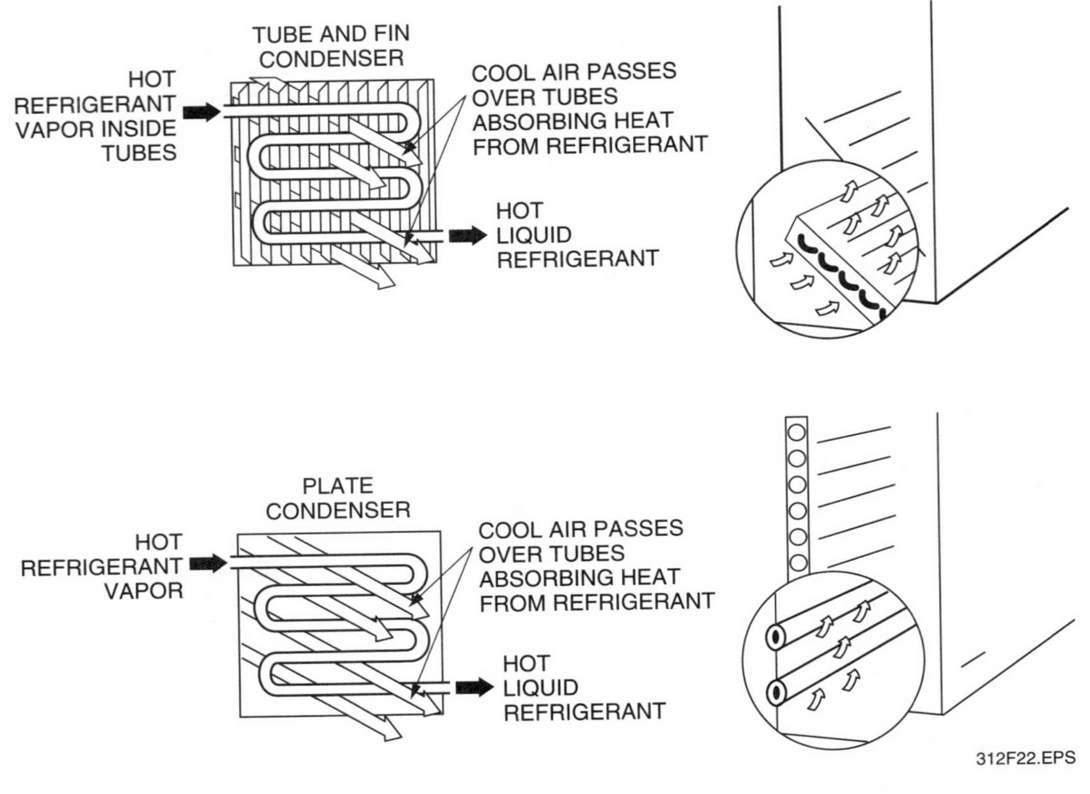

Figure 22. Air-Cooled Condensers

3.4.2 Water-Cooled Condensers

Water-cooled condensers are more complicated, costly, and require more maintenance than air-cooled condensers. However, they are more efficient and operate at much lower condensing temperatures (about 15°F lower). This allows the system compressor to run at lower head pressures, requiring the use of less power. Depending on the type, the velocity of the water flowing in a water-cooled condenser should be between three and 10 feet per second. If it flows too fast, pitting of the tubing may occur. If it flows too slow, scaling will occur. In areas where water is plentiful, the water that flows through the condenser may be used once and then drained into a waste system. Most often, the water portion of a water-cooled condenser is connected via piping to a cooling tower, which is usually located on the roof of the building. In the cooling tower, the heat absorbed by the water in the condenser is rejected from the system into the atmosphere by evaporation. The cooled water is then returned to the system for reuse. As shown in *Figure 23*, there are four types of water-cooled condensers:

- Tube in tube condensers
- Shell and tube condensers
- Shell and coil condensers
- Natural-draft cooling towers

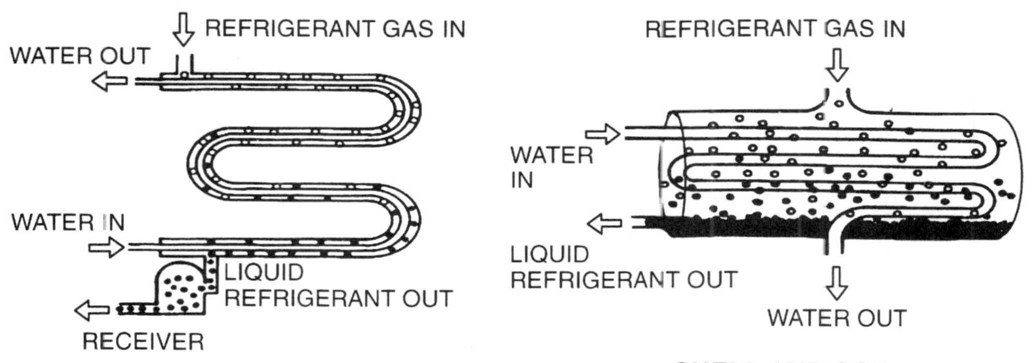

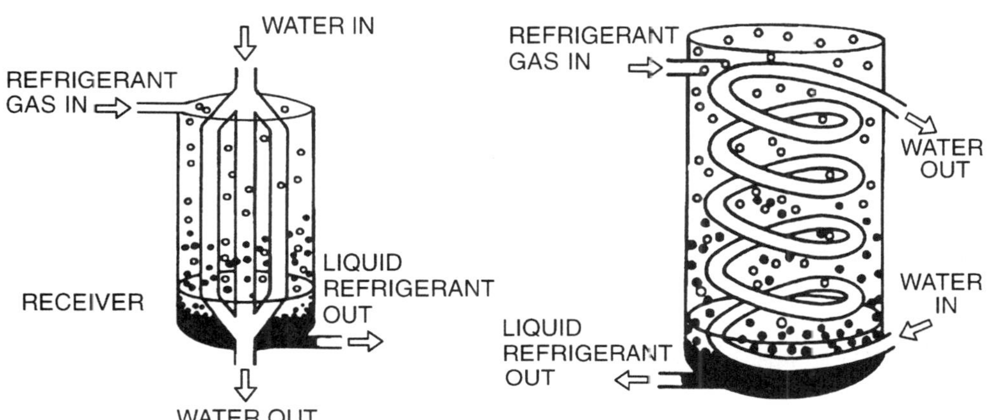

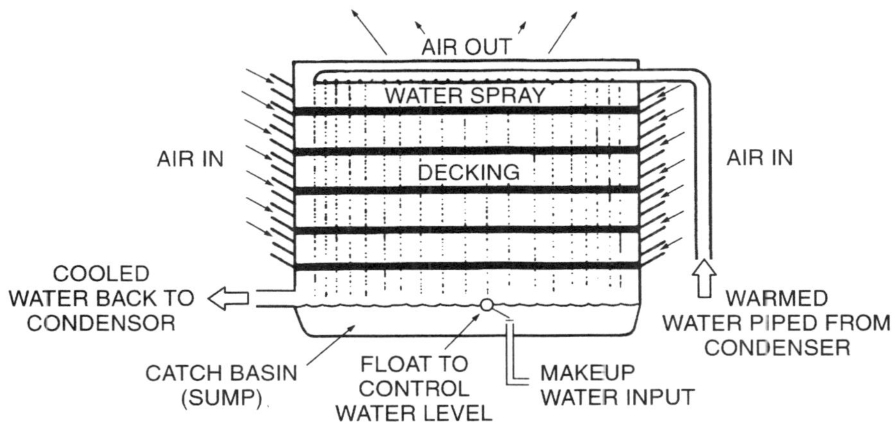

312F23.TIF

Figure 23. Water-Cooled Condensers

3.4.3 Evaporative Condensers

Evaporative condensers first transfer heat to water and then transfer it again from the water to the outdoor air. They combine the functions of a water-cooled condenser and cooling tower in one package. The condenser water evaporates directly off the tubes of the condenser. Each pound of water that is evaporated removes about 1,000 Btu's from the refrigerant flowing through the tubes.

Air enters the bottom of the unit (*Figure 24*) and flows by convection upward over the condensing coil filled with refrigerant. Simultaneously, water is sprayed over the coil. Both the air and the water absorb heat from the refrigerant in the coil. Water eliminators located above the water spray remove water from the rising air. The air is then moved out the top of the unit using one or more fans. Cooled by both air and water, the refrigerant in the coil condenses into a subcooled liquid at the output of the coil.

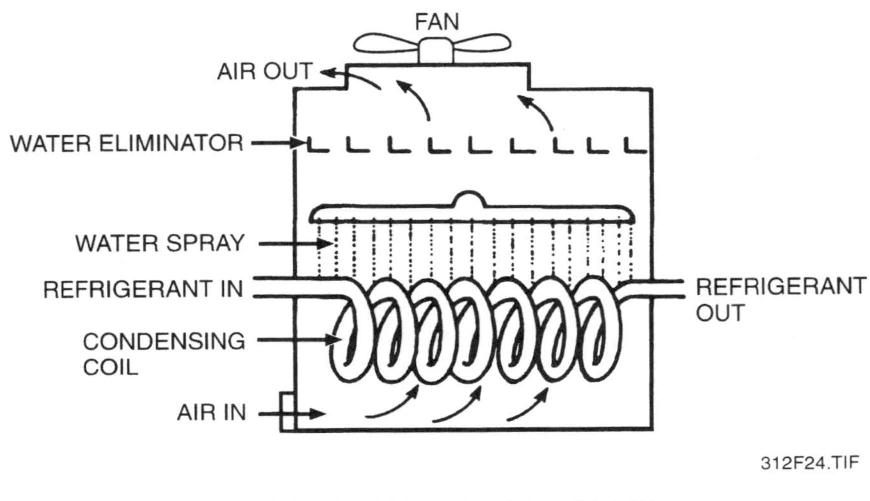

Figure 24. Evaporative Condenser

3.5.0 EVAPORATORS

Evaporators (*Figures 25* and *26*) are used to add heat to the refrigeration system. They take in low-temperature, low-pressure liquid refrigerant from the expansion device and change it into a low-temperature, low-pressure gas. This is done by transferring heat from either air or water to the refrigerant. As the refrigerant flow progresses through the evaporator, the heat in the warmer medium (air or water) causes it to boil (evaporate) and change into a vapor. When this occurs, the refrigerant absorbs heat from the medium being cooled. The amount of heat absorbed depends on how much heat is lost by the medium. The heat gain must equal the heat loss. For example, if the air passing over an evaporator gives up 800 Btu's of heat, then the refrigerant in the evaporator must gain 800 Btu's. Evaporators are of two types: the direct expansion type and the flooded type (*Figure 26*).

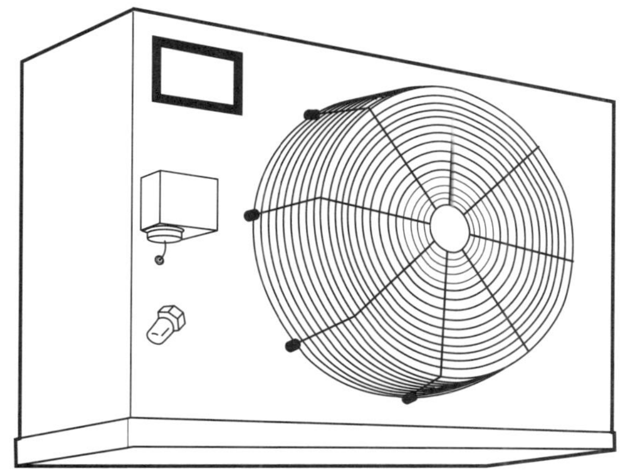

Figure 25. Forced-Draft Evaporator

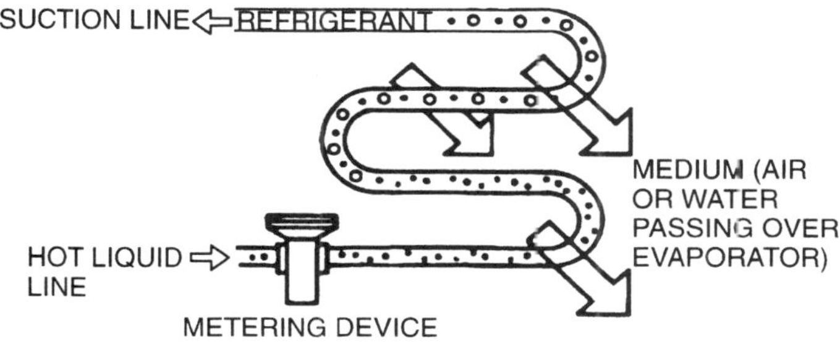

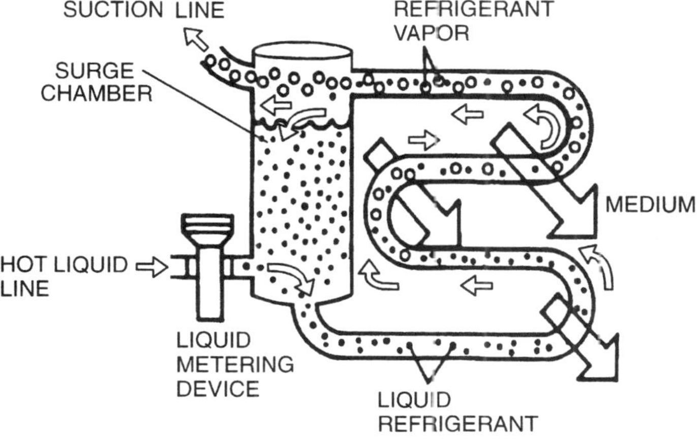

Figure 26. Direct Expansion And Flooded Evaporators

3.5.1 Direct Expansion (DX) Evaporators

Direct expansion (DX) evaporators are the most widely used. DX evaporators have one continuous tube or coil through which the liquid refrigerant flows. The refrigerant, with a small amount of gas mixed in, enters the evaporator and is gradually warmed by the medium until it boils and becomes a vapor near the outlet. The flow of refrigerant into the DX coil is controlled by the expansion device at its input. It supplies just the right amount of refrigerant to the evaporator so that it is all transformed into vapor by the time it reaches the evaporator output. (Actually, the metering devices used with most DX evaporators are designed to produce about a 10°F superheat of the refrigerant vapor at the evaporator output.) The movement of the medium (air or water) over the evaporator can be by natural draft or it can be enhanced using fans or pumps (forced draft).

3.5.2 Flooded Evaporators

In a flooded evaporator, refrigerant can be circulated through the evaporator more than once. A special receptacle known as the *surge chamber* is connected between the evaporator tubing input and output. Liquid refrigerant enters the surge chamber from the metering device, then flows through the evaporator coil, where it boils and then returns to the surge chamber. All of the refrigerant vapor exits through the suction line for input to the compressor. Any refrigerant not changed into a vapor collects in the surge chamber for recycling back through the evaporator. Flooded evaporators are used mainly for cold storage or with systems using ammonia. They are generally not used for air conditioning because they require much more refrigerant than the DX evaporator.

3.5.3 Evaporator Construction

Evaporators are classified by the way they are constructed. These groups are bare tube, finned tube, and plate surface.

- *Bare-tube evaporators* – Bare-tube evaporators (*Figure 27*) are of two types: single circuit (path) or multiple path. Multiple-path evaporators are often used because they save space and reduce the number of metering devices needed. Each is simply a steel or copper pipe shaped in a way that best matches the job. The piping is the only surface used to transfer heat; therefore, these are often called *prime surface coils.*
- *Finned-tube evaporators* – Finned-tube evaporators are a variation of the bare-tube evaporator. Attached to the tubing are thin, spiral-wound or rectangular fins of aluminum or copper like those used with the fin and tube condenser. These fins increase the amount of surface area exposed to the heated medium. This in turn increases the amount of heat that can be transferred to the refrigerant.
- *Plate-surface evaporators* – Plate evaporators are similar to plate condensers. They have a length of tubing weaving through a metal plate. The plate provides greater surface area for heat transfer. This type of evaporator is typically used as a shelf in older upright freezers.

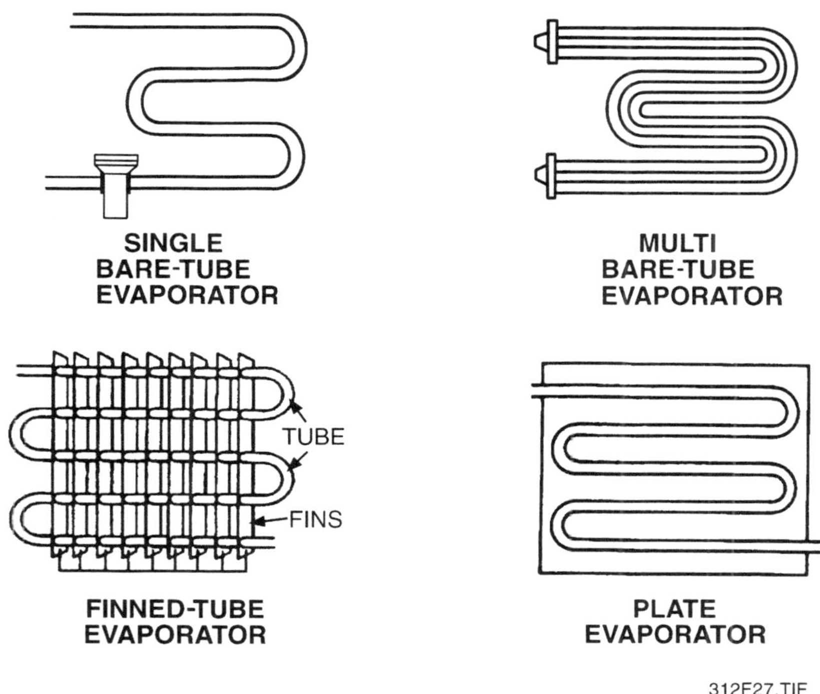

Figure 27. Evaporator Construction Methods

In many large refrigeration and air conditioning installations, cooling coils are installed at some distance apart in the building or complex. Because of the expense and the problems involved with long runs of refrigerant piping, cooling in these remote areas is done with chilled water rather than refrigerant as the medium. This chilled water is called a *secondary refrigerant*. When temperatures are below freezing, brine is used in place of water. A refrigeration system, called the *primary system*, is used to cool the secondary water or brine refrigerant. The primary system generally uses shell and tube or shell and coil evaporators called *chillers* to absorb heat from the water or brine. Like other evaporators, chillers can be of the direct expansion or flooded type. Their construction is similar to that used for shell and tube or shell and coil condensers.

In the direct expansion chiller, the colder liquid refrigerant runs through the tubing, while the warmer secondary refrigerant (water or brine) circulates within the shell around the outside of the tubes. As a result, heat contained in the water or brine is transferred to the primary refrigerant flowing through the tubes. The refrigerant leaves the evaporator as a gas.

In the flooded-type chiller, the water or brine is circulated through the tubing, which is located on the bottom of the evaporator shell. This tubing is submerged below the liquid refrigerant level within the shell (controlled by a float valve). The evaporator shell acts as a surge chamber. The top portion is left vacant so the refrigerant vapor can be properly separated from the liquid refrigerant for output to the suction line as it evaporates.

3.6.0   EXPANSION (METERING) DEVICES

The metering device is located between the condenser outlet and the evaporator inlet. High-pressure, high-temperature liquid refrigerant from the condenser enters the metering device. It leaves as a low-pressure, low-temperature mixture of liquid and vapor. Regardless of the type, the metering device performs two functions:

- It allows the liquid refrigerant to flow into the evaporator at a rate that matches the rate at which the evaporator boils liquid refrigerant into a vapor.
- It provides a pressure drop that lowers the boiling point of the refrigerant.

There are many types of metering devices. They can be divided into two categories: fixed and adjustable.

Fixed metering devices are used mainly in domestic refrigerators and freezers and residential air conditioning units.

Adjustable metering devices are used most often on systems with variable load requirements. This section briefly describes the main types of fixed and adjustable metering devices.

3.6.1   Fixed Metering Devices

Fixed metering devices have a fixed restriction or fixed opening (orifice) size. The capillary tube (*Figure 28*) is the simplest metering device. It is a fixed length, small-diameter copper tube, usually with an inside diameter of $\frac{1}{16}''$ to $\frac{1}{8}''$. Because of its small diameter, it restricts the flow of liquid refrigerant from the condenser to the evaporator. The greater its length or the smaller its diameter, the greater the pressure drop. Capillary tubes are often coiled to conserve space and protect them from damage.

Another type of fixed metering device similar to the capillary tube is the fixed orifice device. This device is a compact and rugged assembly that is installed at the evaporator inlet. It contains a piston. Pistons are made with different-sized orifices to match the capacities of different equipment. The smaller the orifice, the greater the pressure drop. Often, the piston is installed in this type of metering device at the time of system installation in order to match the metering device to the condensing unit.

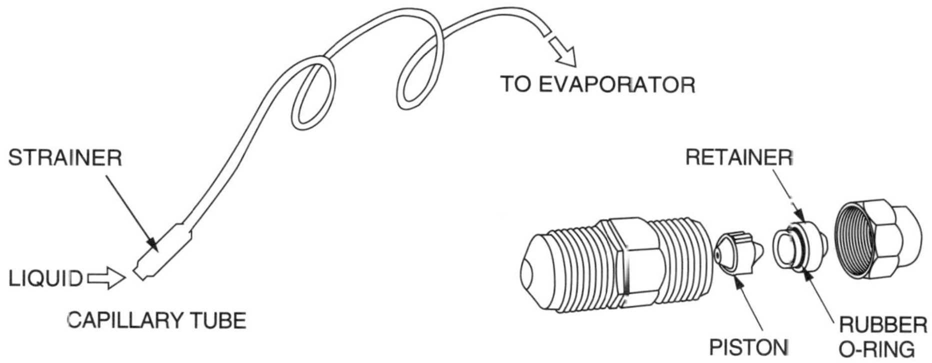

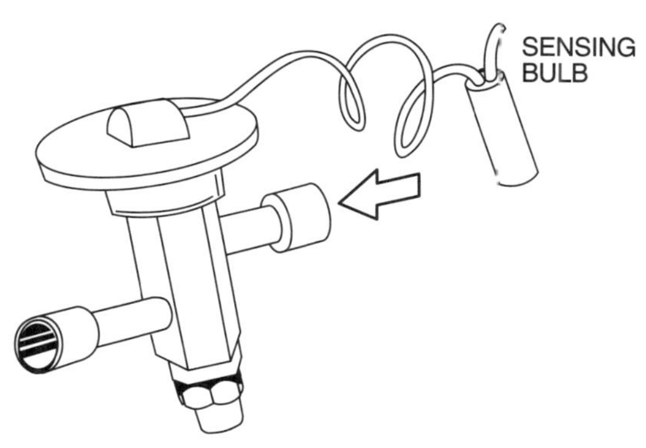

Figure 28. Typical Metering Devices

3.6.2   Adjustable Metering Devices

Adjustable metering devices differ in their mechanisms and how they are controlled (*Figure 29*). They all work to regulate refrigerant flow so that the evaporator capacity matches the cooling load. There are six types of adjustable metering devices in common use:

- Hand-operated **expansion valves**
- Low-side float valves
- High-side float valves
- Automatic expansion valves
- Thermostatic expansion valves
- Electric and electronic expansion valves

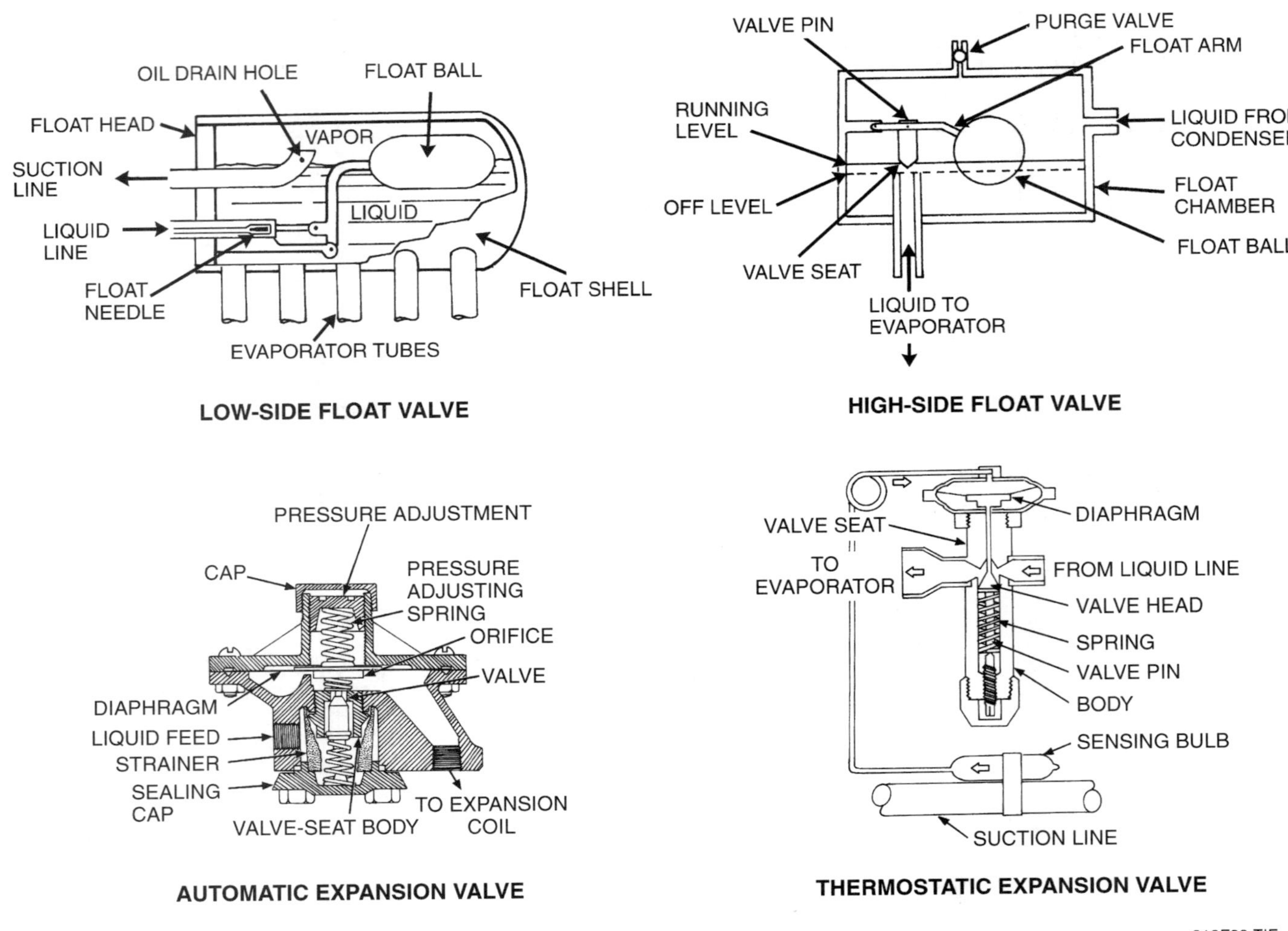

Figure 29. Adjustable Metering Devices

3.7.0 OTHER COMPONENTS

Additional components (*Figure 30*) are usually added to the basic refrigeration system in order to improve safety, endurance, efficiency, or servicing. Some of these components are factory installed, while others may be installed in the field. This section briefly describes the most common components. They include:

- Filter-driers
- Sight glass/moisture-liquid indicators
- Suction line accumulators
- Crankcase heaters
- Oil separators
- Heat exchangers
- Receivers
- Service valves
- Compressor mufflers

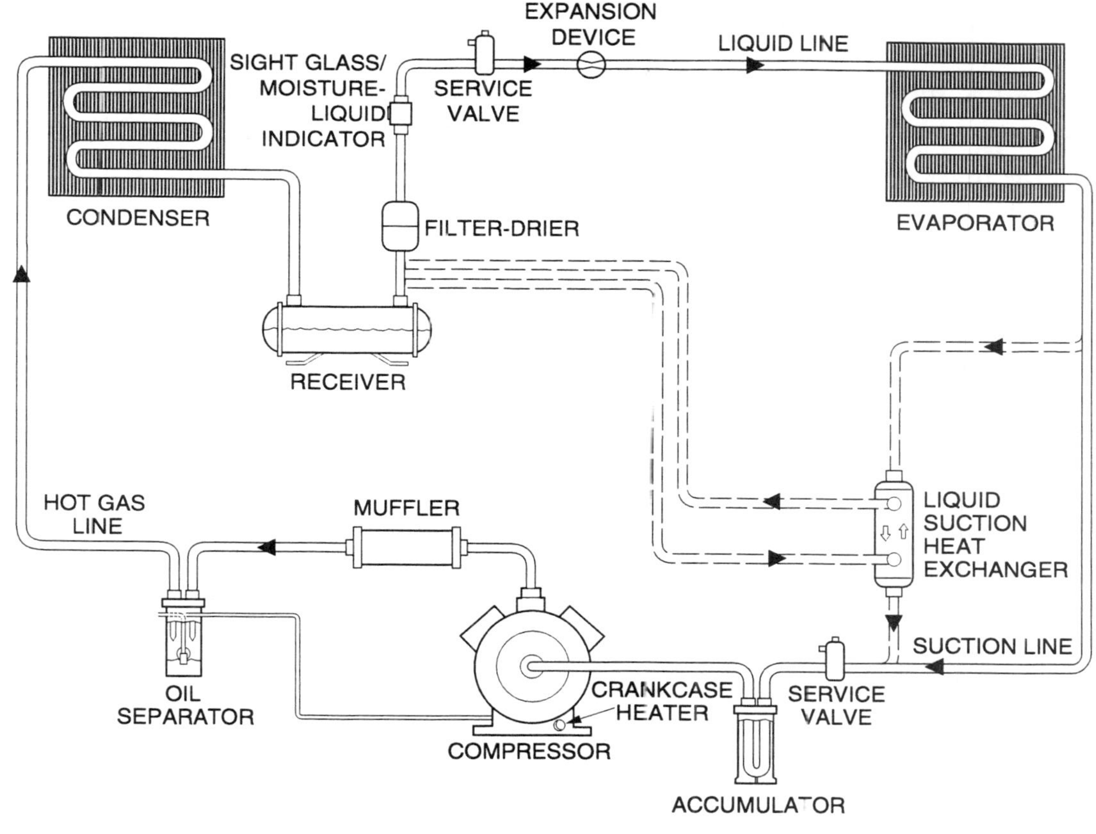

Figure 30. Other Refrigeration System Components

3.7.1 Filter-Driers

The filter-drier or filter-strainer combines the functions of a refrigerant filter and a refrigerant drier in one device. The filter protects metering devices and the compressor from foreign matter such as dirt, scale, or rust. The drier removes moisture from the system and traps it where it can do no harm. Filter-driers are normally installed in the liquid line in front of all metering devices. Filter-driers are replaced periodically during system maintenance or immediately after a system repair, such as a compressor burnout.

3.7.2 Sight Glass/Moisture-Liquid Indicators

The sight glass is like a window that allows the technician to view the condition of the system refrigerant. It is typically used when checking the refrigerant charge. The normal location for the sight glass is in the liquid line, as close to the condenser outlet or receiver as possible. A moisture liquid indicator is a sight glass with a small moisture-indicating device installed in it. This moisture indicator is exposed to the refrigerant and changes color depending on the amount of moisture in the refrigerant. When the moisture is within the limits set by the manufacturer, the indicator is one color. If too much moisture is present, the device will change color.

3.7.3   Suction Line Accumulators

The suction line accumulator is a trap used to prevent the compressor from taking in slugs of liquid refrigerant or compressor oil. If liquid refrigerant is allowed to enter the compressor, noisy operation, high consumption, and compressor damage may result. Accumulators are installed in the suction line as near the compressor suction inlet as possible. At this location, any liquid refrigerant or oil will be trapped temporarily in the accumulator. The trapped refrigerant remains in the accumulator until it is evaporated back into a vapor. Some accumulators have heaters that help to vaporize refrigerant liquid. Trapped oil is usually piped back to the compressor.

3.7.4   Crankcase Heaters

Crankcase heaters are installed on compressors to prevent liquid refrigerant from migrating to the compressor and causing damage. These heaters work by evaporating refrigerant from the oil. They are usually fastened to the bottom of the crankcase or inserted directly into the compressor crankcase (immersion type). Wrap-around or bellyband heaters that encircle the outside shell of welded hermetic compressors are also used.

3.7.5   Oil Separators

Oil is used in a refrigeration system for three purposes:

*   It helps seal the system.
*   It dampens compressor noise.
*   It acts as a coolant for the compressor and compressor motor.

Because there is oil in the compressor, it mixes with the refrigerant and travels with it to other areas of the system. Oil separators minimize the amount of oil that circulates through the system. Oil coats the inside of every component through which it passes. It reduces the heat transfer ability and efficiency of the evaporator and condenser. Another reason for the oil separator is to slow down the accumulation of oil in places from which oil return is difficult.

Oil separators are seldom used on residential or commercial air conditioning systems. Their use is mainly in refrigeration and industrial systems. Typically, they are installed in the hot gas line as close to the compressor discharge as practical. Separators usually have a reservoir (sump) to collect the trapped oil. A float valve in the sump keeps a seal between the high-pressure and low-pressure sides of the system. This valve automatically returns the oil to the compressor through an orifice.

3.7.6 Heat Exchangers

Two types of heat exchangers can be used with refrigeration systems: the liquid-to-suction type and the refrigerant water preheater. The liquid-to-suction heat exchanger transfers some of the heat from the warm liquid refrigerant leaving the condenser to the cool suction gas leaving the evaporator. (See path shown as dashed lines on *Figure 30*.) This increases efficiency and helps subcool the liquid refrigerant. In some applications, it is used to evaporate the small amount of liquid refrigerant expected to return from the evaporator in the suction line to the compressor. Operation of the heat exchanger is similar to that of a water-cooled condenser. The liquid refrigerant leaving the condenser and the cool suction gas leaving the evaporator flow in opposite directions through the heat exchanger. The amount of heat that can be exchanged between the gas and liquid is determined by the temperature difference between the two, the amount of surface area, and how much time there is for heat exchange to occur.

The refrigerant water preheater is used to preheat the water supplied at the input of a hot water heater. In this heat exchanger, heat is transferred from the compressor hot gas line to the water. This reduces energy consumption whenever heat needs to be rejected from the system and helps to de-superheat the discharge gas leaving the compressor. Instead of rejecting heat outdoors, the heat is transferred to the hot water system. Shell and coil and tube in tube heat exchangers are typically used as water preheaters.

3.7.7 Receivers

The receiver is a tank or container used to store liquid refrigerant in the system. This storage is needed on some systems to accommodate changes during operation, to freely drain the condenser of refrigerant, and to provide a place to store the system charge during system service procedures or prolonged shutdowns. The receiver is installed in the liquid line between the condenser and the metering device. Receivers are used to store the excess refrigerant created by varying cooling loads in many systems that use self-adjusting metering devices. Note that some residential and commercial air conditioning equipment store this excess in the condenser. In these cases, the condenser is large enough to hold the excess while delivering less than peak capacity and subcooling.

3.7.8 Service Valves

Service valves enable the service technician to seal off parts of the system while installing gauges and to provide access to the system for servicing. These valves are manually operated and come in several types. Service valves can be installed in any line that may have to be valved off, usually at a place that is easily accessible to the service technician.

3.7.9 Compressor Mufflers

Mufflers are used most often in systems with open or semi-hermetic reciprocating compressors. Reciprocating compressors generate sound that can be transmitted along the piping. A muffler installed in the discharge line, as near the compressor as practical, is used to remove or dampen these pulsations. The muffler lowers the system noise and prevents possible damage from vibration.

3.8.0 TYPICAL AIR CYCLE

Indoor air can be too cold, too hot, too wet, too dry, too drafty, and too still. These conditions are changed by treating the air. Cold air is heated, hot air is cooled, moisture is added to dry air (or removed from damp air), and fans are used to create adequate air movement. Each of these treatments are provided in the air conditioning air cycle (see *Figure 31*).

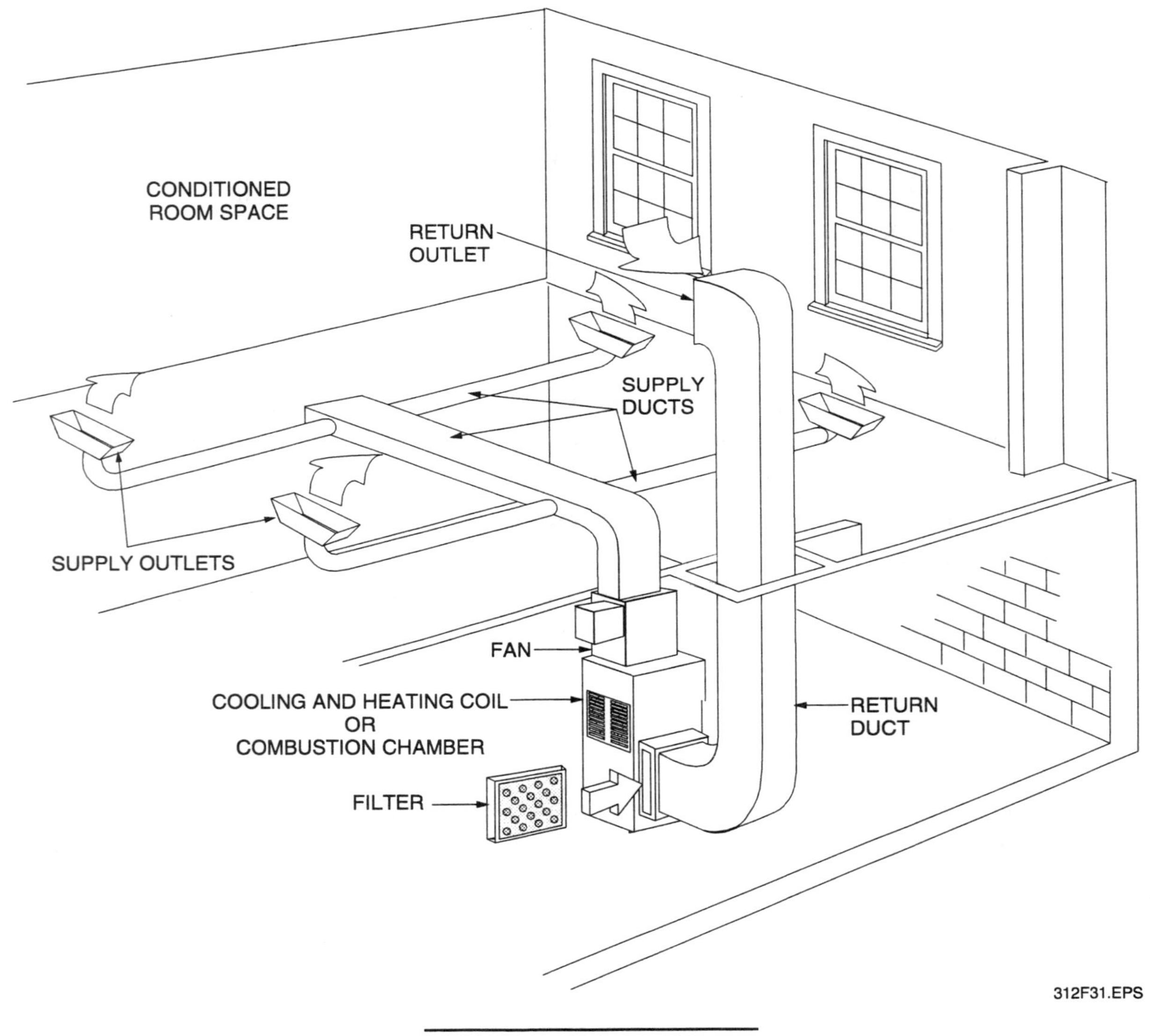

Figure 31. Typical Air Cycle

3.8.1 Air Cycle Description

The air cycle begins with the fan because it is the piece of equipment that starts the air through the cycle. A fan forces air into ductwork connected to openings in the room. These openings are commonly called *outlets* or *terminals*. The ductwork directs the air to the room through the outlets. The air enters the room and either heats it or cools it, as required. Dust particles from the room enter the air stream and are carried along with it.

Air then flows from the room through a second outlet (sometimes called the *return outlet*) and enters the return ductwork, where dust particles are removed by a filter. After the air is cleaned, it is either heated or cooled, depending on the condition in the room. If cool air is required, the air is passed over the surface of a cooling coil; if warm air is required, the air is passed through a combustion chamber or over the surface of a heating coil. Finally, the treated air flows back to the fan and the cycle is completed.

The major components of an air conditioning system are the fan, supply duct, supply outlets, return outlets, return duct, filter, heating chamber, and cooling coil.

- *Fan* – The principal job of the fan is to move air to and from a room. In an air conditioning system, the air that the fan moves is made up of all outdoor air, all indoor or room air (this is also called *recirculated air*), or a combination of outdoor and indoor air. The fan can pull air exclusively from outdoors or from the room, but in most systems, it pulls air from both sources at the same time. Because drafts in the room cause discomfort, and poor air movement slows the body heat rejection process, the amount of air supplied by the fan must be regulated. This regulation is done by choosing a fan that can deliver the correct amount of air and by controlling the speed of the fan so that the air stream in the room provides good circulation without causing drafts. Of course, the fan is only one of the pieces of equipment that contributes to body comfort; others, such as supply and return room outlets and cooling and heating equipment, are described in subsequent paragraphs.
- *Supply duct* – The supply duct directs the air from the fan to the room. It should be as short as possible and have a minimum number of turns so the air can flow freely.
- *Supply outlets* – Supply outlets help to distribute the air evenly in a room. Some outlets fan the air, others direct it in a jet stream, and still others can do a combination of both. Because supply outlets can either fan or jet the air stream, they are able to exert some control over the direction of the air delivered by the fan. This directional control, combined with the location and the number of outlets in the room, contributes a great deal to the comfort or discomfort effect of the air pattern.

- *Return outlets* – Return outlets are openings in the room surface that are used to allow room air to enter the return duct. They are usually located at the opposite extreme of a wall or room from the supply outlet. For example, if the supply duct is on the ceiling or on the wall near the ceiling, the return duct may be located on the floor or on the wall near the floor. This is not true in all cases, however, because some systems have both supply and return outlets near the floor or near the ceiling. Keep in mind that the main function of the return outlet is to allow air to pass from the room.

- *Return duct* – The return duct supplies air to the heating/cooling equipment. It also contains a filter to trap dust particles.

- *Filters* – Filters are usually located at some point in the return air duct. They are made of many materials, from spun glass to composition plastic. Other types operate on the electrostatic principle and actually attract and capture dust and dirt particles through the use of electricity. The end purpose of all filters is to clean the air by removing dust particles.

- *Cooling coil and heating coil or combustion chamber* – The cooling coil and the heating coil or combustion chamber can be located either ahead of or after the fan but should always be located after the filter. A filter ahead of the coil is necessary to prevent excessive dust and dirt particles from covering the coil's surface.

3.9.0 PIPING

Most piping used in refrigeration systems is ACR copper tubing. Aluminum, steel, stainless steel, and plastic tubing may also be used for certain applications. The piping layout is usually made by the system designer. We will cover piping briefly to provide you with an understanding of its purpose from a servicing viewpoint.

A good piping layout should meet the following requirements:

- Provide refrigerant paths
- Avoid excessive pressure drops
- Return oil
- Protect compressors

The purpose of the piping system is to provide a path for the flow of refrigerant from one component to another. Refrigerant flow must be accomplished without excessive pressure drops, such as those caused by friction, long risers, restrictions, and other piping conditions.

Some oil circulates in all refrigeration systems. The piping layout, therefore, must return the oil to the compressor crankcase. Liquid refrigerant or oil entering the compressor in the suction line can seriously damage the compressor. Good piping practices minimize the potential for damage.

In *Figure 32*, the major types of piping in the refrigeration cycle are identified. The suction line carries cold, low-pressure gas from the evaporator to the compressor. The hot gas line carries hot, high-pressure gas from the compressor to the condenser. Where separate receivers are used, a condensate line is installed to drain refrigerant from the condenser to the receiver. The liquid line carries the liquid refrigerant from the receiver to the metering device.

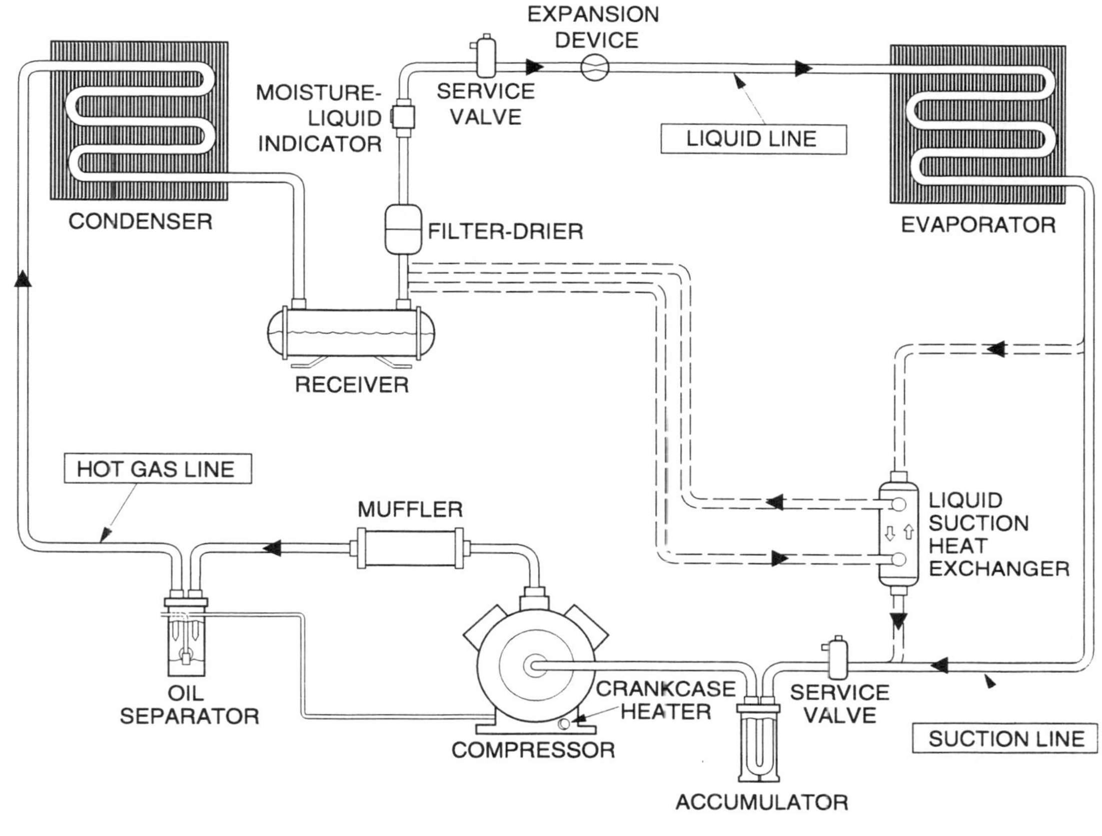

Figure 32. Major Types Of Piping In The Refrigeration System

3.9.1   Insulation

Liquid lines are not normally insulated except where the surrounding temperature is higher than the liquid refrigerant. Hot gas lines are generally above the surrounding temperature and need only be insulated for personnel protection. Suction lines should be insulated to prevent condensation. Some heat absorption is desirable to evaporate any slop-over, but excessive heat gain by the suction gas must be avoided. Suction line insulation must be covered with a vapor barrier and weatherproofed when outdoors.

The three major considerations in refrigerant piping layout are compressor protection, oil return, and pressure drop. *Figure 33* illustrates the methods by which these piping objectives are achieved.

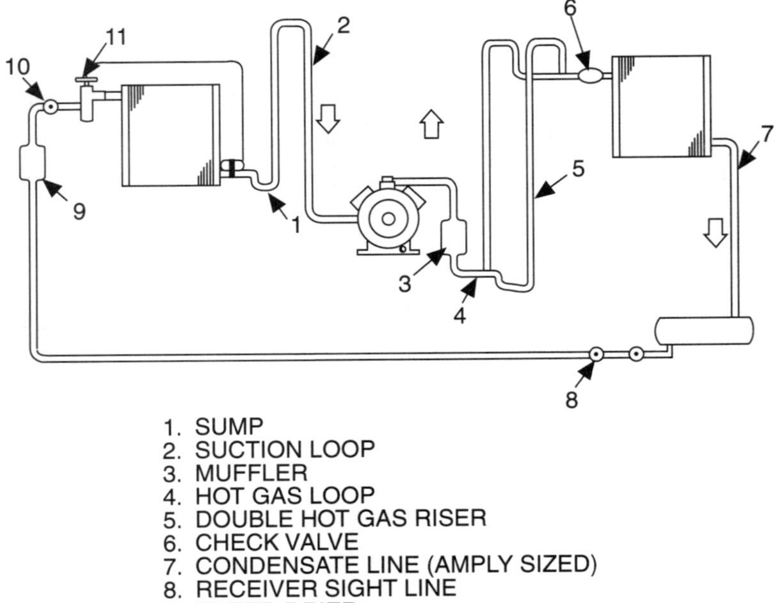

1. SUMP
2. SUCTION LOOP
3. MUFFLER
4. HOT GAS LOOP
5. DOUBLE HOT GAS RISER
6. CHECK VALVE
7. CONDENSATE LINE (AMPLY SIZED)
8. RECEIVER SIGHT LINE
9. FILTER-DRIER
10. SIGHT GLASS
11. METERING DEVICE

312F33.EPS

Figure 33. Piping Layout

3.10.0 HEAT PUMPS

A heat pump is an air conditioner in which the refrigeration cycle is reversed to provide heat. A heat pump has the same components as a cooling system, with the addition of a special switching valve called the *reversing valve* or *four-way valve*. This valve directs the hot, high-pressure refrigerant from the compressor discharge to the indoor coil or outdoor coil, depending on whether the **thermostat** calls for heating or cooling. The coils are called *indoor* and *outdoor coils* because they alternately act as the condenser or the evaporator, depending on whether the unit is providing heating or cooling.

Heat pumps typically use air or water as their heat source. Ground source heat pumps are also used. An air-to-air heat pump is shown in *Figure 34*. This diagram shows air flow in the cooling mode.

A heat pump has the unique ability to furnish more energy than it consumes. This uniqueness is due to the fact that electric energy is required only to move the heat absorbed by the refrigerant. Thus, a heat pump attains a heating efficiency of two or more to one—that is, it will put out an equivalent of 2W or 3W of heat for every watt consumed. For this reason, its use is highly desirable for the conservation of energy.

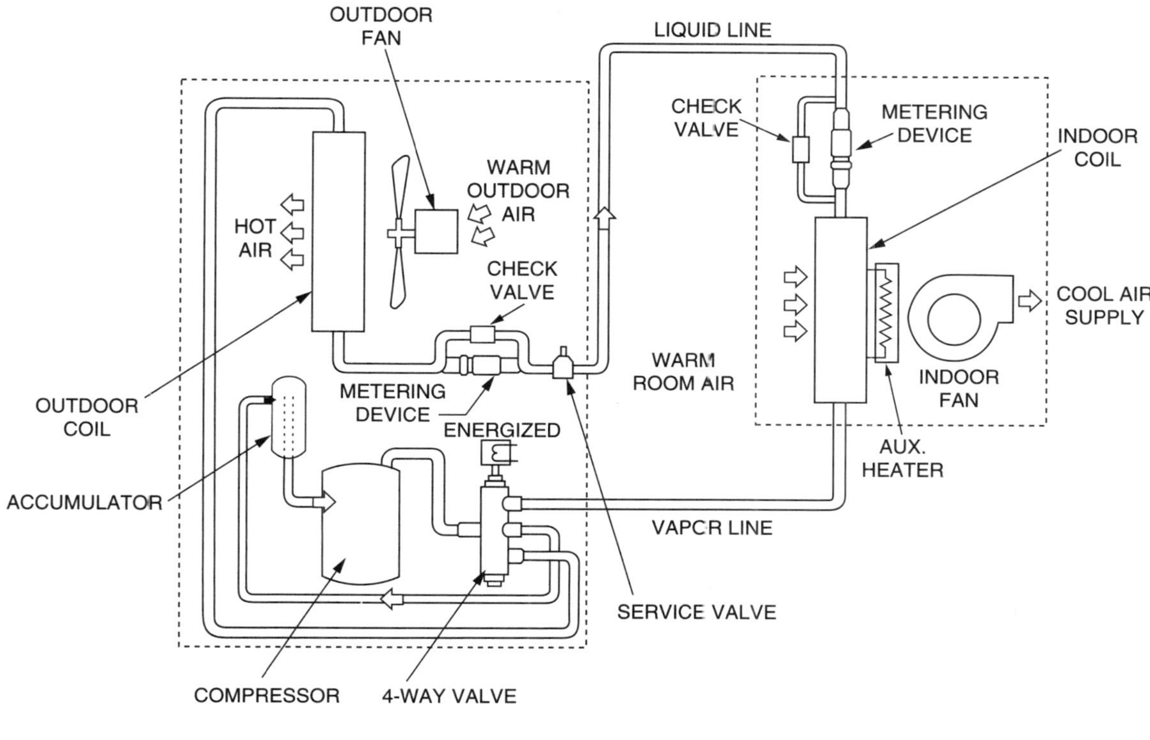

Figure 34. Schematic Of An Air-To-Air Heat Pump

Although air-to-air heat pumps are the most popular type, the water-to-air heat pump is the most efficient. Water-to-air heat pumps have the following advantages over air-to-air heat pumps:

- The pumps can be located anywhere in the building since no outside air is connected to them.
- The outside air temperature does not affect the performance of the heat pump, as it does in an air-to-air heat pump.
- Since the water source of the water-to-air heat pump will seldom vary more than a few degrees in temperature, more consistent performance can be expected.

The schematic drawing in *Figure 35* shows how two heat pumps were connected in parallel for a large residence with an indoor swimming pool; the swimming pool water was used as the means of heat exchange, and since this water was preheated to approximately 78°F, the efficiency of the heat pumps utilizing this same water approached the maximum.

During the warm months, the heat pumps were reversed (cooling cycle) to cool the area. Again, the pool water was used as the heat exchange medium, this time acting as a cooling tower. The air from these heat pumps was distributed by means of underfloor transit ducts with supply **air diffusers** and return air grilles raised above the floor level and mounted in a wainscot around the perimeter of the pool area.

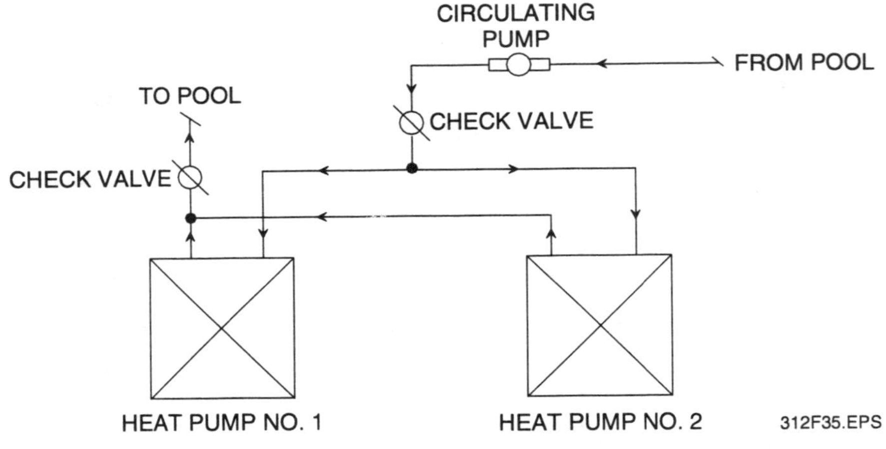

Figure 35. Water-To-Air Heat Pumps

Electric heating is often used to supplement furnaces and heat pumps. In some parts of the country, electricity is inexpensive and the warm climate results in low heating demand. In such situations, electric furnaces, baseboard heaters, and radiant heat are reasonable alternatives to fossil fuel (natural gas or oil) furnaces. In cold and moderate climates, however, electricity is too expensive to be used as the primary source of heat, except as an energy source for a heat pump, unless there is no other heating source available.

Several types of electric heating units are available and a brief description of each type follows. *Figure 36* shows some of these heaters.

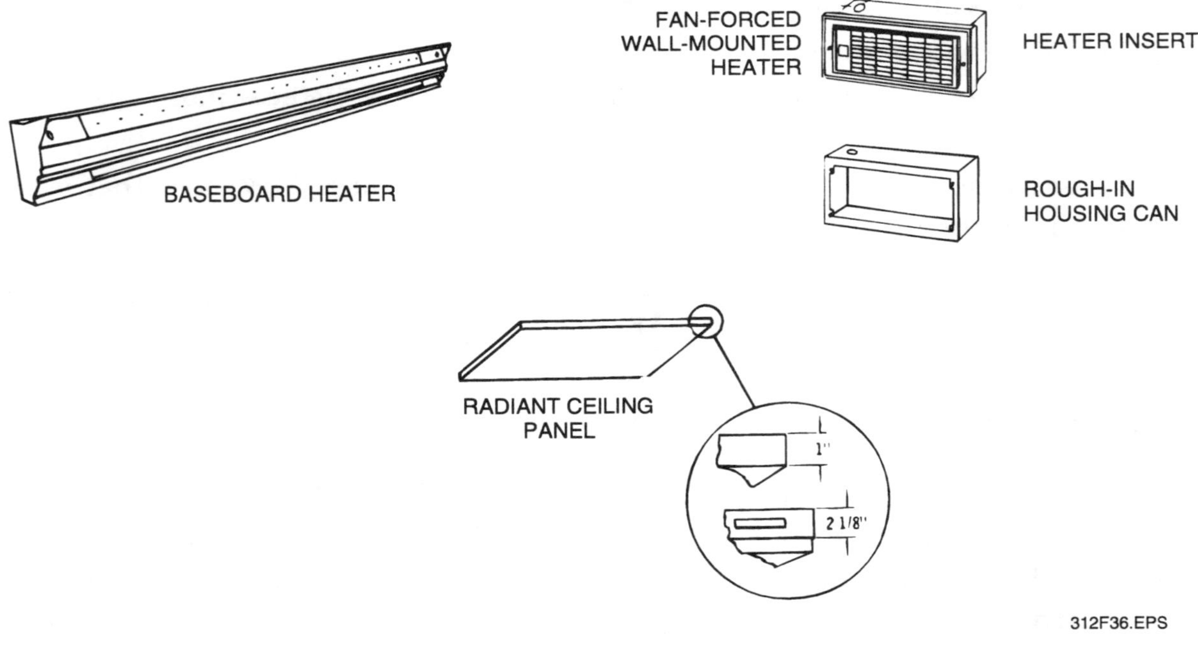

Figure 36. Several Types Of Electric Heating Units

Electric baseboard heaters – Electric baseboard heaters are mounted on the floor along the baseboard, preferably on outside walls under windows for the most efficient operation. They are very quiet (if not completely noiseless) and are the type most often used for heating residential occupancies and for use as supplemental heat in many commercial areas.

Electric baseboard heaters may be mounted on practically any surface (wood, plaster, drywall, and so on), but if polystyrene foam insulation is used near the unit, a ¾" (minimum) ventilated spacer strip must be used between the heater and the wall. In such cases, the heater should also be elevated above the floor or rug to allow ventilation to flow from the floor upward over the total heater space.

One complaint received over the years about this type of heater has been wall discoloration directly above the heating units. When this problem occurred, the reason was almost always traced to one or more of the following:

- High wattage per square foot of heating element
- Heavy smoking by occupants
- Poor housekeeping

Radiant ceiling heaters – Radiant ceiling heaters are often used in bathrooms and similar areas so that the entire room does not have to be overheated to meet the need for extra warmth after a bath or shower. They are also used in larger areas, such as a garage or basement, or for spot-warming a workbench in an otherwise unheated area.

Most of these units are rated from 800W to 1,500W and normally operate on 120V circuits. As with most electric units, they may be controlled by a remote thermostat, but since they are normally used for supplemental heat, a conventional wall switch is often used. They are quickly and easily mounted on an outlet box in much the same way as conventional lighting fixtures. In fact, where a very low wattage is used, ceiling heaters may often be installed by merely replacing the ceiling lighting fixture with a light/heater combination.

Radiant heating panels – Radiant heating panels are commonly manufactured in 2' x 4' sizes and are rated at 500W. They may be located on ceilings or walls to provide radiant heat that spreads evenly through the room. Each room may be controlled by its own thermostat. Since this type of heater may be mounted on the ceiling, its use allows complete freedom for room decor, furniture placement, and drapery arrangement. Most are finished in beige to blend in with nearly any room or furniture color.

The best results are achieved by ceiling-mounted units located parallel to and approximately 2' from the outside wall. However, this type of unit may also be mounted on walls.

Electric infrared heaters – Rays from infrared heaters do not heat the air through which they travel; like the sun, they heat only people and objects that they strike. Therefore, infrared heaters are designed to deliver heat into controlled areas for the efficient warming of people and surfaces both indoors and outdoors (such as to heat people on a patio on a chilly night or around the perimeter of an outdoor swimming pool). This type of heater is excellent for heating a person standing at a workbench without heating the entire room, melting snow from steps or porches, providing sun-like heat over outdoor areas, and similar applications. Some of the major advantages of infrared heat include:

- No warmup period is required; heat is immediate.
- Heat rays are confined to the desired areas.
- They are easy to install (no ducts, vents, etc., are required).

When installing this type of heating unit, never mount the heater closer than 24" from vertical walls unless the specific heating unit is designed for closer installation. Read the manufacturer's instructions carefully.

Note: Infrared quartz lamps provide some light in addition to heat.

Forced-air wall heaters – Forced-air wall heaters are designed to bring quick heat into an area where the sound of a fan will not be disturbing. (Some are very noisy.) Most of these units are equipped with a built-in thermostat with a sensor mounted in the intake air stream. Some types are available for mounting on high walls or even ceilings, but the additional force required to move the air to a usable area produces even more noise.

Floor insert convection heaters – Floor insert convection heaters require no wall space, as they fit into the floor. They are best suited for placement beneath conventional or sliding glass doors to form an effective draft barrier. All are equipped with safety devices, such as a thermal cutout to disconnect the heating element automatically in the event that normal operating temperatures are exceeded.

Floor insert convection heaters may be installed in both old and new homes by cutting through the floor and inserting the metal housing/wiring according to the manufacturer's instructions. A heavy-gauge floor grille then fits over the entire unit.

*Electric kick **space heaters*** – See *Figure 37*. Modern kitchens contain so many appliances and so much cabinet space for the convenience of the owner that there often is no room to install electric heaters except on the ceiling. Therefore, a kick space heater was added to the lines of electric heating manufacturers to overcome this problem.

For optimum comfort, kick space heaters should not be installed in such a manner that warm air blows directly on the occupant's feet. Ideally, the air discharge should be directed along the outside wall adjacent to normal working areas, not directly under the sink.

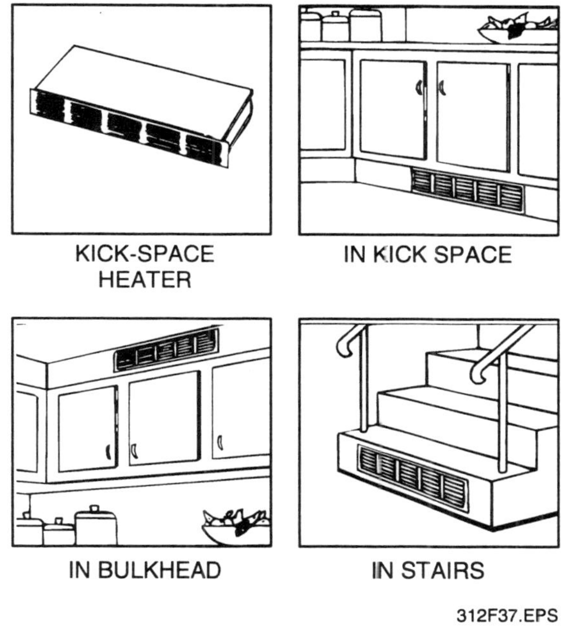

Figure 37. Kick Space Heater Locations

Radiant heating cable – Radiant heating cable provides an enormous heating surface over the ceiling or concrete floor so that the system need not be raised to a high temperature. Rather, gentle warmth radiates downward (in the case of ceiling-mounted cable) or upward (in the case of floor-mounted cable), heating the entire room or area evenly.

There is virtually no maintenance with a radiant heating system, as there are no moving parts and the entire heating system is invisible, except for the thermostat.

Note: When selecting any electric heating units, obtain plenty of literature from suppliers and manufacturers before settling on any one type. In most cases, you are going to get what you pay for, but most contractors and their personnel shop around at different suppliers before ordering the equipment. Delivery of any of these units may take some time, so once the brand, size, and supplier have been selected, the order should be placed well before the unit is actually needed.

Electric furnaces – Electric furnaces are becoming more popular, although they are surpassed by the all-electric heat pump. Most are very compact, versatile units designed for either wall, ceiling, or closet mounting. The vertical model (*Figure 38*) can be flush-mounted in a wall or shelf-mounted in a closet; the horizontal design can be fitted into a ceiling (flush or recessed).

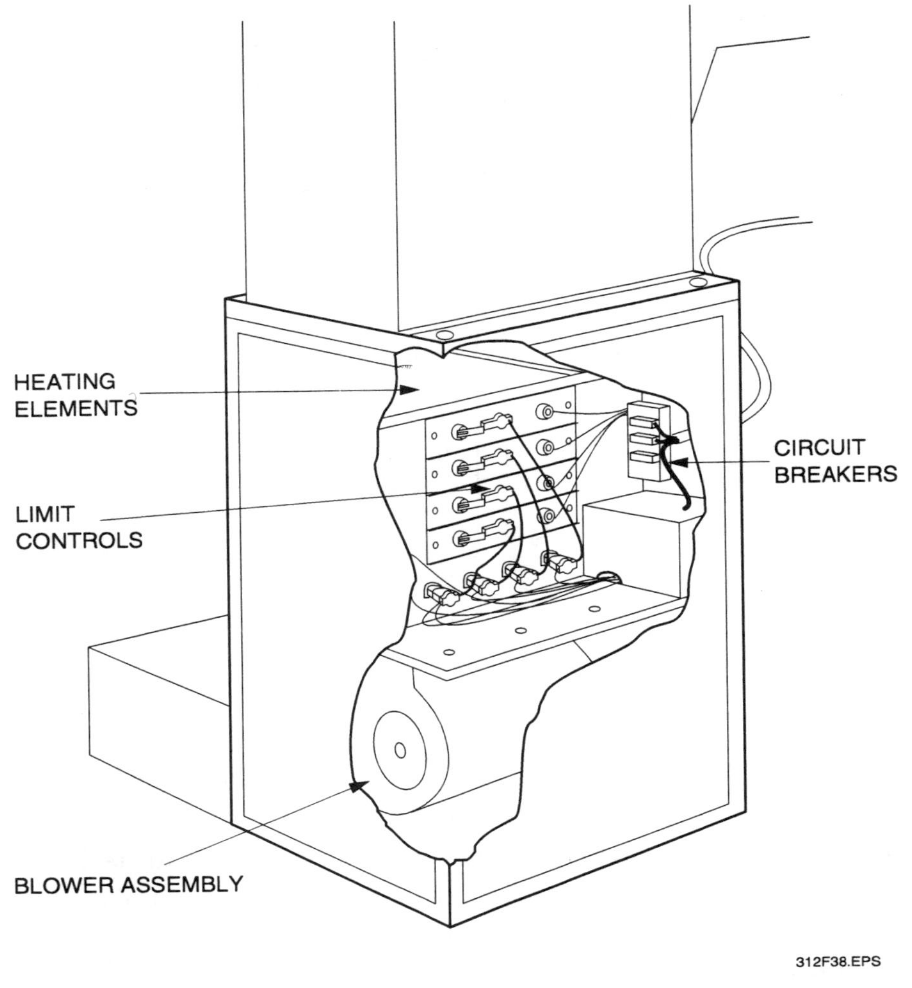

Figure 38. Electric Furnace

Central heating systems of the electrically-energized type distribute heat from a central source by means of circulating air or water. Compact electric boilers can be mounted on the wall of a basement, utility room, or closet with the necessary control and circuit protection, and will furnish hot water to convectors or to embedded pipes. Immersion heaters may be stepped in one at a time to provide heating capacity to match heat loss. The majority of electric furnaces are commonly available in sizes up to 24kW for residential use. The larger boilers with proper controls can take advantage of lower off-peak electricity rates, where they prevail, by heating water during off-peak periods, storing it in insulated tanks, and circulating it to convectors or radiators to provide heat as needed.

Electric hot water systems – A zoned hydronic (hot water) system permits selection of different temperatures in each zone of the home. Baseboard heaters located along the outer walls of rooms provide a blanket of warmth from floor to ceiling; the heating unit also supplies domestic hot water simultaneously through separate circuits. A special attachment coupled to the hot water unit can be used to melt snow and ice on walkways and driveways in winter, and a similar attachment can be used to heat a swimming pool, for example, during the spring and fall seasons.

    ELECTRICAL — TRAINEE TASK MODULE 26312

4.1.0 HEATING CALCULATIONS

Most heating calculations for central systems will be performed by mechanical engineers and installed by mechanical contractors. Highly sophisticated procedures are required for systems of any consequence involving heat loss and heat gain calculations; cost analysis, psychrometrics, and other computations that are outside the realm of this module. Electricians will normally install only the branch circuit or feeder wiring, and sometimes install and connect the control wiring.

However, there may be times when electricians are required to size an electric heater for a commercial or industrial toilet, for example, or perhaps an entire residential system. Therefore, you should have a general knowledge of how simple heating calculations are performed.

The following are the basic goals of an electric heating system:

- Adequate, dependable, and trouble-free service
- Year-round comfort
- Reasonable annual operating cost
- Reasonable installation cost
- Systems that are easy to service and maintain

Heat loss calculations must be made to ensure that heating equipment of proper capacity will be selected and installed. Heat loss is expressed in either Btu's per hour (abbreviated Btuh) or in watts (volt-amperes). Both are measures of the rate at which heat is transferred and are easily converted from one to the other:

$$\text{Watts (volt-amperes)} = \frac{\text{Btuh}}{3.4} \qquad \text{Amps} = \frac{\text{Btuh}}{3.4 \times \text{voltage}}$$

$$\text{Btuh} = \text{watts} \times 3.4$$

Basically, the calculation of heat loss through walls, roofs, ceilings, windows, and floors requires three simple steps:

Step 1 Determine the net **area (A)** in square feet.

Step 2 Find the proper heat loss using appropriate tables.

Step 3 Multiply the area by the factor; the product will be expressed in Btuh. Since most electric heating equipment is rated in watts rather than Btuh, divide this product by 3.4 to convert to watts.

Calculations of heat loss for any building or area may be made more quickly and more efficiently by using a prepared form, such as that shown in *Table 1*. With spaces provided for all necessary data and calculations, the procedure becomes routine and simple.

Heating Load

1. Design Conditions	Dry Bulb (°F)	Specific Humidity (gr./lb.)
Outside		
Inside		
Difference		

2. Transmission Gain (from appropriate tables)

	Sq. Ft. ×	Factor ×	Dry Bulb Temperature Difference =	Heating Load (Btuh)
Windows				
Walls				
Roof				
Floor				
Other				

3. Ventilation or Infiltration (from appropriate tables)

	CFM ×	Dry Bulb Temperature Difference ×	Factor =	
Sensible Load				
	CFM ×	**Specific Humidity Difference ×**	**Factor =**	
Humidification Load				

4. Duct Heat Loss (from appropriate tables)

Heat Loss _________ × Factor for Insulation Thickness _________ × Duct Length (Ft.) ÷ 100 = _________

5. Total Heating Load

= _________________

Table 1. Typical Heat Loss Form

A load estimate is based on design conditions inside the building and outside in the atmosphere surrounding the building. Outside design conditions are the maximum extremes of temperature occurring in a specific locality. The inside design conditions are the temperature and humidity that will give optimum comfort.

4.2.0   ELECTRIC BASEBOARD HEATERS

All requirements of the NEC apply for the installation of electric baseboard heaters, especially *NEC Article 424*, *Fixed Electric Space Heating Equipment*. In general, electric baseboard heaters must not be used where they will be exposed to severe physical damage unless they are adequately protected from such damage. Heaters and related equipment installed in damp or wet locations must be approved for such locations and must be constructed and installed so that water cannot enter or accumulate in or on wired sections, electrical components, or duct work.

Baseboard heaters must be installed to provide the required spacing between the equipment and adjacent combustible material, and each unit must be adequately grounded in accordance with *NEC Article 250*.

Figure 39 summarizes the NEC regulations governing the installation of electric baseboard heaters, while *Figure 40* shows a residential floor plan layout for electric heat.

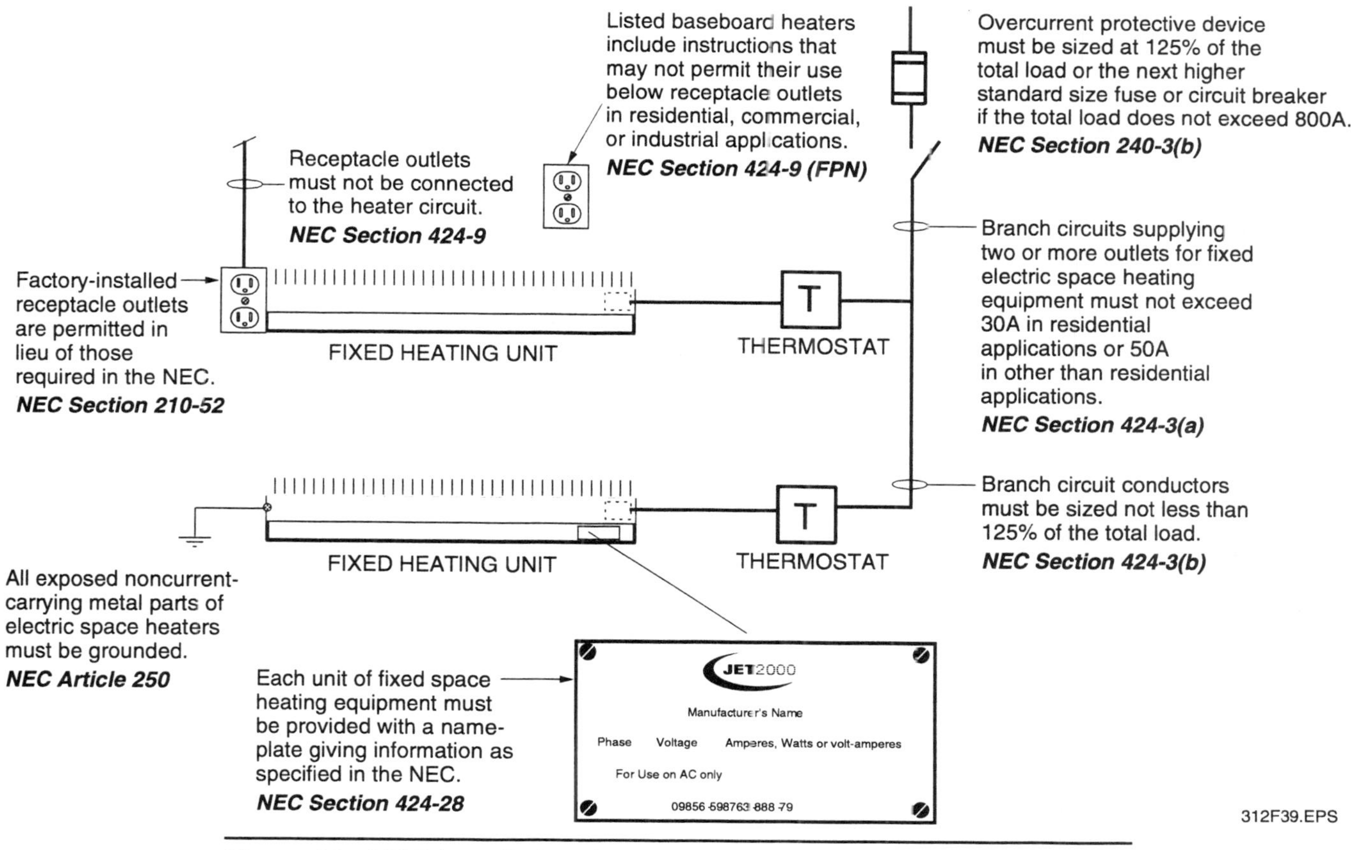

Figure 39. NEC Installation Guidelines For Electric Baseboard Heaters

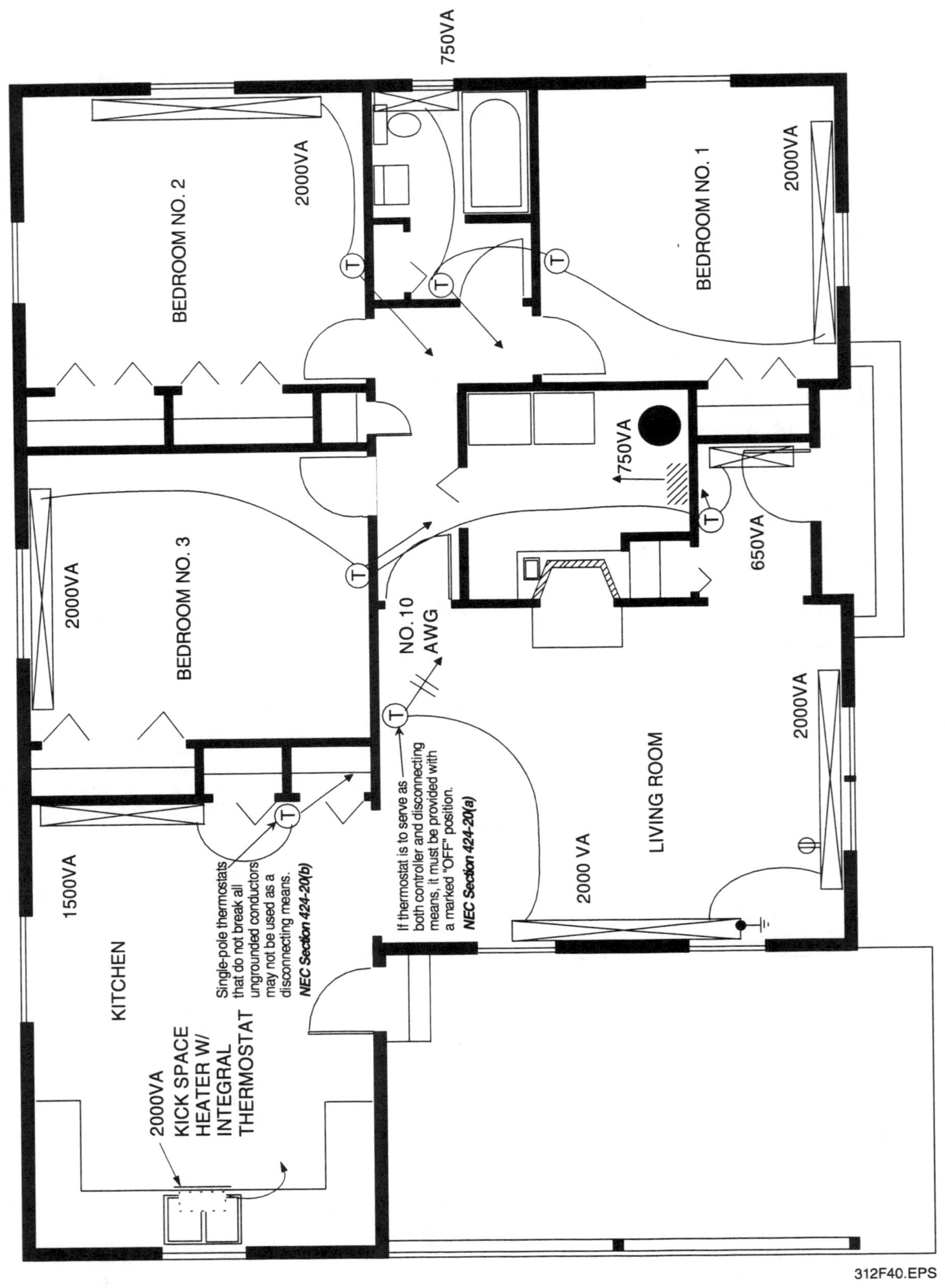

Figure 40. Floor Plan Layout For A Residential Electric Heating Application

4.3.0 ELECTRIC SPACE HEATING CABLES

Radiant heating cable represents a popular new alternative to conventional heating systems and can be installed in either the ceiling or the floor. The enormous heating surface precludes the need for raising air temperatures to a high degree. Rather, gentle warmth flows downward (or upward in the case of cable embedded in concrete floors) from the surfaces, heating the entire room or area evenly, and usually leaving no cold spots or drafts.

There is no maintenance with a radiant heating system as there are no moving parts; nothing to get clogged up; nothing to clean, oil, nor grease; and nothing to wear out.

The installation of this system is within reach of even the smallest electrical contractor. The most difficult part of the entire project is the layout of the system (i.e., how far apart to string the cable on the ceiling or in a concrete slab).

An ideal application of electric radiant heating cable would be during the renovation of an area within an existing residence where the ceiling plaster is beginning to crack and this ceiling will be recovered with drywall or another type of plaster board. Or, perhaps the basement floor needs repair and three inches of additional concrete will be poured over the existing floor.

4.3.1 Installation In Plaster Ceilings

To determine the spacing of the cable on a given ceiling, deduct one foot from the room length and one foot from the room width and multiply this new length by the new width, which will give the usable ceiling area in square feet. Multiply the square footage of the ceiling by 12 to get the ceiling area in inches before dividing by the length of the heating cable. The result will be the number of inches apart to space the cable.

For example, assume that a 14' × 12' room has a calculated heat loss of 2,000W. Therefore, (14' − 1') (12' − 1') × 12" = 13 × 11 × 12 = 1,716. We then look at manufacturers' tables and see that a 2,000W heating cable is 728' in length. Dividing the usable area (1,716 sq. in.) by this length (728), we find that the cable should be spaced 2.3" apart.

Figure 41 shows a floor plan of a typical heating cable installation as suggested by one manufacturer. However, nearly every brand of heating cable will be installed in the same way, and the procedure is as follows:

Step 1 Nail an outlet box on the inside wall approximately 5' above the finished floor for the thermostat location.

Step 2 Drill two holes in the wall plate above this junction box location.

Step 3 Drill two holes through the ceiling lath above the thermostat junction box location.

Step 4 Put the spool of heating cable on a nail, screwdriver, or any type of shaft you have at hand for unwinding the cable from the spool.

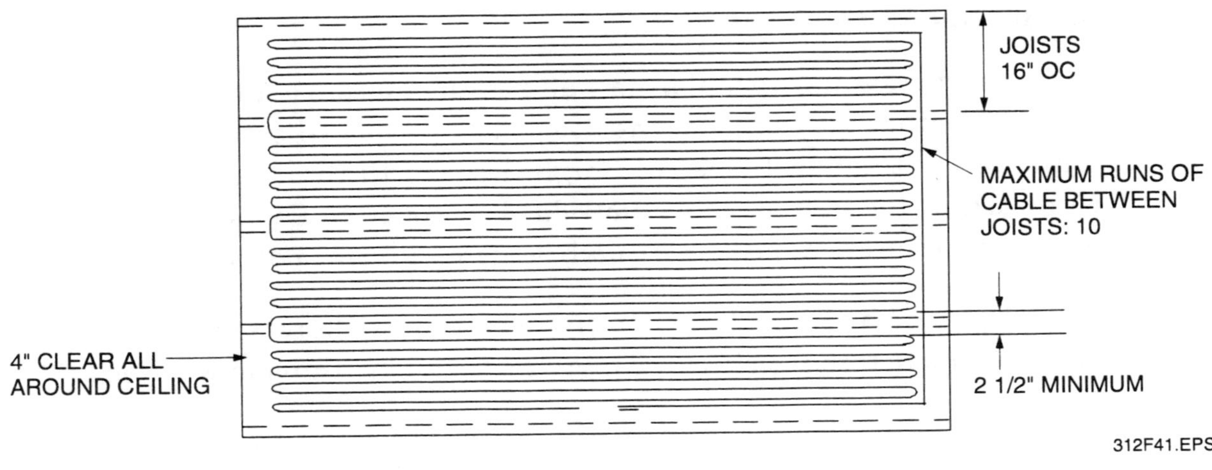

Figure 41. Recommendations For Heating Cable Layout

Step 5 Cover the accessible end of the 8' nonheating lead wire with nonmetallic loom. The loom should be long enough so that at least 2" will go on the ceiling surface and reach to the thermostat outlet box, but leave 6" of lead wire inside of the junction box for viewing the identification tags. Never remove the tags for any reason. Also, do not cut or shorten the nonheating leads.

Step 6 Run the accessible end (loom and all) of your cable through one of the holes in the ceiling, down the wall, through the plate, and into the thermostat outlet or junction box.

Step 7 Pull any slack out of the nonheating leads and staple them securely to the ceiling. Any excess nonheating lead should be covered with plaster the same as the heating cable. Do not staple or bend the cable.

Step 8 Mark a line all the way around the room 6" away from each wall; this accounts for the one foot you deducted from the width and length. A chalkline is best for this. Now take an inexpensive wooden yardstick and notch it for your calculated spacing. Run the cable along the ceiling 6" out from the wall to an outside wall, where it is attached in parallel spacing. In this example, the spacing is 2½". Always keep the cable at least 2" from any metal corner lath or other metal reinforcing.

Step 9 When you are down to the return lead wire, you are back to the starting wall. Cover this lead with the same length of loom as you did the starting lead. Then staple this return lead securely to the ceiling, run it through the other hole in the ceiling, down the wall, and into the thermostat outlet box.

Step 10 Connect the thermostat, which should be fed by a circuit of proper wire size according to the current, in amperes, drawn by the heating cable. Divide the wattage by the rated voltage. Your answer will be the load in amperes. Use *Table 2* to size your wire.

Amps	Type TW Wire
15 or lower	10 AWG
15 to 20	8 AWG
20 to 30	6 AWG
30 to 50	4 AWG

Table 2. Wire Sizes

Always make certain that the heating cable is connected to the proper voltage. A 120V cable connected to a 240V circuit will melt the cable, while a 240V heating cable connected to a 120V circuit will produce only 25% of the rated wattage of the cable. See *Figure 42* for a summary of NEC requirements governing the installation of electric space heating cable.

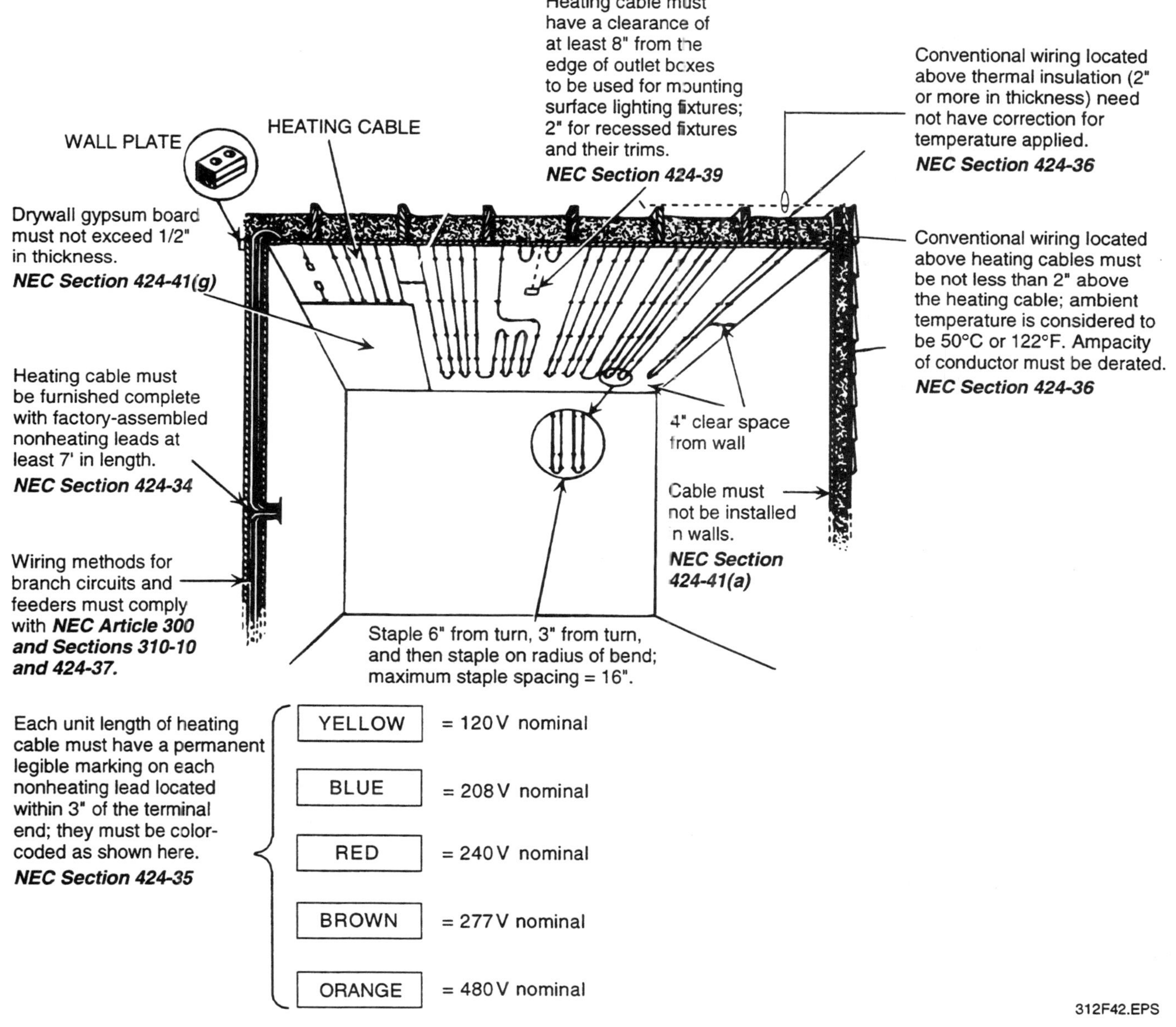

Figure 42. NEC Regulations For The Installation Of Electric Space Heating Cable

4.3.2 Installing Heating Cable In Concrete

The heat loss in concrete is calculated in the same manner as for any other area. For best results, the heating cable should never be spaced less than 2½" apart when installing it in a concrete floor except around outside walls, which may be spaced on 1½" minimum centers for the first 2' out from the wall. The concrete thickness above the cable should be from ½" to 1".

The spacing of the cable is found exactly as previously shown for the spacing of the cable on the ceiling, and then the installation procedure is as follows:

Step 1 Secure a junction box on an inside wall approximately 5' from the finished floor to house the thermostat.

Step 2 Install a piece of rigid conduit from the switch or thermostat junction box to house the nonheating leads between the concrete slab and the switch or thermostat outlet box.

Step 3 Approximately 6" of the lower end of the conduit should be embedded in the concrete, and a smooth porcelain bushing should be installed on this end of the conduit to protect the nonheating leads where they leave the conduit.

Step 4 Place the spool of heating cable on a nail, screwdriver, or any other shaft you have at hand for unwinding the cable from the spool.

Step 5 Run the accessible end of the 8' nonheating lead through the conduit to the thermostat junction box, leaving 6" extending out of the box. Never remove the identification tags or shorten the nonheating leads. They should be embedded in the concrete in the same way as the heating portion of the cable.

Step 6 Run the cable along the floor 6" out from the wall to the outside or exposed walls, fastening the cable to the floor with staples or masking tape.

Step 7 Run the cable. It is usually spaced 1½" apart for the first 2' around the exposed walls and never less than 2½" apart for the remaining area.

Step 8 Run the return nonheating lead wire through the conduit to the thermostat junction box in the same manner as the starting nonheating lead.

In general, the concrete slab should be prepared by applying a vapor barrier of 4" to 6" of gravel. Then pour 4" of vermiculite or other insulating concrete over the gravel after the outside edges of the slab have been insulated, in accordance with good building practice. The heating cable is then installed as described previously.

At this time, inspect and test the cable before the final layer of concrete is installed, because once the concrete is poured, it is an expensive matter to repair. First, visually inspect the cable for any possible damage to the insulation during the application. Then, with a suitable ohmmeter, check for the continuity and capacity of the cable. Concealed breaks may be found by leaving an ohmmeter connected to the cable and then brushing the cable lightly with the bristles of a broom. Any erratic movement of the meter dial will indicate a fault.

During the pouring of the final coat of concrete, it is recommended that the ohmmeter be left connected to the heating cable leads to detect any possible damage to the cable during the pouring of the finish layer of ordinary concrete (do not use insulating concrete). If an ohmmeter is not available, a 100W lamp may be connected in series with the cable to immediately detect any damage during the installation of the concrete. The lamp will glow as long as the circuit is complete and no damage occurs. However, if a break does occur, the lamp will go out and the break can be repaired before the concrete hardens.

Repairs to a broken cable are made by stripping the ends of the broken cable and rejoining the ends with a No. 14 AWG pressure-type connector provided and approved for this purpose. The splice must then be insulated with thermoplastic tape to a thickness equal to the insulation of the cable. Use any thermoplastic tape listed by Underwriters' Laboratories as suitable for a temperature of 176°F.

Once the finish layer of concrete sets, asphalt tile, linoleum, or other approved flooring can be laid on the concrete in the normal manner.

Besides the heating of interior spaces, electric heating cable also has many other uses. It can be embedded in concrete or asphalt surfaces for the removal of ice and snow, provide freeze protection for water pipes exposed to cold weather, provide roof and gutter de-icing, and heat soil in a hotbed or window box, keeping the temperature at a constant 70°F. The cost of heating cable is relatively inexpensive and the installation is relatively quick.

4.4.0 ELECTRIC FURNACES

The electric furnace (*Figure 43*) converts electrical energy directly into heat energy using resistance heaters.

Electric furnaces differ from fuel furnaces in that no combustion is required. Because no fuel is burned, there is no need for a chimney or vent to carry the products of combustion outdoors. This feature allows for greater operational safety and more installation flexibility. The return air from the conditioned space passes directly over the resistance heaters and into the supply air plenum. The amount of heat supplied by an electric furnace depends upon the number and size of the resistance heaters used in the application. To avoid overloading the electrical system on startup, the elements are sequenced on in stages.

The major components of an electric furnace, excluding the controls, are the heating elements, the blower and motor assembly, and the furnace enclosure or cabinet. Accessories such as filters, a humidifier, and a cooling coil may be included.

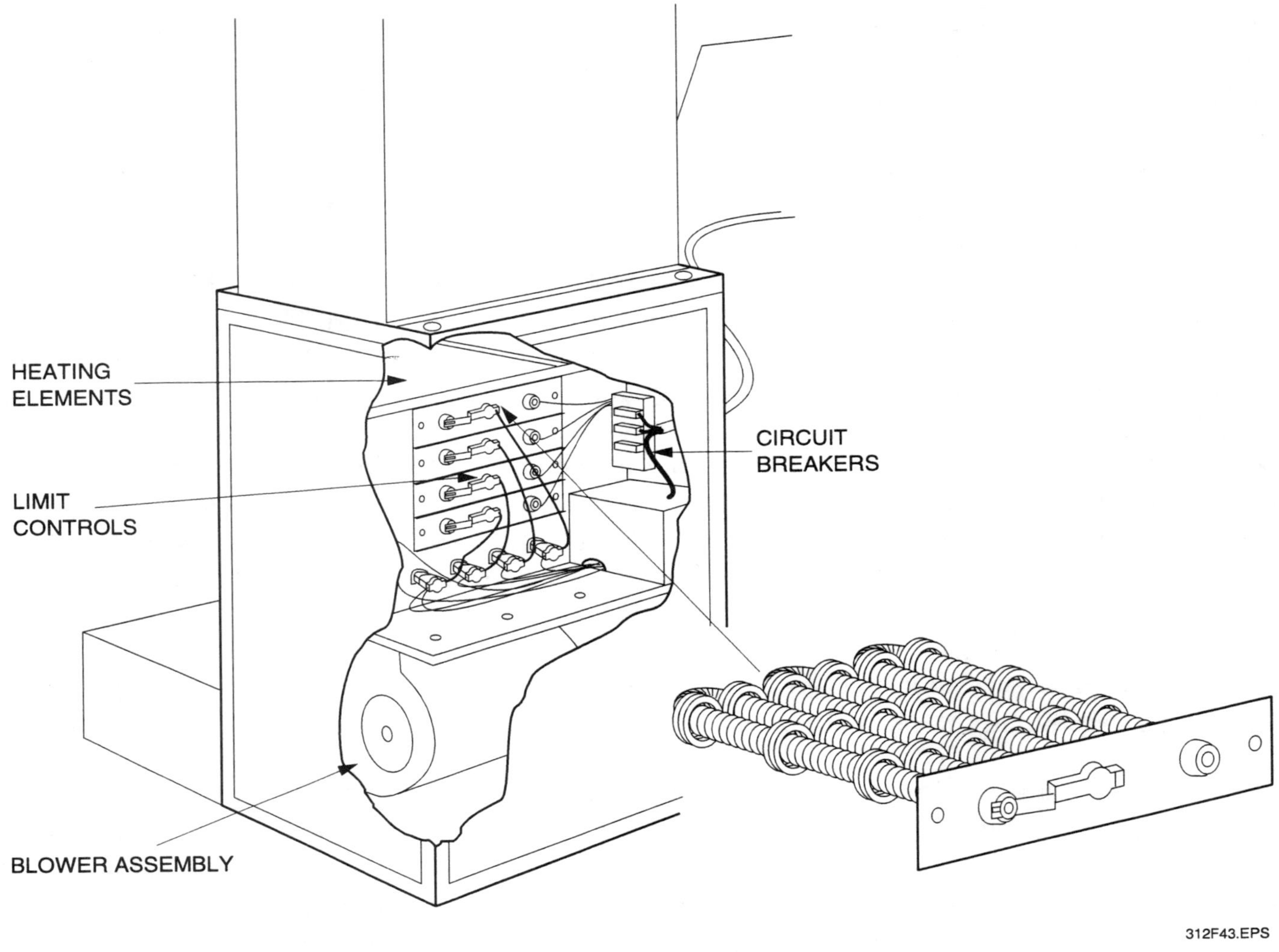

Figure 43. Electric Furnace

The function of the heating element is to provide the heat required for the conditioned space. The heating element wires are made of nickel and chromium (Nichrome). The heating element wire is spiraled and threaded through a metal holding rack which has ceramic insulators that prevent the resistance wires from shorting out on the frame of the rack. The heating elements are similar to those found in small household appliances such as electric clothes dryers and toasters.

The circuit for each heating element contains a fuse (circuit breaker) and a safety limit switch. The fuse backup for the safety limit switch is set to open at a temperature slightly higher than the limit switch. The limit switch is usually set to open at approximately 160°F and close when the temperature drops to 125°F.

The fans used in an electric furnace may be either direct-drive or belt-drive types. When cooling is added to the heating unit, the use of a multi-speed, direct-drive motor may be necessary in order to provide large air quantities.

An electric furnace power supply is usually 208/240V, single-phase, 60Hz alternating current. This type of heating unit is supplied by three wires: two hot and one grounded. The hot lines leading to the furnace contain fused disconnects. All wiring should be enclosed in conduit with the proper connectors as specified by the NEC. The NEC also requires that the furnace unit be grounded. The supply ground is provided for this purpose.

4.5.0 DUCT HEATERS

Duct heater is a term applied to any heating coils mounted in the air stream of a forced-air system. The coils are similar to the heating element shown in *Figure 43*. Duct heaters are used in combination electric heating/cooling systems, and most of the time in heat pumps to provide auxiliary heat when the pumps themselves cannot supply the demand.

In general, heaters installed in an air duct must be identified as suitable for the installation, and some means must be provided to ensure uniform and adequate air flow over the face of the heater in accordance with the manufacturer's instructions. This latter requirement is normally accomplished by air flow controls and other components involving turning vanes, pressure plates, or other devices on the inlet side of the duct heater to ensure an even distribution of air over the face of the heater.

Duct heaters installed closer than 4' to a heat pump or air conditioner must have both the duct heater and the heat pump or air conditioner identified as suitable for such installation and must be so marked.

Duct heaters intended for use with elevated inlet air temperatures must be identified as suitable for use at the elevated temperatures. Furthermore, duct heaters used with air conditioners or other air-cooling equipment that may result in condensation of moisture must be identified as suitable for use with air conditioners.

The NEC requires that all duct heaters be installed according to the manufacturer's instructions. Furthermore, duct heaters must be located with respect to building construction and other equipment so as to permit access to the heater. Sufficient clearance must be maintained to permit replacement of controls and heating elements and for adjusting and cleaning of controls and other parts requiring such maintenance. See *Figure 44*.

Control requirements, including disconnecting means, are specified in **NEC Sections 424-63, 424-64, and 424-65**. A fan circuit interlock is one of the requirements. Such a control ensures that the fan circuit is energized when any heater circuit is energized. It would be a waste of energy, and perhaps also a hazard, if the duct heaters became energized and no air flowed over or through them. However, the NEC permits a slight time- and temperature-delay before the fan may be energized. This prevents the system from blowing cold air into the conditioned space. In other words, such a control gives the duct heaters time to warm up before air is induced in the system.

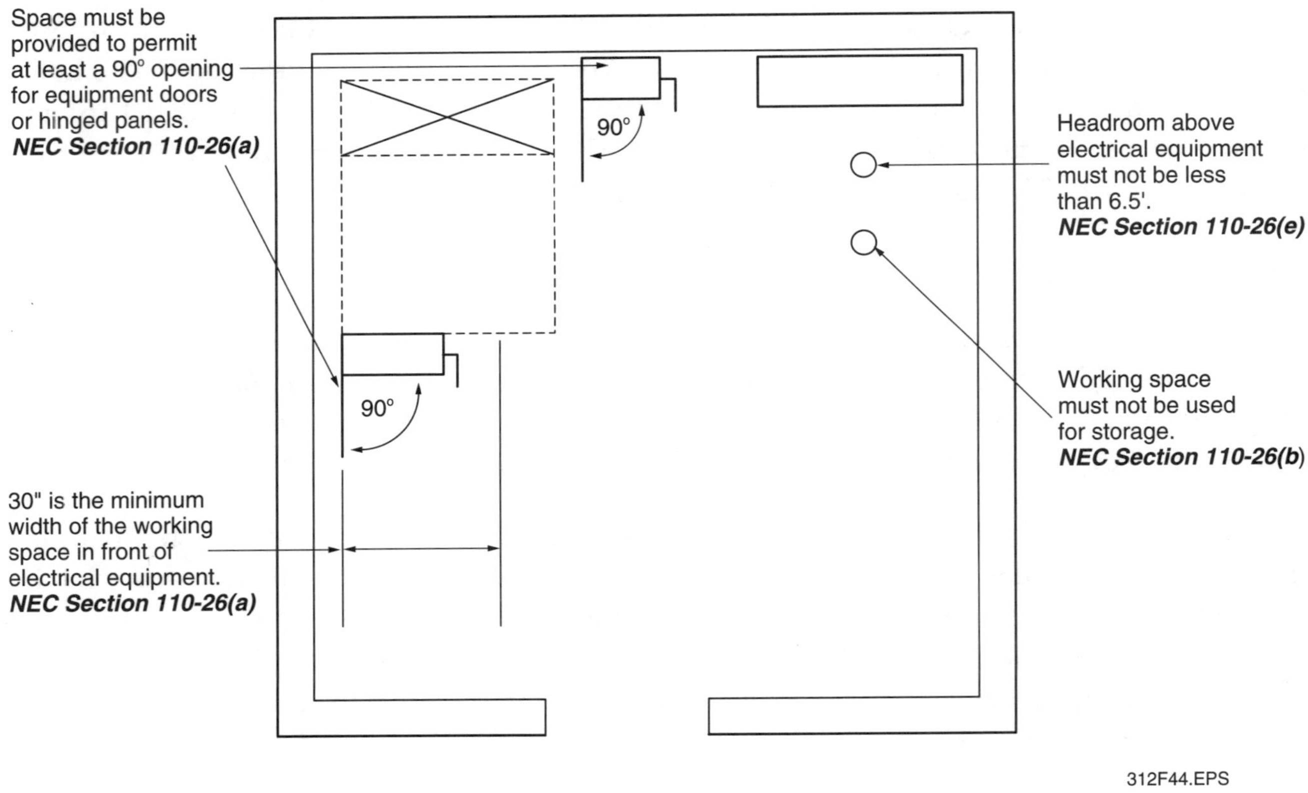

Figure 44. NEC Requirements For Duct Heater Installation

Furthermore, each duct heater must be provided with an automatic reset limit control to deenergize the duct heater circuit(s) in case overheating or other faults occur. In addition, an integral independent supplementary control or controller shall be provided in each duct heater that will disconnect a sufficient number of conductors to interrupt current flow. This device must be manually resettable or replaceable.

The disconnect for duct heaters—the same as for other types of HVAC equipment—must be accessible and within sight of the controller. All control equipment must also be accessible.

Supplementary heating packages for heat pumps and air conditioning air handlers are installed in the field. In the case of a heat pump, the heating coils must provide sufficient heat in the event that the heat pump compressor fails. This is known as *emergency heat* and is discussed later in the module.

The heating coils are usually staged on by multi-stage wall thermostats and outdoor thermostats.

Because of their high current draw, supplementary electric heating packages usually have their own overcurrent protection (either fuses or circuit breakers) which are mounted in the unit, rather than in the service entrance panel.

ELECTRICAL — TRAINEE TASK MODULE 26312

NEC Section 422-11(f) requires that any appliance employing resistance heating elements rated at more than 48A must have the heating elements subdivided. Each subdivided load may not exceed 48A and must be protected at not more than 60A. The overcurrent protection is required to be factory-installed within the enclosure or as a separate assembly. They must be accessible and the conductors supplying these devices are considered to be branch circuit conductors.

4.6.0 AIR FILTERS

Some type of air filter is used on all types of forced-air heating and cooling systems, including air-to-air heat pumps. Individual room air conditioners also use air filters. The filter is placed in the return air duct system to filter all air returning from the conditioned space. Air filters not only provide a cleaner environment, but also prolong the life of the fan coil unit in HVAC systems.

Air filters, as well as insect and bird screens, reduce the free intake area of the vent or ductwork and necessitate a larger overall area for compensation. *Figure 45* shows the effective free area of three types of screening. Choose the appropriate one and multiply the free area by the percent of efficiency to obtain the size needed.

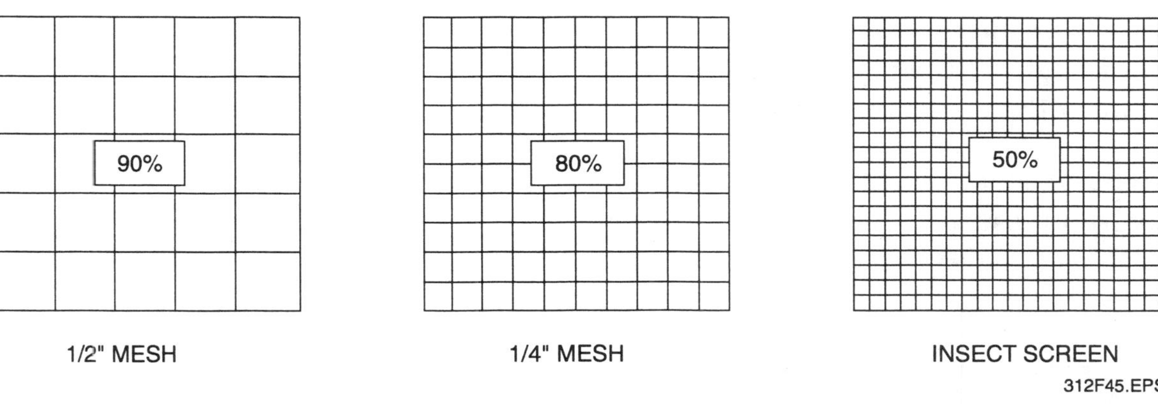

Figure 45. Examples Of Mesh Screening

4.6.1 Electronic Air Cleaners

In systems requiring high air cleaning efficiency, electronic **air cleaners** are used. These devices operate on the principle of passing the airstream through an ionization field where a 12,000V potential imposes a positive charge on all airborne particles. The ionized particles are then passed between aluminum plates, alternately grounded and connected to a 6,000V source, and are attracted to the grounded plates (*Figure 46*).

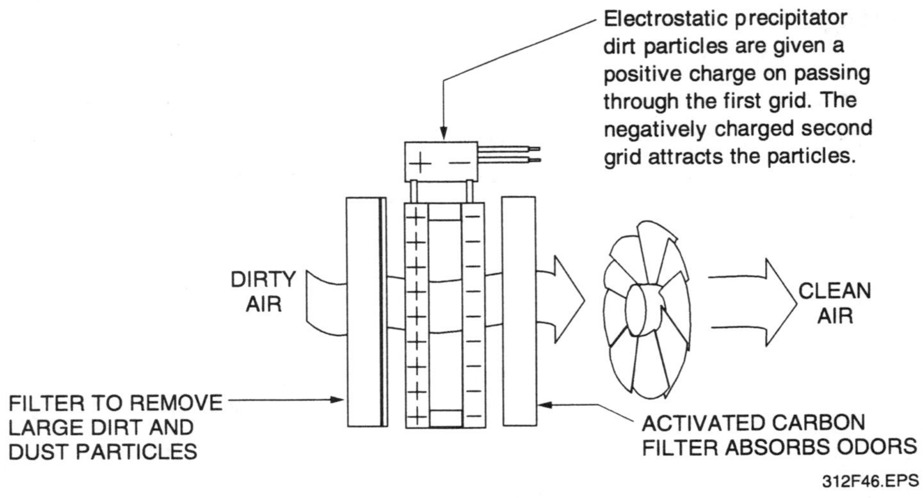

Figure 46. Operating Principles Of Electronic Air Cleaners

The original design of the electronic air cleaner uses a water-soluble adhesive coating on the plates, which holds the dirt deposits until the plates require cleaning. The filter is then deenergized, and the dirt and adhesive films are washed off the plates. Fresh adhesive is applied before the power is turned on again. Newer versions of electronic air cleaners are designed so that the plates serve as agglomerators; the agglomerates of smaller particles are allowed to slough off the plates and are trapped by viscous impingement or duty-type filters downstream of the electronic unit.

The designs of most electronic air cleaners are based on 500 feet per minute (fpm) face velocity, with pressure losses at 0.20" water gauge (w.g.) for the washable type and up to 1.0" w.g. for the agglomerator type using dry-type after-filters. Power consumption is low, despite the 12,000V ionizer potential, because current flow is measured in milliamperes (mA).

5.0.0   HVAC CONTROLS

All of the material described in this module cannot be accomplished without some means of control, if only to stop and start the system. For example, without a controlling mechanism, an air conditioning system would be turned on and run year-round. Even when the space became cool or hot enough, the system would continue to run and make the area more uncomfortable than if it had not been installed in the first place. Therefore, effective control is an important area of comfort conditioning for buildings.

Electronic control circuits are the principal controls used in HVAC systems of any consequence. Not too long ago, their main use was in highly sophisticated commercial and industrial applications, but they are now used in virtually all HVAC applications, from residential to industrial. Electronic controls provide a quick response to temperature changes and temperature averaging is easily accomplished.

Although solid-state controls dominate the field, some of the earlier controls will also be covered, because many are still in use and will remain in use for some time to come.

ELECTRICAL — TRAINEE TASK MODULE 26312

5.1.0 INDOOR THERMOSTAT

HVAC controls can be electric, electronic, or pneumatic. Almost limitless combinations of each type are possible. Therefore, it is not practical to attempt to describe all of the possible combinations in this module. Rather, fundamental terms, functions, operations, and simple maintenance and troubleshooting techniques are presented.

The indoor thermostat (*Figure 47*) is the most easily recognized control device. Such controls can be found in every home utilizing central heating or cooling systems. This section provides an overview of a thermostat used to control an electric heat pump.

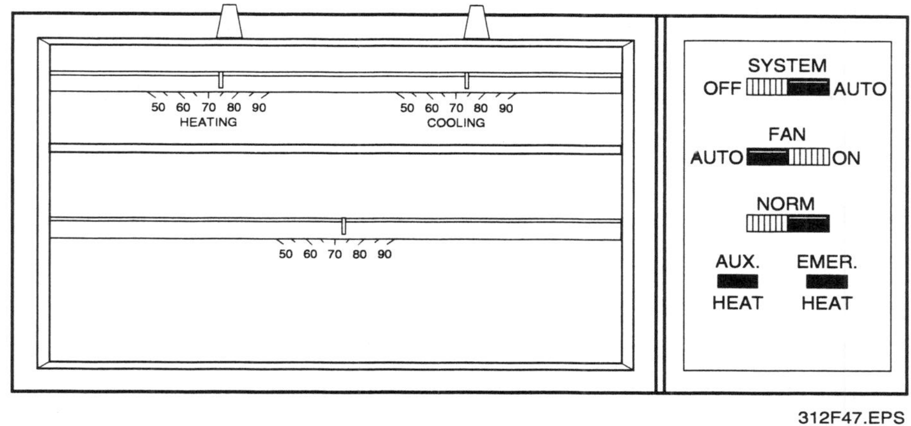

Figure 47. Typical Indoor Thermostat

A two-stage indoor changeover thermostat is the most popular type used to control heat pumps during the heating season. During the cooling season, it functions as a conventional air conditioning thermostat. The first stage of this thermostat controls the heat pump. The second stage (usually preset 1°F to 2°F below the first stage) allows the supplementary heat to be energized.

By placing the selector switch on AUTO, the automatic changeover thermostat switches the system from heating to cooling or cooling to heating automatically. A manual thermostat is also available to offer the option of manually selecting the mode of operation for heating or cooling.

- *Emergency heat switch (EMER. HT.)* – The indoor thermostat should have an emergency heat selector with a light to indicate full use of the supplementary heat when the heat pump is not in operation. If the heat pump should become inoperative, this switch enables bypassing the normal operation of the heat pump and heats the area with the supplementary heat until the problem is corrected. An indicator light mounted on the thermostat will come on when the selector is in the emergency heat position. As soon as the unit has been repaired, return the switch to the normal operating position.

- *Supplementary heat light* – Some thermostats have a light which indicates the supplementary heat is on to assist the heat pump in normal operation. When the outdoor temperature falls below the **balance point** of the heat pump and energizes the supplementary heat, the light will cycle on and off intermittently as the supplementary heat is activated. The temperature range at which the light comes on will vary, depending on the balance point.

5.1.1 Temperature Setting

- *Heating* – The recommended setting for the heating cycle is 68°F. Once the thermostat is set, the best policy is to leave it alone. Raising the thermostat as little as 2°F may cause the supplementary heat to energize, thereby increasing the energy usage.
- *Night setback* – Although night setback is recommended during the winter for most types of heating systems to save energy and reduce costs, it is not generally recommended for a heat pump. When using a heat pump to raise the room temperature in the morning, the supplementary heat may come on, using more energy than was saved during the night. However, thermostat temperature settings for weekend trips or vacations during the heating season should be reduced to save energy.
- *Cooling* – A setting of 78°F or higher is recommended for cooling. For each degree the temperature is set below 78°F, the cooling energy usage will increase by approximately 5%.

Raising the temperature when the room or building is unoccupied is recommended to save energy. If the building will not be occupied for several days, the cooling system can be turned off altogether. However, frequent changes of the thermostat setting reduces the economical operation of the heat pump and tends to shorten the life of the compressor. Many commercial systems use sensors to determine when the building is occupied and adjust the air conditioning.

5.1.2 Fan Operation

Operation of the fan is the same for the automatic or manual changeover thermostat. The fan switch set in the AUTO position provides fan operation only when the unit is actually heating or cooling. In the ON position, the indoor fan will run continuously to provide ventilation. The ON position is recommended to obtain a more even temperature throughout the house. Operating the fan in the ON position may allow the thermostat to be set at a lower temperature or reduce the operating time of the compressor, which may offset the increased cost. It should also increase occupant comfort.

5.1.3 Location

The indoor thermostat should be located on an interior wall in the central portion of the home, approximately five feet above the floor. Electromechanical thermostats must be installed level. The location should be free from drafts, vibrations, and any interior heat sources such as a lamp or television set. Care should be taken to seal behind the wall where the thermostat wire or mounting box penetrates the wall.

5.2.0 BASIC PRINCIPLES OF CONTROL

The circuit in *Figure 48* shows a simple control for an electric resistance-type heater. It consists of a 120V, two-wire circuit feeding the heater and a conventional single-pole toggle switch to interrupt the power supply. A single-pole, 15A circuit breaker is used to protect the circuit against short circuits and ground faults. When the toggle switch is in the ON position, the heater becomes energized; when in the OFF position, the heater is deenergized. Obviously, this is a manual control and leaves much to be desired. For example, once the space to be heated reaches the desired temperature, the toggle switch cannot sense the difference and continues to stay in the ON position until it is manually shut off. If the switch is left on, the space will continue to receive heat, even after the desired temperature has been reached.

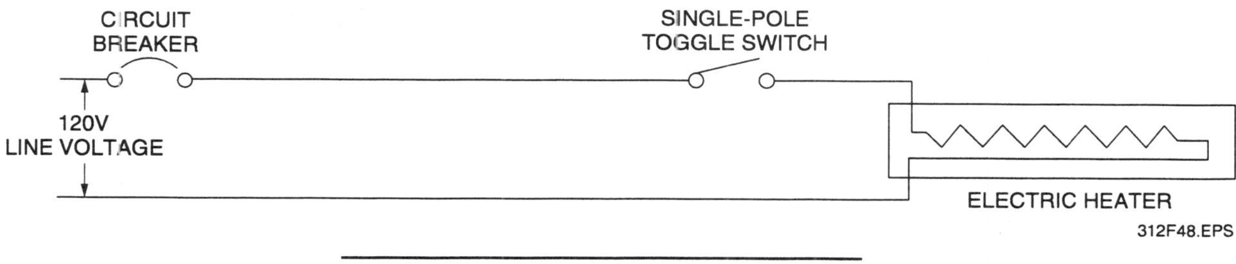

Figure 48. Simple Heater Control Circuit

A better solution is to replace the single-pole toggle switch with a thermostat control. A thermostat utilizing **bimetal** elements is shown in *Figure 49*. The bimetal elements consist of thin strips of two different metals securely attached to each other. Since different metals expand and contract at different rates, the thin strips of metal actually curve toward or away from a given point when there is a change in temperature. In this way, the thermostat makes or breaks its contacts when the temperature changes, providing automatic control of the heater circuit.

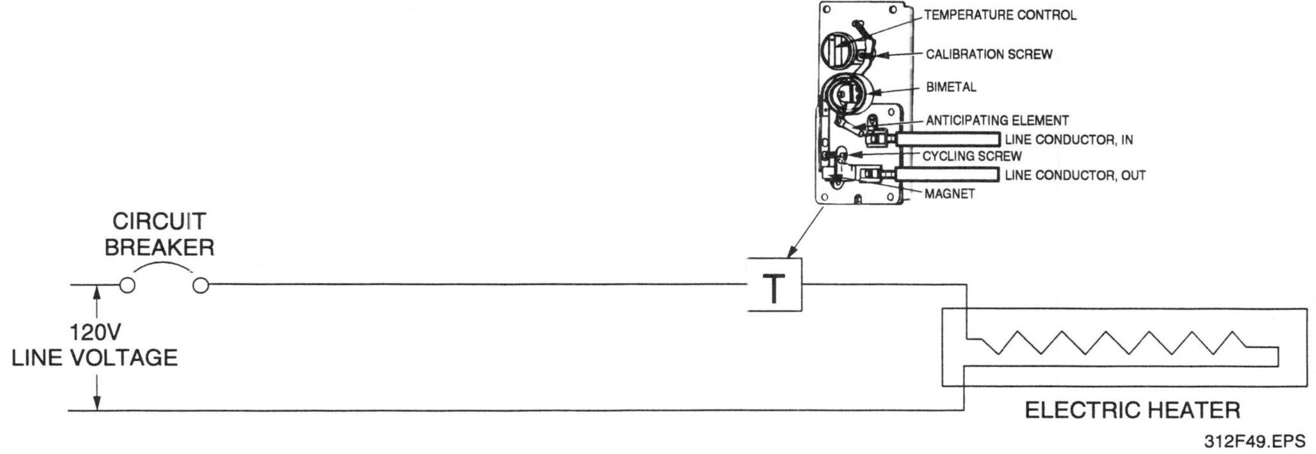

Figure 49. Bimetal Elements In A Line Voltage Thermostat

5.3.0 BASIC ELECTRONIC CONTROLS

The Wheatstone bridge circuit is the basis of many electronic circuits installed in the past couple of decades, and many are still in use. The bridge consists of two sets of two series-wired resistors connected in parallel across a DC voltage source. One set of series-wired resistors is R1 and R2; the second set is R3 and R4 (see *Figure 50*). The voltage source, E, is between points A and B. A sensitive electric current indicator (galvanometer), G, is connected across the parallel sets of resistors at points C and D.

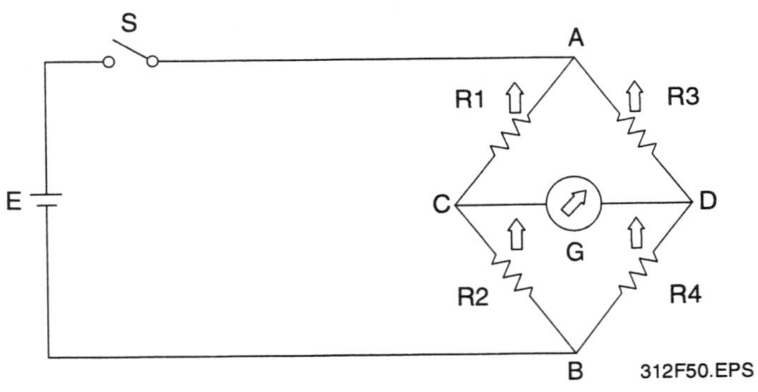

Figure 50. Basic Wheatstone Bridge Circuit

When switch S is closed, the voltage from E flows through both sets of resistors. If the potential at point C is the same as at point D, the galvanometer reads zero. This means that there is no potential difference between the two points and the bridge is balanced.

When any of the four resistors has a different voltage, the galvanometer registers a value other than zero. This indicates that there is a current between points C and D. When this occurs, the bridge is unbalanced. Some control manufacturers have modified this basic bridge circuit and put it to work in electronic circuits. A typical modification is shown in *Figure 51*.

Figure 51 shows that the DC voltage has been replaced by an AC supply. Also, the switch is eliminated and the galvanometer is replaced by an amplifier-switching relay unit. Resistor R2 is replaced by a temperature-sensing element T1.

In this modification, a resistance of $1,000\Omega$ is assigned to each of the three fixed resistors (R1, R3, and R4) and to the thermostat element T1. When conditions in the area to be conditioned are satisfied, the resistance in T1 does not change, and the voltage across the amplifier relay is zero. Because there is no voltage across this amplifier relay, the final control element (motor, valve, etc.) cannot be energized. The bridge circuit is balanced.

When the air temperature in the space changes, the thermostat element senses the change. This causes a corresponding change in the resistance at T1, and the bridge becomes unbalanced. Voltage now flows through the amplifier relay to the final control element. In a heating application, a drop in temperature in the space causes a decrease in resistance at T1.

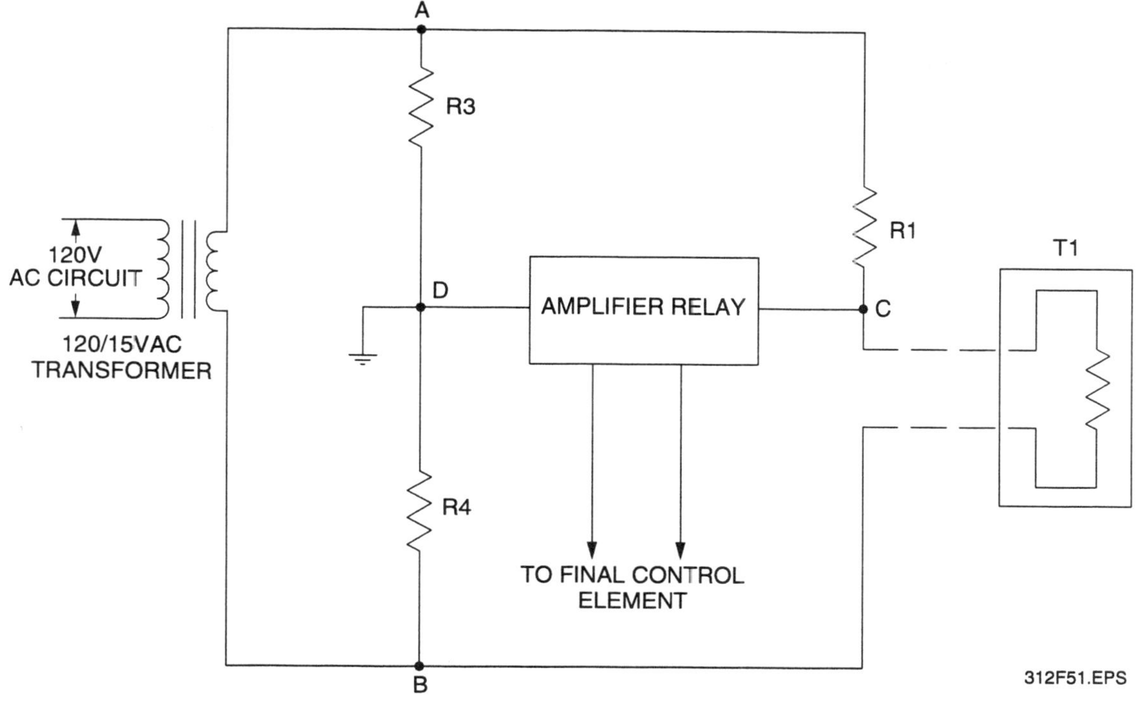

Figure 51. Modified Wheatstone Bridge Circuit

This results in voltage relationships in the bridge circuit that cause the amplifier relay to increase the voltage to the final control element, adding heat to the space. As heat is added, the resistance at T1 increases, and the resulting voltage change in the bridge circuit inactivates the heating action (shuts off the burner).

This modified bridge circuit can also be applied to cooling applications. Depending on whether the bridge voltage fed to the amplifier relay is in phase or out of phase with the supply voltage, the final control element is opened or closed.

5.4.0 TIME-DELAY CIRCUITS

The thermostat or other control for HVAC systems must respond to a gradual or average change in the space to be conditioned. An average change is produced by adding a tiny heater (timing device) near the thermostat temperature-sensing element in electrical controls. Electronic circuits produce an output signal delayed in time by a prescribed and controllable amount in relation to an input waveform in the transmission line or its lumped circuit approximation. More common forms of delay circuits are initiated by a controlling signal and produce an output, not necessarily related to the input in size or shape, at a later time. Usually the input pulses are recurrent at a specific rate, thus the time-displaced output signals are recurrent at the same rate. Such delay circuits are usually designed as linear delay circuits in the sense that a linear variation of some controlling element produces a delay that is a linear variation in time delay (see *Figure 52*).

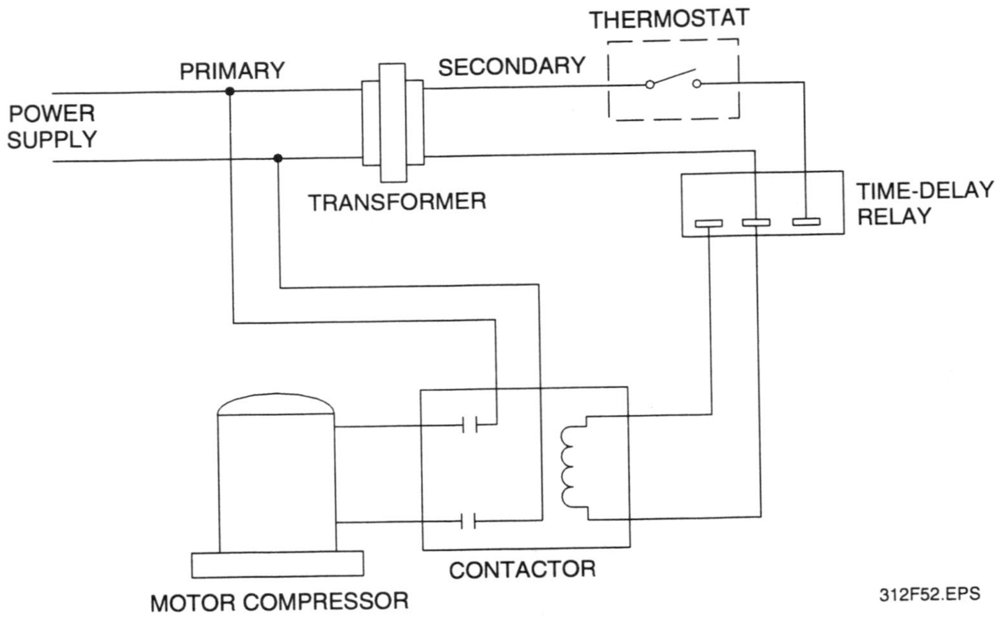

Figure 52. Solid-State Time-Delay Relay Circuit

5.5.0 BASIC CONTROL COMPONENTS

The following is an example of control circuits used in a basic gas furnace (see *Figure 53*). Air conditioning and furnace controls will be covered in more detail in the next level of your training.

Thermostat – In general, low-voltage room thermostats should be used for the best temperature control. Low-voltage thermostats respond much faster to temperature changes than the greater mass line-voltage devices.

From a cost standpoint, the less expensive installation of low-voltage wiring more than offsets the extra cost of the transformer. Also, greater safety is provided by low-voltage thermostats.

The room thermostat includes a heat anticipator connected in series with the rest of the control circuit. These anticipators are made of a resistance-type material that produces heat in accordance with the current drawn through it. Heat anticipators are adjustable and are normally set to correspond with the current rating of the main gas valve, motor starter, or relay. The purpose of these devices is to make the room temperature more stable.

In operation, when the thermostat is calling for heat, the anticipator is also supplying heat to the thermostat. This heating action causes the thermostat to become satisfied before the room actually reaches the set point of the thermostat. Thus, the thermostat stops the flame or deenergizes the motor starter, relay, etc., and the room temperature will not overshoot, or go too high. The remaining heat in the system will then raise the temperature to the desired level.

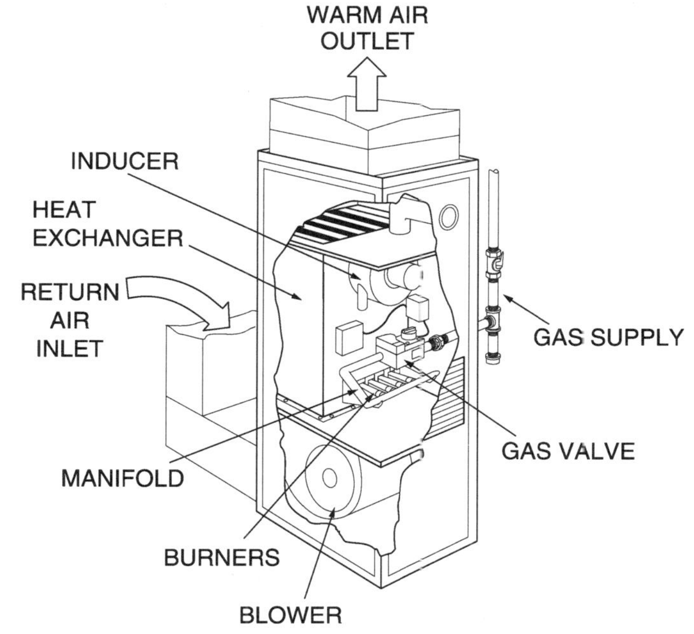

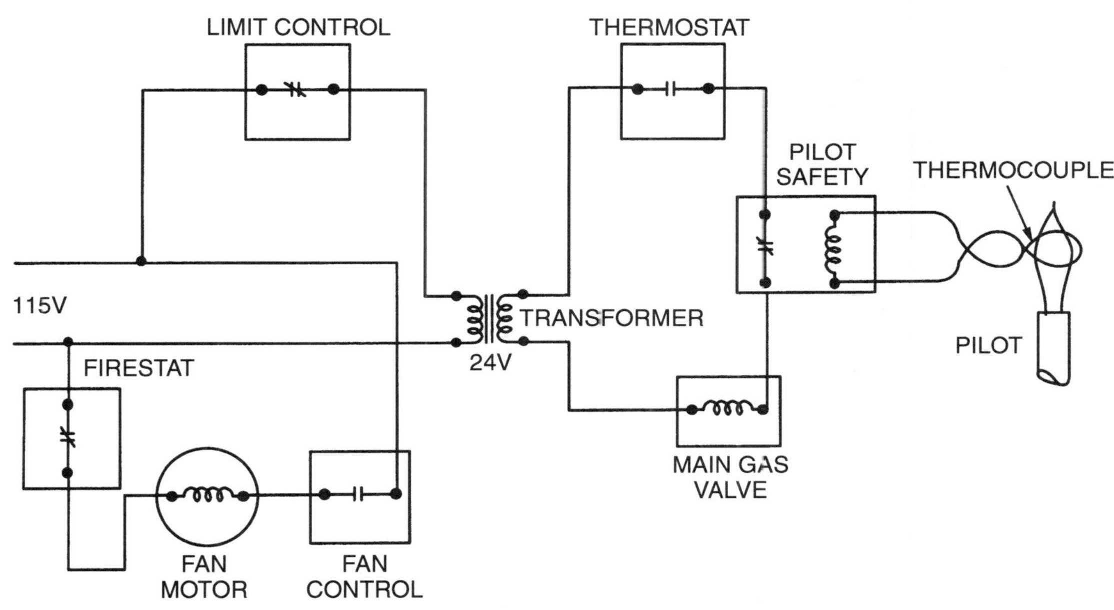

312F53.TIF

Figure 53. Basic Gas Furnace

Transformer – The transformer is a device used to reduce line voltage to a usable control voltage (usually 24V). Transformers must be sized to provide sufficient power to operate the control circuit. Most are sufficiently oversized to provide enough power to also operate an air conditioning control circuit. This rating is usually 40VA for small systems; it is somewhat greater for larger systems.

Fan control – The fan control is a temperature-actuated control that (when heated) will close a set of contacts to start the indoor fan motor. The sensing element of the fan control is positioned inside the heat exchanger where the temperature is the highest.

This control is actuated by a bimetal element that opens or closes the contacts on a temperature change. The fan control is usually set to bring the fan on at about 100°F in the heating mode.

In operation, the burner provides heat to the heat exchanger for a few seconds to warm the furnace before the fan is started. This operation is to prevent blowing cold air into the room on furnace startup. When the thermostat is satisfied, the main burner stops providing heat, but the fan continues to operate until the temperature in the furnace has been reduced, thus removing any excess heat in the furnace.

Limit control – The limit control is also a heat-actuated switch with a bimetal sensing element positioned inside the heat exchanger. This is a safety control that is wired into the primary side of the transformer. If the temperature inside the furnace reaches approximately 200°F, the power to the transformer will be shut off, which also stops all power in the temperature control circuit.

Main gas valve – The main gas valve is the device that acts on demand from the thermostat to either admit gas to the main burners or to stop the gas supply. This valve has many functions. It has a gas pressure regulator, a pilot safety, a main gas cock, a pilot gas cock, and the main gas solenoid all in a single unit—the combination gas control.

As the thermostat calls for heat, energizing the solenoid coil, the valve lever opens the cycling valve. The inlet gas now flows through the control orifice past the cycling valve. At this point, gas flow is in two directions, as follows:

- Part of the flow is to the back of the diaphragm by means of internal passageways. The resulting increase in pressure pushes the main valve to the open position, compressing the diaphragm springs lightly.
- Part of the flow is through the seat of the master regulator into the valve outlet by means of internal passageways. This causes the master regulator to begin to function.

The gas valve remains in this position and the master regulator continues to regulate until the relay coil is deenergized, at which time the cycling valve seals off.

As the cycling valve closes, the regulator spring causes the seat of the master regulator to close off. The function of the bypass orifice is to permit gas in the passageways to escape into the outlet of the valve, thereby causing the main gas valve to close.

Pilot safety – There are two types of pilot safety controls: 90% safe and 100% safe. These two names refer to the amount of gas cut off when the pilot light is unsafe. The 100% safe device is incorporated in the combination main gas valve. The 90% safe device incorporates a set of contacts that open the control circuit during an unsafe condition.

These units are used in conjunction with a **thermocouple** to keep the control contacts closed or the valve open during normal operation. If, at any time, the control drops out (the contacts open), the reset button must be manually reset before operation of the furnace can be resumed.

Thermocouple – The thermocouple is a device that uses the difference in metals to provide electron flow. The hot junction of the thermocouple is put in the pilot flame where the dissimilar metals are heated. When heat is applied to the welded junction, a small voltage is produced. This small voltage is measured in millivolts (mV) and is the power used to operate the pilot safety control. The output of a thermocouple is approximately 30mV. This simple device can cause many problems if the connections are not kept clean and tight.

Firestat – The firestat is a safety device mounted in the fan compartment to stop the fan if the return air temperature reaches about 60°F. It is a bimetal-actuated, normally closed switch that must be manually reset before the fan can operate.

The reason for stopping the fan when high return air temperatures exist is to prevent agitation of any open flame in the house, thus helping to prevent the spreading of any fire that may be present.

The control of electric furnaces is quite different (*Figure 54*). The furnace, as previously shown, usually has several banks of heating elements. These are staged on and off by the thermostat as heating demand increases and decreases. Sequencing relays create stage-to-stage time delays that bring the heating elements on one at a time to prevent current overloads.

The variety of functions performed by a heating system is limited only by the use of controls. The more you know about controls, the easier your job will be when installing or performing electrical troubleshooting of such equipment.

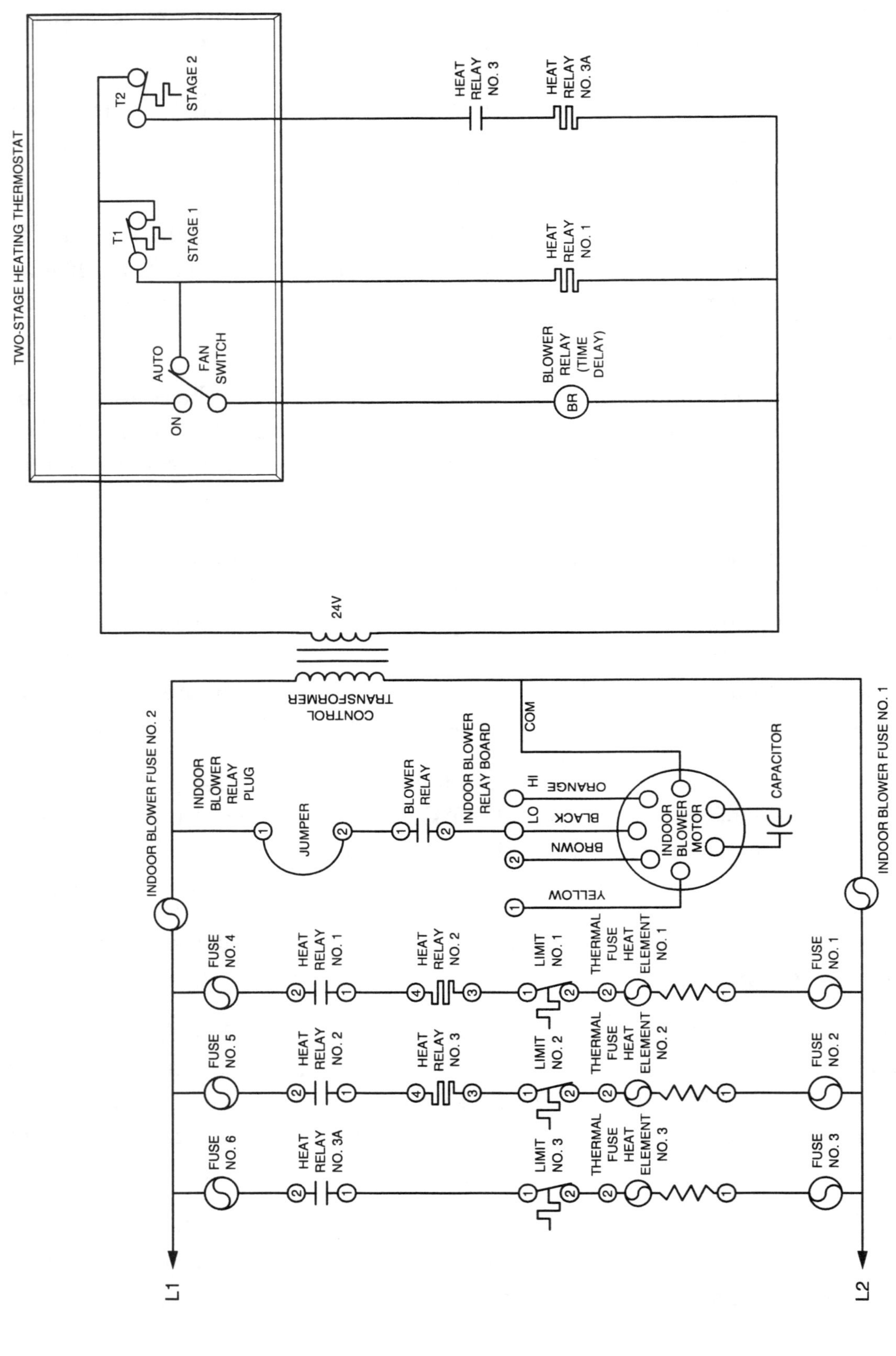

Figure 54. Electric Furnace Controls

ELECTRICAL — TRAINEE TASK MODULE 26312

This section summarizes the NEC requirements for HVAC controls, compressors, and room air conditioners.

6.1.0   NEC REQUIREMENTS FOR HVAC CONTROLS

Several sections of the NEC cover the requirements for HVAC controls. For example, ***NEC Article 424, Part C*** deals with the control and protection of fixed electric space heating equipment; ***NEC Article 440, Part E*** covers requirements for motor compressor controllers; and ***NEC Article 440, Part F*** deals with motor compressor and branch circuit overload protection.

In general, a means must be provided to disconnect heating equipment, including motor controllers and supplementary overcurrent protective devices, from all ungrounded conductors. The disconnecting means may be a switch, circuit breaker, unit switch, or a thermostatically-controlled switching device. Both the selection and use of disconnecting devices are governed by the type of overcurrent protection and the rating of any motors that are part of the equipment.

In certain heating units, supplementary overcurrent protective devices other than the branch circuit overcurrent protection are required. These supplementary overcurrent devices are normally used when heating elements rated at more than 48A are supplied as a subdivided load. In this case, the disconnecting means must be on the supply side of the supplementary overcurrent protective device and within sight of it. This disconnecting means may also serve to disconnect the heater and any motor controllers, provided the disconnecting means is within sight of the controller and heater, or it can be locked in the open position. If the motor is rated over ⅛hp, a disconnecting means must comply with the rules for motor disconnecting means unless a unit switch is used to disconnect all ungrounded conductors.

A heater without supplementary overcurrent protection must have a disconnecting means that complies with rules similar to those for permanently-connected appliances. A unit switch may be the disconnecting means in certain occupancies when other means of disconnection are provided as specified in the NEC.

Figures 55 and *56* summarize some of the NEC requirements for HVAC controls, including thermostats, motor controllers, disconnects, and overcurrent protection. Additional NEC regulations on motor controllers are covered in other modules.

You are also encouraged to study (not just read) ***NEC Sections 424-19 through 424-22***, as well as ***NEC Sections 440-41 through 440-55***. While most of this material has been covered in this module, interpreting these NEC regulations is a good training exercise in itself.

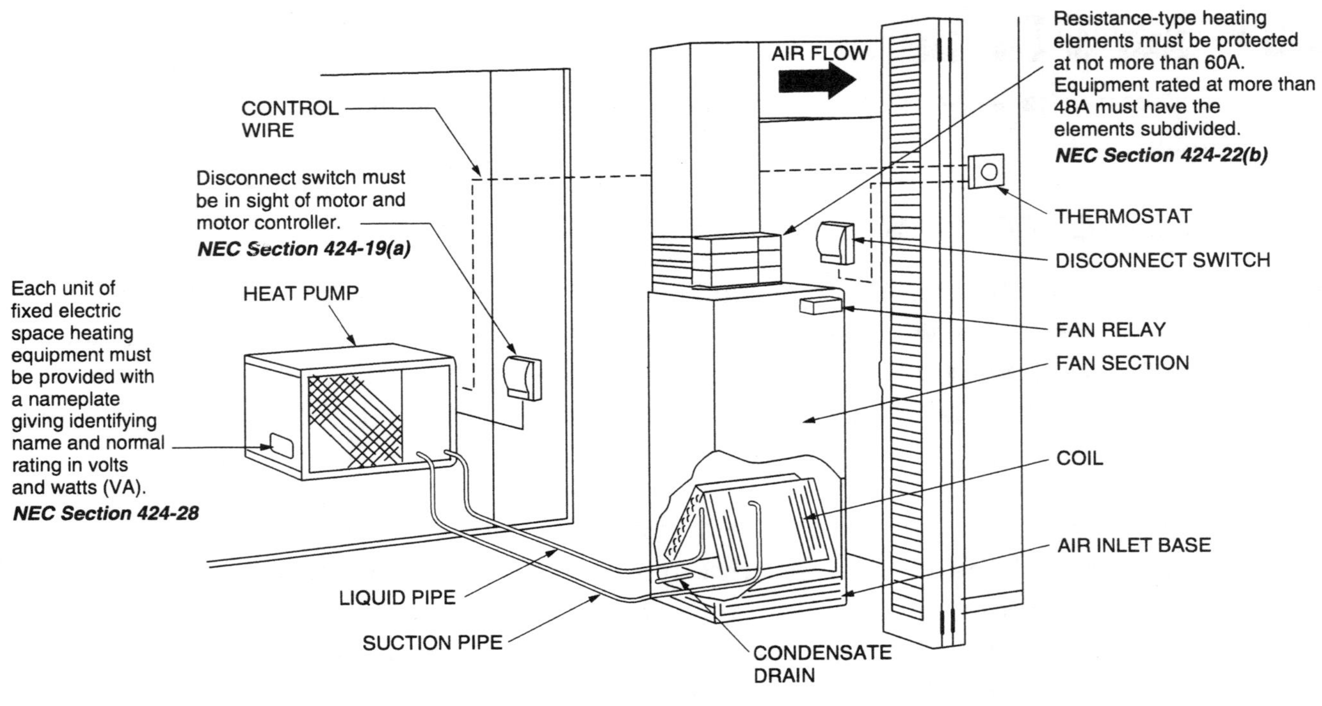

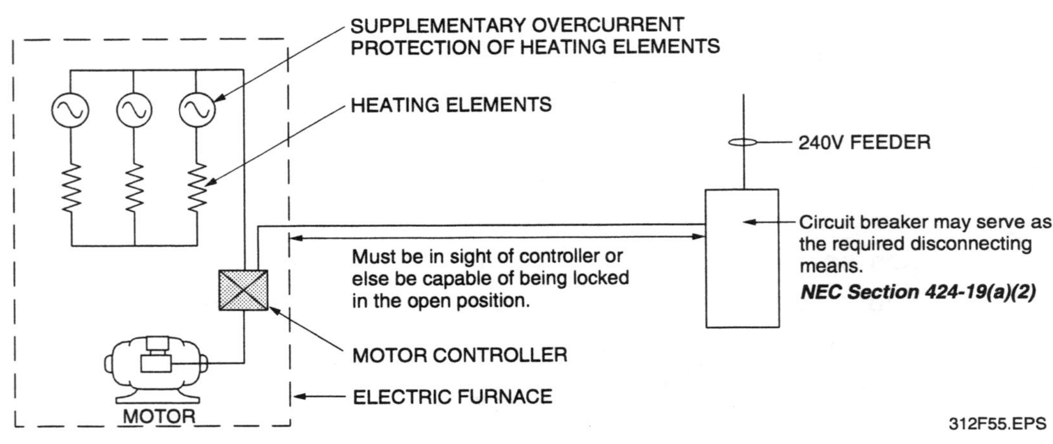

Figure 55. Summary Of NEC Requirements For HVAC Controls

6.2.0 NEC REQUIREMENTS FOR COMPRESSORS

NEC Article 440 contains provisions for motor-driven equipment, and for the branch circuits and controllers for the equipment. It also takes into account the special considerations involved with sealed (hermetic-type) motor compressors in which the motor operates under the cooling effect of the refrigeration.

It must be noted, however, that the rules of ***NEC Article 440*** are in addition to, or are amendments to, the rules given in ***NEC Article 430***. The basic rules of ***NEC Article 430*** also apply to air conditioning and refrigerating equipment, unless exceptions are indicated in ***NEC Article 440***. ***NEC Article 440*** further clarifies the application of NEC rules to this type of equipment.

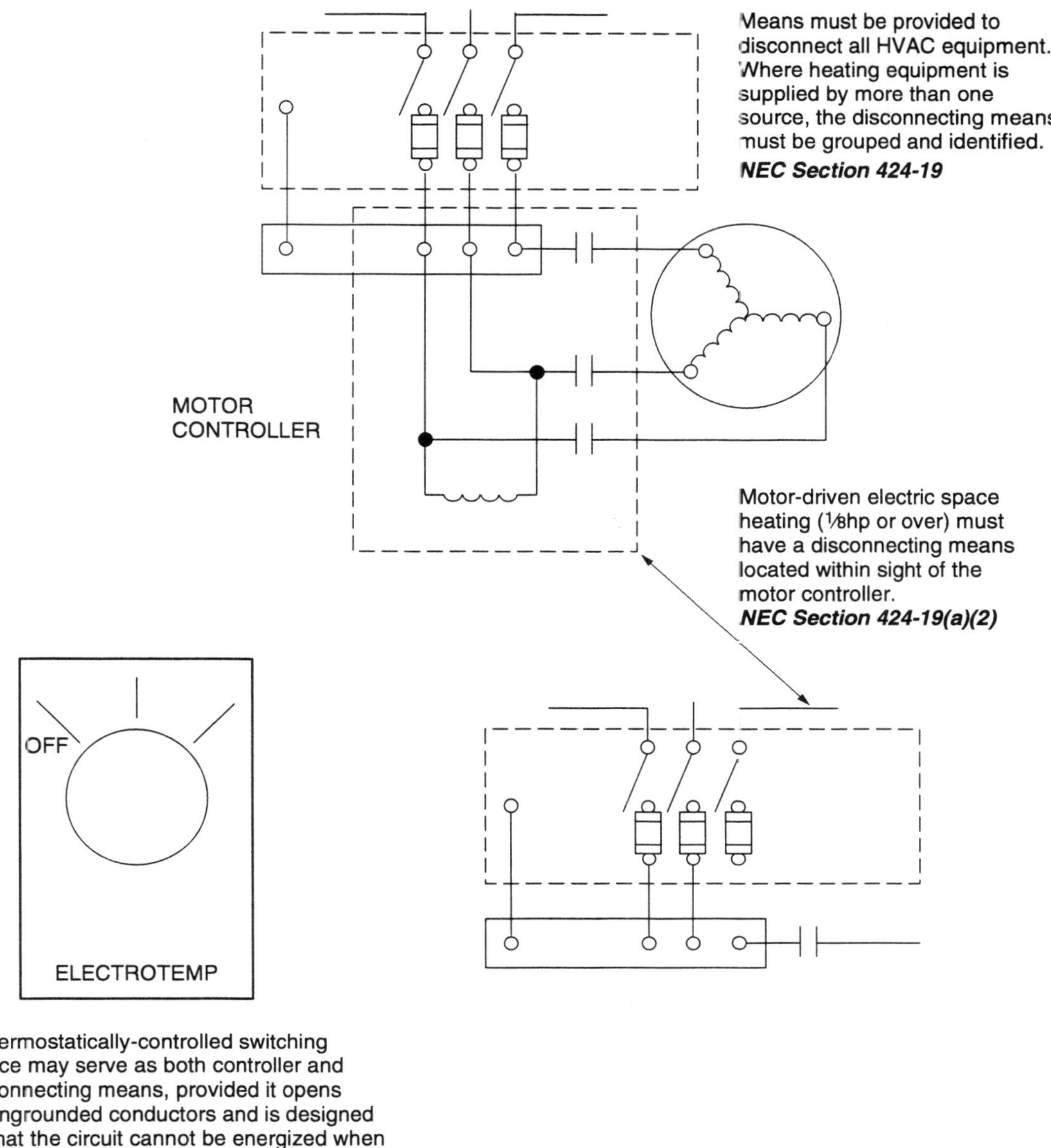

Figure 56. Summary Of NEC Requirements For HVAC Controls

Where refrigeration compressors are driven by conventional motors (not the hermetic type), the motors and controls are subject to *NEC Article 430*, not *NEC Article 440*.

Other NEC Articles that will be covered in this module (besides *NEC Articles 430 and 440*) include:

- *NEC Article 422*, *Appliances*
- *NEC Article 424*, *Space Heating Equipment*

Room air conditioners are covered in *NEC Article 440, Part G*, but must also comply with the rules of *NEC Article 422*.

Household refrigerators and freezers, drinking water coolers, and beverage dispensers are considered by the NEC to be appliances, and their application must comply with *NEC Article 422* and must also satisfy the rules of *NEC Article 440*, because such devices contain sealed motor compressors.

Hermetic refrigerant motor compressors, circuits, controllers, and equipment must also comply with the applicable provisions of the following:

- *NEC Section 460-9*, *Capacitors*
- *NEC Article 470*, *Resistors and Reactors*
- *NEC Articles 500 through 503*, *Hazardous (Classified) Locations*
- *NEC Articles 511, 513 through 517, and 530*, *Special Occupancies*

Table 3 summarizes the requirements of *NEC Article 440*, while *Figures 57* through *60* illustrate many of these requirements.

Application	NEC Regulation	NEC Reference
Marking on hermetic compressors	Hermetic compressors must be provided with a nameplate containing the manufacturer's name, trademark, or symbol, identifying designation, phase, voltage, frequency, rated-load current, locked-rotor current, and the words *thermally protected system*, if appropriate.	**NEC Section 440-4(a)**
Marking on controllers	Controllers serving hermetically-sealed compressors must be marked with the maker's name, trademark, or symbol, identifying designation, voltage, phase, and full-load and locked-rotor currents (or hp rating).	**NEC Section 440-5**
Ampacity and rating	Conductors for hermetically-sealed compressors must be sized according to **NEC Tables 310-16 through 310-19** or calculated in accordance with **NEC Section 310-15**, as applicable.	**NEC Section 440-6**
Highest rated motor	The largest motor is considered to be the motor with the highest rated-load current.	**NEC Section 440-7**
Single machine	The entire HVAC system is considered to be one machine, regardless of the number of motors involved in the system.	**NEC Section 440-8**
Rating and interrupting capacity	The disconnecting means for hermetic compressors must be selected on the basis of the nameplate rated-load current or branch circuit selection current, whichever is greater.	**NEC Section 440-12(a)**
Cord-connected equipment	For cord-connected equipment, an attachment plug and receptacle is permitted to serve as the disconnecting means.	**NEC Section 440-13**

Table 3. Summary Of NEC Requirements For Hermetically-Sealed Compressors (1 Of 2)

Application	NEC Regulation	NEC Reference
Location	A disconnecting means must be located within sight of the equipment. The disconnecting means may be mounted on or within the HVAC equipment.	**NEC Section 440-14**
Short circuit and ground fault protection	Amendments to **NEC Article 240** are provided here for circuits supplying hermetically-sealed compressors against overcurrent due to short circuits and grounds.	**NEC Section 440-21**
Rating of short circuit and ground fault protective device	The rating must not exceed 175% of the compressor rated-load current; if necessary for starting, the device may be increased to a maximum of 225%.	**NEC Section 440-22(a)**
Compressor branch circuit conductors	Branch circuit conductors supplying a single compressor must have an ampacity of not less than 125% of either the motor compressor rated-load current or the branch circuit selection current, whichever is greater.	**NEC Section 440-32**
	Conductors supplying more than one compressor must be sized for the total load plus 25% of the largest motor's full-load amps.	**NEC Section 440-33**
Combination load	Conductors must be sufficiently sized for the other loads plus the required ampacity for the compressor as required in **NEC Section 440-33**.	**NEC Section 440-34**
Multi-motor load equipment	Conductors must be sized to carry the circuit ampacity marked on the equipment as specified in **NEC Section 440-4(b)**.	**NEC Section 440-35**
Controller rating	Must have both a continuous-duty full-load current rating and a locked-rotor current rating not less than the nameplate rated-load current.	**NEC Section 440-41(a)**
Application and selection of controllers	Each motor compressor must be protected against overload and failure to start by one of the means specified in **NEC Section 440-52(a)(1) through (4)**.	**NEC Section 440-52(a)**
Overload relays	Overload relays and other devices for motor overload protection that are not capable of opening short circuits must be protected by a suitable fuse or inverse-time circuit breaker.	**NEC Section 440-53**
Equipment on 15A or 20A branch circuit; time-delay required	Short circuit and ground fault protective devices protecting 15A or 20A branch circuits must have sufficient time delay to permit the motor compressor and other motors to start and accelerate their loads.	**NEC Section 440-54(b)**

Table 3. Summary Of NEC Requirements For Hermetically-Sealed Compressors (2 Of 2)

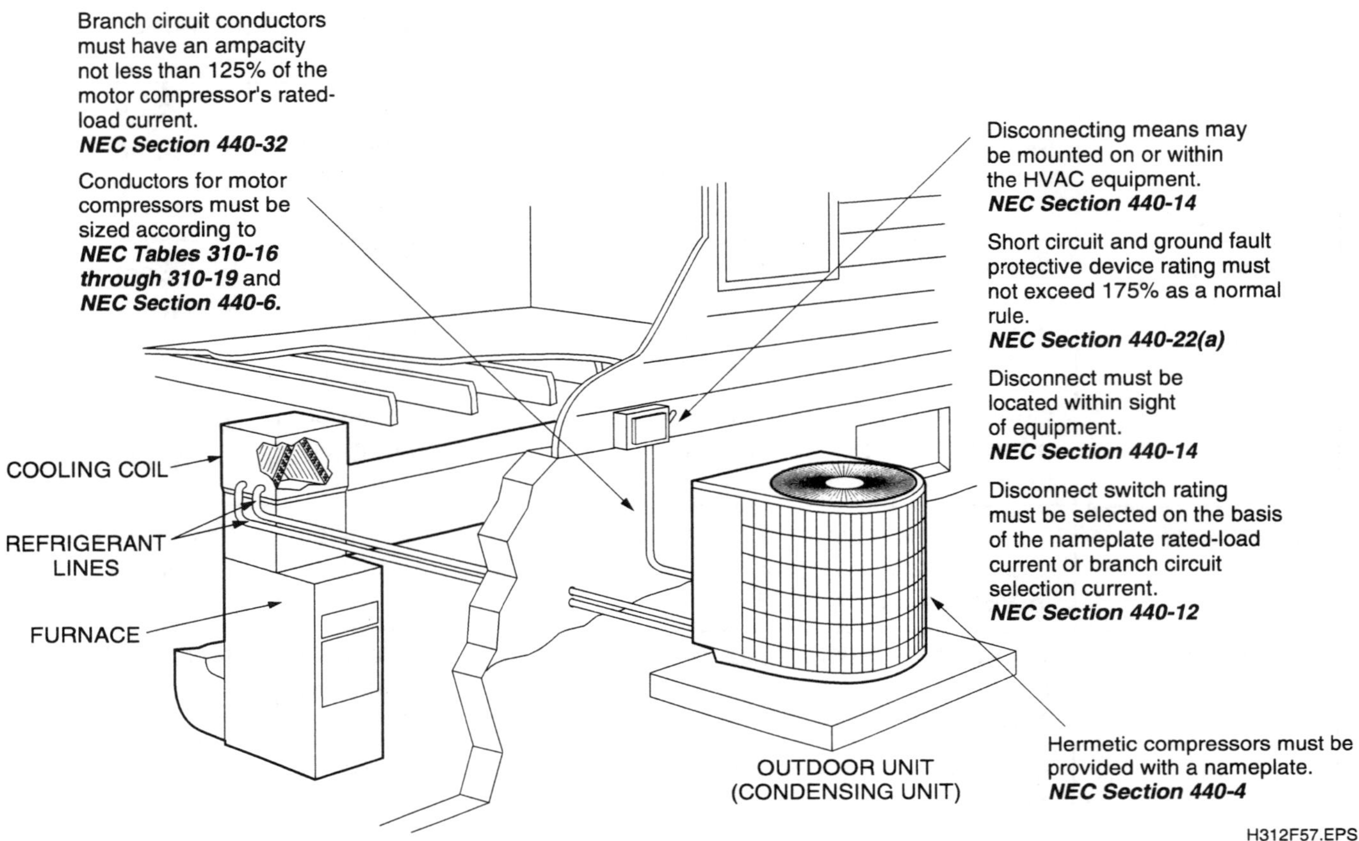

Figure 57. NEC Regulations Governing Motor Compressors

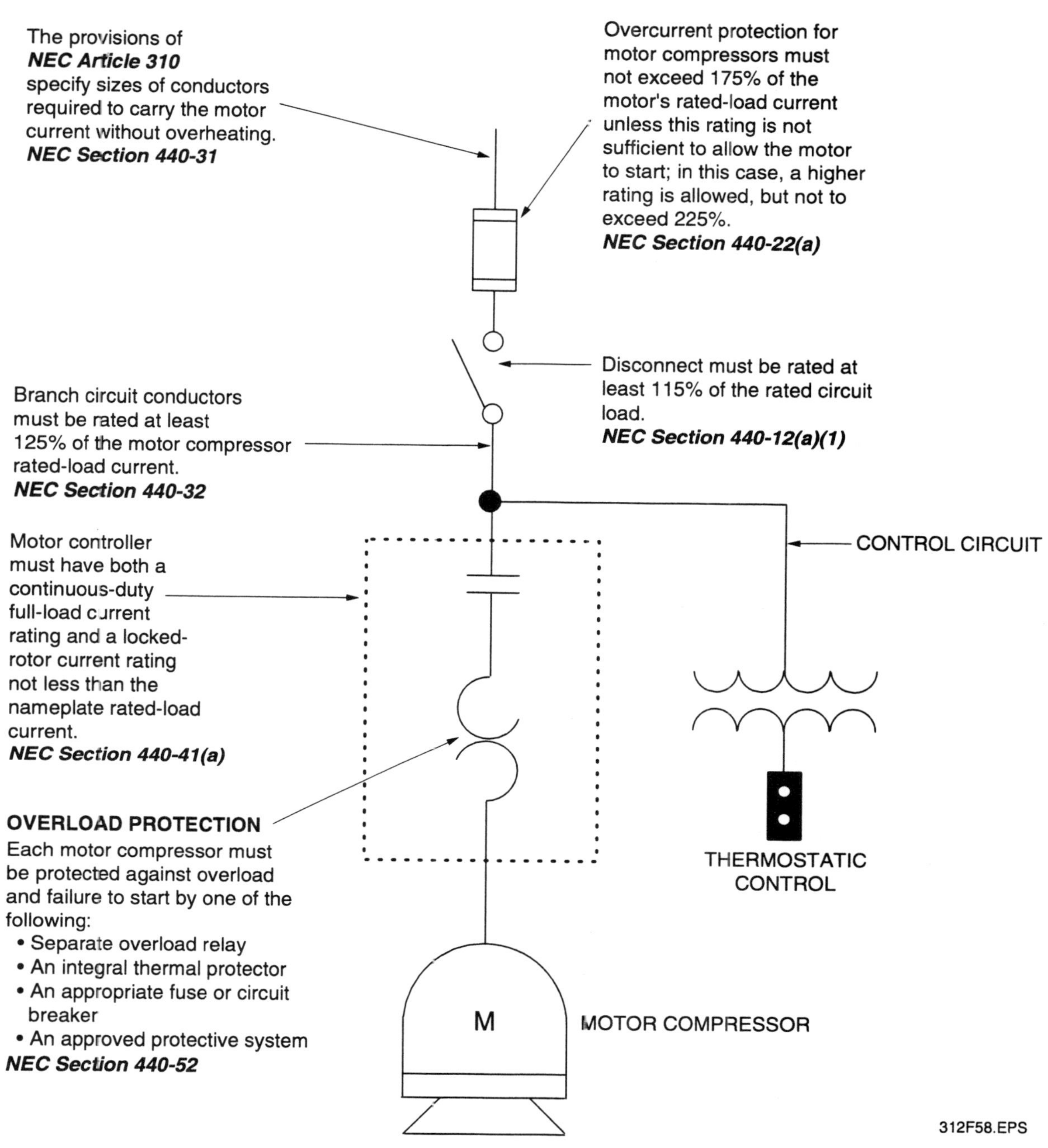

Figure 58. Compressor Branch And Control Circuits

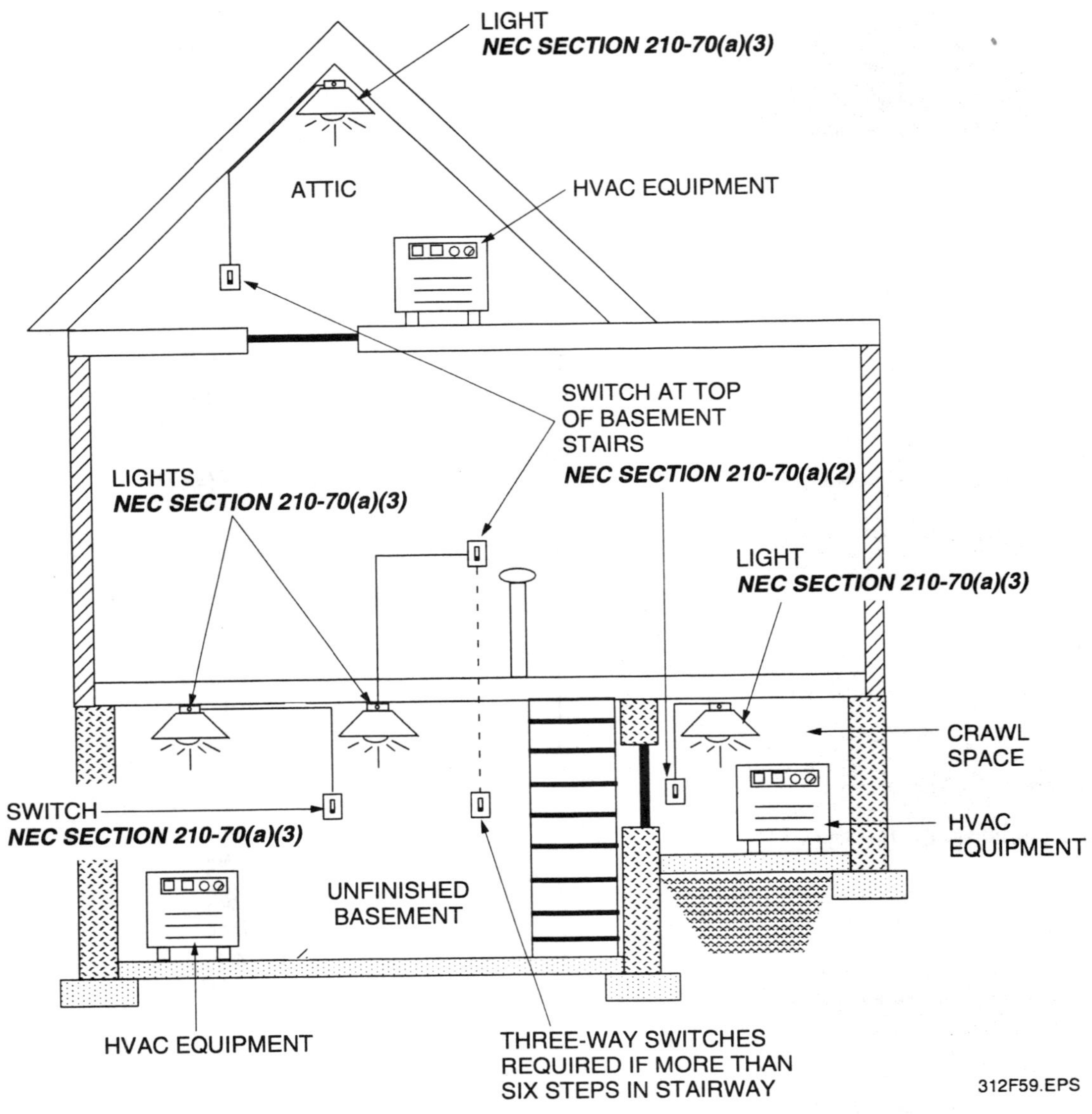

Figure 59. NEC Requirements For Lighting And Switches For HVAC Equipment

6.3.0 NEC REQUIREMENTS FOR ROOM AIR CONDITIONERS

There are millions of room air conditioners in use throughout the United States. Consequently, the NEC deemed it necessary to provide *NEC Article 440, Part G*, beginning with *NEC Section 440-60*, to ensure that such equipment will be installed so as not to provide a hazard to life or property. These NEC requirements apply to electrically-energized room air conditioners that control temperature and humidity. In general, this section of the NEC considers room air conditioners (with or without provisions for heating) to be an alternating current appliance of the air-cooled window, console, or in-wall (through-wall) type that is installed in a conditioned room or space and that incorporates one or more hermetic refrigerant motor compressor(s). Furthermore, this NEC provision covers only equipment rated at 250V or less, single-phase, and such equipment is permitted to be cord- and plug-connected.

ELECTRICAL — TRAINEE TASK MODULE 26312

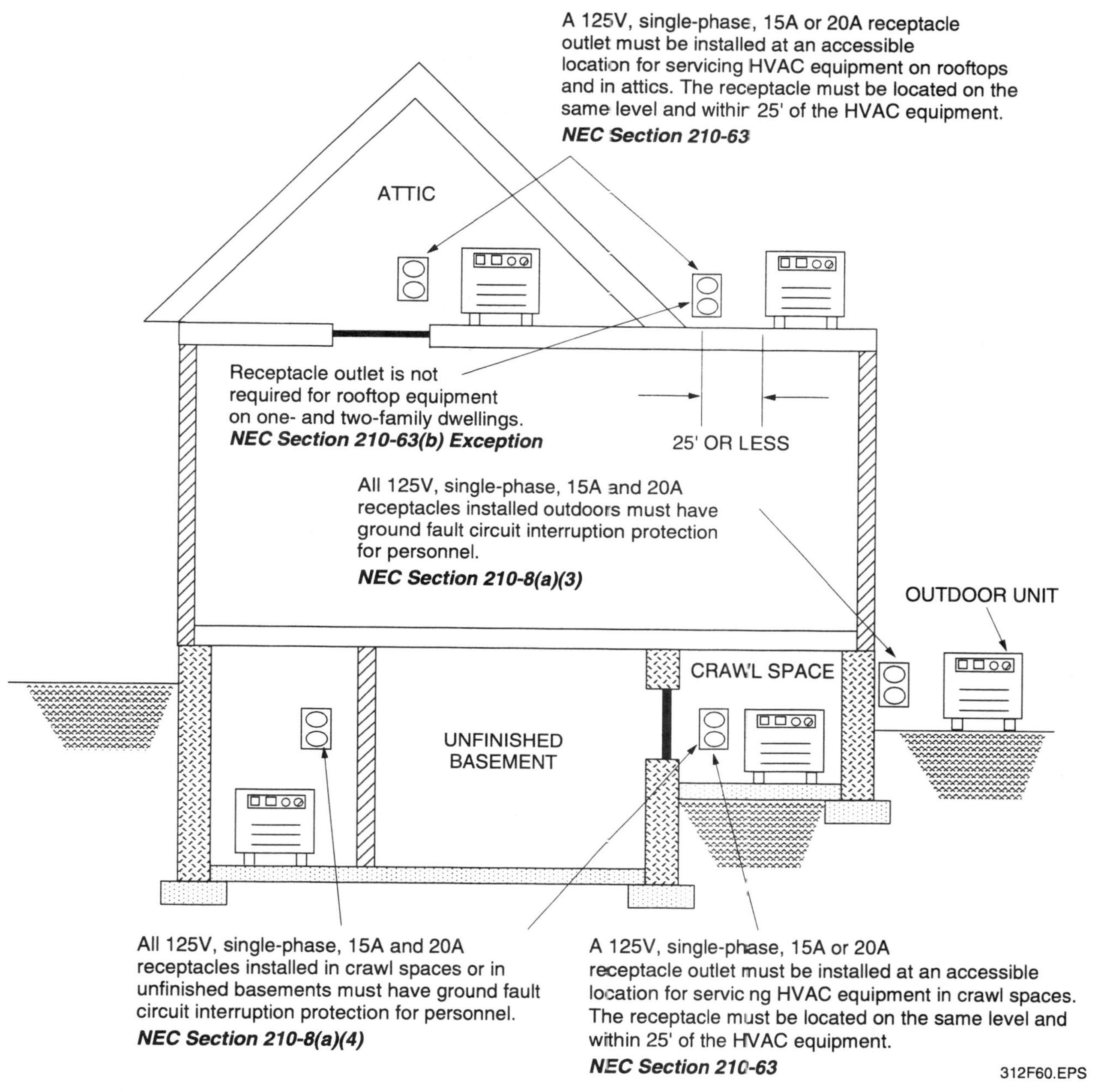

Figure 60. NEC Requirements For Locating 125V Receptacles At HVAC Equipment

Three-phase room air conditioners, or those rated at over 250V, are not covered under *NEC Article 440*. This type of equipment must be directly connected to a wiring method, as described in *NEC Chapter 3*.

The majority of room air conditioners covered under *NEC Article 440* are cord- and plug-connected to receptacle outlets of general-purpose branch circuits. The rating of any such unit must not exceed 80% of the branch circuit rating if connected to a 15A, 20A, or 30A general-purpose branch circuit. The rating of cord- and plug-connected room air conditioners must not exceed 50% of the branch circuit rating if lighting units and other appliances are also supplied.

Figures 61 and *62* depict the NEC application rules for room air conditioners. Note that the attachment plug and receptacle are allowed to serve as the disconnecting means. In some cases, the attachment plug and receptacle may also serve as the controller, or the controller may be a switch that is an integral part of the unit. The required overload protective device may be supplied as an integral part of the appliance and need not be included in the branch circuit calculations.

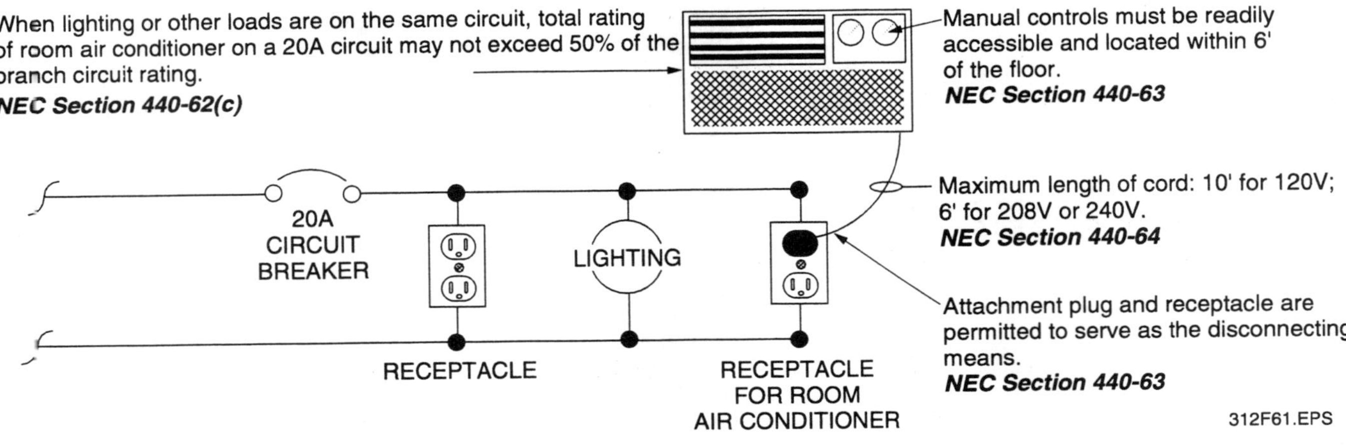

Figure 61. Branch Circuits For Room Air Conditioners

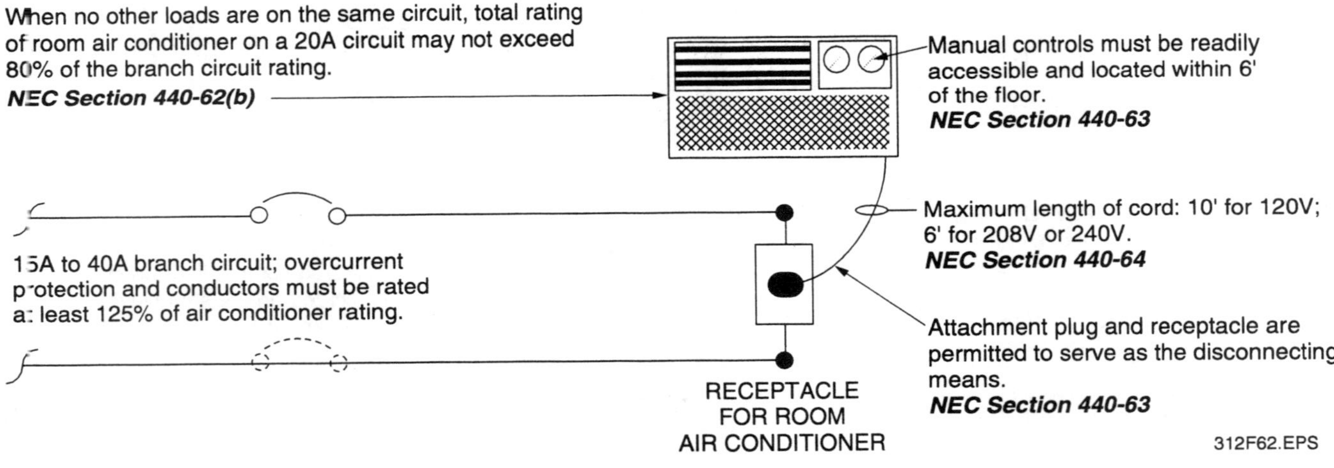

Figure 62. Fixed Air Conditioner Connected To A Branch Circuit

Equipment grounding, as required by **NEC Section 440-61**, may be handled by the grounded receptacle.

7.0.0 TROUBLESHOOTING

Troubleshooting of heating and cooling systems covers a wide range of electrical and mechanical problems, from finding a short circuit in the power supply line, through adjusting a pulley on a motor shaft, to tracing loose connections in complex control circuits. However, in nearly all cases, the electrician can determine the cause of the trouble by using a systematic approach, checking one part of the system at a time in the right order.

Every heating and cooling system problem can be solved, and it is the purpose of this section to show you exactly how to go about solving the more conventional problems in a safe and logical manner.

Table 4 is arranged so that the problem is listed first. The possible causes of the problem are listed in the order in which they should be checked. Finally, solutions to the various problems are given, including step-by-step procedures where necessary.

To better illustrate the use of these solutions to heating and cooling equipment problems, assume that an air conditioner fan or blower motor is operating, but the compressor motor is not. Glance down the left-hand column in the troubleshooting charts until you locate the problem titled *Compressor motor and/or condenser motor will not start, but the blower motor operates*. Begin with the first item under *Probable Cause* which tells you to check the thermostat system switch to make sure it is set to COOL. Finding that the switch is set in the proper position, you continue on to the next item, which is to check the temperature setting. You may find that the temperature setting is above the room temperature so the system is not calling for cooling. Set the thermostat below room temperature and the cooling unit will function.

This example is, of course, very simple, but most of the heating and cooling problems can be just as simple if a systematic approach to troubleshooting is used.

This section provides troubleshooting and repair procedures for common HVAC problems. For more information, also see the module entitled *Motor Controls*. Motor controls are used extensively in HVAC applications, and the information contained in this module can be very helpful to the electrician.

Manufacturers of HVAC equipment also provide troubleshooting and maintenance manuals for their equipment. These manuals can be one of the most helpful tools imaginable for troubleshooting specific HVAC equipment. When unpacking equipment, controls, and other components for the system, always save any manuals or instructions that accompany the items. File them in a safe place so that you and other maintenance personnel can readily find them. Many electricians like to secure these manuals on the inside of a cabinet door within the equipment. This way, they will always be available when needed.

Malfunction	Probable Cause	Corrective Action
Compressor motor and condenser motor will not start, but the blower motor operates.	Check the thermostat system switch to ascertain that it is set to COOL.	Make necessary adjustments to settings.
	Check the thermostat to make sure that it is set below room temperature.	Make necessary adjustments.
	Check the thermostat to see if it is level. Most thermostats must be mounted level; any deviation will ruin their calibration.	Remove cover plate, place a spirit level on top of the thermostat base, loosen the mounting screws, and adjust the base until it is level; then tighten the mounting screws.
	Check all low-voltage connections for tightness.	Tighten.
	Make a low-voltage check with a voltmeter on the condensate float switch; the condensate may not be draining.	The float switch is normally found in the blower unit. Repair or replace.
	Low air flow could be causing the trouble, so check the air filters.	Clean or replace.
	Make a low-voltage check of the antifrost control.	Replace if defective.
	Check all duct connections to the blower unit.	Repair if necessary.
Compressor, condenser, and blower motors will not start.	Check the thermostat system switch setting to ascertain that it is set to COOL.	Adjust as necessary.
	Check the thermostat setting to make sure it is below room temperature.	Adjust as necessary.
	Check the thermostat to make sure it is level.	Correct as required.
	Check all low-voltage connections for tightness.	Tighten.
	Check for a blown fuse or tripped circuit breaker.	Determine the cause of the open circuit and then replace the fuses or reset the circuit breaker.
	Make a voltage check of the low-voltage transformer.	Replace if defective.
	Check the electrical service against minimum requirements (correct voltage, amperage, etc.).	Update as necessary.

Table 4. HVAC Troubleshooting Chart (1 Of 5)

Malfunction	Probable Cause	Corrective Action
Condensing unit cycles too frequently; contactor opens and closes on each cycle and blower motor operates.	Check condensate drain.	Repair or replace.
	Check all low-voltage wiring connections for tightness.	Tighten.
	Check for a defective blower motor.	Test amperage reading while motor is running. Do not confuse the full-load (starting) amperes shown on the motor nameplate with the actual running amperes. The latter should be about 25% less. If the amperage varies considerably from that on the nameplate, check the motor for bad bearings, defective winding insulation, etc.
	Check for low voltage.	Test the circuit for proper voltage.
Inadequate cooling with condensing unit and blower running continuously.	Check all low-voltage connections (control wiring) against the wiring diagram furnished with the system.	Correct if necessary, then call in a qualified HVAC technician to check for leaks in the refrigerant lines.
	Check all joints in the supply and return ductwork.	Make all joints tight.
	The equipment could be undersized. Check heat gain calculations against the output of the unit.	Correct structural deficiencies with insulation, awnings, etc., or install properly sized equipment.
Condensing unit cycles, but the blower motor does not run.	Check all low-voltage connections against the wiring diagram furnished with the system.	Correct if necessary.
	Check all low-voltage connections for tightness.	Tighten.
	Make a voltage check of the blower relay.	Replace if necessary.
	Make electrical and mechanical checks on the blower motor. Check for correct voltage at motor terminals. Mechanical problems could be bad bearings or a loose blower wheel. Bearing trouble can be detected by turning the blower wheel by hand (with the current off) and checking for excessive wear, roughness, or seizure.	Repair or replace defective components.

Table 4. HVAC Troubleshooting Chart (2 Of 5)

Malfunction	Probable Cause	Corrective Action
Unit shows continuous short cycling of blower coil unit and provides insufficient cooling.	Make electrical and mechanical checks.	Repair or replace motor if necessary.
Unit is sweating at the blower coil output or at the electric duct heater outlet.	Check to see if the insulation is installed properly.	Insulate properly.
	Inspect the joints at the duct heater or blower coil receiving collar.	Seal properly.
Thermostat calls for heat, but the blower motor does not operate.	Check all low-voltage connections against the wiring diagram furnished with the system.	Correct if necessary.
	Check all low-voltage connections for tightness.	Tighten.
	Check all low-voltage wiring against the unit nameplate.	Correct if necessary.
	Check all line-voltage connections for tightness.	Tighten.
	Check for blown fuses or a tripped circuit breaker in the line.	Determine the reason for the open circuit and replace the fuses or reset the circuit breaker.
	Check the low-voltage transformer.	Replace if defective.
	Make a low-voltage check of the magnetic relay.	Repair or replace if necessary.
	Make electrical and mechanical checks on the blower motor.	Repair or replace the motor if defective.
Thermostat calls for heat; blower motor operates, but it delivers cold air.	Make a visual and electrical check on the heating elements.	If not operating, continue on to the next check.
	Make an electrical check of the heater limit switch; begin by disconnecting all power to the unit, then use an ohmmeter to check for continuity between the two terminals of the switch.	If the limit switch is open, repair or replace.
	Make an electrical check of the time-delay relay. Most are rated at 24V and have one set of normally open auxiliary contacts for pilot duty.	If the relay heater coil is open or grounded, repair or replace.
	Make an electrical check of the magnetic relay.	Repair or replace if defective.
	Check the electric service entrance and related circuits against the minimum recommendations.	Upgrade if necessary.

Table 4. HVAC Troubleshooting Chart (3 Of 5)

Malfunction	Probable Cause	Corrective Action
Thermostat calls for heat and blower motor operates continuously; system delivers warm air, but the thermostat is not satisfied.	Check all joints in the ductwork for air leaks.	Make all defective joints tight.
	Check the blower outlets for tightness.	Seal where necessary.
	Make a visual and electrical check of the electric heating element.	Repair or replace if necessary.
	Make an electrical check of the heater limit switch as described previously.	Repair or replace.
	Make an electrical check of the heater limit switch.	Repair or replace.
	Check the heating element against the blower unit for the possibility of a mismatch.	Replace if incompatible.
	Check your heat loss calculations. The equipment could be undersized.	If so, correct structural deficiencies by installing more insulation, storm windows and doors, etc., or install properly sized equipment.
Blower unit operates properly and delivers air, but the thermostat is not satisfied.	Check all joints in the ductwork for air leaks.	Repair if necessary.
	Check the air filter.	Clean or replace if necessary. Also check the number of air outlets for adequacy and make sure they are balanced.
	Check for undersized equipment.	Correct structural deficiencies or install properly sized equipment.
Electric heater cycles on limit switches, but the blower motor does not operate.	Make an electrical check of the magnetic relay.	Repair or replace if defective.
	Make electrical and mechanical checks on the blower motor.	Repair or replace if defective.
	Check the line connections against the wiring diagram furnished with the system.	Make any necessary changes.
There is excessive air noise at the terminator.	Duct or outlet undersized; air velocity too great.	Increase size of duct and/or outlet.
	Make an external static pressure check.	Correct restrictions in system if necessary.
	Check for a properly balanced system.	Make corrections if necessary.

Table 4. HVAC Troubleshooting Chart (4 Of 5)

Malfunction	Probable Cause	Corrective Action
There is excessive noise at the return air grille.	Check the return duct to make sure it has a 90° bend.	Correct if necessary.
	Make a visual check of the blower unit to ascertain that all shipping blocks and angles have been removed.	Remove if necessary.
	Check the blower motor assembly suspension and fasteners.	Tighten if necessary.
There is excessive vibration at the blower unit.	Visually check for vibration isolators (which isolate the blower coil from the structure).	If missing, install as recommended by the manufacturer.
	Visually check to ascertain that all shipping blocks and angles have been removed from the blower unit.	Remove if necessary.
	Check the blower motor assembly suspension and fasteners.	Tighten if necessary.

Table 4. HVAC Troubleshooting Chart (5 Of 5)

SUMMARY

This module covered the basic theory behind heating, ventilation, and air conditioning (HVAC) systems, as well as the NEC requirements for the installation of this equipment. A complete understanding of **NEC Articles 422, 424, 430, and 440** is essential to the proper installation of these systems.

References

For advanced study of topics covered in this Task Module, the following books are suggested:

American Electricians' Handbook, Latest Edition, McGraw-Hill, New York, NY.

National Electrical Code Handbook, Latest Edition, National Fire Protection Association, Quincy, MA.

1. The condenser in a refrigeration system _______.

   a. converts the liquid to a gas
   b. transfers the heat in the refrigerant to the surrounding air or to a water supply
   c. sends a liquid-vapor mixture to the compressor
   d. reduces the amount of refrigerant in the system

2. Under normal atmospheric pressure, water boils at _______.

   a. 110°F
   b. 120°F
   c. 212°F
   d. 240°F

3. Heat content is measured in _______.

   a. degrees
   b. psig
   c. in. Hg
   d. Btu's

4. Which of the following is *not* a form of heat transfer?

   a. Radiation
   b. Compression
   c. Convection
   d. Conduction

5. The refrigerant entering the compressor is in the form of a _______.

   a. warm liquid
   b. hot, high-pressure liquid
   c. hot, low-pressure vapor
   d. cold, low-pressure vapor

6. The liquid control valve in a refrigeration system is known as a(n) _______.

   a. expansion valve
   b. LCV
   c. four-way valve
   d. oil-recovery valve

7. Which of these is *not* a common type of compressor?

   a. Rotary
   b. Screw
   c. Evaporative
   d. Scroll

8. A heat pump uses a(n) _____ valve to direct the refrigerant to the appropriate coil for either heating or cooling.

   a. service
   b. four-way
   c. expansion
   d. check

9. A 60,000 Btuh furnace will draw approximately _____ at 240V.

   a. 25A
   b. 40A
   c. 74A
   d. 83A

10. Which of the following contains provisions for fixed electric space heating equipment?
    a. *NEC Article 422*
    b. *NEC Article 424*
    c. *NEC Article 430*
    d. *NEC Article 440*

11. If you are installing a heating cable that draws 18A, you would connect the thermostat with _____ AWG wire.

    a. 10
    b. 8
    c. 6
    d. 4

12. A _____ is a device that uses the difference in metals to provide electron flow.

    a. limit control
    b. thermostat
    c. thermocouple
    d. transformer

13. When installing a disconnecting means for an HVAC system containing a motor controller, the disconnect must ______.
    a.   be within 60' of the motor controller
    b.   be within 75' of the motor and controller
    c.   not be rated more than 80% of the motor's FLA
    d.   be within sight of the motor and controller

14. Overload protection for motor-driven hermetic compressors may *not* exceed ______ current rating.
    a.   150% of the locked-rotor
    b.   175% of the rated-load
    c.   200% of the rated-load
    d.   150% of the rated-load

15. Which of the following contains provisions for hermetic motor-driven equipment?
    a.   ***NEC Article 422***
    b.   ***NEC Article 424***
    c.   ***NEC Article 430***
    d.   ***NEC Article 440***

Answer	**Section Reference**
1. b	1.4.0
2. c	2.1.1
3. d	2.1.2
4. b	2.2.0
5. d	3.2.1
6. a	3.2.2
7. c	3.3.0
8. b	3.10.0
9. c	4.1.0
10. b	4.2.0
11. b	4.3.1/Tab. 2
12. c	5.5.0
13. d	6.1.0
14. b	6.2.0/Fig. 58
15. d	6.2.0

Hazardous Locations

Module 26313

Electrical Trainee Task Module 26313

HAZARDOUS LOCATIONS

NATIONAL
CENTER FOR
CONSTRUCTION
EDUCATION AND
RESEARCH

OBJECTIVES

Upon completion of this module, the trainee will be able to:

1. Identify the various classifications of hazardous locations.
2. Select and install branch circuits and feeders in specific hazardous locations.
3. Select seals and drains for specific hazardous locations.
4. Select wiring methods for Class I, Class II, and Class III hazardous locations.
5. Follow NEC requirements for installing explosionproof fittings in specific hazardous locations.

Prerequisites

Successful completion of the following Task Modules is recommended before beginning study of this Task Module: Core Curricula; Electrical Level 1; Electrical Level 2; Electrical Level 3, Modules 26301 through 26312.

Required Trainee Materials

1. Trainee Task Module
2. Appropriate Personal Protective Equipment
3. Copy of the latest edition of the *National Electrical Code*

Note: The designations "National Electrical Code," "NE Code," and "NEC," where used in this document, refer to the National Electrical Code®, which is a registered trademark of the National Fire Protection Association, Quincy, MA. *All National Electrical Code (NEC) references in this module refer to the 1999 edition of the NEC.*

This course map shows all of the modules in the third level of the Electrical curricula. The suggested training order begins at the bottom and proceeds up. Skill levels increase as a trainee advances on the course map. The training order may be adjusted by the local Training Program Sponsor.

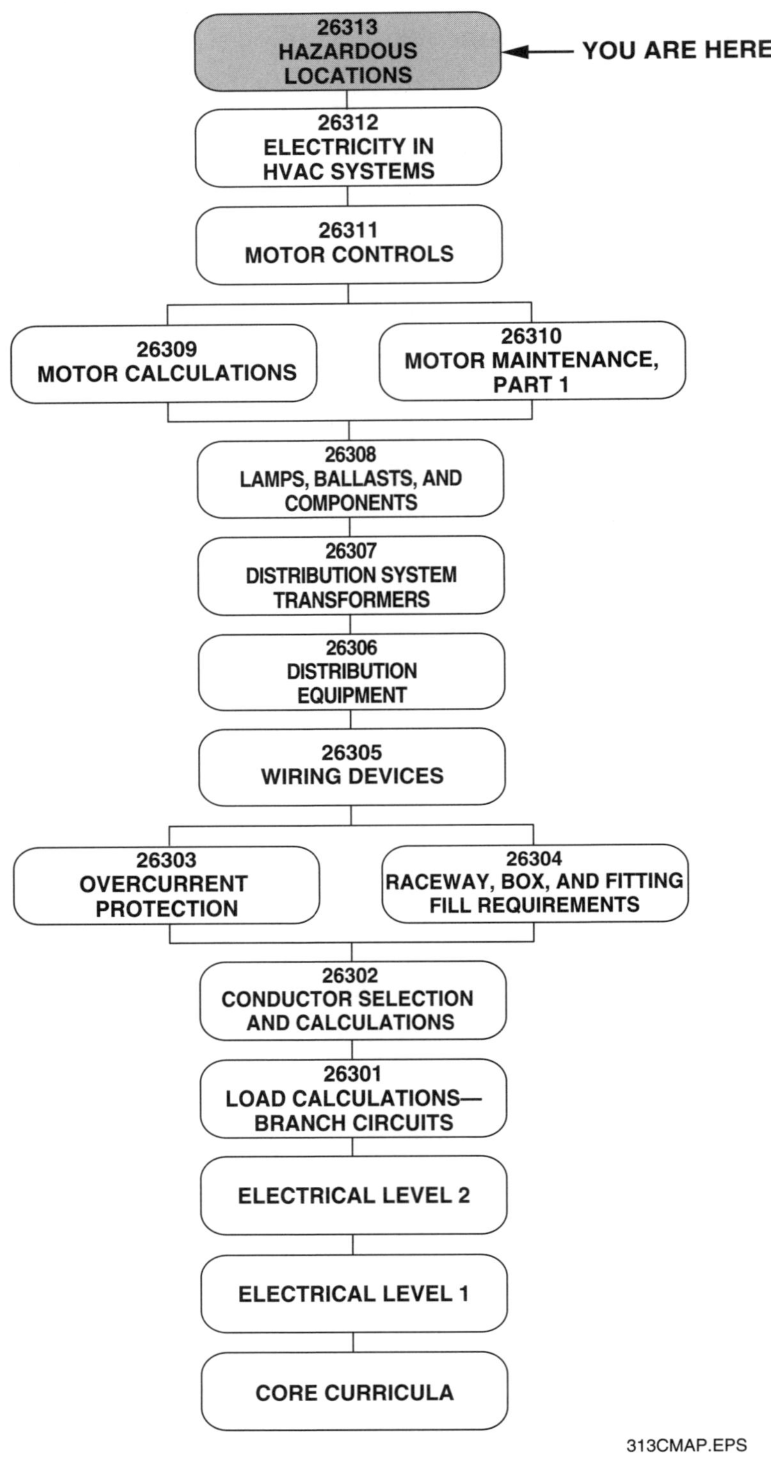

ELECTRICAL — TRAINEE TASK MODULE 26313

TABLE OF CONTENTS

Trade Terms Introduced in This Module

Approved: Acceptable to the authority having jurisdiction.

Conduit: A tubular raceway such as electrical metallic tubing (EMT); rigid metal conduit, rigid nonmetallic conduit, etc.

Conduit body: A separate portion of a conduit or tubing system that provides access through removable covers to the interior of the system at a junction of two or more sections of the system or at a terminal point of the system.

Equipment: A general term including material, fittings, devices, appliances, fixtures, apparatus, and the like used as a part of (or in connection with) an electrical installation.

Explosionproof: Designed and constructed to withstand an internal explosion without creating an external explosion or fire.

Explosionproof apparatus: Apparatus enclosed in a case that is capable of withstanding an explosion of a specified gas or vapor that may occur within it; also capable of preventing the ignition of a specified gas or vapor surrounding the enclosure by sparks, flashes, or explosion of the gas or vapor within; which operates at such an external temperature that a surrounding flammable atmosphere will not be ignited thereby.

Hazardous (classified) location: A location in which ignitable vapors, dust, or fibers may cause a fire or explosion.

Sealing compound: The material poured into an electrical fitting to seal and minimize the passage of vapors.

Seal-off fittings: Fittings required in conduit systems to prevent the passage of gases, vapors, or flames from one portion of the electrical installation to another through the conduit. Also referred to as *seals*.

1.0.0 INTRODUCTION

NEC Articles 500 through 504 cover the requirements of electrical **equipment** and wiring for all voltages in locations where fire or explosion hazards may exist due to flammable gases or vapor, flammable liquids, combustible dust, or ignitable fibers or other flying materials. Locations are classified depending on the properties of the flammable vapors, liquids, gases, or combustible dusts or fibers that may be present, as well as the likelihood that a flammable or combustible concentration or quantity is present.

Any area in which the atmosphere or a material in the area is such that the arcing of operating electrical contacts, components, and equipment may cause an explosion or fire is considered a **hazardous (classified) location**. In all such cases, **explosionproof apparatus**, raceways, and fittings are used to provide an **explosionproof** wiring system.

The NEC divides hazardous materials into three classes (Class I, Class II, and Class III), with two divisions for each class (Division 1 and Division 2). Of these, Class I, Division 1 represents the most hazardous location. These classes have been established on the basis of the explosive character of the atmosphere for the testing and approval of equipment for use in each class. However, it must be understood that considerable skill and judgment must be applied when deciding to what degree an area contains hazardous concentrations of vapors, combustible dusts, or easily ignitable fibers and flying materials. Furthermore, many factors, such as temperature, barometric pressure, quantity of release, humidity, ventilation, distance from the vapor source, etc. must be considered. When information on all factors concerned is properly evaluated, a consistent classification for the selection and location of electrical equipment can be developed.

Appendix A lists all of the flammable gases and combustible dusts which have been classified by the National Fire Protection Association (NFPA), along with their ignition temperatures. This information will prove invaluable when various atmospheres are encountered in your career as an electrician.

NEC Article 505 allows classification and application to international standards, but it will be applied only under engineering supervision. In addition, few American-made products are listed for international application. As a result, this module will not cover **NEC Article 505** in any detail.

1.1.0 CLASS I LOCATIONS

Class I atmospheric hazards are divided into Divisions 1 and 2, and also into four groups (A, B, C, and D). Group A represents the most hazardous location.

Those locations in which flammable gases or vapors may be present in the air in quantities sufficient to produce explosive or ignitable mixtures are identified as Class I locations. If these gases or vapors are present during normal operation, frequent repair or maintenance operations, or where breakdown or faulty operation of process equipment might also cause simultaneous failure of electrical equipment, the area is designated as Class I, Division 1. Examples of such locations are interiors of paint spray booths where volatile, flammable solvents are used, inadequately-ventilated pump rooms where flammable gas is pumped, anesthetizing locations of hospitals (to a height of 5' above floor level), and drying rooms for the evaporation of flammable solvents (see *Figure 1*).

Class I, Division 2 covers locations in which volatile flammable gases, vapors, or liquids are handled either in a closed system or confined within suitable enclosures, or where hazardous concentrations are normally prevented by positive mechanical ventilation. Areas adjacent to Division 1 locations, into which gases might occasionally flow, would also belong in Division 2.

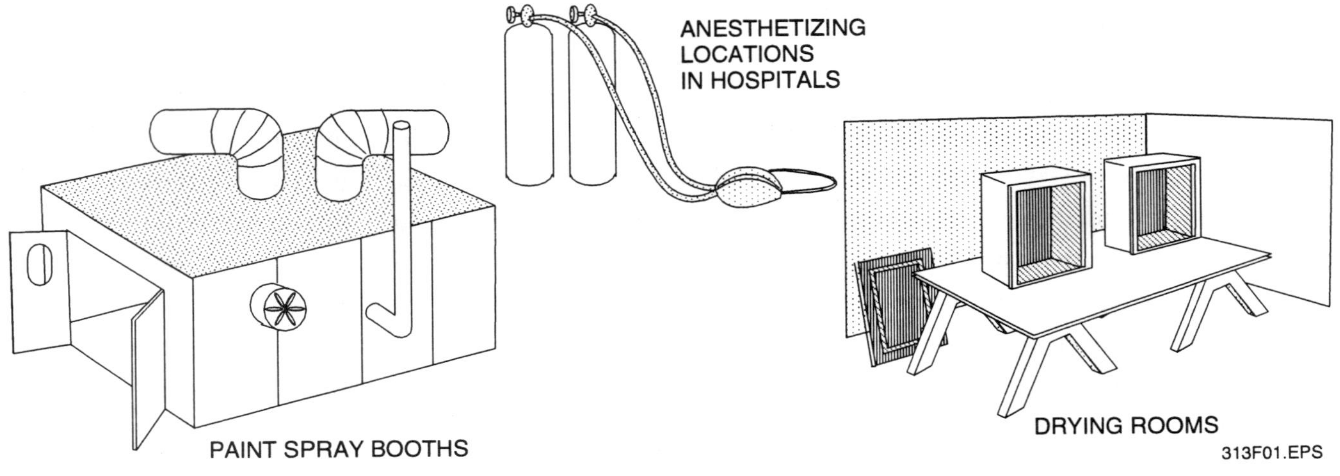

Figure 1. Typical NEC Class I Locations

1.2.0   CLASS II LOCATIONS

Class II locations are those that are hazardous because of the presence of combustible dust. Class II, Division 1 locations are areas in which combustible dust may be present in the air under normal operating conditions in quantities sufficient to produce explosive or ignitable mixtures; examples are working areas of grain-handling and storage plants and rooms containing grinders or pulverizers (*Figure 2*). Class II, Division 2 locations are areas in which dangerous concentrations of suspended dust are not likely, but where dust might accumulate.

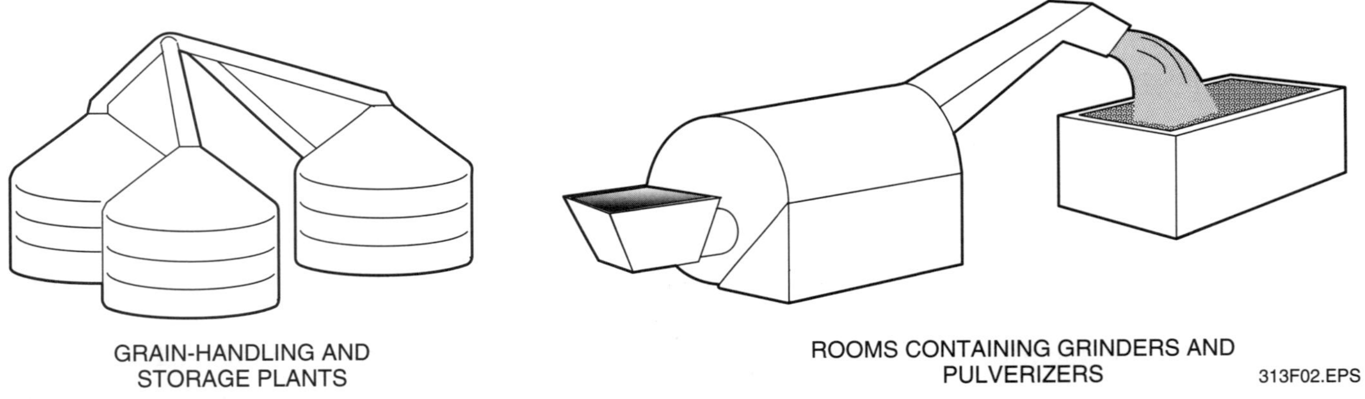

Figure 2. Typical NEC Class II Locations

Besides the two divisions, Class II atmospheric hazards also cover three groups of combustible dusts (E, F, and G). The groupings are based on the resistivity of the dust. Group E is always Division 1. Groups F and G may be either Division 1 or 2, depending on their resistivity. Since the NEC is considered the definitive classification tool and contains explanatory data about hazardous atmospheres, refer to **NEC Section 500-5** for exact definitions of Class II, Divisions 1 and 2.

1.3.0 CLASS III LOCATIONS

These locations are those areas that are hazardous because of the presence of easily ignitable fibers or other flying materials, but such materials are not likely to be in suspension in the air in quantities sufficient to produce ignitable mixtures. Such locations usually include certain areas of rayon, cotton, and textile mills, clothing manufacturing plants, and woodworking plants (*Figure 3*).

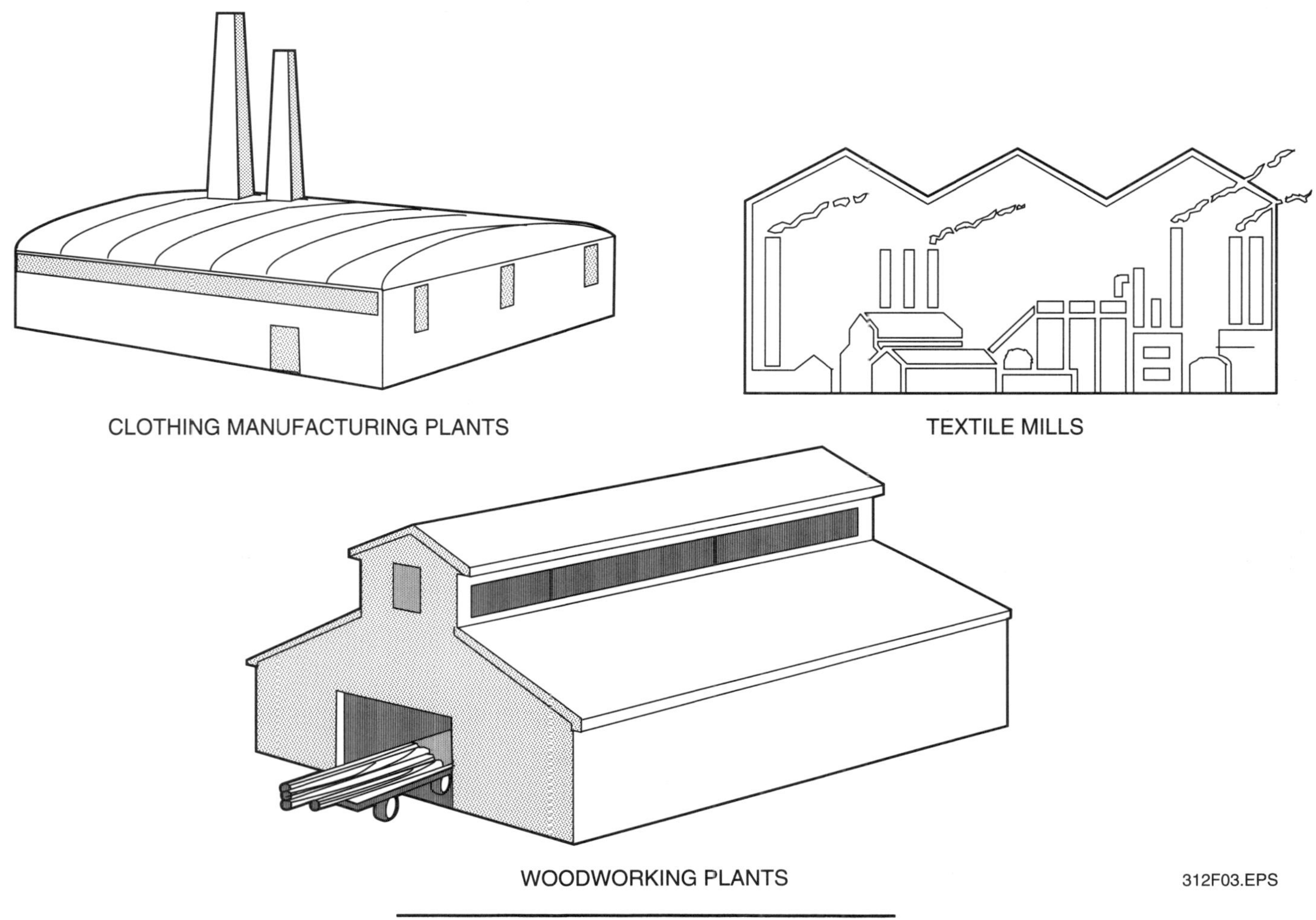

Figure 3. Typical NEC Class III Locations

1.4.0 APPLICATIONS

The application rules for all three classes are summarized in *Table 1*. For a more complete listing of flammable liquids, gases, and solids, see *Classification of Gases, Vapors, and Dusts for Electrical Equipment in Hazardous (Classified) Locations*, National Fire Protection Association Publication No. 497M.

Class	Division	Group	Typical Atmosphere/Ignition Temps.	Devices Covered	Temperature Measured	Limiting Value
I	1	A	Acetylene (305C, 581F)	All electrical devices and wiring	Maximum external temperature in 40C ambient	See *NEC Section 500-5*
Gases, vapors	Normally hazardous	B	1,3-Butadiene (420C, 788F)			
			Ethylene Oxide (429C, 804F)			
			Hydrogen (520C, 968F)			
			Manufactured Gas (containing more than 30% hydrogen by volume)			
			Propylene Oxide (449C, 840F)			
		C	Acetaldehyde (175C, 347F)			
			Diethyl Ether (160C, 320F)			
			Ethylene (450C, 842F)			
			Unsymmetrical Dimethyl Hydrazine (UDMH) (249C, 480F)			
		D	Acetone (465C, 869F)			
			Acrylonitrile (481C, 898F)			
			Ammonia (498C, 928F)			
			Benzene (498C, 928F)			
			Butane (288C, 550F)			
			1-Butanol (343C, 650F)			
			2-Butanol (405C, 761F)			
			n-Butyl Acetate (421C, 790F)			
			Cyclopropane (503C, 938F)			
			Ethane (472C, 882F)			
			Ethanol (363C, 685F)			
			Ethyl Acetate (427C, 800F)			
			Ethylene Dichloride (413C, 775F)			
			Gasoline (280-471C, 536-880F)			
			Heptane (204C, 399F)			
			Hexane (225C, 437F)			
			Isoamyl Alcohol (350C, 662F)			
			Isoprene (220C, 428F)			
			Methane (630C, 999F)			
			Methanol (385C, 725F)			
			Methyl Ethyl Ketone (404C, 759F)			
			Methyl Isobutyl Ketone (449C, 840F)			
			2-Methyl-1-Propanol (416C, 780F)			
			2-Methyl-2-Propanol (478C, 892F)			
			Naphtha (petroleum) (288C, 550F)			
			Octane (206C, 403F)			
			Pentane (243C, 470F)			
			1-Pentanol (300C, 572F)			

Table 1. Summary Of Hazardous Atmospheres (1 Of 2)

Class	Division	Group	Typical Atmosphere/Ignition Temps.	Devices Covered	Temperature Measured	Limiting Value
			Propane (450C, 842F)			
			1-Propanol (413C, 775F)			
			2-Propanol (399C, 750F)			
			Propylene (455C, 851F)			
			Styrene (490C, 914F)			
			Toluene (480C, 896F)			
			Vinyl Acetate (402C, 756F)			
			Vinyl Chloride (472C, 882F)			
			Xylenes (464-529C, 867-984F)			
I	2	A	Same as Division 1	Lamps, resistors, coils, etc., other than arcing devices. (see Div. 1)	Max. internal or external temp. not to exceed the ignition temperature in degrees Celsius (°C) of the gas or vapor involved	See *NEC Section 500-5*
Gases, vapors	Not normally hazardous	B	Same as Division 1			
		C	Same as Division 1			
		D	Same as Division 1			
II Combustible dusts	1 Normally hazardous	E	Atmospheres containing combustible metal dusts regardless of resistivity, or other combustible dusts of similarly hazardous characteristics having resistivity of less than 10^2 ohm-centimeter	Devices not subject to overloads (switches, meters).	Max. external temp. in 40C ambient with a dust blanket	Shall be less than ignition temperature of dust but not more than: No overload: E—200C (392F) F—200C (392F) G—165C (329F) Possible overload in operation: Normal E—200C (392F) F—150C (302F) G—120C (248F) Abnormal E—200C (392F) F—200C (392F) G—165C (329F)
		F	Atmospheres containing carbonaceous dusts having resistivity between 10^2 and 10^8 ohm-centimeter			
		G	Atmospheres containing combustible dusts having resistivity of 10^8 ohm-centimeter or greater			
	2	F	Atmospheres containing carbonaceous dusts having resistivity of 10^5 ohm-centimeter or greater	Lighting fixtures	Max. external temp under conditions of use	Same as Division 1
	Not normally hazardous					
		G	Same as Division 1			

Table 1. Summary Of Hazardous Atmospheres (2 Of 2)

Once the class of an area is determined, the conditions under which the hazardous material may be present determines the division. In Class I and Class II, Division 1 locations, the hazardous gas or dust may be present in the air under normal operating conditions in dangerous concentrations. In Division 2 locations, the hazardous material is not normally in the air, but it might be released if there is an accident or if there is faulty operation of equipment.

Tables 2 through *6* provide a summary of the various classes of hazardous locations as defined by the NEC.

Components	Characteristics	NEC Reference
Boxes, fittings	Explosionproof	*NEC Section 501-4(a)*
Seal-offs	Approved for purpose	*NEC Section 501-5(a)*
Wiring methods	Rigid metal conduit, steel intermediate metal conduit, Type MI cable and, under certain conditions, ITC and MC cable	*NEC Section 501-4(a)(1)*
Receptacles	Explosionproof	*NEC Section 501-12*
Lighting fixtures	Explosionproof	*NEC Section 501-9(a)*
Panelboards	Explosionproof	*NEC Section 501-6(a)*
Circuit breakers	Class I enclosure	*NEC Section 501-6(a)*
Fuses	Class I enclosure	*NEC Section 501-6(a)*
Switches	Class I enclosure	*NEC Section 501-6(a)*
Motors	Class I, totally-enclosed or submerged	*NEC Section 501-8(a)*
Liquid-filled transformers	Installed in approved vault	*NEC Section 501-2(a)*
Dry-type transformers	Class I, Division 1 enclosure	*NEC Section 501-7(a)*
Utilization equipment	Class I, Division 1	*NEC Section 501-10(a)*
Flexible connections	Class I, explosionproof	*NEC Section 501-4(a)(2)*
Portable lamps	Explosionproof	*NEC Section 501-9(a)*
Generators	Class I, totally enclosed or submerged	*NEC Section 501-8(a)*
Alarm systems	Class I, Division 1	*NEC Section 501-14(a)*

Table 2. Application Rules For Class I, Division 1

ELECTRICAL — TRAINEE TASK MODULE 26313

Components	Characteristics	NEC Reference
Boxes, fittings	Do not have to be explosionproof unless current interrupting contacts are exposed	*NEC Section 501-4(b)*
Seal-offs	Approved for purpose	*NEC Section 501-5(c)*
Wiring methods	Rigid metal conduit, steel intermediate metal conduit, or Types MI, MC, MV, TC, ITC, or PLTC cables, or enclosed gasketed busways or wireways	*NEC Section 501-4(b)*
Receptacles	Explosionproof	*NEC Section 501-12*
Lighting fixtures	Protected from physical damage	*NEC Section 501-9(b)(2)*
Panelboards	General purpose with exceptions	*NEC Section 501-6(b)*
Circuit breakers	Class I enclosure	*NEC Section 501-6(b)(1)*
Fuses	Class I enclosure	*NEC Section 501-6(b)(3)*
Switches	Class I enclosure	*NEC Section 501-6(b)(2)*
Motors	General purpose unless motor has sliding contacts, switching contacts, or integral resistance devices; if so, use Class I	*NEC Section 501-8(b)*
Motor controls	Class I, Division 1	*NEC Section 501-10(b)(2)*
Liquid-filled transformers	General purpose	*NEC Section 501-2(b)*
Dry-type transformers	Class I, general purpose except switching mechanism Division 1 enclosures	*NEC Section 501-7(b)*
Utilization equipment	Class I, Division 1	*NEC Section 501-10(b)*
Flexible connections	Class I, explosionproof	*NEC Section 501-4(b)*
Portable lamps	Explosionproof	*NEC Section 501-9(b)(1)*
Generators	Class I, totally enclosed or submerged	*NEC Section 501-8(a)*
Alarm systems	Class I, Division 1	*NEC Section 501-14(b)*

Table 3. Application Rules For Class I, Division 2

Components	Characteristics	NEC Reference
Boxes, fittings	Class II boxes required when using taps, joints, or other connections; otherwise, use dust-tight boxes with no openings	*NEC Section 502-4(a)(1)*
Wiring methods	Rigid metal conduit, steel intermediate metal conduit, or Types MI and, under certain conditions, MC cables	*NEC Section 502-4(a)*
Receptacles	Class II	*NEC Section 502-13(a)*
Lighting fixtures	Class II	*NEC Section 502-11(a)*
Panelboards	Dust/ignitionproof	*NEC Section 502-6(a)*
Circuit breakers	Dust/ignitionproof enclosure	*NEC Section 502-6(a)*
Fuses	Dust/ignitionproof enclosure	*NEC Section 502-6(a)*
Switches	Dust/ignitionproof enclosure	*NEC Section 502-6(a)*
Motors	Class II, Division 1 or totally enclosed	*NEC Section 502-8(a)*
Motor controls	Dust/ignitionproof	*NEC Section 502-6(a)*
Liquid-filled transformers	Install in vault	*NEC Section 502-2(a)*
Dry-type transformers	Class II, vault	*NEC Section 502-2(a)*
Utilization equipment	Class II, Division 1	*NEC Section 502-10(a)*
Flexible connections	Extra hard usage cord, liquid-tight, and others	*NEC Section 502-4(a)(2)*
Portable lamps	Class II	*NEC Section 502-11(a)*
Generators	Class II, Division 1 or totally enclosed	*NEC Section 502-8(a)*

Table 4. Application Rules For Class II, Division 1

ELECTRICAL — TRAINEE TASK MODULE 26313

Components	Characteristics	NEC Reference
Boxes, fittings	Use tight covers to minimize entrance of dust	**NEC Section 502-4(b)(1)**
Wiring methods	Rigid metal conduit, steel intermediate metal conduit, or Types MI, MC, TC, ITC, or PLTC cables, or enclosed dust-tight busways or wireways	**NEC Section 502-4(b)**
Receptacles	Exposed live parts are not allowed	**NEC Section 502-13(b)**
Lighting fixtures	Class II	**NEC Section 502-11(b)**
Panelboards	Dust-tight enclosure	**NEC Section 502-6(b)**
Circuit breakers	Dust-tight enclosure	**NEC Section 502-6(b)**
Fuses	Dust-tight enclosure	**NEC Section 502-6(b)**
Switches	Dust-tight enclosure	**NEC Section 502-6(b)**
Motors	Class II, Division 1 or totally enclosed	**NEC Section 502-8(b)**
Motor controls	Dust-tight enclosure	**NEC Section 502-6(b)**
Liquid-filled transformers	Install in vault	**NEC Section 502-2(b)**
Dry-type transformers	Class II vault	**NEC Section 502-2(b)**
Utilization equipment	Class II	**NEC Section 502-10(b)**
Flexible connections	Extra hard usage cord, liquid-tight, and others	**NEC Section 502-4(b)(2)**
Portable lamps	Class II	**NEC Section 502-11(b)(1)**
Generators	Class II, Division 1 or totally enclosed	**NEC Section 502-8(b)**

Table 5. Application Rules For Class II, Division 2

Components	Characteristics	NEC Reference
Boxes, fittings	Use tight covers to minimize entrance of dust	*NEC Section 503-3(a)(1)*
Wiring methods	Rigid metal conduit, steel intermediate metal conduit, EMT, or Types MI and MC cables, or enclosed dust-tight busways or wireways	*NEC Section 503-3(a)*
Receptacles	Tight with no openings	*NEC Section 503-11*
Lighting fixtures	Tight enclosure with no openings	*NEC Section 503-9*
Panelboards	Dust-tight enclosure	*NEC Section 503-4*
Circuit breakers	Dust-tight enclosure	*NEC Section 503-4*
Fuses	Tight metal enclosure with no openings	*NEC Section 503-4*
Switches	Dust-tight enclosure	*NEC Section 503-4*
Motors	Totally enclosed	*NEC Section 503-6*
Motor controls	Dust-tight enclosure	*NEC Section 503-4*
Liquid-filled transformers	Install in vault	*NEC Section 503-2*
Dry-type transformers	Class II vault	*NEC Section 503-2*
Utilization equipment	Class II	*NEC Section 503-8*
Flexible connections	Extra hard usage cord and other flexible conduit/fittings	*NEC Section 503-3(a)(2)*
Portable lamps	Unswitched, guarded with tight enclosure for lamp	*NEC Section 503-9(d)*
Generators	Totally enclosed	*NEC Section 503-6*

Table 6. Application Rules For Class III, Divisions 1 And 2

2.0.0 PREVENTION OF EXTERNAL IGNITION/EXPLOSION

The main purpose of using explosionproof fittings and wiring methods in hazardous areas is to prevent ignition of flammable liquids or gases and to prevent an explosion.

2.1.0 SOURCES OF IGNITION

In certain atmospheric conditions when flammable gases or combustible dusts are mixed in the proper proportion with air, any source of energy is all that is needed to touch off an explosion.

One prime source of energy is electricity. Equipment such as switches, circuit breakers, motor starters, pushbutton stations, or plugs and receptacles can produce arcs or sparks in normal operation when contacts are opened and closed. This could easily cause ignition.

Other hazards are devices that produce heat, such as lighting fixtures and motors. In this case, the surface temperatures may exceed the safe limits of many flammable atmospheres.

Finally, many parts of the electrical system can become potential sources of ignition in the event of insulation failure. This group would include wiring (particularly splices in the wiring), transformers, impedance coils, solenoids, and other low-temperature devices without make-or-break contacts.

Non-electrical hazards such as sparking metal can also easily cause ignition. A hammer, file, or other tool that is dropped on masonry or on a ferrous surface can cause a hazard unless the tool is made of non-sparking material. For this reason, portable electrical equipment is usually made from aluminum or other material that will not produce sparks if the equipment is dropped.

Electrical safety is of crucial importance. The electrical installation must prevent accidental ignition of flammable liquids, vapors, and dusts released to the atmosphere. In addition, since much of this equipment is used outdoors or in corrosive atmospheres, the material and finish must be such that maintenance costs and shutdowns are minimized.

2.2.0 COMBUSTION PRINCIPLES

Three basic conditions must be satisfied for a fire or explosion to occur:

- A flammable liquid, vapor, or combustible dust must be present in sufficient quantity.
- The flammable liquid, vapor, or combustible dust must be mixed with air or oxygen in the proportions required to produce an explosive mixture.
- A source of energy must be applied to the explosive mixture.

In applying these principles, the quantity of the flammable liquid or vapor that may be liberated and its physical characteristics must be recognized.

Vapors from flammable liquids also have a natural tendency to disperse into the atmosphere and rapidly become diluted to concentrations below the lower explosion limit, particularly when there is natural or mechanical ventilation.

CAUTION: The possibility that the gas concentration may be above the upper explosion limit does not afford any degree of safety, as the concentration must first pass through the explosive range to reach the upper explosion limit.

3.0.0 EXPLOSIONPROOF EQUIPMENT

Each area that contains gases or dusts that are considered hazardous must be carefully evaluated to make certain the correct electrical equipment is selected. Many hazardous atmospheres are Class I, Group D or Class II, Group G. However, certain areas may involve other groups, particularly Class I, Groups B and C. Conformity with the NEC requires the use of fittings and enclosures **approved** for the specific hazardous gas or dust involved.

The wide assortment of explosionproof equipment now available makes it possible to provide adequate electrical installations under any of the various hazardous conditions. However, you must be thoroughly familiar with all NEC requirements and know what fittings are available, how to install them properly, and where and when to use the various fittings. For example, some electricians are under the false impression that a fitting rated for Class I, Division 1 can be used under any hazardous conditions. However, remember the groups. For example, a fitting rated for Class I, Division 1, Group C cannot be used in areas classified as Groups A or B. On the other hand, fittings rated for use in Group A may be used for any group beneath A; fittings rated for use in Class I, Division 1, Group B can be used in areas rated as Group B areas or below, and so on.

WARNING!   Never interchange fittings or covers between one hazardous area and another. Such items must be rated for the appropriate class, division, and group.

Explosionproof fittings are rated for both classification and groups. All parts of these fittings (including covers) are rated accordingly. Therefore, if a Class I, Division 1, Group A fitting is required, a Group B (or below) fitting cover must not be used. The cover itself must be rated for Group A locations. Consequently, when working on electrical systems in hazardous locations, always make certain that fittings and their related components match the condition at hand.

3.1.0 INTRINSICALLY SAFE EQUIPMENT

Intrinsically safe equipment is incapable of releasing sufficient electrical energy under normal or abnormal conditions to cause ignition of a specific hazardous atmospheric mixture in its most easily ignited concentration. The use of intrinsically safe equipment is primarily limited to process control instrumentation, since these electrical systems lend themselves to the low energy requirements.

Installation rules for intrinsically safe equipment are covered in *NEC Article 504*. In general, intrinsically safe equipment and its associated wiring must be installed so that it is positively separated from the non-intrinsically safe circuits, because induced voltages could defeat the concept of intrinsically safe circuits. Underwriters' Laboratories and Factory Mutual list several devices in this category.

     ELECTRICAL — TRAINEE TASK MODULE 26313

3.2.0 EXPLOSIONPROOF CONDUIT AND FITTINGS

A typical floor plan for a hazardous area is shown in *Figure 4*.

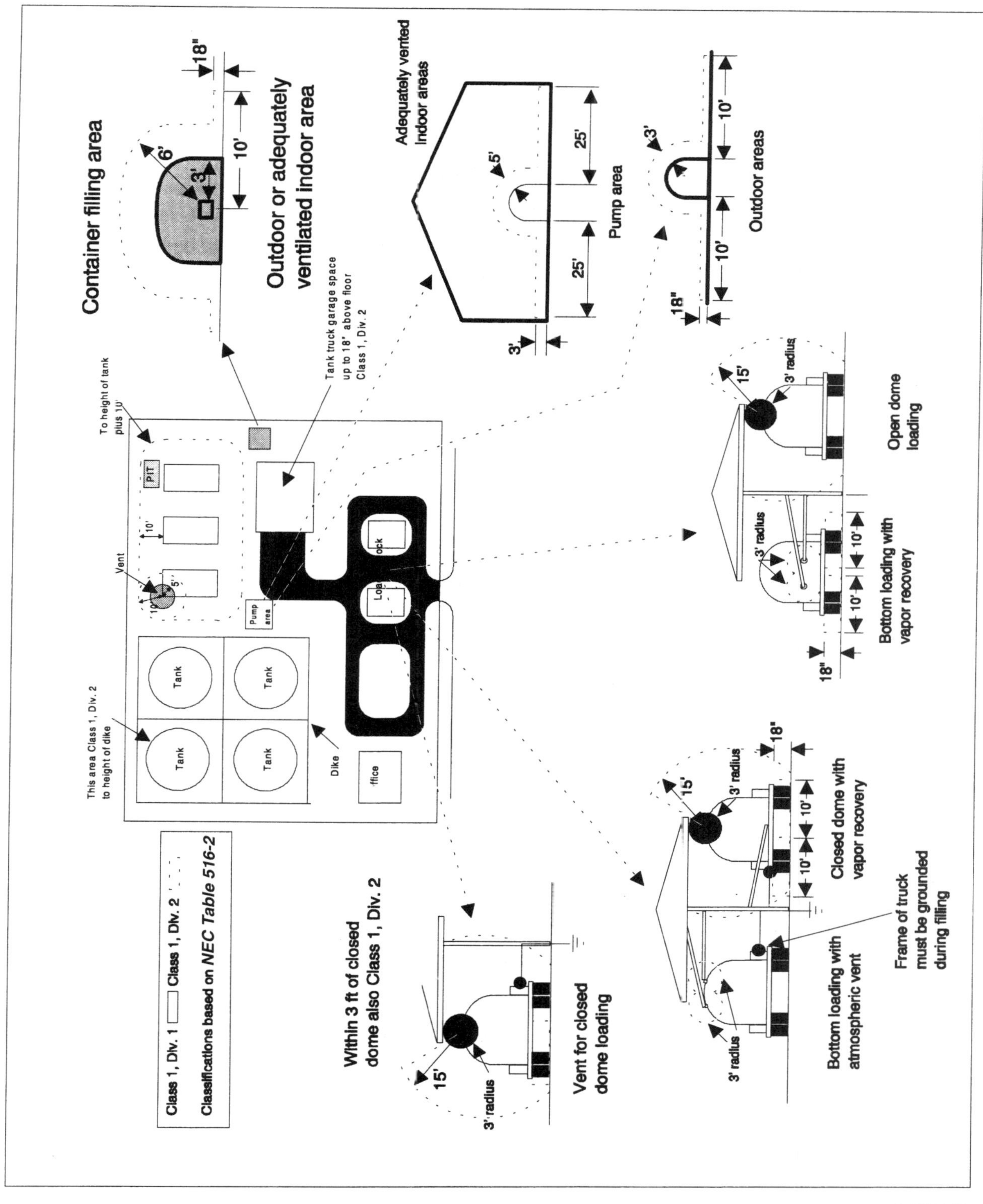

Figure 4. Floor Plan Of A Hazardous Location

In hazardous locations where threaded metal **conduit** is required, the conduit must be threaded with a standard conduit cutting die (*Figure 5*) that provides ¾" taper per foot. The conduit should be made up wrench-tight to prevent sparking in the event fault current flows through the raceway system [***NEC Section 500-3(d)***]. All boxes, fittings, and joints shall be threaded for connection to the conduit system and shall be an approved, explosionproof type (*Figure 6*). Threaded joints must be made up with at least five threads fully engaged. Where it becomes necessary to employ flexible connectors at motor or fixture terminals (*Figure 7*), flexible fittings approved for the particular class location shall be used. Unions are provided to facilitate the installation and removal of equipment.

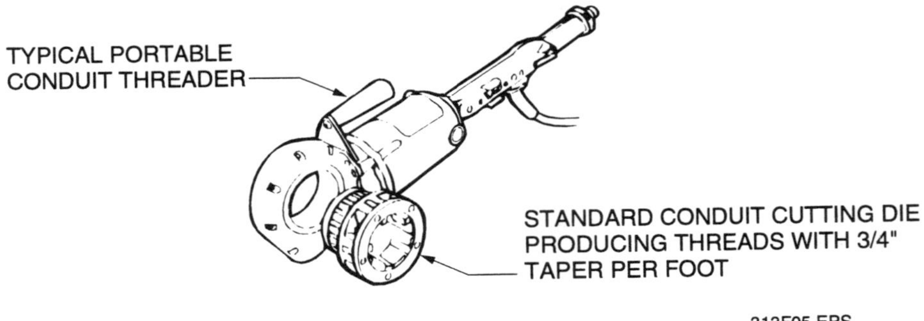

Figure 5. Conduit Body For Use In Hazardous Locations

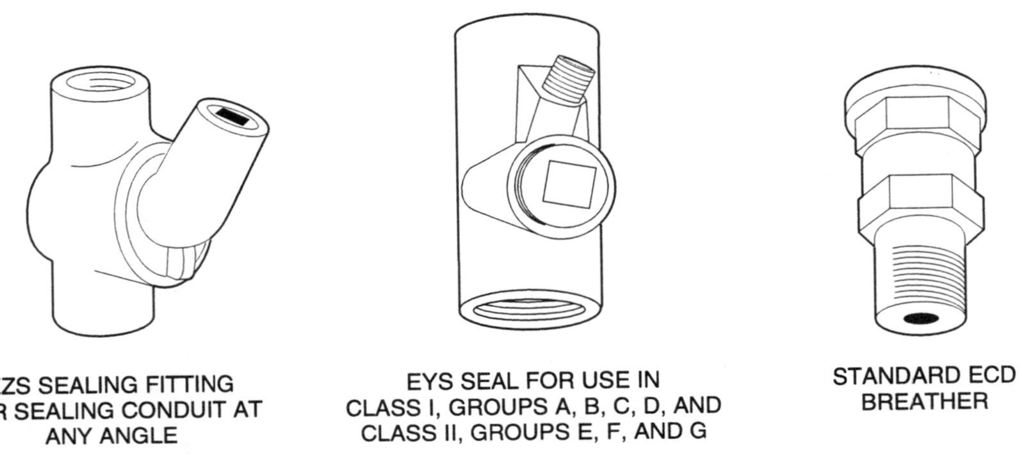

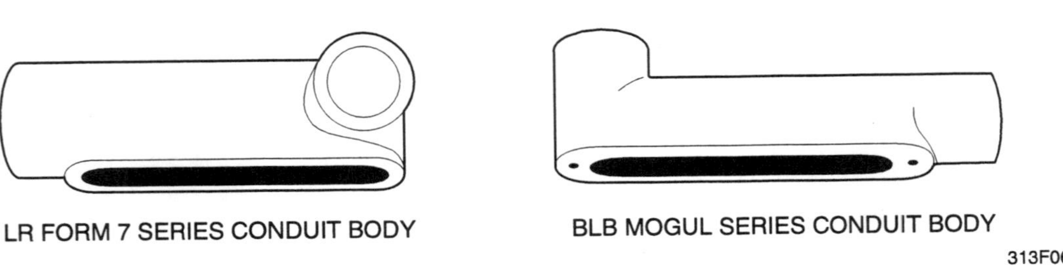

Figure 6. Typical Fittings Approved For Hazardous Areas

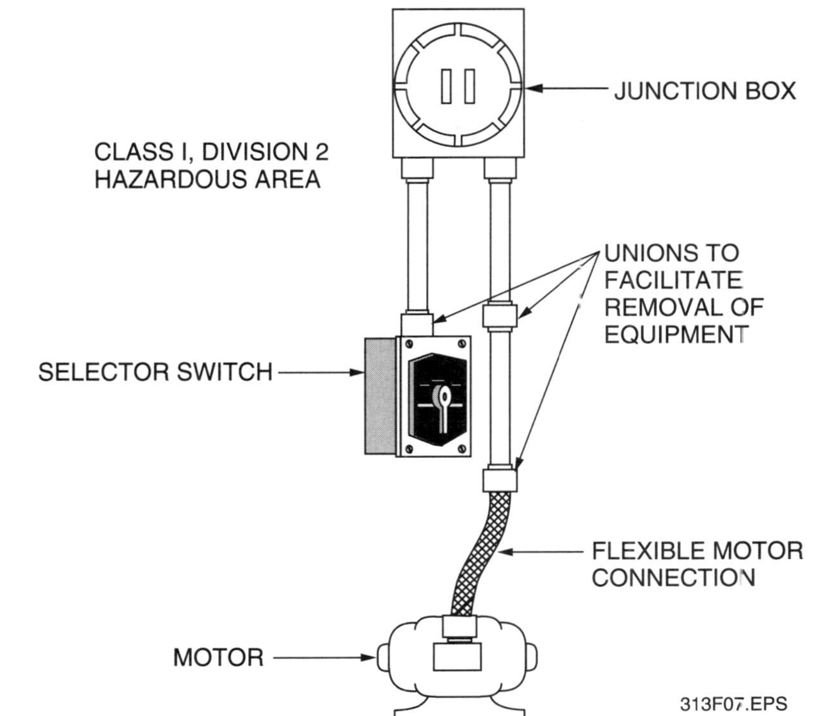

Figure 7. Explosionproof Flexible Connectors Are Frequently Used For Motor Terminations

3.3.0 SEALS AND DRAINS

Seals and drains are both used to protect conduit systems.

3.3.1 Seals

Seal-off fittings or seals (*Figure 8*) are required in conduit systems to prevent the passage of gases, vapors, or flames from one portion of the electrical installation to another at atmospheric pressure and normal ambient temperatures. Furthermore, seal-offs limit explosions to the enclosure and prevent precompression of pressure piling in conduit systems.

For Class I, Division 1 locations, ***NEC Section 501-5(a)(1)*** states that in each conduit run entering an enclosure for switches, circuit breakers, fuses, relays, resistors, or other apparatus which may produce arcs, sparks, or high temperatures, seals shall be installed within 18" from such enclosures. Explosionproof unions, couplings, reducers, elbows, capped elbows, and **conduit bodies** similar to L, T, and cross types shall be the only enclosures or fittings permitted between the sealing fitting and the enclosure. The conduit bodies shall not be larger than the largest trade size of the conduit.

However, one exception to this rule is that conduits are not required to be sealed if the current interrupting contacts are enclosed within a chamber hermetically sealed against the entrance of gases or vapors, immersed in oil in accordance with ***NEC Section 501-6(b)(1)(b)***, or enclosed within a factory-sealed explosionproof chamber within an enclosure approved for the location and marked *FACTORY SEALED* or equivalent.

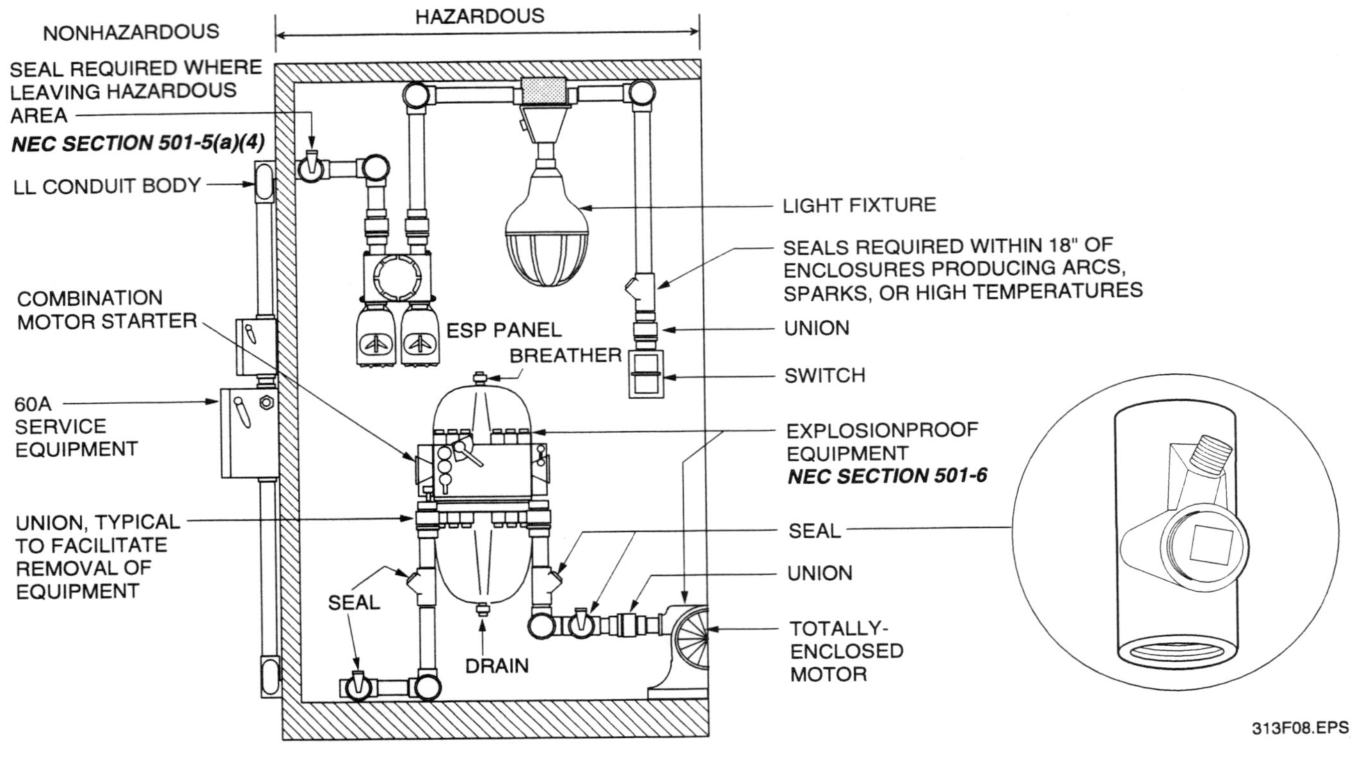

Figure 8. Installation Of Seals In Class I, Division 1 Locations

Seals are also required in Class II locations where a raceway provides communication between an enclosure that is required to be dust/ignitionproof and one that is not (**NEC Section 502-5**).

A permanent and effective seal is one method of preventing the entrance of dust into the dust/ignitionproof enclosure through the raceway. A horizontal raceway, not less than 10' long, is another approved method, as is a vertical raceway not less than 5' long and extending downward from the dust/ignitionproof enclosure.

Where a raceway provides communication between an enclosure that is required to be dust/ignitionproof and an enclosure in an unclassified location, seals are not required.

Where sealing fittings are used, all must be accessible.

While it is not a NEC requirement, many electrical designers sectionalize long conduit runs by inserting seals not more than 50' to 100' apart, depending on the conduit size. This is done in order to minimize the effects of pressure piling.

In general, seals are installed at the same time as the conduit system. However, the conductors are installed after the raceway system is complete and prior to packing and sealing the seal-offs.

ELECTRICAL — TRAINEE TASK MODULE 26313

3.3.2 Drains

In humid atmospheres or wet locations where it is likely that water can gain entrance to the interiors of enclosures or raceways, the raceways should be inclined so that water will not collect in enclosures or on seals, but will be led to low points where it may pass out through integral drains.

Frequently, the arrangement of raceway runs makes this method impractical, if not impossible. In such instances, special drain/seal fittings should be used, such as the type shown in *Figure 9*. These fittings prevent harmful accumulations of water above the seal and meet the requirements of **NEC Section 501-5(f)**.

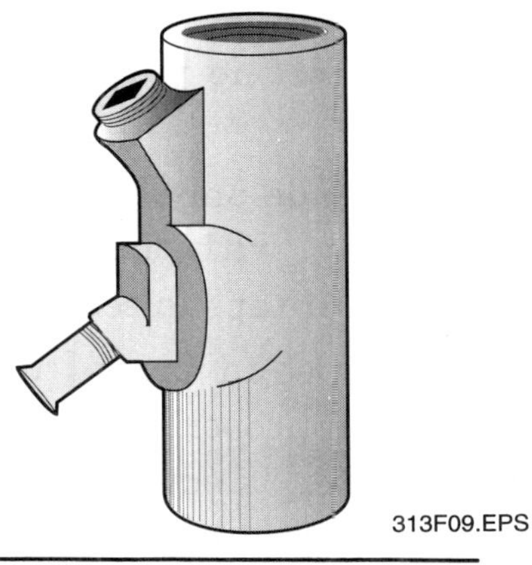

Figure 9. Typical Drain Seal

In locations which usually are considered dry, surprising amounts of water may collect in conduit systems. No conduit system is airtight; therefore, it may breathe. Alternate increases and decreases in temperature and/or barometric pressure due to weather changes or to the nature of the process carried on in the location where the conduit is installed will cause breathing.

Outside air is drawn into the conduit system when it breathes in. If this air carries sufficient moisture, it will be subject to condensation within the system when the temperature decreases and chills this air. Because the internal conditions are unfavorable to evaporation, the resultant water accumulation will remain and be increased by repetitions of the breathing cycle.

In view of this, it is best to ensure against such water accumulations and probable subsequent insulation failures by installing drain/seal fittings with drain covers or fittings with inspection covers, even though prevailing conditions at the time of planning or installation may not indicate a moisture problem.

3.4.0 SELECTION OF SEALS AND DRAINS

The primary considerations for selecting the proper sealing fittings are:

- Select the proper sealing fitting for the hazardous vapor involved (i.e., Class 1, Groups A, B, C, or D).

- Select a sealing fitting for the proper use in respect to its mounting position. This is particularly critical when the conduit runs between hazardous and nonhazardous areas. The improper positioning of a seal may permit hazardous gases or vapors to enter the system beyond the seal and escape into another portion of the hazardous area or enter a nonhazardous area. Some seals are designed to be mounted in any position; others are restricted to horizontal or vertical mounting.

- Install the seals on the proper side of the partition or wall, as recommended by the manufacturer.

- The installation of seals should be made only by trained personnel in strict compliance with the instruction sheets furnished with the seals and **sealing compound**. *NEC Section 501-5(c)(4)* prohibits splices or taps in sealing fittings.

- Sealing fittings are listed by UL for use in Class I hazardous locations with CHICO® A compound only. This compound, when properly mixed and poured, hardens into a dense, strong mass which is insoluble in water, is not attacked by chemicals, and is not softened by heat. It will easily withstand the pressure of the exploding trapped gases or vapors.

- Conductors sealed in the compound may be any approved thermoplastic or rubber insulated type. Both may or may not be lead covered.

3.5.0 TYPES OF SEALS AND FITTINGS

Certain seals, such as Crouse-Hinds EYS seals, are designed for use in vertical or nearly vertical conduit in sizes from ½" through 1". Other styles are available in sizes from ½" through 6" for use in vertical or horizontal conduit. In horizontal runs, these are limited to face-up openings. Various types of seals are shown in *Figure 10*.

Seals ranging in sizes from 1¼" through 6" have extra large work openings and separate filling holes so that fiber dams are easy to make. However, the overall diameters of these fittings are scarcely greater than that of unions of corresponding sizes, permitting close conduit spacing.

Crouse-Hinds EZS seals are for use with conduit running at any angle, from vertical through horizontal.

EYD drain seals provide continuous draining and thereby prevent water accumulation. EYD seals are for vertical conduit runs and range in size from ½" to 4". They are provided with one opening for draining and filling, a rubber tube to form a drain passage, and a drain fitting.

Figure 10. Various Types Of Seals And Related Components

EZD drain seals provide continuous draining and thereby prevent water accumulation. The covers should be positioned so that the drain will be at the bottom. A set screw is provided for locking the cover in this position.

EZD fittings are suitable for sealing vertical conduit runs between hazardous and nonhazardous areas, but must be installed in the hazardous area when it is above the nonhazardous area. They must be installed in the nonhazardous area when it is above the hazardous area.

EZD drain seals are designed so that the covers can be readily removed, permitting inspection during installation or at any time thereafter. After the fittings have been installed in the conduit run and the conductors are in place, the cover and barrier are removed. After the dam has been made in the lower hub opening with packing fiber (discussed later), the barrier must be replaced so that the sealing compound can be poured into the sealing chamber.

EZD inspection seals are identical to EZD drain seals to provide all inspection, maintenance and installation advantages, except that the cover is not provided with an automatic drain. Water accumulations can be drained periodically by removing the cover (when no hazards exist). The cover must be replaced immediately.

In addition to the seals discussed above, Crouse-Hinds also produces GUA Series conduit outlet boxes for use in hazardous areas. These boxes can also be used as sealing fittings (with appropriate covers) and are available in various configurations (GUA, GUAB, GUAC, GUAD, GUAL, GUAM, GUAN, GUAT, GUAW, and GUAX) for use as pull and splice boxes.

Note: When assembled with a sealing-type cover, GUA Series outlet boxes provide adequate sealing for hazardous areas (Class I, Groups C and D; Class II, Groups E, F, and G; and Class III). Seals can be made in either horizontal or vertical positions, and require the use of CHICO® A sealing compound.

CAUTION: Per the NEC, conductor splices or terminations must not be made in enclosures where sealing compound is to be used.

3.6.0   SEALING COMPOUNDS AND DAMS

Poured seals should be made only by trained personnel in strict compliance with the specific instruction sheets provided with each sealing fitting. Improperly poured seals are worthless. Sealing compound must be approved for the purpose, must not be affected by the surrounding atmosphere or liquids, and must not have a melting point of less than 200°F (93°C). The sealing compound and dams must also be approved for the type and manufacturer of the fitting. For example, Crouse-Hinds CHICO® A sealing compound is the only sealing compound approved for use with Crouse-Hinds ECM sealing fittings.

To pack the seal-off, remove the threaded plug or plugs from the fitting and insert the fiber supplied with the packing kit. Tamp the fiber between the wires and the hub before pouring the sealing compound into the fitting, then pour in the sealing cement and reset the threaded plug tightly. The fiber packing prevents the sealing compound from entering the conduit lines in the liquid state.

Sealing compound is poured after the conduit system and seals are installed and the conductors and packing fiber have been installed. Most sealing compound kits contain a powder in a polyethylene bag within an outer container. Remove the bag of powder, fill the outside container, pour in the powder, and mix.

CAUTION: Always make certain that the sealing compound is compatible for use with the packing material, brand and type of fitting, and type of conductors used in the system.

In practical applications, there may be dozens of seals required for a particular installation. Consequently, after the conductors are pulled, each seal in the system is first packed. To prevent the possibility of overlooking a seal, a certain color of paint is normally sprayed on the seal hub to indicate that the seal has been packed. When the sealing compound is poured, a different color paint is sprayed on the seal hub to indicate a finished job. This method permits the job supervisor to visually inspect the conduit run, and if a seal is not painted the appropriate color, he or she knows that the proper installation on this seal was not done; therefore, action can be taken to correct the situation immediately. The seal-off fittings in *Figure 11* are typical of those used. The type in *Figure 11(A)* is for vertical mounting and is provided with a threaded, plugged opening into which the sealing cement is poured. The seal-off in *Figure 11(B)* has an additional plugged opening in the lower hub to facilitate packing fiber around the conductors to form a dam for the sealing cement.

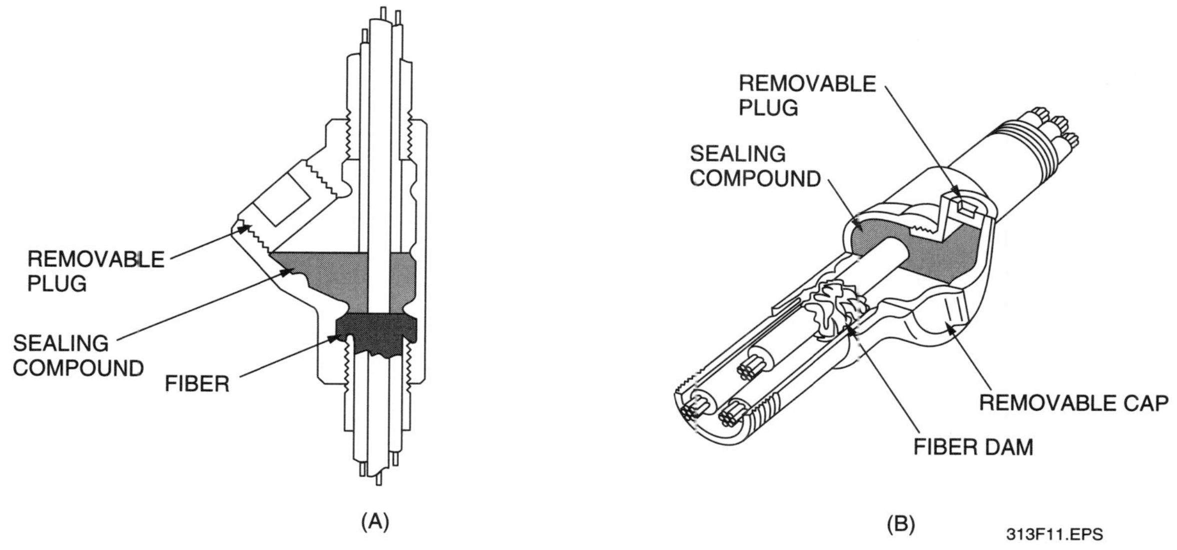

Figure 11. Seals Made With Fiber Dams And Sealing Compound

The following guidelines should be observed when preparing sealing compound:

- Use a clean mix vessel for every batch. Particles of previous batches or dirt will spoil the seal.

- Recommended proportions are by volume—usually two parts powder to one part clean water. Slight deviations in these proportions will not affect the results.

- Do not mix more than can be poured in 15 minutes after water is added. Use cold water; warm water increases the setting speed. Stir immediately and thoroughly.

- If the batch starts to set, do not attempt to thin it by adding water or by stirring. Such a procedure will spoil the seal. Discard the partially set material and make a fresh batch. After pouring, close the opening immediately.

- Do not pour compound in sub-freezing temperatures or when these temperatures are likely to occur during curing.

- Ensure that the compound level is in accordance with the instruction sheet for the specific fitting.

Most other explosionproof fittings are provided with threaded hubs for securing the conduit as described previously. Typical fittings include switch and junction boxes, conduit bodies, unions and connectors, flexible couplings, explosionproof lighting fixtures, receptacles, and panelboard and motor starter enclosures. A practical representation of these and other fittings is shown in *Figures 12* through *14.*

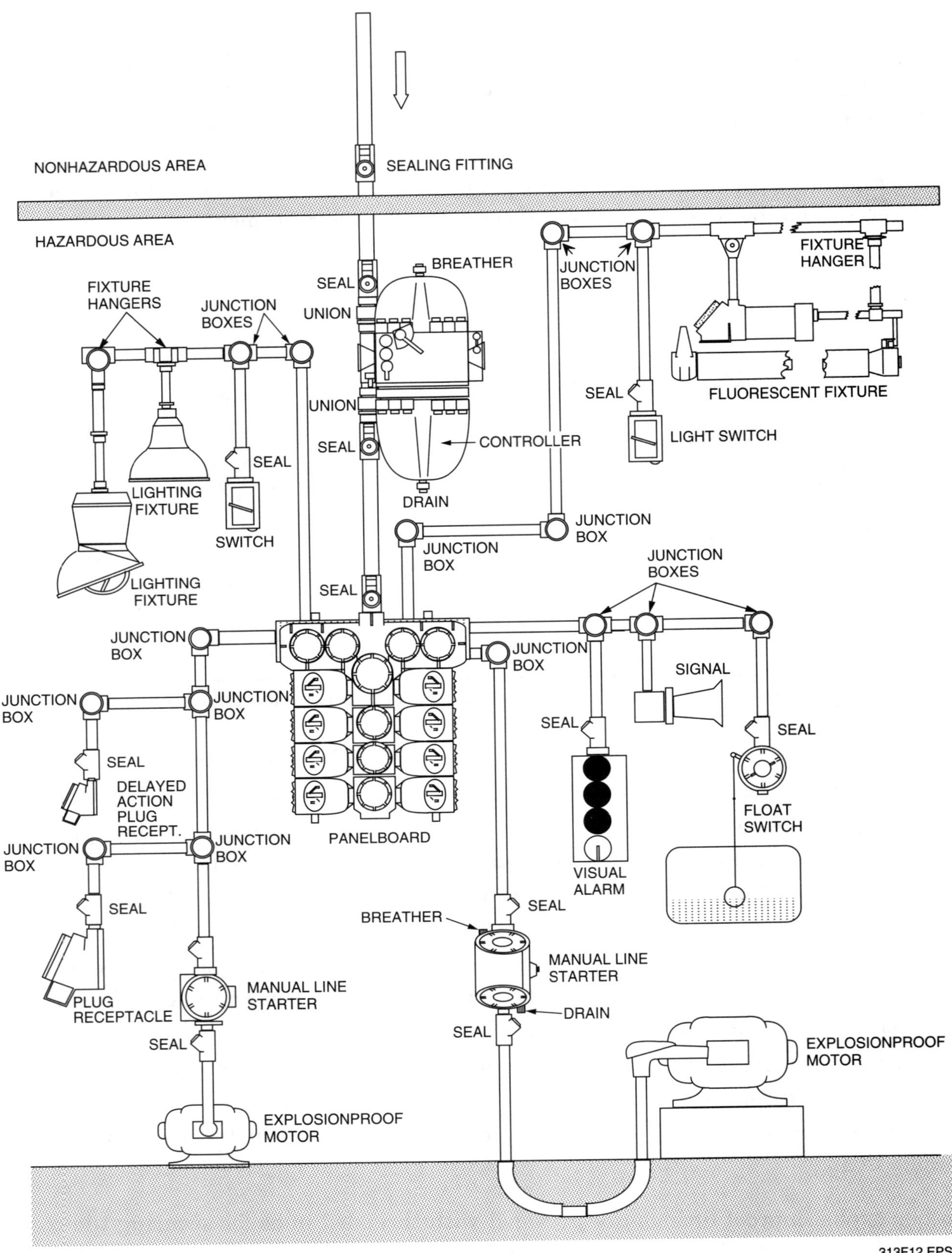

Figure 12. Class I, Division 1 Electrical Installation

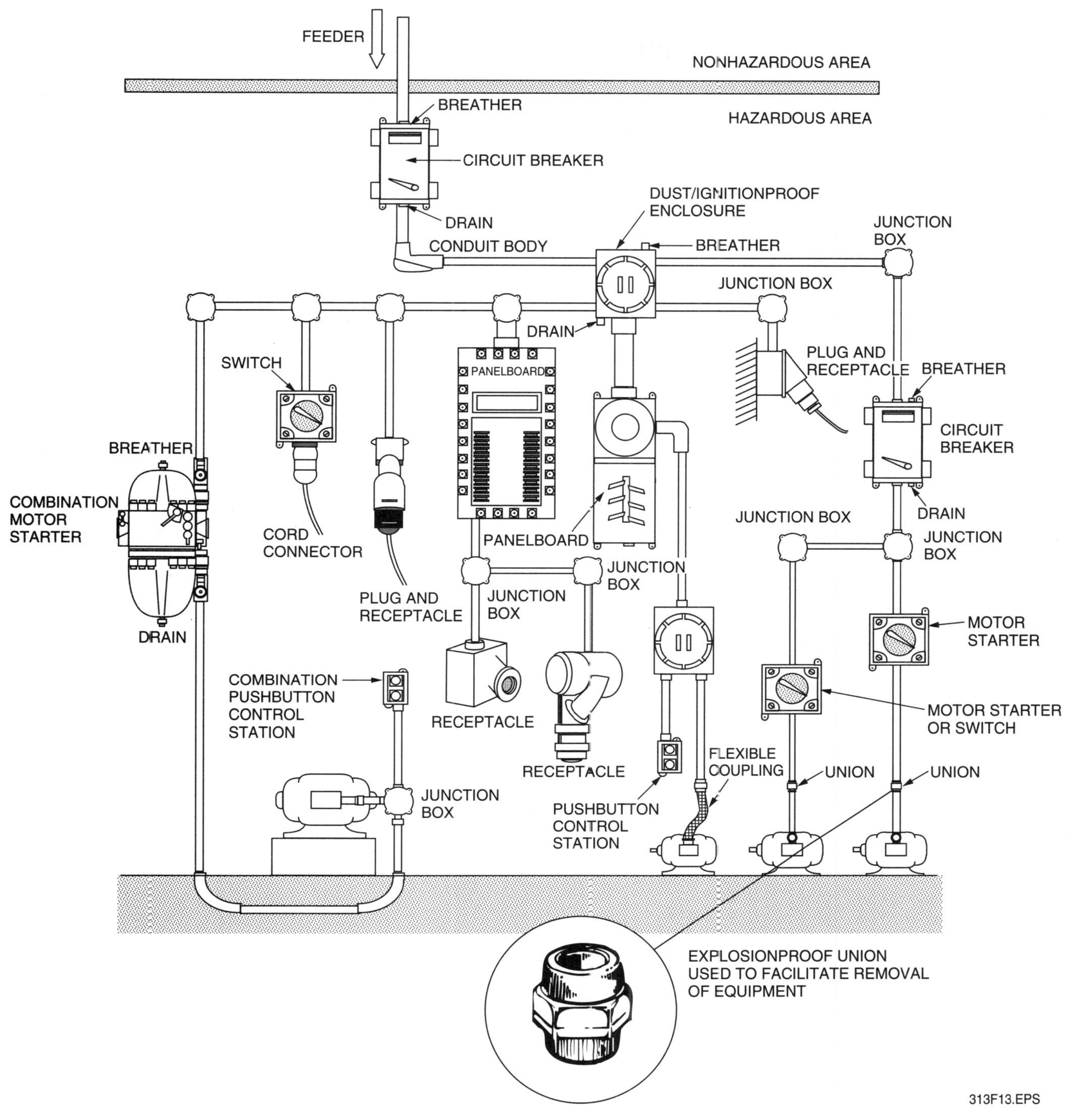

Figure 13. Class II, Division 1 Electrical Installation

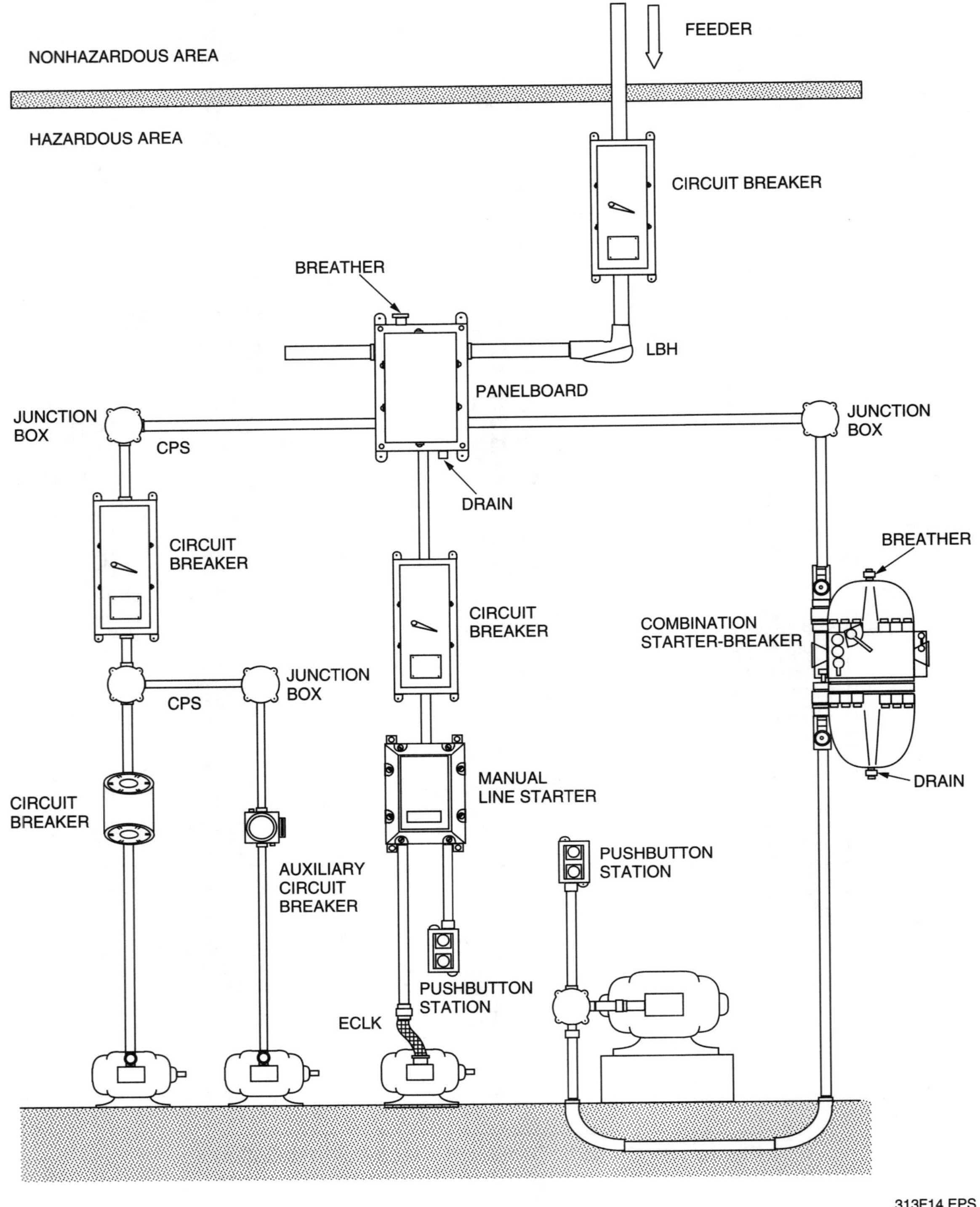

Figure 14. Class II Power Installation

4.0.0 GARAGES AND SIMILAR LOCATIONS

Garages and similar locations where volatile or flammable liquids are handled or used as fuel in self-propelled vehicles (including automobiles, buses, trucks, and tractors) are not usually considered critically hazardous locations. However, the entire area up to a level 18" above the floor is considered a Class I, Division 2 location, and certain precautionary measures are required by the NEC. Likewise, any pit or depression below floor level shall be considered a Class I, Division 2 location, and the pit or depression may be judged as a Class I, Division 1 location if it is unvented.

Normal raceway (conduit) and wiring may be used for the wiring method above this hazardous level, except where conditions indicate that the area concerned is more hazardous than usual. In this case, the applicable type of explosionproof wiring may be required.

Approved seal-off fittings should be used on all conduit passing from hazardous areas to nonhazardous areas. The requirements set forth in **NEC Article 501** apply to horizontal as well as vertical boundaries of the defined hazardous areas. Raceways embedded in a masonry floor or buried beneath a floor are considered to be within the hazardous area above the floor if any connections or extensions lead into or through such an area. However, conduit systems terminating to an open raceway in an outdoor unclassified area shall not be required to be sealed between the point at which the conduit leaves the classified location and enters the open raceway.

Figure 15 shows a typical automotive service station with applicable NEC requirements. The space in the immediate vicinity of the gasoline dispensing island is denoted as Class I, Division 1. The surrounding area, within a radius of 20' of the island, falls under Class I, Division 2 to a height of 18" above grade. Bulk storage plants for gasoline are subject to comparable restrictions.

NEC Article 514 covers gasoline dispensing and service stations, while **NEC Article 511** covers commercial garages.

A summary of NEC rules governing the installation of electrical wiring at and near gasoline dispensing pumps is shown in *Table 7*.

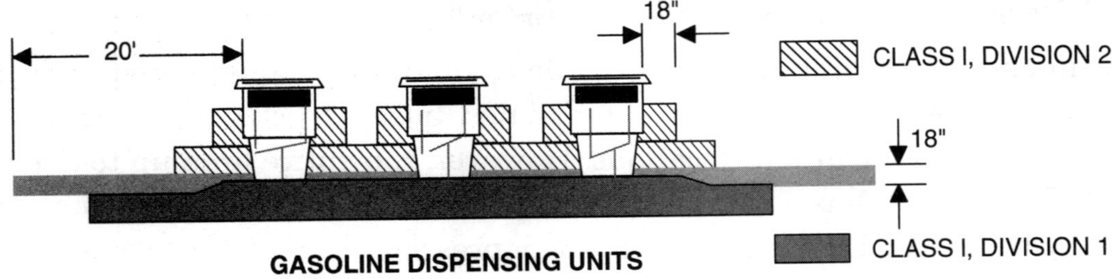

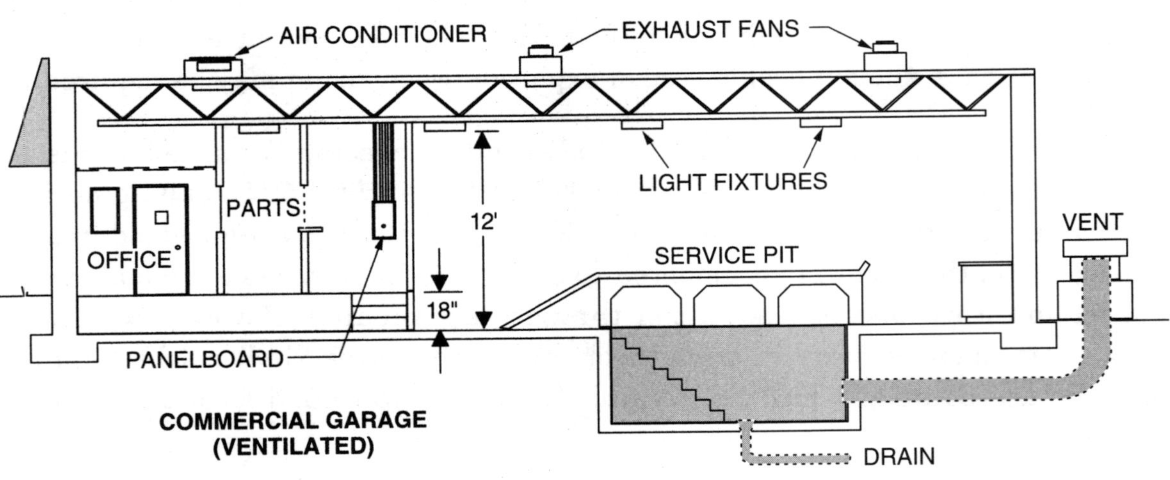

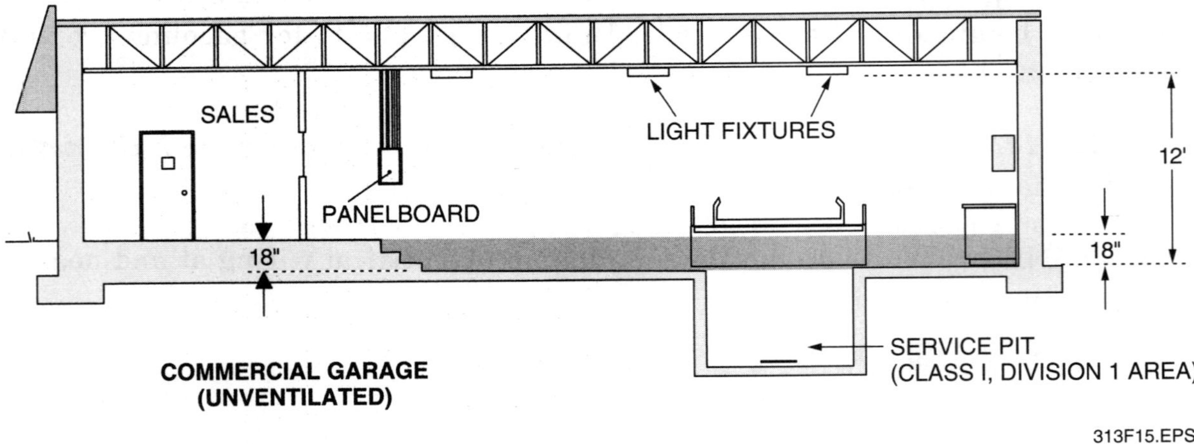

313F15.EPS

Figure 15. Commercial Service Station And Garage Classifications

Application	NEC Regulation	NEC Reference
Equipment in hazardous locations	All wiring and components must conform to the rules for Class I locations.	**NEC Section 514-3**
Equipment above hazardous locations	All wiring must conform to the rules for such equipment in commercial garages.	**NEC Section 514-4**
Gasoline dispenser	A disconnecting means must be provided for each circuit leading to or through a dispensing pump to disconnect all voltage sources, including feedback, during periods of service and maintenance. An approved seal (seal-off) is required in each conduit entering or leaving a dispenser.	**NEC Sections 514-6 and 514-7**
Grounding	Metal portions of all noncurrent-carrying parts of dispensers must be effectively grounded.	**NEC Section 514-16**
Underground wiring	Underground wiring must be installed within 2' of ground level in threaded rigid metal conduit or IMC. If underground wiring is buried 2' or more, rigid nonmetallic conduit may be used along with the types mentioned above; Type MI cable may also be used in some cases.	**NEC Section 514-8**

Table 7. NEC Application Rules For Service Stations

5.0.0 AIRPORT HANGARS

Buildings used for storing or servicing aircraft in which gasoline, jet fuels, or other volatile flammable liquids or gases are used fall under **NEC Article 513**. In general, any depression below the level of the hangar floor is considered to be a Class I, Division 1 location. The entire area of the hangar, including any adjacent and communicating area not suitably cut off from the hangar, is considered to be a Class I, Division 2 location up to a level of 18" above the floor. The area within 5' horizontally from aircraft power plants, fuel tanks, or structures containing fuel is considered to be a Class I, Division 2 hazardous location; this area extends upward from the floor to a level 5' above the upper surface of wings and engine enclosures.

Adjacent areas in which hazardous vapors are not likely to be released, such as stock rooms and electrical control rooms, should not be classified as hazardous when they are adequately ventilated and effectively cut off from the hangar itself by walls or partitions. All fixed wiring in a hangar not within a hazardous area as defined in **NEC Section 513-2** must be installed in metallic raceways or shall be Type MI, TC, or MC cable; the only exception is wiring in nonhazardous locations as defined in **NEC Section 513-3(d)**, which may be of any type recognized in **NEC Chapter 3**. *Figure 16* summarizes the NEC requirements for airport hangars.

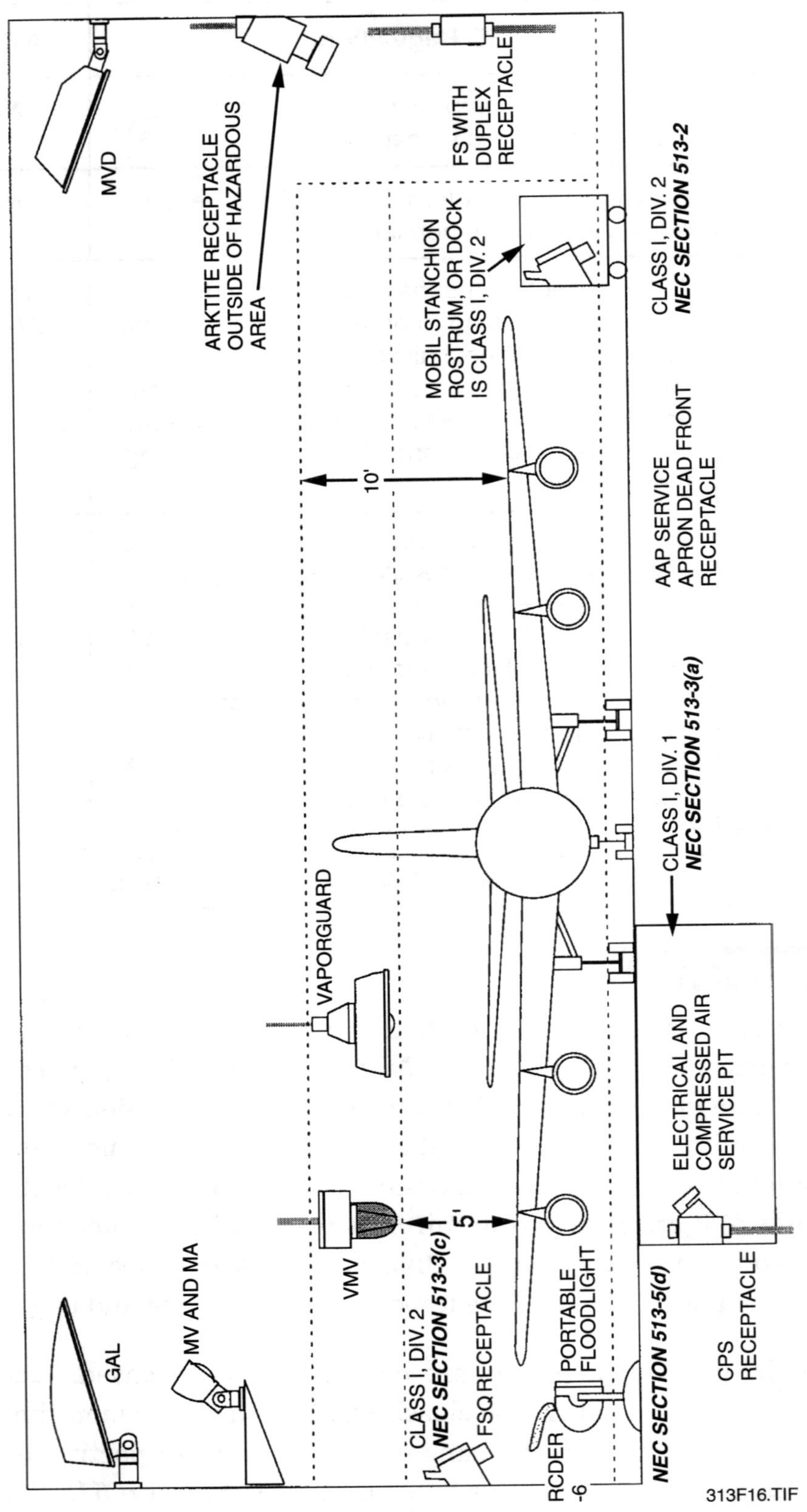

Figure 16. Sections Of An Airport Hangar Showing Hazardous Locations

Hospitals and other healthcare facilities fall under *NEC Article 517*. *NEC Article 517, Part B* covers the general wiring of healthcare facilities. *NEC Article 517, Part C* covers essential electrical systems for hospitals. *NEC Article 517, Part D* gives the performance criteria and wiring methods used in inhalation anesthetizing locations. *NEC Article 517, Part E* covers the requirements for electrical wiring and equipment in X-ray installations. *NEC Article 517, Part F* covers communications, signaling systems, and fire alarm systems. *NEC Article 517, Part G* covers isolated power systems.

Anesthetizing locations of hospitals are considered Class I, Division 1 to a height of 5' above the floor. Gas storage rooms are designated as Class I, Division 1 throughout. Most of the wiring in these areas, however, can be limited to lighting fixtures only—locating all switches and other devices outside of the hazardous area.

The NEC recommends that electrical equipment for hazardous locations be located in less hazardous areas wherever possible. It also suggests that by adequate, positive-pressure ventilation from a clean source of outside air, the hazards may be reduced or hazardous locations limited or eliminated. In many cases, the installation of dust-collecting systems can greatly reduce the hazards in a Class II area.

7.0.0   PETROCHEMICAL HAZARDOUS LOCATIONS

Most manufacturing facilities involving flammable liquids, vapors, or fibers must have their wiring installations conform strictly to the NEC as well as governmental, state, and local ordinances. Therefore, the majority of electrical installations for these facilities are carefully designed by experts in the field—either the plant in-house engineering staff or an independent consulting engineering firm.

Industrial installations dealing with petroleum or some types of chemicals are particularly susceptible to several restrictions involving many governmental agencies. Electrical installations for petrochemical plants will therefore have many pages of electrical drawings and specifications which require approval from all the agencies involved. Once approved, these drawings and specifications must be followed exactly, because any change whatsoever must once again go through the various agencies for approval.

8.0.0   MANUFACTURERS' DATA

Manufacturers of explosionproof equipment and fittings expend a lot of time, energy, and expense in developing guidelines and brochures to ensure that their products are used correctly and in accordance with the latest NEC requirements. The many helpful charts, tables, and application guidelines available from manufacturers are invaluable to anyone working on projects involving hazardous locations. Therefore, it is recommended that you obtain as much of this data as possible. Once obtained, study this data thoroughly. Doing so will enhance your qualifications for working in hazardous locations of any type. Manufacturers' data is usually available to qualified personnel at little or no cost and can be obtained from local distributors or directly from the manufacturer.

SUMMARY

Any area in which the atmosphere or a material in the area is such that the arcing of operating electrical contacts, components, and equipment may cause an explosion or fire is considered a hazardous location. In all such cases, explosionproof equipment, raceways, and fittings are used to provide an explosionproof wiring system.

The wide assortment of explosionproof equipment now available makes it possible to provide adequate electrical installations under any of the various hazardous conditions. However, you must be thoroughly familiar with all NEC requirements and know what fittings are available, how to install them properly, and where and when to use the various fittings.

References

For advanced study of topics covered in this Task Module, the following books are suggested:

American Electricians' Handbook, Latest Edition, McGraw-Hill, New York, NY.

Code Digest, Latest Edition, Crouse-Hinds, Syracuse, NY.

National Electrical Code Handbook, Latest Edition, National Fire Protection Association, Quincy, MA.

REVIEW/PRACTICE QUESTIONS

1. The NEC lists _____ classification(s) of hazardous atmospheres.

   a. 1
   b. 2
   c. 3
   d. 4

2. There are _____ divisions for each classification.

   a. 1
   b. 2
   c. 3
   d. 4

3. How many groups are listed under Class I, Division 1?

   a. 1
   b. 2
   c. 3
   d. 4

4. Which of the following are the groups listed under Class II, Division 1?

   a. A, B, C, and D
   b. E, F, G
   c. H, I, J
   d. L, M, N

5. When installing circuit breakers in Class II, Division 1 hazardous locations, a _____ enclosure must be used.

   a. dust/ignitionproof
   b. dust-tight
   c. tight metal enclosure with no openings
   d. standard enclosure with several openings

6. When rigid metal conduit is required in hazardous locations, the threads must be cut at _____ taper per foot.

   a. ½"
   b. ¾"
   c. 1"
   d. 1¼"

7. The main purpose of a union in conduit runs is to _____.

    a. facilitate the installation and removal of equipment
    b. ensure grounding continuity
    c. seal the system from flammable gases or vapors
    d. form tighter joints in the system

8. When installing switches or other arc-producing apparatus in Class I, Division 1 locations, within what distance of the switch (or other apparatus) must sealing fittings be installed?

    a. 6"
    b. 12"
    c. 18"
    d. 24"

9. The purpose of packing fiber in a sealing fitting is to _____.

    a. identify the type of seal and the sealing compound to use
    b. prevent any liquids, gases, or vapors from passing through the fitting
    c. prevent flammable vapors from mixing with the sealing compound
    d. provide a dam to contain the sealing compound until it hardens

10. Which of the following best describes the time to pour in the sealing compound in a sealing fitting?

    a. Within five minutes after it is installed in a raceway system
    b. After the conduit system and seals are installed and the conductors and packing fiber have been installed
    c. Prior to installing the packing fiber
    d. After the threaded plug is set tight

ANSWERS TO REVIEW/PRACTICE QUESTIONS

<u>Answer</u>	<u>Section Reference</u>
1. c	1.0.0
2. b	1.0.0
3. d	1.1.0
4. b	1.2.0
5. a	1.4.0
6. b	3.2.0
7. a	3.2.0
8. c	3.3.1
9. d	3.6.0
10. b	3.6.0

SUBSTANCES USED IN BUSINESS AND INDUSTRY

Class I Group	Substance	°F	°C	°F	°C	Lower	Upper	Vapor Density (Air Equals 1.0)
C	Acetaldehyde	347	175	-38	-39	4.0	60	1.5
D	Acetic Acid	967	464	103	39	4.0	19.9 @200°F	2.1
D	Acetic Anhydride	600	316	120	49	2.7	10.3	3.5
D	Acetone	869	465	-4	-20	2.5	13	2.0
D	Acetone Cyanohydrin	1270	688	165	74	2.2	12.0	2.9
D	Acetonitrite	975	524	42	6	3.0	16.0	1.4
A	Acetylene	581	305	gas	gas	2.5	100	0.9
B(C)	Acarolein (inhibited)	455	235	-15	-26	2.8	31.0	1.9
D	Acrylic Acid	820	438	122	50	2.4	8.0	2.5
D	Acrylonitrile	898	481	32	0	3.0	17	1.8
D	Adiponitrite	—	—	200	93	—	—	—
C	Allyl Alcohol	713	378	70	21	2.5	18.0	2.0
D	Allyl Chloride	905	485	-25	-32	2.9	11.1	2.6
B(C)	Allyl Glycidyl Ether	—	—	—	—	—	—	—
D	Ammonia	928	498	gas	gas	15	28	0.6
D	n-Amyl Acetate	680	360	60	16	1.1	7.5	4.5
D	sec-Amyl Acetate	—	—	89	32	—	—	4.5
D	Aniline	1139	615	158	70	1.3	11	3.2
D	Benzene	928	498	12	-11	1.3	7.9	2.8
D	Benzyl Chloride	1085	585	153	67	1.1	—	4.4
B(D)	1,,3-Butadiene	788	420	gas	gas	2.0	12.0	1.9
D	Butane	550	288	gas	gas	1.6	8.4	2.0
D	1-Butanol	650	343	98	37	1.4	11.2	2.6
D	2-Butanol	761	405	75	24	1.7 @ 212°F	9.8 @ 212°F	2.6
D	n-Butyl Acetate	790	421	72	22	1.7	7.6	4.0
D	iso-Butyl Acetate	790	421	—	—	—	—	—
D	sec-Butyl Acetate	—	—	88	31	1.7	9.8	4.0
D	t-Butyl Acetate	—	—	—	—	—	—	—
D	n-Butyl Acrylate (inhibited)	559	293	118	48	1.5	9.9	4.4
C	n-Butyl Formal	—	—	—	—	—	—	—
B(C)	n-Butyl Glycidyl Ether	—	—	—	—	—	—	—
C	Butyl Mercaptan	—	—	35	2	—	—	3.1
D	t-Butyl Toluene	—	—	—	—	—	—	—
D	Butylamine	594	312	10	-12	1.7	9.8	2.5
D	Butylene	725	385	gas	gas	1.6	10.0	1.9
C	n-Butyraldehyde	425	218	-8	-22	1.9	12.5	2.5
D	n-Butyric Acid	830	443	161	72	2.0	10.0	3.0
?	Carbon Disulfide	194	90	-22	-30	1.3	50.0	2.6

Class I Group	Substance	°F	°C	°F	°C	Lower	Upper	Vapor Density (Air Equals 1.0)
C	Carbon Monoxide	1128	609	gas	gas	12.5	74.0	1.0
C	Chloroacetaldehyde	—	—	—	—	—	—	—
D	Chlorobenzene	1099	593	82	28	1.3	9.6	3.9
C	1-Chloro-1-Nitropropane	—	—	144	62	—	—	4.3
D	Chloroprene	—	—	-4	-20	4.0	20.0	3.0
D	Cresol	1038-1110	559-599	178-187	81-86	1.1-1.4	—	—
C	Crotonaldehyde	450	232	55	13	2.1	15.5	2.4
D	Cumene	795	424	96	36	0.9	6.5	4.1
D	Cyclohexane	473	245	-4	-20	1.3	8.0	2.9
D	Cyclohexanol	572	300	154	68	—	—	3.5
D	Cyclohexanone	473	245	111	44	1.1 @ 212°F	9.4	3.4
D	Cyclohexene	471	244		-7	—	—	2.8
D	Cyclopropane	938	503	gas	gas	2.4	10.4	1.5
D	p-Cymene	817	436	117	47	0.7 @ 212°F	5.6	4.6
C	C n-Decaldehyde	—	—	—	—	—	—	—
D	n-Decanol	550	288	180	82	—	—	5.5
D	Decene	455	235	â	7	—	—	4.84
D	Diacetone Alcohol	1118	603	148	64	1.8	6.9	4.0
D,o-Dichlorobenzene		1198	647	151	66	2.2	9.2	5.1
D	1,,1-Dichloroethane	820	438	22	-6	5.6	—	—
D	1,,2-Dichloroethylene	860	460	36	2	5.6	12.8	3.4
C	1,,1-Dichloro-1-Nitroethane	—	—	168	76	—	—	5.0
D	1,,3-Dichloropropene	—	—	95	35	5.3	14.5	3.8
C	Dicyclopentadiene	937	503	90	32	—	—	—
D	Diethyl Benzene	743-842	395-450	133-135	56-57	—	—	4.6
C	Diethyl Ether	320	160	-49	-45	1.9	36.0	2.6
C	Diethylamine	594	312	-9	-23	1.8	10.1	2.5
C	Diethylaminoethanol	—	—	—	—	—	—	—
C	Diethylene Glycol Monobutyl Ether	442	228	172	78	0.85	24.6	5.6
C	Diethylene Glycol Monomethyl Ether	465	241	205	96	—	—	—
D	Di-isobutyl Ketone	745	396	120	49	0.8 @ 200°F	7.1 @ 200°F	4.9
D	Di-isobutylene	736	391	23	-5	0.8	4.8	3.9
C	Di-isopropylamine	600	316	30	-1	1.1	7.1	3.5

Class I Group	Substance	°F	°C	°F	°C	Lower	Upper	Vapor Density (Air Equals 1.0)
C	N-N-Dimethyl Aniline	700	371	145	63	—	—	4.2
D	Dimethyl Formamide	833	455	136	58	2.2 @ 212°F	15.2	2,5
D	Dimethyl Sulfate	370	188	182	83	—	—	4.4
C	Dimethylamine	752	400	gas	gas	2.8	14.4	1.6
C	1,,4-Dioxane	356	180	54	12	2.0	22	3.0
D	Dipentene	458	237	113	45	0.7 @ 302°F	6.1 @ 302°F	4.7
C	Di-n-propylamine	570	299	63	17	—	—	3.5
C	Dipropylene Glycol Methyl Ether	—	—	185	85	—	—	5.11
D	Dodecene	491	255	—	—	—	—	—,
C	Epichlorohydrin	772	411	88	31	3.8	21.0	3.2
D	Ethane	882	472	gas	gas	3.0	12.5	1.0
D	Ethanol	685	363	55	1.3	3.3	19	1.6
D	Ethyl Acetate	800	427	24	-4	2.0	11.5	3.0
D	Ethyl Acrylate (inhibited)	702	372	50	10	1.4	14	3.5
D	Ethyl sec-Amyl Ketone	—	—	—	—	—	—	—
D	Ethyl Benzene	810	432	70	21	1.0	6.7	3.7
D	Ethyl Butanol	—	—	—	—	—	—	—
D	Ethyl Butyl Ketone	—	—	115	46	—	—	4.0
D	Ethyl Chloride	966	519	-58	-50	3.8	15.4	2.2
D	Ethyl Formate	851	455	-4	-20	2.8	16.0	2.6
D	2-Ethyl Hexanol	448	231	164	73	0.88	9.7	4.5
D	2-Ethyl Hexyl Acrylate	485	252	180	82	—	—	—
C	Ethyl Mercaptan	572	300		-18	2.8	18.0	2.1
C	n-Ethyl Morpholine	—	—	—	—	—	—	—
C	2-Ethyl-3-Propyl Acrolein	—	—	155	68	—	—	4.4
D	Ethyl Silicate	—	—	125	52	—	—	7.2
D	Ethylamine	725	385		-18	3.5	14.0	1.6
C	Ethylene	842	450	gas	gas	2.7	36.0	1.0
D	Ethylene Chlorohydrin	797	425	140	60	4.9	15.9	2.8
D	Ethylene Dichloride	775	413	56	13	6.2	16	3.4
C	Ethylene Glycol Monobutyl Ether	460	238	143	62	1.1 @ 200°F	12.7 @ 275°F	4.1
D	Ethylene Glycol Monobutyl Ether Acetate	645	340	160	71	0.88 @ 200°F	8.54 @ 275°F	—
C	Ethylene Glycol Monoethyl Ether	455	235	110	43	1.7 @ 200°F	15.6 @ 200°F	3.0
C	Ethylene Glycol Monoethyl Ether Acetate	715	379	124	52	1.7	—	4.72

Class I Group	Substance	°F	°C	°F	°C	Lower	Upper	Vapor Density (Air Equals 1.0)
D	Ethylene Glycol Monomethyl Ether	545	285	102	39	1.8 @ STP	14 @ STP	2.6
B(C)	Ethylene Oxide	804	429	-20	-28	3.0	100	1.5
D	Ethylenediamine	725	385	93	34	4.2	14.4	2.1
C	Ethylenimine	608	320	12	-11	3.6	46.0	1.5
C	2-Ethylhexaldehyde	375	191	112	44	0.85 @ 200°F	7.2 @ 275°F	4.4
B	Formaldehyde (Gas)	795	429	gas	gas	7.0	73	1.0
D	Formic Acid (90%)	813	434	122	50	18	57	—
D	Fuel Oils	410-765	210-407	100-336	38-169	0.7	5	—
C	Furfual	600	316	140	60	2.1	19.3	3.3
C	Furfuryl Alcohol	915	490	167	75	1.8	16.3	3.4
D	Gasoline	536-880	280-471	-36 to -50	-38 to -46	1.2-1.5	7.1-7.6	3-4
D	Heptane	399	204	2.5	-4	1.05	6.7	3.5
D	Heptene	500	260			—	—	3.39
D	Hexane	437	225	-7	-22	1.1	7.5	3.0
D	Hexanol	—	—	145	63	—	—	3.5
D	2-Hexanone	795	424	77	25	—	8	3.5
D	Hexenes	473	245		-7	—	—	3.0
D	sec-Hexyl Acetate	—	—	—	—	—	—	—
C	Hydrazine	74-518	23-270	100	38	2.9	9.8	1.1
B	Hydrogen	968	520	gas	gas	4.0	75	0.1
C	Hydrogen Cyanide	1000	538	0	-18	5.6	40.0	0.9
C	Hydrogen Selenide	—	—	—	—	—	—	—
C	Hydrogen Sulfide	500	260	gas	gas	4.0	44.0	1.2
D	Isoamyl Acetate	680	360	77	25	1.0 @ 212°F	7.5	4.5
D	Isoamyl Alcohol	662	350	109	43	1.2	9.0 @ 212°F	3.0
D	Isobutyl Acrylate	800	427	86	30	—	—	4.42
C	Isobutyraldehyde	385	196	-1	-18	1.6	10.6	2.5
C	Isodecaldehyde	—	—	185	85	—	—	5.4
D	Iso-octyl Alcohol	—	—	180	82	—	—	—
C	Iso-octyl Aldehyde	387	197	—	—	—	—	—
D	Isophorone	860	460	184	84	0.8	3.8	—
D	Isoprene	428	220	-65	-54	1.5	8.9	2.4
D	Isopropyl Acetate,860	460	35	2	1.8 @ 100°F	8	3.5	
D	Isopropyl Ether	830	443	-18	-28	1.4	7.9	3.5
C	Isopropyl Glycidyl Ether	—	—	—	—	—	—	—
D	Isopropylamine	756,402	-35	-37	—	—	2.0	
D	Kerosene	410	210	110-162	43-72	0.7	5	—
D	Liquefied Petroleum Gas	761-842	405-450	—	—	—	—	—

Class I Group	Substance	°F	°C	°F	°C	Lower	Upper	Vapor Density (Air Equals 1.0)
B	Manufactured Gas (containing more than 30% H							
D	Methyl Isobutyl Ketone	840	440	64	18	1.2 @ 200°F. 8.0 @ 200°F 3.5		
D	Methyl Isocyanate	994	534	19	-7	5.3	26	1.97
C	Methyl Mercaptan	—	—	—	—	3.9	21.8	1.7
D	Methyl Methacrylate	792	422	.50	10	1.7	8.2	3.6
D	2-Methyl-1-Propanol	780	416	82	28	1.7 @ 123°F	10.6 @ 202°F	2.6
D	2-Methyl-2-Propanol	892	478	52	11	2.4	8.0	2.6
D	alpha-Methyl Styrene	1066	574	129	54	1.9	6.1	—
C	Methylacetylene	—	—	gas	gas	1.7	—	1.4
C	Methylacetylene-Propadiene (stabilized)	—	—	—	—	—	—	—
D	Methylamine	806	430	gas	gas	4.9	20.7	1.0
D	Methylcyclohexane	482	250	25	-4	1.2	6.7	3.4
D	Methylcyclohexanol	565	296	149	65	—	—	3.9
D	0-Methylcyclohexanone	—	—	118	48	—	—	3.9
D	Monoethanolamine	770	410	185	85	—	—	2.1
D	Monoisopropanolamine	705	374	171	77	—	—	2.6
C	Monomethyl Aniline	900	482	185	85	—	—	3.7
C	Monomethyl Hydrazine	382	194	17	-8	2.5	92	1.6
C	Morpholine	590	310	98	37	1.4	11.2	3.0
D	Naphtha (Coal Tar)	531	277	107	42	—	—	—
D	Naphtha (Petroleum)	550	288		-18	1.1	5.9	2.5
D	Nitrobenzene	900	482	190	88	1.8 @ 200°F —	4.3	
C	Nitroethane	778	414	82	28	3.4	—	2.6
C	Nitromethane	785	418	95	35	7.3	—	2.1
C	1-Nitropropane	789	421	96	36	2.2	—	3.1
C	2-Nitropropane	802	428	75	24	2.6	11.0	3.1
D	Nonane	401	205	88	31	0.8	2.9	4.4
D	Nonene	—	—	78	26	—	—	4.35
D	Nonyl Alcohol	—	—	165	74	0.8 @ 212°F	6.1 @ 212°F	5.0
D	Octane	403	206	56	13	1.0	6.5	3.9
D	Octene	446	230	70	21	—	—	3-9
D	n-Octyl Alcohol	—	—	178	81	—	—	4.5

Class I Group	Substance	°F	°C	°F	°C	Lower	Upper	
D	Pentane	470	243	-40	-40	1.5	7.8	2.5
D	1-Pentanol	572	300	91	33	1.2	10.0 @ 212°F	3.0
D	2-Pentanone	846	452	45	7	1.5	8.2	3.0
D	1-Pentene	527	275	0	-18	1.5	8.7	2.4
D	Phenylhydrazine	—	—	190	88	—	—	—
D	Propane	842	450	gas	gas	2.1	9.5	1.6
D	1-Propanol	775	413	74	23	2.2	13.7	2.1
D	2-Propanol	750	399	53	12	2.0	12.7 @ 200°F	2.1
D	Propiolactone	—	—	165	74	2.9	—	2.5
C	Propionaldehyde	405	207	-22	-30	2.6	17	2.0
D	Propionic Acid	870	466	126	52	2.9	12.1	2.5
D	Propionic Anhydride	545	285	145	63	1.3	9.5	4.5
D	n-Propyl Acetate	842	450	55	13	1.7 @ 100°F	8	3.5
C	n-Propyl Ether	419	215	70	21	1.3	7.0	3.53
B	Propyl Nitrate	347	175	68	20	2	100	—
D	Propylene	851	455	gas	gas	2.0	11.1	1.5
D	Propylene Dichloride	1035	557	60	16	3.4	14.5	3.9
B(C)	Propylene Oxide	840	449	-35	-37	2.3	36	2.0
D	Pyridine	900	482	68	20	1.8	12.4	2.7
D	Styrene	914	490	88	3.1	1.1	7.0	3.6
C	Tetrahydrofuran	610	321	6	-14	2.0	11.8	2.5
D	Tetrahydronaphthalene	725	385	160	71	0.8 @ 212°F	5.0 @ 302°F 4.6	
C	Tetramethyl Lead	—	—	100	38	—	—	6.5
D	Toulene	896	480	40	4	1.2	7.1	3.1
D	Tridecene	—	—	—	—	—	—	—
C	Triethylamine	480	249	16	-9	1.2	7.1	3.1
D	Triethylbenzene	—	—	181	83	—	—	5.6
D	Tripropylamine	—	—	105	41	—	—	—
D	Turpentine	488	253	95	35	0.8	—	—
D	Undecene	—	—	—	—	—	—	—
C	Unsymmetrical Dimethyl Hydrazine (UDMH)	480	249	5	-15	2	95	2.0
C	Valeraldehyde	432	222	54	12	—	—	3.0
D	Vinyl Acetate	756	402	18	-8	2.6	13.4	3.0
D	Vinyl Chloride	882	472	gas	gas	3.6	33.0	2.2
D	Vinyl Toluene	921	494	120	49	—	11.0	4.1
D	Vinylidene Chloride	1058	570	-19	-28	6.5	15.5	3.4
D	Xylenes	867-984	464-529	81-90	27-32	1.0-1.1	7.0	3.7

313F17F.TIF

ELECTRICAL — TRAINEE TASK MODULE 26313

The NCCER makes every effort to keep these manuals up-to-date and free of technical errors. We appreciate your help in this process. If you have an idea for improving this manual, or if you find an error, a typographical mistake, or an inaccuracy in the NCCER's Craft Training Manuals, please write us, using this form or a photocopy. Be sure to include the exact module number, page number, a description of the problem, and the correction, if possible. Your input will be brought to the attention of the Technical Review Committee. Thank you for your assistance.

Instructors – If you found that additional materials were necessary in order to teach this module effectively, please let us know so that we may include them in the Equipment/Materials list in the Instructor's Guide.

Write: Curriculum Development and Revision Department
National Center for Construction Education and Research
P.O. Box 141104
Gainesville, FL 32614-1104

Fax: 352-334-0932

Craft ___________________ Module Name ___________________

Copyright Date __________ Module Number __________ Page Number(s) __________

Description of Problem

____

____

____

____

(Optional) Correction of Problem

____

____

____

(Optional) Your Name and Address

____

____

____

notes